COMPLETE
OUTDOORS
ENCYCLOPEDIA
Revised & Expanded

Revised & Expanded

COMPLETE OUTDOORS ENCYCLOPEDIA

by Vin T. Sparano

*Editor Emeritus/
Senior Field Editor,
Outdoor Life magazine*

THOMAS DUNNE BOOKS

St. Martin's Press ⚏ New York

A THOMAS DUNNE BOOK.
An imprint of St. Martin's Press.

COMPLETE OUTDOORS ENCYCLOPEDIA. Copyright © 1972, 1980, 1988, 1998 by Vin T.
Sparano. All rights reserved. Printed in the United States of America. No part of this book
may be used or reproduced in any manner whatsoever without written permission except
in the case of brief quotations embodied in critical articles or reviews. For information,
address St. Martin's Press, 175 Fifth Avenue, New York, N.Y. 10010.

Library of Congress Cataloging-in-Publication Data

Sparano, Vin T.
    Complete outdoors encyclopedia / by Vin T. Sparano.—1st St.
  Martin's Press ed.
      p. cm.
    "Thomas Dunne books"—T.p. verso.
    Originally published: New York : Outdoor Life Books, c1972.
    Includes index.
    ISBN: 0-312-19190-1
    1. Hunting. 2. Fishing. 3. Camping. 4. Outdoor life.
  I. Title.
  SK33.S646   198
  799'.03—dc21   97-46772
                                   CIP

First published in the United States by Outdoor Life Books

First St. Martin's Press Edition: September 1998

10 9 8 7 6 5 4 3 2 1

To my wife and partner Betty . . .
who demands so little from a
man who chases the seasons

CONTENTS

Part 11
OUTDOOR INFORMATION SOURCES

PREFACE

More than twenty-five years ago, when I wrote the first introduction to this book, I said, "This encyclopedia will provide the outdoorsman with a good working knowledge of all phases of outdoor recreation, including hunting, fishing, camping, boating, archery, and hunting dogs." That First Edition won the Library Association Award for Outstanding Reference Work. I promised the same comprehensive outdoor coverage in 1980 and 1988, when I revised the Second and Third Editions.

You are now holding the Fourth Edition, which has been totally revised and expanded. The basic goal of this encyclopedia has not changed over the years, but nearly all the information here has been updated to keep pace with the remarkable progress we have seen in the outdoors.

This Fourth Edition has more than 1,300 illustrations and diagrams, including nearly 400 new photographs and more than 100 new instructional drawings. All material was selected to illustrate new technology and trends in the outdoors.

To further broaden the scope of the encyclopedia, I have created several brand-new sections and chapters: Survival and Watersports, which includes kayaking, water skiing, and personal watercraft. I have also compiled valuable data with a stronger focus on latest trends,

such as fly fishing, sporting clays, and new first-aid breakthroughs in outdoor emergencies and survival.

Over the years, I have written nearly 1,000 instructional outdoor columns for *Outdoor Life* magazine, the Gannett Newspaper Syndicate, and the *Los Angeles Times* News Service. All of this updated information has been woven into the chapters of this Fourth Edition.

This monumental work is the ultimate one-volume library for anyone interested in the outdoors. The revision took one year of full-time work with a staff of editors, photographers, and artists. I want to thank wildlife photographer William Hartley for his excellent casting pictures. I also want to thank artists Ken Laager and Chris Armstrong for their concise how-to illustrations.

A special thanks goes to Regina Efimchik, a college intern from East Stroudsburg University, who worked at my side for ten months. Regina's energy kept me at my desk when I would have preferred to go fishing. Her editing and organizational skills were a valuable asset in tracking this huge amount of data, which made it possible to meet all my deadlines.

I also want to thank my editors at St. Martin's Press, especially Pete Wolverton, Neil Bascomb, and Kristen Nardullo. I did not envy their positions when I delivered the completed manuscript, photographs, and illustrations in two cardboard cartons that weighed about 50 pounds.

I am also indebted to the outdoor industry and all those people who answered my many requests for photographs and research data on the latest technological advancements that have literally changed the way we enjoy and sometimes cope with the outdoors we love so much. We are, indeed, entering a new age of outdoors sports.

I believe this Fourth Edition of the *Complete*

Outdoors Encyclopedia will prove to be the most effective outdoor reference work ever published and a most valuable guide to the outdoors. For new campers and hikers who want to learn how to identify poison ivy to sportsmen trekking to remote wilderness areas, this huge volume will be the ultimate outdoor guide.

Vin T. Sparano
Editor Emeritus/Senior Field Editor
Outdoor Life

ACKNOWLEDGMENTS

I want to thank the following companies, organizations, and agencies for their permission, cooperation, and assistance in compiling information for this new edition.

Outdoor Life
Bass Pro Shops
Jayco, Inc.
O. Mustad & Son
Northwest Kayaks, Inc.
Marketing Resources Group International, Inc.
Orvis Company, Inc.
Images Group
Camp Trails
Silva
Millett Sights
International Game Fish Association
National Shooting Sports Foundation, Inc.
Recreational Vehicle Industry Association
The Farrell Group
Uncle Josh Bait Company
Walker Agency
Wright & McGill Co.
Bushnell Sports Optics
The Coleman Company, Inc.

Federal Cartridge Co.
Johnson Worldwide Associates, Inc.
Magellan Systems Corporation
Woolrich, Inc.
Imperial Schrade Corporation
Dunham Bootmakers
Cabela's Inc.
Diamond Machining Technology, Inc.
Garmin International
Lowrance Electronics, Inc.
National Rifle Association of America
Outdoor Technologies—Berkeley/ABU Garcia
Penn Fishing Tackle Mfg. Co.
Stren Fishing Lines
Techsonic Industries, Inc.
3M Scientific Anglers
Yamaha Marine Group
H.D. Wood Advertising
Boone & Crockett Club
United States Fish and Wildlife Service
Winchester Operations of Olin Corporation
Remington Arms Company, Inc.
Outboard Marine Corporation
American Water Ski Association
Personal Watercraft Industry Association

PART 1

HUNTING AND SHOOTING

RIFLE ACTIONS

Popular rifle actions used today fall into two broad classifications—the repeating action and the single-shot action. An old but still another action design is the double-barreled rifle. The double rifle is extremely limited in use for a number of reasons which will be discussed in some detail later.

Among the repeaters, the most popular is the bolt-action rifle, which uses a manually operated steel bolt assembly to chamber and seal a cartridge in the breech. Two other repeating rifle mechanisms are the lever and pump, or slide, actions, which are also manually operated to chamber and seal cartridges for firing. Fourth and last of the repeating rifles is the semi-automatic or autoloader, an action that requires only a pull of the trigger to fire a cartridge, eject the spent case, chamber a new cartridge, and cock the rifle for the next shot.

The single-shot rifles come in three designs: The single-shot bolt action, which differs from the repeating bolt action in that it has no magazine or clip. The break action which, in simplest terms, utilizes a lever, usually a thumb lever, to break open the rifle and expose the chamber for loading. The falling-block action, an old design that for all practical purposes was considered dead and obsolete only a few decades ago. The Sturm, Ruger Company brought the strong falling-block design back to life in 1966 with the introduction of the Ruger No. 1 Single Shot. Browning followed with its Model 1885, another single-shot utilizing the falling-block system. Both Ruger and Browning single-shot rifles are available in a variety of calibers from varmint to big-game loads.

These various actions all have advantages and disadvantages. Only by examining each action in detail can hunters and target shooters select the most practical and effective rifle for their particular use.

BOLT ACTION

The most widely used rifle in the field and on the range is the bolt action, and there are several good reasons for this. The bolt action is strong and simple. It disassembles easily for cleaning, an important factor for the hunter in the field. The bolt on most modern rifles can be easily slipped out of the receiver and wiped clean of dirt, sand, or wet snow. With the bolt removed a hunter who has just taken a fall can simply glance through the breech to check for obstructions in the bore.

Because the bolt affords strong hand leverage, this action is also best for the shooter who handloads his own ammunition. The powerful pull of the bolt is an advantage when extracting dirty or stuck cases. Likewise, cases slightly oversize can usually be chambered with a bit more than normal pressure on closing the bolt. Because the bolt locks a cartridge at the head, the cases are not subjected to stretch when fired and only the neck of the cases generally needs to be resized during the reloading process.

NOMENCLATURE OF THE BOLT-ACTION RIFLE

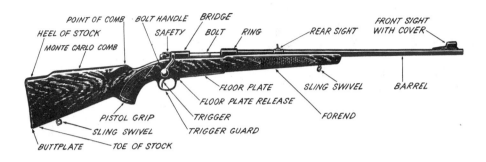

The bolt gun also has a one-piece stock which makes for better bedding of the action and barrel and produces greater accuracy than nearly all other rifle designs.

Who should use the bolt action? Because of its reliability and simplicity, the bolt-action rifle is the logical choice for hunters who prefer to hunt in remote areas, where gunsmiths and spare parts are scarce. Because of its superior accuracy, and the fact that it is chambered for nearly all flat-shooting, high-velocity cartridges, the bolt gun is a favorite among mountain and prairie hunters who are generally forced to take game at long ranges.

The bolt action also comes into its own as a target and benchrest rifle. The solid-locking action and one-piece stock produces accuracy, and the entire rifle is the most adaptable to alterations to satisfy the fancy of the serious target shooter.

Not all bolt-action rifles look alike and handle the same, however. Let's take a look at some typical factory models and learn the reasoning behind their design.

The Ruger Model 77 is typical of the bolt actions built for hunting. It is chambered for a variety of calibers, including the .22/250, 6mm, .243, .308, .220 Swift, .270, .257 Roberts, .280 Remington, .30/06, .25/06 and the 7×57. Magnum calibers include the 7mm Remington, the .375 Holland & Holland, and the .300, .338 and .458 Winchester Magnums. This range of calibers fills the bill for all North American, European, and African game. Other gun companies, such as Remington, Browning, and Winchester, have comparable bolt-action models in many of these calibers.

The .460 Weatherby Magnum rifle fires one of the world's most powerful cartridges. The .460 Weath-erby Magnum cartridge, using a 500-grain bullet, produces a muzzle energy of 8,100 foot-pounds. By comparison, the popular .30/06 with a 180-grain bullet has a muzzle energy of 2,910 foot-pounds. Though the .460 Weatherby Magnum is generally limited to the world's largest and most dangerous game, this rifle and caliber combination does point out that the bolt action's strong design can handle the most potent loads.

The Ruger International Model 77 RSI is a good example of a bolt-action carbine. Keeping barrel length down improves maneuverability in rough terrain and heavy brush. Built with an 18½-inch barrel, it comes in an array of calibers, from .243 to .308. This carbine is full-stocked—a handsome style widely known as Mannlicher-stocked or Mannlicher-style. Several European-made carbines of the same general type—including the Steyr-Mannlicher model—are imported by American distributors.

One of the more specialized bolt actions is the Winchester Model 70 Varmint, designed for shooting woodchucks, coyotes, foxes and any other varmints at long ranges. Its most distinguishing characteristic is the heavyweight barrel, which affords steadier holding and consequently better accuracy. The rifle weighs about 9¾ lbs., roughly 3 pounds more than the average bolt action, and has a 26-inch barrel.

The Model 70 Varmint comes without front and rear sights, as do most varminters, since these rifles invariably are mounted with scopes up to 24×. Bolt guns designated as varmint models are built for maximum range and precision shooting with high velocity cartridges. The Winchester version comes in .223 Remington, .22/250 Rem., .308 and .243 Win. calibers.

HOW A BOLT-ACTION RIFLE WORKS

1. Raising the bolt handle unlocks the bolt head from the barrel chamber. At the same time, notch at bottom of the bolt handle catches and pushes up protruding finger of the firing-pin head, pushing firing pin to rear.

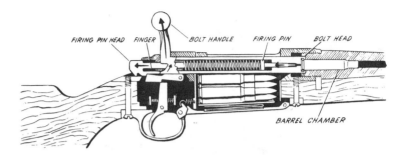

2. Moving bolt assembly back ejects the empty case. A circular spring in the end of the bolt (see detail) exerts pressure on the claw, holding the case tightly. When the mouth of the fired case clears the chamber, the spring-loaded ejector flips the case clear. The pressure of the magazine spring now raises a new cartridge to loading position.

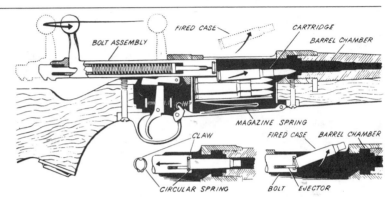

3. Moving bolt handle forward and turning it downward locks the bolt in the chamber and seals in the cartridge. The sear engages notch on firing-pin head, cocking the rifle. (Detail shows how bolt locks into barrel chamber.)

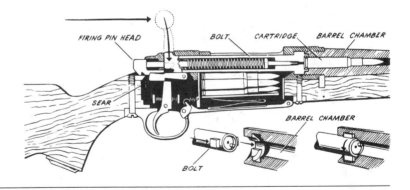

4. Pulling the trigger disengages sear from the notch on the firing-pin head. The main spring forces the firing pin forward, detonating the cartridge.

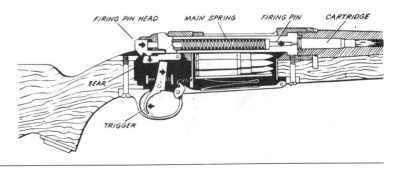

BOLT-ACTION RIFLES

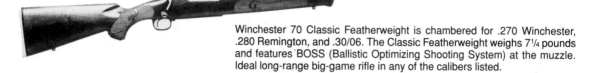

Winchester 70 Classic Featherweight is chambered for .270 Winchester, .280 Remington, and .30/06. The Classic Featherweight weighs 7¼ pounds and features BOSS (Ballistic Optimizing Shooting System) at the muzzle. Ideal long-range big-game rifle in any of the calibers listed.

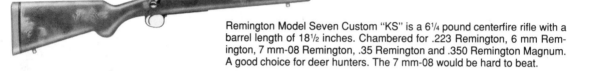

Remington Model Seven Custom "KS" is a 6¼ pound centerfire rifle with a barrel length of 18½ inches. Chambered for .223 Remington, 6 mm Remington, 7 mm-08 Remington, .35 Remington and .350 Remington Magnum. A good choice for deer hunters. The 7 mm-08 would be hard to beat.

Browning A-Bolt II Eclipse Varmint features laminated thumbhole-type stock with a heavy 22-inch barrel. Chambered in short-action calibers .308 Winchester, .22-.250 Remington, and .223 Remington, the model weighs 9 pounds. A well-designed varmint rifle.

Remington 700 MTN DM (Mountain Rifle Detachable Magazine) has a stainless steel detachable magazine and 22-inch barrel. Weighing 6½ pounds, the Model 700 is available from .243 Winchester to .30-.06. A good choice for western big game.

Ruger KM77RSP Mark II is offered in 22- and 24-inch barrel lengths with chambers ranging from .243 Winchester to .338 Winchester Magnum. A fine long-range, synthetic stocked, and stainless steel big-game rifle for all North American species and for all-weather hunting.

Weatherby Mark V Accumark, designed for extended-range accuracy, has a free-floating barrel and a recessed target crown. Weighing 8 pounds, the Mark V is available in Weatherby Magnum calibers from .257 to .340, 7 mm Remington Magnum, and .300 Winchester Magnum. A long-range, all-weather big-game rifle.

Marlin 882 rifle sports a 7-shot clip magazine. Chambered for .22 Magnum with a 22-inch Micro-Groove barrel, the Model 882 has a black walnut stock with Monte Carlo comb and weighs 6 pounds.

Savage 900B Biathlon Rifle, chambered for .22 Long Rifle, features five 5-shot clip magazines, clip holder mounted on stock, carrying and shooting rails, butt hook, and hand stop. This competition model weighs 8¼ pounds. Ideal for aspiring Olympic shooters.

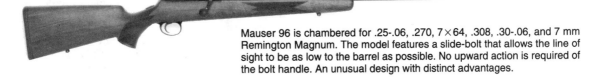

Mauser 96 is chambered for .25-.06, .270, 7×64, .308, .30-.06, and 7 mm Remington Magnum. The model features a slide-bolt that allows the line of sight to be as low to the barrel as possible. No upward action is required of the bolt handle. An unusual design with distinct advantages.

Anschutz Super Match International Model 1813 Free Rifle

For the target shooter, the Anschutz Model 1907 ISU Standard Match is typical of a finely designed target rifle. It is suitable for all National Rifle Association Matches and meets the requirements of the International Shooting Union. The 1907 Match weighs 11 pounds and has fully adjustable trigger pull. Chambered for .22 Long Rifle only, the rifle's receiver is grooved for micrometer iron sights.

Radical in design is the belt-action Anschutz Super Match International Model 1913 which comes under the classification of free-class rifle. Rifles of this type are used in Olympic and world championship shooting. Available in rimfire and centerfire calibers, such rifles have a heavy barrel, adjustable buttplate with hook, and an adjustable palm rest. A free rifle is drilled and tapped for receiver sights.

A shooter looking for a .22 bolt action for informal shooting and small-game hunting will have little trouble finding a model to fill his needs. There are three basic designs for the popular rimfire and the differences deal mainly with cartridge capacity.

The Marlin 15YN Little Buckaroo, for example, is a single-shot rifle ideal for beginners and youngsters. It is extremely safe. When the bolt is operated, the safety goes on automatically. Closing the bolt cocks it, of course, but the safety must then be moved to the off position before the rifle can be fired.

For those who want more ammunition in their guns, there are rifles such as the Ruger Model 77/22 which has a rotary clip magazine with a capacity of 10 cartridges. The bolt is simply operated to eject the spent cartridge and chamber a new round.

Another type of repeating bolt-action .22 employs a tubular magazine. The Marlin Model 881 is typical of this design. The tubular magazine holds 17 Long Rifles. Here again the bolt is operated to eject the empty case and chamber a new round.

Repeating rifles, such as the Marlin and Ruger models, are well suited for small game, varmint shooting, and plinking. The single-shot, which admittedly has limitations, comes into its own as a youngster's first rifle. All of these .22 rifles have a lot going for them. The rimfire cartridge has almost no recoil or loud muzzle blast to unnerve the shooter, making it easy for beginners to learn proper trigger squeeze and sight picture. Since the ammunition is relatively inexpensive, the .22 is also an intelligent investment for anyone who wants a rifle for informal target shooting and plinking.

LEVER ACTION

The lever-action rifle is deeply embedded in American history. Its design produced the first successful repeating rifle in America. It has been labeled "the gun that won the West," and it has become a favorite among deer hunters in the East and Northeast. Today, the smooth and fast lever gun has earned a permanent niche for itself in the hunting clan. Like any rifle design, however, the lever action has advantages and disadvantages. Let's examine the advantages first.

Though the lever gun is not as strong nor as accurate as the bolt-action rifle, it is faster to operate and easier to carry. Its narrow action and smooth lines make it an ideal scabbard gun for western hunters on horseback.

Combine the lever gun's quick handling for snap shots at moving game with the fact that most lever actions are generally chambered for medium-range deer cartridges and it's easy to understand why these rifles have also become a favorite among eastern and northeastern hunters, who get practically all their shots within 50 yards.

Another obvious advantage is that left-handed shooters can operate a lever action just as fast as a right-handed shooter. This is an important factor for the southpaw woods hunter to consider. Though he may have his heart set on a bolt action, he'd be better off with a lever gun, with which he can get off a second or third shot without lowering the rifle from his shoulder.

There are left-hand bolt-action rifles available, but they still cannot be handled from the shoulder as fast as a lever action. The left-handed bolt, however, is a good compromise for the woods hunter who may want to handload his own ammunition and supplement his deer trips with some varmint hunting and target shooting.

There is another advantage, though minor, that should at least be mentioned. The older-type lever actions, such as the Winchester 94 and the Marlin 336, offer an exposed hammer with half-cock safety. The safety is engaged by thumbing the hammer back halfway, where it locks in place. This is a convenient feature for cold-weather hunters who must wear heavy gloves and for left-handed shooters who find other safeties awkward to reach.

To fully cock the gun, the hammer is thumbed back all the way and the rifle is ready to be fired. If a hunter decides to pass up a shot, he simply holds the hammer with his thumb, depresses the trigger and eases the hammer forward to half-cock safety. The simplicity of the exposed hammer design is a distinct advantage to hunters who hunt only a few weeks a year and it's also a safety feature to look for when shopping for a youngster's first deer rifle.

The fast lever-action rifle, however, does have shortcomings. Most lever guns are fitted with two-piece stocks, and in general they are not as accurate as rifles with one-piece stocks. With some exceptions, the older-type lever actions are not strong enough to handle the high pressures of some modern cartridges, and they do not have the camming power to chamber and extract dirty or oversize cartridges.

The breech bolts in most lever guns don't lock at the head of the cartridge and the brass cases invariably stretch on firing. This makes lever actions a poor choice for handloaders. While these faults are of little concern to the occasional hunter, they are important factors to the more avid rifle shooter.

Now that both advantages and disadvantages of lever-action rifles have been discussed, let's talk about some of these typical guns presently on the market and how they may vary slightly in design.

The Winchester 94 is the most familiar lever action to hunters. It features side loading gate, tubular magazine, and exposed hammer with half-cock safety. In the carbine version, it measures 37¾ inches long and weighs about 6½ pounds. It is chambered for the .30/30 Winchester, a medium-class deer cartridge that can generally be expected to group at about 3½ inches at 100 yards. The model 94 is also available in .44 Remington Magnum, 7×30 Waters, .32 Winchester, .307 Winchester, and .356 Winchester.

The Winchester 94 makes a fine saddle gun where long ranges aren't encountered, and it is a handy

HOW A LEVER-ACTION RIFLE WORKS

1. Beginning with the rifle loaded and cocked, pulling the trigger releases the upper end of the trigger from the notch in the hammer, which springs forward and strikes the firing pin, which in turn detonates the cartridge.

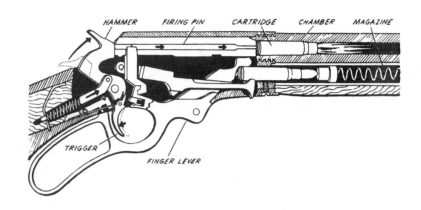

2. Moving the finger lever forward moves the locking bolt downward, disengaging it from the bolt, and the finger-lever tip engages slot in the bolt and moves it rearward. As the bolt slides back, an extractor hook pulls the fired case from the chamber and a spring-loaded ejector on the opposite side of the bolt ejects the case. The magazine spring pushes the cartridge onto the carrier and a cam on the finger lever moves carrier upward toward the barrel chamber.

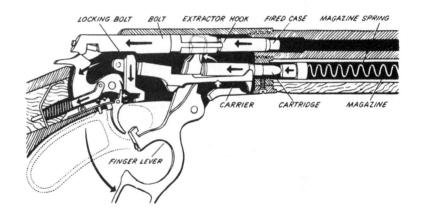

3. As the finger lever is moved to its forwardmost position and returned slightly, it engages a protruding pin on the carrier rocker and cams the carrier fully upward to the barrel chamber. As the finger lever is returned, its tip, which is engaged in the bolt slot, moves the bolt forward, pushing the cartridge into the chamber. Returning the finger lever to the stock raises the locking bolt to a matching notch in the bolt and aligns the safety firing pin (see Figure 1). The gun is now ready for firing.

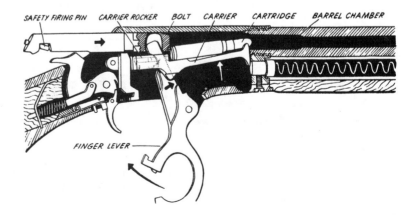

lightweight deer gun in the wooded areas of the East and Northeast where most shots are within 100 yards. The .30/30 is adequate for game the size of whitetails.

The handy little Model 94 that everyone loves to handle and shoot does have some drawbacks. It is not a long-range weapon and is not chambered for most modern high-velocity flat-shooting cartridges. Since cases tend to stretch in the action, it is not a good choice for a hunter who plans to handload his own ammunition. All these factors should be taken into consideration when making a selection.

Another popular lever action is the Marlin 336C. It is chambered for the .30/30 Winchester and .35 Remington, both good brush cartridges that do their work well at medium ranges. In weight, length, and features, the Marlin 336C is similar to the Winchester Model 94. There is, however, one difference. The Marlin has a solid top receiver and ejects its empty cases from the side. This feature permits low scope mounting over the receiver.

The Marlin 336C has roughly the same drawbacks as the Winchester 94. While it is an ideal saddle rifle and deer gun for brush hunters who get most shots at medium-size big game at short ranges, it is not a good choice for the hunter who may want to use his rifle for long shots in prairie and mountain country. Nor is the Marlin 336C chambered for cartridges recommended for big North American game, such as grizzlies, brown bears, moose, and elk.

The Marlin Model 444 should be mentioned here, since it is the world's most powerful lever-action rifle. Using the basic Marlin 336 action design, the rifle is chambered for the .444 Marlin, a shoulderless cartridge which uses a 240-grain bullet and develops a muzzle energy of 3,070 foot-pounds and a muzzle velocity of 2,400 feet per second.

Up to 100–150 yards, the Marlin 444 is deadly on the biggest North American game. At longer ranges, however, both velocity and energy drop rapidly. This comparatively new addition to the Marlin line of lever actions falls into a peculiar position. While it is certainly capable of flattening any vitally hit deer that crosses its path, the awesome cartridge is needlessly powerful for most deer hunters. Because velocity and energy drop off at longer ranges, it does not meet the requirements of a mountain rifle. Perhaps the Marlin 444 is most suitable in such places as Alaska and Canada, where big brown bears, grizzlies, and moose are frequently taken at medium ranges.

LEVER-ACTION RIFLES

Browning Lightning BLR is available in long and short action designs, and in eight calibers from .223 Remington to 7 mm Remington Magnum. Barrel length and weight vary among models. Good timber rifle for big game.

Winchester Model 9422 Trapper is chambered for .22 Long Rifle, but also handles Longs and Shorts interchangeably. Barrel length is 16½ inches. Weight is 5½ pounds. A good choice for small-game hunting, plinking, camping, and survival.

Marlin 1895SS is chambered for .45/70 Government. Weighing 7½ pounds, this model features a 4-shot tubular magazine and a 22-inch barrel with Micro-Groove rifling.

Savage 99C is available in .243 and .308 Winchester, with detachable box magazines. Quick-disconnect swivel studs and a Monte Carlo stock are features of this 7¾-pound model. An old favorite with Eastern deer hunters.

Marlin 39AS has a tubular magazine and is chambered for .22 Short, Long, or Long Rifle. Weighing 6½ pounds, the model has a 24-inch barrel with Micro-Groove rifling. Time-tested model for all small-game hunting and plinking.

Ruger Model 96 .44 Magnum has a detachable rotary magazine. Available in .22 Long Rifle, .22 WMR and .44 Magnum, the model has a 18½-inch barrel and weighs 5⅞ pounds.

Browning BL-22 Grade II is chambered for .22 Long, Short, or Long Rifle. Weight is 5 pounds, and barrel length is 20 inches. A 33-degree lever throw allows for quick chambering. Good for small game and plinking.

Next on the list of popular lever actions is the Savage Model 99, a rifle that is quite different from the Marlin and Winchester lever guns. The Savage 99 uses a rotary magazine and cartridges loaded from the top, much like a bolt action. In the late 1960s, however, Savage introduced one of its Model 99s with a clip magazine that can be removed from the rifle by pushing a release button on the side of the receiver.

The Model 99 ejects spent cartridges to the side, which makes the rifle suitable for scope use. While it is a hammerless lever action, the Model 99 has a cocking indicator forward of the tang safety.

The Model 99 has a very strong action and it was perhaps the first lever action to be offered in a range of calibers that would push bullets faster and flatter than the typical, round-nose deer cartridges.

As early as 1914, the Model 99 offered hunters the .250 Savage, which drove an 87-grain bullet 3,000 feet per second, a sensational speed at that time. At the time of this writing, the Savage Model 99 is being chambered only for the .243 and the .308. Over the years, however, it has been chambered for more than half a dozen calibers. In the future, other calibers will likely be added.

The .243 Winchester cartridge, for example, can be used on medium game in plains or mountain country where flat trajectory and high velocity are an asset.

In the 1970s, Browning introduced its BLR, a lever action with a detachable box magazine. Like the Savage, it could be chambered for a wider variety of cartridges than the more traditional lever actions which employ tubular magazines. A centerfire tubular-magazine lever action is not intended to handle cartridges with pointed bullets because of the possibility, however slim, that such a bullet could strike the cartridge ahead of it in the magazine and cause an accidental discharge if the rifle were dropped or severely jolted.

Moreover, the BLR has a rotary bolt with a very strong locking system that makes possible the chambering of modern high-velocity cartridges. It is now available in more calibers than any other lever action, ranging from .223 Remington to .30/06.

It is sufficient to say here that there are many good .22 lever-action rifles on the market. While they cannot be considered fine target rifles, the .22 lever guns are enjoyable to use for small-game hunting, plinking, and informal target shooting. Choice is largely a matter of personal preference and the price tag.

SLIDE, OR PUMP, ACTION

Stated simply, the slide, or pump, action is operated by a quick backward and forward movement of the forend. This action ejects the spent case, rechambers a fresh cartridge, and cocks the rifle for the next shot.

The pump's obvious advantages are that it can be reloaded manually from the shoulder and that it is faster than a lever action. It is also a handy brush and timber rifle. The hunter accustomed to pump shotguns will also find this type of rifle a natural to use.

The pump has drawbacks, however. It has a two-piece stock and is therefore not as accurate as a bolt action. In addition, the pump's mechanism is not strong enough to chamber and eject handloaded ammunition whose cases have not been resized to original tolerances. The pump is not a good choice for the hunter looking for maximum accuracy and a rifle that will really take all handloads.

This pump is a good choice, though, for the deer hunter who puts a great deal of faith in getting off a fast second shot in heavy cover, does not use handloaded ammunition, and uses a pump shotgun on gamebirds and small game.

Remington is one manufacturer that turns out pump-action rifles in a variety of calibers. Remington offers three grades of its old Model 7600. This model is chambered for .243, .270, .280 Remington, .30/06, and .308. With these calibers, there are pumps suitable for game ranging from coyotes to moose.

This Remington has a detachable four-shot clip magazine and weighs about 7½ pounds. It has a solid top and ejects cases from the side, two features which make this good for scope mounting.

In the .22 class, the pump action has definitely made a place for itself among small-game hunters and plinkers. While it is definitely outclassed on the target range by bolt actions, the little .22 pump and its firepower has taken more than its share of cottontails, squirrels, pests, and other small game. Nearly all of the modern .22 pumps have tubular magazines, side ejection, and are grooved for tip-off scope mounting. These pumps are an excellent choice for hunters who want to add an all-purpose .22 to their gun racks.

HOW A PUMP-ACTION RIFLE WORKS

1. Moving the forend rearward pushes back the action bar and the bolt assembly, which in turn moves the hammer downward and ejects the empty case. Ejection is accomplished by a circular spring in the end of the bolt (see detail, showing top view) with a claw which hooks under rim of the cartridge and pulls it out of the chamber. When the case clears the chamber, the ejector spring in the bolt flips the case out. Then the magazine spring moves a new cartridge upward.

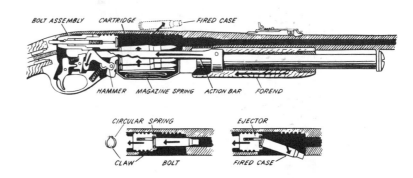

2. Moving the forend forward locks the cartridge in the barrel chamber. The notch in the sear holds the hammer so that the rifle is cocked. As the bolt carrier is moved forward, the threads on the bolt contact the locking lugs (see detail). Continued movement of the bolt carrier causes the cam pin on the carrier to engage a curved slot in the bolt, turning the bolt and threading it into locking lugs.

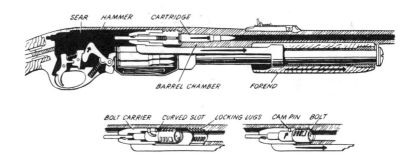

3. Pulling the trigger disengages the sear from notch on the hammer. The main spring forces the hammer against the firing pin, detonating the cartridge. The safety lock and a disconnecting device, which prevents the rifle from going off until the action is closed, is not shown to allow maximum clarity.

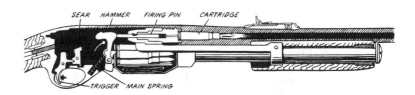

PUMP-ACTION RIFLES

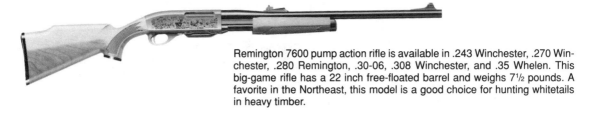

Remington 7600 pump action rifle is available in .243 Winchester, .270 Winchester, .280 Remington, .30-06, .308 Winchester, and .35 Whelen. This big-game rifle has a 22 inch free-floated barrel and weighs 7½ pounds. A favorite in the Northeast, this model is a good choice for hunting whitetails in heavy timber.

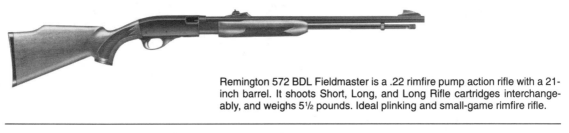

Remington 572 BDL Fieldmaster is a .22 rimfire pump action rifle with a 21-inch barrel. It shoots Short, Long, and Long Rifle cartridges interchangeably, and weighs 5½ pounds. Ideal plinking and small-game rimfire rifle.

Rossi 62 SA pump action is chambered for .22 Long Rifle and .22 WMR. This pump action weighs 6¼ pounds. Features quick takedown 23-inch round or octagonal barrel. A good choice for plinking and small game.

SEMI-AUTOMATIC OR AUTOLOADING RIFLE

The basic requirements of a good hunting rifle are accuracy, reliability, and safety. The semi-automatic or autoloading rifles do not meet these requirements as well as other rifle actions available to shooters.

In discussing the semi-automatics and autoloaders, we shall simply refer to them as automatics, since this is what they are most often called by shooters. It should be made clear, however, that semi-automatics and autoloaders are not fully automatic, which means that they do not continue to fire as long as the trigger is held back. Such a rifle would, in effect, be a machine gun. Fully automatic rifles are not on the sporting market today and their possession by unauthorized personnel is prohibited by federal law.

Since no manual operation of any lever, bolt, or slide is required with an automatic after the first shot, the biggest advantage of such a rifle has to be firepower. Those quick second or third shots can

sometimes mean meat in the pot for hunters in heavy timber or brushy areas. The automatic's usefulness, however, seems restricted to such conditions.

The advantage of firepower can also be a double-edged sword. A big-game hunter, knowing he has only to squeeze the trigger again to send another bullet on its way, may well present a dangerous situation in the woods. For reasons which we will not analyze here, there is a tendency for some users of automatics to empty their clips at fleeing big game after missing that first important shot. This, obviously, is dangerous in thickly wooded areas where other hunters are around. Several states, in fact, prohibit the use of automatics for big-game hunting.

The automatic falls short on other counts. It is not as accurate as the bolt action. It is a poor choice for hunters who may have to take big game or varmints at long range. The automatic design is also tough on cases and tosses them far from the shooter, so it is also a poor choice for the handloader. The gas-operated automatic is not a simple mechanism and is more likely to have malfunctions than other types of rifle actions. The hunter heading into a remote area for an extended hunt would be better off with a bolt action.

While there are some variations to the design of the automatic, these rifles still rely on one of two sources of power for their operation—recoil or gas. Both systems will be explained here very briefly. Readers interested in a detailed treatment of automatic-rifle design can find this information in any specialized gun book.

The recoil system, or blow-back, utilizes a breechblock that is held against the head of the case by a spring. When a cartridge is fired, the breechblock moves to the rear, against spring tension, and ejects the fired case. As the spring moves the breechblock forward, it cocks the rifle and picks up and chambers a fresh round.

Two examples of modern rifles that use this re-

coil, or blow-back, mechanism are the Browning Auto-22, a full-size .22 that holds 15 Long Rifle cartridges in a tubular magazine under the barrel; and the Ruger 10/22, a small-game and plinking rifle that features a 10-shot detachable magazine that fits flush into the stock. Both rifles are effective field guns in the hands of those familiar with firearms. An automatic is not recommended as a young shooter's first gun. It is not for beginners.

Since the blow-back system used in these and nearly all other .22 automatics does not have a locking breechblock, the design is somewhat limited to rimfire and centerfire cartridges that develop low pressures. There are some modified blow-back designs, such as retarded blow-back, short recoil, and long recoil systems. It is sufficient to say here, however, that they all rely on the same basic principle for their operation.

HOW AN AUTOLOADING RIFLE WORKS

1. Beginning with rifle loaded and cocked, pulling the trigger disengages the sear from notch on the hammer. The hammer spring forces the hammer against the firing pin, exploding the cartridge. After the bullet passes the port, residual gases are metered downward through the barrel opening into the impulse chamber located in the forend.

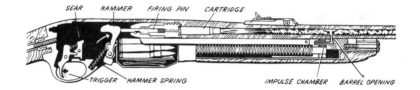

2. Gases force the action bar and bolt assembly rearward, compressing the action spring, pushing down the hammer and ejecting the empty case. Further rearward travel of the bolt permits the next cartridge to raise into the path of the returning bolt. The ejection mechanism (see detail, showing top view) is the same as in the pump action.

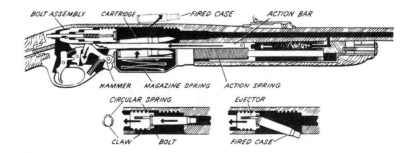

HOW AN AUTOLOADING RIFLE WORKS (Continued)

3. Compressed action spring moves the action bar and bolt assembly forward, causing multiple lugs to lock the bolt into place (see detail also), sealing the cartridge tightly in the barrel chamber. The notch in the sear holds the hammer in cocked position. Pulling the trigger sets the weapon in motion as in the first diagram. The safety lock and a disconnecting device, which prevents the rifle from going off until the action is closed, is not shown to allow maximum clarity.

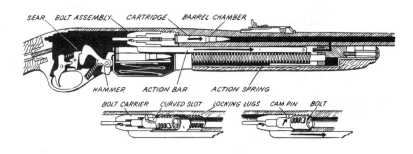

AUTOLOADING RIFLES

Browning Bar Mark II Safari is available in .30-06, .270, .308, and .203 Winchester, and has a 22-inch barrel and weighs 7½ pounds. Magnum Models with 24-inch barrels are chambered for .338 Winchester Magnum, .300 Winchester Magnum, and 7 mm Remington Magnum.

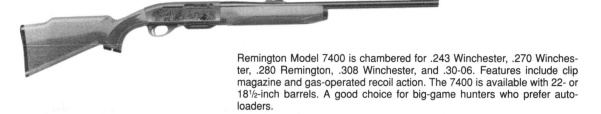

Remington Model 7400 is chambered for .243 Winchester, .270 Winchester, .280 Remington, .308 Winchester, and .30-06. Features include clip magazine and gas-operated recoil action. The 7400 is available with 22- or 18½-inch barrels. A good choice for big-game hunters who prefer auto-loaders.

Savage 64G, chambered for .22 Long Rifle, comes with a 10-shot detachable clip magazine. This semi-automatic model weighs 5½ pounds with a 20¼-inch barrel.

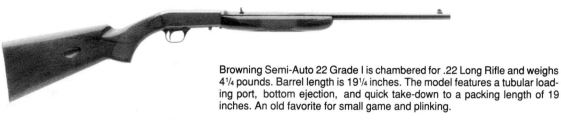

Browning Semi-Auto 22 Grade I is chambered for .22 Long Rifle and weighs 4¼ pounds. Barrel length is 19¼ inches. The model features a tubular loading port, bottom ejection, and quick take-down to a packing length of 19 inches. An old favorite for small game and plinking.

Remington 522 Viper is chambered for .22 Long Rifle. Features 10-round magazine clip, grooved scope mounting rail, and synthetic stock. This autoloader weighs 4⅝ pounds. Good survival gun.

Marlin 60 is chambered for .22 Long Rifle and has a 22-inch barrel. Weighing 5½ pounds, this autoloader features a tubular magazine.

Gas-operated centerfire automatics are quite different in design. In these rifles, a hole is drilled through the barrel to channel off gas from the first shot to provide power to work the action. Here is how it works. After that first bullet passes over the hole in the barrel, gasses enter the hole and go into a piston chamber in the forend. The piston forces a rod that unlocks the breech bolt and pushes it to the rear to eject the spent case and recock the rifle. At this point, a recoil spring takes over. The spring drives the breech bolt, rod, and piston forward. On this forward movement, a new cartridge is picked up and chambered for the next shot.

Because these gas-operated automatics have a breech bolt with lugs that lock at the head of the case, these rifles can handle cartridges that develop very high pressures. One example is the magnum version of the Browning Bar Mark II, which is chambered for the 7mm Remington and .300 Winchester Magnum cartridges. The standard version of this rifle, called the High-Power Auto, is available in .243, .270, and .308 Winchester, as well as .30/06 Springfield.

Remington's Model 7400 is another example of an autoloader designed for high-pressure big-game cartridges. It is chambered for the .270, the .243 and .308 Winchester, and the old standard .30/06. Like

the Browning, it features a detachable box magazine. The Remington is available in a standard and deluxe grade.

If you choose an automatic rifle for big game, after weighing all the advantages and disadvantages, you can't go wrong by selecting one of the rifles covered in this section. All are as reliable and accurate as an automatic can be. Among the various models, you'll also find a range of calibers from flat-shooting high-velocity loads to the big magnums.

SINGLE-SHOTS

The single-shot fills many outdoor needs and it is disappointing to see that so little attention is given to these firearms in the typical gun book. True, the single-shot may never find a place among most hunters of deer and bigger game, but this type of rifle has many uses—and it should be remembered that such activities as one-shot antelope hunts have gained well-deserved prestige and popularity in recent years.

Most, but not all, single-shot rifles are either .22 Rimfire bolt actions or break actions. These .22s come into their own as a beginner's gun, a utility gun, a plinking gun, a trapper's and farmer's gun or, where the laws allow, as part of a camper's gear. Because they are not specialized guns, they fill a variety of needs. Moreover, they are inexpensive. The exceptions to those last two statements are the very specialized and usually expensive .22 single-shot bolt actions used for international target competition—chiefly, free-rifle matches. (The word "free" here refers to a lack of restrictions on sophisticated features such as adjustable buttstock, palm rest, barrel weights, light trigger pull, and so on.)

Of more interest to average American shooters are the ordinary, inexpensive single-shots, some with full-size stocks for adults and others in scaled-down versions for youngsters. Some of these rifles cock when a round is chambered; others must be cocked manually after the action is closed, and some have automatic safeties. The Chipmunk is a bolt-action rifle that features a safety that goes on automatically when the bolt is operated.

Remington's Model 581-S might be called a repeater/single-shot. This .22 Rimfire bolt action is a repeater with a six-shot clip. It comes with a single-shot adapter. With the adapter in place, only one cartridge can be loaded, making it ideal for the novice. After experience has been gained, the 581-S can be converted into a repeater by removing the adapter.

Another type of single-shot manufactured in the United States is the break action, or top-breaking action. Few single-shots of this sort are available today. One is the New England Firearms Handi Rifle, which is available in six rifle calibers and 24 shotgun configurations. These rifle calibers provide more power and longer range than the rimfires, of course, so this model fares well as a versatile, inexpensive gun for a variety of game—birds with the smoothbore; small game, chucks or deer.

Depending on caliber, a single-shot can take small game, pronghorns, deer, sheep, black bears—in fact, quite a few species of game, large and small. The demand for good single-shots in a wide choice of calibers was recognized by the Sturm, Ruger Company back in 1966, when Bill Ruger introduced the No. 1 Single Shot Rifle. Inspired by the fine old Farquharson action, the Ruger No. 1 has an underlever that operates a falling-block action. It is chambered for calibers ranging from .218 Bee to .458 Winchester Magnum.

Models like the Ruger are rugged, accurate rifles. Mounted with carefully selected scope sights, such arms are more than adequate for big game, as well as the varmint species. Traditionally, sheep hunters favor bolt-action repeaters, but some hunters have found these single-shots to be very handy for mountain hunting because, with game such as sheep, the first shot should count.

SINGLE-SHOT RIFLES

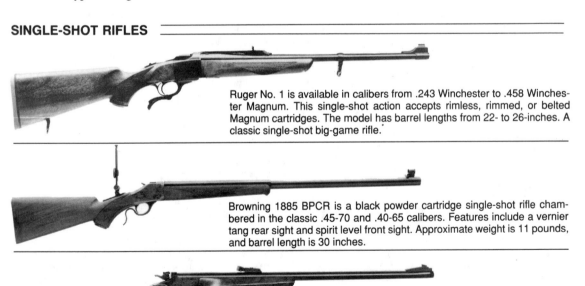

Ruger No. 1 is available in calibers from .243 Winchester to .458 Winchester Magnum. This single-shot action accepts rimless, rimmed, or belted Magnum cartridges. The model has barrel lengths from 22- to 26-inches. A classic single-shot big-game rifle.

Browning 1885 BPCR is a black powder cartridge single-shot rifle chambered in the classic .45-70 and .40-65 calibers. Features include a vernier tang rear sight and spirit level front sight. Approximate weight is 11 pounds, and barrel length is 30 inches.

Thompson/Center Contender Carbine features interchangeable barrels handling up to 12 cartridge options from .22 Long Rifle to .375 Winchester. The standard model has a 21-inch barrel and weighs 5¹/₅ pounds. A good survival and camp gun.

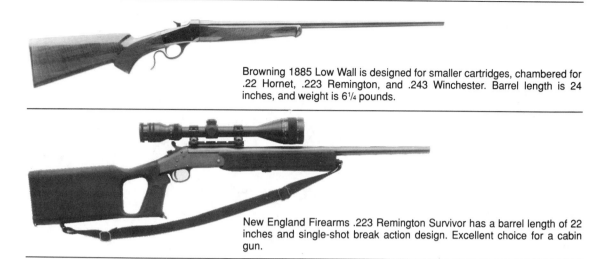

Browning 1885 Low Wall is designed for smaller cartridges, chambered for .22 Hornet, .223 Remington, and .243 Winchester. Barrel length is 24 inches, and weight is 6¼ pounds.

New England Firearms .223 Remington Survivor has a barrel length of 22 inches and single-shot break action design. Excellent choice for a cabin gun.

DOUBLES AND COMBINATION GUNS

The double rifle, in simplest terms, is a double-barreled shotgun action with a strengthened frame, two rifle barrels, and iron sights. It can and has been chambered for a wide range of calibers, from .22 to .470. Because it has no long receiver, the double is short, handy, and fast. In fact, it is the fastest two-shot high-power rifle made.

These features would appear to make the double a dream gun for North American big game taken at medium ranges, but such is not the case. It is extremely unlikely that a double-barreled rifle will ever be manufactured in the United States. Even in England, where most doubles are made, they are generally available only on special order. And in Africa and India, where the double rifle earned a reputation for stopping dangerous game, it has been on the wane for some time. It is being replaced by strong bolt actions, such as the Winchester Model 70 Express Magnum and Remington Model 700 Safari, both chambered for the .458 Winchester Magnum, and the Weatherby Mark V in .460 Magnum.

The biggest reason for the decrease in the double rifle is its high cost of manufacture. Getting both barrels aligned so that they place their bullets at the same point-of-aim, usually 80 or 100 yards, is a tedious and expensive task. It is done by repeated shooting and regulating of a wedge between the barrels until the bullets from both barrels have the same point of impact. The double is also two rifles with two sets of locks and two triggers. What all this means to the hunter is that a good double-bar-reled rifle may have a price tag ranging anywhere from $5,000 to $35,000.

In addition to high cost, the double has other drawbacks. The ejectors frequently lack the power to pull or toss out stretched or dirty cases. And once a double is sighted for one particular load, other loads cannot be effectively used. As for accuracy, the doubles cannot compete with the comparatively new strong bolt-action repeaters built today. The double rifle has a romantic background, but it cannot be considered a practical firearm for the American hunter.

Combination guns are an interesting breed of rifle and shotgun. Longtime favorites in Europe, they are slowly becoming more popular in the United States. In areas where hunting seasons overlap and laws permit, the combination gun can be a good choice. It can also fill in as an off-season gun for plinking, chuck hunting, crow shooting, and so on.

Basically, there are eight types of combination guns: a rifle barrel under two shotgun barrels, an over/under shotgun and rifle combination, a shotgun barrel and two rifle barrels below and to the side, a four-barreled model with two shotgun barrels side by side and two rifle barrels underneath, a double-barreled rifle with a shotgun barrel underneath, an over/under shotgun with a rifle barrel to the side, a side-by-side double-barreled shotgun with rifle barrel on top, and a side-by-side shotgun and rifle combination.

Several of these combination guns are of uncommon design and rarely seen today. They are generally of European origin, most being built in Germany. It is interesting to note, however, that so

COMBINATION-GUN BARREL CONFIGURATIONS

 Over/under, shotgun on top, rifle under.

 Over/under shotgun with rifle at side.

 Shotgun on top with rifles under and at side.

 Side-by-side shotgun with rifle on top.

 Side-by-side rifle and shotgun.

 Side-by-side shotgun with rifle under.

 Side-by-side shotgun with two rifles under.

 Side-by-side double rifle with shotgun under.

DOUBLES AND COMBINATION GUNS

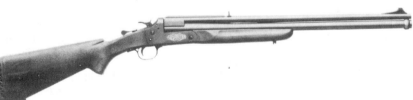

Savage 24F can match a 20 or 12 gauge shotgun with .22 Long Rifle, .22 Hornet, .223 Remington, or .30-30 Winchester. The 12 gauge models come with Full, Modified, and Improved Cylinder choke tubes, and the 20 gauge sports a Modified barrel. Barrel length is 24 inches, and weight is 8 pounds. An excellent choice for an all-around survival and camp gun.

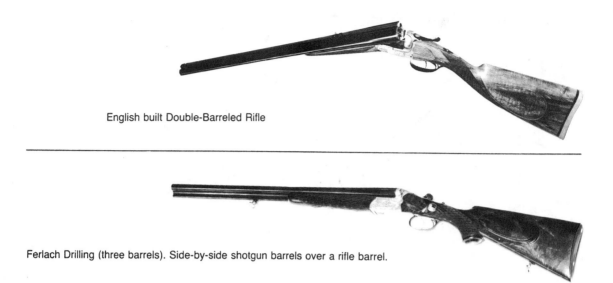

English built Double-Barreled Rifle

Ferlach Drilling (three barrels). Side-by-side shotgun barrels over a rifle barrel.

many combinations have been conceived by gun builders.

Unfortunately, nearly all European combination guns and drillings (any three-barreled combination) are quite expensive. Ferlach, for example, manufactures an over/under offering a choice of three shotgun gauges in the top barrel and more than seven rifle calibers in the bottom barrel. This particular Ferlach, labeled Turkey Gun, can be ordered with 12-gauge barrels on top and a .30/06 barrel underneath. Such a rifle could be quite useful to the deer hunter who may also want to take a grouse or two on the same hunt. Or the shotgun barrel could be loaded with buckshot for the big buck that often bursts out of the brush and offers only a fast snap shot. The chief drawback is that imported combination guns like the Ferlach cost about four times as much as an average American hunter pays for a rifle or shotgun. Ferlach and a few other European firms also build typical drillings—three-barreled combinations, usually with two smoothbores side by side and a rifle barrel underneath.

There are several other European firms offering such combination guns. Hege, a German manufacturer, makes a boxlock over/under and the purchaser can choose between 12- and 20-gauge for the top barrel and .222 or .30/06 for the bottom barrel. Voere makes a combination gun with a single 20-gauge barrel on top and .222, .222 Magnum, or .223 for the bottom barrel. Krieghoff produces a model with side-by-side 12-gauge barrels over a rifle barrel that can be had in .30/06 or 7mm Magnum.

At one time, drillings were made in the United

States, but the manufacture of combination guns in this country has always been limited to very few companies. Savage Arms is the only major American firm that has continued to build and improve an over/under rifle-shotgun combination. Its early models wore a .22 barrel over a .410. Today, Savage has a series of these guns, the Model 24s, with the rifle barrel chambered for .22 Rimfire, .22 Hornet, .223 Remington, and .30/30 Winchester. The lower, smooth-bore barrel is made in 12 and 20-gauge.

A break-action design, the Savage combination is grooved for scope mounts. The older Model 24s have a barrel-selector button on the side of the receiver. Today's 24s have a spur on the hammer for barrel selection. Prices depend on grade and specifications, but all of the 24s are priced far below the European combination guns.

Scope mounted, the Savage 24 makes an ideal turkey and varmint gun. It's fine for plinking and a good gun for camp, one that would earn its keep by providing small game and birds for the pot. For the farmer, it will keep pests under control. And, should the occasion arise, the Savage 24 could fill in as an ideal survival weapon. It provides the shooter with a choice of a bullet or shot to take game. When not in use, the Savage 24 takes down and stows easily.

MUZZLELOADING RIFLE

Muzzleloaders were pushed into obsolescence by breechloaders long before the end of the 19th century, yet the old "frontloaders" were never quite buried by progress. Their revival began in the 1930s,

MUZZLELOADER NOMENCLATURE

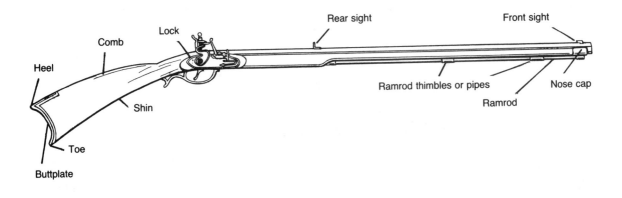

gained staggering momentum in the 1960s, and is still growing at a phenomenal rate. One reason is the interest of many Americans in the ways of our forefathers. Another is the challenge of using "primitive" firearms. Probably most important of all is a kind of sporting contagion—word-of-mouth promotion by people who have discovered the fun of shooting muzzleloaders.

These shooters have their own organization, the National Muzzle Loading Rifle Association, with several hundred affiliated clubs. National and interclub competitions include offhand shooting, shooting from a rest, flintlock matches, even precision shooting with the big benchrest muzzleloading rifles like those of the late 1800s. In addition to rifle matches, there are events for muskets, shotguns, and handguns. Most colorful of all are the primitive matches, in which competitors dress in frontier clothing of a bygone era and test not only their shooting ability but other skills such as tomahawk throwing and firebuilding with flint and steel.

Another form of competition is promoted by the North/South Skirmish Association, which holds regional and national matches. Teams from both sides of the Mason-Dixon Line name themselves after military units that fought the Civil War. There are individual matches, but the most colorful and interesting are the team events. At the bigger shoots, hundreds of participants all fire at the same time, working against the clock to hit a specified number of breakable targets. Cannon competition is a bonus that leaves spectators gaping. The din and smoke are unforgettable.

Hunting with muzzleloaders has also gained im-

mense popularity. Nearly all the states have special deer seasons for muzzleloaders, and other states permit their use during the regular deer season. Many other kinds of game are also hunted with these old-fashioned guns. The muzzleloaders now available are capable of taking all North American game. However, the smaller calibers (.30 to .45) should be limited to small game. Bores from .50 up are best for deer and heavier game such as bears, elk, and moose. Many states stipulate a minimum bore size for deer or big game.

In accuracy, a good muzzleloading rifle is the equal of a cartridge rifle at moderate range, but trajectory is a problem. A typical muzzleloader for deer hunting has a muzzle velocity of about 2,000 feet per second when a .50 caliber ball is seated over 110 grains of black powder. With the rifle sighted-in to zero at 50 yards, this ball will be about 4 inches low at 100 yards. Sighted to hit 2 inches high at 50 yards, it will be a close 2 inches low at 100.

Three basic types of muzzleloaders are in general use today: the flintlock, the caplock or percussion cap, and the in-line ignition system. To load a flintlock, the proper charge of black powder is first poured down the bore. The shooter then seats a precut, lubricated patch and ball over the muzzle. Using a starter—typically a short dowel with a round handle—the patched ball is moved down into the barrel. With a ramrod, it is pushed the rest of the way down until it is seated firmly against the powder. A small amount of very fine black powder (usually the granulation designated as FFFFg) is dropped into the pan; this is the printer. The pan cover, or frizzen, is closed. Instead of the more

FIRING MECHANISM OF A FLINTLOCK

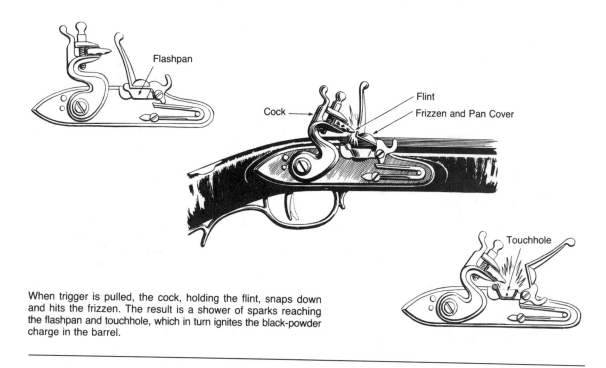

When trigger is pulled, the cock, holding the flint, snaps down and hits the frizzen. The result is a shower of sparks reaching the flashpan and touchhole, which in turn ignites the black-powder charge in the barrel.

Knight MK85 Predator is typical of in-line ignition muzzleloaders. This hunters' model is available in .50 and .54 calibers.

modern hammer, this action employs a flint held in a cock. When the cock is pulled all the way back, it is ready to fire. At the pull of the trigger, the cock is released and the flint strikes the frizzen a glancing blow, producing a shower of sparks to ignite the fine powder in the flashpan. The flash goes through a small touchhole to ignite the main charge and fire the piece.

With a caplock gun, the percussion cap performs the same function as a modern primer in a cartridge. The cap is seated on a nipple at the end of a little tube leading into the barrel. When the hammer falls, it ignites the priming compound in the cap, driving sparks down the tube to the powder charge. The loading process is the same with a percussion gun as with a flintlock, except that the cap replaces the loose priming charge and flashpan—and the hammer

replaces the cock and flint. Caplock rifles are more popular for hunting than flintlocks. The caps are faster and more convenient to use than loose priming powder; there is no need to replace flints; and ignition is faster and surer with a caplock.

Operating the striker mechanism of an in-line ignition muzzleloader is as straightforward as you can get. The striker is cocked and held rearward, locked in place when the thumb safely is in the rearward position. By sliding the thumb safety forward, the striker is free to fire the percussion cap when the trigger is pulled.

A couple of decades ago, most of the muzzleloaders in use were originals, reconditioned and tested for safety and functional reliability. But antique arms are often too valuable to be taken into the field, and the supply of shootable originals dwindled as muzzleloading gained unprecedented popularity. During the 1960s, a few imported replicas became available, and in the United States custom and semicustom makers were busy filling orders for new muzzleloaders. By the early 1970s, muzzle-loaders were being mass-produced both here and abroad. Today the array is staggering. Moreover, many of the guns are available either finished or in kit form for budget-minded do-it-yourselfers. And the custom makers are still producing finely crafted muzzleloaders—both replicas and new but authentically traditional designs.

Among the mass-produced models, the Hawken, made by Thompson/Center Arms, is probably one of the most popular. A very well-made half-stock percussion rifle, it is certainly not a true replica of the famous Hawken for which it's named, but it *is* certainly a rugged, dependable firearm. It's available in .45, .50, or .54 caliber and features a 28-inch octagonal barrel. It weighs about 8½ pounds.

CVA (Connecticut Valley Arms) builds the St. Louis Hawken Classic Rifle in .50 and .54 calibers. Weights are comparable to those of the Hawkens. This rifle, too, has double-set triggers that can be used set or unset.

Dixie Gun Works can be called a pioneer in this field. The company started importing muzzleloaders in the 1950s. Today, the Dixie catalog is crammed with everything a muzzleloading enthusiast would ever need, including accessories, parts, kits, and finished guns. Dixie's Tennessee Mountain Rifle is a full-stock model patterned after the long rifles of the late flint and early percussion era. Its .50 or .32 caliber octagonal barrel is 41½ inches long and ⅞ inch across the flats. Like the originals of this distinctive type, it has browned-iron hardware. You can choose flint or percussion.

Lyman, a company that offers a vast assortment of shooting products, is in this muzzleloading business, too. Lyman's Great Plains Rifle, though not billed as a Hawken replica, is a percussion half-stock that's quite representative of the guns once used by the men engaged in the Western fur trade. It has browned-steel hardware and comes in .50 or .54. A good example of the newer in-line ignition muzzleloaders is Knight's MK-85 Hunter. It weighs seven pounds. The MK-85 is available in .50 and .54 caliber. It is also available blued or in stainless steel and with wood or synthetic stock.

The muzzleloading rifles described here are only a sampling of currently popular models. Companies that make or import muzzleloaders also include Armsport, Euroarms, Mitchell Arms, Shiloh Sharps, Traditions, and Knight.

FIRING MECHANISM OF A CAPLOCK

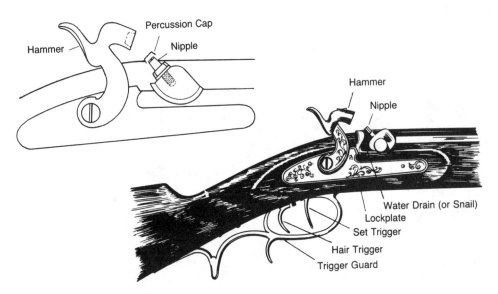

Simplified drawing, above left, shows percussion firing mechanism. When hammer hits percussion cap, the flash travels through hollow nipple to ignite the powder charge.

MUZZLELOADING RIFLES

Remington Model 700 MLS black powder rifle features a modified bolt and an in-line ignition system. The Model 700 has a barrel length of 24 inches and weighs 7¾ pounds. Available in .45, .50, and .54 calibers.

Thompson/Center Renegade Cap Lock Rifle is available in .50 and .54 calibers. Weighing 8 pounds, this big-game model features a 26-inch barrel with a 1 in 48-inch twist. Ideal for hunters who prefer original percussion cap mechanisms.

Dixie Gun Works Deerslayer Rifle has a 28¼-inch barrel that handles .50 caliber balls or conical bullets. Available in flintlock or percussion cap models. One of the few flintlock options available today.

CVA PR4510 Buckmaster is a .50 caliber in-line ignition muzzleloader with a 24-inch barrel. Other features include oversize trigger guard, swivel studs, and camofinish. The Buckmaster weighs 6½ pounds. A good choice for beginners in black-powder hunting.

Thompson/Center .50 caliber rifle with in-line ignition offers a one-piece breech for faster ignition time and a striker handle for simple, quiet action. The model weighs 7 pounds and has a 24-inch barrel.

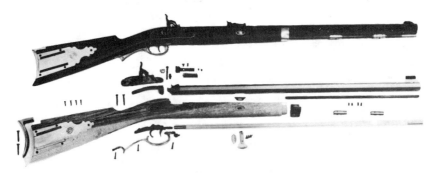

Typical finished gun and kit

Muzzleloading Precautions. Safety is a paramount concern when using any firearm, and extra precautions are mandatory with muzzleloaders. If the shooter wishes to use an old muzzleloader rather than a new one, it should not be fired until it has been inspected for safety—and serviced, if necessary—by a gunsmith who is familiar with black-powder guns. Otherwise, such a gun may be unsafe.

In addition to possibly dangerous defects, an old gun is often encountered with a load left in the barrel. This has even been known to happen with modern muzzleloaders. *Because the load is unknown, it should never be fired*. The bullet or ball should be pulled and the charge removed.

A common practice with percussion guns is to fire a cap, without any powder or ball, to clear the nipple of excess oil; but this should be done only after the barrel is cleared to the breech.

Powder for Muzzleloaders. Another precaution concerns the proper powder. Nothing but black powder or Pyrodex should be used in a muzzleloader. The term "black powder" in this context does not refer to color in the usual sense, because most gunpowder is black or gray. The modern powders used in cartridges can be extremely dangerous in a muzzleloader. The kind to use is the powder that comes in cans labeled "Black Powder" by the manufacturer.

The one exception is Pyrodex, a propellant recently developed for use in black-powder guns. Its burning rate and pressure curve closely follow the characteristics of black powder, but Pyrodex is safer to ship and store, and it has become more readily available through retail outlets. Its only disadvantage is that it doesn't ignite well in flintlocks.

Black powder comes in various granulations. The

HUNTER'S BLACK-POWDER BAG

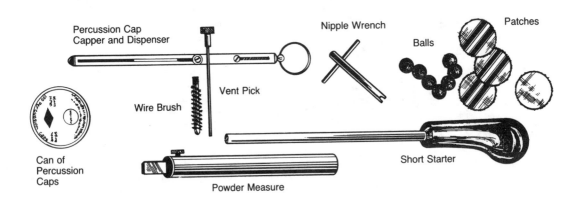

HOW TO LOAD A MUZZLELOADING PERCUSSION CAP OR FLINTLOCK RIFLE

By Rick Hacker

The procedure of loading black-powder rifles can be difficult and time consuming to hunters not familiar with their use. The margin for error is much greater than with modern centerfire rifles—and it may cost you a trophy if you don't load correctly with consistent measures of powder. Follow each of the steps below in the proper sequence. If your muzzleloader is new, read the manufacturer's specific directions for that gun.

1   **2 A**   **2 B**

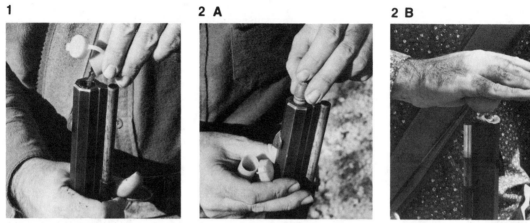

1. After popping a cap or snapping the flintlock on a pan of 4f powder to burn out any excess oil from your *unloaded* rifle, pour a pre-measured charge down the tube. Keep your hand away from the open bore. **2a.** For conical bullets, take a pre-greased conical from your loading tube and press it into the bore, at least up to the first grease groove. Make sure the projectile is not at an angle to the bore. **2b.** For round ball, center the ball over a precut patch or on a piece of pre-lubed patching material. Give a sharp rap to your short starter, which will seat the ball down into the muzzle. If using untrimmed patching material, as shown, trim the excess away with a knife so that the patched ball is flush with the muzzle of the rifle.

3   **4 A**   **4 B**

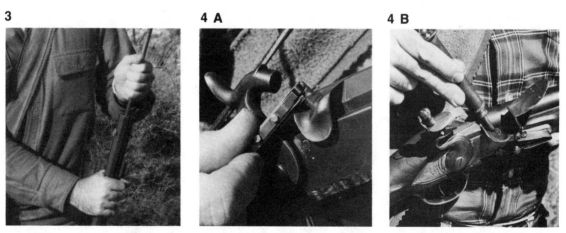

3. Place the buttstock on your foot to avoid damaging the buttplate, and ram the projectile firmly all the way down so that it is resting tightly against your powder charge. Do not leave any air space between the ball and the powder or you could bulge your barrel upon firing. When ramming, keep your hand close to the muzzle to avoid breaking your ramrod. **4a.** For percussions, place a cap firmly on the nipple. You may wish to pinch the ends of the cap slightly to keep it from falling off, but be sure it is not so tight that it cannot be easily removed after firing. **4b.** For flintlocks, the final step before firing is to prime the pan. Put in just enough 4f powder to cover the bottom of the pan, reaching a level slightly below the touchhole.

letters Fg identify the coarsest black powder available. The granulations most commonly used in muzzleloaders are FFg and FFFg. The finest granulation, FFFFg, ignites rapidly and is therefore used to prime the pan of a flintlock.

Accessories. Since a cartridge is literally assembled in a muzzleloader for each shot, a shooter must carry tools and equipment. A small toolbox or tackle box can hold what's needed on a rifle range. Its contents should include:

- Rifle balls or other suitable projectiles
- Percussion caps or flints
- Patches or patch material
- Patch lubricant
- Black powder of suitable granulation or Pyrodex
- Priming powder for a flintlock
- Extra nipples for a caplock
- Adjustable powder measure
- Knife for trimming patches
- Short starter
- Ramrod (extra-long for range use)
- "Worm" for pulling lost patches from bore
- Ball or bullet puller
- Cleaning patches
- Cleaning solvent
- Rust-preventive oil
- Pliers
- Screwdrivers
- Brass or copper drift for sight adjustments
- Light hammer
- Nipple wrench for a caplock

The muzzleloading hunter seldom carries all those items. He wants to travel light, and he's better off carrying his equipment in a shoulder pouch, called a "possibles bag." What it contains is up to the hunter, but only real necessities should be carried. These include enough balls or other projectiles for the day's hunt, a few caps in a capper for a percussion gun, an extra flint or two for a flintlock, patching for both ball and cleaning, a patch knife, and a short starter. In addition, the hunter wants a powder measure and a small powder horn or flask.

With a caplock, a nipple wrench should be added to this list. It's possible (though hardly smart) to forget to put in the powder charge before loading a ball. If this happens, you can remove the nipple and sift in enough powder to blow the "dead ball" out of the barrel.

Muzzleloading Information. Finally, any newcomer to the muzzleloading clan should seek reliable advice and read the loading data available from manufacturers and in black-powder handbooks. There are numerous muzzleloading publications including periodicals. An excellent source of information about muzzleloading skills, products, competitions, hunting news, and so on is the National Muzzle Loading Rifle Association, Box 67, Friendship, IN 47021. Members of this organization receive a monthly magazine, *Muzzle Blasts*.

RIFLE STOCKS

The purpose of a well-designed rifle stock is to put the shooter's eye quickly in line with the sights, enable him to hold the rifle as steady as possible in any position, and to keep the effect of recoil to a minimum. The results are all achieved when the various parts of a rifle stock work in conjunction with one another, and when the shooter feels the stock fits him comfortably.

How can a shooter select a stock that fits him? First, it is sufficient to say here that most factory stocks are well designed for shooters of average build, and tall and short shooters can easily compensate for a stock that does not "feel" exactly right. Most shooters, therefore, are satisfied with a mass-produced stock right from the factory.

Shooters who are more concerned about stock fit can make a selection by following the recommended stock measurements and tolerances which will be discussed later in this chapter. There are also the

problems of specialized stocks for target shooters and benchrest shooters. But first let's look at the typical rifle stock and explain the function of each part.

Basically, four parts of the rifle stock determine fit and feel to the shooter. These are the comb, cheekpiece, pistol grip, and forend. All four parts come in direct contact with the shooter's face and hands.

The comb should be of a height and thickness to insure that the pressure of the cheek against it steadies the shooter's hold and quickly puts his eye in line with the sights. But a comb that is too high and too thick will force a shooter to squeeze his cheek down on the comb to get his eye in line with the sights, and the result is an unnecessary whack on the cheek from the recoil.

Mention should also be made here of the Monte Carlo comb, which is designed to raise and support

RIFLE-STOCK NOMENCLATURE

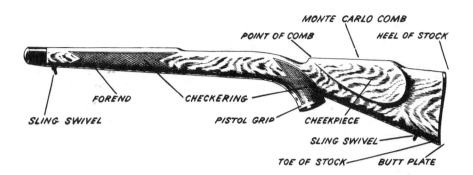

MONTE CARLO COMB

POINT OF COMB

HEEL OF STOCK

FOREND

CHECKERING

SLING SWIVEL

PISTOL GRIP

CHEEKPIECE

SLING SWIVEL

TOE OF STOCK

BUTT PLATE

the shooter's cheek and eye to bring the latter in line with telescopic sights, which are a bit higher than open sights. A Monte Carlo comb may run level toward the butt, then drop rather sharply near the heel of the stock, or it may slope upward toward the butt. The Monte Carlo that slopes slightly upward from front to rear is a good design, because the comb will recoil away from the face.

A good Monte Carlo will help the shooter who uses telescopic sights. On rifles used exclusively with open sights, the Monte Carlo is of little value.

The slope of a comb also determines the drop at heel, which is the distance measured from an imaginary line from the line of sight down to the heel of the stock. In simple words, the greater the drop at

heel the more the recoil will be felt. Likewise, the less the drop at heel the less recoil will be felt. A straight stock, with little or no drop at heel, will bring recoil straight back against the shoulder, minimizing the kick. Excessive drop at heel will cause the stock to thrust upward upon firing and bruise or hit the shooter's cheek.

In terms of actual measurements, the drop at heel for an average shooter using open sights should be 2½ to 2¾ inches. When drop at heel is 3 inches or more on big-bore rifles, the recoil will be uncomfortable. A rifle used with scope sights should have a straighter stock and comb, with less "slope" and less drop at heel—about 2 to 2½ inches is good for the average shooter.

STOCK MEASURING

Here's where to take measurements for drop at heel (**A**) and length of pull (**B**).

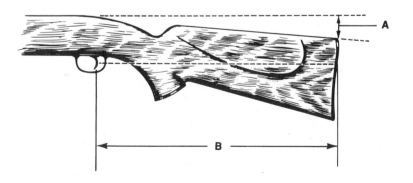

CHEEKPIECE DESIGN

Poor cheekpiece design. Cheek-piece has forward edge to strike shooter's cheek. View from butt also shows it is excessively rounded into comb. not giving full support to face.

Good cheekpiece design. Note forward portion blends into comb, leaving no edge to hit cheek. Butt view also shows it is flat, which gives maximum support to face.

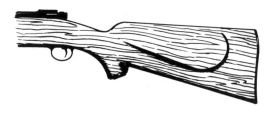 

½″

The cheekpiece is an additional aid in supporting the face. Cheekpieces come in all sizes and shapes, but a well-designed and functional cheekpiece is simple and has clean lines. The bottom of the cheekpiece should not extend more than ½ to ⅝ inch from the stock. The forward portion should flow or merge smoothly into a well-rounded comb. It should be flat, giving support to a good portion of the face.

Next of the important parts of a stock is the pistol grip, which should be shaped to enable the shooter to brace the butt against his shoulder while leaving the trigger finger free to squeeze off the shot. It should be curved so that the shooter has no stress or strain on the trigger. One rule of thumb in determining a properly curved grip is that the point of the comb should be directly and vertically over the center of the pistol-grip cap.

The circumference of the pistol grip should afford a firm and comfortable hold, without cramping the fingers. For the average shooter, a pistol grip should be round and about 4½ inches in circumference. Shooters with large hands may prefer a grip closer to 5 inches, but anything over 5 inches is too much wood for comfortable and steady shooting.

The butt of the stock should be wide and flat, to distribute recoil over a large area of the shoulder.

FOREND DESIGN

Round or oval-shaped forends are best for hunting rifles. Either type will fill the hand, give good control, and keep the fingers from barrel.

Triangular-shaped or square slab-sided forends are poor for hunting rifles, though their flat bottoms may prove of some use in benchrest shooting.

RIFLE-STOCK DESIGN

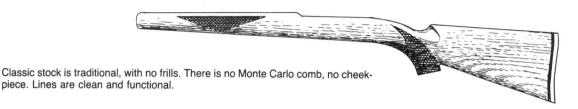

Classic stock is traditional, with no frills. There is no Monte Carlo comb, no cheek-piece. Lines are clean and functional.

Well-designed, functional stock for a hunting rifle. This one has a cheekpiece and moderate Monte Carlo (raised comb) configuration.

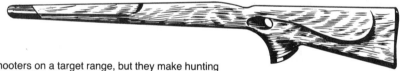

A target stock is very straight with full pistol grip and wide, heavy forend. These features make more body-to-stock contact for steadier holding.

This thumbhole stock may help shooters on a target range, but they make hunting rifles slow to handle and awkward to carry.

Designed for International Match Shooting, this specialized stock has no place in the field but excells on the target range. It has thumbhole, thumbrest, and handrest which adjusts in height. Bottom of forend has an inlaid rail which is the base for the sling swivel, hand stop, and palm rest. These accessories can be moved along the stock to suit the individual shooter. The buttplate can be adjusted for both height and length. Such specialized stocks usually come fitted with two buttplates—one for standing and the other one for use when in the kneeling and prone shooting positions.

The curved narrow butts, frequently seen on muzzleloaders and early breechloaders, can make the recoil of big-bore rifles quite painful.

The forend of a rifle stock has two purposes: 1) control over the rifle and 2) to keep fingers away from a hot barrel. To accomplish these two objectives, the forend should be rounded to fit the contour of the cupped hand and full to keep fingers from making contact with the barrel.

When the palm and fingers of the hand are turned inward, as if to grip a baseball bat or tennis racket, they naturally form a circle or oval—this shape, therefore, is undoubtedly the best for a forend. The forend can be held fully, the shooter has maximum control, and there are no gaps between the wood and hand. Forends that are trianglular in cross-section, have squared jutting "jaws," or slab sides are not only unappealing to the eye, but are awkward to hold.

Length of pull, the measurement between the trigger and butt, is another very important factor in stock design since it determines how quickly and comfortably a shooter will be able to shoulder his rifle firmly and reach the trigger with his finger. Because all men and women are not the same size with same length arms, the length of pull varies. It should be emphasized here, however, that factory stocks generally have a length of pull of 13½ inches, which is a good compromise for average shooters for all-round use. With the exception of very big shooters with long arms or very short shooters, a pull of 13½ inches should prove adequate.

For the more serious shooter who may want to alter his factory rifle or is planning to invest in a custom-built rifle, the following chart will be helpful:

Size	Recommended Length of Pull
Tall men (6'1" to 6'3")	13¾" to 14"
Average men (5'8" to 6')	13¼" to 13½"
Short men, average women	13" to 13¼"
Short women, youngsters	12¾"

Checkering on a rifle stock definitely has a function, in addition to making a stock attractive. For the hunter, checkering means a non-slip grip on his rifle in wet weather or while wearing gloves. It keeps both hands from sliding or moving on the pistol grip and forend, making for a more rigid hold.

Unfortunately, most modern factory stocks now come with checkering that is not really checkering at all. It is merely a design impressed into the wood by machine. This is a step down from the earlier factory stocks which had true checkering, even though most of the work was carelessly done. In those days, most factory stocks were checkered from 14 to 18 lines to the inch.

Custom rifle builders of today still do all their checkering by hand. It is long tedious work, which is one reason for the high cost of custom firearms. These men, who use good hard wood, checker about 24 to 26 lines to the inch. Precision checkering with sharp diamonds is one indication that the stock-maker is a master of his trade.

The features of a rifle stock mentioned thus far pertain to a sporter or hunting rifle. There are exceptions, such as target stocks, thumbhole stocks, stocks with rollover cheekpieces, and so on. Some of these exceptions are legitimate and aid the shooter, but most just make the rifle awkward to handle. Any hunter who sticks to the functional stock design described in this chapter is sure to find himself with a comfortable and good-handling field rifle.

WOODS FOR RIFLE STOCKS

The strength and "eye-appeal" of a finished stock depends on several factors. A stock that has considerable figure or "burl" generally comes from a piece of wood cut from where roots and limbs branch out from the trunk of a tree. While this wood may look attractive, it is not necessarily the best for a rifle stock, particularly a one-piece stock. Because there is considerable figure in the wood, it is prone to warping with climatic changes and such warping in the forend of a rifle can throw off accuracy under hunting conditions. Such wood is better for shotgun stocks.

The one-piece rifle stock should be straight grained, with the grain running parallel to the direction of the grip and the grain in the forend slightly diagonal to the barrel. This keeps warping in the forend to a minimum. The grip should never be cut cross-grain, since this would dangerously weaken the stock at a critical point.

It is sufficient to say here that a good stock should have a drying out period of about four or five years, that is from the time it is cut from the tree until it is finally turned into a finished gunstock. The drying period, naturally, allows the wood to lose all its moisture, keeping warping to a minimum in the finished product.

The most common wood used for factory gunstocks is American walnut. Though it generally lacks the fancy figure of other woods, it is a good stock wood. It is most often straight grained, but occasionally a factory stock of American walnut will show up with attractive burl figure. The configuration depends from which part of the tree the stock

DESIGN OF SYNTHETIC GUNSTOCKS

Typical of the breed of rifles with synthetic stocks is this Remington Model 700 with a Kevlar Aramid Fiber stock. It comes in a range of calibers from .223 to .350 Remington Magnum.

blank is cut. If cut from crotch of limbs or roots, the finished stock will nearly always have a fancy figure. American walnut, though not as hard a stock material as European walnut, holds checkering well.

There are many other woods used to make gunstocks. Some are soft, some hard. Some have good figure, others are straight grained.

SYNTHETIC GUNSTOCKS

Although wood is the traditional material for making gunstocks, synthetics have come on strong. There are many advantages to these space-age materials. Fiberglass and Kevlar, for example, are tough and light. They resist weather and freezing temperatures without swelling or warping and pushing the barrel and action enough to shift a rifle's zero. These stocks are also strong enough to take the hard knocks and falls of mountain hunting.

The early synthetic stocks included Charter's AR-7 with a plastic called Cycolac. Back in 1959, Remington brought out its Model 66 rifle, which has a stock of structural nylon. These stocks can be made in any color and checkering is molded in.

In the mid-1980s, synthetic stocks began to show up on big-game rifles from other manufacturers. Currently, nearly all gun makers offer models in a variety of synthetic stock styles and colors, including camouflage. These stocks are durable and unaffected by climate or weather conditions. Synthetic stocks combined with stainless steel mechanisms and barrels are totally weatherproof and a good choice for hunters who care more for ruggedness than aesthetics.

FINISHING THE WOOD GUNSTOCK

The best finish for a wood rifle stock is a straight oil finish, nearly always with boiled linseed oil. It

is a durable finish and one that can be easily maintained by simply hand-rubbing on another coat of oil. And it does not crack or peel, which can and does happen with factory stocks finished with varnish or lacquer.

Sanding is the first step to putting a good oil finish on a bare stock. Before any oil is applied, the wood must be made as smooth as possible. After an initial sanding with No. 180-grit sandpaper, wet the wood with a cloth. The moisture will cause the grain to raise and become rough. After the wood has dried, use No. 180 sandpaper again and sand the stock as smooth as possible. Follow this same procedure, using No. 180 sandpaper, one more time.

The next step is to progress to a finer sandpaper, such as No. 240 grit. Once again, wet the stock, allow the grain to raise and the wood to dry, then sand as smooth as possible with the No. 240 paper. When this is done, follow the same procedure again, only this time use No. 320-grit paper. Continue to wet and sand with the No. 320 paper until the grain will no longer raise when wet.

When sanding is completed, the actual oil finish can be applied. If the wood appears quite porous, however, a filler should be used before the oil is rubbed on. Commercial fillers are available, but an excellent filler can be concocted by mixing equal parts of white shellac and alcohol. This should be applied with a brush or cloth, allowed to dry, then sanded off. Depending on the wood, several coats of filler may be necessary. Remember to always allow the filler to dry thoroughly and sand between coats. The stock is now ready for the oil.

There are several commercial oil finishes on the market and any one of them will do a good job if directions are followed carefully. Some of the finishing kits available also provide shortcuts for the refinisher. One method is to add a bit of spar varnish to the oil to bring a fast sheen to the wood. Lacquer and plastic finishes are also available for a fast finishing job.

Let's assume here, however, that a straight boiled linseed oil finish is desired. Properly done, a pure oil finish is extremely durable and, most important, easily maintained. The first step is to apply a fairly heavy coat of linseed oil to the wood and set the stock aside for a day or two, allowing the wood to absorb the oil and dry thoroughly. When this is done, rub the stock down with fine steel wool. You'll note that the wood is taking on a light satin sheen.

Now comes the hard part. Start to apply thin coats of the oil and rub them well into the wood. The harder the oil is rubbed into the stock the better. After each thin coat of oil is rubbed into the wood, wipe off the excess oil and allow the remaining oil to dry thoroughly. If this is not done, the coats of oil that are not dry will begin to build up gummy deposits on the wood. If this happens, the only alternative is to sand the stock down to bare wood and start the job all over again. It is, therefore, *very* important for a coat of oil to dry thoroughly before another is applied. There is no set number of coats of oil to be rubbed into a stock. The process is simply repeated until the desired finish is obtained. The idea is to build up many thin coats of oil on the wood until the stock takes on a rich satin finish that will resist rain, snow, heat, and so on.

One of the biggest advantages to a good oil finish is that if the stock is lightly scratched in the field or marred in any way, another coat of oil, applied as described here, will bring the finish back to its original condition.

Naturally, the above method is for a stock of bare wood with no finish at all. If it is a factory stock that is to be refinished, the old factory finish, usually varnish or lacquer, must first be removed and the bare wood made as smooth as possible. This is done simply by brushing the stock with commercial varnish remover and waiting for the stock to blister and peel. The old finish can then be scraped off with a knife or razor blade. This is a messy but necessary job and it is not uncommon to use more than one coat of varnish remover to get all of the old finish off the wood. Once this is done, start with the sanding process described above to get a new oil finish.

Getting a good oil finish on a gunstock is not a difficult job, but it is a long and tedious project. The results, however, make the effort worthwhile.

RIFLE BARRELS

The modern rifle barrel has come a long way since the time of the twist or Damascus barrels of the 19th century. During those early years, barrels were made by twisting and welding strips of iron around a mandrel to form a hollow tube. Such barrels were fine during the black-powder era when pressures were comparatively low and lead bullets were used.

But then came smokeless powder and with it higher temperatures and higher pressures than the black-powder barrels could handle. The high-velocity smokeless-powder cartridges also used metal-jacketed bullets which caused too much abrasion in barrels made of iron or mild steel, a low carbon alloy.

Progress by steel makers and a great deal of experimenting by gun companies resulted in the steel rifle barrel of today. The modern rifle barrel is tough, but it can still be machined easily. It can resist erosion and withstand the stresses and strains created by high pressures. The steel is tough enough so that rifling holds up under the abrasion of metal-jacketed bullets.

The majority of barrels for high-power rifles are made of chrome molybdenum steel. Some barrels are made of stainless steel, which meets all the requirements of a good barrel material and has the additional virtue of being rustproof. One reason stainless steel is not used for all barrels is that it is difficult to machine.

Gun manufacturers get their barrels in the form of long steel bars, which are cut to desired lengths. The bar is then ready for drilling and reaming. Drilling is done by a deep-hole drill, a long rod with a V-cut running its entire length. One edge of this V does all the cutting. The barrel rotates at high speed while the deep-hole drill, which remains stationary and does not spin, bores a hole from breech to muzzle.

Once the initial hole is cut, a series of reamers, usually three or more, are used to ream the hole to the desired bore diameter. These reamers make the bore as smooth as possible and ready the barrel for rifling.

RIFLING

Rifling, put simply, is a system of spiral grooves cut into the bore to make the bullet spin and stabilize it on its way to the target.

Before going into a discussion of the various forms of rifling, let's first learn the meaning of bore diameter, groove diameter, and lands. These terms will make rifling and rifling methods easier to understand.

Grooves are the spiral cuts running the length of the barrel. The distance from the bottom of one groove to the bottom of the opposite groove is called *groove diameter*. *Lands* refers to the portion of the bore left between the rifling grooves. The measurement between lands is called *bore diameter*.

There are various forms of rifling, but the type most commonly used today has square-cut lands and grooves. These grooves, which spiral to the right and are always cut opposite one another, usually number four or six in most factory guns. One exception is Marlin's Micro-Groove barrel, which has 16 shallow grooves cut into the bore. The theory behind many shallow grooves is that it minimizes bullet distortion and increases accuracy.

There are several other forms of rifling, but none, to this writer's knowledge, are used today. One type of rifling, called either segmental or Metford, has lands and grooves with rounded-off edges. It was used in Europe for black-powder guns because it made barrels easier to keep clean. The black powder was not apt to foul the barrel quickly since there were no sharp edges in the rifling to catch particles.

Another form of rifling is the oval bore, which, as its name implies, has an out-of-round bore. The oval actually turns as it moves down the length of the barrel and spins the bullet. At one time, oval-bore rifling was used both in England and the United States.

Still another type of rifling is the parabolic pattern, which gives a pinwheel appearance when looking down the barrel. This type of rifling was used in some rifles around 1920.

Methods of putting rifling into a barrel vary, and this has been particularly true within the past 20 years. At one time, all manufacturers cut rifling into a barrel by the same process, and that was cutting one groove at a time. The cutter bit made one com-

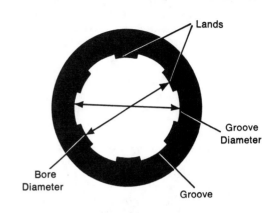

The most common type of rifling has lands and grooves that are square cut.

plete pass through the barrel, while at the same time the barrel rotated at a predetermined speed to give the rifling the desired amount of twist. Then, if the barrel was to have four-groove rifling, the barrel was given a quarter turn and another groove cut. These steps continued until all grooves were cut. It is important to note here that the bit could not cut a groove to its proper depth on a single pass, so a number of shallow cuts had to be made until the groove reached correct depth.

Cutting one groove at a time was obviously slow, and this brought about the use of broaches. A broach is a steel tool with several cutting edges. When the tool is pushed or pulled through the bore, each cutting edge removes slightly more steel than the one preceding it. All the rifle grooves are cut in a single

MORE TYPES OF RIFLING

Segmental or Metford Rifling

Oval Bore Rifling

Parabolic Rifling

operation. Though these broaching tools are expensive and costly to repair, this method is certainly much faster than cutting one groove at a time.

Still another method of putting rifling in a barrel, called cold forming, was developed during World War II. This procedure involves placing the barrel over a mandrel or carbide die that has the reverse impression of rifling on it. Barrel and mandrel are then placed in a forging machine which pounds the outside of the barrel until the rifling is formed inside the barrel.

Another rifling process involves the use of a carbide rifling button to form the rifling in a bore. The torpedolike carbide button has reverse spiral grooves machined into it. When pushed or pulled through a bore, the button compresses and forms rifling rather than cutting it. The operation is done by one pass through the barrel and production goes faster. Most manufacturers now use this button-rifling method. But most important to the shooter is the fact that button-rifled barrels tend to be more accurate than those rifled by other methods.

RATES OF TWIST

The rate of twist of the rifling is directly related to the bullet weight (and velocity) which that particular firearm can handle with accuracy. Heavier (longer) bullets in a given caliber require a faster rifling twist.

A good example of this is the .30/06 and the .308 Winchester. Both rifles use the same diameter (.308 inch) bullets which are available in a wide assortment of weights ranging from 110 grains up to 220 grains. While both of these rifles turn in excellent results with all of the medium weight (150 and 180 grains) bullets, their abilities differ when it comes to the very heavy or the very light.

The .30/06 will handle 220-grain bullets better because it has a faster twist of one turn in 10 inches. On the other hand, the .308 Winchester turns in better results with the light 110-grain bullets due to its slower twist of one turn in 12 inches.

When extremely light bullets are used in a barrel with a fast twist, they may accelerate too rapidly and deform themselves. The weight, length and shape of the bullet are important to accuracy. The length of the projectile must be compatible with the rifling twist and velocity, or the bullet may become erratic in flight.

Keep in mind that you may obtain good results in your firearm with a supposedly less-than-optimum bullet weight simply by reducing or increasing the velocity a bit.

Don't be discouraged from experimenting with various bullet weights. However, always stay within safe pressure limits.

RATES OF TWIST

In a given caliber a heavier or longer bullet will require a faster spin to stabilize it in flight.

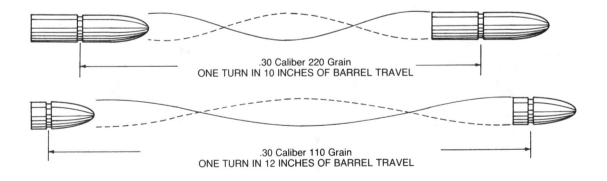

.30 Caliber 220 Grain
ONE TURN IN 10 INCHES OF BARREL TRAVEL

.30 Caliber 110 Grain
ONE TURN IN 12 INCHES OF BARREL TRAVEL

CHAMBER

The oversize portion at the breech end of the barrel is called the chamber of the rifle. It is designed to hold the cartridge that is to be fired. The chamber must be slightly bigger than the cartridge to allow the brass case to expand slightly from the pressure of the exploding powder and contract sufficiently for ejection of the spent case from the chamber.

The throat or neck of the chamber, which encircles the case neck, should likewise be oversize to allow the case neck to expand enough to release the bullet for its flight through the barrel.

HEADSPACE

Any definition or description of a chamber automatically leads into the subject of headspace. To make headspace easier to understand, let's first define a couple of terms: (1) *Headspace* is the distance between the head of a cartridge case and the face of a closed and locked bolt. (2) *Headspace measurement* is the distance between the face of a closed bolt and the point of contact on the cartridge case that controls the distance the case will go into the chamber. Consequently, headspace measurement determines headspace.

Headspace measurement would be simple if all cartridges chambered the same way, but there are four types of cartridges (rimmed, rimless, belted, rimless pistol), and headspace is measured differently for each type. The accompanying drawings clearly illustrate the headspace measurement for each class or type of cartridge. The drawings also illustrate how each type of cartridge fits in the chamber, showing the contact points between the case and chamber that hold the cartridge in place.

Obviously, since all chambers and cartridges cannot be made exactly alike, there is always some space between the bolt face and the head of the car-

HEADSPACE

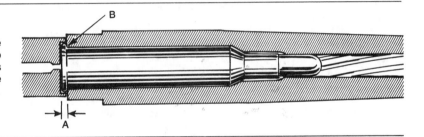

Rimmed Cartridge. Headspace (**A**) is measured from bolt face to front edge of rim. Rim (**B**) holds cartridge in place and stops the travel of the case into the chamber.

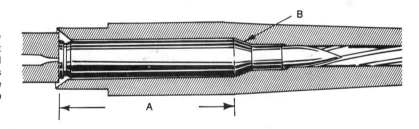

Rimless Cartridge. Headspace (**A**) the distance between the bolt face and case head, is determined by the case shoulder. On rimless cartridges, the shoulder of the case (**B**) stops travel of the cartridge into the chamber.

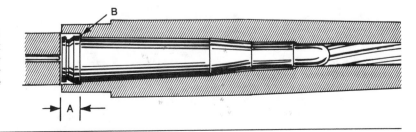

Belted Cartridge. Headspace (**A**) is measured from bolt face to front edge of belt. The belt on the case (**B**) seats against a shoulder in the chamber and stops travel of the cartridge into the chamber.

HEADSPACE (Continued)

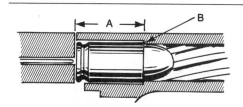

Rimless Pistol. Headspace (**A**) for rimless pistol cartridges is measured from bolt face to edge of case mouth (**B**), which seats against shoulder in the chamber and stops travel of the cartridge into the chamber.

tridge. In modern high-power rifles, the acceptable tolerance between the bolt face and head of a maximum gauge used to determine headspace is 6/1,000 inches.

If there is too much space between the cartridge head and bolt face, a condition known as *excessive headspace* exists. If there is not enough space between the cartridge head and bolt face, the problem of *insufficient headspace* exists. Either of these conditions in a rifle handling high-powered cartridges can be dangerous if it goes unchecked.

How does a shooter determine whether his rifle has excessive or insufficient headspace? There are several symptoms to look for: When a shooter has difficulty chambering a cartridge or getting the bolt to close or lock, his rifle may have insufficient headspace. Another indication is shiny score marks on the head of the case, which may be the result of the bolt closing too tightly on the cartridge and creating friction between the head of the case and the bolt face. Any of these signs may indicate insufficient headspace. This means pressures may run abnormally high when the rifle is fired.

A shooter who recognizes these signs should not automatically assume his rifle has an insufficient headspace problem. The chamber may be normal and the problem may lie with the cartridges being used, particularly reloaded ammunition. As mentioned above, it is almost impossible for all cartridges of one caliber to have exactly the same dimensions.

If insufficient headspace is suspected, it is best to take the rifle to a gunsmith and have it checked with headspace gauges. If the problem does exist, it can often be corrected by reaming out the chamber

to an acceptable tolerance.

In rifles with excessive headspace, there is too much room between the head of the cartridge and the bolt face. When such a rifle is fired, the head of the cartridge face comes back against the bolt face and the case expands beyond normal limits. The case may stretch or crack near the head or pull itself apart completely.

Determining the possibility of excessive headspace in a rifle is done by examining the spent cases for the following telltale signs:

1. A partial crack or rupture near the head of the case.

2. A stretched ring mark on the brass near the head of the case. This can be considered a warning of possible complete separation of the head from the case.

3. When firing reduced loads in a rimless case, a protruding primer is an indication of excessive headspace.

4. In rimfire cartridges, excessive headspace will produce a bulge near the rim.

5. Total case separation. In this extreme situation, the cartridge pulls apart completely, usually near the head, and only the rear section of the case ejects.

Here again, signs of excessive headspace may not necessarily mean a chamber problem. The symptoms may be the result of the ammunition being used, particularly reloads. A full-length resizing die, for example, may shorten a case and create excessive headspace in a normal chamber. The best bet is to take both rifle and ammunition to a gunsmith and have him check the firearm with headspace and case gauges. Sometimes the problem can be corrected by changing ammunition or resizing it.

CARTRIDGES

Let's get off to a good start by calling a cartridge by its right name. It's a "cartridge," and calling it anything else is wrong. It's not a bullet, a slug, a

shell, nor anything else that does not adequately describe a cartridge. A cartridge is not a single item or unit, but a combination of various components, which include a bullet, case, powder, and primer. Put these four basic components together and you have a "cartridge."

It's not all that simple, however, since cartridges are broken down into types. Among metallic rifle cartridges, there are two basic categories—the rimfires and the centerfires.

The common rimfire cartridge has its primer sealed in and around the entire rim. The firing pin striking the rim anywhere around the edge of the cartridge will ignite the charge. Examples of rimfire cartridges are the .22 Short, the .22 Long, the .22 Long Rifle, the .22 Magnum, and the 5mm Remington Rimfire Magnum.

The centerfire cartridges have a primer in the center of the base of the cartridge case. The firing pin striking the primer ignites the primer and sets off the powder charge via a flash hole in the brass case. The centerfires make up the bulk of modern sporting ammunition.

THE CENTERFIRE CARTRIDGE

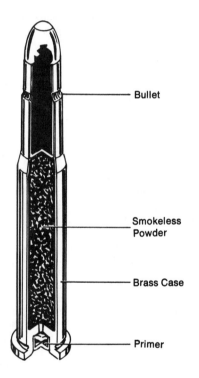

- Bullet

- Smokeless Powder

- Brass Case

- Primer

CARTRIDGE CASE

Just about all modern rifle cartridge cases are made of brass, which is most suitable for reloading. There are still some plated steel cases in use around, but brass is still the first choice. The cartridge case has a number of important jobs. It houses the powder charge, and it holds the primer and bullet firmly in place. Upon firing a cartridge, the case also seals off gases from escaping from the breech.

There are various parts of a cartridge case and the accompanying drawings cover them all.

Cartridge cases fall into five categories or types: rimmed, semi-rimmed, rebated case, rimless, and the belted case.

The rimmed cases are an old design and are still very much in use today. The .30/30 Winchester, for example, uses a rimmed cartridge case. The rim of the cartridge is the contact point which keeps the cartridge from entering the chamber.

A semi-rimmed case is one that has a rim a bit bigger in diameter than the body of the case, and the extraction groove is cut under the rim. The semi-rimmed cases are not too common today and the .225 Winchester may be the only current cartridge using this type of case.

The rebated cartridge case is one of the easiest to spot. The rim is smaller in diameter than the base of the case body. The extraction groove is cut under

TYPICAL CENTERFIRE CARTRIDGE CASE

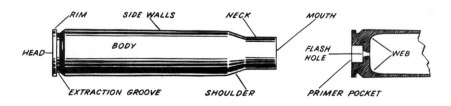

TYPES OF CARTRIDGE CASES

Rimmed Case   Semi-Rimmed Case   Rimless Case   Rebated Case   Belted Case

the rim. An old design, it was apparently revived in the .284 Winchester cartridge.

The rimless case is the design most widely used today. The rim diameter and the diameter of the case body are nearly identical and the extraction groove is cut into the head of the case. The classic .30/06 utilizes the rimless case.

The belted case has become synonymous with the magnum calibers. The design makes it possible to build the strongest case. The belt acts as a reinforcing band and the extraction groove is cut into the belt.

THE BULLET

A bullet is simply a component of a cartridge and a nonspherical projectile that is fired through a rifle barrel. But there the simplicity ends. Bullet design differs, depending on whether the bullet is to be used for long-range varmint shooting, brush hunting for whitetails, bear hunting, or hunting thick-skinned dangerous game.

For example, bullets designed for varmint shooting, generally in the .17 to .24 caliber class, are constructed with soft lead cores, thin metal jackets, and

PARTS OF A TYPICAL BULLET

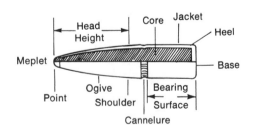

can be either soft or hollow pointed. They are usually sharp pointed to enable them to retain velocity better, which means a flatter trajectory. This design, however, causes them to expand quickly and disintegrate when they hit.

Such varmint bullets are fine for long-range shooting where there are no obstructions, but they rank a poor second on bigger game, because they are easily deflected by the smallest twig in their path and they go to pieces before good penetration occurs. While it is true that varmint cartridges have taken numerous heads of big game, the fact remains that these bullets are not suitable for big game.

On thin-skinned big game, ranging from deer to moose, bullets are larger in diameter, heavier in weight, and made with soft lead cores and thin jackets. They differ from varmint bullets in that plenty of lead is exposed at the point to give good even expansion or "mushrooming" and reliable penetration. Bullets in this category may also use methods other than exposed lead at the tip to control expansion. Remington, for example, uses a bronze wedgelike point which is driven to the rear on impact and "mushrooms" the bullet. Another Remington design features a scalloped jacket to insure uniform expansion. Winchester covers its lead point with soft aluminum which extends back and under the jacket cover. Whatever the design, the ultimate goal is dependable penetration and controlled expansion.

Finally, there are the bullets built for thick-skinned dangerous game. These bullets are invariably full-jacketed with no lead exposed. Their purpose is to penetrate thick hide and smash bone. No appreciable mushrooming is expected of them. These "solid" bullets are best jacketed in steel and have round or flattened points. Such bullets are for massive African game, such as Cape buffalo and elephants, where a hunter may need fast and deep penetration to stop a charge. They are not practical for any North American big-game animals.

A bullet designed with a point at both ends would be best aerodynamically, since it would reduce wind

MODERN BULLET DESIGNS

Full-jacketed or nonexpanding solid bullet. Only opening in jacket is at base of bullet.

Expanding bullet with round nose and soft point. Large area of lead exposed at tip with one-piece jacket covering sides and base of bullet. Cannelure aids in crimping cartridge case neck into the bullet.

Expanding bullet with round nose and soft point. One-piece jacket has slits in forward portion to weaken nose and bring on quick-controlled expansion.

Hollow-point expanding bullet. Jacket encloses sides and base but is weakened by knurling near tip to promote quick expansion.

Nosler Partition bullet has metal jacket open at both ends to expose lead. Partition strengthens base of bullet and jacket decreases in thickness toward tip. One of the best expanding-bullet designs.

Boattail bullet is tapered at base to reduce air drag. A top bullet design for long-range shooting.

Winchester Silvertip has a copper jacket that covers the side and base of the bullet. Tip is covered with a soft aluminum case that extends back and under the copper jacket. The Silvertip has good "expanding" qualities.

Remington Bronze-Point has a bronze wedge in tip that produces good expansion when it is driven to the rear of the bullet on impact.

Remington Core-Lokt is a soft-point, round-nose bullet. Forward edge of jacket has scalloped edge to insure uniform mushrooming. Bullet is strengthened by increased jacket thickness near base.

Hornady pointed soft-point expanding bullet has lead core exposed at the tip. One-piece jacket covers base and side of bullet. Note pronounced thinning of jacket in nose section.

RWS H-Mantle bullet is a semi-fragmenting bullet design. Outer jacket is steel covered with cupro-nickle alloy. Tip cap enclosing internal cavity is copper. Jacket is indented at halfway point to separate the frangible forward section from the base.

Remington hollow-point Core-Lokt has shallow tip cavity to lessen quick expansion. Jacket is purposely thin at nose to weaken it.

resistance and air drag, but such a bullet, for obvious reasons, is not feasible. The closest we can come to it, however, is the boattail bullet, which tapers slightly at the rear. This is the best choice for long-range shooting. Combine the boattail design with a spire point or spitzer point, and the result is a bullet with top-flight characteristics.

Such pointed bullets, however, have disadvantages. First, they cannot be safely used in rifles with tubular magazines, because recoil may drive the sharp nose of such a bullet into the primer of the cartridge in front of it. Secondly, sharp-pointed bullets have less shocking power on big game than round-nose bullets, because tissue, like air, offers less resistance to the sharp-pointed bullets. For this reason, the sharp-pointed bullets designed for hunting will nearly always have soft or hollow points.

A term that is mentioned when the subject of bullets comes up is "sectional density," which is the ratio of a bullet's diameter to its weight. The sectional density of a bullet is figured by dividing the bullet's weight in pounds by the square of the diameter. Unless a shooter is good at math, he'll have trouble with the formula. It is important to remember, however, that bullets with a low sectional density are short and fat and velocity is lower than bullets with a high sectional density. Bullets with high sectional density are long, slim and retain velocities well over long ranges.

What does this mean to the average hunter? In simple terms, a bullet with a high sectional density, such as a 130-grain .270, would be fine for game taken at long ranges. For the brush hunter, however, a chunky .35 caliber deer-class bullet with a low sectional density would be okay in wooded areas where ranges are not extreme.

Still another term that frequently gets tossed around is "ballistic coefficient," which is a complicated principle that relates a bullet's sectional density to the bullet's shape and measures its ability to overcome air resistance.

Unless a shooter plans to get involved in handloading his own ammunition for hunting, there is really no need for him to learn the aerodynamic principles and formulas of bullet design and weight. Firearms manufacturers have gone into extensive research to produce the best bullets for various hunting conditions. Check the table "Modern Bullet Designs" on the previous page before buying ammunition for a hunting trip.

THE PRIMER

The primer of a cartridge is frequently referred to as the spark plug of the cartridge, and one would be hard put to find a better description. The primer

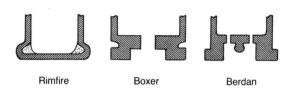

Rimfire   Boxer   Berdan

Cutaways of cartridge case heads show three basic designs for primers. **Rimfire** has priming compound completely around rim. Firing pin striking rim anywhere ignites cartridge. **Boxer primer** fits into the primer pocket. Firing pin striking primer ignites mixtures and sets off cartridge via flash hole. Case for **Berdan primer** has built-in anvil. When the firing pin strikes the primer, the cartridge is set off via flash holes around anvil.

contains a highly explosive compound which, when struck by the firing pin, ignites the cartridge's powder charge via a flash hole in the brass case.

Thanks to modern manufacturing techniques, the chances of primer malfunction are rather remote. When a malfunction does occur it is generally because of a weak firing pin or because oil, grease, or water has worked its way into the primer. If you're a handloader, keep the primer dry and clean and don't handle it if your fingers have even a trace of lubricant.

The typical American primer for a centerfire cartridge is actually an assembly of several components, including an anvil, a cup, paper, and the priming mixture. The paper lies between the mixture and the anvil. The primer ignites when the firing pin crushes the explosive mixture against the anvil. Just about all primers made in the United States use chemicals which are noncorrosive and nonmercuric.

There are basically two types of primers in use today: the Boxer and Berdan. The Boxer primer has a built-in anvil, which means it can be punched out of a spent case with a decapping pin. This is a great advantage to handloaders.

The Berdan primer does not have a built-in anvil. Instead, the anvil is an integral part of the cartridge case. This makes removal of the primer difficult, which accounts for the increased usage of the Boxer primer throughout the world. To a limited degree, the Berdan primer is still used in Europe.

The difference in reliability between the Boxer and Berdan primers is almost nonexistent—both are dependable. Cartridge cases using the Boxer primer utilize one large flash hole in the primer pocket, while the Berdan primer ignites the powder charge through several small holes around the built-in anvil in the case. The Boxer primer is most widely used because it is a boon to handloaders.

Boxer primers are made in two different sizes and six types, as the following list shows:

Primer	Diameter (inches)
Large rifle	.210
Large rifle magnum	.210
Large pistol	.210
Large pistol magnum	.210
Small rifle	.175
Small rifle magnum	.175
Small pistol	.175
Small pistol magnum	.175

The large rifle primers are used with cartridges such as the .270, .308, .30/06, and similar calibers. The large pistol primers are used in such calibers as the .45 Auto, the .44 Special, and so on.

The small rifle primers are used in the .22 Hornet, the .222 Remington, and similar cartridges. The small pistol primers are used in the .32 Smith & Wesson, the .38 Special, and similar cartridges.

The magnum primers, as the above list indicates, are the same in diameter as the other primers. The difference lies in their chemical structure. These magnum primers are built to provide long sustained heat to insure complete ignition when large quantities of powder are used.

There are at least eight manufacturers producing dependable primers for handloaders. If you're going to try your hand at handloading, you'll find that all handloading manuals will list the correct primer size for your cartridge.

Rimfire cartridges, such as the .22s, use a much different priming design. The priming mixture in these small cartridges is distributed completely around the rim of the case. The firing pin, striking anywhere around the rim, will ignite the priming mixture and fire the cartridge.

THE POWDER

When was the first time a gunpowder was used in a firearm? That's a tough, if not impossible, question to answer. It's generally accepted that the Chinese developed black powder (a mixture of sulphur, charcoal, and potassium nitrate) for use in fireworks and a man named Roger Bacon adapted it to firearms around 1265.

During the pioneer era, before the advent of smokeless powder, black powder was used in muzzleloading rifles and cap-and-ball pistols. Black powder is not an ideal propellant and no factory cartridges today are loaded with it. Small batches

are still produced, however, for the growing number of gun enthusiasts who enjoy shooting and hunting with muzzleloaders.

Black powder has more than a few disadvantages, which we should explain before discussing the development of smokeless powder. First, black powder is explosive and consequently presents a potential danger to the user. If a spark or hot ash should hit a pound of black powder on your reloading bench it could result in a serious explosion. And in spite of the fact that it is an explosive, it burns at a constant rate and it takes a great deal of it to produce enough gas to get a bullet up to acceptable velocity. This was one reason the old muzzleloaders had long barrels; they were needed to give the black powder enough time to burn and build up pressure. Black powder also gives off great clouds of smoke from the muzzle of an old front-loading gun and fouls a barrel badly. To maintain any kind of accuracy, muzzleloaders had to be cleaned frequently.

So, unless you're a muzzleloading enthusiast, forget black powder. It was used at a time when there was nothing else to do the job. Now we have smokeless powder, which is far superior in all respects.

Our modern smokeless powders stem from the discovery of nitroglycerin and guncotton. Nitroglycerin is a liquid that results from the action of nitric and sulphuric acids on glycerin. Guncotton is formed by the action of the same acids on various kinds of cellulose and cotton. Perhaps the single most important fact about smokeless powder is that the rate of burning can be controlled so that its use can be boosted to maximum efficiency in various types of firearms.

It is difficult to categorize smokeless powders because they come in almost endless varieties and shapes, but there are basically two groups—double-base powders and single-base powders.

A double-base powder is made when guncotton and nitroglycerin are mixed. Cordite, for example, is a well-known double-base powder. Double-base powder burns quite hot, but gives high velocity with low pressure.

Single-base powders contain no nitroglycerin and are formed by dissolving guncotton in a mixture of alcohol and ether.

As mentioned above, the burning rate of smokeless powder can be controlled and this is done by one of two methods—size of granulation of the powder and coating the grains with a retardant substance. Either of these two methods produces "progressive-burning powder."

To put it simply, the smaller the grains of powder the faster the burning rate; the bigger the grains the slower the burning rate. When a retardant coating

RECOMMENDED CALIBERS AND BULLET WEIGHTS FOR GAME

FOR VARMINTS

Cartridge	Bullet Weight (grs.)	Muzzle Velocity (f.p.s.)	Cartridge	Bullet Weight (grs.)	Muzzle Velocity (f.p.s.)
.17 Remington	25	4020	.257 Weatherby	87	3825
.5 mm. Remington Magnum	38	2100	.220 Swift	48	4110
.22 Long Rifle	40	1145	.225 Winchester	55	3650
.22 Long Rifle	40	1335	.243 Winchester	80	3500
.22 Long Rifle H. P.	37	1365	.25-06 Remington	90	3500
.22 W.R.F. (.22 Rem. Spl.)	45	1450	.25-06 Remington	100	3300
.22 Win. Automatic	45	1055	.6 mm. Remington	80	3544
.22 Win. Mag. Rimfire	40	2000	.25-20 H.V.	60	2250
.218 Bee	46	2860	.256 Win. Mag. (rifle)	60	2800
.22 Hornet	45	2690	.250 Savage	87	3030
.22 Hornet	46	2690	.257 Roberts	87	3200
.222 Remington	50	3200	.264 Win. Mag.	100	3700
.222 Remington Mag.	55	3300	.270 Weatherby	100	3760
.22-250 Remington	55	3810	.270 Winchester	100	3480
.223 Remington	55	3300	.284 Winchester	125	3200
.224 Weatherby	50	3750	.308 Winchester	110	3340
.240 Weatherby	70	3850	.30-06 Springfield	110	3370

FOR BIG GAME

Cartridge	Bullet Weight (grs.)	Muzzle Energy (ft.-lbs.)	Cartridge	Bullet Weight (grs.)	Muzzle Energy (ft.-lbs.)
†.243 Winchester	100	2090	.307 Winchester	180	2510
.250 Savage	100	1760	†*.308 Winchester	180	2720
†6 mm Remington	100	2260	*.308 Winchester	200	2670
†.25-06 Remington	120	2590	.32 Winchester Special	170	1960
.25-35 Winchester	117	1370	.32 Remington	170	1700
†6.5 mm Remington Magnum	120	2780	*8mm Mauser (8 × 57; or 7.9)	170	2490
†.240 Weatherby	100	2554	8mm Remington Magnum	185	3896
.257 Roberts	117	1820	†*.338 Winchester Magnum	200	4000
†.264 Winchester Magnum	140	3180	*.338 Winchester Magnum	300	4000
†*.270 Weatherby	150	3501	†*.340 Weatherby	200	4566
†*.270 Winchester	150	2800	*.348 Winchester	200	2840
†*.280 Remington	165	2910	.35 Remington	200	1950
†*.284 Winchester	150	2800	.350 Remington Magnum	200	3261
*7 mm Mauser	175	2410	.351 Winchester Self Loading	180	1370
7/30 Waters	120	1940	.356 Winchester	200	2460
7mm/08 Remington	140	2542	.356 Winchester	250	2160
†*7mm Remington Magnum	175	3660	*.358 Winchester	200	2840
†*7mm Weatherby	154	3406	*.358 Winchester	250	2810
.30/30 Winchester	170	1860	.375 Winchester	200	2150
.30 Remington	170	1700	*.375 Holland & Holland	270	4500
*.30/40 Krag	180	2440	*.375 Holland & Holland	300	4330
*.30/40 Krag	220	2360	*.416 Rigby Solid	410	2370
*.300 Savage	180	2240	*.416 Rigby Trophy Bonded Sledgehammer	400	2370
†*.30/06 Springfield	180	2910	.44 Magnum	240	1630
*.30/06 Springfield	220	2830	*.444 Marlin	240	3070
†*.300 Winchester Magnum	180	3770	.45/70 Government	405	1570
†*.300 Weatherby	180	4201	*.470 Nitro Express	500	2150
.303 Savage	190	1650			
*.303 British	180	2580			
.307 Winchester	150	2760			

*Suitable for heavy game, such as elk or moose, as well as for lighter species such as deer.

†For long-range plains or mountain hunting where flat trajectory is important (e.g. sheep, goat).

FOR DANGEROUS GAME

Cartridge	Bullet Weight (grs.)	Muzzle Energy (ft.-lbs.)	Cartridge	Bullet Weight (grs.)	Muzzle Energy (ft.-lbs.)
*7 mm. Remington Magnum	175	3660	†.375 Holland & Holland	300 Solid	4330
*.30-06 Springfield	220	2830	†.378 Weatherby	300 Solid	5700
*.300 Holland & Holland	180	3400	‡.416 Rigby	410 Solid	2370
**.300 Holland & Holland	220	3350	.416 Remington	400 Solid	2400
*.300 Winchester Magnum	180	3770	*.444 Marlin	240	3070
**.300 Weatherby	220	4123	**.458 Winchester Magnum	510	5140
8mm. Remington Magnum	220	3912	‡.458 Winchester Magnum	500 Solid	5040
*.338 Winchester Magnum	250	4050	‡.460 Weatherby	500 Solid	8095
**.338 Winchester Magnum	300	4000	‡.470 Nitro Express	500 Solid	2150
**.340 Weatherby	200	4566			
*.350 Remington Magnum	250	3220			
*.358 Winchester	250	2810			
*.375 Holland & Holland	270	4500			
**.375 Holland & Holland	300	4330			

*Only for such North American species as Alaskan bear and moose.
**Not for elephants or rhino, but suitable for large Asiatic and African cats.
†Adequate for elephant, rhino, and buffalo.
‡Recommended for toughest, most dangerous game.

is used, this coating must first be burned off before the powder burns. The purpose is to get the powder to start burning slowly, then increase the rate of burning as the bullet starts its trip through the barrel. The result is a continuous accelerating thrust pushing the bullet.

How can we apply this "progressive-burning" principle to cartridges? A few examples should make it clear. Light bullets require less gas pressure to start them moving in a barrel than heavier bullets. Using the .308 as an example, a fast-burning powder can be used with the 110-grain bullet but a slow-burning powder with the heavier 200-grain bullet.

Let's carry this a step further and take a look at rifle and handgun ammunition. A rifle may have a barrel up to 22 or 24 inches, which means more time is available for a powder to build up pressure, so

one of the slower burning powders can be used. In a handgun, however, where peak velocity must be reached quickly because of the short barrel, a very fast powder must be used.

If you're a handloader, the importance of correct powder selection cannot be overemphasized, since it will have a direct bearing on velocity. You'll be confronted with powder in various forms, including circular flakes, small cylinders, and small spheres. A good handloading manual, however, will recommend what kind of powder to use and what velocity you can expect with various bullet weights.

If you're not a handloader but an average hunter, there's no need to worry about the gunpowder in the factory ammunition you buy at your favorite gunshop. If it's from a reputable manufacturer, you can be sure you're getting the right powder.

CARTRIDGE SELECTION

It is just about impossible to talk about cartridge selection without also covering the subject of ballistics (velocity, trajectory, and energy), since a shooter must obviously know how a particular cartridge will perform before he makes his choice.

Let's first start out with a basic premise. Game is killed by a good combination of rifle, cartridge, and shooter. The most important is the shooter. The most efficient rifle and cartridge is nearly worthless unless the hunter can comfortably handle his gun and confidently place his bullet in a vital area. If a hunter can't kill a deer with a .30/30, there is no

reason to believe he will do much better with a .338 Winchester Magnum.

When a hunter using a deer-class cartridge finds himself wounding and missing game with any amount of frequency, the problem is usually with the hunter behind the gun . . . not the gun. The solution to such a problem is more time on the range, where a shooter can find where his bullets are going and make the necessary sight adjustments. He should also put in as much practice as possible to develop a steady hold and good smooth trigger squeeze.

DEER HUNTING IN BRUSH

Basically, however, there are some guidelines a hunter can follow in selecting a cartridge for his brand of hunting. If he's a typical deer hunter who takes his game in wooded country where ranges are not extreme, he'd be wise to pick a caliber between .25 and .35 handling bullets weighing from 120 to 200 grains. This would give him a fairly heavy bullet pushed along at a not-too-fast velocity that would give it good timber qualities. You don't want a very high-velocity bullet that will go through a deer at short range and exit before it can properly expand. A heavy medium-velocity bullet would also be less apt to be deflected by brush and, if properly constructed, would not disintegrate on impact. A bullet that goes to pieces when it strikes is all right for varminters, but not for big-game hunters who need bullets that will provide good penetration.

Another fact to keep in mind is that the typical deer hunter, unless he plans to hunt moose or bears as well, should not overpower himself with the mighty magnums, such as the .300 and .338 Winchester cartridges. These big belching berthas can be a definite handicap. Because of their uncomfortable recoil and muzzle blast, these rifles are not fired as often as a hunting rifle should be and the result is that the shooter does not become familiar with his rifle and may also develop a flinch or become "afraid" of his rifle—something that is sure to mean missed or wounded game.

So if you're a deer hunter in brush country, stick to the calibers you can handle comfortably and confidently. A well-placed shot with a .30/30 will kill cleaner than a sloppy shot with one of the big magnums. As mentioned earlier, the deer-class cartridges between .25 and .35 calibers are good choices. A few excellent cartridges for brush hunting are the old-time .308 Winchester, the .35 Remington, .30/06, .300 Savage, .356 Winchester, .358 Winchester, .32 Special, and .375 Winchester.

WESTERN DEER HUNTING

The deer hunter in the West has a different problem. He needs a cartridge that will produce high velocity and flat trajectory for the long 200-yard-plus shots he will encounter in mountain and prairie country. He also needs a quick-expanding bullet that is fairly light.

Generally, the Western hunter chooses from the .25 to .30 caliber range of cartridges. Because of the long shooting distances involved, bullet weights are more important here since they will affect trajectory and bullet drop. The proven cartridges for western

hunting include the .270 with the 150-grain bullet, the .243 with the 100-grain bullet, the .25/06 with the 120-grain bullet, the .264 Winchester Magnum with the 140-grain bullet, the 7mm/.08 Remington with the 140-grain bullet, the 7mm Remington Magnum with the 175-grain bullet, the .280 Remington with the 165-grain bullet, the .30/06 with the 180-grain bullet, and any of the .300 Magnums.

It certainly is not unusual for western hunters to include such game as antelope, sheep, and goats in some of their hunts. These medium-size game animals all have one thing in common—they are generally taken at long range. Any of the cartridges and bullet weights listed above for the western hunter will do the job on these animals.

BIG GAME/VARMINT CARTRIDGES

We've covered cartridges for deer-size game in the West and East, but how about hunters looking for a big-game cartridge that can also be used during the off-season for varmints? If this is the case, any selection will have to be a compromise. The ideal deer cartridge can never be a top-flight woodchuck or varmint load. The best solution is to favor the lighter, high-velocity cartridges that will reach out for chucks but also be adequate for deer. Such compromise cartridges include the .243 Winchester with the 80-grain bullet for varmints and the 100-grain bullet for deer, the .25/06 Remington with the 90-grain bullet for varmints and the 120-grain bullet for deer, and the .250/3000 with the 87-grain bullet for varmints and the 100-grain for deer. Similar combinations include the .257 Roberts, the .270, and the 6mm Remington. In a pinch, the .308 and .30/06 with light bullets can also prove adequate for long-range woodchuck shooting.

We're assuming, of course, that a shooter following these recommendations is shopping for a rifle that will work on both deer and varmints. If a hunter, however, already owns a .270 or .30/06, it would be poor economics for him to unload it and buy another rifle that would be closer to a deer-and-varmint combination gun. It would be much wiser to simply use lighter bullets on varmints and heavier bullets on deer-size game. The .30/06, for example, offers a range of bullet weights from 110 to 220 grains. The .308 offers nearly the same range of bullet weights.

Perhaps another point to keep in mind before possibly swapping your rifle is that most hunters who suddenly become addicted to varmint shooting will invariably end up with one of the specialized high-velocity flat-shooting varmint cartridges, such as the .17 Remington, the .222 Remington, the .223 Remington, or the .22/250 Remington.

One of the most perplexing yet most interesting problems is the search for the all-round cartridge, one that can fill in during the summer months for chucks, take deer on those annual hunts, and also be put to use on occasional trips for such big game as elk, moose, caribou, and brown and grizzly bears.

Such an all-round cartridge has to be a compromise. No single cartridge does the job well on all game, from chucks to moose. If you choose a powerful cartridge, you must cope with heavy recoil, muzzle blast, and noise, even if you just want to bang away at chucks on a Saturday afternoon. If you choose a lighter cartridge, it may fall slightly short of acceptable power for game such as elk or moose.

But if a hunter can afford just one gun for all game, the old .30/06 is most often recommended. With a 110-grain bullet, it produces a velocity of 3,370 fps (feet per second), which makes it a more than adequate varmint load. The deer or sheep hunter can use the 180-grain bullet, which leaves the muzzle at 2,700 fps. For bigger game, the 220-grain bullet leaves the muzzle at 2,410 fps and packs 2,830 foot-pounds of energy.

The .30/06 has become more versatile than ever with the introduction of the Remington Accelerator cartridge, which is designed to make a .30/06, .308, or .30/30 rifle into a passable varmint rig. It employs a .224 bullet encased in a .30 caliber plastic vehicle called a sabot. On leaving the muzzle, the sabot and the bullet separate. When fired from a .30/06, the small .224 bullet is then traveling at over 4,080 fps. The same bullet and sabot loaded in a .30/30 case will be moving at 3,400 fps. Accuracy is as good as the rifle from which the Accelerator is fired. If your .30/06 produces 1-inch groups at 100 yards with a standard 165-grain load, the Accelerator will probably do likewise. But if your rifle delivers 4-inch groups, it will probably continue to do so with the Accelerators.

Most .30/30s are lever actions and not noted for pinpoint accuracy, so the value of the Accelerators in this caliber may be questionable. However, you may be lucky enough to own one of the Remington Model 788 bolt actions that were once chambered for this round. The Accelerators would make it an outstanding combination for deer and varmint shooting.

If the .30/06 is the best all-round load, it isn't the only one. The .308 Winchester is available with bullets weighing 110, 125, 150, 180, and 200 grains. Bullets for the .270 Winchester come in 100, 130, and 150 grains. The .280 Remington and 7mm Mauser can also do far more than one job—as can the 7mm Remington Magnum for a hunter who can take recoil. All these cartridges have a good variety of bullet weights and good retention of velocity and energy.

CARTRIDGES FOR DANGEROUS GAME

For heavy and dangerous game, the choice of a cartridge is not difficult because there are not that many American-made cartridges available for such animals. For Alaskan bears, Cape buffalo, and the big Asian and African cats, a hunter can use such cartridges as the .300 Holland & Holland, the .338 Winchester Magnum, the .300 and .340 Weatherby Magnums, or the .375 Holland & Holland. For the toughest game, such as elephant and rhino, a hunter should use solid bullets in such cartridges as the .378 Weatherby Magnum, the .375 Holland & Holland, the .458 Winchester Magnum, the .460 Weatherby Magnum, the .416 Rigby, the .470 Nitro Express, and the .416 Remington Magnum.

The tables on pages 42–43 show recommended calibers and bullet weights for game will prove valuable to shooters looking for the all-round cartridge or the hunter who wants to add another rifle to his battery, whether it be for woodchucks or Alaskan brown bears. Note that muzzle velocity is listed for varmint cartridges, since a flat trajectory is important for this type of long-range shooting. For big game, however, muzzle energy is listed, since knockdown power is needed for the bigger animals.

BALLISTICS

Ballistics, which is a study of what happens to a bullet in flight when it leaves the muzzle of a rifle, is an extremely valuable aid to a shooter in selecting and comparing the pros and cons of various cartridges. Without getting too technical, ballistics covers trajectory, velocity, and muzzle energy of a cartridge. Before going any further, we should know what these terms mean.

Trajectory is the curved path the bullet takes from muzzle to target. No bullet will travel a flat path to the target—even if velocity were pushed to more than 4,000 feet per second and the range was only 10 yards. A bullet, because of gravitational pull, begins to drop the instant it leaves the barrel. It is the degree of the trajectory curve that is of key importance to the shooter, and this is determined by initial muzzle velocity and bullet shape.

The faster a bullet leaves the muzzle the shallower the trajectory curve or, in other words, the "flatter" the path of the bullet. As mentioned above, bullet shape also has an effect on the trajectory curve. Long sharp-pointed bullets handle wind resistance better, retain velocity longer than chunky round-nose bullets and will produce a flatter bullet path.

Velocity is simply the speed at which a bullet travels, and this is usually measured in feet per second. Generally, the abbreviation "fps" is used after the digits. On nearly all published ballistic charts, figures on velocity are given at the muzzle and at ranges of 100, 200, and 300 yards. The purpose is to tell how well or how poorly a particular cartridge retains its speed. Such figures, as we shall see, are valuable in cartridge and bullet weight selection.

Muzzle energy is a measurement expressed in foot-pounds of the impact by a bullet as it leaves the muzzle of a rifle. Ballistic charts nearly always give energy figures for bullets at the muzzle and at ranges of 100, 200, and 300 yards. These figures are useful in determining how rapidly various loads and bullets lose impact power in flight.

What do trajectory, velocity, and energy mean to a hunter or target shooter? The answer is the difference between missing and hitting. Trajectory figures will tell you which cartridges shoot "flatter" than others, though there is really no such thing as a flat-shooting cartridge. The trajectory curve (flight path of a bullet) has often been compared with a baseball player throwing a ball. The farther he must toss a ball, the higher he must throw it to make it reach its target. The same applies to a bullet. The farther the target, the higher the muzzle of a rifle

must be raised, by adjusting the rear sight upward, to make the bullet travel a greater distance.

The accompanying sketch clearly shows trajectory in relation to line of sight and line of bore. Since the bullet never goes above the line of bore and begins to drop the instant it leaves the muzzle, the rear sight must be adjusted to compensate for the bullet drop.

Published ballistic tables also almost always show trajectory figures, which indicate a bullet's flight path from muzzle to target. The figures, given in inches, indicate the rise or drop of a bullet from the line of sight. Let's take, for example, the .30/06 with a 180-grain bullet. Sighted-in at 200 yards, the bullet will hit 2.4 inches high at 100 yards and 9 inches low at 300 yards. Obviously the midrange figures are valuable when trying to figure out the best range to sight-in your hunting rifle, and they also tell you where to hold at ranges closer or farther than the distance for which your rifle is sighted.

The table "Recommended Calibers and Bullet Weights for Game" (page 42) is a compilation of ballistic figures from various ammunition makers. Studying these tables will give you a good insight into how various cartridges perform and how they compare with one another. Use these tables when trying to pick a varmint load that shoots the flattest, or when trying to find the load that offers the widest range of bullet weights for all-round hunting. And if someone says his .270 packs more energy at 100 yards than your .308, you will find that answer there, too.

In order to make this ballistic section as complete as possible, figures on handgun cartridges have also been included, although a description of handguns themselves begins on page 156.

The accompanying photos show the most popular American and European cartridges. (Note: Owing to technical limitations in photo resizing, these cartridges are uniformly shown slightly smaller than actual, though relative sizes are close to actual.)

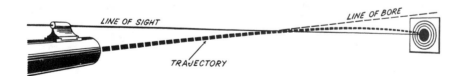

Trajectory, or path of the bullet, never rises above line of bore, but crosses line of sight. To compensate for bullet drop, the bore must be pointed upward and this is done by adjusting rear sight so it is higher than front sight.

RIFLE CARTRIDGES

.17 Remington

.218 Bee

.22 Hornet

.220 Swift

.222 Remington

.222 Remington Magnum

.223 Remington

.22/250 Remington

.224 Weatherby Magnum

.225 Winchester

.240 Weatherby Magnum

.243 Winchester

6mm Remington &
.244 Remington

(Continued next page)

RIFLE CARTRIDGES (Continued)

.25/20 Winchester

.250/3000 Savage

.257 Roberts

.257 Weatherby Magnum

.25/06 Remington

6.5 × 54mm
Mannlicher-Schoenauer

6.5 Japanese

6.5 × 55mm (Swedish)

.264 Winchester Magnum

6.5 Remington Magnum

.270 Winchester

.270 Weatherby Magnum

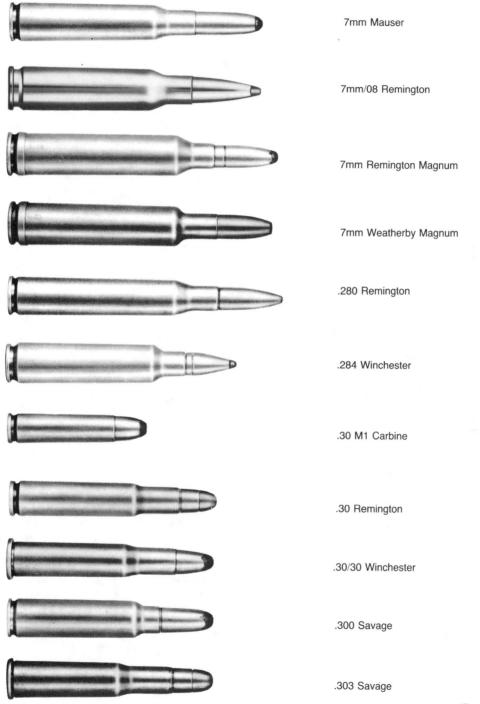

7mm Mauser

7mm/08 Remington

7mm Remington Magnum

7mm Weatherby Magnum

.280 Remington

.284 Winchester

.30 M1 Carbine

.30 Remington

.30/30 Winchester

.300 Savage

.303 Savage

(Continued next page)

RIFLE CARTRIDGES (Continued)

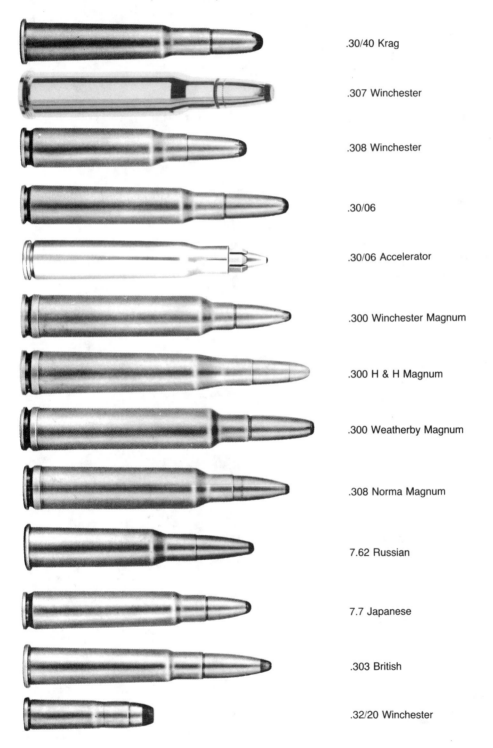

.30/40 Krag

.307 Winchester

.308 Winchester

.30/06

.30/06 Accelerator

.300 Winchester Magnum

.300 H & H Magnum

.300 Weatherby Magnum

.308 Norma Magnum

7.62 Russian

7.7 Japanese

.303 British

.32/20 Winchester

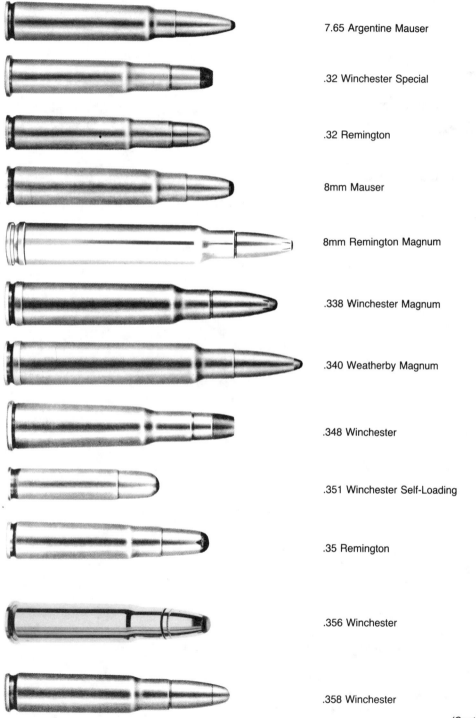

7.65 Argentine Mauser

.32 Winchester Special

.32 Remington

8mm Mauser

8mm Remington Magnum

.338 Winchester Magnum

.340 Weatherby Magnum

.348 Winchester

.351 Winchester Self-Loading

.35 Remington

.356 Winchester

.358 Winchester

(Continued next page)

RIFLE CARTRIDGES (Continued)

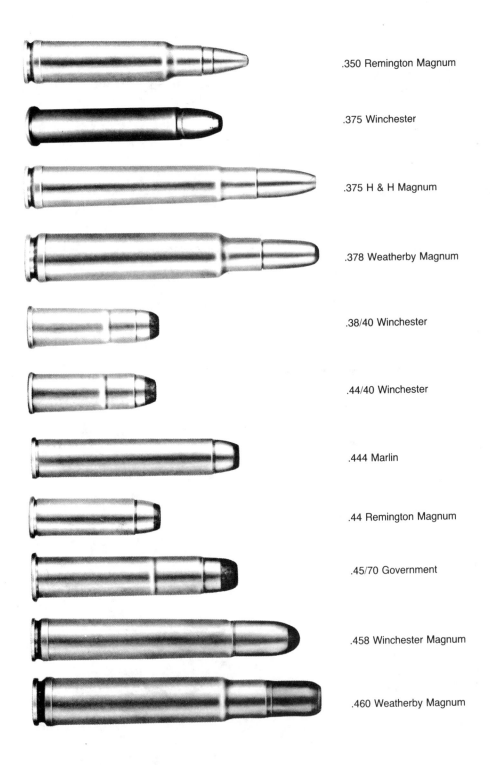

.350 Remington Magnum

.375 Winchester

.375 H & H Magnum

.378 Weatherby Magnum

.38/40 Winchester

.44/40 Winchester

.444 Marlin

.44 Remington Magnum

.45/70 Government

.458 Winchester Magnum

.460 Weatherby Magnum

PISTOL CARTRIDGES

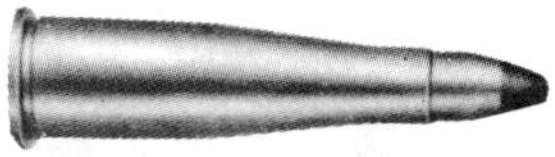

.22 Remington Jet

.221 Remington Fireball

.25 Automatic Pistol

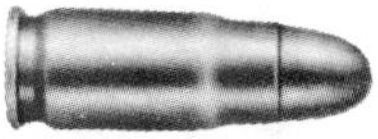

.30 Luger

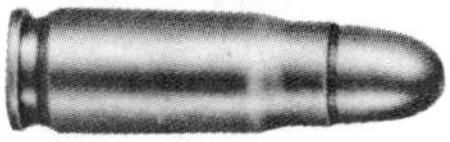

.30 Mauser

.32 A.C.P.

.32 Smith & Wesson

.32 Smith & Wesson Long

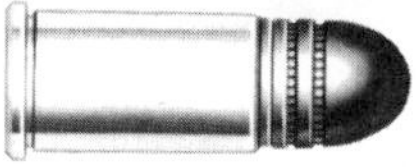

.32 Short Colt

.32 Long Colt

9mm Luger

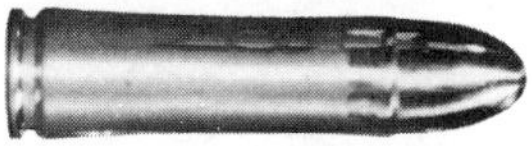

9mm Winchester Magnum

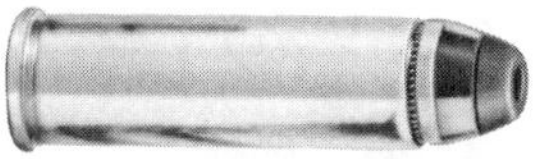

.32 H & R Magnum

.357 Magnum

.357 Remington Maximum

.380 Auto

(Continued next page)

PISTOL CARTRIDGES (Continued)

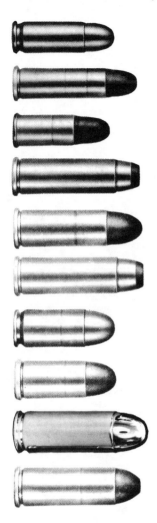

.38 Super Auto

.38 Special

.38 Smith & Wesson

.41 Remington Magnum

.44 Special

.44 Remington Magnum

.45 A.C.P.

.45 Auto Rim

.45 Winchester Magnum

.45 Colt

CARMICHEL'S GUIDE TO HUNTING CARTRIDGES

By Jim Carmichel (Courtesy of *Outdoor Life* magazine)

The debate never ends. Knockdown power, bullet energy—what are they? How do we compare one cartridge or bullet to another and determine which is better for killing big game?

Ever since hunters first observed the awesome effect of a powder-driven projectile, they've never tired of speculating on the relative effectiveness of bullets of different sizes and weights traveling at different speeds. The very earliest firearms literature, as you might guess, is filled with all sorts of opinions about killing energy. The speculations are based on everything from black magic to the alignment of stars and other heavenly bodies.

During this century, there have been some notable attempts to categorize cartridge performance. One much-discussed example is John Taylor's tables of "Knock Out," or "KO," values, in which he attempted to index the relative punch of dangerous-game cartridges.

Ballisticians prefer the foot-pound system for comparing cartridge performance for some very good reasons. First of all, it is the industry standard of comparison. Second, it is easily calculated. Third, the relative energy levels of various cartridges tend to correspond to actual performance in the field. The foot-pound energy index is not without a host of critics, however, especially shooters who prefer large-diameter, slow-moving bullets. As these critics very correctly point out, the foot-pound system is heavily skewed in favor of high-velocity cartridges. With the accepted formula for calculating bullet energy, if you double the weight of the bullet, leaving all else the same, you merely double the energy level. But if you double the velocity, you *quadruple* the energy. That's why big-bore fanciers stomp and sputter and dream up calculations that favor heavy bullets. One such set of calculations I saw led to the conclusion that a thrown brick would be the surest way to stop a charging Cape buffalo!

A once-popular means of comparing cartridge effectiveness that was favored by fans of large, heavy bullets was the so-called, and often confusing, "pounds-feet" theory. Obviously, one reason it was so confusing was that it was frequently confused with foot-pounds of kinetic energy because of the similarity of names. The pounds-feet theory does not favor velocity as much as kinetic-energy calculations do. For example, when using standard kinetic foot-pounds calculations, a 180-grain bullet from a .30/06 leaving the muzzle at 2,700 feet per second develops 2,913 foot-pounds of energy at the muzzle. By comparison, a 405-grain .45/70 bullet that leaves the muzzle at 1,330 fps has only 1,590 foot-pounds of energy. But if we apply the pounds-feet theory, the .45/70 has a relative index of 76.95 compared with 69.40 for the .30/06.

The pounds-feet theory was done asunder by the arrival of modern cartridges, which demonstrated that the shock generated by a relatively small but high-velocity bullet was a better killer than the big holes made by old-fashioned, slow-moving bullets.

Back in the early 1960s, P.O. Ackley, the well-known gunsmith and cartridge experimenter, wrote a book called *Handbook for Shooters & Reloaders* which includes a chapter on killing power. Ackley discusses the various theories of bullet energy, and also includes a section by Paul Van Rosenberg on the relative effectiveness of different cartridges on big game. Ackley describes Van Rosenberg as an experienced big-game hunter and ballistics engineer, and Van Rosenberg's comments indicate he was indeed. Among Van Rosenberg's recommendations is establishment of more-or-less specific energy levels that a cartridge must provide to perform well on game. He feels that 1,200 foot-pounds of energy is adequate for game such as deer, antelope, sheep, and goats. For elk and small bears, he recommends 2,000 foot-pounds, and he sets 2,800 as adequate for large bears and moose. Of course, Van Rosenberg speaks of the *remaining energy at the target,* not at the muzzle.

By necessity, Van Rosenberg's recommendations must be regarded as generalizations, and there are plenty of exceptions to them. For example, the energy level of the .30/30 Winchester with a 170-grain bullet drops below 1,200 foot-pounds inside 150 yards. Yet, we know by experience that a .30/30 easily kills deer at 200 yards and even a bit beyond. Just the same, we can make some interesting comparisons of different cartridges and bullet weights by imposing Van Rosenberg's performance levels and seeing how—or, rather, where (at what ranges)—they stack up.

The accompanying table, computed at *Outdoor Life's* Briarbank Ballistic Laboratory, shows the critical ranges for 100 cartridges and bullet weights. By comparing the different energy/range figures, you'll get a pretty fair idea of what to expect in *relative* performance on big game at different ranges.

The table shows the 3-inch (plus or minus) point-

POINT-BLANK TRAJECTORIES AND REMAINING ENERGY LEVELS
OF 100 POPULAR RIFLE CARTRIDGES

Caliber	Bullet Weight (Grains)	Bullet Type*	Muzzle Velocity (Feet Per Second)	50 Yards	100 Yards	150 Yards	200 Yards	250 Yards	300 Yards	350 Yards	Range at Which Bullet Is Three Inches Low	1,200 Foot-Pounds (Deer, Antelope)	2,000 Foot-Pounds (Elk, Bears to 600 Pounds)	2,800 Foot-Pounds (Large Bears, Moose)
.223 Remington	55	HPPL	3,240	1.0	2.6	3.0	2.1	0.4	4.8		282	0	0	0
.22/250 Remington	55	HPPL	3,730	0.7	2.3	3.0	2.7	1.4	1.2	5.3	324	100	0	0
.224 Weatherby Mag.	55	PE	3,650	0.8	2.3	3.0	2.7	1.3	1.4	5.5	322	120	0	0
.220 Swift	52	HPST	4,000	0.6	2.1	2.9	2.9	2.1	0.3	2.6	355	170	0	0
.243 Winchester	80	HPPL	3,350	0.9	2.5	3.0	2.4	0.5	2.8	7.9	302	200	0	0
.243 Winchester	100	PSPCL	2,960	1.1	2.6	3.0	2.0	0.5	4.5		284	250	0	0
6mm Remington	80	HPPL	3,470	0.9	2.4	3.0	2.6	0.9	2.1	6.7	311	220	0	0
6mm Remington	100	PSPCL	3,130	1.0	2.5	3.0	2.3	0.3	3.1		299	300	0	0
.240 Weatherby Mag.	87	PE	3,500	0.8	2.3	3.0	2.7	1.3	−1.3	5.2	324	320	85	0
.240 Weatherby Mag.	100	PE	3,395	0.8	2.4	3.0	2.6	1.2	−1.4	5.3	322	415	140	0
.250 Savage	87	PSP	3,030	1.1	2.6	3.0	1.9	−0.8	−5.3		278	155	0	0
.250 Savage	100	PSP	2,820	1.2	2.7	2.9	1.4	−1.8	−7.1		263	160	0	0
.257 Roberts	87	PSP	3,170	1.0	2.6	3.0	2.2	−0.1	−4.0		289	190	0	0
.257 Roberts	117	SPCL	2,650	1.4	2.9	2.7	0.5	−3.8				140	0	0
.25/06 Remington	87	HPPL	3,440	0.9	2.4	3.0	2.5	0.6	−2.7	−7.9	303	225	50	0
.25/06 Remington	100	PSPCL	3,230	1.0	2.5	3.0	2.3	0.4	−3.1		299	285	65	0
.25/06 Remington	120	PSPCL	3,010	1.1	2.6	3.0	2.1	−0.2	−4.0		289	360	95	0
.257 Weatherby Mag.	87	PE	3,825	0.7	2.1	2.9	2.9	2.0	0.0	−3.0	351	415	175	5
.257 Weatherby Mag.	100	PE	3,555	0.8	2.3	3.0	2.8	1.6	−0.7		335	455	190	1
.257 Weatherby Mag.	117	NP	3,300	0.9	2.4	3.0	2.5	0.9	−1.9	−6.1	315	465	195	5
6.5 mm Remington Mag.	120	PSPCL	3,210	1.0	2.5	3.0	2.4	0.5	−2.9	−7.7	302	390	155	0
.264 Winchester Mag.	100	PSP	3,320	0.9	2.5	3.0	2.4	0.4	−3.1		299	270	80	0
.264 Winchester Mag.	140	PSPCL	3,030	1.1	2.6	3.0	2.2	0.0	−3.6		299	475	205	10
.270 Winchester	100	PSP	3,480	0.3	2.4	3.0	2.6	0.9	−2.1	−6.7	311	295	85	0
.270 Winchester	130	BP	3,110	1.0	2.5	3.0	2.3	0.3	−3.1		299	435	170	0
.270 Winchester	150	SPCL	2,900	1.2	2.7	2.9	1.6	−1.6	−6.7		266	295	115	15
.270 Weatherby Mag.	130	PE	3,375	0.8	2.4	3.0	2.6	1.2	−1.4	−5.3	323	570	295	95
.270 Weatherby Mag.	150	NP	3,245	0.9	2.4	3.0	2.5	0.9	−1.9	−6.0	316	690	380	155
.284 Winchester	125	PP(SP)	3,140	1.0	2.5	3.0	2.2	0.1	−3.5		294	370	150	0
.284 Winchester	150	PP(SP)	2,860	1.2	2.7	2.9	1.7	−1.1	−5.6		274	395	155	0
7/30 Waters	120	FP	2,680	1.4	2.9	2.7	6.5	−3.9	−11.2		242	145	0	0
7mm Mauser	140	PSP	2,660	1.3	2.8	2.8	1.2	−2.1	−7.4		260	325	55	0
7mm/08 Remington	140	PSP	2,860	1.2	2.7	2.9	1.8	−0.8	−5.1		278	410	140	0
.280 Remington	150	PSPCL	2,970	1.1	2.6	3.0	2.0	−0.5	−4.5		284	435	195	25
.280 Remington	165	SPCL	2,820	1.2	2.7	2.9	1.4	−1.8	−7.0		264	355	160	15
7mm Remington Mag.	125	PP(SP)	3,310	0.9	2.4	3.0	2.5	0.7	−2.5	−7.1	307	410	195	40
7mm Remington Mag.	150	PSPCL	3,110	1.0	2.5	3.0	2.2	0.2	−3.4	8.5	296	485	245	75
7mm Remington Mag.	175	PSPCL	2,860	1.2	2.7	2.9	1.9	−0.7	−4.8		281	575	285	80
7 mm Weatherby Mag.	139	PE	3,300	0.9	2.4	3.0	2.5	1.0	−1.8	−6.0	316	570	300	110
7 mm Weatherby Mag.	154	PE	3,160	1.0	2.5	3.0	2.4	0.6	−2.4		307	625	340	130
7 mm Weatherby Mag.	175	RN	3,070	1.0	2.5	3.0	2.3	0.3	−3.0	−7.8	300	660	380	175
.30 Carbine	110	SP	1,990	2.1	2.9	0.1	−7.1				176	0	0	0
.30 Remington	170	ST	2,120	1.9	3.0	1.5	−3.1				199	115	0	0

Caliber	Bullet Weight (Grains)	Bullet Type*	Muzzle Velocity (Feet Per Second)	50 Yards	100 Yards	150 Yards	200 Yards	250 Yards	300 Yards	350 Yards	Range at Which Bullet Is Three Inches Low (Deer, Antelope)	1,200 Foot-Pounds	2,000 Foot-Pounds (Elk, Bears to 600 Pounds)	2,800 Foot-Pounds (Large Bears, Moose)
.30/30 Winchester	150	SPCL	2,390	1.7	3.0	2.1	−1.6	−8.7			212	120	0	0
.30/30 Winchester	170	SPCL	2,200	1.8	3.0	1.8	−2.3	−9.6			206	140	0	0
.300 Savage	150	SPCL	2,630	1.4	2.9	2.6	0.3	−4.4			238	280	65	0
.300 Savage	180	PSPCL	2,350	1.6	2.9	2.4	−0.2	−5.2			231	305	50	0
.300 Savage	180	RM	2,350	1.7	2.3	2.2	−1.1	−7.3			218	300	35	0
.30/40 Krag	180	PSPCL	2,430	1.5	2.9	2.5	0.2	−4.3			238	345	90	0
.30/40 Krag	220	ST	2,160	1.8	3.0	1.9	−1.7	−8.1			214	330	85	0
.30/06 Springfield	110	PSP	3,380	1.0	2.5	3.0	2.2	−0.2	−4.5		285	225	85	0
.30/06 Springfield	150	BP	2,910	1.1	2.7	2.9	1.9	−0.7	−4.9		280	435	185	5
.30/06 Springfield	165	PSPCL	2,800	1.2	2.7	2.9	1.5	−1.5	−6.4		268	405	180	15
.30/06 Springfield	180	PSPCL	2,700	1.3	2.8	2.8	1.3	1.9	7.0		263	460	205	20
.30/06 Springfield	220	SPCL	2,410	1.6	2.9	2.4	−0.3	5.5			229	330	140	5
.300 Winchester Mag.	150	PSPCL	3,290	0.9	2.5	3.0	2.4	0.6	2.7	7.5	304	465	260	115
.300 Winchester Mag.	180	PSPCL	2,950	1.1	2.6	3.0	2.1	−0.1	3.8		291	645	355	145
.300 Winchester Mag.	220	ST	2,680	1.3	2.8	2.8	1.3	2.0	7.3		261	540	300	125
.300 H&H Mag.	150	ST	3,130	1.0	2.6	3.0	2.2	0.1	3.6		294	460	245	90
.300 H&H Mag	180	PSPCL	2,880	1.2	2.7	2.9	1.8	−0.7	5.0		279	535	280	95
.300 H&H Mag.	220	ST	2,580	1.4	2.9	2.7	0.8	−3.0	9.0		250	490	260	95
.300 Weatherby Mag.	150	PE	3,545	0.8	2.3	3.0	2.7	1.5	−0.8	4.3	334	645	400	225
.300 Weatherby Mag.	180	PE	3,245	0.9	2.4	3.0	2.5	0.9	−1.9	6.0	315	750	465	265
.303 Savage	190	ST	1,940	2.1	2.9	0.6	−5.4				184	70	0	0
.307 Winchester	150	FP	2,760	1.3	2.8	2.7	0.6	3.8	−11.1		243	205	70	0
.307 Winchester	180	FP	2,510	1.5	2.9	2.5	0.0	−5.1	−13.0		232	250	80	0
.303 British	180	SPCL	2,460	1.6	2.9	2.4	−0.4	−5.8			227	230	65	0
.308 Winchester	110	PSP	3,180	1.1	2.6	3.0	1.8	−1.1	−6.3		271	200	60	0
.308 Winchester	125	PSP	3,050	1.1	2.6	3.0	1.9	−0.6	−5.0		280	295	105	0
.308 Winchester	150	PSPCL	2,820	1.2	2.7	2.9	1.5	−1.5	−6.5		267	345	130	0
.308 Winchester	180	PSPCL	2,620	1.4	2.8	2.8	1.1	−2.5	−8.1		256	425	170	0
.32 Winchester Special	170	SPCL	2,250	1.8	3.0	1.9	−2.0	−9.2			209	145	0	0
8mm Mauser	170	SPCL	2,360	1.7	3.0	2.0	−1.6	−8.6			212	150	15	0
8mm Remington Mag.	185	PSPCL	3,080	1.1	2.6	3.0	2.1	−0.2	−4.1		287	490	290	150
8mm Remington Mag.	220	PSPCL	2,830	1.2	2.7	2.9	1.7	−1.1	−5.7		273	580	345	180
.338 Winchester Mag.	200	PP(SP)	2,960	1.1	2.7	3.0	1.9	−0.8	−5.1		278	495	295	150
.338 Winchester Mag.	225	SP	2,780	1.2	2.7	2.9	1.7	−1.1	−5.6		274	680	400	205
.338 Winchester Mag.	250	ST	2,660	1.3	2.8	2.8	1.0	−2.6	−8.3		255	700	320	175
.340 Weatherby Mag.	200	PE	3,210	0.9	2.5	3.0	2.4	0.7	−2.4	−6.9	308	695	455	280
.340 Weatherby Mag.	250	NP	2,850	1.2	2.7	2.9	1.6	−1.3	−6.1		270	530	360	220
.35 Remington	150	PSPCL	2,300	1.8	3.0	1.8	−2.5	−10.8			203	95	0	0
.35 Remington	200	SPCL	2,080	2.0	3.0	1.0	−4.8				188	115	0	0
.351 Remington SL	180	RN	1,850	2.2	2.8	−0.1	−7.3	−19.6			174	40	0	0
.356 Winchester	200	FP	2,460	1.6	2.9	2.4	−0.5	−6.0	−14.8		226	255	95	0
.356 Winchester	250	FP	1,160	1.8	3.0	1.8	−2.1	−9.0	−19.5		208	300	105	0
.358 Winchester	200	ST	2,490	1.5	2.9	2.5	−0.1	−5.1			232	290	115	0

*HPPL, Hollow Point-Lokt; PE, Pointed Expanding; HPBT, Hollow Point Boat Tail; PSPCL, Pointed Soft Point Core-Lokt; PSP, Pointed Soft Point; SPCL, Soft Point Core-Lokt; NP, Nosier Partition; BP, Bronze Point; PP(SP), Power-Point (Soft Point); FP, Flat Point; RN, Round Nose; SP, Soft Point; ST, Silver Tip; SJHP, Semijacketed Hollow Point; FMJ, Full Metal Jacket.

(Continued next page)

(CARMICHEL'S CARTRIDGE GUIDE Continued)

| Caliber | Bullet Weight (Grains) | Bullet Type* | Muzzle Velocity (Feet Per Second) | Trajectory (inches) | | | | | | | Ranges at Which Cartridges Retain Three Levels of Energy (Yards) | | | |
				50 Yards	100 Yards	150 Yards	200 Yards	250 Yards	300 Yards	350 Yards	Range at Which Bullet Is Three Inches Low	1,200 Foot-Pounds (Deer, Antelope)	2,000 Foot-Pounds (Elk, Bears to 600 Pounds)	2,800 Foot-Pounds (Large Bears, Moose)
.358 Winchester	250	ST	2,230	1.7	3.0	2.1	−1.4	−7.6			216	355	105	0
.350 Remington Mag.	200	PSPCL	2,710	1.3	2.8	2.8	1.1	−2.5	−8.3		255	395	205	65
.375 Winchester	200	FP	2,200	1.8	3.0	1.6	−2.9	−11.1	−23.9		201	160	20	0
.375 Winchester	250	FP	1,900	2.1	2.9	0.5	−5.6	−16.0	−31.3		183	175	2	0
.375 H&H Mag.	270	SP	2,690	1.3	2.8	2.8	1.1	−2.4	−8.0		257	550	345	200
.378 Weatherby Mag.	300	NP	2,925	1.2	2.7	2.9	1.8	−1.0	−5.5		275	640	440	310
.38/40 Winchester	180	SP	1,160	3.0	−0.2	−12.1					116	0	0	0
.38/55 Winchester	255	SP	1,320	2.8	1.5	−5.9					135	0	0	0
.44 Remington Mag.	240	SJHP	1,760	2.4	2.6	−1.7	−11.8				159	65	0	0
.444 Marlin	240	SP	2,350	1.8	3.0	1.6	−3.3				197	170	80	0
.444 Marlin	265	SP	2,120	1.9	3.0	1.1	−4.3				191	190	70	0
.45/70 Government	405	SP	1,330	2.8	1.4	−6.3					134	110	0	0
.458 Winchester Mag.	500	FMJ	2,040	1.9	3.0	1.5	−3.0	−10.8			200	640	360	220
.460 Weatherby Mag.	500	FMJ	2,700	1.3	2.8	2.8	1.1	−2.4	−8.0		257	827	575	445

*HPPL, Hollow Point-Lokt; PE, Pointed Expanding; HPBT, Hollow Point Boat Tail; PSPCL, Pointed Soft Point Core-Lokt; PSP, Pointed Soft Point; SPCL, Soft Point Core-Lokt; NP, Nosier Partition; BP, Bronze Point; PP(SP), Power-Point (Soft Point); FP, Flat Point; RN, Round Nose; SP, Soft Point; ST, Silver Tip; SJHP, Semijacketed Hollow Point; FMJ, Full Metal Jacket.

blank range of most American big-game calibers. By 3-inch point-blank range, we mean that, within the recommended ranges, the bullet never rises above or falls below 3 inches of your line of sight. From a hunter's standpoint, this is more than adequate bullet placement because it is well within the vital-area size of all big-game and many varmints.

These figures are the best-ever means of comparing the useful hunting ranges of various cartridges. All data are based on a line of sight 1½ inches above the bore line. This is typical of most scope-sighted rifles. To make use of the table, simply sight your rifle in at any of the ranges shown so that the bullet impact, in relation to point of aim, matches the impact point at that distance (assuming that you're using factory-loaded ammunition and a rifle that is in good condition).

For example, the table shows that the .270 Winchester with a 130-grain Bronze Point bullet is 2.5 inches high at 100 yards. Accordingly, simply adjust the sight on your .270 so that the bullet hits 2.5 inches above point of aim at 100 yards. From that point on, the bullet will hit within 3 inches (vertically) of where you aim out to more than 250 yards.

One column of the table lists the range at which the bullet is 3 inches below line of sight. All the way out to that range, stated in yards, you can hold dead on and forget about trajectory when you're big-game

hunting or when you're shooting most varmints.

By consulting the retained-energy figures and the point-blank ranges, you can provide yourself with a very good idea of the performance of any listed cartridge. Some have such a looped trajectory that the practical hunting ranges at which they can be used are very short. At the other extreme are some of the magnums that retain, for instance, enough energy to kill deer dead at very long ranges. But at those ranges (over 300 yards), even expert riflemen would seldom attempt a shot. In other words, by using both sets of figures, you can quite closely determine how far you can kill efficiently in terms of both on-target energy and ability to make a hit. Perhaps best of all, the combined figures give someone who's buying a new rifle a reliable means of determining which cartridge or cartridges are best suited to his form of hunting.

Hitting what you shoot at is the big weakness in the assumptions behind most cartridge-performance tables. Argue as we may about the relative performance of various cartridges, the major factor is the man behind the gun. When it comes to killing game, I give bullet placement a relative importance of 70 percent. The other 30 percent can be divided between bullet energy and terminal bullet performance any way you want to split it up. As for myself, I long ago decided not to agree with anyone.

MANUFACTURER BALLISTIC DATA

BALLISTICS FOR HUNTERS

The following ballistic tables from various ammunition manufacturers will provide a good insight into how various cartridges perform and how they compare with one another.

These tables will be an aid in cartridge selection—for instance, in trying to pick a varmint load that shoots flattest at long range, or trying to pick a load that offers the widest range of bullet weights for all-round hunting.

INTERCHANGEABILITY TABLE

Cartridges within groups shown are interchangeable. Other substitutions should not be made without specific recommendation of the firearms manufacturer since improper combinations could result in firearm damage or personal injury. **Note A:** *High-speed cartridges must not be used in revolvers. They should be used only in rifles made especially for them. **Note B:** Ammunition with (+ P) on the case headstamp is loaded to higher pressure. Use only in firearms designated for this cartridge and so recommended by the gun manufacturer. **Note C:** Not for use in revolvers chambered for .32 S&W or .32 S&W Long. **Note D:** All .38 Special cartridges can be used in .357 Magnum revolvers but not conversely. **Note E:** 9mm sub-machine gun cartridges should be used in handguns. **Note F:** .44 Russian and .44 S&W Special can be used in .44 Remington Magnum revolvers but not conversely. **Note G:** Not to be used in Win. M-66 and M-73. (This table courtesy of Remington.)

RIMFIRE
.22 W.R.F.
.22 Remington Special
.22 Win. M/1890 in a .22 Win. Magnum Rimfire but not conversely

CENTERFIRE
.25/20 Remington
.25/20 W.C.F.
.25/20 Win.
.25/20 Win. High Speed
.25/20 Marlin
.25 W.C.F.

6mm Rem. (80 & 90 grain)
.244 Rem.

.25 Automatic
.25 Auto. Colt Pistol (ACP)
.25 (6.35mm) Automatic Pistol
6.35 mm Browning

7mm Express Rem.
.280 Rem.

.30/30 Sav.
.30/30 Win.
.30/30 Win. "Accelerator"
.30/30 Marlin
.30/30 Win. High Speed
.30 W.C.F.

.32 Colt Automatic
.32 Auto. Colt Pistol (ACP)
.32 (7.6mm) Automatic Pistol
7.65mm Automatic Pistol

7.65mm Browning (not interchangeable with 7.65mm Luger)

.32 Short Colt in 32 Long Colt but not conversely
SEE NOTE C

.32 S. & W. in 32 S. & W. Long but not conversely

.32 S. & W. Long
.32 Colt New Police
.32 Colt Police Positive

.32 W.C.F.*
.32 Win.*
.32/20 Win. High Speed*
SEE NOTE A

.32/20 Colt L.M.R.
.32/20 W.C.F.
.32/20 Win. and Marlin
SEE NOTE G

.38 S. & W.
.38 Colt New Police
.380 Webley

.38 Colt Special
.38 S. & W. Special
.38 Targetmaster
.38 S. & W. Special Mid-Range
.38 Special (+ P)
.38/44 Special (+ P)
.38 Special
.38 Special Flat Point
SEE NOTES B & D

.38 Short Colt in .38 Long Colt but not conversely. Both can be used in .38 Special

38 Marlin
38 Win.*
SEE NOTE A

.38 Remington*
.38/40 Win.
.38 W.C.F.*
SEE NOTE A

.38 Automatic in .38 Super (+ P) but not conversely

.380 Automatic
9mm Browning Short (Corto Kurz)

9mm Luger
9mm Parabellum
SEE NOTE E

.44 S. & W. Special
SEE NOTE F

.44 Marlin
.44 Win.
.44 Remington
.44/40 Win.
.44 W.C.F.

.45/70 Government
.45/70 Marlin, Win.
.45/70-405

WINCHESTER CENTERFIRE RIFLE BALLISTICS

Cartridge	Game Selector Guide	CXP Guide Number	Bullet Wt. Grs.	Bullet Type	Barrel Length (In.)	Muzzle	100	200	300	400	500
218 Bee	V	1	46	Hollow Point	24	2760	2102	1550	1155	961	850
22 Hornet	V	1	45	Soft Point	24	2690	2042	1502	1128	948	840
22 Hornet	V	1	46	Hollow Point	24	2690	2042	1502	1128	948	841
22-250 Remington	**V**	**1**	**52**	**Hollow Point Boattail**	**24**	**3750**	**3268**	**2835**	**2442**	**2082**	**1755**
22-250 Remington	V	1	55	Pointed Soft Point	24	3680	3137	2656	2222	1832	1493
222 Remington	V	1	50	Pointed Soft Point	24	3140	2602	2123	1700	1350	1107
222 Remington	V	1	55	Full Metal Jacket	24	3020	2675	2355	2057	1783	1537
223 Remington	V	1	53	Hollow Point	24	3330	2882	2477	2106	1770	1475
223 Remington	V	1	55	Pointed Soft Point	24	3240	2747	2304	1905	1554	1270
223 Remington	V	1	55	Full Metal Jacket	24	3240	2877	2543	2232	1943	1679
223 Remington	D	2	64	Power-Point®	24	3020	2656	2320	2009	1724	1473
223 Remington Match	**—**	**M**	**69**	**Hollow Point Boattail**	**24**	**3060**	**2740**	**2442**	**2164**	**1904**	**1665**
225 Winchester	V	1	55	Pointed Soft Point	24	3570	3066	2616	2208	1838	1514
243 Winchester	V	1	80	Pointed Soft Point	24	3350	2955	2593	2259	1951	1670
243 Winchester	D,O/P	2	100	Power-Point	24	2960	2697	2449	2215	1993	1786
243 Winchester	**D,O/P**	**2**	**100**	**Soft Point Boattail**	**24**	**2960**	**2712**	**2477**	**2254**	**2042**	**1843**
6mm Remington	D,O/P	2	100	Power-Point	24	3100	2829	2573	2332	2104	1889
25-06 Remington	V	1	90	Positive Expanding Point	24	3440	3043	2680	2344	2034	1749
25-06 Remington	D,O/P	2	120	Postive Expanding Point	24	2990	2730	2484	2252	2032	1825
25-20 Winchester #	V	1	86	Soft Point	24	1460	1194	1030	931	858	798
25-35 Winchester	D	2	117	Soft Point	24	2230	1866	1545	1282	1097	984
250 Savage	D,O/P	1	100	Silvertip®	24	2820	2467	2140	1839	1569	1339
257 Roberts + P	D,O/P	2	117	Power-Point	24	2780	2411	2071	1761	1488	1263
264 Winchester Mag.	D,O/P	2	140	Power-Point	24	3030	2782	2548	2326	2114	1914
6.5 × 55 Swedish	D,O/P	2	140	Soft Point	24	2550	2359	2176	2002	1836	1680
270 Winchester	D,O/P	2	130	Power-Point	24	3060	2802	2559	2329	2110	1904
270 Winchester	D,O/P	2	130	Silvertip	24	3060	2776	2510	2259	2022	1801
270 Winchester	**D,O/P**	**2**	**140**	**Silvertip Boattail**	**24**	**2960**	**2753**	**2554**	**2365**	**2183**	**2009**
270 Winchester	**D,O/P,M**	**3**	**140**	**Fail Safe®**	**24**	**2920**	**2671**	**2435**	**2211**	**1999**	**1799**
270 Winchester	D,M	3	150	Power-Point	24	2850	2585	2336	2100	1879	1673
280 Remington	D,O/P	2	140	Power-Point	24	3050	2705	2428	2167	1924	1698
280 Remington	**D,O/P**	**3**	**160**	**Silvertip Boattail**	**24**	**2840**	**2637**	**2442**	**2256**	**2078**	**1909**
280 Remington	**D,O/P,M**	**3**	**160**	**Fail Safe**	**24**	**2840**	**2600**	**2372**	**2156**	**1951**	**1759**
284 Winchester	D,O/P,M	3	150	Power-Point	24	2860	2595	2344	2108	1886	1680
7mm Mauser (7×57)	D	2	145	Power-Point	24	2660	2413	2180	1959	1754	1564
7mm Remington Mag.	D,O/P,M	2	150	Power-Point	24	3110	2830	2568	2320	2085	1866
7mm Remington Mag.	**D,O/P,M,L**	**3**	**160**	**Silvertip Boattail**	**24**	**2950**	**2745**	**2550**	**2363**	**2184**	**2012**
7mm Remington Mag.	**D,O/P,M,L**	**3**	**160**	**Fail Safe**	**24**	**2920**	**2678**	**2449**	**2331**	**2025**	**1830**
7mm Remington Mag.	D,O/P,M.L	3	175	Power-Point	24	2860	2645	2440	2244	2057	1879
7.62 × 39mm Russian	D,V	2	123	Soft Point	20	2365	2033	1731	1465	1248	1093
30 Carbine #	V	1	110	Hollow Soft Point	20	1990	1567	1236	1035	923	842
30-30 Winchester	D	2	150	Hollow Point	24	2390	2018	1684	1398	1177	1036
30-30 Winchester	D	2	150	Power-Point	24	2390	2018	1684	1398	1177	1036
30-30 Winchester	D	2	150	Silvertip	24	2390	2018	1684	1398	1177	1036
30-30 Winchester	D	2	170	Power-Point	24	2200	1895	1619	1381	1191	1061
30-30 Winchester	D	2	170	Silvertip	24	2200	1895	1619	1381	1191	1061
30-06 Springfield	V	1	125	Pointed Soft Point	24	3140	2780	2447	2138	1853	1595
30-06 Springfield	D,O/P	2	150	Power-Point	24	2920	2580	2265	1972	1704	1466
30-06 Springfield	D,O/P	2	150	Silvertip	24	2910	2617	2342	2083	1843	1622
30-06 Springfield	**D,O/P,M**	**2**	**165**	**Silvertip Boattail**	**24**	**2800**	**2597**	**2402**	**2216**	**2038**	**1869**
30-06 Springfield	**D,O/P,M**	**3**	**165**	**Fail Safe**	**24**	**2800**	**2540**	**2295**	**2063**	**1846**	**1645**
30-06 Springfield	D,O/P,M	2	165	Pointed Soft Point	24	2800	2573	2357	2151	1956	1772
30-06 Springfield	**D,O/P,M,L**	**3**	**180**	**Fail Safe**	**24**	**2700**	**2486**	**2283**	**2089**	**1904**	**1731**
30-06 Springfield	D,O/P,M	2	180	Power-Point	24	2700	2348	2023	1727	1466	1251
30-06 Springfield	D,O/P,M,L	3	180	Silvertip	24	2700	2469	2250	2042	1846	1663
30-06 Springfield	M,L	3	220	Silvertip	24	2410	2192	1985	1791	1611	1448
30-40 Krag	D	2	180	Power-Point	24	2430	2099	1795	1525	1298	1128
300 Winchester Mag.	D,O/P	2	150	Power-Point	24	3290	2951	2636	2342	2068	1813
300 Winchester Mag.	**D,O/P,M**	**3**	**165**	**Fail Safe**	**24**	**3120**	**2807**	**2515**	**2242**	**1985**	**1748**
300 Winchester Mag.	**M,L**	**3D**	**180**	**Fail Safe**	**24**	**2960**	**2732**	**2514**	**2307**	**2110**	**1923**
300 Winchester Mag.	O/P,M,L	3	180	Power-Point	24	2960	2745	2540	2344	2157	1979
300 Winchester Mag.	M,L,XL	3D	220	Silvertip	24	2680	2448	2228	2020	1823	1640
300 H&H Magnum	**M,L**	**3D**	**180**	**Fail Safe**	**24**	**2880**	**2628**	**2390**	**2165**	**1952**	**1752**
300 H&H Magnum	O/P,M,L	3	180	Silvertip	24	2880	2640	2412	2196	1991	1798
300 Savage	D,O/P	2	150	Power-Point	24	2630	2311	2015	1743	1500	1295

	Energy in Foot Pounds (ft-lbs.)					Trajectory, Short Range Yards						Trajectory, Long Range Yards						
Muzzle	100	200	300	400	500	50	100	150	200	250	300	100	150	200	250	300	400	500
778	451	245	136	94	74	0.3	0	-2.3	-7.2	-15.8	-29.4	1.5	0	-4.2	-12.0	-24.8	-71.4	-155.6
723	417	225	127	90	70	0.3	0	-2.4	-7.7	-16.9	-31.3	1.6	0	-4.5	-12.8	-26.4	-75.6	-163.4
739	426	230	130	92	72	0.3	0	-2.4	-7.7	-16.9	-31.3	1.6	0	-4.5	-12.8	-26.4	-75.5	-163.3
1624	**1233**	**928**	**689**	**501**	**356**	**0.1**	**0**	**-0.7**	**-2.4**	**-5.1**	**-9.1**	**1.2**	**1.1**	**0**	**-2.1**	**-5.5**	**-16.9**	**-36.3**
1654	1201	861	603	410	272	0.2	0.5	0	-1.6	-4.4	-8.7	2.3	2.6	1.9	0	-3.4	-15.9	-38.9
1094	752	500	321	202	136	0.5	0.9	0	-2.5	-6.9	-13.7	2.2	1.9	0	-3.8	-10.0	-32.3	-73.8
1114	874	677	517	388	288	0.5	0.9	0	-2.2	-6.1	-11.7	2.0	1.7	0	-3.3	-8.3	-24.9	-52.5
1305	978	722	522	369	256	0.3	0.7	0	-1.9	-5.3	-10.3	1.7	1.4	0	-2.9	-7.4	-22.7	-49.1
1282	921	648	443	295	197	0.4	0.8	0	-2.2	-6.0	-11.8	1.9	1.6	0	-3.3	-8.5	-26.7	-59.6
1282	1011	790	608	461	344	0.4	0.7	0	-1.9	-5.1	-9.9	1.7	1.4	0	-2.8	-7.1	-21.2	-44.6
1296	1003	765	574	423	308	0.1	0.7	0	-2.1	-5.8	-11.4	1.7	1.6	0	-3.2	-8.2	-25.1	-53.6
1435	**1151**	**914**	**717**	**555**	**425**	**-0.2**	**0**	**-0.9**	**-3.1**	**-6.8**	**-12.1**	**1.6**	**1.4**	**0**	**-2.9**	**-7.4**	**-22.3**	**-46.7**
1556	1148	836	595	412	280	0.2	0.6	0	-1.7	-4.6	-9.0	2.4	2.8	2.0	0	-3.5	-16.3	-39.5
1993	1551	1194	906	676	495	0.3	0.7	0	-1.8	-4.9	-9.4	2.6	2.9	2.1	0	-3.6	-16.2	-37.9
1945	1615	1332	1089	882	708	0.5	0.9	0	-2.2	-5.8	-11.0	1.9	1.6	0	-3.1	-7.8	-22.6	-46.3
1946	**1633**	**1363**	**1128**	**926**	**754**	**0.1**	**0**	**-1.3**	**-3.8**	**-7.8**	**-13.3**	**1.9**	**1.6**	**0**	**-3.0**	**-7.6**	**-22.0**	**-44.8**
2133	1777	1470	1207	983	792	0.4	0.8	0	-1.9	-5.2	-9.9	1.7	1.5	0	-2.8	-7.0	-20.4	-41.7
2364	1850	1435	1098	827	611	0.3	0.6	0	-1.7	-4.5	-8.8	2.4	2.7	2.0	0	-3.4	-15.0	-35.2
2382	1985	1644	1351	1100	887	0.5	0.8	0	-2.1	-5.6	-10.7	1.9	1.6	0	-3.0	-7.5	-22.0	-44.8
407	272	203	165	141	122	0	-4.1	-14.4	-31.8	-57.3	-92.0	0	-8.2	-23.5	-47.0	-79.6	-175.9	-319.4
1292	904	620	427	313	252	0.6	0	-3.1	-9.2	-19.0	-33.1	2.1	0	-5.1	-13.8	-27.0	-70.1	-142.0
1765	1351	1017	751	547	398	0.2	0	-1.6	-4.9	-10.0	-17.4	2.4	2.0	0	-3.9	-10.1	-30.5	-65.2
2009	1511	1115	806	576	415	0.8	1.1	0	-2.9	-7.8	-15.1	2.6	2.2	0	-4.2	-10.8	-33.0	-70.0
2854	2406	2018	1682	1389	1139	0.5	0.8	0	-2.0	-5.4	-10.2	1.8	1.5	0	-2.9	-7.2	-20.8	-42.2
2022	1731	1473	1246	1048	878	0	0	-1.5	-4.8	-9.8	-16.9	2.4	2	0	-3.9	-9.7	-28.1	-56.8
2702	2267	1890	1565	1285	1046	0.4	0.8	0	-2.0	-5.3	-10.1	1.8	1.5	0	-2.8	-7.1	-20.6	-42.0
2702	2225	1818	1472	1180	936	0.5	0.8	0	-2.0	-5.5	-10.4	1.8	1.5	0	-2.9	-7.4	-21.6	-44.3
2724	**2356**	**2029**	**1739**	**1482**	**1256**	**0.1**	**0**	**-1.2**	**-3.7**	**-7.5**	**-12.7**	**1.8**	**1.5**	**0**	**-2.9**	**-7.2**	**-20.6**	**-41.3**
2651	**2218**	**1843**	**1519**	**1242**	**1007**	**-0.2**	**0**	**-1**	**-3.4**	**-7.2**	**-12.6**	**1.7**	**1.5**	**0**	**-3**	**-7.6**	**-22.3**	**-45.7**
2705	2226	1817	1468	1175	932	0.6	1.0	0	-2.4	-6.4	-12.2	2.2	1.8	0	-3.4	-8.6	-25.0	-51.4
2799	2274	1833	1461	1151	897	0.5	0.8	0	-2.2	-5.8	-11.1	1.9	1.6	0	-3.1	-7.8	-23.1	-47.8
2866	**2471**	**2120**	**1809**	**1535**	**1295**	**0.1**	**0**	**-1.4**	**-4.1**	**-8.3**	**-14.0**	**2.1**	**1.7**	**0**	**-3.2**	**-7.9**	**-22.6**	**-45.4**
2866	**2402**	**2000**	**1652**	**1353**	**1100**	**-0.2**	**0**	**-1.1**	**-3.7**	**-7.7**	**-13.5**	**1.8**	**1.6**	**0**	**-3.2**	**-8**	**-23.5**	**-48.2**
2724	2243	1830	1480	1185	940	0.6	1.0	0	-2.4	-6.3	-12.1	2.1	1.8	0	-3.4	-8.5	-24.8	-51.0
2279	1875	1530	1236	990	788	0.2	0	-1.7	-5.1	-10.3	-17.5	1.1	0	-2.8	-7.4	-14.1	-34.4	-66.1
3221	2667	2196	1792	1448	1160	0.4	0.8	0	-1.9	-5.2	-9.9	1.7	1.5	0	-2.8	-7.0	-20.5	-42.1
3093	**2679**	**2311**	**1984**	**1694**	**1439**	**0.1**	**0**	**-1.2**	**-3.7**	**-7.5**	**-12.8**	**1.9**	**1.5**	**0**	**-2.9**	**-7.2**	**-20.6**	**-41.4**
3030	**2549**	**2131**	**1769**	**1457**	**1190**	**-0.2**	**0**	**-1**	**-3.4**	**-7.1**	**-12.5**	**1.7**	**1.5**	**0**	**-2.9**	**-7.5**	**-22**	**-44.9**
3178	2718	2313	1956	1644	1372	0.6	0.9	0	-2.3	-6.0	-11.3	2.0	1.7	0	-3.2	-7.9	-22.7	-45.8
1527	1129	818	586	425	327	0.5	0	-2.6	-7.6	-15.4	-26.7	3.8	3.1	0	-6.0	-15.4	-46.3	-98.4
967	600	373	262	208	173	0.9	0	-4.5	-13.5	-28.3	-49.9	0	-4.5	-13.5	-28.3	-49.9	-118.6	-228.2
1902	1356	944	651	461	357	0.5	0	-2.6	-7.7	-16.0	-27.9	1.7	0	-4.3	-11.6	-22.7	-59.1	-120.5
1902	1356	944	651	461	357	0.5	0	-2.6	-7.7	-16.0	-27.9	1.7	0	-4.3	-11.6	-22.7	-59.1	-120.5
1902	1356	944	651	461	357	0.5	0	-2.6	-7.7	-16.0	-27.9	1.7	0	-4.3	-11.6	-22.7	-59.1	-120.5
1827	1355	989	720	535	425	0.6	0	-3.0	-8.9	-18.0	-31.1	2.0	0	-4.8	-13.0	-25.1	-63.6	-126.7
1827	1355	989	720	535	425	0.6	0	-3.0	-8.9	-18.0	-31.1	2.0	0	-4.8	-13.0	-25.1	-63.6	-126.7
2736	2145	1662	1269	953	706	0.4	0.8	0	-2.1	-5.6	-10.7	1.8	1.5	0	-3.0	-7.7	-23.0	-48.5
2839	2217	1708	1295	967	716	0.6	1.0	0	-2.4	-6.6	-12.7	2.2	1.8	0	-3.5	-9.0	-27.0	-57.1
2820	2281	1827	1445	1131	876	0.6	0.9	0	-2.3	-6.3	-12.0	2.1	1.8	0	-3.3	-8.5	-25.0	-51.8
2873	**2421**	**2114**	**1799**	**1522**	**1280**	**0.1**	**0**	**-1.4**	**-4.3**	**-8.6**	**-14.6**	**2.1**	**1.8**	**0**	**-3.3**	**-8.2**	**-23.4**	**-47.0**
2873	**2365**	**1930**	**1560**	**1249**	**992**	**-0.1**	**0**	**-1.2**	**-3.9**	**-8.2**	**-14.4**	**2.0**	**1.7**	**0**	**-3.4**	**-8.6**	**-25.3**	**-52.3**
2873	2426	2036	1696	1402	1151	0.7	1.0	0	-2.5	-6.5	-12.2	2.2	1.9	0	-3.6	-8.4	-24.4	-49.6
2914	**2472**	**2083**	**1744**	**1450**	**1198**	**-0.1**	**0**	**-1.3**	**-4.1**	**-8.6**	**-14.9**	**2.1**	**1.8**	**0**	**-3.5**	**-8.7**	**-25.5**	**-51.8**
2913	2203	1635	1192	859	625	0.2	0	-1.8	-5.5	-11.2	-19.5	2.7	2.3	0	-4.4	-11.3	-34.4	-73.7
2913	2436	2023	1666	1362	1105	0.2	0	-1.6	-4.8	-9.7	-16.5	2.4	2.0	0	-3.7	-9.3	-27.0	-54.9
2837	2347	1924	1567	1268	1024	0.4	0	-2.2	-6.4	-12.7	-21.6	1.5	0	-3.5	-9.1	-17.2	-41.8	-79.9
2360	1761	1288	929	673	508	0.4	0	-2.4	-7.1	-14.5	-25.0	1.6	0	-3.9	-10.5	-20.3	-51.7	-103.9
3605	2900	2314	1827	1424	1095	0.3	0.7	0	-1.8	-4.8	-9.3	2.6	2.9	2.1	0	-3.5	-15.4	-35.5
3567	**2888**	**2319**	**1842**	**1445**	**1120**	**-0.3**	**0**	**-0.8**	**-2.9**	**-6.4**	**-11.4**	**1.5**	**1.3**	**0**	**-2.7**	**-7.0**	**-20.9**	**-43.6**
3503	**2983**	**2528**	**2129**	**1780**	**1478**	**-0.2**	**0**	**-1.0**	**-3.2**	**-6.8**	**-11.8**	**1.6**	**1.4**	**0**	**-2.8**	**-7.1**	**-20.7**	**42.1**
3501	3011	2578	2196	1859	1565	0.5	0.8	0	-2.1	-5.5	-10.4	1.9	1.6	0	-2.9	-7.3	-20.9	-41.9
3508	2927	2424	1993	1623	1314	0.2	0	-1.7	-4.9	-9.9	-16.9	2.5	2.0	0	-3.8	-9.5	-27.5	-56.1
3316	**2762**	**2284**	**1873**	**1523**	**1227**	**-0.2**	**0**	**-1.1**	**-3.5**	**-7.5**	**-13.2**	**1.8**	**1.6**	**0**	**-3.1**	**-7.9**	**-23.2**	**-47.6**
3315	2785	2325	1927	1584	1292	0.6	0.9	0	-2.3	-6.0	-11.5	2.1	1.7	0	-3.2	-8.0	-23.3	-47.4
2303	1779	1352	1012	749	558	0.3	0	-1.9	-5.7	-11.6	-19.9	2.8	2.3	0	-4.5	-11.5	-34.4	-73.0

WINCHESTER CENTERFIRE RIFLE BALLISTICS (Continued)

Cartridge	Game Selector Guide	CXP Guide Number	Bullet Wt. Grs.	Bullet Type	Barrel Length (In.)	Muzzle	100	200	300	400	500
300 Savage	D,O/P	2	150	Silvertip	24	2630	2354	2095	1853	1631	1434
300 Savage	D	2	180	Power-Point	24	2350	2025	1728	1467	1252	1098
303 Savage	D	2	190	Silvertip	24	1890	1612	1372	1183	1055	970
303 British	D	2	180	Power-Point	24	2460	2233	2018	1816	1629	1459
307 Winchester	D,M	2	180	Power-Point	24	2510	2179	1874	1599	1362	1177
308 Winchester	**D,O/P**	**2**	**150**	**Silvertip Boattail**	**24**	**2820**	**2559**	**2312**	**2080**	**1861**	**1659**
308 Winchester	**D,O/P,M**	**3**	**150**	**Fail Safe**	**24**	**2820**	**2533**	**2263**	**2010**	**1775**	**1561**
308 Winchester	D,O/P	2	150	Power-Point	24	2820	2488	2179	1893	1633	1405
308 Winchester	D,O/P	2	150	Silvertip	24	2820	2533	2263	1774	1560
308 Winchester Match	**—**	**M**	**168**	**Hollow Point Boattail**	**24**	**2680**	**2485**	**2297**	**2118**	**1948**	**1786**
308 Winchester	**D,O/P,M,L**	**3**	**180**	Fail Safe	24	**2590**	**2357**	**2137**	**1929**	**1734**	**1555**
308 Winchester	D,O/P,M	2	180	Power-Point	24	2620	2274	1955	1666	1414	1212
308 Winchester	M,L	3	180	Silvertip	24	2620	2393	2178	1974	1782	1604
32 Win Special	D	2	170	Power-Point	24	2250	1870	1537	1267	1082	971
32 Win Special	D	2	170	Silvertip	24	2250	1870	1537	1267	1082	971
32-20 Winchester #	V	1	100	Lead	24	1210	1021	913	834	769	712
8mm Mauser (8 × 57)	D	2	170	Power-Point	24	2360	1969	1622	1333	1123	997
338 Winchester Mag.	D,O/P,M,L	3	200	Power-Point	24	2960	2658	2375	2110	1862	1635
338 Winchester Mag.	M,L,XL	3D	225	Soft Point	24	2780	2572	2374	2184	2003	1832
338 Winchester Mag.	**M,L,XL**	**3D**	**230**	**Fail Safe**	**24**	**2780**	**2573**	**2375**	**2186**	**2005**	**1834**
35 Remington	D	2	200	Power-Point	24	2020	1646	1335	1114	985	901
356 Winchester	D,M	2	200	Power-Point	24	2460	2114	1797	1517	1284	1113
357 Magnum #	V,D	2	158	Jacketed Soft Point	20	1830	1427	1138	980	883	809
358 Winchester	D,M	3	200	Silvertip	24	2490	2171	1876	1610	1379	1194
375 Winchester	D,M	2	200	Power-Point	24	2200	1841	1526	1268	1089	980
375 H&H Magnum	**L,XL**	**4**	**270**	**Fail Safe**		under development					
375 H&H Magnum	M,L,XL	3D	300	Silvertip	24	2530	2268	2022	1793	1583	1397
375 H&H Magnum	XL	4	300	Full Metal Jacket	24	2530	2171	1843	1551	1307	1126
38-40 Winchester #	D	2	180	Soft Point	24	1160	999	901	827	764	710
38-55 Winchester	D	2	255	Soft Point	24	1320	1190	1091	1018	963	917
44 Remington Magnum #	V,D	2	210	Silvertip Hollow Point	20	1580	1198	993	879	795	725
44 Remington Magnum #	D	2	240	Hollow Soft Point	20	1760	1362	1094	953	861	789
44-40 Winchester #	D	2	200	Soft Point	24	1190	1006	900	822	756	699
45-70 Government	D,M	2	300	Jacketed Hollow Point	24	1880	1650	1425	1235	1105	1010
458 Winchester Magnum	L, XL	3D	510	Soft Point	24	2040	1770	1527	1319	1157	1046

Game Selector	CXP Class	Examples
V-Varmint	1	Prairie dog, coyote, woodchuck
D-Deer	2	Antelope, deer, black bear
O/P-Open or Plains	3	Elk, moose
M-Medium Game	3D	All game in category 3 plus large dangerous game (i.e. Kodiak bear)
L-Large Game	4	Cape Buffalo, elephant
XL-Extra Large Game	M	Match

#Acceptable for use in pistols and revolvers also.
Bold type indicates Supreme® product line

*Intended for use in fast twist barrels (e.g., 1 in 7 to 1 in 9).
Slower twist barrels may not sufficiently stabilize bullet.

Energy in Foot Pounds (ft-lbs.)						Trajectory, Short Range Yards						Trajectory, Long Range Yards						
Muzzle	100	200	300	400	500	50	100	150	200	250	300	100	150	200	250	300	400	500
2303	1845	1462	1143	886	685	0.3	0	−1.8	−5.4	−11.0	−18.8	2.7	2.2	0	−4.2	−10.7	−31.5	−65.5
2207	1639	1193	860	626	482	0.5	0	−2.6	−7.7	−15.6	−27.1	1.7	0	−4.2	−11.3	−21.9	−55.8	−112.0
1507	1096	794	591	469	397	1.0	0	−4.3	−12.6	−25.5	−43.7	2.9	0	−6.8	−18.3	−35.1	−88.2	−172.5
2418	1993	1627	1318	1060	851	0.3	0	−2.1	−6.1	−12.2	−20.8	1.4	0	−3.3	−8.8	−16.6	−40.4	−77.4
2519	1898	1404	1022	742	554	0.3	0	−2.2	−6.5	−13.3	−22.9	1.5	0	−3.6	−9.6	−18.6	−47.1	−93.7
2649	2182	1782	1441	1154	917	0.2	0	−1.5	−4.4	−9.0	−15.4	2.2	1.8	0	−3.5	−8.7	−25.5	−52.3
2649	2137	1706	1346	1049	812	−0.1	0	−1.2	−3.9	−8.4	−14.7	2.0	1.7	0	−3.4	−8.8	−26.2	−54.6
2648	2061	1581	1193	888	657	0.2	0	−1.6	−4.8	−9.8	−16.9	2.4	2.0	0	−3.8	−9.8	−29.3	−62.0
2648	2137	1705	1344	1048	810	0.2	0	−1.5	−4.5	−9.3	−15.9	2.3	1.9	0	−3.6	−9.1	−26.9	−55.7
2680	2303	1970	1674	1415	1190	−0.1	0	−1.3	−4.1	−8.6	−14.9	2.1	1.8	0	−3.4	−8.7	−25.1	−50.7
2682	2222	1826	1487	1202	966	0	0	−1.5	−4.8	−9.9	−18.2	2.4	2.1	0	−4.0	−10.0	−29.4	−60.3
2743	2066	1527	1109	799	587	0.3	0	−2.0	−5.9	−12.1	−20.9	2.9	2.4	0	−4.7	−12.1	−36.9	−79.1
2743	2288	1896	1557	1269	1028	0.2	0	−1.8	−5.2	−10.4	−17.7	2.6	2.1	0	−4.0	−9.9	−28.9	−58.8
1911	1320	892	606	442	356	0.6	0	−3.1	−9.2	−19.0	−33.2	2.0	0	−5.1	−13.8	−27.1	−70.9	−144.3
1911	1320	892	606	442	356	0.6	0	−3.1	−9.2	−19.0	−33.2	2.0	0	−5.1	−13.8	−27.1	−70.9	−144.3
325	231	185	154	131	113	0	−6.3	−20.9	−44.9	−79.3	−125.1	0	−11.5	−32.3	−63.6	−106.3	−230.3	−413.3
2102	1463	993	671	476	375	0.5	0	−2.7	−8.2	−17.0	−29.8	1.8	0	−4.5	−12.4	−24.3	−63.8	−130.7
3890	3137	2505	1977	1539	1187	0.5	0.9	0	−2.3	−6.1	−11.6	2.0	1.7	0	−3.2	−8.2	−24.3	−50.4
3862	3306	2816	2384	2005	1677	1.2	1.3	0	−2.7	−7.1	−12.9	2.7	2.1	0	−3.6	−9.4	−25.0	−49.9
3948	3382	2881	2441	2054	1719	−0.1	0	−1.2	−3.8	−7.9	−13.7	1.9	1.7	0	−3.2	−8.1	−23.4	−47.4
1812	1203	791	551	431	360	0.9	0	−4.1	−12.1	−25.1	−43.9	2.7	0	−6.7	−18.3	−35.8	−92.8	−185.5
2688	1985	1434	1022	732	550	0.4	0	−2.3	−7.0	−14.3	−24.7	1.6	0	−3.8	−10.4	−20.1	−51.2	−102.3
1175	715	454	337	274	229	0	−2.4	−9.1	−21.0	−39.2	−64.3	0	−5.5	−16.2	−33.1	−57.0	−128.3	−235.8
2753	2093	1563	1151	844	633	0.4	0	−2.2	−6.5	−13.3	−23.0	1.5	0	−3.6	−9.7	−18.6	−47.2	−94.1
2150	1506	1034	714	527	427	0.6	0	−3.2	−9.5	−19.5	−33.8	2.1	0	−5.2	−14.1	−27.4	−70.1	−138.1
4263	3426	2723	2141	1669	1300	0.3	0	−2.0	−5.9	−11.9	−20.3	2.9	2.4	0	−4.5	−11.5	−33.8	−70.1
4263	3139	2262	1602	1138	844	0.3	0	−2.2	−6.5	−13.5	−23.4	1.5	0	−3.6	−9.8	−19.1	−49.1	−99.5
538	399	324	273	233	201	0	−6.7	−22.2	−47.3	−83.2	−130.8	0	−12.1	−33.9	−66.4	−110.6	−238.3	−425.6
987	802	674	587	525	476	0	−4.7	−15.4	−32.7	−57.2	−89.3	0	−8.4	−23.4	−45.6	−75.2	−158.8	−277.4
1164	670	460	361	295	245	0	−3.7	−13.3	−29.8	−54.2	−87.3	0	−7.7	−22.4	−44.9	−76.1	−168.0	−305.8
1650	988	638	484	395	332	0	−2.7	−10.2	−23.6	−44.2	−73.3	0	−6.1	−18.1	−37.4	−65.1	−150.3	−282.5
629	449	360	300	254	217	0	−6.5	−21.6	−46.3	−81.8	−129.1	0	−11.8	−33.3	−65.5	−109.5	−237.4	−426.2
2355	1815	1355	1015	810	680	0	−2.4	−8.2	−17.6	−31.4	−51.5	0	−4.6	−12.8	−25.4	−44.3	95.5	—
4712	3547	2640	1970	1516	1239	0.8	0	−3.5	−10.3	−20.8	−35.6	2.4	0	−5.6	−14.9	−28.5	−71.5	−140.4

REMINGTON RIFLE BALLISTICS

Caliber	Bullet Wt.(grs.)	Style	Primer No.	Muzzle	100 Yds.	200 Yds.	300 Yds.	400 Yds.	500 Yds.
						Velocity—Feet Per Second			
17 Rem.	25	Hollow Point Power-Lokt®	7½	4040	3284	2644	2086	1606	1235
22 Hornet	45	Pointed Soft Point	6½	2690	2042	1502	1128	948	840
	45	Hollow Point	6½	2690	2042	1502	1128	948	840
220 Swift	50	Pointed Soft Point	9½	3780	3158	2617	2135	1710	1357
222 Rem.	50	Pointed Soft Point	7½	3140	2602	2123	1700	1350	1107
	50	Hollow Point Power-Lokt®	7½	3140	2635	2182	1777	1432	1172
222 Rem. Mag.	55	Pointed Soft Point	7½	3240	2748	2305	1906	1556	1272
223 Rem.	55	Pointed Soft Point	7½	3240	2747	2304	1905	1554	1270
	55	Hollow Point Power-Lokt®	7½	3240	2773	2352	1969	1627	1341
	55	Metal Case	7½	3240	2759	2326	1933	1587	1301
	60	Hollow Point Match	7½	3100	2712	2355	2026	1726	1463
22-250 Rem.	55	Pointed Soft Point	9½	3680	3137	2656	2222	1832	1493
	55	Hollow Point Power-Lokt®	9½	3680	3209	2785	2400	2046	1725
243 Win.	80	Pointed Soft Point	9½	3350	2955	2593	2259	1951	1670
	80	Hollow Point Power-Lokt®	9½	3350	2955	2593	2259	1951	1670
	100	Pointed Soft Point Core-Lokt®	9½	2960	2697	2449	2215	1993	1786
	105	Extended Range	9½	2920	2689	2470	2261	2062	1874
6MM Rem.	80	Pointed Soft Point	9½	3470	3064	2694	2352	2036	1747
	100	Pointed Soft Point Core-Lokt®	9½	3100	2829	2573	2332	2104	1889
	105	Extended Range	9½	3060	2822	2596	2381	2177	1982
6MM BR Rem.	100	Pointed Soft Point	7½	2550	2310	2083	1870	1671	1491
25-20 Win.	86	Soft Point	6½	1460	1194	1030	931	858	797
250 Sav.	100	Pointed Soft Point	9½	2820	2504	2210	1936	1684	1461
257 Roberts	117	Soft Point Core-Lokt®	9½	2650	2291	1961	1663	1404	1199
	122	Extended Range	9½	2600	2331	2078	1842	1625	1431
25-06 Rem.	100	Pointed Soft Point Core-Lokt®	9½	3230	2893	2580	2287	2014	1762
	120	Pointed Soft Point Core-Lokt®	9½	2990	2730	2484	2252	2032	1825
	122	Extended Range	9½	2930	2706	2492	2289	2095	1911
6.5 x 55 Swedish	140	Pointed Soft Point Core-Lokt®	9½	2550	2353	2164	1984	1814	1654
264 Win. Mag.	140	Pointed Soft Point Core-Lokt®	9½M	3030	2782	2548	2326	2114	1914
270 Win.	100	Pointed Soft Point	9½	3320	2924	2561	2225	1916	1636
	130	Pointed Soft Point Core-Lokt®	9½	3060	2776	2510	2259	2022	1801
	130	Bronze Point	9½	3060	2802	2559	2329	2110	1904
	150	Soft Point Core-Lokt®	9½	2850	2504	2183	1886	1618	1385
	140	Swift A-Frame® PSP	9½	2925	2652	2394	2152	1923	1711
	135	Extended Range	9½	3000	2780	2570	2369	2178	1995
	140	Extended Range Boat Tail	9½	2960	2749	2548	2355	2171	1995
7MM BR Rem.	140	Pointed Soft Point	7½	2215	2012	1821	1643	1481	1336
7MM Mauser (7 x 57)	140	Pointed Soft Point	9½	2660	2435	2221	2018	1827	1648
7 x 64	140	Pointed Soft Point	9½	2950	2714	2489	2276	2073	1881
	175	Pointed Soft Point Core-Lokt®	9½	2650	2445	2248	2061	1883	1716
7MM-08 Rem.	140	Pointed Soft Point	9½	2860	2625	2402	2189	1988	1798
	120	Hollow Point	9½	3000	2725	2467	2223	1992	1778
	154	Extended Range	9½	2715	2510	2315	2128	1950	1781
280 Rem.	140	Pointed Soft Point	9½	3000	2758	2528	2309	2102	1905
	150	Pointed Soft Point Core-Lokt®	9½	2890	2624	2373	2135	1912	1705
	165	Soft Point Core-Lokt®	9½	2820	2510	2220	1950	1701	1479
	165	Extended Range	9½	2820	2623	2434	2253	2080	1915
7MM Rem. Mag.	150	Pointed Soft Point Core-Lokt®	9½M	3110	2830	2568	2320	2085	1866
	175	Pointed Soft Point Core-Lokt®	9½M	2860	2645	2440	2244	2057	1879
	140	Pointed Soft Point	9½M	3175	2923	2684	2458	2243	2039
	160	Swift A-Frame™ PSP	9½M	2900	2659	2430	2212	2006	1812
	165	Extended Range	9½M	2900	2699	2507	2324	2147	1979
7MM Wby. Mag.	140	Pointed Soft Point	9½M	3225	2970	2729	2501	2283	2077
	175	Pointed Soft Point Core-Lokt®	9½M	2910	2693	2486	2288	2098	1918
	165	Extended Range	9½M	2950	2747	2553	2367	2189	2019
30 Carbine	110	Soft Point	6½	1990	1567	1236	1035	923	842
30 Rem.	170	Soft Point Core-Lokt®	9½	2120	1822	1555	1328	1153	1036
30-30 Win. Accelerator®	55	Soft Point	9½	3400	2693	2085	1570	1187	986
30-30 Win.	150	Soft Point Core-Lokt®	9½	2390	1973	1605	1303	1095	974
	170	Soft Point Core-Lokt®	9½	2200	1895	1619	1381	1191	1061
	170	Hollow Point Core-Lokt®	9½	2200	1895	1619	1381	1191	1061
	160	Extended Range	9½	2300	1997	1719	1473	1268	1116
300 Savage	180	Soft Point Core-Lokt®	9½	2350	2025	1728	1467	1252	1098
	150	Pointed Soft Point Core-Lokt®	9½	2630	2354	2095	1853	1631	1432

Energy—Foot-Pounds						Short Range[1] Trajectory*						Long Range[2] Trajectory*							Barrel Length
Muzzle	100 Yds.	200 Yds.	300 Yds.	400 Yds.	500 Yds.	50 Yds.	100 Yds.	150 Yds.	200 Yds.	250 Yds.	300 Yds.	100 Yds.	150 Yds.	200 Yds.	250 Yds.	300 Yds.	400 Yds.	500 Yds.	
906	599	388	242	143	85	0.1	0.5	0.0	-1.5	-4.2	-8.5	2.1	2.5	1.9	0.0	-3.4	-17.0	-44.3	24″
723	417	225	127	90	70	0.3	0.0	-2.4	-7.7	-16.9	-31.3	1.6	0.0	-4.5	-12.8	-26.4	-75.6	-163.4	24″
723	417	225	127	90	70	0.3	0.0	-2.4	-7.7	-16.9	-31.3	1.6	0.0	-4.5	-12.8	-26.4	-75.6	-163.4	
1586	1107	760	506	325	204	0.2	0.5	0.0	-1.6	-4.4	-8.8	1.3	1.2	0.0	-2.5	-6.5	-20.7	-47.0	24″
1094	752	500	321	202	136	0.5	0.9	0.0	-2.5	-6.9	-13.7	2.2	1.9	0.0	-3.8	-10.0	-32.3	-73.8	24″
1094	771	529	351	228	152	0.5	0.9	0.0	-2.4	-6.6	-13.1	2.1	1.8	0.0	-3.6	-9.5	-30.2	-68.1	
1282	922	649	444	296	198	0.4	0.8	0.0	-2.2	-6.0	-11.8	1.9	1.6	0.0	-3.3	-8.5	-26.7	-59.5	24″
1282	921	648	443	295	197	0.4	0.8	0.0	-2.2	-6.0	-11.8	1.9	1.6	0.0	-3.3	-8.5	-26.7	-59.6	
1282	939	675	473	323	220	0.4	0.8	0.0	-2.1	-5.8	-11.4	1.8	1.6	0.0	-3.2	-8.2	-25.5	-56.0	24″
1282	929	660	456	307	207	0.4	0.8	0.0	-2.1	-5.9	-11.6	1.9	1.6	0.0	-3.2	-8.4	-26.2	-57.9	
1280	979	739	547	397	285	0.5	0.8	0.0	-2.2	-6.0	-11.5	1.9	1.6	0.0	-3.2	-8.3	-25.1	-53.6	
1654	1201	861	603	410	272	0.2	0.5	0.0	-1.6	-4.4	-8.7	2.3	2.6	1.9	0.0	-3.4	-15.9	-38.9	24″
1654	1257	947	703	511	363	0.2	0.5	0.0	-1.5	-4.1	-8.0	2.1	2.5	1.8	0.0	-3.1	-14.1	-33.4	
1993	1551	1194	906	676	495	0.3	0.7	0.0	-1.8	-4.9	-9.4	2.6	2.9	2.1	0.0	-3.6	-16.2	-37.9	
1993	1551	1194	906	676	495	0.3	0.7	0.0	-1.8	-4.9	-9.4	2.6	2.9	2.1	0.0	-3.6	-16.2	-37.9	24″
1945	1615	1332	1089	882	708	0.5	0.9	0.0	-2.2	-5.8	-11.0	1.9	1.6	0.0	-3.1	-7.8	-22.6	-46.3	
1988	1686	1422	1192	992	819	0.5	0.9	0.0	-2.2	-5.8	-11.0	2.0	1.6	0.0	-3.1	-7.7	-22.2	-44.8	
2139	1667	1289	982	736	542	0.3	0.6	0.0	-1.6	-4.5	-8.7	2.4	2.7	1.9	0.0	-3.3	-14.9	-35.0	
2133	1777	1470	1207	983	792	0.4	0.8	0.0	-1.9	-5.2	-9.9	1.7	1.5	0.0	-2.8	-7.0	-20.4	-41.7	
2183	1856	1571	1322	1105	916	0.4	0.8	0.0	-2.0	-5.2	-9.8	1.7	1.5	0.0	-2.7	-6.9	-20.0	-40.4	
1444	1185	963	776	620	494	0.3	0.0	-1.9	-5.6	-11.4	-19.3	2.8	2.3	0.0	-4.3	-10.9	-31.7	-65.1	15″
407	272	203	165	141	121	0.0	-4.1	-14.4	-31.8	-57.3	-92.0	0.0	-8.2	-23.5	-47.0	-79.6	-175.9	-319.4	24″
1765	1392	1084	832	630	474	0.2	0.0	-1.6	-4.7	-9.6	-16.5	2.3	2.0	0.0	-3.7	-9.5	-28.3	-59.5	24″
1824	1363	999	718	512	373	0.3	0.0	-1.9	-5.8	-11.9	-20.7	2.9	2.4	0.0	-4.7	-12.0	-36.7	-79.2	24″
1831	1472	1170	919	715	555	0.3	0.0	-1.9	-5.5	-11.2	-19.1	2.8	2.3	0.0	-4.3	-10.9	-32.0	-66.4	
2316	1858	1478	1161	901	689	0.4	0.7	0.0	-1.9	-5.0	-9.7	1.6	1.4	0.0	-2.7	-6.9	-20.5	-42.7	
2382	1985	1644	1351	1100	887	0.5	0.8	0.0	-2.1	-5.6	-10.7	1.9	1.6	0.0	-3.0	-7.5	-22.0	-44.8	24″
2325	1983	1683	1419	1189	989	0.5	0.9	0.0	-2.2	-5.7	-10.8	1.9	1.6	0.0	-3.0	-7.5	-21.7	-43.9	
2021	1720	1456	1224	1023	850	0.3	0.0	-1.8	-5.4	-10.8	-18.2	2.7	2.2	0.0	-4.1	-10.1	-29.1	-58.7	24″
2854	2406	2018	1682	1389	1139	0.5	0.8	0.0	-2.0	-5.4	-10.2	1.8	1.5	0.0	-2.9	-7.2	-20.8	-42.2	24″
2448	1898	1456	1099	815	594	0.3	0.7	0.0	-1.8	-5.0	-9.7	2.7	3.0	2.2	0.0	-3.7	-16.6	-39.1	
2702	2225	1818	1472	1180	936	0.5	0.8	0.0	-2.0	-5.5	-10.4	1.8	1.5	0.0	-2.9	-7.4	-21.6	-44.3	
2702	2267	1890	1565	1285	1046	0.4	0.8	0.0	-2.0	-5.3	-10.1	1.8	1.5	0.0	-2.8	-7.1	-20.6	-42.0	24″
2705	2087	1587	1185	872	639	0.7	1.0	0.0	-2.6	-7.1	-13.6	2.3	2.0	0.0	-3.8	-9.7	-29.2	-62.2	
2659	2186	1782	1439	1150		0.6	0.9	0.0	-2.3	-6.0	-11.5	2.0	1.7	0.0	-3.2	-8.1	-23.8	-48.9	
2697	2315	1979	1682	1421	1193	0.5	0.8	0.0	-2.0	-5.3	-10.1	1.8	1.5	0.0	-2.8	-7.1	-20.4	-41.0	
2723	2349	2018	1724	1465	1237	0.5	0.8	0.0	-2.1	-5.5	-10.3	1.9	1.5	0.0	-2.9	-7.2	-20.7	-41.6	
1525	1259	1031	839	681	555	0.5	0.0	-2.7	-7.7	-15.4	-25.9	1.8	0.0	-4.1	-10.9	-20.6	-50.0	-95.2	15″
2199	1843	1533	1266	1037	844	0.2	0.0	-1.7	-5.0	-10.0	-17.0	2.5	2.0	0.0	-3.8	-9.6	-27.7	-56.3	24″
2705	2289	1926	1610	1336	1100	0.5	0.9	0.0	-2.1	-5.7	-10.7	1.9	1.6	0.0	-3.0	-7.6	-21.8	-44.2	24″
2728	2322	1964	1650	1378	1144	0.2	0.0	-1.7	-4.9	-9.9	-16.8	2.5	2.0	0.0	-3.9	-9.4	-26.9	-54.3	
2542	2142	1793	1490	1228	1005	0.6	0.9	0.0	-2.3	-6.1	-11.6	2.1	1.7	0.0	-3.2	-8.1	-23.5	-47.7	
2398	1979	1621	1316	1058	842	0.5	0.8	0.0	-2.1	-5.7	-10.8	1.9	1.6	0.0	-3.0	-7.6	-22.3	-45.8	24″
2520	2155	1832	1548	1300	1085	0.7	1.0	0.0	-2.5	-6.7	-12.6	2.3	1.9	0.0	-3.5	-8.8	-25.3	-51.0	
2797	2363	1986	1657	1373	1128	0.5	0.8	0.0	-2.1	-5.5	-10.4	1.8	1.5	0.0	-2.9	-7.3	-21.1	-42.9	
2781	2293	1875	1518	1217	968	0.6	0.9	0.0	-2.3	-6.2	-11.8	2.1	1.7	0.0	-3.3	-8.3	-24.2	-49.7	
2913	2308	1805	1393	1060	801	0.2	0.0	-1.5	-4.6	-9.5	-16.4	2.3	1.9	0.0	-3.7	-9.4	-28.1	-58.8	24″
2913	2520	2171	1860	1585	1343	0.6	0.9	0.0	-2.3	-6.1	-11.4	2.1	1.7	0.0	-3.2	-8.0	-22.8	-45.6	
3221	2667	2196	1792	1448	1160	0.4	0.8	0.0	-1.9	-5.2	-9.9	1.7	1.5	0.0	-2.8	-7.0	-20.5	-42.1	
3178	2718	2313	1956	1644	1372	0.6	0.9	0.0	-2.3	-6.0	-11.3	2.0	1.7	0.0	-3.2	-7.9	-22.7	-45.8	24″
3133	2655	2240	1878	1564	1292	0.4	0.7	0.0	-1.8	-4.8	-9.1	2.6	2.9	2.0	0.0	-3.4	-14.5	-32.6	
2987	2511	2097	1739	1430	1166	0.6	0.9	0.0	-2.2	-5.9	-11.3	2.0	1.7	0.0	-3.2	-7.9	-23.0	-46.7	
3081	2669	2303	1978	1689	1434	0.5	0.9	0.0	-2.1	-5.7	-10.7	1.9	1.6	0.0	-3.0	-7.5	-21.4	-42.9	
3233	2741	2315	1943	1621	1341	0.3	0.7	0.0	-1.7	-4.6	-8.8	2.5	2.8	2.0	0.0	-3.2	-14.0	-31.5	
3293	2818	2401	2033	1711	1430	0.5	0.9	0.0	-2.2	-5.7	-10.8	1.9	1.6	0.0	-3.0	-7.6	-21.8	-44.0	24″
3188	2765	2388	2053	1756	1493	0.5	0.8	0.0	-2.1	-5.5	-10.3	1.9	1.6	0.0	-2.9	-7.2	-20.6	-41.3	
967	600	373	262	208	173	0.9	0.0	-4.5	-13.5	-28.3	-49.9	0.0	-4.5	-13.5	-28.3	-49.9	-118.6	-228.2	20″
1696	1253	913	666	502	405	0.7	0.0	-3.3	-9.7	-19.6	-33.8	2.2	0.0	-5.3	-14.1	-27.2	-69.0	-136.9	24″
1412	886	521	301	172	119	0.4	0.8	0.0	-2.4	-6.7	-13.8	2.0	1.8	0.0	-3.8	-10.2	-35.0	-84.4	24″
1902	1296	858	565	399	316	0.5	0.0	-2.7	-8.2	-17.0	-30.0	1.8	0.0	-4.6	-12.5	-24.6	-65.3	-134.9	
1827	1355	989	720	535	425	0.6	0.0	-3.0	-8.9	-18.0	-31.1	2.0	0.0	-4.8	-13.0	-25.1	-63.6	-126.7	24″
1827	1355	989	720	535	425	0.6	0.0	-3.0	-8.9	-18.0	-31.1	2.0	0.0	-4.8	-13.0	-25.1	-63.6	-126.7	
1879	1416	1050	771	571	442	0.5	0.0	-2.7	-7.9	-16.1	-27.6	1.8	0.0	-4.3	-11.6	-22.3	-56.3	-111.9	
2207	1639	1193	860	626	482	0.5	0.0	-2.6	-7.7	-15.6	-27.1	1.7	0.0	-4.2	-11.3	-21.9	-55.8	-112.0	24″
2303	1845	1462	1143	806	685	0.3	0.0	-1.8	-5.4	-11.0	-18.8	2.7	2.2	0.0	-4.2	-10.7	-31.5	-65.6	

FEDERAL CLASSIC® HUNTING RIFLE

Usage Key: ① = Varmints, predators, small game ② = Medium game ③ = Large, heavy game ④ = Dangerous game ⑤ = Target shooting, training, practice

Usage	Caliber	Bullet Wgt. In Grains	Bullet Wgt. In Grams	Bullet Style**	Factory Primer No.	Velocity in Feet Per Second (To Nearest 10 FPS) Muzzle	100 Yds.	200 Yds.	300 Yds.	400 Yds.	500 Yds.	Energy in Foot-Pounds (To Nearest 5 Foot-Pounds) Muzzle	100 Yds.	200 Yds.	300 Yds.	400 Yds.	500 Yds.
①	222 Rem. (5.56×43mm)	50	3.24	Hi-Shok Soft Point	205	3140	2600	2120	1700	1350	1110	1095	750	500	320	200	135
⑤	222 Rem. (5.56×43mm)	55	3.56	Hi-Shok FMJ Boat-tail	205	3020	2740	2480	2230	1900	1780	1115	915	750	610	485	385
①	223 Rem. (5.56×45mm)	55	3.56	Hi-Shok Soft Point	205	3240	2750	2300	1910	1550	1270	1280	920	650	445	295	195
⑤	223 Rem. (5.56×45mm)	55	3.56	Hi-Shok FMJ Boat-tail	205	3240	2950	2670	2410	2170	1940	1280	1060	875	710	575	460
①	22-250 Rem.	55	3.56	Hi-Shok Soft Point	210	3680	3140	2660	2220	1830	1490	1655	1200	860	605	410	270
①	243 Win. (6.16×51mm)	80	5.18	Sierra Pro-Hunter SP	210	3350	2960	2590	2260	1950	1670	1995	1550	1195	905	675	495
②	243 Win. (6.16×51mm)	100	6.48	Hi-Shok Soft Point	210	2960	2700	2450	2220	1990	1790	1945	1615	1330	1090	880	710
①	6mm Rem.	80	5.18	Sierra Pro-Hunter SP	210	3470	3060	2690	2350	2040	1750	2140	1665	1290	980	735	540
②	6mm Rem.	100	6.48	Hi-Shok Soft Point	210	3100	2830	2570	2330	2100	1890	2135	1775	1470	1205	985	790
②	25-06 Rem.	117	7.58	Sierra Pro-Hunter SP	210	2990	2730	2480	2250	2030	1830	2320	1985	1645	1350	1100	885
②	6.5×55 Swedish	140	9.07	Hi-Shok Soft Point	210	2600	2400	2220	2040	1860	1700	2100	1795	1525	1285	1080	900
②	270 Win.	130	8.42	Hi-Shok Soft Point	210	3060	2800	2560	2330	2110	1900	2700	2265	1890	1565	1285	1045
②	270 Win.	150	9.72	Hi-Shok Soft Point RN	210	2850	2500	2180	1890	1620	1390	2705	2085	1585	1185	870	640
②	7mm Mauser (7×57mm Mauser)	175	11.34	Hi-Shok Soft Point RN	210	2440	2140	1860	1600	1380	1200	2315	1775	1340	1000	740	565
②	7mm Mauser (7×57mm Mauser)	140	9.07	Hi-Shok Soft Point	210	2660	2450	2260	2070	1890	1730	2200	1865	1585	1330	1110	930
②	280 Rem.	150	9.72	Hi-Shok Soft Point	210	2890	2670	2460	2260	2060	1880	2780	2370	2015	1695	1420	1180
②	7mm Rem. Magnum	150	9.72	Hi-Shok Soft Point	215	3110	2830	2570	2320	2090	1870	3220	2670	2200	1790	1450	1160
③	7mm Rem. Magnum	175	11.34	Hi-Shok Soft Point	215	2860	2650	2440	2240	2060	1880	3180	2720	2310	1960	1640	1370
①	30 Carbine (7.62×33mm)	110	7.13	Hi-Shok Soft Point RN	205	1990	1570	1240	1040	920	840	965	600	375	260	210	175
②	7.62×39mm Soviet	123	7.97	Hi-Shok Soft Point	210	2300	2030	1780	1550	1350	1200	1445	1125	860	655	500	395
②	30-30 Win.	150	9.72	Hi-Shok Soft Point FN	210	2390	2020	1680	1400	1180	1040	1900	1355	945	650	460	355
②	30-30 Win.	170	11.01	Hi-Shok Soft Point RN	210	2200	1900	1620	1380	1190	1060	1830	1355	990	720	535	425
①	30-30 Win.	125	8.10	Hi-Shok Hollow Point	210	2570	2090	1660	1320	1080	960	1830	1210	770	480	320	260
②	300 Savage	150	9.72	Hi-Shok Soft Point	210	2630	2350	2100	1850	1630	1430	2305	1845	1460	1145	885	685
②	300 Savage	180	11.66	Hi-Shok Soft Point	210	2350	2140	1940	1750	1570	1410	2205	1825	1495	1215	985	800
②	308 Win. (7.62×51mm)	150	9.72	Hi-Shok Soft Point	210	2820	2530	2260	2010	1770	1560	2650	2140	1705	1345	1050	810
②	308 Win. (7.62×51mm)	180	11.66	Hi-Shok Soft Point	210	2620	2390	2180	1970	1780	1600	2745	2290	1895	1555	1270	1030
②	30-06 Springfield (7.62×63mm)	150	9.72	Hi-Shok Soft Point	210	2910	2620	2340	2080	1840	1620	2820	2280	1825	1445	1130	875
③	30-06 Springfield (7.62×63mm)	180	11.66	Hi-Shok Soft Point	210	2700	2470	2250	2040	1850	1660	2915	2435	2025	1665	1360	1105
①	30-06 Springfield (7.62×63mm)	125	8.10	Sierra Pro-Hunter SP	210	3140	2780	2450	2140	1850	1600	2735	2145	1660	1270	955	705
③	30-06 Springfield (7.62×63mm)	220	14.25	Sierra Pro-Hunter SP RN	210	2410	2130	1870	1630	1420	1250	2835	2215	1705	1300	985	760
③	30-06 Springfield (7.62×63mm)	180	11.66	Sierra Pro-Hunter SP RN	210	2700	2350	2020	1730	1470	1250	2915	2200	1630	1190	860	620
③	300 Win. Magnum	180	11.66	Sierra Pro-Hunter SP	215	2960	2750	2540	2340	2160	1980	3500	3010	2580	2195	1860	1565
②	300 Win. Magnum	150	9.72	Sierra Pro-Hunter SP	215	3280	3030	2800	2570	2360	2160	3570	3055	2600	2205	1860	1560
②	303 British	180	11.66	Sierra Pro-Hunter SP	210	2460	2230	2020	1820	1630	1460	2420	1995	1625	1315	1060	850
②	303 British	150	9.72	Hi-Shok Soft Point	210	2690	2440	2210	1980	1780	1590	2400	1980	1620	1310	1055	840
②	32 Win. Special	170	11.01	Hi-Shok Soft Point	210	2250	1920	1630	1370	1180	1040	1910	1395	1000	710	520	410
②	8mm Mauser (8×57mm JS Mauser)	170	11.01	Hi-Shok Soft Point	210	2360	1970	1620	1330	1120	1000	2100	1465	995	670	475	375
③	338 Win. Magnum	225	14.58	Hi-Shok Soft Point	215	2780	2570	2370	2180	2000	1830	3860	3305	2815	2380	2000	1670
②	357 Magnum	180	11.66	Hi-Shok Hollow Point	100	1550	1160	980	860	770	680	960	535	385	295	235	185
②	35 Rem.	200	12.96	Hi-Shok Soft Point	210	2080	1700	1380	1140	1000	910	1920	1280	840	575	445	370
③	375 H&H Magnum	270	17.50	Hi-Shok Soft Point	215	2690	2420	2170	1920	1700	1500	4340	3510	2810	2220	1740	1355
④	375 H&H Magnum	300	19.44	Hi-Shok Soft Point	215	2530	2270	2020	1790	1580	1400	4265	3425	2720	2135	1665	1295
②	44 Rem. Magnum	240	15.55	Hi-Shok Hollow Point	150	1760	1380	1090	950	860	790	1650	1015	640	485	395	330
②	45-70 Government	300	19.44	Sierra Hollow Point FN	210	1880	1650	1430	1240	1110	1010	2355	1815	1355	1015	810	680

*Only for use in barrels intended for .323 inch diameter bullets. Do not use in 8×57mm J Commission Rifles (M1888) or in sporting or other military arms of .318 inch bore diameter.
**RN = Round Nose   SP = Soft Point   FN = Flat Nose   FMJ = Full Metal Jacket

| Wind Drift in Inches 10 MPH Crosswind | | | | | Height of Bullet Trajectory in Inches Above of Below Line of Sight if Zeroed at ⊕ Yards. Sights 1.5 Inches Above Bore Line. | | | | | | | | | | Test Barrel Length Inches |
| | | | | | Average Range | | | | Long Range | | | | | | |
100 Yds.	200 Yds.	300 Yds.	400 Yds.	500 Yds.	50 Yds.	100 Yds.	200 Yds.	300 Yds.	50 Yds.	100 Yds.	200 Yds.	300 Yds.	400 Yds.	500 Yds.	
1.7	7.3	18.3	36.4	63.1	−0.2	⊕	−3.7	−15.3	+0.7	+1.9	⊕	−9.7	−31.6	−71.3	24
0.9	3.4	8.5	16.8	26.3	−0.2	⊕	−3.1	−12.0	+0.6	+1.6	⊕	−7.3	−21.5	−44.6	24
1.4	6.1	15.0	29.4	50.8	−0.3	⊕	−3.2	−12.9	+0.5	+1.6	⊕	−8.2	−26.1	−58.3	24
0.8	3.3	7.8	14.5	24.0	−0.3	⊕	−2.5	−9.9	+0.3	+1.3	⊕	−6.1	−18.3	−37.8	24
1.2	5.2	12.5	24.4	42.0	−0.4	⊕	−2.1	−9.1	+0.1	+1.0	⊕	−6.0	−19.1	−42.6	24
1.0	4.3	10.4	19.8	33.3	−0.3	⊕	−2.5	−10.2	+0.3	+1.3	⊕	−6.4	−19.7	−42.2	24
0.9	3.6	8.4	15.7	25.8	−0.2	⊕	−3.3	−12.4	+0.6	+1.6	⊕	−7.5	−22.0	−45.4	24
1.0	4.1	9.9	18.8	31.6	−0.3	⊕	−2.2	−9.3	+0.2	+1.1	⊕	−5.9	−18.2	−39.0	24
0.8	3.3	7.9	14.7	24.1	−0.3	⊕	−2.9	−11.0	+0.5	+1.4	⊕	−6.7	−19.8	−40.6	24
0.8	3.4	8.1	15.1	24.9	−0.2	⊕	−3.2	−12.0	+0.6	+1.6	⊕	−7.2	−21.4	−44.0	24
0.8	3.4	8.0	14.8	24.1	−0.1	⊕	−4.5	−16.2	+1.1	+2.3	⊕	−9.4	−27.2	−55.0	24
0.8	3.2	7.6	14.2	23.3	−0.2	⊕	−2.9	−11.2	+0.5	+1.5	⊕	−6.8	−20.0	−41.1	24
1.2	5.3	12.8	24.5	41.3	−0.1	⊕	−4.1	−15.5	+0.9	+2.0	⊕	−9.4	−28.6	−61.0	24
1.5	6.2	15.0	28.7	47.8	−0.1	⊕	−6.2	−22.6	+1.6	+3.1	⊕	−13.3	−40.1	−84.6	24
1.3	3.2	8.2	15.4	23.4	−0.1	⊕	−4.3	−15.4	+1.0	+2.1	⊕	−9.0	−26.1	−52.9	24
0.7	3.1	7.2	13.4	21.9	−0.2	⊕	−3.4	−12.6	+0.7	+1.7	⊕	−7.5	−21.8	−44.3	24
0.8	3.4	8.1	15.1	24.9	−0.3	⊕	−2.9	−11.0	+0.5	+1.4	⊕	−6.7	−19.9	−41.0	24
0.7	3.1	7.2	13.3	21.7	−0.2	⊕	−3.5	−12.8	+0.7	+1.7	⊕	−7.6	−22.1	−44.9	24
3.4	15.0	35.5	63.2	96.7	+0.6	⊕	−12.8	−46.8	+3.9	+6.4	⊕	−27.7	−81.8	−167.8	18
1.5	6.4	15.2	28.7	47.3	+0.2	⊕	−7.0	−25.1	+1.9	+3.5	⊕	−14.5	−43.4	−90.6	20
2.0	8.5	20.9	40.1	66.1	+0.2	⊕	−7.2	−26.7	+1.9	+3.6	⊕	−15.9	−49.1	−104.5	24
1.9	8.0	19.4	36.7	59.8	+0.3	⊕	−8.3	−29.8	+2.4	+4.1	⊕	−17.4	−52.4	−109.4	24
2.2	10.1	25.4	49.4	81.6	+0.1	⊕	−6.6	−26.0	+1.7	+3.3	⊕	−16.0	−50.9	−109.5	24
1.1	4.8	11.6	21.9	36.3	0	⊕	−4.8	−17.6	+1.2	+2.4	⊕	−10.4	−30.9	−64.4	24
1.1	4.6	10.9	20.3	33.3	+0.1	⊕	−6.1	−21.6	+1.7	+3.1	⊕	−12.4	−36.1	−73.8	24
1.0	4.4	10.4	19.7	32.7	−0.1	⊕	−3.9	−14.7	+0.8	+2.0	⊕	−8.8	−26.3	−54.8	24
0.9	3.9	9.2	17.2	28.3	−0.1	⊕	−4.6	−16.5	+1.1	+2.3	⊕	−9.7	−28.3	−57.8	24
1.0	4.2	9.9	18.7	31.2	−0.2	⊕	−3.6	−13.6	+0.7	+1.8	⊕	−8.2	−24.4	−50.9	24
0.9	3.7	8.8	16.5	27.1	−0.1	⊕	−4.2	−15.3	+1.0	+2.1	⊕	−9.0	−26.4	−54.0	24
1.1	4.5	10.8	20.5	34.4	−0.3	⊕	−3.0	−11.9	+0.5	+1.5	⊕	−7.3	−22.3	−47.5	24
1.4	6.0	14.3	27.2	45.0	−0.1	⊕	−6.2	−22.4	+1.7	+3.1	⊕	−13.1	−39.3	−82.2	24
1.5	6.4	15.7	30.4	51.2	−0.1	⊕	−4.9	−18.3	+1.1	+2.4	⊕	−11.0	−33.6	−71.9	24
0.7	2.8	6.6	12.3	20.0	−0.2	⊕	−3.1	−11.7	+0.6	+1.6	⊕	−7.0	−20.3	−41.1	24
0.7	2.7	6.3	11.5	18.8	−0.3	⊕	−2.3	−9.1	+0.3	+1.1	⊕	−5.6	−16.4	−33.6	24
1.1	4.5	10.6	19.9	32.7	0	⊕	−5.5	−19.6	+1.4	+2.8	⊕	−11.3	−33.2	−68.1	24
1.0	4.1	9.6	18.1	29.9	−0.1	⊕	−4.4	−15.9	+1.0	+2.2	⊕	−9.4	−27.6	−56.8	24
1.9	8.4	20.3	38.6	63.0	+0.3	⊕	−8.0	−29.2	+2.3	+4.0	⊕	−17.2	−52.3	−109.8	24
2.1	9.3	22.9	43.9	71.7	+0.2	⊕	−7.6	−28.5	+2.1	+3.8	⊕	−17.1	−52.9	−111.9	24
0.8	3.1	7.3	13.6	22.2	−0.1	⊕	−3.8	−13.7	+0.8	+1.9	⊕	−8.1	−23.5	−47.5	24
5.8	21.7	45.2	76.1	NA	⊕	−3.4	−29.7	−88.2	+1.7	⊕	−22.8	−77.9	−173.8	−321.4	18
2.7	12.0	29.0	53.3	83.3	+0.5	⊕	−10.7	−39.3	+3.2	+5.4	⊕	−23.3	−70.0	−144.0	24
1.1	4.5	10.8	20.3	33.7	−0.4	⊕	−5.5	−18.4	+1.0	+2.4	⊕	−10.9	−33.3	−71.2	24
1.2	5.0	11.9	22.4	37.1	+0.5	⊕	−6.3	−21.2	+1.3	+2.6	⊕	−11.2	−33.3	−69.1	24
4.2	17.8	39.8	68.3	102.5	⊕	−2.2	−21.7	−67.2	+1.1	⊕	−17.4	−60.7	−136.0	−250.2	20
1.7	7.6	18.6	35.7	NA	⊕	−1.3	−14.1	−43.7	+0.7	⊕	−11.5	−39.7	−89.1	−163.1	24

These trajectory tables were calculated by computer using the best available data for each load. Trajectories are representative of the nominal behavior of each load at standard conditions (59°F temperature:barometric pressure of 29.53 inches; altitude at sea level). Shooters are cautioned that actual trajectories may differ due to variations in altitude, atmospheric conditions, guns, sights, and ammunition.

WEATHERBY BALLISTICS CHART

Suggested Usage	Cartridge	Bullet Weight Grains	Bullet Type	Ballistic Coefficient	Velocity in Feet per Second						Energy in Foot-Pounds						Path of Bullet Above or below line-of-sight of riflescopes mounted 1.5" above bore				
					Muzzle	100 Yards	200 Yards	300 Yards	400 Yards	500 Yards	Muzzle	100 Yards	200 Yards	300 Yards	400 Yards	500 Yards	100 Yards	200 Yards	300 Yards	400 Yards	500 Yards
V	.224 WM	55	Pt-Ex	.235	3650	3192	2780	2403	2057	1742	1627	1244	944	705	516	370	2.8	3.7	0.0	−9.7	−27.7
V	.240 WM	87	Pt-Ex	.327	3523	3198	2888	2595	2317	2055	2398	1975	1612	1301	1037	816	2.7	3.4	0.0	−8.6	−23.7
M		100	Pt-Ex	.381	3406	3116	2844	2588	2346	2117	2577	2156	1796	1488	1222	996	2.8	3.5	0.0	−8.6	−23.6
		100	Partition	.384	3406	3136	2881	2641	2413	2196	2577	2184	1843	1549	1293	1071	2.7	3.5	0.0	−8.3	−22.7
V	.257 WM	87	Pt-Ex	.322	3825	3456	3118	2803	2511	2236	2827	2308	1878	1518	1218	966	2.1	2.8	0.0	−7.2	−20.0
M		100	Pt-Ex	.357	3602	3280	2980	2701	2438	2190	2882	2389	1973	1620	1320	1065	2.4	3.2	0.0	−7.8	−21.6
		117	Pt-Ex	.391	3402	3134	2878	2632	2397	2173	3007	2552	2151	1799	1493	1227	2.8	3.5	0.0	−8.5	−23.1
		120	Partition	.391	3305	3045	2800	2568	2348	2139	2911	2472	2090	1758	1469	1219	3.0	3.7	0.0	−8.8	−24.0
V	.270 WM	100	Pt-Ex	.307	3760	3380	3033	2712	2412	2133	3139	2537	2042	1633	1292	1010	2.3	3.0	0.0	−7.8	−21.6
M		130	Pt-Ex	.409	3375	3100	2842	2598	2367	2147	3287	2773	2330	1948	1616	1331	2.9	3.6	0.0	−8.7	−23.7
		130	Partition	.416	3375	3127	2893	2670	2458	2257	3287	2822	2415	2058	1714	1470	2.8	3.5	0.0	−8.3	−22.4
		150	Pt-Ex	.462	3245	3019	2803	2598	2402	2215	3507	3034	2617	2248	1922	1634	3.0	3.7	0.0	−8.9	−23.8
		150	Partition	.465	3245	3029	2823	2627	2439	2259	3507	3055	2655	2298	1981	1699	3.0	3.7	0.0	−8.7	−23.3
M	7MM WM	139	Pt-Ex	.392	3340	3082	2838	2608	2389	2180	3443	2931	2486	2099	1761	1467	2.9	3.6	0.0	−8.7	−23.6
		140	Partition	.434	3303	3069	2847	2636	2434	2241	3391	2927	2519	2159	1842	1562	2.9	3.6	0.0	−8.6	−23.1
		154	Pt-Ex	.433	3260	3022	2797	2583	2379	2184	3633	3123	2675	2281	1934	1630	3.0	3.7	0.0	−9.0	−24.1
		160	Partition	.475	3200	2991	2791	2600	2417	2241	3637	3177	2767	2401	2075	1784	3.1	3.8	0.0	−8.9	−23.8
B		175	Pt-Ex	.462	3070	2855	2649	2449	2258	2075	3662	3168	2726	2331	1981	1672	3.5	4.2	0.0	−10.0	−27.0
M	.300 WM	150	Pt-Ex	.349	3600	3297	3016	2751	2502	2266	4316	3621	3028	2520	2084	1709	2.4	3.1	0.0	−7.7	−21.0
		150	Partition	.387	3600	3319	3057	2809	2575	2353	4316	3669	3111	2628	2208	1843	2.4	3.0	0.0	−7.5	−20.1
		165	Boat Tail	.435	3450	3207	2973	2748	2531	2324	4361	3768	3238	2766	2347	1978	2.6	3.3	0.0	−7.9	−21.2
B		180	Pt-Ex	.425	3300	3064	2841	2629	2426	2233	4352	3753	3226	2762	2352	1992	2.9	3.6	0.0	−8.6	−23.2
		180	Partition	.474	3300	3085	2881	2686	2499	2319	4352	3804	3317	2882	2495	2150	2.8	3.5	0.0	−8.3	−22.3
		220	Rn-Ex	.300	2905	2498	2125	1787	1491	1250	4122	3047	2206	1560	1085	763	5.3	6.6	0.0	−17.6	−51.3
B	.340 WM	200	Pt-Ex	.361	3260	2977	2708	2451	2206	1975	4719	3937	3255	2667	2162	1732	3.2	4.0	0.0	−9.8	−26.8
		210	Partition	.400	3250	3000	2763	2539	2325	2122	4924	4195	3559	3004	2520	2098	3.1	3.8	0.0	−9.2	−24.9
		225	Pt-Ex	.307	3105	2854	2614	2385	2166	1957	4816	4070	3414	2841	2343	1914	3.6	4.3	0.0	−10.5	−28.4
		250	Pt-Ex	.291	3002	2672	2365	2079	1814	1574	5002	3963	3105	2399	1827	1375	1.7	0.0	−7.9	−24.0	−50.7
		250	Partition	.473	2980	2780	2588	2404	2228	2059	4931	4290	3719	3209	2756	2354	3.7	4.4	0.0	−10.3	−27.5
B	.378 WM	270	Pt-Ex	.380	3180	2915	2661	2419	2189	1970	6062	5094	4246	3509	2872	2326	1.3	0.0	−6.2	−18.4	−37.9
																	3.4	4.2	0.0	−10.1	−28.0
		300	Rn-Ex	.250	2925	2545	2191	1864	1564	1292	5699	4314	3199	2315	1629	1111	2.0	0.0	−9.3	−28.6	−62.3
A		300	FMJ	.275	2925	2580	2262	1972	1710	1482	5701	4434	3408	2592	1949	1463	1.84	0.0	−8.6	−26.1	−55.9
A	.416 WM	400	Swift A	.391	2650	2411	2185	1971	1770	1585	6239	5165	4242	3450	2783	2233	5.4	6.3	0.0	−15.1	−41.7
																	2.2	0.0	−9.5	−27.7	−57.5
		400	Rn-Ex	.311	2700	2406	2129	1869	1626	1399	6475	5141	4025	3102	2347	1739	5.6	6.6	0.0	−16.7	−46.6
																	2.3	0.0	−10	−30	−63.2
		400	**Mono Solid®	.304	2700	2397	2115	1852	1613	1402	6474	5104	3971	3047	2310	1747	5.7	6.7	0.0	−17.0	−47.4
																	2.3	0.0	−10.1	−30.4	−64.3
A	.460 WM	500	RNSP	.287	2600	2289	1998	1726	1474	1247	7505	5816	4430	3308	2414	1727	2.6	0.0	−11.4	−34.5	−73.7
		500	FMJ	.295	2600	2297	2013	1747	1501	1276	7505	5858	4498	3390	2501	1807	2.6	0.0	−11.2	−33.9	−72.0

Legend: PT-EX = Pointed Expanding   Rn-Ex = Round nose-Expanding   FMJ = Full Metal Jacket   A = Divided Lead Cavity or "H" Type

Note: These tables were calculated by computer using a standard modern scientific technique to predict trajectories and recoil energies from the best available data for each cartridge. The figures shown are expected to be reasonably accurate of ammunition behavior under standard conditions. However, the shooter is cautioned that performance will vary because of variations in rifles, ammunition, atmospheric conditions and altitude.

B.C.: Ballistic Coefficients used for these tables were supplied by the bullet manufacturers.

Listed velocities were determined using 26-inch barrels. Velocities from shorter barrels will be reduced by 30 to 65 feet per second per inch of barrel removed.

Trajectories were computed with the line-of-sight 1.5 inches above the bore centerline.

*Partition is a registered trademark of Nosler, Inc.

**Monolithic Solid is a registered trademark of A-Square, Inc.

Usage: V-Varmint   M-Medium Game (Deer, Sheep, Pronghorn, Black Bear)   B-Big Game (Elk, Moose, Grizzly)   A-African Big Game (Elephant, Cape Buffalo, Rhino, Lion)

FEDERAL CLASSIC® AUTOMATIC PISTOL

Usage Key: 1 = Varmints, predators, small game   2 = Medium game   3 = Self-defense   4 = Target shooting, training, practice

Usage	Caliber	Bullet Wgt. In Grains	Bullet Wgt. In Grams	Bullet Style*	Factory Primer No.	Velocity in Feet Per Second (To Nearest 10 FPS) Muzzle	25 Yds.	50 Yds.	75 Yds.	100 Yds.	Energy in Foot-Pounds (To Nearest 5 Foot-Pounds) Muzzle	25 Yds.	50 Yds.	75 Yds.	100 Yds.	Mid-Range Trajectory 25 Yds.	50 Yds.	75 Yds.	100 Yds.	Test Barrel Length Inches
3, 4	25 Auto (6.35mm Browning)	50	3.24	Full Metal Jacket	200	760	750	730	720	700	65	60	55	55	55	0.5	1.9	4.5	8.1	2
3, 4	32 Auto (7.65mm Browning)	71	4.60	Full Metal Jacket	100	910	880	860	830	810	130	120	115	110	105	0.3	1.4	3.2	5.9	4
3, 4	380 Auto (9×17mm Short)	95	6.15	Full Metal Jacket	100	960	910	870	830	790	190	175	160	145	130	0.3	1.3	3.1	5.8	3¾
3, 4	380 Auto (9×17mm Short)	90	5.83	Hi-Shok JHP	100	1000	940	890	840	800	200	175	160	140	130	0.3	1.2	2.9	5.5	3¾
3, 4	9mm Luger (9×19mm Parabellum)	124	8.03	Full Metal Jacket	100	1120	1070	1030	990	960	345	315	290	270	255	0.2	0.9	2.2	4.1	4
3	9mm Luger (9×19mm Parabellum)	115	7.45	Hi-Shok JHP	100	1160	1100	1060	1020	990	345	310	285	270	250	0.2	0.9	2.1	3.8	4
3	9mm Luger (9×19mm Parabellum)	147	9.52	Hi-Shok JHP	100	980	950	930	900	880	310	295	285	265	255	0.3	1.2	2.8	5.1	4
3	357 Sig	125	8.10	Truncated FMJ	100	1350	1270	1190	1130	1080	510	445	395	355	325	0.2	0.7	1.6	3.1	4
3	40 S&W	180	11.06	Hi-Shok JHP	100	990	960	930	910	890	390	365	345	330	315	0.3	1.2	2.8	5.0	4
3	40 S&W	155	10.04	Hi-Shok JHP	100	1140	1080	1030	990	950	445	400	365	335	315	0.2	0.9	2.2	4.1	4
3	10mm Auto	180	11.06	Hi-Shok JHP	150	1030	1000	970	950	920	425	400	375	355	340	0.3	1.1	2.5	4.7	5
3	10mm Auto	155	10.04	Hi-Shok JHP	150	1330	1230	1140	1080	1030	605	515	450	400	360	0.2	0.7	1.8	3.3	5
3	45 Auto	230	14.90	Full Metal Jacket	150	850	830	810	790	770	370	350	335	320	305	0.4	1.6	3.6	6.6	5
4	45 Auto	185	11.99	Hi-Shok JHP	150	950	920	900	880	860	370	350	335	315	300	0.3	1.3	2.9	5.3	5
3	45 Auto	230	14.90	Hi-Shok JHP	150	850	830	810	790	770	370	350	350	335	300	0.4	1.6	3.7	6.7	5

*JHP = Jacketed Hollow Point   FMJ = Full Metal Jacket

FEDERAL CLASSIC® REVOLVER

Usage Key: ① = Varmints, predators, small game   ② = Medium game   ③ = Self-defense   ④ = Target shooting, training, practice

Usage	Caliber	Bullet Wgt. In Grains	Grams	Bullet Style**	Factory Primer No.	Velocity in Feet Per Second (To Nearest 10 FPS) Muzzle	25 Yds.	50 Yds.	75 Yds.	100 Yds.	Energy in Foot-Pounds (To Nearest 5 Foot-Pounds) Muzzle	25 Yds.	50 Yds.	75 Yds.	100 Yds.	Mid-Range Trajectory 25 Yds.	50 Yds.	75 Yds.	100 Yds.	Test Barrel Length Inches
④	32 S&W Long	98	6.35	Lead Wadcutter	100	780	700	630	560	500	130	105	85	70	55	0.5	2.2	5.6	11.1	4
④	32 S&W Long	98	6.35	Lead Round Nose	100	710	690	670	650	640	115	105	100	95	90	0.6	2.3	5.3	9.6	4
③	32 H&R Magnum	95	6.15	Lead Semi-Wadcutter	100	1030	1000	940	930	900	225	210	195	185	170	0.3	1.1	2.5	4.7	4½
③	32 H&R Magnum	85	5.50	Hi-Shok JHP	100	1100	1050	1020	970	930	230	210	195	175	165	0.2	1.0	2.3	4.3	4½
③,④	38 Special	158	10.23	Lead Round Nose	100	760	740	720	710	690	200	190	185	175	170	0.5	2.0	4.6	8.3	4-V
③,④	38 Special	158	10.23	Lead Semi-Wadcutter	100	760	740	720	710	690	200	190	185	175	170	0.5	2.0	4.6	8.3	4-V
①,③	38 Special (High-Velocity+P)	125	8.10	Hi-Shok JHP	100	950	920	900	880	860	250	235	225	215	205	0.3	1.3	2.9	5.4	4-V
①,③	38 Special (High-Velocity+P)	110	7.13	Hi-Shok JHP	100	1000	960	930	900	870	240	225	210	195	185	0.3	1.2	2.7	5.0	4-V
①,③	38 Special (High-Velocity+P)	158	10.23	Semi-Wadcutter HP	100	890	870	860	840	820	280	265	260	245	235	0.3	1.4	3.3	5.9	4-V
①,③	38 Special (High-Velocity+P)	158	10.23	Lead Semi-Wadcutter	100	890	870	860	840	820	270	260	260	245	235	0.3	1.3	3.3	5.9	4-V
①,③	38 Special (High-Velocity+P)	125	8.10	Hi-Shok JSP	100	950	920	900	880	860	250	235	225	215	205	0.3	1.3	2.9	5.4	4-V
②,③	357 Magnum	158	10.23	Hi-Shok JSP	100	1240	1160	1100	1060	1020	535	475	430	395	365	0.2	0.8	1.9	3.5	4-V
②,③	357 Magnum	125	8.10	Hi-Shok JHP	100	1450	1350	1240	1160	1100	580	495	430	370	335	0.1	0.6	1.5	2.8	4-V
①,③	357 Magnum	158	10.23	Lead Semi-Wadcutter	100	1240	1160	1060	1040	1020	535	475	430	395	365	0.2	0.8	1.9	3.5	4-V
①,③	357 Magnum	110	7.13	Hi-Shok JHP	100	1300	1180	1090	1040	990	410	340	290	260	235	0.2	0.8	1.9	3.5	4-V
②,③	357 Magnum	158	10.23	Hi-Shok JHP	100	1240	1160	1100	1060	1020	535	475	430	395	365	0.2	0.8	1.9	3.5	4-V
②,③	357 Magnum	180	11.66	Hi-Shok JHP	100	1090	1030	980	930	890	475	425	385	350	320	0.2	1.0	2.4	4.5	4-V
②,③	357 Magnum	140	9.07	Hi-Shok JHP	100	1360	1270	1200	1130	1080	575	500	445	395	360	0.2	0.7	1.6	3.0	4-V
①,③	41 Rm. Magnum	210	13.60	Hi-Shok JHP	150	1300	1210	1130	1070	1030	790	680	595	540	495	0.2	0.7	1.8	3.3	4-V
①,③	44 S&W Special	200	12.96	Semi-Wadcutter HP	150	900	860	830	800	770	360	330	305	285	260	0.3	1.4	3.4	6.3	6½-V
②,③	44 Rem. Magnum	240	15.55	Hi-Shok JHP	150	1180	1130	1090	1050	1010	740	675	625	580	550	0.2	0.9	2.0	3.7	6½-V
①,②	44 Rem. Magnum	180	11.66	Hi-Shok JHP	150	1610	1480	1370	1270	1180	1035	875	750	640	555	0.1	0.5	1.2	2.3	6½-V
①,③	45 Colt	225	14.58	Semi-Wadcutter HP	150	900	880	860	840	820	405	385	370	355	340	0.3	1.4	3.2	5.8	5½

+ P ammunition is loaded to a higher pressure. Use only in firearms so recommended by the gun manufacturer. "V" indicates vented barrel to simulate service conditions. *Also available in 20-round box (A44B20).

** JHP = Jacketed Hollow Point HP = Hollow Point   JSP = Jacketed Soft Point

FEDERAL CLASSIC® 22

Usage Key: ① = Varmints, predators, small game   ② = Medium game   ③ = Large, heavy game   ④ = Dangerous game   ⑤ = Target shooting, training, practice

Usage	Cartridge Per Box	Caliber*	Bullet Wgt. In Grains	Bullet Style**	Velocity in Feet Per Second (To Nearest 10 FPS) Muzzle	50 Yds.	100 Yds.	150 Yds.	Energy in Foot-Pounds (To Nearest 5 Foot-Pounds) Muzzle	50 Yds.	100 Yds.	150 Yds.	Wind Drift in Inches 10 MPH Crosswind 50 Yds.	100 Yds.	150 Yds.	Height of Bullet Trajectory in Inches Above or Below Line of Sight If Zeroed at ⊕ Yards. Sights 1.5 Inches Above Bore Line. 50 Yds.	100 Yds.	150 Yds.	Above Bore Line. 50 Yds.	100 Yds.	150 Yds.
①, ⑤	50	22 Long Rifle HV	40	Solid, Copper Plated	1260	1100	1020	940	140	110	90	80	1.5	5.5	11.4	⊕	-6.5	-21.0	+2.7	⊕	-10.8
①, ⑤	100	22 Long Rifle HV	40	Solid, Copper Plated	1260	1100	1020	940	140	110	90	80	1.5	5.5	11.4	⊕	-6.5	-21.0	+2.7	⊕	-10.8
①, ⑤	50	22 Long Rifle HV	38	HP Copper Plated	1280	1120	1020	950	140	105	90	75	1.6	5.8	12.1	⊕	-6.3	-20.6	+2.7	⊕	-10.6
①, ⑤ NEW	50	22 Long Rifle HV†	31	HP Copper Plated	1550	1280	1100	980	165	115	85	65	1.7	7.0	15.5	⊕	-3.8	-14.7	+1.9	⊕	-9.0
①	50	22 Long Rifle Bird Shot	25	No. 12 Lead Shot	—	—	—	—	—	—	—	—	—	—	—	—	—	—	—	—	—

*HV = High Velocity HV† = Hyper Velocity **HP = Hollow Point These ballistic specifications were derived from test barrels 24 inches in length.

FEDERAL CLASSIC® 22 MAGNUM

Usage Key: ① = Varmints, predators, small game   ② = Medium game   ③ = Large, heavy game   ④ = Dangerous game   ⑤ = Target shooting, training, practice

Usage	Cartridge Per Box	Caliber	Bullet Wgt. In Grains	Bullet Style*	Velocity in Feet Per Second (To Nearest 10 FPS) Muzzle	50 Yds.	100 Yds.	150 Yds.	Energy in Foot-Pounds (To Nearest 5 Foot-Pounds) Muzzle	50 Yds.	100 Yds.	150 Yds.	Wind Drift in Inches 10 MPH Crosswind 50 Yds.	100 Yds.	150 Yds.	Height of Bullet Trajectory in Inches Above or Below Line of Sight If Zeroed at ⊕ Yards. Sights 1.5 Inches Above Bore Line. 50 Yds.	100 Yds.	150 Yds.	Above Bore Line. 50 Yds.	100 Yds.	150 Yds.
①, ⑤	50	22 Win. Magnum	50	Jacketed HP	1650	1450	1280	1150	300	235	180	145	1.1	4.5	10.3	⊕	-3.6	-12.5	+1.3	⊕	-6.5
①, ⑤	50	22 Win. Magnum	40	Full Metal Jacket	1910	1600	1330	1140	325	225	155	115	1.3	5.7	13.4	⊕	-2.9	-10.7	+1.0	⊕	-5.8
①, ⑤	50	22 Win. Magnum	30	Jacketed HP	2200	1750	1380	1120	320	205	125	85	1.4	6.4	15.8	⊕	-1.4	-7.4	+0.7	⊕	-5.3

*HP = Hollow Point These trajectory tables were calculated by computer using the best available data for each load. Trajectories are representative of the nominal behavior of each load at standard conditions (59°F temperature; barometric pressure of 29.53 inches; altitude at sea level). Shooters are cautioned that actual trajectories may differ due to variations in altitude, atmospheric conditions, guns, sights, and ammunition.

REMINGTON PISTOL AND REVOLVER AMMUNITION BALLISTICS

Caliber	Primer No.	Weight (grs.)	Bullet Style	Velocity (ft./sec.) Muzzle	50 Yds.	100 Yds.	Energy (ft.-lb.) Muzzle	50 Yds.	100 Yds.	Mid-range Trajectory 50 Yds.	100 Yds.	B.L.
221 REM. FIREBALL	7½	50	Pointed Soft Point	2650	2380	2130	780	630	505	0.2″	0.8″	10″
25 (6.35MM) AUTO. PISTOL	1½	50	Metal Case	760	707	659	64	56	48	2.0″	8.7″	2″
6MM BR REM.	7½	100	Pointed Soft Point									
7MM BR REM.	7½	140	Pointed Soft Point									
32 S. & W.	1½	88	Lead	680	645	610	90	81	73	2.5″	0.5″	3″
32 S. & W. LONG	1½	98	Lead	705	670	635	115	98	88	2.3″	10.5″	4″
32 (7.65MM) AUTO. PISTOL	1½	71	Metal Case	905	855	810	129	115	97	1.4″	5.8″	4″
357 MAG.	5½	110	Semi-Jacketed H.P.	1295	1094	975	410	292	232	0.8″	3.5″	4″
Vented Barrel Ballistics	5½	125	Semi-Jacketed H.P.	1450	1240	1090	583	427	330	0.6″	2.8″	4″
	5½	125	Brass-Jacketed Hollow Point	1220	1095	1009	413	333	283	0.8″	3.5″	4″
	5½	165	JHP Core-Lokt®	1290	1189	1108	610	518	450	0.7″	3.1″	8⅜″
	5½	130	TEMC, Lead-Lokt™	1400	1239	1116	566	443	360	0.6″	2.8″	4″
(Refer to page 42 for test details)	5½	158	Semi-Jacketed H.P.	1235	1104	1015	535	428	361	0.8″	3.5″	4″
	5½	158	Soft Point	1235	1104	1015	535	428	361	0.8″	3.5″	4″
	5½	158	Semi-Wadcutter	1235	1104	1015	535	428	361	0.8″	3.5″	4″
	5½	140	Semi-Jacketed H.P.	1360	1195	1076	575	444	360	0.7″	3.0″	4″
	5½	180	Semi-Jacketed H.P.	1145	1053	985	524	443	388	0.9″	3.9″	8⅜″
	5½	125	Semi-Jacketed H.P. (Med. Vel.)	1220	1077	984	413	322	269	0.8″	3.7″	4″
357 REM. MAXIMUM*	7½	158	Semi-Jacketed H.P.	1825	1588	1381	1168	885	669	0.4″	1.7″	10″
9MM LUGER	1½	115	Jacketed H.P.	1155	1047	971	341	280	241	0.9″	3.9″	4″
	1½	124	Jacketed H.P.	1120	1028	960	346	291	254	1.0″	4.1″	4″
AUTO. PISTOL	1½	124	Metal Case	1110	1030	971	339	292	259	1.0″	4.1″	4″
	1½	115	Metal Case	1135	1041	973	329	277	242	0.9″	4.0″	4″
	1½	88	Jacketed H.P.	1500	1191	1012	440	277	200	0.6″	3.1″	4″
	1½	115	Jacketed H.P. (+P)‡	1250	1113	1019	399	316	265	0.8″	3.5″	4″
	1½	147	Jacketed H.P. (Subsonic)	990	941	900	320	289	264	1.1″	4.9″	4″
	1½	147	Metal Case (Match)	990	941	900	320	289	264	1.1″	4.9″	4″
	1½	115	TEMC, Lead-Lokt™	1135	1041	973	329	277	242	0.9″	4.0″	4″
	1½	147	TEMC, Lead-Lokt™	990	941	900	320	289	264	1.1″	4.9″	4″
	1½	124	Brass-Jacketed Hollow Point	1125	1041	963	349	293	255	1.0″	4.0″	4″
	1½	147	Brass-Jacketed Hollow Point	990	941	900	320	289	264	1.1″	4.9″	4″
	1½	124	BJHP (+P)‡	1180	1089	1021	384	327	287	0.8″	3.8″	4″
380 AUTO. PISTOL	1½	95	Metal Case	955	865	785	190	160	130	1.4″	5.9″	4″
	1½	88	Jacketed H.P.	990	920	868	191	165	146	1.2″	5.1″	4″
	1½	102	BJHP	940	901	866	200	184	170	1.2″	5.1″	4″
38 SUPER AUTO. COLT PISTOL (A)	1½	115	Jacketed H.P. (+P)‡	1300	1147	1041	431	336	277	0.7″	3.3″	5″
38 S. & W.	1½	146	Lead	685	650	620	150	135	125	2.4″	10.0″	4″
38 SPECIAL	1½	95	Semi-Jacketed H.P. (+P)‡	1175	1044	959	291	230	194	0.9″	3.9″	4″
Vented Barrel Ballistics	1½	110	Semi-Jacketed H.P. (+P)‡	995	926	871	242	210	185	1.2″	5.1″	4″
	1½	110	Semi-Jacketed H.P.	950	890	840	220	194	172	1.4″	5.4″	4″
	1½	125	Semi-Jacketed H.P. (+P)‡	945	898	858	248	224	204	1.3″	5.4″	4″
	1½	130	TEMC, Lead-Lokt™	950	901	859	261	235	213	1.4″	5.0″	4″
	1½	125	Brass-Jacketed Hollow Point (+P)	975	929	885	264	238	218	1.0″	5.2″	4″
	1½	148	Targetmaster Lead W.C. Match	710	634	566	166	132	105	2.4″	10.8″	4″
	1½	158	Targetmaster Lead	755	723	692	200	183	168	2.0″	8.3″	4″
	1½	158	Lead (Round Nose)	755	723	692	200	183	168	2.0″	8.3″	4″
	1½	158	Semi-Wadcutter (+P)‡	890	855	823	278	257	238	1.4″	6.0″	4″
	1½	158	Semi-Wadcutter	755	723	692	200	183	168	2.0″	8.3″	4″
	1½	158	Lead H.P. (+P)‡	890	855	823	278	257	238	1.4″	6.0″	4″
38 SHORT COLT	1½	125	Lead	730	685	645	150	130	115	2.2″	9.4″	6″
40 S. & W.	5½	155	Jacketed H.P.	1205	1095	1017	499	413	356	0.8″	3.6″	4″
	5½	180	Jacketed H.P.	1015	960	914	412	368	334	1.3″	4.5″	4″
	5½	180	TEMC, Lead-Lokt™	985	936	893	388	350	319	1.4″	5.0″	4″
	5½	165	Brass-Jacketed Hollow Point	1150	1040	964	485	396	340	1.0″	4.0″	4″
	5½	180	Brass-Jacketed Hollow Point	1015	960	914	412	368	334	1.3″	4.5″	4″
10MM AUTO	2½	200	Metal Case	1050	994	948	490	439	399	1.0″	4.2″	5″
	2½	180	Jacketed H. P. (Subsonic)	1055	997	951	445	397	361	1.0″	4.6″	5″
	2½	180	Jacketed H. P. (High Vel.)	1160	1079	1017	538	465	413	0.9″	3.8″	5″
41 REM. MAG.	2½	210	Soft Point	1300	1162	1062	788	630	526	0.7″	3.2″	4″
Vented Barrel Ballistics	2½	210	Lead	965	898	842	434	376	331	1.3″	5.4″	4″
	2½	170	Semi-Jacketed H.P.	1420	1166	1014	761	513	388	0.7″	3.2″	4″
44 REM. MAG.	2½	180	Semi-Jacketed H.P.	1610	1365	1175	1036	745	551	0.5″	2.3″	4″
Vented Barrel Ballistics	2½	240	Lead Gas Check	1350	1186	1069	971	749	608	0.7″	3.1″	4″
	2½	240	Soft Point	1180	1081	1010	741	623	543	0.9″	3.7″	4″
	2½	240	Semi-Jacketed H.P.	1180	1081	1010	741	623	543	0.9″	3.7″	4″
	2½	240	Lead (Med. Vel.)	1000	947	902	533	477	433	1.1″	4.8″	6½″
	2½	210	Semi-Jacketed H.P.	1495	1312	1167	1042	803	634	0.6″	2.5″	6½″
	2½	275	JHP Core-Lokt™	1235	1142	1070	931	797	699	0.8″	3.3″	6½″
44 S. & W. SPECIAL	2½	246	Lead	755	725	695	310	285	265	2.0″	8.3″	6″
	2½	200	Semi-Wadcutter	1035	938	866	476	391	333	1.1″	4.9″	6″
45 COLT	2½	250	Lead	860	820	780	410	375	340	1.6″	6.6″	5″
	2½	225	Semi-Wadcutter (Keith)	960	890	832	460	395	346	1.3″	5.5″	5″
45 AUTO.	2½	185	Targetmaster M.C. W.C. Match	770	707	650	244	205	174	2.0″	8.7″	5″
	2½	185	Jacketed H.P.	1000	939	889	411	362	324	1.1″	4.9″	5″
	2½	230	Metal Case	835	800	767	356	326	300	1.6″	6.8″	5″
	2½	185	Jacketed H.P. (+P)‡	1140	1040	971	534	445	387	0.9″	4.0″	5″
	2½	230	TEMC, Lead-Lokt™	835	800	767	356	326	300	1.6″	6.8″	5″
	2½	185	Brass-Jacketed Hollow Point	1015	951	899	423	372	332	1.1″	4.5″	5″
	2½	230	Brass-Jacketed Hollow Point	875	833	795	391	355	323	1.5″	6.1″	5″

*Will not chamber in 357 Mag. or 38 Special handguns. ‡Ammunition with (+P) on the case headstamp is loaded to higher pressure. Use only in firearms designated for this cartridge and so recommended by the gun manufacturer. §Subject to stock on hand. (A)Adapted only for 38 Colt Super and Colt Commander pistols. Not for use in sporting, military and pocket models.

CENTERFIRE HANDGUN BALLISTICS

Cartridge	Bullet Wt. Grs.	Type	Velocity (fps) Muzzle	50 Yds.	100 Yds.	Energy (ft-lbs.) Muzzle	50 Yds.	100 Yds.	Mid Range Traj. (In.) 50 Yds.	100 Yds.	Barrel Length Inches
25 Automatic	45	Expanding Point**	815	729	655	66	53	42	1.8	7.7	2
25 Automatic	50	Full Metal Jacket	760	707	659	64	56	48	2.0	8.7	2
30 Luger (7.65mm)	93	Full Metal Jacket	1220	1110	1040	305	255	225	0.9	3.5	4½
30 Carbine #	110	Hollow Soft Point	1790	1601	1430	783	626	500	0.4	1.7	10
32 Smith & Wesson	85	Lead-Round Nose	680	645	610	90	81	73	2.5	10.5	3
32 Smith & Wesson Long	98	Lead-Round Nose	705	670	635	115	98	88	2.3	10.5	4
32 Short Colt	80	Lead-Round Nose	745	665	590	100	79	62	2.2	9.9	4
32 Automatic	60	Silvertip® Hollow Point	970	895	835	125	107	93	1.3	5.4	4
32 Automatic	71	Full Metal Jacket	905	855	810	129	115	97	1.4	5.8	4
38 Smith & Wesson	145	Lead-Round Nose	685	650	620	150	135	125	2.4	10.0	4
380 Automatic	85	Silvertip-Hollow Point	1000	921	860	189	160	140	1.2	5.1	3¾
380 Automatic SXT®	**95**	SXT	955	889	835	192	167	147	1.3	5.5	3¾
380 Automatic	95	Full Metal Jacket	955	865	785	190	160	130	1.4	5.9	3¾
38 Special	110	Silvertip Hollow Point	945	894	850	218	195	176	1.3	5.4	4V
38 Special Super Unleaded®	130	Full Metal Jacket Encapsulated	775	743	712	173	159	146	1.9	7.9	4V
38 Special Super Match®	148	Lead-Wad Cutter	710	634	566	166	132	105	2.4	10.8	4V
38 Special	158	Lead-Round Nose	755	723	693	200	183	168	2.0	8.3	4V
38 Special	158	Lead-Semi Wad Cutter	755	721	689	200	182	167	2.0	8.4	4V
38 Special + P	95	Silvertip Hollow Point	1100	1002	932	255	212	183	1.0	4.3	4V
38 Special + P#	110	Jacketed Hollow Point	995	926	871	242	210	185	1.2	5.1	4V
38 Special + P#	125	Jacketed Hollow Point	945	898	858	248	224	204	1.3	5.4	4V
38 Special + P#	125	Silvertip Hollow Point	945	898	858	248	224	204	1.3	5.4	4V
38 Special + P# SXT	**130**	SXT	925	887	852	247	227	210	1.3	5.5	4V
38 Special + P Subsonic®	147	Jacketed Hollow Point	860	830	802	241	225	210	1.5	6.3	4V
38 Special +P Super Unleaded	**158**	Full Metal Jacket-Encapsulated	890	864	839	278	262	249	1.4	5.8	4V
38 Special +P	**158**	Lead-Semi Wad Cutter Hollow Point	890	855	823	278	257	238	1.4	6.0	4V
38 Special +P	**158**	Lead-Semi Wad Cutter	890	855	823	278	257	238	1.4	6.0	4V
9mm Luger Super Unleaded	**115**	Full Metal Jacket Encapsulated	1155	1047	971	341	280	241	0.9	3.9	4
9mm Luger	**115**	Full Metal Jacket	1155	1047	971	341	280	241	0.9	3.9	4
9mm Luger	**115**	**Silvertip Hollow Point**	1225	1095	1007	383	306	259	0.8	3.6	4
9mm Luger SXT	**147**	SXT	990	947	909	320	293	270	1.2	4.8	4
9mm Luger Super Unleaded	147	Full Metal Jacket-Encapsulated	990	945	907	320	292	268	1.2	4.8	4
9mm Luger Subsonic	147	Jacketed Hollow Point	990	945	907	320	292	268	1.2	4.8	4
9mm Luger	147	Silvertip Hollow Point	1010	962	921	333	302	277	1.1	4.7	4
9mm Luger Super Match	147	Full Metal Jacket-Truncated Cone-Match	990	945	907	320	292	268	1.2	4.8	4
38 Super Automatic + P*	125	Silvertip Hollow Point	1240	1130	1050	427	354	306	0.8	3.4	5
38 Super Automatic + P*	130	Full Metal Jacket	1215	1099	1017	426	348	298	0.8	3.6	5
357 Magnum #	110	Jacketed Hollow Point	1295	1095	975	410	292	232	0.8	3.5	4V
357 Magnum #	125	Jacketed Hollow Point	1450	1240	1090	583	427	330	0.6	2.8	4V
357 Magnum #	145	Silvertip Hollow Point	1290	1155	1060	535	428	361	0.8	3.5	4V
357 Magnum	158	Lead-Semi Wad Cutter**	1235	1104	1015	535	428	361	0.8	3.5	4V
357 Magnum #	158	Jacketed Hollow Point	1235	1104	1015	535	428	361	0.8	3.5	4V
357 Magnum #	158	Jacketed Soft Point	1235	1104	1015	535	428	361	0.8	3.5	4V
40 Smith & Wesson	155	Silvertip Hollow Point	1205	1096	1018	500	414	357	0.8	3.6	4
40 Smith & Wesson Super Match	155	Full Metal Jacket-Truncated Cone-Match	1125	1046	986	436	377	335	0.9	3.9	4
40 Smith & Wesston SXT	**165**	SXT	1110	1020	960	443	381	338	1.0	4.2	4
40 Smith & Wesson Super Unleaded	165	Full Metal Jacket-Encapsulated	1110	1020	960	443	381	338	1.0	4.2	4
40 Smith & Wesson Super Unleaded	180	Full Metal Jacket-Encapsulated	990	933	886	392	348	314	1.2	5.0	4
40 Smith & Wesson SXT	**180**	SXT	1015	959	912	412	367	333	1.1	4.7	4
40 Smith & Wesson Subsonic	180	Jacketed Hollow Point	1010	954	909	408	364	330	1.1	4.8	4
10mm Automatic	175	Silvertip Hollow Point	1290	1141	1037	649	506	418	0.7	3.3	5½
10 mm Automatic Subsonic	180	Jacketed Hollow-Point	990	936	891	390	350	317	1.2	4.9	5
41 Remington Magnum #	175	Silvertip Hollow Point	1250	1120	1029	607	488	412	0.8	3.4	4V
41 Remington Magnum #	210	Jacketed Hollow Point	1300	1162	1062	788	630	526	0.7	3.2	4V
44 Smith & Wesson Special #	200	Silvertip Hollow Point	900	860	822	360	328	300	1.4	5.9	6½
44 Smith & Wesson Special	246	Lead-Round Nose	755	725	695	310	285	265	2.0	8.3	6½
44 Remington Magnum #	210	Silvertip Hollow Point	1250	1106	1010	729	570	475	0.8	3.5	4V
44 Remington Magnum #	240	Hollow Soft Point	1180	1081	1010	741	623	543	0.9	3.7	4V
45 Automatic	185	Silvertip Hollow Point	1000	938	888	411	362	324	1.2	4.9	5
45 Automatic Super Match	185	Full Metal Jacket-Semi Wad Cutter	770	707	650	244	205	174	2.0	8.7	5
45 Automatic SXT	**230**	SXT	880	846	816	396	366	340	1.5	6.1	5
45 Automatic Super Unleaded	230	Full Metal Jacket-Encapsulated	835	800	767	356	326	300	1.6	6.8	5
45 Automatic Subsonic	230	Jacketed Hollow Point	880	842	808	396	363	334	1.5	6.1	5
45 Automatic	230	Full Metal Jacket	835	800	767	356	326	300	1.6	6.8	5
45 Colt #	225	Silvertip Hollow Point	920	877	839	423	384	352	1.4	5.6	5½
45 Colt	255	Lead-Round Nose	860	820	780	420	380	345	1.5	6.1	5½
45 Winchester Magnum #	260	Hollow Soft Point	1250	1137	1053	902	746	640	0.8	3.3	5

+ P Ammunition with (+ P) on the case head stamp is loaded to higher pressure. Use only in firearms designated for this cartridge and so recommended by the gun manufacturer.

V-Data is based on velocity obtained from 4" vented test barrels for revolver cartridges (38 Special, 357 Magnum, 41 Rem. Mag. and 44 Rem. Mag.)

Specifications are nominal. Test barrels are used to determine ballistics figures. Individual firearms may differ from test barrel statistics.

Specifications subject to change without notice.

**Lubaloy® Coated

*For use only in 38 Super Automatic Pistols.

#Acceptable for use in rifles also.

UNSAFE ARMS AND AMMUNITION COMBINATIONS

Ammunition used in a firearm must be the same caliber or gauge as that marked on the firearm by its manufacturer.

If the firearm is not marked as to caliber or gauge, or if it appears that the original marking has been overprinted or changed, it is the responsibility of the gun user to have a qualified person determine what cartridge or shell can safely be used in the firearm.

The firing of a cartridge or shell other than that for which the firearm is chambered can result in the cartridge or shell rupturing and releasing high-pressure gas that can damage or destroy the firearm and kill or seriously injure the shooter and persons nearby.

There are countless combinations of specific cartridges and firearm chambers which are unsafe. Many of these unsafe combinations are recognizable because of significant dimension differences between the cartridge and the firearm chamber. Dangerous combinations may also have similar chamber and cartridge dimensions. It is not possible to list every unsafe combination; therefore, in the interest of safety, use only the cartridge (or shell) designated by the firearm or ammunition manufacturer for use in a specific firearm. The cartridge caliber or shotshell gauge must be marked on the firearm frame, receiver or barrel by its manufacturer.

The practice of rechambering firearms is not guided by industry standards. It is possible that a firearm which has been rechambered may not be rechambered properly or the rechambered caliber may not be marked on the firearm. The firearm user is responsible for finding out from a qualified person the cartridge caliber or shell gauge for which the firearm has been rechambered.

---

* +P ammunition is loaded to a higher pressure, as indicated by the +P marking on the cartridge case headstamp, for use only in firearms especially designed for this cartridge and so recommended by the manufacturer.

UNSAFE ARMS AND AMMUNITION COMBINATIONS

RIMFIRE RIFLE

In Rifles Chambered For	Do Not Use These Cartridges
.22 WRF	.22 BB, .22 CB .22 Short .22 Long .22 LR .22 LR Shot
.22 WMRF	.22 BB, .22 CB .22 Short .22 Long .22 LR .22 LR Shot
.22 Win Auto	.22 BB, .22 CB .22 Short .22 Long .22 LR .22 LR Shot
5mm Rem RF Magnum	.22 BB, .22 CB .22 Short .22 Long .22 LR .22 LR Shot .22 Win Auto
.25 Stevens Long	5mm Rem RF Magnum

RIMFIRE PISTOL & REVOLVER

In Handguns Chambered For	Do Not Use These Cartridges
5mm Rem RF Magnum	.22 BB, .22 CB .22 Short .22 Long .22 LR .22 LR Shot .22 Win Auto
.22 WRF	.22 BB, .22 CB .22 Short .22 Long .22 LR .22 LR Shot
.22 WMRF	.22 BB, .22 CB .22 Short .22 Long .22 LR .22 LR Shot
.25 Stevens Long	5mm Rem RF Magnum

CENTERFIRE PISTOL & REVOLVER

In Handguns Chambered For	Do Not Use These Cartridges
.32 S&W	.32 Auto .32 Long Colt .32 Short Colt
.32/20 Win	.32/20 High Velocity
.38 Auto	.38 Super Auto +P*
.38 S&W	.38 Auto .38 Long Colt .38 Short Colt .38 Special
.38 Special	.357 Magnum .380 Auto
.38/40 Win	.38/40 High Velocity
.44/40 Win	.44/40 High Velocity
.45 Auto	.38/40 Win .44 Rem Magnum .44 Special .44/40 Win
.45 Colt	.38/40 Win .44 Rem Magnum .44 S&W Special .44/40 Win

CENTERFIRE RIFLE

In Rifles Chambered For	Do Not Use These Cartridges
6mm Remington (244 Rem)	.250 Savage
6.5mm Remington Magnum	.300 Savage
7mm Express Remington	7mm Mauser (7 × 57) .270 Winchester .30 Remington .30/30 Winchester .300 Savage .308 Winchester .32 Remington .375 Winchester .38/55 Winchester
7mm Mauser (7 × 57)	300 Savage
7mm Remington Magnum	7mm Express Remington 7mm Mauser (7 × 57) 7mm Weatherby Magnum .270 Winchester .280 Remington

In Rifles Chambered For	Do Not Use These Cartridges
	.303 British .35 Remington .350 Remington Magnum .375 Winchester .38/55 Winchester
8mm Mauser (8 × 57)	7mm Mauser (7 × 57) .35 Remington
8mm Remington Magnum	.338 Winchester Magnum .350 Remington Magnum .358 Norma Magnum .375 Winchester .38/55 Winchester
.17 Remington	.221 Remington Fireball .30 Carbine
.17/223	.17 Remington .221 Remington Fireball .30 Carbine
.223 Remington	5.56mm Military .222 Remington
.243 Winchester	.225 Winchester .250 Savage .300 Savage
.257 Roberts	.250 Savage
.264 Winchester Magnum	.270 Winchester .284 Winchester .303 British .308 Winchester .350 Remington .375 Winchester .38/55 Winchester
.270 Winchester	7mm Mauser (7 × 57) .30 Remington .30/30 Winchester .300 Savage .308 Winchester .32 Remington .375 Winchester .38/55 Winchester
.280 Remington	7mm Mauser (7 × 57) .270 Winchester .30 Remington .30/30 Winchester .300 Savage .308 Winchester .32 Remington .375 Winchester .38/55 Winchester

UNSAFE ARMS AND AMMUNITION COMBINATIONS (Continued) ⎯⎯⎯⎯⎯⎯⎯

In Rifles Chambered For	Do Not Use These Cartridges	In Rifles Chambered For	Do Not Use These Cartridges
.284 Winchester	7mm Mauser (7 × 57) .300 Savage	.300 Winchester Magnum	8mm Mauser Rd. Nose Bullet .303 British .350 Remington Magnum .375 Winchester .38/55 Winchester
.30/06 Springfield	8mm Mauser (8 × 57) .32 Remington .35 Remington .375 Winchester .38/55 Winchester		
		.303 British	.32 Winchester Special
		.303 Savage	.32 Winchester Special .32/40 Winchester
.30/40 Krag (.30 Govt.)	.303 British .303 Savage .32 Winchester Special	.308 Winchester	.300 Savage
.300 Holland & Holland Magnum	8mm Mauser (8 × 57) .30/06 Springfield .30/40 Krag .375 Winchester .38/55 Winchester	.338 Winchester Magnum	.375 Winchester .38/55 Winchester
		.348 Winchester	.35 Remington
		.375 Winchester	.38/55 Winchester .41 Long Colt
.300 Weatherby Magnum	.338 Winchester Magnum	.375 H&H Magnum	.375 Winchester .38/55 Winchester
		.38/55 Winchester	.375 Winchester .41 Long Colt

RIFLE SIGHTS ⎯⎯⎯⎯⎯⎯⎯⎯⎯⎯⎯⎯⎯⎯⎯⎯⎯⎯⎯⎯

IRON SIGHTS

Mass-produced rifles usually come with a plain open rear sight and bead-type front sight. Few hunters are satisfied with these sights, which really are suitable only for auxiliary use in case a scope becomes inoperative. However, many manufacturers have improved the sights they install. In former years, a low semi-buckhorn rear sight came on almost all rifles, even if the stock had a high Monte Carlo comb for use with a scope. Today, most factory rifles with high combs have appropriately higher open sights, and many of these sights also feature adjustments that permit more precise alignment. The improvements are welcome, but for most purposes open sights still can't match a telescopic sight or an aperture (peep) sight. These rifles are drilled and tapped for scope mounting, and big-game models are rarely seen afield without a scope.

There are two basic types of open sights—the V- or U-notch and the patridge, which has a square notch used with a square blade front sight.

In the first category, there is some controversy about the shape and size of the V- or U-notch, which may take the form of a shallow V, a deep V, or a V with "ears" and is called the buckhorn.

The worst of the lot is the buckhorn with its "ears" that blot out more than half of the target when the sights are lined up. Fortunately, very few guns now come equipped with buckhorn sights, but there are still enough around to cause problems. One can replace it, of course, but the sight can be partly fixed or improved by filing down the ears to the top of the V.

The deep V is a big improvement over the buckhorn sight, but it also has a drawback. A hunter will most likely sight-in his rifle by carefully placing the front bead down into the V-notch, which is the correct way to do it. This works well on the range where the shooter has plenty of time to zero in, but prob-

Buckhorn

Shallow-V

Peep, or Aperture

Patridge

Basic types of iron sights. The buckhorn is the worst of the lot since it covers too much of the animal. The shallow-V is an improvement as it allows a hunter to see more of the game he's shooting at. The aperture or peep sight is the best choice for hunting because it's fast, lets in plenty of light and landscape, and hunter simply puts bead where he wants to hit and squeezes off. The patridge sight is actually the most accurate, but it's a difficult one to use on game and should be used only for target shooting.

lems come up in the field. Shooting at game during the poor light of dusk or dawn or taking snap shots at spooked whitetails, a hunter may not seat the front bead as deep or as carefully in the V as he did on the range. This means he will shoot high and miss his target.

The shallow V is the best compromise for an open rear sight. The absence of any kind of ears means at least half of the target can be seen. The shooter has more light to work with, and the shallow V-notch literally doesn't leave much room for error in seating the bead. Some manufacturers place a white diamond or triangle at the bottom of the V, and this certainly helps to quickly center the bead. If an open sight must be used, the shallow V is the best choice.

Front bead sights for the above, incidentally, come in a variety of colors, including gold, ivory, or red plastic. Some show up better than others under certain lighting conditions, but the gold bead has been proven the best for all conditions.

Assuming you're a target shooter and not a hunter, the patridge sight with its square-cut notch rear sight and square blade front sight is actually more accurate and a better choice than the sights utilizing a bead front sight. With this sight, the front blade is centered in the square notch of the rear sight and a 6 o'clock hold is taken. That is, the front blade is placed at the bottom edge of the bull's-eye. The sight picture should look like an apple sitting on a fence post. This sight combination is surprisingly accurate for target work, but a difficult one to use on game.

The biggest problem with open sights is adjustment, or we should say lack of dependable adjustment. If bullets consistently hit left, the rear sight in its dovetail mount must be tapped to the right—

not a very precise technique. If bullets consistently hit high or low, the rear sight must be moved accordingly on the notched bar, to a lower notch to lower the point of impact and to a higher notch to raise it. Sometimes a rifle will shoot high with the sight in its lowest notch. This leaves us with two choices: file down the notch or look for a better sight.

Another problem with open sights is that they require the shooter to focus on three things at once: the rear sight, the front bead, and the target. This is not a simple trick even for the best pair of eyes. A shooter trying to keep everything in focus at the same time will find himself shifting focus back and forth between rear and front sights and his target, and such an arrangement will mean misses.

APERTURE OR PEEP SIGHT

The peep sight is far superior to the best open sight ever designed. The peep is mounted on the receiver of the rifle, only a few inches from the eye, and the shooter looks through it, not at it. The peep sight works on the principle that the eye will automatically center the front bead in the hole. Many hunters and shooters find this hard to believe, but there is no doubt that it works.

It's important to remember not to try to focus on the aperture itself. It's supposed to look slightly blurred. Simply look through the hole and pick up the front bead. Your eye will automatically center it in the hole and all you have to do is put the bead on your target.

The peep sight also offers the important feature of positive adjustment. The aperture can be adjusted

APERTURE (PEEP) SIGHTS

Left: The Lyman 57 Universal Receiver Sight is fairly typical of high-quality aperture sights for hunting rifles. Its mount hugs the receiver. (Another version, the 66, is made for autos, pumps, and lever actions with flat receivers.) Elevation and windage are adjustable, with audible ¼-minute clicks. Release button permits quick removal of the slide assembly so rifle can be used with scope or open sights. **Right:** The Williams Receiver Sight can be bought with target knobs (as shown) or without them. Protruding adjustment knobs are excellent for target work, but on a hunting rifle they tend to get in the way and snag twigs.

Typical Metallic Target Receiver Sight (right) is popular for several types of competitive shooting at paper targets as well as metallic game-silhouette matches. It's shown with a full complement of fronts, which accept a wide variety of sign inserts.

Palma Metallic Target Sight

International Small-Bore Front

International Big-Bore Front

Olympic Front

No. 60 Series Globe Fronts

for both windage and elevation by means of screws that provide corrections of ¼ to ½ inch at 100 yards.

All peep sights come with insert discs for target shooting. The hole through these discs is generally very small, and they're fine for shooting at paper on the range. Hunters, however, should take this disc and throw it away. It's not needed and only decreases the size of your sight picture.

The peep sight is the fastest of all iron sights for hunting. It lets you see plenty of light, landscape, and nearly all of a game animal when shooting. It may be hard to believe, but a hunter can pick up a running whitetail faster through a peep sight than an open sight . . . then it's just a matter of putting the bead on the animal and squeezing off.

TELESCOPIC SIGHTS

Most hunting rifles today have telescopic sights mounted on them. Hunters and shooters have come to realize that these riflescopes are not the fragile optical instruments they were in the 1920s. The modern scope is a rigid dependable sight that under almost all conditions is far superior to any other sight. Its advantages are many; its disadvantages few.

Hunters who are getting on in years and beginning to have difficulty with iron sights when trying to focus rear sight, front sight, and target at the same time, can eliminate this problem with a scope. With a scope the image of the target or game is placed right on the crosshairs, and when the hunter focuses on the crosshairs he will find his target is also automatically in focus. Elderly hunters with failing eyesight can often stretch their hunting years by using a scope.

Another advantage is that game that may ordinarily go unnoticed in protective cover can often be picked up in the magnification of a riflescope. Scopes also add a margin of safety to hunting. What may look like a deer with the naked eye may well turn out to be another hunter through a 4× scope. A scope will also lengthen your hunting day by enabling a hunter to see well enough to shoot in the poor light of dawn and dusk.

Disadvantages of a scope are few. A scope will add weight to a rifle, anywhere from 6 ounces to maybe more than a pound. A scope also adds bulk, which sometimes creates a minor problem when carrying the rifle. Rain or snow can also put a scope temporarily out of commission, unless it is equipped with scope caps of some sort. A scope can also be a handicap for short-range snap shooting at game in thick cover. But all these problems can be solved to a degree.

Scopes are perhaps best classified by type: (1) hunting scopes; (2) scopes for .22 rifles; (3) target and varmint scopes.

HUNTING SCOPES

Hunting scopes are available with fixed powers from 1.5× to 12× and with variable powers offering a variety of magnifications of 1.5×–4× up to 6×–24×. In buying a scope, the shooter has to decide what power to choose and whether to spend extra money for a variable model. The answers depend on the hunting to be done. The highest-powered scopes listed above may be wanted for varminting but are not really suitable for most hunting.

High magnification can actually be a drawback. The greater the magnification, the smaller is the field of view (the width of area visible through the scope). Moreover, high power increases the apparent tremors in the sight picture. With a smaller field of view plus the problem of holding steady, lining up

A MODERN SCOPE

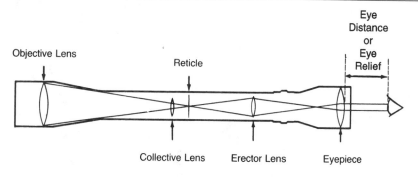

Objective Lens · Reticle · Eye Distance or Eye Relief · Collective Lens · Erector Lens · Eyepiece

on moving game can be difficult. Sometimes a shooter can't even find the game in his scope before it disappears into thick cover.

Although fixed-power scopes have by no means become obsolete, variables have been so greatly improved in recent years that they are now more popular among big-game hunters. If your hunting is mostly in woods and brush, your best bet is a variable in the $1.5 \times -5 \times$ class. Many of the newer scopes, including variable models, feature an extra-wide field of view. With a wide-field $1.5 \times -5 \times$ scope cranked down to the lowest setting, the field of view is about 70 feet at 100 yards. At the top setting, it's about 27 feet. A wide-field $2\frac{1}{2} \times$ fixed-power scope has a field of view of more than 50 feet at 100 yards.

But the variable has just as wide a field at a comparable setting, so it's ideal for hunting whitetails in brush country.

Among fixed-power scopes, the most popular magnification is $4 \times$. But for all-round hunting, a $2 \times -7 \times$ compact variable is probably best. Although the $3 \times -9 \times$ is extremely popular, its slightly increased magnification isn't really worth the extra bulk and weight if the scope is to be used for a wide variety of hunting. If you use just one rifle and your hunting ranges from Eastern whitetails to Colorado mule deer, either a fixed-power $4 \times$ or a $2 \times -7 \times$ variable would be your best choice. If your hunting is strictly eastern, you want a wide field of view and you don't need as much power, so the choice is be-

SCOPES

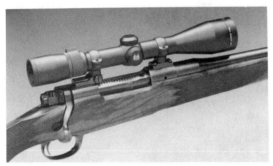

Nikon Monarch UCC 3-9×40 Riflescope. Available in matte, silver, or lustre, this scope features a wide field of view at lower settings and powerful high magnification.

Bushnell Trophy 3-9×40 Light Sight offers wide angle field of view and an illuminated reticle with back-up crosshairs.

Bausch & Lomb Elite 4-16×50 Matte Finish. A good choice for varmint and precision shooting.

Weaver Handgun Scopes. Available in 2×, 4×, 1.5-4×, and 2.5-8× (not pictured). These models are nitrogen-charged, fogproof, waterproof, and multi-coated to protect against flare and internal reflections.

Bushnell 2×-6× (32mm) Silver Trophy Handgun Scope needs only 18 inches of eye relief.

Bushnell HOLOsight gun sight with interchangeable reticles. Holographic technology and 20 brightness settings are features of this electronic targeting system. Works well on handguns, rifles, and shotguns, including clay-bird shooting.

Millet Redot electronic Red Dot Sights offer a wide field of view and precision click adjustments. Magnification is 1 ×.

Steiner Hunting Z Series, available in 1.5-5 × 20, 2.5-8 × 36 and 3.5-10 × 50 in Duplex and European reticles. Windage and elevation adjustments are hand adjustable.

Pentax Lightseeker SG Plus Scope 2.5 × Advantage in Mossy Oak finish measures 10 inches and weighs 9 ounces.

Leupold Vari-X II 6-18 × 40mm Scope, available in matte and silver is designed for long-range big-game hunting and varmint shooters.

Tasco ProPoint Plus was designed for competitive shooting. This Plus model has a brighter and larger dot than standard ProPoint models.

Burris Electro-Dot Scopes in 3 × -9 × Signature, 6 × -24 × Signature, and 3 × -9 × Fullfield. Each scope has a lighted dot roughly half the diameter of a human hair for precise shooting in poor light.

tween a 1.5×–5× variable and a 2½× or 3× fixed-power scope. The variable has the edge, though it costs more.

The famous drawbacks of the variable models no longer apply. By comparison with fixed-power scopes, they used to be longer, heavier, and less sturdy than they should have been, and they offered a smaller field of view. But now they've been trimmed, strengthened, and so improved optically that they provide just as wide a field—wider at the lowest settings. A bonus is that they can do special jobs at the high settings, such as spotting holes in a target or picking a trophy head out of a herd.

SCOPES FOR .22s

Most .22 rifles are used for plinking and hunting small game and it's hard to imagine such a rimfire gun without a scope. The bulk of the .22s available today come equipped with cheap iron sights that can rarely be adjusted for accurate shooting. A receiver or peep sight is certainly an improvement, but a scope will turn most .22s into accurate firearms.

Cost should not be a critical factor here, since scopes for .22 rifles generally run up to $100. and they are a good investment. The low cost of these scopes is due mainly to their construction. First, their optics are not as highly corrected as the scopes for big-game rifles. Second, they are usually not constructed strong enough to take the recoil of the big centerfire cartridges.

It's wise here to mention that under no circumstances should one of these scopes be mounted on a high-powered rifle, since it could result in a serious eye injury. These inexpensive scopes for .22s have an eye relief (distance between eye and ocular lens that gives the shooter maximum field of view) of about 3 inches. A .22 has just about no recoil, so the eye being this close to the ocular lens presents no problems. Put the same scope on a high-powered rifle with heavy recoil, however, and the scope tube could be driven into the shooter's eye.

The best power for a scope to be used on a .22 is not as important as it is with big-game rifles. For general use, a 4× scope is fine. For target and squirrel hunting, a 6× would be better. If you can't make up your mind, pick up one of the variables. You can't go wrong putting one of these inexpensive scopes on a .22 rifle, especially since cost of mounting the scope is nonexistent. Just about all .22 rifles are grooved for tip-off mounts and the price of the scope usually includes the tip-off mount.

TARGET AND VARMINT SCOPES

Scopes for long-range varmint shooting and for benchrest and other serious target competition are a special breed. Until a few years ago, the necessary accuracy was obtained only with scopes over 2 feet long that had fragile adjustments in the mounts. Now, with very few exceptions, powerful and precise target scopes employ internal adjustments, and they measure no more than about 18 inches long. The very long, slender, externally adjusted target/varmint scope is a dying breed. However, the Unertl high-power target and varmint scopes, which are among the best made, still employ external windage and elevation adjustments. But Bausch & Lomb, Burris, Leupold, Redfield and a few others offer rugged, precise, internally adjusted target scopes that look like hunting models.

The field of view is smaller than the field in a lower-powered hunting scope, but this doesn't matter in a scope to be used strictly for varminting or target work. Serious varmint shooters generally use scopes with 10× to 15× magnification, though some of them favor even greater power. For target shooting, 15× and 20× scopes are preferred, and benchresters use 20× and even 25× scopes.

A relatively new type of target competition requires the shooter to knock down metallic game silhouettes at various ranges. Accuracy and power are essential, but the rules call for a scoped rifle weighing no more than 10 pounds 2 ounces. For this competition, both fixed-power and variable scopes are used. The favorites are in the 8× to 12× range. A good silhouette scope is essentially a very precise hunting-type scope. The adjustments are internal but the knobs are not enclosed in protective caps. They must be quick and convenient to use, easy to grasp and read.

An advantage of these scopes is "zero repeatability"—a feature they share with other fine, relatively expensive target scopes and even with some of the better hunting scopes. Ordinary scopes may have a bit of slack in the threads of the adjustment screws. To sight-in such a scope very precisely, you must take up the slack by turning the adjustment a trifle too far and then turning it back against the load of the reticle cell. A scope with zero repeatability has no slack. Move an adjustment dial four ¼-inch clicks, and you move the point of impact *precisely* 1 inch at 100 yards. You get what you read on the adjustment dial. Silhouette-target scopes are marketed by Redfield, Tasco, Beeman, Bushnell, Leupold, Simmons, and Bausch & Lomb.

RETICLE OPTIONS

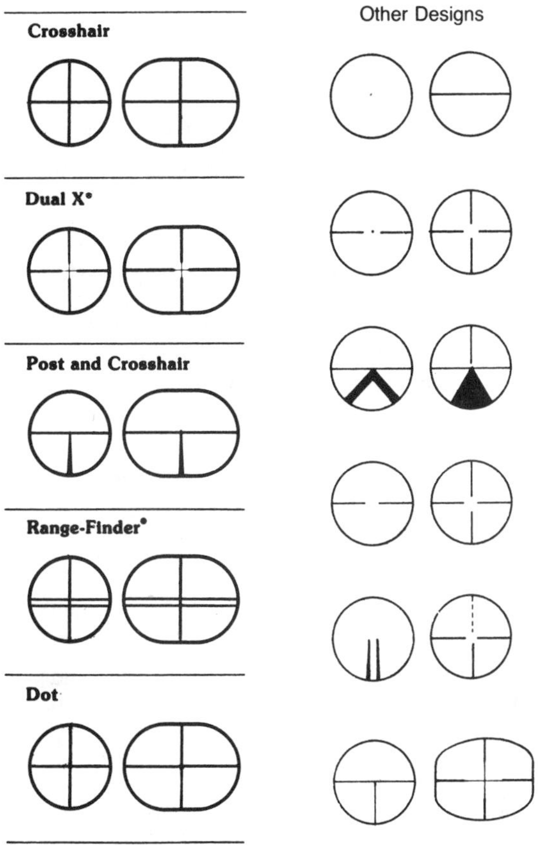

Crosshair

Dual X°

Post and Crosshair

Range-Finder°

Dot

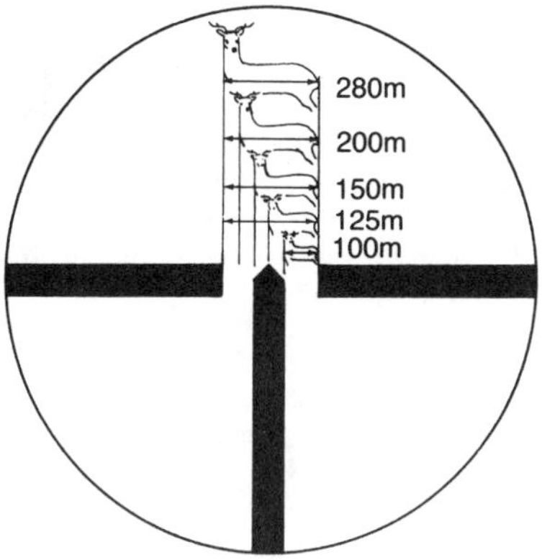

Other Designs

280m
200m
150m
125m
100m

There is a wide range of scope reticles shown here, from American reticles to those by European and Japanese makers. These represent most of the types available today. Some of the reticles are shown both in standard form and wide-view models. The bottom scope assists in range determination.

ELECTRONIC SIGHTS

Bushnell's HOLOsight is a unique electronic sight that utilizes holographic technology. Adapting jet fighter holographic display capabilities, the HOLOsight produces a reticle pattern that appears in a display window. When illuminated by a laser light, a holographic image becomes visible at the target and remains in focus with the target. Since critical eye alignment is not required, multi-plane focusing error is eliminated. The HOLOsight, powered by two 3-volt lithium batteries, is adaptable to any rifle, handgun, or shotgun.

Aimpoint is another electronic sight. Shooter puts a small luminious red dot on his target and that's his point of impact at the distance to which he has sighted in his rifle. Basic model has no power magnification, but attachments are available to convert the sight to $3\times$. Aimpoint does not require shooter to focus dot in the center of the eyepiece. No matter where the shooter sees the dot in the eyepiece, it's on the target.

THE SCOPE RETICLE

A scope reticle is simply a fixed or suspended device in a scope tube which marks the aiming point. Reticles come in many sizes and shapes, and they can be confusing to a hunter who is worried about laying out considerable cash for a scope and then discovering the reticle is wrong for him.

The drawings on the previous page show most reticle types, including the traditional plain crosshair, post and crosshair, dot, rangefinding gadgets, and dual-thickness (heavy and thin) crosswire. Most reticles are wire, though some makers in the past used animal hairs, etched glass, or spider silk.

The simpler the reticle, the easier it is to aim with. A sight picture cluttered with multiple crosshairs or other rangefinding devices can sometimes be more trouble than it's worth. As with scope power, the best type of reticle depends on the hunting for which it's most often used.

Technology developed during World War II resulted in a blossoming of new designs and optical systems. For years, however, the most popular reticle remained the standard crosshair, sometimes tapered toward the center but usually of uniform thickness. This type was and still is offered with fine wire for target or varmint shooting or heavier wire for big game.

For aiming at moving game in woods and brush, a good variation is the post and crosswire. The vertical post is usually tapered and flat-topped. In variable-power scopes, it generally comes up exactly to the horizontal crosswire. In fixed-power scopes, it generally extends a trifle above the horizontal wire. In either case, its top is the aiming point. The crosswire is merely a horizontal reference line to help the hunter keep from canting his rifle. Such a reticle works well for relatively fast shooting in poor light, because the thick-bottomed post is so easy to see.

But at long range, a post covers too much of the target—as do the coarse crosshairs that have been traditional in many big-game scopes. One solution is the use of fine crosshairs, and another is the combination of a center dot and fine or tapered crosshairs. Many target and varmint shooters like the dot and fine crosshair. For big game in open country, a suspended dot (without crosshair) was at one time quite popular. It's fast to use. This type of dot isn't good for target work, as it covers the bull's-eye. Even in hunting, the size of the dot is important. A 2-minute dot, for example, covers 2 inches at 100 yards, a 4-minute dot covers 4 inches, and so on. Choose one that won't cover too much of the target in your type of hunting, and remember that knowing its size will help you estimate range. A varmint hunter with a $6\times$ or $8\times$ scope wouldn't want more than a 1-minute dot, but a big-game hunter in open country might want a 2- or even 4-minute dot.

The standard crosshair, post, and dot reticles are no longer as popular as they once were, because a relatively new type has gained eminence for many shooting purposes. This is the dual-thickness crosswire. Leupold introduced it in the late 1960s and called it the Duplex. Now, many makers offer it under different names: the Leupold Duplex, Bushnell Multi-X, Redfield 4-Plex, Burris Plex, and so on.

This type of reticle employs rather heavy vertical and horizontal crosswires that abruptly become fine near the center. Even in poor light, the shooter's eye quickly picks up the coarse wires, and the fine center wires allow precise aiming—even at a small target. If there's one all-round hunting reticle, this is it.

With a bit of practice, such a reticle also permits fast range estimation. Let's say, for instance, that you're hunting deer with a wide-view scope, either $4\times$ or $1.5\times-4.5\times$ variable at the high setting. In either case, the space between the points of the heavy outer wires at 100 yards is 22 inches. A mature deer's body is only about 18 inches deep, from the top of the back to the belly (a fact that seems to surprise many hunters). If the deer's body, from top to bottom, fills the vertical space between the wires, the deer is about 80 yards away. If it fills half the space, it's 160 yards away. To get the knack of judging range with your reticle, just practice on stationary targets of known size at known distances.

The dual-thickness reticle is so practical and popular that it has replaced the ordinary crosshair as the "standard" type. If you order a scope without specifying the reticle, chances are you'll get the dual design.

SCOPE ADJUSTMENT

This is simple and easy to understand, but still bears brief explanation. All scopes are adjustable for windage and elevation by two dials on the scope tube. The only exception is with externally adjustable scopes, in which case the windage and elevation dials are a part of the mount. Scopes are adjustable in graduations of $\frac{1}{4}$-, $\frac{1}{2}$-, or 1-minute clicks, which means one click will move the point of impact $\frac{1}{4}$, $\frac{1}{2}$, or 1 inch at 100 yards respectively.

MOUNTING THE SCOPE

There are several factors to consider before mounting a scope. By discussing the various types of mounts, it will become evident which is the best scope mount for your gun and use.

Bridge or top mount.

The bridge mount is chiefly for a hunter who plans to stick a scope on his rifle and leave it there. It's a sturdy mount, suitable for saddle-scabbard carrying and other jolting treatment. One major disadvantage is that the mounting blocks are screwed into the top of the receiver so that, with many rifles, the iron sights can't be used if the scope is damaged and has to be removed. The mount bases hide the open sights. However, this is no longer a problem on many modern rifles that have higher-than-normal factory-installed sights for use with a high-combed stock. Also, some mounts are grooved to allow sighting with the scope removed. With or without these improvements, a sturdy top mount is a good choice for target shooting or hunting in which a scope is just as important as an accurate rifle.

See-through bridge mount.

The see-through mount is an old but yet a recently revived idea. This is essentially a bridge mount with a peep hole through the bases so the shooter can also use his iron sights in a pinch. The see-through mount should be particularly appealing to the brush hunter who is never quite sure whether he'll need a scope for a long shot or iron sights for a close quick shot. The basic idea is good and the mount satisfies many hunters. It does have disadvantages, however. For one thing, the scope must necessarily

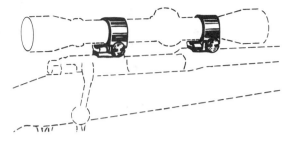

Scope with typical bridge, or top, mount.

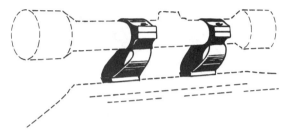

Basic design of a see-through scope mount. Scope is high enough for hunter to use iron sights through openings.

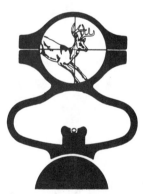

Another version of the see-through mount is Clear View's Broad View. It allows a wide viewing area, but it may make gun carrying awkward for extended periods.

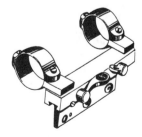

Quick-detachable side mount.

be mounted high, which means the shooter will have to crane his neck upward slightly to get a good sight picture through the tube. This is a good case for only putting these mounts on rifles with Monte Carlo combs or fairly high rollover cheekpieces. Also, because the scope is mounted high, it makes a bulky package and the sight is more accident prone. Some of these mounts, however, are designed to permit easy sighting through especially low see-through design.

All factors considered, the see-through mount is a fair compromise for the hunter who wants instant choice of scope or iron sights. But he will have to accept the fact that the scope will not be mounted in the best possible position, which is as low as possible and directly over the receiver.

Quick-detachable mount.

This mount is the best and only choice for a hunter who occasionally wants to remove his scope and use iron sights, or who wants to use his scope in conjunction with a receiver or peep sight. The base portion of this mount is generally screwed and pinned to the side or top of the receiver, so that when the scope and ring portion of the mount is removed, there are no obstructions along the top of the barrel and iron sights can be used.

As mentioned above, the quick-detachable mount can also be effectively used in conjunction with a receiver or peep sight that has a removable slide. The scope can quickly be removed and the slide of the receiver sight slipped in. This makes it a fine choice for the hunter heading into a remote area. If the scope should accidentally get knocked out of commission, he can remove it and have a reliable receiver sight to fall back on.

Two excellent side mounts are the Griffin & Howe and the Jaeger. Both mounts will keep the scope on zero, regardless of how many times the scope is taken off and put back on the base mount. Either of these side mounts is a good bet for the brush hunter who wants both scope and iron sights at his disposal. On stand at dawn and dusk, he can use the scope. Stillhunting during the day, he can remove the scope and use open sights or a receiver sight.

Swing or pivot mount.

Still another version of the side mount is the swing mount, which is basically a hinged bracket screwed to the side or top of the receiver. With this arrangement, a hunter confronted with a quick shot at close range has only to swing the scope out of the way and use the iron sights. Makers claim a scope will maintain its zero when swung back and forth.

Offset mount.

This mount, which is literally offset to the side of the receiver, has only one practical application—and that's for rifles that eject fired cases from the top of the receiver. It is somewhat awkward to use, since the shooter must cock his head over the comb to see through the scope. But if a hunter has a top-ejection rifle and wants to put a scope on it, he doesn't have much choice and he must consider the offset mount. It does, however, also offer the instant choice of iron or scope sights.

Another alternative for top-ejection rifles is special scopes with long eye relief—from 10 to 24 inches. These scopes are mounted forward of the top ejection port in the traditional over-the-bore position. While a scope mounted this way looks a bit awkward, the rig is apparently satisfactory.

Basic design of swing or pivot mount.

Typical side mount.

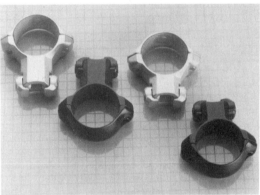

Millet .22 Caliber Scope Rings, available in smooth, engraved, nickel, and matte styles, are windage adjustable.

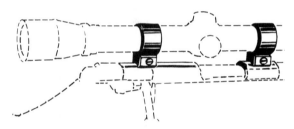

This scope is mounted to a .22 rifle with typical tip-off mount. Note ring bases fasten to grooved receiver of rifle.

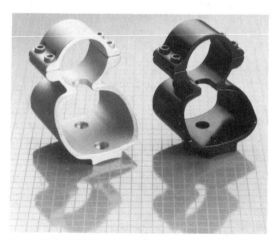

Millet See-Thru Mounts have a three-point design that accommodates variations in the radius of the receiver. A good choice for big-game hunters who still want the option of instant iron sights for quick shots.

Tip-off mount.

The tip-off mount, because it is not designed as rigidly as other mounts, is relegated to the .22 rifles. The tip-off mount should not be cut short, however. It works fine, is inexpensive, and can be clamped on a .22 rifle in minutes by someone who knows almost nothing about guns.

Whereas most modern high-power rifles come factory drilled and tapped for scope bases, the .22s have the male portion of a dovetail machined into the top of the receivers. The female portion of the tip-off mount, which holds the scope, is simply fastened in place on the receiver with coin-slotted screws.

Generally, the cost of putting a scope on a .22 is nonexistent, since nearly all new .22s have grooved receivers and the inexpensive .22 scopes come equipped with the complete tip-off mount.

William Sight-Thru Mount, and 2×−6× scope mounted on Remington Model 700 bolt action. With this type of installation, you can use scope or see through the mount base to use open sights.

SIGHTING-IN A RIFLE

Sighting-in a rifle isn't difficult, it's just time-consuming, and shortcuts will only work against you. Follow the correct procedure step-by-step and you'll reap the rewards in the field.

Start by bore sighting the rifle. This gives you a baseline from which all other adjustments can be made. Bore sighting is best done at 25 yards. You'll find this relatively short range is particularly helpful when sighting-in a new rifle or a gun you're using for the first time. It virtually assures that you'll at least put your first bullet on the paper.

With that first bullet on target, it's easy to subsequently adjust for windage and elevation, and to fine-tune your sights for any range you choose. Conversely, when you attempt to sight-in at 100 or 200 yards, you can use up a lot of ammunition and patience trying to find out where your bullets are going.

Bore sighting is simple with a bolt-action rifle. You have to use some sort of benchrest—a cardboard carton with notches carved at both ends will do. Remove the bolt from the rifle and put it securely on your rest, or cradle it in the notches of the cardboard box. Look through the bore at the target (Fig. 1) and move the rifle—and rest—until the target is centered in the bore.

Then look through your scope and see where the crosshairs fall. If the crosshairs don't intersect on the target center, adjust the windage and elevation until they do. When the crosshairs and bore are both perfectly centered (Fig. 2), you've created a proper baseline. (The procedure is similar for iron sights: Just remember that the goal is to get the sight picture and the bore sight both centered on the target.)

How do you bore sight a lever-action pump gun or autoloader? You have to use a "bore sighter," a device that aligns either scope or iron sights without the need for looking down the bore. You might be

1

The first step is to remove the bolt from your rifle, look through the bore, and center both the rifle bore and crosshairs on a target at 25 yards. Use a rock-steady rest.

2

After your rifle is bore sighted **(above)**, squeeze off three rounds to check where they group.

you've done this, you've effectively moved the sights to where the rifle is shooting. Three more rounds should confirm that you are sighted-in at 25 yards or very close to it.

Why 25 yards? The typical centerfire rifle sighted-in at 25 yards will also be sighted-in for about 200 yards because of the bullet's trajectory (Fig. 4), and about two to three inches high at 100 yards, which is perfect for most deer hunters. Trajectory and point of impact will vary slightly depending on the specific ammunition and bullet weight you select. Once you're happy with a brand of ammunition and bullet weight, try to stick with the combination. When necessary, manufacturers provide ballistics charts to help in switching between ammo for different types of hunting.

The final step in sighting is shooting at 100 yards and 200 yards to confirm the actual point of impact and make your final click adjustments for elevation and windage. These adjustments might vary depending on the brand of scope you use, but generally one click will move the point of impact a quarter of an inch at 100 yards.

As a practical rule, sight-in for the longest possible range that won't cause mid-range misses (because of the arc of the bullet's trajectory). If you're planning a hunt that will require long-range shooting, it's a good idea to fire a few additional shots at targets set at 250, 275, and 300 yards to get a precise idea of where the bullets are hitting and what your aiming point should be.

able to beg or borrow one from a local gun shop, but consider buying your own. Although the cost is about $100, having a bore sighter can be invaluable, particularly when you need to double-check the sights after a rifle has suffered some hard knocks on a plane or in a saddle scabbard.

With your rifle bore sighted, squeeze off three shots at the center of the target. Note the location of your three-shot group and aim again at the center of the target. Only this time don't shoot. Hold the rifle as steady as possible on the center of the target and move the crosshairs both vertically and horizontally until they're centered on your shot group. Once

3

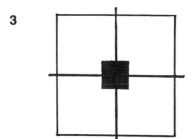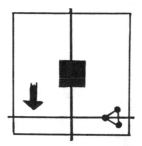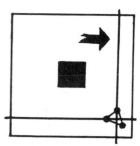

Any target will do, but a black one-inch square works best. Let's assume those first three shots at 25 yards grouped in the lower right of your target. Your next step is to aim precisely at the black square again and, holding your rifle steady, adjust the crosshairs vertically and then horizontally (see drawings) until the crosshairs are centered on the three-shot group.

4

The trajectory, or path, of the bullet never rises above the "line of bore," but it can cross the "line of sight." To compensate for bullet drop, the bore must be pointed upward—this is done by adjusting the rear sight so it is higher than the front sight.

To align crosshairs in scope with bores of lever actions, pump rifles, and autoloaders, use the Bushnell Bore Sighter (detail shown in insert). A cardboard carton with notches in ends will keep rifle from shifting.

BULLET IMPACT WITH RIFLE SIGHTED-IN AT 25 YARDS
(ALL MEASUREMENTS IN INCHES)

Caliber	Bullet Wt.	25 yd.	50 yd.	100 yd.	200 yd.	250 yd.
.222 Rem.	50	0	+¾	+2¼	+½	-2½
.243 Win.	100	0	+¾	+2	+1¾	-½
6mm Rem.	100	0	+¾	+1¾	+2	0
.256 Win. Mag.	60	0	+¾	+1¼	-3	-8½
6.5mm Rem. Mag.	120	0	+¾	+2	+½	-2¼
.264 Win. Mag.	140	0	+¾	+2½	+2	0
.270 Win.	150	0	+1	+1¾	-½	-4
.284 Win.	150	0	+1	+2½	+1¼	-1
7mm Rem. Mag.	150	-¼	+¾	+1¾	+1¼	-½
7mm Rem. Mag.	175	0	+½	+1¼	0	-2½
.30/30 Win.	150	0	+1	+2¾	-¾	-5

Caliber	Bullet Wt.	25 yd.	50 yd.	100 yd.	200 yd.	250 yd.
.30/30 Win.	170	+¼	+1¼	+2¾	-2½	-10
.30/06	150	0	+1	+2¼	+1¼	-1½
.30/06	180	0	+1	+2¼	+¾	-2½
.300 Win. Mag.	150	0	+¾	+2¼	+1¾	0
.300 Sav.	150	0	+1	+1¾	-½	-4
.300 Sav.	180	0	+1¼	+2¾	-½	-5½
.308 Win.	150	0	+1	+2¼	+½	-2½
.308 Win.	180	0	+1	+1¾	-½	-4
.308 Win.	200	0	+1	+2	-1	-7
.338 Win. Mag.	200	0	+¾	+2½	+1½	-2
.35 Rem.	200	+¼	+1½	+3	-3	-13
.358 Win.	250	0	+1¼	+2½	0	-4½
.44 Rem. Mag.	240	+½	+2	+2¾	-10½	—
.444 Marlin	240	+¼	+1½	+2½	-2	-9½

RIFLE ACCESSORIES

When a hunter finally feels he has put together a winning combination of cartridge, rifle, and sights, he'll find there are a few extra items he'll need to round out his rig. Here we'll cover the most important in detail.

SLINGS

Anyone who has ever hunted with a rifle knows the value of a sling, whether it's a simple carrying sling or the military-type target sling. A sling means a rifle can be carried on the shoulder or across the back, leaving both hands free for climbing, dragging out game, and so on. And, of course, the sling is used to help steady your hold for a shot.

Three types of slings are available to the hunter— the military sling, the Whelen-type sling, and the carrying sling.

The military sling is fine for match shooting, but it is generally too heavy and wide (1¼ inches) for most hunting rifles. If you're turned on by the military sling, however, some are manufactured that are lighter and narrower.

A better choice for a hunting rifle is the one-piece Whelen sling, which has a single claw hook to lengthen or shorten it. This sling is about 50 to 55 inches long and measures ¾ to 1 inch wide, just about right for a hunting rifle.

The Whelen sling can be adjusted to a comfortable carrying length that will also work out well if the hunter wants to use the "hasty sling" position to steady his rifle.

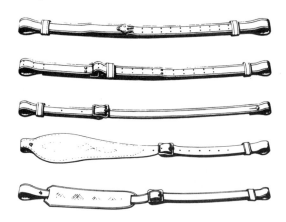

Basic sling designs. From top, military sling, Whelen sling, plain carrying strap, cobra sling, and straight strap with sliding shoulder pad.

Most hunting rifles wear a simple carrying sling, or strap. There are two basic versions—a straight strap and the popular "cobra" sling which widens at the forend, like a cobra's hood, so that it won't dig into the shoulder. A lining patch of suede, sheepskin, or rough leather prevents it from slipping. Some straight slings have a sliding pad that works as the cobra design does, to distribute the load and prevent the strap from slipping off the shoulder. Fastenings on both straight and cobra slings include claws, leather thongs, buckles, and even Velcro hook-and-pile closures. The cobra type is excellent for general use on a hunting rifle, and a plain one works just as well as an expensive one with decorative tooling.

SWIVELS

Swivels come in two basic types—those that mount permanently to the rifle and the quick-detachable models.

The permanent types are fine if you're going to put a sling on a rifle and leave it there. But for a few extra dollars, the quick-detachable swivels are a better bargain. The bases of the swivels are mounted on the rifle and the sling-holding portion of the swivel has a spring catch that quickly detaches from the base. This means a hunter can have bases installed on several rifles and use the same sling on all of them. Another advantage is that the brush hunter who finds his sling getting in the way in thick cover can remove the sling and carry it in his pocket. When he's walking out on a woods road, he can snap it back on.

Two types of sling swivels. Permanent swivels, left, are fine if sling is rarely taken off rifle. The quick-detachable swivels, right, are a better choice for hunting rifles, since sling can be removed easily and used on different rifles.

RECOIL PADS

Nearly all factory rifles in magnum calibers come equipped with rubber recoil pads to cushion the jolt of the gun's recoil. Most other high-power rifles, however, come with steel, aluminum, or plastic buttplates. These are fine, but do nothing to soften recoil. The hunter who uses his rifle during cold-weather hunting seasons when he's wearing heavy clothing does not need a rubber recoil pad, but a shooter who uses his rifle year-round would be well-advised to have one installed on his rifle. Recoil can easily bruise a shoulder while target shooting or varmint hunting during the summer months while wearing only a light shirt.

Recoil pads also serve another purpose. They can shorten or lengthen a stock by as much as an inch or so. If you're a six-footer with long arms, have the pad installed without the stock being cut. This

Three recoil pad designs. Vented pad, left, is preferred when stock is to be lengthened. Slip-on pad, middle, has detachable as well as recoil absorbing feature. Solid pad, right, is preferred for rifles with magnum recoil.

will lengthen the stock an inch or more than the standard 13½-inch length of pull on most factory rifles. If you're a short person with short arms and the butt catches under your arm when mounting the gun, have the stock cut and a recoil pad installed for a length of pull from 12 to 12½ inches.

There are three types of recoil pads and selection is mostly a matter of personal preference. All three types serve the same function—absorb recoil.

The side-vented pad, which is generally found on more shotguns than rifles, is good and perhaps a preferred choice if a stock is to be lengthened. The solid rubber pad is usually factory installed on guns that pack a magnum recoil.

The slip-on pad can be put on and taken off a rifle butt in seconds. It's a good bet for a youngster who is beginning to outgrow his youth's model rifle. The slip-on pad will lengthen the stock and he can get a few more years use out of the gun.

GUN CASES AND SADDLE SCABBARDS

It's poor economics to put a $400 rifle and scope rig in a cheap plastic case and expect it to survive unscathed the bumps and jolts of a rough trip. The

better protected a rifle and sights, the more likely the sights will remain zeroed in. The rifle itself will also be saved from unnecessary scratches and gouges.

The type of case depends on the hunting done. The average hunter who almost always uses his car to get to his hunting grounds can get by with a good-grade gun case made of canvas, vinyl, Cordura nylon, or leather. Pick a case that has a heavy rubber tip protector at the muzzle and one that's lined with flannel or fleece. Leather is the best protector in this type of case, but also the most expensive. A good compromise is a lined heavy-duty vinyl or nylon case that has a zipper at least one-third the way down from the butt end. If it has a compartment for a cleaning rod, all the better.

If a hunter travels to far-off places, he should pick one of the hard plastic or aluminum gun cases lined with polyurethane foam. The rifle and scope are held firmly in place while it bumps its way through airline and train depots. Here again, cost is a factor. The best cases of this type are expensive. Generally, however, one can get a good multi-ribbed hard plastic case with foam lining for about $50 to $75. And remember that these same cases can also be used for fishing tackle during the off-season.

Hunters who seek their game from the back of a horse need saddle scabbards. Always made of a good-grade thick leather because of the rugged use they get on mountain trails, these scabbards also make good cases for transporting guns in cars, buses, trains, and so on. Since scabbards are expensive, select one carefully.

Nylon scabbards are also available and considerably less expensive than leather. They are constructed of Cordura nylon with a closed-cell foam and nylon lining. This nylon-foam laminate, unlike leather, will not absorb moisture, so a rifle can be carried for days, or even stored, without danger of rust or chemical reaction to the gun's bluing.

A good scabbard should cover the rifle completely, but still leave enough of the rifle butt exposed so that it can be quickly hauled out for a quick dis-

Uncle Mike's Sidekick scabbard (above and below) is made of Cordura nylon and foam laminate. It has a "memory" that makes it return to its original shape after the rifle is removed. This means that one scabbard will hold different rifles and won't take a "set."

mount and shot. It should also have a boot that can be buckled on during transportation and bad weather, yet can be easily removed during the hunt. The two straps that hold it to the saddle should be 40 to 45 inches long and strong.

One excellent example of a rifle scabbard is manufactured by the George Lawrence Company. Originally designed by the late Jack O'Connor, well-known shooting editor of *Outdoor Life*, the scabbard has a removable boot and adjustable saddle straps.

THE RIFLE CLEANING KIT

The cost of a cleaning kit is minimal when compared with the price of a good rifle, yet such a kit could keep a rifle from rusting and perhaps from becoming inoperable.

The basic cleaning kit should have the following:

- A cleaning rod of proper size to fit bore diameter
- A bristle brush, either brass or hard nylon
- Cloth cleaning patches
- Gun solvent
- Gun oil
- Linseed oil

Any centerfire rifle using jacketed bullets should be cleaned after each shooting session. First run the bristle brush, soaked with solvent, through the bore. Follow with about two dry cleaning patches, then one clean patch coated with oil. It doesn't take long, but it will keep your bore in top shape.

If you're shooting a .22 Rimfire with waxed or grease-coated bullets, such as Remington's Kleanbore ammunition, there's no need to clean the rifle. The bullet's coating is actually a rust preventative and the rifle can be fired indefinitely without cleaning.

This Cabela rifle vise and cradle makes gun cleaning, scope mounting, and repair work convenient and prevents damage to the stock and metal parts. The vise can be adjusted to hold any rifle or shotgun.

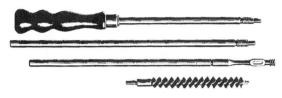

Cleaning rod with attachments for holding a cloth patch and for a wire brush.

Once the bore is taken care of, wipe all metal parts with an oily rag or a silicone-treated gun cloth. This will keep rust from forming on exposed parts.

A lightly oiled rag can also be used on the stock to remove fingerprints or smudges, since such stocks are generally varnished or lacquered. If the stock is deeply scratched, however, rub the wood with linseed oil. The oil will help coat the scratch. This is the next best thing to refinishing the entire stock.

SHOOTING POSITIONS: HUNTING/COMPETITION

Competition shooting knows no boundaries. It pits man against man, state against state, and nation against nation. It is a world-wide activity. Matches are governed by the rules and regulations of such organizations as the National Rifle Association and the International Shooting Union. The variety of events in these matches are many and diversified, but most include shooting from the basic positions of standing, prone, kneeling, and sitting.

The photos on upcoming pages illustrate in detail the technique of getting into and shooting from the accepted positions. The model is Matt Sparano, an accomplished marksman and hunter.

The hunter would also do well to study each position carefully and adapt his shooting style to them. The human body is a shaky shooting platform at best and these positions have been internationally proven to be the steadiest.

Outdoor Life Shooting Editor Jim Carmichel makes some final adjustments before trying to shoot as small a group as possible from a benchrest with his 7mm Remington. (Carmichel photo)

BENCHREST SHOOTING

Contributed by Mike Walker, benchrest expert and rifle designer, courtesy of National Shooting Sports Foundation

The idea behind benchrest target shooting is simple. The shooter tries to put each bullet into the hole made by its predecessor. Five shots but only one hole. Needless to say, that's easier to say than it is

to do; and that's where the simplicity of benchrest ends and the challenge begins.

The name "benchrest" comes from the fact that the rifle is supported on a bench during shooting. Two sandbags, one at the forend and one at the toe of the stock, hold it steady.

Benchrest shooting has several classes of competition, each with different rules on what guns may

THE PRONE POSITION

Below left: Oblique view of prone position. Angle made by shooter's spine and rifle will vary from less than 30 degrees up to 45 degrees depending on type of rifle and shooter's conformation. Comfort is the key. Note that left elbow is under the rifle to give maximum support and help reduce fatigue. **Below right:** This shows shooter's body straight, with feet spread out and heels flat for solid support. Position should be adjusted for comfort. **Bottom:** In this view, note that shooter has elected to draw his right leg up. This frequently improves comfort. Also, when firing points are inclined, the drawn up right leg elevates the right shoulder. (Robert T. Otto photos)

THE STANDING POSITION

Below left: In the standing position, the shooter faces about 85 degrees from the line of aim. Feet are spread comfortably apart. Left hand grasps forearm of rifle at a point giving steadiest feel. The butt is tucked into the pocket of the shoulder. Left elbow should be under the forearm of rifle, but not so far under that the arm feels strained or twisted. **Below right:** This is a familiar position among competition shooters, but it's also very valuable for hunters when there is no other shooting support available. Here the left elbow rests on the hip for extra support. The weight of the rifle is supported by fingertips of left hand with thumb under trigger guard and the rest of the fingers contacting the bottom of the stock. **Bottom:** Front view of standing position, also shown at left, shows that left elbow is not directly under the forearm of the rifle, contrary to an old rule that fortunately has died. Otherwise, to cock the elbow under the forearm of the rifle, the shooter would be also twisting his shoulder, which would cause discomfort while failing to provide stability.

THE SITTING POSITION

Top: The sitting position is often preferred to the prone in varmint hunting because vegetation can otherwise block the line of sight. In the sitting position, the shooter bends slightly forward from the waist. Right elbow is positioned against inside of the right knee. Left elbow should rest comfortably against left knee. Feet are spread slightly farther apart than knees. **Below left:** The cross-legged sitting position is sometimes preferred by shooters with lighter and thinner physical frames. Note that elbows are positioned solidly against knees, and legs are crossed and braced solidly. **Below right:** Front view of cross-legged shooting position shows that shooter is in solid contact with the ground. (Robert T. Otto photos)

THE KNEELING POSITION

Top: The kneeling position is not as steady as the sitting position, which is preferred by hunters. In the kneeling position, the shooter keeps his right heel under his right buttock and keeps his left elbow braced over his left knee. Torso is slightly forward with most of the weight resting on the left knee. **Bottom:** Front view of kneeling position shows shooter's left leg nearly vertical under the rifle for maximum support. Left toe should either be pointing in the same direction as the muzzle or turned inward slightly.

THE HASTY SLING TECHNIQUE

Many hunters have slings on their rifles, but surprisingly few use the hasty sling technique, which greatly helps steady a rifle. Here's how to use the hasty sling in three easy steps. **Top left:** Put your arm through the sling as shown. Place the sling midway between elbow and shoulder. **Right:** Bring left hand around sling and between sling and forearm of the rifle. **Bottom left:** Finally, shoulder the rifle. If sling is adjusted properly, the rifle will come up snug and steady. Left hand should be against sling and sling swivel.

be used. The most popular division is the Heavy Varmint Class. Rifles used in this class must be of a centerfire caliber and weigh a maximum of 13½ pounds. The rules are intended to restrict contestants to a gun that could very well be used for varmint hunting.

The most exotic form is called Benchrest Unlimited Class. Rifles in this class are often called "shooting machines" because they are very heavy and usually mounted on steel rails which are in turn mounted on a short and very sturdy tripod. Favorite calibers in this class are .222 Remington and .308 Winchester, although any caliber may be used. Other classes include Light Varmint and Sporter, which place additional restrictions on rifle weight and caliber.

Scoring is done on the basis of group size. There is no bull's-eye per se; the idea is that all shots be close together and not necessarily in the middle of the target. The shooter producing the smallest average group resulting from five shots at five different targets at a given range wins. Targets are shot at 100 and 200 yards; the average groups at 100 yards are now running a quarter of an inch or less. There is one class that does use a bull's-eye target—but the bull's-eye is a ¹⁄₁₆-inch dot at 100 yards!

For more information write to: National Bench Rest Shooters of America, 5735 Sherwood Forest, Akron, OH 44319.

METALLIC SILHOUETTE SHOOTING

Americans who enjoy the shooting sports have invented some unique and challenging games over the years to test their shooting skills. But one of the most challenging of all has come to us from our neighbors in Mexico—and it has caught on with a bang—and a clang.

Metallic silhouette shooting is one of the most exciting things to happen to rifle and handgun shooters since the invention of rifled barrels and telescopic sights.

With silhouette targets of chickens, pigs, turkeys, and sheep that are shot at ranges up to 500 meters with centerfire rifles, metallic silhouette shooting offers the ultimate test of the shooter's skill—and the ideal practice and training for hunting and other shooting sports.

The first time you level your sights on the silhouette of a sheep 500 meters away, squeeze off a shot and see that sheep topple off his stand—you'll be hooked. And you'll be in good company. Thousands of rifle and handgun shooters have caught silhouette fever in the last few years.

With special versions at different ranges for largebore, smallbore, handgun and air-gun shooters, silhouette shooting offers fun and challenge for shooters of all ages, sizes and inclinations.

Let this text introduce you to the excitement of this fast-growing shooting sport.

Metallic silhouette shooting caught hold north of the border as recently as 1973. Yet today, "silueta" has become one of the fastest growing of all the shooting sports. There has to be a reason for the phenomenal enthusiasm and interest shown in this new shooting game on the part of thousands of shooters across the country. And there is. The reason, like the game itself, is simple. Metallic silhouette shooting is both fun and challenging.

Action is a big part of metallic silhouette shooting, and that's where the fun comes in. Instead of trying to find a hole in a paper target with a spotting scope, most every shot fired at metallic silhouette targets produces a clearly visible—and if you score a hit, audible—sensation. Chicken silhouettes, depending on where they are hit, may spin wildly or turn end over end. Rams, when hit, often seem to hang for a moment before majestically toppling over. Even misses are easily seen, usually raising a cloud of dust behind the silhouette. This kind of action has helped make silhouette shooting both a popular family and spectator sport.

Part of the fun, too, is in the straightforward and uncomplicated nature of the game itself—and the equipment needed. Suffice it to say that even the first-time shooter will have no trouble understanding match procedures or the scoring system.

All metallic silhouette shooting, whether bigbore or smallbore rifle, handgun or air gun, is fired without any means of artificial support, such as adjustable or hook buttplates, palm rests, shooting coats or slings. In other words, the only equipment you need is the appropriate rifle, handgun or air gun for the type of metallic silhouette shooting that interests you. In most cases, the rifle or handgun you normally hunt with will do just fine.

There's plenty of challenge in metallic silhouette shooting, even for top-flight rifle and pistol competitors. When you consider the difficulty in having to knock over a 50-pound steel ram at 500 meters (546.8 yards) firing a high-power rifle from an off-hand position, the challenge of this game is easy to understand. But in silhouette shooting, you don't have to worry about missing a few targets. To knock down more than half the targets in a complete round is considered good shooting. In fact, no one has ever fired a perfect score in high-power rifle competition. The world record for sanctioned high-power rifle silhouette, which was set in 1978, was 88 out of 120—or an average of 29 knockdowns out of each 40 target rounds.

It may not be easy to describe the fun and challenge of metallic silhouette shooting to someone who has not tried it. But once you try it, you'll know exactly what we're talking about.

Essentials

Silhouette shooting involves firing at steel silhouette targets of chickens, pigs, turkeys and sheep (set up on stands) at increasing distances from the firing line. The object of the game is to knock down as many targets as possible.

The procedures for silhouette shooting are essentially the same for all forms of silhouette competition. The basic difference among the various versions of metallic silhouette is the distance at which the targets are set up and, in some versions, the size of the target.

A silhouette match consists of 40 rounds. Ten rounds are first fired at the chicken targets, followed by 10 rounds each at the pig, turkey, and finally the ram targets. Firing is done in five-round stages, with each competitor having a bank of five targets to fire against. Targets are shot in left-to-right order, and only one shot at each target is allowed.

In order to score a hit, a silhouette target must be knocked down from its rest. Turning a target sideways on the stand does not count. Hits out of sequence (i.e., third shot hitting fourth target) are counted as misses.

A match begins when competitors are called to the firing line and go to their assigned firing points. Competitors must place their guns and ammunition on the shooting stand bench or pad provided at each firing point and may not touch them again until the command "Ready" (Listo) is given. After that command has been given, shooters may pick up their guns and load. Fifteen seconds for rifle and 30 seconds for pistol are allowed for loading prior to the command to commence firing, "Fire" (Fuego), is given.

Each competitor may have one coach with him on the firing line who may have a scope or binocular and advise the shooter where shots are going, keep time and the like. However, the coach may not touch the shooter during firing time. Each shooter's coach also acts as a scorer.

High-Power Rifle

High-power rifle, the original "Siluetas Metalicas," is fired with a hunting-type rifle that must be of 6mm or larger caliber.

A match consists of 40 rounds fired in the following sequence:*

• 10 chicken (gallina) targets at 200 meters (218.7 yards)
• 10 pig (javelina) targets at 300 meters (328 yards)
• 10 turkey (guajalote) targets at 385 meters (421 yards)
• 10 sheep (borrego) targets at 500 meters (546.8 yards)

For each five-round stage (one shot, left to right, at each target in a bank of five), a shooter is allowed a maximum of 2½ minutes.

The beginning shooter will be at no disadvantage if he, or she, starts off with a favorite hunting rifle, such as a bolt-action .30/06 caliber with a 4× scope and a couple of boxes of factory 150- or 180-grain loads. While the 6mm is the smallest caliber allowed, experience has shown that the 6mm bullet cannot always be relied on to knock the sheep target—at 500 meters—off its stand. Today, the most popular high-power caliber is the .308 Winchester, followed by the venerable .30/06. Other calibers that have been used with some success include the .25/06, .243 Winchester, 6mm Remington, .257 Roberts, .270 Winchester, 7×57mm Mauser and some wildcats, mostly in 7mm. Although magnum calibers are not specifically prohibited, many clubs disallow their use because of greater damage to the silhouette targets.

Most all silhouette shooters use scopes, with those in 10 or 12× the most popular among serious competitors. Though there are no restrictions on the magnification allowed in scopes, a high-powered target scope can be more of a handicap than an aid, since it will magnify any unsteadiness in the shooter's holding ability in the offhand position.

The trend among avid competitors has been toward rifles that feature heavy barrels and stocks custom designed for offhand shooting. The tremendous growth of the high-power game has prompted several major manufacturers to offer a centerfire, bolt-action model specifically designed for metallic silhouette shooting.

Whether you use your favorite deer rifle or a more specialized silhouette model, the following rules and equipment restrictions apply to high-power rifle competition:**

• You must use a hunting-type rifle of 6mm or larger

---

*In some cases, the firing sequence (i.e., chicken, pig, turkey, sheep) may be altered due to the number of shooters at a match and range facilities.

**The above rules and regulations are intended to provide you with the basic guidelines of the sport. For the official rules and regulations governing high-power metallic silhouette shooting, you should write to the National Rifle Association, Silhouette Department, 1600 Rhode Island Avenue, N.W., Washington, DC 20036.

caliber. The maximum allowable weight of the rifle, including sights, is 10 pounds, 2 ounces.
• You may use any sights, telescopic or metallic.
• You may not use any device (such as a sling or adjustable or hooked buttplate) or clothing (such as a shooting coat) that provides artificial support.
• You may fire your rifle from any standing position without artificial support.

Smallbore Rifle

Smallbore rifle silhouette is simply a miniature version of the high-power game, with target distance and target size scaled down to one-fifth the size. Rifles must be chambered for unmodified .22 caliber Rimfire Short, Long or Long Rifle. The new ultra-high-velocity .22 Rimfire loads may not be used.

As in the high-power version, a smallbore rifle match consists of 40 rounds fired in the following sequence:

• 10 chicken (gallina) targets at 40 meters (43.7 yards)
• 10 pig (javelina) targets at 60 meters (65.6 yards)
• 10 turkey (guajalote) targets at 77 meters (84.2 yards)
• 10 sheep (borrego) targets at 100 meters (109.4 yards)

For each five-round stage (one shot, left to right, at each target in a bank of five), a shooter is allowed a maximum of 2½ minutes.

Smallbore rifle silhouette has really caught on with shooters of all ages throughout the country. On many of the old 100-yard smallbore ranges, the backstop is short of 100 meters (109.4 yards). However, in accordance with the current NRA rules, where available range distances do not permit placing targets at their maximum specified distances, tournament sponsors may use targets scaled to proportional distances. Alternate range distances may not be used for establishing national records.

Toppling a sheep target at 100 meters with a .22 calls for the same steady offhand marksmanship as needed in the high-power rifle game. As low-cost, practical training for the small- or big-game hunter, it's hard to imagine a more helpful shooting game than smallbore silhouette.

Except for the restriction to .22 Rimfire caliber, all equipment requirements for smallbore rifle silhouette are the same as for the high-power rifle silhouette. The official rules and regulations for smallbore rifle silhouette competition are available from the National Rifle Association, Silhouette Department, 1600 Rhode Island Avenue, N.W., Washington, DC 20036.

Handgun

Although formal competition in handgun metallic silhouette shooting only began in 1975, the pistol game has had a phenomenal growth rate and offers handgunners of almost every persuasion perhaps the ultimate test of their shooting skills.

There are two sanctioning bodies for handgun competition, the International Handgun Metallic Silhouette Association (IHMSA) and the National Rifle Association. Rules established by both organizations for corresponding classes are similar, with some exceptions. A major difference between IHMSA and NRA is that scopes are allowed in NRA competition but not in IHMSA.

Both IHMSA and NRA long-range handgun matches consist of 40 rounds fired with centerfire handguns in the following sequence:

• 10 chicken (gallina) targets at 50 meters (54.7 yards)
• 10 pig (javelina) targets at 100 meters (109.4 yards)
• 10 turkey (guajalote) targets at 150 meters (164 yards)
• 10 sheep (borrego) targets at 200 meters (218.7 yards)

For each five-round stage (one shot, left to right, at each target in a bank of five), a shooter is allowed a maximum of 2 minutes.

Two shooting positions are allowed, freestyle and standing. Freestyle includes any safe position without artificial support, with the most common position being the Creedmoor. The gun may not touch the ground or ground mat. In the standing position, the gun may be held in one or both hands; but the shooter may not brace his arm, or arms, on other parts of the body.

IHMSA has two long-range classes, production and unlimited. Both are fired with centerfire handguns. The production class is limited to handguns that are, or were, a catalog item as of January 1, 1977, or before, and were readily available to the general public. Barrel length may not exceed 10¾ inches, and the gun cannot weigh more than 4 pounds, unloaded with magazine. Handguns manufactured after January 1, 1977, are subject to examination by the IHMSA evaluating committee.

Handguns in the IHMSA unlimited class are those other than a production gun with a maximum barrel length and sight radius of 15 inches and a maximum weight of 4½ pounds, unloaded with magazine.

Scopes, or any optical device, are not allowed in either class. Nor are artificial rests, supports, slings, or padded clothing also are not permitted.

IHMSA has also begun a new competition for production .22 caliber handguns. The rimfire version is divided into three categories, one for semi-automatic handguns, one for revolvers and one for single-shot handguns. The .22 Rimfire Long Rifle is the only cartridge allowed in this competition.

Targets are three-eighths the size of the full-size silhouette for centerfire handguns. All other IHMSA rules apply to this competition, except that targets are set at the following distances:

• 10 chicken (gallina) targets at 25 yards
• 10 pig (javelina) targets at 50 yards
• 10 turkey (guajalote) targets at 75 yards
• 10 sheep (borrego) targets at 100 yards

As with smallbore rifle, a .22 handgun silhouette range can easily be set up at a standard 100-yard rifle range.

For more detailed information on the rules and regulations governing IHMSA competition and IHMSA membership, write to: IHMSA, Box 1609, Idaho Falls, ID 83401.

NRA long-range centerfire handgun classes include conventional long range, modified conventional long range and unlimited long range.

The conventional long-range class is similar to the IHMSA production category. It includes guns that are, or have been, catalog items readily available to the general public with a maximum barrel length of 10¾ inches and a maximum weight of 4 pounds.

The NRA's modified conventional long-range class allows a variety of modifications to conventional long-range guns. For example, production sights and grips may be replaced, target-style hammers and triggers may be installed and barrels may be gas vented. Maximum weight in this class is 3 pounds, 12 ounces, not including scope or mounts.

The NRA's unlimited long-range class is similar to IHMSA's unlimited category. It includes guns with a maximum barrel length of 15 inches and a maximum weight of 4½ pounds.

The last version of handgun metallic silhouette, hunter's pistol, is sanctioned by the NRA only. A match consists of 40 rounds fired on targets that are one-half the size of the standard high-power rifle targets in the following sequence:

• 10 chicken (gallina) targets at 25 meters (27.3 yards)
• 10 pig (javelina) targets at 50 meters (54.7 yards)
• 10 turkey (guajalote) targets at 75 meters (82 yards)
• 10 sheep (borrego) at 100 meters (109.4 yards)

The restrictions on handguns allowed in hunter's pistol are similar to conventional long-range handgun; however, the weight of the gun cannot exceed 3 pounds, 12 ounces, and barrel length is set at a maximum of 10 inches. Also, only the following

pistol cartridges are permitted: .22 Rimfire, .32 and .32/20, .380, 9mm, .38ACP, .38 Special, .357, .41, .44, and .45 caliber. Scopes, or any metallic sights, are allowed. Standing position only is permitted in hunter's pistol.

For more information on the rules and regulations governing conventional long range, modified long range, unlimited, write to: National Rifle Association, Silhouette Department, 1600 Rhode Island Avenue, N.W., Washington, DC 20036.

Air Guns

The newest version of silhouette competition is for both air rifles and air pistols with targets one-tenth the size of the full-size templates.

An air-rifle match consists of 40 rounds as follows:

• 10 chicken (gallina) targets at 15 meters (16.4 yards)
• 10 pig (javelina) targets at 20 meters (21.9 yards)
• 10 turkey (guajalote) targets at 35 meters (38.2 yards)
• 10 sheep (borrego) targets at 40 meters (43.7 yards)

There are classes for both precision target air rifles and sporter-type air rifles. Match procedures and other regulations are similar to rifle silhouette competition.

Competition for air pistols also consists of 40 rounds fired as follows:

• 10 chicken (gallina) targets at 10 meters (10.9 yards)
• 10 pig (javelina) targets at 15 meters (16.4 yards)
• 10 turkey (guajalote) targets at 20 meters (21.9 yards)
• 10 sheep (borrego) targets at 25 meters (27.3 yards)

Any air pistol capable of firing .177 or .22 caliber pellets is allowed. Match procedures and regulations are similar to pistol silhouette competition.

For the complete rules and regulations governing air-gun silhouette shooting, write to: National Rifle Association, Silhouette Department, 1600 Rhode Island Avenue, N.W., Washington, DC 20036.

More Information

With the nationwide interest being shown in both rifle and handgun silhouette, ranges have been established in many parts of the country. For information about silhouette clubs in your area, write to the National Rifle Association or to the International Handgun Metallic Silhouette Association, P.O. Box 1609, Idaho Falls, ID 83401.

Both the NRA and IHMSA also have a wealth of information for clubs that want to develop their own silhouette facilities and put on silhouette matches.

SHOTGUN ACTIONS

The modern shotgun of today falls into one of four basic designs—the break action, which includes the single-shot, the side-by-side double and over/under double; the pump action; the autoloader, which includes gas- and recoil-operated models; and the bolt action.

Selection of a shotgun differs slightly from that of a rifle in that personal preference and cost play a more important role. But there are still some guidelines to follow when choosing one of these smoothbore scatterguns for your game.

BREAK-ACTION SINGLE-SHOT

The single-shot break action is the cheapest and simplest shotgun available today. But, like a good ax or knife, it can do many jobs. Made with or without exposed hammer and in all popular gauges and chokes, this single-shot has taken game from squirrels with No. 6 shot to black bears with rifled slugs.

While not the ideal scattergun for hunting, it makes a fine first shotgun for youngsters. Safe and simple to use, a youngster can use it to break his first clay pigeon, bag his first cottontail, and even accompany dad with it on his first deer hunt.

There are some factors to consider, however. This single-shot is a light weapon and has a fair amount of recoil in the bigger gauges. If the gun is for a youngster, pick a 20-gauge with a 26-inch Modified Choke barrel. The recoil of a 12-gauge may be too

much for some youngsters to handle. The 20-gauge also gets the nod over the .410 as a hunting load. With a bit of practice, a youngster can knock over rabbits consistently with a 20-gauge. But with a .410 it generally takes a good shot, and this is so particularly on winged game.

It seems to be a popular idea to buy a .410 for a youngster's first shotgun, but I wonder how many fathers would want to take out after pheasants and grouse with a .410? So why harness a youngster with such a gauge? The .410 shotgun can be an effective hunting arm, but only in the hands of an exceptionally skilled shot. The 20-gauge is a better choice and if the gun is fitted with a recoil pad the recoil can generally be handled by youngsters of average build.

The single-shot break action also makes a good camper's gun and is a long-time favorite of the farmer. The camper can use the gun for claybird shooting or taking a rabbit for the pot, if he's camping during small-game season. The break action has a quick take-down feature, which means the gun can be stored conveniently in a camper.

For the farmer, such a gun becomes more of a tool than a sporting arm. He uses it to knock off marauding crows or a fox or two raiding his chicken house. The farmer is better off with a 12-gauge, since he can also use it come deer season. The camper, however, would do well to stick to a 20-gauge, so the entire family can comfortably shoot the gun.

As for safety, the break action can't be beat.

SINGLE-SHOT SHOTGUNS

Remington 90-T Super Single Trap Gun with high post adjustable rib. Available with 32- or 34-inch barrel.

Harrington & Richardson Topper Deluxe 12 Gauge Slug Gun. A fully rifled 24-inch barrel with 1 in 35-inch twist, fully adjustable sights, and 3-inch chambering. Also available in a Topper Jr. Youth Model. A sound choice for young hunters or hunters on a budget.

SINGLE-SHOT SHOTGUNS (Continued)

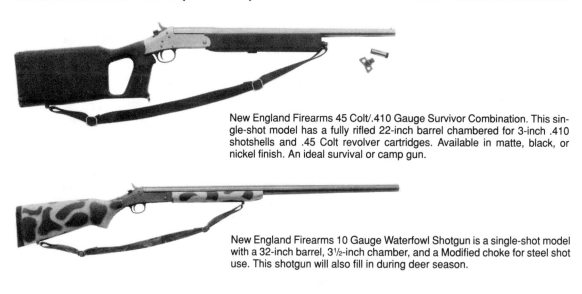

New England Firearms 45 Colt/.410 Gauge Survivor Combination. This single-shot model has a fully rifled 22-inch barrel chambered for 3-inch .410 shotshells and .45 Colt revolver cartridges. Available in matte, black, or nickel finish. An ideal survival or camp gun.

New England Firearms 10 Gauge Waterfowl Shotgun is a single-shot model with a 32-inch barrel, 3½-inch chamber, and a Modified choke for steel shot use. This shotgun will also fill in during deer season.

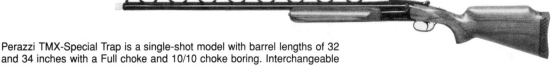

Perazzi TMX-Special Trap is a single-shot model with barrel lengths of 32 and 34 inches with a Full choke and 10/10 choke boring. Interchangeable custom-made stock, adjustable trigger, and high tapered rib are featured. Gold Grade retails for more than $22,000.

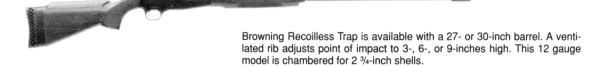

Browning Recoilless Trap is available with a 27- or 30-inch barrel. A ventilated rib adjusts point of impact to 3-, 6-, or 9-inches high. This 12 gauge model is chambered for 2 ¾-inch shells.

Simply break it open and you can carry it around with no fear of an accidental discharge.

Another type of single-shot break action which we will mention briefly is the specially designed trap gun. These guns are fitted with ventilated ribs and are precision bored. They are very expensive and should only be considered by the serious trapshooter.

A number of companies, including Beretta, Krieghoff, Tikka (formerly Valmet), and Winchester, also make over/unders with interchangeable barrels, including optional single barrels for trap. Most also include screw-in choke tubes.

SIDE-BY-SIDE AND OVER/UNDER DOUBLE

These side-by-side and over/under doubles are so similar in basic design that they should be discussed together. The side-by-side, as its name indicates, wears its barrels next to each other. The over/under has its two barrels stacked vertically, one on top of the other.

As a good, safe, and dependable hunting arm, the double is near the top of the list. The traditional doubles have two triggers, one for each barrel, or a nonselective single trigger. On the single-nonselective-trigger models, the barrel with the more open choke always fires first. On a double-choked Modified and Full, for example, the trigger will always fire the Modified barrel first. Incidentally, these doubles, which are not too expensive, also have a matted rib and extractors, which means the fired shell must be removed manually.

The better and more expensive doubles have single selective triggers, which means the hunter can choose the barrel he wants to fire first. These doubles are generally equipped with automatic ejectors and frequently with ventilated ribs, particularly on the over/unders.

As we mentioned above, the double is a traditional hunting arm and a top choice for small game, upland game, and waterfowl. Its advantages are many. First, it is the safest hunting gun. To tell if it is loaded, simply break it and take a glance. When hunting in wet and sloppy weather you can also tell at a glance if the bores are obstructed in any way. If you have to jump a small creek or cross a fence, just break the action and the gun will not fire. You also have the choice of two chokes to control shot pattern. And another factor to keep in mind is that for the same barrel length, the overall length of the double is a few inches shorter than autoloaders and pumps. It also balances better because there is more weight between the hands.

Actual selection of a double depends a great deal on your budget. The better doubles with the more desirable features cost more. There are some basic guidelines to follow, however. If you're an average hunter who gets out about a half-dozen times a year and who sticks mainly to rabbits and pheasants, one of the cheaper doubles should fill the bill. If choice of barrel chokes to be fired first is important to you, get a double-trigger model. Otherwise a single nonselective trigger will work just as well.

Some hunters claim the single nonselective trigger is a handicap, since you have no choice of which barrel to shoot first. But, looking at the problem realistically, 9 times out of 10 a hunter will want to shoot the open-choke barrel first anyway, since small game and birds are likely to be close when he gets that first shot.

The double-trigger model does have one edge over the single nonselective trigger, and that's for the hunter who occasionally shoots trap with the tighter-choked barrel.

If you can afford the extra cash, you can avoid making the above decision of getting a double with a single selective trigger. Then, by manipulating a button near the tang safety, you have a quick choice of which barrel to shoot first—open or tight choke. If you do a great deal of small-game hunting, from cottontails to waterfowl, with some trap and skeet tossed in, it would be worth the extra money to pick a scattergun with a selective trigger.

Should your gun be a side-by-side or an over/under? Here again, it's largely a matter of personal preference. Some shooters like the single sighting plane of the over/under. If you have spent a great

DOUBLE-BARRELED SHOTGUNS

Citori Lightning Sporting Clay model has a rounded pistol grip and lightning-style forearm. The 12 gauge models are available with either 28- or 30-inch barrels, and are chambered for 3-inch shells.

Remington Peerless Over and Under Shotgun. Available in 26-, 28-, or 30-inch barrel lengths with interchangeable REM choke. The model has 3-inch chambers and weighs 7½ pounds.

DOUBLE-BARRELED SHOTGUNS (Continued)

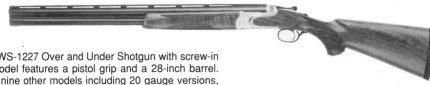

Ruger Woodside Model KWS-1227 Over and Under Shotgun with screw-in chokes. This 12 gauge model features a pistol grip and a 28-inch barrel. Woodside series includes nine other models including 20 gauge versions, barrel lengths of 26-, 28-, and 30-inches, and English straight stock. A good upland game gun.

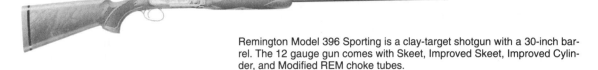

Remington Model 396 Sporting is a clay-target shotgun with a 30-inch barrel. The 12 gauge gun comes with Skeet, Improved Skeet, Improved Cylinder, and Modified REM choke tubes.

Beretta S687EELL Diamond Pigeon is chambered for 2¾- and 3-inch shells. Weighing 6½ pounds, the model is available in 12, 20, and 28 gauge.

IGA Side-By-Side Youth Model Shotgun is a double-trigger .410 gauge. This lightweight shotgun has a 13-inch stock for young hunters. Its 24-inch barrels are bored modified and full, and both barrels will handle 2½- or 3-inch shells. One of the few double-barreled guns with youth-size stocks.

Citori Special Trap is available in eight Monte Carlo or an adjustable conventional stock version. The model is chambered for 2¾-inch shells. Barrel lengths are 30- and 32-inches.

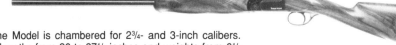

Perazzi MX20C Game Model is chambered for 2¾- and 3-inch calibers. Available with barrel lengths from 26 to 27½ inches and weights from 6½ to 7¼ pounds. High grade models can run as high as $34,000.

deal of time shooting a rifle or pump shotgun, you may prefer the over/under. Other hunters like the traditional quick-handling feel of a side-by-side. Best bet is to handle both types of gun and let "feel" be the deciding factor.

THE PUMP SHOTGUN

The pump gun is likely the most popular scattergun for hunting, though in the past decade it has been getting some stiff competition from the increasing number of doubles introduced to the shooting public.

This manually operated repeater, however, has some distinct advantages. Since it is cheaper to manufacture, the pump can be sold at a lower price—usually less than a good double. Some hunters, particularly waterfowlers, like the magazine capacity of three or more shells. It's also fast and offers a single sighting plane. Fit a pump with a variable choke, and it becomes a good all-round gun. Most well-known manufacturers, in fact, produce shotguns with screw-in choke tubes, so the choke on your shotgun can be changed quickly and easily in the field. If you don't like the choke device on your muzzle, you can always get a pump that will take interchangeable barrels. A pump with a couple

of interchangeable barrels makes a dandy combination. For example, there isn't much that a shotgun hunter can't handle if he has one 28-inch Full Choke barrel and one 26-inch Improved Cylinder barrel. By simply switching barrels, he'll do well on the trap range with the tight choke and do equally well with the open choke on upland game.

Those who prefer the doubles will point out that pumps are too long, muzzle heavy, and don't have the slim feel and handling qualities of a fine double. This is all true to a degree, but it actually all boils down to the fact that you can get an extremely well-made pump shotgun for the price of a fair double.

THE AUTOLOADER

The autoloading, or automatic, shotgun works on one of two principles—recoil or gas. The accompanying sketches show step by step how each type of mechanism works. Both types work well and both are equally acceptable in the field. Remington uses gas operation in its Model 1100, while Browning has the Model 500. Most other autos are gas operated.

The autoloading shotgun has all the advantages

NOMENCLATURE FOR THE PUMP-ACTION SHOTGUN

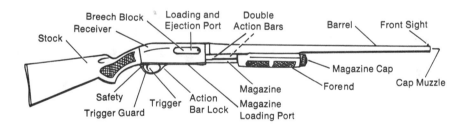

NOMENCLATURE FOR THE AUTOLOADING SHOTGUN

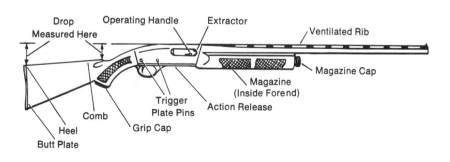

HOW A PUMP-ACTION SHOTGUN WORKS

1. With the gun loaded and cocked, pulling the trigger trips the sear, releasing the hammer to strike the firing pin and fire the shell.

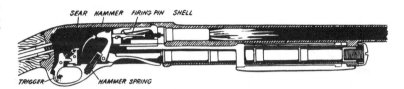

2. Pulling the forend rearward moves the action bar and bolt assembly toward the rear, ejecting the fired shell (see also top-view detail of ejection), pressing the hammer down into cocked position, and moving the new shell onto the carrier.

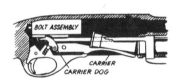
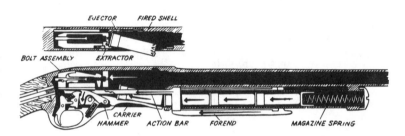

3. Detail of the carrier mechanism (near drawing) shows how the bolt assembly at its rearmost position engages the carrier dog. As the bolt assembly moves forward (right), it moves the carrier dog downward, pivoting the carrier and new shell up into loading position. At the same time the shell latch moves to the right to hold the remaining shells in the magazine.

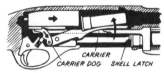

4. As the forend action bar and bolt assembly continue to move forward, the new shell is pushed into the chamber, and the sear engages the hammer, locking it. At the final movement of the forend, the slide continues forward, pushing the locking block up to lock the action for firing.

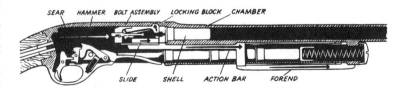

PUMP-ACTION SHOTGUNS

Remington 870 Wingmaster is a 12 gauge pump action shotgun that handles all 2¾- and 3-inch Magnum shells. A Light Contour 30-inch barrel and REM choke system are features. Also available in 20 gauge with 26- or 28-inch barrels.

Browning BPS Upland Special is chambered for 3-inch shells and has a 22-inch barrel. The model comes with an Invector-Plus choke and three choke tubes: Full Choke, Modified, and Improved Cylinder.

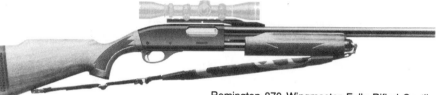

Remington 870 Wingmaster Fully Rifled Cantilever Deer Gun. 12 gauge pump action, Monte Carlo-style stock, and Cordura sling are features of this model. Barrel length is 20 inches. A good choice for deer hunters in shotgun-only regions.

The 20 gauge Mossberg 500 Bantam is a pump gun featuring top receiver safety, twin extractors, anti-jam elevator system, and 3-inch chamber. A good moderately priced starter shotgun.

Browning BPS Game Gun Deer Special is a 12 gauge model chambered for 3-inch shells. Features include a heavy 20½-inch barrel, adjustable rear sights and rifled choke tube. Also comes with an extra-full turkey choke tube. A good combination shotgun for big game and turkeys.

Remington 870 SPS-T-CAMO is a 12 gauge pump action turkey gun with synthetic stock in Mossy Oak and Greenleaf camouflage finish. The model has a vent rib 21-inch barrel and a Turkey Super Full REM choke.

HOW A GAS-OPERATED SHOTGUN WORKS

1. Starting with the gun cocked and loaded, squeezing the trigger releases the hammer, which strikes the firing pin and fires the shell.

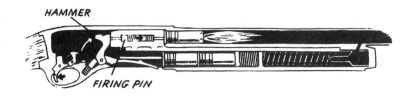

2. The gas generated by the fired shell is metered down through the gas port in the barrel into the cylinder. The pressure of the gas in the cylinder then pushes the piston and connecting rod rearward, moving the bolt from the chamber. As the bolt travels rearward, it recocks the hammer and opens the carrier lock.

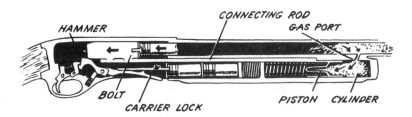

3. Further rearward travel of the bolt ejects the spent shell through the side opening, and the magazine spring pushes a fresh shell onto the carrier.

4. The piston spring starts the piston forward, moving the bolt forward, and pivoting the carrier to bring the new shell into loading position. As bolt moves all the way forward, it loads the new shell into the chamber. Spent gas escapes through the port.

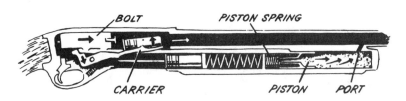

HOW A RECOIL-OPERATED SHOTGUN WORKS

1. Starting with the gun cocked and loaded, squeezing the trigger causes the hammer to hit the firing pin and fire the shell.

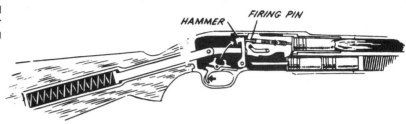

2. Backward force of the recoil moves the chamber and bolt 1/10 inch, kicking the inertia rod pin so that the rod travels rearward. As it travels backward the inertia rod recocks the hammer.

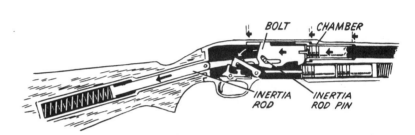

3. Full rearward travel of the inertia rod pulls back the bolt, and the ejector pin throws out the spent shell through the side opening. Carrier lock pivots, admitting new shell onto carrier.

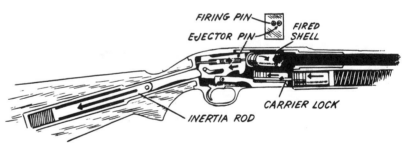

4. The spring at the base of the inertia rod starts the rod returning, moving the bolt forward. As the bolt begins to move, it pivots the carrier, which lifts the new shell into loading position. Full forward movement of the bolt carries new shell into chamber.

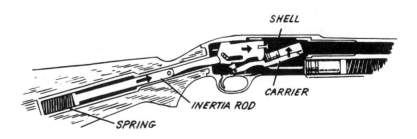

AUTOLOADING SHOTGUNS

Remington Model 11-87 SP Magnum Autoloading Shotgun. Chambered for all 2¾- and 3-inch Magnum shells, the model features interchangeable chokes. A good choice for waterfowl.

Browning Gold Hunter Semi-Automatic Shotgun. Chambered for 3-inch shells, 12 and 20 gauge models are available with barrels from 26- to 30-inches. the self-regulating gas system shoots all loads interchangeably.

Remington SP-10 Magnum-CAMO. This 10 gauge autoloader has a 23-inch vent rib barrel with Mossy Oak Bottomland Camo pattern. Features a Turkey Extra Full REM Choke. A fine turkey gun for those who can handle recoil.

Browning Auto-5 Autoloading Shotgun. Available in 17 models with chambers from 2¾- to 3-inches, all models have the Invector-Plus choke tube system. An old time-tested favorite for small-game, upland game, and waterfowl.

Beretta Pintail, a short recoil semiautomatic 12 gauge shotgun, is available with 24- or 26-inch barrels. Chambered for 2¾- and 3-inch loads, this model weighs approximately 7 pounds.

Remington Model 1100 LT-20 autoloader is a 20 gauge lightweight shotgun with interchangeable REM chokes. Its 26-inch vent rib barrel extends its use from skeet shooting to hunting and sporting clays as well.

and disadvantages of the pump. The only difference is that manual operation after each shot is eliminated with the autoloader, which means faster firepower.

When is this fast firepower really needed? It's difficult to say. The average small-game hunter can get by without an automatic and, actually, he's better off with a gun that requires some manual manipulation between shots for safety's sake. The rabbit and pheasant hunter rarely gets the chance to cut loose with more than two shots and the speed with which he gets off those two shots is not as critical as some hunters believe.

The autoloader, however, may be preferred for waterfowlers and skeetshooters. Duck hunters often have the chance to get off extra shots and they want to fire those second and third shots fast when a mallard discovers he's been had and retreats like a turpentined cat. And the skeetshooter who is having trouble dusting doubles will appreciate the autoloader since all he has to do is squeeze the trigger to get off a second shot.

THE BOLT ACTION

As far as fast-handling qualities on small game and birds, bolt actions are bottom on the list. Their most important features are that they are cheap and strong. They work out best where fast shooting isn't involved. Hunters in states where rifles are not allowed for deer hunting, for example, may find one of these inexpensive bolt actions a good choice. It's an effective combination when fitted with iron sights and used with shotgun slugs. It's also a more than

adequate choice for farmers who want an inexpensive shotgun to protect crops and stock from predators and pests.

MUZZLELOADING SHOTGUN

Muzzleloading shotguns, though not as popular as muzzleloading rifles and handguns, have claimed a growing number of enthusiasts in recent years. Quite a few shooters hunt with them—though such guns are slow to load—and quite a few compete in muzzleloading trap and skeet matches. The supply of shootable antiques began to dwindle quite some time ago, and most of the muzzleloading smoothbores in use today are new, factory-made guns. Now and then you may see a flintlock, but caplocks are the general rule, and they're designed after the good English, French, and American ones made in the 19th century.

A few are single barreled, which means they're single-shots, of course, but most are side-by-side doubles. Quality varies widely, and it's true that you get what you pay for. Some of the surprisingly inexpensive, low-grade ones are unreliable or even of questionable safety. Good ones, mostly imported, cost no more (sometimes less) than breechloading shotguns of comparable quality, and are available from CVA, Dixie, Navy, and a few other companies.

Navy Arms imports several good ones, including a classic side-by-side reminiscent of fine English and French doubles of the 1840s. It has 12-gauge barrels, 28 inches long. Flintlock shotguns are avail-

BOLT-ACTION SHOTGUNS

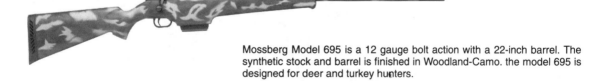

Mossberg Model 695 is a 12 gauge bolt action with a 22-inch barrel. The synthetic stock and barrel is finished in Woodland-Camo. the model 695 is designed for deer and turkey hunters.

Marlin Model 55 Goose Gun is a 12 gauge with a 36-inch full choke barrel. The model will handle 2¾- and 3-inch Magnum shells, as well as rifled slugs and buckshot. A good inexpensive choice for waterfowl.

HOW TO LOAD A MUZZLELOADING SHOTGUN

By Rick Hacker

1. Left: After cleaning excess oil out of the twin bores and popping at least three caps on each nipple to clear them, this double is ready for first loading of the day. Pour a measured charge of powder down bore. **2.** Middle: Thick core over-powder wad is placed in the bore. Try to keep it square with the centerline of the barrel. **3.** Right: Short starter is used to push the wad 5 or 6 inches down the barrel.

4. Ramrod is used to firmly seat the wad on the powder charge. You may hear a rush of air as the wad moves down the bore.

5. Left: A measured charge of shot is then poured down the barrel. **6.** Right: A thin cardboard over-shot wad is firmly seated on top of the shot with short starter (if necessary) and ramrod.

7. After both barrels of a double have been loaded with powder, shot, and wads, the twin nipples are capped. Never leave a cap on the nipple of one barrel while you load the other barrel. If you are loading a fired barrel, take the cap off the loaded barrel's nipple. If you don't do this, accidental discharge of the loaded barrel could cause severe injury.

MUZZLELOADING SHOTGUNS

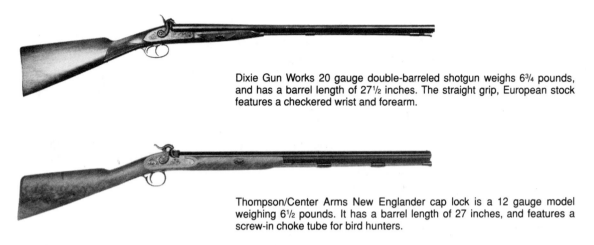

Dixie Gun Works 20 gauge double-barreled shotgun weighs 6¾ pounds, and has a barrel length of 27½ inches. The straight grip, European stock features a checkered wrist and forearm.

Thompson/Center Arms New Englander cap lock is a 12 gauge model weighing 6½ pounds. It has a barrel length of 27 inches, and features a screw-in choke tube for bird hunters.

able from some builders, but they are difficult to buy because demand for them is so limited. Dixie's percussion doubles include 10- and 12-gauge models with 28-inch blued barrels, case-hardened locks, and a stock with a checkered wrist. Shop around and you should find what you want. Most but not all of the muzzle-loaders are 12-gauge.

Before loading such a shotgun, all oil should be removed with a dry patch, and the nipple—or nipples if it's a double—should be cleared by firing several caps to remove any residual oil from the breech area. Then, you pour the powder charge down the barrel. If you're using a 12-gauge for upland hunting, this would be a 3-dram charge of FFg black powder or a bulk charge of Pyrodex from the same measure setting. Most shotgunning is done with loads measured in drams but, in case you're wondering, 82 grains is the same as 3 drams. The traditional wad column consists of an over-powder

card, a couple of filler wads, the load of shot, and an over-shot wad. In this upland load, 1 to 1¼ ounces of shot will work well.

Some shooters use one-piece plastic wads, but you'll get better results with the traditional wad column or a combination of the traditional and contemporary. If you choose the latter, use the over-powder wad and fillers for a cushion but top these with a plastic shot pouch. This will tighten your pattern. After pouring in the shot, you still use an over-powder wad, of course, to hold the load in. Then, with the nipples capped, just cock the gun and fire away.

To obtain information about muzzleloading trap and skeet shoots, as well as many details about hunting and competitive shooting, contact the National Muzzle Loading Rifle Association, Box 67, Friendship, IN 47021.

GAUGE AND SHOT SIZE

The system of referring to shotguns by gauges was started many years ago. The inside diameter of a shotgun's bore was designated by the number of lead balls that would fit the bore and would make up 1 pound. For example, a round lead ball that would fit the bore of a 12-gauge should weigh one-twelfth of a pound, and 12 of these balls would weigh 1 pound. A 20-gauge would take 20 lead balls that

would weigh 1 pound, and so on. The .410 is the only departure from this system. The .410 is not a gauge at all, but the actual measurement in inches of the diameter of the bore.

The accompanying chart shows in actual size the diameters of shotgun bores in the common gauges. Gauge is also converted into measurement in inches.

BORE DIAMETERS OF SHOTGUN GAUGES

10-gauge
.775 inch

12-gauge
.730 inch

16-gauge
.670 inch

20-gauge
.615 inch

28-gauge
.550 inch

.410 bore
.410 inch

THE 12, AN ALL-ROUND GAUGE

The typical hunter looks for one shotgun that he can shoot well and use on all game from squirrels to deer. There is no doubt that such an all-round shotgun has to be a 12-gauge. In the very early 1900s the 10-gauge with 1¼ ounces of shot was a hot item and considered a good choice for an all-round gauge. But modern shotshells have changed the scene. Today the 12-gauge can do anything the 10-gauge did, and sometimes do it better.

Gunning for small game and upland birds, a hunter can get by very well with the standard 2¾-inch 12-gauge shotshell loaded with 1¼ ounces of shot. The waterfowl hunter who takes his birds at greater range should use the 12-gauge 2¾-inch magnum load with 1½ ounces of shot or the 3-inch magnum load with 1⅜ to 1⅞ ounces of shot. If it's deer you're after, use the 2¾-inch magnums loaded with 12 pellets of 00 buckshot, or the 3-inch magnum with 15 pellets of 00 buckshot.

The 12-gauge, then, is a good choice for the one-gun shooter who hunts small game, birds, and deer. He merely varies shotshell loads to do the different jobs.

A typical 12-gauge shotgun, however, is heavier and bulkier than guns in the smaller gauges. The ammunition is also bigger and heavier to carry. This may not mean much to the duck hunter sitting in a blind, but the upland gunner who carries his scattergun all day may find the smaller gauges more suitable.

THE 16-GAUGE

The 16-gauge simply refuses to die, even though the 12-gauge has it beat as an all-round gauge and the 20-gauge comes off a better choice for a light, quick-handling scattergun for small game and birds. Some hunters claim the 16-gauge is a good compromise between the 12- and 20-gauges, but this is a tough argument to prove.

The standard 16-gauge load carries 1⅛ ounces of shot, exactly the same as the 20-gauge 2¾-inch magnum load, and ⅛ ounce less than the standard 12-gauge load. The 2¾-inch 16-gauge magnum shell has 1¼ ounces of shot, the same as the standard 12-gauge field load and the 20-gauge 3-inch magnum.

True, the 16-gauge gun is a bit lighter than a 12, but it's not as light as a 20. What does all this mean? If you have a 16-gauge, keep it and you will be happy with it. But if you're buying a new shotgun, you're better off narrowing your selection down to the 12- or 20-gauge.

THE 20-GAUGE

The 20-gauge makes the grade as a top choice for all-round upland gunning and waterfowl shooting over decoys. It's lighter and slimmer than the 12-gauge, which makes it a faster handling gun and a more comfortable one to carry in pheasant fields and through briar patches. The ammunition is also lighter to carry.

And it's a fact that most upland game is shot at under 30 yards, so the 20 has more than adequate killing range. The standard 20-gauge load carries 1 ounce of shot, which is enough for just about all upland hunting. If a hunter expects to take birds under tougher conditions, he can use the 20-gauge 2¾-inch magnum load with 1⅛ ounces of shot. For ducks over decoys, the 20-gauge 3-inch magnum is the ticket. In fact, the 3-inch magnum load will also do the job at pass-shooting.

SHOTGUN

In Shotgun Chambered For	Do Not Use These Shells
10-Gauge	12-Gauge
12-Gauge	16-Gauge
12-Gauge	20-Gauge
16-Gauge	20-Gauge
20-Gauge	28-Gauge

In Shotgun Chambered For	Do Not Use These Centerfire Metallic Cartridges
.410 Bore	Any

With any gauge, shotshells of a given nominal length should not be fired in a gun the chamber length of which is shorter than the fired shell length, such as a 3-inch (75mm) shell fired in a 2¾-inch (70mm) chamber.

THE SHOTSHELL SELECTOR
(LEAD SHOT UNLESS INDICATED "STEEL")

	Type of Shell	Size
DUCKS	Magnum or Hi-Power	4, 5, 6 Steel 2, 4
GEESE	Magnum or Hi-Power	BB, 2, 4 Steel BB, 1, 2,
PHEASANTS	Magnum or Hi-Power	5, 6, 7½
QUAIL	Hi-Power or Field Load	7½, 8, 9
RUFFED GROUSE & HUNGARIAN PARTRIDGE	Hi-Power or Field Load	6, 7½, 8
OTHER GROUSE, CHUKAR PARTRIDGE	Hi-Power or Field Load	5, 6, 7½
DOVES & PIGEONS	Hi-Power or Field Load	6, 7½, 8, 9
RABBITS	Hi-Power or Field Load	4, 5, 6, 7½
WOODCOCK, SNIPE, RAIL	Field Load	7½, 8, 9
SQUIRRELS	Hi-Power or Field Load	4, 5, 6
WILD TURKEY	Magnum or Hi-Power	2, 4, 5, 6
CROWS	Hi-Power or Field Load	5, 6, 7½
FOX	Magnum or Hi-Power	BB, 2, 4

SHOT SIZES AND DIAMETER IN INCHES

No. 9	8½	8	7½	6	5	4	2	1	BB
.08	.085	.09	.095	.11	.12	.13	.15	.16	.18

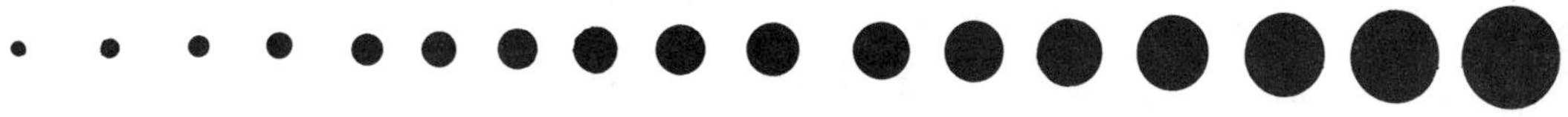

BUCKSHOT SIZES AND DIAMETER IN INCHES

No.4	No.3	No.2	No.1	No.0	No.00	No.000
.24	.25	.27	.30	.32	.33	.36

APPROXIMATE NUMBER OF PELLETS IN A GIVEN CHARGE

Shot Size	2 oz.	1⅞ oz.	1⅝ oz.	1½ oz.	1⅜ oz.	1¼ oz.	1⅛ oz.	1 oz.	⅞ oz.	¾ oz.	½ oz.
#2	180	169	146	135	124	113	102	90	79	68	45
#4	270	253	221	202	185	169	152	135	118	101	67
#5	340	319	277	255	234	213	192	170	149	128	85
#6	450	422	396	337	309	281	253	225	197	169	112
#7½	700	656	568	525	481	437	393	350	306	262	175
#8	820	769	667	615	564	513	462	410	359	308	205
#9	1170	1097	951	877	804	731	658	585	512	439	292

Note: The exact number of pellets can vary depending upon brand and lot.

Hunters who have both 12- and 20-gauge guns in their racks admit that most often they will pick the 20 when heading for favorite rabbit patches and woodcock covers.

THE 28-GAUGE AND .410

The 28-gauge seems to have a growing number of fans. For the average upland gunner, the 28-gauge may not be big enough. The skilled shooter, however, should take a closer look. The 28 is available in a load with 7/8 ounces of shot, which makes it adequate for woodcock, quail, doves, and similar birds.

The .410 is another load that has limited use. It's fine for the smaller species that can be taken at close range, but it's not recommended for anything else. True, at one time or another, we've all seen a hunter knock down pheasants with a .410—but these men are generally skilled shotgunners. The average hunter would be far better off with a 12- or 20-gauge. The same reasoning can be used to discourage a parent from buying his child a .410. A wiser choice for a youngster would be a light 20-gauge.

GAUGES FOR TRAP AND SKEET

When it comes to shooting claybirds, whether on official trap and skeet ranges or in a wooded area with a buddy tossing the birds out with a hand trap, almost any shotgun can be pressed into service for fun and practice. But the serious trap- and skeet-shooters stick to proven combinations.

On the trap range, for example, nearly all shooting is done with a 12-gauge gun. The barrel is 30 inches long, bored Full Choke, and wears a ventilated rib.

The skeetshooter goes to the opposite extreme. He generally starts with a 12-gauge gun, the most popular for the beginner at skeet. But he can vary his gauges, since regulated skeet matches are broken down into four events: the 12-gauge, the 20-gauge, the 28-gauge smallbore, and the .410 sub-smallbore. As the skeetshooter improves at the game, he feels obliged to go to the smaller gauges.

The most common skeet gun has a 26-inch barrel that is bored "Skeet," which is a choke that falls between Improved Cylinder and Cylinder.

SELECTING SHOT SIZE— LEAD SHOT

Shot (the pellets in a shotshell) is normally made of lead, a relatively cheap metal and one that's soft enough so it won't score gun barrels or damage choke construction. Being heavy, it has good ballistic qualities. It's an ideal metal for the pellets used in most types of shotgunning. Everyone agrees about that, but the subject of best shot size for a given type of game often starts arguments. Some grouse hunters, for example, prefer shot as large as No. 7½ or even No. 6, claiming the larger sizes plow through foliage well. Others prefer shot as small as No. 9 since a lot more No. 9s go into a shell, and a dense pattern of shot is more likely to put some pellets into the mark.

An accompanying chart, "The Shotshell Selector," offers advice formulated by experts. Another chart shows the comparative shot sizes, plus the average number of pellets per ounce.

SELECTING SHOT SIZE—STEEL SHOT, BISMUTH, AND TUNGSTEN

Lead shot has one serious drawback. The fired pellets fall into marshes and fields, where they are picked up as grit by feeding waterfowl. The ingested lead is poisonous. Retained in the gizzards of the birds, it kills large numbers of ducks and geese. In some areas, the problem is insignificant. The diet of the birds is one factor. The hardness of the marsh is another, since lead sinks into soft mud and the birds cannot get it. All the same, widespread poisoning of waterfowl by lead shot has mandated the use of a substitute material in shotshells for duck and goose shooting. No truly ideal nontoxic substitute has yet been found, but steel shot—the subject of research and development programs at ammunition companies for a number of years—has been significantly improved and is now supplied by the major manufacturers in waterfowl loads.

Since steel is only about 70 percent as heavy as lead, it requires more space in a shell than an equal weight of lead. Whereas an average of 135 No. 4 lead pellets make an ounce, you need about 192 steel pellets of the same size to make an ounce. A 1¼-ounce load of steel shot takes up so much more space in a shotshell that the makers have developed new powders that take less space, as well as a special plastic wad that merely acts as a gas seal and shot cup. There is no cushion section, and the shot cup is long enough to cover the entire length of the shot column. This protects the walls of the gun barrel from the hard steel pellets as they travel through the bore.

Because steel is lighter than lead, it is less efficient ballistically. To offset the loss of retained velocity and energy, larger shot must be used. The manufacturers have developed roughly equivalent steel loads in which there is only a small sacrifice in the number of pellets. In an ounce of No. 4 lead shot, for instance, there are 135 pellets; in an ounce of No. 2 steel shot there are 125. A 2¾-inch 12-gauge shell has an average of 169 pellets in a 1¼-ounce No. 4 lead load, 156 pellets in a 1¼-ounce No. 2 steel load. Laboratory and field tests by Remington, Winchester, and Federal have shown that appropriate steel loads (No. 2 steel as a substitute for No. 4 lead, for instance) lose more velocity and energy than lead shot at 40 and 50 yards, but the difference isn't drastic. Three-inch magnum 12-gauge shells with steel shot have become available, but you need not switch to long magnum steel loads in a situation that would call for 2¾-inch lead-shot loads. Assuming you have a gun chambered for 3-inch shells, you use such steel-shot loads only where you would use 3-inch magnum loads of lead shot. Where standard lead-shot loads are used, standard steel-shot loads have power enough.

However, the appropriate shot size obviously differs with steel. From tests by the manufacturers, rules of size have been formulated for switching to steel shot. Essentially, you go up one size for a given use. Shells are commonly available with four sizes of steel shot—No. 4, 2, 1, and BB. The three smallest sizes—No. 4, 2, and 1—are most often used. Generally speaking, the BB size is used only by expert gunners for ultra-long-range pass-shooting at geese. That makes the guidelines easy: Where you would use No. 5 or 6 lead shot, use No. 4 steel; where you would use No. 4 lead shot, use No. 2 steel; where you would use No. 2 lead shot, use No. 1 steel. To put it another way, use No. 4 steel for ducks over decoys; No. 2 steel for close-range shooting at geese over decoys and for longer-range pass-shooting at ducks; and No. 1 steel for pass-shooting at geese, or the BB size at extremely long range.

Although steel is ballistically inferior to lead, it has one advantage. Because the pellets are so hard, they suffer very little deformation as they pass through a gun's bore. Therefore, they produce slightly tighter patterns than lead. Some hunters have found that they get better results with steel by switching from Full Choke to Modified for pass-shooting, except when the range is quite long. As for the power of steel shot at waterfowling ranges, field tests have proved that it will bring down ducks and geese at 50 yards or so just as well as lead if the pattern is properly centered on the target. The average shotgunner shouldn't be trying for ducks or geese at ranges much beyond 50 yards.

A widely publicized drawback is the supposed harm that steel shot will do to a shotgun barrel. It is true that double-barreled guns and even some of the older repeaters with relatively thin or soft steel barrels can suffer minor damage—either barrel rings or bulges in the choke area. While these effects aren't hazardous, such guns should be reserved for other kinds of hunting. Most modern guns will not be harmed by steel shot. If in doubt, consult the manufacturer of your shotgun.

Tungsten and Bismuth are two newcomers in the search for a non-toxic shot with ballistics comparable to lead. Tungsten shot was introduced by Federal in 1997. It is actually tungsten-iron shot, a blend of two metal powders, 40 percent tungsten and 60 percent iron, pressed into the shape of a sphere. The pellets are then sintered or bonded together by a heating process. The shot is then coated with a rust inhibitor. Tungsten is harder than lead, steel, and bismuth. Tungsten-iron shot is 30 percent denser than steel, 94 percent as dense as lead, and 10 percent denser than bismuth.

Bismuth shot is another non-toxic shot available to waterfowl hunters. Bismuth shot is formed from an alloy composed of 97 percent bismuth and 3 percent tin. Bismuth is found in deposits with tin, copper, tungsten, gold, silver, and lead. Bismuth is separated during a refining process. Bismuth shot is 91 percent as dense as lead, a considerable improvement over steel's 71 percent.

Both bismuth and tungsten show a ballistic improvement over steel shot for waterfowl. The only rub is cost. These new non-toxic loads may cost you about $18 a box.

SHOTGUN BARREL AND CHOKE

THE BARREL

Not too long ago the most popular shotgun had a 30-inch Full Choke barrel. Today, because of modern shotshells with plastic shot collars and protectors which give tighter patterns, the No. 1 choice is a 28-inch barrel with Modified Choke. And upland gunners are even swinging to 24-, 25-, and 26-inch barrels with Improved Cylinder choke. All this makes sense. A shorter barrel means a lighter gun that is easier to carry and faster to shoot in thick upland cover.

Many years ago, a great number of shotgunners believed that barrels 36 inches and longer shot harder and farther than shorter barrels. This was true in the black-powder days when long barrels were required for full velocity to develop before the shot reached the muzzle. Now, with our modern smokeless powder, full velocity is reached in less than 24 inches. In fact, velocity in a 36-inch barrel is slowed down a bit because once the powder is burned and full velocity is reached within 24 inches, friction takes over between shot charge and bore, which decreases velocity.

If some hunters are still convinced they can knock down more game with long barrels, it is only because such barrels give a longer sighting plane and afford better balance and steadiness of swing. This is one reason for the popularity of 30- and 32-inch barrels on the trap range. Velocity has nothing to do with it.

As a general rule, a hunter is better off using as short a barrel as possible without sacrificing balance. Manufacturers know this and build their guns accordingly. Next column shows recommended barrel lengths for various types of shooting:

Types of Shooting	Barrel Length
Long-range duck, goose	30″ or 32″
Waterfowl over decoys	28″ or 30″
Pheasant, grouse	25″ to 28″
Rabbits, squirrels	25″ to 28″
Quail, doves, woodcock	24″ to 28″
Turkey	28″ or 30″
Deer	22″ to 28″
Trap shooting	30″ to 32″
Skeet shooting	25″ to 28″
All-round shooting	28″
Sporting clays	28″ to 32″

THE CHOKE

The choke on a shotgun is the amount of constriction in the bore of the barrel that is used to control the spread of the shot charge. The greater the constriction, which starts about 3 inches from the muzzle, the tighter the concentration of pellets during flight. Likewise, the less the constriction, the greater or wider the spread of pellets in flight.

The choke principle is easily understood by comparing it with a garden hose. Tighten the garden-hose nozzle and you'll get a narrow, heavy stream of water. Open it up and you'll get a wide spray. The choke and the garden-hose nozzle work on basically the same principle.

Chokes on today's shotgun barrels range from Full Choke, which has the most constriction and con-

sequently throws the tightest concentration of shot, to Cylinder, which means no choke at all—that is, no constriction at any point in the bore. Listing them by their common names, the popular range of chokes include Full Choke, Improved Modified, Improved Cylinder, Skeet, and Cylinder.

The constriction in the bore is generally accomplished by reaming or swagging, but much more important than the method is the amount of constriction and its effect on shot spread and pattern. Choke is the difference between bore diameter and muzzle diameter measured in one-thousandths of an inch. This measurement is also referred to as points. For example, the bore of a 12-gauge barrel will measure .730 inches and a constriction of .035 near the muzzle will make it a Full Choke barrel. We can also say the barrel has a 35-point constriction.

Unfortunately, bore diameters and constriction diameters often vary from manufacturer to manufacturer. For example, two 20-gauge guns, both stamped Modified Choke but turned out by two different gunmakers, may have a constriction difference of as much as .025 or 25 points. The result is, of course, that not all guns of the same choke will shoot identical patterns. One manufacturer's Full Choke may throw a Modified pattern and vice versa. The only foolproof way of determining the choke of a shotgun is to pattern it.

Before patterning a shotgun, we should know that the choke of a shotgun is determined by the percentage of pellets from the particular shotshell load that fall within a 30-inch circle at 40 yards. The following figures are generally accepted as standard guidelines in determining a barrel's choke:

Choke	Percentage of Shot in 30-Inch Circle at 40 Yd.
Full Choke	70–80
Improved Modified	65–70
Modified	55–60
Quarter Choke	50–55
Improved Cylinder	45–50
Skeet No. 2	50–60
Skeet No. 1 (Cylinder)	35–40

So if you're having trouble with your shotgun, either missing birds with it or getting more than your share of cripples, it would be wise to pattern your gun and see exactly what choke you have and whether your pattern is too dense or sparse for the ranges you're shooting at.

To pattern a shotgun, simply tack up a piece of paper 40 inches by 40 inches. Draw a small bull's-eye in the center of the paper, then inscribe a 30-inch circle around it. Now check the shotshell load you normally use and compute the number of pellets in it (see table above on shot percentages). Take a shot at 40

PERCENTAGE OF PELLETS AT VARIOUS RANGES

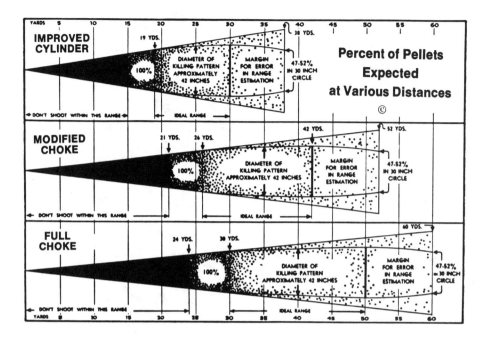

yards at the bull's-eye, count the pellet holes within the circle, and figure out the percentage that landed in the circle. Check this figure with the above listings and you'll be able to determine the true choke of your shotgun, regardless of the size hole in the barrel or what is stamped on the barrel. Patterning your shotgun and knowing exactly what pattern it throws can be just as important as sighting-in a rifle, and no deer hunter should go afield without sighting-in his rifle.

It's important to note that these patterns are taken at 40 yards and that most game is taken at considerably closer ranges. In fact, the majority of small game and upland birds are shot at 30 yards or less. So that Full Choke spread that looks great on paper at 40 yards would actually be much smaller and the pellets much more concentrated at, say, 25 yards. To the grouse hunter who rarely shoots his birds at more than 25 yards, this would mean two things: a lot of misses or, if he was an excellent shot, birds shot to pieces. What all this means is that the choke you select depends on the game you're hunting.

The hunter after grouse, rabbits, quail, and woodcock—which are all taken in fairly heavy cover—should use a Modified or Improved Cylinder choke, preferably the latter. If he's a waterfowl gunner, he should use a Modified or Full Choke.

Though most duck hunters would feel handicapped with a Modified Choke, this would probably be a better choice. For game such as turkeys, usually taken at greater ranges, a Full Choke is the top choice. For all-round small game and bird hunting, the Improved Cylinder or Modified Choke comes off as the best compromise.

For a more detailed patterning procedure, see the following illustrated instructions.

HOW TO PATTERN A SHOTGUN

Imagine this upland hunting situation: A bird dog locks up on point and a pheasant hunter moves in for the shot. When he gets within 10 feet or so of the dog, a ringneck flushes straight up. Startled, the hunter immediately nails the bird with his shotgun. At such short range, the bird catches the full load of pellets from a Modified Choke barrel. The result? The pheasant is raked so badly with pellets that it cannot be salvaged for the table.

This situation occurs all too frequently and pretty much for the same reason: Many hunters simply do not know how their shotguns will pattern at various ranges. The result is that they will either miss long shots at game or blast birds apart at close ranges. They also assume that a barrel will throw a Modified pattern because it is stamped "Modified." This isn't always true. There is only one way to find out what your shotgun will do at different ranges and that is to take your gun out and pattern it on paper. It's a simple job, and the results may surprise you.

The photos on pages 144–145 show patterns shot with a 12-gauge Remington Model 870 pump. Three interchangeable barrels were used and they were choked Modified, Improved Cylinder and Cylinder. Patterns were shot at 40, 30, and 15 yards.

These photographs show patterns shot with various combinations of range and choke. The comparisons are interesting. But DON'T expect these exact patterns from your shotgun. Patterns differ slightly, depending on manufacturer's choke specifications. Even among the same chokes, patterns are likely to be different.

The choke on a shotgun is the amount of constriction in the muzzle of the barrel that is used to control the spread of the shot charge. The greater the constriction the tighter the concentration of pellets during flight. The lesser the constriction, the greater the spread of pellets during flight. And the degree of choke is determined by the percentage of pellets from a particular shotshell load that hit within a 30-inch circle at 40 yards.

Even the percentages used to measure choke vary among some manufacturers. Generally, though, the following figures can be used:

Choke	Percentage of Shot in 30-inch Circle at 40 yards
Full	70–80
Improved Modified	65–70
Modified	55–60
Improved Cylinder	45–50
Skeet No. 2	50–60
Skeet No. 1 (Cylinder)	35–40

The range to begin patterning is 40 yards. The only exceptions are the 28-gauge, the .410, and skeet chokes of all gauges—which should be patterned at 25 yards. You'll note, however, that one of the barrels patterned here at all ranges was straight Cylinder, which means no choke constriction at all. This was done to learn just how well a 20-inch Cylinder-Choke barrel would stack up against the other more popular chokes.

To pattern your shotgun, you'll also have to know the approximate number of pellets in the shotshells you're using. You should always pattern your shotgun with the hunting loads you ordinarily use. The patterns here were shot with Remington Express loads with 1¼ ounces of No. 6 shot, which throws a charge of about 276 pellets. You can get the num-

ber of pellets from most firearm catalogs or you can actually cut open a couple of shotshells and count them.

Targets are available with a printed 30-inch circle and a claybird for an aiming point. Such targets,

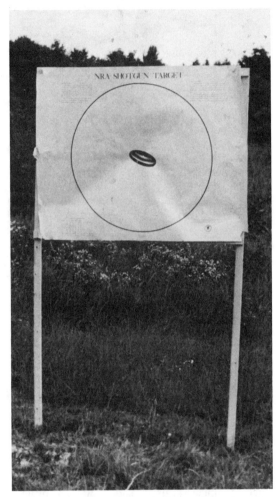

Front view of shotgun target and target frame I used to pattern my scattergun.

however, are not necessary. Any sheet of paper measuring 4 feet by 4 feet will do. Just mark a spot in the center of the paper to use as an aiming point. You can make the frame of your target from 6-foot firing strips. The two uprights, which are sharpened and driven into the ground, measure a full 6 feet. The three cross members are 45 inches across. Use ordinary bulletin board push pins to hold the targets in place.

After shooting is done, I mark and count pellet holes in 30-inch circle with felt-tip marker. Note that I've marked range and pertinent shotshell data in lower right-hand corner.

Actual patterning is simple. Mark each target with range and pertinent data about the hunting load you're using. For example, mark your targets as follows: 40 yards, Remington Express, 12-gauge, Modified, No. 6, 1¼ ounces.

Fire at least five shots, at a new target each time, at 40, 30, and 15 yards. Do this with each choke. After all the shooting is done, use a felt-tip marker and mark and count each pellet hole within the 30-inch circle. When you get this figure, divide it by the number of pellets in the shot charge and multiply it by 100. The answer will be your pattern percentage. Next, figure the average percentage of your five shots with each choke.

An important factor should be mentioned here. The 30-inch circle must encompass the most pellet holes on the paper. If you're lucky, the aiming point on your target will result in putting the most pellets in the printed circle. If the densest part of your pattern is *not* within the circle, you must make a second circle encompassing the most pellet holes. Count the holes within this second circle and figure out the percentage.

For example, Remington Express 12-gauge loads with 1¼ ounces of No. 6 shot were used here. The ammo maker says that this load has 276 pellets. At 40 yards, the Modified barrel put 131 pellets into a 30-inch circle. Divide 276 into 131, multiply the answer by 100, and you'll get 47 percent.

Now this is where the whole patterning business gets tricky and why it is so important to pattern your own gun. According to firearm manufacturers, a Modified Choke throws a 55–60 percent pattern at 40 yards. Yet this particular barrel patterned 47 percent at 40 yards, roughly 10 percent less. Your Modified barrel may pattern at exactly 55 percent, or it may throw a denser pattern. Patterns will vary among the same chokes and even when you change shot size.

Here are the results of patterning this particular 12-gauge pump with Remington Express loads with 1¼ ounces of No. 6 shot:

Range (yards)	Choke	Percent
40	Modified	47
40	Improved Cylinder	40
40	Cylinder	37
30	Modified	80
30	Improved Cylinder	58
30	Cylinder	47
15	Modified	96
15	Improved Cylinder	95
15	Cylinder	95

It's obvious, by comparing percentages, that these barrels do not jibe with some of the percentages listed by firearm manufacturers. At 40 yards, for example, Modified and Improved Cylinder patterned more open than anticipated. This was especially surprising, because the Remington loads used the Power Piston wad and shot collar, which protects the shot from deformation as it travels through the barrel. These shot collars will frequently make a Modified Choke throw a tight Modified or Full pattern. This, however, does not happen in all cases.

What conclusions can you draw from this patterning session? First, don't shoot game too close or you will needlessly load birds with too many pellets. If you shoot a lot of game over dogs, stick with Improved Cylinder or even Cylinder Choke and let the birds get out at least 30 yards before shooting.

And you can gain a great deal of new respect for Cylinder Choke. It threw a good pattern and put only 11 pellets less than the Improved Cylinder in a 30-inch circle at 30 yards. And the 20-inch Cylinder barrel will make the gun a charm to handle in grouse country.

At 40 yards, which is a long shot in anyone's book, both the Modified and Improved Cylinder chokes threw killing patterns. This means that occasional misses at long ranges are probably the shooter's fault and not the gun's. The reason for misses on those long shots is easy to figure out: The shooter is not leading the birds enough and the shot charge is passing harmlessly behind them.

What all this means is that we are probably hunting with guns choked too tight. Most shooters should use their Modified barrels for claybird shooting and pass-shooting at waterfowl. For pheasants, gunning over dogs, where a hunter has a chance to let the birds get out to 30 yards, stick with the Improved Cylinder barrel. When hunting grouse and woodcock in thick cover, use the 20-inch Cylinder barrel.

If you take the time to pattern your shotgun, you will know what your barrels and chokes will do. I strongly recommend that you go out and see how your scattergun stacks up on paper. There may be some surprises in store for you.

PATTERN YOUR SHOTGUN FOR TURKEYS

Turkeys make a tough target. They are difficult to see and even harder to kill. The head and neck are the only vital areas that insure a fast, clean kill, but this will only happen if your shotgun throws a tight, dense shot pattern.

The best shotgun choice for turkeys is a 12-gauge magnum, though the 10-gauge is gaining some ground among turkey hunters. The best shot sizes are No. 2, 4, 5, or 6. The best shotgun chokes are full, extra full, and super-full.

Patterning your shotgun for turkey hunting is simply a matter of shooting your shotgun with various shot sizes at different ranges to determine the most effective combination. If you have different choke tubes available, try them all and pick the one that gives you the best pattern.

To pattern your shotgun, you will need two loads of each shot size and six targets that show the full-size head and neck of a gobbler. Start by taking one shot at each target at 15, 25, and 40 yards.

With each load and choke combination, count the number of pellets in the vital areas of the gobbler's head. Opinions vary on the number of pellets you will need in a vital area to put a turkey down. You will need at least six pellets in the vital area to kill a turkey. Some experienced hunters, however, claim that a turkey hunter will need up to 30 pellets in a vital area to kill a gobbler quick and clean.

After you have tried all the different loads at 15, 25, and 40 yards, analyze your targets and count the pellets in the vital area. Determine which load gives you the densest pattern in the gobbler's head and neck. That's the load to use.

Remember that 40 yards is about maximum shotgun range on gobblers, regardless of your choke and load combination. Any turkey farther than 40 yards is not in killing range and you should not take the shot.

SHOTGUN PATTERNS

40-Yard Modified, 12-Ga., 1¼ oz. No. 6. A good 40-yard killing pattern.

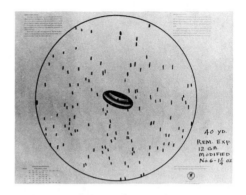

40-Yard Improved Cylinder, 12-Ga., 1¼ oz. No. 6. Another good 40-yard pattern. A more evenly spread pattern than that from Modified Choke.

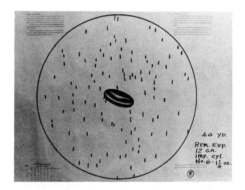

40-Yard Cylinder, 12-Ga., 1¼ oz. No. 6. A somewhat surprising 40-yard pattern from Cylinder bore. It has some holes in it, but it is still good enough for most upland game.

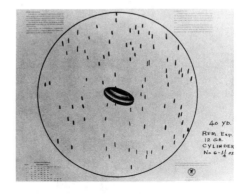

30-Yard Modified, 12-Ga., 1¼ oz. No. 6. Much too tight a pattern for most upland game.

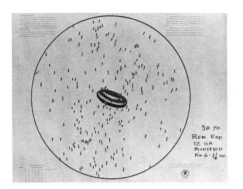

15-Yard Modified, 12-Ga., 1¼ oz. No. 6. This pattern is positively too dense for any gamebird, yet many hunters take game at this range with the popular Modified Choke. A bird caught in this pattern would be inedible.

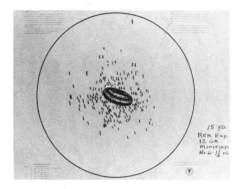

30-Yard Improved Cylinder, 12-Ga., 1¼ oz. No. 6. A good 30-yard pattern for almost all bird shooting. If anything, it might still be too dense.

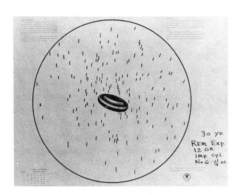

15-Yard Improved Cylinder, 12-Ga., 1¼ oz. No. 6. This pattern is still too dense for hunting. At 15 yards, the shot charge still hasn't had much chance to open up into an even pattern. The circled hole is where the combination wad and shot protector went through the paper.

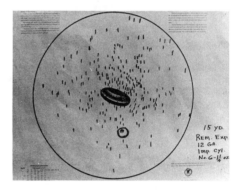

30-Yard Cylinder, 12-Ga., 1¼ oz. No. 6. This pattern is pretty close to ideal for 30 yards, the range at which game is most often shot.

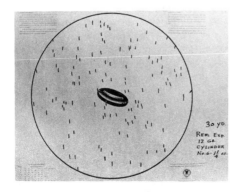

15-Yard Cylinder, 12-Ga., 1¼ oz. No. 6. Even with Cylinder Choke, 15 yards is still a bit too close to shoot game. The circled hole in target is where the combination wad and shot protector went through the paper.

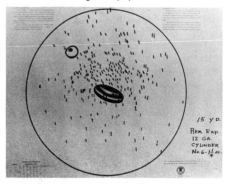

VITAL AREAS

 Bony skull and vertebrae
(penetration will immobilize)

 Aiming point and center of pattern

NON-VITAL AREAS
A-Esophagus (gullet)
B-Trachea (windpipe)
C-Wattles
D-Snood (dew bill)
E-Loose neck skin
This Winchester patterning target shows the head and
neck of an adult gobbler. Vital and non-vital areas are
based on an X-ray of an actual turkey.

If you decide to use a scope on your shotgun this
season, remember that you are dealing with magnification. A gobbler will look bigger and closer in a
scope. Make sure your turkey is in range.

There was a time when duck hunting was considered the most dangerous form of hunting. That's no
longer true. Turkey hunting now accounts for most
accidents. There are some good rules for turkey
hunters to keep in mind.

Never wear red, white, black, or light blue clothing that could be visible to other hunters. These are
the colors of a spring gobbler.

Wear full camouflage but avoid white socks or
T-shirts, which might look like the white part of a
gobbler.

Use your turkey call in terrain where you can see
at least 50 yards in every direction. Keep your back
against a tree trunk, stump, or boulder that is higher
than your head.

If you see another turkey hunter approaching you,
stay still and whistle or shout loudly.

Never sneak in on a turkey that is gobbling, and
avoid using a call when hunters are nearby. There is
always the chance that you are approaching another
hunter, or roles could be reversed.

If you use a decoy, position it so that you are not
in any possible line of fire with it. Position the
decoy so it can be seen from the sides, not from in
front or behind you. Use only hen decoys, never a
fake gobbler.

SOLVING SHOTGUN PROBLEMS

Knowing the right barrel length and choke for your
hunting is fine if you're in the process of buying a
new gun. But what about the chap who already has
a gun and is dissatisfied because the barrel is too
long or the pattern it throws is too dense or too
sparse. Suppose his favorite grouse gun has a 26-
inch barrel with Improved Cylinder choke and he
suddenly decides he wants to take up duck hunting.
How does he get a tighter pattern out of it? Or suppose he wants to take his Full-Choke duck gun
grouse hunting and wants a wider pattern, but is
unwilling to have the shotgun bored out to Improved
Cylinder. All these problems can be solved one way
or another. Let's take them one by one.

First, let's talk about the fellow who was told that
a 30-inch barrel and Full Choke was the greatest
combination going. But now he discovers that his
barrel is hanging up on limbs and brush in heavy
cover while hunting rabbits and grouse and that he's
either missing his target or shooting it to pieces. He
knows he needs a shorter barrel and a more open
choke. There are a few ways he can solve his problem. One way that would involve no expense is to
use brush loads (also called scatter loads), a special
shotshell that has dividers separating the shot
charge. At one time, manufacturers supplied these
loads, but they are now hard to find. They can,
however, be handloaded. Such a shotshell would
open his choke one step. That means his Full Choke
could be turned into a Modified Choke by simply
changing ammunition. But, unfortunately, brush
loads are usually available in one shot size, generally
No. 8. And our hunter still has the problem of the
long barrel.

A better alternative would be to have his barrel
cut down to 28 inches and bored Improved Cylinder

APPARENT SIZES OF DUCKS AT VARIOUS DISTANCES

20 YDS.   30 YDS.   40 YDS.   50 YDS.   60 YDS.

It is generally accepted among duck and goose hunters that a good killing range with a shotgun is about 35 yards. Many hunters, however, have difficulty judging distance. These drawings show what a duck looks like over your shotgun barrel at 20, 30, 40, 50 and 60 yards. Another good rule of thumb is that if your shotgun bead obliterates the duck's head or if the bead looks bigger than the duck's head, the bird is probably out of effective killing range. (Courtesy of Browning Arms.)

or Modified. Generally, taking 2 inches off a barrel will still leave enough constriction to enable a gunsmith to open the choke. If the hunter wants to cut his 30-inch barrel down to 26 inches, he has a bigger problem. Taking 4 inches off a barrel will remove all constriction and he'll have a Cylinder bore, which may or not be too open for his kind of hunting. We should mention here that some hunters who have chopped 4 inches off their shotguns have found them to be deadly on upland game, probably because they were consistently shooting their game a lot closer than they realized. But if a hunter finds a complete loss of choke in his gun is a handicap he has no choice but to install a variable-choke device, which we'll discuss later on.

As for the grouse hunter who has a 26-inch barrel with an Improved Cylinder choke and wants to start duck hunting, he has no choice but to install a variable-choke device. The same applies to the duck hunter with a Full Choke gun who wants a more open choke for upland game but still wants to be able to fall back on a Full Choke for ducks. He can switch to brush loads, but a better solution is a variable choke. This explains the enormous popularity of the screw-in choke tubes that are now available on most shotguns.

The only exception to the above cases are the shotguns produced to accept interchangeable barrels. With these, a hunter can buy a variety of barrels to suit his needs until his money runs out.

VARIABLE-CHOKE SELECTORS

A variable choke is a mechanical device fitted to the muzzle of a shotgun that enables the shooter quickly and simply to change the choke from Full to Cylinder, with a variety of settings in between. They are available in two basic designs—the interchangeable tube type and the collet type.

The Cutts Compensator is a typical example of the interchangeable tube-type choke device. The main body of the device, which also serves as a muzzle brake and reduces recoil, is fitted to the muzzle. A hunter who wants to change his choke merely screws in tubes of various degrees of constriction to give different patterns.

The collet-type variable choke uses an adjustable nozzle-like affair on the muzzle to change choke setting. The hunter simply turns a knurled ring to increase or decrease the constriction at the muzzle to change his choke and pattern.

The newer screw-in choke tubes have become enormously popular and most major gunmakers now offer them on shotguns under a variety of names. Winchester calls its choke-tube system Winchoke, Remington calls it Rem Choke, Weatherby names it Multi-choke, Browning has Invector, and Mossberg offers Accu-Choke. All systems work basically the same way. The choke tube is threaded and is seated in the muzzle with a wrench. Extra tubes

DESIGNS OF VARIBLE CHOKES

Various screw-in choke tube devices from some major gun manufacturers.

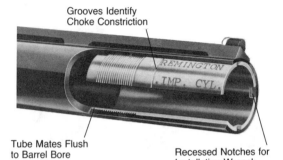

Grooves Identify
Choke Constriction

Tube Mates Flush
to Barrel Bore

Recessed Notches for
Installation Wrench

Remington Rem Choke

Browning Invector System

Beretta Screw-In Choke

Winchester Winchoke

Weatherby Multi-Choke

Cutts Compensator comes with variety of tubes to change choke, as well as wrench to screw tubes into muzzle brake, which also reduces recoil as much as 35 percent with 12-gauge high-velocity loads.

with different chokes can be easily carried and replaced quickly in the field.

If you think these variable-choke devices are a good deal, you're right. Hunters who can't make up their minds about the best choke for their gun, or who are determined to use one gun for all game, will find a variable choke a good deal. With a variable choke, they can use the same gun for pass-shooting at waterfowl at 50 yards and quail gunning at 20 yards.

These variable chokes offer another advantage. They give the hunter the option of having his barrel cut down to as much as 24 or 26 inches. This is a definite asset, since there is no reason for a pump or autoloader to have a barrel longer than 26 inches. And a 24-inch barrel is fast and deadly on game such as quail and woodcock.

Even though these variable-choke devices have the settings clearly indicated on them, it's still a good idea to check the pattern at each setting to make sure it's doing the job it's supposed to do.

Collet-type variable-choke device fitted to the muzzle of a shotgun.

SHOTGUN STOCKS

The shotgunner, unlike the rifle shooter who generally has plenty of time to snuggle up comfortably to his stock and squeeze off a careful shot, has a different set of problems to cope with. His game is almost always moving—running on the ground or taking to the air in a burst of wingbeats. He rarely has time to mount his gun carefully and shoot slow-

ly. He is forced to focus on his target, snap the shotgun to his shoulder, start his swing, determine lead, and slap the trigger. Human reaction time, from the point of mounting the gun to pulling the trigger, has been clocked at .25 seconds. For the average gunner, that's fast shooting.

What all this means is that the stock fit of a shot-

PARTS AND BASIC MEASUREMENTS OF A SHOTGUN STOCK

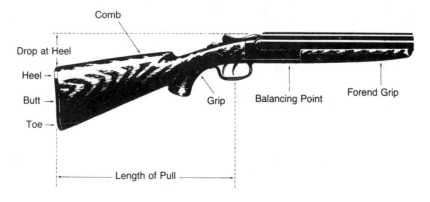

gun is very important, perhaps more so than with a rifle. It seems strange then that many hunters will go to great lengths to get a rifle stock that fits their physical frame, yet will grab any scattergun out of the rack and take it out for a day of grouse shooting.

Shotgunners should take the fit of their smooth-bores more seriously. We should first understand that a skilled wing shot actually "points" with the position of his feet and head before he even brings the shotgun to his shoulder. If the stock fits his frame, the gun will almost automatically be on target when he mounts it. If it's a poor fit, he'll likely shoot over, under, in front of, or behind the bird.

If you're a wealthy shooter who can afford to have shotguns custom built and the stocks shaped to exacting dimensions by means of a complicated "try gun," your problem is simple. The custom gun-builder will see that your stock fits properly.

But the majority of hunters have to solve their own problems of shotgun stock fit and the first step is a basic understanding of various measurements and how they will affect shooting in the field.

LENGTH OF PULL

Length of pull is the distance between the butt and trigger. If this measurement is too long, the shooter will catch the heel of the stock on his clothes or under his armpit. If length of pull is too short, the shooter will find that he will be smacking his nose with the thumb of his right hand when he pulls the trigger and the gun recoils. The proper length of pull, then, is one that will enable a shooter to mount the gun easily, clearing his clothes and keeping the thumb a safe distance from his nose.

The typical factory shotgun comes off the line with a length of pull of about 14 inches, which is usually all right for men 5 feet 8 inches to 5 feet 10 inches tall. A man over 6 feet tall will generally do better with a length of pull of 14¼ to 14½ inches. A boy, woman, or short man about 5½ feet tall, should look for a length of pull of about 13½ inches. The important factor is that the shooter should be able to mount his gun quickly and comfortably.

DROP AT COMB

Drop at comb is the distance from the top of the forward edge of the comb and the line of sight. This is an important measurement since the comb, in a sense, is the rear sight of a shotgun because it positions and lines up the eye with the front bead sight. If the comb is too high, it will raise the eye of the shooter. This means he will see more barrel and point the barrel up. When this happens, the shot charge will go higher and he'll likely shoot over his birds.

If the drop at comb is too low, the reverse happens—the gunner will shoot under his birds.

The typical factory-made shotgun has a drop at comb of 1½ inches, which is suitable for a man 5 feet 7 inches to 5 feet 11 inches tall. A 6-footer, however, needs less drop at comb. Thickness of the comb is also a factor. A thick comb will position the eye higher than a low comb.

This business of comb height is perhaps the most common reason for misses. If a hunter sees too much barrel when he quickly mounts his gun and feels he is getting more than his share of misses, it's a good bet that he's overshooting his target. If a hunter feels he must raise his cheek a bit to get a clear view of the front bead, chances are the comb is too low and he'll shoot under some of his birds.

The one exception to this is the trapshooter, who consistently shoots at a fast-rising target and wants to keep the claybird in sight at all times. He uses a special trap stock with a drop at comb of about 1⅜ inches. This will give him a high comb, which means his shot charge will fly higher. In effect, he has a built-in lead when he shoots directly at a claybird tossed straightaway.

The hunter, however, gets most of his shots at 20 to 25 yards and frequently prefers to blot out his game at closer ranges. If his gun has a high comb, like the trapshooter's, he'll shoot over the bird.

Firearm manufacturers have accounted for these differences and turn out shotguns labeled field models and trap models. The difference lies mainly in stock dimensions.

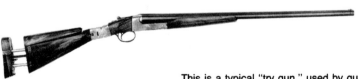

This is a typical "try gun," used by gunmakers to build custom stocks designed to fit their clients' body proportions. Such try guns are adjustable for drop at comb, drop at heel, length of pull, and pitch.

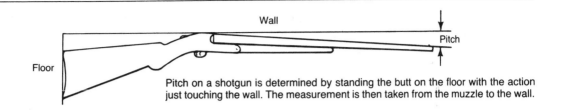

Pitch on a shotgun is determined by standing the butt on the floor with the action just touching the wall. The measurement is then taken from the muzzle to the wall.

DROP AT HEEL

Drop at heel is the distance between the heel of the stock and the line of sight. Here again, this measurement depends on the shooter's physical frame. The typical factory shotgun has a drop at heel of 2½ inches, which is fine for all-round use. A squarely built man, however, might prefer less drop at heel—which means a straighter stock. A round-shouldered and bull-necked shooter would be better off with a greater drop at heel.

It's a generally accepted fact that the less drop at heel—the straighter the stock—the easier the gun will be to mount and shoot. Recoil is also felt less with a straight stock, since the gun will recoil more directly into the shoulder.

PITCH

Pitch is the angle of the buttplate on the butt and is measured from the muzzle. To determine pitch, a shotgun is stood on its butt with the action touching a wall. The measurement is then taken from the muzzle to the wall. The drawing above illustrates it clearly.

Pitch is important in shotguns, since the point of impact can be raised or lowered by changing the angle of the butt. Its major function is to keep the butt solidly against the shooter's shoulder. With too little downward pitch, the butt may slip down and point the gun up, which will make the shot charge fly high. With too much downward pitch, the stock may ride up the shoulder and the shot charge will fly low. A pitch of about 2 to 3 inches is about right for a shotgun with 28-inch barrels.

CAST-OFF

Hunters who stick to American-made guns need not be concerned with "cast-off," since guns made in the U.S. rarely have this feature. Cast-off means that, for a right-handed shooter, the butt is angled slightly to the right of the line of sight. Or slightly to the left for a left-handed shooter. Cast-off is supposed to make the gun easier to mount and swing. It is common on British-made shotguns.

This drawing shows proper cast-off on a double-barreled shotgun for a right-handed shooter. Note that the butt angles to the right of line of sight. Cast-off is rarely designed into American-made guns.

STOCK STYLE

Shotgun stocks come in two basic designs—pistol-grip stock and English straight stock. The English straight stock looks neater and has a trimmer appearance. This straight stock design is popular in Europe, and it also seems to have periods of popularity in North America.

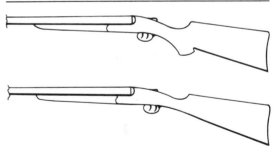

Here are the two basic stock designs for shotguns—the pistol-grip stock (top) and the English straight stock.

The modern American shotgun has a pistol grip, which puts the wrist in a comfortable position and affords better control when swinging the gun and shooting. The original purpose of the straight stock was to allow the hand to flow more quickly when pulling the second trigger on a double-barreled shotgun, but this is not needed with a single-trigger gun. Some shooters feel they have better control with a pistol grip. Still, the appearance of the straight stock is again winning favor. And Remington, for example, offers a straight-stocked Special Field version of its widely used Model 870 pump and Model 1100 autoloader.

SHOTSHELL SELECTION AND BALLISTICS

The changes in shotshell construction within two decades or so have been phenomenal. Most hunters over 40 years old can probably remember when just about all shotshells were made of paper impregnated with wax. A look inside these shells was often bewildering. They generally had about 10 to 12 components, including brass cup, primer, paper case, base wad, shot, over-powder wad, filler wads, over-shot wads, and so on.

In those days, ammunition makers ran those components through a complicated process before turning out the finished shell. These shells had several drawbacks. They could not be reloaded more than several times, water would eventually get into the paper body and the case would slowly deteriorate, and the shot charge would frequently deform when it came into contact with the bore.

Things started to change around 1960, when Remington introduced the plastic shell, which was waterproof and offered longer case life for those shooters who handloaded their own shotshells. Then came the plastic shot sleeve or collar, which surrounded and protected the pellets from becoming deformed as the shot charge traveled through the barrel. Many plastic shot sleeves now also form the over-powder wad. Winchester made shotshell construction even simpler when it designed its plastic shells in such a way that made even base wads unnecessary. The over-shot wad was eliminated when the star-crimp came into standard use. The star-crimp utilizes the shell case itself to seal off the top of the completed shotshell. This type of crimp also made reloading easier and less expensive.

The shotshells of today are more durable, more uniform, produce denser patterns, and can be reloaded many more times at less cost than the shotshells of a decade or so ago.

A more recent innovation is the all-plastic shotshell case without a brass head. Pioneers in manufacturing such a shotshell had two problems. First, shooters felt a brass head was needed for safety and strength. Second, the extractor sometimes broke through the rim of early shotshells of this type. Both problems appear to have been solved. The plastic

PARTS OF SHOTSHELLS

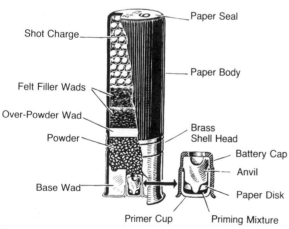

Parts of a shotshell produced in the 1950s.

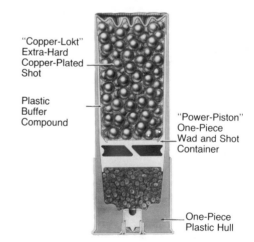

Remington 12-Gauge 2¾-inch Magnum

High-speed photography shows the shot collar separating from the shot charge after it has protected pellets from deforming while traveling through barrel. (Photo couresty of Winchester-Western.)

head and rim are reinforced. One leader in this field, Activ, is currently producing shotshells of this type.

STANDARD SHELLS

American-made shotguns are chambered for the standard 2¾-inch shotshell. We should mention here, however, that the shell labeled "2¾ inches" is not 2¾ inches long, but about ¼ inch shorter. The 2¾-inch measurement is taken when the case is open, before crimping. The chamber of the shotgun, on the other hand, *is* 2¾ inches. This difference in measurements is to allow enough room in the gun's chamber for the crimp to unfold completely.

The difference in shell length and chamber length should make it obvious that hunters should not attempt to shoot the 3-inch magnum shotshells in guns chambered for the 2¾-inch standard loads, in spite of what some shotgunners claim. It's all right to shoot a shell that is shorter than the gun is chambered for, but it is dangerous to shoot long shells in guns chambered for shorter shells. The chamber does not allow enough room for the crimp to unfold completely and excessive pressure can build up when the shot charge forces its way through a not-completely-open crimp.

THE MAGNUMS

Magnum shotshells are available in both 2¾- and 3-inch size. Just about all shotguns chambered for the 2¾-inch standard shells will take the 2¾-inch magnum shells. The 3-inch magnum shells, however, needs guns chambered to handle the longer shells.

Magnum shotshells have more powder and shot than standard field loads, but do not expect them to perform miracles. The extra powder and shot will increase effective range on game because of the extra number of pellets, but the muzzle velocity of a magnum shell is nearly the same as that of a standard high-velocity load.

Magnums, however, do give the hunter an extra edge when gunning for deer and tough game, such as turkeys and geese.

BRUSH LOADS

Brush loads, also called scatter or spreader loads, are shotshells that have a divider of sorts separating the shot charge into three or four separate sections. When the shell is fired, these partitions spread the shot charge into a more open pattern, in spite of the gun's designated choke. Generally, a brush load will, in effect, open the choke of a gun one setting. Fired in a Full Choke gun, for example, a brush load will throw a Modified pattern. Used in a Modified Choke barrel, a brush load will produce an Improved Cylinder pattern, and so on.

Even though these brush loads are available in one or two shot sizes, generally No. 8, it's surprising they aren't used more by hunters after the smaller gamebirds in thick cover, such as woodcock and quail. A hunter with a double-barreled shotgun choked Full and Modified, for example, can get Modified and Improved Cylinder patterns out of his scatterguns by simply changing loads. And the shooter with a Modified Choke pump gun would fare much better with brush loads when gunning for quail.

These brush loads are sometimes difficult to find. Not all manufacturers load them. They can, however, be handloaded by using a spreader device in the shot charge, usually a partitioned piece of cardboard forming an X.

The duplex, another unique shotshell, is loaded with both large and medium size pellets. The theory is that the large pellets retain maximum energy for long range and the smaller pellets make the pattern denser at close range. The duplex shotshell loads are usually designed for turkey hunters with a mix of No. 2 and 6 shot sizes. Some hunters can get the same results by first loading their gun with a smaller pellet size load for a close range dense pattern, and following-up with a larger shot size load for retained energy and longer range.

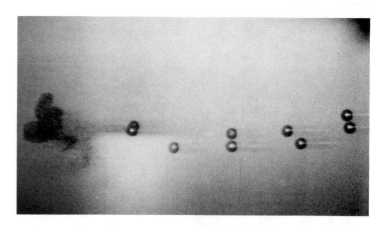

Above left: High-speed photo shows Federal 00 Buckshot load 12 inches from the muzzle as pellets and buffer emerge from the shot cup. **Above right:** At 6 feet from the muzzle, the nine pellets show little dispersion. **Right:** With Full Choke, here's the pattern at 40 yards in a 15-inch circle. This is an excellent pattern for a 00 Buckshot load.

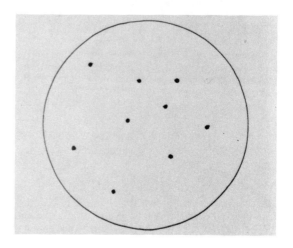

RIFLED SLUGS

Shotgun slug loadings were developed to give the scattergunner big-game capability at short range in areas which were too densely populated for safe use of rifles. Slugs didn't really enjoy a great reputation for accuracy and it seems only recently that the problem has been properly addressed.

Slugs, in their variations, are elongated (conical) projectiles. The best way to make such projectiles shoot accurately is to fire them from a rifled barrel. However, shotguns are smoothbored and have no rifling. This one factor automatically limits us to close- or medium-range shooting—not much over 100 yards in typical hunting situations.

Presently there is no choice but to fire the soft lead slug from an unrifled shotgun barrel. Since we can do nothing about that, our attention should move to those areas where we have some control: Shells, projectile, wadding and sights.

A brief examination of interior ballistics points up the general lack of understanding of what is needed, in principle, to obtain optimum accuracy. Basically, a slug must be kept centered in the bore without being tilted, deformed or similarly abused. Wadding beneath the slug should fully seal the bore and provide a rigid base for the slug to rest upon.

Often, a slug will be considerably undersize for the bore through which it is fired. In this case, the slug literally bounces from side to side as it travels toward the muzzle. After every contact with the

The Brenneke slug, specially designed for shotgun hunting of big game. The slug and wad are joined to form one long projectile, which increases ballistic performance and accuracy. Keyholing is eliminated.

bore wall the slug sustains a bit of deformation and tilts to a new angle before going over to bounce against the other side of the bore.

However, the worst happens at the muzzle as the slug departs. Since its wanderings within the bore are of a random nature, a slug will contact the choke taper of the muzzle in a different spot nearly every shot. You can imagine how the point of impact is affected by the first shot which strikes the choke at 6 o'clock, the second striking the choke at 12 o'clock, and so forth.

The worst offenders, generally speaking, are those slugs which are not securely attached to their wad columns and thus centered in the bore. When fired in "standard" shotgun barrels (not special slug barrels) the over-powder felt cushion wad topped by a thick nitro card tend to seal the bore pretty well and keep propellant gases where they belong—behind the projectile. However, nothing keeps the slug centered and stationary in the bore's center and so our slug bounces from side to side on the way out the muzzle.

Although the common slug sports a hollow base and is cast of soft lead, there seems to be a real advantage to protecting the hollow base from damage due to wads forcing themselves into the base— that's why a sturdy nitro card often proves to be a real group-tightener when seated over the felt cushion wad. The nitro card keeps the felt wad out of the slug base, minimizing projectile deformation.

Projectiles like the Brenneke and Vitt slugs which have the over-powder wad and/or plastic obturating cup securely attached to the slug proper seem to perform consistently well. No doubt part of this can be attributed to the relative stability of the slug atop the wads but the "weathervane" effect of the attached wads is perhaps the prime stabilizing agent.

When a shooter thinks of a shotshell slug, the first image that comes to mind is that of a fat chunk of lead with a hollow base only slightly greater in length than width. Our shooter probably sees this slug with deep grooves on its exterior which strongly resemble rifling marks although smooth-sided projectiles are available to the casting reloader.

This slug derives any performance from the "shuttlecock" weight distribution—a heavy nose pulling along the rest of the body. Once it is clear of the gun muzzle the slug settles down and flies with fine stability. The Brenneke and Vitt slugs work on the same general shuttlecock principle but rely on the attached base wad to "weathervane" and further prevent gross deviation in flight.

When the early slugs proved somewhat less than wonderfully accurate, the firearms industry pondered on the problem, and among other things, the rifled slug was announced. The fairly logical reasoning was that, through the use of rather large spiral lands and grooves, the slug would be spun by air resistance during flight. Thus stabilized the slug would be notably more accurate. After all, the fletching on arrows causes a rotation of the shaft, increasing the arrow's accuracy, doesn't it?

It would seem the theory didn't work all that well by itself. Reloaders' demand for slug rifling dies fell off and even Lyman has not offered them for some time—although molds in 12- and 20-gauge are available for casting smooth-side slugs.

Rifled slugs can be a benefit, though, particularly when the "lands" extend from the projectile circumference. These lands, acting like fenders, serve to keep the slug centered in the bore and thus produce a more accurate shot.

The Brenneke and descendant Vitt slugs feature projectiles nearly bore size. Not only are these slugs stabilized perhaps a bit better but slug contact with the bore wall is reduced and thus friction, pressure and bore leading.

In the final analysis experimentation is the only answer. There are specially bored shotguns made for slug shooting. However, many older or "regular" shotguns will do an excellent job. Try slug loads in your gun. If you have several sets of barrels, change off and duplicate the test.

Once you have a gun, regardless of choke, printing a reasonable group (say 4 inches at 50 yards) the next step is to fit good rifle sights—either metallic operation or a low-powered scope. In almost all cases a shotgun will throw slugs to a different impact point than shot and the shooter should be able to properly zero the gun.

Finally, as hunting season rolls around, load up a goodly number of slugs and head for the range. Sight-in off the bench, then expend the remaining rounds in either the offhand or sitting position—get to know the gun and what it will do to 100 yards and beyond.

POWDER

The designation "dram equivalent" on a box of shotshells still confuses some shooters. The term is actually a throwback to the old black-powder days, when the standard load had a powder charge of about 3 drams. Today, of course, shotshells are loaded with modern smokeless powder.

The dram equivalent label, however, is still used by many manufacturers. When you pick up a box of shotshells and see it stamped "3¼ dram equivalent," this means that the amount of smokeless powder in the loads will produce the same amount of pressure and velocity as the designated drams of black powder. It's worth noting here that a charge

RIFLED SLUGS (APPROXIMATE BALLISTICS COURTESY OF FEDERAL CARTRIDGE)

Gauge	Weight (Ounces)	Velocity (Feet Per Second) Muzzle	50 yds.	Energy (Foot-Lbs.) Muzzle	50 yds.	Drop (Inches) 50 yds.	100 yds.	Barrel* Length
10	1¾	1280	1080	2785	1980	2.9	13.2	32
12	1¾	1490	1240	2695	1865	2.3	9.8	30
12	1	1560	1175	2365	1340	2.0	9.0	30
16	⅘	1600	1175	1990	1070	2.1	10.4	28
20	¾	1600	1270	1865	1175	1.9	9.5	26
410	⅕	1830	1335	650	345	1.6	8.2	26

*All calculations based on Full Choke barrels of this length.

BUCKSHOT (Courtesy of Federal Cartridge)

Gauge	Per Box	Length (Inches)	Dram Equiv.	Shot Sizes
10	5	3½	Mag.	00 Buck/18 Pellets
10	5	3½	Mag.	4 Buck/54 Pellets
12	5	3	Mag.	000 Buck/10 Pellets
12	5	3	Mag.	00 Buck/15 Pellets
12	5	3	Mag.	1 Buck/24 Pellets
12	5 }	3	Mag.	4 Buck/41 Pellets
12	25 }			
12	5	2¾	Mag.	00 Buck/12 Pellets
12	5	2¾	Mag.	1 Buck/20 Pellets
12	5 }	2¾	Mag.	4 Buck/34 Pellets
12	25 }			
12	5	2¾	Max.	000 Buck/ 8 Pellets
12	5	2¾	Max.	00 Buck/ 9 Pellets
12	5	2¾	Max.	0 Buck/12 Pellets
12	5	2¾	Max.	1 Buck/16 Pellets
12	5	2¾	Max.	4 Buck/27 Pellets
16	5	2¾	Max.	1 Buck/12 Pellets
20	5	3	Mag.	2 Buck/18 Pellets
20	5	2¾	Max.	3 Buck/20 Pellets

LEAD AND STEEL PELLET ENERGY COMPARISON

Muzzle velocity of the lead pellets is figured at 1330 feet per second. Muzzle velocity of the steel pellets is figured at 1365 feet per second.

PELLET ENERGY IN FOOT-POUNDS AT RANGE (YARDS)

Shot Type/Size	30	40	50
lead 6	3.0	2.3	1.7
steel 4	3.5	2.5	1.8
lead 4	5.6	4.4	3.4
steel 2	6.0	4.4	3.4
lead 2	9.5	7.5	6.1
steel BB	11.6	9.0	7.1

PELLETS PER OUNCE

Shot Size	Steel	Lead
BB	72	50
1	103	N/A
2	125	87
4	192	135
6	315	225

Shot sizes should be adjusted to compensate for steel's lighter weight. When switching from lead to steel, larger shot sizes should be selected. With the increased initial velocity of steel, this will provide adequate downrange pellet energy. However, hunters have their own preferred shot size and load and should experiment with different loads to determine which is best for their type of hunting.

SHOTGUN SHELL BALLISTICS

Gauge	Type load	Shot size	MV fps[1]	Pellet ME fp[2]	Vel. (60 yds.)
10	High Vel.	4	1330	12.7	685
12	Std. Vel.	6	1255	6.8	610
12	High Vel.	6	1330	7.6	630
12	HV 3" Mag.	6	1315	7.4	625
16	Std. Vel.	6	1185	6.0	595
16	High Vel.	6	1295	7.2	620
20	Std. Vel.	6	1165	5.8	590
20	High Vel.	6	1220	6.4	605
20	HB 3" Mag.	6	1315	7.4	625
28	High Vel.	6	1300	7.3	620
410	HV 3"	6	1260	6.8	612

Above ballistics are average. There is some variation between brands and different sizes and weights of shot. The heavier the pellet the greater the remaining energy and velocity at 60 yards.

[1]Muzzle velocity in feet per second.

[2]Muzzle energy, in foot pounds, of one pellet.

RANGE—Waterfowl hunting usually involves the longest distances for shotgun shooting. The practical range for taking ducks and geese is 35 to 50 yards. Individual pellets, however, may travel great distances. For safety when hunting, consider these possible extreme ranges.

00 Buck	610 yds.
No. 2 Shot	337 yds.
No. 6 Shot	275 yds.
No. 9 Shot	225 yds.

Courtesy of Federal Cartridge

AVERAGE PELLET COUNT—LEAD SHOT
Weight of Shot in Ounces (Grams) (3% Antimony)

Shot Size	1/2 (14.17)	11/16 (19.49)	3/4 (21.25)	7/8 (24.80)	1 (28.35)	1-1/8 (31.89)	1-1/4 (35.44)	1-3/8 (38.98)	1-1/2 (42.52)	1-5/8 (46.06)	1-7/8 (53.15)	2 (56.70)	2-1/4 (63.78)
9	292	402	439	512	585	658	731	804	877	951	1097	1170	1316
8½	249	342	373	435	497	559	621	683	745	808	932	994	1118
8	205	282	307	359	410	461	512	564	615	666	769	820	922
7½	175	241	262	306	350	394	437	481	525	569	656	700	787
6	112	155	169	197	225	253	281	309	337	366	422	450	506
5	85	117	127	149	170	191	212	234	255	276	319	340	382
4	67	93	101	118	135	152	169	186	202	219	253	270	304
2	43	60	65	76	87	98	109	120	130	141	163	174	196
BB	25	34	37	44	50	56	62	69	75	81	94	100	112

AVERAGE PELLET COUNT—STEEL SHOT
Weight of Shot in Ounces (Grams)

Shot Size	3/4 (21.25)	15/16 (26.58)	1 (28.35)	1-1/8 (31.89)	1-1/4 (35.44)	1-3/8 (38.98)	1-1/2 (42.52)	1-9/16 (44.30)	1-5/8 (46.06)
7	316	395	422	475	527	580	633	659	685
6	236	295	315	354	394	433	472	492	512
5	182	228	243	273	304	334	364	380	395
4	144	180	192	216	240	264	288	300	312
3	118	143	158	178	197	217	237	247	257
2	94	117	125	141	156	172	187	195	203
1	77	97	103	116	129	142	154	161	167
BB	54	67	72	81	90	99	108	112	117
BBB	46	58	62	70	77	85	93	97	101
T	39	49	52	58	65	71	78	81	84
F	30	37	40	45	50	55	60	62	65

STEEL SHOT VELOCITIES

Gauge	Length (Inches)	Dram Equiv.	Ounces Shot	Shot Sizes	Muzzle Velocity Feet Per Second
10	3½	4¼	1⅝	BB, 2	1350
12	3	3½	1⅜	BB,1,2,4	1265
12	3	Max.	1¼	BB,1,2,4	1450
12	2¾	3¾	1¼	BB,1,2,4	1325
12	2¾	3¾	1⅛	2,4,6	1365
20	3	3¼	1	4,6	1330
20	2¾	3¼	¾	4,6	1425

of smokeless powder may be less than half the weight of the dram equivalent.

Rifle shooters, realizing the importance of velocity, energy, and trajectory, take a great interest in ballistics, but most shotgunners pay little attention to how hard a shot charge moves once it leaves the barrel. Such information provides a better understanding of how a gun and ammunition will perform at typical or long ranges and on various kinds of game.

With regard to steel shot for waterfowling, published figures have been controversial—even contradictory in some cases—as the manufacturers have continually sought to improve the powders and other components used with steel pellets. As explained in the section on gauge and shot size, steel No. 2s are the correct substitute for lead No. 4s.

For the waterfowler, exact figures on steel shot velocity and energy are less important than the knowledge that steel does slow down at a considerably greater rate than lead, and it packs less energy at equal range. Although very skillful gunners can kill geese at more than 60 yards even with steel, the average hunter should not attempt shots at ranges much beyond 50 yards. Even at that distance—and here's an important fact that seems to have eluded many hunters—it's necessary to swing the gun farther ahead of a duck or goose when using steel shot than when using lead, in order to compensate for the relatively slow travel of the shot string.

Slug shooters seem to devote more time to studying the performance of their loads than do other shotgunners, but they too would do well to pay more attention to ballistics. The tables on the previous two pages provide data for rifled slugs as well as standard lead- and steel-shot loads.

SHOT SIZE COMPARISON

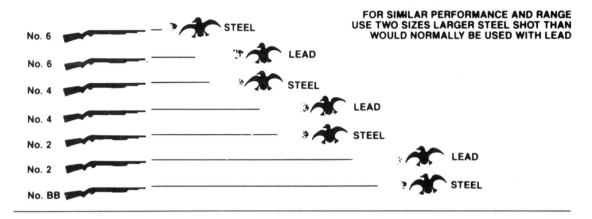

No. 6 — STEEL

No. 6 — LEAD

No. 4 — STEEL

No. 4 — LEAD

No. 2 — STEEL

No. 2 — LEAD

No. BB — STEEL

FOR SIMILAR PERFORMANCE AND RANGE USE TWO SIZES LARGER STEEL SHOT THAN WOULD NORMALLY BE USED WITH LEAD

TRAPSHOOTING

A trap field consists of a trap situated in a trap house and five shooting positions spaced 3 yards apart. All five positions are 16 yards from the trap. Five shots are taken by each shooter at each of the five positions. This makes a total of 25 shots and this is referred to as a round of trap. Each shooter takes his turn in shooting and upon completion of his five shots moves to the next position. Each time the shooter on the fifth position completes his five shots he goes to the first position, and so on.

TRAPSHOOTING AT EACH STATION

 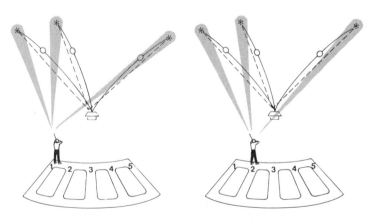

At **Station 1,** your feet should be placed as shown with your left foot pointed toward the left corner of the trap house. Your gun should point at the left corner of the trap house. Solid lines indicate the flight angles of three typical targets you may encounter; dotted lines indicate the swing and follow-through of your gun as well as the target breaking point. At **Station 2,** your feet should be placed as indicated with your left foot pointed one quarter of the way in from the left corner of the trap house. Point the gun halfway between left corner and center of the trap house.

Targets are thrown from the trap and must go a minimum of 48 yards and not over 52 yards. The targets must be thrown between 8 to 12 feet high at 10 yards in front of the trap. Each of these traps moves automatically to a position unknown to the shooter; therefore, the shooter never knows where the target will be thrown. In singles shooting, the trap shall be so adjusted that within the normal distribution of angles as thrown by the trap, the right angle shall not be less than straightaway from position one.

There are three different events held in trapshooting. The first type is known as the "16-yard event." This event is held in classes and each shooter is placed in a class according to his ability.

The second event, probably the most popular, is known as "handicap shooting." Each shooter is given a shooting position at a certain distance from the trap. These distances are from 18 to 27 yards, depending on the shooter's ability. The intent of this handicapping is to make the shooters compete on an equal basis. There are no classes in these events and all shooters are competing against each other.

The third type of shooting is known as "doubles." This is a most difficult event as two targets are thrown simultaneously. Unlike 16-yard and handicap shooting, the flight of these targets is fixed, and the left and right targets follow the path of the extreme left and right 16-yard targets.

Almost all shooting is done with the 12-gauge gun. There are no minimum restrictions but the maximum is no more than 1⅛ ounces of shot and no more than 3 drams of powder. No shot larger than 7½s nor any gun larger than a 12-gauge may be used.

All traps must throw unknown angles. Some do this by mechanical means and are powered by electrical motors. The most modern traps load the targets and reset the angles automatically.

Clay pigeons are all of a standard size. They are basically black with a yellow, orange, or white trim. Some are made all black. These color variations are used depending on which has the best visibility. This varies at different gun clubs based on the background of each field.

An area of 1,000 feet deep by 1,000 feet wide is sufficient for safety purposes for a trap field.

TECHNIQUES OF TRAPSHOOTING

To be a fine trap shot you must point the shotgun. Some persons believe that because of the pattern the shot throws that this should be fairly simple. Once he has tried it he will discover there is a lot of room around the moving target.

Targets are thrown at varying angles; consequently, the shooter must be prepared to shoot any-

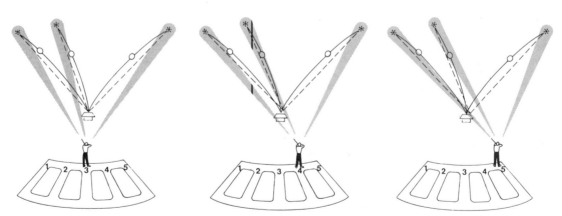

At **Station 3,** your left foot should be pointed slightly to the left of the center of the trap house. Your gun should be pointed toward center of trap house. At **Station 4,** your feet should be placed as indicated with your left foot pointed one-quarter of the way in from the right corner of the trap house. Point your gun halfway between the center and right corner of trap house. At **Station 5,** your feet should be placed as shown with the left foot pointed toward the right corner of the trap house. Point your gun at the right corner of the trap house. (Adapted from Winchester News Bureau drawings)

where within that given area. The first thing a shooter does when he prepares to shoot is to plant his feet properly. He must be able to turn to the right or left with ease in order to hit targets flying in different directions. A shooter shooting at the first station will get no more than a straightaway target for his extreme right. He can also get an extremely wide angle to the left. Knowing this he should face halfway in between both extremes. Obviously, a shooter should face in the center of both extreme right and left targets on all five stations. If for some reason or another he faces too far in one direction, he will find his body winding up like a spring when he tries to move to the opposite direction. This causes him to slow down or even stop his swing, and he misses or barely hits the target.

The next step in shooting is for the shooter to start his gun in the proper place. The gun should be started halfway between the two extreme angles of the targets. At station one the gun should be pointed on the left corner of the trap house, at station two halfway between the left corner and the center of the trap house, on station three the center of the trap house, on station four halfway between the center and the right corner, and on station five on the right corner of the trap house. Under certain conditions it is advisable to start the gun higher because of wind conditions. A target will sometimes climb considerably even though it is thrown from the trap at the legal height. The amount the gun should be raised should be determined by the shooter based on the amount of climb of the target. There are many shooters who normally start higher simply because they have to move the gun less to get to the target and it is easier for them to shoot in this manner.

Most new shooters are more concerned with the recoil of the gun than anything else. Their first thought is to get the gun on their shoulder comfortably so it won't kick. They place the gun on their shoulder, then try to bring their head down on the stock of the gun. This tends to stretch the neck muscles and pulls the head off the stock. The proper way is to bring the gun up to the face and line up the gun with the eye. Then the shoulder is raised to the gun. With constant practice this becomes a natural act.

When the shooter has accomplished the foregoing, he calls for the target. As he does not know in which direction the target will fly, he must let it get a sufficient distance from the trap house before starting to move the gun. He must never try to guess where the target is going.

Once the direction of the target is determined the next step is to visualize where you want to poin' the gun in order to break the target. The gun should be held firmly but not tightly by the hand on the grip. The other hand should grip the forend lightly, and the arms should be relaxed. Too tight a grip causes a jerky swing on the target. Trap targets take very little lead and the amount of this lead can only be determined by the shooter through his experience. Of course, the targets flying straightaway from the shooter take no lead at all. I have known some very fast shooters who claim they do not lead any target.

Never try to hold a certain lead on the target. The instant you have the gun pointed where you want it, pull the trigger. If you stay with the target, it will drop away from you and you will shoot over it. Try to swing the gun smoothly up to the target.

Eventually you will develop a sense of timing and you will shoot at your targets with a fairly consistent rate of speed. This varies with each person depending on how well coordinated he may be. Most beginning shooters shoot too slow; but by shooting with faster shots, they will eventually increase their speed. Unlike upland gamebirds, trap targets are moving at their fastest rate of speed when they leave the trap house. This does not leave much time to think about a shot. Gamebirds start slowly and increase their speed as they go giving the shooter more time.

One of the most common errors is to raise one's head off the gunstock. Sometimes this is caused by shooters wanting to get a better look at the target and sometimes by not bringing the gun tight enough into the face. In either case it causes the shooter to shoot over the target.

Handicap trap is the same as 16 yards except the ranges are greater—depending on the shooter's ability. Everything that applies to 16-yard shooting applies to handicap. The gun is moved to a lesser degree but you have to point finer on the targets. You can be a little sloppy in your 16-yard shooting and still get some fair hits but that same sloppiness will cost you targets when shooting at the longer ranges. The more your skill increases the farther back you will want to shoot. The wind, if it is a strong one, can even blow the target away from where you may have pointed before the shot even gets there. Most good handicap shooters who shoot from 23 to 27 yards are fast shooters. Their speed gives them better chances at these long ranges. As you increase your range yard by yard in handicap, you have to learn to make slight changes in your shooting. Your mental attitude may become a problem, too, just because you know its tougher to shoot from the new distance than it was a yard closer. Handicap shooting takes a lot of practice and most regular trapshooters realize this and do most of their practicing there.

Shooting doubles is the most challenging phase of trapshooting. First of all, you must face in a direction equally distant from both targets. You have the advantage of knowing where both of these targets are going so you are able to do this without any difficulty. Because you know where the target will be, you can start your gun much higher, which will give you a very short swing. This enables you to move to your second target much faster than you would if you started your gun where you would when shooting singles on that particular station. All of the top doubles shooters are fast shooters. Remember, you are shooting at two targets both going away from you, and the more time you take in shooting, the farther away they will be. Most doubles shooters widen their stance and point their toes farther apart. This prevents their knees from locking the body and preventing their swing to either side.

INTERNATIONAL TRAP

Virtually everywhere except in the United States, the so-called "International" methods, equipment, procedures, and rules govern trapshooting. International trap differs in three primary ways from the American version. First, you get two shots at each bird, and if you miss with the first but hit with the second, it counts as a hit. That may make the International version sound easier, but in reality it's much harder. The second and third differences are the reasons why.

The trap mechanism for the International game is set to fling targets through the air at a significantly greater velocity than in the American version. Try hitting a claybird as it zips through the air at about 100 miles per hour and you'll begin to appreciate the second difference.

The third involves angle and height. In International trap, targets go out at random angles, as in American trap, and you may get some straightaway birds, but the trap mechanism is also set to throw them at much more acute angles—much farther to the left or right. And it may throw one very high and then throw the next one about as low as a fleeing rabbit. You never know whether your next target will be a towering one, or will go out at moderate height, or will be a "grasscutter" streaking away just a few inches off the ground.

Americans trying this competition for the first time invariably find it extremely difficult—and disconcerting. They very quickly come to understand why a second shot is permitted. And that second shot can be all the tougher because the speeding target is so far away by then. Expect embarrassingly low scores at first.

By the way, a good International trapshooter always fires his second shot, even if he doesn't need it. This is because he develops a very helpful rhythm, or sense of timing, in getting off two shots. Failing to fire the second breaks the rhythm.

A great many renowned experts—Jim Carmichel and Bob Brister, to mention a couple—feel that the International version is closer to field shooting because of the angle-and-height variations, and is thus a better way to improve your wing shooting for hunting purposes.

SKEETSHOOTING

Skeet fields were originally full semicircle, but it was necessary to make some changes for the safety of the shooters. The fields are now altered slightly and the targets are thrown at a slight angle from each trap house. A target must travel a minimum of 55 yards.

There are two trap houses. One is known as the high house and is located immediately behind station one. The targets emerge from this trap house at a height of 10 feet. The other trap is known as the low house and the target emerges from a height of 3½ feet.

There are eight stations marked out on the field. Seven are an equal distance apart (26 feet, 8 inches) and are placed on the semicircle. The eighth station is in the center of the field midway between the two trap houses. Each shooting station is 3 feet square. Any part of both of the shooter's feet must touch the station.

A single shot is taken at targets from both houses on all eight stations. A target from the high house is always shot first. After finishing the single shots, doubles are fired. At stations one, two, six and seven, two targets are thrown simultaneously and the going-away target is fired upon with the first shot and the incoming target with the second shot. This makes a total of 24 shots. The 25th shot is taken immediately following the first target missed and the identical shot must be made. If no misses occur, the shot is taken from low eight.

Shooting is conducted with groups of five persons or less. Each group is known as a squad. Each

SKEETSHOOTING AT EACH STATION

The following illustrations show the shooter's position, aiming point, and suggested lead for each station on a skeet field. The path of the gun's swing is indicated by a dotted line, and the point at which the target is broken is indicated by a star. (All drawings adapted from Winchester News Bureau drawings.)

STATION 1 HIGH HOUSE   Lead 6 inches under.

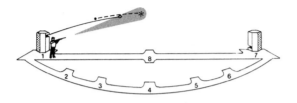

STATION 1 LOW HOUSE   Lead 1 foot.

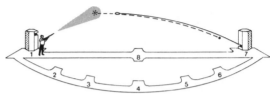

STATION 2 HIGH HOUSE   Lead 1 foot.

STATION 2 LOW HOUSE   Lead 1½ feet.

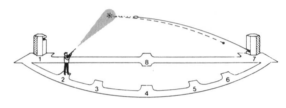

STATION 3 HIGH HOUSE   Lead 1½ feet.

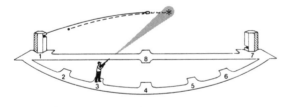

STATION 3 LOW HOUSE   Lead 3 feet.

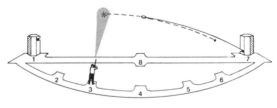

STATION 4 HIGH HOUSE   Lead 2½ feet.

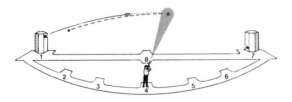

STATION 4 LOW HOUSE   Lead 2½ feet.

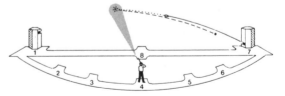

STATION 5 HIGH HOUSE   Lead 3½ feet.

STATION 5 LOW HOUSE   Lead 1½ feet.

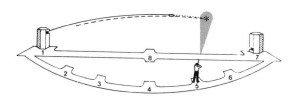
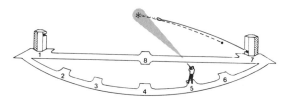

STATION 6 HIGH HOUSE   Lead 1½ feet.

STATION 6 LOW HOUSE   Lead 1 foot.

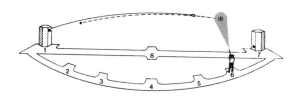
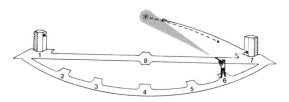

STATION 7 HIGH HOUSE   Lead 1 foot.

STATION 7 LOW HOUSE   Aim point blank.

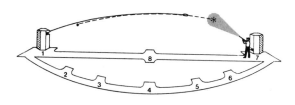
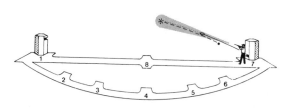

STATION 8 HIGH HOUSE   Aim: Blot out target with muzzle and slap trigger at same time.

STATION 8 LOW HOUSE   Aim: blot out target with muzzle and slap trigger at same time.

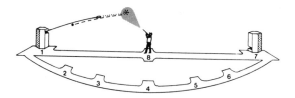

(Continued on next page)

SKEET DOUBLES

In doubles, targets emerge from both houses, requiring
that you decide which to shoot first.

STATION 1 DOUBLES   Break High House target first.

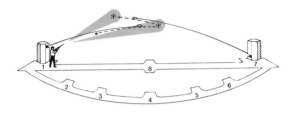

STATION 2 DOUBLES   Break High House target first.

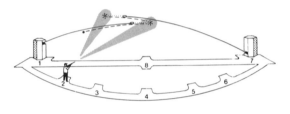

STATION 6 DOUBLES   Break Low House target first.

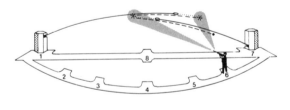

STATION 7 DOUBLES   Break Low House target first.

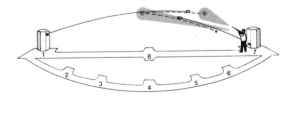

shooter takes his turn on each station in the order
in which they are signed up and continue in that
order.

Each group of 25 shots is known as a round and
is also the amount of shells in each box.

For safety reasons it is considered necessary to
have an area 1,000 feet deep and 2,000 feet long for
a skeet field. No No. 9 shot can travel this far and
this amount of room is more than ample.

There are two types of traps available. One type
is handloaded and the other is automatically loaded.
Most targets used are black with a yellow, orange,
or white band.

TECHNIQUES OF SKEETSHOOTING

Skeet offers a greater variety of shots than any other
shotgun game. You know where each target is going;
but, in spite of that advantage, you still have to hit
them. The beginner has to learn he cannot break
targets by shooting at them. After he learns to break
a few he gets the general idea that you must shoot
in front of each target in order to break it. Lead is
the common term for this. The next step is to learn
just how much lead for each shot. This will come
from practice and from help of other shooters. Try
to learn to master one shot at a time, but this is
possible only if you can get a skeet field to yourself.

It is reasonable to assume that a target flying at
a given rate of speed and a load of shot fired from
a shotgun at a given range will meet *if* the proper
amount of lead is given. The confusing thing to many
new shooters is what amount of lead is necessary
for each shot. Years ago shooters' reaction time was
checked by one of the universities and they found
that it took approximately two-fifths of a second
from the time the mind registered that that was the
proper time to pull the trigger to the time the shot
left the end of the shotgun barrel. Obviously a fast-
swinging shooter is going to move that gun barrel
farther in that period of time than a slow-swinging
shooter. Because of this we get different answers
from different shooters on just how much a target
must be led.

Although getting the proper lead on each target
is the ultimate objective, attention must be paid to
stance and proper gun mounting. Position the feet
correctly for each shot by facing the general area
where you expect to break the target. The next step
is to place the gun at a position in front of the trap
house. Many new shooters will place the gun directly even with the trap house. This results in the
shooter having to move the gun too fast in order to
catch up with the target and he ends up with very

poor control of the shotgun. As a rule of thumb a spot approximately one-third of the distance from the trap house to eight post would be about right. Some youngsters with very fast reactions can come in a little closer to the trap house, whereas some of us who are considerably older and find our reactions are slowing down must do just the opposite. The height of the gun should be approximately a couple of feet below the path of the target. This will allow ample room to see a target go downward if the wind happens to push it below its regular flight. Going up with a target that rises presents no problem; but if the target gets below the gun, we lose sight of it entirely.

After we get our feet placed right for the shot we are making and the gun started in the right place in relation to the trap house, the last thing that comes into our mind is to get the correct lead for the shot we are about to make. These three steps are the basic steps for each shot.

Next we must call for the target; the word "pull" is used by most shooters. Do not start the gun moving until the target appears. Bring the gun up to the shoulder at the same time you are moving the gun after the target. It is best to try to keep the gun moving with the target and continue moving out to the correct lead. The instant this lead is reached pull the trigger. Never try to hold a lead in order to break a target at a certain spot on the field. Pull that trigger the instant that lead is reached. One of the two most common faults of experienced shooters is to stop swinging their gun after the lead is reached. You are not apt to make this mistake if you do not try to hold the lead. It is always best to "follow through" with your swing just like the golfers, tennis players, and baseball players do. Beware of the shooter who advises you that the shot you just missed was the result of shooting behind the target. This leads you to believe you did not have enough lead when in reality you stopped swinging your gun.

The other common fault of the experienced shooter is that sometimes he does not "get his head down on the stock." This means he is looking above his barrel instead of down the barrel. This results in shooting over the top of the target.

It is impossible to learn all of these steps at one time. If you try to, you will only confuse yourself. Learn them one at a time. These are the basic steps of becoming a good shooter. Try to memorize the leads for each shot and in time you will automatically remember them. This will also help tremendously with your field shooting. Every shot you make at skeet with the exception of those at eight post are identical to shots you will make in upland bird shooting. It will surprise you how much your field shooting will improve after a few rounds of skeet.

INTERNATIONAL SKEET

International skeet, like International trap, is unquestionably more demanding than the American form. For one thing, the trap-spring is set to throw the bird considerably faster—and just think what that does to a station eight shot! For another, you cannot shoulder the gun before calling for the bird. You must keep the stock down at waist level, as if you were hunting and about to mount the gun while your dog points. The butt must touch your hipbone.

Finally—and probably most disconcerting of all for Americans unfamiliar with the International competition—a target does not necessarily fly out the instant you call "Pull!" It may go out on the instant of demand, but it may also be delayed for an unknown time, up to three full seconds.

That makes it very much like a live bird flushing, and the game in general is enormously beneficial in improving your performance in the field.

CLAY TARGET GAMES

In recent years, shotgunners (and their gun clubs) have developed a great number of variations on trap and skeet—plus some target games with little or no resemblance to those traditional shoots. The unconventional exercises and competitions have several special attractions. In some instances, the necessary equipment and layout may be inexpensive compared to the investment needed to set up a regulation trap or skeet field. In other instances, the attraction is informality and/or a chance for gunners of unequal skill to compete on a more or less equal footing. One very strong appeal is the similarity of some of the games to field shooting. Artificial situations are concocted that imitate real hunting situations—the sudden and unexpected sight of game, an explosive flush, shots made at tough angles, and variations in target speed. All of this adds up to great practice, a lot of misses, plenty of fun, and occasional hilarity. Here are some of the more common nontraditional games, beginning with Hunter's

Clays—the most popular of all. Known in England and elsewhere as Sporting Clays, this is a game that has rapidly won adherents on both sides of the Atlantic.

SPORTING CLAYS

This is a clay target game designed to simulate shooting situations and target angles encountered when hunting with a shotgun. It is a flexible, easily changed game aimed at duplicating the hunting shots and angles most commonly encountered while hunting in the state where the Sporting Clays layout is located.

Shooting stations are often in woods or brush where the target must be broken quickly before it disappears from view.

In short, it is truly a hunter's game where shooters can gather and have fun while improving their hunting skills.

Although it began and has evolved into the most popular clay target game in England, it has also become highly popular in the U.S.

The primary advantage is lower shooting cost because fewer shots are required to complete a round. It is difficult because, as in hunting, the shooter is never sure precisely when the target will appear. This is particularly true in the "walk-up" events simulating upland bird shooting.

Some targets are very high overhead incomers, simulating doves, ducks or other high-flying game. Others are fast going-away challenges resembling upland birds. No two Sporting Clays ranges need be quite the same, and competition can be made as difficult or as easy as desired by location of the shooting positions relative to the location of the trap machines (which ideally are out of view of the shooter).

Ordinary clay targets are used, and shooters move in squads from one shooting location, or "stand," to the next. Each shooter faces the same basic challenge and will receive essentially the same targets at the same approximate speed, angle and height. But variations of wind, slight differences in how a target may be placed on the throwing arm of the trap and variances in time of appearance of the target offer many of the variables of field hunting.

Normally, squads of six shooters go from one stand to the next. They are told by the referee what basic target to expect (singles, doubles, high, low, walk-up, or waiting), and each shooter has the opportunity to view at least one set of targets, either in advance if he is the squad leader or by watching other shooters perform.

The largest layouts might involve 100 targets shot at from 10 stands; small shooting layouts sometimes have as few as three stands, and 25 or 30 targets can make up the contest. But invariably the shooter will be confronted by some very high or long shots and some close, fast ones. Some will be going away; some, incoming.

One shooter at a time stands at the shooting station with gun in a "low gun" position, similar to the way the gun is carried when hunting. When the shooter calls "pull," the target may appear instantly or at any time up to three seconds later. He may not shoulder the gun until the target appears. No more than two targets will appear at one time, and guns may contain no more than two shotgun shells. Two shots are permitted at singles, one each at doubles.

Hits or misses are scored by the referee; to score a hit, the target must be broken.

There is virtually no angle encountered in field shooting that cannot, to a very realistic degree, be simulated by Sporting Clays. As a result, shooters gain not only the excitement and fun of the shooting but usually become much better game shots.

Perhaps more important than the competitive angle is the excellent game shooting practice at informal "fun shoots" arranged by the participants to suit their own needs. Regularly used field hunting shotguns and a minimum of equipment expense can lead to much better game shooting the next hunting season.

Almost anywhere it is safe to hunt or to fire a shotgun, some sort of Sporting Clays layout can be accommodated. The important requirement is that there be a "safety zone" of at least 300 yards in the direction the shooter must fire from each shooting station.

Farms, ranches, gun clubs, hunting clubs and even unused areas around golf courses can be utilized as long as there is no danger of pellets striking people, livestock, or buildings.

The best and most attractive layouts are usually in wooded areas featuring some hill or ridge from which high targets can be launched. If the terrain is suitable, the trap machines that launch the targets should be hidden from the shooter's view. It is much more like game shooting when a target suddenly appears over trees or from behind a clump of brush.

On flat land, some sort of tower is usually required to house one or two trap machines. The high target is a very important part of Sporting Clays because it simulates a situation so often encountered in dove and waterfowl hunting and because the high incomer or crosser is not effectively simulated by trap or skeet. If building a tower is not possible, barns, windmills and water tanks may substitute or the shooter can be down on a riverbed with the trap on a high bank above him.

Several shooting stations can be set up to utilize a single tower. Situated in front of the tower, the shooter gets the high overhead incomer. Moved to the right or left, he gets high crossing targets. Moved directly beneath the tower, he gets high going-away "birds" similar to the angles presented by high ducks passing over from behind the blind.

On flat land, it is often possible to obscure the origin of low targets by putting up trees, brush, hay bales or some sort of cover around each shooting station, in effect making it more like a blind.

It is important, if manually operated traps are used, that the trap operator be protected from pellets. This can be done by situating the traps behind a ridge or hill or by erecting some sort of protection for the trapper. Bales of hay are often effective as are corrugated heavy metal sheets.

Operators of traps, like competitors, should wear shooting glasses for added protection against the odd "flyer" or stray pellet.

Trap machines can be simple, inexpensive devices manually operated or the most sophisticated automatic loading, oscillating types. The only real requirement is that the machine be capable of throwing a target sufficiently fast that it is not a cinch to hit. Sporting Clays is a difficult game, intentionally so because it simulates the difficulties of hunting. Properly set up, competent shooters can expect to score on only about 80 to 85 percent of the targets shot at.

The amount and type of equipment depends upon the size of the layout and how many shooting stations will be set up. Ideally, there should be a minimum of five stations, and some more elaborate layouts might offer 10 or more. But that doesn't mean a separate trap for each station. By drawing up the course in such a way that a shooter fires at the same target, but from a different angle, the effect is of an

RABBIT RUN

If your gun club has trap houses with roofs strong enough to support a shooter's weight, here's a good game to lend variety to your program. Shooters stand atop the house and fire at targets which skim a foot or so above the ground. They appear underfoot and depart at various angles at great speed. The trap throwing angle is depressed and spring tension is increased to pitch targets low to the ground that will reach out 40 yards or more from the trap house.

WALK-UP SKEET (OR TRAP)

In this game the shooter takes his place at station four and starts to walk toward station eight. He may receive a target from either high or low house at the puller's option, and unknown to the shooter. The target is thrown at any time during the shooter's walk toward station eight but before he reaches that post.

A similar game is played on a standard trap field, with the gunner beginning the long walk toward the traphouse at the 27-yard marker. Targets fly at unknown angles, of course, appearing at the option of the puller. At some clubs, walk-up skeet or trap is played with doubles being thrown. The club that has its trap field superimposed on the skeet field can add still more variety to the game using all three machines.

entirely different "bird." A minimum of three traps is usually recommended; these can be turned to throw a different direction or angle and can accommodate up to 10 shooting stations.

The most effective trap to be used in a tower is an oscillating machine (like the ones used in American trapshooting) and preferably an autoloading model. This eliminates the need for a trapper in the tower and the problem of protecting him from shot pellets. However, manual traps mounted in towers and operated by the trapper at the sound of the referee's whistle or call are perfectly feasible. The trap boys are protected by corrugated metal shields.

There are many inexpensive portable trap machines on the U.S. market and, if mounted on an automobile spare tire and wheel, they can be rolled to different locations. The spare tire, laid flat on the ground, then serves as a sturdy base for the trap and helps protect the trap from jolts and vibrations of operation. Wooden pallets also can make an inexpensive, easily moved base for traps. A steel oil drum filled with concrete makes an excellent base for a trap.

The only other major item of equipment is some form of enclosure for the shooter (usually made of "chicken wire" with wooden framework) which prevents him from swinging around to the rear and thus possibly endangering spectators. Sporting Clays is an interesting spectator sport, and the gallery is perfectly safe if the shooter is enclosed. On individual farm or hunting club layouts, however, such protective "cages" may not be necessary. Much depends upon the experience of the shooter and the nature of the layout.

If possible, the "cages" should be made portable for the times when other angles and shooting positions are desired.

Gun clubs can utilize existing 16-yard trap layouts as one of several shooting stations, either as a "walk-up" (having the shooter walk toward the trap and releasing the bird at an unknown time and yardage) or as the "flushing pheasant" event. For this one, the trap machine would be set to throw its highest possible targets, and the shooter stands on the 16-yard line in gun-down position.

The first rule in the international Sporting Clays rule book (FITASC—Federation International de Tir aux Armes Sportive de Chasse) is that shooting be made as near as possible to game shooting. The whole idea is to simulate local hunting and the shots most frequently encountered while in the field.

Shooting stands or "stations" are preferably located in woods, brush or utilizing terrain in such a way that the trap machines which launch targets are hidden from the shooter's view.

Squads of up to six shooters move from one shooting stand to another, and one shooter at a time stands waiting with toe of butt touching his waistline. At his call of "ready," the target may be launched instantly or up to three seconds later; the shooter may not shoulder the gun until the target appears.

Twelve-gauge guns or smaller, loaded with no more than 1¼ ounces of shot, are used. No special

CRAZY QUAIL

This is an exciting clay target game that was developed in Texas. Targets are thrown from a single trap in a 360-degree circle, where there are safe distances.

No shooter can outguess the person operating the trap. He deliberately tries to confuse the shooter by changing the angle of rotation after each shot. Also, he may use one-second or 10-second delays in releasing after the shooter yells "Pull."

Crazy Quail is a combination of skeet and trap.

For instance, a target may be thrown back at the shooters similar to a skeet station eight, or a target may be thrown away from the shooter similar to regulation trap. The setup is also convenient for teaching a beginning shooter, as spring tension can be eased for a slower target and the trap held at a constant angle; also, the shooter can move close to the release point.

Crazy Quail is a great fun game where shooters can easily make up their own rules and create new versions of the game. It is also an excellent warm-up for the hunting season.

360° Circle

Trap located in bottom of 7 × 7-foot square pit.

16 yards

Crazy Quail is most often set up with the trap in a pit. A mound of dirt is usually built to act as a safe barrier between the releaser and the shooter. Where there is poor drainage, the trap can be set up at ground level and a higher mound built for safety purposes. If your Crazy Quail setup is in a pit, be sure you consider drainage problems.

A practice trap is welded onto a vertical shaft. A seat for the releaser, attached to the shaft, swings in a complete circle. The shooters usually stand 16 yards behind the trap, but they may wish to vary this. Be sure that in any direction you will be shooting there is safe clearance for 300 yards.

Many clubs build their own release setup. There is one manufacturer in the United States who makes the complete unit. Information is available by writing Valentine Equipment Co., 2630 West Arthington St., Chicago, IL 60612.

Shooter's position in start at 16 yards from center of pit.
Walkway graduated back to 27 yards for a variety of shooting and handicapping.

spreader loads are permitted.

Shooters must not load until they are in position at the shooting stand, and the gun must be unloaded and open any time the shooter turns toward the referee or crowd. The sequence of targets at each shooting station is announced in advance and is the same for each shooter. Normally, each shooter finishes his single targets; then, in the same squad order, doubles are shot if that particular station offers doubles.

Guns may be loaded with no more than two shells. On single targets, two shots are permitted, and scoring is the same whether the bird is broken on the first or second shot. On doubles, the shooter may fire twice at the same target (if he misses the first shot) or may switch to the other. Should both targets break with one shot, they are scored as both dead, exactly as would be the case if two game birds were taken with one shot.

The number of targets shot at each shooting station varies, but a big shoot will usually be 10 targets from each of 10 stations. For informal shooting, it's up to the group as long as everyone shoots the same number of birds from the same station.

The important thing is to get hunters improving their shooting skills in the off-season. Hunting and shooting clubs can and should set up their own shoots with their own rules and have fun. Simulate your own game shooting situations and keep practicing with your favorite hunting shotgun. You'll be amazed at the improvement in your shooting skill during the hunting season.

RIVERSIDE SKEET

This clay target game was developed in 1948 by shooters at the Riverside Yacht Club, in Riverside, Connecticut. It is known in southern Connecticut as that "Blankity Blank Riverside Skeet." There are five stations, arranged similarly to standard trap. A trap is safely located at each end of the line. The traps are angled so that when doubles are thrown the targets cross at about 25 yards.

The shooter at station one gets a left-hand single, then a right-hand single. His third shot is a single at the option of the releaser, the idea being to confuse the shooter. After the third shot, the shooting rotates to station two and the other stations. After each shooter has fired three rounds, station one then fires a double. After all stations have fired a double, which totals fives shots per person, all shooters rotate the same as in standard trap.

Shooters can work out many variations of the game. The trap angles can be varied to make the shooting more difficult. Since the game was first started at the Riverside Yacht Club, there have been only 12 scores of 25×25.

Riverside Skeet can easily be set up at an existing trap or skeet club. Ideally, the shooters would face north or northeast, as this is the optimum direction to keep the sun out of their eyes. The traps should be controlled electrically by the releaser who stands behind the shooters. Manual traps can be used, but in the long run it might be cheaper to use autoloading traps.

The stations are located 3 to 4 yards apart. For your installation, the diagram at the left is a suggestion for a starter. You may wish to try variations periodically to make the shooting more challenging.

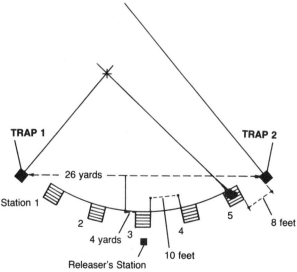

Anyone with access to sufficient land and financing for enough traps can set up a Sporting Clays layout. It can be as simple or as elaborate as desired. It is perfect for the small hunting club or syndicate that has leased hunting property.

Sporting Clays is a natural for hunting clubs, particularly those in areas where waterfowl hunting is permitted mornings only. Sporting Clays practice could be an excellent way to utilize those open afternoons and also make better duck and goose hunters of the membership. The improvement in hitting long crossing and high overhead shots can be phenomenal, mainly because no other target game in the U.S. (other than a few club tower shoots) has offered the opportunity to practice these shots. But any hunting club can improve interest and off-season use of the club (as well as in-season use, too) with a Sporting Clays setup.

Sporting Clays would seem an ideal "interest builder" for a trap or skeet club with some space not being utilized. Since a Sporting Clays shoot requires from 25 to 100 shells, unlike big trap and skeet shoots which require up to 500, this could be an excellent way of getting new hunter-members out to utilize club facilities. Sporting Clays is also an excellent way of getting potential new members to visit the club. An "open shoot" just prior to the beginning of bird hunting season would seem almost certain to bring out hunters and spectators, and some of those spectators may ultimately become members. A special "Hunter's Division" for visitors who don't compete at trap or skeet could be a big incentive to getting new shooters interested.

Another version of Sporting Clays is Five-Stand Sporting. Usually set-up in a five-station trap field format, this game uses six to eight automatic traps at different locations. There are three levels of difficulty: Level I, five single targets with full use of the gun for scoring; Level II, three single and a simultaneous pair; Level III, one single and two simultaneous pairs. Shooters, usually a squad of five, can move from station to station with a predetermined menu of shots and combinations. Five-Stand Sporting can also be shot without the shooters knowing any clay bird sequence or pattern.

Sporting Clays could be an excellent means of providing corporate entertainment on some farm, ranch or hunting lease. And since the only permanent facility required would be a tower (and often not even that), the investment is virtually nil except for a few relatively inexpensive traps.

It is possible to install a high trap on a windmill or any other high structure, including the top of a barn.

In the U.S., a leading trap company is developing new models capable of throwing the fast targets best utilized at Sporting Clays. However, there is no rule that specifies target speed or distance because, as yet, there are no hard-and-fast rules. Even inexpensive traps throwing relatively slow targets can offer better practice than none at all.

A number of manual traps from various countries are available for less than $400 each and will throw targets almost 100 yards. In general, a target that will travel 75 yards is considered ideal.

One of the concerns about hunter safety in America today is that many hunters have so little opportunity to learn the safe ways of gun handling, the instant decisions that must be made as to whether to shoot or not to shoot.

These things cannot be learned on a skeet or trap range where guns are never carried loaded even from one station to the next.

But shooting Sporting Clays can involve walking with a loaded gun (in the walk-up event only), and it also deals with shooting in wooded areas, possibly from positions of somewhat unsure footing, and, in short, simulates many of the situations of field shooting where safety is a major consideration.

Practice at walking with other hunters (or walking from one Sporting Clays station to the next) is a good way to learn very quickly if one has careless gun handling habits. Sporting Clays participants are sticklers for gun safety and proper gun-carry positions.

Sporting Clays layouts could well be utilized by state shooting program instructors because they offer a more realistic environment than a classroom or traditional skeet and trap fields. Proper field procedures can be demonstrated and practiced with the help and direction of hunter safety instructors.

HANDGUN ACTIONS

MECHANISMS

Before discussing the various sporting uses of the handgun, let's talk about the different types of actions. Apart from a few single-shot models, there are only two basic designs—the semi-automatic and the revolver. The semi-automatic comes in two versions, the blow-back and breechblock design, which are similar to the mechanisms used in semi-automatic rifles. A detailed explanation of these actions begins on page 12.

Briefly, the semi-automatic uses gas pressure from the powder to operate the mechanism. The first step in firing an automatic is to pull the slide back and then release it. As the slide moves forward, it will pick up and chamber a cartridge from the magazine, as well as cock the handgun. When the trigger is pulled and that first round is fired, the energy from the explosion drives the slide backward, ejecting the empty case. As the slide automatically moves forward again, it picks up and chambers the next round and the gun is ready to fire again.

The revolver also comes in two versions—the single action and double action. The single action, put simply, means the hammer must be pulled back for every shot. In effect, it must be cocked manually each time. While cocking the single action, a spur also engages a notch in the cylinder, rotating it to the next loaded chamber.

The double action only requires the trigger to be pulled each time to fire the cartridges in the cylinder. Pulling the trigger moves the hammer back to full cock, rotates the cylinder, releases the sear and fires another round.

REVOLVER OR SEMI-AUTOMATIC?

Revolver and semi-automatic handguns seem to have an equal number of fans. Ask the owner of a revolver what kind of handgun to buy and he'll tell you a revolver. And the owner of a semi-automatic pistol will swear by his type of gun. There are some basic comparisons between the two designs, however, that hold true.

The revolver is inherently safer because more manual operation is required between shots. But the

A TYPICAL DOUBLE-ACTION REVOLVER

Schematic drawing shows parts of High Standard's Crusader, an innovative double-action design employing side-plate construction, segmented gears, and hammer travel on an eccentric, permitting a light double-action trigger pull. No rebound system or transfer bar is used because none is needed. When hammer is down, it rests safely on the frame and cannot touch the firing pin, so accidental discharge is prevented.

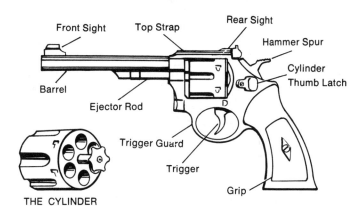

THE CYLINDER

A TYPICAL SEMI-AUTOMATIC PISTOL

The semi-automatic may be less safe than a revolver because of its lighter trigger squeeze and capacity for faster fire. Yet its lighter trigger squeeze is preferred by many target shooters. Also many "automatics" feel better balanced because the weight of the magazine and most of the gun is concentrated in the hand.

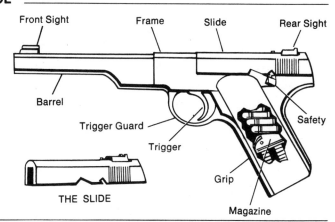

THE SLIDE

RUGER SINGLE-ACTION REVOLVER

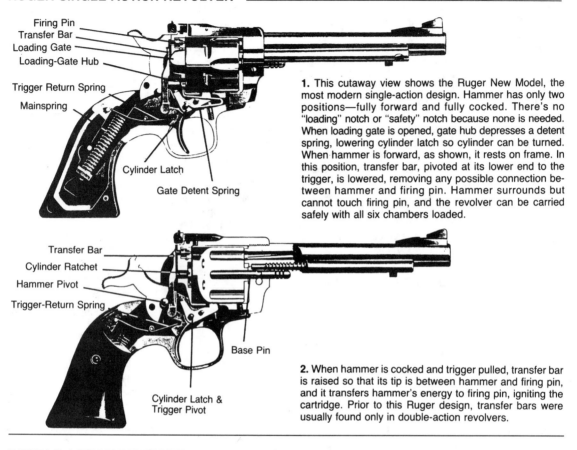

Firing Pin
Transfer Bar
Loading Gate
Loading-Gate Hub

Trigger Return Spring

Mainspring

Cylinder Latch

Gate Detent Spring

1. This cutaway view shows the Ruger New Model, the most modern single-action design. Hammer has only two positions—fully forward and fully cocked. There's no "loading" notch or "safety" notch because none is needed. When loading gate is opened, gate hub depresses a detent spring, lowering cylinder latch so cylinder can be turned. When hammer is forward, as shown, it rests on frame. In this position, transfer bar, pivoted at its lower end to the trigger, is lowered, removing any possible connection between hammer and firing pin. Hammer surrounds but cannot touch firing pin, and the revolver can be carried safely with all six chambers loaded.

Transfer Bar

Cylinder Ratchet

Hammer Pivot

Trigger-Return Spring

Base Pin

Cylinder Latch &
Trigger Pivot

2. When hammer is cocked and trigger pulled, transfer bar is raised so that its tip is between hammer and firing pin, and it transfers hammer's energy to firing pin, igniting the cartridge. Prior to this Ruger design, transfer bars were usually found only in double-action revolvers.

DOUBLE ACTION REVOLVER

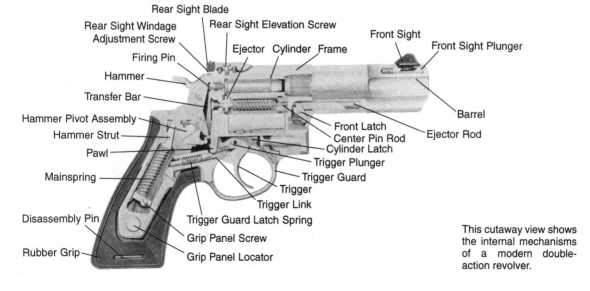

Rear Sight Blade
Rear Sight Windage
Adjustment Screw
Rear Sight Elevation Screw
Firing Pin
Ejector   Cylinder   Frame
Front Sight
Front Sight Plunger
Hammer
Transfer Bar
Hammer Pivot Assembly
Hammer Strut
Pawl
Front Latch
Center Pin Rod
Cylinder Latch
Barrel
Ejector Rod
Trigger Plunger
Mainspring
Trigger Guard
Trigger
Trigger Link
Disassembly Pin
Trigger Guard Latch Spring
Grip Panel Screw
Rubber Grip
Grip Panel Locator

This cutaway view shows the internal mechanisms of a modern double-action revolver.

THE .22 SEMI-AUTOMATIC

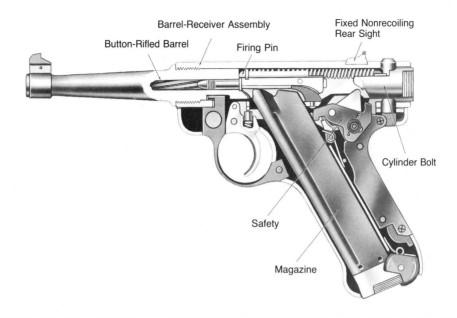

Barrel-Receiver Assembly

Button-Rifled Barrel

Firing Pin

Fixed Nonrecoiling Rear Sight

Cylinder Bolt

Safety

Magazine

Left: Correct way to hold and load most single-action revolvers. Hammer is in half-cock position so cylinder will rotate. Hinged loading gate is down, and thumb rotates cylinder as cartridges are placed in chambers. This does not apply to New Model Rugers shown on previous page. With these, hammer is lowered rather than half-cocked, and gate will not open unless hammer is down. Opening gate locks hammer, trigger, and transfer bar in position, while a gate hub depresses a spring to allow cylinder rotation. **Right:** Correct and safe way to hold and load a double-action revolver. Place fingers through frame and around cylinder as cartridges are loaded into chambers. If you should be required to leave your revolver unattended at a shooting range, always leave it with cylinder swung out for safety.

semi-automatics, which we'll call automatics from here on, will fire more rapidly. The automatics have a larger magazine capacity and are more compact than the typical revolver of the same caliber, but revolvers will handle some ammunition interchangeably. The .357 Magnum, for example, will accept the .38 Special, but not conversely. The automatic may be faster to reload, but the revolver is more rugged and requires little maintenance.

Examining these comparisons, it does become apparent that the revolver makes a better handgun for hunting, plinking, and informal target shooting. It is dependable, needs little care, and has some built-in safety features. A fairly hard trigger pull is needed to cock, rotate the cylinder, and fire additional rounds. With an automatic, once the first shot is fired, only a light trigger pull will discharge another round. The revolver is obviously safer.

The revolver is also easier for the novice to understand and learn how to shoot. Granted, the automatic provides more rapid firepower, but there is no outdoor sport where such firepower is needed. For hunting and plinking, then, the revolver gets the nod.

The automatic does have its fans, however. Roughly half of all handgun matches are won with automatics and the military forces of the United States, and most others, use the automatic. This is probably so for a number of reasons. When it comes to target shooting, the automatic is a better balanced firearm, since most of the weight of the gun and the loaded magazine is concentrated in the hand. A target shooter who competes in rapid-fire matches will find he can get his shots off quicker and more smoothly with an automatic. As for the military, its main concern is defense, and rapid firepower is an important consideration. The handgun hunter is generally not concerned with defense in the field and almost never will he need rapid firepower.

This is all boiled down to a few basic conclusions. For hunting and plinking, the revolver is the best choice. The serious target shooter, who gets involved in official matches, should look to the automatic. If a shooter is involved in all three—hunting, plinking, target shooting—the choice will have to be one of personal preference. Select the handgun that you feel safe and comfortable with.

SELECTING THE HANDGUN

Now that we know the basic mechanics of revolvers and semi-automatic handguns, the question of sights, barrel length, and caliber arises. A shooter may have decided on a revolver, for example, but now he must select a caliber, sights, and so on. If he wants to hunt squirrels, he certainly wouldn't choose a .357 Magnum. And if target shooting is his primary interest, he'll obviously steer clear of fixed sights.

The best way to handle this problem of selection is to choose the gun to fit the sport. Let's discuss them one by one.

HUNTING

It takes a skilled marksman to master the handgun, so anyone who decides to hunt with a sidearm needs all the help he can get. One of the important differences between a handgun for hunting and a precision target pistol is weight. The hunter's gun should be lighter, simply because he has to carry it around with him.

Weight, however, helps any shooter to maintain a steadier hold, so the problem is a bit of a double-edged sword. A good rule is to pick a hunting handgun that is not in the featherweight class but is not excessively heavy either. For a .22 handgun, one that weighs from 25 to 35 ounces is about right. For the heavier calibers, such as the .357, .41, and .44 magnums, a handgun should weigh between 40 and 45 ounces.

Sights, as indicated earlier, should be the best available and always with a rear sight that is adjustable for windage and elevation. Micrometer sights usually found on quality target pistols work fine in the game field. A handgun hunter, like the rifle shooter, must sight-in his firearm and know the point of impact at various ranges. This is only possible with adjustable sights. Fixed sights, such as those generally found on service revolvers, have no place in the field.

The handgun hunter does have another choice when it comes to sights. He can mount a scope on the gun. In addition to magnification, a scope on a handgun serves a very important function. It puts the crosshairs and target in one optical plane so that both are in sharp focus. Without the scope, it is impossible for shooters to bring both sights and target into sharp focus, and this problem gets more acute as handgunners get on in years. Handgun scopes solve this frustrating problem. These special scopes have a long eye relief, generally 10 to 24 inches.

Magnification is usually 1.3× to 4×, fixed and variable 1.5 to 4×.

Barrel length is still another factor to consider. The handgun used for hunting should have a long barrel, and one from 6 to 10 inches is a good handling length. There are several reasons for avoiding the short-barreled models. First, and most important, is that they do not give a long enough sight radius for good accuracy. It's an accepted fact that the longer the distance between the front and rear sights the greater the accuracy potential. In the magnum calibers, the short barrels also give off greater muzzle flash and noise, both of which could bring on a case of flinches.

With short-barreled handguns in the big calibers there is also the problem of loss of velocity. A .41 Magnum cartridge, for example, will leave the muzzle of an 8⅜-inch barrel at 1,500 feet per second, but only 1,250 fps from the muzzle of a 4-inch barrel. A short barrel is simply not long enough for full thrust to take place behind the bullet. This situation is particularly important if the shooter handloads his ammunition to maximum charges.

Picking the right caliber depends on the size of the game being hunted. For small game, such as rabbits, squirrels, sitting grouse, and the smaller varmints, a handgun chambered for the .22 Long Rifle is adequate. It's accurate and ammunition is inexpensive (which means plenty of practice shooting at low cost). Revolvers are also available chambered for the .22 Winchester Magnum, which is nothing more than a souped-up .22. The .22 Magnum gives an edge to the hunter after slightly larger small game, such as raccoons, bobcats, possibly foxes. The one drawback is that the .22 Magnum is not interchangeable with the .22 Long Rifle. Buying a handgun chambered for the .22 Magnum means ammunition will be more expensive and the gun will likely not be used often for extended shooting sessions and practice. But if the idea of a .22 Magnum appeals to you, there is a solution. Ruger's Single Six Convertible is equipped with two interchangeable cylinders, one chambered for the standard .22, the other for the .22 Magnum. The shooter uses the .22 Magnum cylinder for hunting and switches to the standard .22 cylinder for target practice and plinking.

Another interesting development in recent years has been the revival of single-shot pistols. They've become particularly popular for varminting at longer ranges than the usual handgunning distances, so their owners often scope them. A famous gun of this sort is Remington's XP-100, a bolt-action pistol chambered for the .221 Fireball, a good varminting cartridge. The other single-shots are generally break actions. Best known is the Thompson/Center Contender, which comes in a wide variety of calibers, from .22 Rimfire, both standard and Magnum, to powerful centerfire calibers suitable for big game. Included are a number of good varminting cartridges such as .218 Bee, .22 Hornet, .221 and .222 Remington, and so on. Magnum Research also makes a single-shot handgun with calibers up to .444 Marlin. A few big-game hunters use single-shots, but most of them prefer repeaters. Revolvers are the favorites, at least partly because they come in very popular calibers.

For big game, the centerfire magnums take the lead, though other calibers will do in a pinch. The .45 Auto, the .44 Special, and the .45 Colt will work on deer-size animals if range is not excessive, say 100 feet or so. Beyond that range, you're pushing your luck and it's best to rely on the magnums.

The big four magnums are the .357, .41, .44, and .45. The .357 Magnum, the smallest of the big four with its 158-grain bullet, develops a muzzle energy of 845 foot-pounds and a muzzle velocity of 1,550 feet per second. Recoil is heavy, but not enough to shake up the average shooter. The .357 is fine for deer, mountain lions, coyotes, and bobcats. It also makes a dandy rig for varmints. The .357 has taken bigger game, such as bears, but using it on animals over 200 pounds is stretching the cartridge beyond its limits.

One very big advantage in selecting a .357 Magnum is that the handgun will also accept the .38 Special, a popular target load. (*Caution:* The .38 Special can be fired in guns chambered for the .357 Magnum—but the .357 Magnum *cannot* be fired in a gun chambered for the .38 Special.) The .357 Magnum, then, is a good combination rig for hunting. The magnum loads are adequate for deer and smaller game. Switch to the .38 Special cartridge and the gun can be used for target shooting and plinking. This is a particularly good combination for the reloader, since the .38 Special is an inexpensive round to turn out.

A more recently introduced handgun magnum cartridge is the .357 Maximum which is factory-loaded with 158- or 180-grain bullets. The lighter bullet has a muzzle velocity of 1,825 fps and muzzle energy of 1,168 foot-pounds. The heavier bullet leaves the muzzle at 1,555 fps with 966 foot-pounds of energy. Both have more velocity and energy than the .357 Magnum not only at the muzzle but as far out as 100 yards. This cartridge cannot be chambered in a .357 Magnum or .38 Special handgun.

Next in size is the .41 Magnum, which would probably be considered an excellent load for big game if the .44 Magnum wasn't around. The .41 Magnum was designed to fill the gap between the .357 and .44 magnums, but it hasn't quite turned out

REVOLVERS

Smith & Wesson 629 Classic DX is chambered for .44 Magnum and .44 Special. The single and double action model with adjustable sights is available in barrel lengths of 6½ and 8⅜ inches. An excellent handgun choice for big game.

Ruger Blackhawk is a single action chambered for .44 Magnum and .44 Special. This revolver has a 5½-inch barrel. A good camp and back-up hunting gun.

Colt Realtree Anaconda is chambered for .44 Remington Magnum and has a barrel length of 8 inches. It was specifically designed for big-game hunting.

Ruger GP 100 is a double action revolver chambered for .357 Magnum. The model features a long ejector shroud for steady hold and pointing.

Smith & Wesson LadySmith Model 60LS is chambered for .357 Magnum and .38 Special. With a barrel length of 2 inches, this single and double action model has adjustable sights.

Ruger Fixed Sight Model Single-Six is chambered for .22 Short, .22 Long, and .22 Long Rifle. Barrel length is 5½ inches, with a weight of 2 pounds.

Harrington and Richardson Sportsman 999 is a top-break revolver with a 9-shot capacity. Chambered for .22 Short, Long and Long Rifle, the model is good for hunting, plinking, and target shooting.

that way. The .41 offers slightly less velocity and energy than the .44, but recoil is still considerable.

The .44 Remington Magnum and .45 Winchester Magnum take top honors for big-game hunting. Their big bullets don't travel quite as fast as the .357 Magnum or the .357 Maximum, but both have a muzzle velocity in excess of 1,450 fps, and they develop nearly double the foot-pounds of energy of the .357 Magnum. The .357 Maximum, however, vies with both the .41 and .44 magnums in velocity and energy. Out to 100 yards, a skilled shooter can take big game with any of these three cartridges. All are ideal for deer and black bears. They would also be good insurance when traveling in grizzly country.

However, these very hefty magnums are not for inexperienced or weak-handed shooters. They're the most powerful factory-loaded handgun cartridges made, and they produce the recoil and muzzle blast that must be expected from such cartridges.

TARGET SHOOTING

The shooter who wants to take up target shooting with a handgun should definitely start out with a .22 Rimfire. Because recoil is almost nonexistent with a .22, the shooter can concentrate on developing good shooting habits, such as proper trigger squeeze, grip, stance, and so on. Theoretically, after a training period with a .22 Rimfire, a shooter should be able to progress to larger calibers without letting heavier recoil and muzzle blast affect his shooting style.

As mentioned earlier, the revolver is simpler and safer to use. But since the safety factor is not as critical on a supervised target range as it is in the field, a shooter can select either a revolver or automatic. Both are accurate handguns and, under target-range conditions, both are equally reliable.

Barrel length for a target pistol should not be less than 6 inches. The only exceptions to this barrel-

length rule are the few specially designed target pistols, such as the .45 caliber Colt Gold Cup National Match, which has a 5-inch barrel. But because there aren't many handguns of this quality around, it's best to stick to barrels that fall between 6 and 9 inches for serious target shooting.

Target guns should be heavier than sidearms used for hunting. Target shooters do not have to carry their guns great distances, so weight is not a burden. A heavier gun means a steadier hold on the range and this is important in competition. Generally, a target handgun should weigh between 38 and 48 ounces, but a handgun chambered for the .38 Special or .45 Auto usually weighs a bit more.

When a shooter moves from the .22 Rimfire to the bigger calibers, he'll have to choose between a revolver and automatic. The two most popular centerfire target cartridges are the .38 Special and the .45 Auto. One factor to keep in mind is that you'll have a wider selection of handguns to choose from with the .38 Special. The .38 Special also kicks less than the .45 Auto.

And if you want to get involved in both hunting and target shooting, the .38 Special is by far a better choice since it can also be fired in .357 Magnum revolvers. A good combination, then, would be a match-grade .357 Magnum, such as the Colt Python. The .357 Magnum cartridges can be used for both hunting and target work. If you find the .357 too much gun for the target range, simply switch to the .38 Special loads and use the same gun.

Needless to say, all target handguns must have the best sights available, and these are generally Micrometer sights with solid adjustments for windage and elevation.

In addition to these conventional target handguns, there are much more specialized types that are useful only for specific—and very sophisticated—target events. There are .22 Long Rifle free pistols (single-

SEMI-AUTOMATIC HANDGUNS

Beretta 92-F is a 9mm model that takes a 15-round maga-zine. Features include combat style frame, non-glare fin-ish, and open slide design. Ideal for police application or home defense.

Ruger MK-4B .22 compact pistol. The model has a 4-inch bull barrel with adjustable target sights, an overall length of 8³/₁₆ inches and a weight of less than 2¹/₂ pounds.

Beretta 89 is chambered for .22 Long Rifle. With a barrel length of 6 inches, this target pistol features interchange-able front sights and adjustable rear sights.

Magnum .50 Caliber Desert Eagle is one of the six guns and three calibers that can be created by switching barrels and magazines on a single component system. Barrels accommodate scope rings, and are available in lengths of 6 and 10 inches.

Smith & Wesson 622 VR is chambered for .22 Long Rifle. This autoloader has adjustable sights and a 6-inch barrel. Good for hunting, target shooting, and plinking.

Ruger KP95D is chambered for 9mm Luger/9 × 19 mm Parabellum. This semi-automatic model has a barrel length of 3⁹/₁₀ inches. A good choice for home defense.

Magnum Baby Eagle FS is a double action semi-automatic pistol chambered for 9mm Parabellum. The model has a 4³/₄-inch barrel.

shots called "free" in reference to the lack of restrictions on weight, sight radius, trigger pull, types of grips, and so on). There are .22 Long Rifle automatics with adjustable grips, weights, and other features for "standard" international matches. For rapid-fire international matches, there are special automatics chambered for the .22 Short. And there are specially modified revolvers for Police Course matches as well as revolvers and automatics for other combat-style target competitions.

One new target event calls for knocking over metallic game silhouettes at 50, 100, 150, and 200 meters with a handgun or at 200, 300, 385, and 500 meters with a rifle. The handgunning version is divided into two classes, Production and Unlimited. The production guns are what you might expect— the S&W Model 29 and Ruger Super Blackhawk in .44 Remington Magnum, the Thompson/Center Contender with a 10-inch barrel, not only in .44 Magnum and .45 Magnum but also in less familiar handgun calibers like .30/.30, .357 Herrett, and .35 Remington. The guns may have production-line actions and contours, but special barrels and wildcat calibers are common. In the unlimited class, the guns are even more specialized. You see bolt-action pistols like the Remington XP-100 chambered for cartridges like the .308 and .358 Winchester. The Thompson/Center Super 14 Contender—with a 14-inch bull barrel—is really a production gun but is fired in the Unlimited Class. And many custom and semi-custom guns are popular for this competition.

Among rifles, too, there are specialized models for sophisticated matches—game-silhouette rifles,

free rifles, highly tuned sporters for running-game targets, and so on. A good source of information on competitive shooting with both handguns and rifles is the National Rifle Association of America, 1600 Rhode Island Ave., N.W., Washington, DC 20036.

PLINKING

Plinking means shooting at tin cans, paper targets, stationary claybirds, or any other safe target. Plinking has also turned beginners into skilled shooters. In short, it's an ideal and informal way of learning how to safely handle and shoot guns.

The ideal handgun for plinking is the .22 Rimfire, since ammunition is cheap and plinking usually involves a lot of shooting. The .22s recoil is nil, which means the entire family can get involved. A revolver is the best bet for this type of informal shooting, since it is the safest to handle.

Adjustable sights are advisable even on guns for plinking, though fixed sights are sometimes adequate for busting tin cans.

Theoretically, any gun you happen to have in your hand at the moment can be used for plinking. If you can stand the cost of the more expensive centerfire ammunition, that's fine. But the .22 Rimfire is the ideal plinker and also a good choice for the camper who can legally take a handgun along on his trips.

A complete listing of rimfire and centerfire handgun cartridges, as well as data on bullet weights, velocity, and energy, is included in the ballistics section beginning on page 45.

SINGLE-SHOT HANDGUNS

Magnum Lone Eagle single-shot pistol accommodates 14 interchangeable barrels and calibers from .22/250 Remington to 7mm. The model features an ambidextrous grip.

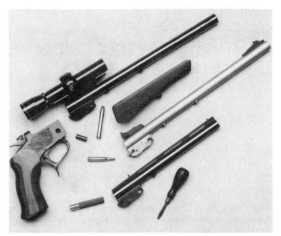

Thompson/Center Contender pistol is chambered for 17 cartridges from .22 Long Rifle to .45/70, plus the .410 shotgun shell. It's available in 4 barrel lengths: 10, 12, 14, and 16¼ inches.

MUZZLELOADING HANDGUN

Among muzzleloading handguns there are replica and nonreplica revolvers, replica and nonreplica single-shots. Of the replica revolvers, copies of the old Colts exceed all others in number. Most of them are used for plinking or informal target shooting. A few shooters also use such guns for hunting. For competitive target shooting, the solid-frame replicas such as the Remington Model 1858 and the Rogers & Spencer are a better choice. These are customized for competition by adding adjustable target sights and improved grips, and the actions are smoothed and adjusted. Many of these replicas are imported by the same companies listed in the section on muzzleloading rifles.

For shooters who want truly authentic Colts of the colorful 1850–1870 era, they're now available from at least half a dozen makers. The 1860 Army, the Dragoons, and the 1851 Navy are among currently available models.

The revolvers are all percussion guns, of course. Single-shots come in flintlock as well as percussion versions. The flintlocks are less popular, but they're available from Navy, Dixie, Connecticut Valley Arms, and a few other companies. These pistols are replicas or near-replicas of late 18th- and early 19th-century guns. They're mostly used for plinking, although flintlock target matches are sometimes con-ducted. Some models are available in kit form as well as finished.

Some of the same single-shot pistols, or guns very much like them, are available in caplock versions from the same makers or importers, as well as from most of the other companies engaged in the muzzleloading business. A few of the one-shot caplocks, such as the Thompson/Center .45 Patriot, are popular among serious muzzleloading target shooters. The T/C Patriot isn't a true replica but is modeled after the very fine dueling pistols of the percussion era.

A flintlock pistol is loaded in the same manner as a flintlock rifle (see the section on muzzleloading rifles) except that a pistol charge is considerably lighter than the charge for a rifle of the same caliber. The charge for a percussion pistol is also much lighter than for a rifle of the same caliber, and the loading procedure requires a few words of advice here.

First, clean all the oil from the bore—and from the cylinder if the gun is a revolver. Then fire a couple of caps to clear the nipple (or each nipple of a revolver) to clear out any residual oil. From this point on, the procedures differ for the single-shot and the revolver. Let's take the single-shot first.

Place the hammer at half cock and pour the correct measure of powder down the barrel. If the gun is a .45, a suitable charge is 30 grains FFFg black

BLACK-POWDER HANDGUNS

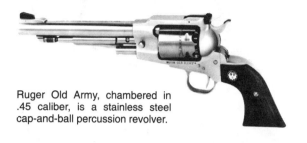

Ruger Old Army, chambered in .45 caliber, is a stainless steel cap-and-ball percussion revolver.

Thompson/Center Scout is chambered for .50 and .54 caliber and has an in-line ignition system.

powder or Pyrodex, Follow it with a patched ball, in this case a .440 ball of pure lead. Good patch material is tightly woven cotton, 0.15 inch thick. You'll have to give the starter a good bump with the heel of your hand, but a tight-fitting ball is vital for accuracy. After starting it, use the ramrod to push it all the way to the powder. Seat it firmly but don't pound on it. Now, when you seat a percussion cap over the nipple, the gun is ready to fire.

Loading a cap-and-ball revolver begins in the same way—by cleaning out the oil and clearing the nipples. Next, move the hammer to half cock. The cylinder can then be turned by hand. From a powder measure, drop a proper charge into one chamber and place an unpatched ball over the powder at the mouth of the chamber. If the gun is the Ruger Old Army .44 or another gun of that caliber, a good charge is 25 grains of FFFg black powder, and a .457 round ball is recommended. Cap-and-ball revolvers have built-in ramming systems, and you now turn the cylinder until the loaded chamber is under the rammer. Lower the ramming level to seat the

ball against the powder. Repeat these operations until all the chambers are loaded, and then fill the mouth of each chamber with grease. Lubricants are available for this, but ordinary vegetable shortening works well, and so does automotive water-pump grease. Plugging the chamber mouths with grease is insurance against a multiple discharge, and it also softens fouling. Having done this, just cap the nipples and the gun is ready to fire.

Black-powder guns require a thorough cleaning after a firing session and, for best results, quick cleanings during a session. With a single-shot, just use a damp patch followed by a dry one after each shot and your score will improve. With a revolver, you should use the same treatment after firing the full cylinder.

As with muzzleloading long guns, the National Muzzle Loading Rifle Association provides members with news and information regarding matches, gun shows, and other activities, as well as products. For more information, the address of the NMLRA is Box 67, Friendship, IN 47021.

SHOOTING THE HANDGUN

Of all sporting arms, the handgun is the most difficult to master. An outstretched arm, with a couple of pounds of gun, at the end, becomes a shaky mass of nerves and muscle. And the short sight radius of the handgun doesn't help matters.

Perhaps the most common mistake made by novice handgunners is that they try too hard to steady their arm. They squeeze the grip harder, which only results in a worse case of the trembles and makes matters worse. The handgun should be held firmly, but not tightly. Don't fight the wandering front sight; let it move back and forth across the target. The secret is the trigger squeeze. First take a deep breath, let out half of it, then aim. When the sights

cross the bull's-eye, start the trigger squeeze. When it wanders past the bull's-eye, stop the squeeze but maintain pressure on the trigger. Continue the squeeze when the sights cross the target again. Continue to do this and, eventually, the gun will fire at a point when the sights are on target. You should not be aware of when the gun will go off. Just concentrate on a slow, determined trigger squeeze.

In all likelihood, your handgun will have the common patridge sight. The correct way to use this sight is to center the post of the front sight in the square notch of the rear sight. The top of the front post should be level with the top of the rear notch. The accompanying drawing shows the correct sight picture with the patridge sight. The bull's-eye should look like an apple sitting on a fence post.

Novice handgunners also make the mistake of trying to keep both sights and target in focus at the same time, which is impossible. When shooting a handgun, keep the sights in focus. The target should and will be slightly blurred.

The serious target shooter will stick to his one-hand hold, because it is traditional among paper-target shooters and also because regulated competition matches may require it. But the hunter is not shooting at paper. He is shooting at game and a poor shot may well mean a wounded animal or a miss. The handgun hunter needs all the help he can get to steady his hold. In the field, he should always use a two-hand hold, and steady his sights even more by using a rest whenever possible.

The accompanying photographs illustrate the various handgun grips and shooting positions that have proven the steadiest under most conditions. The model is Matt Sparano, an accomplished marksman and handgun hunter.

The correct one-hand hold for a double-action revolver. Hold the grip firmly, but not tightly.

The correct one-hand hold for a heavy single-action revolver with factory grips. Note the little finger is curled and braced under the grip. Though this grip may look awkward, the little finger provides additional support.

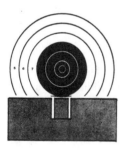

This is how your sight picture should look when using the patridge sight, the most common and best iron sight for a handgun. While the drawing shows both sight and target in focus, this is impossible to see sharply with the human eye. Keep the sights pretty much in focus. The target will and should be slightly blurred.

The correct two-hand hold for revolvers. This is the hold hunters should learn well, since it's foolish to use the less-steady one-hand hold when shooting at live game.

OFFHAND HANDGUN STANDING POSITIONS

Offhand Target, right: This offhand position is for target shooting at paper only. Space your feet comfortably, arm extended straight at target. Lean slightly toward the target, inserting your free hand in pocket, rather than letting it dangle freely at side. Under controlled range conditions a shooter can fire amazing offhand groups. But a hunter has no business shooting at game from this position. Here use a two-hand hold and a rest whenever possible. **Offhand Hunting, left:** This two-hand offhand position is for hunters when no other rest is available. Cup your left hand slightly around the gun butt, which should be resting in the palm of your left hand. Extend your arms but not so straight that you begin to shake. Relax and be comfortable.

THE PRONE POSITION

This is the steadiest of all handgun positions. Simply lie flat on the ground, feet comfortably spaced, arms fully extended, and elbows resting on the ground. The line of sight should run directly down the center of your back. A handgun hunter should use this position when possible.

THE KNEELING POSITION

Use this position when grass or brush is too high for the steadier sitting position, shown on the upcoming pages. Both heels are in line with the target, and buttock rests on heel. Elbow is bent slightly and rests on knee.

THE SITTING POSITION

This sitting position is best for high grass when no rest is available. Facing the target, lean forward, and rest your elbows on your knees. Keep both arms relatively straight if possible, but a slight bend in the arms is okay. The most important thing is to support both elbows comfortably on your knees. **Front view** shows feet spread slightly farther apart than knees, both elbows resting comfortably on the knees. Note the two-handed grip with the left hand cupped around the right hand. Gun butt is supported in palm of left hand.

SITTING WITH ARM REST

Though this sitting position may look strange at first, it is very steady when no other rest is available. This position has become popular with long-range silhouette shooters. Note that every part of the body is supported and braced. The buttocks are on the ground, the gun hand rests on the knee, and the shooter's back is braced by the left arm on the ground. **Front view** of this unique shooting position clearly shows that the shooter can relax and squeeze off his shot comfortably. No part of his body is strained or twisted.

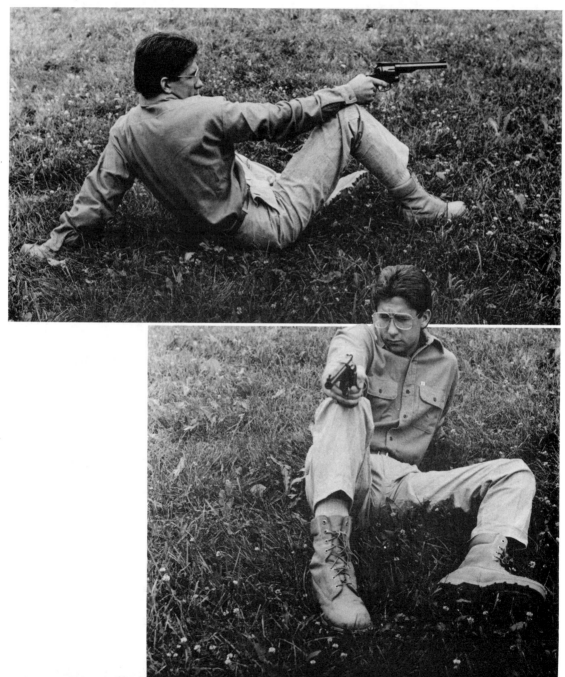

SUPPORTED HANDGUN POSITIONS

Sitting with Backrest: This is an excellent position for big-game hunters on stand in wooded areas. Sit facing the target and rest your back against the support, so that your forearms are supported by both knees and you can extend your arms.

Arm Rest: As a handgun hunter, you owe it to the game you hunt to make sure your shot counts. Utilize every possible rest or prop. If there's a tree or post available, brace your left arm against it as shown, and support your gun hand on your left wrist.

Post Rest: Steady those sights whenever and wherever possible. Use posts, stumps, rocks, anything to steady your handgun. Always hold the gun with two hands.

HANDLOADING

RIFLE CARTRIDGES

If you are considering reloading, it is safe to assume that you have already had considerable shooting experience. Certainly, you have purchased, and fired, a good many rounds of factory-loaded ammunition. Hence you are equipped with a working knowledge of the various caliber designations and cartridge shapes, and you have learned to recognize the correct cartridge for your particular rifle. Probably many readers will have an overall understanding of shooting that extends beyond these simple basics. However, for the benefit of the uninitiated, we'll begin at this point.

Each factory-loaded cartridge that we purchase and fire represents extensive thought and care on the part of its manufacturer. If we are to reload a fired cartridge, and duplicate, if possible, the original factory loading, we must first learn to appreciate some of the intricacies of ammunition design. For instance, the fired cartridge case is the most important reloading component. The function of the case, how it is constructed, and its condition after firing, are important considerations to reloaders.

The Cartridge Case

The chief function of a cartridge case is to seal off the breech at the time of firing. To accomplish this, the case walls must expand freely so that they are tight against the sides of the chamber. This sealing action prevents the hot powder gases from leaking back around the cartridge and out through the action. Along with this, the cartridge case must withstand the chamber pressure that is built up during firing. To achieve this, the case requires a structural strength of its own—plus the additional supporting strength supplied by the bolt face and chamber walls. In essence, the case functions as an intrinsic part of the rifle. A rifle is no stronger than the case that is used in it—nor is the case stronger than the rifle.

Cartridge brass is carefully tempered in its final manufacture. The head of the case is thick and tough which gives it the strength and rigidity necessary to resist the force of the chamber pressure. The forward section of the case (neck, shoulder and body) is considerably thinner than the head section. In manufacture, these portions are given an anneal which leaves them soft and ductile. The obvious advantage is that the case walls and neck will now expand freely to release the bullet and seal the chamber while the cartridge is fired.

As shooters, we may have been rather casual in our regard for empty brass cases, but as reloaders we soon come to think differently. Without a quantity of strong and serviceable cases, we would not get far in reloading ammunition for old Betsy. The most usual way for a reloader to obtain serviceable cases is to purchase factory-loaded ammunition. After this "store bought" ammo has been fired, the empty cases are retained for future reloading. The reloader may also purchase new cases from his component dealer.

To make sure your cases are in prime condition, we recommend you start with either new or once-fired cases. Never use brass of unknown origin such as that found on a shooting range.

Each firing and resizing has an influence on the serviceability of the case. The battering of chamber pressure, and the forces applied by the resizing die eventually work-harden the forward portion of the case and destroy its usefulness. When cases have deteriorated due to excessive reloading, they are referred to as "fatigued brass" and must be discarded. To make sure the cases are in good condition, inspect them before each reloading.

Carefully inspect your cases before each reloading. If your cases are new, or once fired, they will not reveal fatigue at the first reloading. However, fatigue signs will show up in subsequent loading, so you must learn to look for them. Check your cases for splits or cracks in the neck, shoulder or body. Reject all cases that show signs of defects, but before discarding them flatten them with a pair of pliers to prevent their reuse.

We suggest that you separate your cartridge cases into lots and keep a record of their history. For example, if you purchase two boxes of factory-loaded cartridges on a given date, keep all 40 rounds together and load them as one lot. Maintaining a record of the brand name, date of purchase, and the number of times you loaded the cases will be helpful in determining your case life, and you will benefit later on when trimming is required.

Trimming is necessary when your cases have lengthened after numerous firings.

When loading new or once-fired cases, it is necessary to remove the sharp inside edges of the case mouth. This operation is called chamfering and its purpose is to ease the insertion of the new bullet. Chamfering is required only for the first reloading of a new or once-fired case. An inexpensive hand reamer chamfers a case easily and with uniformity. Hold the case in one hand, while you lightly turn the reamer in the case mouth with the other hand.

All photos and portions of text furnished by Lyman Reloading Products, Middlefield, Connecticut.

FATIGUED BRASS CASES

The condition pictured above illustrates case fatigue. Note how the cracks run lengthwise. Sometimes only pinhole cracks are noticeable. But, for the sake of safety, such cases must be discarded.

The condition pictured in this example is quite different from case fatigue. This crack runs around the circumference of the case and indicates an excessive headspace. Never use any rifle which shows signs of excessive headspace.

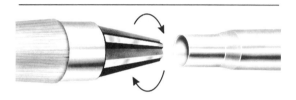

When chamfering turn the reamer lightly, removing very little case material.

Remove very little material and do not cut a sharp knife edge on the case.

Choosing a Load

To select the proper components, study a reloading handbook that lists your specific cartridge. Make a note of the bullet diameter and primer size required for this cartridge. This information will be needed when you purchase components. For example, if your cartridge were a .218 BEE, you would look under the specifications for that cartridge and take note of the following information:

EXAMPLE (.218 BEE)

CARTRIDGE SPECIFICATIONS:
Bullet Dia. Jacketed and Cast . . . . .224"
Maximum Case Length . . . . 1.345"
Trim-to Length . . . . 1.335"
Maximum Overall Length (w/Bullet) . . . . 1.680"
Primer Size . . . . Small Rifle
Lyman Shell Holder Number 10

Now, you must also decide on a bullet weight and a type of powder. For the time being, we suggest that you select a jacketed bullet of a weight with which you are familiar, and that you restrict yourself to the "starting load" shown for this bullet weight. Let's suppose you are still using the .218 BEE cartridge and that you have decided to use a 50-grain jacketed bullet with IMR 4198 powder. You would make note of your load as shown below and then be able to purchase the proper components from your dealer.

EXAMPLE (.218 BEE)

50 Grain Jacketed

Powder	Sug. Starting Grains	Velocity F.P.S.	Max. Grains	Velocity F.P.S.
2400	10.0	2331		
IMR 4227	11.0	2331		
IMR 4198	12.0	2105		

Basic Mechanics

Before getting into the actual loading of a cartridge case, it may be wise to show the reloading procedure in a simplified graphic form. Picturing reloading in this manner will enable you to quickly grasp the fundamentals and to understand why each operation is necessary.

Actually, there are only SIX basic mechanical operations required to reload a cartridge. FOUR of them are performed by the reloading dies. As you read through the text and take note of the illustrations, you will see how a set of only two reloading dies can accomplish all four of these operations.

RELOADING OPERATIONS (RIFLE CARTRIDGES)

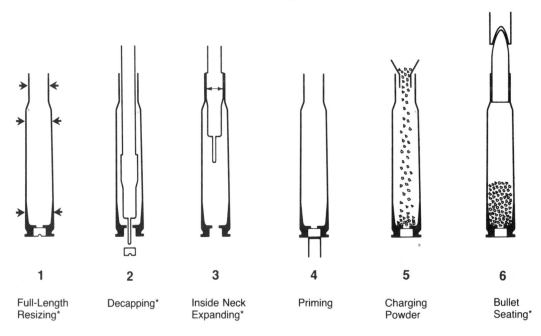

1	2	3	4	5	6
Full-Length Resizing*	Decapping*	Inside Neck Expanding*	Priming	Charging Powder	Bullet Seating*

*Operations 1,2,3, and 6 are performed by reloading dies.

Later on in reloading, you will hear of three- and even four-die sets. The difference is that two- and three-die sets combine some of the operations, whereas a four-die set accomplishes each operation separately.

1. Full-Length Resizing: When a cartridge is fired, the neck, shoulder and body of the case expand to seal the chamber and release the bullet. These portions of the case remain pretty much at their expanded size and do not snap back to their original dimension. Since all chambers are not identical, cases fired in one rifle may not chamber in another unless their walls are reduced to a standard diameter that is acceptable to all rifles. This operation is called resizing.

2. Decapping: This operation consists of simply removing the old or fired primer.

3. Inside Neck Expanding: After a case has been resized, the inside diameter of its neck will be too small to accept the new bullet. Inside neck expanding enlarges the diameter of the neck to a size that will receive and hold the bullet securely.

4. Priming: This operation consists of inserting a new primer into the primer pocket.

5. Charging Powder: This operation consists of carefully weighing out and pouring the appropriate powder charge into the case.

6. Bullet Seating: The last operation in the reloading process is the seating of a bullet into the case.

Making Cartridges

Now, if your cases have been properly inspected and you've selected a load, and purchased the necessary components (primers, powder and bullets), you are ready to begin. Your reloading press should be assembled and mounted according to the instructions supplied with the tool. Many reloading presses may be assembled to function either on the up-, or on the downstroke of the handle. The press pictured in our illustrations (next page) is operating on the downstroke. First, lubricate your cases by wiping them with a cloth sparingly greased with a case lubricant. Use care for too much lubricant will trap air in the die and cause "lube dents." Cases dented in this manner may be used for reloading, for the dents will be ironed out in firing. It is not considered good reloading practice, however, and care should be exercised.

Screw the Full-Length Resizing Die into the head of your press and adjust it according to the instructions supplied with the die.

1. Full-Length Resizing and Decapping: Slide the head of your cartridge case into the shell holder, as pictured in the illustration, and pull the press handle down all the way. If the die is adjusted properly, the entire cartridge case will enter the die flush to the shell holder. Note in the cutaway drawing how two of the original six reloading operations (full-length resizing and decapping) are accomplished simultaneously by this step.

2. Inside Neck Expanding and Priming: As your case is withdrawn from the resizing die, two further operations are accomplished. The expanding button will automatically enlarge the neck, as shown in the cutaway drawing, and the priming punch will seat the new primer. As the expanding action of the button is automatic, you need not be concerned with it. You must, however, place the new primer (cup side up) into the priming punch sleeve. Push the priming arm forward (toward the press) and pull up on the press handle. As the ram is lowered, the priming arm will enter the slot in the side of the ram and seat the primer.

3. Charging Powder: For the weighing of powder, you will require an accurate powder scale. The data

MAKING CARTRIDGES, STEP 1: RESIZING AND DECAPPING

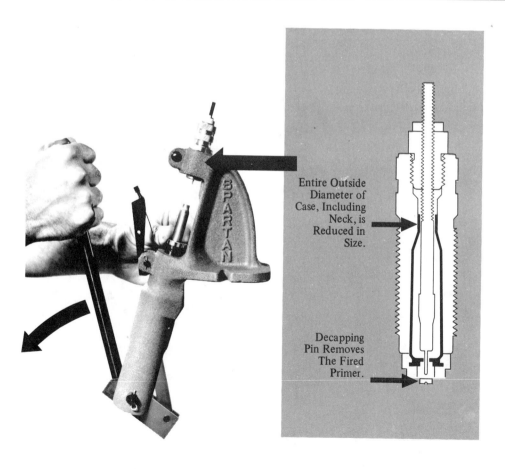

Entire Outside Diameter of Case, Including Neck, is Reduced in Size.

Decapping Pin Removes The Fired Primer.

section in a reloading handbook specifies the powders that are appropriate for your particular cartridge. It also lists a suggested weight of the powder charge in grains and in fractions of grains. For example, 9.5 grains woud be read as NINE and FIVE TENTHS grains, 10.0 grains would be read as TEN grains. We recommend that the novice restrict himself to the suggested starting load. Carefully level the powder scale as explained in the scale instructions and set it to weigh your required charge. The illustration on page 194 explains how to adjust the scale.

Slowly sprinkle small amounts of powder into the scale pan until the beam comes into balance. The beam is in balance when the pointed end (extreme left) is exactly on the zero mark.

Carefully remove the pan and pour its contents into the cartridge case. Use a powder funnel to make sure all the powder enters the case. To avoid the

CONVERSION TABLE OUNCES TO GRAINS

Oz.	Grains	Oz.	Grains	Oz.	Grains
½	218.8	1⅛	492.2	1¾	765.6
9/16	246.1	1 3/16	519.5	1 13/16	793.0
⅝	273.4	1¼	546.9	1⅞	820.3
11/16	300.8	1 5/16	574.2	1 15/16	847.7
¾	328.1	1⅜	601.6	2	875.0
13/16	355.5	1 7/16	628.9	2 1/16	902.3
⅞	382.8	1½	656.3	2⅛	929.7
15/16	410.2	1 9/16	683.6	2 3/16	957.0
1	437.5	1⅝	710.9	2¼	984.4
1 1/16	464.8	1 11/16	738.3		

MAKING CARTRIDGES, STEP 2: NECK EXPANDING AND PRIMING

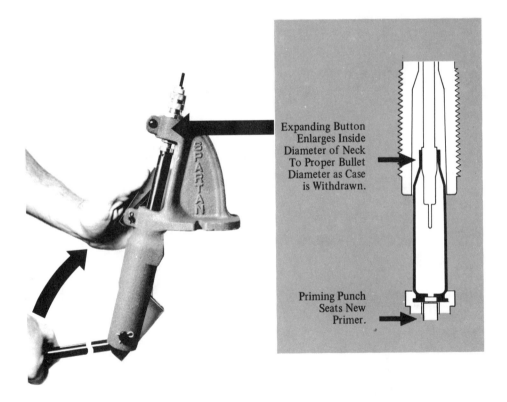

Seating Primers: Primers are seated mainly by feel. The bottom of the anvil *must bottom* in the primer pocket. Use care and do not crush the primer. Crushed primers give erratic ignition, or fail to fire.

CONVERSION FACTORS

Multiply	×	by	=	To Obtain
Pounds per square inch		0.07032		Kilograms per cm²
Drams		1.772		Grams
Drams		0.0625		Ounces
Grains (Troy)*		1		Grains (Avoirdupois)**
Grains		0.0648		Grams
Grams		15.43		Grains
Grams		0.03527		Ounces
Kilograms		1000		Grams
Ounces		16		Grams
Ounces		437.5		Grains
Ounces		0.0625		Pounds (Avoirdupois)**
Ounces		28.35		Drams
Pounds		7000		Grains
Pounds		453.6		Grams

Multiply	×	by	=	To Obtain
Pounds		16		Ounces
Centimeters		0.3937		Inches
Centimeters		0.01		Meters
Centimeters		10		Millimeters
Inches		2.540		Centimeters
Meters		100		Centimers
Meters		3.281		Feet
Meters		39.37		Inches
Meters		1.094		Yards
Feet per Second		0.3048		Meters per Second
Feet per Second		0.6818		Miles per Hour
Meters per Second		3.281		Feet per Second
Miles per Hour		1.467		Feet per Second

*Troy: Weight based on a pound of 12 ounces and an ounce of 480 grains.

**Avoirdupois: Weight based on a pound of 16 ounces and an ounce of 16 drams.

MAKING CARTRIDGES, STEP 3: CHARGING POWDER

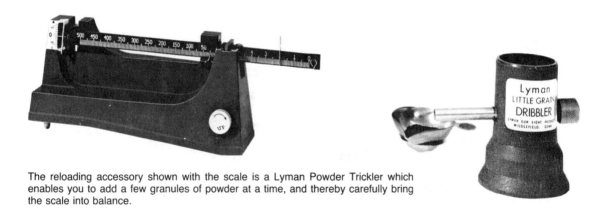

The reloading accessory shown with the scale is a Lyman Powder Trickler which enables you to add a few granules of powder at a time, and thereby carefully bring the scale into balance.

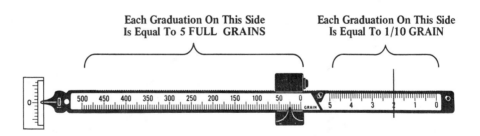

This illustration shows the beam of a modern reloading scale. Note how it is graduated on both sides of the pivot point. The scale is set by moving the two weights (poise) to the proper graduations. The large poise (on the left) is used to obtain multiples of FIVE GRAINS, while the small poise (on the right) is used for ¹/₁₀ FRACTIONS of a grain, or SINGLE grains from one to five. **EXAMPLE:** The illustration shows a setting of 27.0 grains. If you wanted to decrease this ¹/₁₀ grain, you would simply move the small poise one notch to the right.

possibility of accidentally "Double Charging" a cartridge, you should develop a foolproof system of loading. A suggested method is to place all the un-charged cases on your left. As you pick up each case for charging, turn it upside down and shake it. This will insure that the case is empty. Turn the case right-side up, charge it and place it carefully on your right. Take care not to accidentally move the poise when removing or replacing the scale pan.

4. Bullet Seating: The last step in reloading a cartridge is seating the new bullet. Make certain that the overall length of the finished round is not longer than the MAXIMUM OVERALL LENGTH specified for the particular cartridge. Adhering to this

measurement will insure that the cartridge will function through the magazine of your rifle. Also, a bullet that is not seated to the proper depth can engage the rifling and build up pressure upon firing.

This illustration shows how a bullet is seated. Screw the bullet seating die into the head of the press and adjust it according to the instructions supplied with the die. Place a primed, charged cartridge case in the shell holder and a bullet on the mouth of the case. Hold the bullet in place as you pull the press handle all the way down. As the case enters the die, the bullet will be pushed firmly into the neck of the case. Adjusting the seating screw controls the depth to which the bullet is seated. Adjusting the die body controls the crimp.

MAKING CARTRIDGES, STEP 4: SEATING BULLETS

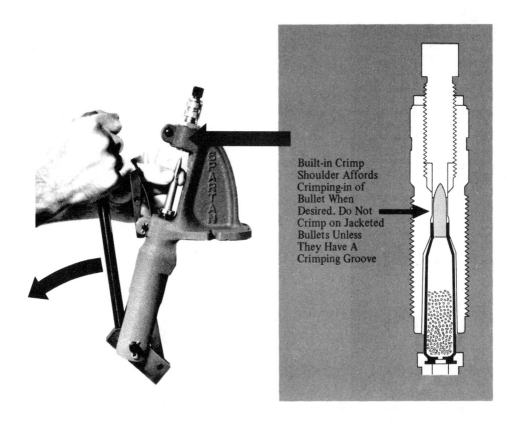

Built-in Crimp Shoulder Affords Crimping-in of Bullet When Desired. Do Not Crimp on Jacketed Bullets Unless They Have A Crimping Groove

CRIMPING

Crimping is a matter of choice and the seating die may be adjusted to crimp, or not to crimp as you desire. If you are loading hunting loads that will see hard usage in the magazine, it is wise to crimp-in the bullet. This prevents the bullets from unseating when the rifle is under recoil. Best accuracy, however, is usually obtained by not crimping-in the bullet. Target, or varmint loads, are best left uncrimped.

CAUTION: AFTER RELOADING AND BEFORE FIRING, WIPE YOUR CASES TO REMOVE ALL SIZING LUBRICANT. THE PRESENCE OF OIL OR GREASE ON A CARTRIDGE MAY DANGEROUSLY INCREASE THRUST ON THE BOLT FACE.

PISTOL CARTRIDGES

In the rifle section, we stated that the empty cartridge case is our most important reloading component. This statement applies to handgun cartridges as well. The fired case must be strong and in good condition in order to function properly, and to fulfill its task of sealing the chamber and withstanding chamber pressure. Generally speaking, most handgun cases do not take as severe a battering from chamber pressure and from resizing as do most rifle cases. The wear they do experience, however, will eventually destroy their usefulness. Case life is a relative thing which varies with the pressure of the load. Heavy magnum loads destroy cases rapidly, while the same cases loaded with light midrange loads may last almost indefinitely.

The Case as a Component

The reloader soon learns to think of his cartridge case as an intrinsic and functional part of the firearm itself. After all, if the case is to rely on the supporting strength of the chamber walls and bolt face, then its dimensions must remain close to those of the gun chamber. In other words, the cartridge case must be designed and manufactured with the same care and skill as the firearm. Inasmuch as the safety of the load depends on both the strength of the firearm and the case, one is no stronger than the other. To be sure your cases are in good condition, we recommend that you start with either new or once-fired cases. Never use brass of unknown origin such as that found on shooting ranges. You should inspect your cases for signs of case fatigue before each reloading. If, as suggested, the cases are new, or once fired, they will not show fatigue at this first reloading. However, the first fatigue signs are bound to reveal themselves in subsequent loading, so you should learn to watch for them.

It is a wise practice to separate your cases into lots and to keep a record of their history. For example, if you purchase two boxes of factory-loaded cartridges on a certain date, keep all 100 rounds together and load them as one lot. Record the brand name, the date of purchase, and the number of times you loaded these cases. Maintaining a record will be helpful in determining your case life, and you will benefit later on when trimming is required.

Trimming is necessary when the cases have been lengthened after numerous firings.

After you have inspected your cases and culled out the rejects, you are ready to go on to the next step. Before you dispose of the defective cases, however, it is a good idea to flatten them with a pair of pliers to prevent their reuse.

When loading new or once-fired cases, it is necessary to remove the sharp edges inside the case mouth. This operation is called chamfering and its purpose is to ease the insertion of the new bullet. Chamfering is needed only for the first reloading of a new or once-fired case. An inexpensive hand reamer chamfers a case easily and with uniformity. Hold the case in one hand, while you lightly turn the reamer in the case mouth with the other hand. Remove very little material and do not cut a sharp knife edge on the case.

Choosing a Load

To select the proper components, refer to the data pages of a reloading handbook that lists your cartridge. Make a note of the bullet diameter and primer size specified for this cartridge. This information will be needed when you purchase components. For example, if your cartridge was a .38 Special, you would look under the specifications for that cartridge and take note of the following data:

EXAMPLE (.38 SPECIAL)

SPECIFICATIONS:

Bullet Dia. Jacketed & Cast . . . . .354'' to .360''*
Maximum Case Length . . . . 1.155''
Trim-to Length . . . . 1.149''
Maximum Overall Length (w/Bullet) . . . . 1.550''
Primer Size . . . . Small Pistol
Lyman Shell Holder Number 1

*The correct bullet diameter is related to the groove diameter of your particular handgun. With handguns, this dimension can vary from one handgun to another. The only way to be certain of your exact groove diameter is to slug the barrel.

Now, you must decide on a bullet weight and a type of powder. You will note, in most pistol calibers, that a selection of bullet types (cast, jacketed and half-jacketed) is available.

If you should decide to use either a jacketed or a half-jacketed bullet, then these bullets may be purchased from your component dealer. Jacketed or half-jacketed bullets are manufactured to a standard diameter which may vary from the groove diameter of your pistol. The starting loads for these bullet types take into consideration these possible variations, and they will be safe to use in your handgun.

If you should decide to use a cast bullet, however, then you must purchase a mold for the bullet specified. The loads shown for cast bullets are quite specific and the correct bullet number and alloy must be used. These bullets should be sized to the groove diameter of your handgun for which a sizing die is available.

Basic Mechanics

Reloading a pistol cartridge requires a series of SIX basic mechanical operations. So that you will understand the fundamentals of each operation, we will first treat them graphically and then explain why each operation is necessary. Four out of the six operations are performed by the reloading dies.

1. Full-Length Resizing: When a cartridge is fired, the side walls of the case expand to the chamber

EXAMPLE (.38 Special)
158 Grain Jacketed

Powder	Sug. Starting Grains	Velocity F.P.S.	Max. Grains	Velocity F.P.S.
Unique	4.6	688		
2400	9.5	785		

141 Grain Cast
BULLET #358495 (#2 ALLOY)

Powder	Sug. Starting Grains	Velocity F.P.S.	Max. Grains	Velocity F.P.S.
Bullseye	2.0	568		
Unique	3.5	739		
2400	8.0	794		
SR 7625	3.1	550		
SR 4756	4.0	562		
IMR 4227	7.0	550		

RELOADING OPERATIONS (HANDGUN CARTRIDGES)

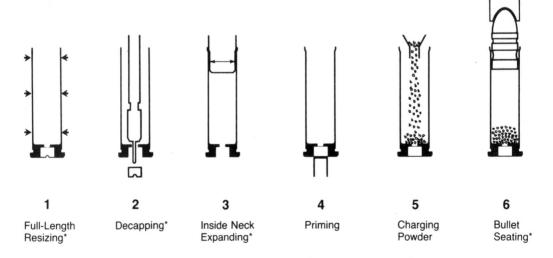

1	2	3	4	5	6
Full-Length Resizing*	Decapping*	Inside Neck Expanding*	Priming	Charging Powder	Bullet Seating*

*Operations 1, 2, 3, and 6 are performed by the reloading dies.

size of the handgun. This is necessary for the case to function properly and seal the chamber. These walls remain pretty much at their expanded size and do not snap back to original dimensions. Since all pistol chambers are not identical, cases fired in one pistol may not chamber in another. Even the chambers of a revolver cylinder will, in fact, vary from one to another. For this reason, it is necessary to compress the walls of the case to a standard diameter that is acceptable to all handguns. This operation is called resizing.

2. Decapping: This operation consists of simply removing the old or fired primer.

3. Inside Neck Expanding: After the case has been resized, the inside diameter of the neck will be too small to accept the bullet. Inside neck expanding enlarges the inside diameter of the neck to a size which will receive and hold the bullet securely. For pistol cases, a two-step expanding plug is used to open up the inside of the case neck. The first step on this plug is slightly smaller than bullet diameter, while the second step is a few thousandths larger. The idea behind this is to allow the bullet to enter the case freely without shaving lead. The actual difference between the two steps is not visually apparent. The illustrations on the previous page have been exaggerated for purposes of clarification.

4. Priming: This operation consists of inserting a new primer into the primer pocket.

5. Charging Powder: This operation consists of carefully weighing out and pouring the appropriate powder charge into the case.

6. Bullet Seating: The last operation in the reloading process is seating a new bullet into the case, again, as shown on the previous page.

MAKING CARTRIDGES, STEP 1: RESIZING AND DECAPPING

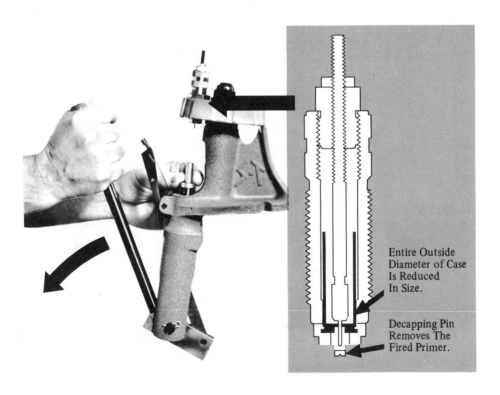

Entire Outside Diameter of Case Is Reduced In Size.

Decapping Pin Removes The Fired Primer.

In the preceding text we covered reloading graphically and have given the reader a general idea of what is required. Now by employing photographs we will explain the actual reloading of a cartridge. You will note that we are using a set of three reloading dies to perform four of the six operations. Further along in reloading you will hear of two-die sets and even four-die sets. The difference is that two- and three-die sets combine some of the operations, while a four-die set performs each operation separately. Due to their shape, most pistol cartridges require the use of a three-die set.

Making Cartridges

We now assume that your cases have been properly inspected, that you have selected a load, and purchased the necessary components. Your reloading press should be assembled and mounted according to the instructions supplied with it. Many reloading presses may be assembled to function on either the up-, or downstroke of the handle. The press illustrated here is operating on the downstroke. First, lubricate your cases by wiping them with a cloth sparingly greased with a case lubricant. This special lubricant will cut friction to a minimum and ease the sizing operation. Apply a very thin coat, for too much grease will trap air in the die and cause "lube dents." Although cases dented in this manner may be used for reloading, as the dents are ironed out in firing, it is not considered good reloading practice. Screw your Full-Length Resizing Die into the head of the press, adjust it according to the instructions furnished, and you are ready to commence loading.

1. Full-Length Resizing and Decapping: Slide the head of your cartridge case into the shell holder as illustrated, and pull your press handle down all the way. If the die is adjusted properly, the entire cartridge case will enter the die flush to the shell holder.

MAKING CARTRIDGES, STEP 2: NECK EXPANSION

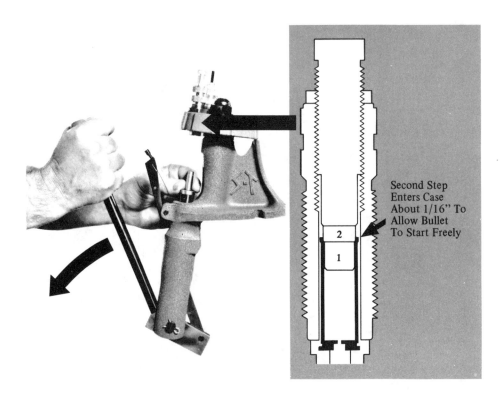

Second Step Enters Case About 1/16" To Allow Bullet To Start Freely

2

1

Note, in the cutaway drawing, how two of the original six reloading operations (full-length resizing and decapping) are accomplished by this step. Pull up on the press handle to remove the case from the die.

2. Inside Neck Expanding: Screw the neck expanding die into the turret head and adjust it according to the instructions supplied with the die. Place the resized cartridge case into the shell holder and pull down on the press handle. Note (drawing on previous page) how the two-step plug enters and expands the case neck. Actually, there is only a few thousandths difference in diameter between the first and second steps on the plug. This difference is so slight that it is not visually apparent. The illustration has been exaggerated for clarification.

3. Priming: The priming operation takes place as your case is withdrawn from the neck expanding die. Place the new primer (cup side up) into the priming punch sleeve. Push the primer arm forward (toward the press) and pull up on the press handle. As the ram is lowered, the priming arm will enter the slot in the side of the ram and seat the primer.

4. Charging Powder: For the weighing of powder, you require an accurate powder scale. The data section in a handbook specifies the powders appropriate for your particular cartridge. It also lists a suggested weight of the charge in grains and in fractions of grains. For example, 2.2 would be read as TWO and TWO TENTHS grains, 3.0 would be read as THREE grains. We recommend that the novice restrict himself, at least temporarily, to the sug-

MAKING CARTRIDGES, STEP 3: PRIMING

Seating Primers: Primers are seated mainly by feel. The bottom of the anvil *must bottom* in the primer pocket. Depending on the brand of case and primer being used, this usually works out so that the primer is fully seated when the top of the primer is flush with the head of the case, or a few thousandths below the head. Under no circumstances should primers protrude from the head of the case. Use care not to crush the primer. Crushed primers give erratic ignition, or fail to fire.

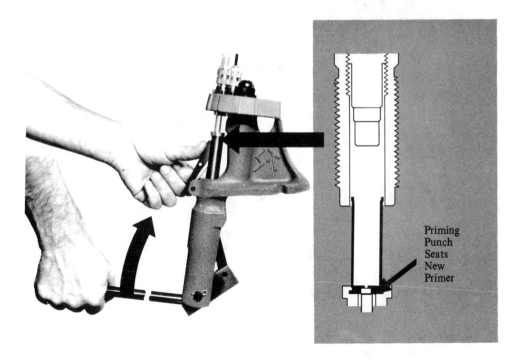

Priming Punch Seats New Primer

gested starting load. Carefully level the powder scale as explained in the instructions and set it to weigh your required charge. The illustration below explains how to adjust the scale.

Slowly trickle small amounts of powder into the scale pan until the beam comes into balance. The beam is in balance when the pointed end (extreme left) is exactly on the zero mark.

Carefully remove the pan and pour its contents into the cartridge case. Use a powder funnel to make sure all the powder enters the case. Because pistol powders are comparatively fast burning, most normal charges take up very little room in the cartridge case. In other words, it is possible to accidentally double charge, or even triple charge many pistol cases. This, of course, would prove extremely dangerous and a foolproof system of loading must be

developed. A suggested method is to place all the uncharged cartridge cases on your left. As you pick up each case for charging, turn it upside down and shake it. This will insure that the case is empty. Turn the case right-side up, charge it and place it carefully on your right. Take care, when removing or replacing the scale pan, that the poise are not accidentally moved.

5. Bullet Seating: The last operation in reloading a cartridge case is seating the new bullet. Be sure the overall length of the finished round is not longer than the MAXIMUM OVERALL LENGTH specified for the particular cartridge. Adhering to this measurement will make certain that the finished round will function properly in your magazine or cylinder. Also, a bullet not seated to the proper

MAKING CARTRIDGES, STEP 4: CHARGING POWDER

The reloading accessory pictured with the scale is a Lyman Powder Trickler. With a Trickler you can add a few granules at a time, and carefully bring the scale into balance.

The illustration below shows the beam of a modern reloading scale. Note how it is graduated on both sides of the pivot point. The scale is set by moving the two weights (poise) to the proper graduations. The large poise (on the left) is used to obtain multiples of FIVE GRAINS, while the small poise (on the right) is used for FRACTIONS of a grain or SINGLE grains from one to five. **EXAMPLE:** The illustration shows a setting of 3.0 grains. If you wish to increase this to 8.0 grains, simply move the large poise one notch to the left.

Each Graduation On This Side
Is Equal To 5 FULL GRAINS

Each Graduation On This Side
Is Equal To 1/10 GRAIN

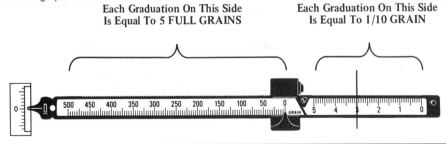

depth can engage the rifling in an autoloading pistol, and build up pressure upon firing.

This illustration shows how a bullet is seated. Screw the bullet seating die into the head of the press and adjust it according to the instructions supplied. Place a primed, charged cartridge case in the shell holder and start a bullet in the mouth of the case. Pull your press handle all the way down, so when the case enters the die, the bullet will be pushed firmly into the neck of the case. Adjusting the seating screw controls the depth to which the bullet is seated. Adjusting the die body controls the crimp.

Letter "A" indicates headspace in first example below. If case of this type is crimped, it can shorten

the overall length of the case and create an excessive headspace condition. Rimmed cases of the "B" type may be crimped if desired. Magnum cartridges, due to their heavy recoil, require the use of a crimp to hold the bullet securely.

CASTING BULLETS

Text and illustrations courtesy of Lyman Products Corp.

Never before have metallic cartridge reloaders had such an array of jacketed and cast bullets from which to choose. Until fairly recently most reloaders used jacketed bullets in their guns. That is still the case, but cast bullets are once again working their way back into the shooter's reloading repertoire.

Properly made cast bullets can do many things the jacketed bullet can do. Reloaders, aware of the increasing cost of jacketed bullets, have found that cast bullets are good to use for recreational shoot-

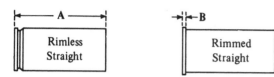

MAKING CARTRIDGES, STEP 5: SEATING BULLETS

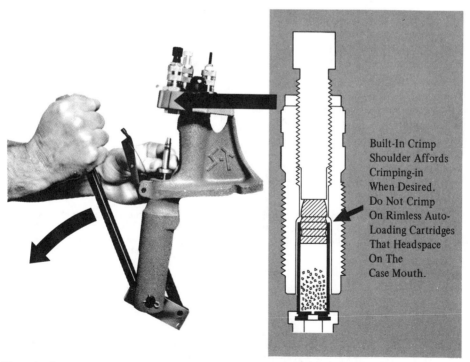

Built-In Crimp Shoulder Affords Crimping-in When Desired. Do Not Crimp On Rimless Auto-Loading Cartridges That Headspace On The Case Mouth.

CAUTION: After reloading and before firing, wipe your cases to remove all sizing lubricant. The presence of oil or grease on a cartridge may dangerously increase thrust on the bolt face.

ing—and even for hunting in .30 caliber and above. Besides, a cast bullet will cost approximately one-fifth as much as a corresponding jacketed bullet—and not a premium bullet, either!

There are several factors to consider when selecting a bullet besides having carefully tested load data for a given projectile weight:

1. Weight: For optimum potential accuracy the bullet must fall within a range peculiar to a given caliber. Also, the velocity at which that bullet will be driven is a factor. The whole idea is to properly blend the three (weight, rate of twist and velocity) to produce the results satisfying you, the reloader. Weight is important to the target shooter for its effect upon sectional density; hunters are concerned with weight for its implications to penetration on game.

2. Base Design: There are two types: flat base and boattail. Of the two, the boattail has the most po-

tential for accuracy in that the base can be more precisely made. Also, the boattail will produce less aerodynamic drag than will an otherwise identical projectile with a flat base. This means the boattail design will shoot flatter at extended range than will a flat base; all other variables being equal.

3. Point Design: There are various configurations within a given caliber, ranging from aerodynamically sleek spitzer points for minimum drag to round noses particularly suited for short-range hunting loads. These point shapes can also incorporate an exposed lead nose, hollow-point or full-coverage jacket.

The one firm rule for a cast bullet is that it must fit the bore of the gun in which it will be used. These lead alloy bullets, even the harder ones of Linotype or heat-treated wheelweights, are much easier to damage in firing than their jacketed descendants. They must fit precisely; otherwise they cannot be expected to perform at their best.

DESIGN FEATURES OF CAST BULLETS

These four shapes are basic to cast bullet design. Actual bullets may vary to some extent, but, generally, they fall into one of these four categories.

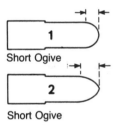

1

Short Ogive

2

Short Ogive

Ideal Designs: Bullets that conform to either of these general shapes have performed very well in testing. Due to their short ogive, the greatest weight mass bears on some portion of the rifling. The driving bands bear directly on the groove, while the nose acts as a pilot to align the bullet in the throat and bore.

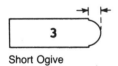

3

Short Ogive

Loverin Design: Bullets having this general shape have performed extremly well in testing. Due to their short ogive, the greatest weight mass bears directly on the groove. While the design does not always provide for a section of the bullet to bear on the lands, the many driving bands of groove diameter keep them well aligned.

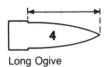

4

Long Ogive

Bullets of this general shape have proved to be the worst performers in testing. Their long flowing ogives leave a portion of the bullet unsupported by the rifling. Cast bullets of this general shape can easily misalign themselves as they enter the throat and bore.

There is, even now, detectable variation in the bore and groove measurements of modern centerfire firearms. Cast bullets which do not fit properly are inaccurate and contribute to leading.

One last thing to remember about jacketed bullets is that the actual jacket material and projectile bearing surface will vary between manufacturers for bullets of identical weight and similar design.

Getting Started

Bullet casting is rather easy and not all that expensive considering that you'll be deriving additional enjoyment of your hobby—plus increased per-shot economy which quickly defrays equipment cost. If you are a muzzleloader, your start-up costs will be greatly reduced by the elimination of sizing and lubricating equipment.

The key to an easy introduction is starting out with the proper equipment. The beginning caster needs the following basic casting equipment to obtain good initial results: mold and handles, melting pot, pouring ladle, casting mallet (with which to strike the mold's sprue plate to cut off the bullet's sprue), ingot mold and a lubricator/sizer fitted with appropriate top punch and sizing die. Muzzleloaders excused on the last item, as noted.

Additionally, every caster should wear basic safety garb. We recommend that no casting be done unless the caster is protected by sturdy gloves and safety glasses. An accident with molten lead can have serious consequences.

One last item for riflemen, essential to successful initial efforts, is a die which flares the case mouth just a bit. This makes seating the cast bullet undamaged that much easier. (Lyman pistol die sets include this type of expander.)

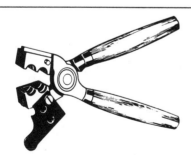

Typical bullet mold for casting bullets. Before using a new mold, clean it in alcohol, or other suitable solvent to remove protective coating of oil. Casting bullets with oil still in the mold will leave an undesirable residue. Molds are available in single, double (as shown) or four-cavity models.

Bullets can be cast and processed in the same area in which you reload. All primers and propellant should be cleaned up, containers sealed and put away. There are no special fixtures needed. A folded towel will cushion the bullets as they fall from the mold. An old box will serve to catch sprue and rejects.

Venturing into bullet casting is really a rather simple task. Sure, there are plenty of variables with which to wrestle, but excellent results can be had right from the first by choosing good equipment and following the instructions for its use.

Melting and Fluxing Bullet Metal: When working with bullet metal, one of the first requirements is a suitable heat source capable of heating the metal to about 750° or 800° Fahrenheit. A simple cast iron pot to hold the metal and most any heat source (kitchen stove, etc.) will suffice. Improved equipment, such as the Lyman Electric Furnace, is more desirable. The electric furnace is cleaner, safer and more convenient. Its adjustable thermostat allows best control of the melt temperature. Whether you are blending the various metals into an alloy or actually casting bullets, the same melting and fluxing procedure is followed.

Heat the metal for about 20 minutes until it be-

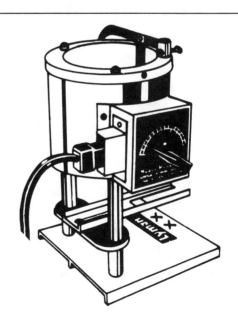

Typical bullet-casting furnace.

comes a free-flowing liquid ready for fluxing.

To flux the metal merely drop a small bit of tallow, beeswax or bullet lubricant into the mixture. A smoky gas will rise from the top of the pot and should be immediately ignited with a match to eliminate the smoke.

A more modern and much more pleasant fluxing procedure is to use a dry substance, such as the product called MARVELUX. Smoke and greasy fumes are eliminated—an important benefit to those casters with wives and/or mothers in residence—and a good flux is obtained. This method is much preferable to the foregoing traditional technique.

Whichever flux substance you choose, be sure to stir the mixture with the dipper. As you stir, hold the dipper so the cup side is down and raise it out of the metal with each stirring stroke. This seems to help the flux.

Metal that has been properly fluxed will leave the surface almost mirror-bright and flecked with small particles of black and brown impurities. Skim off and discard these impurities. Flux the metal whenever, by its appearance, it seems to need it. While the dipper is not in use, it should be left in the molten metal to keep it hot.

Casting Bullets: After the metal has been fluxed and is hot enough to pour through the dipper, it is ready for casting. In addition to the mold, you should have on hand a hardwood stick (about 10 inches long) to be used for opening the mold. Also, pad a small area of your bench with an old piece of cloth or carpet. This will soften the fall of the hot bullets as they drop from the mold and prevent them from being damaged.

While there is no set way to dipper-cast good bullets, the following method is suggested. Fill the dipper with metal and place the spout of the dipper against the pouring hole in the mold's sprue plate. Holding the mold and dipper together, slowly turn them to a vertical position with the dipper above the mold.

Casting via the bottom-pour valve on your electric furnace may require a slightly different technique. Instead of holding the mold tight against the external bottom pour valve and lifting the operating lever to release molten lead, it is often better to leave a little space between the mold and the bottom-pour valve—no more than an inch.

The latter method allows a good sprue puddle to form and, in some instances, may enhance the escape of air from the mold as the molten lead pours in.

If you find the lead is solidifying in the bottom-pour valve, increase the pot temperature. Keep an ingot mold handy to catch drips.

The extra metal that runs over the top of the mold is called sprue. When it hardens, which takes several seconds, pick up the hardwood stick and tap the sprue cutter sharply. This will separate the sprue from the base of the bullet. Drop the sprue into a cardboard box, or other receptacle. Open the mold and let the bullet fall to the pad. If the bullet does not drop out readily, use the stick to rap the hinge pivot sharply. Use only wood for this purpose and never strike the mold blocks themselves.

It is very important to pour a generous sprue and allow it to harden. As the bullet cools, it draws down metal from the molten sprue. If it cannot (i.e. the sprue has already hardened or is of insufficient size), then internal voids will form.

Further, cutting a still-molten sprue damages the bullet's base and often creates a buildup of smeared alloy between the cutoff plate and mold blocks.

As the mold will be cool, your first bullets will be imperfect. Casting bullets, one after the other, will bring the mold to the proper temperature. If you wish, the mold can be preheated by placing it on the rim of your furnace, or alongside your lead pot on the stove. Never dunk the mold in the molten metal or subject it to direct flame.

Wrinkled bullets indicate that the mold, and/or metal, is too cool. Frosted bullets indicate that the mold, and/or metal, is too hot. Good bullets should be clean, sharp and fill the mold. Imperfect bullets should be collected and, along with the sprue, returned to the pot.

Bullets selected for accuracy shooting should be carefully weighed on the reloading scale. This reveals air pockets that may have formed in the bullet, lightening or unbalancing it. The actual weight of your bullets will depend pretty much on the composition of your bullet metal, which may vary slightly from lot to lot. Rejected bullets may be saved and recast.

Sizing and Lubrication: The sizing process is merely a method of swaging cast bullets to a diameter that corresponds to, or slightly exceeds, the groove diameter of your gun. Bullet sizing also ensures that the bearing bands of each and every bullet in the group are made perfectly round. As no metal is removed from the bullet (bullet is swaged to shape and size), sizing does not alter the bullet's as-cast weight.

Generally speaking, the less a bullet must be sized, the more accurately it will shoot. Some cast bullet shooters feel that .002 inches is the most a bullet can be sized and retain the ability to perform accurately.

Whether .002 inches is, indeed, the magic number is only part of the overall question.

The real questions are the true dimensions of your gun. Rifles should be measured both at the muzzle and just past the chamber mouth.Handguns should receive the same bore measurements while revolvers should have each chamber mouth measured. The results of these tests should show you where to start.

To obtain these measurements you must drive a pure lead slug into the barrel or chamber mouth. Use two slugs on the barrel (revolver owners may want to use just one; maneuvering around the frame to introduce that second slug is tough) and a separate one for each chamber in a revolver's cylinder and identify them with the cylinder they came from.

Normally, you define your initial "size to" diameter as one which will match, or slightly exceed, the groove diameter just ahead of the chamber. Sometimes revolver shooters have the matter confused by having a groove diameter larger than that of their chamber mouths. They should select their first sizing die on the basis of barrel, not chamber, dimensions.

Bullet casters should expect to experiment with several sizing diameters, just as they'll use several types of propellant, in a given load-development program. Normally, these other diameters will be greater than the groove diameter as discussed above. To shoot an undersize cast bullet is to invite almost certain leading and inaccuracy.

Lyman plans the "as-cast" diameter of each caliber grouping to permit maximum utility within reasonable sizing ranges. The company does not claim that Lyman molds will cast to a single guaranteed diameter or that said cast bullets will be perfectly round, but does state that each mold is manufactured to cast a specified size in #2 Alloy with a manufacturing tolerance for both diameter variation and out-of-roundness.

The production of molds to a customer's specification is the domain of the custom mold maker—and there are few (if any) who will guarantee a perfectly round cast bullet from their mold. Of course, the cost of such a custom mold is much greater than those produced for general consumption.

So the bullet which drops from a mold is intended to be reduced in diameter and trued up by the sizing process.

Sizing the cast bullet has been done a number of ways over the years. Today all sizing dies feature tapered leads which allow excess metal to be swaged, rather than shaved, into dimensional conformity.

Lubricant, applied to the grooved body of a given bullet design, provides a film between the bullet metal and the walls of the bore. This film greatly reduces friction as the bullet travels down the barrel and either eliminates or minimizes leading.

LYMAN BULLET DESIGNS

Lyman molds can turn out a variety of cast bullets ranging from .22 to .44 caliber. Here are some Lyman bullets in a variety of sizes and weights.

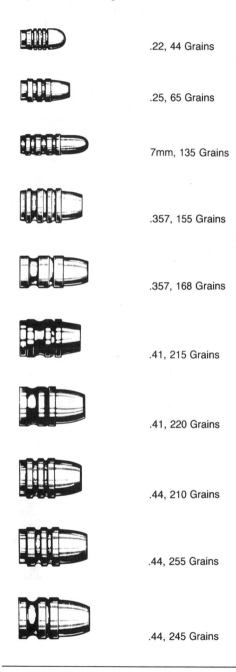

.22, 44 Grains

.25, 65 Grains

7mm, 135 Grains

.357, 155 Grains

.357, 168 Grains

.41, 215 Grains

.41, 220 Grains

.44, 210 Grains

.44, 255 Grains

.44, 245 Grains

SHOTSHELLS

Case Inspection

Repeated firing and reloading will eventually wear out your cases, so develop the habit of inspecting them carefully before each reloading, and be fussy with them. Check each case for defects in the inner base wad.

At one time we recommended that a small dowel be used as a depth gauge to check the inside of each case. However, this does not always work, because sometimes only small portions of the base wad are blown away, and the dowel method of checking is not exact enough to pick up such small defects.

Discard cases that have torn, split, or blown-away mouths. Such cases will not crimp properly. Check the case walls for pinhole burns. Also, twist the case head slightly in your fingers to see if it has loosened from the case body.

While the foregoing pre-loading inspection is adequate to make sure your cases are in good condition, you should also keep alert to case defects that show up in loading. For instance, if a spent primer decaps too easily, or a new primer seats too easily, then it is an indication that the primer pocket has stretched due to fatigue. This condition can sometimes be picked up in your pre-loading inspection by looking for dark smudges around the primer. Such cases should also be thrown away.

Basic Mechanics

To the novice who has never reloaded his own ammunition, the mechanical procedure of shotshell reloading may at first appear to be somewhat difficult. Actually, it is so amazingly simple that all of the eight basic operations can be learned in a matter of minutes. Let's run through them briefly and see what they consist of.

Loading Shotshells

You will require a shotshell reloading tool equipped with dies to accommodate your gauge. The basic tool will supply the leverage, while the dies will perform the varied operations required to reload a shotshell.

STATION 1. (Decapping): The very first operation is to push out the old or fired primer. Select a fired casing and slip the case up over the decapping punch as illustrated. Hold the case in position with your hand as you pull down on the press handle. The punch will move downward and carry the case along with it. Added pressure on the handle at the bottom of the stroke will pop out the spent primer. Raise the handle and remove the casing. It is now ready for the next station.

STATION 2. (Priming and Charging of Powder): On this station we complete two of the eight operations by putting a new primer and a measured powder charge into the case. The new primer is placed (flange down) into the priming base as illustrated on page 210. Now, place the head of the shotshell in the circular recess over the primer. As you pull down lightly on the press handle, you will notice that the powder drop tube will enter the case and

SHOTSHELL RELOADING OPERATIONS

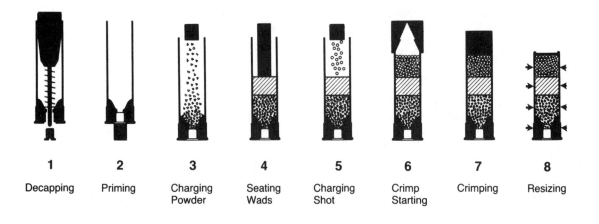

1	2	3	4	5	6	7	8
Decapping	Priming	Charging Powder	Seating Wads	Charging Shot	Crimp Starting	Crimping	Resizing

force it down over the primer. The pressure applied to the handle should be only hard enough to seat the new primer, and no more. Hold the handle in the down position as you operate the powder slide. Pull the slide out and push it smoothly with a single stroke in each direction. Your shell is now primed and charged with powder. Raise the press handle and remove the case. It is ready for station three.

STATION 3. (Seating Wads and Charging Shot): Once the case has been primed and charged with powder, it advances to station three where we insert the wads and drop in a charge of shot. Here again we perform two loading operations at a single station. In order that the wads may enter the case easily, the case is first inserted into a wad chamber, as shown in the illustration. Start the wads into the chamber by hand and then set the wad chamber (with the case still inside) into the base collar over the pressure gauge.

Pull down on the press handle and the wad will seat firmly against the powder. A glance at the pressure gauge will tell you how much wad pressure you are applying. Hold the handle down as you operate the shot slide. Pull the slide out and push it in smoothly with a single stroke in each direction.

Raise the press handle and remove your case from the wad chamber. It is now ready for crimping.

STATION 4. (Starting the Crimp): The plastic used in today's shotshell cases is a tough material that will not bend into a crimp form as readily as the old paper cases. Therefore, it is necessary to complete the crimp in two stages. The first stage is called crimp starting.

Depending on brand and style, cases vary in the number of folds or pleats, which are used to close the crimp. Some cases require eight folds, others six. Make sure that your crimp starter is equipped

STATION 1: DECAPPING

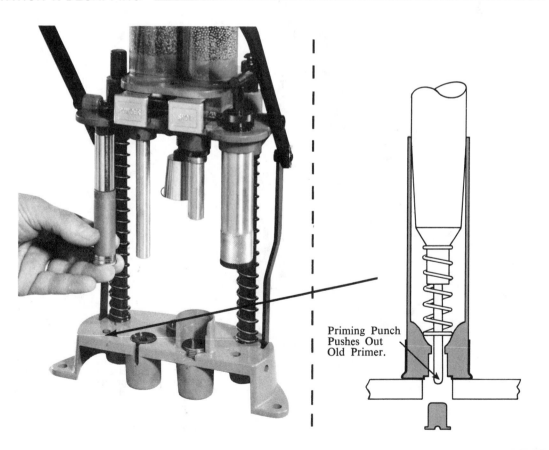

Priming Punch
Pushes Out
Old Primer.

with the appropriate head for the case.

To use the crimp starter, simply place your charged case in the alignment base under the starter as shown in the illustration and pull down the handle. The self-aligning arm will pivot the starter head so that it meshes exactly to the existing folds in the case mouth.

STATION 5. (Crimping and Sizing): This is the final operation in loading a shotshell. At this station we close the mouth of the case with a good firm crimp and resize the walls so that the case will chamber freely.

Slip your shotshell up into the crimping and sizing die as shown in the illustration, and pull the press handle all the way down. Allow the handle to rise slowly. Now, firmly force the press handle up so that the ejector rod contacts the ejector stop. This action will automatically free your finished reload from the die.

STATION 2: PRIMING AND CHARGING POWDER

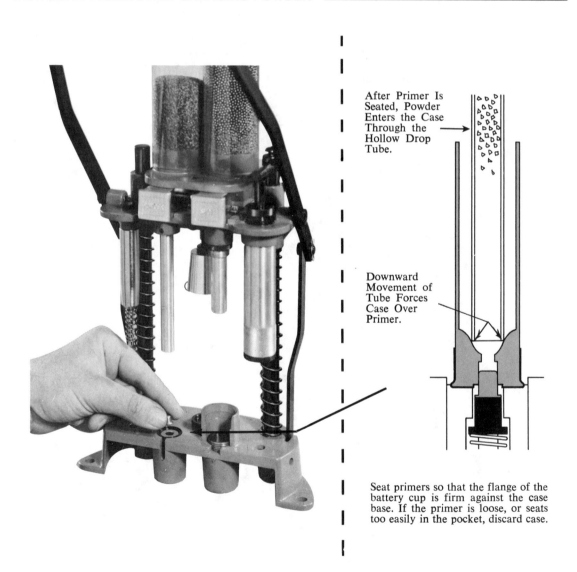

After Primer Is Seated, Powder Enters the Case Through the Hollow Drop Tube.

Downward Movement of Tube Forces Case Over Primer.

Seat primers so that the flange of the battery cup is firm against the case base. If the primer is loose, or seats too easily in the pocket, discard case.

STATION 3: SEATING WADS AND CHARGING SHOT

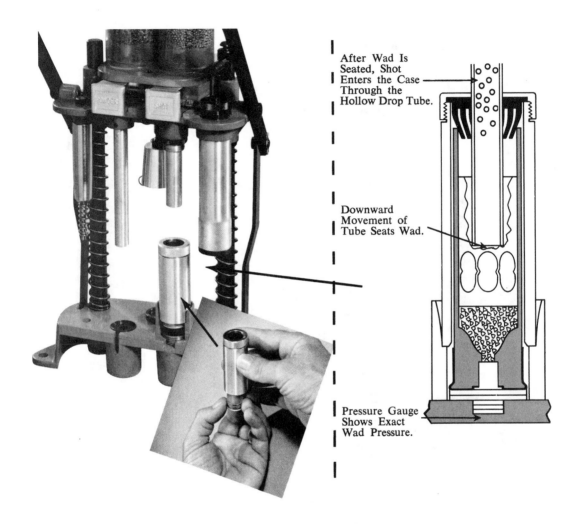

After Wad Is Seated, Shot Enters the Case Through the Hollow Drop Tube.

Downward Movement of Tube Seats Wad.

Pressure Gauge Shows Exact Wad Pressure.

STATION 4: STARTING THE CRIMP

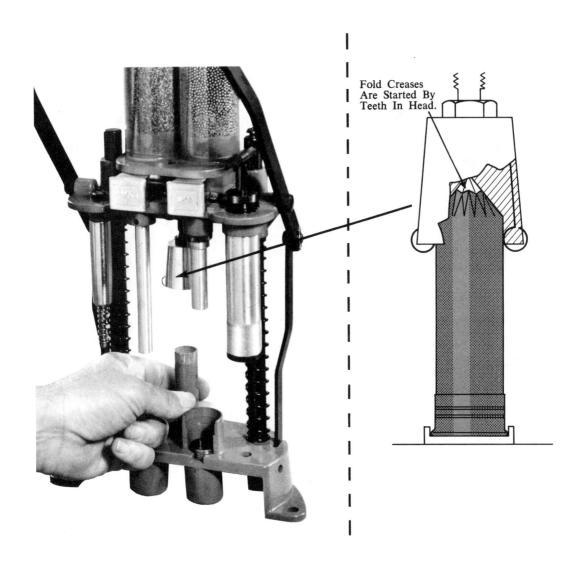

Fold Creases
Are Started By
Teeth In Head.

STATION 5: CRIMPING AND SIZING

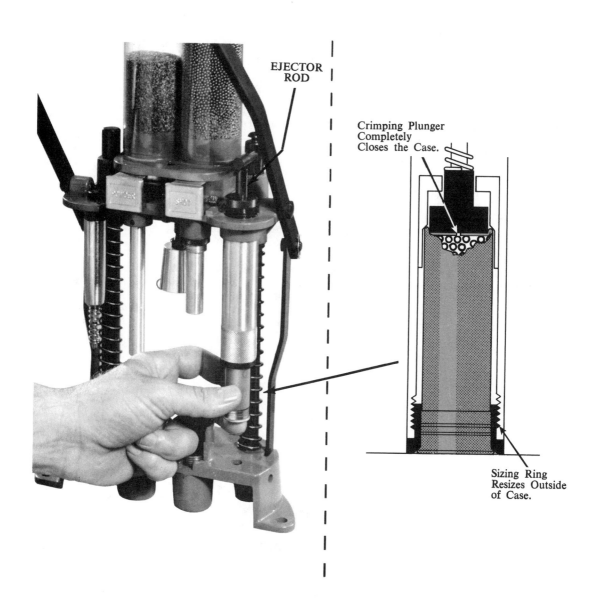

EJECTOR ROD

Crimping Plunger
Completely
Closes the Case.

Sizing Ring
Resizes Outside
of Case.

WHERE TO HIT BIG GAME

The most important factor in killing big game quickly and cleanly is bullet placement. Even a .375 Magnum won't knock down a small whitetail for keeps unless the deer is hit in a vital organ. Caliber means little if a hunter doesn't put the bullet where it will be most effective. You'll minimize chances of losing wounded game if you take time to study the animals you hunt and learn the location of vital organs.

The accompanying drawings show the anatomy of popular big game and the aiming points that are important. The information should also benefit the bowhunter, whose arrow kills by hemorrhage. He should note especially the location of main arteries.

Though the most vital organ in any animal is the brain, you should rule out a brain shot 98 percent of the time. The brain is a small target and easy to miss. A brain shot is also a poor choice for a trophy hunter. A brain shot on a deer, for example, will shatter the base of the skull, making a head mount nearly impossible. Bears are scored by skull dimensions, and any head shot on a bruin will smash the skull and make scoring impossible. When is a brain shot justified? Only on dangerous game when it is charging. In North America, this means bears. Aim

to hit two inches above center of the eyes of a bear, and you should hit the brain.

Neck shots involve some risk of wounding antlered game because the spinal column in the neck is only about two inches in diameter. If you hit neck muscles and arteries but miss the spine, your deer may run a fair distance before dropping. A neck shot is a fair choice only at close range, where you can be reasonably sure of putting your bullet into the spinal column.

What is the best shot? Let's talk in terms of vital areas as opposed to vital organs. The forward one-third of a deer is a vital area since it houses the heart, lungs, several major arteries, spine, and shoulder. Any bullet hitting these organs will bring down a big-game animal.

The best shot, then, is at a vital organ in a vital area—specifically the heart. Though a heart shot frequently will not drop an animal in its tracks, it is always a fatal shot, and tracking a heart-shot animal is not difficult. One big advantage of aiming for the heart is that a miss will generally still hit some other vital organ.

A shot at the heart, for example, will likely put the bullet into the lungs also. A hit in the lungs may

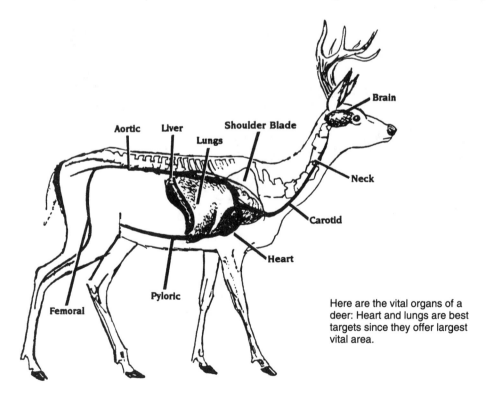

Here are the vital organs of a deer: Heart and lungs are best targets since they offer largest vital area.

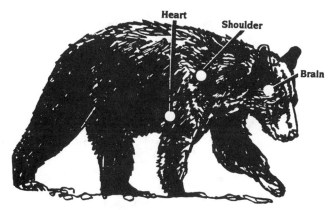

If bear is unaware of your presence, try a heart or a shoulder shot. Shoulder may be best, as it's likely to drop bruin

A brain shot should be taken only when a bear is charging. Shoulder is a better and larger target area

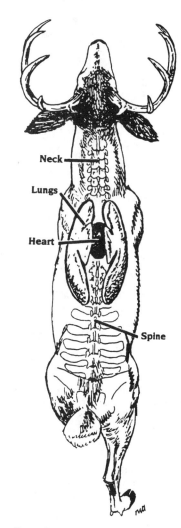

knock a deer down through shock. If not, the animal will eventually die through hemorrhaging.

No animal can survive a bullet through the lungs, but it may sometimes travel a good distance. If you spot blood on brush a few feet off the ground and to the side of the tracks, blood is coming from the sides of the deer—a good indication of a lung hit. The deer will be bleeding freely, and tracking should not be difficult. Frothy blood is another sign of a lung hit.

Recognizing blood and hair signs can be useful to hunter. Bright red blood generally means a heart or lung shot. A deer shot in the heart, however, may not start to bleed immediately, so follow the tracks until you can confirm a miss or hit. If you spot brown-yellow blood, particularly if bits of white

If buck walks under your tree stand, aim between shoulder blades to put your bullet into the heart and lungs

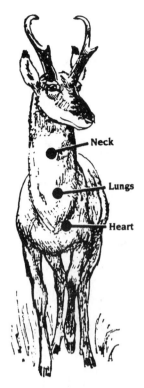

Aiming points for vital organs on frontal shot: try for upper part of heart so bullet will also hit lungs

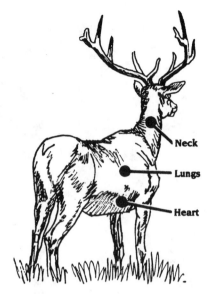

When animal is quartering away, aim farther back; drive bullet at angle

hair are in it, you can be reasonably sure that the deer is gut shot. This is unfortunate since a gut-shot animal can travel a great distance before dying. If you've gut-shot an animal, stick with the track. You'll get it eventually, but it won't be easy.

The track itself can be a tip-off to the location of a wound. A broken leg will show as drag marks in snow or mud. Blood in or right next to the tracks may mean a leg wound.

If your initial shot is high, missing both heart and lungs, your bullet may still hit a vital spot. Such a shot may shatter the shoulder, breaking the animal down and rendering it helpless.

The only time a hunter should intentionally aim for the shoulder is on dangerous game. A bear hunter, for example, wants to knock down and immobilize a bruin quickly, especially if it's charging. A shoulder shot will do it (if a brain shot is considered too risky), and the hunter can then put in a killing shot with little danger.

Once you know where the vital organs are, you must also know where to put your rifle sights in relation to the animal's position.

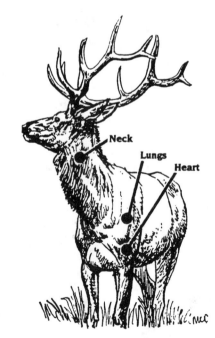

Game quartering toward you presents similar situation. Note aiming points

To hit the heart when an antlered animal is broadside, put your sights just above where the foreleg joins the body. Aim a big high, so that if you miss the top portion of the heart you will still hit the lungs.

If a buck is facing you, put your sights just below dead center on its chest. If your shot is a good one, you'll hit the top of the heart as well as the lungs.

If you are in a tree stand and a buck walks under you, a somewhat different problem arises. Since less heart and lung area is available, the best aim is right between the shoulder blades for a hit in heart and lungs. Remember that you are shooting from above and various angles must be taken into account.

Quartering animals present some problems. Excited hunters frequently assume that a quartering animal presents the same target as a broadside. But on a deer quartering away, your points of aim should be farther back on the body.

GETTING BIG GAME HOME

If you're one of the lucky big-game hunters, you will have to haul a sizable animal out of the woods and safely home.

Handling big game requires some planning. First, make sure you are carrying the right gear. In a small day pack or in your pockets, you should be carrying a 10 or 12 foot length of rope, a small bone saw, and a knife. If you're planning to hunt elk or moose in a remote area where you might have to quarter an animal to carry it out, I would also include a small pulley and a hand ax.

The easiest and best way to get a deer out of the field is to drag it out. On snow or leaves, a deer will slide easy. If the terrain is rough, however, drag your deer out on a small piece of tarp. Make sure the head or rack is securely tied to one end of the tarp, which will act as a sled.

Two men can easily drag out a deer, but you can do it alone if you don't rush and stop to rest often. After you have field-dressed the deer, tie the front legs behind the head with your drag line and then loop it around the deer's muzzle. When you pull your deer, it will be more streamlined and slide without hanging up on rocks and shrubs.

If you're alone, make a loop in your drag line and wrap it around your body like a harness. You will get more leverage if you use your body rather than your arms to drag a deer. Your drag line should also be short enough to lift the deer's head off the ground when you're dragging it.

A small field-dressed deer will weigh under 100 pounds and can probably be carried out by one hunter. Simply lash all four feet together and carry it on one shoulder with the head to the rear. With your hand on the opposite side, reach around, grab the head and hold it to your side. For safety, always wrap a red bandana or a blaze orange vest around the carcass when carrying it out.

When you have a heavy deer or a black bear, tie its legs together and then run a thick tree limb between its legs and as close to the body as possible. Two men can place the pole on their shoulders and carry it out. Always remember to tie a red or orange bandana to the carcass. If you and a friend are carrying out a deer, talk loudly so other hunters will hear you. If you're alone, whistle as loud as you can.

Once you get your deer to your car, you will have a different set of problems. If practical, haul it back on the roof of your vehicle. Your deer should be protected inside your vehicle, but not the back seat. The trunk is the best place because it's unheated. With the threat of Lyme disease from deer ticks, it's also a good idea to keep the carcass away from car heaters and your own body.

If you must transport a deer outside your vehicle, wrap it in blankets and tie it on the roof of your car. Never haul it on a fender or hood, where engine heat may "cook" the meat by the time you get home.

When you're forced to quarter an animal, leave the hide on. If you want to save the hide for tanning, then you should make sure someone has some plastic bags to protect the meat in transit. Once you get to camp, however, take the meat out of the plastic bags and hang it to air dry. If there are flies around, sprinkle the meat with black pepper. In fact, any game meat hanging in camp during warm weather should be coated with black pepper to keep the bugs off.

THE GAME PROCESSORS

Every fall hunters spend thousands of dollars on big game hunts. If they are lucky, they will take a trophy whitetail or an elk or a moose. Whatever the trophy, these hunters will look for a reliable butcher to process and ship their meat home.

The averge bull elk may weigh from 500 to 600 pounds. That's a lot of meat and it represents a sizable investment. When you turn it over to a butcher, make sure it's the right man. First, don't be taken in by the processor who advertises the most. Many good game processors don't advertise at all. Based on their good reputation, word-of-mouth recommendations produce more business than they can handle.

It's important to remember that wild-game processing is basically exempt from USDA regulations, which means that temperature control, cleanliness, and packing are pretty much left to the discretion of the processor or butcher. You will have to determine the cleanliness of the cutting tables, knives, grinders, saws and other equipment.

If you're planning to hunt out-of-state, plan to arrive a couple of days before your hunt. In addition to scouting and setting up camp, the extra time will give you a chance to find the right processor. Start by inquiring at sporting goods stores, game wardens, gas stations, and cafés. If one person is recommended by different people, plan to pay him a visit.

Use common sense. If a processing plant has a foul smell, find out why, but be fair. The smell may be coming from meat that was already contaminated before it was brought into the place. Look around the floor. Are there fresh meat scraps on the floor or have they been there awhile. Check the saw. If it's not cleaned regularly, it will smell. Brown stains around a meat grinder are a good sign that the processor doesn't clean his place regularly.

It is not unreasonable to ask a processor to see his cooler. If game is skinned and field-dressed properly, the meat doesn't smell, so be suspicious of a cooler that has a questionable odor. If a cooler is overloaded with game, it will run several degrees warmer than the preferred 36 to 38 degrees. If you're not sure, don't leave your animal there. Remember that the stench of overaged (rotting) meat can't be disguised.

If you have to rely on an outfitter, ask him for the name of his processor long before your hunt. Call him and ask for references. If he procrastinates or refuses to cooperate, look elsewhere. In the West, you will be charged by hanging weight, so insist that any processor weighs your meat in front of you. And stay there until he tags the carcass with your name before placing it in cold storage.

If you're not sure how you want the meat cut, tell your processor to butcher it into steaks, chops, roasts, and leave the tenderloin whole. The burger trim should be ground into hamburger or made into sausage (fresh, summer, or smoked).

THE BEST VENISON

It's true that venison should be allowed to cure for at least a week before eating, but this is not true of the tenderloins and liver, which can be eaten soon after a deer or elk is brought into camp. Prepared properly, the tenderloins and liver can be turned into delicious dinners in camp or at home.

The tenderloins are two small strips of meat, measuring one to two inches in diameter and about 12 to 15 inches long. They are located on both sides of the backbone inside the upper chest cavity. The tenderloins can only be removed from inside the chest cavity. Don't confuse the tenderloins with the backstraps, which are cut away from both sides of the backbone from outside the carcass. Backstraps, incidentally, produce your venison filet mignon. But even the backstraps cannot compare with the tenderloins, the tenderest part of a deer.

As soon as you field-dress that deer, cut out the tenderloins. Do it before the air has a chance to toughen the meat's surface. Use a small knife to separate the tenderloins from the cavity. Once the initial cut is made, you may be able to pull the tenderloins free. But do it carefully because the meat is so tender it may tear.

Cooking the tenderloins back in camp or at home is easy. Because the meat is tender and tasty, a simple recipe that will not alter the flavor is best. In deer camp, where you want to keep cooking time down to a minimum, cut the tenderloins into medallions about one-half inch thick and coat them with salt, pepper, and a touch of garlic powder. Then sauté the pieces in a hot skillet greased with butter until the meat is rare and pink inside.

At home, marinate the tenderloins in Italian salad dressing for an hour or so, then put them on a hot grill and only allow the charcoal to sear the exterior.

When the inside of the tenderloins are pink, take them off the grill and slice them into medallions. The tenderloins are a perfect first fare for those people who have traditionally refused to eat venison.

In deer camp, the tenderloins are always the appetizer and the liver is the main course. When you take the liver out of your deer during the field-dressing operation, wipe it clean and put it in a plastic bag. Back in damp, soak it in a pan of water with a cup of salt. Keep changing the water until the liver is thoroughly purged of blood, then pat dry.

Preparing liver is just as easy as the tenderloins. All you need is about a pound of bacon, four or five onions, flour and butter. First, fry the bacon in a skillet. In a second skillet sauté the sliced onions with butter until the onions are soft and transparent. When both bacon and onions are done, set them aside. Now flour the liver, which you've already cut into slices one-half inch thick, and fry them in the skillet with the bacon drippings. Serve the bacon and onions over the liver.

VENISON JERKY

When frontiersmen headed west and mountain men ran traplines in the Rockies, these adventurers had a common problem: no refrigerators or freezers. The only way they could preserve meat was to dry it. We don't have those problems today, but sportsmen still enjoy making and eating dried meat. We prefer to make it from venison and we call it jerky. It's a great trail food and it's easy to make in your kitchen.

Jerky is nothing more than lean raw meat with all the moisture removed. Round steak from a deer, elk, moose, caribou, or antelope makes the best jerky. Fatty meat, such as bear and wild boar, does not make very good jerky.

You can also use domestic beef to make jerky. Just make sure the meat is very lean. You must also trim away all fat, sinew, and gristle—too much fat in jerky can cause rancid meat.

You can use the sun to dry meat, but it's safer and more convenient to use your kitchen oven or a fruit dehydrator. Always remember that you are drying the meat and not cooking it.

First, cut the venison with the grain into strips about six inches long, one-inch wide and one-quarter-inch thick. Next, coat the meat with salt and pepper, then brush heavily with Liquid Smoke, which you can find in any supermarket. Let the meat marinate overnight in your refrigerator.

The next day, drain the meat on paper towels and place the strips in your oven. It's best to run a toothpick through the end of a strip and hang it from your oven rack. Put a tray under the meat to catch the drippings. Most ovens will handle about two dozen strips.

Now set your oven at about 130 degrees or its lowest setting. Use a meat thermometer to make sure the oven stays at 130 degrees. Drying time may vary slightly, but most of the time it takes about 10 to 12 hours. It's important to leave the oven door slightly open to allow moisture to escape.

If it has dried properly, the meat will be dark with no moisture in its center. You should also be able to bend the strips of meat without breaking.

You can store the meat in any moisture-proof containers. Any jar with a tight lid of a ziplock-type plastic bag will do. You can eat jerky anytime. Just bite off a piece and start chewing. The saliva from your mouth will reconstitute the dried meat into tasty food.

There are all kinds of variations to making jerky. If you don't like the Liquid Smoke taste, marinate the venison in equal parts of soy sauce and Worcestershire sauce and one-quarter teaspoon of garlic powder. If you like it hot, substitute cayenne pepper for garlic powder. You can also rub the meat with sugar cure before drying, then coat the meat completely after drying with steak sauce.

There is also no need to limit yourself to venison. You can just as easily make turkey or pheasant jerky. Because you will need strips, the meat must come from the breasts of these birds. Cut the strips two or three inches long with the grain of the meat running lengthwise. Season the breast meat the same as the venison meat. The drying process, however, may take less time. Depending on the thickness of the cuts, four to six hours in your oven, set on the lowest temperature, should do it.

FIELD CARE OF GAMEBIRDS

Many pheasants, grouse, chukars, and other game-birds have been ruined between the time of the kill and the time they reached the table. Some hunters will put a bird into a hot, rubber-lined game pocket, leaving it there to "cook" and perhaps to spoil by the day's end.

Other hunters may field-dress a bird, let it hang a couple of days, and then try to dry pluck it. The usual result is that pieces of the skin are torn away and the bird is a mess.

Here's sound advice from more than a few shooting preserve operators who have literally cleaned thousands of pheasants and other gamebirds. These experts agree on the right way to handle a bird in the field.

Obviously, a pheasant should be field-dressed soon after it is shot, particularly in warm weather. Field-dressing is a simple operation. Make the initial cut from breast bone to anal opening carefully so that no organs are cut or broken, which can taint the meat. First, lay the bird on its back and pull the feathers off from below the breast bone to anal opening, clearing the area for the first cut. Make the cut from the soft area below the breast bone down to the anal opening. First cut the skin; then cut through the meat. Reach in and take out the viscera, pulling down toward the anal opening. Now remove the windpipe and crop.

During warm weather, pack the empty cavity with dry grass and then press the sides of the opening tightly together. The grass will absorb blood in the cavity and will keep insects from entering it. This is not necessary in cold weather, when you can leave the cavity open and let the meat cool, free of insects.

You can expedite cooling in winter by placing some snow in the body cavity. Both dry grass and snow can also be used with equal effectiveness on furred small game such as rabbits and squirrels.

Many hunters believe it is a crime to skin a bird, but some prefer to skin pheasants. One reason for skinning is because of the critical conditions necessary for effective plucking. You can easily pluck a bird immediately after it is shot and the body is warm. The feathers will pull out with little trouble, and the skin will not tear. But some hunters dislike stopping a hunt after each kill so that you can pluck a bird. Also, once a bird is plucked in the field, the bare skin is exposed to dirt and bacteria.

Once the body has cooled, a pheasant cannot be dry plucked without being torn up. It must be dipped in hot water (180 degrees). If the water is cooler or warmer than 180 degrees, the skin will tear. Because of the difficulty of maintaining the correct water temperature, this method isn't recommended. If you plan to pluck pheasants, though, remember this temperature factor.

The best bet is to field-dress the bird as soon as possible after it is shot and skin it when you get home. If you prefer, you can hang your birds in a cool dry place for a couple of days before skinning. This aging process has some merit for slightly tenderizing old cock birds, but you will generally be unable to detect any difference in taste between birds skinned at once and those skinned a few days later.

Skinning a bird is easy. Slit the skin lengthwise, keeping the cutting edge along the center of the breast bone. Now peel the skin away from the breast, down to the legs and up to the neck. Work the skin over each thigh and upper leg, stopping when you reach the leg joint. At this point, bend each leg backward until the joint cracks, and then cut off the leg. With breast and both legs now free of skin, cut the tail off at its base.

Now take each wing and bend them backward at the first joint until it cracks. Cut off the wing tips and the head. Finally, peel the skin down toward the neck and off the bird.

If you freeze your birds after skinning, make sure there are no air pockets in the package, since these air traps can cause freezer burn. When you plan to eat a bird, let it thaw slowly in the refrigerator. Don't rush it on the kitchen counter.

The absence of skin on your birds should not bother you, and it doesn't affect the table quality of the birds. Gamebirds are generally dry and must be basted frequently while cooking. Cover the birds with bacon strips. The bacon creates a "skin" for the birds, retaining body juices and adding moisture and taste.

FIELD-DRESSING YOUR BUCK

Dick Fagan, of the Pennsylvania game department, guided artist Ken Laager in the preparation of these drawings. (This series courtesy of *Outdoor Life* magazine)

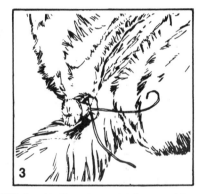

1. Remove penis and scrotum with shallow cuts. Do not pierce body cavity. **2.** With tip of knife, cut completely around the rectum to free it from rest of skin. **3.** Pull rectum outside body and tie off to prevent feces from reaching meat.

4. Open abdomen from rear to sternum (where last ribs join). Hold intestines down with fingers and back of hand so that you do not cut or pierce the intestinal tract or paunch. **5.** Cut the bladder out very carefully. Try not to spill urine.

FIELD-DRESSING YOUR BUCK (Continued)

 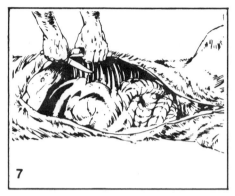 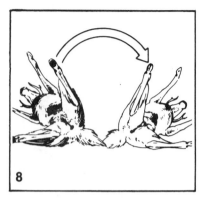

6. Pull rectum inside cavity and cut tissue holding it in place. **7.** With deer lying on one side, cut all tissues that hold the intestines in place all the way down to animal's spine. **8.** The next step is to rotate the deer over so that you can free the intestines from the other side.

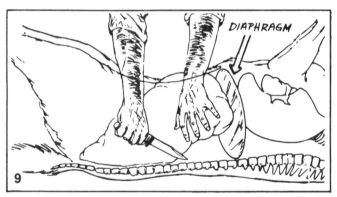 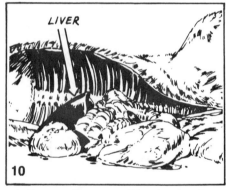

9. Repeat Step 7. Little cutting is needed. Then sever gullet in front of stomach. Do not spill contents. If you do, wipe clean. **10.** Contents of abdomen come out in one big mass. Retrieve liver and cool it quickly in open air or water.

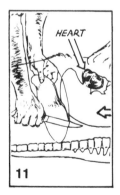 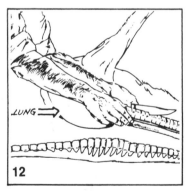 

11. Cut out diaphragm (wall from abdomen to chest.) **12.** Reach up inside chest and sever gullet and windpipe. Pull them out with lungs, heart. **13.** Wipe dry. If it's hot, it's better to split the breast, open neck and cut out rest of windpipe and gullet to avoid spoilage. If, however, head is to be mounted, "cape out" (skin) neck first.

SKINNING YOUR DEER

Dick Fagan, of the Pennsylvania game department, guided artist Ken Laager in the preparation of these drawings.

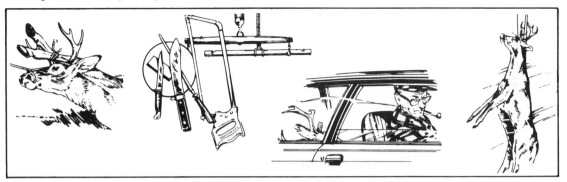

After field-dressing, tie forefeet over neck. Drag out with rope around antlers and half-hitch around upper jaw. Never subject carcass to heat. Don't user car heater; keep windows open. Hang deer in cool place (41° to 45°) for a week with hide still on to tenderize meat and enhance flavor before skinning. Methods shown result in rawhide suitable for tanning. For head and shoulders mount see Step 13.

1. With point of knife, cut hide from abdominal cut to just below both joints. Don't touch leg glands. **2.** Skin out both thighs. Try not to cut meat or inner side of skin. **3.** With deer still lying on the floor, skin out thighs to top of legs. **4.** Saw off lower legs just below the joints. Use a meat-cutting saw or crosscut wood saw.

5. Hang deer with gambrel or stick in each leg between bone and tendon. **6.** If it wasn't done during field-dressing, cut H-bone of pelvis with your saw. **7.** Continue skinning. Leave tail on hide by tunneling under it between hide and back. **8.** Hide in this area usually comes off quite easily. Pull on hide and then cut.

SKINNING YOUR DEER (Continued)

(Courtesy of *Outdoor Life* magazine)

9. Sever tail near body inside hide. This avoids cutting the hair, which you'd have to pick off meat. **10.** Use knife to separate hide from thin muscles near the abdominal lengthwise incision. **11.** Hoist deer higher. Pull with one hand and "fist" hide. **12.** Saw off forelegs. Split breast and neck and cut out the gullet.

13. Slit skin of forelegs to breast cut. (If you want deer-head mounted, by taxidermist, inset shows cuts for caping out neck. Unless you are skilled enough for meticulous skinning of eyes, ears, and nose, cut off head. Refrigerate or freeze if there is delay in delivery to taxidermist.) **14.** Skin out legs and neck. Neck is hardest area to skin. **15.** Pull hide down and then use knife. Continue to base of skull. **16.** Saw off head. Again, doing it this way avoids cutting the hair.

17. Remove dirt and debris. Cut out and discard bloodshot meat around bullet holes. Pick off all deer hair, which otherwise lends bad taste to meat when cooked. **18.** Hide still has head and tail attached. Cut head off. Wipe inside of hide dry with cloth. **19.** Sprinkle borax or salt on inside of hide. Fold lengthwise, hair out, roll it up and tie. Send hide to taxidermist/ tanner at once or store in refrigerator or freezer until you can do so.

BUTCHERING YOUR DEER

Dick Fagan, of the Pennsylvania game department, guided artist Ken Laager in the preparation of these drawings.

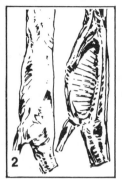
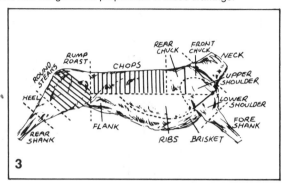

1. Cut the spine in half lengthwise. The cut *can* be corrected if it wanders. **2.** With a meat-cutting saw or fine carpenter's saw, cut the carcass into two sides. Start where the tail was severed. **3.** Dotted lines show major cuts. Solid lines indicate secondary cuts that divide roasts into two or separate steaks and chops. This drawing shows the right-hand side. After cutting the whole side, repeat cuts on the left side.

4. Divide haunch from loin. With all cuts, use knife first. If you hit bone, use saw to complete cut. A cleaver is handy but not essential. **5.** Cut rump roast off haunch. Make a neat straight cut because it determines angle of cuts for round steaks. **6.** Cut thin or thick round steaks as you prefer, but keep cuts parallel. **7.** Down toward joint, meat is tough. There, take off a chunk called the heel, usually used for stew.

8. Now for the front part. Cut entire shoulder and foreleg off the side where the shoulder joins the body. Knife blade is horizontal. **9.** There is no ball-and-socket joint, so this cut is easy. **10.** Separate shoulder from shank at joint or close to it. You need the saw for this cut. The shank is used as chop meat. **11.** The shoulder is usually divided into two separate pieces for pot roasts or stew meat.

BUTCHERING YOUR DEER (Continued)

(Courtesy of *Outdoor Life* magazine)

12. Cut off the neck. Neck is tough like shank or shoulder and is best as chop meat or stew. **13.** Saw ribs off. This long, angled cut is made where thin meat between ribs thickens toward spine. **14.** Separate chuck (under the meat cutter's left hand) from the loin. The loin is cut into chops; chuck is usually cut into two roasts. **15.** Cut the loin into chops, as thick as you like. They resemble lamb chops. These cuts are started with the knife and completed with saw.

  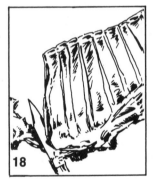 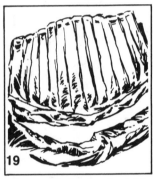

16. Trim thick fat off chops. Heavy fat should be trimmed off all cuts. It has an unpleasant flavor. **17.** Cut the chuck into two equal portions. It's too big to cook whole (usually as pot roast) unless you have a big family. **18.** This long cut starts parallel to first rib and outside it and then circles around the tips of ribs. **19.** The cut completed. It separates brisket and flank from ribs. Brisket and flank go into chop meat.

 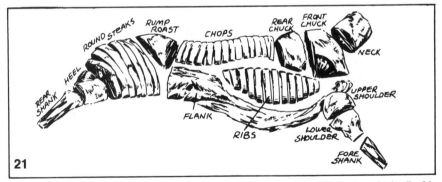

20. Separate ribs. Knife slides along bone to one side so all the meat between two ribs stays attached to single rib. **21.** Here are all the cuts from right side, properly trimmed. If you do mangle a piece, remember that you can always bone it out and grind it up for chop meat or mince meat or chop it up into chunks for stew.

BONING YOUR DEER

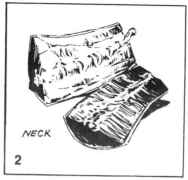

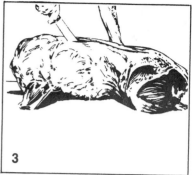

1. Begin the boning process by cutting the neck off the skinned carcass. Be sure to first cut off the meatless lower legs. **2.** Split the neck and unroll meat from the neck bone. A small knife will help. Neck meat makes good stew and roasts. **3.** The next cut, to remove backstrap, should be made from in front of the pelvic bone to the shoulder. Cut along the spine, two inches deep.

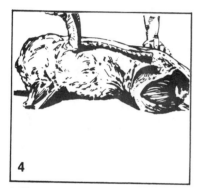

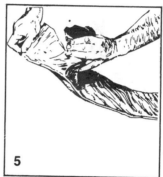

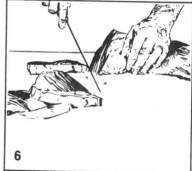

4. To extract backstrap, cut along side of ribs over the point where ribs curve down to join backbone. Loosen with fore and aft cross cuts. **5.** Repeat procedure to extract second fillet. Pull and rip the layer of fat and tissue from fillet. **6.** Many claim that this is the finest meat on the deer. Cut the trimmed loin into steaks about three-quarters to one-inch thick.

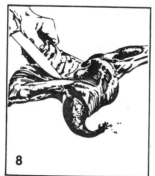

7. Remove shoulders by working your knife through tissue between leg and ribs. Detach by cutting at top of shoulder blade. **8.** Bone shoulder for use as stew meat or rolled for roast, or simply cut into three pieces. **9.** Remove shoulder roast from leg by severing at upper joint. Separate arm roast from shank with saw. Shank makes excellent venison soup.

(Courtesy of *Outdoor Life* magazine)

BONING YOUR DEER (Continued)

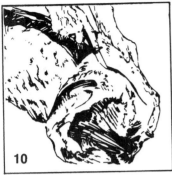

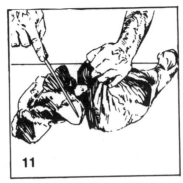

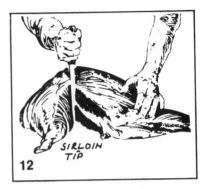

10. To detach the ham, start your cut near the tail bone. Slice the tissue and tendons, and then detach with a saw or by twisting the ball joint. **11.** The rump roast is at the top part of the ham. To remove it, make your cut as vertical as possible, leaving enough meat for a meal. **12.** Lay the hind leg on the table and remove the sirloin tip by using the leg bone to guide the knife. Start at the kneecap and work up.

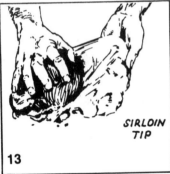

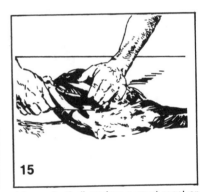

13. Once sirloin tip has been removed, trim scrap and tissue. This piece, resembling a football, makes a great roast or can be cut into steaks. **14.** In removing bone from the remaining piece (round), cut tissue separating shank from round and bone. **15.** Shave and cut meat loose from the leg bone. This will take maneuvering around the joints, but keep cutting.

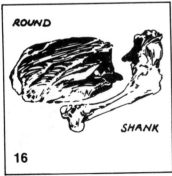

16. Here's what the finished product should look like. Now separate the round into its individual muscle pieces, each encased in tissue. **17.** Divide by cutting connective membrane. Avoid cutting into meat. Trim scrap for grinding or stew. **18.** Chunks of trimmed round can be sliced thin for use as steaks and made on the barbecue or cooked whole as roasts.

PART 2
GAME ANIMALS
AND BIRDS

BIG-GAME ANIMALS

All photos by Leonard Rue Enterprises

Grizzly Bear (*Ursus arctos*)

RANGE: Mostly in inland Alaska, though there are small herds of grizzlies in the Rocky Mountains. A variety of the grizzly, the Alaska brown bear, once considered to be a separate species, inhabits the Alaska Peninsula to its southernmost point. Limited sections of British Columbia, the Yukon Territory, and nearby islands are also inhabited by the brown bear.

IDENTIFICATION: The grizzly bear has a compact, powerful frame, with long thick hair ranging from dark brown through shades of tan to almost yellow. The tips of the hairs are grizzled; hence the bear's name. The grizzly has sharply curved claws, 3¾ inches long, which it uses for fighting and digging. The grizzly has a prominent shoulder hump, a feature which distinguishes it from the black and polar bears.

SIZE: The typical grizzly is 6 to 8 feet long; the distance from its foot to the top of its hump is about 3½ feet. Average weight is 800 pounds, though some grizzlies have gone as high as 1,100.

The world-record grizzly, whose skull was picked up in Bella Coola Valley, British Columbia, in 1970, scored 27⁷⁄₁₆ points in the Boone and Crockett competition. The record skull measured 17⁹⁄₁₆ inches long and 9¹²⁄₁₆ inches wide.

The brown bear, largest of the carnivorous, land-based mammals, reaches 8 to 10 feet in length and stands 4½ feet at the top of its shoulder. The average male weighs 1,000 pounds, the female rarely more than 800. Some browns on record have weighed over 1,500 pounds.

The world-record Alaska brown bear, killed by Roy Lindsley on Kodiak Island in 1952, scored

GRIZZLY BEAR

BLACK BEAR

POLAR BEAR

30¹²⁄₁₆ points in the Boone and Crockett Club competition. The record male's skull measured 17¹⁵⁄₁₆ inches long and 12¹³⁄₁₆ inches wide.

FOOD: The grizzly is classified as a carnivore, but because grasses, sedges, roots, and tubers of plants are readily available, the grizzly has omnivorous tendencies. Salmon, mice, snakes, and frogs also supplement this bear's diet.

EDIBILITY: Indians and outdoorsmen used to eat the flesh in early times, but the grizzly bear is primarily a trophy animal today.

Black Bear (*Ursus americanus*)

RANGE: Every Canadian province and Alaska are populated with black bears, as are substantial portions of the United States from Montana south through Arizona and New Mexico. Sections of the northeastern, northwestern and Gulf Coast states are inhabited by the species, along with northern Mexico and northeastern Arkansas.

IDENTIFICATION: Shiny black hair covers a major part of the body, but turns lighter about the eyes and muzzle. A blaze of white adorning the chest is a distinguishing characteristic, as is the absence of the conspicuous shoulder hump of the Alaska brown bear and the grizzly bear.

SIZE: A prime male averages between 300 and 400 pounds; a female far less. Some black bears on record have scaled more than 600 pounds. The average animal stands 3 feet high at the shoulder and measures 5½ feet in length.

The world-record bear, a skull picked up in San Pete County, Utah, in 1975, scored 23¹⁰⁄₁₆ points in the Boone and Crockett competition. The skull measured 14¹²⁄₁₆ inches long and 8¹⁴⁄₁₆ inches wide.

FOOD: The black bear tends to be omnivorous, eating grasses, fruits, berries, buds, fish, rodents, and sedges. Dead bears, ants, and bees are also on its menu.

EDIBILITY: The meat is dark and tends to be coarse. But it is very good when handled and prepared properly.

Polar Bear (*Ursus maritimus*)

RANGE: Polar bears are found predominantly in regions of the Arctic coast, ranging from Labrador west to Alaska's Seward Peninsula, and south along the Hudson Bay and James Bay shore.

IDENTIFICATION: The polar bear's body is almost completely covered by long, thick, yellow-white fur during the entire year. Only the lips, eyes, nose and toenails are black. The head is small and tapering, the neck long and muscular, and the body somewhat pear-shaped.

SIZE: Though the male averages 1,000 pounds, some have been reported as heavy as 1,600 pounds. A prime male stands 4 feet high at the shoulder, usually measuring 8 feet in length. Females tend to be smaller.

The world-record polar bear was taken by Shelby Longoria in 1963 off Kotzebue, Alaska. The male had a Boone and Crockett Club score of $29^{15}/_{16}$ points, with a skull measuring $18^{8}/_{16}$ inches in length and $11^{7}/_{16}$ inches in width. The polar bear is currently ineligible, until further notice, for the North American Big Game competition.

FOOD: The most carnivorous bear of all, the polar bear dines on seals, foxes, mollusks, lemmings, birds, caribou, and dead or helpless whales. Often, however, this species eats seaweed, grasses, and roots.

EDIBILITY: The meat is the main staple in the diet of the Eskimos, but the liver can be poisonous due to excessive amounts of Vitamin A within.

Whitetail Deer
(*Odocoileus virginianus*)

RANGE: The whitetail deer inhabits a vast section of North America, from southern Canada down through the southern border of the United States. Only a few dry regions of western North America are devoid of whitetails.

IDENTIFICATION: In spring the whitetail sports a bright brownish-red coat made up of thin hair. With the coming of winter a new coat grows, long, kinky hair, varying in color from brownish-gray to blue. The nose is pure black with two white bands behind it. The face is brown and the eyes are circled with white. The darkest part of the body is the middle of the back. Though gradually lighter on other parts of the body, the coloring turns an abrupt white at the stomach. The antlers consist of two main beams that grow outward, backward, and then sweep forward.

SIZE: A typical whitetail is slightly taller than 3 feet at the shoulder, measures 5 to 6 feet in length, and weighs about 150 pounds. The largest whitetail ever recorded, however, weighed 425 pounds.

WHITETAIL DEER

The world-record whitetail deer, according to the Boone and Crockett Club ratings, scored $213^{5}/_{8}$ points. Taken by Milo Hanson on November 3, 1993 in Saskatchewan, the rack's inside spread is $27^{2}/_{8}$ inches.

FOOD: Most types of vegetation are included in the whitetail's diet, which changes with both the season and the area of the country inhabited. Tops on the menu are white cedar, white acorns, witchhazel, pine, red maple, apples, dogwood, oak, sweetfern, sumac, wintergreen, bearberry, Oregon grape, hemlock, willow, greenbriar, snowberry, and arborvitae. Among the cultivated crops it seeks out are soybeans, trefoil, rye, alfalfa, corn, rape, cabbage, clover, and lespedeza.

EDIBILITY: Whitetail venison, if treated like good beef, will taste delicious. Prompt and proper field-dressing insures fine meat.

Mule Deer *(Odocoileus hemionus)*

RANGE: The overall area encompassed by the mule deer extends from southeastern Alaska to Mexico, east to west Texas, Minnesota, and Hudson Bay. Those muleys inhabiting the coastal area from Alaska to mid-California are properly termed blacktail deer.

IDENTIFICATION: The mule deer's basic coloring in summer is a brownish-red, changing to a brownish-gray come winter. The nose and the band around the muzzle are black, the face and a section about the eyes are white. Its throat has two white patches separated by a dark bar, its belly and the inside of its legs are whitish, and its hoofs are jet black. The tail is round and white but becomes black about 2 inches from its tip. The ears often reach 11 inches in total length. A buck's antlers, very large and heavy, divide into two main beams. Each beam forks into two tines.

Though closely related to the mule deer, the blacktail does have some distinctions. The ears measure 6½ inches and are narrower, and the tail is dark on top with a white underside. But like the muley the blacktail's coloring is brownish-red in summer and brownish-gray in winter.

SIZE: This species stands about 3½ feet high at the shoulder, measures close to 6½ feet in length, and averages between 175 and 200 pounds in weight. The blacktail is slightly smaller on the average. One

MULE DEER

mule deer that was recorded weighed 480 pounds.

The world-record mule deer, according to the Boone and Crockett Club record book, was killed in Dolores County, Colorado, in 1972 by Doug Burris, Jr. Scoring 226⁴/₈ points, the rack's right main beam, sporting 6 points, measures 30¹/₈ inches, its left, sporting 5 points, measures 28⁶/₈ inches. The rack's inside spread is 30⁷/₈ inches.

The world-record Columbia Blacktail Deer, according to the Boone and Crockett Club record book, scored 182²/₈ points. It was taken by Lester H. Miller in Lewis County, Washington, in 1953. The right beam measures 24²/₈ inches, the left 24⁵/₈ inches. Both have 5 points. The rack's inside spread is 20²/₈ inches.

FOOD: In summer, grasses play an important role in the mule deer's diet: rice grass, needlegrass, grama grass, wheat grass, bluegrass, fescue grass, and bromegrass. In winter, when grasses are scarce, browse takes over: mountain mahogany, cliffrose, sagebrush, poplar, bitterbrush, jack pine, sunflower, cedar, oak, snowberry, bearberry, fir, and serviceberry. Although the deer eat almost any vegetation, they prefer fungus, nuts, cactus fruit, acorns, wildflowers, ferns, and berries.

Rating high on the blacktail's menu are wild oats, manzanita, ceanothus, chamise, buckthorn, buttercup, bromegrass, and fescue grass. Cactus fruit, nuts, wildflowers, acorns, fungus, berries, and acorns are also preferred foods.

EDIBILITY: Deer venison, though drier than beef, is delicious.

Elk *(Cervus canadensis)*

RANGE: The bulk of the elk population is in the Rocky Mountains, ranging from British Columbia to New Mexico and Arizona. Herds are also found in some midwestern and eastern states. Alberta, Saskatchewan, and Manitoba also have fair-size elk populations.

IDENTIFICATION: The elk's normal winter coat is brown-gray with long chestnut-brown hair on its head and neck. Legs are dark and belly nearly black. The rump patch and short tail are yellow-white. Cow elk are lighter than bulls. In summer the elk's coat turns reddish.

SIZE: Bull elk range in weight from 600 to as much as 1,000 pounds. Cows are smaller, averaging about 600 pounds. A good-size bull may stand 5 feet tall at the shoulder and measure 10 feet in length. Antlers

Moose *(Alces alces)*

RANGE: The Alaska-Yukon moose is found in the Alaska and Yukon peninsulas; the Canada moose is found in every Canadian province and in sections of northern Minnesota, Wisconsin, and Maine; the Wyoming, or Shiras, moose inhabits the area from the Rocky Mountain region of northern Colorado and Utah northward to the border between Canada and the United States.

IDENTIFICATION: The moose is a large, antlered, ungraceful-looking creature. The primary color is black, though shades of dark brown and russet have been spotted. The nostrils, circles about the eyes, inner parts of the ear, and lower portions of the legs are whitish-gray. The hindquarters are much more tapered than the forequarters, and together they hold the moose's belly approximately 40 inches from the ground. The immense antlers weigh in the area of 90 pounds and often reach 6 feet in length. The tail is 3 inches long and stublike. The ears are large, and the long face finishes up in a wide, down-turned muzzle.

SIZE: A typical large bull is from 6½ to 7½ feet tall at the shoulder, measures 8½ to 10½ feet in length, and scales between 1,300 and 1,400 pounds. Several

MOOSE

of a prime bull will grow up to 5 feet above its head, with each antler sporting from 5 to 7 points and measuring 60 inches or more along the beam.

The world-record head, taken in 1899 in Dark Canyon, Colorado, by John Plute, had a Boone and Crockett Club score of 442⅜ points. The beams measured 55⅝ and 59⅝ inches long. The right beam had 8 points, the left 7 points. Inside spread measured 45½ inches.

FOOD: The diet consists mainly of grasses and browse. Some of the prime foods are pinegrass, bluegrass, blue bunchgrass, sweet vernal grass, and wheatgrass. Elk eat nearly all the conifers, aspen, and willows. Their diet may also include alder, maple, blackberry, and serviceberry.

EDIBILITY: The meat is dark and much like beef in taste and texture. Elk is generally considered to be very good eating.

recorded bulls have weighed in at as high as 1,800 pounds.

The world-record Alaska-Yukon moose scored 255 points in the Boone and Crockett Club competition. Killed by Kenneth Best in 1978 at McGrath, Alaska, the trophy's greatest spread measures 77 inches. Its right palm is 49⅝ inches long, its left 49⅝ inches long.

The world-record Canada moose, according to the Boone and Crockett Club rating system, scored 242 points. Killed by Michael E. Laub in 1980 near Grayling River, British Columbia, the trophy has a right palm measuring 44⅝ inches long with 15 points and a left palm measuring 45 inches long with 16 points. The greatest spread is 63 inches.

The world-record Wyoming moose, killed by John M. Oakley at Green River Lake, Wyoming, in 1952, scored 205⁴⁄₈ points in the Boone and Crockett Club competition. Its greatest spread is 53 inches, its right palm 38⁶⁄₈ inches long, and its left palm 38⅝ inches long. Both palms sport 15 points.

FOOD: A favorite food is dwarf willow, as are white birch, aspen, and balsam fir in forested sections. Come summer the moose seeks shelter from the heat and insects at lakes, where it dines on eelgrass, sedges, pondweeds, and water lilies. Red osier, alder, honeysuckle, chokecherry, striped maple, spiraea, snowberry, dwarf birch, current, elder, cranberry, mountain ash, and cottonwood are also preferred items.

EDIBILITY: Though a bit darker and drier than beef, moose meat is very similar to it in taste.

Bighorn Sheep *(Ovis canadensis)*

RANGE: The Rocky Mountain bighorn is found in remote areas from central British Columbia down through the northern Rocky Mountains. The desert bighorn inhabits a good portion of the southeastern United States and northern Mexico.

IDENTIFICATION: The bighorn has a well-muscled, finely proportioned body set atop stout, strong legs. The head and heavy majestic horns are supported by a rather sturdy neck. The horns, dark brown in color, have conspicuous growth rings and may weigh over 20 pounds. The Rocky Mountain bighorn is dark brown, the desert bighorn pale buff, but the tail is black. White is the color of the animal's muzzle, a patch around the eye, a rump patch, and an edging running along the back of each leg. The ears, though small, are alert.

BIGHORN SHEEP

SIZE: An average ram stands 3 to 3½ feet tall at the shoulder, measuring 5 to 6 feet in length. The ram weighs about 200 pounds. Some on record have surpassed 300 pounds. Ewes are usually a bit less than three-quarters the size of rams.

The world-record Rocky Mountain bighorn sheep, according to the Boone and Crockett Club, was taken by Fred Weiller in Blind Canyon, Alberta, in 1911. The trophy scored 208⅛ points, the right horn being 44⅞ inches long and the left horn being 45 inches long.

The world-record desert bighorn scored 205⅛ points in the Boone and Crockett Club competition. Taken by an Indian in Lower California, Mexico, in 1940, the trophy's right horn measured 43⅜ inches and the left measured 43⁶⁄₈ inches. The greatest spread came to 25⅝ inches.

FOOD: Grasses comprise the bulk of the bighorn's diet. They include fescue, wheatgrass, sedges, rushes, horsetail, little ricegrass, pentstemon, June grass, and vetch. When the grasses are snow-covered come winter, browse—sagebrush, willow, alder, chokeberry, bitterbrush, rabbitbrush, greasebrush, and mountain mahogany—takes a prominent place on the menu.

EDIBILITY: Many big-game hunters rate bighorn sheep as the finest of all wild-game meat.

Dall Sheep *(Ovis dalli)*

RANGE: This species inhabits the mountainous regions of northern Alaska, east to the western Mackenzie Mountain range.

IDENTIFICATION: Dall rams and ewes are practically snow white except for a few black hairs in their tails. The horns, a bit lighter than those of the Stone ram, have a conspicuous flare that keeps them away from the ram's eyes. Also, the light-yellow horns show well-defined yearly growth marks that depict the animal's age. Ewes have horns that usually resemble thin spikes and rarely grow beyond 15 inches in length. In winter the waxy hair covering the body reaches 3 inches in length, but this is shed before summer and replaced by a shorter coat.

SIZE: A typical Dall ram weighs between 180 and 200 pounds, stands slightly above 3 feet high at the shoulder, and measures approximately 6 feet in length.

The world-record Dall sheep, killed by Harry L. Swank Jr. in Alaska's Wrangell Mountains in 1961, polled 189⅝ points in the Boone and Crockett Club competition. The right and left horns measure 48⅝

DALL SHEEP

and 47⅞ inches respectively. The greatest spread is 34⅜ inches.

FOOD: Forbes and grasses make up the bulk of the Dall sheep's diet, though it will eat browse, especially the dwarf willow.

EDIBILITY: Most hunters rate the meat far better than that of the domestic sheep. In fact, they consider it the finest in the world.

Stone Sheep *(Ovis dalli stonei)*

RANGE: This subspecies of the Dall is found in northern British Columbia.

IDENTIFICATION: Stone sheep have colorings varying from gray-blue to blue-black to black. Stones do, however, have a light belly, a white rump patch, and a white edging down the rear of each leg. There is also a sort of whitish blotch on the face, which tends to enlarge with age. The horns of the Stone ram are a bit heavier than those of the Dall ram. The coat covering the body measures 3 inches, but it is shed when summer approaches and is replaced by a shorter coat.

SIZE: An average Stone ram scales between 180 and 200 pounds, measures 6 feet in length, and stands just above 3 feet tall at the shoulder.

The world-record Stone sheep, killed by L. S. Chadwick on the Muskwa River of British Columbia in 1936, scored 196⅝ points in the Boone and Crockett Club competition. The right horn is 50⅛ inches long and the left is 51⅝ inches long. The greatest spread is 31 inches.

FOOD: Grasses and forbes comprise the major portion of the Stone sheep's diet. It does dine on browse, however, especially the dwarf willow.

EDIBILITY: The meat of the domestic sheep can't compare with that of this fine specimen. Many hunters rate its meat as the finest in the world.

Rocky Mountain Goat *(Oreamnos americanus)*

RANGE: The species inhabits the steep slopes of the western mountains from Washington and Idaho up through central Yukon and southern Alaska.

IDENTIFICATION: The mountain goat's body is a

ROCKY MOUNTAIN GOAT

wheatgrass, purple milk vetch, green lily, strawberry, alpine sorrel, and alpine equisetum. In winter goats switch to aspen, red osier, bearberry juniper, willow, dwarf birch, and balsam fir. Lichens and mosses are year-round favorites.

EDIBILITY: The meat of a trophy billy is usually rather tough as the animal is getting on in years. The meat of the younger animals, though, is used for food.

Caribou *(Rangifer tarandus)*

RANGE: There are four varieties of caribou, formerly classified as subspecies but now considered to be of the same species, for which *Rangifer tarandus* is the accepted scientific name. The mountain caribou inhabits the tundra and coniferous forests of Canada and Alaska; the Barren Ground caribou summers from Canada and northern Alaska to the far north, until the land runs out. In winter, it migrates to the south as far as Saskatchewan and northern Manitoba. The woodland caribou is found in forested areas between northern Idaho and Great Slave Lake and from Newfoundland to the Alaska-Yukon border. Fourth is the Quebec-Labrador.

IDENTIFICATION: The caribou has a dark neck and a long mane running under the neck from chin to chest. In the summer the fur is dark brown, but becomes brown-gray in winter. The belly, rump patch, feet and short tail vary in color from pale gray to yellow-white throughout the year. A wide

CARIBOU

short, blunt, boxlike structure, and except for the bottom 8 inches of each leg, it is covered by an abundance of hair. The shoulders are humped and the head is long and narrow. Its lengthy hair is pure white save for a yellow tint, but pure black is the color of its horns, nose, eyes, and hoofs. The horns, rising from the rear of the head, are slender and curve backward. Both the billy and the nanny sport horns and beards. In the billy the horns average 12 inches; in the nanny 9 inches.

SIZE: A typical mountain goat stands just over 3 feet high at the shoulder and measures 5 to 6 feet in length. Though the species averages between 150 and 300 pounds, the heaviest on record weighed just over 500 pounds.

   The world-record mountain goat, killed by E. C. Haase in 1949 in British Columbia's Babine Mountains, scored 56⅛ points in the Boone and Crockett Club competition. Both the male's horns measure 12 inches long; the greatest spread between them is 9⅞ inches.

FOOD: In summer the goat's diet consists of grasses, browse, and forbes; specifically bluegrasses,

muzzle circled with white hairs, long fur, and a main beam that sweeps backward, upward, and outward, finishing in a flat palm, typify the species. The mountain caribou is the largest and darkest of the four types. The Barren Ground is the smallest and palest; its neck is a very bright white. Both the male and female of the species have antlers, the male shedding his in December or January, the female during the fawning period in May and June.

SIZE: An average mountain caribou bull measures 7½ to 8 feet in length, close to 4 feet from foot to shoulder, and scales between 500 and 600 pounds. Some recorded mountain caribou have weighed in the vicinity of 700 pounds. Females are smaller and lighter.

The world-record mountain caribou, killed by Garry Beaubien in 1976 on the Turnagain River, British Columbia, scored 452 points in the Boone and Crockett Club competition. The right beam has 22 points, and measures 43⅛ inches; the left has 19 points and measures 42²⁄₈ inches. The greatest inside spread measures 30⅜ inches.

A typical Barren Ground bull is 6½ feet long, 3½ feet high from toe to shoulder, and averages 375 pounds. Females are smaller and weigh less. The world-record Barren Ground caribou, killed by Roger Hedgecock at Mosquito Creek, Alaska, in 1987, scored 465⅛ points in the Boone and Crockett Club competition. The right beam measures 50⁶⁄₈ inches and has 24 points; the left measures 49⅞ inches and has 23 points. The greatest inside spread between beams is 40⅛ inches.

A typical woodland caribou bull is about 8 feet long, measures 4 feet from foot to shoulder, and weighs approximately 400 pounds. Females tend to be smaller in both total weight and size. The world-record woodland caribou was killed sometime prior to 1910 in Newfoundland, scoring 419⅝ points in the Boone and Crockett Club competition. The left beam measures 47⅜ inches and has 18 points, the right 50⅛ inches and has 19 points. The greatest inside spread is 43²⁄₈ inches between beams.

Another category has been added to the Boone and Crockett listings—the Quebec-Labrador caribou—because racks from that region are so impressive. The world record, taken in 1931 by Zack Elbow at Nain, Labrador, scored 474⁶⁄₈ points. Its right beam is 60⁴⁄₈ inches and has 22 points. Its left is 61⅛ inches and has 30 points. The inside spread is 58²⁄₈ inches.

FOOD: Caribou favor lichens as their main food, but also eat grasses, twigs, shrubs, flowers, moss, and practically any other plant matter available.

EDIBILITY: Caribou meat is rated excellent.

Pronghorn Antelope *(Antilocapra americana)*

RANGE: The pronghorn is located in the region from southern Saskatchewan south through the western United States to the Mexican plains.

IDENTIFICATION: The pronghorn is similar to a small deer in body structure and coloring. Both male and female have similar markings—two black horns (both of which are longer than the ears), a bright tannish-red hue on the upper body and the outside of legs. The inside of the legs and underparts are a strong white, as is the rump patch. The necks of both sexes are streaked by two thick brown bands. The buck, however, has a wide black band that extends from the nose to just below the eyes.

PRONGHORN ANTELOPE

SIZE: A full-grown male may reach 3½ feet in height at the shoulder, and 5 feet in length, with an average weight of between 100 and 140 pounds. Does usually peak at 80 pounds. The world-record head, taken in Coconino County, Arizona, in 1985, polled 93⁴⁄₈ points in the Boone and Crockett Club competition. The right horn measured 17⁶⁄₈ inches, the left horn 17⁴⁄₈ inches, and the inside spread was 12⅝ inches.

FOOD: Diet consists chiefly of vegetable substances such as saltbrush, onion, western juniper, sage-brush, and bitterbrush.

EDIBILITY: Hunters rate the meat very good.

Bison *(Bison bison)*

RANGE: The wild bison no longer exists in the United States, and those of the species that remain are located in national parks, wildlife refuges, and private ranches in North America. Yellowstone and South Dakota's Wind Cave National Parks, Montana's National Bison Range, and Oklahoma's Wichita Wildlife Refuge have bison, as do Big Delta, Alaska and northern Alberta's Wood Buffalo Park.

IDENTIFICATION: The bison has a humped back, and is the largest wild animal on the North American continent. Lengthy hair, reaching 8 inches in winter and 4 inches in summer, covers its head, neck, shoulders, and forequarters. The hair on the rear section of the bison usually measures one-half the length of the hair on the front section. Hair color ranges from dark brown to black, but the sun often bleaches it to a dark tan. Both male and female have two thick horns, each of which is sharply upturned.

SIZE: A large bull may measure 11½ to 12 feet in length and stands 6 feet high from his foot to the apex of his hump. Bulls usually weigh about 2,000 pounds, while cows are much smaller, scaling 800 to 900 pounds. Records indicate that some bison have reached weights of nearly 3,000 pounds.

The world-record bison, killed by S. Woodring in Yellowstone National Park, Wyoming, in 1925, scored 136⅛ points in the Boone and Crockett Club competition. Its right horn measured 21⅞ inches; its left, 23⅞ inches. The greatest spread between the record's horns is 35⅜ inches.

FOOD: As the bison hasn't any teeth in the front of its upper jaw its diet consists of grasses such as tumbleweed, gramagrass, dropseed grass, and buffalo grass. Using its tongue and lower incisors, the bison snips off the grasses.

EDIBILITY: When bison weren't as scarce, people raved about the fine flavor of its meat. The bison's tongue and hump meat were considered delicacies. Some bison meat is available today from specimens killed on private ranches.

Mountain Lion *(Felis concolor)*

RANGE: This species, which is also known as the cougar, puma, painter, panther, catamount, and American lion, is distributed throughout western North America, from northern British Columbia south to Mexico, east to the Rocky Mountains and Saskatchewan, and along the Gulf Coast states to Mississippi. Southern Florida also features the mountain lion.

IDENTIFICATION: The body color is practically uniform, though it may vary from russet to a near-gray. The fur measures a uniform 1 inch all over the body, dark near the eyes and upper muzzle, and off-white at the forepart of the mouth, lower flanks, and belly. The eyes are frequently yellow, the ears pronounced but well-rounded. Its prominent whiskers tend to be white. The tail, measuring from 2 to 3 feet, has a dark tip. The rounded head appears small in comparison to the body.

SIZE: The mountain lion is the largest North American unspotted cat. A mature adult measures 7 to 9½ feet in length, stands 26 to 31 inches at the shoulder, and scales up to 275 pounds. Most lions are far lighter, and females are usually two-thirds the weight of males. The heaviest cat weighed over 300 pounds before evisceration.

The world-record cougar, according to the Boone and Crockett Club records, was taken by Douglas E. Schuk in Tatlayoko Lake, British Columbia, in

BISON

MOUNTAIN LION

JAGUAR

1979. Scoring 16⁴/₁₆ points, the skull measured 9⁹/₁₆ inches long and 6¹¹/₁₆ inches wide.

FOOD: Mule deer in particular are the staple of the mountain lion's diet, though he prefers all species of deer. Horses and steers are also preyed upon, colts being a favorite. Chickens, pigs, goats, turkeys, and sheep also have their places on the menu.

EDIBILITY: The meat is reminiscent of lamb or veal in flavor, texture, and taste. The relative lack of fat, however, makes it somewhat dry.

Jaguar *(Felis onca hernandesii)*

RANGE: Quite rare in the United States, the jaguar is located from Mexico southward to Central and South America.

IDENTIFICATION: The body, compact and enormously muscled, is coated with spots. This coat, basically yellow shading to tawny, features small spots around the head, large spots on the legs, and an intermixing of the two across the chest. The spots are actually rosettes, square in shape. The back and sides are covered with large, black rosettes with yellow middles and a black spot in the center. The tail measures just 30 inches long, shorter than the cougar's. The predominantly white feet have tiny black spots. The head is round, the ears short and finely rounded, and the whiskers long, white and highly prominent.

SIZE: The jaguar is the Western Hemisphere's largest cat, usually measuring 6 to 9 feet in overall length, 2⅓ feet high at the shoulder, and scaling from 200 to 250 pounds. Some specimens have been reported at over 350 pounds.

The world-record skull scored 18⁷/₁₆ points in the Boone and Crockett Club competition. Taken by C. J. McElroy in 1965 in Sinaloa, Mexico, the jaguar's skull measured 10¹⁵/₁₆ inches in length and 7⁸/₁₆ inches in width.

FOOD: Monkeys, parrots, coatis, and turkeys form a part of the jaguar's diet, as do peccaries, cattle, sea turtles, and man himself.

Collared Peccary *(Tayassu tajacu)*

RANGE: The peccary, or javelina, resides in arid, brushy regions and scrub oak forests along the border between the United States and Mexico, extending from eastern Texas west to Arizona.

IDENTIFICATION: The collared peccary resembles a pig in that it has a lengthy snout with a tough disc at its tip, along with a very short neck, short but stout legs, and a somewhat arched back. Also, its ears are small, erect, and pointed. Though the eyelids have long lashes, the eyes themselves are small. The body is covered with 2-inch-long, bristly, salt-and-pepper gray hair. A thin, white band begins under the animal's throat and joins on its back. Eight

COLLARED PECCARY   ·

IDENTIFICATION: Thin and muscular (unlike its domesticated relative), the wild boar has tusks measuring up to 9 inches in length. Its snout is long and saucerlike, its eyes rather small, and its always-erect ears about 5 inches long. The wild boar is usually pure black, but, on occasion, its bristly guard hairs may be white. The species' long legs give it nearly the swiftness of a deer.

SIZE: A typical adult measures 30 inches in height at the shoulder and is 4 to 5 feet long. In North America a big boar may weigh from 300 to 350 pounds. Some European wild boars, however, have been recorded at close to 600 pounds.

FOOD: During the warmer months wild boars feed on roots, tubers, fruits, berries, and grasses. The menu also ranges from fawns to nuts, including rabbits, mice, frogs, beechnuts, and even rattlesnakes (to whose poison the wild hog appears to be immune).

EDIBILITY: The wild boar is hunted chiefly for sport and trophies, as its meat is reputed to be tough.

inches above its short tail, on the center of its back, is a gaping musk gland.

SIZE: A typical member of this species is 2½ feet in length, measures 22 inches high at the shoulder, and averages between 40 and 65 pounds in total weight.

FOOD: Prickly pears—fruit and spines—are the peccary's favorite food. It eats roots, tubers, acorns, nuts, fruits, and berries. Being omnivorous the species also dines on insects, the young and eggs of ground-nesting birds, amphibians, and reptiles. Snake meat is a special treat.

EDIBILITY: Peccary meat, dry in texture and light in color, is considered tasty by some people; others tend to disagree.

European Wild Hog *(Sus scrofa)*

RANGE: The species is far from numerous in the United States. To find European wild hogs, hunters must go to the areas of initial releases (e.g., Tennessee's Great Smoky Mountains and North Carolina's Hooper's Bald) to find them.

EUROPEAN WILD HOG

KNOW YOUR BIG-GAME TRACKS

It's hard to imagine a big-game hunter in the woods not scanning the ground carefully for animal tracks. Even during the off-season it's a wise use of time to study tracks: They will tell you what big-game animals live in your favorite hunting areas.

The animal tracks shown here will help you identify big game. The dimensions given will also be helpful, but regard them only as benchmarks. The track sizes here are for average adult animals. Obviously, smaller tracks are made by young animals and oversize tracks by exceptionally large ones.

Identifying tracks is largely a process of elimination. For example, if you find a single-file pad track, you can eliminate all hoofed animals and animals that leave a double or side-by-side track. Animals that leave a single-gait track include wolves and lions. Also, if the track has claw prints, you can probably eliminate the mountain lion, which normally keeps its claws retracted. After you have narrowed tracks down to a couple of species, final indentification should be easy.

When you've identified the species, you may also be able to determine its size by the depth of the track. If possible, compare them with others of the same species over the same terrain: If one deer track is an inch deep and another of the same size is two inches deep, it follows that the deeper track belongs to a heavier deer—possibly a big buck.

Study animal tracks every time you're in the woods, and learn to identify the animals that left them. It will lend you insight into the wildlife around you and make you a better hunter.

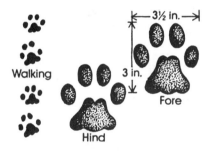

MOUNTAIN LION
A mountain lion's forepaws are larger than its hind feet; claws are retracted and rarely show in the track.

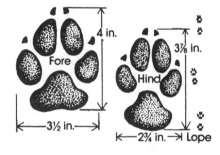

WOLF
Wolf tracks are similar to a large dog's. Forepaw is typically wider than rear paw.

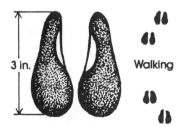

BIGHORN SHEEP
A bighorn has blunt toes and a slight hollow on the outer edges of a widely split hoof.

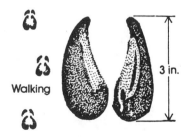

MOUNTAIN GOAT
Look for a widely splayed hoof and soft-edged print from the rubberlike hoof.

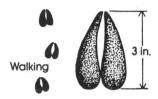

WHITETAIL DEER
A buck's tracks are longer and wider than a doe's tracks. Dewclaws seldom show.

MULE DEER
The track of the mule deer is very similar to that of a white-tail.

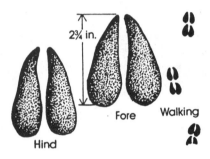

ANTELOPE
Dewclaws are absent in the track of a prong-horn antelope. The forehoof is also wider than the hind hoof.

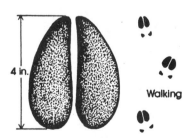

ELK
Bull elk usually show blunt toes; cows leave a track with pointed toes. Dewclaws also show in elk tracks.

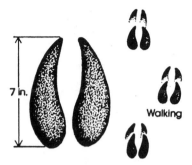

MOOSE
Moose have pointed hooves; hind hooves often overlap tracks of front hooves.

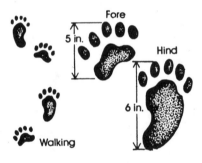

BLACK BEAR
The black bear's claws are shorter than a grizzly's (about 1½") and rarely show in tracks.

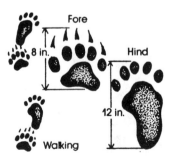

GRIZZLY
The grizzly's forepaws have exceptionally long claws—sometimes more than 3" long in a full-grown adult.

SMALL-GAME ANIMALS

Cottontail Rabbit *(Sylvilagus)*

RANGE: Combined, the four species of the cottontail, which include the Eastern cottontail *(Sylvilagus floridanus)*, mountain cottontail *(S. nuttali)*, desert cottontail *(S. auduboni)*, and New England cottontail *(S. transitionalis)*, inhabit much of the United States, except for some sections of the Far West.

IDENTIFICATION: The body pigment is basically brown with the possibility of a reddish or buff cast. Guard hairs with black tips are scattered about, but the belly, chin, and undersides of the legs are white. The underside of the tail is also white, resembling a cotton ball when the rabbit is scampering about—hence, its name. A majority of cottontails have a white spot on the forehead between the eyes. The whiskers, though long, are light and relatively inconspicuous. The ears, 2½ to 3 inches long, are bare on the inside but lightly furred on the outside.

SIZE: The cottontail is from 14 to 19 inches long and stands 6 to 7 inches at the shoulder. Females tend to be a bit larger than males. Weights vary from 2½ to 3½ pounds, the latter being the top weight that has ever been recorded.

FOOD: The diet of the cottontail consists of crabgrass, bluegrass, and other grasses, all kinds of fruits and berries; such cultivated crops as clover, alfalfa, lettuce, beans, wheat, soybeans, and cabbage; weeds such as yarrow and goldenrod; sheep sorrel, wild cherry, and wild shrubs. Sumac is a favorite food come winter.

EDIBILITY: The meat, lightly colored and finely textured, is delicious.

Varying Hare *(Lepus americanus)*

RANGE: The varying hare inhabits the tree limits of Alaska and Canada, south through New England and the Appalachians, to Tennessee in the east. In the Rockies, it ranges to northern New Mexico, and to mid-California.

COTTONTAIL RABBIT

VARYING HARE

IDENTIFICATION: The hare's coat acts as an excellent camouflage costume. Though brown in summer, the coat is shed come winter for a white one. A dark line runs down the center of its back, ending in a dark rump and tail top. The chin, belly, and the undersides of the tail are white, but the throat is a brownish-red. The feet are huge and hairy.

SIZE: A typical member of this species stands 8 to 9 inches at the shoulder and measures 21 inches in length. Though weights vary from 3 to 4½ pounds, the heaviest varying hare ever recorded scaled 5¼ pounds.

FOOD: Almost any vegetation appeals to the hare, but he has his preferences—succulent grasses and the tender tips of woody plants in summer, and dead grasses, buds, and bark in winter. White cedar is a favorite.

EDIBILITY: As the varying hare usually lacks any fat, the meat is dry.

Jackrabbit *(Lepus)*

RANGE: The whitetail jackrabbit (*Lepus townsendii*) inhabits the sagebrush regions and grasslands from northern New Mexico north to southern Alberta, and from Lake Michigan west to the Sierras.

IDENTIFICATION: The whitetail jackrabbit's tail is white on both top and bottom. Its conspicuous ears measure 5 to 6 inches in length. In summer, the coat is a light grayish-brown over the sides and back, but the belly is lighter. The ear tips are black. When winter arrives, the coat is completely white or, on occasion, a buff-white. The blacktail's rump is black, as is the top of its tail. Its ears are longer than the whitetail's by an inch or so. The underside of the tail is white, as is the belly. The ears are white outside, brown inside, and black-tipped. Though the whitetail sheds twice annually, the color change is relatively insignificant.

SIZE: A typical whitetail jackrabbit measures between 22 and 26 inches long and weighs from 6 to 10 pounds. The average blacktail jackrabbit is 18 to 24 inches long and scales between 4 and 7½ pounds.

The heaviest jackrabbit on record was a whitetail which tipped the scales at 13 pounds.

The blacktail jackrabbit (*Lepus californicus*) lives in the deserts and open grasslands of the western United States from mid-Arkansas to the Pacific Coast, north to southeastern Washington in the west, and to mid-South Dakota in the east.

JACKRABBIT

FOOD: Though jackrabbits eat practically all kinds of vegetation in their diets, shrubs, weedy plants, and grasses make up the bulk of it. Main food items include spiderling, snakeweed, mesquite, gramagrass, rabbitbrush, sagebrush, greasewood, filaree, prickly pears, eriogonum, and saltbrush.

EDIBILITY: Whitetail meat is said to be far preferable to the meat of the blacktail. Younger jackrabbits are more palatable than their elders.

Arctic Hare *(Lepus arcticus)*

RANGE: The Arctic hare is found in the tundra region of northern Canada, from Newfoundland to the Mackenzie River. The Alaskan hare (*Lepus othus*) inhabits the area west of the Mackenzie Delta along the coast of Alaska to the Alaska Peninsula.

IDENTIFICATION: The hare's fur is pure white in winter, except for the black-tipped ears. In summer the hare's coat becomes brown. There is no lag in the transition from white to brown of the coat in relation to the land. For example, when patches of white and brown are mixed on the coat, the ground is still covered with snow patches.

SIZE: The largest of the North American hares, the Arctic hare measures up to 28 inches long, stands close to 1 foot high at the shoulder, and weighs from 6 to 12 or more pounds.

FOOD: The basic food of the Arctic hare is the dwarf willow—its buds, leaves, catkins, bark, and even roots. Berries, mosses, herbs, and grasses are also eaten.

EDIBILITY: All those who have eaten the meat regard it highly.

European Rabbit
(Oryctolagus cuniculus)

RANGE: Sometimes called the San Juan rabbit after the islands off the coast of Washington where it still runs wild, the European hare is more commonly found in captivity today. As a game animal it has been a failure.

IDENTIFICATION: Somewhat similar to the cottontail in pigmentation, the European rabbit's hair is a light brown, intermingled with black. The nape of this rabbit's neck is buff, however, while our cottontail has a reddish nape. The tail, belly, and insides of the legs are white, but the tips of the 3½-inch ears are black.

SIZE: Larger than the cottontail, this species can reach some 18 inches in length and scale a top of 5 pounds in weight.

FOOD: The preferred foods are herbs and grasses, but the European hare won't turn away from coarse vegetation when its favorites are scarce.

EDIBILITY: The meat, light in color, is quite tasty.

Gray Squirrel (Sciurus)

RANGE: The eastern gray (*Sciurus carolinensis*) is located in hardwood forests from eastern Texas and eastern Saskatchewan to the Atlantic Coast, and from the Gulf of Mexico to southern Canada. The Arizona gray (*Sciurus arizonensis*) inhabits pine and oak forests in southeastern and central Arizona. The western gray (*Sciurus griseus*) is also found in oak

GRAY SQUIRREL

and pine forests, but in the region from southern California north to Washington.

IDENTIFICATION: The gray squirrel's coloring is a salt-and-pepper gray. The body's underfur is solid gray with guard hairs that go from gray at the base to buff-brown to black, and finish off in a white tip. The small hairs of the face, muzzle, and ears are a yellow-tan, while those under the throat, its underparts, and the insides of its legs are a rich white.

SIZE: A large adult measures between 17 and 20 inches depending upon its range, the tail taking up approximately 8 to 8½ inches of that length. Males and females tend to weigh the same—slightly over 1 pound. The heaviest gray squirrel recorded scaled 1½ pounds.

FOOD: Nuts are a staple in the squirrel's diet and are cached for later use. They also feed on buds, berries, tree blossoms, fruit, fungi, and field corn, as well as eggs and baby birds.

EDIBILITY: The quality and flavor of squirrel meat are generally regarded as excellent.

Fox Squirrel *(Sciurus)*

RANGE: The eastern fox squirrel (*Sciurus niger*) inhabits the open woods from the Canadian border to the Gulf of Mexico, and from the Atlantic Coast to eastern Colorado. New England is free of the species. The Apache fox squirrel (*Sciurus apache*) resides in southeastern Arizona's Chiricahua Mountains, and in Mexico.

IDENTIFICATION: Northeastern squirrels are frequently gray, and resemble oversize gray squirrels except for the rusty flank markings. In the West, bright rust is the dominant color, and black is the main pigment in the South. The hair tips of the tail are an orange color. The ears are round and large, the whiskers long and conspicuous. The plane from the ear to the nose is straighter than that of the gray squirrel.

SIZE: The typical fox squirrel weighs from 1½ to 3 pounds, the latter being exceptional for the species. Females tend to weigh a bit more than males. The total length is usually 28 inches (1 foot of which is a plumed tail), and the height at the shoulder is between 3½ and 4 inches.

FOOD: Like the gray squirrel, the fox squirrel rates nuts—especially acorns—an important item in its diet. The most important are the nuts of the white oak, black oak, and red oak. Hickory nuts, beech-nuts, hazelnuts, black walnuts, butternuts, and pecans are runners-up. Osage oranges are a wintertime treat, and blossoms, the fruit of maples, domesticated and wild fruits and berries, and fungi are favorites during other seasons. The fox squirrel also has a penchant for field corn.

EDIBILITY: The meat of the fox squirrel is highly palatable.

Raccoon *(Procyon lotor)*

RANGE: The raccoon inhabits nearly all of the United States, parts of Mexico, and extreme southern Canada, northward along the border between Saskatchewan and Alberta.

IDENTIFICATION: Though this species varies in size and color depending on its location, two conspicuous features distinguish it—(1) the black mask across the eyes and (2) the ringed tail. The latter is usually 10 inches long. The dense underfur is a brownish-red. Guard hairs are tipped with white but come in shades of black, red, yellow, and gray. The white face and ears offer sharp contrast to the black nose and mask. The soles of the feet are jet black, the topsides light.

SIZE: An average male measures 34 inches in length and stands from 9 inches to a foot high at the shoul-

FOX SQUIRREL

RACCOON

der. A typical adult weighs from 12 to 16 pounds, but some males exceed 25 pounds. The heaviest coon ever recorded tipped the scales at 62 pounds, 6 ounces, and measured 55 inches from tail tip to nose tip.

FOOD: Wild raccoons eat snakes, eggs, baby birds, baby mice, baby rabbits, mussels, fish, frogs, grapes, berries, apples, and acorns. Crayfish is a delicacy to the raccoon, and both sweet corn and field corn are very important in the diet.

EDIBILITY: Hunters have long considered raccoon meat a delicacy.

Woodchuck, Groundhog
(*Marmota monax*)

RANGE: Five-hundred-million woodchucks are said to inhabit North America, ranging from eastern Alaska to Labrador, south in the central and eastern United States to Arkansas and Alabama, respectively, and to northern Idaho in the West.

IDENTIFICATION: The round, barrellike body is supported by short, though powerful, legs. Brown

WOODCHUCK, GROUNDHOG

is the basic body color, but shades of red to near-black are fairly common. The guard hairs are silver-tipped, giving the animal a grizzled look. The ears are short and round, and the black eyes stick out above its flattened skull.

SIZE: A large male may measure up to 26 inches in length (5 or 6 inches of which is its tail), often stands 6 to 7 inches high at the shoulder, and averages 10 pounds in weight. Females tend to be a bit smaller. The heaviest recorded chuck scaled 15¾ pounds.

FOOD: Woodchucks are 99 percent vegetarian, feeding on soybeans, corn, alfalfa, beans, peas, clover, and lettuce among the cultivated crops. Bark, twigs, and buds of low-growing bushes like the sumac and wild cherry are also part of the diet. Fruits and berries, all types, are frequently consumed.

EDIBILITY: Woodchuck meat, particularly that of the young, makes very good eating.

Prairie Dog *(Cynomys)*

RANGE: The whitetail species (*Cynomys gunnisoni, C. leucurus,* and *C. parvidens*) are found in mountainous valleys from central Arizona and New Mexico to southern Montana. The blacktail prairie

PRAIRIE DOG

dog (*Cynomys ludovicianus*), though once found in the high plains from southern Alberta and Saskatchewan to the Mexican border, and from the eastern Rocky Mountains to eastern Kansas and Nebraska, is relatively extinct. A small number of them, however, are located in national parks and monuments.

IDENTIFICATION: Unlike its name, the prairie dog is a rodent rather than a dog. The tag comes from its yapping bark. The head comes to a flat surface, and the whiskers are prominent. The ears are short and rounded, and the black eyes are encircled in white. The body hair tends to be short, ranging in color from dark brownish-red to light gray. The animal's underparts are light. The slender tail differentiates between the blacktail and whitetail prairie dogs. In the former, the tail has a black terminal tip and measures about 3½ inches in length. The latter's tail is a bit shorter (perhaps 2½ inches long), with a white tip.

SIZE: An adult measures some 15 inches in length, stands 5 inches high at the shoulder, and scales between 1½ and 3 pounds.

FOOD: Vegetation is readily available to the prairie dog, and he takes advantage of it. The blacktail favors gramagrass, wheatgrass, fescue grass, Russian thistle, bromegrass, and bluegrass. The whitetail also dines on Russian thistle and wheatgrass, but adds saltbrush, sagebrush, wild onion, dandelion, and nightshade to the menu. Insects, especially grasshoppers, whet the prairie dog's appetite. They eat meat (e.g., ground-nesting birds) once in a while.

EDIBILITY: Though the Indians enjoyed the meat, today's hunters dislike the "earthy" flavor.

Opossum (*Didelphis marsupialis*)

RANGE: The opossum is found in woods and agricultural regions from Ontario west to eastern Colorado, and east to Florida. Many inhabit the Pacific Coast stretch from Canada through California.

IDENTIFICATION: This species is the only marsupial (pouched animal) in North America, housing its somewhat underdeveloped young in a pouch where they are nourished through the mother's nip-

OPOSSUM

ples until they can seek out their own food. The animal's ears are black, though often white-rimmed, as are the eyes, legs, and feet. The face and toes are white, while the nose is pink. Because of the silver-tipped guard hairs, the opossum's fur appears salt-and-pepper gray, but the underfur is cotton-white. A white-yellow stain is apparent on the throat due to a gland secretion. The lengthy, whitish tail tends to be practically bare of hair.

SIZE: A typical opossum may measure up to 3 feet in length, 12 to 15 inches of which is the animal's tail. Though this marsupial generally weighs 5 or 6 pounds, one recorded male scaled 14 pounds.

FOOD: Persimmons are one of the opossum's favorite treats, but its diet ranges from mice, ground-nesting birds, moles, shrews, and rabbits to dead and crippled game to fruits and green vegetation. Earthworms, grains, reptiles, and amphibians round out the menu.

EDIBILITY: Those hunters who have eaten opossum meat claim it is tasty.

PREDATORS

North American Wolf (*Canis*)

RANGE: The gray wolf (*canis lupus*) is located in the tundra and forests in a major portion of Canada from the United States border north to the Arctic and Alaska, and also in the northern sections of Michigan, Minnesota and Montana. The red wolf (*canis niger*) recently clung to existence in western Louisiana and eastern Texas. But the populations died off there. Efforts are under way to stock red wolves elsewhere.

NORTH AMERICAN WOLF

IDENTIFICATION: The wolf is large and doglike in appearance, so much so that its head somewhat resembles that of a German shepherd. There is an immense color range that may run the gamut from practically pure white to coal black. The legs and underparts are lighter than the remainder of the body. A scent gland is found at the base of its tail above the anus.

SIZE: A mature male stands up to 38 inches high at the shoulder, measures 6 feet in length, and weighs 100 pounds or more. The heaviest recorded male tipped the scales at 175 pounds. Females tend to be lighter than males.

FOOD: The wolf preys on large game such as caribou, mountain sheep, moose, and deer, as well as marmots, varying hares, grouse, ptarmigan, small birds, eggs, mice, ducks, and geese among the small game. During the salmon runs, the wolf may be found in the vicinity.

Coyote (*Canis latrans*)

RANGE: This species is located throughout western North America from the Arctic Ocean to Mexico, east to James Bay, southern Quebec, and Vermont, and south to the Mississippi River. Other eastern states either have the coyote naturally or through introduction.

IDENTIFICATION: The face of the coyote is sharp, reminiscent of a wild dog with a shaggy coat and erect ears. Its nose pad is black, but the upper face, the top of the head, and the outer portion of the ears are a sandy grayish-red with black hairs intermingled. The area about the mouth and throat, and the inside of the ears, is white. The eyes are yellow, the pupils black. Basically the body color varies from gray to dull yellow. The rough-textured pelage is dark on the back, but gets whiter on the belly. The tail is 2 inches in length and ¼ inch in width, ending in a dark tip.

SIZE: An average male coyote weighs between 18 and 30 pounds, stands approximately 2 feet tall at the shoulder, and measures 44 to 54 inches in length (of which 12 to 16 inches is its tail). Females tend to be four-fifths the weight and size of the males. The heaviest coyotes on record have weighed as much as 75 pounds.

COYOTE

BOBCAT

FOOD: The coyote preys on rabbits, antelope, ground squirrels, mice, rats, prairie dogs, livestock, and poultry. Rating second to the initial list are fruits, berries, and melons, both domesticated and wild.

EDIBILITY: Though the Indians ate coyote meat, it is rarely considered table fare nowadays.

Bobcat *(Lynx rufus)*

RANGE: Bobcats are found from the Maritime Provinces westward across southern Canada to southern British Columbia, and southward from the latter to Mexico and the Gulf of Mexico. Except for the area along the Mississippi and Ohio rivers and in the Appalachian Mountains, the cat, which is also called the wildcat, catamount, tiger cat, bay lynx, lynx cat and red lynx, is absent from a considerable portion of the eastern and central United States.

IDENTIFICATION: The bobcat varies in coloration, depending upon its location: the cats in the southwestern desert regions are the palest, while those in the northern, forested regions are the dark-

est. The nose is a pinkish-red, and the base color of the face, back, and sides is yellowish, gray, or brownish-red. A checkering of black or a darker color than that of the base accompanies the face and the body. White is the color under the chin, throat, belly, and tail, and also around the eyes. The 4- to 7-inch tail, however, has a black spot over the tip. The fur, although brittle, is quite long and luxurious. This predator's face seems wide due to its face ruff, and slight tufts of hair stand up from the tips of its ears. The eyes are yellow, the pupils black. In comparison to its body size, the bobcat's legs are long, its large paws well furred.

SIZE: A typical bobcat measures approximately 50 inches in length, stands 22 inches high at the shoulder, and weighs between 18 and 25 pounds. Female cats tend to be a bit smaller and lighter than their male counterparts. Bobcats in the North are larger than those in the South. Though there are many cases of these predators weighing in the 40- to 45-pound class, one of 76 pounds and another of 69 pounds have been recorded.

FOOD: The main staples in the diet of this species are the rabbit and the hare. The animal also preys readily on squirrels, rats, mice, porcupines, and chipmunks. Ruffed grouse is its favorite among the ground-nesting birds, though all types are eligible for its menu. Deer and wild turkeys at times make this list.

EDIBILITY: The meat is eaten very frequently, and its taste is reminiscent of veal.

Lynx *(Lynx lynx)*

RANGE: The lynx, also known as the Canadian lynx, lucivee, wildcat, catamount, and loup-cervier, is distributed from Newfoundland west to the Arctic Ocean in Alaska, south to the northern United States in Minnesota, Wisconsin, Michigan, and New England, and in the Rocky Mountain areas of Wyoming and Utah. It resides as far south as mid-Washington and Oregon and in western Montana. *Lynx subsolanus,* another subspecies, is found solely on the island of Newfoundland.

IDENTIFICATION: This predator's main features are its large, padded feet and its 2-inch-long, black ear tufts. A smoky gray is the lynx's basic color, often intermixed with a tan shading. The large face ruff is white with black barring, and the sharp tips practically meet under its chin. White also appears around the animal's muzzle, inside its ears, beneath its eyes, and on the insides of its legs. The body, though compact, is supported by unusually long legs, and is spotted or barred with a black coloring. The tail, often 4 inches long, is light in color and has a jet-black tip.

SIZE: A typical adult lynx measures between 3 and 3⅓ feet in length, stands from 1½ to 2 feet high at the shoulder, and tips the scale at from 12 to 25 pounds. The heaviest lynx on record weighed 40 pounds.

FOOD: The varying hare is at the top of this predator's mealtime menu, with squirrels, mice, voles, lemmings, beavers, and both spruce and ruffed grouse taking relatively minor roles. The lynx's predatory link with the varying hare is so intense that the former's population is uncannily proportional to that of the latter. Records prove this out.

EDIBILITY: Lynx meat is light in color and is said to have a flavor similar to chicken.

Gray Fox *(Urocyon cinereoargenteus)*

RANGE: This species inhabits the open forests and brush country across the southern United States, northward in the West to the state of Washington and northern Colorado, and to southern Canada in eastern and central North America. *Urocyon littoralis,* a second species, is found on a couple of

LYNX

GRAY FOX

the channel islands off the coast of southern California.

IDENTIFICATION: The top of the animal's head and back is a salt-and-pepper gray, but the flanks, the ears, and the area just below them are a rust-red color. Belly, chest, throat, and the inner side of the legs are whitish. The 12- to 15-inch tail is gray with a prominent black mane running to the black tip. A 4½-inch musk gland is visible on the top of the tail.

SIZE: A typical adult stands 15 inches high at the shoulder, is up to 45 inches from nose tip to tail tip, and scales between 8 and 11 pounds. The heaviest recorded gray fox weighed 19 pounds.

FOOD: Gray foxes prey heavily upon rabbits and ruffed grouse. And, depending on the abundance of the prey animal, fish, snakes, rats, mice, and insects. Dead and crippled animals are easy game for the wary gray fox.

Red Fox *(Vulpes vulpes)*

RANGE: The red fox is distributed from Alaska and northern Canada south to the Gulf of Mexico (except under the fall line of the southeastern states). Though it is found southward to the border of Mexico in places in the West, it is absent in the high plains from Mexico to central Alberta.

IDENTIFICATION: The red fox is slightly built, and resembles a domesticated dog. There are considerable color variations. This species ranges from a dark russet-red to a light yellowish-blond. The nose pad and the outside of the ear tips are black, the upper face rusty, the throat and cheeks white. The bushy tail, somewhat cylindrical in shape, is usually colored the same as the back (the darkest part of the animal), and has a light underside and a huge white tip. The belly tends to be white.

SIZE: A mature red fox is 3 to 3½ feet long (13 to 15 inches of which is tail), stands 16 inches high at the shoulder, and weighs from 6 to 15 pounds. The latter is the top weight recorded.

FOOD: Ranking at the top of the list is the meadow mouse, a plentiful and nutritious animal. The red fox also favors rabbits, ruffed grouse, quail, pheasants, muskrats, squirrels, hares, chipmunks, and groundhogs. Preying on poultry yards is frequent. Add weasels, snakes, shrews, beetles, moles,

RED FOX

crickets, and grasshoppers to this fox's menu, along with corn, melons, berries, and fruits.

Northwestern Crow *(Corvus caurinus)*

RANGE: Found along the coasts and islands from Kodiak Island to western Washington, the Northwestern crow wanders inland in Washington and Oregon.

IDENTIFICATION: The Northwestern crow tends to be a small replica of the common crow, also having a predominantly black body with a purple gloss. Its nostrils are barely visible due to the bristlelike feathers that rise from its forehead. It has large, strong feet, a sturdy bill, and long, thick feet. All are black.

SIZE: The northwestern crow rarely grows longer than 16 or 17 inches.

FOOD: The diet consists of shellfish, other invertebrates, insects, offal, seashore carrion, plus some seeds and berries.

FLIGHT SPEED: The norm here is from 20 to 30 mph, but crows have been known to reach speeds of 40 to 45 mph.

Common Crow (*Corvus brachyrhynchos*)

RANGE: Breeding takes place from northern British Columbia, northern Saskatchewan, northern Manitoba, northern Ontario, central Quebec, and southern Newfoundland south to northern Baja California, central Arizona, central New Mexico, Colorado, central Texas, the Gulf Coast, and southern Florida.

IDENTIFICATION: The common crow is a large, predominantly black bird with a purple gloss. The sturdy bill, the long, thick legs, and the large, strong feet are also black. The bird's nostrils are hidden by bristlelike feathers that rise from its forehead. The tail is gently rounded but has a somewhat square tip.

SIZE: This predator measures from 17 to 21 inches in length.

FOOD: Over 650 different items have been discovered in the diet, 70 percent of which is vegetable matter—large amounts of corn and other cultivated crops, as well as wild fruits and seeds. The remainder consists of insects, spiders, reptiles, amphibians, snails, birds and their eggs, carrion, crustaceans, and small mammals.

FLIGHT SPEED: Though the crow usually averages between 20 and 30 mph in flight, he has been known to attain speeds of from 40 to 45 mph.

Fish Crow (*Corvus ossifragus*)

RANGE: The locale for this bird is from the coast of Rhode Island to the coast of southern Florida, west along the Gulf Coast to southeast Texas, and inland along the major waterways.

IDENTIFICATION: The fish crow highly resembles the common crow in that it is also mostly black with a purple gloss, has feathers rising from its forehead that tend to hide its nostrils, and has a sturdy bill, long, thick legs, and large, strong feet, all of which are black. The fish crow, however, is smaller and slimmer than the common crow, and its wings are broader at the base and more pointed at the tips. The tail is gently rounded.

SIZE: This predator averages between 16 and 20 inches in length.

FOOD: Being omnivorous, the fish crow's diet ranges from primarily marine invertebrates, offal, bird's eggs, seashore carrion, and insects to seeds, fruit, and berries.

FLIGHT SPEED: Though the crow can reach speeds of from 40 to 45 mph in flight, its usual speed ranges from 20 to 30 mph.

UPLAND GAMEBIRDS

Ruffed Grouse (*Bonasa umbellus*)

RANGE: Locale for this bird includes the Yukon and Porcupine river valleys of Alaska and the Yukon. In addition, they are found throughout Canada and the U.S. Pacific Northwest, northern Rocky Mountain states and the Middle Atlantic region.

IDENTIFICATION: The ruffed grouse has a large, square, reddish-brown or gray tail with thin, dark barring, followed by narrow, light barring, followed by a broader black band, and terminating in a light band. A ruff composed of blackish feathers appears on both sides of the bird's neck. The upper parts range in color from gray to brown, mottled with darker colors. The undersides tend to be lighter, on occasion buffy, and are barred with black and dark browns. The head is crested; and a small, bare, red patch appears above each eye. The West Coast members of this species are reddish, those of the Rocky Mountains grayish. Eastern ruffed grouse are brownish. Females and young are duller colored, with less prominent ruffs.

SIZE: Adult ruffed grouse usually from 16 to 19 inches in length.

RUFFED GROUSE

BLUE GROUSE

FOOD: About 90 percent of the diet consists of leaves, buds, fruits, seeds, and nuts. The remaining 10 percent is made up of insects.

Blue Grouse
(Dendragapus obscurus)

RANGE: This gamebird is found from southeastern Alaska down through western Canada and California to northwest New Mexico.

IDENTIFICATION: This gamebird has distinctive large feet, short legs, and a short, stout bill. Its plumage tends to be dusky or grayish-blue in color, and its tail is square-tipped and black. However, some members of the species have a wide terminal band of light color on their tails, while others have a narrow band or no band at all. The male has whitish feathers under its tail and on its throat. Above the eyes is a small bare patch of orange or yellow skin. The female is black with brown bars and mottling and sports a dark though light-tipped tail.

The male has smallish inflatable air sacs at the sides of his throat to assist in vocalization.

SIZE: This western grouse measures from 15½ to 21 inches in length.

FOOD: A major portion (approximately 90 percent) of the diet is composed of leaves, seeds, and berries. The remainder consists of animal matter such as insects and spiders.

Spruce Grouse
(Canachites canadensis)

RANGE: This bird, also called Franklin's grouse, is found in Alaska, Canada, and along the entire U.S.-Canadian border, from Washington to Maine.

IDENTIFICATION: In the male, this gamebird's throat, undersides, and tail are black. The upperparts are brown, barred with darker brown, and marked with white at the flanks and the sides of the throat. A small, bright-red patch of bare skin is found just above the eyes of the male. The female lacks this red spot, and the black coloring of the male is replaced by browns in the female.

SIZE: The spruce grouse averages between 15 and 17 inches in length.

FOOD: Its diet consists of buds and needles of the spruce and other conifers, along with berries and vegetable matter. Some insects are included.

SPRUCE GROUSE

Greater Prairie Chicken
(*Tympanuchus cupido*)

RANGE: Western Canada and the southern United States are the two areas where this gamebird may be found.

IDENTIFICATION: In general, the prairie chicken, or pinnated grouse, is brown, buff, and barred dark brown above, and a lighter brown and whitish below. On each side of the bird's throat is a cluster of slender black pinnate feathers. In the vicinity of this cluster in the male are large orange air sacs that are inflatable. The tail is short, rounded, and very dark.

SIZE: This grouse measures from 16½ to 18 inches in length.

FOOD: Eighty-five percent of the diet consists of all forms of vegetable matter. Insects, particularly grasshoppers, comprise the remainder.

Sage Grouse
(*Centrocercus urophasianus*)

RANGE: This species is found in parts of the western United States and minute sections of southeastern Alberta and southwestern Saskatchewan.

IDENTIFICATION: This gamebird is the only grouse that has a black belly. Its tail feathers are long and pointed, its throat black with a tiny white necklace. The white breast features prominent feathers, and the remainder of the plumage is mottled or barred with white, black, dark brown, and light brown. Yellow is the color of the small, bare-skinned patch above the eye. The hen is mottled and barred in black, browns, and white over most of its body, but, as in the male, the belly is black, flanked by white.

SIZE: The sage grouse is the largest of all grouse, measuring 22 to 30 inches in length. The average female is 22 inches, the average male 28 inches.

FOOD: Its diet consists of tender, succulent vegetation and some insects. Adults eat the leaves of the sage, but their gizzards and stomachs are not constructed to accept harsh foods.

Sharp-Tailed Grouse
(*Pedioecetes phasianellus*)

RANGE: This species is located in vast sections of southern Canada, and in several parts of the northern United States south through Nevada, Utah, and Colorado.

IDENTIFICATION: This gamebird has a long, pointed tail, and its body is barred light brown with dark brown and black above. Below, it is whitish. The breast is scaled with brown and the flank is barred with brown and black. The wings are grayish on top, spotted with white. The long central tail feathers are the same color as the bird's back; the remainder of the tail is white. An air sac and a small crest appear on the throat, but the side of the neck is devoid of long feathers.

SIZE: The sharp-tailed grouse measures from 15 to 20 inches in length. Though the same size as the ruffed grouse, it is a bit slimmer.

FOOD: Ninety percent of the menu consists of leaves, grass, fruits, and seeds. Grasshoppers and other insects comprise the rest.

Chukar Partridge
(*Alectoris graeca*)

RANGE: The semiarid mountain regions of the western United States, specifically parts of Wash-

CHUKAR PARTRIDGE

ington, Idaho, Nevada, Wyoming, Colorado, and California, are this bird's haunts.

IDENTIFICATION: The chukar partridge has a short tail which is brownish-gray above. The wings are the same color. Two black lines that begin at the forehead, run through the eyes and then turn downward, form a "V" on the upper breast which fully encloses the yellow throat and cheeks. The lower breast is gray; the rest of the underside (the dark-barred flanks inclusive) is yellowish. Red or pink is the color of the legs, bill, and feet. Immature birds are usually duller in color.

SIZE: This gamebird, on the average, measures 13 inches in length.

FOOD: Fruit, seeds, and leaves comprise 60 percent of the diet, the rest being insects and spiders.

Hungarian Partridge
(Perdix perdix)

RANGE: This gamebird breeds in large sections of southern Alberta and southern Saskatchewan, plus small sections of Manitoba and Ontario. Practically every northern U.S. state has border representatives of this species, down through the northern portions of California, Nevada, Utah, Iowa, Illinois, and Indiana.

IDENTIFICATION: The Hungarian partridge has a gray nape and breast, and a brownish-red face and throat. Its cape, wings, and tail are black. The back, also black, is barred with a brownish-red. The wings have white spots. Undersides are buffy; flanks buffy-gray, barred with a reddish-brown. In the center of the breast a dark brown spot is conspicuous. Gray is the color of the bill, feet, and legs.

SIZE: This species measures between 12 and 14 inches.

FOOD: Leaves and shoots of grasses and clover, seeds, berries, grain, spiders, and insects all are part of this gamebird's diet.

Ring-Necked Pheasant
(Phasianus colchicus)

RANGE: The ring-necked pheasant ranges from southern Canada down through Baja California and northern Mexico, and can be found in parts of Texas, Oklahoma, Kansas, Missouri, Illinois, Indiana, Ohio, and Maryland.

IDENTIFICATION: The cock is more colorful than the hen. It has a head and neck which are a dark metallic green, separated from the rest of the body by a white ring. A bright red patch of bare skin is conspicuous about the eye and on the cheek. The lengthy feathers above the eye form a double crest. The plumage of the underparts, upper back, and shoulders is a rich, bronzy red-brown with dark-brown, black, and white markings. The feathers of the rump and up the lower back are grayish-green; the flank feathers are a light golden brown with dark-brown streaks. The slender, pointed feathers of the tail are dull bronze barred with dark brown, and cover over one-half the length of the body. Legs and feet are gray, the bill is yellowish. The hen is brownish and much paler below, marked with darker browns and black above. Darker brown and whitish bars streak the lengthy yellow-brown tail.

SIZE: This gamebird measures between 21 and 36 inches in length, depending upon sex. The cock tends to be about 10 inches longer than the hen.

FLIGHT SPEED: The ring-necked pheasant flies between 35 and 40 mph.

RING-NECKED PHEASANT

BOBWHITE QUAIL

FOOD: Twenty-five percent of the diet consists of insects, the remainder being shoots, nuts, and fruit.

Bobwhite Quail
(Colinus virginianus)

RANGE: This species is sparse out West, located only in parts of southern British Columbia, Washington, Oregon, Idaho, Arizona, and Mexico. But moving eastward, this bird is far more abundant and is found from southeast Wyoming, eastern Colorado, and eastern New Mexico all the way to the Atlantic, save for the New England states.

IDENTIFICATION: The bobwhite quail is a chicken-like bird with strong, lengthy legs; a stout bill; and a short, dark, strong tail. Its color tends to vary depending upon its range, but in general the bird is brownish—barred with white and lighter below. Above, it has brown marked with darker brown; frequently, these dark browns have random whitish spots. The dark-brown head is slightly crested, featuring white eye stripes. Many—but not all—members of the species have a white throat as well. The female tends to be dull yellow or buff in color.

SIZE: Measuring 8½ to 10½ inches in length, this gamebird is smaller than the average quail.

FLIGHT SPEED: Over short distances, the bob-

white's flight is strong and rapid, often reaching speeds of 40 to 45 mph.

FOOD: Eighty-five percent of its diet consists of all types of plant life; the remainder is primarily insects.

Harlequin Quail
(Cyrtonyx montezumae)

RANGE: This gamebird, also known as Mearn's quail, inhabits the far southwestern United States, ranging from Arizona, New Mexico, and Texas down through the less arid and more mountainous areas of southern Mexico.

IDENTIFICATION: The breast and undersides of the harlequin quail are reddish-brown; the flanks and sides of the neck are gray with conspicuous round, white spots. Long buff feathers comprise the crest at the back of the head, accentuating the head's large appearance. The stocky bird's head is white, and is separated from the breast by a black ring at the neck. Mustaches, earmarks, and a black throat patch are additional features. The wings, tail, and back are variegated designs of black, white, and brown. On the distaff side, the browns are duller, and the female is more lightly colored below and on the throat and head. In addition, there are dark markings behind the eye and at the lower edge of the throat.

SIZE: Measuring 8 to 9½ inches in length, the harlequin is similar in size to the bobwhite quail.

FLIGHT SPEED: The quail clocks 40 to 45 miles an hour, but can sustain this speed only over rather short distances.

FOOD: Acorns, piñon nuts, other seeds and grasses and leaves comprise the harlequin's diet. Insects are rarely eaten.

Gambel's Quail
(Lophortyx gambelii)

RANGE: The arid Southwest is the bird's haunt, from New Mexico, Colorado, Utah and Nevada through northeastern Baja California.

IDENTIFICATION: The males of the species feature a black forehead that lacks the white spots of the California quail. They also have a buff-colored belly with a big, centrally located black spot. The flank feathers are reddish-brown with white streaks and slashes. The hens are similar to the males in that they also have a buff-colored belly and white streaks across their reddish-brown flanks.

SIZE: The Gambel's quail reaches lengths of from 10 to 11½ inches in length.

FLIGHT SPEED: Forty to 45 miles an hour is the speed of this quail. Though strong and rapid, its flight is usually over short distances.

FOOD: A mere 2 percent of the diet consists of insects; the major portion consists of leaves, seeds, plant shoots, fruit, and grain.

Mountain Quail (Oreortyx pictus)

RANGE: This upland bird resides on the coastal ranges from southern Vancouver Island in British Columbia down to northern Baja California, and in the Sierra Nevada and other ranges of eastern Nevada and California. Introductions into the western states of Washington, Idaho, Oregon and Nevada have been successful.

IDENTIFICATION: The mountain quail's head, shoulders, lower breast, and crest are a grayish blue. A long, pointed, stiff plume rises from its head. The upper breast and throat are reddish-brown. The neck, also a grayish blue, is separated from the upper

breast by a white line. There is also some white around the eyes and about much of the face. The flanks are colored reddish-brown with an upper edging of white, and a series of wide, rounded bars (also white) cover the bottom part of the back. Wings and tail are a neutral brown.

SIZE: This gamebird measures 10½ to 11½ inches in length.

FLIGHT SPEED: Though it has a strong, rapid 40- to 45-mile-an-hour speed, the quail usually flies but short distances.

FOOD: Buds, seeds, fruit, flowers, leaves, and plant shoots comprise most of the diet. An insignificant number of insects is also consumed.

Scaled Quail (Callipepla squamata)

RANGE: This bird is found only in Texas north to Colorado, west to Arizona and south to Mexico.

IDENTIFICATION: Dark-edged gray-and-white scales appear to coat the breast, neck, and shoulders of this species. A white topknot caps the gray head. A medium brownish-gray colors the back, wings, and tail; the feet and legs are a blue-gray. Both sexes are alike in coloration.

SIZE: This species measures 10 to 12 inches in length, this being generally a couple of inches longer than the bobwhite quail.

SCALED QUAIL

FLIGHT SPEED: The quail moves rapidly and strongly over short distances, hitting speeds of from 40 to 45 miles an hour.

FOOD: Insects comprise approximately 30 percent of the diet, with buds, seeds, leaves, and other plant material making up the rest.

California Quail
(*Lophortyx californicus*)

RANGE: This quail ranges from southwestern British Columbia to the southern tip of Baja California, and inland from the Pacific to western Nevada. In recent years the species has been introduced in parts of Utah, Nevada, Idaho, Oregon, and Washington.

IDENTIFICATION: The adult male of this species has a long, large-tipped black plume that curves forward from the forepart of its dark reddish-brown cap. The forehead, as well as a line that extends from it to the back of the head above the eye, is white. The necklace beginning behind the eye and bordering the black throat and face is also white. The breast is grayish-blue, as is the back of the neck, the nape of which is spotted with white. The belly feathers are white with black edging, save for the middle of the abdomen—there, they're reddish-brown. The back and tail are medium brown; so, too, are the flanks, which feature white slashes. The hen does not have the reddish-brown patches and the white-and-black patterned head. Her plume

tends to be browner and her face whitish with dull brown marks and spots. Otherwise, she highly resembles the male.

SIZE: At from 9½ to 11 inches in length, the California quail is just a bit larger than the bobwhite.

FLIGHT SPEED: Though frequently attaining speeds of 40 to 45 miles per hour, the quail usually travels only very short distances.

FOOD: Leaves, grain, fruit, seeds, and grass make up about 95 percent of the diet, with insects and other animal matter comprising the remainder.

Wild Turkey
(*Meleagris gallopavo*)

RANGE: The wild turkey has six subspecies: the eastern (most of eastern U.S.), the Florida (basically Florida), the Merriam (mostly western U.S.), the Mexican (central Mexico), the Rio Grande (of U.S. Southwest), the Gould (northwestern Mexico).

IDENTIFICATION: The wild version of the turkey is slimmer and has longer legs than the domestic variety. Its wattles, neck, and head are reddish, grading to a blue. The attractive plumage is an iridescent bronze with black bars; the tail tips are buff. The male has a long hank, consisting of hairlike feathers hanging from its breast; the hen usually lacks this "beard." The wings are round and short;

CALIFORNIA QUAIL

WILD TURKEY

the feet and legs are large and strong. The large, sturdy bill appears to be hooked.

SIZE: This gamebird measures from 36 to 48 inches long, with the hen usually averaging some 10 inches shorter than the cock. The average weight of these gobblers is between 15 and 20 pounds.

FLIGHT SPEED: Though the species cannot fly long distances, it can attain speeds of 30 to 35 miles per hour when it does take flight.

FOOD: Twigs, fruit, seeds, and nuts make up 85 percent of the wild turkey's menu; the rest is insects.

EDIBILITY: Turkey meat, traditionally served at the Thanksgiving table, is rich in protein and the B vitamins. Though it's usually fattier than chicken, turkey meat has less fat than that of the duck.

Band-Tailed Pigeon
(Columba fasciata)

RANGE: The band-tailed pigeon breeds from southwest British Columbia to the mountains of Baja California and northern Nicaragua. It winters from California, Arizona, and New Mexico southward.

IDENTIFICATION: The band-tailed pigeon's head, foreneck, and complete breast are a pinkish-gray. A conspicuous narrow white bar separates the head from the cape. The latter is a metallic, black-bordered grayish-yellow that fades into a greenish-gray black. Rump and wings are gray and flight feathers are almost totally black. The gray-green tail is centrally barred with dark gray. Undertail plumage and belly are white, while the legs, feet, and bill (which ends in a black tip) are yellow. The red-rimmed eyes are also yellow.

SIZE: This gamebird averages between 14 and 15½ inches in length.

FOOD: This species favors nuts, especially acorns. But berries, flowers, fruit, grain, and other seeds and vegetables also make their way into its diet.

Willow Ptarmigan
(Lagopus lagopus)

RANGE: Large groups are found in the wide-open areas of Canada and Alaska, though some have

WILLOW PTARMIGAN

wandered down into the northern United States east of the Rocky Mountains.

IDENTIFICATION: In summer, the male's belly, feet, legs, and wings are white. Its rather small tail and its bill are black, and the remainder of its plumage is a reddish-brown, including the throat. A "comb," or tiny patch of bare skin located above the eye, is a strong scarlet. The hen, on the other hand, is mottled a buff-brown, and is white above. Her feet, legs, and belly are whitish; the rest of the undersides are wavy-barred with whitish, buff, and brown colorings. In winter, however, both male and female are totally white save for the tail and bill, which remain black.

SIZE: The willow ptarmigan measures from 15 to 17 inches in length.

FOOD: Fruit, buds, leaves, and insects are consumed through the warmer months; in winter, the twigs of shrubs and trees are added to the diet.

EDIBILITY: Ptarmigan flesh is dry in winter, but turns tender and develops an aromatic flavor with the advent of summer.

Mourning Dove
(*Zenaidura macroura*)

RANGE: The species breeds throughout North America and southern Canada, and winters from the Great Lakes south to Panama.

IDENTIFICATION: The mourning dove has a smallish black spot behind and below its dark eyes. The tail is wedge-shaped and slender, the feathers being white-tipped except for the longer central ones. The plumage is buff-brown with a metallic purplish sheen at the side of the neck. The wings are gray with a purple tinge to them, though the flight feathers are somewhat darker. Occasionally,

MOURNING DOVE

the back will be sparsely covered with very dark brown spots.

SIZE: The mourning dove averages between 11 and 13 inches in length.

FLIGHT SPEED: The mourning dove has been clocked at between 60 to 65 miles per hour.

FOOD: Seeds (mainly those of weeds) practically make up this bird's entire menu. Minute amounts of other vegetable matter are eaten.

White-Winged Dove
(*Zenaidura asiatica*)

RANGE: Though this bird is found mainly in the Southwest, there are members of the species throughout the continental U.S. and parts of southern Canada.

IDENTIFICATION: The plumage is predominantly brown-buff, with some purplish tinges (particularly around the head). A conspicuous white patch is visible on the wing. The flight feathers are practically black, and white patches are evident on the partly rounded tail. The orange eye features a minute black spot behind and below it. The feet and legs are red, the bill black.

SIZE: The white-winged dove measures from 11 to 12½ inches in length.

FOOD: Shrubs and cacti, the fruit of trees, grain, and other vegetable matter comprise this gamebird's diet.

American Woodcock
(*Philohela minor*)

RANGE: In warmer weather, this bird is found from southeastern Manitoba down through the eastern tip of Texas, and throughout the entire eastern United States. In winter, it is concentrated in the southeastern United States, spreading a bit farther into

WOODCOCK

Texas, Oklahoma, Arkansas, Alabama, Georgia, and Florida.

IDENTIFICATION: The American woodcock has a straight bill that is twice the size of its head. Its neck is rather short, as is its tail. Above the coloring is a variegated pattern of black, grays, and browns; below, it is rufous. There is a trio of wide, black bands separated both from one another and from the gray forehead by thin, rufous bands. The legs, feet, and bill are a dark flesh color.

SIZE: This species measures 10 to 12 inches in length.

FOOD: Earthworms make up the bulk of the diet, but occa seeds, berries, and insect larvae are significant components of the diet.

WATERFOWL

Barnacle Goose *(Branta leucopsis)*

RANGE: This species is located along the coastal regions of North America from Labrador down to North Carolina, as well as inland as far as Ohio.

IDENTIFICATION: The barnacle goose's head, bill, and chest are black; in contrast, its face, cheeks, and upper throat are white. The remainder of the bird's upperparts is dark-slate or brownish. Underparts are white. The bird's neck, also black, is rather long.

SIZE: Medium-sized for a goose, this bird averages between 24 and 27 inches in length.

FLIGHT SPEED: Though geese usually fly at speeds of 55 to 60 miles an hour, they are capable of reaching 65 to 70 mph.

FOOD: Grass is the primary dish on the menu.

BLUE GOOSE

Blue Goose *(Chen caerulescens)*

RANGE: The Gulf Coast of eastern Texas and Louisiana is the habitat of this bird.

IDENTIFICATION: The blue goose features a white head, upper neck, and throat. Its back and a major portion of its body are a dark brown-gray. The flight feathers on the wing are black; the tail and the feathers below the wing are white. Though the edge of the bill is black, the rest of the bill and the legs are pinkish. Immature blue geese have dark bills and lack the white heads of their parents.

SIZE: This species is medium-size, measuring from 25 to 30 inches long.

FLIGHT SPEED: Geese can attain speeds of 65 to 70 miles per hour, but they'll average between 55 and 60 mph.

FOOD: The menu consists of sedges, grain, grasses, and waterweeds.

Common Canada Goose *(Branta canadensis)*

RANGE: The breeding range is from northern Canada down to central California. There are a couple of colonies south of this line. In the winter, the species travels down to the southern United States and even into northeastern Mexico.

CANADA GOOSE

IDENTIFICATION: The body is brownish while the head, tail, neck, feet, and bill are black. Several white patches are apparent on the cheeks. The throat and underrump are also white.

SIZE: This species varies widely in size, measuring from 22 to 40 inches in length.

FLIGHT SPEED: Fifty-five to 60 miles per hour is the norm for geese, but they can fly as fast as 65 to 70 mph.

FOOD: The common Canada goose feasts on aquatic vegetation, grain, and grass.

Emperor Goose
(Philacte canagica)

RANGE: Winters are spent primarily in the Aleutian Islands, but Hawaii and California also feature the species. On rare occasions, some will be found in Oregon.

IDENTIFICATION: The main body coloring is a grayish-blue, but the bird's head and rear portion of its neck are white. The throat is black. The wings and the body feathers are dark-edged, giving this species a scaly appearance. The very young birds have a grayish-blue coloring spotted with white on their heads and necks.

SIZE: Medium-size for a goose, this bird is from 26 to 28 inches in length.

FLIGHT SPEED: The norm for the goose is from 55 to 60 miles an hour, but full speed nears the 70-mph mark.

FOOD: Shellfish and seaweeds comprise the bulk of the diet. In tundra regions, however, berries and grasses are eaten.

Snow Goose *(Chen hyperborea)*

RANGE: The most abundant of all North American geese, this species inhabits northern Baja California, Mexico, the Gulf Coast, and the Atlantic Coast from New Jersey down through the Carolinas.

IDENTIFICATION: Though predominantly white, the snow goose has black flight feathers. The black-edged bill and the legs of the species are pink. Immature snow geese are gray above, with somewhat blackish bills.

SNOW GOOSE

SIZE: The snow goose is medium size, measuring 25 to 38 inches long.

FLIGHT SPEED: Fifty-five to 60 miles an hour is the usual speed for geese, but they have been known to reach 65 to 70 mph.

FOOD: Waterweeds, sedges, grain, and grasses rank high on the menu.

Ross' Goose *(Chen rossii)*

RANGE: Though it breeds in a tiny section of the coastal tundra in northwestern Keewatin and northeastern Mackenzie, it relocates in winter in California's Central Valley.

IDENTIFICATION: The Ross' goose resembles the snow goose in that it is white and has black flight feathers on the wings. It differs, however, in that its pink bill is not black-edged. The legs are pink. The bill is relatively rough, and has warts at its base.

SIZE: At 20 to 26 inches in length, this is the smallest American goose.

FLIGHT SPEED: Sixty-five to 70 miles an hour is full speed for the goose, but it cruises at 55 to 60 mph.

FOOD: The menu consists of grasses, sedges, grain, and waterweeds.

BRANT

White-Fronted Goose *(Anser albifrons)*

RANGE: The western United States breeds most of these birds. They are also found occasionally along the Atlantic Coast.

IDENTIFICATION: Body coloring is a grayish-brown. The feet tend to be either orange or yellow, the forward section of the face white. Young white-fronted geese do not have white faces, although they do have light-colored bills.

SIZE: Ranging from medium to large among geese, this species measures between 26 and 34 inches long.

FLIGHT SPEED: Though geese have topped 65 miles per hour, their usual speed is 55 to 60 mph.

FOOD: The bulk of the diet is composed of berries, nuts, leaves, grain, and grasses. On occasion, aquatic insects are consumed.

Brant *(Branta bernicla)*

RANGE: The brant usually spends its winters along the Pacific Coast from Baja California north to British Columbia, and along the Atlantic Coast from North Carolina up through Massachusetts. However, this far-ranging species is often found farther north or south of these haunts.

IDENTIFICATION: The brant's short neck is black, as are its head, bill, and chest. On the upper neck of the adult there appears a partial white necklace. The remainder of the species' upperparts are brownish or a dark-slate color. The American subspecies has small, light-gray markings on the front section of its white underparts.

SIZE: Twenty to 24 inches in length, the brant is smallish to medium-size among geese.

FLIGHT SPEED: Geese travel at speeds of 55 to 60 miles an hour, but can attain 70 mph if necessary.

FOOD: Sea lettuce and eelgrass are the main foods. Small insects are also occasionally consumed.

Black Brant *(Branta nigricans)*

RANGE: Breeding area includes the coasts of the Canadian Arctic east to longitude 110° W. Winters are spent on the Pacific Coast south to Baja California and inland to Nevada.

BLACK DUCK

IDENTIFICATION: The black brant has a black breast that extends into a blackish belly. Unlike the brant, this species has a complete, rather than partial, white collar around its neck. The forepart of the undersides is also much darker, making the bird appear blacker.

SIZE: A typical member of this species is about 24 inches long.

FLIGHT SPEED: Geese can attain speeds of 65 to 70 miles per hour, though the norm is 55 to 60 mph.

FOOD: Like the brant, this species primarily eats eelgrass, but also dines on sea lettuce.

Black Duck *(Anas rubripes)*

RANGE: Breeding range includes central Canada east to northern Labrador and Newfoundland, and down to the Great Lakes region and eastern North Carolina. In winter, the bird ranges from the southern edge of the breeding area to the Gulf Coast and southern Florida. Its distribution is rather spotty.

IDENTIFICATION: Both sexes appear similar, having very dark brown bodies with paler cheeks and throat. The black-bordered speculum is purple. The yellowish-to-greenish bill has a black knob at its tip. The legs are red or dusky. The underparts appear nearly black when the duck is in flight.

SIZE: The black duck measures from 21 to 26 inches in length.

FLIGHT SPEED: Though it can get up to speeds of 65 to 70 miles an hour, the duck's norm is 55 to 60 mph.

FOOD: Three-quarters of the black duck's diet is vegetable matter, mainly grasses and aquatic plants. The remainder consists of animal matter—specifically crustaceans, insects, mollusks, and small fish.

Black-Bellied Tree Duck *(Dendrocygna autumnalis)*

RANGE: Though native to southern Texas, this bird has strayed into Arizona and California.

IDENTIFICATION: The bill of this species is a bright pink, the legs a pale pink. The breast is brownish, as are the upperparts. The black-bellied tree duck, as its name indicates, has a black belly. The throat and cheeks are gray, the wings mantled dark.

SIZE: The black-bellied duck reaches from 20 to 22 inches in length.

FLIGHT SPEED: The norm for ducks is 55 to 60 miles an hour. They can attain speeds of 65 to 70 mph.

Bufflehead *(Bucephala albeola)*

RANGE: The bufflehead breeds across much of Canada and Alaska. It winters in Mexico and along the Gulf Coast.

IDENTIFICATION: The male has a large, blackish head that is overlayed with a purplish-green iridescence. Above and behind the eye, a white quarter-circle patch is conspicuous. The tail and back are black; the rest of the plumage is white, including a prominent upper-wing patch that is very noticeable when the duck is swimming. The female features a grayish-brown back and head, and lighter-colored flanks that are whitish below. On the lower rear quarter of the head a tiny white spot can be seen.

SIZE: The smallest of the diving ducks, the bufflehead measures 12 to 16 inches long.

FLIGHT SPEED: The duck's normal speed is 55 to

60 miles per hour, but it can reach 65 to 70 mph at times.

FOOD: Eighty percent of the menu is fish, mollusks, insects and crustaceans. Aquatic plants make up the remainder.

Canvasback *(Aythya valisineria)*

RANGE: This species winters in British Columbia, Montana, Colorado, the eastern Great Lakes, and eastern Massachusetts down to central Mexico, the Gulf Coast states, and northern Florida. Breeding takes place from central Alaska to Manitoba and south through California, Utah, Colorado, Nebraska, and Minnesota.

IDENTIFICATION: The back and flanks of the male are whitish, and the head and bill appear longer than those of the Redhead. Where the head and bill merge, there is a slight concave curvature. The female has a brownish breast and head, a whitish belly and flanks, and a light-gray back.

SIZE: The canvasback averages between 19 and 24 inches in length.

FLIGHT SPEED: This bird has been clocked at 72 miles an hour.

FOOD: Eighty percent of the diet is composed of vegetable matter—primarily aquatic plants and wild celery of the genus *Vallisneria*. Fish, insects, and mollusks are sometimes eaten.

American Coot
(Fulica americana)

RANGE: The main breeding area extends in Canada from New Brunswick to British Columbia. In addition, there are colonies in Florida, along the Gulf Coast, and in Panama, Nicaragua, and Baja California. In winter, the bird relocates in southern British Columbia, the American Southwest, the Ohio River Valley, and Maryland down to Panama, the Greater Antilles, and the Bahamas.

IDENTIFICATION: The plumage of the American coot is a darkish gray that becomes a bit lighter below. Beneath the short tail, a patch of white is visible. The eye is red; the feet and legs are a shade of green. The bill, on the stout side and conical, is the color of white china. The downy young are

AMERICAN COOTS

blackish and feature an orange bill; in addition, the feathers about the shoulders, neck, and head are either orange or orange-tipped.

SIZE: Similar in size to a small chicken, this species is 13 to 16 inches long.

FLIGHT SPEED: Though they usually fly at speeds of from 55 to 60 miles an hour, ducks can at times attain 65 to 70 mph.

FOOD: Being omnivorous, the American coot dines on all classes of vegetable matter, as well as crustaceans, worms, snails, tadpoles, and fish.

European Coot *(Fulica atra)*

RANGE: Breeding occurs throughout Europe, save for the northernmost areas. Some stragglers have been sighted in Greenland, Labrador, and Newfoundland.

IDENTIFICATION: The European coot is almost an exact replica of the American coot, except for the fact that the feathers located below the tail are slate-gray instead of white.

SIZE: Similar in size to the American coot, this species is from 14 to 16 inches long.

FLIGHT SPEED: Ducks travel at an average pace of 55 to 60 miles an hour. However, speeds of 65 to 70 mph are attainable.

FOOD: This species feeds on plant food and tiny animals. In shallow-water regions, the coot dives for water plants, which it picks clean of snails and other small aquatic animals.

Common Eider
(Somateria dresseri)

RANGE: The Aleutian Islands, southwestern Alaska, most of Canada, and Maine comprise this species' breeding range. Winters are spent at the southern tip of the ice pack and southward to British Columbia, Washington, Middle Atlantic states.

IDENTIFICATION: There is a conspicuous amount of white on the back and wings of the male. The white head features a black cap and a pair of pale-green patches at the rear. The flight feathers of the wings, the rump, the tail, and the undersides are black; the breast is pinkish. The feet are greenish-gray. The bill tends to be either orange or yellow. The female's bill, however, is grayish, and her body is a light brown with black and dark-brown barrings.

SIZE: The largest of the eiders, the common eider measures 21 to 27 inches in length.

FLIGHT SPEED: Speeds of 65 to 70 miles per hour are attainable, but the norm is 55 to 60 mph.

FOOD: Mollusks make up 80 percent of the American eider's diet. Tiny crustaceans, fish, echinoderms (sea urchins and starfish), and small amounts of plant food are also eaten.

King Eider
(Somateria spectabilis)

RANGE: This species breeds on the islands and Arctic coasts from northwestern Alaska to Hudson and James bays and northern Labrador. In winter, this eider is located in the Aleutian Islands, southern Alaska, California, the Great Lakes, New Jersey, and Newfoundland.

IDENTIFICATION: From a distance, the forward half of the male king eider seems white, the rear half black. The crown is gray, the breast pinkish. Traces of pale green are visible on the face, and there is a tiny black crescent beneath each eye. A prominent white patch can be seen on the wing and also on the bottom part of the rump. A black-edged frontal knob at the tip of the orange bill flares out over the forehead. The hen is a browner red than the American eider hen.

SIZE: The king eider is 18 to 24 inches long.

FLIGHT SPEED: Ducks can reach 65 to 70 miles per hour, but normally their pace is 55 to 60 mph.

FOOD: The menu includes mollusks (predominantly mussels), starfish, sea urchins, crustaceans, and insects. A small percentage of the diet is composed of seaweeds and eelgrass.

Spectacled Eider
(Lampronetta fischeri)

RANGE: The principal breeding region is the Aleutians, but some members of the species are found on rare occasions on Kodiak Island.

IDENTIFICATION: The male spectacled eider's neck, throat, and upperparts are white; its underparts are black. The head is a pale green, and a large white area edged with black—the spectacles—appears around the eyes. The female has brownish plumage and lighter-brown "spectacles."

SIZE: This species is from 20 to 23 inches long.

FLIGHT SPEED: Ducks average 55 to 60 miles an hour, but can reach a top of 70 mph when necessary.

FOOD: This diving duck feasts on crowberries, sedges, pondweeds, and algae (seaweeds).

EDIBILITY: The meat of this duck is reputed to be one of the favorite foods of the Aleutians.

Steller's Eider (Polysticta stelleri)

RANGE: Breeding area includes the Arctic coasts and islands of Alaska. A number of these eiders are also found in Maine and Quebec.

IDENTIFICATION: This bird has a thick body and

a rather short neck. The drake features a white head with a tiny gray crest at the back. The throat is black, as is the eye-ring. The back, tail, feathers beneath the tail, and neck-ring are black. The breast and remainder of the undersides are reddish-brown. The flank, as well as a major portion of the wing feathering visible from the sides, is white. The feet and bills of both sexes are blackish. The female has a whitish and dark-brown eye-ring and a white-bordered blue wing speculum.

SIZE: At from 17 to 19 inches in length, the Steller's eider is small for a diving duck.

FLIGHT SPEED: Ducks reach a top speed of 70 miles an hour, but the norm is 55 to 60 mph.

FOOD: A major portion of the diet consists of fish, worms, insects, mollusks, and crustaceans. The remaining percentage is made up of plant food—algae and pondweeds.

Fulvous Tree Duck
(Dendrocygna bicolor)

RANGE: This duck resides in California, New Mexico, Texas, and southern Louisiana. Some strays have been sighted around the Great Lakes as far north as Nova Scotia.

IDENTIFICATION: This species has a grayish bill and grayish feet; its head, breast, and underparts are tawny-brown, or fulvous, in color. The back and rear of the neck are a dark brown. The throat features a buffy patch and a series of white slashes that are underlined with dark brown at the side.

SIZE: The smallest of the tree ducks, the fulvous tree duck measures 18 to 21 inches in length.

FLIGHT SPEED: Top speed for the duck is 70 miles per hour, but the normal pace is 55 to 60 mph.

FOOD: The diet consists primarily of grasses, seeds, and weeds. But on several occasions, this duck has been sighted gleaning cornfields.

Gadwall (Anas strepera)

RANGE: Breeding occurs in most of western North America and in some of the Middle Atlantic states. For winter, gadwalls usually migrate to southern Mexico or to Florida.

GADWALL

IDENTIFICATION: The breeding plumage of the male is gray; the neck and head are brownish. Black feathers are apparent above and below the gray tail. The prominent white speculum is bordered with black. At the bend of the wing, there is a chestnut-brown patch. The belly is white, the feet yellowish, and the bill dark. The female's body is almost completely dull brown save for the whitish upperparts and white speculum.

SIZE: The gadwall is from 19 to 23 inches long.

FLIGHT SPEED: Speeds of 55 to 60 miles an hour are normal for the duck, but 70 mph is its peak.

FOOD: Approximately 90 percent of the diet consists of aquatic plants, grasses, grains, nuts, and acorns. The remaining 10 percent is animal matter, primarily insects and crustaceans.

Common Golden-Eye
(Bucephala clangula)

RANGE: This duck breeds in the northern coniferous forest, from the tree line down, in southern Alaska and along the entire U.S.-Canadian border. The bird winters from the bottom edge of the breeding region to the southern United States.

COMMON GOLDENEYE

IDENTIFICATION: The drake features a glossy dark-green head with a circular white patch just before, and slightly under, its golden eyes. The breast, neck, flanks, and underside are white. The dark-gray back is broadly hatched with white at the sides. The young and the females have red-brown heads, and their neck, breast, and undersides are white. The flanks and a bar across the top of the breast are gray, as is the back. The white on the wing of the drake is more prominent than on the wing of the hen.

SIZE: The common, or American, golden-eye measures 15 to 21 inches in length.

FLIGHT SPEED: Ducks average between 55 and 60 miles an hour, but can attain a top speed of 70 mph.

FOOD: Predominantly animal matter comprises this duck's diet—mollusks, insects, fish, and crustaceans. During the breeding seasons, plants are also consumed.

Barrow's Golden-Eye
(Bucephala islandica)

RANGE: The breeding area in western North America is shaped like an inverted "V," beginning in southeastern Alaska and northwestern British Columbia; one arm extends south to California's High Sierras, the other southeast to the Colorado mountains. Some breeding also takes place in northern Quebec. Winters are spent on the Pacific shores from southern Alaska to central California, and on the Atlantic from Long Island, New York, to the mouth of the St. Lawrence River.

IDENTIFICATION: The Barrow's golden-eye is remarkably similar to the American golden-eye, except for the fact that the female has a shorter bill. The head of the drake is glossed with purple, and there is a white crescent between the bill and the eye.

SIZE: This species is 16 to 20 inches in length.

FLIGHT SPEED: The norm for ducks is 55 to 60 miles an hour; the top speed is 70 mph.

FOOD: Seventy-five percent of the diet is animal matter, principally mollusks. This species consumes more insects than the American golden-eye.

Harlequin Duck
(Histrionicus histrionicus)

RANGE: Breeding area extends from south-central and southern Alaska (including the Aleutian Islands) south and southeast to British Columbia, the mountains of California, and Colorado. Some breeding takes place in Quebec and Labrador, as well as in Maryland.

IDENTIFICATION: The body of the drake is medium blue-gray except for the reddish-brown flanks. A patch of white is conspicuous in the front of the eyes. Behind the eyes, there is a tiny circular spot and a vertical white line. There are also a pair of white slashes radiating from the back onto the breast. A heavy white bar followed by smaller white bars is visible on the wing when the bird is at rest. There is also a reddish-brown streak on the crown. Both male and female have legs, feet, and bills that are grayish-blue. The female's body is medium brown save for the lighter belly and a trio of white spots on the head—two in front, one behind.

SIZE: The harlequin duck's length range is from 14½ to 21 inches.

FLIGHT SPEED: The typical cruising speed for these ducks is 55 to 60 miles an hour, with recorded bursts of up to 70 mph.

FOOD: Animal matter—insects, crustaceans, fish, mollusks, and sea urchins—comprises 97 percent of the diet. The rest is vegetation.

Red-Breasted Merganser
(Mergus serrator)

RANGE: Breeding occurs near the tree line in Canada, Alaska, and along the U.S.-Canadian border. In winter, this merganser stays in the coastal regions from southeastern Alaska to Baja California, as well as along the Atlantic Coast.

IDENTIFICATION: Both sexes have ragged crests, with eyes, bills, legs, and feet that are red. The drake features a metallic-green head. The forward and lateral sections of the neck are white, as are the undersides and breast. The breast is crossed by a wide, dark-buff band that is haphazardly streaked with dark brown. The back and parts of the wings are black, the speculum white. There are some white patches on the wings which, like the tail, are shaded dark gray. The flanks and the feathers above and below the tail are finely barred with black.

SIZE: The red-breasted merganser is 19 to 26 inches long; it is smaller than the common merganser.

FLIGHT SPEED: The mergansers can attain speeds of 100 miles an hour.

FOOD: Their diet consists of fish, crustaceans, mollusks, and aquatic insects.

Common Merganser
(Mergus merganser)

RANGE: Breeding occurs in southern Alaska, across Canada, in the mountains of central California, Arizona, and New Mexico, and east to the Great Lakes region and northern New England. Wintering spots are southerly to New Mexico, the western Gulf Coast, northern Georgia, and South Carolina.

IDENTIFICATION: The drake lacks a crest; its neck and head are dark metallic green. Its bill is a bright red, its back black, its tail gray, its feet orange, and its breast white. The undersides and the flanks usually have a bright pink tinge to them. The female, on the other hand, has a rough crest at the back of its reddish-brown head. The neck is the same color as the head, while the throat is white. The tail and back are medium gray, the flanks light gray. The

black and gray wings feature a white speculum. The undersides tend to be whitish.

SIZE: Relatively large for a duck, the common merganser measures 21 to 27 inches in length.

FLIGHT SPEED: Mergansers have been clocked at speeds as fast as 100 miles an hour.

FOOD: A major section of the diet consists of fish, but tiny mollusks, insects, aquatic plants, and crustaceans are also eaten.

Hooded Merganser
(Lophodytes cucullatus)

RANGE: This species breeds from southeastern Alaska and southern Canada down through the whole of the United States save the southwestern quarter. Winters are passed in the region encompassed by southern British Columbia and Massachusetts south through mid-Mexico, the Gulf Coast, and Florida.

IDENTIFICATION: The drake features a large crest; its head, neck, back, and tail are black. A white quarter-circle is very conspicuous just below and to the rear of the eye. The breast and underparts are white, and a pair of black fingers stretches from the back over to the breast. The feet are a dusky-yellow, the bill blackish, and the eyes yellow. The female has a smaller crest. Her back, tail, and wings are dark gray; in addition, each wing is patched with

HOODED MERGANSER

white. The flanks and upper breast are medium gray; the remainder of the upperparts is whitish. The face is a dusky grayish-red that fades to a dusky brownish-red at the crest and at the back of the head. The female's bill and feet are a dusk-yellow and her eyes are yellow.

SIZE: The smallest and slimmest of the mergansers, the hooded merganser measures 16 to 20 inches long.

FLIGHT SPEED: Mergansers can attain speeds of approximately 100 miles an hour.

FOOD: The hooded merganser primarily eats animal matter—fish, insects, crustaceans, and amphibians. Small amounts of grasses, pondweeds, grain, and other vegetable foods make up the rest of the menu.

Green-Winged Teal (*Anas carolinensis*)

RANGE: This bird's breeding area is enclosed in a triangular region of North America from west-central Alaska and northwestern Mackenzie south to lower California and east to Newfoundland. Winters are spent in southern British Columbia and through most of the United States.

IDENTIFICATION: Both male and female feature bright, glossy-green speculums. The male's head is a bright reddish-brown with a wide, bright-green band beginning around the eyes and continuing to the back of the head. The buffy breast is spotted with black. The feathers below the tail are buffy and edged with black. The belly is white; the remainder of the plumage is grayish. The female is grayish-brown, though lighter below. Her feet and bill are grayish.

SIZE: This teal measures 12 to 16 inches in length.

FOOD: Plants (chiefly the aquatic type, but including grasses) comprise 80 percent of the diet. Insects, mollusks, and maggots dining on rotting fish are also consumed.

Blue-Winged Teal (*Anas discors*)

RANGE: Breeding occurs throughout most of Canada and also throughout the U.S. Southwest and Middle Atlantic states.

IDENTIFICATION: Many of the tiny feathers atop the wing are a very pale blue. Both sexes feature lengthy, bright-green speculums. The drake has a large white face crescent that can be at times indistinct. His bill is blue-black, his head blue-purple. The breast, flanks and underparts are dullish brown; the back is a darker brown. Feathers above and below the tail are black, and just forward of the tail is a white patch. The female is brownish; her dusky bill is edged with pink. Her legs are yellowish.

SIZE: This teal measures 14 to 17 inches long.

FOOD: Though primarily a mix of aquatic plants, rice, corn, and grasses, the diet does include about 30 percent animal matter—mollusks, crustaceans, and insects.

Cinnamon Teal (*Anas cyanoptera*)

RANGE: Breeding range is from southwestern Canada and Wyoming south to northern Mexico. In winter, this teal is found from the southwestern United States through Central America and northwestern South America. Some members of this species are occasionally found in the eastern United States.

IDENTIFICATION: The hens and drakes are so similar in appearance that they are nearly impossible to tell apart. Practically all of the plumage is a rich cinnamon-brown hue. Back and wings lack such coloring, and instead resemble those of the blue-winged teal.

SIZE: This duck measures 16 inches in length.

FOOD: Eighty percent of the diet consists of grasses, weeds, and aquatic plants; the remainder is insects and mollusks.

Common Teal (*Anas crecca*)

RANGE: Found mainly in Africa and Eurasia, the common teal is also found along the eastern coast of North America as far south as South Carolina.

IDENTIFICATION: The male common teal resembles its green-winged counterpart in almost every way. There are two main differences: the common drake has a horizontal white stripe on its back above the folded wings, and it does not have the vertical white crescent behind the breast. The female is indistinguishable from the female green-winged teal.

SIZE: This species measures 13 to 16 inches in length.

FOOD: About 80 percent of the diet is plant matter—mainly aquatic, but some grasses. This teal also eats insects, mollusks, and the maggots that dine on rotting fish.

American Widgeon
(Mareca americana)

RANGE: Breeding occurs in Alaska, western Canada and the American Northwest. Wintering spots reach from southern Alaska, the central United States, and New England south to Costa Rica and the West Indies.

IDENTIFICATION: The male of the species features a gray head with a glaring white cap and a metallic-green band that extends from just in front of each eye to the rear of the head. The breast is pink, while the flanks tend to be whitish, the wings dark. Each wing has a bright-green speculum and a conspicuous white patch on top. The gray tail has black feathers both above and below. Preceding these feathers is a white mark that extends up from the belly. The female widgeon is recognized by her grayish head, brownish back, and tannish-red flanks and breast. The white patch on the male wing is, in the female, light gray. The feet and bills of both sexes are blue-gray.

AMERICAN WIDGEON

WOOD DUCK

SIZE: Somewhat larger than the European widgeon, the American widgeon measures 18 to 23 inches long.

FLIGHT SPEED: Ducks average between 55 and 60 miles an hour, but can reach 65 to 70 mph.

FOOD: Over 90 percent of the diet consists of vegetable matter, the remainder being insects and mollusks.

Wood Duck *(Aix spousa)*

RANGE: Breeding ranges stretch from central British Columbia to central California, and are also located in such disparate areas as the Great Lakes, New England, Northeast Canada, the Gulf Coast and Cuba. Winters are spent in the United States, and as far south as mid-Mexico.

IDENTIFICATION: This species is considered one of the most beautiful of all native American ducks. It has a big crest and a chunky body. The drake's head is a mix of iridescent green and blackish purple. On each side of the head there is a pair of thin white lines—one curving over the eye from the bill to the terminal point of the crest, and the other running parallel to it, but beginning behind the eye. The throat is white, with one finger stretching to just beneath the eyes and the other to the back of the head. Red, black, and white colorings comprise the variegated bill. The neck and breast are a bright reddish-brown. The back is of a dark iridescence, and the flanks are a creamy buff with black-and-white vertical lines separating them from the breast. The upperparts are whitish. The female of the species has a grayish head that features a whitish ring around the eye. Her throat is white and her back is a moderate brown-gray. The breast and flanks are brownish.

SIZE: The wood duck is 17 to 21 inches long.

FOOD: Mainly a vegetarian, this species dines on shrub and tree seeds, grasses, and aquatic plants. Some insects and tiny spiders are also consumed.

Masked Duck *(Oxyura dominica)*

RANGE: This species is found in Vermont, Massachusetts, Maryland, Louisiana, Wisconsin, Florida, and Texas.

IDENTIFICATION: The drake has a reddish-brown head and a black mask about the entire face. The upperparts are buffy and there are dark spots on the flanks. The wings and tail are dark, and the wings feature a large, white speculum. The black back has red-brown spots. The hen is dark buff in color, with dark-brown spots and scales. She sports a cap as well as a pair of streaks below it. Her wings and tail are the same color as the male's.

SIZE: The masked duck measures 9 to 11 inches long.

FLIGHT SPEED: The peak among ducks is 65 to 70 miles per hour, the norm 55 to 60 mph.

Mottled Duck *(Anas fulvigula)*

RANGE: This species inhabits the Gulf Coast from Texas to Mississippi, as well as the Florida peninsula.

IDENTIFICATION: True to its name, the mottled duck is pale brown, mottled with black, and its speculum is a bluish green.

SIZE: The mottled duck, also called the dusky duck, is about 20 inches in length.

FOOD: Though the majority of the diet consists of acorns, berries, grains, grasses, sedges, and aquatic vegetables, tiny amounts of insect material and mollusks are consumed.

Oldsquaw *(Clangula hyemalis)*

RANGE: Breeding takes place in the Arctic tundra from western Alaska through northern Canada. Winters are spent along the coasts from the breeding places to California in the West and North Carolina in the East. An additional wintering area is the Great Lakes.

IDENTIFICATION: The drake alternates between a pair of distinct, rich plumages every year. The hen also has differing summer and winter plumages. In summer, the male's head, neck, breast, and tail are a dull-glossed black; in addition, there is a large, pale-gray patch above the eyes. The dark feathers of the back are bordered with a light brown. The upperparts and huge areas of the wings are white, the feet a grayish-blue. The pinkish bill has a dark tip, a white edge, and a blue patch in the vicinity of its base. Come winter, the upper breast, neck, and head become white, with a black patch under and to the back of the eye. A grayish area is visible about the eye. The forecrown is a buffy-yellow. The rest of the tail, breast, and most of the back, as well as several wing feathers, are black. The remainder of the undersides and the wings are white. All plumages feature distinctively long tail feathers.

In summer, the hen's back and legs resemble the male's, but the head and neck are a grayish-blue, and the eye-ring is white. A white streak, beginning in the back of the eye, runs down the neck, widening near the brown breast. The flanks are a brownish gray, the underparts a light gray. In winter, the female's head and neck turn whitish, as do the flanks and undersides. A gray patch is visible to the back of, and below, the eye, and gray stretches from the cap down the rear of the neck. The bill tends to be grayish despite the season.

SIZE: The oldsquaw measures 14 to 23 inches in length, approximately one-third of which is its tail.

FOOD: Mostly mollusks, crustaceans, insects, and fish are consumed, along with tiny amounts of pondweeds and grasses.

Mallard *(Anas platyrhynchos)*

RANGE: This surface-feeding species is located throughout a major portion of the temperate Northern Hemisphere (save for northeastern Canada).

IDENTIFICATION: The adult male features a metallic-green head and neck that are separated from its bright-chestnut breast by a thin, white ring. The underparts are a light gray, the upperparts a dark gray. The tail is both black and white, with conspicuously curled feathers on top. The dark wings have a band of rich iridescent blue; the band is edged on each side first by a thin, black band and then a thin, white band. These bands, called speculums, are partly visible when the bird is at rest. The female also has a speculum, but it is predominantly dark or mottled brown and bordered by white. She has a tiny dark cap and an eye stripe, and lacks the

curled tail feathers of the male. The male's bill is yellow, the female's orange. Orange feet are common to both sexes.

SIZE: The mallard ranges from 16 to 27 inches in length.

FOOD: Aquatic vegetables, acorns, berries, sedges, grains, and grasses are consumed, as well as small amounts of mollusks and insects.

Ring-Necked Duck *(Aythya collaris)*

RANGE: Breeding takes place from southern British Columbia to the Maritime Provinces and in the northern parts of the U.S. Winters are spent along the coasts to Massachusetts and southwestern British Columbia.

IDENTIFICATION: The ring-necked duck features a glossy purple head, a black breast, a dark, greenish-glossed back, gray flanks, and white upperparts. The grayish bill has a black tip; the two colors are separated by a thin, white ring. The breast and neck are separated by a brown ring. The female is brownish and has a white ring above the eye and a slender, white line leading from this ring to the back of the head. Male and female both have a conspicuous pale-blue patch on the wing.

SIZE: This species measures 14 to 18½ inches in length.

FOOD: Four-fifths of the diet revolves around vegetable matter—mainly sedges, grasses, and aquatic plants. The remainder consists of mollusks and insects.

Ruddy Duck *(Oxyura jamaicensis)*

RANGE: Breeding extends from central British Columbia and the Canadian Prairie Provinces down to Guatemala and the Bahamas. In winter, they relocate to southern British Columbia, the south-central United States, Pennsylvania, and Massachusetts.

IDENTIFICATION: In summer, the drake has a reddish-brown back, neck, and flanks. His cheeks are white, but his cap, spikelike tail, and the flight feathers on the wings are blackish. The bill is a rich blue; the upperparts are whitish and barred lightly

MALLARD

with browns. Come winter, the drake is similar to the female, but he retains the white cheeks. The hen features a dark brownish-gray cap, neck, upper breast, back, wings, and tail. Horizontal brown streaks run through her whitish cheeks. The feet, legs, and bill are gray, the undersides whitish, and the flank and lower breast excessively barred with black.

SIZE: The ruddy duck is from 14 to 17 inches long.

FOOD: Approximately 75 percent of the diet consists of wild celery, sedges, pondweeds, and grasses; the remainder includes such animal matter as insects and tiny shellfish.

Pintail *(Anas acuta)*

RANGE: This bird breeds in western and north-central North America, New England and eastern Canada. Winters are spent northerly to southeastern Alaska, along the Gulf Coast and in Massachusetts.

IDENTIFICATION: The male features a rather long, pointed tail which, when in full plumage, accounts for his large size range. The lengthy, slender tail and neck are quite distinctive. His back and flanks are grayish, but he is blackish beneath the tail and on the wing. The head and throat are a bright

purple-brown; this color also proceeds down the rear of the neck. The forward part of the neck and the undersides are white, as well as a finger that extends from the throat first into the brown area of the head and then to behind the eye. A patch at the rear of the flanks is also white. The feet and the bill are bluish-gray.

SIZE: As mentioned above, the pintail's length varies extensively, depending on tail size. Adults average between 20 and 29 inches in length.

FOOD: The menu reads as follows: aquatic plants, weeds, small mollusks, grasses, crustaceans, grains, and insects.

Redhead *(Aythya americana)*

RANGE: The breeding range encompasses a triangular area from eastern British Columbia south to lower California, and from there east to the Great Lakes. Come winter, the redhead resides from southwestern British Columbia east to Maryland, and south to lower Baja California, central Mexico, the Gulf Coast, and Florida.

IDENTIFICATION: The male's back, wings, flanks, and tail are gray; the breast is blackish; the head is reddish-brown. The bill and legs of both

PINTAIL

REDHEAD

sexes are grayish-blue. The bill's black tip is separated from the remainder of the bill by a thin, whitish line. The male breast is white. The female is buffy brown and also has a white breast.

SIZE: The redhead is 18 to 22 inches in length.

FOOD: Ninety percent of the diet is aquatic plants; the remainder is mollusks and insects.

Greater Scaup *(Aythya marila)*

RANGE: The scaup breeds in central and south-central Alaska through the Yukon into western Mackenzie. In winter, it relocates from southeastern Alaska down to southern California, and from the eastern Great Lakes and the Canadian Maritime Provinces south to Florida and the Gulf Coast.

IDENTIFICATION: The greater scaup is quite similar to the redhead in appearance except for the fact that the male of this species features a metallic-green head with a purplish cast, and the female greater scaup has a dark-brown head with a conspicuous white feather patch. Also, at the bottom of the blue-hued bill the whiteness extends farther into the wing as a gradually thinning, blurry line. The "nail" at the bill's tip is much larger in the greater scaup than in the lesser scaup.

SIZE: This species measures from 15 to 21 inches in length.

FOOD: The menu is an omnivorous one, being 50 percent vegetable (aquatic plants and grasses) and 50 percent animal (crustaceans, insects, and mollusks).

Lesser Scaup *(Aythya affinis)*

RANGE: This scaup breeds from central Alaska and the tree limits of Mackenzie and Keewatin southerly, east of the Coast Ranges to central British Columbia and Idaho, and east of the Rocky Mountains to Colorado, Nebraska, and Iowa; and a bit farther east. In winter, it is found northerly along the coasts to British Columbia and Connecticut, and in the interior to southern Arizona, southern New Mexico, central Texas, Missouri, and the southern Great Lakes area.

IDENTIFICATION: This species has less white in the wing than does the greater scaup, and a smaller

dark-colored "nail" at the tip of the bill. The head is often glossy purple rather than green, giving the scaup the appearance of having a slight crest.

SIZE: The lesser scaup measures 14 to 19 inches in length.

FOOD: Being more of a vegetarian than the greater scaup, this species favors aquatic plants and grasses. It does, however, also consume crustaceans, insects, and mollusks.

Common Scoter *(Oidemia nigra)*

RANGE: Breeding areas include western and southern Alaska and the Aleutian Islands. In winter, the species relocates to the Great Lakes, and along the Atlantic from Newfoundland to South Carolina.

IDENTIFICATION: The common scoter's entire plumage is slightly glossy and blackish. The bright-orange bill features a grayish "lip." The feet and legs are gray-green. The female is dark brown, but has whitish cheeks and a whitish throat; her bill is a gray-blue. The immature scoter looks like the female, but is lighter below. The eyes of this species are dark.

SIZE: Moderate-size for a diving duck, this scoter measures 17 to 21 inches long.

FOOD: Mollusks are the preferred dish, with crustaceans, fish, and insects the runners-up. About 10 percent of the diet is made up of plant matter.

Surf Scoter *(Melanitta perspicillata)*

RANGE: Breeding occurs from northeastern Alaska to the western half of Mackenzie and on islands in James Bay. Some have also been seen in central Labrador. Come winter, this scoter resides along the Pacific Coast from the eastern Aleutians to Baja California and on the Atlantic Seaboard from Nova Scotia to North Carolina.

IDENTIFICATION: The male's plumage is black but there is one white patch at the back of the head and another at the forehead. The large, swollen bill consists of white, red, bluish-gray, and yellow colorings in a variegated pattern. The eyes are white. Both sexes have dusky-yellow feet and no trace of

SURF SCOTERS

white at all on the wings. The female is dark brown, and has white patches on the head not unlike those of the white-winged scoter. But the surf scoter has an additional white patch at the back of the head.

SIZE: Medium-size among diving ducks, this scoter measures between 17 and 21 inches.

FOOD: Sixty percent of this bird's diet consists of mollusks, and another 10 percent is vegetable matter. Scallops and oysters are also consumed.

White-Winged Scoter
(*Melanitta deglandi*)

RANGE: This species breeds in west-central Alaska, northwestern Mackenzie and along the Rocky Mountains. In summer, the bird ranges from eastern Canada south to Massachusetts. In winter, it moves on to the Great Lakes and along the temperate Atlantic and Pacific coasts.

IDENTIFICATION: This scoter features a glossy-purplish plumage that is punctuated by a white speculum and a tiny patch of white about the eyes. The bill is orange, lightening to yellow at the tip. There is a black knob at the base of the bill. The female's body is dark brown, her upperparts white. A pair of white spots are located beneath the eyes, one is forward, the other at the back. Her bill is gray-blue. The feet of both sexes are a dusky-pink, the eyes white. Immature scoters resemble the female.

SIZE: A medium-size diving duck, this scoter measures between 19 and 23 inches in length.

FOOD: Approximately 75 percent of the diet is composed of mollusks, mussels, clams, and oysters.

The remainder is crustaceans, a small amount of plant matter, and insects.

Shoveler (*Spatula clypeata*)

RANGE: The breeding area encompasses Alaska, central and southeastern Canada, both coasts and the Great Lakes area. In winter, the species spreads eastward.

IDENTIFICATION: This species has a wide spatulate bill that is quite distinct among North American birds; this bill is longer than the bird's head. The drake's breeding plumage consists of a metallic-green head and neck. The breast, upperparts, tail, and the forepart of the back are white. A wide, red-brown band stretches across the belly from flank to flank. The remainder of the back and the feathers above and below the tail are blackish-green or black. The female is reminiscent of the female cinnamon teal, even to the horizontal, pale-blue line above the wing. The eye of the hen is dull brown, that of the drake a rich yellow.

SIZE: The shoveler averages some 20 inches in length.

FOOD: Primarily grasses and aquatic plants. In addition, large amounts of vegetable debris which are strained from the ooze at marsh and pond bottoms. Small amounts of mollusks, aquatic insects, and fish are also eaten.

SHOVELER

SHOREBIRDS

Purple Gallinule
(Porphyrula martinica)

RANGE: Mainly inhabiting coastal lowlands and large river basins in the triangle formed by Tennessee, Louisiana, and South Carolina, this shorebird has also found its way throughout most of the United States and into southeastern Canada.

IDENTIFICATION: The purple gallinule sports extremely flamboyant colors. A deep, rich purple coats the head, neck, and undersides, while the back, wings, and upper tail feathers are dark greenish with a bronzelike sheen. The feathers below the short tail are white, while the feet and legs are a prominent yellowish-green. The bill is bright red at the base and bright yellow at the tip. A tough, fleshy casque begins at the bottom of the upper bill and flares out to the middle of the head. Immature gallinules are light gray and white below, dark gray above. Their casques and bills are a dull gray. The chicks are glossy black with white bristles on their cap, cheeks, chin, and forehead.

SIZE: Medium-size for a rail, the purple gallinule measures 13 inches in length (the same size as the Florida gallinule).

FOOD: The menus consists of rice, grain, seeds, insects, small mollusks, and amphibians.

Common Gallinule
(Gallinula chloropus)

RANGE: This bird is found in southern Canada, throughout much of the United States and in such South American countries as Peru, Argentina, and Brazil.

IDENTIFICATION: The common gallinule resembles the purple gallinule in general appearance, but it is dark gray instead of purple. The yellow-tipped bill and the casque are bright red, and the legs and feet are greenish-yellow. The top edge of the flank is white, and it appears as a white streak down the side when the bird is swimming. The central feathers of the undertail are dark gray. The downy young are glossy black, and the skin at the bottom of the black-tipped, reddish bill is a bright red. The chin feathers are curled and stiff, the forehead white.

SIZE: Like the purple gallinule, this shorebird is about 13 inches in length.

FOOD: Though consisting primarily of underwater plants, the diet also features herbs, grasses, seeds, and berries. This gallinule also eats insects, snails and worms.

Carolina Rail (Porzana carolina)

RANGE: The Carolina rail breeds throughout lower Canada, Saskatchewan and Manitoba. In the U.S., it can be found in the Southwest, Plains states and the Midwest.

IDENTIFICATION: Typically, this rail has a body that is compressed laterally. Its cap, nape, tail, back, and wings are brown. In addition, the back and wings are spotted and marked with black and buff coloring. There is irregular barring below that is composed of thin, white lines on medium gray. The rest of the head and breast are a warmish-gray, but the face and bib are black. The short, yellowish bill features a blackish tip; the feet and legs are a greenish-yellow. The adult's eye is vermilion, but the eye is yellow in the duller, browner, immature bird. The downy young are a glossy black with curled, stiff chin feathers of a rich orange. Their yellowish bills are enlarged and reddish at the base.

SIZE: A smallish rail, this bird—also called the sora—is only 8 to 10 inches long.

FOOD: The sora eats more vegetation than is the norm for a rail. The diet consists primarily of aquatic plants, but the consumption of small mollusks, insects, and worms is also high, particularly in the spring.

Virginia Rail (Rallus limicola)

RANGE: This shorebird breeds from Guatemala north to southern Canada.

IDENTIFICATION: The Virginia rail has a long bill and very gray cheeks. On its underparts, there are wide, black lines that alternate with thin, wavy white lines. The feet, legs, and bill are pink. The young are nearly black.

SIZE: A medium-size rail, this bird measures from 8½ to 10½ inches in length.

FOOD: The diet consists of worms, mollusks, aquatic insects, amphibians, and small fish. On occasion, seeds are included.

Greater Yellowlegs
(*Totanus melanoleucus*)

RANGE: The breeding grounds are from central Alaska east to Labrador and Newfoundland; the wintering areas are from southwestern British Columbia through the West Indies and Latin America.

IDENTIFICATION: The greater yellowlegs has a slender but sturdy, slightly upturned, blackish bill that is approximately 50 percent longer than the head. The upperparts are dark brown, the outer flight feathers black. The tail (lightly barred) and the back are also black. The bill of this species is proportionately longer and stockier than the bill of the lesser yellowlegs.

SIZE: This shorebird is 12½ to 15 inches long.

FOOD: This bird's menu consists of small fish, insects (primarily aquatic), worms, small mollusks, and crustaceans.

Lesser Yellowlegs
(*Totanus flavipes*)

RANGE: This species breeds from north-central Alaska east to Quebec. Winters are spent along the coastal lowlands from Mexico, the Gulf Coast and South Carolina down through Central America and the West Indies.

IDENTIFICATION: The lesser yellowlegs is practically identical to the greater yellowlegs, except for the fact that the bill of this species is much more slender and, lacking the upturn, much straighter.

SIZE: This shorebird is smaller than the greater yellowlegs, measuring 9½ to 11 inches in length.

FOOD: Like the greater yellowlegs, the lesser yellowlegs consumes insects, small fish, mollusks, and crustaceans.

Wilson's Snipe (*Gallinago delicata*)

RANGE: Though this shorebird breeds in the Arctic tundra down to New York and the mountains of California, it winters from the Gulf Coast states southward to Brazil and Columbia.

IDENTIFICATION: The upperparts of this, the only North American species of snipe, are blackish with buff mottlings. A pair of conspicuous buff stripes are located along the back, and another down the center of the crown. The body is whitish below, but brown-spotted on the throat and tail. The latter is black with a red tip.

SIZE: The Wilson's snipe measures some 11 inches in length, 3 inches of which is its tail.

FOOD: Its menu consists of worms, snails, and insects.

EDIBILITY: The flavor of the flesh is, as the bird's scientific name implies, delicate.

GREATER YELLOWLEGS

PART 3
FISHING

SPINNING

Spinning became popular in America in the late 1940s. It is unique because the reel is mounted on the underside of the rod rather than on top, as in other methods, and because the reel spool remains stationary (does not revolve) when the angler is casting and retrieving.

In operation, the weight and momentum of the lure being cast uncoils line (usually monofilament) from the reel spool. Unlike conventional revolving-spool reels, in which the momentum of the turning spool can cause backlashes, the spinning-reel user has no such problem, for the line stops uncoiling at the end of the cast. The beginner can learn to use spinning gear much faster than he can master conventional tackle. Still another advantage of spinning gear is that it permits the use of much lighter lines and smaller, lighter lures than can be cast with conventional equipment.

THE REEL

On a standard open-face spinning reel, the pickup mechanism is usually of a type called the bail—a metal arm extending across the spool's face. To cast a lure or bait, the angler opens the bail by swinging it out and down. This frees the line which, as a rule, he momentarily controls with his index finger. He casts and then cranks the reel handle—not a full turn but just a small fraction of a turn. This snaps the bail closed, engaging the line.

In place of a manually opened bail, an open-face reel can be designed with an automatic pickup and a lever, or trigger, control. When you begin the cast with this reel, instead of working the bail you pull a

Abu Garcia Cardinal is a typical open-face spinning reel.

long trigger with your casting hand, then cast in the normal manner and simply release the trigger to stop the line automatically. A smoothly functioning pickup mechanism—whether it employs a conventional bail or a lever control—is an extremely important part of the spinning reel.

Other devices on a spinning reel include the drag and the antireverse lock. The drag, an adjustable mechanism usually consisting of a series of discs and friction washers, is fitted on the outer (forward) face of the spool or at the rear of the gear housing in most reels. The drag permits a hooked fish to take out line without breaking off, while the reel handle remains stationary. The antireverse lock, usually a lever mounted on the gear-housing cover, prevents the reel handle from turning in reverse at

SPINNING REEL PARTS

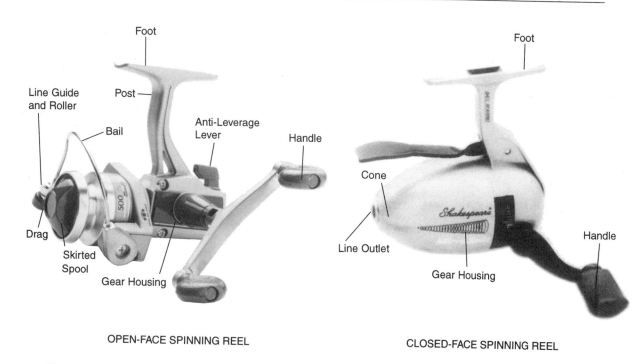

Foot

Foot

Line Guide
and Roller

Post

Anti-Leverage
Lever

Handle

Bail

Cone

Drag

Handle

Skirted
Spool

Line Outlet

Gear Housing

Gear Housing

OPEN-FACE SPINNING REEL

CLOSED-FACE SPINNING REEL

such times as when a hooked fish is running out or when you are trolling.

Spinning reels are designed for all types of fishing. How does the beginner select the right one for his particular needs? A reel's weight and line capacity are the major determining factors.

For ultralight fishing with tiny lures (¹⁄₁₆ to ⁵⁄₁₆ ounce), a reel weighing 6 to 10 ounces and holding 100 yards of 1¼- to 3-pound-test line is the ticket. Reels for light freshwater use weigh 10 to 12 ounces and hold up to 200 yards of 6- or 8-pound-test line. Reels for general freshwater and light saltwater use weigh 12 to 18 ounces and hold up to 250 yards of 8- to 15-pound-test line. Heavy surf-spinning reels weigh upwards of 18 ounces and hold a minimum of 250 yards of 15-pound-test line.

In addition to the open-face spinning reel, there is a closed-face design. This type, too, is mounted under the rod. Its spool and working parts are enclosed in a hood, with the line running through an opening at the front. The pickup mechanism is normally an internal pin, and there's no need for a bail since line control is accomplished by other means. In some of these reels, which were fairly common

at one time, line was disengaged from the pickup by backing the handle a half-turn. In others, it was accomplished by pushing a button, working a lever or disc, or pressing the front reel plate. Closed-face reels are no longer common.

Besides eliminating the bail, closed-face reels give the spool and other parts some protection from the elements and help to keep out sand, dirt, and such. Some fishermen, however, dislike the fact that the line is choked through the constriction at the point of the cone, feeling that this arrangement somewhat limits casting range and accuracy. Another drawback is that the hood enclosing the spool hides the line from the angler's view, preventing him from seeing line tangles, whether the line is uncoiling smoothly, and such.

Mainly because of the simplicity of spinning reels, there has been little gadgeteering by manufacturers. However, some unusual wrinkles have appeared in recent years. These include bails that open automatically, self-centering (self-positioning) bails, rear drags, and skirted spools, which prevent line from getting behind the spool—a problem that crops up occasionally and is particularly vexing.

HOW TO MATCH UP SPINNING TACKLE

This table is meant only as a general guide aimed at helping you put together, in proper balance, the basic elements of a spinning outfit tailored for fish of a particular weight category. Specific conditions—and your ability and personal preferences—should also be considered.

SPECIES OF FISH	REEL	ROD ACTION, LENGTH (Ft.)	LINE (Lb. test)	LURES (Oz.)
Trout, small bass, grayling, panfish	Ultra-light	Ultralight 4 to 6	2, 3	$1/16$ to $5/16$
Smallmouth, large-mouth, and white bass; pickerel, trout, grayling	Light	Light $5^{1}/_{2}$ to $6^{1}/_{2}$	4 to 8	$1/4$ to $3/8$
Large bass and trout, walleye pickerel, pike, snook, landlocked salmon	Medium	Medium 6 to $7^{1}/_{2}$	6 to 10	$3/8$ to $5/8$
Salmon, lake trout, muskellunge, pike, bonefish, tarpon, striped bass, bluefish	Heavy	Heavy 7 to $8^{1}/_{2}$	10 to 15	$1/2$ to $1^{1}/_{2}$
General saltwater use (surf and boat)	Extra-heavy	Extra-heavy 9 to 13	12 and up	1 and up

SPINNING REELS

Daiwa Emblem-X-H is a surf casting reel that weighs 22.4 ounces. It is available in three line capacities up to 220 yards of 30-pound-test line.

Sigma Intrepid features two ball bearings and removable trigger with self-centering bail. Available in ultra-light, light, medium, and freshwater models.

Penn 9500 SS features four stainless steel ball bearings and an oversized drag with a single washer behind the spool for smooth stopping power. Weighing 32 ounces, it will hold 300 yards of 30-pound-test line. A good choice for saltwater fishing.

Quantum Energy Metal Spinning Series offers a one-piece, no-torque aluminum frame and up to seven bearings. Available in three sizes up to light saltwater use.

Fin-Nor Ahab Spinning Reel has a no-wobble spool. Available in four saltwater models from 19.3 ounces and line capacity of 200 yards of an 8-pound-test line, to 32 ounces with a line capacity of 250 yards of a 20-pound-test line.

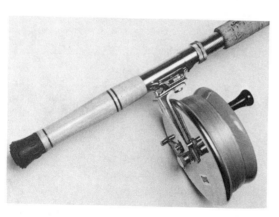

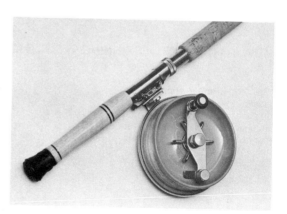

Alvey reel, made in Australia, is a combination spinning and conventional reel that pivots into two positions. During the cast, the spool faces forward and line peels off just as it would peel from a standard open-faced spinning reel. For retrieving, the spool is turned 90° and line is cranked in just as it would be wound on a revolving-spool (baitcasting) reel. With this reel, developed for surf fishing, casts of more than 200 yards are possible.

THE ROD

There are spinning rods designed for every conceivable kind of sport fishing. They come in lengths of from 4 to 13 feet and weigh from 2 to about 30 ounces. Most are constructed of fiberglass, graphite, boron, and even Kevlar, though a few are made of bamboo. Construction is one, two, or three piece; however, spinning rods designed for backpackers may have as many as a half-dozen or more sections.

Spinning rods fall into five general categories: ultralight, light, medium, heavy, and extra-heavy. They are further broken down according to type of reel and design of hand grip.

TRADITIONAL SPINNING ROD DESIGNS

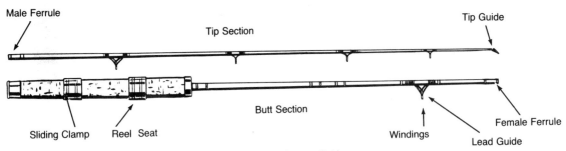

Male Ferrule

Tip Section

Tip Guide

Sliding Clamp

Reel Seat

Butt Section

Windings

Female Ferrule

Lead Guide

Sliding-clamp reel seat. Ultralight to medium actions, for freshwater fishing.

Fixed reel seat. Light to medium actions, general freshwater and light saltwater fishing.

Fixed reel seat with heavy foregrip. Medium to extra-heavy actions, saltwater fishing.

HOW TO CAST WITH SPINNING TACKLE (Captions by Joe Brooks)

The Grip: Proper grip for open-face spinning reel puts two fingers on each side of the reel's supporting shank. With a closed-face reel **(far right)**, proper grip is ahead of the reel seat.

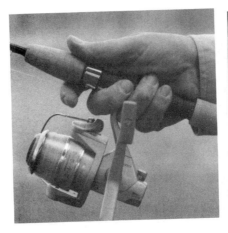

Line Control, Bail: First step in preparing for a cast with an open-face spinning reel is to catch line where it leaves the reel spool with the crooked first finger of right hand **(right)**. Then the left hand flips the line-holding bail to one side, leaving line free to curl off the reel spool when the crooked finger lets it go. **(far right)** Caster's finger holds the line until the rod is whipped through the casting arc and aimed toward target. Then the crooked finger releases the line to let it curl off the reel spool and flow through rod guides for distance cast. The spool of a spinning reel doesn't turn during the cast.

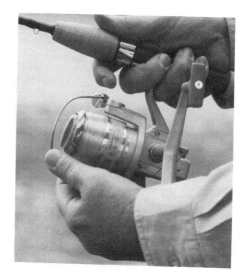

Line Control, Closed Face: A closed-face reel needs a different line-holding system to control the line prior to the cast. Line is run from the reel over the back of the rod-holding hand and pressed against the cork rod grip with the thumb of the rod-holding hand. With line held firmly in place with right hand, the left hand is used to push the reel handle into a position that unlocks the line-holding bail inside the reel. The thumb will release the line for the cast.

To Stop the Lure: There are two methods of stopping forward flight of a lure after the cast. With a spinning reel **(right)**, turn the reel handle forward to engage the line with reel bail. **(far right)** Using an open-face reel, you can also control the cast distance by fingering line as it curls off the reel spool. Turning the handle of an open-face reel will close the bail and engage the line.

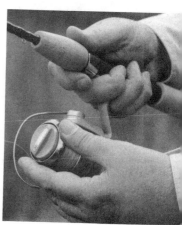

STRAIGHTAWAY CAST

Here are three steps in making a straight-ahead cast where there are no special problems or obstructions. **(left)** The photo shows the starting position: thumb holding the line as the rod points forward and up at about 45 degrees. **(center)** Then the rod is swung back smoothly to the position shown. All done with smoother and faster motion than stop-action photos suggest. **(right)** Then the rod is powered forward and held at the angle shown, while the lure sails to the target.

COPING WITH WIND

These photos show how to cope with the wind. With the wind at your back, let the line shoot forward with the rod tip high. This way the wind can carry the lure the added distance. Casting into the wind, sweep the rod forward and down to minimize wind drift as the lure shoots low over the water.

SIDEARM CAST

The sidearm cast is a good wind-bucker, and useful when overhead foliage makes a conventional forward cast difficult. The cast starts with the rod low and angled forward (**right**). Then comes a backswing and forward sweep that ends with the rod pointing toward the target (**far right**). The line is released just before the rod points toward the target. The rod's follow-through motion curves the bait or lure to the target. Sidearm casts are particularly useful when wading narrow, tree-bordered streams or in boats holding two or more anglers. There's plenty of room for casts with sidearm motion.

UNDERHAND LOB

This underhand cast is made much like a sidearm cast, except that the rod tip is lower on the backswing and higher on the forward sweep. A lure given an underhand lob will sail in a high, soft arc and will hit the water gently. This makes a good cast for the clear and shallow runs where a splashy cast would scare fish. The underhand lob is also useful when there's foliage blocking overhead casts.

FLIP CAST

This short-range, cramped-quarters cast depends on an upward flip of the rod to toss the lure. Start the flip cast by dipping the rod tip sharply **(left)**. After that quick downswing bends the tip of the rod, add to the rod spring with a sharp lifing motion. If the cast is to be short, release the line as the upsweeping rod nears a horizontal position **(center)**. For a longer flip cast, bring the rod up to position shown in photo before releasing the line **(right)**.

BACKHAND LOB

If overhanging limbs block the area over your head and to your right, the backhand job will throw the lure a fair distance. To make the cast, swing the rod to the position shown **(right)**. Then power the rod tip up and toward the target. A high arc drops the lure with a minimum of splash—a good approach for clear, shallow water.

BOW AND ARROW

This is a trick that anglers walking banks can use to shoot a lure through holes in streamside brush. The photos show the same cast from two positions. The technique is the same: Grasp the bend of the lowest hook on the lure so that it will clear your fingers smoothly and safely. Then shoot the lure like an arrow, releasing line at the rod grip as the lure shoots forward.

RETRIEVE

This is the proper stance for a routine retrieve **(left)**. The rod is high enough that its bend will absorb the shock of a hard strike by a big fish. The position is good for hook setting. Note that the angler holds his left hand on the reel handle to keep the line under constant control **(center)**. The rod butt is braced against his body. This photo shows how to gain clearance when playing fish in very shallow, snag-filled water **(right)**.

FLY FISHING

The art of fly fishing dates back to at least the 3rd century A.D. and so is one of the oldest forms of sport fishing. Its adherents—and they are legion—say that it is also the most artistic form of the sport.

Fly fishing is unique in two basic ways: In all other forms of fishing, the weight of the lure or bait is what enables the angler to cast; in fly fishing, the weight of the line itself is cast. In spinning, spincasting, and baitcasting, for the most part, a natural bait or a lure or plug imitating a natural bait is offered to the fish; the fly fisherman's offering is a near-weightless bit of feathers and hair that imitates some insect in one of its forms of life (though some flies—streamers and bucktails—imitate baitfish).

THE REEL

It is generally agreed that the reel is the least important item of fly-fishing tackle, and yet without it the angler would find himself amid a tangle of line and leader. The fly reel is mounted below the rod grip and close to the butt end of the rod. In most kinds of fishing the reel's main function is to store line that is not being used. In handling large fish, however, the workings of the fly reel come into play.

There are two basic types of fly reels, the single action and the automatic.

The single-action reel, which is best when the quarry is either small or quite heavy fish, is so named because the spool makes one complete turn for each turn of the handle. The spool is deep and narrow. The beginner should make sure that the reel has a strong click mechanism to prevent the line from overrunning, and if he'll be tangling with sizable strong-running fish such as striped bass or salmon, he should get a reel with an adjustable drag.

The standard (trout size) single-action fly reel weighs 3 to 5½ ounces and has a spool diameter of

FLY REELS

SINGLE-ACTION FLY REEL

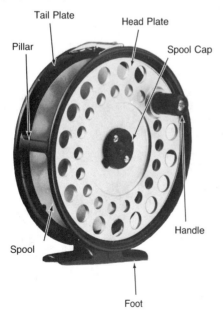

Tail Plate
Head Plate
Pillar
Spool Cap
Handle
Spool
Foot

AUTOMATIC FLY REEL

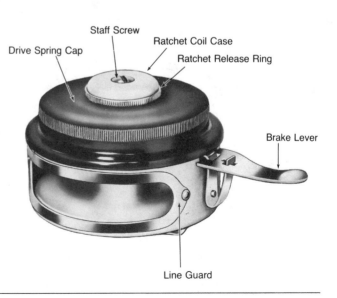

Staff Screw
Drive Spring Cap
Ratchet Coil Case
Ratchet Release Ring
Brake Lever
Line Guard

FLY REEL PARTS

Pflueger Supreme Model 1798, with externally mounted adjustable drag system and easy right-to left-hand conversion. Weighs 7.6 ounces, and holds 90 yards of up to 12-weight line.

Penn International fly reels feature an anti-reverse system that prevents the handle from turning backward when a fish takes line against the drag. International fly reels come in a range of sizes designed to handle lines from weights 6 to 12 with room for plenty of backing.

Pflueger Automatic Model 1195 features stainless steel main spring, foot and line guard. Weighing 9 ounces, it holds 30 yards of up to 8-weight line.

Fin-Nor Ahab Tarpon Buster is an anti-reverse fly reel built to hold a weight 12 fly line and 400 yards of 30-pound-test Dacron backing. The Tarpon Buster easily converts from right to left hand with a few turns of a screwdriver.

Orvis Odyssey fly reels are available in four sizes covering the complete range of fly line weights from 3 to 14. The biggest Odyssey will handle 300 yards of 30-pound-test Dacron backing, ideal for billfish and all other saltwater species.

FLY REEL PARTS (Continued)

Fin-Nor Fast Retrieve fly reels come in three models designed for line weights 8 to 12. All models feature direct drive.

3 to 3½ inches. The spool should be filled with enough line (the fly line itself, usually 30 yards, plus sufficient "backing" line) to reach within about ⅜ inch of the reel's cross braces. Many of the best fly fishermen like 15-pound-test braided nylon or monofilament as backing.

The chief advantages of the single-action fly reels are that they weigh considerably less than the automatics and that they can hold much more line (backing)—an important factor in handling large fish.

The automatic fly reel has a spring-operated spool that retrieves line automatically when the angler activates the spool-release lever. The spring is wound up as line is pulled from the reel, but line may be stripped from the reel at any time, even when the spring is tightly wound.

Though heavier than the single action (weight range is 5 to 10 ounces), the automatic greatly facilitates line control. Instead of having to shift the rod from the right to the left hand (assuming the user is right-handed) to reel in line, as the user of the single-action reel must do, the automatic user simply touches the release lever with the little finger of his right hand.

THE ROD

The rod is of paramount importance to the fly caster. It must be suited to the kind of fishing he does (dry fly, wet fly, bass bugging, and so on), and it must be matched with the proper fly line.

Fly rods are made of either fiberglass, graphite, boron, or bamboo. Graphite and boron are comparatively new developments. Though expensive, graphite fly rods are faster and more sensitive than fiberglass rods. And, ounce for ounce, graphite is twice as strong as glass. What length rod should the beginner select? A good all-purpose length, according to the recommendations of casting instructors and tackle manufacturers, is 8 to 8½ feet with a weight of about 5 ounces. Such a rod should have fast action.

Action, briefly, is a measure of a rod's flexibility, and it determines the use for which the rod is suited. In fast-action rods, best suited for dry-fly fishing, most of the flex (or bend) is at the tip. Medium-action rods, often used for wet-fly and nymph fishing, bend down to about the middle. Slow-action rods, designed for fishing streamers, bass bugs, and the like, bend well down to and even into the butt.

Good fly rods have a screw-lock reel seat, which holds the reel securely. Line guides are usually made of stainless steel, except that the tip guide and sometimes the stripper guide (the one nearest the reel) may be chrome or highly durable carboloy steel. The largest fly rods, those designed for taking tarpon and other large saltwater fish, have an extension butt or a fore-end grip, which gives the angler more leverage in fighting the big ones.

FLY ROD PARTS

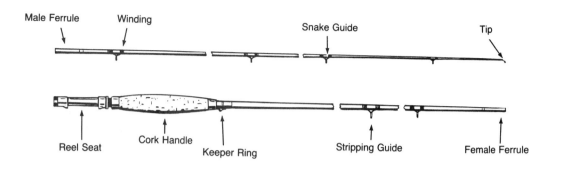

Male Ferrule   Winding   Snake Guide   Tip

Reel Seat   Cork Handle   Keeper Ring   Stripping Guide   Female Ferrule

HOW TO MATCH UP FLY TACKLE

This table is meant only as a general guide for helping you put together, in proper balance, the basic elements of a fly-fishing outfit tailored for fish of a particular weight category. Specific conditions and your ability and personal preference should also be considered.

SPECIES OF FISH	REEL	ROD LENGTH (Ft.)	LEVEL	LINES DOUBLE-TAPER	WEIGHT-FORWARD
Trout, small bass, grayling, panfish	Single-action, auto	6½ to 7½	L4 or L5	DT4F or DT5F; DT6S	———————
Smallmouth, large-mouth, and white bass; pickerel; trout; grayling	Single-action, auto	7½ to 8½	L6 or L7	DT6F or DT7F; DT8S	WF6F; WF8S
Large bass and trout, landlocked salmon, walleye, pickerel, pike,	Single-action	8½ to 9	L8 or L9	DT8F or DT9F; DT9S	WF9F; WF10S
Salmon, lake trout, muskellunge, pike, bonefish, tarpon, striped bass, blue-fish	Single-action	9½	L10	DT10F	WF10F; WF10S

KEY TO LINE DESIGNATIONS: L-Level   DT-Double-Taper   WF-Weight-Forward   F-Floating   S-Sinking

Note: The line sizes above are given in the number system of the American Sportfishing Association. These line sizes are meant only as a general guide, and the newcomer to fishing should note that there is a wide range of conditions and circumstances that determines the correct line weight for a given rod.

HOW TO USE FLY TACKLE (Written by and featuring Joe Brooks)

Gripping the Rod: There are several ways to grip a fly rod, but only two of them give the wrist freedom you need for good fly casting. The grips I like are shown in the **first two photos below.** The main difference in them is that in the first the thumb is extended along the top of the cork; whereas in the second it is curved around the cork. I find this second hand position, with the thumb curved over to meet my forefinger, a bit more free and easy than the extended-thumb grip. It also helps put more power into a conventional overhead cast because it places the back of the hand in a position to exert more force on the rod. The **bottom photo** shows how lightly the rod is held as it pivots in the hand during casting motion. The grip should be comfortable, natural. Pick the rod up between thumb and first finger and let it settle gently into place.

SWITCHING OUT LINE

Before any cast can be made, a working length of line must be switched out through the rod guides. Start by grasping the fly at the hook bend **(below right)** and pulling a little more than a rod's length of line and leader through the guides. Letting that line dangle from the rod tip, pull more line off the reel **(center)** and switch the rod forward and back to pull the slack through the guides. Continue pulling off line and false casting **(bottom left)** until you have enough line working back and forth through the air for a forward cast. Drive the rod forward with extra power when you're ready to deliver the fly.

WRIST POSITION

The wrist of the casting arm should never bend back farther than the position shown when making a normal overhead backcast. Many beginners handicap themselves by breaking the wrist backward, which allows rod and line to fall so low behind them that a good forward toss is almost impossible. An extreme backward bend of the wrist will let the line and rod tip bog down in the water behind you. You'll sometimes see tournament casters tip their rods way back, but that's an expert's stunt. The average angler should stop the rod at 1 or 2 o'clock, as shown.

AIMING YOUR CAST

An important thing to remember in making the forward throw is not to aim the cast directly at the point where you want the fly to hit. Aim a few feet above that point, so the fly will stop above the target and fall gently to the surface. If the cast is aimed too low it will drive line and leader down into the water. This shortens the cast and sometimes tangles the leader.

BACKCAST KNOW-HOW

Backcast Elbow Position: Your elbow should be high for the backcast. Your elbow is lowered smoothly as you power the rod forward. Your elbow should remain at chest height while line snakes out to drop the fly on target. The wrist, which is held stiff during the backcast, is flexed forward and down when the backcast line straightens behind you. The forward motion of wrist and forearm is much like the slow, powerful swing you'd use to hammer a nail into a wall at shoulder height. The rod should go forward to about the 10 o'clock position, then hold steady there as fly, leader, and line fall to the water. The left hand controls slack line.

Incorrect Wrist-Broken Backcast: In these two photos there is deliberate tipping of the wrist in the backcast to show how that common fault can get fly casters in trouble. The rod tips so low that line curls down into the water, where it either bogs down completely or drags enough to ruin the forward cast. Line falling very low behind the angler adds extra weight to the rod and upsets the correct balance of rod power and line weight that's required for good fly casting. To make the backcast properly, stop the rod at the 1 or 2 o'clock position with a firm wrist. That keeps the line high and roughly parallel with the water—in ideal position for the forward cast.

HOW TO PICK UP LINE AND FLY

Beginners often scare fish by yanking a great length of floating line and leader off the water when they're ready to start a new cast. Avoid that commotion by lifting the rod slightly and gently stripping-in line with your left hand. This photo shows proper rod grip and position for this maneuver—wrist at shoulder height and above the rod grip. This position allows the angler to strike if a fish hits the fly at the last second. Slowly strip-in all but 30 or 35 feet of line and leader; then flip the rod up and back to the 1 or 2 o'clock position. That starts the backcast that precedes the new forward throw.

HOW TO RETRIEVE

For all-around efficiency, the strip method of retrieving line is best. As shown here, you do this by extending thumb and finger of your rod hand to form an extra guide for the incoming line as you strip it in with your left hand. Guiding thumb and finger of your rod hand can be clamped on the line instantly if a fish strikes, giving you positive control of the line while you retrieve it. This method also leaves you ready to pick up line for a new cast at any moment. Your rod should be pointed at the fly, but with the tip slightly elevated. In this position, the tip will offer shock-absorbing spring if a fish is hooked.

THE ROLL CAST

The easily learned roll cast pays off heavily when the fisherman has some barrier behind him that prevents a normal backcast. In fact, the roll is a quick way to make a new cast under almost any circumstances. To execute this cast, bring the line in until only 25 feet of line and leader remain on the water **(below left)**. Then move the rod back to the 2 o'clock position and drive it sharply forward and down **(bottom photo)**. The line rolls up from the surface and curls forward to drop fly and leader as neatly as a conventional forward cast. **Photo at right** shows rear view of the roll cast just as the rod is being powered forward. Note the smooth forward "roll" of rod tip and line. With a weight-forward tapered fly line, it's possible to shoot out as much as 25 feet of slack line in the final phase of a roll cast, adding that much distance to cast.

ROLL CAST PICKUP

The first three photos show how to use a roll to pick up line as it drifts down after an upstream cast. You merely lift the rod to a vertical position as line floats near you, then drive the rod forward. You can either let the line roll on out for a short upstream cast or—if more distance is needed—the forward-rolling line can be whipped into a backcast just at it straightens, then shot upstream in a routine forward cast. The **fourth photo** shows how swift current can sweep line down to an angler faster than he can strip it in, leaving him in an awkward position that would be a serious handicap in starting a new cast or striking at a fish. This contorted posture can be avoided by making a quick roll cast to pick up the line.

OVERHAND ROLL CAST

This cast is for small, brush-rimmed pools where a routine roll cast started on the surface would frighten fish. It's also useful when a strong tail wind defeats a regular backcast. Just pull leader and several feet of line from rod tip and false cast into the air with ordinary roll-cast motion, but rotate your wrist to keep the airborne line rolling while you strip more line off the reel and feed it through the guides. With 25 or 30 feet of line rolling like a hoop to your right, make the forward cast and follow through **(right-hand photo)**, driving the rod well down. This variation on the basic roll is ideal for high wind or tight quarters because the line starts in the air close to you and stays there until you're ready to deliver the fly.

BACKHAND ROLL CAST

The backhand version of ordinary roll cast is useful when wading along a shoreline that has trees or brush crowding your right arm. This position gives unobstructed casting room over the water.

HIGH-BANK ROLL CAST

Many times the angler finds himself on a high bank with trees close behind him, blocking the backcast. This calls for a variation of the roll cast. Holding the rod out over the high bank, switch out a working length of line and start a routine roll cast by bringing the rod back to 2 o'clock and then driving it forward. The high-bank variation comes as the rod goes forward. Drive the rod tip farther down than usual to straighten the line.

HORIZONTAL CAST

The horizontal cast is another brush-dodger, one that's particularly useful when angler is wading a stream that has trees leaning low over the water from both banks. Fish in such streams often feed close to the shore, under the low roof of tree limbs. The angler's problem is to get a backcast beneath the overhanging foliage behind him and then drive his forward cast under the foliage that forms a canopy over the rising fish. The horizontal cast, made by holding the rod low and parallel with the water, will get a fly under such obstacles. Line speed is the main trick in this cast. Considerable velocity is needed to keep the low-flying line from sagging into the water. Otherwise the cast is much the same as an overhead throw.

THE "S" CAST

This cast drops the line on moving water in curves that will straighten slowly. That gives the fly a long, natural float, whereas a straighter line on the surface would quickly transmit the motion of the current to the fly, dragging it over the water in a way that spooks fish. There are two good ways to make the "S" cast. One is to shoot the forward cast a bit harder than needed and then stop it abruptly when it's above the target. The other is to wiggle the rod tip from side to side as the line shoots forward.

CASTING OVER OBSTRUCTIONS

You'll often get into a situation where a log or a slab of partially submerged rock separates you from a good fish rising in a pool beyond. In this case, just toss a regular forward cast over the obstruction, aiming a bit high to let the fly fall gently. Line will drape smoothly over the obstruction as shown in these photos. When a fish hits **(bottom photo)** strike with rod high. That tightens line, lifts slack off the obstruction. While playing the fish, steer him around the obstacle.

DOUBLE-HAUL CAST

This technique was originated by tournament casters who used it to set distance records. It makes long tosses easy. The key to the double haul is that it adds the power of the left hand to the force exerted by the rod hand. Start by grabbing line near the rod grip with the left hand and pulling down sharply **(top left)** as line is picked up for backcast. As line sails back **(bottom left)** the left hand is raised to head level to let several feet of line feed into the backcast. Then the left hand pulls line forcefully **(right)** as the forward cast is started. As the forward cast straightens, the left hand releases line to let slack shoot through guides and adds distance to the forward cast.

HOW TO WADE A RIVER

Wading looks easy enough, but it can turn into a dangerous situation if you are swept off your feet in the swift current. The rules for safe wading are simple. First, never take a step in any direction unless your rear or anchor foot is firmly planted. Next, *slide* your lead foot forward until it is secure. When your lead foot is firmly planted, then slide your anchor foot ahead. Never try to wade by lifting your feet. The current will swing your leg out from under you and throw you off balance. Avoid wading big, wide stretches of river. It is safer to wade from pool to pool, taking advantage of slower current to rest. There are several other points to remember when wading:

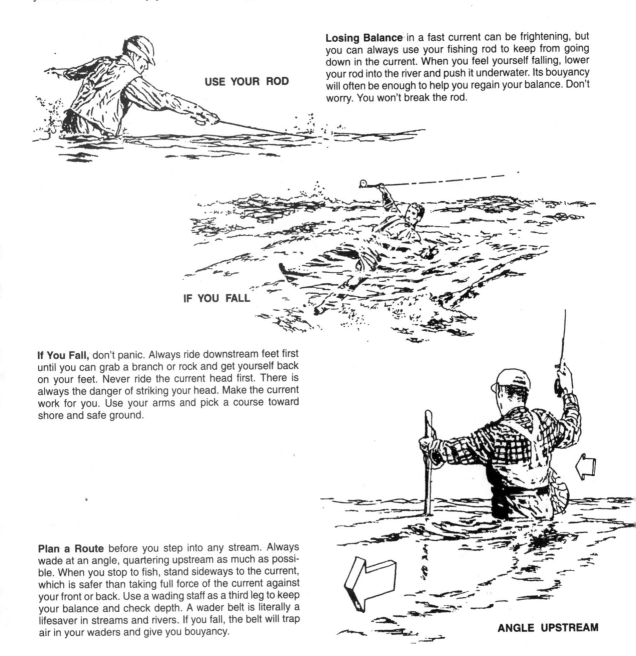

USE YOUR ROD

IF YOU FALL

ANGLE UPSTREAM

Losing Balance in a fast current can be frightening, but you can always use your fishing rod to keep from going down in the current. When you feel yourself falling, lower your rod into the river and push it underwater. Its bouyancy will often be enough to help you regain your balance. Don't worry. You won't break the rod.

If You Fall, don't panic. Always ride downstream feet first until you can grab a branch or rock and get yourself back on your feet. Never ride the current head first. There is always the danger of striking your head. Make the current work for you. Use your arms and pick a course toward shore and safe ground.

Plan a Route before you step into any stream. Always wade at an angle, quartering upstream as much as possible. When you stop to fish, stand sideways to the current, which is safer than taking full force of the current against your front or back. Use a wading staff as a third leg to keep your balance and check depth. A wader belt is literally a lifesaver in streams and rivers. If you fall, the belt will trap air in your waders and give you bouyancy.

BAITCASTING

Baitcasting is a method of fishing distinguished by the use of a revolving-spool reel. Originally intended by its 19th-century creators as a means of casting live baitfish, baitcasting tackle today is used to present all sorts of offerings—from worms and minnows to spoons and huge jointed plugs—to gamefish in both fresh and salt water. This method is also known as plugcasting.

Before the advent of spinning gear, baitcasting was the universally accepted tackle for presenting bait or lure. Even today many anglers, especially those who grew up with a baitcasting outfit in their hands, prefer this method, even though the revolving-spool reel is more difficult to use than fixed-spool spinning and spincasting reels.

The confirmed baitcaster feels that his gear gives him more sensitive contact with what is going on at the end of his line. He feels that he can manipulate a lure better on baitcasting gear and have better control over a hooked fish. Most fishermen agree that when the quarry is a big, strong fish such as muskies, northern pike, and the tackle-straining largemouth bass found in the southern states, a baitcasting outfit gets the nod over spinning or spincasting tackle.

Baitcasting tackle is often preferred for trolling, too, for the revolving-spool reel makes it easy to pay out line behind the moving boat, and the rod has enough backbone to handle the big water-resistant lures used in many forms of trolling.

THE REEL

The reel is by far the most important part of a baitcasting outfit, and the budding baitcaster would do well to buy the best reel he can afford.

The main distinguishing feature of baitcasting reels is that the spool revolves when line is cast out or reeled in, while in spinning and spincasting reels the spool remains stationary.

Baitcasting reels have a relatively wide, shallow spool, and most have multiplying gears that cause the spool to revolve several times (usually four) for each complete turn of the reel handle. There is also

BAITCASTING REEL PARTS

The cub-drag handle **(middle drawing)** is a friction drag adjusted by six external screws. On star-drag reels **(shown at right)**, drag is set by the friction of washers on brake linings.

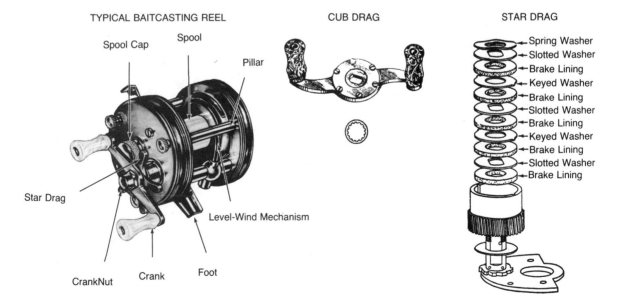

TYPICAL BAITCASTING REEL — Spool Cap, Spool, Pillar, Star Drag, Level-Wind Mechanism, CrankNut, Crank, Foot

CUB DRAG

STAR DRAG — Spring Washer, Slotted Washer, Brake Lining, Keyed Washer, Brake Lining, Slotted Washer, Brake Lining, Keyed Washer, Brake Lining, Slotted Washer, Brake Lining

some kind of drag mechanism, which is helpful in fighting big fish. These range from a simple click mechanism to a screw-down nut to a star drag. Some reels have what is called a cub drag, which is adjusted by turning six screws on the base of the handle.

Almost all of today's good baitcasting reels have an important device called a level-wind. It usually takes the form of a U-shaped loop of heavy wire attached to a base that travels from one side of the spool to the other by means of a wormlike gear. The device permits line to be wound evenly on the spool and thus is a big help in preventing backlashes, which are often caused by line "lumping up" on the spool. A backlash occurs when the speed of the revolving spool is faster than that of the outgoing line, resulting in a "bird's nest."

More and more baitcasting reels are being made with antibacklash devices. These employ either centrifugal force or pressure on the spool axle or flange to slow down the spool during a cast. Some reels utilize magnets to slow down the spool during a cast. However, though these antibacklash devices are helpful, the user of a baitcasting reel must still learn to apply thumb pressure to the spool if he is to prevent backlashes under all conditions. Only experience can teach him how much thumb pressure is needed under any given set of circumstances.

A breakthrough development in baitcasting was the free-spool reel. Without this feature, the cast lure not only pulls out line and turns the spool but also turns the gears, the level-wind, and the reel handle. All those moving parts tend to shorten the cast. But in the free-spool reel, most of the gearing is disconnected from the spool before a cast is made, and only the spool (and sometimes the level-wind) turns. That makes it easier to start and stop the turning of the spool and so permits the use of lighter lures than can be cast with a standard baitcasting reel. Longer casts are also possible. A turn of the handle reengages the gears of the free-spool reel so that the retrieve can be made.

Until recently, free-spool reels usually were heavier than standard models and required more skill and thumb control to cast without backlashes. Now, however, free-spool reels are available in light, easy-handling models as well.

BAITCASTING REELS

Browning Vectra baitcast reels are available in four and five bearing models that weigh 8.9 ounces and hold 145 yards of 14-pound-test line. Features include variable six-post centrifugal brake system and continuous anti-reverse.

Quantum 1310 MG Series has one-piece metal frames for precision alignment and durability. Weighs 9 ounces. Two models handle up to 200 yards of 12-pound-test line.

Abu Garcia Ambassadeur Black Max 3600 weighs 9.5 ounces and has a 6.3:1 gear ratio. Features include centrifugal and mechanical spool controls.

Team Daiwa Technique-Specific Longcast Spool TD-S100HI features bronze alloy drive gear with a brass shaft. The reel weighs 9.7 ounces, and handles 140 yards of 16-pound-test line.

Shimano Calcutta CT-100 is a palm-size version of a traditionally styled reel. It weighs 8.8 ounces, has a gear ratio of 5.8:1, and handles up to 120 yards of 12-pound-test line.

Penn Levelmatic 940 is designed for a range of light tackle duties in fresh and saltwater. Weighing 11.5 ounces, the 940 handles 225 yards of 12-pound-test line. Features include a level wind system.

Sigma Baitcast SS430 has unilock anti-reverse and three stainless steel ball bearings. This medium freshwater class reel holds 120 yards of 14-weight line.

THE ROD

Most baitcasting rods are now made of fiberglass, or graphite, or a composite material called Kevlar, or a very light metallic filament called boron—or a combination of these substances. Such materials—especially graphite, Kevlar, and boron—boast light weight, strength, and sensitivity in desirable proportions, though arguments persist as to which is best for most fishing (or for a given kind of fishing).

Rod lengths range from about 4 to more than 7 feet. Some, obviously, are most suitable for specific purposes. The most popular length—because it works well for many kinds of fishing—is 5½ feet.

Manufacturers generally classify their rods according to their action, which refers to the lure weights that a rod handles efficiently. Generally, Extra-Light rods can handle lures weighing ¼ ounce or less. Light rods can handle ¼ to ½ ounce. Medium rods are better at·handling ⅝ to ¾ ounce, and Heavy rods are for ¾ ounce and more.

Baitcasting rods have either a straight handle or an offset handle. The offset-handle type has a depressed reel seat and is recommended for beginners because it places the reel at an above-the-rod level that is most comfortable for thumbing the spool. There is also a double-offset handle, in which the reel seat is depressed and the butt grip is canted

TYPICAL BAITCASTING RODS

Casting Rod-Pistol Grip

Casting Rod-Straight Handle

HOW TO PLUG CAST

The Grip advocates a relaxed natural grip. Thumb on the reel spool controls the line. The reel is tipped so the spool is almost vertical with the handles up. This cuts down spool friction.

BASIC FORWARD CAST

With thumb holding the reel spool to prevent premature turning, he sights the target, and then swings the rod up and back with a smooth, forceful motion.

Alternate Spincast Reel: The fixed-spool, or spincasting reel, will do about the same job as the revolving-spool bait reels. Mechanically, this reel is much like a spinning reel, except that it has push-button line control. Spincast reels are very good when used with monofilament line to cast light lures. They're easier to master than revolving-spool bait reels. Many beginners like them.

BASIC FORWARD CAST (Continued)

Left: Never taking his eyes off the target, he lets his rod tip whip down to horizontal behind him, then starts to drive it forward with speed and power. **Right:** Thumb pressure used to hold the reel spool is released as the rod points toward the target. Very light thumbing will control the lure's flight.

HOW TO MATCH UP BAITCASTING TACKLE

This table is meant only as a general guide aimed at helping you put together, in proper balance, the basic elements of a baitcasting outfit. Specific conditions—and your ability and personal preferences—should also be considered.

SPECIES OF FISH	REEL	ROD LENGTH (Ft.)	LINES (Lb. Test)	LURE WEIGHTS (Ounces)
Panfish; small bass, pickerel, trout	Multiplying-gear with level-wind	6 to 6½ (Extra-light action)	6 to 8	⅛ to ¼
Bass, pickerel, walleye, small pike, trout	Multiplying-gear with level-wind	5½ to 6½ (Light action)	6 to 12	¼ to ½
Large bass, wall-eyes, pike, lake trout, muskie, striped bass	Multiplying-gear with stardrag	5 to 6 (Medium action)	10 to 20	⅝ to ¾
Muskie, steel-heads, lake trout, salmon, striped bass, bluefish, tarpon, snook	Multiplying-gear with star drag	4½ to 7 (Heavy action)	18 to 25	¾ and up

downward. This type makes accurate casts almost as simple as pointing your finger.

Other features of baitcasting rods are a finger hook on the underside of the reel seat and various reel-holding devices, including a spring-loaded locking mechanism and a screw-lock.

Baitcasting rods are of one- or two-piece construction. Some have ferrules about midway up the rod, while others have only a detachable handle.

In heavier baitcasting rods, there are two types—the popping rod and the muskie rod. Popping rods have a straight handle, unusually long butt section,

a foregrip usually made of cork, and a rubber butt cap. Well suited for heavy freshwater and light salt-water use, popping rods can handle an extensive range of lure weights for various species of fish.

Muskie rods generally have an offset or double-offset handle, cork foregrip, long butt section, and the backbone needed to handle that toothy terror of the North, the muskellunge. The most popular lengths are 5 and 5½ feet, and they can handle lures ranging in weight from ¾ ounce to 3 ounces, with a few of these rods capable of handling monster plugs up to 6 ounces.

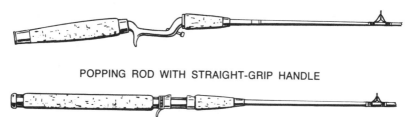

HEAVY MUSKIE ROD WITH FOREGRIP

POPPING ROD WITH STRAIGHT-GRIP HANDLE

Typical casting rod handles. Pistol grip **(top)** is for one-handed casting. Straight grip design **(bottom)** is for two-handed casting. The longer handle, originally built for bigger fish, is now finding favor with bass fisherman. Two-handed casting is less tiring and makes longer casts possible.

PLUG RETRIEVE

Proper moves in retrieve are shown in these photos. After the lure hits, he quickly moves the rod to his left hand, in order to control the line better as he reels it back onto the spool with his right hand. Note that he raises the rod to about 45 degrees, and then he presses its butt against his body as he reels it in. This keeps the outfit steady and ready for quick strike.

BACKHAND CAST

The backhand cast is used to get the lure out when some obstacle behind you blocks a routine backswing. Start the cast as shown. A strong snap of the wrist brings the rod forward. Note that the reel is always in a handle-up position as the line is released; the reel spool spins better that way.

SIDEARM CAST

The sidearm cast, shown in these three photos, is a powerful toss that is good for long-range work and casts into the wind. It saves the day when overhead foliage prevents a vertical backswing for a conventional forward cast. The casting motions follow the one, two, three pattern: sight at target, swing rod back, whip it forward. The casting arm remains straight, and points at the target until the lure is well on its way.

CASTING INTO THE WIND

Left: Even with a heavy lure, it takes extra power to cast into strong wind. He makes his backswing with the rod angled off to his right, which will keep the rod tip lower than usual throughout casting motion. **Right:** In forward motion, he releases the reel spool to let the line out when the rod is parallel with the water, and then follows through until rod tip is almost in the water.

SILENT-DIVE CAST

The main purpose of the silent-dive cast is to drop the lure with a light splat, rather than with a heavy splash. A small splat, like that made by a minnow surfacing, may attract fish that would be spooked by a loud splash. The forward cast is halted in air above the target by reel thumbing and haul-back on the rod. A braked lure hits more softly.

UNDERHAND LOB

This cast is a short-range toss with a dual purpose: It will work where there's little room for a backcast, and it drops a lure gently. The rod tip is kept below parallel during the backswing. The forward swing is aimed upward to loft the lure. A soft, underpowered lob is good for small pockets of water.

FLIPPING

Flipping is a comparatively new technique among bass fishermen. It's a simple, but deadly, technique for presenting a lure in and around brush, standing timber, grass, logs, lily pads and heavy vegetation.

For flipping, most bass fishermen prefer 7- to 8-foot, stiff casting rods with 25- to 30-pound-test line. Lure selections are usually sparse—jigs and plastic worms. The fisherman usually ties on a black, blue or brown ½-ounce "living rubber" jig. He protects the large hook with a fiber guard, and tips it with an Uncle Josh pork frog. This is especially deadly in the cooler springtime waters.

Flipping allows you to keep the lure close to cover constantly, thus allowing the fish to bite with very little effort or movement. The angler starts with about 8 to 9 feet of line from rod tip to lure. Then, he strips off an arm's length of line. Using his wrist

Matt Sparano demonstrates flipping into a pocket of water. The accompanying drawings clearly show the complete technique in detail.

and not the shoulder or elbow, he begins swinging the lure like a pendulum. Never let the lure come too far back. The swing should be smooth. When the lure reaches the back of its arc closest to you, a slight flick of the wrist (pretend you're only using the rod tip to do the work) will aim the lure toward the target. At this point, the line should be allowed to slide through your hand and the rod tip lowered to steer the lure to the desired spot.

A silent entry is essential. Never release the line until the lure reaches the water, because you want to control the lure. Once in the water, the jig or worm should fall freely to the bottom. Then your task is to climb and wriggle the lure up and over every limb, root and stem, carefully watching the line for the slightest nibble.

FLIP CAST

Ever find yourself in a spot where there seems to be no room for any kind of cast? The flip cast shown here can be made when you're brushed in on both sides with branches above you. The rod tip is dipped sharply toward angler's feet, snapped up to aim at the target as the thumb releases the reel spool.

SPINCASTING

Spincasting is a method of fishing that, in effect, combines a "pushbutton"-type spinning reel with a baitcasting-type rod. This tackle efficiently handles lures and baits of average weight—say, ¼ ounce to ¾ ounce. With lighter or heavier lures, its efficiency falls off sharply. Spincasting is ideal for newcomers to fishing, for it is the easiest casting method to learn and is the ticket for lots of trouble-free sport.

THE REEL

Spincasting reels, like spinning reels, operate on the fixed-spool principle—that is, the weight of the lure or bait being cast uncoils the line from the stationary spool. Most spincasting reels are of the closed-face type, the spool and gearing being enclosed in a cone-shaped hood.

The major factor distinguishing the spincasting reel from the spinning reel is that spincasting action is controlled by a thumb-activated "trigger" (a pushbutton or a lever) mounted either on the reel or on the butt of the rod. In operation, the spincaster holds his thumb down on the trigger until the rod is about halfway through the forward-cast motion. He then releases thumb pressure on the trigger, which frees the line and feeds it through a small hole in the center of the cone, sending the lure on its way.

Spincasting reels have various kinds of adjustable drag mechanisms. In one kind, the drag is set by rotating the cone that surrounds the spool. Other reels have star drags such as those found on baitcasting reels. The drag in still other reels is activated by turning the reel handle.

There are two kinds of spincasting reels, those mounted atop the rod and those mounted below it.

Most spincasting reels are of the top-mounted type and are designed for rods having an offset reel seat. They can be mounted on straight-grip rods, but this combination is uncomfortable to use since the caster must reach up with his thumb to activate the reel trigger.

Below-the-rod spincasting reels are a quite recent development. They look much like the standard semiclosed-face (also called semiopen-face) spinning reels. However, instead of the spinning reel's internal line-pickup pin, these spincasting reels (actually sold as rod-and-reel combinations) have a line-controlling pushbutton built into the rod butt.

Spincast reels are ideal for night fishing because

SPINCASTING GRIP AND REEL PARTS

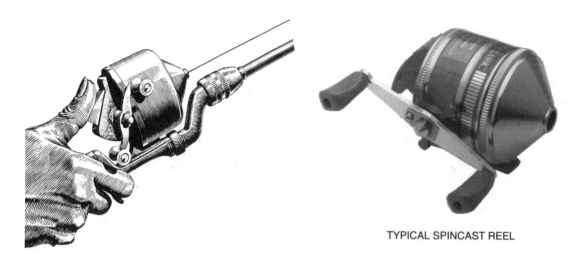

TYPICAL SPINCAST REEL

The grip for the spincasting reel is similar to that used with a baitcasting reel. The thumb depresses the control lever during the backcast, checking the line, and releases pressure as the rod whips forward.

TYPICAL SPINCASTING ROD

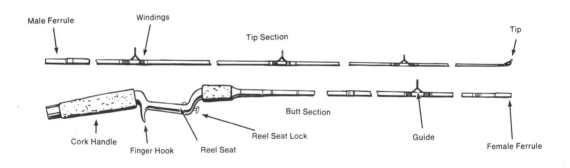

Male Ferrule   Windings   Tip Section   Tip

Cork Handle   Finger Hook   Reel Seat   Reel Seat Lock   Butt Section   Guide   Female Ferrule

of their trouble-free operation. However, besides the fact that they can handle a rather limited range of lure weights, if very light line is used on these reels the line has a tendency to foul in the housing.

THE ROD

Spincasting rods are basically the same as those designed for baitcasting, but there are a few dif-

ferences. In general, spincasting rods average a bit longer (most popular lengths are 6 and 6½ feet) than baitcasting rods. They have flexible, more-responsive tips, and guides are usually of the larger spinning-rod type. They may have both a detachable handle and a ferrule-jointed upper section.

HOW TO MATCH UP SPINCASTING TACKLE

This table is meant only as a general guide aimed at helping you put together, in proper balance, the basic elements of a spincasting outfit tailored for fish of a particular weight category. Specific conditions—and your ability and personal preferences—should also be considered.

SPECIES OF FISH	REEL	ROD LENGTH (Ft.)	LINES (Lb. Test)	LURE WEIGHTS (Ounces)
Panfish, small trout and bass, pickerel	Lightweight	6½ to 7 (Light action)	4 to 8	⅛ to ⅜
Trout, bass, pickerel, pike, landlocks, walleye	Medium-weight	6 to 7 (Medium action)	6 to 12	⅜ to ⅝
Pike, lake trout, steelhead, muskie, salmon, striped bass, snook, bonefish	Medium-heavy, with star drag	6 to 6½ (Medium-heavy action)	10 to 15	½ to ¾

CONVENTIONAL TACKLE FOR SALTWATER TROLLING AND CASTING

A host of saltwater gamefish—from half-pound snapper bluefish to 40-pound yellowtails to bluefin tuna weighing nearly half a ton—draw millions of fishermen to the briny each year. They stand in crashing surf and on jetties and piers, and they sail for deeper waters aboard boats of almost every description.

Because of the great differences in weights of saltwater fish, it is important for the fisherman to be armed with balanced tackle that is suited for the particular quarry he is after. Just as the freshwater muskie angler wouldn't use bluegill tackle, the person who's trolling for, say, blue marlin wouldn't use a jetty outfit designed for striped bass.

Balanced tackle—in which rod, reel, line, and other items are all in reasonable proportion to one another—is important for a number of reasons.

For one, a properly balanced outfit—for example, a 9-foot surf rod with a good casting reel and 15- to 25-pound-test line—is a joy to use. Conversely, if you substituted a 5-foot boat rod for the 9-footer in the above outfit and tried to cast, you would soon be turning the air blue. Besides the casting advantage, properly balanced gear makes hooking and playing a fish easier and more effective.

There is still another reason for using balanced tackle. Every fisherman, beginner and expert alike, who tosses or trolls lure or bait in the salt has a chance to sink a hook into a record-size gamefish. The rules of the International Game Fish Association, keeper of the official records of marine gamefish, require that any fish submitted for a record be caught on tackle that is "in reasonable proportion . . . to the line size."

Let's take a detailed look at the various kinds of conventional saltwater gear and how to match up the component parts.

TROLLING REELS

Trolling is the method of fishing in which a lure or bait is pulled along behind a moving boat. It is also a method in which the reel is of paramount importance.

Saltwater trolling reels are designated by a simple and yet not completely reliable numbering system. This system employs a number followed by a diagonal (/) and then the letter "O," which merely stands for "ocean." The numbers run from 1 to 16, with each one representing the line capacity of the

SALTWATER REEL PARTS

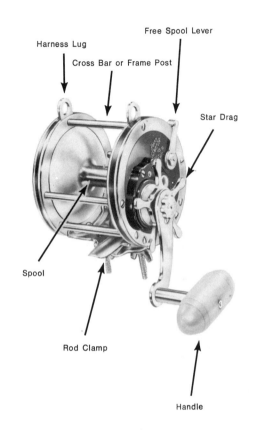

Harness Lug

Cross Bar or Frame Post

Free Spool Lever

Star Drag

Spool

Rod Clamp

Handle

reel. The higher the number, the larger the reel's line capacity.

It should be noted, however, that these numbers are not standardized—that is, one manufacturer's 4/O trolling reel may have a smaller capacity than another maker's 4/O. A prospective reel buyer would do well to check manufacturers' catalogs to make sure of a reel line's capacity.

Trolling reels are the heavyweights among saltwater reels. Weighing from 18 ounces (for the 1/O size) up to nearly 11 pounds (for the 16/O), they are designed primarily for handling the largest of gamefish (sailfish, marlin, bluefin tuna, swordfish) but are also effective for bluefish, stripers, channel bass, albacore, dolphins, and the like.

These reels have no casting features (such as anti-backlash devices), since their sole function is trolling. Spools are smooth-running, usually operating on ball bearings. The reels are ruggedly built and, of course, corrosion resistant. Unique features include lugs on the upper part of the sideplate for attachment of a big-game fishing harness worn by the fisherman, a U-shaped clamp for more secure union of rod and reel, and, in the largest reels, a lug-and-brace arrangement for extra rigidity.

By far the most important feature on a trolling reel is the drag. If a reel is to handle the sizzling runs and line-testing leaps of fish weighing hundreds of pounds, its drag must operate smoothly at all times. And the drag must not overheat or it may bind, causing the line to break.

In most reels the drag is of the star type and consists of a series of alternating metal and composition (or leather) washers. In more expensive trolling reels the drag is an asbestos-composition disc that applies pressure directly to the reel spool.

Some quite expensive trolling reels have not one but two drag controls. One is a knob-operated device that lets you preset drag tension to a point below the breaking strength of the line being used. The other is a lever, mounted on the sideplate, that has a number of positions and permits a wide range of drag settings, from very light up to the safe maximum for the line in use. This lever, when backed off all the way, throws the reel into free-spool.

Trolling-reel spools are made of metal, usually either machined bronze or anodized aluminum, and range in width from 1⅝ inches (for the 1/O size) to 5 inches (for the 16/O).

Some trolling reels are designed especially for wire and lead-core lines. They have narrow but deep spools and extra-strong gearing.

Other features of trolling reels include free-spool lever mounted on the sideplate, a single oversize handle grip, and gear ratios ranging from 1.6:1 to 3½:1.

TROLLING RODS

Big-game trolling rods have the strength and fittings to withstand the power runs and magnificent leaps of such heavyweights as marlin, sailfish, and giant tuna. The great majority of these rods are of fiberglass and graphite construction, though a few bamboo models are still being used.

Almost all blue-water rods have a butt section and a tip section—that is, they seldom have ferrules fitted midway along the "working length" of the rod. In most rods the tip section is about 5 feet long, while butt lengths vary from 14 to 27 inches, depending on the weight of the tip. Tip sections are

TROLLING REELS AND LINE CAPACITIES (In Yards)

LINES	REELS									
	1/0	2/0	3/0	4/0	6/0	9/0	10/0	12/0	14/0	16/0
20-lb. mono-filament	350	425								
30-lb. mono-filament	200	275	375							
36-lb. mono-filament				350	600					
45-lb. mono-filament				275	500					
54-lb. mono-filament				200	400					
72-lb. mono-filament					350	500	850			
90-lb. mono-filament						400	600	800	1100	1400
108-lb. mono-filament						300	500	600	1000	1200
20-lb. Dacron	225									
30-lb. Dacron	200	275	350	450						
50-lb. Dacron			200	250	400					
80-lb. Dacron				150	250	400	650	800	1050	1250
130-lb. Dacron						300	450	550	850	1000

usually designated by weight, ranging from about 3 ounces to as heavy as 40 ounces, depending on the line being used and the fish being sought.

Trolling rods are rated according to the line-strength classes of the International Game Fish Association. The eight I.G.F.A. classes are: 6-pound line, 12-pound (line testing, when wet, up to and including 12 pounds), 20-pound (line testing, when wet, more than 12 pounds and up to and including 20 pounds), 30-pound (line testing, when wet, more than 20 pounds and up to and including 30 pounds); 50-pound, 80-pound, 130-pound, and 180-pound.

No rod used in catching a fish submitted for an I.G.F.A. record can have a tip length of less than 5 feet. In the 12-, 20-, and 30-pound classes, a rod's butt length can be no more than 18 inches. In the 50- and 80-pound classes, butt length can be no more than 22 inches. In the 130- and 180-pound classes, butt length can be no more than 27 inches.

The fittings on trolling rods include strong, high-quality guides. The first guide above the reel (called the stripping guide) and the tip guide are of the roll-

TYPICAL SALTWATER TROLLING ROD

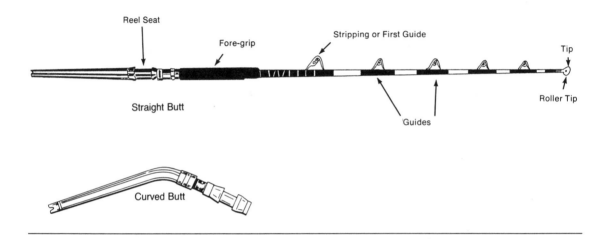

HOW TO MATCH UP OFFSHORE TROLLING TACKLE

This table is meant only as a general guide aimed at helping you put together, in proper balance, the basic elements of a bluewater trolling outfit tailored for fish of a particular weight category. Specific conditions—and your ability and personal preferences—should also be considered.

SPECIES OF FISH	REEL	ROD (Tip-Section Weight, in oz.)	LINE (Lb. Test)
Striped bass, dolphin, wahoo, yellowtail, king-fish, salmon, barracuda, tarpon, school tuna	1/0 to 3/0	3 to 9	12 to 30
Atlantic sailfish, Pacific sailfish, white marlin	3/0 to 6/0	6 to 18	30 to 50
Striped marlin	4/0 to 9/0	6 to 20	30 to 80
Black marlin, blue marlin, swordfish, sharks	6/0 to 14/0	9 to 30	30 to 130
Giant bluefin tuna	9/0 to 16/0	16 to 30	50 to 130

er type (either single-roller or double-roller). The middle guides, usually numbering four or five, are of the ring type and are made either of heavily chromed stainless steel or of tungsten carbide (carboloy), which is the most durable material. In some rods all of the guides are rollers. Most roller guides have self-lubricating bearings that can be disassembled for cleaning.

Other features of trolling rods include extra-strong, locking reel seats, and gimbal fittings in the end of the butt that enable the rod to be fitted into a socket on a boat's fighting chair or into a belt harness worn by the fisherman.

CASTING AND BOAT REELS

Conventional (revolving-spool) reels in this category are widely used by saltwater fishermen who cast lures and baits from piers, bridges, jetties, and in the surf, and by sinker-bouncers (bottom fishermen) in boats. Actually an outgrowth and refinement of freshwater baitcasting reels, these reels fill the gap between those freshwater models and big-game trolling reels.

Many surf and jetty casters, especially those who are after big fish, prefer a conventional reel (and rod) over a spinning outfit because the conventional

rig is better able to handle heavy lures and sinkers. And a vast majority of bottom fishermen lean toward the revolving-spool reel.

Conventional reels designed for casting, often called squidding reels, have wide, light spools (a heavy spool makes casting difficult) of either metal or plastic (metal is preferred for most uses), and gear ratios ranging from 2:1 to 4½:1. Weights range from about 12 to 22 ounces. In most models the drag is of the star type and there is a free-spool lever mounted on the sideplate. Some of these reels have level-wind mechanisms.

Line capacities range from about 250 yards of 12-pound-test monofilament to 350 yards of 36-pound-test mono. For most surf, jetty, and pier situations, 250 yards of line is sufficient.

A few of these reels have a mechanical brake, magnets, or a thumbing device to help prevent the spool from overrunning during a cast and causing a backlash. In most models, however, as in freshwater baitcasting reels, thumb pressure against the spool is required to control the cast.

Conventional reels designed for deep-sea bottom fishing are quite similar to the casting models but are somewhat heavier and have narrower, deeper spools. They also have larger line capacities and can take heavier lines.

SALTWATER CASTING AND BOAT REELS

Penn Super Level Wind Reel 345 GTi is built for heavy duty, high-line capacity applications. Weighing 34 ounces, the reel holds 375 yards of 50-pound-test line, and has a gear ratio of 3.25-1.

Shimano Tiagra TI-50 big-game reel. Features include a torque-resistant frame 7 mm. thick, and a hydrothermal drag system, which keeps drag pressure consistent. The reel holds 600 yards of 50-pound-test line, and weighs 80.1 ounces.

Penn 80STW International II is a two-speed reel that features a power handle and adjustable clicker that lets an angler set the amount of tension for the fishing being done. It holds 950 yards of 80-pound-test line, and weighs 118 ounces.

Quantum IR4 Baitcast Reel. Handles 125 yards of 12-pound-test line, and weighs 9.6 ounces. Has four stainless steel ball and roller bearings, continuous anti-reverse, and 5.2 to 1 retrieve.

Penn Special Senator 113 HLW holds 600 yards of 30-pound-test line. Weighing 32 ounces, the model has a lightweight, one piece graphite composite frame that locks into a one piece stainless steel stand.

Fin-Nor Ahab 2-Speed Big-Game Reel. Available in five models handling 12, 20, 30, 50, and 80-pound-test lines.

Shimano Calcutta 400S has a wide-open spool for casting control and line access, designed primarily for live bait anglers and surf casting. The reel has a 4.7:1 gear ratio and weighs 10.7 ounces. It will handle 320 yards of 12-pound-test, 260 yards of 14-pound-test, 210 yards of 17-pound, and 160 yards of 20-pound.

ELEC-TRA-MATE 312-HS is an electric drive system created to fill a need for a lightweight power-driven reel with level wind feature. Weighing 28.5 ounces, the model is easily handled by women, children, senior citizens, and physically challenged anglers. Various optional switches, 322 feet per minute retrieval speed, line capacity of 320 yards of 20-pound-test, and an optional portable 12 Volt DC battery are features of this drive. Available for the Penn 320 GTi Super Level Wind Reel.

CASTING AND BOAT RODS

In choosing a conventional casting rod, more so than with boat (bottom-fishing) rods, the type of fishing to be done and the fish being sought are critical factors. For casting in the surf, for example, the rod must be long enough so that the fisherman can make lengthy casts and hold the line above the breakers. A rod for jetty use, on the other hand, need not be so long. And if you'll be fishing mainly from piers and bridges, you'll need a rod with enough backbone to lift hefty fish from the water and up over the rail.

However, the beginning fisherman can get a casting rod that will handle most of the situations he'll be facing. A good choice would be one that is 8½ to 9 feet in overall length, of tubular fiberglass (rather than solid fiberglass), and has a rather stiff tip. The stiff tip of a conventional rod lets the angler use a wide range of lure weights and enables him to have more control over big fish.

Conventional casting rods are available in lengths from about 8 to 11½ feet and even longer. A few split-bamboo models are still kicking around the beaches, but most are now made of fiberglass, graphite, Kevlar, or a combination thereof. Recent developments in graphite show that rods of this material can carry an exceptionally wide range of lure weights. In tests, weights of 18 ounces were cast

with graphite rods. A majority of these rods are of two-piece construction, breaking either at the upper part of the butt or about midway up the working length of the rod.

These rods are distinguished by the number and arrangement of their guides. In most models, there are only three or four guides, including the tip guide, and all are located in the upper half of the tip section. Why this arrangement? Because these rods are stiffer than most others, fewer guides are required to distribute the strain along the length of the rod. The guides are bunched near the tip because that's where most of the bend occurs when a fish is being played.

Conventional casting rods have sturdy salt-resistant reel seats, usually of anodized aluminum, and butts of hickory, other sturdy woods, or cork.

Boat, or bottom-fishing, rods, as their name implies, are designed for noncasting use aboard boats—party boats, charter craft, and private boats. They are also used on piers and bridges, in situations in which lure or bait is simply dropped down to the water.

Boat rods are considerably shorter than casting rods, running from about 4½ to 6½ feet in overall length, with a good average length being about 5½ feet. Their shortness makes them highly maneuverable, a factor of more than a little importance aboard a crowded party boat, and makes it easier

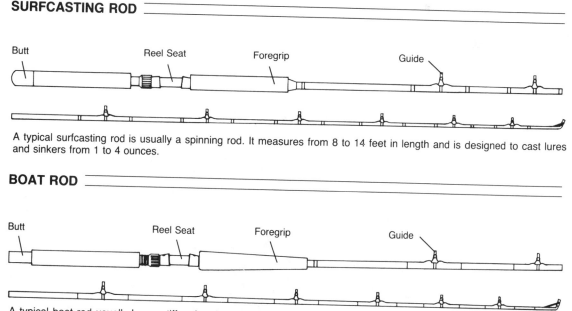

SURFCASTING ROD

Butt   Reel Seat   Foregrip   Guide

A typical surfcasting rod is usually a spinning rod. It measures from 8 to 14 feet in length and is designed to cast lures and sinkers from 1 to 4 ounces.

BOAT ROD

Butt   Reel Seat   Foregrip   Guide

A typical boat rod usually has a stiff action. It measures from 5 to 7 feet and is generally designed for noncasting use, such as on party boats and charter craft.

to handle, say, a 30-pound cod while trying to remain upright on a pitching deck.

As with most other modern rods, boat rods are mostly of fiberglass construction with a growing number of graphite models available. Most are two-piece, with tip section and detachable butt. The number of guides on a boat rod depends on length, but there are seldom more than five. Some of these rods, designed for large fish, have a roller tip. Other boat-rod features are similar to those of casting rods.

HOW TO MATCH UP SALTWATER CASTING TACKLE

This table is meant only as a general guide aimed at helping you put together, in proper balance, the basic elements of a saltwater casting outfit tailored for fish of a particular weight category. Specific conditions—and your ability and personal preferences—should also be considered.

SPECIES OF FISH	REEL	ROD TYPE & LENGTH (In Feet)	LINES (Lb. Test)	LURE WEIGHTS (Ounces)
Small stripers, bluefish, weakfish, snook, bonefish, redfish, salmon, pompano, jacks	Light (with star drag)	Popping 6 to 7	8 to 15	1/2 to 1
Stripers, big bluefish, school tuna, albacore, bonito, salmon, dolphin, wahoo	Medium	Medium-action 6 1/2 to 8	12 to 30	3/4 to 3
Channel bass, black drum, tarpon, dolphin, big kingfish, sharks	Heavy	Heavy-action 7 to 8 1/2	18 to 50	1 1/2 to 5
Surf species (bluefish, stripers, drum, channel bass, etc.)	Squidding (Surf-casting)	Surf 8 to 11 1/2	18 to 45	1 1/2 to 6

HOW TO SURF CAST WITH A CASTING REEL

Fit of Rod and Reel: This shows how the butt of a surf rod should just reach the caster's armpit when held with thumb on reel spool. A shorter butt section will lack leverage to handle the long rod, while a too long butt adds needless weight. Proper butt length allows the comfortable and powerful two-handed grip shown in photo. The thumb must be in easy reach of the reel spool for casts with this type of reel, for it's thumb pressure on the spool that regulates outgoing line.

HOW TO SURF CAST WITH A CASTING REEL

Advance Adjustments: The time to set the star drag properly is before the cast is made **(right)**. That way the drag is right if the fish hits the lure the instant it touches the water. Test the drag adjustment by pulling line from the reel **(far right)**. Drag should be tight enough to set the hook in a striking fish, but at the same time loose enough to feed out line to a big fish making a determined run. Also adjust spool end caps so that your lure will drop slowly when reel is in free spool. This adjustment will vary with lure weight, but it is an important adjustment to avoid backlashes.

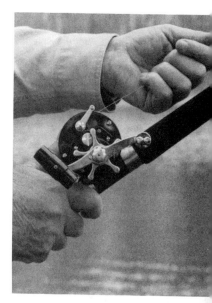

Flip to Free Spool: Once the drag is set, the caster holds the reel spool with one thumb and uses the other to flip the free-spool lever, which will let the spool spin freely during the cast. Some levers move forward, some back. This depends on the design of the reel. This is the last mechanical adjustment needed.

HOW TO SURF CAST WITH A CASTING REEL (Continued)

Thumbing the Spool: The angler's thumb is placed on the reel spool with firm pressure at the start of the cast to hold the spool during the backsweep of the casting motion. As the rod is powered forward, the thumb is lifted to let the weight of the lure or sinker take out line. Very light thumbing as line goes out will prevent backlash. The most common thumbing position is shown. A good alternate position is shown where the thumb is pressed against the side of the reel spool instead of on the line-covered spool core.

STARTING THE CAST

This photo shows details of grip and reel position as a surf caster prepares to sail his bait or lure far out over the ocean breakers.

Since hooks on a heavy lure can be dangerous, your first move should always be a look behind you to be sure your backswing won't hook another angler. Then start your cast from the stance shown. Note that the handle of the reel is down, the dangling lure just above the sand as the rod is held parallel to the beach.

THE CASTING MOTION

These photos show a smooth, powerful cast from beginning to end. With his feet set in wide stance for balance, he pulls the rod butt powerfully with his left hand and pushes at the grip behind the reel with his right hand. The handle of the reel remains down until the rod tip is overhead. The reel spool is locked by thumb pressure until the rod tip snaps forward. Then a very light touch of the thumb on the reel spool prevents line snarl as the outgoing line spins the reel spool. The thumb brakes the spool again at the end of the cast.

"FISHING" THE CAST

When the lure hits the water, as quickly as possible he gets his gear set to handle a fish. The rod butt is lowered at once and held steady between the legs **(top left)**. With thumb holding the reel spool, the angler quickly flips the free-spool lever of the reel to engage the reel's mechanical drag. The lever is flipped with the left hand **(top right)**. The left hand is then moved to the grip ahead of the reel **(bottom left)**. The left hand then holds the rod at about 45 degrees, while the right hand reels in the lure or plays a hooked fish. If the lure comes in close to the angler without being hit by a fish, the rod is gradually angled to the right. This is to allow rod spring and a safe striking position if the fish hits in the final feet of retrieve. The danger in striking at fish close in, with the rod in front of you, is that the lure may jerk loose and sail straight back into your face. The typical surf lure is heavy enough to do considerable damage with its sharp hooks. With the rod held to one side, a missed strike with a short line will only send the lure flying harmlessly back on the beach behind you **(bottom right)**.

HOW TO SURF CAST WITH A SPINNING REEL (Captions by the late Joe Brooks) ————

Proper Grip: A spinning reel on a surf rod is gripped with the two fingers of the right hand on each side of the metal shank that supports the reel. The left hand may be farther down the rod butt than shown when cast is started. **Far right:** This photo shows how the forefinger of the right hand is extended to hold line running between the spool and guides.

STARTING THE CAST ————

The actual cast with a surf-size spinning tackle, as shown, is very similar to the rod work with a reel that has a revolving spool. The main difference is that the line from the fixed-spool spinning reel is held by the angler's crooked forefinger until the rod tip snaps forward toward the target. Then the line is allowed to slip off the fingertip, and coil off the reel spool, as the lure drives out over the water.

SURF SPINNING CAST (Continued)

After cocking the rod, the angler powers it forward with pull on the butt and push on the grip at the reel seat. He aims at a distant target as the rod tip starts to pass over his head. His finger releases the line when the rod is at about a 45 degree angle in front of him. He can catch the line again by feathering the spool with his fingers, if he wants to stop the cast before the lure travels the maximum distance.

RETRIEVING THE LURE

The caster now steadies the butt of the rod between his legs and reels in. Most spinning reels are designed for reeling with the left hand, while revolving-spool, surf reels generally are set up for right-handed reeling. The angler will angle the rod to his right, as the lure he's retrieving enters the shallows. This allows a safe jerk at late-striking fish in case the hook breaks free and flies toward the caster. This also puts the rod in position for a new cast.

HOW TO SET DRAG

Drag is what keeps a fish from breaking your line. That sounds simple, but fishermen sometimes lose big fish because they do not know or understand a few basic facts about the drag on their reel.

Many anglers, for example, tighten their drag when a big fish makes a long run and strips off a lot of line. This is wrong. The drag should actually be lightened, because a lot of line in the water as well as a smaller spool diameter will increase the drag. Unfortunately, the reaction of most fishermen is to tighten the drag and stop the fish. Often the result is a lost trophy.

Drag is the resistance of a reel against the fighting pull of a fish, and drag is set at a strain the line can endure without breaking. The drag mechanism usually consists of a series of metal (stainless steel, aluminum, or chromed brass) and composition (leather, cork, plastic, fiber) washers. The washers are stacked, alternating metal and composition, and the friction between the surface areas of the washers creates "drag."

When an angler tightens the drag on his reel, he compresses these washers, creates more friction, and increases drag. Conversely, when he backs off the drag, he lessens friction and lightens drag.

If the size of a fish was the only factor in setting drag, the job would be easy. But there are other considerations, such as the friction of the line against the rod guides, resistance of the line being pulled through the water, and the amount of line remaining on the reel spool after a long run.

In addition, not all drags are created equal. They should be smooth, but many are sticky and jerky. In fact, it often takes as much as double the force of the drag setting to get the drag moving. For example, a drag set at 5 pounds may actually take up to 10 pounds of pull before the drag starts moving. It's obvious, therefore, that if you're using 8-pound-test line you should set your drag at about 2 pounds to allow for "starting your drag."

The amount of line on your spool is another factor affecting drag. When the outside diameter of line on your spool is reduced by half, the drag tension is doubled. For example, if your drag is set at 2 pounds with a full spool, it will be increased to 4 pounds when a fish makes a long run and strips off half your line.

Long, fast runs will also generate friction and heat

between drag washers. This will frequently tighten a drag and add even more tension.

It's also important to remember that a rod held at about 45 degrees will add about 10 percent to the drag you get with the rod pointed directly at the fish. This increased drag is due to friction between your line and the rod guides. If the rod is held at about 90 degrees, drag will increase about 35 percent of the initial setting.

This is why it is important to lighten the drag and, when possible, point the rod at the fish when it is about to be netted or gaffed. If you hold your rod high and keep a tight drag, a sudden lunge by a fish could break your line. But point the rod tip at the fish and the line will run off the spool more easily, even with the same drag setting.

This technique of lowering the rod is also used when handling thrashing or jumping fish, such as tarpon and marlin. Lowering the rod will lighten drag tension and "cushion" the line from the shock of a jumping fish. This is called "bowing." It's part of the technique that makes it possible to land 100-pound tarpon on 10-pound line.

Taking all the above factors into consideration, how does an angler set his drag so that he can feel reasonably secure when he hooks a trophy fish? The first step is to determine the minimum and maximum range of drag for the various pound-test lines (see accompanying table). By minimum drag, I mean "starting drag," the amount of pull needed to get the drag moving. If the minimum drag seems light for the pound-test line, remember that there will be other factors increasing your drag beyond this setting, such as rod angle, spool diameter, and amount of line in water. Maximum drag means the heaviest setting you should use while fighting a fish. Never go beyond the maximum for your line class.

Let's take 12-pound-test line and see what factors come into play. Minimum drag is set at 4 pounds, but 8 pounds of pull will likely be required to get that drag started. If the angler holds his rod at 45 degrees or higher, he can add another 10 percent, which brings the drag to 9 pounds. To this figure we also have to add water resistance or line drag,

Line	Min. Drag (in lbs.)	Max. Drag (in lbs.)
6-lb.-test	1½	4
8-lb.-test	2	5
10-lb.-test	3	6
12-lb.-test	4	8
20-lb.-test	6	12
30-lb.-test	8	15
50-lb.-test	12	25
80-lb.-test	20	40
130-lb.-test	30	50

which varies according to amount of line in the water, line diameter, and speed of the fish. With 12-pound line and a fast fish, it can amount to as much as 2 pounds, which brings us up to 11 pounds of drag on our 12-pound line. With only 1 pound of drag to spare, a big fish would likely break the line. It's obvious that you're far better off with a very light drag setting.

The first step is to set your drag at the minimum setting. This is easily done at dockside with a reliable fish scale and the help of a friend. Run your line through the guides and tie it to the scale. Ask your friend to hold the scale and back off about 30 feet. Tighten your drag and begin to apply pressure as you would when fighting a fish. Now adjust the drag so that it comes into play when the scale reads the correct minimum drag weight. For example, if you're using 12-pound line, the drag should begin to slip when you apply enough pressure to pull the scale indicator to the 4-pound mark.

Now, with your drag set at 4 pounds, slowly tighten your drag until it comes into play at 8 pounds, which is the maximum setting. Note how many turns of the star drag or spool cap are required to bring your drag to maximum setting. Play with the drag, setting it back and forth from 4 to 8 pounds. Do this several times and get the feel of the resistance and pressure you're putting on the line. With enough practice, you'll be able to safely lighten and tighten the drag while fighting a fish.

An easier technique is to leave your drag set at the minimum setting and use your hand or fingers to apply more drag. This is a method many anglers use and it works well. You can practice with your buddy and the scale. With drag at the minimum setting, cup your hand around the spool (assuming you're using an open-face spinning reel), grip it so that the drag does not slip, and apply just enough pressure to pull the scale indicator to the maximum figure. Practice this technique and you'll soon be able to bear down on a fish and gain line without even touching the drag knob.

As mentioned above, you can also cup your hand around the spool of an open-face spinning reel to apply more drag. With conventional reels, use your thumb against the spool and hold the lines against the rod. Make sure you lift your finger when a big fish begins a run, or else you'll get a bad line burn.

Learn to combine this hand technique with "pumping" and you will be able to land big fish on light lines. Pumping a big fish in is not difficult. Let's assume you're using an open-face spinning reel with a light drag. Put your hand around the spool, apply pressure, and ease your rod back into a vertical position. Now drop the rod tip and reel in the slack. Repeat the process and you'll eventually have your fish at boatside. Always be ready, however, to lower the rod tip and release hand pressure from the spool when you think the fish is about to make a run. When he stops, you begin to pump once again.

One last point: At the end of the day, back off the drag and release all pressure on the washers, or they will lose their physical characteristics and take a set. If this happens, the drag will become jerky and unpredictable. If the washers do take a set, replacing them is then the only solution.

SETTING THE DRAG

Top left: *Outdoor Life* Fishing Editor Jerry Gibbs puts pressure on a 30-pound-test outfit while the author of this Encyclopedia, Vin Sparano, checks the indicator on a fish scale. At this point, Gibbs was pulling about 16 pounds. Note the bend in the rod. **Top right:** Here's a scale used to set drag as well as weigh fish. The indicator and numbers are large enough to read without getting too close.

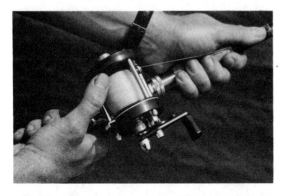

Left: With conventional gear, such as this popping outfit, the best way to apply drag pressure is to thumb spool and hold the line under the other thumb. When a fish makes a run, move your thumbs quickly or else you'll get a bad line burn. **Right:** 10-pound line is used on a 13-pound albacore off Montauk Point, New York. Drag is set at about 4 pounds and author Sparano used his left hand to hold the fixed spool to increase drag and to pump the fish in. On the same trip, he took striped bass and bluefish up to 20 pounds on the same line and drag.

ICE FISHING

Ice fishing differs greatly from open-water fishing. And it is a demanding sport. It demands an understanding of and an ability to cope with winter weather, it demands a knowledge of the cold-weather habits of the fish, and it demands the use of an unusual assortment of gear, most of it unique to ice fishing.

There are two basic ice-fishing methods: tip-up fishing and jigging. In general, tip-ups are usually used on larger fish—pike, pickerel, walleyes, trout, and such—that prefer bait and require that the angler play the waiting game. Jigging is usually preferred for smaller fish that tend to school up—bluegills, perch, crappies, and the like.

But it should be remembered that those are merely

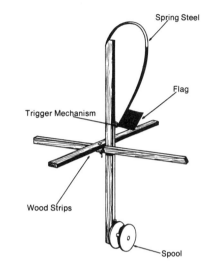

The typical ice fishing tip-up. Shown in cocked position, this model places the reel underwater, thereby preventing freeze-up of the line.

Insulated and waterproof clothing, portable heaters, and modern tents have increased the fun and reduced the rigors of ice fishing for those who would rather not rough it.

generalizations, not hard and fast rules. For example, jigging (sometimes called chugging) is often quite productive on big lake trout and salmon in the Great Lakes.

TIP-UPS

Also called tilts, these come in various styles, but they all perform two basic functions: they hold a

baited line leading from a revolving-type reel spool, and they signal the bite of a fish. The most common type of tip-up consists of three strips of wood, each about 18 inches long. Two are cross-pieces that form an X as they span the ice hole. The third piece is an upright; at its bottom end is attached a simple line-holding spool, while the upper end holds the signaling device. The signal is usually a piece of very flexible spring steel with a red (some anglers prefer black) flag on the end. After the hook is baited and lowered to the desired depth, the steel arm is "cocked"—bent over and down and hooked onto a "trigger." When a fish strikes, an arm on the revolving spool releases the steel arm and it flies erect.

In this tip-up the reel is positioned underwater. In other variations the reel is positioned above the ice. Each type has its advantages. The above-the-ice reel can be more sensitively adjusted for light-biting fish, but the line tends to freeze on the reel once it gets wet. The underwater reel largely eliminates the problem of freeze-up, but the fisherman must remove the tip-up from the hole before he can grab the line.

Baits for tip-up fishing are usually of the live variety. In general, it pays to match the size of the bait to the size of the fish you're after. Baits range

JIGGING RODS

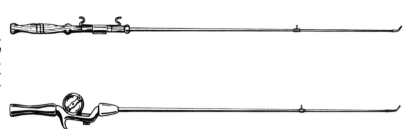

Two types of ice-fish jigging rods. The rod at top utilizes two wire hooks on handle to hold the line. The model below uses an inexpensive reel on a short, baitcasting-type rod.

from tiny maggots (often called mousies) and grubs for panfish, to worms and small minnows for walleyes, and up to 6-inch baitfish for northern pike.

JIGGING RODS

As done by ice fishermen, jigging is simply a method of imparting an up-and-down movement to a lure and/or bait. Jigging can be—and is—done with any sort of line-holding rod or stick.

Some jigging rods—more appropriately called sticks—are simply pieces of wood 18 inches or so long, with U-shaped notches in each end. The line—10-pound monofilament is very popular—is wound lengthwise onto the stick around the U-shaped notches and is paid out as needed. There are other types of jigging sticks of varying design, and many ice anglers use standard spinning or spincast rods or the butt half of a fly rod.

Rods made specially for ice jigging are simple affairs consisting of a fiberglass tip section 2 or 3 feet long seated in a short butt. The butt may have a simple revolving-spool reel or merely a pair of heavy-wire projections around which the line is wound. The tip section may have two to four guides including the tip guide. The shortness of such a rod lets the user fish up close to the hole and have better control over the lure or bait at the end of his line.

What sort of enticements does a jigger lower into those frigid depths?

JIGGING LURES AND BAITS

These are many and varied, but flashiness is built into most of them. Others produce best when "sweetened" with bait. Two popular jigging lures are: 1) an ungainly looking critter with a heavy body shaped and painted to resemble a baitfish, a hook at each end and a treble hook in the middle of its

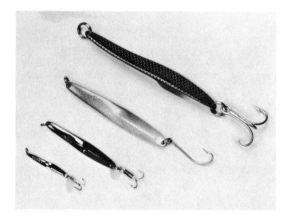

Above are various metal, jigging lures that employ the treble hook at the "tail." Below are Rapala jigging lures, designed to be suspended from a loop at the position normally occupied by the dorsal fin of a minnow. Here hooks abound—fore, aft, and underneath.

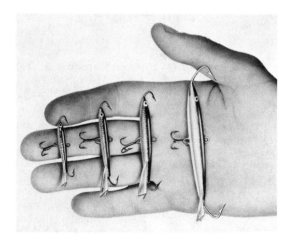

ICE-FISHING ACCESSORIES

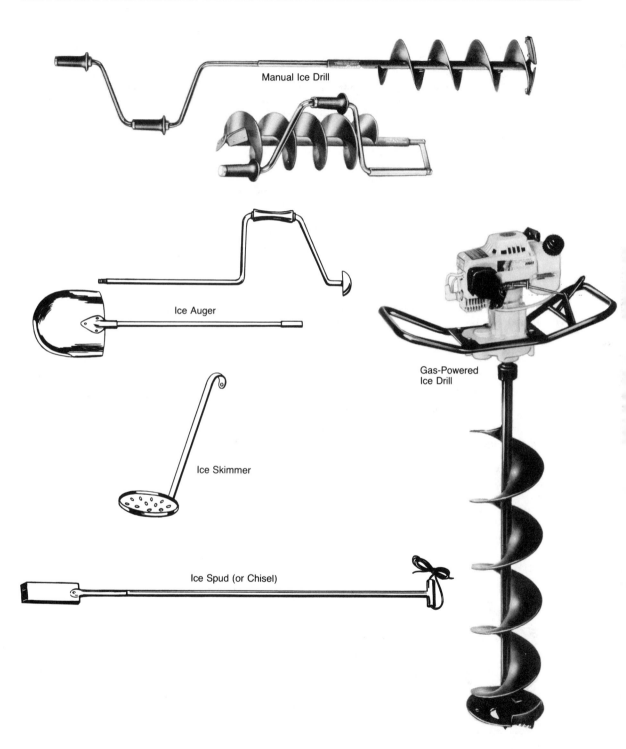

Manual Ice Drill

Ice Auger

Ice Skimmer

Ice Spud (or Chisel)

Gas-Powered
Ice Drill

underside, and a line-tie ring in the middle of its upper surface; and 2) a long, slim, three- or four-sided, silvery model with a treble hook at one end and a line-tie ring at the other,.

Jigging methods vary with the fisherman and with the fish being sought. However, a productive way to fish many jigging lures, especially flasher types, is to twitch the lure slightly and then jerk it suddenly upward with a quick upward movement of the arm. The proper interval between jerks is learned with experience.

Favorite jigging baits include a single perch eye (either impaled on a small hook or used to sweeten a tiny hair or rubber-bodied ice fly), worms, grubs, maggots, insect larvae, minnows, and cut bait (pieces of skin or flesh cut from the tail or body of such fish as smelt and perch).

Jiggers tend to move about more than tip-up fishermen, boring holes in different areas until they find a productive spot.

OTHER EQUIPMENT

Like most other forms of fishing, ice angling requires some auxiliary equipment. Most ice anglers prefer to keep such gear to a minimum, for they have to haul it with them wherever they go on the ice.

If you're going to fish through holes in the ice, you need something to make those holes. The ice auger is a popular tool for this job. Augers come in different designs. One has a long handle with a U-shaped bend at the top, and a rounded cutting blade at the bottom. The handle is turned much like that of a manual drill, and the blade cuts a round hole through the ice. Another type looks like a giant ice drill with sharp widely spaced threads. It is used in the same way. Gasoline-powered ice drills are also available.

Then there's the ice spud or chisel. This is a heavy metal handle with a large chisel-type blade at the bottom. The spud's weight helps the angler punch

down through the ice, but the user must shape the hole once he has broken through.

An indispensable item of accessory gear is the ice skimmer, a ladle-type device that is used to keep the hole clear of ice chips and chunks and skim ice.

Many ice anglers like to use an ice sounder, which consists of a lead weight and an attached spring clip. It is attached to the fishing line and used to determine the water depth—an important factor because in winter most gamefish are found on or near bottom. A heavy sinker will serve the same purpose.

ICE SAFETY

Winter is the time of year when icefishermen venture out onto frozen waters. Most will have fun, but a few will get into trouble because they don't know how to make sure that the ice is safe. The first rule is never take changes. There are two periods when accidents are likely to happen: early in the season when slush ice doesn't freeze uniformly and late in the season when ice melts at an uneven rate. It takes prolonged periods of freezing to make ice safe. Here are some rules to remember:

- Be cautious of heavy snowfalls while ice is forming. Snow acts as an insulator. The result is a layer of slush and snow on top of treacherous ice.
- Clear solid river ice is 15 percent weaker than clear lake ice.
- River ice is thinner in midstream than near the banks.
- River mouths are dangerous because currents create pockets of unsafe ice.
- When walking with friends, stay 10 yards apart.
- Lakes that have a lot of springs have weak spots of ice.

IF A FRIEND FALLS THROUGH THE ICE, never approach him upright. Toss him a rope, branch or jacket to pull him from the water. Lay flat on your stomach and slide toward your friend. When he has taken hold, slide backward. He can assist with a flutter kick to propel himself out of the hole.

IF YOU'RE ALONE, carry "ice claws" that can help you crawl onto safe ice. They can be made from two awls or stove bolts filed to points. The sharp points can be shielded by corks, and holes drilled in the ends so they can be carried on lanyards. If you don't have ice claws, carry 10-penny nails or even car keys that you can dig into the ice and pull yourself out.

ICE SAFETY CHART

Ice (In inches)	Maximum Safe Load
2	One person on foot
3	Group in single file
7½	Cars (two tons gross weight) snowmobiles
8	Light truck (2½ tons)
10	Medium truck (3½ tons)
12	Heavy truck (eight tons)

*This chart, prepared by Lumberman's Safety Association, gives general ice thickness and weight loads they can safely support. These figures apply only to clear blue lake ice. For early winter slush ice or late season ice, the thickness should be doubled.

LINES AND LEADERS

No fisherman is stronger than the line that connects him and his quarry. Fishing lines are made of a wide variety of natural and synthetic materials and as a result differ widely in their characteristics and the uses to which they can be put. No two types of lines, for example, have the same degree of elasticity, abrasion resistance, water absorption, weight, and diameter.

Let's take a look at the physical characteristics of the various lines and the uses for which they are best suited.

Monofilament (single-strand nylon). By far the most widely used fishing line today. It is suitable for everything from blue-water trolling to surf casting to freshwater spinning, and it is the universal material for leaders in both fresh water and salt because of its near-invisibility in water. It is extremely strong and light for its diameter, and it absorbs very little water (3 to 12 percent of its own weight). About the only drawback of monofilament is its relatively high rate of stretch (15 to 30 percent when dry, 20 to 35 percent when wet). For that reason it is not the best choice for such uses as deep-water bottom fishing, in which large fish must be reeled up from considerable depths.

Dacron. A DuPont trademark for a synthetic fiber that is made into a braided line. It is nearly as strong as monofilament but does not stretch so much (about 10 percent). It has virtually the same characteristics whether wet or dry. Its visibility in water is greater than that of monofilament. Dacron's widest use is as trolling line.

Linen. A braided line made from natural fibers and rated according to the number of threads, with each thread having a breaking strength of 3 pounds (6-thread linen has a breaking strength of 18 pounds, 15-thread tests 45 pounds, and so on). This material absorbs considerable water and is stronger when wet. Linen line is subject to deterioration and is heavy and bulky. Very little linen fishing line is made or used today, but because of its negligible stretch and good abrasion resistance it is still preferred by some big-game fishermen.

Cuttyhunk. A braided linen line originally created in the 1860s for the Cuttyhunk Fishing Club on Cuttyhunk Island, Massachusetts. The word Cuttyhunk is often used to denote any linen line.

Silk. Before World War II fly-fishing lines were

made of silk and had an oily coating to make them water resistant. Modern materials have made the silk line obsolete, and very few are in use today.

Braided Nylon. Extensively used on revolving-spool reels in fresh and salt water, and sometimes used on spinning reels. Braided nylon's main advantage over monofilament is that it is extremely limp and so is less likely to backlash on conventional reels. It is often preferred over monofilament for fishing with surface lures. But it is less durable than mono-filament, has less abrasion resistance, absorbs more water, and is more visible in water.

Lead-Core. This type of line is made by sheathing a flexible lead core in a tightly braided nylon sleeve. It's suitable for deep trolling in both fresh and salt water, and is especially useful for quickly getting a bait or lure down deep without bulky, heavy sinkers or planers. It's color-coded in 10-yard segments for precise depth control.

Wire. These lines, too, are designed for deep trolling in both fresh and salt water. They're made of stain-less steel, Monel (nickel alloy), bronze, or copper. Wire is popular for downrigger fishing, but because it's heavy enough to sink on its own, it's also used without downriggers and in many cases eliminates the need for a cumbersome drail weight or planer. Since it has no stretch, the angler can jig the rod and give movement to a bait or lure. However, wire is somewhat tricky until a fisherman gets used to it. Kinks can develop, causing weak spots or pos-sibly cutting an unwary angler's hand. Wire line is generally available in a wider range of test weights than lead-core line.

Wire leaders, usually sleeved in plastic, are widely used to prevent line-cutting when fishing for such toothy battlers as pike, muskellunge, and many saltwater species.

BRAIDED FISHING LINES

An ideal fishing line that has a small diameter, mini-mum stretch, and a good knot strength. The new high-tech synthetic braided lines get a high score on two out of three. If you want to use a braided line, you had better listen to some sound advice on knots.

There are more than a dozen manufacturers of these new space-age braided lines, and they all claim their lines are three times as strong as mono-filament lines of the same diameter. This means, of course, that you can get three times as much line on your reel. The smaller diameter also means easier casting with lighter lures. So far so good.

Braided lines have a stretch factor of less than 5 percent. Monofilament has a stretch factor of about 25 percent, depending on the manufacturer. Mini-mum stretch is a big deal in fishing. It means sensi-tivity and fast hook-ups.

So where's the rub with braided lines? It's in the knots! With braided lines, you may only get about 75 percent knot strength and that's only if you use the right knot. With monofilament, you can get nearly 100 percent with the right knot. Unless you take certain precautions tying knots, the strength-to-diameter ratio of braided lines isn't such a big deal.

Berkley, a line manufacturer that has done a great deal of research on testing the new braided lines, admits that knots may be the weak link. Good knots are difficult to tie. They are tough to cinch up tight and they tend to slip.

After considerable research, Berkley recom-mends the Palomar Knot and the Trilene Knot (see Knots, pg. 406). The Palomar and Trilene knots are used to tie fishing line to swivels, snaps, hooks, and lures. It's extremely important to wet braided lines before cinching the knot tight. Also, take care to keep the wraps from crossing over one another, and double the length of the tag line.

Stren has another answer to the knot problem in braided Kevlan lines. This company recommends a glue called Stren Lok-Knot. A drop or two of this adhesive will literally weld a poorly-tied knot and eliminate slippage. Stren feels so strongly about the strength of Lok-Knot that it even recommends it for totally knotless connections.

Braided lines have a lot going for them, including small diameters, minimal stretch, and the sensitivity to transmit the slightest nibble. Learning to use tie and the right knots should eliminate any knot problem.

Remember to double the tag end. In fact, it's wise to double braided line before tying any knot. Braided lines are also sharp and hard. Joining braided lines with monofilament may not be such a good idea, though further testing may prove other-wise.

FLY LINES

Ever since the time of Izaak Walton, anglers have been using special lines designed to present insect imitations to trout, salmon, and other fish. The ear-liest fly lines were made of braided horsehair. Then came oiled silk lines, which were standard until the late 1940s.

Today's fly lines are basically a synthetic coating over a braided core. They are made in various shapes and weights. Some are constructed so that

WEIGHT STANDARDS FOR FLY LINES

*WEIGHT IN GRAINS				+ ALLOWABLE TOLERANCES					
Code	*Weight	+ Range	Code	*Weight	+ Range	Code	*Weight	+ Range
1	60	54-66	5	140	134-146	9	240	230-250
2	80	74-86	6	160	152-168	10	280	270-290
3	100	94-106	7	185	177-193	11	330	318-342
4	120	114-126	8	210	202-218	12	380	368-392

FISHING LINE TROUBLESHOOTING CHART

This chart was designed to help you quickly find and correct line troubles when you can least afford to have them—on the water. Keep this handy chart in your tackle box.

Symptoms	Possible Causes	Recommended Cures
Unexplained line breaks under low stress loads.	a. Nicks or abrasion. If smooth surface and shiny, failure may be line fatigue.	a. Strip off worn line or retie line more frequently.
	b. If surface dull, faded and fuzzy, failure due to sunlight or excessive wear.	b. Replace line.
	c. Wear or stress points on guides and/or reel.	c. Replace worn guides.
Line usually sticky and stretchy.	Line stored in area of high heat. Line damaged by chemicals.	Replace line and change storage areas.
Line has kinks and flat spots.	a. Line spooled under excessive tension.	a. Use lower spooling tension. Make one final cast and rewind under low tension.
	b. Line stored on reel too long without use.	b. Strip out and soak last 50 yards in water.
Excessive curls and backlashes.	Using too heavy mono for reel spool diameter.	Use a more flexible mono or one with a lower pound test or smaller diameter.
Mono stiff and brittle; dry, powdery surface.	Improper storage in either wet or too warm conditions.	Replace line and change storage area.
Line looks good, but losing too many fish.	Faulty or improperly set reel drag. Using too light a break strength for conditions.	Check reel drag. Lubricate or replace washers. Refill with line of higher break strength.
Reel casts poorly.	Not enough line on spool or line is too heavy for reel.	Fill spool with additional line. Use lighter, more limp monofilament.
Line is hard to see.	Line has faded due to excessive exposure to sunlight. Using wrong color line.	Replace line. Switch to high visibility line.

they float (primarily for dry-fly fishing), and others are made to sink (for wet-fly and nymph fishing). A fairly recent development is the floating-sinking, or intermediate, line, the first 10 to 30 feet of which sinks while the rest floats.

The illustrations on page 325–327 show the basic types of fly lines and explain how you should select the proper one.

It is impossible to overemphasize the importance to the fly fisherman of balanced tackle. And the most vital element in a fly-fishing outfit is the line. It must "fit" the rod if casting is to be accurate and efficient.

A line that is too heavy for the rod causes sloppy casts, poor presentation of the fly, and lack of accuracy, and it makes it difficult to manipulate the fly once it is on the water. An angler who uses a line that's too light for his rod must flail the rod back and forth during repeated backcasts in order to get out enough line to make his cast, and even then his forward cast might not "turn over" and the line may fall onto the water in a jumbled mass of coils.

Before 1961, fly lines were identified by a system of letters—A to I—with each letter representing a line diameter. For example, an "A" line measured .060 inch in diameter, an "I" line .020 inch.

But when modern fly lines replaced silk after World War II, weight, rather than diameter, became the critical factor in matching a fly line with a rod. So, in 1961 manufacturers adopted a universally accepted fly-line identification code. Its three elements give a complete description of a fly line.

The first part of the code describes the line type: L stands for level, DT means double-taper, and WF means weight-forward. The second element, a number, denotes the weight (in grains) of the line's first 30 feet. The third element tells whether the line is floating (F), sinking (S), or floating/sinking (F/S). Therefore, a DT-6-F, for example, is a double-taper, weight-6, floating line.

Many fly-rod manufacturers today are eliminating the angler's problem of proper line choice by imprinting on the rod itself, usually just above the butt, the proper line size for that particular rod.

However, there are other, general, ways to pick the right fly line. Rod length is one determining factor. These general recommendations may help:

ROD LENGTH	PROPER LINE
7½	DT-4-F or WF-4-F to WF-6-F
8	DT-5-F or WF-5-F to WF-8-F
8½	DT-6-F or WF-6-F to WF-9-F
9 and 9½	DT-8-F or WF-8-F to WF-12-F

Another determining factor is the type of water the angler will be fishing. Here's how to select a line on that basis:

TYPE OF WATER	SUITABLE LINE WEIGHTS
Very small streams	4 and 5
Small and medium streams	5 to 8
Large streams	7 to 11
Lakes (light outfits)	5 to 7
Lakes (heavy outfits)	8 to 11
Salt water	9 to 15

TAPER DESIGN: THE KEY TO CASTING PERFORMANCE

Courtesy of *Scientific Anglers*

The fly line's shape, or taper, determines how energy is transmitted and dissipated during casting. By varying the lengths and diameters of the various parts of a line, specific performance attributes can be accentuated. The parts of the fly line taper are:

Tip — the short (usually six inch) level front end section of line primarily intended to protect the front taper. When changing leaders a small part of the fly line is cut off. The level tip allows changes to be made without shortening the front taper and thus altering the way the line casts.

Front Taper — in conjunction with the diameter of the line's tip, the length of a line's front taper determines how powerfully or delicately a fly is delivered. Longer tapers dissipate more casting energy, enabling a more delicate presentation, while shorter tapers provide a much more powerful delivery.

Belly — this, the line section with the greatest diameter and length, carries most of the casting energy.

Rear Taper — this section decreases in diameter from the belly to the much thinner running section of the line in a WF line. It is this transition that is the key to casting smoothness. Lines with short rear tapers cast quickly, but casting smoothness and control are sacrificed. Longer tapered lines cast more smoothly and are easier to control.

Head — this term is applied to the combination of the front taper, belly, and rear taper. Generally, the length of the head section dictates the effective casting and control range of a line. Short heads cast quickly but don't cast well for distance. Long heads cast and control well at longer ranges, but require more false casting to clear the head from the rod.

Running Line — this section exists primarily to make distance casting easier. The running line on a WF line is small in diameter and creates less friction in the guides than a DT. Running lines are also very lightweight. This is important because the energy stored in the head of the line during casting must pull the running line through the guides.

LINE WEIGHT VS. HEAD LENGTH

Some weight forward lines have group tailored head lengths which match the lengths of the heads to the distances normally fished with each line size. The lighter lines are delicate; the heavier lines are more powerful.

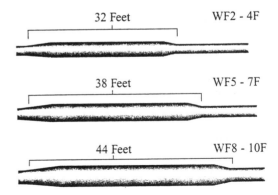

32 Feet   WF2 - 4F

38 Feet   WF5 - 7F

44 Feet   WF8 - 10F

Courtesy of *Scientific Anglers*

TAPER TYPES

Fly lines are typically tapered so that they will deliver a leader and a fly appropriately. There are four basic taper types: Level (L), Double Taper (DT), Weight Forward (WF), and Shooting Taper (ST).

Level—these untapered lines are the same diameter from end to end. The lack of a taper makes them more difficult to cast accurately and control on the water.

Double Taper—best for short to medium casts in the 20–50 foot range, these lines have extra long bellies with identical tapers at either end. The tapers serve to dissipate casting energy, resulting in a delicate presentation. They don't, however, cast long distances as easily as WF lines.

Weight Forward—these lines are designed to fish well at short to long ranges. They cast farther and more easily than DT lines because their small diameter running line offers less resistance in the rod guides.

Shooting Tapers—best to use when maximum distance is needed, and control and accuracy are less important. Also called "shooting heads," they are commonly 30 feet long. They attach to a very small diameter "shooting line" that offers less resistance in the rod guides. This results in maximum length casts.

TAPER DESIGN: A COMPARISON

In addition to standard tapers, there is a wide range of Specialty Tapers. These lines are designed to increase your effectiveness by providing performance characteristics to match situations you'll encounter when fishing for specific species. When extra large flies are used, more powerful tapers work best, such as Bass Bug or Saltwater. When extra line control is needed, Steelhead or Spey/Salmon tapers are the best choice.

Using two different WF8F lines—a standard Scientific Angler Ultra 3 and a Bass/Saltwater—let's compare how we use taper design to give you lines with different performance advantages.

Front Taper—the standard Ultra line has a 6.6 foot front taper while the Bass/Saltwater has a 3.5 foot front taper. As a result, the Bass design transfers more energy from the belly to the tip, providing the power to turn over large, wind resistant flies. Conversely, the longer taper of the standard line allows for a more delicate presentation of smaller flies.

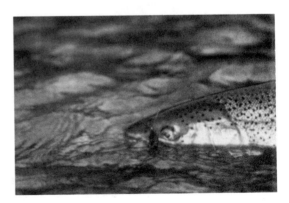

Ultra 3 (standard taper)

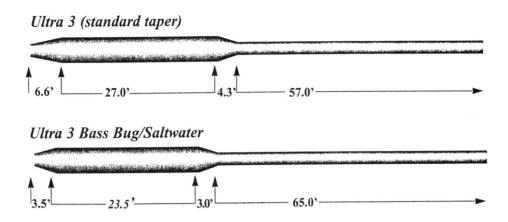

6.6'   27.0'   4.3'   57.0'

Ultra 3 Bass Bug/Saltwater

3.5'   23.5'   3.0'   65.0'

Rear Taper—the short rear taper of the Bass line allows you to cast quickly because the thin running line is in the guides sooner. The longer rear taper of the standard line gives you more distance and line control due to the smoother transmission of energy from the running line to the belly.

Belly—longer bellies, like those of the standard line, are best suited where longer, more accurate casts are required. For middle distances, the shorter belly of the Bass line is better. In these shorter casting situations, the belly section is out of the rod guides after a couple of false casts. As a result, they shoot better, but at the expense of accuracy.

LEADERS

There are two basic leader materials, wire and monofilament (single-strand nylon).

Wire leaders—either piano wire (high-carbon or stainless steel) or braided wire—are used generally to protect the line from sharp underwater obstacles and from the teeth, gill plates, and other sharp appendages of both freshwater and saltwater fish.

Some wire leaders, particularly the braided type, are enclosed in a "sleeve" of nylon, which prevents the wire strands from fraying and eliminates kinking.

Some monofilament leaders perform a similar function. Called shock tippets, they are short lengths (6 feet or shorter in most cases) of strong mono testing up to about 100 pounds depending on the size of the fish being sought. Shock tippets protect the line from sharp objects and sharp teeth, but they are also able to withstand the sledgehammer strikes of large fish. Shock tippets are especially important to tarpon fishermen.

The main purpose of most monofilament leaders, however, is to provide an all-but-invisible link between the end of the line and the lure, bait, or fly. In spinning and spincasting, a leader is seldom necessary, for the line itself is monofilament. But in baitcasting, in which highly visible braided line is sometimes used, a monofilament leader at least 6 feet long is a big advantage.

Fly fishing is perhaps the form of the sport in which the leader is most critical. Today's trout, salmon, and other fly-caught fish—both stocked and wild—are far more wise to the ways of the angler than they once were. When you go for these fish, a sloppy cast, a too-short leader, or an improperly presented fly seldom brings a strike.

Though some fly fishermen feel they can get by with a level leader (one whose diameter is the same throughout its length), a tapered leader makes casting far more pleasant and efficient and brings far more strikes.

A tapered leader must be designed so as to transmit the energy of the cast from the line right down to the fly. But because the fly fisherman's offerings range from dry flies to wet flies to streamers and bucktails to bass bugs, tapered leaders differ too. The proper leader is also determined by water conditions and the size of the fish.

The makeup of a tapered leader starts with the butt section, which is tied to the end of the fly line. The diameter of the tapered leader should be approximately one-half to two-thirds the diameter of the end of the line. The leader then progresses through progressively lighter (and thinner) lengths down to the tippet, to the end of which the fly is itself tied.

Most popular leader lengths are 7½ and 9 feet, but under some conditions—such as when casting to trout in low, clear water—leaders of 12, 15, or more feet may be necessary.

TYPICAL LEADER AND FLY SIZE RECOMMENDATIONS—9 FEET AND 12 FEET

Size	7X	6X	5X	4X	3X	2X	1X	0X
Tippet Diameter	.004	.005	.006	.007	.008	.009	.010	.011
Butt Diameter	.020	.020	.022	.022	.022	.022	.022	.022
Test lbs.	2	3	4	5	6	7	9	10
Fly Size**	18–28	14–22	10–18	6–14	4–10	2–8	2–6	1/0–6

**Fly size is suggested range only

HEAVY FRESHWATER LEADER—9 FEET

Size	8lb	10lb	12lb	14lb
Tippet Diameter	.009	.011	.013	.014
Butt Diameter	.026	.026	.026	.026
Fly Size**	2–8	1/0–6	2/0–4	3/0–2

**Fly size is suggested range only

SALTWATER LEADER—9 FEET AND 12 FEET

Size	8lb	10lb	12lb	16lb
Tippet Diameter	.009	.011	.013	.015
Butt Diameter	.026	.026	.026	.026
Fly Size**	2–8	1/0–6	2/0–4	4/0–1/0

**Fly size is suggested range only

RECOMMENDED TIPPET STRENGTH FOR VARIOUS SPECIES

FRESH WATER

Bream, Sunnies, other small fish	3-pound test
Smallmouth Black Bass	4- to 6-pound test
Largemouth Black Bass	6- to 8-pound test
Brown Trout	3-pound test
Brown Trout using Streamers	5-pound test
Sea run Brown Trout	10-pound test
Brook Trout	3-pound test
Brook Trout using Streamers	5-pound test
Sea run Brook Trout	6-pound test
Cutthroat Trout	3-pound test
Sea Run Cutthroat, called Bluebacks, Harvest Trout	4-pound test
Grayling	3-pound test
Rainbow Trout	4-pound test
Steelhead (sea run Rainbow Trout)	10-pound test
Winter Steelhead	12-pound test

SALT WATER

Mangrove or Gray Snapper	8-pound test
Bonefish	6- or 8-pound test
Tarpon, baby (under 20 pounds)	8-pound test
Tarpon, big (over 20 pounds)	12-pound test
Channel Bass (Redfish)	10-pound test
Striped Bass (to 10 pounds)	8-pound test
Striped Bass (over 10 pounds)	12-pound test
Jack Crevalle	10-pound test
Horse-Eye Jack	10-pound test
Ladyfish	8-pound test
Snook	12-pound test
Spotted Seatrout	10-pound test
Barracuda	12-pound test

SALTWATER FISH IN DEEP WATER, BY CHUMMING OR SIGHTING

Dolphin	10-pound test
Mackerel	10-pound test
False Albacore	10-pound test
Bonito	10-pound test
Grouper	10-pound test
Yellowtail	10-pound test
Bermuda Chub	10-pound test

Bluefish 10-pound test with 12 inches #4 wire leader added
Sailfish 12-pound test with 12 inches 80-pound-test nylon added
Marlin 12-pound test with 12 inches 100-pound-test nylon added
Tarpon 12-pound test with 12 inches 100-pound-test nylon added
Tuna 12-pound test with 12 inches 100-pound-test nylon added
Barracuda 12-pound test with 12 inches #5 wire leader added
Sharks 12-pound test with 12 inches #5 or #7 heavier wire
  leader added

You can buy tapered leaders, either knotless or with the various sections knotted together. Each time you change flies, however, you must snip off a bit of the tippet, so it pays to carry small spools of leader material in various strengths so that you can tie on a new tippet when necessary. You can also tie your own tapered leaders.

Leader material is classified according to "X" designations (1X, 2X, 3X, and so on), with the number representing the diameter of the line. Tapered leaders are classified the same way, with the number representing the diameter of the tippet.

FISHHOOKS

Modern hook design and manufacture has come a long way since the first Stone Age bone hooks found by archeologists and dating back to more than 5,000 B.C. Today's fishhooks come in hundreds of sizes, shapes, and special designs. They're made from carbon steel, stainless steel, or some rust-resistant alloy. They're hardened and tempered, then plated or bronzed to meet special specifications. Some are thin steel wire for use in tying artificial flies; others are thick steel for big-game fish that prowl offshore waters.

There is no such thing as an all-purpose hook. Fishermen must carry a variety of patterns and sizes to match both tackle and size of fish being hunted. Let's start from the beginning by learning the basic nomenclature of a typical fishhook, illustrated in the accompanying drawing.

Even the various parts of a typical fishhook may vary in design to meet certain requirements. There are sliced shanks to better hold bait on the hook, forged shanks for greater strength in marine hooks, tapered eyes to reduce weight of hooks used in tying dry flies, and so on.

HOOK WIRE SIZE

The letter X and the designations "Fine" or "Stout" are used to indicate the weight or diameter of a hook. For example, a 2X Stout means the hook is made of the standard diameter for a hook two sizes larger,

PARTS OF A FISHHOOK

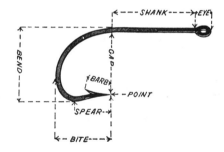

and a 3X Stout is made of the standard diameter for a hook three sizes larger.

When we go to lightweight hooks, the designations are reversed. For example, a 2X Fine means that the hook is made of the standard diameter for a hook two sizes smaller, and so on.

Obviously, the angler seeking the big fish should lean toward the stout hooks, which are not apt to bend or spring when striking the bigger fish that swim our waters, particularly salt water.

Fishermen who use live bait will want the fine-wire hooks, which will not weigh down the bait. The use of flies, particularly dry flies, also requires fine-wire hooks, since their light weight will enable a fly to float more easily.

SHANK LENGTH

The letter X and the designations "Long" or "Short" are used to specify shank length of a hook. The formula for determining shank length is similar to that used for wire sizes. A 2X Long means the shank of the hook is the standard length for a hook two sizes larger, and a 4X Long for a hook four sizes larger. A 2X Short is a hook that has a shank as short as the standard length of a hook two sizes smaller, and 4X Short for a hook four sizes smaller, and so on.

Picking a hook with the correct shank length depends on the type of fishing you plan to undertake. A short-shank hook is preferred for baitfishing, since it can be hidden in the bait more easily. The long-shank hook is at its best when used for fish with sharp teeth. A bluefish, for example, would have a tough time getting past the long shank and cutting into the leader. Long-shank hooks are also used in tying streamers and bucktails.

HOOK SIZE

Attempts have been made to standardize hook sizes, but none have been very successful. The problem has been that a hook actually has two measurements—the gap and the length of the shank, both of which vary from pattern to pattern.

Only by studying the various patterns and sizes in the accompanying charts (hooks are shown actual size) can an angler become sufficiently familiar with hook patterns to pick the right hook for the job.

As a guide, refer to Natural Saltwater Baits on page 389, and note the hook sizes recommended for various species of fish. Match those recommendations with the hook sizes on these pages and compare the differences. With this information, it is not difficult to choose the correct size hook for your type of fishing.

HOOK CHARACTERISTICS

In addition to size and shank length, there are other characteristics of hooks to consider when selecting a hook for a specific purpose. The barb, obviously, is a critical part of the hook. A short barb is quick to set in the mouth of a fish, but it also gives a jumping fish a greater chance of dislodging it. A long barb, on the other hand, is more difficult to set but it also makes it a lot tougher for a fish to shake it loose.

So what guidelines should an angler follow? Let's list some basic recommendations. The all-round saltwater fisherman can't go wrong by using the O'Shaughnessy, Kirby, Sproat, or Siwash patterns.

And if you happen to have some Salmon hooks, they're perfectly all right to use with a wire leader for barracuda and other toothy fish.

TWO TYPES OF WEEDLESS HOOKS

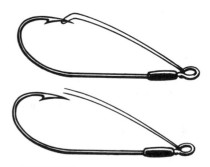

HUMP-SHANKED HOOK

BARBLESS HOOK

If you're a flounder fisherman, you'll find that the Chestertown and Carlisle patterns are your best bet. The long-shanked Chestertown makes it especially easy to unhook flounders, which may well be a primary reason for using them when fishing for these flatfish.

If you're a baitfisherman, use the sliced shanked Mustad-Beak or Eagle Claw patterns. Those extra barbs on the shanks do a good job keeping natural baits secured to the hook.

Fishermen can also become confused when they see hooks with straight-ringed eyes, turned-up eyes, and turned-down eyes. This should not present a

HOOK PART VARIATIONS

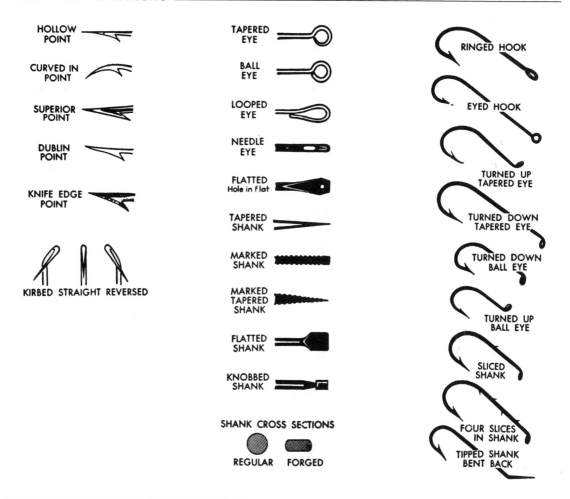

problem. If you're replacing hooks on lures or attaching hooks to spinners, use a straight-ringed eye. If you're tying short-shanked artificial flies, pick the turned-up eye, which will provide more space for the hook point to bite into the fish. The turned-down eye is the best bet for standard flies and for baitfishing, since it brings the point of the hook closest to a straight line of penetration when striking a fish.

Curved shanks also lead to some confusion.

Without getting into specific details, let's say simply that a curved shank, curved right or left, has its place in baitfishing. The offset point has a better chance of hitting flesh when a strike is made.

When you are casting or trolling with artificial lures or spinners, however, the straight-shanked hook is a better choice, since it does not have a tendency to spin or twist, which is often the case with curved-shanked hooks.

HOOK STYLES AND SIZES

Below and on upcoming pages, you will find various styles of hooks. In most cases, the smallest and largest of hooks in these styles are shown, with intermediate hook sizes indicated by means of horizontal lines and corresponding hook numbers. To match the name and size of an unknown hook, just compare yours to the drawings. (Chart concept by Jeff Fitschen)

SUPERIOR MUSTAD-LIMERICK

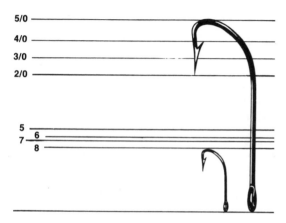

SUPERIOR MUSTAD-SPROAT
FLY HOOK, TURNED DOWN BALL EYE

HOLLOW POINT MUSTAD-LIMERICK
FLY HOOK, TURNED DOWN TAPERED EYE

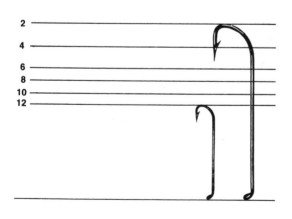

HOLLOW POINT
MUSTAD-SPROUT WORM HOOK

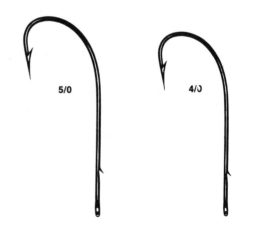

SUPERIOR MUSTAD-CARLISLE

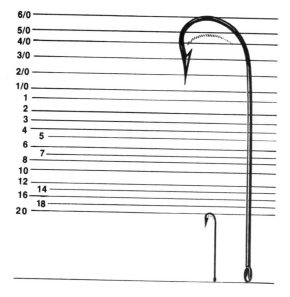

HOLLOW POINT MUSTAD-WIDE GAP HOOK

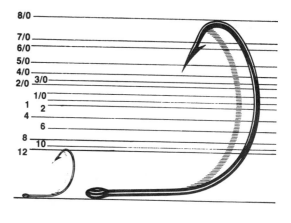

SUPERIOR MUSTAD-ABERDEEN
CRICKET HOOK

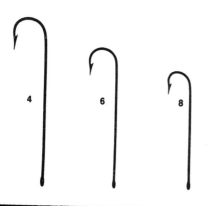

SUPERIOR MUSTAD-O'SHAUGHNESSY

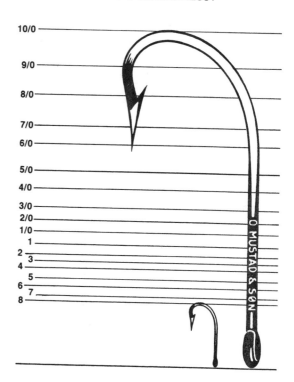

SHANK BENT ASIDE MUSTAD-LIMERICK

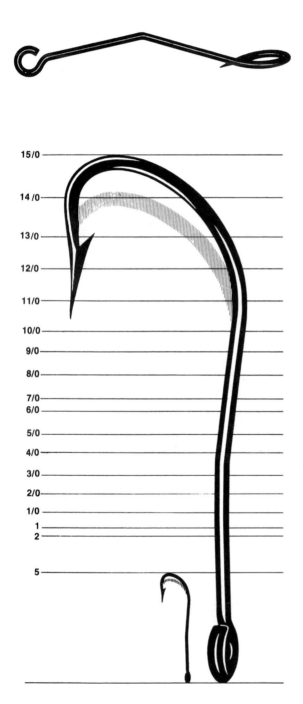

15/0
14 /0
13 /0
12/0
11/0
10/0
9/0
8/0
7/0
6/0
5/0
4/0
3/0
2/0
1/0
1
2

5

SHANK BENT DOWN MUSTAD-O'SHAUGHNESSY

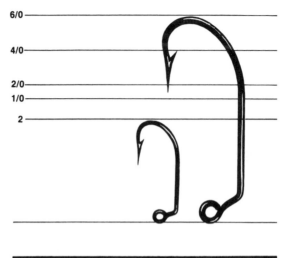

6/0
4/0
2/0
1/0
2

HOLLOW POINT MUSTAD-CENTRAL DRAUGHT

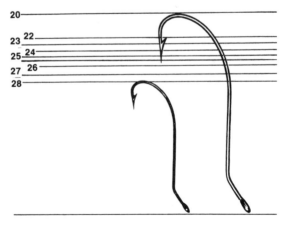

20
23 22
25 24
27 26
28

**SUPERIOR MUSTAD-PACIFIC BASS,
TURNED DOWN BALL EYE**

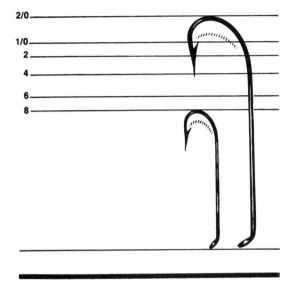

2/0
1/0
2
4
6
8

**HOLLOW POINT MUSTAD-VIKING
FLY HOOK, 2X LONG SHANK,
TURNED DOWN TAPERED EYE**

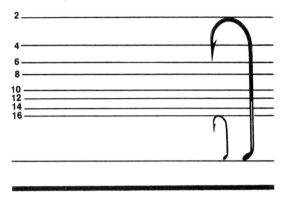

2
4
6
8
10
12
14
16

**HOLLOW POINT MUSTAD-VIKING
FLY HOOK, 5X SHORT SHANK,
TURNED DOWN TAPERED EYE**

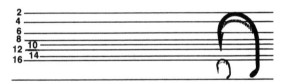

2
4
6
8
12 10
16 14

**MUSTAD-KINK SHANK
(HUMP SHANK)**

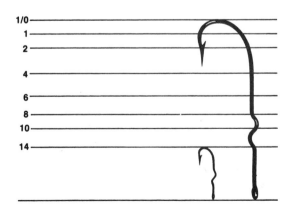

1/0
1
2
4
6
8
10
14

**HOLLOW POINT MUSTAD-BEAK,
TURNED DOWN TAPERED EYE**

3/0
2/0
1/0
1   2
3   4
5
9   8
11 10
13 12

HOLLOW POINT MUSTAD-BEAK,
TURNED DOWN TAPERED EYE,
TWO SLICES IN SHANK

HOLLOW POINT MUSTAD-BEAK
FLOUNDER HOOK, SPECIAL LONG SHANK

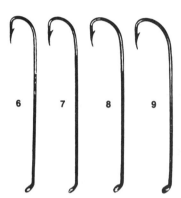

MUSTAD-PIKE HOOK

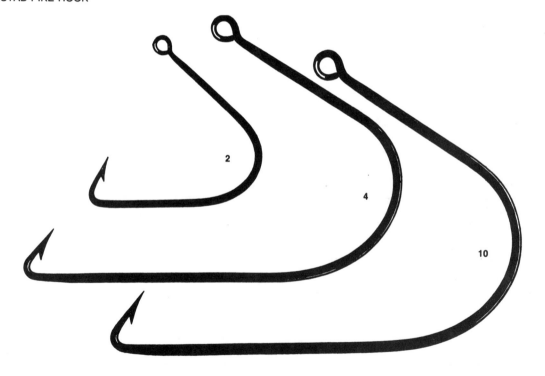

HOLLOW POINT
MUSTAD-SALMON HOOK, 3X STOUT

KNIFE EDGE POINT MUSTAD-SEA HAWK

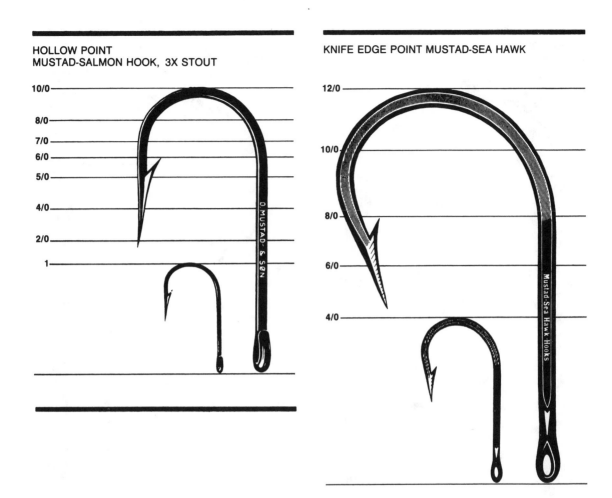

MUSTAD-SHARK HOOK

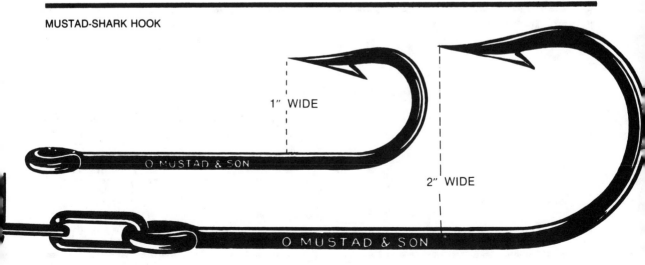

KNIFE EDGE POINT
MUSTAD-SEA DEAMON

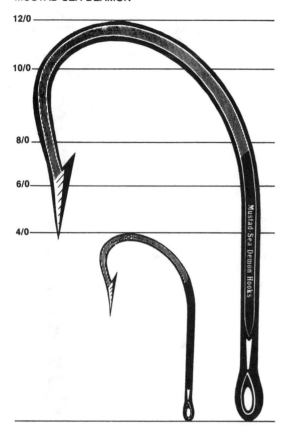

KNIFE EDGE POINT
MUSTAD-SOUTHERN & TUNA HOOK

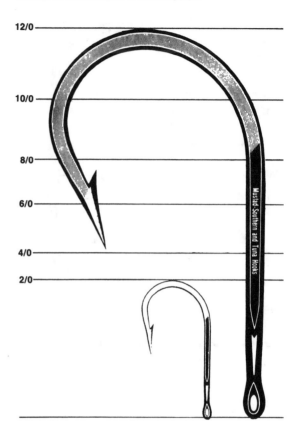

SUPERIOR MUSTAD-DOUBLE HOOK,
BRAZED SHANK

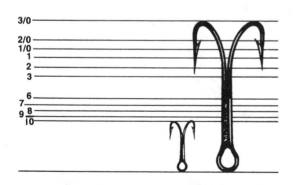

SUPERIOR MUSTAD-DOUBLE HOOK,
LOOSE, RINGED

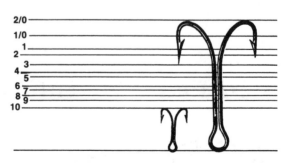

MUSTAD-TUNA CIRCLE HOOK

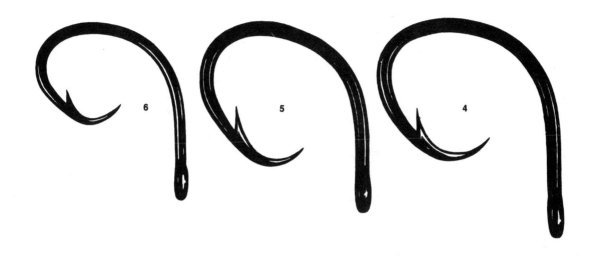

**HOLLOW POINT MUSTAD-DOUBLE HOOK,
UNIVERSAL DOUBLE BAIT,
NEEDLE EYE, ROD ATTACHED**

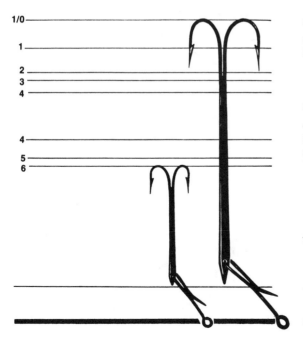

**SUPERIOR MUSTAD-TREBLE
HOOK, SPROAT BEND**

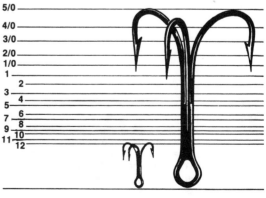

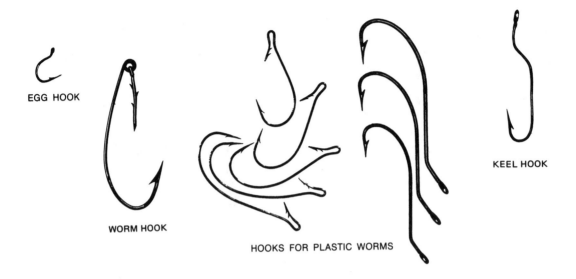

EGG HOOK

WORM HOOK

HOOKS FOR PLASTIC WORMS

KEEL HOOK

HOOKS FOR FLY FISHING

HOOK EYES

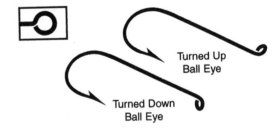

Turned Up
Ball Eye

Turned Down
Ball Eye

Ball Eye: A strong untapered eye, it is the simplest eye form. It is available turned up and turned down. Considered too heavy for dry flies, hooks with ball eyes are used for wet flies.

Tapered Eye: Also produced turned up and turned down. The tapered eye is made to maintain a full inner diameter while at the same time it features a reduced outer diameter. This is achieved because the diameter of the wire decreases as the eye closes. The larger diameter makes for easier insertion of leader material in the eyes of the hooks. The tapered eye also lightens the weight of the hook and, when turned up, faces away from the point of the hook, leaving the gap clear and enhancing the chances of the small hook setting firmly and quickly when hit. Tapered eye hooks are used for dry flies, wet flies, and streamers.

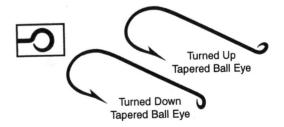

Turned Up
Tapered Ball Eye

Turned Down
Tapered Ball Eye

Looped Eye: Properly referred to as the looped eye because of its construction, this eye has been a traditional characteristic of salmon fly hooks. It is a strong fly hook, easily tied to leaders and is less likely to fray them than ball and tapered eyes. In addition to dry and wet salmon hook patterns, the looped eye is available in a barbless dry fly pattern and in a long-shanked steamer hook. Available turned up and turned down.

Oval Eye: This eye takes its name from its obvious shape. A characteristic found on many traditional salmon fly hooks as well as numerous treble hooks. The oval eye is used to achieve a slimmer profile than an eyed hook.

HOOK SIZES

Every fly has a size number which is determined by the hook pattern (name) and which is stated in the terms of the width of the gap between the hook point and the hook shank. The gap width of the given size in one particular pattern or family of hooks . . . for example, the Viking . . . for the most part does not vary. One might note slight deviations in gap width among the same family. Between different hook families, there is little compatibility in gap width.

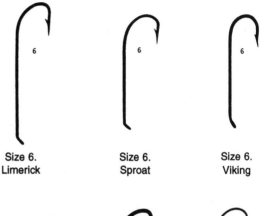

Size 6.   Size 6.   Size 6.
Limerick   Sproat   Viking

HOOK SHAPES AND BENDS

This display illustrates some of the variations in shapes and bends which help identify hook patterns used in fly tying.

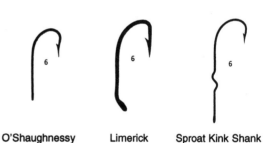

O'Shaughnessy   Limerick   Sproat Kink Shank

ARTIFICIAL LURES

Fishing with bait is enjoyable, certainly, but there's something about fooling a fish with an artificial that gives most anglers a special charge.

A neophyte fisherman who visits a well-stocked sporting-goods store or tackle shop is confronted with a bewildering array of plugs, spoons, spinners, jigs, flies, bugs, and others. Some artificials look like nothing that ever swam, crawled, or flew, and yet they catch fish.

Let's look at each type of artificial and see how and why it works and how it should be fished.

PLUGS

Plugs are lures designed to imitate small fish for the most part, though some plugs simulate mice, frogs, eels, and other food on which gamefish feed. Plug action—meaning the way it moves when retrieved by the angler—is important and is something on which manufacturers expend much money and time. Many plugs, particularly the divers, are known as crankbaits because every crank of the reel handle imparts some sort of diving or darting action.

The type, size, and weight of the plug you select is determined by the fish you are after and the kind of fishing outfit you are using. The charts, found elsewhere in this book, on how to match up various kinds of fishing tackle will help the beginner choose the right weight plugs.

There are five basic types of plugs: popping, surface, floating-diving, sinking (deep-running), and deep-diving.

Popping. These plugs float on the surface and have concave, hollowed-out faces. The angler retrieves a popping plug by jerking the rod tip back so that the plug's face digs into the water, making a small splash, bubbles, and a popping sound. Some make a louder sound than others. This sound is especially attractive to largemouth bass, pike, muskies, and some inshore saltwater species, such as striped bass. Most popping plugs (and most other plugs) have two sets of treble hooks. Popping plugs are most productive when the water surface is calm or nearly so. They should usually be fished very slowly.

Surface. These plugs float on the surface, but they can be fished with various kinds of retrieves and create a different kind of surface disturbance than poppers do. Designed with an elongated, or bullet-shaped, head, they create surface disturbance by various means, including propellers (at the head or at both head and tail), a wide metal lip at the head, and hinged metal ''wings'' just behind the head. They can be twitched so that they barely nod, retrieved steadily so that they chug across the water, or skimmed across the top as fast as the angler can turn his reel handle. The proper retrieve depends on the lure's design and, of course, on the mood of the fish. It's best to try different retrieves until you find one that produces.

Floating-Diving. These plugs are designed to float when at rest and dive when retrieved. Some float horizontally while others float with the tail hanging down beneath the surface. They are made to dive by an extended lip at the head. The speed of the retrieve determines the depth of the dive. The faster the retrieve, the deeper the dive. Most of these plugs have a side-to-side wobbling action. An erratic retrieve—dive, surface, dive, surface—is often productive, and these plugs are also effective when made to swim just above a submerged weed bed, rock pile, and so on.

Sinking (deep-running). These plugs sink as soon as they hit the water and are designed for deep work. Some sink slower than others and can be fished at various depths, depending on how long the angler waits before starting his retrieve. Most of these plugs have some sort of wobbling action, and some fairly vibrate when retrieved. Some have propellers fore and aft.

These plugs are excellent fish-finders: the fisherman can start by bouncing them along bottom, and if that doesn't work, he can work them at progressively shallower depths until he finds at what depth the fish are feeding. It should be remembered that deep-running plugs don't have to be fished in deep water; for example, in small sizes they're tops for river smallmouths.

Deep-Diving. These plugs may float or sink, but all are designed with long and/or broad lips of metal or plastic that cause the plugs to dive to depths of 30 feet or more as the angler reels in. As with other diving plugs, the faster the retrieve, the deeper the dive. Most of these lures have some sort of wobbling action. They are ideally suited for casting or trolling in deep lakes and at the edges of dropoffs, and they work best in most waters when the fish are holding in deep holes, as fish usually do during the midday in July and August.

FRESHWATER POPPING PLUGS

Hula Popper: Hollow or cupped face imparts popping and surface commotion when retrieved in short jerks. An effective surface plug for bass, particularly at night when fished close to shore.

Storm Rattlin' Chug Bug: Top-water popper that will pop, chug, and dart in response to wrist movements. Available in large sizes for saltwater.

SALTWATER POPPING PLUGS

Mirrolure Surface Poppers: Create a rattling and popping sound when retrieved along or just below the surface. The 109MR, 7 inches and 2 ounces, creates a surface commotion when trolled or cast-and-retrieved. The 44MR, 3½ inches and ½ ounce, tempts snook and redfish from the mangroves.

Pencil Popper: Good casting plug because of its heavier tail section. This lure floats at an angle and should be retrieved in short jerks. A favorite in northeastern coastal waters for school stripers and bluefish.

Mann's Chug-N-Spit: Deep mouth throws water forward while the head hole squirts water upward. Good choice for surface feeding inshore and offshore species.

SURFACE PLUGS

Sputterbug: Spinner at head of plug churns surface as it is retrieved fast. A slow retrieve produces a paddling noise. A good producer of bass, muskies, pickerel. Fish it along the edge of reed beds and near lily pads.

Jitterbug: Swimming animal lure with side-by-side crawling action. This lure emits gurgling sounds and leaves a V-wake of bubbles on surface. It's an effective lure for bass, pike, muskies, pickerel.

Crazy Crawler: A top bass lure for dawn, dusk, and night-time fishing. Retrieve it just fast enough for the two metal arms to paddle water. Stop it occasionally, pause, twitch it once or twice, then resume retrieve. Designed to simulate a swimming animal.

Mirrolure (Float Model): Rests on top, but dips below surface when jerked. Action must be imparted by rod tip, but plug is productive on bass, pike, muskies, pickerel, and small saltwater species.

Luhr Jensen Dalton Special: A classic wood topwater plug for bass and pike.

Tiny Torpedo: Rests on surface, but tail propeller creates noisy bubbling action when lure is jerked. Designed to imitate a wounded minnow, the plug will take bass, pickerel, muskies, pike.

Zara Spook: A torpedo-type lure that darts, dives, bobs when jerked. While good for bass, pike, muskies, and pickerel, it has proven particularly productive in Florida's mangrove waters for snook and tarpon.

FLOATING-DIVING PLUGS

Luhr Jensen Kwikfish: A good trolling lure for salmon and steelhead. Particularly effective when back trolled. Available up to 5½-inches long.

Rapala Husky Jerks: Available in sizes from 3⅛ to 5½ inches. Can dive and hold practically motionless until twitched. Good lure for all fresh and saltwater species.

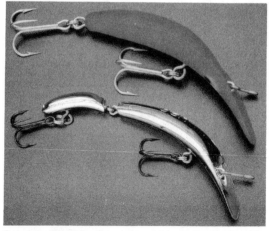

Cabela's Flatfish: On a slow retrieve, the lure's wide wobble will catch salmon, walleyes, lake trout, pike, muskies, and bass.

SALTWATER DIVING PLUGS

Mirrorlure 112MR Trolling Lure: Shape, flash, diving action, and rattle produce large saltwater game fish. Effective when trolled at high speeds for tuna, dolphin, and wahoo.

Mann's Stretch 25 + : Dives to a depth of 25 feet almost vertically for maximum time at its running depth. A good striped bass lure.

Stan Gibbs Darter: Heavy tail section makes this plug easy to cast far out. It floats at rest, but darts side-to-side when retrieved. From beach, boat, or jetty, this plug will get strikes from nearly all saltwater inshore species. It's a favorite of the striped-bass fisherman.

DEEP-DIVING AND SINKING PLUGS

Mann's Stretch 15 + : Dives almost vertically to depths of 15 feet. Good for smallmouth bass and trout.

Mann's Wally-Trac: Self-centering line-tie design guarantees a straight-running lure. A good trolling lure. Three models dive down to 11–13 feet.

River Runt: Sinks slowly and dives deeper with side-to-side action when retrieved. Faster the retrieve, deeper plug will run. Effective on bass, pickerel, pike, walleyes, muskies.

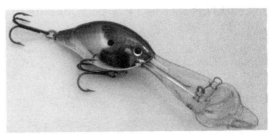

Luhr Jensen Deep Secret: Allows an angler to go deep with a smaller lure and not fatigue from cranking and pumping the lure to the surface, despite the large diving lips.

Mirrolure: This plug sinks when it hits the surface and dives deeper on retrieve. Can be cast or trolled and comes in various sizes for fish from crappies to bass and pike.

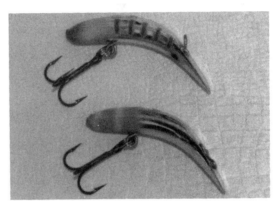

Worden's Flatfish: Slow retrieve motion. Available in 14 sizes up to 6 inches. A good lure for all species.

SALTWATER SINKING PLUGS

Needlefish: In bay waters, from the surf, and off jetties, this sinking plug has taken its share of striped bass, bluefish, weakfish. Has no built-in action. Lure must be retrieved with jerks.

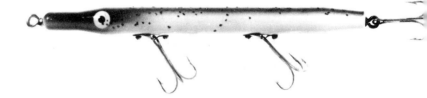

Boone T.D. Special: A sinking plug that can be worked at any depth. Equally effective on New Jersey striped bass and Florida's tarpon and snook.

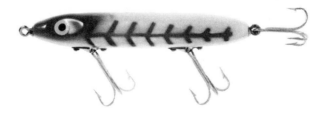

SALTWATER SINKING PLUGS (Continued)

Mirrolure (Sinking Model): A big weighted lure that casts easy and sinks fast. Has little, if any, built-in action. Lure must be worked with a jerk-and-crank retrieve. Lack of built-in action is no handicap, however. This shiny-sided plug draws strikes from striped bass, bluefish, tarpon, snook, barracuda, and similar inshore species.

SPOONS

Spoons are among the oldest of artificials. If you cut the handle off a teaspoon, you'd have the basic shape of this lure.

Spoons are designed to imitate small baitfish of one kind or another, so flash is an important feature in many of these lures. Most spoons have a wobbling side-to-side action when retrieved.

Many spoons have a silver or gold finish, while others are painted in various colors and combinations of colors. Most have a single free-swinging treble hook at the tail; others have a single fixed hook. Weedless arrangements are becoming more and more popular on both types.

In general, the smaller spoons are better in streams and ponds, while the larger ones are a good choice for lakes. However, the angler must remember that with two spoons of equal weight but different size, the smaller one will cast easier in wind and sink faster, while the larger one will sink slower and swim at shallower depths.

What's the best retrieve for a spoon? Again, that depends on weather and water conditions and other circumstances, including the mood of the fish. But generally, an erratic retrieve, with twitches and jerks of the rod tip, is better than a steady retrieve because it makes the spoon look like an injured baitfish. Attaching a strip of pork rind to a spoon often adds to its fish appeal.

SPOONS

Dardevle: This spoon can be cast or trolled for pike, muskies, salmon, steelhead. Available in a variety of patterns, the Dardevle is also effective in saltwater.

Doctor Spoon: Heavier than most freshwater spoons, this lure is used by trollers. It's productive on salmon, lake trout, pike, muskies. Also available with chemical light.

Finsel Spoon: Fins give this spoon a darting action. Good casting lure for pike, muskies, pickerel, trout.

Red Eye Wiggler: A wobbler that imparts good action at any speed of retrieve. Cast or trolled, an effective lure for pike, muskies, pickerel, lake trout.

Johnson's Silver Minnow: An old favorite wobbling spoon. With a strip of pork rind on its weedless hook, it can be fished in weed- and brush-infested waters. Excellent for pickerel, pike, muskies, trout, coho salmon.

Mr. Champ: A wobbling spoon that won't spin or twist line. Serves well for casting, jiggling, trolling. Will take most species, such as bass, panfish, trout, pickerel, pike.

Limper: A darting spoon that can be used for jigging as well as casting and trolling. Good for pickerel, pike, muskies, bass, trout. Available with single hook for coho salmon.

Al's Goldfish: An effective wobbler that can be cast or trolled for trout and salmon. Al's Goldfish works equally well for bass, pickerel, pike.

Tony Accetta Pet: Also available with weedless hook, this wobbling spoon is best fished with a strip of pork rind. Can be cast or trolled for trout, salmon, bass, pickerel, pike.

Sidewinder: Has a side-to-side action in addition to its wobble. A good fast-water lure for trout and salmon, as well as a good choice for most warm-water species.

Phantom Wobbler: A slab of pearl-like material is added to this wobbling spoon. Fine choice for trout and salmon, and should prove effective on bass, pike, and pickerel.

SALTWATER SPOONS

Dardevle: Big mackerel-finish spoon has action similar to the well-known Dardevle, except it is designed for casting and trolling in coastal waters. Trolled deep on wire line it will take bluefish. When it is cast from surf or boat it will take stripers.

Acme Kastmaster: Produces action without line twist. Available from $\frac{1}{12}$ ounce to 4 ounces. A good casting lure for surf and jetty fishermen.

Reed R.T. Flash: Well-designed spoon that can be cast, trolled, jigged. Good lure in coastal waters for tinker mackerel, snappers, weakfish, kingfish. Trolled off shore with wire line or trolling lead, it takes bigger inshore species.

Wob-L-Rite: A heavy brass spoon, is easy to cast far distances. Wobbles on steady retrieve or can be jigged. Good choice for deep jigging reef species or surf and boat casting.

Tony Accetta Spoon: Available in various sizes, this spoon has proven itself in coastal waters. Usually rigged with pork rind strip, as shown here, it is an effective trolling and casting lure for nearly all inshore game fish.

SPINNERS

Spinners, like spoons, are designed to imitate baitfish, and they attract gamefish by flash and vibration. A spinner is simply a metal blade mounted on a shaft by means of a revolving arm or ring called a clevis. Unlike a spoon, which has a wobbling action, a spinner blade rotates around the shaft when retrieved.

Other parts of a simple spinner include a locking device to accommodate a hook at one end of the shaft, a metal loop to which the line is tied at the other end of the shaft, and a series of metal or plastic beads that separate the blade from—and keep it from jamming against—the locking device and loop. In some spinners, notably the Colorado, the blade is mounted on a series of swivels instead of on a shaft.

Most spinners have either one or two blades. However, in some forms of fishing, particularly deep-water trolling for lake trout, eight or more spinner blades are mounted in tandem on a length of wire.

Most spinner blades have either a silver or a gold finish. Some, however, are painted in various colors, including black, yellow, and white, while others are striped and still others are made of simulated pearl. In general, the brighter finishes are best in shaded or discolored water and on overcast days, while the darker finishes are better in very clear water under bright skies.

Spinner blades have various shapes and other physical characteristics. Both shape and thickness determine how the blade reacts when retrieved. To illustrate this point, let's take a look at a few types of simple spinners, often used with bait, that have proven their worth over the years.

Colorado. Has a wide, nearly round blade that rotates well out from the shaft. Because it has considerable water resistance and spins relatively slowly, it is best suited for use in lakes and in streams with slow currents. A Colorado spinner used with a worm is a proven taker of trout, walleyes, and other fish.

Willow Leaf. Has a long, narrow blade that spins fast and close to the shaft. Having minimum water resistance, it is well suited for use in fast-flowing water. A willow-leaf spinner is often used with a worm, minnow, and other natural baits.

June Bug. Unusual in that the blade is attached directly to the shaft (there is no clevis), has a sort of "leg" that braces the blade against the shaft, and has a hole in the middle. A June Bug spinner with its hook sweetened by a nightcrawler is a potent combination for trout, walleyes, and many other gamefish. The June Bug comes in various designs.

Spinner-blade sizes are usually classified by numbers. But the numbers vary with the manufacturers and are not a reliable guide for the buyer. It's easy enough to simply look over a selection of spinners and select the size that seems right for your particular purpose.

Many spinner-type lures are produced today and are extremely popular, especially among freshwater fishermen. In all of them, the basic attracting element is a revolving spinner blade. Most have some sort of weight built in along the shaft and a treble hook at the tail. In many, the treble hook is hidden or at least disguised with bucktail, feathers, or a skirt of rubber or plastic strands. Weedless hooks are becoming increasingly popular on these lures.

BUZZ BAITS

Buzz baits are spinner baits incorporating a wide propeller that churns a substantial surface commotion. Shown here are typical buzz baits (A) Doodle Buzz and (B) Lindy Clacker.

BASIC TYPES OF SPINNERS

Willow Leaf Spinner: A single or double-hook rig can be attached to this spinner to make it a good trolling lure. Used with worms or minnows, it takes fish in both fresh and salt water. Particularly effective when trolling blood or sandworms for striped bass.

BASIC TYPES OF SPINNERS (Continued)

Colorado Spinner: Old favorite that fills a variety of needs. Can be cast or trolled, with or without natural bait on tail treble hook. Small sizes can be effectively used with a fly rod in streams for trout. A worm or salmon egg on the tail hook frequently makes spinner extra attractive to fish. Good for just about all freshwater species.

Indiana Double-Blade: A multi-purpose spinner rig, this can be cast or trolled with a single or double-hook fixed to its shaft. Can be used as attractors when trolling for pike, pickerel, muskies, and similar freshwater species. This Indiana spinner has even been used on party boats drifting cut bait along the bottom for fluke and flounder.

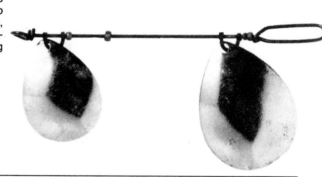

June Bug Spinner: One of the most versatile spinners, it is available with one or two blades, with weighted or unweighted shaft. As with other spinner rigs, it can be used with a single or double hook. The June Bug is especially effective when trolled with a nightcrawler or baitfish for pike, pickerel, walleyes, perch, muskies, and bass.

BUZZ BAITS

Mann's Undulator: A segmented blade flaps up and down rather than spins for more flash and vibration on the drop and retrieve.

Moss Master Buzzbait: A floating, weedless bass target when buzzed in short bursts or ripped in long sweeps.

Worden's Buzz Tail: Combines Worden's Spin-N-Glo winged drift bobber that spins and buzzes with a pulsating hackle tail. Available in 90 color combinations.

SPINNER BAITS

Typical safety-pin spinner baits.

WEIGHTED SPINNERS

Mepps Black Fury

Mepps Aglia Plain

Rooster Tail: These spinners have a painted glitter blade to match the shimmer tail, creating added sparkle as the lure moves through the water. Good choice for trout and smallmouth.

WEIGHTED SPINNERS (Continued)

Mepps Aglia
with squirrel tail

Mepps Aglia Comet with
plastic minnow

WEEDLESS SPINNER-TYPE LURES

Sputterfuss

Shimmy Wiggler

DEEP-WATER TROLLING RIGS

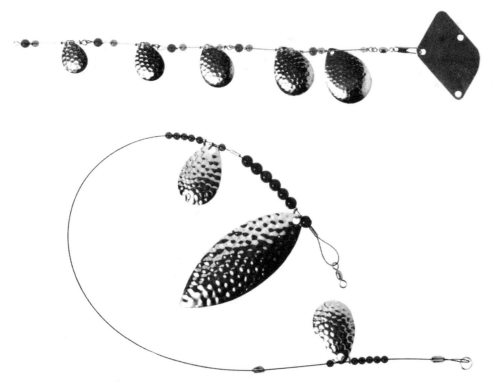

Typical trolling rigs for lake trout and other deep-running fish are the Webertroll **(top photo)** and the Dave Davis Spinner.

JIGS

Generally speaking, a jig is any lure with a weighted head (usually lead), a fixed hook, and a tail of bucktail, feathers, nylon, or similar material. Jigs are made in sizes of 1/16 ounce to 6 ounces and even heavier, and they will take just about any fish that swims in fresh water and salt. Jigs imitate baitfish, crustaceans, and other gamefish forage. In some jigs, the hook rides with the point up, to minimize the chance of snagging.

Jigs, and related lures, take many forms. Here's a look at the most popular types.

Feathered Jig. Often called Japanese feathers, this jig is commonly used in saltwater trolling and casting. It consists of a heavy metal head with eyes. Through the head runs a wire leader, to the end of which the hook is attached. Running from the head down to the hook is a long tail, usually of feathers. A plastic sleeve covers the feathers for about half their length.

Bonito Jig. Similar to the feathered jig but smaller and having a fixed hook embedded in the metal head. Line is tied to ring on head. Used for saltwater trolling and casting.

Bucktail Jig. Consists of a lead head, embedded hook, and trailing tail of bucktail. Head has ring to which line is attached. Head is painted, with the most popular colors being white, red, yellow, and combinations of those colors. The most popular member of the jig family, bucktail jigs are used on a wide variety of freshwater and saltwater gamefish, especially largemouth and smallmouth bass, walleyes, pike, striped bass, bluefish, and many other bottom-feeders.

Bullet Bucktail Jig. Same as standard bucktail jig except that head is bullet-shaped, coming to a blunt point.

Shad Dart. Small jig (usually weighing about 1/4 ounce) with relatively long, narrow head, flat face, and short tail of bucktail or similar material. Usually painted in two colors, with most popular combinations being red and white, yellow and white, and red and yellow. An extremely popular lure for American (white) shad in East Coast rivers.

Metal (Block-Tin) Squids. Falling under the general category of jigs are these lures, which are used mostly in salt water for striped bass, bluefish, and the like. Made to resemble baitfish, they have a long,

SALTWATER JIGS

Metal (Block-Tin) Squid with free-swinging feathered hook.

Hopkins hammered steel jig.

Metal (Block-Tin) Sand Eel with single free-swinging feathered hook.

Bullet or Torpedo bucktail jig with single fixed hook.

Hammered steel jig with treble feathered hook.

Upperman bucktail jig with single fixed hook.

narrow body of block tin, stainless steel, chrome, or nickel-plated lead and either a single fixed hook or a free-swinging treble hook, with or without a tail of bucktail. Most metal squids range in length from 3 to 6 inches. All have bright finishes, usually silvery; in some the finish is smooth, while others have a hammered finish that gives a scalelike appearance. Among the most popular metal squids are types such as the Hopkins (which has a hammered finish; a long, narrow, flat body; and a free-swinging treble hook), the diamond jig (four-sided body, treble hook), and the sand eel (long, rounded, undulating body). A strip of pork rind often adds to the effectiveness of metal squids.

Jig and Eel. Consists of a small metal squid onto which is rigged a common eel, either the real McCoy (usually dead and preserved) or a plastic artificial. These rigged eels range in length from about 6 inches up to a foot or longer. The jig and eel is a deadly combination for striped bass, big snook, redfish, and sea trout. Best retrieve depends on various conditions, but usually a slow, slightly erratic swimming motion is best.

How do you fish a jig? Most jigs—except the jig-and-eel combination and those designed for trolling—should be retrieved with sharp upward jerks of the rod tip so that they look like fleeing darting bait. Most jigs have little action of their own (though some are designed to wiggle when retrieved), so the angler must impart fish-attracting motion.

JIGS AND JIG-AND-EEL RIGS

Acme Fiord With Tube Tail: Good for casting or vertical jigging, the fluorescent tube tail creates flash and eel-like wiggle. Produces bluefish, stripers, weakfish, jacks, and other saltwater game fish.

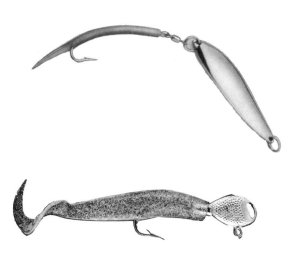

Acme Need-L-Eel: Imitates the shape and flash of sand eels with slim profile and slow wobble when cast or trolled. Good casting distance for surf or jetty fishing.

Bead Jigs-for-Rigs: Features a hooking setup developed for large fish found off oil rigs, such as gulf coast Amberjack. Available in weights from 3 to 16 ounces.

Block-Tin Squid: An old favorite, shown here with a pork rind strip, has proven itself a good casting and trolling rig for stripers, bluefish, and other inshore species.

SALTWATER TROLLING LURES

Cow Killer: An artificial eel with lead head and double hooks. Weighing six ounces and measuring 18 inches, it's the heaviest artificial eel made. Excellent for big striped bass and other large saltwater gamefish.

Barracuda Jig: A rig more commonly known as Japanese feathers, it is basically a trolling lure for offshore work on billfish, tuna, albacore, and bluefish.

Tony Accetta Pet Spoon: Big with a single fixed hook, this type of lure is more commonly known as a bunker spoon. It can be trolled with large strip of pork rind or an eel. One of the most effective lures for striped bass.

Plastic Squid: With long wire leader running through body and attached to single hook, this rig is designed for offshore trolling for billfish, tuna, albacore, bluefish, and similar species.

SALTWATER TROLLING LURES (Continued)

Plastic Trolling Lures: A variety of soft and hard-headed ones for canyon and offshore fishing. All are effective for marlin, sailfish, tuna and other bluewater species.

Umbrella Rig: A fishing lure with four wire arms, each supporting two or three surgical-tube lures. A single tube is trailed from the center. Designed to imitate a school of sand eels or baitfish, the umbrella rig is extremely effective on the East Coast for saltwater fish, especially bluefish. The umbrella rig is always trolled.

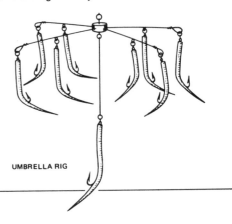

UMBRELLA RIG

PLASTIC LURES

Hundreds of years from now the history books may refer to our era as the Age of Plastic. And fishermen haven't escaped the gaze of the plastic manufacturers.

On the market today are soft-plastic lures that imitate just about anything any fish will eat. There are plastic worms, eels, snakes, crickets, crawfish, minnows, shrimp, hellgrammites, mullet, flies, beetles, grasshoppers, frogs, and many, many more. Even salmon eggs!

Surprisingly, a good many of these synthetic creations catch fish. A prime example is the plastic worm, which came into its own in the mid and late 1960s. It has accounted for some eye-popping stringers of largemouth bass, especially in big southern lakes. A plastic worm threaded on a weedless hook and slithered through lily pads or an underwater weed bed is a real killer. Some plastic worms come with a weighted jig-type head and/or a spinner at the front.

Cork   3/0 Hook

RIGGING PLASTIC WORMS

The plastic worm can be fished on the bottom, above the bottom, on the surface and through thick weeds. It comes in different lengths, shapes, colors, flavors, and scents. The fake night crawler is so versatile it has spawned specialized hooks and a separate vocabulary. Here's how to tie the basic worm rigs, as well as when and where to fish them—and, just so there's no confusion, what they're called.

Floating Worm Rig: This is the simplest of all worm rigs. Thread a worm on a hook, push it up to the hook-eye and the rig is complete. You can buy floating worms (usually molded with air chambers), or you can make any worm a floater by threading a piece of cork on your line in front of the hook. You can also try "larding" the worm with bits of Styrofoam (cut from a plate or coffee cup). Some fishermen buy injectors—they look like miniature basketball pumps—to float worms, lizards, or any other soft-plastic lure. A floating worm works best at dusk or dawn. It's especially effective during spawning season, when bass are protective of their beds: Cast the worm near a bass bed, swim it slowly, pause and allow it to hang directly above the bed . . . and hang on.

Carolina Rig: This rig is designed to be fished deep, but not on the bottom. The principal difference between the Carolina and Texas rigs is that in the Carolina the sinker, usually a slip sinker, is placed two to three feet ahead of a floating worm. The sinker is held in position with a swivel (and often a bead). Use a bullet- or egg-shaped sinker; either will slide over most obstructions. The rig allows a bass to pick up the bait without immediately feeling the weight of a sinker, and it makes the worm more visible to suspended fish. The Carolina rig is another good summer lure for deep water. Depending on the amount of vegetation, the hook can be left exposed or buried in the worm.

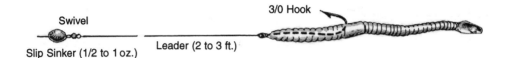

Swivel
Slip Sinker (1/2 to 1 oz.) Leader (2 to 3 ft.) 3/0 Hook

Texas Rig: The Texas rig is a brush-buster. In its most common variant, a bullet-shaped sinker is threaded on the line just ahead of the worm, and the point of the hook is buried in it. This requires that the worm be carefully measured so it will hang straight when the hook point is inserted (it takes some practice). If the worm is "scrunched" on the shank of the hook, it won't be nearly as effective. The Texas rig is designed to be fished through weeds and brush and around stumps, and crawled along snag-infested bottoms. It's particularly effective on hot summer days when bass seek out brushy, shaded shorelines or hang very deep in cool water.

3/0 Hook
Slip Sinker (1/2 to 1 oz.)

Worm Hooks

 Weighted shank with free-swinging keeper at the eye to hold worm.

 Wide-gap hook with weighted keeper. Worm is snugged against eye; point is buried.

 Kink in shank holds worm securely and helps it hang straight.

 Worm is treaded on keeper, ultrawide gap reduces chance of a thrown hook.

PLASTIC LURES AND BAITS

Mister Twister Worm: Twisted tail imparts a wiggle and vibration when retrieved in erratic speeds. Good worm lure for bass.

PLACTIC LURES AND BAITS (Continued)

Creme Tru-Lur Baits: Hand-crafted baits with lifelike feel, coloration, size, shape, and appearance. More than 20 species available, including frogs, crickets, crawdads, grasshoppers, and worms.

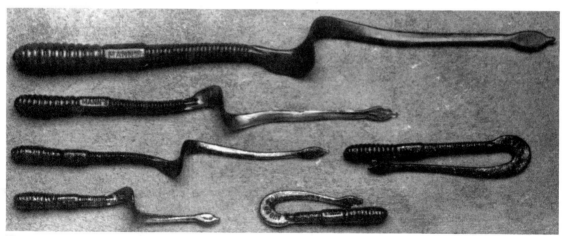

Mann's Augertail: The lure's "auger" feature makes the tail kick around with bass-attracting action. Ideal for Carolina and Texas rigs.

PORK RIND

Pork rind, as used by fishermen, is the skin from the back of a hog. It is sold in jars containing a liquid preservative to prevent spoilage and to retain the rind's flexibility.

It used to be that pork rind was used only as an addition to a spoon or other lure. For example, a single-hook spoon with a 2- or 3-inch strip of pork rind was—and still is—a popular combination for pickerel, pike, and the like.

Pork rind is still widely used that way today. It is sold in many shapes and sizes, from tiny half-inch V-strips for panfish up to 6-inch strips for muskies and saltwater gamefish. It comes in many colors.

But in recent years a number of all-pork-rind lures have appeared. They take such forms as spring lizards, worms, and jointed eels. These pork-rind lures, many of them black, can be extremely effective. This may be because they give off an aroma or taste that fish like.

FLIES

An artificial fly is a combination of feathers, hair, floss, tinsel, and other materials tied to a hook in such a way as to imitate a natural insect (dry and wet flies, including nymphs) or a baitfish (streamer flies and bucktails). Flies are used to take many gamefish but are designed principally for trout and salmon. There are four basic kinds of artificial flies: dry, wet (including nymph), streamer, and bucktail.

PORK RIND DESIGNS

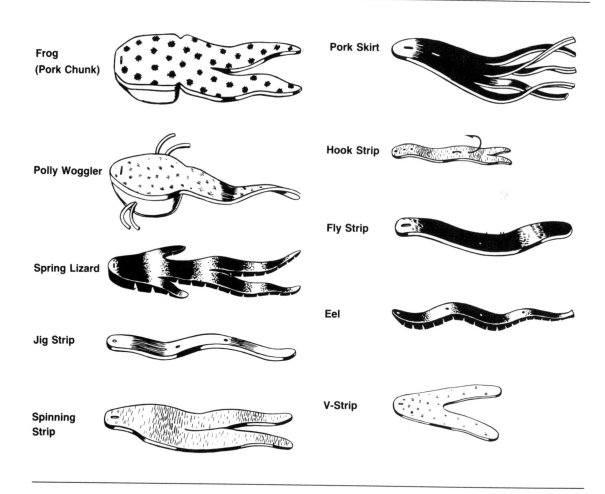

Frog (Pork Chunk)

Polly Woggler

Spring Lizard

Jig Strip

Spinning Strip

Pork Skirt

Hook Strip

Fly Strip

Eel

V-Strip

TYPICAL FLY AND PART NAMES

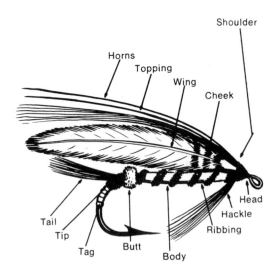

Shoulder

Horns

Topping

Wing

Cheek

Head

Hackle

Ribbing

Tail

Tip

Tag

Butt

Body

Dry Flies

The dry fly, designed to imitate a floating insect, is tied so that the fibers of the hackles (feathers) used stick out at approximately right angles to the shank of the hook. A properly tied dry fly sits high and lightly on the tips of its hackles, riding the surface of the water.

There are countless dry-fly patterns, but almost all of them fall into one of nine basic types. Here is a brief description of each type:

Downwing (or Sedge). Has a built-up body, hackle, and wings lying flat along the shank of the hook. It floats with hook underwater.

Divided Wing. The standard dry-fly type. Has two erect separated wings of feather fibers, hackle, tapered body, and stiff, slender tail. It floats with hook above or partly underwater.

Hairwing. Has upright wings made of deer hair, as well as hackle, tapered body, and stiff tail. Floats with hook above or partly underwater.

Fanwing. Has large, flat, erect wings; hackle, body, and a stiff tail. Floats with hook above or partly underwater. The large wings make this fly readily visible to angler.

Bivisible. Has no wings. White hackle is wound on body at the fly's head, and hackle of another color

(brown, gray, and black are most popular) covers most of the remainder of body. The tail is stiff. Floats high, with hook above water, and is highly visible to angler.

Spentwing. Has slender wings that stick out horizontally from a tapered body, hackle, and stiff tail. Floats on wings and body with bend of the hook underwater.

Spider. Has no wings. The hackle is extra long and stiff. There is no body in the smaller sizes, a tinsel or herl body in the larger sizes. Stiff, extra-long tail. Floats on hackle tips and tail with hook well out of the water.

Variant. Has upright divided wings, extra-long and stiff hackle, very light body (or none at all), and stiff, extra-long tail. Floats on hackle tips and tail with hook well out of water.

Hair Body. Has upright divided wings, hackle, body of clipped deer hair or similar material, and a stiff tail. Floats with hook partly underwater.

Keel Fly. Shank of the hook is weighted, causing the fly to ride upright in the water. The keel principle also has been applied to wet flies and streamers.

The budding fly fisherman who walks into a fishing-tackle store is sure to be overwhelmed by the display of artificial flies. Which patterrns are best for his

BASIC DRY FLIES

SPIDER

DOWNWING

DIVIDED WING

VARIANT

HACKLE

FANWING

HAIRBODY

BIVISIBLE

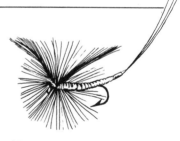

SPENTWING

GAUZE WING

KEEL FLY

PARACHUTE FLY

particular needs? Only experience can answer that question. However, here are 10 basic dry-fly patterns—and the most productive sizes—that should be found in every trouter's fly box:

- Light Cahill, Size 16
- Gray Midge Hackle, Size 20
- Black Flying Ant, Size 20
- Red Variant, Size 14
- Black Gnat, Size 12
- Gray Wulff, Size 10
- Blue Dun, Size 16
- Adams, Size 12
- Quill Gordon, Size 14
- Jassid, Size 20

Wet Flies

Wet flies are tied to imitate submerged insects, either those that have fallen to the surface and drowned or those that are rising from the stream or lake bottom to the surface to hatch. Nymphs, which are classified as wet flies, are imitations of the larval or nymphal stages of underwater insects that rise to the surface before hatching.

As with dry flies, there is a bewildering number of wet-fly patterns. However, most of them fall into one of four basic types. Here's a brief description of each type:

Divided Wing. Two prominent separated wings tied at about a 30-degree angle from the shank of the hook. A wisp of hackle, body, stiff tail.

Hairwing. Wing of deer hair extending over shank of hook, wisp of hackle, body, tail.

Featherwing. Swept-back wing of feather fibers, soft hackle, tapered body, sparse tail.

Hackle. Soft hackle tied on at head and extending back over built-up body all around fly. Sparse tail.

Here are 10 wet-fly patterns that should produce well for the trout fisherman:

- Gray Hackle, Yellow Body, Size 10
- Brown Hackle, Size 10
- Coachman, Size 12
- Royal Coachman, Size 12
- Black Gnat, Size 14
- Quill Gordon, Size 14
- Blue Dun, Size 16
- Light Cahill, Size 16
- March Brown, Size 12
- Ginger Quill, Size 16

Nymphs

It is impossible to break down the various nymph patterns into broad classifications. However, most nymphs have the following basic characteristics: no wings; wisps of soft hackle at head; tapered body, usually of dubbed fur; sparse tail of a few feather fibers.

Here are 10 nymph patterns that no trout fisherman should be without:

- March Brown, Size 12
- Ginger Quill, Size 14
- Yellow May, Size 12
- Freshwater Shrimp, Size 8
- Light Mossback, Size 6
- Large Stone Fly, 2X Long-Shank, Size 8
- Large Mayfly, 2X Long-Shank, Size 10
- Caddis, 2X Long-Shank, Size 10
- Dark Olive, 2X Long-Shank, Size 12
- Montana, Size 4

BASIC WET FLIES

DIVIDED WING   HAIRWING   FEATHERWING   HACKLE

OTHER WET FLIES

WOOLY WORM

GAUZE WING

KEEL FLY

SPIDER

BASS FLY

PANFISH TEASER

TYPES OF NYMPHS

DARK HENDRICKSON

STONEFLY CREEPER

MAYFLY NYMPH

STONEFLY NYMPH

MARCH BROWN

Streamers and Bucktails

Streamer flies and bucktails are tied to imitate a minnow or other baitfish on which gamefish feed. They are widely used in both fresh water and salt. Many saltwater streamers and bucktails, and some used in fresh water, have two hooks—the main hook, on which the dressings are tied, and a trailer hook. Streamers and bucktails are well known for producing big fish.

Streamers are tied with long wings of feathers. Bucktails are similar—but more durable—flies tied with wings of hair, usually deer hair. Most streamers and bucktails are tied on Size 8 and Size 10 long-shank hooks. Some have bodies that hide the shank

TYPES OF STREAMERS

BUCKTAIL

FEATHER STREAMER

MARIBOU

MUDDLER MINNOW

of the hook, but in others the bare shank shows.

Here is a list of 10 of the most productive streamer patterns and 10 top bucktail patterns (best hook sizes are 6 to 12, unless otherwise noted):

Streamers

- Black Ghost
- Gray Ghost
- Supervisor
- Mickey Finn
- Black-Nosed Dace
- Red and Yellow
- Colonel Fuller
- Red and White Multiwing, Size 1
- Black Marabou
- White Marabou

Bucktails

- Black Prince
- Brown and White
- Black and White
- Red and White
- Mickey Finn
- Platinum Blonde, Size 1/0
- Strawberry Blonde, Size 1/0
- Brown Muddler Minnow, Sizes 1/0 to 10
- White Muddler Minnow, Sizes 1/0 to 10
- White Marabou Muddler, Sizes 1/0 to 6

Terrestrials

A class of artificial flies that is unique and deserves special mention is the terrestrials—a group of flies, both wet and dry, that are tied to imitate insects that are born on land and then fly, jump, fall, crawl, or are blown into the water and become food for trout and other fish. Such insects include ants, grasshoppers, inchworms, beetles, houseflies, and others.

Among the most popular and productive terrestrial patterns are the Inchworm, the Black Ant (especially in very small sizes), and the Jassid. The Jassid is a relatively new fly that was developed in Pennsylvania and is particularly effective in limestone streams. It is tied on tiny hooks, with best sizes being 18, 20, and 22.

Choosing the Right Fly

Selecting the correct fly to use at any given time is a problem that has both delighted and dumbfounded anglers since the dawn of this sport. Dry fly or wet? What color? What size?

The answers to those questions can often be found in the water at your feet. Study it carefully, both at the surface and underneath. If insects are flying from the surface, you are in the middle of a hatch, and you should select a dry fly that imitates as closely as possible the color and size of the natural insects. If you see subsurface insects, choose a wet fly or

TYPES OF TERRESTRIALS

ANT

BEETLE

GRASSHOPPER

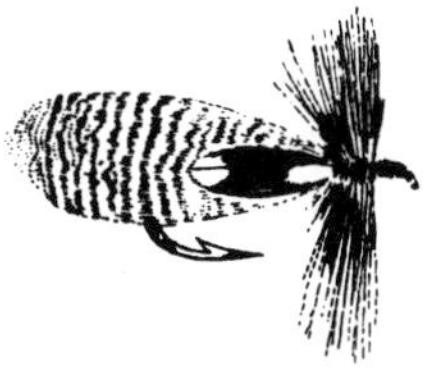

HORNBERG

INCH WORM

JASSID

SALTWATER FLIES

Offshore Angler Tube Fly: A good example of a typical big-game fly. Also available pre-rigged, the unrigged flies can be rigged as single or double streamers. A top choice for catching sailfish, marlin, tuna, and other offshore species.

nymph of similar size and color.

However, spotting and identifying the natural may be difficult, due to water conditions, the minute size of the insects, and the sparseness of the hatch (a "hatch" occurs when aquatic insects rise from the stream or lake bottom and change from the larval stage to winged adult flies). Also, the fisherman may not have the right size and color of artificials in his fly box.

The following table will aid the angler in solving the problem of fly choice. It gives the approximate date on which each insect can be expected to emerge, or hatch, from the water and the general localities in which these hatches occur.

Ruoff's Barracuda Fly™

Clouser Minnow™

Curcione's Bonito Buster™

Skipping Bug

Ruoff's Backcountry Popper™

Huff Backcountry Fly™

Bonito Bunny

Curcione's Sardina™

Curcione's Tuna Tonic™

Bruun's Mangrove Midget™

Huff's Ballyhoo Tarpon Fly™

Tabory's Slab Fly™ JO580-00

Mark's Baby Bunker

Peterson's Tinker Mackerel™

Tabory's Sand Lance™

Tabory's Big Eye Spearing™

Peterson's Baby Bunker™

Ruoff Lay-up Tarpon Fly™

Tabory's Sea Rat™

Martha's Vineyard Squid Fly™

Kirk's Rattle Rouser™

Winslow's Afternoon Delight™

Tabory's Snake Fly™

Woolhead Mullet

Winslow's Whisper™

Bruun's Mangrove Minnow™

Steve Huff Tarpon Fly™

SALTWATER FLIES

TROUT STREAM INSECT EMERGENCE TABLES

COMMON NAME	SCIENTIFIC NAME	HABITAT	EMERGENCE DATE
Little Black Stonefly (3)	*Taeniopteryx maura*	Pa., W. Va., Tenn., Mass., N. Y., Minn., Mo., Md., Kan.	Apr. 15
Red Quill (1)	*Ephemerella subvaria*	N. Y., Pa., N. J., Ont., Quebec	Apr. 16
	Epeorus pleuralis, iron fraudator		Apr. 17
Little Black Caddis (2)	*Chimarra aterrima*	Pa., Can., N. Y., N. J., Del., Ind., Ga., Fla., Washington	May 1
Red Legged March Fly (5)	*Bibio femoratus*	Pa., N. Y., N. J.	May 1
Smokey Alderfly (5)	*Sialis infumata*	Que., N. S., N. Y., New England, N. J., Pa., Wash., Mich., Ill., Minn., Calif.	May to Sept.
Black Midge (5)	*Glyptotendipes lobiferus*	Pa., N. Y., N. J., Ont.	May 1
Light Stonefly (3)	*Isoperla signata*	Pa., N. Y., N. S.	May 8 to May 25
Penns Creek Caddisfly (2)	*Brachycentrus numerosus*	Well distributed through the northern hem.	May 15
Black Quill (1)	*Leptophlebia cupida*	Pa., Ohio, N. S., Nfld., Ill., Can., N. Y., N. H., N. C., R. I., N. J., Ont., Quebec, Mass.	May 16
Early Brown Spinner (1)	*Leptophlebia cupidus*	Same as above	May 15
Yellow Spider (4)	*Antocha saxicola*	Well distributed throughout the northern hem.	May 15
Stonefly (3)	*Neophasganophora capitata*	Pa., N. Y., Md., Mass., Minn., Quebec, N. S., Ind., Ill., Mich., Kan., Tenn., N. C.	May 16
Spotted Sedge (2)	*Hydropsyche slossonae*	Pa., N. Y., N. H., Ill.	May 20
Pale Evening Dun (1)	*Ephemerella dorothea and rotunda*	Pa., N. Y., Can.	May 20
March Brown (1)	*Stenonema vicarium*	Pa., N. Y., N. B., N. H., Quebec, Tenn.	May 21
Great Red Spinner (1)	*Stenonema vicarium*	Same as above	May 21
Green Caddis (2)	*Rhyacophila lobifera*	Pa., N. Y., Ill.	May 21
Dark Green Drake (1)	*Hexagenia recurvata*	Pa., N. Y., Mass., Me., W. Va., Mich.	May 23
Brown Drake (1)	*Hexagenia recurvata*	Same as above	May 24
Ginger Quill Dun (2)	*Stenonema fuscum*	Pa., N. Y., Ont., Que., New Brunswick	May 25
Pale Evening Spinner (1)	*Ephemerella dorothea and rotunda*	Same as Pale Evening Dun	May 26
Ginger Quill Spinner (1)	*Stenonema fuscum*	Same as Ginger Quill Dun	May 26
Fish Fly (5)	*Chauliodes serricornis*	Pa., N. Y., Md., Ga., Ohio, Minn.	May 26
Green Drake (1)	*Ephemera guttulata*	Pa., N. Y., Tenn., Ont., Quebec	May 28
Black Drake (1)	*Ephemera guttulata*	Same as Green Drake	May 28
Gray Drake (1)	*Ephemera guttulata*	Same as Green Drake	May 28
Iron Blue Dun (1)	*Leptophlebia johnsoni*	Pa., N. Y., N. H., Que., Ontario	May 28
Grannon (5)	*Brachycentrus fuliginosus*	Pa., N. Y., Wash., Ontario	May 29
Jenny Spinner (1)	*Leptophlebia johnsoni*	Same as Iron Blue Dun	
Brown Quill (1)	*Siphlonurus quebecensis*	Pa., N. Y., N. C., Ont., Quebec	June 1
Green bottle or Blue bottle fly (5)	*Lucilia casear*	Commonly distr.	Variable
Whirling Cranefly (4)	*Tipula bella*	Pa., N. Y., N. J.	June 1
Orange Cranefly (4)	*Tipula bicornis*	Same as above	June 1
Golden Eyed Gauze Wing (5)	*Chrysopa occulata*	Commonly distr.	Variable
White Mayfly (1)	*Stenonema rubromaculatum*	Pa., N. Y., Mass., Ill., Ont., Quebec, N. B., N. S.	June 2
White Gloved Howdy (1)	*Isonychia albomanicata*	Pa., N. Y., Ont., N. C.	June 27
Yellow Sally (3)	*Isoperla spp.*	Commonly distr.	June 28
Golden Spinner (1)	*Potomanthus distinctus*	Pa., N. Y., W. Va., Ohio	June 28
Willow or Needle Stonefly (3)	*Leuctra grandis*	Pa., N. Y., N. J., North Carolina	June 28
Stonefly Nymph (3)	*Acroneuria lycorias*	Pa., N. H., N. Y., Mass., Me., W. Va., Mich., Wisc., Que.	June 29
Brown Silverhorns (2)	*Athripsodes wetzeli*	Pa., N. Y. Similar species in Wisc. and Ontario	June 30
Big Orange Sedge (2)	*Neuronia postica*	Pa., Ga., Mass., Wisc., Newfoundland and Washington, D. C.	July 1
Yellow Drake (1)	*Ephemera varia*	Pa., N. Y., Mich., N. H., Ont.	July 1
White Caddis (2)	*Leptocella exquisita, leptocella albida, leptocella spp.*	Florida to Canada	July 1
Deer Fly (5)	*Chrysops vittatus*	Eastern and Northern States	Variable
Green Midge (5)	*Chironomus modestus*	Pa., N. Y., N. J., Ontario	July 4

NOTE. The number in parentheses following the common name of the insect indicates the following: 1. Mayfly; 2. Caddisfly; 3. Stone- fly; 4. Cranefly; 5. Miscellaneous.

Bass Bugs

If any form of fly fishing approaches the thrill of taking a wary trout on a dry fly, it is having a belligerent largemouth or smallmouth bass burst through the surface and engulf an enticingly twitched bass bug.

Bass bugs are fly-rod lures created to imitate such bass morsels as frogs, bees, dragonflies, and mice. Because of the size of a bass's mouth, these surface lures are tied on large hooks—No. 4 to 2/0 in most cases. However, smaller versions of these bugs are made for panfish.

Most bass bugs fall into one of two categories: those with solid bodies (usually of cork, plastic, or balsa wood) and those with bodies of deer hair.

Many cork or balsa bugs have some hackle or bucktail at the tail to partly disguise the hook. Some have a perpendicular hollowed-out face so that when the angler jerks the rod tip the bug makes a popping sound that often brings a bass charging out of his lair. These bugs are called poppers. Others have a more streamlined body and are really designed to be twitched slowly rather than jerked.

Deer-hair bugs are, as you might expect, made of deer hair wound onto a hook and clipped to form the body shape of a mouse, large insect, and such. These bugs are best fished very slowly.

Weedless arrangements, usually stiff monofilament or light wire, are becoming more and more popular on bass bugs today.

DEEP-HAIR BUGS

Hair Bug: Made of carefully trimmed deer hair, this bug is at its best when twitched in glass-smooth water. Tied especially for bass.

Henshall Lure: Trimmed deer-hair bug with hair dyed for special effect. Tops for bass.

Hair Mouse: Tied with deer hair and trimmed to imitate a mouse, this bug will work on bass, pickerel, and pike.

SOLID-BODY BUGS

Fly Rod Popper: Hollowed-out face makes popping sound when jerked. Good dawn and dusk lure for smallmouth and largemouth bass and other warm-water fish.

Dylite Nitwit: A slim, rubber-legged bug for panfish.

Dylite Slim Bug: Small popper for both bass and panfish.

Mountain Hopper: This is good deer-hair bug for bass, trout, and panfish.

NATURAL FOODS AND THEIR IMITATIONS

Fly tying is the art of imitating or suggesting numerous food forms . . . insects, minnows, crustaceans, and similar forage eaten by fishes . . . by dressing hooks with feathers, fur, wool, tinsel, latex, wire and other suitable materials.

The following text provides a breakdown of the basic food forms fly tiers try to imitate. Get to know them. Know their habits, when and where to find them, how they act in their own environment and for which fishes they form partial or principal diets. You don't have to be an entomologist to be a successful fly fisherman, but the more you know about these basic foods, the more fish you are going to find in your creel or live box.

Larva. The immature, wingless and often wormlike forms in which certain insects hatch from the egg, and in which they remain until the pupa or chrysalis stage. Grubs, caterpillars and maggots are examples. Wet fly larval imitations are fished under water.

Pupae. The intermediate, usually dormant form assumed by insects after the larva stage, and maintained until the beginning of the adult (dun or subimango) stage. Wet fly pupa imitations are fished under water.

Nymphs. The nymph, in the strictest sense, is that stage in the development of an insect, when the rudimentary wings of the adult (imago or spinner) becomes visible. It is common practice, however, to use the word "nymph" to cover all forms of developing, underwater insects. Normally fished below the surface as a wet fly, some nymph patterns are dressed to float.

Adult Insects. Imitations of adult insects (imagoes or spinners) generally have wings and are tied in dry fly patterns for surface fishing and in wet fly patterns for use underwater. "Wets" also are dressed to resemble small fishes and other natural foods.

Terrestrials. Among the lesser fish foods, terrestrials are land insects which, through one misadventure or another, wind up in the water to become forage for hungry fish. As a group, they include grasshoppers, beetles, ants, crickets, crane flies, inchworms, leafhoppers, and spiders. Imitations are fished on or in the surface film.

Midges. Entomologists use the word "midge" to identify a special order (Diptera) or minute, two-winged insects which include flies, mosquitos, jassids and gnats. To a fly fisherman, however, it refers to any very small artificial fly. Thus, it becomes a catch-all term for tiny caddis nymphs, mayflies, some of the terrestrials and other minutiae. Midges are dressed in both wet and dry patterns.

Crustaceans. Since they form an important part of the diet of a number of fresh and salt water fish, these little creatures deserve attention. They include crabs, crayfish, prawns, scuds, sandbugs, shrimps, and sowbugs. Imitations are fished under water.

Bait Fishes. Bait fishes fall into the collective term "minnows", which includes shiners, chubs, dace, silversides, darters, and sculpins. They are an extremely important source of food for sport and game fish. Bucktail and streamer imitations are built on hooks running from standard length to 8 extra long shanks. Although some patterns can be worked on the surface with good results, they are normally fished under water.

Other Fish Foods. This category is a smorgasbord of such goodies as mice, moths, frogs, eels, bloodsuckers, worms, dragonflies and bees. Imitations are made of hollow deer, elk and caribou hair, cork, Balsa wood, pre-cast plastic, and mylar tubing. For the most part, these are fished on the surface.

TYING FLIES AND BUGS

There are few pleasures in the sport of fishing that can match that of taking a trout, salmon, or other fish on a fly of your own creation. And there are other reasons for taking up this ancient art. On winter evenings, with the snow piled high outside and a bitter wind rattling the shutters, you can sit at the tying bench, reliving past fishing experiences and putting together the ingredients for future ones. And of course, once you get the hang of it, you can tie respectable flies for a very small fraction of what you would pay for them in a store.

TOOLS

The fly-tyer needs only a few inexpensive tools. Let's take a look at each one and its use:

Vise. The most important device in the fly-tyer's workshop, the vise is used to hold a hook securely and in the best position for the tyer to work around it. Most popular vise is the lever-and-cam type.

Hackle Pliers. Used to hold the tips of hackle feathers so that the tyer can wind the feathers onto the hook. Squeezing the sides of the pliers opens the jaws. There are two types: rubber-cushioned and English style. Both work well. A surgeon's artery forceps also makes an adequate hackle pliers.

Scissors. Best type is a pair of sharp fine-point scissors with either straight or curved blades. Larger scissors are helpful for making hair bugs. Scissors are used to cut thread and other dressing materials and perform other auxiliary duties.

Bobbin. A device that holds the spool of tying thread and hangs down from the hook, providing necessary tension on the thread, while the tyer is at work. Most bobbins have a tube through which the thread is fed. The bobbin saves thread, and it is especially useful to tyers who have rough hands that tend to fray the thread.

Dubbing Needle. A large, fairly heavy, sharp steel needle set in a handle of wood or plastic. It performs many duties, including picking out fur bodies to make them fuzzier, picking out wound-under hackle, dividing wings, separating strands of floss and the like, applying head lacquer, and making the whip finish.

Other helpful fly-tying tools and auxiliaries include tweezers, hackle gauge, magnifying glass, hackle cutter, hackle clip, hackle guards, whip finisher, head lacquer, and thread wax.

HOW TO TIE FLIES

The following information from well-known fisherman and fly-tyer Tom McNally, and the accompanying drawings, show the simple step-by-step procedure involved in tying the basic flies—streamers, nymphs, dry flies, wet flies.

BASIC FLY-TYING TOOLS

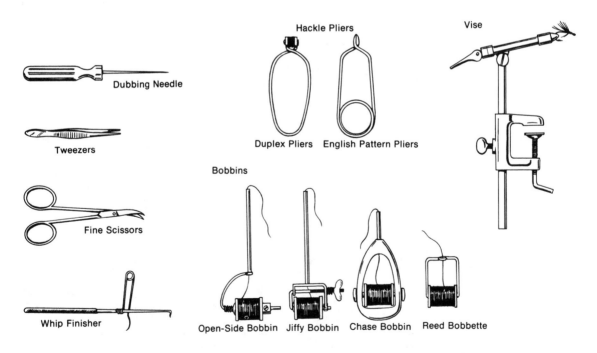

Dubbing Needle

Tweezers

Fine Scissors

Whip Finisher

Hackle Pliers

Duplex Pliers   English Pattern Pliers

Vise

Bobbins

Open-Side Bobbin   Jiffy Bobbin   Chase Bobbin   Reed Bobbette

Writing of fly tying, a friend of mine described this ancient art as "the technique of fastening various materials on a hook to suggest real or fancied insects or food for the purpose of deceiving fish." I like that definition. It clears fly tying of the mysticism with which many would like to bury it. Actually, it's not difficult to turn out handsome, fish-catching flies. Anyone with a yen to learn can become a reasonably accomplished fly-tyer. Persons with special aptitude learn how to do it almost overnight.

Many years ago I taught my wife to tie flies after three evening sessions at my worktable. Today, she shows me a trick or two. Some years ago I taught my mother—who was looking for a hobby—to make shad flies and popping bugs. Those she produced were sold in tackle stores. I don't know how many friends I've introduced to fly tying, and none failed eventually to turn out flies that were both attractive and fishable.

Fly tying was going on in Macedonia 2,000 years ago. A wasplike insect called hippuras was imitated by dressing a hook with purplish yarn and creamy hackles. The flies were floated, dry-fly fashion, on the Astraeus River. Ever since then, anglers have been using artificial flies—many of them tying their own. Judging from the growing interest in fly tying, fishermen will continue dressing their own hooks so long as there's fishing to be done. One doesn't have to be a watchmaker, a surgeon, or an engineer to tie flies. All that's needed is a little common sense—and practice.

To become a professional or recognized fly-tyer, of course, takes experience. And the intricacies of producing masterful flies would require a book-length treatise. But any beginner who absorbs the details here and studies the illustrations, should be able to tie the simpler flies. Once big streamers and wet flies are mastered, and once you get the "feel" of the materials, the smaller and more complicated dry flies and nymphs can be attempted. The techniques are basically the same.

Why is fly tying growing in popularity? Because tyers save money? No, it's because fly tying is fun. Fishermen get more personal satisfaction out of gilling a bonefish or netting a trout with a hook they themselves stuck into a vise and dolled up with feathers, tinsel, and fur.

Dollars can be saved by home-tying, of course. A fly that would cost $2 at the tackle shop can be self-made for less than 50¢. You can get a start in the fly-tying game for less than $100. Your hunting friends will add duck, goose, turkey, pheasant, and grouse feathers to your stock of materials, as well as rabbit, fox, squirrel, and skunk fur. Deer, moose, elk, and bear skins are useful. The hair or feathers from almost any wildlife can be utilized by the fly-tyer.

The tyer's mainstay, however, is the common barnyard chicken. Its hackles are used in nearly every fly. The great bulk of fly-tying materials comes from material houses, but even direct purchase is inexpensive. If you wind up like most tyers, thoroughly wrapped up in the hobby, you'll take on enough materials in a few years to open your own supply house. But like other fly-tyers, you wouldn't part with a hair of your motley assortment.

To begin, you'll need a few basic tools: vise, hackle pliers, scissors, razor blade. In the early days, flies were tied by holding the hook between one's fingers, but in 1897 D. H. Thompson ended this by producing a lever-and-cam type vise—the style most widely used and copied today. The vise is your most important single piece of equipment, and a good one should be purchased. Fine-pointed scissors will run a dollar or two, the hackle pliers about $1.50. You may want a bobbin to hold your spool of tying thread. It's inexpensive, frequently replaces hackle pliers, saves thread, and generally makes fly tying easier.

A beginner's basic materials should include thread (size 00 nylon), lacquer or head cement, hooks, hackles (neck, back, and breast feathers from roosters or gamecocks), duck wing quills, mallard breast feathers, golden-pheasant tippets, assortments of silk floss and chenille (a kind of tufted cord), tinsel, and peacock herl from the "eyed" tail feathers of peacocks, as well as Mylar, a shiny metallic material that comes in narrow strips and in tube form. These materials, and more, usually are stocked by better sports and hobby stores. Some firms that deal in fly-tying material supply catalogs, generally with photographs, that describe and price materials. The hook is the most important single factor in fishing, so tie your flies with the best.

STREAMERS

Although you may have no use for large streamer flies, they are easy-to-tie jobs that are ideal for your first lessons in fly tying. Stick to streamers until you get the knack of handling the tools and materials. It won't be necessary to follow a standard pattern in tying one of these big streamers, so the need for specific materials is lessened.

Always prepare your working area, tools, and materials, before starting a fly. Rig a bright lamp on your desk, and place a large sheet of white cardboard or white paper under your vise to provide a white background while you work on the fly. That makes the fly easier to see, materials simpler to locate. You'll need a short length of chenille, floss, or wool for the body of your streamer. Preferred colors are black, white, yellow, or red. About six hackles 3 to 4 inches long will make the wing, and they can be one of the colors mentioned, mixed colors, or natural brown or barred-grizzly feathers from Plymouth Rock chickens. Two or three extra hackles, colored differently than ones used in the wing, also will be needed.

Mount your vise at a comfortable height and clamp a No. 2 hook on it. The tying thread must be started on the hook. Most tyers first wax the thread since this waterproofs it, helps it hold to the hook, and generally produces a stronger fly. However, waxing takes time, and I doubt that it's vital to the durability of a fly. I haven't waxed thread for years, yet my flies stay together. I apply a generous portion of fly-tying cement to the hook shank, then wind the tying thread from the hook eye to the bend. The cement waterproofs the thread and locks it to the hook.

When you've reached the hook bend with your thread, (see drawing 1 on the next page) cut off any excess, then tie in one end of the chenille (floss or wool) by looping the tying thread over it tightly (drawing 2). Wind the thread back to the hook eye, and let the bobbin hang or attach hackle pliers to the thread to keep it taut. The body material can be wound to within $\frac{1}{16}$ inch of the hook eye (drawing 4), and tied off with the thread (drawing 5). The thread is looped in tight turns over the material to keep it in place. Be careful not to bring the body material all the way out to the hook eye or you'll have no room to tie off other materials or to form the fly's head. Excess body material is clipped off. Now comes the most difficult part of fly tying—attaching wings. Whether the fly is a streamer, nymph, wet, or dry, beginners usually have most trouble with wings.

Choose from four to six hackles and use your fingernails to clean off some of the fuzzy fibers from the stems at the butt end of the feathers. Now group the feathers in streamer-wing fashion and—holding them securely between two fingers of the left hand—place them in position on top of the hook, with the webby butts extending beyond the eye. They're tied in with tight loops of thread (drawing 6). Be sure to hold them tightly while tying. Otherwise the hackles will turn on the hook and go in cockeyed. After making several tight turns over the butts, you can clip off the surplus (drawing 7).

The final step is hackling the head of the fly. The hackle feather (two or more may be needed to make a bushy fly) is wound around the hook so that the separate fibers flare outward like bristling hairs. This is the technique used in putting hackles on wet and dry flies. Good hackles are especially important on a dry fly because they make it float. Strip the web from the hackle feather, place it against the head of the fly at an angle (drawing 8), and secure with a few tight loops of thread. The hackle, gripped at the loose end by hackle pliers, should be turned around the fly two or three times. Then the thread can be wound over it once or twice, and the hackle tips cut off (drawing 10). Now the fly head is finished with several turns of tying thread (drawing 11), and the thread knotted off with a series of half-hitches. Cement the head of the fly (drawing 12) to waterproof it and keep knots secure. The whip-finish knot—identical to the one rodmakers use in attaching guides—is better than half-hitches, but it's a little beyond the beginning stage. Actually half-hitches, properly knotted and cemented, will keep a fly together indefinitely. The whip finish can be executed either manually or with the aid of a device called a whip finisher. For a look at both methods, see end of this section.

The streamer is now finished, unless you'd like to paint "eyes" on it. This is easy to do with red, yellow, white, or black lacquer. You can buy small bottles of lacquer that have tiny brushes fixed to the caps. Most fly-tyers paint their fly heads black. Lacquer dries in a few minutes. The fly's "eyes" are put on over the black base by dipping the blunt end of a finishing nail or wood match in light-colored lacquer and touching it to the head of the fly. As soon as that dries, a dark "pupil" is added. It's my opinion that such dolling up adds nothing to a fly's fish-appeal, but it makes a fly more attractive to fishermen.

When you can tie one of these large streamers so it's proportioned correctly and won't come apart if you tug at a feather, you've mastered the fundamentals of fly tying. Methods you've learned in making this fly apply to any other pattern, including wets, nymphs, and dries.

The better streamers have tails, tinsel bodies, tinsel over chenille, wool or floss, perhaps colorful "cheeks" and "topping." The tying in of all these extras can be learned by following an advanced book on fly tying or watching some experienced tyer.

Large streamers can be made with marabou feathers, bucktail hair, or saddle hackles. Either way, they're good for large trout, black bass, pike, walleyes, and saltwater species such as bonefish, striped bass, snook, and tarpon.

TYING A STREAMER FLY (See also text on facing page.)

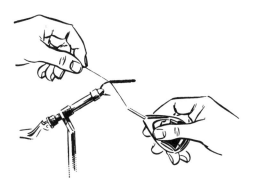

1. Tying thread held in the bobbin is first wrapped on the shank of a vise-held hook.

2. Yarn (floss or wool) that will form the body is tied in place with tight half hitches of thread.

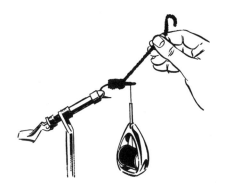

3. The tying thread is advanced to the hook eye, and the yarn is wound on evenly.

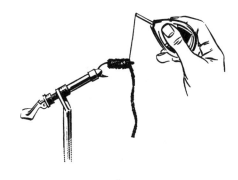

4. Body yarn is wound to within $\frac{1}{16}$ inch of the hook eye and tied off with several wraps of nylon thread.

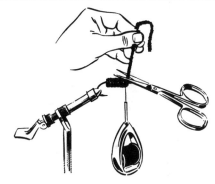

5. After thread tie-off, surplus yarn is snipped off close with a fine-pointed scissors.

6. Next, matched streamer feathers (four in this case) are tied in as shown here.

TYING A STREAMER FLY (Continued)

7. After making several tight turns over the feather butts, clip off excess butts. Weight of bobbin holds thread taut.

10. Give the hackle feather two or three turns, tie end once or twice, and cut off surplus hackle tips.

8. Hackle feathers make flies float. Two are needed for a bushy fly. Tie them in securely.

11. Use wraps of thread to create a streamer head. Cinch the head with half hitches or a whip finish.

9. Holding the hackle feather edgewise with the hackle pliers, wind the feather around the hook.

12. A light coat of lacquer on the fly head serves both to cement the thread and to waterproof it.

WET FLIES

A wet fly, whether bass- or trout-size, is tied much like a streamer, except that wing material is usually cut from duck wing quills or large turkey quills. Turkey quills are used in the typical wet fly shown in the accompanying illustrations. Other materials in this fly are red duck quill, silver tinsel, black silk floss, and red hackles.

Start your tying thread the same as to tie a streamer, only continue wrapping it around the hook to build up a tapered body (see wet-fly drawing 1). Cut a small section from the red duck quill and bind it down at the bend of the hook (drawing 2) with a few turns of thread. Be sure the tail is tied in tightly and is centered on top of the hook. Drawing 3 shows the finished tail, with excess cut off. Next tie in a length of silver tinsel and several strands of black floss. The tying thread should be brought to the eye of the hook, floss wrapped over the body, followed by the tinsel (drawing 4). Floss and tinsel are secured by thread at the head of the fly, and the surplus is trimmed off (drawing 5).

Attaching the wing is next. Select a pair of turkey quills and cut sections, one from each side of a feather, approximately half an inch wide. Place the two wing sections together, tips matched, curved sides facing. Grasp them firmly between thumb and forefinger and place them on the shank behind the eye, as in drawing 6. (Pinching the wings firmly during the tying-on can't be overemphasized. When wings are poorly done, it's usually because they were not held firmly while being tied.) Bring the tying thread over the wings and down on the opposite side sliding it slightly back between the fingers. Pinching the wings tightly, pull the thread down, following with several turns over the butts. Now the wing should appear as in drawing 7 with butts ready to be trimmed. The final step is tying soft red hackle behind the fly head, just as was done with the big streamer. Drawings 9 through 11 show this step. Tying thread should be half-hitched (drawing 12) and lacquered (drawing 13).

NYMPHS

Nymphs are the trout-catchingest flies made, good also for smallmouth bass and panfish. One of the simplest to make is the "attractor" type—which doesn't imitate any particular live nymph but suggests several kinds of real nymphs.

Begin the nymph by tying in a "tail" (see typical-nymph drawing 1). Tail material can be fibers from a feather, sections of peacock herl, deer, or boar hairs. Pig bristle makes an excellent tail because it

isn't broken easily by fish. A narrow section cut from a turkey feather, or olive or black duck quill, will serve to make the nymph's back or wing case. Tie it in just above the tail (drawing 2). A short length of tinsel and some wool yarn, chenille, or floss (drab colors) are put on next (drawing 3). Wind the tying thread back and forth over the shank, making a tapered body form, then wind on the body material and tinsel (drawing 4), tying them off near the hook eye. The quill section is brought forward, covering the top half of the nymph's body, tied down at the hook eye with a few tight turns of thread (drawing 5), and surplus is trimmed. Spin a small, webby hackle around the head, tie off, and trim so fibers extend only from the underside of the nymph to simulate legs. I usually lacquer a nymph's head, but some tyers lacquer the body too.

DRY FLIES

The bivisible—invented by the late Edward R. Hewitt—is the easiest dry fly to build. The bivisible is made by winding stiff, dry-fly-quality rooster neck hackles along the shank of a hook. Usually two or three hackles are needed to give a bivisible bulk enough to float well. The simplest way to start a bivisible is by tying in the tip sections of a couple of hackles at the bend of a hook, allowing the tips to extend backward to form a tail. The tying thread is then brought forward to the hook eye, the hackles turned around the hook tightly and finally tied down at the hook eye. That's all there is to this all-hackle dry fly. You'll find that it's a fish-catcher, too.

Excluding salmon flies, dry flies with upright wings are the most difficult flies to tie. Don't attempt them until you've had experience at tying the other types, and then start by making simple patterns. If you concentrate on large dries, no smaller than hook size 6 or size 8, the work will come to you faster.

The materials used for dry flies are selected for flotation, and for resistance to water absorption. Chenille, for example, becomes heavy with water, so it's never used in a good dry fly. The hackles and tail are what float a fly, so the finest quality gamecock or rooster neck hackles should be used. Common dry-fly body materials include floss, raffia (fiber from the raffia palm), deer or moose hair, quill, peacock herl, and muskrat fur.

To make a Black Gnat dry fly (see typical dry-fly illustrations) start the tying thread as usual. Cut a narrow section from each side of a matched, slate-colored, duck wing quill. Place the wing sections together, curved sides out. Grasping them firmly between thumb and forefinger, place them on the hook over the eye (drawing 1 on the next page) and

TYING A WET FLY (See also "Wet Flies" text on previous page.)

1. Start the wet fly by wrapping thread so as to build up a tapering rounded body.

4. After bringing tying thread to eye of hook, wrap floss and hold it by a thread loop while you wind tinsel.

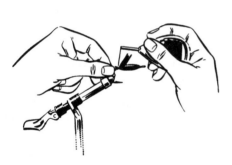

2. The tail of the fly is cut from a duck's wing feather and tied centered on top of the hook.

5. Tie down the floss tinsel with thread near the hook eye. Then snip off surplus.

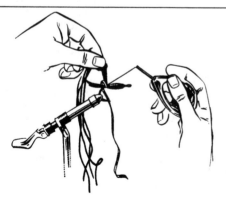

3. The tail is shown finished here. The body material ready for use includes one strand of tinsel and three threads of black floss.

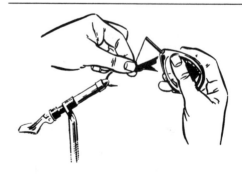

6. For wings, cut two matched sections from each side of a turkey wing feather and then tie with tips matched (hidden by thumb here).

7. After pinching the wings firmly, use several wraps of thread to cinch the fly wings in place.

8. Snip off the butt fragments of the turkey-feather wings close to the shank of the hook.

9. Tie a soft red hackle feather at head and then wind it on edgewise as shown next.

10. Hackle pliers grip feather tight for edgewise winding.
11. Tie down stem of hackle feather and cut off excess.

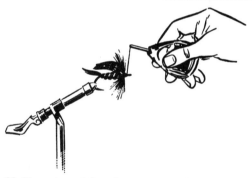

12. Use wraps of thread to wind and tie off head. Cinch with half hitches or a whip finish.

13. A light coat of lacquer serves both to cement the thread and to waterproof it.

TYING A TYPICAL NYMPH

1. Tie in three strands of peacock herl for the tail.

2. Piece of turkey feather represents folded wing.

3. Body materials: Dark wool yarn and silver tinsel.

4. Wind on tinsel last to get the rib effect shown.

5. Tie down wing, add wisp of hackle and make thread head.

bring the thread over the sections and down, taking several tight turns. Still holding the sections firmly between the fingers, raise them erect, bring the tying thread in front of them, and make enough turns against the wing bases to keep them upright, as shown in drawing 2. Spread the wings apart, and wrap thread between them to the opposite side of the hook, reversing to describe a figure 8 between the sections. Tie in a few stiff black hairs or some suitable hackle fibers for a tail (drawing 2). Cut off the excess tail fibers, then tie in black silk floss (drawing 3) and bring the tying thread forward to front of wings. A glossy-black hackle feather (two may be needed) is tied in front of the wings as shown in drawing 4. Secure the hackle feather with several turns of thread. Then use hackle pliers to grasp the tip of the hackle and take a turn or two in front of the wings and two or three turns in back. Catch the hackle tip with tying thread and bind it down. Cut off the surplus end of the hackle feather. Finish the fly with a small, neat head made with the tying thread. Lacquer the head. That's all. Your first winged dry fly is finished. Your second dry fly will

be easier than the first, the third easier still, and so on until you begin to feel skilled.

CORK BUG

You can buy cork bodies in many different shapes and sizes, or you can shape and size your own from a large piece of cork, using a razor blade and an emery board or small file. Be sure to sand the body smooth so that you get a good finish when you paint it.

Here are the basic steps in making a cork-bodied bug:

Place a hump-shanked hook (available at most tackle-supply outlets) in the vise, coat the shank with liquid cement, and wrap the part that is to be covered by the cork body with tying thread. With a razor blade make a slit in the cork body, fill the slit with cement, and press the cork into position on the hook shank (drawing 1 on the next page).

Give the cork body two coats of liquid cement, clear enamel, or wood sealer, and let dry.

TYING A DRY FLY (Black-gnat pattern)

1. Wrap hook shank with thread and then tie on wings.

2. Turns of thread anchor the wings. Now tie on tail.

3. Next tie in black yarn and wind it forward to the wings.

4. Tie on the hackle feather and wind it on edgewise.

5. Trim off surplus hackle, and tie and lacquer the fly head.

TYING A TYPICAL CORK BUG

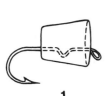  

1   2   3

Tie to the shank of the hook, behind the cork body, four or six neck hackles (badger is a good choice) so that they flare out well and thus give a lifelike action when on the water (drawing 2).

Wind on two or three soft hackle feathers to form the collar, tie them off, and cement the windings. Paint cork body with enamel of whatever color suits you, and paint on eyes (drawing 3).

TYING THE WHIP FINISH

Budding fly-tyers who are confronted with drawings of how to tie the whip finish may be inclined to switch to golf. But though this knot looks complicated, it can be mastered in about 10 minutes of practice, once the basic steps have been learned. The whip finish is undoubtedly the neatest way to finish off a fly. It is practically invisible, even on tiny dry flies.

There are two ways to make the whip finish—manually (that is, with the fingers alone) and with the aid of an ingenious little device called the whip finisher.

Without a Tool. Here's how to do it manually (for purposes of clarity, the sketches on the next page show the knot itself, without the finger manipulations, which are impossible to show in detail and which the tyer will pick up with a bit of practice):

Grasp thread (which is hanging down from hook) with the last three fingers of the left hand, about 6 inches below the hook. Position the right hand so that its back is facing the tyer, and grasp the thread 2 inches down from the hook with the first two fingers and thumb. Twist the right hand to the right and forward so that the palm is facing upward. There is now a loop in the thread, as shown in drawing 1.

With the left thumb and forefinger (which are free), grasp the left-hand side of the loop, and begin to wind it around both the hook and the return portion of the loop (drawing 2). Use the right hand to help the left in making one complete turn around the hook (drawing 3).

Make about six complete turns around the hook and the return part of the loop, making the first half of each turn with the left hand and the last half with the right hand.

After the last turn is completed, hold the loop

MAKING THE WHIP FINISH WITHOUT A TOOL

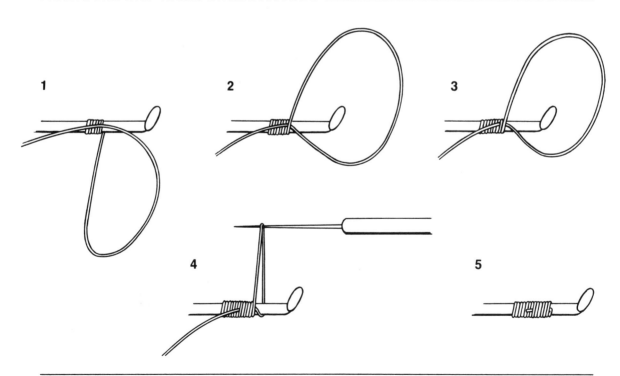

1

2

3

4

5

USING THE WHIP-FINISH TOOL

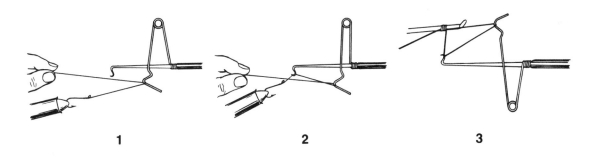

1   2   3

vertically taut with the left hand, and with the right hand insert into the loop, parallel with the hook, a dubbing needle (or a toothpick). Raise the dubbing needle until the loop is held taut by it (drawing 4).

Then, with the left hand, pull on the free end of the thread, contracting the loop unitl the needle rests on the head of the fly. Remove the needle, pull the thread tight, and clip it off close (drawing 5). The whip finish is now complete. Winding should be coated with head cement.

With the Tool. The whip finisher ties the same exact knot but eliminates the somewhat complicated finger manipulations. Here is how to use it:

Take the tool in the right hand, and place it near the hook and parallel with the hook shank. Run the thread from the hook around the spring retainer at Point A (drawing 1, bottom of next page).

Bring the end of the thread back near the fly, and with the tool's nose hook pick up the thread between the fly and Point A (drawing 2).

Now, keeping the thread taut with the left hand and in line with the fly, position the nose of the tool as close to the fly hook as possible—in fact, the fly hook can rest in the curve at the base of the tool's nose hook (for clarity, shown away from it).

Rotate the tool clockwise around the hook shank, causing the thread to wind around both the hook and itself. Try to keep the windings tight up against one another. Make about six such turns as illustrated in drawing 3.

Keeping the thread taut, remove it from the tool's nose hook, and pull the thread with your left hand until the spring retainer is drawn up to the hook. Remove the retainer, pull the thread tight, trim it off close to the windings. Apply head cement.

NATURAL FRESHWATER BAITS

Live bait is the real thing! Even the most avid purist would concede that live bait, when properly presented, is one of the deadliest of all lures. Many times, however, live bait is incorrectly rammed onto a hook. When this happens, the bait does not act naturally, may die quickly, and will likely turn away lunkers that grew big by learning how to recognize food that "doesn't look right."

Live bait will only appear natural if placed on the hook correctly, and this depends on how you plan to fish it. You wouldn't, for example, hook a minnow behind the dorsal fin if you plan on trolling. Minnows just don't swim backwards. Let's take a

look at the popular baits and learn how to hook them.

Even though garden worms and nightcrawlers will take most species of fish, they must still be presented differently. A worm washed into a stream, for example, would drift with the current, so it should also be fished that way. Hook it once through the collar or girdle with both ends free to drift naturally, fish it with no line drag, and let the current do the work. The worm should look strung out, bouncing along quickly through riffles and slowly through pools.

Using worms for panfish requires a different tack. Generally, the panfisherman is stillfishing, so natural

NATURAL FRESHWATER BAITS

Minnows	Largemouth and smallmouth bass, trout, pickerel, pike, walleyes, perch, crappies, rock bass	**Frogs**	Largemouth and smallmouth bass, pickerel, pike, muskies, walleyes
Earthworms	Trout, white bass, rock bass, perch, crappies, catfish, sunfish, whitefish	**Wasp larvae**	Perch, crappies, sunfish, rock bass
		Suckers	Pike, muskies, smallmouth and largemouth bass
Nightcrawlers	Largemouth and smallmouth bass, trout, pickerel, pike, walleyes, muskies, catfish, sturgeon	**Mice**	Largemouth and smallmouth bass, pike, muskies
Crickets	Trout, crappies, perch, rock bass, sunfish	**Freshwater shrimp (scud)**	Trout, smallmouth and largemouth bass, perch, crappies, rock bass, sunfish
Grubs	Trout, crappies, perch, rock bass, sunfish	**Dragonflies**	Largemouth and smallmouth bass, crappies, white bass, rock bass
Caterpillars	Trout, largemouth and smallmouth bass, crappies, perch, rock bass, sunfish	**Darters**	Trout, smallmouth and largemouth bass, walleyes, pickerel, crappies, rock bass
Crayfish	Smallmouth bass, walleyes, trout, catfish	**Sculpins**	Largemouth and smallmouth bass, walleyes, pickerel, rock bass
Hellgrammites	Trout, largemouth and smallmouth bass, walleyes, catfish, rock bass	**Salmon eggs**	Trout, salmon
Nymphs (mayfly, caddisfly, stonefly, and others)	Trout, landlocked salmon, perch, crappies, sunfish	**Cut bait (perch belly, etc.)**	Pickerel, pike, muskies, largemouth and smallmouth bass, walleyes
Grasshoppers	Trout, largemouth and smallmouth bass, perch, crappies	**Doughballs**	Carp, catfish
Newts and salamanders	Largemouth and smallmouth bass, trout, pickerel, rock bass, walleyes, catfish		

presentation is less important. A single worm should be used and threaded about three times on the hook. If you're bothered by nibblers, use only a piece of worm and thread it on the hook, covering the point and barb completely.

Nightcrawlers are effective on bass, and many fishermen stillfish for bass with the big worms the same way they would for panfish. Actually, bass prefer a moving bait and anglers would catch more lunkers if they casted and retrieved nightcrawlers slowly along the bottom. Hook the worm by running the point of the hook into the worm's head, bringing the point and barb out an inch below the head. Rigged this way and retrieved slowly, a nightcrawler will appear to be crawling on the bottom.

Next on the list of most common live baits are the minnows, from 1-inchers for panfish to 8-inchers for big fish. There are two ways of hooking a live minnow and how an angler intends to fish determines which one to use.

When trolling or fishing from a drifting boat, run the hook upward and through both lips of the minnow. The lip-hooked bait will move through the water on an even keel and look natural.

If you're stillfishing from an anchored boat or shoreline, hook the minnow just behind the dorsal fin. Be careful not to run the hook too deep or it will hit the spine and kill the bait. Hooked just behind the fin, a minnow can swim freely and for a surprisingly long time. There is no hook weight near its head or tail to throw it off balance.

Frogs rank as another excellent bait. Stick with the small frogs, however, such as the leopard and green frogs. An old sock makes a fine frog carrier, and frogs are easy to find along any shoreline or riverbank during summer.

SOME NATURAL FRESHWATER BAITS

Cricket

Grasshopper

Grub

Caterpillar

Mayfly Nymph

Stone Fly Nymph

Caddis Fly Larva

Dragonfly Nymph

Mayfly

Stone Fly

Caddis Fly

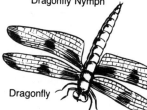
Dragonfly

Freshwater Shrimp (Scud)

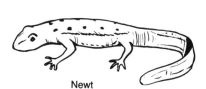
Newt

Wasp Larvae

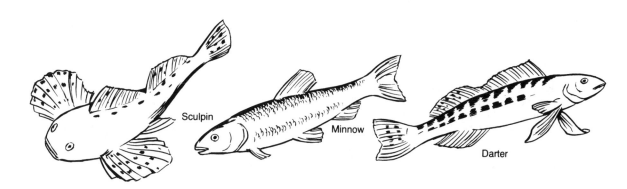
Sculpin

Minnow

Darter

WORM RIGS

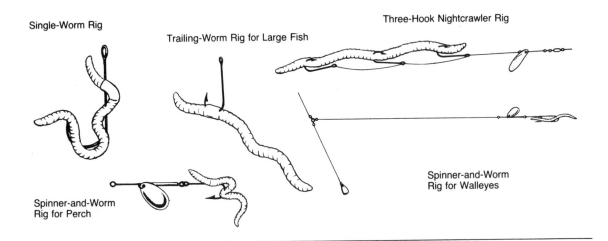

Single-Worm Rig

Trailing-Worm Rig for Large Fish

Three-Hook Nightcrawler Rig

Spinner-and-Worm
Rig for Walleyes

Spinner-and-Worm
Rig for Perch

There is only one good way to hook a live frog and that is under the jaw and up through both lips. Cast it out and let the frog swim freely, or use a twitch and pause retrieve. A lip-hooked frog will stay alive for a long time.

A frog can also be hooked through one of its hind legs. A hook through a frog's leg, however, will destroy some leg muscles, limiting its natural movements.

The crayfish, often called crawfish, is another top bait for bass and trout. The problem is that crayfish are often difficult to find. Best way to hunt them is at night in shallow water that has a rocky or gravel bottom. A crayfish's eyes will glow reddish in the beam of a flashlight. The light seems to freeze them and they can be easily picked up.

The best way to hook a crayfish is to run the hook up, through, and out the top of its tail. Cast into rocky shorelines or streams, they'll account for big trout and bass.

Salamanders or newts also take bass, trout, and similar species. Finding salamanders isn't hard. They like small springs and streams. They're active at night and easily spotted with a flashlight.

Salamanders are fragile and must be hooked carefully. Use a thin-wire hook and run it through the lips or the tail. Salamanders produce best when drifted along stream and river bottoms.

We've covered the popular live baits, but there are still others worth mentioning. The hellgrammite, for example, ranks high with bass and trout. Water insects, hellgrammites average 1 to 2 inches long and can be caught in most streams by simply turning over rocks and holding a net just downstream from

the rock. The hellgrammite has a hard collar just behind the head and this is where the hook should be run through.

The nymph, an underwater stage of the aquatic fly, is still another top bait, particularly for trout. Nymphs differ in the way they behave. Some crawl

CRAYFISH AND HELLGRAMMITES

Tail-Hook Rig for Crawfish

Hellgrammite Hooked Through Collar

MINNOW RIGS

Two Methods of Hooking Minnows

Two Methods of Sewing on Minnows

BENT-MINNOW HARNESS

Pass hook and leader through bait's mouth and out gill on one side, then through mouth again and out gill on other side. Pull leader fairly taut and hook near tail. This will bend minnow, imparting a crippled swimming motion.

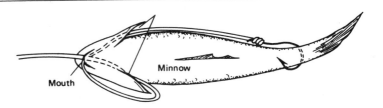

SUCKER-IN-HARNESS RIG FOR MUSKELLUNGE

1. Tie a double strand knot on the hook.

2. Tie the knot right on top of the nose.

3. Tie the knot behind the back of the lower fin.

4. Wrap line around body and tie on top of "neck."

on rocks, others climb shoreline growths, and still others float downstream. They will all eventually hatch into flies, but it is during this nymphal period that they can be effectively used for bait. There are two ways to put nymphs on a hook. They can be completely threaded, running the hook from the rear, through the body, and up to the head. Or they can be simply hooked once just behind the head.

Grasshoppers also work well, and finding them is no problem. Most grassy fields are loaded with 'hoppers. Using a butterfly net, you should be able to fill a box quickly. It's easier to catch them at dawn and dusk. During midday, they are most active and spooky. There are several varieties of grasshoppers and nearly all take fish. It's best to use a thin-wire hook, running it down and through, behind the head.

How you rig a natural bait depends to a large degree on how you are going to fish it. For that reason, the sketches show more than one way to rig some of the popular baits.

BIG SHINERS FOR BIG BASS

Nearly all bass experts agree that fishing a live shiner is one of the most effective ways to catch the biggest bass of your life. Like most things, however, it's not as easy as it sounds.

Your first problem may be finding 10- to 12-inch shiners. If your bait shop doesn't have them, you'll have to catch them in back bays and river pools. You can chum for shiners with oatmeal and bread crumbs and catch them with doughballs on a No. 12 or No. 14 hook. You'll need at least two dozen for a day of bass fishing.

Shiners are most productive when fished along shorelines or close to floating vegetation such as lily pads or hyacinths. The standard rig will have two hooks—a treble hook through the lips of the shiner, and a trailing single or treble hook in the tail of the bait or held alongside the tail with a rubber band. A bobber big enough to keep an active shiner from dragging it under water should be placed three to four feet above the bait.

Don't try to cast this half-pound bait overhand. Lob it underhand against shoreline vegetation and let the shiner take over. The fish will try to seek cover in the growth, and its movements will be telegraphed through the action of the bobber. When your shiner is motionless, jerk it back into action with a twitch or two of your rod tip.

If the bobber starts to bounce and jump on the surface, you'll know a big bass is after the shiner. Do *nothing* until that bobber goes down and stays down. A bass will grab the shiner around the middle and slowly swim away.

Begin counting as you watch your line move toward open water. As you count, slowly begin to reel in all slack until your rod tip is pointing in the

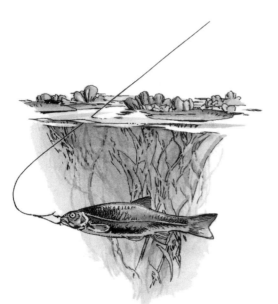

Under some conditions, you can liveline shiners beneath vegetation. Use a single weedless hook through the lips and let the shiner swim freely under weeds with no bobber to interfere with its movements.

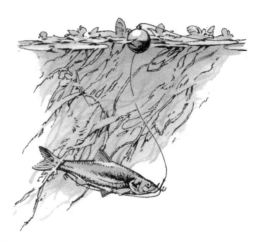

This bobber rig uses two 5/0 hooks: a treble hook through the lips of the shiner and a single or treble hook in the tail. The bobber should be about four feet from the bait.

direction the line is moving. Use your judgment here, but when your count is between 20 and 30 and all slack is out of your line, set the hook solidly.

Don't try to set the hook too quickly—you'll jerk the bait away from the bass. You have to allow enough time for the bass to pick up the shiner, swim away from weed growth and turn the shiner around in its mouth. Bass, like most other fish species, will swallow a live bait head first.

You're after big bass, so leave your light spinning tackle at home. Use a stiff popping rod and a conventional reel loaded with 20- to 30-pound test line.

THE BEST TRACKING LINE

You may find it easier to track a shiner if you use a leader and a white level fly line with some backing on your conventional reel. The floating white fly line will be much more visible than monofilament.

OTHER FRESHWATER BAIT RIGS

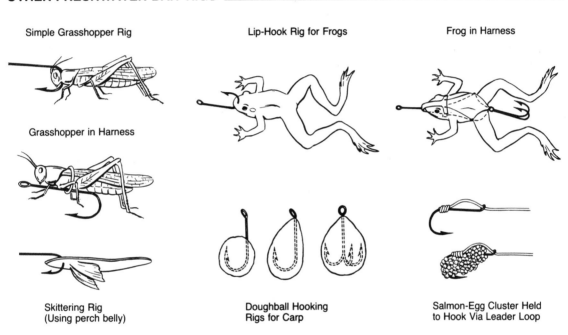

Simple Grasshopper Rig

Lip-Hook Rig for Frogs

Frog in Harness

Grasshopper in Harness

Skittering Rig
(Using perch belly)

Doughball Hooking
Rigs for Carp

Salmon-Egg Cluster Held
to Hook Via Leader Loop

MORE BASIC RIGS

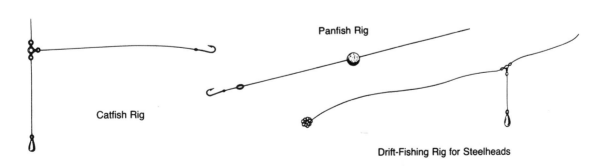

Panfish Rig

Catfish Rig

Drift-Fishing Rig for Steelheads

NATURAL SALTWATER BAITS

Natural baits are no less important in salt water than they are in fresh water. That fact is well known to anyone who has seen a school of ravenous bluefish slash viciously into a horde of spearing, mossbunkers, or the like.

What natural saltwater baits should you use and when? Those are questions that only time and experience can help you answer accurately. Generally, you will find that it pays to use any bait that is prevalent when and where you are fishing. A few discreet questions at a bait shop in the fishing area will go a long way toward helping you choose a productive bait.

How you rig a saltwater bait can be a vital factor. The primary consideration in rigging most baits is to make them appear as lifelike as possible, whether they are to be trolled, cast out and retrieved, or bounced on the bottom. The upcoming drawings show proven ways to prepare and rig the most popular baits used in salt water.

NATURAL BAITS FOR SALTWATER FISH

SPECIES OF FISH	NATURAL BAITS AND LURES	RECOMMENDED METHODS	HOOKS
Albacore	Feather lures	Trolling	7/0
Amberjack	Strip baits, feathers, spoons, plugs	Trolling, casting	6/0 to 9/0
Barracuda	Bait fish, plugs, feathers, spoons	Trolling, casting	1/0 to 8/0
Bass, California kelp	Sardines, anchovies, clams, mussels, sea worms, shrimp	Trolling, casting, still-fishing	1 to 1/0
Bass, channel	Mullet, mossbunker, crab, clam, spoons, plugs	Casting, still-fishing, trolling	6/0 to 10/0
Bass, giant sea	Cut bait, mullet, mackerel, sardines	Still-fishing, trolling	12/0 to 14/0
Bass, sea	Squid, clam, sea worm, crab, killie	Drifting, still-fishing	1/0 to 5/0
Bass, striped	Sea worm, clam, eel, metal squids, plugs, jigs, live mackerel	Casting, trolling, drifting, still-fishing	2/0 to 8/0
Billfish (sailfish, marlin, swordfish)	Balao, mackerel, squid, bonito, strip baits, feathered jigs	Trolling	4/0 to 12/0
Bluefish	Rigged eel, cut bait, butterfish, plugs, spoons, feathers	Trolling, casting, drifting, still-fishing	3/0 to 8/0
Bonefish	Cut bait (mainly sardine and conch), flies, plugs, spoons	Casting, drifting, still-fishing	1/0 to 4/0
Bonito	Feather lures, spoons	Trolling	4/0 to 6/0
Codfish	Clam, crab, cut bait	Still-fishing, drifting	7/0 to 9/0
Croaker	Sand bugs, mussels, clam, sardine, sea worm	Still-fishing, casting,	1/0 to 6/0
Dolphin	Bait fish, feather lures, spoons, plugs, streamer flies	Trolling, casting	2/0 to 6/0
Eel	Killie, clam, crab, sea worm, spearing	Still-fishing, drifting, casting	6 to 1/0
Flounder, summer	Squid, spearing, sea worm, clam, killie, smelt	Drifting, casting, still-fishing	4/0 to 6/0
Flounder, winter	Sea worm, mussel, clam	Still-fishing	6 to 12 (long-shank)
Grouper	Squid, mullet, sardine, balao, shrimp, crab, plugs	Still-fishing, casting	4/0 to 12/0
Grunt	Shrimp, crab, sea worm	Still-fishing	2 to 1/0
Haddock	Clam, conch, crab, cut bait	Still-fishing	1/0 to 4/0
Hake	Clam, conch, crab, cut bait	Still-fishing	2/0 to 6/0
Halibut	Squid, crab, sea worm, killie, shrimp	Still-fishing	3/0 to 10/0

SPECIES OF FISH	NATURAL BAITS AND LURES	RECOMMENDED METHODS	HOOKS
Jack Crevallé	Bait fish, cut bait, feathers, metal squid, spoons, plugs	Trolling, still-fishing, casting, drifting	1/0 to 5/0
Jewfish	Mullet, other bait fish	Still-fishing	10/0 to 12/0
Ladyfish	Killie, shrimp, flies, spoons, plugs	Trolling, casting, still-fishing, drifting	1/0 to 5/0
Ling	Clam, crab, cut bait	Still-fishing	4 to 2/0
Mackerel	Bait fish, tube lures, jigs, spinners, streamer flies	Trolling, still-fishing, casting drifting	3 to 6
Perch, white	Sea worm, shrimp, spearing, flies, spoons	Still-fishing, casting	2 to 6
Pollack	Squid strip, clam, feather lures	Still-fishing, trolling	6/0 to 9/0
Pompano	Sand bugs, jigs, plugs, flies	Trolling, casting, drifting, still-fishing	1 to 4
Porgy	Clam, squid, sea worm, crab, mussel, shrimp	Still-fishing	4 to 1/0
Rockfish, Pacific	Herring, sardine, mussel, squid, clam, shrimp	Still-fishing, drifting	1/0 to 8/0
Snapper, mangrove	Cut bait, shrimp	Trolling, still-fishing, drifting	1/0 to 6/0
Snapper, red	Shrimp, mullet, crab	Trolling, still-fishing, drifting	6/0 to 10/0
Snapper, yellowtail	Shrimp, mullet, crab	Trolling, still-fishing	4 to 1/0
Snook	Crab, shrimp, bait fish, plugs, spoons, spinners, feathers	Casting, drifting, still-fishing	2/0 to 4/0
Sole	Clam, sea worm	Still-fishing	4 to 6
Spot	Crab, shrimp, bait fish, sea worm	Still-fishing	8 to 10
Tarpon	Cut bait, bait fish, plugs, spoons, feathers	Trolling, casting, drifting, still-fishing	4/0 to 10/0
Tautog (blackfish)	Clam, sea worm, crab, shrimp	Still-fishing	6 to 2/0
Tomcod	Clam, mussel, shrimp	Still-fishing	6 to 1/0
Tuna, bluefin	Mackerel, flying fish, bonito, squid, dolphin, herring, cut bait, feathered jigs	Trolling	6/0 to 14/0
Wahoo	Bait fish, feather jigs, spoons, plugs	Trolling, casting	4/0 to 8/0
Weakfish	Shrimp, squid, sea worm	Still-fishing, casting, drifting, trolling	1 to 4/0
Whiting, northern	Sea worm, clam	Still-fishing, drifting, casting	4 to 1/0
Yellowtail	Herring, sardine, smelt, spoons, metal squids, feather lures	Trolling, casting, still-fishing	4/0 to 6/0

HOW TO RIG SALTWATER BAITS

Two Ways to Hook Live Baitfish

HOW TO RIG SALTWATER BAITS (Continued)

Two-Hook Baitfish Rig
for Short-Striking Fish

Hooking Half a Baitfish

Rigging a Mullet or Grunt
for Bottom Fishing

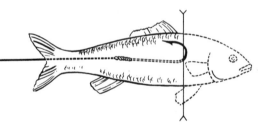

Front part of fish is discarded. Hook with wire leader is threaded through body, and the hook is embedded at the front with its point exposed.

Plug-Cut Baitfish

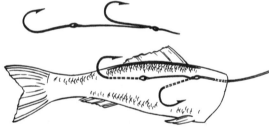

Can be cast out and retrieved like a plug. Especially productive for big snook and tarpon.

Preparing and Using
Menhaden as Cut Bait

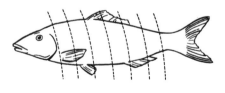

Hooking a Whole Crab

Hooking Half a Crab

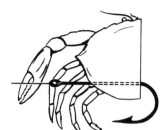

Rigging a Dead Soft-Shell Crab

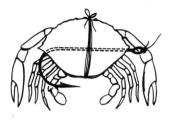

Hooking a Sand Shrimp

Rigging a Single Shrimp

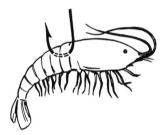

Rigging Two Shrimp on Single Hook

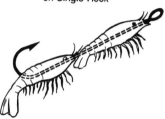

Hooking a Sandworm or Bloodworm

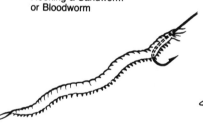

Mooching Rig with Keel Sinker

Mooching is drift-fishing with bait. The keel sinker prevents the line from twisting, but the swivel at its terminal end permits the bait to spin.

SALTWATER BAIT RIGS

Rigging a Whole Unweighted Eel

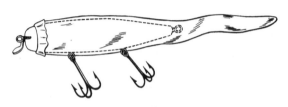

Hooks are attached to light chain or heavy monofilament, or they can be attached to linen line.

Rigging an Eelskin with Metal Squid

To a Montauk or Belmar-type metal squid, a ring is attached, onto which the eelskin is tied.

Rigging an Eelskin with Plug

Eelskin is slipped over the plug, whose tail treble hook has been removed. Bottom treble hooks protrude as shown, and skin is tied on at the plug's head.

Two Ways to Hook a Live Eel

Hooking a Squid Head

Squid and Leadhead Jig

Hooking Whole Squid for Bottom Fishing

Three-Hook Squid Rig

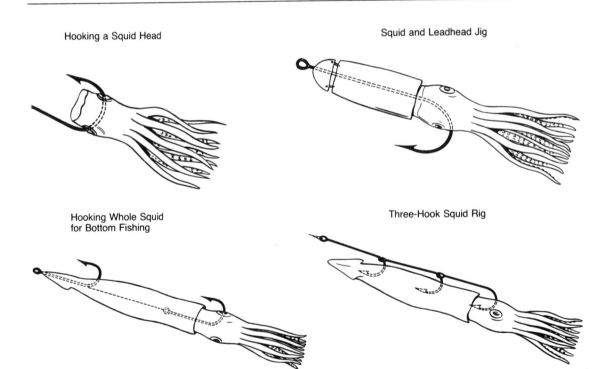

SALTWATER TROLLING RIGS

Rigging a Mullet for Trolling

Herring for Trolling

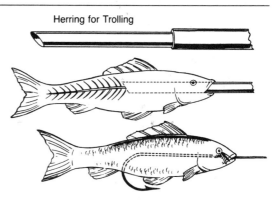

Fish is split down the back, and the backbone and entrails are removed and discarded. Hook is run through body and out vent. Eye of hook and fish's mouth are sewn together, and the back is sewn up.

Fish is first deboned by running a hollow metal tube, its tip sharpened and cut at an angle, through mouth and over backbone. Deboning makes herring more flexible and life-like. Hook as shown.

Two Ways to Rig Balao for Big-Game Trolling

Bait-and-Plug Rig for Trolling

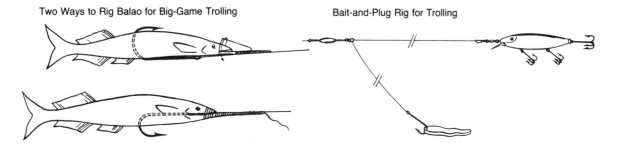

Rigging a Whole Eel with Tin Squid for Trolling and Casting

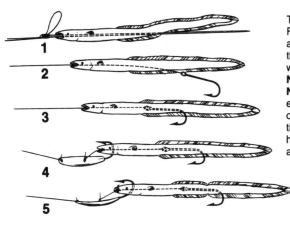

To rig an eel this way, you'll need a long needle with an eye. Form a loop in some relatively heavy line (about 36-pound-test) and run the loop through the needle's eye. Run the needle through the eel from mouth to vent **(Drawing No. 1)**. Pull the loop all the way through the eel, and attach to it a 6/0 to 8/0 hook **(Drawing No. 2)**. Draw protruding line and hook shank into eel **(Drawing No. 3)**. Take a small block-tin squid, and run its hook through the eel's head (or lips) from bottom to top, and tie the line to the eye on the flat surface of the squid **(Drawing No. 4)**. With light line, tie eel's mouth shut, make a tie around the eel's head where the hook protrudes to prevent the hook from ripping out, and make a similar tie around the vent **(Drawing No. 5)**.

MORE SALTWATER TROLLING RIGS

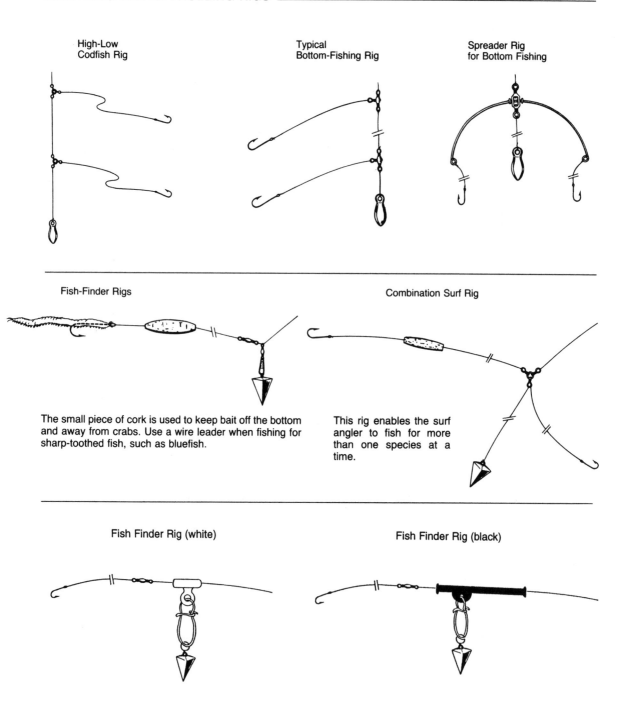

High-Low
Codfish Rig

Typical
Bottom-Fishing Rig

Spreader Rig
for Bottom Fishing

Fish-Finder Rigs

Combination Surf Rig

The small piece of cork is used to keep bait off the bottom
and away from crabs. Use a wire leader when fishing for
sharp-toothed fish, such as bluefish.

This rig enables the surf
angler to fish for more
than one species at a
time.

Fish Finder Rig (white)

Fish Finder Rig (black)

HOW TO CATCH BAIT AND KEEP IT FRESH

Anglers are often puzzled if they have to catch and keep something other than a dozen worms for a day's fishing. Catching the various baits and keeping them alive and kicking is not difficult.

WORMS

Worms, whether earthworms or nightcrawlers, are the most popular live baits. Nightcrawlers get their name from the fact that they come to the surface at night. They like warm and wet weather. Wait until it has been dark at least two to three hours, then prowl around your lawn, a golf course or a park. Use a flashlight, but not one with a bright beam. If the beam is too bright, cover the lens with red cellophane. When you spot a worm, grab it by the head (the thicker end) with your fingers. If the worm tries to shoot back into the hole, hold onto one end until the worm releases tension and is free of the hole.

If you can't find nightcrawlers at night, it's probably too dry for them to come to the surface. You can wait for rain or water your lawn in the afternoon and go worm hunting that night.

If you're after the common earthworm, which is smaller than a nightcrawler, you'll have to dig for

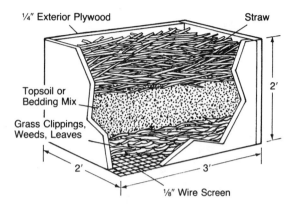

The homemade worm box will hold about 700 nightcrawlers. It can be kept above ground and set into the ground with about 2 inches protruding. Of course, the box must be placed in a shady area.

A day's supply of worms can easily be kept in a can of this size. The metal top and bottom of the can are removed and replaced with plastic lids that manufacturers supply with such cans. Worms always crawl to the bottom, so this double lid makes worms at bottom easily accessible. Punch holes into the plastic top lid and carry the can in a burlap pouch. Every so often, dip the whole thing into water. The wet burlap will help keep the worms cool and fresh.

them. Concentrate on compost heaps, vegetable gardens, and stream banks.

A day's supply of worms can be carried in a few inches of damp soil in a coffee can from which both ends have been removed. Punch holes in the plastic lids that come with the can. With two of these lids in place, it can be opened from either end for easy access to the worms on the bottom. If you keep this container in a burlap pouch and dip it occasionally in a cool creek, the worms will stay fresh all day.

Commercial boxes for worms, as well as other baits, are available. Most are made of porous fiberboard, which insulates the box and keeps the inside cool and humid.

If you want to keep a good supply of worms on hand, build a worm box. In a box of 2 feet × 3 feet × 2 feet you can house 600 or 700 nighcrawlers. Sink the box in a shady spot, allowing 2 inches of the box above ground. Damp and cool are the key words in keeping worms fresh. A wet burlap bag over some straw will work well. You might also try spreading out a few handfuls of ice cubes on the straw every two or three days. The ice will keep the soil damp and cool as it melts. Food is no problem, since worms eat almost anything. You can feed them coffee grounds, breadcrumbs, and cornmeal.

Ice cubes, incidentally, can be used effectively when transporting and keeping worms on an ex-

Here's how to transport a lot of worms in an Oberlin Bait Canteen, designed for lengthy fishing trips. The jar in the center of the bedding is full of ice cubes and sealed in a plastic bag. The plastic bag keeps condensation from getting into the bedding and making it too soggy. The ice will keep the worms cool and fresh. You'll notice that worms will gather around the jar. If you're making a long car trip, drop a few ice cubes on top of the bedding too. The ice will provide additional cooling and yield moisture to the bedding as the ice melts.

tended fishing trip. Try the following method on your next trip. In the center of your bait box, which should measure about 12 inches × 12 inches × 8 inches deep if you're carrying 400 or so worms, clear a space in the bedding. Next, fill a glass jar or plastic container with ice cubes, screw the cap back on, and put it in a plastic bag. Place the container in the center of the box and push the bedding or soil around it.

The ice will keep the soil cool and damp and it will stay that way until the cubes melt. In hot weather, worms will actually crowd around the jar. The purpose of the plastic is to seal in condensation. Without the plastic, the soil would become too soggy for worms.

SEA WORMS

Sea worms, such as blood- and sandworms, are delicate and should be kept in damp seaweed. If they are to be kept for a week or so, spread them out in seaweed and keep them refrigerated. Blood- and sandworms are enemies and should be kept separate. Use a wood partition to divide your bait box into two compartments.

MINNOWS

Minnows rank second as the most popular bait, and they can be caught almost as easily as worms. There are several ways to collect minnows: minnow trap, drop or umbrella net, minnow seine, or the cast net.

Caution: A fishing license is usually required to take bait in fresh water, and many states set limits on the number of baitfish that may be kept. Check the fishing regulations of your state before netting or trapping.

The minnow trap requires the least skill to use. It works on the principle that a small fish will swim into the funnellike openings after food and be unable to find its way out. For bait, you should wet oatmeal or cornmeal and roll it into balls the size of golfballs. The meal will break up gradually in the trap and provide bait for long periods.

The best place to set the trap is in shallow water near a dock or boathouse. On streams, set it near the head or side of a pool where the current is slow.

The drop or umbrella net, which measures 36 inches × 36 inches, gets more immediate results but may be more difficult to use. Lower it into the water just deep enough so that you can still lift it fast.

HOW TO TRAP AND KEEP MINNOWS

Left: Easier to use than nets is the minnow trap. Minnows swim into the funnellike openings at either end but can't find their way out. Place the trap near docks or wherever current is weak. Bait it with a paste mix of oatmeal and water rolled golfball-size. **Right:** Michael Sparano uses a drop (umbrella) net. He'll lower it beneath the surface, sprinkle bread crumbs over it, and wait for baitfish to start feeding. Then he'll lift the net up fast and collect his bait.

These two fellows are working a minnow seine in a tidal bay. The net, which can measure from 10 to 20 feet long, is 4 feet high and weighted at the bottom. The men will sweep the net toward shore and thereby trap a variety of bait.

Left: Of long-established design, this minnow bucket has a vented insert that can be suspended into lake or river water, assuring that the minnows have a continuous fresh change of water. *Caution:* Avoid abrupt changes in water temperature. **Middle:** This trolling bucket makes it possible to keep your bait in the water while your boat is moving. The bucket floats on its side, as shown, and has openings that help aerate water. **Right:** This 10-gallon bait can is aerated by battery and pump. Large bait containers with powered aerators are helpful for big baits, such as live mackerel, shiners, or herring.

Sprinkle breadcrumbs over it and let them sink. When minnows begin to feed on the crumbs, lift the net fast. With practice, you'll make good hauls every time.

A minnow seine not only produces a lot of bait, but is fun to use, especially in bays and tidal rivers. A seine is usually 4 feet high and anywhere from 10 to 50 feet long, with lead weights along the bottom and floats on top. A 20-footer is a good size for most purposes. Seining is easy. Two people carry the seine about 100 feet from shore or until depth hits 4 feet or so. Keeping the weighted end of the seine on the bottom, the people sweep toward shore. The seine will belly out, catching everything in its path and carrying bait up on shore, where it can be picked up.

The cast net, shown on page 402, is one of the most useful tools of both the freshwater and saltwater angler because he can use it to get the bait that he can't buy, and to obtain forage baitfish native to the water that he's fishing—which is the best bait to use under most circumstances.

A few states prohibit the use of cast nets, or restrict sizes or materials. Again, check the fishing regulations of your state before netting.

Monofilament nets, because their nylon strands are stiff, open better than nets made of braided threads. Mono nets also sink faster and are less visible after they're thrown into the water. Generally, they catch more fish, but they're also more expensive.

Cast nets are available in various sizes and types. Experts throw 16-foot and larger nets, but anglers who would only use them occasionally are better off getting one that measures 8 to 10 feet. Bridge nets, popular in the Florida Keys, are short nets with extra lead weights around the bottom. When the net is dropped off a bridge into deep water, its added weight allows it to sink quickly and hold baitfish before they dive and escape.

A plastic bucket is the best storage container for a net. All nets should routinely be rinsed with clean water and cleared of debris.

The proper gripping technique is just as important as the method you use to throw the net (see drawings on page 402). If you're right-handed, you should coil the throwing line and loop it in your right hand. Stretch the net full-length, and grab the net two-thirds of the way down with your left hand. Then bring your right hand (which is still holding the coils) just below your left hand and grasp the net, with your thumb pointing outward. Reach down to the bottom of the net with your left hand, pick up the weighted line at the bottom of the net, and drape the *inside* of the net over your right shoulder.

Gather about two-thirds of the net in your left

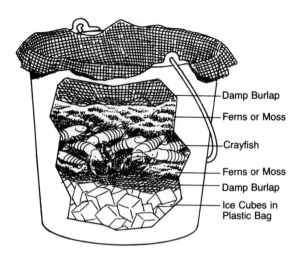

A crayfish bucket with ice will keep crayfish alive and active. Note that the crayfish are sandwiched between fern insulation that helps keep them cool top and bottom.

hand, and with your feet pointing in the direction in which you'll throw the net, rotate the upper half of your body to the right. You're now ready to cast—just throw the net straight out in front of you.

The next problem is keeping the minnows alive and fresh. The water must be aerated to keep enough oxygen in the bucket for survival, and this can be done in several ways. Water can be aerated by battery-powered devices. You can also aerate the water manually with a tin can. Scoop up a canful of water and pour it back into the bucket from a height of 2 feet. Doing this a dozen times every 15 minutes should provide sufficient oxygen for a couple of dozen minnows.

Bait water must be kept at a constant temperature. In summer, add ice cubes to the water before transporting them. As the ice melts, it will cool the water and add oxygen. Take care, however, not to cool the water too fast.

It is important to avoid abrupt temperature changes, which will kill minnows.

If you plan to troll, keep bait in a bucket designed for trolling. This bucket, built to float on its side, will take water at an angle and aerate it.

If you're stillfishing, use the traditional bucket, which is actually two buckets. The outer bucket is used when transporting minnows. When you start fishing, lift out the insert and lower it into the water. The insert, which floats upright, is vented so that water is constantly changed.

CRAYFISH

Crayfish make excellent bait, but they can some-times be difficult to find. You'll do best at night along gravely shorelines. Crayfish feed in the shallows and you can spot them with a flashlight. Their eyes re-flect reddish in the beam. When you locate one, hold a dip net behind it and touch its head with your hand or a stick. If you're lucky, it will swim backwards into the net. If you're fast, you can try grabbing a crayfish from behind with your hand.

Keeping crayfish fresh in hot weather can be a problem. You can use an "ice-bucket" setup. In the bottom of a pail, place two dozen ice cubes in a plastic bag. Cover the ice with a layer of burlap, followed by a few inches of moss or ferns. Next, spread out the crayfish and cover them with another layer of moss or ferns. Cover this top layer with another piece of wet burlap. Crayfish will stay in fine shape in this insulated pail during the hottest weather. Keep that top piece of burlap wet.

FROGS

Few anglers will question the value of a lively frog as a bait. Look for them along the grassy banks of creeks, ponds, and lakes. Catching them is not hard. You can catch a fair number during the day, but you can collect more at night with a flashlight and a long-handled small-mesh net. Frogs will remain still in the beam of a flashlight and you should have

This commercially made frog box consists of fiber, wire screen, and a rubber-slot top opening.

no trouble netting them.

Keeping a day's supply of frogs is no problem. Commercial frog boxes are available, or you can make your own.

Only the popular baits are covered here. As you collect these, you'll soon discover that there are other baits available such as grasshoppers, crickets, hellgrammites, lizards, and so on. Sometimes catching bait is as much fun as the fishing.

HOW TO MAKE A FROG BOX

A frog box is easy to make. It's also effective, and it will last for years.

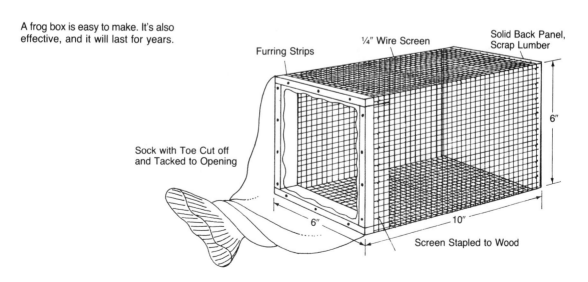

HOW TO THROW A CAST NET

TERMINAL-RIG ACCESSORIES

The items of fishing gear covered in this chapter are various components of the rigs shown in previous chapters. These accessories are as important as links in a chain, so buy the best you can afford. A well-constructed snap swivel of the correct size, for example, won't literally come apart at the seams under the surge of a good muskie, as has happened to this writer.

Swivels come in many forms and sizes, but basically a swivel consists of two or three round metal eyes connected in such a way that each eye can rotate freely and independently of the others. Swiv-

els perform such functions as preventing or reducing line twist, enabling the angler to attach much more than one component (sinker and bait, for example) to his line, and facilitating lure changes.

Sinkers, like swivels, come in many shapes and weights. Usually made of lead, they are used to get a bait (or lure) down to the desired depth.

Floats are lighter-than-water devices that are attached to the line. They keep a bait at a predetermined distance above the bottom and signal the strike of a fish. Floats are usually made of cork or plastic and come in many forms.

SWIVEL DESIGNS

Barrel Swivel   Big-Game Swivel   Snap Swivel

The basic **barrel swivel** is used to join line and leader. The **big-game swivel** is for heavy fish. It also comes with locking snap. The **snap swivel** is used to join line and lure.

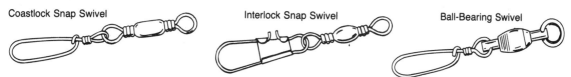

Coastlock Snap Swivel   Interlock Snap Swivel   Ball-Bearing Swivel

Coastlock snap swivel's end of wire snap hooks around itself, and spring tension keeps the snap locked. This is preferred over the standard snap swivel for sizable fish. The **interlock snap swivel** is stronger than the standard swivel. A **ball-bearing swivel** is less apt to bind than a standard swivel.

Connecting Link   Three-Way Swivel   Cross-Line Swivel

The **connecting link** is used to attach a sinker to a terminal rig and can also be used as a component in a fishfinder rig.

SWIVEL DESIGNS (Continued)

McMahon Snap Swivel   Corkscrew Snap Swivel   Duolock Snap Swivel   Cross-Lok Snap Swivel

SINKER DESIGNS

Split-Shot Sinker   Egg Sinker   Clincher Sinker

With the **split-shot sinker,** line is inserted in slot, and split is pinched on. Split-shot sizes range from BB to OO. Split shot finds widest use in freshwater. With the **egg sinker,** line goes through a hole drilled through the core; can be used as basis of a fish-finder rig since line slides freely through the hole. With the **clincher sinker,** line is inserted in the slot, and the "wing" on each end is pressed over the line.

Pyramid Sinker   Bank Sinker   Dipsey Sinker   Diamond Trolling Sinker

Sharp edges on a **pyramid sinker** dig into sand and mud, resisting pressures of tidal currents and wave action and helping the angler "hold bottom." A **bank sinker** is preferred for fishing when and where tide and waves are no problem; also good for fishing from rocks and jetties, for its rounded edges are apt to slide over rock crevices rather than hang up.

Trolling Drail   Keel Swivel Sinker   Trolling Lead

Trolling drail eliminates line twist, gets bait down deep. **Keel swivel sinker,** used for trolling, eliminates line twist.

TROLLING DEVICES

The trolling planer is a heavily weighted device with metal or plastic "wings" that permit trolling at considerable depths. The bait-walker sinker keeps the bait moving near the bottom but not dragging on the bottom. The downrigger assembly shown has a terminal rig with cable, cannon ball, and multi-bead release.

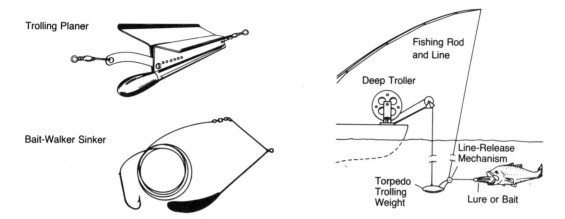

Trolling Planer

Bait-Walker Sinker

Fishing Rod and Line

Deep Troller

Line-Release Mechanism

Torpedo Trolling Weight

Lure or Bait

FLOAT DESIGNS

Plastic Ball Float

Cork Ball Float

Caro-Line Float

In the **plastic ball float,** a spring-loaded top section, when depressed, exposes a small U-shaped "hook" at the bottom into which line is placed. Releasing the top section reseats the "hook" holding the line fast. The **Caro-line cork float** has a doubled length of line running through it lengthwise. The fishing line is run through the loop, and then the loop is pulled through the cork body, seating the line. The Caro-line float is generally used in surf fishing to keep a bait off the bottom and away from crabs.

Teeter Float

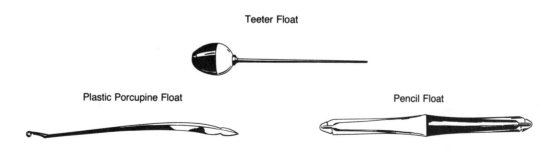

Plastic Porcupine Float

Pencil Float

The **plastic porcupine float** is light and highly sensitive to the strike of a fish. The **teeter float** has a slender section that floats perpendicular to the water and is highly sensitive to the strike of a fish. With the **pencil float,** line is attached at both ends. A strike causes one end to lift from the surface.

KNOTS

Anyone who aspires to competence as a fisherman must have at least a basic knowledge of knots. Most anglers know and use no more than half a dozen knots. However, if you fish a lot, you are sure to run into a situation that cannot be solved efficiently with the basic ties. The aim of this chapter is to acquaint you with knots that will help you handle nearly all line-tying situations.

All knots reduce—to a greater or lesser degree, depending upon the particular knot—the breaking strength of the line. Loose or poorly tied knots reduce line strength even more. For that reason, and

to avoid wasting valuable fishing time, it is best to practice tying the knots at home. In most cases, it's better to practice with cord or rope; the heavier material makes it easier to follow the tying procedures.

It is important to form and tighten knots correctly. They should be tightened slowly and steadily for best results. In most knots requiring the tyer to make turns around the standing part of the line, at least five such turns should be made.

Now let's take a look at the range of fishing knots. Included are tying instructions, the uses for which each knot is suited, and other information.

BLOOD KNOT

Used to connect two lines of relatively similar diameter. Especially popular for joining sections of monofilament in making tapered fly leaders.

1. Wrap one strand around the other at least four times, and run the end into the fork thus formed.

2. Make the same number of turns, in the opposite direction, with the second strand, and run its end through the opening in the middle of the knot, in the direction opposite that of the first strand.

3. Hold the two ends so they do not slip (some anglers use their teeth). Pull the standing part of both strands in opposite directions, tightening the knot.

4. Tighten securely, clip off the ends, and the knot is complete. If you want to tie on a dropper fly, leave one of these ends about 6 to 8 inches long.

STU APTE IMPROVED BLOOD KNOT

Excellent for joining two lines of greatly different diameter, such as a heavy monofilament shock leader and a light leader tippet.

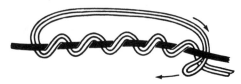

1. Double a sufficient length of the lighter line, wrap it around the standing part of the heavier line at least five times, and run the end of the doubled line into the "fork" thus formed.

2. Wrap the heavier line around the standing part of the doubled lighter line three times, in the opposite direction, and run the end of the heavier line into the opening, in the direction opposite that of the end of the doubled line.

3. Holding the two ends to keep them from slipping, pull the standing parts of the two lines in opposite directions. Tighten the knot completely, using your fingernails to push the loops together if necessary, and clip off the ends.

DOUBLE SURGEON'S KNOT

Used to join two strands of greatly unequal diameter.

1. Place the two lines parallel, with ends pointing in opposite directions. Using the two lines as a single strand, make simple overhand knot, pulling the two strands all the way through loop, and then make another overhand knot.

2. Holding both strands at each end, pull the knot tight and clip off the ends.

IMPROVED CLINCH KNOT

Used to tie flies, bass bugs, lures, and bait hooks to line or leader. This knot reduces line strength only slightly.

1. Run the end of the line through the eye of the lure, fly, or hook, and then make at least five turns around the standing part of the line. Run the end through the opening between the eye and the beginning of the twists, and then run it through the large loop formed by the previous step.

2. Pull slowly on the standing part of the line, being careful that the end doesn't slip back through the large loop and that the knot snugs up against the eye. Clip off end.

DOUBLE-LOOP CLINCH KNOT

Same as Improved Clinch Knot except that line is run through eye twice at the beginning of the tie.

TRILENE® KNOT

Used in joining line to swivels, snaps, hooks and artificial lures, the Trilene Knot is a strong, all-purpose knot that resists slippage and premature failures. It is easy to tie and retains 85–90 percent of the original line strength. The double wrap of monofilament line through the eyelet provides a protective cushion for added safety.

1. Run the end of the line through the eye of the hook or lure and double back through the eye a second time.

2. Loop around the standing part of the line five or six times.

3. Thread the tag end back between the eye and the coils as shown.

4. Pull up tight and trim the tag end.

SHOCKER KNOT

Used to join two lines of unequal diameters.

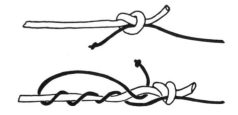

JANSIK SPECIAL KNOT

This is a terminal-tackle connecting knot that is popular with muskie anglers.

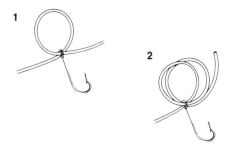

1. Run about 5 inches of line through eye of hook on lure; bring it around in a circle and and run it through again. **2.** Make a second circle, parallel with the first, and pass end of line through eye a third time.

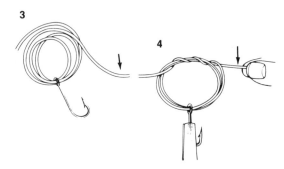

3. Bend standing part of line (identified by arrows) around the two circles. Bring tag end around in a third circle and wrap it three times around the three parallel lines. **4.** Hold hook, swivel, or lure with pliers. Hold standing line with other hand and tag end in teeth. Pull all three to tighten.

ARBOR KNOT

The Arbor Knot provides the angler with a quick, easy connection for attaching line to the reel spool.

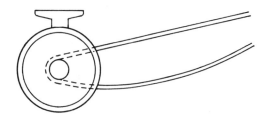

1. Pass line around reel arbor.

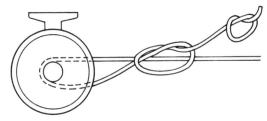

2. Tie an overhand knot around the standing line. **3.** Tie a second overhand knot in the tag end.

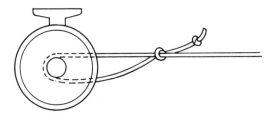

4. Pull tight and snip off excess. Snug down first overhand knot on the reel arbor.

MULTIPLE CLINCH KNOT

Used to join line and leader, especially in baitcasting. This knot slides through rod guides with a minimum of friction.

A loop is tied in the end of the line. Then leader is run into the loops, around the entire loop four times, and then back through the middle of the four wraps.

DOUBLE IMPROVED CLINCH KNOT

Same as Improved Clinch Knot except that line is used doubled throughout entire tie.

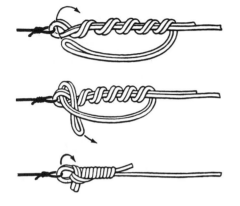

PALOMAR KNOT

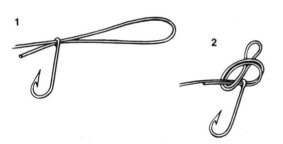

1. Pass line or leader through the eye of the hook and back again to form 3- to 5-inch loop. 2. Hold the line and hook at the eye. With the other hand, bring the loop up and under the double line and tie an overhand knot, but do not tighten.

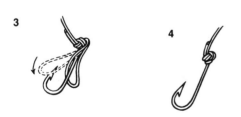

3. Hold the overhand knot. With the other hand, bring the loop over the hook. 4. Pull the line to draw the knot to the top of the eye. Pull both tag end and running line to tighten. Clip tag end off about ⅛ inch from knot.

KING SLING KNOT

This offers the angler an easy-to-tie end loop knot that is used primarily as a connection for crank baits. This knot allows the lure to work freely, making it more lifelike, and resulting in more strikes.

1. Insert tag end of line through artificial bait so that it extends 8 to 10 inches.

2. Hold the tag end and the standing line in your left hand, and form a loop.

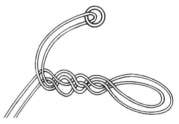

3. With the bait in your right hand make four turns around the tag end and the standing line above the loop.

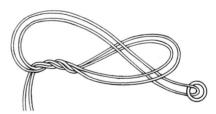

4. Bring the bait down and through the loop.

5. To tighten, hold line above the bait at desired loop length and pull the tag end and the standing line at the same time. 6. Trim the tag end.

DOUBLE SURGEON'S LOOP

This is a quick, easy way to tie a loop in the end of a leader. It is often used as part of a leader system because it is relatively strong.

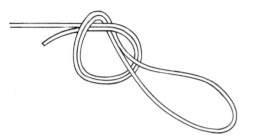

1. Double the tag end of the line. Make a single overhand knot in the double line.

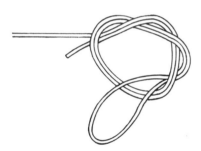

2. Hold the tag end and standing part of the line in your left hand and bring the loop around and insert through the overhand knot again.

3. Hold the loop in your right hand. Hold the tag end and standing line in your left hand. Moisten the knot (don't use saliva) and pull to tighten.

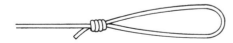

4. Trim off the tag end.

WORLD'S FAIR KNOT

An easy-to-tie terminal tackle knot for connecting line to swivel or lure.

1. Double a 6-inch length of line and pass the loop through the eye.

2. Bring the loop back next to the doubled line and grasp the doubled line through the loop.

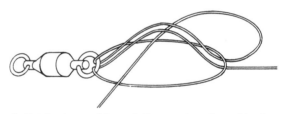

3. Put the tag end through the new loop formed by the double line.

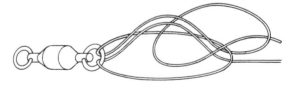

4. Bring the tag end back through the new loop created by Step 3.

5. Pull the tag end snug, and slide the knot up tight. Clip the tag end.

PERFECTION LOOP KNOT

Used to make a loop in the end of line or leader. Make one turn around the line and hold the crossing point with thumb and forefinger **(Drawing 1)**. Make a second turn around the crossing point, and bring the end around and between loops A and B **(Drawing 2)**. Run loop B through loop A **(Drawing 3)**. Pull upward on loop B **(Drawing 4)**, tightening the knot **(Drawing 5)**.

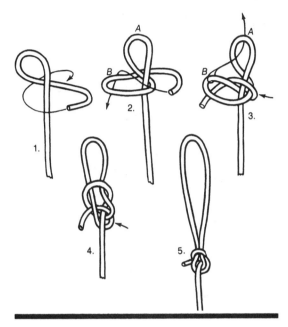

TUCKED SHEET BEND

Joins fly line and leader when leader has an end loop.

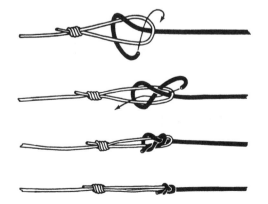

TURLE KNOT

Used to tie a dry or wet fly to a leader tippet. Not as strong as the Improved Clinch Knot, but it allows a dry fly's hackle points to sit high and jauntily on the surface of the water.

1. Run end of leader through eye of hook toward the bend, and tie a simple overhand knot around the standing part of the line, forming a loop.

2. Open the loop enough to allow it to pass around the fly, and place the loop around the neck of the fly, just forward of the eye.

3. Pull on the end of the leader, drawing the loop up tight around the neck of the fly.

4. Tighten the knot completely by pulling on the main part of the leader.

DROPPER LOOP KNOT

This knot is frequently used to put a loop in the middle of a strand of monofilament.

1. Make a loop in the line and wrap one end overhand several times around the other part of the line. Pinch a small loop at point marked X and thrust it between the turns as shown by the simulated, imaginary needle.

2. Place your finger through the loop to keep it from pulling out again, and pull on both ends of the line.

3. The knot will draw up like this.

4. Finished loop knot.

OFFSHORE SWIVEL KNOT

1. Slip loop of double-line leader through the eye of the swivel. Rotate loop ½ turn to put a single twist between loop and swivel eye.

2. Pass the loop with the twist over the swivel. Hold the loop end, together with both strands of double-line leader, with one hand. Let the swivel slide to the other end of the double loops now formed.

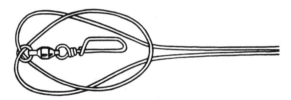

3. Still holding loop/lines, use other hand to rotate swivel through center of both loops. Repeat at least five times.

4. Continue holding strands of double-line leader tightly, but release the end of the loop. As you pull on swivel, loops of line will begin to gather.

5. To draw knot tight, grip the swivel with pliers and push the loops toward eye with fingers, still keeping strands of leader pulled tight.

NAIL KNOT

This is the best knot for joining the end of a fly line with the butt end of a fly leader. The knot is smooth, streamlined, and will run freely through the guides of the fly rod. *Caution:* This knot is designed for use with the modern synthetic fly lines; do not use it with an old silk fly line, for the knot will cut the line.

1. Place the end of the fly line and the butt end of the leader—pointing in opposite directions—along the length of a tapered nail. Allow sufficient overlap.

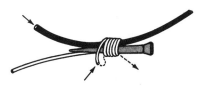

2. Wrap leader five or six times around itself, the nail, and the fly line, keeping windings up against one another. Run butt end of leader back along the nail, inside the wraps.

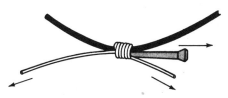

3. Pull both ends of the leader tight, and then remove the nail and tighten again by pulling on both ends of the leader.

4. Pull on both line and leader to test the knot, and clip off ends, completing the knot.

NAIL KNOT (Alternate)

Tying procedures are the same as for the standard Nail Knot, except that in place of the nail, use an air-inflation needle like those used to inflate basketballs and footballs. The tip of the needle must be cut or filed off so that the tube is open at both ends. A large hypodermic needle with its point snipped off also works well. In tying Step No. 3, the butt end of the leader—after having been wrapped five or six times around the fly line, leader, and tube—is simply run back through the tube (needle). Then the knot is tightened, the tube removed, and the final tightening done.

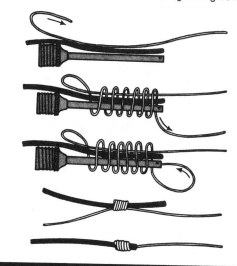

DOUBLE NAIL KNOT

Used to join leader sections of the same or slightly different diameters. This is especially useful in saltwater fly fishing and in making heavy salmon leaders.

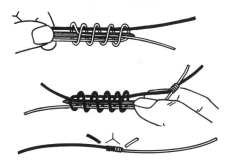

Tying procedure involves making two Nail Knots, one around each of the two leader sections. As each knot is formed, it is tightened only enough to prevent it from unraveling. When both are formed, each leader is pulled slowly so that the knots tighten together securely.

THE UNI-KNOT SYSTEM

The Uni-Knot System consists of variations on one basic knot that can be used for most needs in freshwater and saltwater. The system was developed by Vic Dunaway, editor of *Florida Sportsman* magazine and author of numerous books. Here's how each variation is tied, step by step.

A. TYING TO TERMINAL TACKLE

1. Run line through eye of hook, swivel, or lure at least 6 inches and fold it back to form two parallel lines. Bring the end of the line back in a circle toward the eye.

2. Turn the tag end six times around the double line and through circle. Hold double line at eye and pull tag end to snug up turns.

3. Pull running line to slide the knot up against the eye.

4. Continue pulling until knot is tight. Trim tag end flush with last coil of the knot. This basic Uni-Knot will not slip.

B. LOOP CONNECTION

Tie the same basic Uni-Knot as shown above—up to the point where coils are snugged up against the running line. Then slide knot toward eye only until the desired loop size is reached. Pull tag end with pliers to tighten. This gives a lure or fly free, natural movement in the water. When fish is hooked, knot slides tight against eye.

C. JOINING LINES

1. With two lines of about the same diameter, overlap ends for about 6 inches. With one end, form Uni-Knot circle and cross the two lines at about the middle of the overlap.

2. Tie basic Uni-Knot, making six turns around the lines.

3. Pull tag end to snug the knot.

4. Use loose end of the overlapped line to tie second Uni-Knot and snug it up in the same manner.

5. Pull the two lines in opposite directions to slide the two knots together. Pull tight and snip tag ends close to outermost coils.

D. JOINING LEADER TO LINE

1. Using leader no more than four times the pound-test of the line, double the end of line and overlap with leader for about 6 inches. Make Uni-Knot circle with the doubled line.

2. Tie a Uni-Knot around leader with the doubled line, but use only three turns. Snug up.

3. Now tie a Uni-Knot with the leader around doubled line, again using only three turns.

4. Pull knots together tightly. Trim tag ends and loop.

E. JOINING SHOCK LEADER TO LINE

1. Using leader of more than four times the pound-test of the line, double the ends of both leader and line back about 6 inches. Slip line loop through leader loop far enough to permit tying Uni-Knot around both strands of leader.

2. With doubled line, tie a Uni-Knot around doubled leader, using only four turns.

3. Put finger through loop of line and grasp both tag end and running line to pull knot snug around leader loop.

4. With one hand, pull long end of leader (not both strands). With the other hand, pull both strands of line (as arrows indicate). Pull slowly until knot slides to end of leader loop and slippage is stopped.

F. DOUBLE-LINE SHOCK LEADER

1. As a replacement for Bimini Twist or Spider Hitch, first clip off amount of line needed for desired length of loop. Tie the two ends together with an overhand knot.

2. Double the end of the running line and overlap it 6 inches with knotted end of the loop piece. Tie a Uni-Knot with the tied loop around the double running line, using four turns.

3. Now tie a Uni-Knot with the doubled running line around the loop piece, again using four turns.

4. Hold both strands of double line in one hand, both strands of loop in the other. Pull to bring knots together until they barely touch.

5. Tighten by pulling both strands of loop piece (as two arrows indicate) but only main strand of running line (as single arrow indicates). Trim off both loop tag ends, eliminating overhand knot.

G. SNELLING A HOOK

1. Thread line through the hook eye for about 6 inches. Hold line against hook shank and form Uni-Knot circle. Make as many turns as desired through loop and around line and shank. Close knot by pulling on tag end.

2. Tighten by pulling running line in one direction and hook in the other. Trim off tag end.

LOOP KNOT

Tie overhand knot in line, leaving loop loose and sufficient length of line below loop to tie rest of knot. Run end through hook eye and back through loop in line, and then tie another overhand knot around standing part. Pull tight.

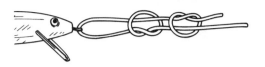

DAVE HAWK'S DROP LOOP KNOT

Used to attach lure to line or leader via a nonslip loop that will permit freer lure action than would a knot snugged right up to the eye of the lure.

1. Tie overhand knot about 5 inches from end of line, pull tight, and run end through the lure eye.

2. Bring end back parallel with standing part of line, bend end back toward lure, and then make two turns around the parallel strands.

3. Slowly draw the knot tight, and then pull on the lure so that the jam knot slides down to the overhand knot.

END LOOP

Used to form a loop in the end of a line.

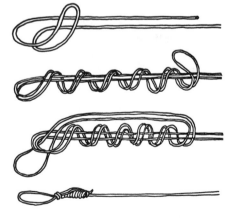

BUFFER LOOP

Used to attach lure to line or leader via a nonslip loop.

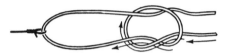

1. Tie simple overhand knot in line, leaving loop loose and leaving end long enough to complete the knot, and then run end through eye of lure.

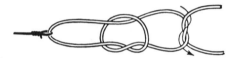

2. Run end back through loose loop, and make another overhand knot, using end and standing part of line.

3. Tighten overhand knot nearest to lure eye, and then tighten second overhand knot, which, in effect, forms a half hitch against first knot.

4. Finished knot.

KNOTTING BACKING LINE TO FLY LINE

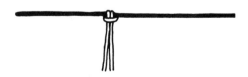

1. Double the end of the backing line, make one wrap around the fly line, and pull all of the backing line through loop at its doubled end so lines appear as in drawing.

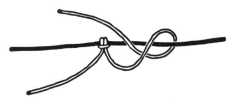

2. With end of the backing line, make a half hitch around the fly line, and pull it tight against the original knot.

3. Continue making such half hitches (eight or ten should be enough) until the tie appears as in drawing.

4. Wrap the entire tie with nylon thread, including part of the end of the backing line. This step is simplified by placing the fly line in a fly-tying vise.

5. Give the entire tie a good coat of lacquer.

FLY-LINE SPLICE

This is used to join two fly lines.

Remove the coating from 2¼ inches of the end of each line, and fray about 1 inch **(Drawing 1)**. Enmesh the frayed ends of one line with those of the other, and wrap most of this joint with nylon thread **(Drawing 2)**. Then make another series of wrappings over the entire splice **(Drawing 3)**. Finish the job with coats of varnish.

ALBRIGHT KNOT (MONO TO MONO)

Used to join lines of dissimilar diameter, such as fly line to leader and heavy shock leader to finer leader tippet.

Double the end of the heavier line, forming a long U. Bring the lighter line up into the U, and make about 10 wraps— in the direction of the bottom of the U—around the U and the standing part of the lighter line, bringing the end of the lighter line out the bottom of the U **(Drawing 1)**. Pull slowly and evenly until the knot is tight **(Drawing 2)**.

ALBRIGHT KNOT (MONO TO WIRE)

Used when short length of wire leader is needed below monofilment leader tippet to prevent sharp-toothed fish from biting through the leader. The fly is attached to the wire leader with a brass crimping sleeve. Also used to tie mono leader to wire or lead-core line so that knot will pass through guides and tip tops smoothly. Eliminates need for swivel.

Bend end of wire leader into a U or open-end loop. Run end of monofilament into the tip of the U, make about 7 wraps around the doubled wire, and run the end of the monofilament back out through the tip of the U **(Drawing 1)**. Hold both leaders to prevent the knot from slipping, and slowly draw the wraps of monofilament tight **(Drawing 2)**. Clip off ends, and the knot is finished **(Drawing 3)**.

BIMINI TWIST

Used to create a loop or double line without appreciably weakening the breaking strength of the line. Especially popular in bluewater fishing for large saltwater fish. Learning this knot requires practice.

1. Double the end of the line to form a loop, leaving yourself plenty of line to work with. Run the loop around a fixed object such as a cleat or the butt end of a rod, or have a partner hold the loop and keep it open. Make 20 twists in the line, keeping the turns tight and the line taut.

2. Keeping the twists tight, wrap the end of the line back over the twists until you reach the V of the loop, making the wraps tight and snug up against one another.

3. Make half hitch around one side of loop and pull tight.

4. Then make a half hitch around the other side of the loop, and pull this one tight.

5. Now make a half hitch around the base of the loop, tighten it, clip off excess line at the end, and the Bimini Twist is complete.

SPIDER HITCH

Serves same function as the Bimini Twist. But many anglers prefer the Spider Hitch because it's easier and faster to tie—especially with cold hands—and requires no partner to help, nor any fixed object to keep the loop open. And it's equally strong.

1. Make a long loop in the line. Hold the ends between thumb and forefinger, with first joint of thumb extending beyond your finger. Then use other hand to twist a smaller reverse loop in the doubled line.

2. Slide your fingers up line to grasp small reverse loop, together with long loop. Most of small loop should extend beyond your thumb tip.

3. Wind the doubled line from right to left around both thumb and small loop, taking five turns. Then pass remainder of doubled line (large loop) through the small loop.

4. Pull the large loop to make the five turns unwind off thumb, using a fast, steady pull—not a quick jerk.

5. Pull the turns around the base of the loop tight and then trim off the tag end.

HAYWIRE TWIST

Used to tie wire to hook, lure, or swivel, or make loop in end of wire.

Run about 4 inches of the end of the leader wire through the eye of the hook, lure, or swivel, and then bend end across standing part of wire as in **Drawing 1**. Holding the two parts of the wire at their crossing point, bend the wire around itself, using hard, even, twisting motions. Both wire parts should be twisted equally **(Drawing 2)**. Then, using the end of the wire, make about 10 tight wraps around the standing part of the wire **(Drawing 3)**. Break off or clip end of wire close to the last wrap so that there is no sharp end, and job is complete **(Drawing 4)**.

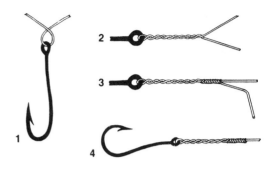

AVOIDING LINE TWIST

Winding new line on your reels is a fairly simple job, but if you do it wrong you'll end up with twists that will pose big problems from your first cast.

OPEN-FACE SPINNING REEL

First, attach the reel to a rod. Any rod will do, but never try winding line on a spool by holding the reel in your hands. Next, string the line through the guides, open the bail and knot the line to the pool. Now flip the bail closed.

The line should spiral off the supply spool in the *same* direction it is going onto the reel spool. Keep the rod tip several feet from the supply spool and maintain tension on the line by holding it between the thumb and forefinger of your rod-holding hand.

If you're alone, place the spool label side up on the floor and wind about 10 feet of line under tension on your reel. Now drop the rod tip. If the slack line between the rod tip and reel immediately starts to twist, you're putting the line on wrong. Flip the spool label side down and start again. The line should now wind on your reel correctly.

You should fill an open-face spinning reel slightly below the spool lip. When the line drops more than ¼ inch below the spool lip, it's time to put on new line.

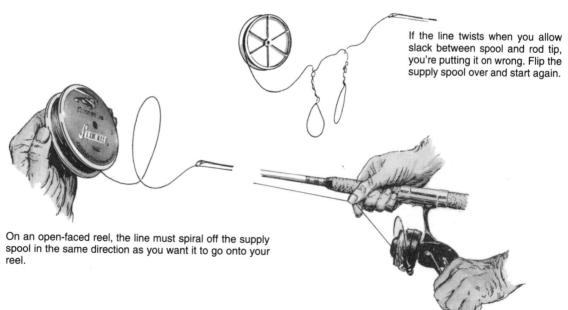

If the line twists when you allow slack between spool and rod tip, you're putting it on wrong. Flip the supply spool over and start again.

On an open-faced reel, the line must spiral off the supply spool in the same direction as you want it to go onto your reel.

REVOLVING-SPOOL REEL

If you're filling a revolving spool reel, start by pushing a pencil through the center of the supply reel. Have a friend hold both ends of the pencil and exert pressure inward on the supply spool with his hand to put tension on the line.

The line will go on evenly from side to side if the reel has a level wind. If not, make sure you wind the line on evenly. You can also use your index finger and thumb of your holding hand to maintain additional tension. Fill the spool to within 1/8 inch of the spool lip.

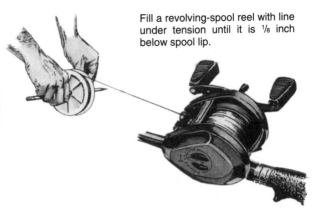

Fill a revolving-spool reel with line under tension until it is 1/8 inch below spool lip.

SPINCAST REEL

With closed-face spincast reels, use nearly the same method as for open-face spinning reels, except remove the nose cone and hold it in front of the reel while winding on line. Most spincast reels have narrow, deep spools, which means you'll lose casting distance if the line level drops below 1/8 inch on the spool.

When filling a spincast reel, slip the nose cone forward as you wind line, exposing the spool. Don't overfill the spool.

CARE AND REPAIR OF FISHING TACKLE

There's more than a germ of truth in the old saying, "A fisherman is no better than his tackle." Of course, that has also been said of quarterbacks!

Seriously, though, it pays in more ways than one to keep your gear in good working order. For one thing, proper maintenance can add a good many years to the working life of rods, reels, and other tackle on which hard-earned money has been spent. And legions of fishermen have discovered, to their chagrin, that unoiled reels can "freeze up," neglected rods can snap, and rusty lure hooks can give out—just when that lunker comes along.

The following tackle-care tips should help to prevent such problems.

CARE OF RODS

Today's rods are designed for long life, but they still require some basic maintenance. The steps recommended below should keep any rod in good working order. How often they should be applied depends upon how often the rods are used and whether they are used in fresh or salt water. It should be remembered that saltwater rods—in fact, all saltwater gear—requires much more care than freshwater rods. Even the best of tackle cannot withstand the corrosive action of salt.

1. Wash the rod, including the guides, thoroughly with soap and fresh water, rinse it with hot water, and let it dry completely. If the rod is used in salt water, this step should be taken after each use.
2. Clean the ferrules well, and give them a very light coating of grease to help prevent oxidation of the metal.
3. Apply a light coating of wax (automobile wax does a good job) to the entire rod—excluding cork handle, if the rod has one, and guides.
4. At least once each season, varnish the rod. Two thin coats are better than one heavy coat.

To avoid creating bubbles in the varnish, apply it with a finger or a pipe cleaner.

5. Put the rod into its container, and store it in a dry, safe place. If the rod is bamboo, it must be placed so that it lays flat; if stored on end, it may develop a ''set'' or permanent bend. Caution: never store in a rod case a cork-handled rod whose handle is wet, or mildew will form on the cork.

CARE OF LINES

Check each line for cracking, aging, wear, and rot. If the entire line is no longer serviceable, discard it. If one end has taken all the use, reverse the line. Fly lines tend to crack at the business end after considerable use. If the cracking is confined to the last foot or so, clip off the damaged section or, if the line is a double-taper, reverse it. If the damage is more widespread, replace the line.

Check particularly for nicks and other weak spots in monofilament, and test its breaking strength. If it's weak, replace it.

With braided line, check for dark spots, signifying rot, and test the breaking strength. Replace if weak.

CARE OF REELS

Reels are the most important item of fishing gear and must be cared for properly. The following checklist should be followed:

1. Rinse reel thoroughly with hot fresh water. If used in salt water, do this after each trip.
2. Oil sparingly.
3. Release drag tension to eliminate spring fatigue.
4. Check reel's operation. Replace worn or missing parts, and send reel to manufacturer for repair if necessary.
5. Cover reel with very light coating of oil, and store in a safe, dry place, preferably in a cloth bag (cloth permits air to enter and escape). Leather cases lock out air.

CARE OF TACKLE ACCESSORIES

Accessory equipment deserves equal time from the fisherman. Saltwater lures, for example, are expensive, so take a few minutes to rinse them off with hot fresh water after each use so that they don't corrode. The same goes for swivels, hooks, and other saltwater accessories.

The following checklist covers a general overhaul of a tackle box and its contents:

1. Remove the contents of the box, and place the items in some kind of order on a table rather than simply dumping them in a pile.
2. Use a vacuum cleaner to remove dust and dirt and other loose particles. If the box is metal, wipe the inside with an oily rag, and lubricate the hinges. If it is plastic, wash it with soap and water.
3. Examine the hooks and lures, and discard rusty hooks and all lures that are beyond repair. Make a list of those lures you'll need to restock the box while they are fresh in your mind.
4. Repair salvageable lures. A soft-wire soap pad can be a great help in sprucing up dingy plug bodies and restoring the finish on spinner blades and spoons. Check for broken, rusty, or dull lure hooks, replacing the hooks if necessary or sharpening them with a small whetstone.
5. Sharpen all hooks, and give them a light coating of oil to prevent rust.
6. Wash the bag of your landing net with a mild detergent.
7. Patch all holes and weak spots in hipboots and waders, and store them in a dark, cool spot. The best way to store boots is to hang them upside down by the boot feet. A sturdy heavy-wire coat hanger, cut in the middle of the bottom section and bent judiciously, makes an excellent and inexpensive boot-hanger.

ROD-WRAPPING TRICKS OF THE TRADE

Guides and Tension: Guides should be purchased in matched sets to assure uniformity. Feet of guides should be dressed with a file to a fine taper. Next sight your rod; you will note a slight bend, or offset. Apply guides opposite the bend; this will bring it into a straight position. Guides should be affixed with snug wrapping tension, so that you may sight after wrapping and make slight guide adjustments before applying color preserver. Do not wrap guides to the absolute breaking point of the thread. Remember, 10 or 20 wraps of thread exert very heavy presure on feet of guides. It is is possible to damage a blank by wrapping too tight.

Threads: Sizes 2/0 to E are most commonly used. Size 2/0 or A for fly, casting, or spinning rods. Size E for the heavier freshwater spinning or saltwater rods. Naturally the finer size 2/0 thread will make a neater job, but, being lighter, it is not quite as durable.

HOW TO WRAP GUIDES

1. Start by wrapping over the end of the thread toward the guide so thread end is held down by the wrapping. Using the tension from whatever type tension device you are using to hold the wrapping tight, continue to turn the rod so that each thread lies as close as possible to the preceding turn.

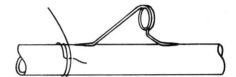

2. About 5 to 8 turns from the finish of the wrap, insert the loop of tie-off thread. (This can be 6 inches of heavier thread or a fine piece of nylon leader material.) Finish the wrap over this tie-off loop.

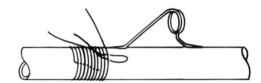

3. Holding wrap tightly, cut the wrapping thread about 4 inches from your rod. Insert this cut end through the tie-off loop. Still holding onto the wrapping thread, pull cut off thread under the wraps with tie-off loop.

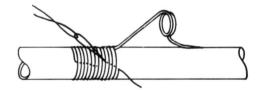

4. With a razor blade, trim cut-off end as close as possible to the wrap. With the back of a knife or your fingernail, push wrapping up tight so that it appears solid, and none of the rod or guide shows through.

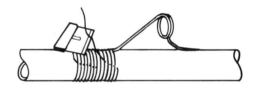

Trim: You may trim the basic color of your wrap with 5 to 10 turns of another color thread. This is done just as outlined in instructions for basic wrap.

Color Preserver and Rod Varnish: Good color preserver has plastic in it, and should be quite thin in order to penetrate the wrappings. Good-grade varnish is essential to durability of finish. A brush may be used to apply both the color preserver and rod varnish; however, air bubbles are usually present when a brush is used. To maintain a smooth finish, make certain these bubbles are out. A very satisfactory method of minimizing air bubbles is to apply both the color preserver and rod varnish with your

index finger. Usually color preserver can be worked in with index finger. This will prevent any shading of the wrapping color.

SELECTING THE TIP TOP AND OTHER GUIDES

The rod-builder, like just about everyone else, gets what he pays for. It doesn't pay to skimp on rod guides, especially if the rod is to be used in salt water or for heavy freshwater fish such as pike, muskies, and salmon.

ROD GUIDE DIAMETERS

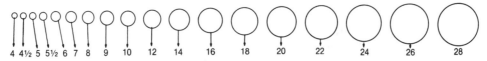

4 4½ 5 5½ 6 7 8 9 10 12 14 16 18 20 22 24 26 28

ACTUAL SIZES OF TIP GUIDES IN 1/64″

TYPES OF ROD GUIDES

Snake (Fly Rod)

Ring (Baitcasting/Spincasting)

BRIDGE (Baitcasting Spincasting)

Spinning

Loop or Foulproof (Spinning)

Roller (Big Game)

Fuji (Big Game)

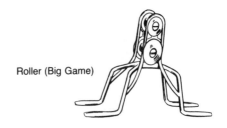

Roller (Big Game)

Guides are made of various metals, including hardened stainless steel, chrome (or chrome-plated Monel), agate, and tungsten-carbide, with the carbide types being the most durable. Roller guides for heavy saltwater fishing are usually made of stainless steel, Monel, or nickel alloy.

The rod-builder should note that the guides are available in sets tailored to particular rod types and lengths.

The tip top must fig snugly over the end of the rod, and so its selection is sometimes a problem. The chart below will help the rod-builder overcome this problem. It shows the actual sizes, in 64ths of an inch, of the inside diameters of a wide range of tip-top guides. To determine what size tip top you need, simply place the end of the rod tip over the circles until you find the correct size.

SELECTING ROD FERRULES

Many older rods still in use today utilize a ferrule system, jointlike devices inserted along the working length of a fishing rod that enables the rod to be dismantled into two or more sections. Ferrules are generally made of metal (nickel, brass, or aluminum), fiberglass, graphite, or a synthetic.

A ferrule set consists of two parts, the male ferrule and the female ferrule. The male section should fit snugly into the female section.

What size ferrule do you need for your rod? The chart at right will help you find out. It shows the actual sizes, in 64ths of an inch, of the inside diameters of a wide range of ferrules. To determine the correct ferrule for your rod, simply place the upper end of the butt section (if it is a two-piece rod) over the circles until you find the right fit.

FERRULE DIAMETERS

INSIDE DIAMETER OF FERRULES

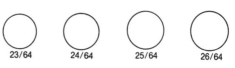

11/64   12/64   13/64   14/64   15/64   16/64   17/64

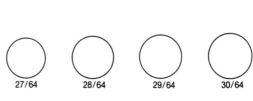

18/64   19/64   20/64   21/64   22/64

23/64   24/64   25/64   26/64

27/64   28/64   29/64   30/64

TYPES OF ROD TIPS

Ring with Support
(Spinning, Baitcasting, Spincasting)

Fly Rod

Foulproof (Spinning)

Fuji (Big Game)

Roller (Big Game)

SPACING OF ROD GUIDES

Whether you are building a fishing rod from scratch (that is, taking a fiberglass blank and adding butt, reel seat, and guides) or refinishing an old favorite, you must pay close attention to the placement of the guides along the working length of the rod.

Putting too many or too few guides on a rod, or placing them improperly, may detract from proper rod action and put undue strain on the line and the rod.

The chart below gives the correct number of guides—and exact spacing measurements—for most spinning, baitcasting, spincasting, and fly rods.

SUGGESTED GUIDE SPACING TABLE

All measurements are from tip of rod down. Figures indicate measurements at the guide ring.

	Rod Length & Type	Lure-Weight Range	Fly-Line Weights	1st	2nd	3rd	4th	5th	6th	7th	8th
Spincasting, Baitcasting	5½-ft.	⅛ to ⅓ oz.		4½"	12"	23"	36"				
	6-ft.	⅛ to ⅜ oz.		4	10	18	28	40			
	6-ft.	¼ to ¾ oz.		4	8¼	13	18	24½	32⅛	42	
	6-ft.	⅜ to 1¼ oz.		3½	7½	12	17⅜	23⅝	31⅞	42½	
	6-ft. 4-in.	1/16 to ¼ oz.		4	10	18½	28½	41			
	6-ft. 4-in.	⅜ oz.		4	10	18½	28½	41			
	6-ft. 4-in.	⅛ to ½ oz.		4	10	18½	28½	41			
	6-ft.	⅜ to ⅝ oz.		4	10	18	28	40			
	6-ft. 4-in.	¼ to ⅝ oz.		4	10	18½	28½	41			
Fly Rods	5-ft. 5-in.		5 F, 6 S	5	13	25	40				
	6-ft.		5 F, 6 S	3	7½	12	17¾	25	33	42½	
	7½-ft.		6 F, 7 S	6	13	21	30	41½	60		
	7-ft. 8-in.		6 or 7 F, 7 S	6	13	21	30	43	62		
	8-ft.		6 or 7 F, 7 S	6	13	21	30	41	52	66	
	8-ft.		7 F, 7 S	6	13	21	30	40	53	66	
	8-ft.		7 or 8 F, 7 or 8 S	6	13	21	30	41	53	66	
	8½-ft.		7 or 8 F, 7 or 8 S	6	13	21	30	40	56	73	
	8½-ft.		7 F, 7 S	6	13	21	30	40	56	73	
	8½-ft.		8 or 9 F, 8 or 9 S	6	13	21	30	40	56	73	
	9-ft.		7 or 8 F, 7 or 8 S	5	11	18	26	35	45	58½	73
	9-ft.		8 or 9 F, 8 or 9 S	5	11	18	26	35	45	58½	73
	10-ft.		9 or 10 F, 9 or 10 S	6	13	22	32	43	54½	66½	80½
Spinning Rods	6-ft.	up to ¼ oz.		5½	15½	27½	40½				
	6-ft.	up to ⅜ oz.		3½	10	19	29¼	41½			
	6½-ft.	1/16 to ¼ oz.		3½	8½	15	23	33	46		
	6½-ft.	⅛ to 1 oz.		5	10⅜	16⅜	23⅜	31⅞	44		
	6½-ft.	⅛ to ⅜ oz.		3½	8½	15	23	33	46		
	7-ft.*	1/16 to ⅜ oz.	5 or 6 F, 6 S	4	10	18	27½	38½	52½		
	7-ft.	1/16 to ⅜ oz.		4	10	18	27½	38½	52½		
	6½ ft.	¼ to ⅝ oz.		3½	8½	15	23	33	46		
	7-ft.	up to 1½ oz.		4	10	18	27½	38	51		

F = Floating   S = Sinking   * = Combination spin/fly rod

FISHING FOR THE RECORD BOOK ⸻

Where was the record largemouth bass caught? What's the weight of the biggest striped marlin ever taken? Where does a fisherman enter his catch for consideration as a possible record?

Answers to these questions and just about any other on fish records can be found in the following lists of records compiled and kept by the International Game Fish Association, 1301 East Atlantic Boulevard, Pompano Beach, Florida 33060.

The International Game Fish Association, keeper of marine gamefish world records for sport fishermen and women since 1939, assumed responsibility for maintaining records for saltwater fly fishing and freshwater angling in 1978.

The Association, long known for its development of ethical marine angling practices and promotion of the wise use of fishery resources, entered the freshwater arena when *Field & Stream* magazine transferred its 68 years of records to IGFA in March 1978. Following this lead, the Saltwater Flyrodders of America, International, designated IGFA as the official keeper of world saltwater fly-fishing records,

and the International Spin Fishing Association entrusted IGFA with their historical record files.

"IGFA's goal is to bring all sport fishing records and gamefishing data under one roof, forming a central information center for anglers, scientists, and other fishing interests throughout the world," says IGFA.

Current record programs include all-tackle records for both freshwater and saltwater fishing (on upcoming pages), as well as saltwater line class records and tippet class records for saltwater fly fishing.

While record-keeping is an important aspect of IGFA's activities, it is a relatively small part of this nonprofit organization's programs in behalf of recreational fishermen. Financed by its membership, the association also works toward fair oceanic legislation and wise fishery management. It also maintains an international library of fish and fishing. It is developing and maintaining a history of angling. It supports scientific data collection programs on gamefish resources. And it generally works to preserve the quality of sport fishing.

IGFA FRESHWATER AND SALTWATER ALL-TACKLE WORLD RECORDS ⸻

All-tackle records are kept for the heaviest fish of each species caught by an angler in any line class category up to 60 kg (130 lb). All-tackle record applications are being accepted for species not currently included on this list. See requirements beginning at the end of this table.

Species	Scientific Name	Weight	Place	Date	Angler
Albacore	*Thunnus alalunga*	40.00 kg 88 lb 2 oz	Gran Canaria Canary Islands	Nov. 19, 1977	Siegfried Dickemann
Amberjack, greater	*Seriola dumerili*	70.59 kg 155 lb 10 oz	Challenger Bank Bermuda	June 24, 1981	Joseph Dawson
Amberjack, Pacific	*Seriola colburni*	47.17 kg 104 lb	Rocas Alijos Baja Calif., Mexico	July 4, 1984	Richard W. Cresswell
Barracuda, great	*Sphyaena barracuda*	38.55 kg 85 lb	Christmas Island Rep. of Kiribati	Apr. 11, 1992	John W. Helfrich
Barracuda, Mexican	*Sphyraena ensis*	9.52 kg 21 lb	Phantom Isle Costa Rica	Mar. 27, 1987	E. Greg Kent
Barracuda, pickhandle	*Sphyraena jello*	7.85 kg 17 lb 4 oz	Sitra Channel Bahrain, Arabian Gulf	Nov. 21, 1985	Roger J. Cranswick
Barramundi	*Lates calcarifer*	28.65 kg 63 lb 2 oz	Normah River, Normahton Queensland, Australia	Apr. 28, 1991	Scott Barnsley
Bass, barred sand	*Paralabrax nebulifer*	5.98 kg 13 lb 3 oz	Huntingdon Beach California, USA	Aug. 29, 1988	Robert Halal
Bass, black sea	*Centropristis striata*	4.30 kg 9 lb 8 oz	Virginia Beach Virginia, USA	Dec. 22, 1990	Jack G. Stallings, Jr.

Species	Scientific Name	Weight	Place	Date	Angler
Bass, European	*Dicentrarchus labrax*	9.40 kg 20 lb 11 oz	Stes Maries de la Mer 13 France	May 6, 1986	Jean Baptiste Bayle
Bass, giant sea	*Stereolepis gigas*	255.60 kg 563 lb 8 oz	Anacapa Island California, USA	Aug. 20, 1968	James D. McAdam, Jr.
Bass, largemouth	*Micropterus salmoides*	10.09 kg 22 lb 4 oz	Montgomery Lake Georgia, USA	June 2, 1932	George W. Perry
Bass, peacock	*Cichla spp.*	12.24 kg 27 lb	Rio Negro Brazil	Dec. 4, 1994	Gerald "Doc" Lawson
Bass, redeye	*Micropterus coosae*	3.99 kg 8 lb 3 oz	Apalatchicola River Florida, USA	Jan. 28, 1995	Carl W. Davis
Bass, rock	*Ambloplites rupestris*	1.36 kg 3 lb	York River Ontario, Canada	Aug. 1, 1974	Peter Gulgin
Bass, smallmouth	*Micropterus dolomieui*	5.41 kg 11 lb 15 oz	Dale Hollow Lake Kentucky, USA	July 9, 1955	David L. Hayes
Bass, spotted	*Micropterus punctulatus*	4.28 kg 9 lb 7 oz	Pine Flat Lake California, USA	Feb. 25, 1994	Bob E. Shelton
Bass, striped	*Morome saxatilis*	35.60 kg 78 lb 8 oz	Atlantic City New Jersey, USA	Sept. 21, 1982	Albert R. McReynolds
Bass, striped (landlocked)	*Morone saxatilis*	30.61 kg 67 lb 8 oz	O'Neill Forebay San Louis, California, USA	May 7, 1992	Hank Ferguson
Bass, Suwannee	*Micropterus notius*	1.75 kg 3 lb 14 oz	Suwannee River Florida, USA	March 2, 1985	Ronnie Everett
Bass, white	*Morone chrysops*	3.09 kg 6 lb 13 oz	Lake Orange Orange, Virginia, USA	July 31, 1989	Ronald L. Sprouse
Bass, whiterock	*Morone saxatilis x Morone chrysops*	10.97 kg 24 lb 3 oz	Leesville Lake Virginia, USA	May 12, 1989	David N. Lambert
Bass, yellow	*Morone mississippiensis*	1.02 kg 2 lb 4 oz	Lake Monroe Indiana, USA	March 27, 1977	Donald L. Stalker
Blackjack	*Caranx lugubris*	9.50 kg 20 lb 15 oz	Cocos Islands Costa Rica	Feb. 15, 1985	Carlos M. Barrantes R.
Bluefish	*Pomatomus saltatrix*	14.40 kg 31 lb 12 oz	Hatteras North Carolina, USA	Jan. 30, 1972	James M. Hussey
Bluegill	*Lepomis macrochirus*	2.15 kg 4 lb 12 oz	Ketona Lake Alabama, USA	April 9, 1950	T. S. Hudson
Bocaccio	*Sebastes paucipinis*	9.63 kg 21 lb 4 oz	Swiftsure Bank, Neah Bay Washington, USA	July 29, 1986	Terry Rudnick
Bonefish	*Albula vulpes*	8.61 kg 19 lb	Zululand South Africa	May 26, 1962	Brian W. Batchelor
Bonito, Atlantic	*Sarda sarda*	8.30 kg 18 lb 4 oz	Fayal Island Azores	July 8, 1984	D. Gama Higgs
Bonito, Pacific	*Sarda spp.*	6.69 kg 14 lb 12 oz	San Benitos Island Baja, Calif., Mexico	Oct. 12, 1980	Jerome H. Rilling
Bowfin	*Amia calva*	9.75 kg 21 lb 8 oz	Florence South Carolina, USA	Jan. 29, 1980	Robert L. Harmon
Bream, bronze	*Arbramis brama*	6.01 kg 13 lb 3 oz	Hagbyan Creek Sweden	May 11, 1984	Luis Kilian Rasmussen
Buffalo, bigmouth	*Ictiobus cyprinellus*	31.89 kg 70 lb 5 oz	Bussey Brake, Bastrop Louisiana, USA	April 21, 1980	Delbert Sisk

(Continued next page)

ALL-TACKLE WORLD RECORDS (Continued)

Species	Scientific Name	Weight	Place	Date	Angler
Buffalo, black	*Ictiobus niger*	25.17 kg 55 lb 8 oz	Cherokee Lake Tennessee, USA	May 3, 1984	Edward H. Mc Lain
Buffalo, smallmouth	*Ictiobus bubalus*	31.07 kg 68 lb 8 oz	Lake Hamilton Arkansas, USA	May 16, 1984	Jerry L. Dolezal
Bullhead, black	*Ictalurus melas*	3.62 kg 8 lb	Lake Waccabuc New York, USA	Aug. 1, 1951	Kani Evans
Bullhead, brown	*Ictalurus nebulosus*	2.59 kg 5 lb 11 oz	Cedar Creek Florida, USA	Mar. 28, 1995	Robert Bengis
Bullhead, yellow	*Ictalurus natalis*	1.92 kg 4 lb 4 oz	Mormon Lake Arizona, USA	May 11, 1984	Emily Williams
Burbot	*Lota lota*	8.27 kg 18 lb 4 oz	Pickford Michigan, USA	Jan. 31, 1980	Thomas Courtemanche
Cabezon	*Scorpaenichthys marmoratus*	10.43 kg 23 lb	Juan De Fuca Strait Washington, USA	Aug. 4, 1990	Wesley S. Hunter
Carp	*Cyprinus carpio*	34.35 kg 75 lb 11 oz	Lac De St. Cassien France	May 21, 1987	Leo van der Gugten
Catfish, blue	*Ictaluru furcatus*	49.55 kg 109 lb 4 oz	Cooper River, Moncks Corner South Carolina, USA	Mar. 14, 1991	George A. Lijewski
Catfish, channel	*Ictalurus punctatus*	26.30 kg 58 lb	Santee-Cooper Res. South Carolina, USA	July 7, 1964	W. B Whaley
Catfish, flathead	*Pylodictis olivaris*	41.39 kg 91 lb 4 oz	Lake Lewisville Texas, USA	March 28, 1982	Mike Rogers
Catfish, gafftopsail	*Bagre marinus*	3.96 kg 8 lb 12 oz	Indian River Stuart, Florida, USA	Mar. 30, 1991	Jack Leadbeater
Catfish, tiger	*Pseudoplatystoma fasciatum*	16.55 kg 36 lb 8 oz	Rupinuni River Karanambo, Guyana	Dec. 4, 1981	William T. Miller
Catfish, white	*Ictalurus catus*	8.56 kg 18 lb 14 oz	Withlacoochee River Inverness, Florida, USA	Sept. 21, 1991	Jim Miller
Char, Arctic	*Salvelinus alpinus*	14.77 kg 32 lb 9 oz	Tree River Canada	July 30, 1981	Jeffery L. Ward
Cobia	*Rachycentron canadum*	61.50 kg 135 lb 9 oz	Shark Bay Western Australia	July 9, 1985	Peter William Goulding
Cod, Atlantic	*Gadus morhua*	44.79 kg 98 lb 12 oz	Isle of Shoals New Hampshire, USA	June 8, 1969	Alphonse J. Bielevich
Cod, Pacific	*Gadus macroephalus*	13.60 kg 30 lb	Andrew Bay Alaska, USA	July 7, 1984	Donald R. Vaughn
Conger	*Conger conger*	60.44 kg 133 lb 4 oz	Berry Head South Devon, England	June 5, 1995	Vic Evans
Corvina, orangemouth	*Cynoscion xanthulus*	24.60 kg 54 lb 3 oz	Sabana Grande Guayaquil, Ecuador	July 29, 1992	Felipe Estrada E.
Crappie, black	*Pomoxis nigromaculatus*	2.05 kg 4 lb 8 oz	Kerr Lake Virginia, USA	March 1, 1981	L. Carl Herring, Jr.
Crappie, white	*Pomoxis annularis*	2.35 kg 5 lb 3 oz	Enid Dam Mississippi, USA	July 31, 1957	Fred L. Bright
Cusk	*Brosme brosme*	15.15 kg 33 lb 6 oz	Langesund Norway	Aug. 5, 1994	Kent Ake Mikael Hakanss

Species	Scientific Name	Weight	Place	Date	Angler
Dentex	*Dentex dentex*	9.85 kg 21 lb 11 oz	Cecina Secche DiVada, Italy	May 21, 1993	Ermini Sergio
Dolly Varden	*Salvelinus malma*	8.41 kg 18 lb 9 oz	Mashutuk River Alaska, USA	July 13, 1993	Richard B. Evans
Dolphin	*Coryphaena hippurus*	39.46 kg 87 lb	Papagallo Gulf Costa Rica	Sept. 25, 1976	Manuel Salazar
Dorado	*Salminus spp.*	23.30 kg 51 lb 5 oz	Toledo (Corrientes) Argentina	Sept. 27, 1984	Armando Giudice
Drum, black	*Pogonias cromis*	51.28 kg 113 lb 1 oz	Lewes Delaware, USA	Sept. 15, 1975	Gerald M. Townsend
Drum, freshwater	*Aplodinotus grunniens*	24.72 kg 54 lb 8 oz	Nickajack Lake Tennessee, USA	April 20, 1972	Benny E. Hull
Drum, red	*Sciaenops ocellata*	42.69 kg 94 lb 2 oz	Avon North Carolina, USA	Nov. 7, 1984	David G. Deuel
Eel, marbled	*Anguilla marmorata*	16.36 kg 36 lb 1 oz	Hazelmere Dam Durban, South Africa	June 10, 1984	Ferdie Van Nooten
Eel, American	*Anguilla rostrata*	3.88 kg 8 lb 8 oz	Cliff Pond, Brewster Massachusetts, USA	May 17, 1992	Gerald G. Lapierre, Sr.
Flounder, southern	*Paralichthys lethostigma*	9.33 kg 20 lb 9 oz	Nassau Sound Florida, USA	Dec. 23, 1983	Larenza W. Mungin
Flounder, summer	*Paralichthys dentatus*	10.17 kg 22 lb 7 oz	Montauk New York, USA	Sept. 15, 1975	Charles Nappi
Gar, alligator	*Lepisosteus spatula*	126.55 kg 279 lb	Rio Grande Texas, USA	Dec. 2, 1951	Bill Valverde
Gar, Florida	*Lepisosteus platyrhincus*	9.61 kg 21 lb 3 oz	Boca Raton Florida, USA	June 3, 1981	Jeff Sabol
Gar, longnose	*Lepisosteus osseus*	22.82 kg 50 lb 5 oz	Trinity River Texas, USA	July 30, 1954	Townsend Miller
Gar, shortnose	*Lepisosteus platostomus*	2.60 kg 5 lb 12 oz	Rend Lake Illinois, USA	July 16, 1995	Donna K. Willmert
Gar, spotted	*Lepisosteus oculatus*	4.44 kg 9 lb 12 oz	Lake Mexia Mexia, Texas	Apr. 7, 1994	Rick Rivard
Goldeye	*Hiodon alosoides*	1.72 kg 3 lb 13 oz	Pierre South Dakota, USA	Aug. 9, 1987	Gary Wayne Heuer
Grayling, Arctic	*Thymallus arcticus*	2.69 kg 5 lb 15 oz	Katseyedie R. N.W.T., Canada	Aug. 16, 1967	Jeanne P. Branson
Grouper, dusky	*Epinephelus guaza*	21.25 kg 46 lb 13 oz	Porto Cervo Sardinia, Italy	Nov. 15, 1990	Luca Bonfanti
Grouper, red	*Epinephelus morio*	17.91 kg 39 lb 8 oz	Port Canaveral Florida, USA	June 11, 1991	David Lee Fox
Grouper, white	*Epinephelus aeneus*	6.85 kg 15 lb 1 oz	Dakar Senegal	Jan. 24, 1984	Michel Calendini
Haddock	*Melanogrammus aeglefinus*	5.30 kg 11 lb 11 oz	Perkins Cove Ogunquit, Maine, USA	Sept. 12, 1991	Jim Mailea
Halibut, Atlantic	*Hippoglossus hippoglossus*	115.78 kg 255 lb 4 oz	Gloucester Massachusetts, USA	July 28, 1989	Sonny Manley

(Continued next page)

ALL-TACKLE WORLD RECORDS (Continued)

Species	Scientific Name	Weight	Place	Date	Angler
Halibut, California	*Paralichthys californicus*	24.17 kg 53 lb 4 oz	Santa Rosa Island California, USA	July 7, 1988	Russell J. Harmon
Halibut, Pacific	*Hippoglossus stenolepis*	166.92 kg 368 lb	Gustavus Alaska, USA	July 5, 1991	Celia H. Dueitt
Herring, skipjack	*Alosa chrysochloris*	1.70 kg 3 lb 12 oz	Watts Bar Lake Kingston, Tennessee, USA	Feb. 14, 1982	Paul D. Goddard
Hind, red	*Epinephelus guttatus*	2.74 kg 6 lb 1 oz	Dry Tortugas Florida, USA	Jan. 23, 1993	Capt. Mark Johnson
Hogfish	*Lachnolaimus maximus*	8.84 kg 19 lb 8 oz	Daytona Beach Florida, USA	April 28, 1962	Robert E. Batson
Houndfish	*Tylosurus crocodilus*	2.35 kg 5 lb 3 oz	Grand Bahama Island Bahamas	April 5, 1984	Todd Patton
Huchen	*Hucho hucho*	34.80 kg 76 lb 11 oz	Gemeinde Spittal/Drau Osterreich, Austria	Feb. 19, 1985	Hans Offermanns
Inconnu	*Stenodus leucichthys*	24.04 kg 53 lb	Pah River Alaska, USA	Aug. 20, 1986	Lawrence E. Hudnall
Jack, almaco (Atlantic)	*Seriola rivoliana*	35.38 kg 78 lb	Argus Bank Bermuda	July 11, 1990	Joey Dawson
Jack, almaco (Pacific)	*Seriola rivoliana*	59.87 kg 132 lb	La Paz Baja Calif., Mexico	July 21, 1964	Howard H. Hahn
Jack, cottonmouth	*Uraspis secunda*	2.04 kg 4 lb 8 oz	Cat Island Bahama	May 17, 1991	Linda R. Cook
Jack, crevalle	*Caranx hippos*	26 kg 57 lb 5 oz	Barra do Kwanza Angola	Oct. 10, 1992	Cam Nicolson
Jack, horse-eye	*Caranx latus*	11.11 kg 24 lb 8 oz	Miami Florida, USA	Dec. 20, 1982	Tito Schnau
Jack, Pacific crevalle	*Caranx caninus*	13.38 kg 29 lb 8 oz	Playa Zancudo Costa Rica	Jan. 1, 1994	Ronald C. Snody
Jack, yellow	*Caranx bartholomaei*	8.81 kg 19 lb 7 oz	Alligator Light Islamorada, Florida, USA	Sept. 14, 1985	Peter Lee Ernst
Jewfish	*Epinephelus itajara*	308.44 kg 680 lb	Fernandina Beach Florida, USA	May 20, 1961	Lynn Joyner
Kahawai	*Arripis trutta*	8.74 kg 19 lb 4 oz	Currarong Australia	Apr. 9, 1994	Stephen Muller
Kawakawa	*Euthynnus affinis*	13.15 kg 29 lb	Isla Clarion Revillagigedo Islands, Mexico	Dec. 17, 1986	Ronald Nakamura
Kokanee	*Oncorhynchus nerka*	4.27 kg 9 lb 6 oz	Okanagan Lake Vernon, Canada	June 18, 1988	Norm Kuhn
Ling	*Molva molva*	37.20 kg 82 lb	Langesund Norway	May 4, 1993	Peter Arvidsson
Lingcod	*Ophiodon elongatus*	31.29 kg 69 lb	Langara Island Canada	June 16, 1992	Murray M. Romer
Mackerel, cero	*Scomberomorus regalis*	7.76 kg 17 lb 2 oz	Islamorada Florida, USA	Apr. 5, 1986	G. Michael Mills
Mackerel, frigate	*Auxis thazard*	1.35 kg 2 lb 15 oz	Fish Rock Australia	March 12, 1994	Wayne Colling
Mackerel, king	*Scomberomorus cavalla*	40.82 kg 90 lb	Key West Florida, USA	Feb. 16, 1976	Norton I. Thomton

Species	Scientific Name	Weight	Place	Date	Angler
Mackerel, Pacific sierra	*Scomberomorus sierra*	8.16 kg 18 lb	Isla de la Plata Ecuador	Mar. 24, 1990	Jorge Begue W.
Mackerel, Pacific sierra	*Scomberomorus sierra*	8.16 kg 18 lb	Salinas Ecuador	Sept. 15, 1990	Luis Alberto Flores A.
Mackerel, queen (spotted)	*Scomberomorus plurilineatus*	8.75 kg 19 lb 4 oz	Umzimkulu, Natal Rep. of South Africa	July 1, 1985	Dick Smith
Mackerel, serra Spanish	*Scomberomorus brasiliensis*	6.10 kg 13 lb 7 oz	Maracaibo Venezuela	May 12, 1985	Edgar C. Jimenez
Mackerel, Spanish	*Scomberomorus maculatus*	5.89 kg 13 lb	Ocracoke Inlet North Carolina, USA	Nov. 4, 1987	Robert Cranton
Mackerel, spotted	*Scomberomorus munroi*	5.20 kg 11 lb 7 oz	Grassy Head New South Wales, Australia	April 7, 1983	David J. Payne
Mahseer	*Barbus tor*	43.09 kg 95 lb	Cauvery River India	March 26, 1984	Robert Howitt
Margate, white	*Haemulon album*	6.57 kg 14 lb 8 oz	South Shore Bermuda	Nov. 24, 1986	J. Henry Gill
Marlin, black	*Makaira indica*	707.61 kg 1560 lb	Cabo Blanco Peru	Aug. 4, 1953	Alfred C. Glassell, Jr.
Marlin, blue (Atlantic)	*Makaira nigricans*	636 kg 1402 lb 2 oz	Vitoria Brazil	Feb. 29, 1992	Paulo Roberto A. Amorim
Marlin, blue (Pacific)	*Makaira nigricans*	624.14 kg 1376 lb	Kaaiwi Pt. Kona, Hawaii, USA	May 31, 1982	Jay Wm. deBeaubien
Marlin, striped	*Tetrapturus audax*	224.10 kg 494 lb	Tutukaka New Zealand	Jan. 16, 1986	Bill Boniface
Marlin, white	*Tetrapturus albidus*	82.50 kg 181 lb 14 oz	Vitoria Brazil	Dec. 8, 1979	Evandro Luiz Coser
Meagre	*Argyrosomus regius*	48 kg 105 lb 13 oz	Nouadhibou Mauritania	Mar. 30, 1986	Laurent Morat
Moi threadfin	Polydactylus sexfilis	3.17 kg 7 lb	Hanalei Hawaii, USA	Sept. 3, 1988	Harry H. Paik
Mullet, thin lipped	*Liza ramada*	2.38 kg 5 lb 4 oz	River Taw Barnstaple, England	June 14, 1984	Raymond John White
Muskellunge	*Esox masquinongy*	30.60 kg 67 lb 8 oz	Lake Court Oreilles Hayward, Wisconsin, USA	July 24, 1949	Cal Johnson
Muskellunge, tiger	*Esox masquinongy x Esox lucius*	23.21 kg 51 lb 3 oz	Lac Vieux-Desert Wis./Mich., USA	July 16, 1919	John A. Knobla
Needlefish, Mexican	*Strongvlura fodiator*	5.72 kg 12 lb 10 oz	Isla Coiba Panama	Aug. 19, 1979	Robert L. Spaulding
Payara	*Hydrolicus scomberoides*	15.76 kg 34 lb 12 oz	La Paragua River Lodge Paragua, Venezuela	Apr. 11, 1994	Lee Thill
Perch, white	*Morone americana*	2.15 kg 4 lb 12 oz	Messalonskee Lake Maine, USA	June 4, 1949	Mrs. Earl Small
Perch, yellow	*Perca flavescens*	1.91 kg 4 lb 3 oz	Bordentown New Jersey, USA	May, 1865	Dr. C. C. Abbot
Permit	*Trachinotus falcatus*	24.15 kg 53 lb 4 oz	Lake Worth Florida, USA	Mar. 25, 1994	Roy Brooker
Pickerel, chain	*Esox niger*	4.25 kg 9 lb 6 oz	Homerville Georgia, USA	Feb. 17, 1961	Baxley McQuaig, Jr.

(Continued next page)

ALL-TACKLE WORLD RECORDS (Continued)

Species	Scientific Name	Weight	Place	Date	Angler
Pickerel, redfin	*Esox americanus americanus*	.87 kg 1 lb 15 oz	Redhook New York, USA	Oct. 16, 1988	William G. Stagias
Pike, Northern	*Esox lucius*	25 kg 55 lb 1 oz	Lake of Grefeern West Germany	Oct. 16, 1986	Lothar Louis
Pollack	*Pollachius pollachius*	12.41 kg 27 lb 6 oz	Salcombe, Devon England	Jan. 16, 1986	Robert Samuel Milkins
Pollock	*Pollachius virens*	21.14 kg 46 lb 10 oz	Perkins Cove Ogunquit, Maine, USA	Oct. 24, 1990	Linda M. Paul
Pompano, African	*Alectis ciliaris*	22.90 kg 50 lb 8 oz	Daytona Beach Florida, USA	Apr. 21, 1990	Tom Sargent
Pompano, Florida	*Trachinotus carolinus*	3.67 kg 8 lb 1 oz	Flagler Beach Florida, USA	March 19, 1984	Chester E. Dietrick
Queenfish	*Scomberoides commersonianus*	15.60 kg 34 lb 6 oz	Daintree River N. Queensland, Australia	July 14, 1985	Peter Richard Cooper
Ray, eagle	*Myliobatidae*	17.23 kg 38 lb	River Gambia Gambia, West Africa	Jan. 14, 1985	John Prescott
Ray, painted (small-eyed)	*Raja microocellata*	4.50 kg 9 lb 15 oz	Jersey Channel Islands, England	Aug. 2, 1988	Andrew R. J. Mitchell
Ray, spiny butterfly	*Gymnura altavela*	60.00 kg 132 lb 4 oz	Nouadhibou Mauritania	May 5, 1984	Robin Michel
Redfish (Ocean perch)	*Sebastes marinus*	4.69 kg 10 lb 5 oz	Sorvfer Finnmark, Norway	July 16, 1990	Ole-Einar Jakobsen
Redhorse, golden	*Moxostoma erythrurum*	1.22 kg 2 lb 11 oz	French Creek, Franklin Pennsylvania, USA	April 26, 1992	Kristen E. Faler
Redhorse, river	*Moxostoma carinatum*	2.52 kg 5 lb 9 oz	Limestone Creek Mooresville, Alabama, USA	March 27, 1985	Don Hale
Redhorse, shorthead	*Moxostoma macrolepidotum*	2.16 kg 4 lb 12 oz	Island Park Elkhart, Indiana, USA	May 18, 1984	William A. Merrick
Redhorse, silver	*Moxostoma anisurum*	5.18 kg 11 lb 7 oz	Plum Creek Wisconsin, USA	May 29, 1985	Neal D. G. Long
Roach	*Rutilus rutilus*	1.84 kg 4 lb 1 oz	Colwick Nottingham, England	June 16, 1975	R. G. Jones
Rockfish, black	*Sebastes melanops*	4.56 kg 10 lb	Puget Sound Washington, USA	July 20, 1986	William J. Harris, DDS
Rockfish, vermillion	*Sebastes miniatus*	5.45 kg 12 lb	Depoe Bay Oregon, USA	June 2, 1990	Joseph William Lowe
Rockfish, yelloweye	*Sebastes ruberrimus*	11.90 kg 26 lb 4 oz	Dickson Island, Wells Passage Canada	Nov. 8, 1993	Alan Mace
Roosterfish	*Nematistius pectoralis*	51.71 kg 114 lb	La Paz Baja Calif., Mexico	June 1, 1960	Abe Sackheim
Runner, blue	*Caranx crysos*	3.83 kg 8 lb 7 oz	Port Aransas Texas, USA	Feb. 13, 1995	Allen E. Windecker
Runner, rainbow	*Elagatis bipinnulata*	17.05 kg 37 lb 9 oz	Isla Clarion Revillagigedo Island, Mexico	Nov. 21, 1991	Tom Pfleger
Sailfish, Atlantic	*Istiophorus platypterus*	61.40 kg 135 lb 5 oz	Lagos Nigeria	Nov. 10, 1991	Ron King
Sailfish, Pacific	*Istiophorus platypterus*	100.24 kg 221 lb	Santa Cruz Island Ecuador	Feb. 12, 1947	C. W. Stewart

Species	Scientific Name	Weight	Place	Date	Angler
Salmon, Atlantic	*Salmo salar*	35.89 kg 79 lb 2 oz	Tana River Norway	1928	Henrik Henriksen
Salmon, chinook	*Oncorhynchus tshawytscha*	44.11 kg 97 lb 4 oz	Kenai River Alaska, USA	May 17, 1985	Les Anderson
Salmon, chum	*Oncorhynchus keta*	14.51 kg 32 lb	Behm Canal Alaska, USA	June 7, 1985	Fredrick E. Thynes
Salmon, coho	*Oncorhynchus kisutch*	15.08 kg 33 lb 4 oz	Salmon River Pulaski, New York, USA	Sept. 27, 1989	Jerry Lifton
Salmon, pink	*Oncorhynchus gorbuscha*	5.94 kg 13 lb 1 oz	St. Mary's River Ontario, Canada	Sept. 23, 1992	Ray Higaki
Salmon, sockeye	*Orcorhynchus nerka*	6.88 kg 15 lb 3 oz	Kenai River Alaska, USA	Aug. 9, 1987	Stan Roach
Sauger	*Stizostedion canadense*	3.96 kg 8 lb 12 oz	Lake Sakakawea North Dakota, USA	Oct. 6, 1971	Mike Fischer
Scamp	*Mycteroperca phenax*	14.17 kg 29 lb	Dauphin Island Alabama, USA	June 2, 1995	Brett Rutledge
Scup	*Stenotomus chrysops*	2.06 kg 4 lb 9 oz	Nantucket Sound Massachusetts, USA	June 3, 1992	Sonny Richards
Seabass, Japanese (suzuki)	*Lateolabrax spp.?*	8.70 kg 19 lb 2 oz	Kano River, Numazu-shi Shizuoka, Japan	Nov. 26, 1988	Yasuaki Ohshio
Seabass, white	*Atractoscion nobilis*	37.98 kg 83 lb 12 oz	San Felipe Mexico	March 31, 1953	L. C. Baumgardner
Seatrout, spotted	*Cynoscion nebulosus*	7.25 kg 16 lb	Mason's Beach Virginia, USA	May 28, 1977	William Katko
Seventyfour	*Polysteganus undulosus*	16.00 kg 35 lb 4 oz	Mapuzi, Transkei Republic of South Africa	Aug. 17, 1985	Nolan Sparg
Shad, American	*Alosa sapidissimal*	5.10 kg 11 lb 4 oz	Connecticut River S. Hadley, Mass., USA	May 19, 1986	Bob Thibodo
Shark, blacknose	*Carcharhinus acronotus*	18.86 kg 41 lb 9 oz	Little River South Carolina, USA	July 30, 1992	Jon-Paul Hoffman
Shark, blue	*Prionace glauca*	198.22 kg 437 lb	Catherine Bay N.S.W., Australia	Oct. 2, 1976	Peter Hyde
Shark, bull	*Carcharhinus leucas*	222.26 kg 490 lb	Dauphin Island Alabama, USA	Aug. 30, 1986	Phillip Wilson
Shark, dusky	*Carcharhinus obscurus*	346.54 kg 764 lb	Longboat Key Florida, USA	May 28, 1982	Warren Girle
Shark, Greenland	*Somniosus microcephalus*	775 kg 1708 lb 9 oz	Trondheimsfjord Norway	Oct. 18, 1987	Terje Nordtvedt
Shark, hammerhead	*Sphyrna spp.*	449.50 kg 991 lb	Sarasota Florida, USA	May 30, 1982	Allen Ogle
Shark, lemon	*Negaprion brevirostris*	183.70 kg 405 lb	Buxton N. Carolina, USA	Nov. 23, 1988	Colleen D. Harlow
Shark, mako	*Isurus spp.*	505.76 kg 1115 lb	Black River Mauritius	Nov. 16, 1988	Patrick Guillanton
Shark, porbeagle	*Lamna nasus*	230 kg 507 lb	Pentland Firth Caithness, Scotland	Mar. 9, 1993	Christopher Bennet

(Continued next page)

ALL-TACKLE WORLD RECORDS (Continued)

Species	Scientific Name	Weight	Place	Date	Angler
Shark, reef white-tip	*Triaenodon obesus*	18.25 kg 40 lb 4 oz	Isla Coiba Panama	Aug. 8, 1979	Jack Kamerman
Shark, sand tiger	*Odontaspis taurus*	158.81 kg 350 lb 2 oz	Charleston Jetty South Carolina, USA	Apr. 29, 1993	Mark Thawley
Shark, six-gilled	*Hexanchus griseus*	485 kg 1069 lb 3 oz	Faial Azores	Oct. 18, 1990	Capt. Jack Reece
Shark, spinner	*Carcharhinus brevipinna*	86.18 kg 190 lb	Flagler Beach Florida, USA	Apr. 3, 1986	Mrs. Gladys Prior
Shark, spiny dogfish	*Squalus acanthias*	3.62 kg 8 lb	Cape Cod Bay Massachusetts, USA	Aug. 26, 1977	David E. Singer
Shark, thresher	*Alopias spp.*	363.80 kg 802 lb	Tutukaka New Zealand	Feb. 8, 1981	Dianne North
Shark, tiger	*Galeocerdo cuvieri*	807.40 kg 1780 lb	Cherry Grove S. Carolina, USA	June 14, 1964	Walter Maxwell
Shark, white	*Carcharodon carcharias*	1208.30 kg 2664 lb	Ceduna South Australia	April 21, 1959	Alfred Dean
Sheepshead	*Archosargus probatocephalus*	9.63 kg 21 lb 4 oz	Bayou St. John New Orleans, LA, USA	April 16, 1982	Wayne Desselle
Skate	*Raja batis*	97.07 kg 214 lb	Scapa Flow Orkney, Great Britain	July 16, 1968	Jan A. E. Olsson
Skate, starry	*Raja radiata*	4.25 kg 9 lb 5 oz	Hvasser Norway	Oct. 10, 1982	Knut Hedlund
Skipjack, black	*Euthynnus lineatus*	11.79 kg 26 lb	Thetis Bank Baja Calif., Mexico	Oct. 23, 1991	Clifford K. Hamaishi
Smooth hound, Starry	*Mustelus asterias*	4.76 kg 10 lb 8 oz	Nab Rocks Isle of Wight, England	July 18, 1984	Sylvia M. Steed
Snapper, greenbar	*Hoplopagrus guntheri*	9.58 kg 21 lb 2 oz	Solmar Beach Baja Calif., Mexico	June 15, 1994	Walt Geiger
Snapper, cubera	*Lutjanus cyanopterus*	55.11 kg 121 lb 8 oz	Cameron Louisiana, USA	July 5, 1982	Mike Hebert
Snapper, Pacific cubera	*Lutjanus novemfasciatus*	35.72 kg 78 lb 12 oz	Bahia Pez Vela Costa Rica	Mar. 23, 1988	Steven C. Paull
Snapper, gray	*Lutjanus griseus*	7.71 kg 17 lb	Port Canaveral Florida, USA	June 14, 1992	Steve Maddox
Snapper, yellowtail	*Ocyurus chrysurus*	3.85 kg 8 lb 8 oz	Gulf of Mexico, Ft. Myers Florida, USA	July 24, 1992	Suzanne Axel
Snook	*Centropomus undecimalis*	24.32 kg 53 lb 10 oz	Rio de Parasmina Costa Rica	Oct. 18, 1978	Gilbert Ponzi
Snook, fat	*Centropomus parallelus*	3.28 kg 7 lb 4 oz	Jupiter Florida, USA	Nov. 3, 1994	Theodore M. Barrick
Snook, Pacific black	*Cetropomus nigrescens*	26.19 kg 57 lb 12 oz	Rio Naranjo Quepos, Costa Rica	Aug. 23, 1991	George Beck
Spearfish	*Tetrapturus spp.*	41.20 kg 90 lb 13 oz	Madeira Island Portugal	June 2, 1980	Joseph Larkin
Splake	*Salvelinus namaycush x. S. fontinalis*	9.39 kg 20 lb 11 oz	Georgian Bay Ontario, Canada	May 17, 1987	Paul S. Thompson
Spurdog	*Squalus acanthias*	4.64 kg 10 lb 4 oz	Tobermory, Isle of Mull Argyll, Scotland	Nov. 20, 1984	Duncan Swinbanks

Species	Scientific Name	Weight	Place	Date	Angler
Steenbras, red	*Petrus rupestris*	56.60 kg 124 lb 12 oz	Aston Bay, Eastern Cape Coast, S. Africa	May 8, 1994	Terry Colin Goldstone
Sturgeon	*Acipenseridae*	212.28 kg 468 lb	Benicia California, USA	July 9, 1983	Joey Pallotta, III
Sturgeon, shovelnose	*Scaphirhynchus platorynchus*	4.88 kg 10 lb 12 oz	Missouri River Loma, Montana, USA	June 14, 1985	Arthur James Seal
Sucker, longnose	*Catostomus catostomus*	2.49 kg 5 lb 8 oz	St. Joseph River Benton Harbor, Mich., USA	Feb. 19, 1983	Ben Knoll
Sucker, spotted	*Minytrema melanops*	1.23 kg 2 lb 11 oz	Hall's Lake Rome, Georgia, USA	March 6, 1985	J. Paul Diprima, Jr.
Sucker, white	*Catostomus commersoni*	2.94 kg 6 lb 8 oz	Rainy River, Loman Minnesota, USA	April 20, 1984	Joel M. Anderson
Sunfish, green	*Lepomis cyanellus*	0.96 kg 2 lb 2 oz	Stockton Lake Missouri, USA	June 18, 1971	Paul M. Dilley
Sunfish, longear	*Lepomis megalotis*	0.79 kg 1 lb 12 oz	Elephant Butte Lake New Mexico, USA	May 9, 1985	Patricia Stout
Sunfish, pumpkinseed	*Lepomis gibbosus*	0.63 kg 1 lb 6 oz	Mexico New York, USA	April 27, 1985	Heather Ann Finch
Sunfish, redbreast	*Lepomis auritus*	0.79 kg 1 lb 12 oz	Suwannee River Florida, USA	May 29, 1984	Alvin Buchanan
Sunfish, redear	*Lepomis microlophus*	2.35 kg 5 lb 3 oz	Folsum South Canal Sacramento, California, USA	June 27, 1994	Anthony H. White, Sr.
Surubi	*Pseudoplatystoma fasciatum*	6.75 kg 14 lb 14 oz	Vallemi, Paraguay River Paraguay	Dec. 5, 1984	Jorge E. Xifra
Swordfish	*Xiphias gladius*	536.15 kg 1182 lb	Iquique Chile	May 7, 1953	L. Marron
Tanguigue	*Scomberomorus commerson*	44.90 kg 99 lb	Scottburgh Natal, South Africa	March 14, 1982	Michael John Wilkinson
Tarpon	*Megalops atlanticus*	128.50 kg 283 lb 4 oz	Sherbro Island Sierra Leone	Apr. 16, 1991	Yvon Victor Sebag
Tautog	*Tautoga onitis*	10.88 kg 24 lb	Wachapreague Virginia, USA	Aug. 25, 1987	Gregory Robert Bell
Tench	*Tinca tinca*	4.64 kg 10 lb 3 oz	Ljungbyan Sweden	July 2, 1985	Dan Dellerfjord
Tigerfish, giant	*Hydrocynus goliath*	44 kg 97 lb	Zaire River Kinshasa, Zaire	July 9, 1988	Raymond Houtmans
Tilapia	*Tilapia spp.*	2.86 kg 6 lb 5 oz	Lake Arenal Costa Rica	Feb. 10, 1995	Marvin C. Smith
Tolstolob	*Hypophthalmichthys spp.*	16.00 kg 35 lb 4 oz	Danube River Austria	Nov. 10, 1983	Josef Windholz
Tope	*Galeorhinus spp.*	32.50 kg 71 lb 10 oz	Knysna Rep. of South Africa	July 10, 1982	William F. DeWet
Trevally, bigeye	*Caranx sexfasciatus*	8.19 kg 18 lb 1 oz	Clipperton Island France	May 12, 1990	Rebecca A. Mills
Trevally, bluefin (Omilu)	*Caranx melampygus*	43.54 kg 96 lb	Christmas Island Rep. of Kiribati	Dec. 19, 1987	Harvey K. Minatoya, MD
Trevally, giant	*Caranx ignobilis*	65.99 kg 145 lb 8 oz	Makena, Maui Hawaii, USA	Mar. 28, 1991	Russell Mori

(Continued next page)

ALL-TACKLE WORLD RECORDS (Continued)

Species	Scientific Name	Weight	Place	Date	Angler
Trevally, golden	*Gnathanodon speciosus*	10.40 kg 22 lb 14 oz	Exmouth Australia	Aug. 17, 1990	Keith C. Deimel
Trevally, thicklip	*Carangoides orthogrammus*	2.55 kg 5 lb 10 oz	Christmas Island Kiribati	Aug. 12, 1982	Derek Dunn Rankin
Triggerfish	*Balistes vetula*	5.44 kg 12 lb	Ponce Inlet Florida, USA	Aug. 11, 1985	Cindy Pitts
Triggerfish, gray	*Balistes capriscus*	6.15 kg 13 lb 9 oz	Murrells Inlet South Carolina, USA	May 3, 1989	Jim Hilton
Tripletail	*Lobotes surinamensis*	19.20 kg 42 lb 5 oz	Zululand South Africa	June 7, 1989	Steve Hand
Trout, Apache	*Salmo apache*	2.36 kg 5 lb 3 oz	White Mt. Apache Res. Arizona, USA	May 29, 1991	John (TRES) Baldwin
Trout, brook	*Salvelinus fontinalis*	6.57 kg 14 lb 8 oz	Nipigon R. Ontario, Canada	July, 1916	Dr. W. J. Cook
Trout, brown	*Salmo trutta*	18.25 kg 40 lb 4 oz	Little Red River Herber Springs, Arkansas, USA	May 9, 1992	Howard L. (Rip) Collins
Trout, bull	*Salvelinus confluentus*	14.51 kg 32 lb	Lake Pond Orielle Idaho, USA	Oct. 27, 1949	N. L. Higgins
Trout, cutthroat	*Salmo clarki*	*18.59 kg* *41 lb*	*Pyramid Lake* *Nevada, USA*	*Dec., 1925*	*John Skimmerhorn*
Trout, golden	*Salmo aguabonita*	4.98 kg 11 lb	Cooks Lake Wyoming, USA	Aug. 5, 1948	Chas. S. Reed
Trout, lake	*Salvelinus namaycush*	30.16 kg 66 lb 8 oz	Great Bear Lake N.W.T., Canada	July 19, 1991	Rodney Harback
Trout, ohrid	*Salmo letnica*	6.46 kg 14 lb 4 oz	Watauga Lake, Hampton Tennessee, USA	Mar. 28, 1986	Richard L. Carter
Trout, rainbow	*Salmo gairdneri*	19.10 kg 42 lb 2 oz	Bell Island Alaska, USA	June 22, 1970	David Robert White
Trout, tiger	*Salmo trutta x Salvelinus fontinalis*	9.44 kg 20 lb 13 oz	Lake Michigan Wisconsin, USA	Aug. 12, 1978	Pete M. Friedland
Tuna, bigeye (Atlantic)	*Thunnus obesus*	170.32 kg 375 lb 8 oz	Ocean City Maryland, USA	Aug. 26, 1977	Cecil Browne
Tuna, bigeye (Pacific)	*Thunnus obesus*	197.31 kg 435 lb	Cabo Blanco Peru	April 17, 1957	Dr. Russel V. A. Lee
Tuna, blackfin	*Thunnus atlanticus*	19.05 kg 42 lb	Challenger Bank Bermuda	July 18, 1989	Gilbert C. Pearman
Tuna, blackfin	*Thunnus atlanticus*	19.05 kg 42 lb	Bermuda	June 2, 1978	Alan J. Card
Tuna, bluefin	*Thunnus thynnus*	679.00 kg 1496 lb	Aulds Cove Novia Scotia, Canada	Oct. 26, 1979	Ken Fraser
Tuna, dogtooth	*Gymnosarda unicolor*	131.00 kg 288 lb 12 oz	Kwan-Tall Island N. Cheju-Do, Korea	Oct. 6, 1982	Boo-Il Oh
Tuna, longtail	*Thunnus tonggol*	35.90 kg 79 lb 2 oz	Montague Island N.S.W., Australia	April 12, 1982	Tim Simpson
Tuna, skipjack	*Euthynnus pelamis*	19 kg 41 lb 14 oz	Pearl Beach Mauritius	Nov. 12, 1985	Edmund K. R. Heinzen

Species	Scientific Name	Weight	Place	Date	Angler
Tuna, southern bluefin	*Thunnus maccoyi*	158.00 kg 348 lb 5 oz	Whakatane New Zealand	Jan. 16, 1981	Rex Wood
Tuna, yellowfin	*Thunnus albacares*	176.35 kg 388 lb 12 oz	San Benedicto I. Mexico	April 1, 1977	Curt Wiesenhutter
Tunny, little	*Euthynnus alletteratus*	15.95 kg 35 lb 2 oz	Cap de Garde Algeria	Dec. 14, 1988	Jean Yves Chatard
Vimba (Zahrte)	*Vimba vimba*	1.14 kg 2 lb 8 oz	Olandsan, Sweden	May 1, 1990	Sonny Petterson
Wahoo	*Acanthocybium solanderi*	70.53 kg 155 lb 8 oz	San Salvador Bahamas	Apr. 3, 1990	William Bourne
Walleye	*Stizostedion vitreum vitreum*	11.34 kg 25 lb	Old Hickory Lake Tennessee, USA	April 1, 1960	Mabry Harper
Warmouth	*Lepomis gulosus*	1.10 kg 2 lb 7 oz	Guess Lake, Yellow River Holt, Florida, USA	Oct. 19, 1985	Tony David Dempsey
Weakfish	*Cynoscion regalist*	8.67 kg 19 lb 2 oz	Jones Beach Inlet Long Island, New York, USA	Oct. 11, 1984	Dennis Roger Rooney
Weaver, greater	*Trachinus draco*	1.67 kg 3 lb 11 oz	Gran Canaria Canary Islands	March 31, 1984	Arild J. Danielsen
Whitefish, broad	*Prosopium nasus*	4.08 kg 9 lb	Tozitna River Alaska, USA	July 17, 1989	Al Mathews
Whitefish, lake	*Coregonus clupeaformis*	6.52 kg 14 lb 6 oz	Meaford Ontario, Canada	May 21, 1984	Dennis M. Laycock
Whitefish, mountain	*Prosopium williamsoni*	2.43 kg 5 lb 6 oz	Rioh River Saskatchewan, Canada	June 15, 1988	John R. Bell
Whitefish, river	*Coregonus lavaretus*	5.06 kg 11 lb 2 oz	Skrabean Nymoua, Sweden	Dec. 9, 1984	Jorgen Larsson
Whitefish, round	*Prosopium cylindraceum*	2.72 kg 6 lb	Putahow River Manitoba, Canada	June 14, 1984	Allan J. Ristori
Wolffish, Atlantic	*Anarhichas lupus*	23.58 kg 52 lb	George's Bank Massachusetts, USA	June 11, 1986	Frederick Gardiner
Wolffish, northern	*Anarhichas denticulatus*	17.00 kg 37 lb 7 oz	Holsteinsborg Greenland	Aug. 19, 1982	Jens Ploug Hansen
Wolffish, spotted	*Anarhichas minor*	23.35 kg 51 lb 7 oz	Holsteinsborg Greenland	Aug. 20, 1982	Jens Ploug Hansen
Wrasse ballan	*Labrus bergylta*	4.35 kg 9 lb 9 oz	Clogher Head Co. Kerry, Ireland	Aug. 20, 1983	Bertrand Kron
Wreckfish	*Poliprion americanus*	48.50 kg 106 lb 14 oz	S. Miguel Azores Islands, Portugal	Aug. 2, 1985	Friedrich Schopf
Yellowtail, Asian	*Seriola lalandei aureovittata*	18.30 kg 40 lb 5 oz	Miyake Island Tokyo, Japan	Oct. 23, 1982	Masahiko Kuwata
Yellowtail, California	*Seriola lalandrei dorsalis*	35.97 kg 79 lb 4 oz	Alijos Rocks Baja Calif., Mexico	July 2, 1991	Robert I. Welker
Yellowtail, southern	*Seriola lalandei lalandei*	52.00 kg 114 lb 10 oz	Tauranga New Zealand	Feb. 5, 1984	Mike Godfrey
Zander	*Stizostedion lucioperca*	11.42 kg 25 lb 2 oz	Trosa Sweden	June 12, 1986	Harry Lee Tennison

INTERNATIONAL ANGLING RULES

The following angling rules have been formulated by the International Game Fish Association to promote ethical and sporting angling practices, to establish uniform regulations for the compilation of world game fish records, and to provide basic angling guidelines for use in fishing tournaments and any other group angling activities.

The word "angling" is defined as catching or attempting to catch fish with a rod, reel, line, and hook as outlined in the international angling rules. There are some aspects of angling that cannot be controlled through rulemaking, however. Angling regulations cannot insure an outstanding performance from each fish, and world records cannot indicate the amount of difficulty in catching the fish. Captures in which the fish has not fought or has not had a chance to fight do not reflect credit on the fisherman, and only the angler can properly evaluate the degree of achievement in establishing the record.

Only fish caught in accordance with IGFA international angling rules, and within the intent of these rules, will be considered for world records.

Following are the rules for freshwater and saltwater fishing and a separate set of rules for fly fishing.

Rules for Fishing in Fresh and Salt Water

(Also see *Rules for Fly fishing*)

Equipment Regulations

A. Line

1. Monofilament, multifilament, and lead core multifilament lines may be used. For line classes, see *World Record Requirements*.
2. Wire lines are prohibited.

B. Line Backing

1. Backing not attached to the fishing line is permissible with no restrictions as to size or material.
2. If the fishing line is attached to the backing, the catch shall be classified under the heavier of the two lines. The backing may not exceed the 130 lb (60 kg) line class and must be of a type of line approved for use in these angling rules.

C. Double Line

The use of a double line is not required. If one is used, it must meet the following specifications:
1. A double line must consist of the actual line used to catch the fish.

2. Double lines are measured from the start of the knot, braid, roll, or splice making the double to the farthermost end of the knot, splice, snap, swivel, or other device used for securing the trace, leader, lure or hook to the double line.

Saltwater species: In all line classes up to and including 20 lb (10 kg), the double line shall be limited to 15 feet (4.57 meters). The combined length of the double line and leader shall not exceed 20 feet (6.1 meters).

The double line on all classes of tackle over 20 lb (10 kg) shall be limited to 30 feet (9.14 meters). The combined length of the double line and leader shall not exceed 40 feet (12.19 meters).

Freshwater species: The double line on all classes of tackle shall not exceed 6 feet (1.82 meters). The combined length of the double line and the leader shall not exceed 10 feet (3.04 meters).

D. Leader

The use of a leader is not required. If one is used, it must meet the following specifications:
1. The length of the leader is the overall length including any lure, hook arrangement or other device. The leader must be connected to the line with a snap, knot, splice, swivel, or other device. Holding devices are prohibited. There are no regulations regarding the material or strength of the leader.

Saltwater species: In all line classes up to and including 20 lb (10 kg), the leader shall be limited to 15 feet (4.57 meters). The combined length of the double line and leader shall not exceed 20 feet (6.1 meters).

The leader on all classes of tackle over 20 lb (10 kg) shall be limited to 30 feet (9.14 meters). The combined length of the double line and leader shall be limited to 40 feet (12.19 meters).

Freshwater species: The leader on all classes of tackle shall be limited to 6 feet (1.82 meters). The combined length of the double line and leader shall not exceed 10 feet (3.04 meters).

E. Rod

1. Rods must comply with sporting ethics and customs. Considerable latitude is allowed in the choice of a rod, but rods giving the angler an unfair advantage will be disqualified. This rule is intended to eliminate the use of unconventional rods.
2. The rod tip must be a minimum of 40 inches (101.6 cm) in length. The rod butt cannot exceed 27 inches (68.58 cm) in length. These measurements must be made from a point directly beneath the center of the reel. A curved butt is measured in a straight line. (The above measurements do not apply to surf casting rods.)

F. Reel

1. Reels must comply with sporting ethics and customs.

2. Power driven reels of any kind are prohibited. This includes motor, hydraulic, or electrically driven reels, and any device which gives the angler an unfair advantage.

3. Ratchet handle reels are prohibited.

4. Reels designed to be cranked with both hands at the same time are prohibited.

G. Hooks For Bait Fishing

1. For live or dead bait fishing no more than two single hooks may be used. Both must be firmly imbedded in or securely attached to the bait. The eyes of the hooks must be no less than a hook's length (the length of the largest hook used) apart and no more than 18 inches (45.72 cm) apart. The only exception is that the point of one hook may be passed through the eye of the other hook.

2. The use of a dangling or swinging hook is prohibited. Double or treble hooks are prohibited.

3. A two-hook rig for bottom fishing is acceptable if it consists of two single hooks on separate leaders or drops. Both hooks must be imbedded in the respective baits and separated sufficiently so that a fish caught on one hook cannot be foul-hooked by the other.

4. All record applications made for fish caught on two-hook tackle must be accompanied by a photograph or sketch of the hook arrangement.

H. Hooks And Lures

1. When using an artificial lure with a skirt or trailing material, no more than two single hooks may be attached to the line, leader, or trace. The hooks need not be attached separately. The eyes of the hooks must be no less than an overall hook's length (the overall length of the largest hook used) apart and no more than 12 inches (30.48 cm) apart. The only exception is that the point of one hook may be passed through the eye of the other hook. The trailing hook may not extend more than a hook's length beyond the skirt of the lure. A photograph or sketch showing the hook arrangement must accompany a record application.

2. Gang hooks are permitted when attached to plugs and other artificial lures that are specifically designed for this use. Gang hooks must be free-swinging and shall be limited to a maximum of three hooks (either single, double, or treble, or a combination of any three). Baits may not be used with gang hooks. A photograph or sketch of the plug or lure must be submitted with record applications.

I. Other Equipment

1. *Fighting chairs* may not have any mechanically propelled devices which aid the angler in fighting a fish.

2. *Gimbals* must be free swinging, which includes gimbals that swing in a vertical plane only. Any gimbal that allows the angler to reduce strain or to rest while fighting the fish is prohibited.

3. *Gaffs and nets* used to boat or land a fish must not exceed 8 feet (2.44 meters) in overall length. In using a flying or detachable gaff the rope may not exceed 30 feet (9.14 meters). The gaff rope must be measured from the point where it is secured to the detachable head to the other end. Only the effective length will be considered. If a fixed head gaff is used, the same limitations shall apply and the gaff rope shall be measured from the same location on the gaff hook. Only a single hook is permitted on any gaff. Harpoon or lance attachments are prohibited. Tail ropes are limited to 30 feet (9.14 meters). (When fishing from a bridge, pier, or other high platform or structure, this length limitation does not apply.)

4. *Floats* are prohibited with the exception of any small flotation device attached to the line or leader for the sole purpose of regulating the depth of the bait. The flotation device must not in any way hamper the fighting ability of the fish.

5. *Entangling devices,* either with or without a hook, are prohibited and may not be used for any purpose including baiting, hooking, fighting, or landing the fish.

6. *Outriggers, downriggers, and kites* are permitted to be used provided that the actual fishing line is attached to the snap or other release device, either directly or with some other material. The leader or double line may not be connected to the release mechanism either directly or with the use of a connecting device.

7. *A safety line* may be attached to the rod provided that it does not in any way assist the angler in fighting the fish.

Angling Regulations

1. From the time that a fish strikes or takes a bait or lure, the angler must hook, fight, and land or boat the fish without the aid of any other person, except as provided in these regulations.

2. If a rod holder is used and a fish strikes or takes the bait or lure, the angler must remove the rod from the holder as quickly as possible. The intent of this rule is that the angler shall strike and hook the fish with the rod in hand.

3. In the event of a multiple strike on separate lines being fished by a single angler, only the first fish fought by the angler will be considered for a world record.

4. If a double line is used, the intent of the regulations is that the fish will be fought on the single line most of the time that it takes to land the fish.

5. A harness may be attached to the reel or rod, but not to the fighting chair. The harness may be replaced or adjusted by a person other than the angler.

6. Use of a rod belt or waist gimbal is permitted.

7. When angling from a boat, once the leader is brought within the grasp of the mate, or the end of the leader is wound to the rod tip, more than one person is permitted to hold the leader.

8. One or more gaffers may be used in addition to persons holding the leader. The gaff handle must be in hand when the fish is gaffed.

9. The angling and equipment regulations shall apply until the fish is weighed.

Any of the following will disqualify a catch:

1. Failure to comply with equipment or angling regulations.

2. The act of persons other than the angler in touching any part of the rod, reel, or line (including the double line) either bodily or with any device, from the time a fish strikes or takes the bait or lure, until the fish is either landed or released, or in giving any aid other than that allowed in the rules and regulations. If an obstacle to the passage of the line through the rod guides has to be removed from the line, then the obstacle shall be held and cut free. The line may not be held or touched by anyone other than the angler during the process.

3. Resting the rod in a rod holder, on the gunwale of the boat, or any other object while playing the fish.

4. Handlining or using a handline or rope attached in any manner to the angler's line or leader for the purpose of holding or lifting the fish.

5. Shooting, harpooning, or lancing any fish (including sharks and halibuts) at any stage of the catch.

6. Chumming with or using as bait the flesh, blood, skin, or any part of mammals other than hair or pork rind used in lures designed for trolling or casting.

7. Using a boat or device to beach or drive a fish into shallow water in order to deprive the fish of its normal ability to swim.

8. Changing the rod or reel while the fish is being played.

9. Splicing, removing, or adding to the line while the fish is being played.

10. Intentionally foul-hooking a fish.

11. Catching a fish in a manner that the double line never leaves the rod tip.

12. Using a size or kind of bait that is illegal to possess.

13. Attaching the angler's line or leader to part of a boat or other object for the purpose of holding or lifting the fish.

14. If a fish escapes before gaffing or netting and is recaptured by any method other than as outlined in the angling rules.

15. When a rod breaks (while the fish is being played) in a manner that reduces the length of the tip below minimum dimensions or severely impairs its angling characteristics.

16. Mutilation to the fish, prior to landing or boating the catch, caused by sharks, other fish, mammals, or propellers that remove or penetrate the flesh. (Injuries caused by leader or line, scratches, old healed scars, or regeneration deformities are not disqualifying injuries.) Any mutilation on the fish must be shown in a photograph and fully explained in a separate report accompanying the record application.

17. When a fish is hooked or entangled on more than one line.

Rules for Fly Fishing

Equipment Regulations

A. Line

Any type of fly line and backing may be used. The breaking strength of the fly line and backing are not restricted.

B. Leader

Leaders must conform to generally accepted fly fishing customs.

A leader includes a class tippet and, optionally, a shock tippet. A butt or taper section between the fly line and the class tippet shall also be considered part of the leader and there are no limits on its length, material, or strength.

A class tippet must be made of nonmetallic material and either attached directly to the fly or to the shock tippet if one is used. The class tippet must be at least 15 inches (38.10 cm) long (measured inside connecting knots). With respect to knotless, tapered leaders, the terminal 15 inches (38.10 cm) will also determine tippet class. There is no maximum length limitation. The breaking strength determines the class of the tippet.

A shock tippet, not to exceed 12 inches (30.48 cm) in length, may be added to the class tippet and tied to the lure. It can be made of any type of material, and there is no limit on its breaking strength.

ILLUSTRATED GUIDE TO EQUIPMENT REGULATIONS

DOUBLE LINES AND LEADERS

Double lines are measured from the start of the knot, braid, roll or splice making the double to the farthermost end of the knot, splice, snap, swivel or other device used for securing the trace, leader, lure or hook to the double line. For saltwater species the double line shall be limited to 15 feet (4.57 meters) for all line classes up to and including 20 lb (10 kg); and shall be limited to 30 feet (9.14 meters) for line classes over 20 lb (10 kg). For freshwater species the double line on all classes of tackle shall not exceed 6 feet (1.82 meters).

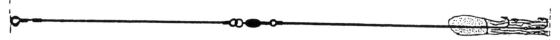

The leader shall be limited to 15 feet (4.57 meters) for saltwater species in line classes up to 20 lb (10 kg), and 30 feet (9.14 meters) for all line classes over 20 lb (10 kg). For freshwater species the leader on all classes of tackle shall be limited to 6 feet (1.82 meters).

The length of the leader is the overall length including any lure, hook arrangements or other device.

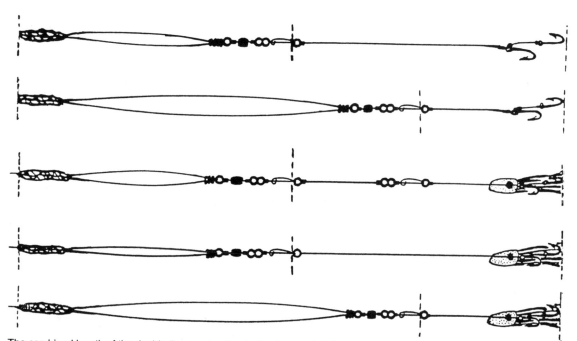

The combined length of the double line and leader shall not exceed 20 feet (6.1 meters) in line classes up to and including 20 lb (10 kg) and 40 feet (12.19 meters) in line classes over 20 lb (10 kg) for saltwater species. The combined length of the double line and leader shall not exceed 10 feet (3.04 meters) for freshwater species.

HOOKS

LEGAL if eyes of hooks no more than 18 inches (45.72 cm) apart in baits and no more than 12 inches (30.45 cm) apart in lures. ILLEGAL if eyes further apart than these distances.

NOT LEGAL in bait or lures as eyes of hooks are less than hook's length (the length of the largest hook) apart.

LEGAL as eyes of hooks are no less than a hook's length apart and no more than 18 inches (45.72 cm) in baits and 12 inches (30.45 cm) in lures.

LEGAL in bait and lures. The point of one hook is passed through the eye of the other hook.

LEGAL as eyes of hooks are no less than a hook's length apart and no more than 12 inches (30.45 cm) apart, and the trailing hook does not extend more than a hook's length beyond the skirt.

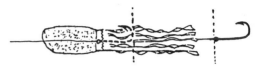

NOT LEGAL as the second or trailing hook extends more than the hook's length beyond skirt. See also two hook rigs.

LEGAL as hook is contained within skirt.

NOT LEGAL as the single hook extends more than its length beyond the skirt.

NOT LEGAL as back hook is not firmly imbedded in or securely attached to bait and is a dangling or swinging hook.

LEGAL as both hooks are firmly imbedded or securely attached to bait. Would not be legal if eyes of hooks were more than 18 inches (45.72 cm) apart.

GAFFS

LEGAL on boats if effective length does not exceed 30 feet (9.14 meters).

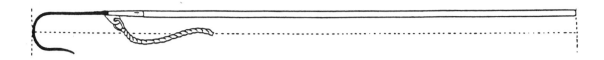

LEGAL on boats if overall length does not exceed 8 feet (2.43 meters).

The shock tippet is measured from the eye of the hook to the single strand of class tippet and includes any knots used to connect the shock tippet to the class tippet. In the case of a tandem hook fly, the shock tippet shall be measured from the eye of the leading hook.

C. Rod

Regardless of material used or number of sections, rods must conform to generally accepted fly fishing customs and practices: A rod shall not measure less than 6 feet (1.82 meters) in overall length. Any rod that gives the angler an unsporting advantage will be disqualified. Extension butts are limited to 6 inches (15.24 cm).

D. Reel

The reel must be designed expressly for fly fishing. There are no restrictions on gear ratio or type of drag employed except where the angler would gain an unfair advantage. Electric or electronically operated reels are prohibited.

E. Hooks

A conventional fly may be dressed on a single or double hook or two single hooks in tandem. The second hook in any tandem fly must not extend beyond the wing material. The eyes of the hooks shall be no farther than 6 inches (15.24 cm) apart. Treble hooks are prohibited.

F. Lures

The lure must be a recognized type of artificial fly, which includes streamer, bucktail, tube fly, wet fly, dry fly, nymph, popper, and bug. Only one fly is allowed. The use of any other type of lure or natural or preserved bait, either singularly or attached to the fly, is expressly prohibited. The fact that a lure can be cast with a fly rod is not evidence in itself that it fits the definition of a fly. The use of any lure designed to entangle or foul-hook a fish is prohibited.

G. Gaffs & Nets

Gaffs and nets used to boat or land a fish must not exceed 8 feet (2.44 meters) in overall length.

(When fishing from a bridge, pier, or other high structure, this length limitation does not apply.) The use of a flying gaff is not permitted. Only a single hook is permitted on any gaff. Harpoon or lance attachments are prohibited. A rope or any extension cannot be attached to the gaff.

Angling Regulations

1. The angler must cast, hook, fight, and bring the fish to gaff or net unaided by any other person. No other person may touch any part of the tackle during the playing of the fish or give aid other than taking the leader for gaffing or netting purposes.

2. Casting and retrieving must be carried out in accordance with normal customs and generally accepted practices. The major criterion in casting is that the weight of the line must carry the lure rather than the weight of the lure carrying the line. Trolling a lure behind a moving water craft is not permitted. The craft must be completely out of gear both at the time the fly is presented to the fish and during the retrieve.

3. Once a fish is hooked, the tackle may not be altered in any way, with the exception of adding an extension butt.

4. Fish must be hooked on the lure in use. If a small fish takes the lure and a larger fish swallows the smaller fish, the catch will be disallowed.

5. One or more people may assist in gaffing or netting the fish.

6. The angling and equipment regulations shall apply until the fish is weighed.

Any of the following will disqualify a catch:

1. Failure to comply with equipment or angling regulations.

2. The act of persons other than the angler in touching any part of the rod, reel, or line either bodily or with any device during the playing of the fish, or in giving any aid other than that allowed in the rules and regulations. If an obstacle to the passage of the line through the rod guides has to be removed from the line, then the obstacle shall be held and cut free. Under no circumstances should the line be held or touched by anyone other than the angler during this process.

3. Resting the rod on any part of the boat, or any other object while playing the fish.

4. Handlining or using a handline or rope attached in any manner to the angler's line or leader for the purpose of holding or lifting the fish.

5. Intentionally foul-hooking or snagging a fish.

6. Shooting, harpooning, or lancing any fish (including sharks and halibut) at any stage of the catch.

7. Chumming with the flesh, blood, skin, or any part of mammals.

8. Using a boat or device to beach or drive a fish into shallow water in order to deprive the fish of its normal ability to swim.

9. Attaching the angler's line or leader to part of a boat or other object for the purpose of holding or lifting the fish.

10. If a fish escapes before gaffing or netting and is recaptured by any method other than as outlined in the angling rules.

11. When a rod breaks (while the fish is being played) in a manner that reduces its length below minimum dimensions or severely impairs its angling characteristics.

12. When a fish is hooked or entangled on more than one line.

13. Mutilation to the fish, prior to landing or boating the catch, caused by sharks, other fish, mammals, or propellers that remove or penetrate the flesh. (Injuries caused by leader or line, scratches, old healed scars or regeneration deformities are not considered to be disqualifying injuries.) Any mutilation on the fish must be shown in a photograph and fully explained in a separate report accompanying the record application.

ESTIMATING FISH WEIGHT

You've just caught a big northern pike. In fact it goes 40 inches, according to the stick-on tape measure you got free from the bait shop. Now you want to know how much that pike weighs . . . but you don't have a scale.

Over the years, fishermen have come up with several ways to estimate fish weight without a scale. Some proved to be fairly accurate, some didn't even come close. Eventually, the generally accepted formula became:

Length times Girth squared divided by 800 equals Weight
or, $L \times G^2 \div 800 = W$

Using this formula is supposed to bring you within 10 percent of a fish's actual weight. The only problem is that the formula doesn't differentiate between fat fish (such as bass or tuna) and elongate fish (pike or barracuda).

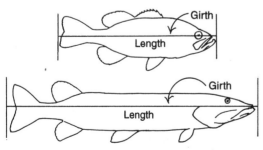

The traditional formula for determining the weight of a fish didn't take into account its shape—either elongate (above) or round (above left). The old equation could be off by as much as 10 percent.

Doug Hannon, a renowned Florida bass fisherman, has developed a more precise calculation specifically for bass and similarly shaped "round" fish. In addition to being more accurate, it requires only one measurement. Hannon's formula is:

Length cubed divided by 1,600 equals Weight
or, $L^3 \div 1,600 = W$

If you caught a 20-inch bass, for example, the math would be $20 \times 20 \times 20$ (8,000), divided by 1,600. Congratulations, that's a nice five-pounder.

With the widespread adoption of catch-and-release, fishermen have developed modifications of the "length cubed" formula that work well with

other species. For pike, muskies, and other elongate fish:

$$L^3 \div 3500 = W$$

In other words, that 40-inch pike you caught would weigh about 18.3 pounds. (Actually it's 18.28, but any fisherman is allowed to round up to the higher tenth.)

If you're a panfish specialist, the formula you want to use is:

$$L^3 \div 1200 = W$$

An eight-inch bluegill, for example, would weigh 0.42 pounds. And if walleyes are your target, the formula changes slightly to:

$$L^3 \div 2700 = W$$

This means the 22-inch walleye you boasted was a 10-pounder really weighed about four pounds.

FIELD CARE AND DRESSING OF FISH

If you sit down at the dinner table and bite into a poor-tasting bass or walleye fillet from a fish you caught, there's a good chance that the second-rate taste is your own fault. In all probability, the fish was not handled properly from the moment it came out of the water. Fish spoil rapidly unless they are kept alive or quickly killed and put on ice.

Here are the necessary steps involved in getting a fresh-caught fish from the water to the table, so that it will retain its original flavor.

First, the decision to keep a fish dead or alive depends on conditions. For example, if you're out on a lake and have no ice in your boat, you'll want to keep all fish alive until it's time to head home. Under no circumstances should you toss fish into the bottom of the boat, let them lie there in the sun, then gather them up at the end of the day. If you try that stunt, the fillets will reach your table with the consistency of mush and a flavor to match. Instead, put your fish on a stringer as quickly as possible and put them back into the water, where they can begin to recover from the shock of being caught.

Use the safety-pin type stringer and run the wire up through the thin almost-transparent membrane just behind the fish's lower lip. This will enable the fish to swim freely, and the fish will recover from this minor injury should you decide to release it at the end of the day.

Do NOT shove the stringer under the gill cover and out of the mouth. This damages gills and kills fish fast. Also avoid cord stringers, where all fish are bunched in a clump at the end of the cord. This is perhaps acceptable on short trips for small panfish, which are generally caught in big numbers and quickly cleaned. But if you're after bigger fish and want to keep them alive and fresh, either for the table or release at the end of the day, use the safety-pin stringer. It does its job well.

If you're rowing or trolling slowly, you can probably keep the stringer in the water. If you have a big boat and motor, however, it's a good idea to take the stringer into the boat for those fast runs to

With a safety-pin stringer, run the clip through the thin membrane behind the lower lip. This lets the fish swim freely and won't injure the fish should you decide to release it.

other hotspots. If the run is fairly long, wet down the fish occasionally. But don't tow a fish in the water at high speed—you'll drown it.

If you're several miles from camp, use the following technique to get fish back alive. When returning to camp with a stringer of fish, stop your boat every half mile or so and ease the fish over the side. Let the fish swim around for 5 minutes or so before hauling them back into the boat and continuing the trip to camp. This way, you should have no trouble reaching camp with lively walleyes to be put in your shoreline live box. Keeping fish alive is especially important on extended trips to remote areas, where ice in sufficient quantity isn't generally available.

On the subject of lengthy fishing trips to remote areas where ice is not available, you can still keep fish alive for a week or more. Your best bet is to use a homemade collapsible fish box, which can be weighted with a rock in a foot of water on shore or floated in deep water (see photo). Either way, the fish will stay alive until the end of the trip. Keeping fish alive for lengthy periods in remote areas is impossible without such a box. Keeping fish on a stringer at dockside will *not* work for long periods. With some wood and wire mesh, a fish box is easy to build. The box in these photos will give you a rough idea of size and construction.

We're assuming, of course, that a fish has been unhooked and is placed in the fish box in good condition. If it has been deeply hooked and appears to be dying slowly, however, it's best to kill the fish immediately, gut it, and keep it on ice.

Killing a fish quickly is simple. Holding the fish upright, impale it between the eyes with the point of your knife or rap it on the head with a heavy stick. The important factor is killing it quickly, since the more slowly it dies the more rapidly the flesh will deteriorate.

If you're a stream fisherman, it's wise to carry your catch in a canvas or wicker creel. The canvas creel works fine, so long as it is occasionally immersed in water. The traditional wicker creel will work just as well, but it should be lined with ferns, leaves, or wet newspaper.

If you're a surf fisherman, you can bury your catch in the damp sand. Just remember to mark the spot. A burlap sack occasionally doused in the surf also makes a practical fish bag. The important factor is to keep the fish cool and out of the sun.

Regardless of the various ways to keep fish cool, they should first be cleaned properly. With a bit of practice and a sharp knife, the job can be done in less than a minute.

Take a sharp knife, and insert it in the anal opening on the underside of the fish. Slit the skin forward from there to the point of the V-shaped area where the forward part of the belly is attached to the gills. Put your finger into the gills and around that V-shaped area, and pull sharply to the rear. You will thus remove the gills and all or most of the entrails. Then, with the fish upside down, put your thumb into the body cavity at the anal opening, and press the thumbnail up against the backbone. Keeping the nail tight against the bone, run your thumb forward to the head, thereby removing the dark blood from the sac along the backbone.

HOW TO KEEP FISH ALIVE

This is a collapsible live box for use on long trips where ice is not available in camp. Floated in deep water, the box will keep a goodly number of fish alive over an extended period. The box need not be floated in deep water. It can also be weighted with a rock along shoreline, so fish can be dropped in without the need to haul the box out of the water.

That completes the cleaning process—unless you want to remove the fins. This is easily done with a knife but is even easier with a small pair of wire clippers or scissors.

One more tip. More good fish meat is probably ruined during the drive home than during any other point in the trip from the water to the plate. Take the time to ice the fish properly for the drive home. Here's how:

Don't pack the fish in direct contact with the ice. The ice is sure to melt, and the fish, lying in the water, might well deteriorate, becoming soft and mushy. It's far better to put the fish in plastic bags, seals the bags so that they are watertight, and then pack the bags in the ice. The fish will stay cool—and dry—until you get home.

When you get the fish home, scale or skin them. If they are freshwater fish, wash them thoroughly, inside and out, in cool tap water. If they are salt-water fish, prepare a heavy brine solution, and brush them thoroughly (a pastry-type brush works well) with the brine until they are clean.

Separate the fish into lots, each of which will make a meal for yourself or your family, and wrap each lot in good freezer paper, sealing tightly to prevent freezer burn. Freeze the fish as quickly as possible.

Some fishermen prefer not to field-dress their fish, but to fillet and skin them. This method, which appears difficult but is actually quite simple, has a number of advantages. First, gutting the fish is not necessary since entrails are left intact and never touched with a knife. Second, messy scaling is also an eliminated step because the fillet is skinned and the skin discarded, scales and all. Finally, and perhaps most important, the fillets are bone free.

Filleting fish is also a good idea for fishermen on extended trips, where sizable quantities of fish are to be packed out or transported home. Head, entrails, fins, and skin are left behind and only clean and meaty fillets are brought home.

The accompanying photographs show how to quickly and easily fillet a fish from start to finish.

Pickerel and Boney Fish. Too many fish in the pickerel family are being wasted because anglers do not know how to cope with the Y-bones. *Bone-free* fillets of pickerel, pike and muskellunge are delicious. Give it a try!

To bake the fish whole, first scale the fish; then follow steps 1 through 4, but leave fillets *attached* to the skin. Then skewer or sew skin together to form a pocket for stuffing.

Pan frying or baking: No need to scale it, just wet the scales and work scaleside down on dry newspapers. No slipping. Follow steps 1 through 4; then with a thin, flexible knife, press the blade flat against the skin and with a sawing motion, slide the knife

along, freeing fillets from the skin. Your efforts should result in four bone-free fillets ready for the frying pan or for dusting with prepared baking mix before placing them in the oven.

The narrow strips along each side of the back can be rolled up pinwheel-fashion and held together with an hors d'oeuvre toothpick run through flatwise. If you like this system, strip the flank flesh and make pinwheels of all of it. The pinwheels come out with a handle for easy eating or dipping in sauces.

Caution: Cuts at (2) and (4) in the drawing below are made only down *to* the tough skin, not through it.

Notes on the Y-bone cuts (4): Until you have dressed a few, run the tip of an index finger along the fish to locate the line of the butts of the Y-bones. Ease the knife through the flesh on these cuts, slightly twisting the blade away from the bones. The knife is pushed through, as opposed to regular cutting action. It will follow the bone-line easily. If it catches a bone, back up, increase the angle and continue. The Y-bone strip and the backbone will rip out in single strips if pinched between the thumb and index finger next to the skin to lift the head end from the skin. Grasp the lifted portion and rip out toward the tail.

EASY FISH RELEASE

Effective catch-and-release fishing is a critical factor for the future of fish stocks in both fresh and salt water. A simple wire dehooker device is amazingly effective in releasing lip-hooked fish without harm and in a matter of seconds. The device, shown in

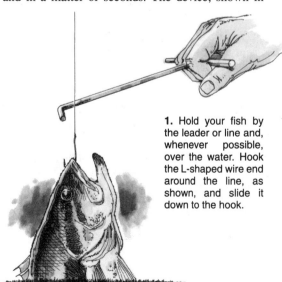

1. Hold your fish by the leader or line and, whenever possible, over the water. Hook the L-shaped wire end around the line, as shown, and slide it down to the hook.

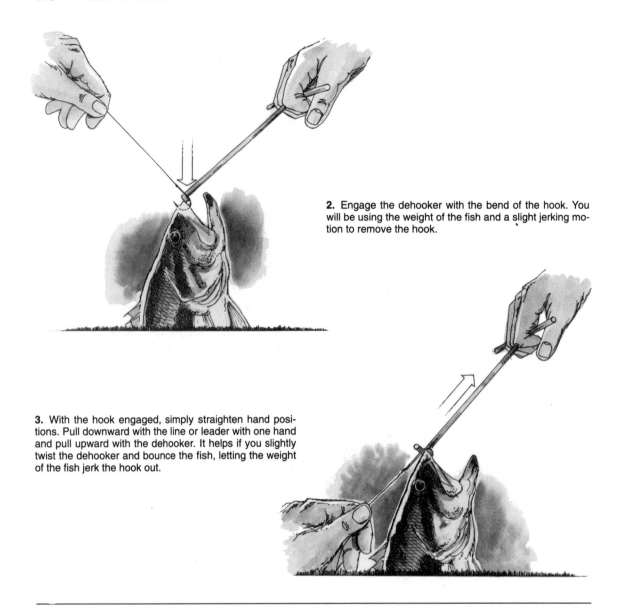

2. Engage the dehooker with the bend of the hook. You will be using the weight of the fish and a slight jerking motion to remove the hook.

3. With the hook engaged, simply straighten hand positions. Pull downward with the line or leader with one hand and pull upward with the dehooker. It helps if you slightly twist the dehooker and bounce the fish, letting the weight of the fish jerk the hook out.

these sketches, is a wire with an L-shaped hook formed on the end. Using this type of dehooker, you can release a fish over water without touching it. The fish will drop safely back into the water.

If you must touch or net a fish, wear wet cotton gloves and always avoid touching the gills. If you regularly net your fish before release, use a smooth rubber mesh net, such as the nets used in fish hatcheries. Avoid nets with knots, which will break through the fish's protective coat of slime and make it vulnerable to fungus infection.

You can make this catch-and-release device for lip-hooked fish from a length of heavy wire.

KEEPING YOUR CATCH COOL

Left: The wicker creel still does it's job well. Lined with wet ferns or grass or with wet newspapers, as shown here, it will keep fish reasonably cool on the hottest days. **Right:** Canvas creels are simple to use. Occasionally dipping the entire creel in a stream, wetting it thoroughly, will keep the fish inside in good shape during a day-long trip.

Left: Surf fishermen should bury their catch in damp sand. This will keep fish cool and out of the sun. But remember to mark the spot! **Right:** A couple of plastic bags work fine when an ice chest is not available. Put ice in one bag and your fish in the other. Then place the bagged fish in the bag with the ice. Your fish will be iced but *not* in direct contact with ice, where they would otherwise get soggy in meltwater.

HOW TO FIELD-DRESS A FISH

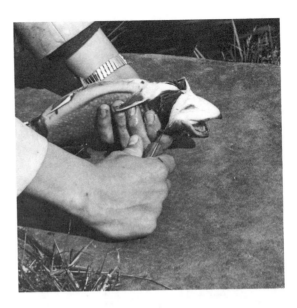

With practice, proper field-dressing of a fish will literally take only seconds. **Left:** With fish belly up, make a cut from the anal opening to gills. **Right:** Make two cuts at the gills, one below and one above the gills where they form a V.

Left: Next, stick a finger into the gullet (as shown) and begin to pull downward. Gills and entrails should come out easily. With entrails out, run your thumbnail along the backbone to break and clean the blood sac. **Right:** Wash the fish. Once is enough because the less water coming into direct contact with the meat, the firmer the flesh when you eat it.

HOW TO FILLET A FISH

1. Using sharp fillet knife, hold fish upright and make a cut as close as possible to the dorsal fin. The cut should run lengthwise from base of tail to back of fish's head and as deep as backbone or spine. **2.** Right: Turn fish over and make an identical cut on the other side.

3. For purposes of illustration, the fish here is held upright to show the two initial cuts. **4.** Next lay the fish flat and make another cut as shown, diagonally from behind the head to just behind the entrail sac, which holds the stomach and other organs. Take care not to break the sac.

5. Now work the knife blade down into the two cuts and begin to carefully slice fillet away from body. Hold knife blade flat against rib cage to avoid wasting meat. **6.** Below right: Still holding blade flat, slice through the underside skin and free fillet from the fish. (Continued on next page)

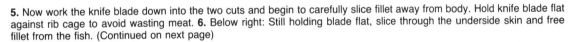

 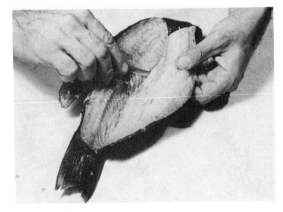

FILLETING A FISH (Continued)

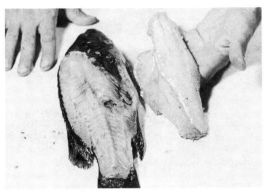

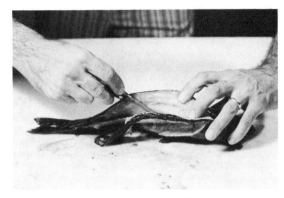

7. This is how the fillet should look when cut from side of fish. Note fillet was cut as close as possible to the rib cage, keeping waste to a bare minimum. The entrail sac is also intact. There are no broken organs, digestive juices, nor blood to taint the fillet. **8.** Right: Turn the fish over and remove the fillet from the other side of the fish exactly the same way.

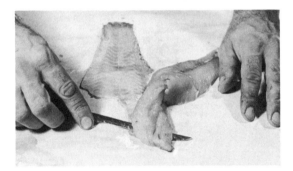

9. Next step is skinning the fillets. Place them, flesh side up, flat on table. Work knife blade between meat and skin, holding skin down firmly with fingers. If skin is too slippery to be held effectively with fingers, try using tines of ordinary kitchen fork. **10.** Right: With a sawing motion, holding blade flat and down against skin, cut meat free of skin. The fillets and skins will separate surprisingly easily.

11. Here's what you should now have: The fish with entrail sac and skeleton, along with skins, ready for the trash can. In center of the photograph are the two neatly cut fillets. Obviously, with this method, there is no need to scale the fish. **12.** Below right: The finished product—two boneless smallmouth bass fillets ready for the pan. Note entire operation only slightly soiled table. With little practice, this filleting method takes less than five minutes per fish.

HOW TO FILLET PICKEREL AND OTHER BONY FISH

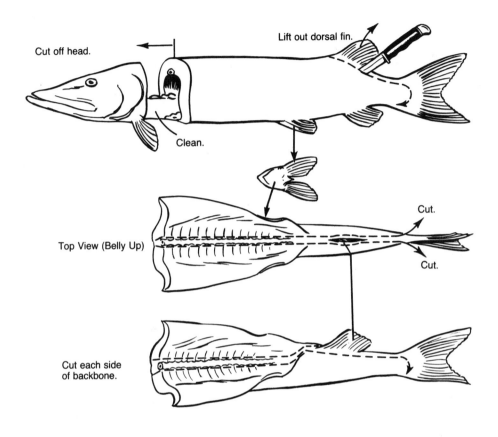

Cut off head.

Lift out dorsal fin.

Clean.

Top View (Belly Up)

Cut.

Cut.

Cut each side of backbone.

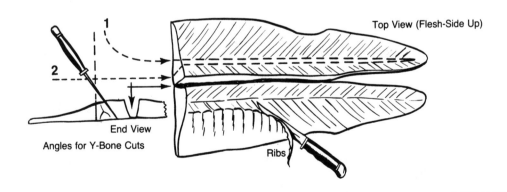

1

2

Top View (Flesh-Side Up)

End View

Angles for Y-Bone Cuts

Ribs

SMOKING YOUR FISH

Smoking your catch is simple, and you can easily turn out great-tasting smoked fish of a variety of species, from salmon to tuna. You can make your own smoker, but it may be more practical to buy a manufactured model. The method described here is "hot" smoking, which produces smoked fish that should be eaten within several days.

Before any fish is smoked, it must be brined. The brine solution will put salt into your fish to increase preservation, leech out blood, and intensify the smoke flavoring. Commercial brine solutions are available, or you can mix your own.

Fish fillets are the easiest to smoke. Make sure all bones are removed, cut the fillets into sections, and rinse them off with water. Next, soak fillets in brine for four to six hours in your refrigerator. If fillets are thick, keep them in the brine for up to 10 hours. Use a glass, stainless steel, or plastic bowl. *Do not use aluminum, which will affect flavor.*

After brining, pat fillets dry and let them air-cool for 30 minutes or so. When a glaze forms on the surface, the fillets are ready to smoke. Use good-flavor wood and keep your smoker at about 160° to 180°. Your smoked fish should be ready in six to eight hours.

Mixing the Brine

Commercial brine solutions are available, but here is a basic do-it-yourself mix.

> 1 gallon water
> 4 cups salt
> 2 cups brown sugar
> 2 tablespoons crushed black pepper
> 2 tablespoons crushed bay leaves

Best Woods for Smoking

Luhr-Jensen, which manufactures smokers and smoking equipment, recommends the following woods for all fish and game.

ALDER	The sportsman's favorite. A good flavor for all fish and seafood.
CHERRY	Distinctive and delicious. Excellent for all dark meats and game. Combine it with other woods for new flavors.
APPLE	The sweetest and mildest of all flavors. Has a subtle, velvety flavor.
HICKORY	The commercial favorite and famous for flavoring hams and bacons.
MESQUITE	Western favorite. Hearty, clean, smoky flavor. Especially good for meat and poultry.

HOW TO FREEZE FISH

The biggest problem in freezing fish is preventing "freezer burn." That's when all of the moisture has been drawn out of the flesh and you are left with dried-out fillets. It is more likely to occur in "frost-free" freezers because they are designed to pull moisture from the air inside the freezer.

The best way, and perhaps the only way, to guard against freezer burn is to freeze your fish in a block of ice. When your fish is completely encased in ice, no air can get at it. Freezing fish in this manner ensures maximum storage life for your fish. You can keep fish frozen in ice for up to two years without much flavor loss. The only disadvantage of container freezing is that it takes up more freezer space than wrapped packages. If freezer space is at a premium, double-wrap your fish for the freezer, which will maintain quality and flavor for up to six months. Here are the two best ways to freeze your fish.

WRAPPER FREEZING

Step 1—First wrap fillets or steaks in clear plastic. Make sure that all of the air is forced out and there are no open spaces between the fish and plastic.

Step 2—Aluminum foil makes a good second wrap because it is moisture-resistant and lies snugly against the fish. Any good freezer paper will also work, but make certain you are not trapping air in the package. Tape the package securely and label it with the species of the fish and the date of freezing.

CONTAINER FREEZING

Step 1—Place fillets or steaks in waterproof container (a clean milk carton is ideal). Add a few drops of lemon juice. Fill container with water to within one inch of the top (to allow for expansion).

Step 2—You can safely run water over the container to break the block of ice, but then the fish should thaw overnight at room temperature.

SKIN A FISH FOR MOUNTING

You're on a remote river in Alaska and you've just caught a giant sockeye salmon that's perfect for your wall back home. Freezers are in short supply and the closest taxidermist is unknown to you, expensive, and may get around to your fish when things get slow at his day job. You've got a problem.

We've got a solution: You can preserve your trophy by skinning and salting it in the field. Once home, you'll have plenty of time to find a reputable taxidermist, since the salted skin can be frozen indefinitely.

Some planning is required. You'll need to pack a few plastic trash bags, cotton, cardboard and paper clips. Anything else you need—such as table salt (two to four pounds) and scissors—can be found in most fishing camps.

1. Make a lateral cut along the back side of the fish, where it will not show. Cut through the skin from gill plate to tail. Use scissors to cut cleanly through bony substance at the gill plate.

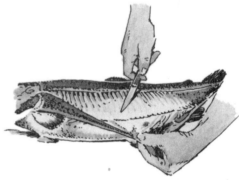

2. Using a small knife, pare the skin away from the body. Work slowly, being careful not to tear the skin. Be particularly careful in the area around the gills.

It's a good idea to practice this method before you go. Lay the fish on a piece of cardboard and position it exactly as you want it mounted. Trace the outline of the fish on the coardboard with a pencil. Then, at three spots along the length of the fish, measure its girth (or cut exact lengths of mono wrapped around it at these points). Save these dimensions with the outline. Also, take a few color photos of your catch as soon as possible, to help your taxidermist recreate true-to-life colors.

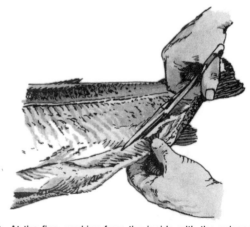

3. At the fins, working from the inside with the scissors, cut the meat free. At the base of the tail, turn the knife and cut directly through the flesh. Take care not to cut the skin on the other side.

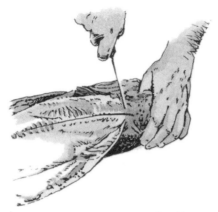

4. Working back from tail to head, cut the skin away from the body on the other side. When the skin is completely freed, sever the backbone, leaving head attached to the skin.

6. Free the gills and remove all flesh from inside the head, including the eyes. During the entire skinning process, make sure you don't break or split any fins.

5. Holding the skin with one hand, use a spoon to gently scrape the remaining meat from the skin. Remove all the cartilage from below and behind gill plates.

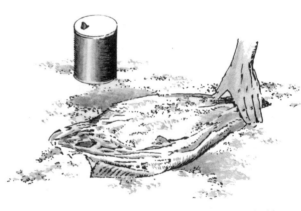

7. Rub liberal amounts of table salt into the skin, inside the head and into the base of all fins. Use plenty of salt and work it in thoroughly, but gently.

8. Wrap the fins in wet cotton. Place pieces of cardboard, held by paper clips, over the cotton. Wrap the fish in a plastic bag. Your trophy is now ready for the taxidermist.

WATER TEMPERATURE AND FISH

There is no doubt left in anglers' minds of the importance of water temperature and its direct bearing on the activities of fish. Water temperature will tell you where the fish gather and where they feed at various times of the year.

It is a scientifically proven fact that every species of fish has a preferred temperature zone or range and it will stay and generally feed in this zone. Smallmouth bass, for example, prefer water 65 to 68 degrees Fahrenheit. During spring, this temperature range may be in shallow water, and in hot midsummer weather this range may be in depths of 30 feet or more. In other words, locate the depth that reads 65 to 68 degrees and you're sure to find smallmouths.

Taking temperature readings of water is not difficult, whether you use a sophisticated electronic thermometer or an inexpensive water thermometer lowered into the water on a fishing line. One electronic thermometer has a probe attached to a cable that is marked at regular intervals, so depth and temperature can be read simultaneously.

The inexpensive water thermometers can also do the job, and many also indicate depth by inserting a water pressure gauge in the thermometer tube. With these thermometers, allow at least 30 seconds to 1 minute for a reading. Also, the fishing line attached to it should be marked off in regular intervals, say 5 feet, so you can determine just how deep you are lowering the thermometer in the water.

The accompanying Preferred Temperature Table shows popular fresh- and saltwater gamefish and baitfish and their preferred temperature zones. Look up the fish you are seeking and the water temperature it prefers. Then begin taking temperature readings from the surface on down, at 5-foot intervals, until you locate the correct zone and depth. Concentrate your efforts at that depth and you'll soon come to discover how important this water temperature business is.

PREFERRED TEMPERATURE

FRESHWATER GAMEFISH

Species	Lower Avoidance	Optimum	Upper Avoidance
American shad (Alosa sapidissima)		66°	86°
Atlantic salmon (Salmo salar)		62° (17 C)	
Atlantic sturgeon (Acipenser oxyrhynchus)	56°	66° (18.9 C)	70°
Black crappie (Pomoxis nigromaculatus)	60°	70° (21.1 C)	75°
Bloater (Coregonus hoyi)	43°		50°
Bluegill (Lepomis macrochirus)	58°	69° (21 C)	75°
Brook trout (Salvelinus fontinalis)	44°	59° (15 C)	70°
Brown bullhead (Ictalurus nebulosus)		74° (23.3 C)	
Brown trout (Salmo trutta)	44°	55°–65° (13–18 C)	75°
Buffalo species (Ictiobus sp.)	81°		94°
Burbot (Lota lota maculosa)		52° (11.1 C)	
Carp (Cyprinus carpio)	75°	84° (28.9 C)	88°
Chain pickerel (Esox niger)	60°	66° (19 C)	74°
Channel catfish (Ictalurus punctutatus)	55°	82°–89°	
Chinook salmon (Oncorhynchus tshawytscha)	44°	54° (12.2 C)	60°
Chum salmon (Oncorhynchus keta)		57° (14.1 C)	
Cisco (Coregonus artedii)		52°–55° (11–13 C)	
Coho salmon (Oncorhynchus kisutch)	44°	54° (12.2 C)	60°
Flathead catfish (Pylodictus olivaris)	81°		90°
Freshwater drum (Aplodinotus grunniens)		74° (23.1 C)	
Grass pickerel (Esox americanus vermiculatus)		78° (26 C)	
Grayling (Thymallus arcticus)			64°
Green sunfish (Lepomis cyanellus)	73°	87° (30.6 C)	91°
Goldeye (Hiodon alosoides)	72°		83°
Kamloops trout (Salmo gairdneri)	46°	47°–54° (8–12 C)	
Kokanee (Oncorhynchus nerka kenerlyi)		52°–55° (11–13 C)	
Lake trout (Salvelinus namaycush)	42°	50°–59°	
Lake whitefish (Coregonus clupeaformis)	43°	51° (10.5 C)	
Landlocked Atlantic salmon (Salmo salar sebago)		50°–58°	65°

Species	Lower Avoidance	Optimum	Upper Avoidance
Largemouth bass (*Micropterus salmoides*)	60°	80° (21–23 C)	
Longnose gar (*Lepisosteus osseus*)		92° (33.3 C)	
Longnose sucker (*Catostomus catostomus*)		53° (11.7 C)	
Mooneye (*Hiodon tergisus*)	72°		81°
Muskellunge (*Esox masquinongy*)	55°	63° (17.2 C)	72°
Northern pike (*Esox lucius*)	56°	63° (17.2 C)	74°
Pink salmon (*Oncorhynchus gorbuscha*)		49° (9.4 C)	
Pumpkinseed (*Lepomis gibbosus*)		82° (27.8 C)	
Rainbow trout (*Salmo gairdneri*)	44°	48°–65° (9–18 C)	75°
Redhorse suckers (*Moxostoma sp.*)	72°		79°
Rock bass (*Ambloplites rupestris*)		70°	
Round whitefish (*Prosopium cylindraceum*)		63° (17.2 C)	
Sauger (*Stizostedion canadense*)	55°	67° (19.4 C)	74°
Shortnose gar (*Lepisosteus platostomus*)	81°		94°
Smallmouth bass (*Micropterus dolomieui*)	60°	65°–68° (18–20 C)	73°
Sockeye salmon (*Oncorhynchus nerka*)		55° (13 C)	
Spotted bass (*Micropterus punctulatus*)	71°	75° (24.4 C)	80°
Steelhead trout (*Salmo gairdneri*)	38°	48°–52° (9–11 C)	
Sunfishes (*Centrarchidae*)	50°	58° (14.4 C)	68°
Tench (*Tinca tinca*)			79°
Walleye (*Stizostedion vitreum*)	50°	67°	76°
White bass (*Morone chrysops*)	62°	70° (21 C)	78°
White crappie (*Pomoxis annularis*)		61° (16.1 C)	
White perch (*Morone americana*)		89° (32 C)	
White sucker (*Catostomus commersoni*)		72° (22.2 C)	
Yellow bass (*Morone mississippiensis*)		81° (27.2 C)	
Yellow bullhead (*Ictalurus natalis*)		83° (28.3 C)	
Yellow perch (*Perca flavescens*)	58°	65° (18.3 C)	74°

FRESHWATER BAITFISH

Species	Lower Avoidance	Optimum	Upper Avoidance
Alewife (*Alosa pseudoharengus*)	48°	54° (12 C)	72°
Bitterling (*Rhodeus sericeus*)		77° (25.0 C)	
Bluehead chub (*Nocomis leptocephalus*)	50°	59° (15.0 C)	63°
Bluntnose minnow (*Pimephales notatus*)	70°	84° (28.9 C)	88°
Desert pupfish (*Cyprinodon macularius*)	71°		78°
Emerald shiner (*Notropis atherinoides*)		61° (16.1 C)	
Fathead minnow (*Pimephales promelas*)	77°	84° (28.9 C)	90°
Fourhorn sculpin (*Myoxcephalus quadricornis*)	39°		
Gizzard shad (*Dorosoma cepedianum*)		69° (20.5 C)	
Golden shiner (*Notemigonus crysoleucas*)		70° (21.1 C)	
Goldfish (*Carassius auratus*)		77° (25.0 C)	
Guppy (*Poecilia reticulata*)		84° (28.9 C)	
Lake chub (*Couesius plumbeus*)		48°–52° (9–11 C)	
Longjaw mudsucker (*Gillichthys mirabilis*)	48°	72° (22.2 C)	
Moapa dace (*Moapa coriacea*)		85° (29.4 C)	
Mosquitofish (*Gambusia affinis*)		81° (27.2 C)	85°
Mottled sculpin (*Cottus bairdi*)		48°–52° (9–11 C)	
Mozambique mouthbrooder (*Tilapia mossambica*)		83° (28.3 C)	92°
Nine-spine stickleback (*Pungitius pungitius*)		48°–52° (9–11 C)	
Quillback (*Carpiodes cyprinus*)		72° (22.2 C)	
Rainbow smelt (*Osmerus mordax*)	43°	50° (10.0 C)	57°
River carpsucker (*Carpoides carpio*)	79°		94°
Rosyface shiner (*Notropis rubellus*)	70°	80° (26.7 C)	88°
Slimy sculpin (*Cottus cognatus*)	39°		43°
Spotfin shiner (*Notropis spilopterus*)	79°	85° (29.4 C)	95°
Spottail shiner (*Notropis hudsonius*)		54° (12.2 C)	
Stonecat (*Notorus flavus*)		59° (15.0 C)	
Stoneroller (*Campostoma anomalum*)	75°	84° (28.9 C)	91°
Trout-perch (*Percopsis omiscomaycus*)	50°		61°
White River killfish (*Crenichthys baileyi*)		85° (29.4 C)	

(Continued next page)

SALTWATER GAMEFISH

Species	Lower Avoidance	Optimum	Upper Avoidance
Albacore (Thunnus alalunga)	59°	64° (17.8 C)	66°
Amberjack (Seriola dumerili)	60°	65° (18.3 C)	72°
Atlantic bonito (Sarda sarda)	60°	64° (17.8 C)	80°
Atlantic cod (Gadus morhua)	31°	44°–49° (6–8 C)	59°
Atlantic croaker (Micropogon undulatus)			100°
Atlantic mackerel (Scomber scombrus)	45°	63° (17 C)	70°
Barracuda (Sphyraena barracuda)	55°	75°–79° (24–26 C)	82°
Big-eye tuna (Thunnus obesus)	52°	58° (14.4 C)	66°
Blackfin tuna (Thunnus atlanticus)	70°	74° (23.3 C)	82°
Black marlin (Makaira indica)	68°	75°–79° (24–26 C)	87°
Bluefin tuna (Thunnus thynnus)	50°	68° (20 C)	78°
Bluefish (Pomatomus saltatrix)	50°	66°–72° (19–22 C)	84°
Blue marlin (Makaira nigricans)	70°	78° (26 C)	88°
Bonefish (Albula vulpes)	64°	75° (23.9 C)	88°
Dolphinfish (Coryphaena hippurus)	70°	75° (23.9 C)	82°
Fluke or summer flounder (Paralichthys dentatus)	56°	66° (18.9 C)	72°
Haddock (Melanogrammus aeglefinus)	36°	47° (8 C)	52°
Horn shark (Heterodontus francisci)		75° (24 C)	
Kelp bass (Paralabrax clathratus)	62°	65° (18.3 C)	72°
King mackerel (Scomberomorus cavalla)	70°		88°
Opaleye (Girella nigricans)		79° (26.1 C)	86°
Permit (Trachinotus falcatus)	65°	72° (22.2 C)	92°
Pollock (Pollachius virens)	33°	45° (8.3 C)	60°
Red drum (Sciaenops ocellata)	52°	71° (22 C)	90°
Red snapper (Lutjanus blackfordi)	50°	57° (13.8 C)	62°
Sailfish (Istiophorus platypterus)	68°	79° (26 C)	88°
Sand seatrout (Cynoscion arenarius)	90°	95° (35.0 C)	104°
Sea catfish (Arius felis)			99°
Skipjack tuna (Euthynnus pelamis)	50°	62° (16.7 C)	70°
Snook (Centropomus undecimalis)	60°	70°–75° (21–24 C)	90°
Spotted seatrout (Cynoscion nebulosus)	48°	72° (22 C)	81°
Striped bass (Morone saxatilis)	61°	68°	77°
Striped marlin (Tetrapturus audax)	61°	70° (21 C)	80°
Swordfish (Xiphias gladius)	50°	66° (19 C)	78°
Tarpon (Megalops atlantica)	74°	76° (24.4 C)	90°
Tautog (Tautoga onitis)	60°	70° (21 C)	76°
Weakfish (Cynoscion regalis)		55°–65°	78°
White marlin (Tetrapturus albidus)	65°	70° (21.1 C)	80°
White sea bass (Cynoscion nobilis)	58°	68° (20.0 C)	74°
Winter flounder (Pseudopleuronectes americanus)	35°	48°–52° (9–11 C)	64°
Yellowfin tuna (Thunnus albacares)	64°	72° (22.2 C)	80°
Yellowtail (Seriola dorsalis)	60°	65° (18.3 C)	70°

SALTWATER BAITFISH

Species	Lower Avoidance	Optimum	Upper Avoidance
Atlantic silverside (Menidia menidia)			90°
Atlantic threadfin (Polydactylus octonemus)			92°
Bay anchovy (Anchoa mitchilli)		82° (27.8 C)	92°
California grunion (Leuresthes tenuis)	68°	77° (25.0 C)	93°
Gulf grunion (Leuresthes sardina)	68°	89° (32 C)	98°
Gulf menhaden (Brevoortia patronus)			86°
Pacific silversides such as jacksmelt and topsmelt (Atherinopsis sp)	72°	77° (25 C)	82°
Rough silverside (Membras martinica)			91°
Skipjack herring (Alosa chrysochloris)	72°		84°
Spot (Leiostomus xanthuras)			99°
Tidewater silverside (Menidia beryllina)			93°

PART 4

GAME FISH

FRESHWATER SPECIES

Atlantic Salmon

SCIENTIFIC NAME: *Salmo salar.*

DESCRIPTION: Atlantic salmon are anadromous fish, meaning that they are spawned in freshwater rivers and then migrate to the ocean to spend most of their lives before returning to fresh water to spawn themselves. When fresh from the sea, Atlantics are steel blue on top and silvery on sides and belly, and have dark spots on their sides. As their stay in fresh water lengthens, the colors become darker, with the sides taking on a pinkish hue as spawning time arrives. Very young salmon are called parrs. Parrs have distinctive dark vertical bars called parr markings. Unlike Pacific salmon, all of which die after spawning, about 15 percent of Atlantic salmon survive the spawning act and return to sea.

RANGE: The highly prized Atlantic salmon once ranged from Delaware north through Quebec and the Canadian Maritime provinces to Greenland, and in the western Atlantic Ocean in the British Isles and parts of Scandinavia. But today, because of "progress"—meaning dams, pollution, and urban and suburban sprawl—the range of the Atlantic salmon in the U.S. is restricted to a handful of rivers in Maine, though efforts are being made to restore this fine gamefish to the Connecticut and other northeastern rivers.

HABITAT: In fresh water, the Atlantic salmon must have clean, flowing, cold water. In upstream spawn-ing areas, shallow water over a gravel bottom is a must so that the fish can create "redds," or spawning beds. When in the ocean, these salmon range over vast areas but tend to concentrate on feeding grounds, which are only recently being discovered.

SIZE: Mature Atlantic salmon weigh from 9 to about 75 pounds, with the average being about 12. Their size depends on how many years they have spent in the sea, where their growth is fast. Salmon that return to fresh water after only one or two years at sea are called grilse and weigh up to about 6 or 8 pounds.

FOOD: These fish feed on small baitfish and such when in the ocean, but upon entering fresh water they stop feeding almost completely. And yet they can be induced to strike an artificial lure, particularly dry and wet flies.

Landlocked Salmon

COMMON NAMES: Landlocked salmon, landlock, ouananiche, Sebago salmon.

SCIENTIFIC NAME: *Salmo salar sebago.*

DESCRIPTION: The landlocked salmon is very similar in coloration and general appearance to the Atlantic salmon, of which the landlock is a subspecies. It is assumed that the subspecies descended from Atlantic salmon trapped in freshwater lakes

461

thousands of years ago. As their name suggests, landlocks do not spawn in the sea. They either spawn in their home lakes or descend outlet streams to spawn.

RANGE: Landlocks range over much of New England (they are most numerous in Maine), in Quebec and other parts of eastern Canada, and north to Labrador. They have been introduced in New York and other eastern states and in South America.

HABITAT: The landlock survives best in deep, cold lakes that have a high oxygen content.

SIZE: Most landlocks average 2 to 3 pounds, but a 6-pounder is not unusual, and an occasional 10-pounder is caught. Maximum weight is about 30 pounds.

FOOD: Landlocks feed mostly on small baitfish, particularly smelt.

Chinook Salmon

COMMON NAMES: Chinook salmon, king salmon, tyee salmon, blackmouth (immature stage).

SCIENTIFIC NAME: *Oncorhynchus tshawytscha.*

DESCRIPTION: The chinook, like all other Pacific salmon, is anadromous and seems to prefer the largest of Pacific Coast rivers for spawning. Chinooks have a dark-blue back that shades to silver on the sides and to white on the belly. Small dark spots, barely noticeable in fish fresh from the sea, mark the upper part of the body.

RANGE: Chinook salmon range from southern California to northern Alaska, being more numerous in the northern part of that area. They often travel enormous distances upriver to spawn; in the Yukon River, for example, chinooks have been seen 2,000 miles from the sea.

HABITAT: Chinooks prefer large, clean, cold rivers, but often enter small tributary streams to spawn in shallow water over gravel bottom.

SIZE: The chinook is the largest of the Pacific salmon, reaching weights of over 100 pounds. Rarely, however, does a sport fisherman catch one of more than 60 pounds, and the average size is about 18 pounds.

FOOD: Chinooks eat ocean baitfish (herring, sar-dines, candlefish, anchovies), freshwater baitfish, and fish roe.

Dog Salmon

COMMON NAMES: Dog salmon, chum salmon.

SCIENTIFIC NAME: *Oncorhynchus keta.*

DESCRIPTION: The dog salmon closely resembles the chinook salmon but has black-edged fins and lacks the chinook's dark spots on back, dorsal fin, and tail. During spawning, the male dog salmon often exhibits red or green blotches on its sides. The dog salmon is rarely taken by sport fishermen.

RANGE: One of the five species of Pacific salmon, the dog salmon is found from central California north to Alaska, but is far more numerous in Alaska than farther south. In their sea migrations, dog salmon travel as far as the Aleutians, Korea, and Japan.

HABITAT: Like all other salmon, the dog spawns in gravel in freshwater rivers, usually spawning in the lower reaches of the parent streams but occasionally found far upstream.

SIZE: Dog salmon reach weights of 30 pounds or a bit more but average 6 to 18 pounds.

FOOD: The diet of dog salmon consists mainly of baitfish and crustaceans.

Sockeye Salmon

COMMON NAMES: Sockeye salmon, red salmon, blueback salmon.

SCIENTIFIC NAME: *Oncorhynchus nerka.*

DESCRIPTION: The sockeye is similar to the chinook but has a small number of gill rakers and has tiny spots along the back. When spawning, sockeye males turn a dark red, with the forward parts of the body being greenish. Females range in color from olive to light red. Sockeyes are more often caught by sport fishermen than are dog salmon, and they will take artificial flies and are good fighters.

RANGE: Sockeyes are found from California to Japan but few are encountered south of the Columbia River. A landlocked strain of the sockeye (see Kokanee Salmon), originally found from British Columbia south to Oregon and Idaho, is being stocked in freshwater lakes in various areas of the U.S.

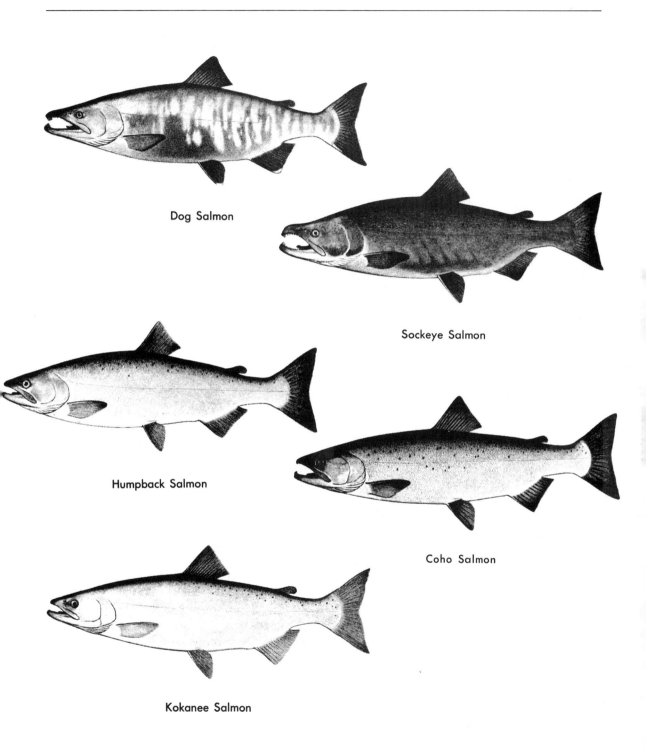

Dog Salmon

Sockeye Salmon

Humpback Salmon

Coho Salmon

Kokanee Salmon

HABITAT: Spawns over gravel in freshwater lakes, especially those fed by springs.

SIZE: Sockeyes reach a maximum weight of about 15 pounds, but the average is 4 to 9 pounds.

FOOD: Sockeyes feed mainly on crustaceans but also eat small baitfish.

Humpback Salmon

COMMON NAMES: Humpback salmon, pink salmon.

SCIENTIFIC NAME: *Oncorhynchus gorbuscha.*

DESCRIPTION: Similar to the other salmons but smaller, the humpback has small scales, and its caudal fin (tail) has large, oval, black spots. At maturity, or at spawning time, the males develop a large, distinctive hump on their backs. The humpback is among the most commercially valuable of the Pacific salmons and is becoming more popular with sport fishermen.

RANGE: The humpback is found from California to Alaska and as far away as Korea and Japan.

HABITAT: Spawns over gravel in freshwater rivers, usually near the sea.

SIZE: Smallest of the Pacific salmon, the humpback averages 3 to 6 pounds, attaining a maximum weight of about 10 pounds.

FOOD: Humpbacks subsist largely on a diet of crustaceans, baitfish, and squid.

Coho Salmon

COMMON NAMES: Coho salmon, silver salmon, hooknose.

SCIENTIFIC NAME: *Oncorhynchus kisutch.*

DESCRIPTION: The coho is generally silvery with a bluish back and has small dark spots along the upper part of the sides and tail. When the spawning urge takes hold, the males assume a reddish coloration, but when they enter fresh water they become almost black. The coho is highly prized as a sport fish, striking artificials readily and leaping breathtakingly when hooked.

RANGE: The coho is found from California to Alaska and as far from the U.S. West Coast as Japan. It has also been transplanted with unprecedented success to the Great Lakes, and at present attempts are being made to establish the coho in large freshwater lakes in many other parts of the U.S.

HABITAT: Spawns in gravel in freshwater rivers, either near the sea or far upstream.

SIZE: Cohoes reach weights approaching 30 pounds but average 6 to 12 pounds.

FOOD: A coho's diet is mainly baitfish, squid, crustaceans, and crab larvae.

Kokanee Salmon

COMMON NAMES: Kokanee, silver trout, blueback, little redfish, Kennerly's salmon, landlocked sockeye, redfish, silversides.

SCIENTIFIC NAME: *Oncorhynchus nerka kennerlyi.*

DESCRIPTION: The kokanee is a landlocked strain of the anadromous sockeye salmon. Biologically identical with the true sockeye (though much smaller), the kokanee is silvery on sides and belly, but during spawning the males have reddish sides and the females slate-gray sides. Kokanees resemble some trout but differ from all trout in that they have more than 12 rays in the anal fin. The kokanee is the only Pacific salmon that matures in fresh water. Much prized by sport fishermen.

RANGE: The kokanee's original range extended from Idaho and Oregon north to Alaska, but it has been introduced in recent years in lakes as far south as New Mexico and as far east as New England.

HABITAT: Spawns in gravel, both in lakes and in tributary streams, and ranges throughout lakes at other times.

SIZE: Much smaller than the true sockeye salmon, the kokanee reaches a maximum weight of about 4 pounds. Average length varies greatly, depending upon water and food conditions. In some places they never exceed 10 inches, while in other places—California's Donner Lake, for example—their average length is over 18 inches.

FOOD: Kokanees feed almost exclusively on tiny forage—minute crustaceans and other plankton.

Arctic Char

COMMON NAMES: Arctic char, arctic trout, alpine trout, Quebec red trout.

SCIENTIFIC NAME: *Salvelinus alpinus.*

DESCRIPTION: The arctic char is a far-north salmonid whose colors vary greatly. Sea-run char are quite silvery as they enter freshwater rivers, but their freshwater colors soon predominate, turning the char into a stunning fish, with sides ranging in color from pale to very bright orange and red. Char are usually spotted in red, pink, or cream and have the white-edged fins of the brook trout. But they lack the brook trout's vermiculations (wormlike markings) on the back. There are both anadromous and landlocked strains of arctic char.

RANGE: Arctic char are found in northern Canada, Alaska, Iceland, Greenland, Scandinavia, England, Ireland, Scotland, Europe, and the Soviet Union.

HABITAT: As its range indicates, the char thrives in very cold clean water, preferring fast shallow river water near the mouths of tributary streams. Relatively little is known about the nomadic movements of anadromous char, but they apparently spend the summer near the mouths of rivers, where they feed heavily before moving inland.

SIZE: Arctic char reach weights of nearly 30 pounds, but the average weight is 2 to 8 pounds.

FOOD: Char feed on a species of smelt called capelin and on sand eels, various baitfish, some crustaceans, and occasionally on insects.

Brook Trout

COMMON NAMES: Brook trout, speckled trout, speck, squaretail.

SCIENTIFIC NAME: *Salvelinus fontinalis.*

DESCRIPTION: This best-loved of American native fish is not a true trout but actually a member of the char family. It is a beautiful fish, having a dark back with distinctive wormlike markings (vermiculations), sides marked with yellow spots and with red spots encircled in blue, a light-colored belly (bright orange during spawning), and pink or red lower fins edged in white. Wherever they are found, brook trout willingly take the offerings of fly, bait, and lure fishermen alike, a fact that has contributed to their de-

crease in many areas, though pollution has done far more to decimate populations of native brookies.

RANGE: Originally native only to northeastern North America from Georgia to the Arctic, the brook trout is now found in suitable waters throughout the U.S., Canada, South America, and Europe. Stocking maintains brook trout in many waters, but true native brookies are becoming rare.

HABITAT: Brook trout must have clean cold water, seldom being found in water warmer than 65°F. They spawn both in lakes and in streams, preferring small spring-fed brooks.

SIZE: Though the rod-and-reel record for brook trout is 14½ pounds, fish half that size are a rarity today. In fact, a 5-pounder is an exceptional brook trout, and fish of that size are seldom found anywhere but in Labrador, northern Quebec and Manitoba, and Argentina. Native brook trout caught in streams average 6 to 12 inches in length.

FOOD: Brook trout eat worms, insects, crustaceans, and various kinds of baitfish.

Sunapee Trout

COMMON NAMES: Sunapee trout, Sunapee golden trout.

SCIENTIFIC NAME: *Salvelinus aureolus.*

DESCRIPTION: This attractive fish—which may be a member of the char family or a distinct species of trout (there is some disagreement on the subject)—has a dark-bluish back that lacks the wormlike markings of the brook trout. Its sides have spots of pinkish white, yellow, or red, and the yellowish or orange fins are white-edged.

RANGE: Originating in New Hampshire, principally in Sunapee Lake, the Sunapee trout is exceedingly rare, being found only in Sunapee Lake and in a few lakes and ponds in northern New England. The introduction of lake trout in Sunapee and other lakes has had a deteriorating effect on populations of Sunapee trout.

HABITAT: Little is known about the wanderings of this attractive fish, but it is known that in Sunapee Lake these trout move into the shallows in spring and fall, while in summer they are found in the deepest parts of the lake—way down to 60 to 100 feet, where the water is quite cold.

SIZE: Many years ago 10- and 12-pound Sunapees were taken in the lake from which they derive their name, but today the fisherman is lucky to catch a 15-incher.

FOOD: Smelt makes up the majority of the Sunapee trout's diet.

Dolly Varden Trout

COMMON NAMES: Dolly Varden trout, Dolly, western char, bull trout, salmon trout, red-spotted trout.

SCIENTIFIC NAME: *Salvelinus malma.*

DESCRIPTION: This member of the char family somewhat resembles the brook trout but lacks the brookie's wormlike back markings and is usually more slender. It has red and yellow side spots and the white-edged fins typical of all chars. In salt water the Dolly is quite silvery. The Dolly, said to have been named after a Charles Dickens character, is not so popular in some parts of its range as are the other trout species, possibly because it is not as strong a fighter.

RANGE: Occurring from northern California to Alaska and as far from the U.S. as Japan, the Dolly is found in both fresh water and, in the northern part of its range, in salt water.

HABITAT: Dolly Vardens spawn in gravel in streams. At other times of year, stream fish are likely to be found in places similar to those preferred by brook trout, such as under rocks, logs, and other debris and lying in deep holes. In lakes they are likely to be found near the bottom near reefs and dropoffs. They are seldom found near the surface.

SIZE: Dolly Vardens reach weights of upwards of 30 pounds. Average size is 8 to 18 inches in some places (usually streams), 3 to 6 pounds in other spots (usually lakes).

FOOD: These are primarily bottom-feeders, though in streams they feed heavily on insects and may be taken on flies. Large fish feed heavily on baitfish, including the young of trout and salmon. It has been said that these trout will eat anything, and that may be true, considering that in some areas fishermen shoot ground squirrels, remove the legs and skin them, and use the legs for Dolly Varden bait!

Lake Trout

COMMON NAMES: Lake trout, togue, mackinaw, gray trout, salmon trout, forktail, laker.

SCIENTIFIC NAME: *Salvelinus namaycush.*

DESCRIPTION: More somberly hued than most other trout, the laker is usually a fairly uniform gray or blue-gray, though in some areas he is a bronze-green. He has irregular pale spots over head, back, and sides and also has the white-edged fins that mark him as a char.

RANGE: The lake trout is distributed throughout Canada and in the northern U.S., principally in New England, New York's Finger Lakes, the Great Lakes, and many large western lakes. Stockings have widened the laker's range considerably and have restored the species to portions of the Great Lakes where an incursion of lamprey eels decimated the laker populations in the 1950s and early 60s.

HABITAT: Lake trout are fish of deep, cold, clear lakes, though in the northern part of their range they are found in large streams. Lakers prefer water temperatures of about 45°F and are rarely found where water rises above 70°. In the southern part of their range they are usually found only in lakes that have an adequate oxygen supply in the deeper spots.

SIZE: The lake trout is the largest of our trout species, reaching weights of more than 100 pounds. Their average size often depends on the size, depth, and water quality of a given lake.

FOOD: Though the young feed on insects and crustaceans, adult lake trout eat primarily fish such as smelt, small kokanee salmon, ciscoes, whitefish, and sculpin.

Rainbow Trout

COMMON NAMES: Rainbow trout, steelhead, Kamloops rainbow, Kamloops trout, redsides.

SCIENTIFIC NAME: *Salmo gairdneri.*

DESCRIPTION: This native American trout takes three basic forms: the nonmigratory rainbow, which lives its entire life in streams and/or lakes; the steelhead, which is spawned in freshwater rivers, migrates to the sea, and returns to the rivers to spawn (large rainbows that live in the Great Lakes and

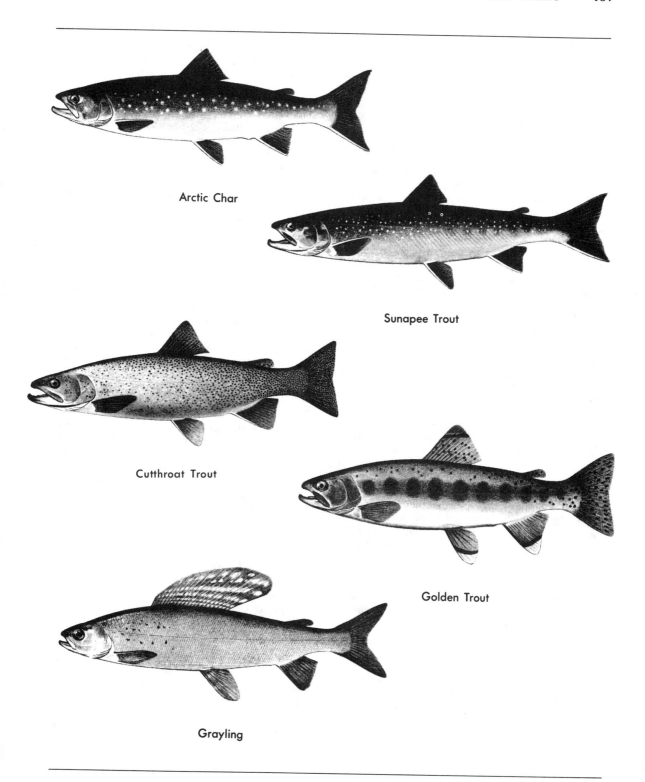

Arctic Char

Sunapee Trout

Cutthroat Trout

Golden Trout

Grayling

elsewhere in the eastern U.S. also are called steel-heads but are not true members of the steelhead clan); and the Kamloops rainbow, a large subspecies found mostly in interior British Columbia. Though the rainbow's colors vary greatly, depending upon where he is found, the fish generally has an olive or lighter green back shading to silvery or white on lower sides and belly. There are numerous black spots on the upper body from head to tail and a distinctive red stripe along the middle of each side. Sea-run and lake-run rainbows are usually quite silvery, with a faint or nonexistent red stripe and few spots. The rainbow is an extremely important sport fish and will take flies, lures, and bait willingly. It usually strikes hard and is noted for its wild leaps.

RANGE: The natural range of the rainbow trout is from northern Mexico to Alaska and the Aleutian Islands, but stocking programs have greatly widened that range so that it now includes most of Canada, all the northern and central states, and some of the colder waters in such southern states as Georgia, Tennessee, Arkansas, and Texas.

HABITAT: The rainbow, like all trout, must have cold, clean water, though it does fairly well under marginal conditions. It is found in shallow lakes and deep lakes, in small streams and large ones. It may be found at the surface one day, feeding on the bottom the next. The rainbow's universality is due partly to the fact that it can do well in a wide variety of environments.

SIZE: The average nonmigratory stream rainbow runs from 6 to 18 inches in length, though some much larger specimens are occasionally taken. Nonmigratory lake fish tend to run considerably larger—up to 50 pounds and more. An average migratory steelhead runs from 8 to 12 pounds, but this strain reaches 35 pounds or so.

FOOD: Rainbows feed heavily on insect life but also eat baitfish, crustaceans, worms, and the roe of salmon and trout. The diet of the Kamloops rainbow is mainly kokanee salmon.

Cutthroat Trout

COMMON NAMES: Cutthroat trout, cut, native trout, mountain trout, Rocky Mountain trout, black-spotted trout, harvest trout, Montana black-spotted trout, Tahoe cutthroat, Yellowstone cutthroat.

SCIENTIFIC NAME: *Salmo clarki.*

DESCRIPTION: Occurring in both nonmigratory and anadromous forms, the cutthroat trout gets its common name from the two slashes of crimson on the underside of its lower jaw. Its scientific name honors William Clark of the famed Lewis and Clark expedition. The cutthroat is often mistaken for the rainbow, but it lacks the rainbow's bright-red side stripe, and its entire body is usually black-spotted, while the rainbow's spots are usually limited to the upper half of the body. The cutthroat usually has a greenish back, colorful gill plates, sides of yellow or pink, and a white belly. Coastal cutthroats are greenish blue with a silvery sheen on the sides and heavy black spots. The cutthroat is a fine sport fish, taking flies—particularly wet flies—readily and showing an inordinate liking for flashy spoons.

RANGE: The cutthroat is found from northern California north to Prince William Sound, Alaska, and inland throughout the western U.S. and Canada.

HABITAT: A fish of clean, cold water, the cutthroat frequents places like those preferred by the brook trout—undercut banks, deep holes, logs, and other debris. They prefer quiet water, generally, in streams. Unlike other trout that go to sea, anadromous cutthroats do not range widely in the ocean depths. Instead, they remain in bays at the mouths of their home streams or along the nearby ocean shores.

SIZE: Though cutthroats of up to 41 pounds have been caught by anglers, they seldom exceed 5 pounds and average 2 to 3 pounds. Four pounds is large for a sea-run cutthroat.

FOOD: Young cutthroats feed mainly on insect life, while adults eat insects, baitfish, crayfish, and worms.

Golden Trout

COMMON NAMES: Golden trout, Volcano trout, Sierra trout.

SCIENTIFIC NAME: *Salmo aguabonita.*

DESCRIPTION: This rare jewel of the western high country is the most beautiful of all trout. The golden trout has an olive back, crimson gill covers and side stripes, while the remainder of the body ranges from orange-yellow to gold. The dorsal fin is orange-tipped, and the anal and ventral fins are white-edged. Each side contains about 10 black parr markings. The coloring differs from lake to lake. The golden is a rarely caught but highly prized sport fish.

RANGE: Originally found only in the headwaters of California's Kern River, the golden is now present in high-mountain lakes in many western states, including California, Wyoming, Idaho, Washington. Modern fish-breeding and stocking techniques have extended the range of the golden—or, rather, a golden-rainbow trout cross—to the eastern states, including West Virginia and New Jersey.

HABITAT: The true golden trout is found in small, high lakes and their tributary streams at elevations of 9,000 to 12,000 feet. The water in these lakes is extremely cold, and weed growth is minimal or nonexistent. Because of the golden's spartan habitat, he can be extremely moody and difficult to catch.

SIZE: Golden trout are not large, a 2-pounder being a very good one, though some lakes hold fair numbers of fish up to 5 pounds. Maximum size is 11 pounds.

FOOD: Golden trout feed almost exclusively on minute insects, including terrestrial (land) insects, but also eat tiny crustaceans and are sometimes caught by bait fishermen using worms, salmon eggs, and grubs.

Brown Trout

COMMON NAMES: Brown trout, German brown trout, Loch Leven trout.

SCIENTIFIC NAME: *Salmo trutta.*

DESCRIPTION: Introduced in North America in the 1880s, the brown trout is a top-notch dry-fly fish, and yet its daytime wariness and whimsy can drive fishermen to the nearest bar. The brown trout is generally brownish to olive brown, shading from dark brown on the back to dusky yellow or creamy white on the belly. Sides, back, and dorsal fin have prominent black or brown spots, usually surrounded by faint halos of gray or white. Some haloed red or orange spots are also present. Sea-run browns and those in large lakes are often silvery and resemble landlocked salmon.

RANGE: The brown is the native trout of Europe and is also found in New Zealand, parts of Asia, South America, and Africa. It is found in the U.S. from coast to coast and as far south as New Mexico and Arkansas and Georgia.

HABITAT: The brown trout can tolerate warmer water and other marginal conditions better than the other trout species can. It is found in both streams and lakes, preferring hiding and feeding spots similar to those of brook trout. It often feeds on the bottom in deep holes, coming to the surface at night.

SIZE: Brown trout have been known to exceed 40 pounds, though one of more than 10 pounds is exceptional. Most browns caught by sport fishermen weigh ½ to 1½ pounds.

FOOD: Brown trout feed on aquatic and terrestrial (land) insects as well as worms, crayfish, baitfish, and fish roe. Large specimens will eat such tidbits as mice, frogs, and small birds.

Grayling

COMMON NAMES: Grayling, Arctic grayling, Montana grayling.

SCIENTIFIC NAME: *Thymallus arcticus.*

DESCRIPTION: Closely related to the trouts and whitefishes, the grayling's most distinctive feature is its high, wide dorsal fin, which is gray to purple and has rows of blue or lighter dots. Its back is dark blue to gray, and the sides range from gray to brown to silvery, depending upon where the fish lives. The forepart of the body usually has irregularly shaped dark spots. The grayling is a strikingly handsome fish and a fly-fisherman's dream.

RANGE: The grayling is abundant in Alaska, throughout northern Canada from northern Saskatchewan westward, and northward through the Northwest Territories. It is less common in the U.S., ranging in high areas of Montana, Wyoming, and Utah. Recently developed grayling-breeding procedures are extending the range of this fish into Idaho, California, Oregon, and other mountain states.

HABITAT: The grayling is found in both lakes and rivers but is particularly at home in high and isolated timberline lakes. In lakes, schools of grayling often cruise near shore. In rivers, the fish are likely to be found anywhere, but they usually favor one type of water in any given stream.

SIZE: Maximum weight of grayling is 20 pounds or a bit heavier, but in most waters, even in the Arctic, a 2-pounder is a good fish. In U.S. waters, grayling seldom top 1½ pounds.

FOOD: The grayling's diet is made up almost entirely of nymphs and other insects and aquatic larvae. However, this northern fish will also readily eat worms and crustaceans.

Rocky Mountain Whitefish

COMMON NAMES: Rocky Mountain whitefish, mountain whitefish, Montana whitefish.

SCIENTIFIC NAME: *Prosopium williamsoni.*

DESCRIPTION: The Rocky Mountain whitefish resembles the lake whitefish, though its body is more cylindrical. Coloration shades from brown on the back to silver on the sides to white on the belly. The dorsal fin is large but not nearly as large as that of the grayling. Where it competes with trout in a stream, the Rocky Mountain whitefish is considered a nuisance by many anglers, though it fights well and will take dry and wet flies, spinning lures, and bait.

RANGE: The Rocky Mountain whitefish is endemic to the western slope of the Rocky Mountains from northern California to southern British Columbia.

HABITAT: Found in cold, swift streams and in clear deep lakes, these whitefish school up in deep pools after spawning in the fall and feed mostly on the bottom. In spring the fish move to the riffles in streams and the shallows in lakes.

SIZE: Rocky Mountain whitefish reach 5 pounds, but a 3-pounder is an exceptional one. Average size is 11 to 14 inches and 1 pound.

FOOD: These fish feed almost entirely on such insects as caddis and midge larvae and stonefly nymphs. They also eat fish eggs, their own included.

Lake Whitefish

COMMON NAMES: Lake whitefish, common whitefish, Great Lakes whitefish, Labrador whitefish, Otsego bass.

SCIENTIFIC NAME: *Coregonus clupeaformis.*

DESCRIPTION: Similar in appearance—though only distantly related—to the Rocky Mountain whitefish, the lake whitefish has bronze or olive shading on the back, with the rest of the body being silvery white. It has rather large scales, a small head and mouth, and a blunt snout. Large specimens appear humpbacked. Lake whitefish, because they spend much of the year in very deep water, are not important sport fish.

RANGE: Lake whitefish are found from New En-gland west through the Great Lakes area and throughout much of Canada.

HABITAT: These fish inhabit large, deep, cold, clear lakes and are usually found in water from 60 to 100 feet deep, though they will enter tributary streams in spring and fall. In the northern part of their range, however, lake whitefish are often found foraging in shallow water, and they will feed on the surface when mayflies are hatching.

SIZE: Lake whitefish reach weights of a bit more than 20 pounds, but their average size is something less than 4 pounds.

FOOD: Lake whitefish feed primarily on small crustaceans and aquatic insects but will eat baitfish.

Cisco

COMMON NAMES: Cisco, herring, lake herring, common cisco, lake cisco, bluefin, Lake Erie cisco, tullibee, shortjaw chub, grayback.

SCIENTIFIC NAME: *Coregonus artedii* (and others).

DESCRIPTION: Though the cisco superficially resembles members of the herring family, it is not a herring but rather a member of the whitefish family. The cisco has a darker back (usually bluish or greenish) than the true whitefish. The body is silvery with large scales. There are more than 30 species and subspecies of ciscoes in the Great Lakes area alone, and all of them look and act alike. Ciscoes occasionally provide good sport fishing, particularly on dry flies, but they are more important commercially.

RANGE: The various strains of ciscoes occur from New England and New York west through the Great Lakes area and range widely through Canada. Their center of concentration seems to be the Great Lakes area.

HABITAT: Ciscoes prefer large, cold, clear lakes, usually those having considerable depth. Little is known of the wanderings of these fish; some species are found from the surface to several hundred feet down. They spawn in July and August over hard bottom. In summer ciscoes often come to the surface to feed on hatching insects, usually at sundown.

SIZE: The size of a cisco depends on its species. Some average only a few ounces in weight, while

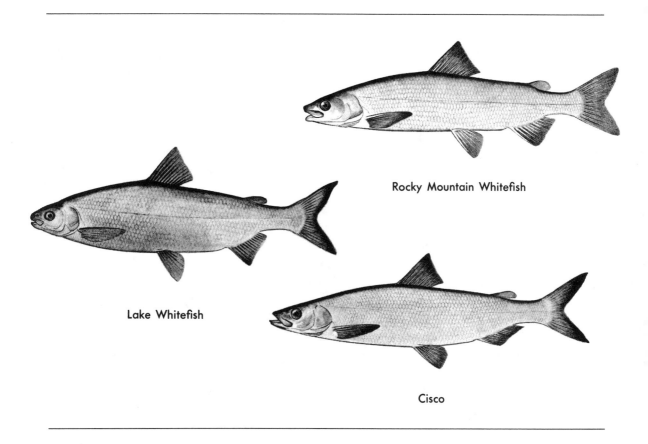

Rocky Mountain Whitefish

Lake Whitefish

Cisco

the largest attain a maximum weight of about 7 pounds. Average length is about 6 to 20 inches.

FOOD: Insect life—mainly bottom-dwelling types—is the blueplate special of the cisco, though it sometimes feeds on surface insects and on minute crustaceans and worms.

American Shad

SCIENTIFIC NAME: *Alosa sapidissima.*

DESCRIPTION: The American shad is an anadromous fish—meaning one that ascends coastal rivers to spawn but spends much of its life in salt water. A member of the herring family, the shad has a greenish back, with the remainder of the body being silvery. There are usually a few indistinct markings on the forebody. Shad put up a no-holds-barred

battle on hook and line and are important sport and commercial fish, though pollution is putting a dent in their population in some areas.

RANGE: American shad were originally native only to the Atlantic but were introduced in the Pacific in the 1870s. On the Atlantic coast they are found from Florida to the Gulf of St. Lawrence, while in the Pacific they range from San Diego, California, to southern Alaska. They are also found in Scandinavia, France, Italy, Germany, Russia, and elsewhere.

HABITAT: American shad swarm up large coastal rivers to spawn in the spring—from March to May, depending upon the location of the river. They are particularly susceptible to anglers below dams and in holes and slow runs just upstream of riffles, where they tend to rest before continuing upriver. They generally spawn in the main river.

SIZE: The average weight of an American shad is 3 to 5 pounds, while maximum weight is 12 to 13 pounds. Egg-laden females are usually heavier than males.

FOOD: While in the ocean American shad feed almost exclusively on plankton, so far as is known. After they enter fresh water on the spawning runs, these fish apparently do not feed at all. Curiously, however, they will strike at a small variety of artificial lures, including small, sparsely dressed wet flies and leadhead jigs tied on a gold hook and having a wisp of bucktail at the tail.

Largemouth Bass

COMMON NAMES: Largemouth bass, bigmouth bass, black bass, green trout, Oswego bass, green bass.

SCIENTIFIC NAME: *Micropterus salmoides.*

DESCRIPTION: The largemouth bass is among the most important of this continent's freshwater gamefish. In physical makeup it is a chunky fish, with coloration ranging from nearly black or dark green on the back, through varying shades of green or brownish green on the sides, to an off-white belly. The largemouth's most distinctive marking, however, is a horizontal dark band running along the side from head to tail. In large, old bass particularly, the band may be almost invisible. There are two reliable ways to distinguish the largemouth from its close relative and look-alike, the smallmouth bass: 1) the largemouth's upper jaw (maxillary) extends back behind the eye, while the smallmouth's does not; 2) the spiny part of the largemouth's dorsal fin is almost completely separated from the softer rear portion, while in the smallmouth the two fin sections are connected in one continuous fin.

RANGE: The largemouth is native to or stocked in every state in the "lower 48" and is found as far south as Mexico and as far north as southern Canada.

HABITAT: Largemouths are found in slow-moving streams large and small and in nonflowing waters ranging in size from little more than puddles to vast impoundments. It thrives best in shallow, weedy lakes and in river backwaters. It is a warm-water fish, preferring water temperatures of 70°F to 75°. Largemouths never venture too far from such areas as weed beds, logs, stumps, and other sunken debris, which provide both cover and food. They are usually found in water no deeper than 20 feet.

SIZE: Largemouth bass grow biggest in the southern U.S., where they reach a maximum weight of a little over 20 pounds and an 8- or 10-pounder is not a rarity. In the north largemouths rarely exceed 10 pounds and a 3-pounder is considered a good catch.

FOOD: The largemouth's diet is as ubiquitous as the fish itself. These bass eat minnows and any other available baitfish, worms, crustaceans, a wide variety of insect life, frogs, mice, ducklings.

Smallmouth Bass

COMMON NAMES: Smallmouth bass, black bass, bronzeback.

SCIENTIFIC NAME: *Micropterus dolomieui.*

DESCRIPTION: A top gamefish and a flashy fighter, the smallmouth bass is brownish, bronze, or greenish brown in coloration, with the back being darker and the belly being an off-white. The sides are marked with dark, vertical bars, which may be indistinguishable in young fish. (For physical differences between the smallmouth bass and its look-alike relative, the largemouth bass, see Largemouth Bass.) The smallmouth is not as common as, and is a wilder fighter than, the largemouth.

RANGE: The smallmouth's original range was throughout New England, southern Canada, and the Great Lakes area, and in large rivers of Tennessee, Arkansas, and Oklahoma. However, stocking has greatly widened this range so that it now includes states in northern and moderate climates from coast to coast.

HABITAT: Unlike the largemouth bass, the smallmouth is a fish of cold, clear waters (preferring water temperatures of no higher than 65°F or so). Large, deep lakes and sizable rivers are the smallmouth's domain, though he is often found in streams that look like good trout water—that is, those with numerous riffles flowing over gravel, boulders, or bedrock. In lakes, smallmouths are likely to be found over gravel bars, between submerged weedbeds in water 10 to 20 feet deep, along dropoffs near shale banks, on gravel points running out from shore, and near midlake reefs or shoals. In streams they often hold at the head of a pool where the water fans out, and in pockets having moderate current and nearby cover.

SIZE: Maximum weight attained by smallmouth bass is about 12 pounds. In most waters, however, a 4- or 5-pounder is a very good fish, and average weight is probably 1½ to 3 pounds.

FOOD: Smallmouths eat baitfish and crayfish mainly, though they also feed on hellgrammites and other insect life, worms, small frogs, and leeches.

Redeye Bass

COMMON NAMES: Redeye bass, Coosa bass, shoal bass, Chipola bass.

SCIENTIFIC NAME: *Micropterus coosae.*

DESCRIPTION: Given full status as a distinct species in about 1940, the redeye bass is a relative of the smallmouth. Though this fish is often difficult to identify positively, especially in adult form, the redeye young have dark vertical bars (which become indistinct with age) and brick-red dorsal, anal, and caudal fins. This fin color, and the red of its eyes, are the redeye's most distinctive physical traits. The redeye is a good fighter and is good-eating.

RANGE: An inhabitant of the southeastern states, the redeye bass is found mainly in Alabama, Georgia, and South Carolina. It is also found in the Chipola River system in Florida.

HABITAT: The redeye bass is mainly a stream fish,

usually inhabiting upland parts of drainage systems. They often feed at the surface.

SIZE: Maximum weight of the redeye is 6 pounds, but, in Alabama at least, the average weight is about 12 ounces.

FOOD: A large portion of the redeye's diet is insects, but it also feeds on worms, crickets, and various baitfish.

Spotted Bass

COMMON NAMES: Spotted bass, Kentucky bass, Kentucky spotted bass.

SCIENTIFIC NAME: *Micropterus punctulatus.*

DESCRIPTION: The spotted bass, recognized as a distinct species only since 1927, is quite similar in appearance to the largemouth bass and has characteristics of both the largemouth and the smallmouth. The spotted bass is olive-green on the back with many dark blotches, most of which are diamond-shaped. A series of short blotches form a horizontal dark band along the sides which is somewhat more irregular than that of the largemouth. Spots below the lateral line distinguish the spotted bass from the largemouth, and that spotting, plus

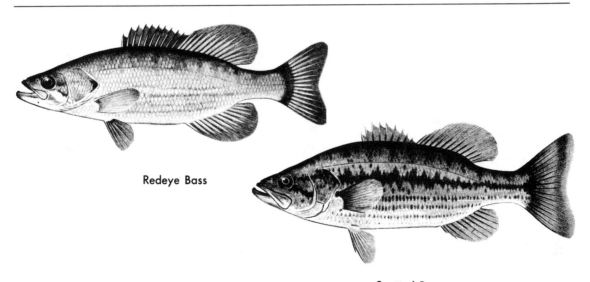

Redeye Bass

Spotted Bass

the lack of vertical side bars, distinguishes it from the smallmouth bass.

RANGE: The spotted bass is found in the Ohio-Mississippi drainage from Ohio south to the states bordering the Gulf of Mexico, western Florida, and west to Texas, Oklahoma, and Kansas.

HABITAT: In the northern part of its range, the spotted bass prefers large, deep pools in sluggish waters. Its preferred habitat in the southern part of its range is quite different, consisting of cool streams with gravel bottoms and clear spring-fed lakes. In lakes, spotted bass are sometimes found in water as deep as 100 feet.

SIZE: Maximum weight of spotted bass is 8 pounds, but few specimens top 4 or 5 pounds.

FOOD: Spotted bass, like most other members of the bass family, feed on various baitfish and insects, frogs, worms, crustaceans, grubs, and the like.

Bluegill

COMMON NAMES: Bluegill, bluegill sunfish, bream, sun perch, blue perch, blue sunfish, copperbelly, red-breasted bream, copperhead bream, blue bream.

SCIENTIFIC NAME: *Lepomis macrochirus.*

DESCRIPTION: Many's the fisherman who cut his angling teeth on the bluegill, most widely distributed and most popular of the large sunfish family. The color of the bluegill varies probably more than that of any other sunfish, ranging in basic body color from yellow or orange to dark blue. The shading goes from dark on the back to light on the forward part of the belly. The sides of a bluegill are usually marked by six to eight irregular vertical bars of a dark color. A bluegill's prominent features are a broad black gill flap, and long, pointed pectoral fins. Bluegills are excellent fighters, and if they grew to largemouth-bass size, they would break a lot of tackle.

RANGE: The bluegill's range just about blankets the entire 48 contiguous states.

HABITAT: The bluegill prefers habitat very much like that of largemouth bass—that is, quiet, weedy waters, in both lakes and streams, where they can find both cover and food. In daytime, the smaller bluegills are usually close to shore in coves, under overhanging trees, around docks. The larger ones

are usually nearby but in deeper water, moving into the shallows early and late in the day.

SIZE: Maximum size of bluegills is about 4½ pounds in weight and 15 inches in length, but average length is 4 to 8 inches.

FOOD: A bluegill's food consists chiefly of insect life and vegetation. Other items on the diet include worms, grubs, small baitfish, crustaceans, small frogs, grasshoppers, and the like.

Redear Sunfish

COMMON NAMES: Redear sunfish, redear, shellcracker, stumpknocker, yellow bream, chinquapin.

SCIENTIFIC NAME: *Lepomis microlophus.*

DESCRIPTION: A large and very popular sunfish in the South, the redear has a small mouth, large and pointed pectoral fins, and a black gill flap with a whitish border (the bluegill lacks the white gill-flap border). The body color is olive with darker olive spots, and the sides have five to 10 dusky vertical bars. The redear is distinguishable from the pumpkinseed—the member of the sunfish family that it most closely resembles—by the lack of spots on the dorsal fin.

RANGE: The redear sunfish ranges from southern Illinois and southern Indiana south to Florida and the other Gulf states and westward to Texas and New Mexico. Its heaviest concentration is in Florida.

HABITAT: The redear sunfish shows a definite liking for large, quiet waters, congregating around logs, stumps, and roots. It will, however, frequent open waters and seems to require less vegetation than other sunfish.

SIZE: The redear is more likely to run to large size than is most any other sunfish. Three pounds seems to be maximum weight, but 2-pounders are not uncommon.

FOOD: Redears depend mainly on snails for food, but will eat other mollusks, crustaceans, worms, and insects.

White Crappie

COMMON NAMES: White crappie, papermouth, bachelor perch, papermouth perch, strawberry bass, calico, calico bass, sago, grass bass.

SCIENTIFIC NAME: *Pomoxis annularis*.

DESCRIPTION: This popular freshwater panfish is a cousin to the true sunfish. In coloration, its back is an olive green and the sides silvery olive with seven to nine dark vertical bands, while the sides of the very similar black crappie (which see) have irregular dark mottlings. Another, more reliable way to tell the white crappie from the black is the number of spines in the dorsal fin: the white has six while the black has seven or eight. The white is more elongated in general shape, while the black, by comparison, has a high, rather arched back.

RANGE: Original range of the white crappie extended from Nebraska east to the Great Lakes, south through the Mississippi and Ohio river systems, and throughout most of the South as far north as North Carolina. Stocking has greatly extended that range, though the white crappie is predominantly a southern species.

HABITAT: The white crappie can live under more-turbid conditions than can the black crappie—in fact, it prefers silty rivers and lakes to clear water and is common in southern impoundments and cypress bayous, warm and weedy ponds, slow streams. The ideal home for these schooling fish is a pile of sunken brush or a submerged treetop. In summer crappies often seek such a spot in deep holes, moving into the shallows in the evening to feed.

SIZE: White crappies average 6 to 10 inches in length and less than a pound in weight. However, individuals of more than 5 pounds have been caught by sport fishermen, and 2- or 3-pounders are not rare.

FOOD: White crappies eat baitfish for the most part—gizzard shad is their blueplate special in southern lakes—but also feed on worms, shrimp, plankton, snails, crayfish, and insects.

Black Crappie

COMMON NAMES: Black crappie, calico, calico bass, papermouth, grass bass.

SCIENTIFIC NAME: *Pomoxis nigromaculatus*.

DESCRIPTION: This near-identical twin of the white crappie is dark olive or black on the back. Its silvery sides and its dorsal, anal, and caudal fins contain dark and irregular blotches scattered in no special pattern. (For physical differences between black and white crappie, see White Crappie.)

Though it is a school fish like the white crappie, the black crappie does not seem to populate a lake or stream so thickly as does the white.

RANGE: The black crappie, though predominantly a northern-U.S. fish, is found from southern Manitoba to southern Quebec, and from Nebraska to the East Coast and south to Texas and Florida. However, stocking has widened this range to include such places as British Columbia and California.

HABITAT: The black crappie prefers rather cool, clear, weedy lakes and rivers, though it often shares the same waters with the white crappie. The black is a brush-lover, tending to school up among submerged weed beds and the like. It occasionally feeds at the surface, particularly near nightfall.

SIZE: Same as white crappie.

FOOD: Same as white crappie.

White Bass

COMMON NAMES: White bass, barfish, striped bass, streak.

SCIENTIFIC NAME: *Morone chrysops*.

DESCRIPTION: This freshwater member of the ocean-going sea-bass family has boomed in popularity among sport fishermen in recent years, thanks to its schooling habits, eagerness to bite, tastiness of its flesh, and increase in its range. The white bass is a silvery fish tinged with yellow toward the belly. The sides have about 10 narrow dark stripes, the body is moderately compressed, and the mouth is basslike. The white bass may be distinguished from the look-alike yellow bass (which see) by its unbroken side stripes (those of the yellow bass are broken) and by its projecting lower jaw (the upper and lower jaws of the yellow are about even). The white bass is astonishingly prolific.

RANGE: White bass are found in the St. Lawrence River area and throughout the Mississippi and Missouri river systems, west into Texas, and in most of the other southern and southwestern states.

HABITAT: The white bass lives in large lakes and rivers but appears to prefer large lakes containing relatively clear water. The burgeoning number of large, deep reservoirs constructed recently in the South and Southwest are tailor-made for the white bass. These fish like large areas of deep water and need gravel or bottom rubble for spawning. Schools of whites can often be seen feeding voraciously on or near the surface, particularly in the evening.

SIZE: Maximum size of white bass is about 6 pounds, but average size is ½ to 2 pounds. A 3- or 4-pounder is an excellent specimen.

FOOD: Baitfish, particularly gizzard shad, form the main part of the white bass's diet, though it will also eat crustaceans, worms, and insect life.

Yellow Bass

COMMON NAMES: Yellow bass, barfish, brassy bass, stripe, striped bass, streaker.

SCIENTIFIC NAME: *Morone mississippiensis.*

DESCRIPTION: Quite similar in appearance to the white bass (for physical differences, see White Bass), the yellow bass has an olive-green back, silvery to golden-yellow sides with six or seven dark, horizontal, broken stripes, and a white belly. Like the white bass, the yellow is a member of the sea-bass family. It is a school fish, but its population levels tend to fluctuate drastically from year to year.

RANGE: The range of the yellow bass is quite restricted, being mainly the Mississippi River drainage from Minnesota to Louisiana and eastern Texas, plus the Tennessee River drainage, plus Iowa. Even within its range, the yellow is found only in scattered lakes and streams.

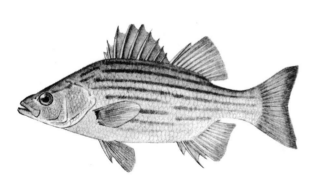

Yellow Bass

HABITAT: One of the yellow's primary habitat requirements is wide, shallow, gravelly areas and rocky reefs. This fish prefers large lakes and large rivers, especially those with clear water. Yellow-bass schools tend to roam in deep water in daytime, coming into the shallows to feed late and very early.

SIZE: Most yellow bass caught by sport fishermen range from 8 to 11 inches, or ¼ to ¾ pound. Maximum size is probably about 3 pounds.

FOOD: Yellow bass feed almost exclusively on baitfish, but occasionally take crustaceans and insects.

White Perch

COMMON NAMES: White perch, silver perch, sea perch.

SCIENTIFIC NAME: *Morone americanus.*

DESCRIPTION: This fish is not a perch but rather a bass. And though it is often found in fresh water, it is not a freshwater bass. It is a member of the sea-bass family and superficially resembles one other member of that family, the saltwater striped bass, though it is much smaller. The white perch is greenish to blackish green on the back and silvery on the sides, particularly when living in salt water (freshwater individuals are usually darker). Young white perch have indistinct stripes on the sides, but adult fish lack them.

RANGE: In salt water, white perch range along the Atlantic Coast from Nova Scotia to North Carolina. They are found inland as far as the Great Lakes and are especially abundant in New York State and New England.

HABITAT: In salt water, white perch are most likely to be found in brackish ponds and backwaters formed by coastal sandbars. Anadromous members of the clan run up rivers to spawn. In inland lakes, these fish usually lie in deep water over a sand or gravel bottom during the day, sometimes at 50 feet or deeper, but often come into shoreside shallows in evening and at night to feed. At those times, and on dark days, schools of white perch may be seen breaking the surface.

SIZE: White perch seem to run larger in salt and brackish water than in fresh water. Average size, generally, is 8 to 10 inches, though 2-pounders are not rare. They seldom exceed 4 pounds.

FOOD: In salt water, white perch forage on small fish, shrimp, squid, crabs, and the like. In fresh water, their diet includes larval and other insect forms, crustaceans, baitfish, and worms.

Yellow Perch

COMMON NAMES: Yellow perch, ringed perch, striped perch, coon perch, jack perch.

SCIENTIFIC NAME: *Perca flavescens.*

DESCRIPTION: The yellow perch, in no way related to the white perch, is an extremely popular freshwater panfish. Though its colors may vary, the back is generally olive, shading to golden yellow on the sides and white on the belly. Six to eight rather wide, dark, vertical bands run from the back to below the lateral line. Though the body is fairly elongated, the fish has a somewhat humpbacked appearance.

RANGE: The yellow perch is a ubiquitous species, being found in most areas of the U.S. It is most common from southern Canada south through the Dakotas and Great Lakes states into Kansas and Missouri, and in the East from New England to the Carolinas. Stockings have established it in such places as Montana and the Pacific slope.

HABITAT: The yellow perch is predominantly a fish of lakes large and small, though it is also found in rivers. It prefers cool, clean water with plenty of sandy or rocky bottom areas, though it does well in a wide variety of conditions. As a very general rule, the best perch lakes are large and have only moderate weed growth. These fish feed at various levels, and the fisherman must experiment until he finds them.

SIZE: The average yellow perch weighs a good deal less than a pound, though 2-pounders aren't uncommon. Maximum weight is about 4½ pounds.

FOOD: Yellow perch eat such tidbits as baitfish (including their own young), worms, large plankton, insects in various forms, crayfish, snails, and small frogs.

Walleye

COMMON NAMES: Walleye, walleyed pike, pike, jack, jackfish, pickerel, yellow pickerel, blue pickerel, dore, pikeperch.

SCIENTIFIC NAME: *Stizostedion vitreum.*

DESCRIPTION: The walleye is not a pike or pickerel, as its nicknames might indicate, but rather the largest member of the perch family. Its most striking physical characteristic is its large, almost opaque eyes, which appear to be made of glass and which reflect light eerily. The walleye's colors range from dark olive or olive-brown on the back to a lighter olive on the sides and to white on the belly. Here's how to tell the walleye from its look-alike relative, the sauger: (1) the lower fork of the walleye's tail has a milky-white tip, absent in the sauger; (2) the walleye's dorsal-fin foresection has irregular blotches or streaks, unlike the definite rows of spots found on the sauger's dorsal. The walleye isn't the best fighter among gamefish, but he makes up for that shortcoming by providing delectable eating.

RANGE: The walleye is found in most of Canada as far north as Great Slave Lake and Labrador. Its original U.S. range was pretty much limited to the northern states, but stocking has greatly widened this range to include all of the East and most of the far-west and southern states.

HABITAT: The walleye loves clear, deep, cold, and large waters, both lakes and rivers, and prefers a sand, gravel, or rock bottom. He is almost always found on or near the bottom, though during evening and night hours he may move into shallow water to feed. Once you find a walleye hole, you should catch fish there consistently, for walleyes are schooling fish and are unlikely to move their places of residence.

SIZE: Top weight of walleyes is about 25 pounds, but a 6- to 8-pounder is a brag fish. Most walleyes that end up on fishermen's stringers weigh 1 to 3 pounds.

FOOD: Walleyes feed primarily on small fish and crayfish. Strangely enough, though they don't often eat worms, nightcrawlers are a real walleye killer, especially when combined with a spinner.

Sauger

COMMON NAMES: Sauger, sand pike, gray pike, river pike, spotfin pike, jack fish.

SCIENTIFIC NAME: *Stizostedion canadense.*

DESCRIPTION: The sauger is very much like the walleye in all important respects, except that it is quite a bit smaller. It is olive or olive-gray on back and sides and has a white belly. Its large glassy eyes are very much like those of the walleye. (For phys-

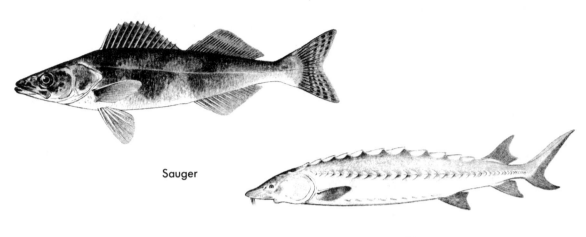

Sauger

White Sturgeon

ical differences between the sauger and the walleye, see Walleye.)

RANGE: The sauger's range is generally a blueprint of the walleye's. However, sauger are most common in the Great Lakes, other very large lakes in the northern U.S. and southern Canada, and in the large rivers (and their tributaries) such as the Mississippi, Missouri, Ohio, and Tennessee.

HABITAT: In this category, too, the sauger is much like the walleye, though the sauger can tolerate siltier or murkier water than can the walleye and tends to stick to deeper waters. A good place to look for sauger is in tailwaters below dams.

SIZE: The sauger's maximum weight is about 8 pounds. Average size is 1 to 2 pounds.

FOOD: Same as the walleye.

White Sturgeon

SCIENTIFIC NAME: *Acipenser transmontanus*.

DESCRIPTION: This huge, primitive throwback to geological history is one of 16 species of sturgeon in the world, seven of which occur in the U.S. It is the largest fish found in this country's inland waters and the only member of the sturgeon family that is considered a gamefish. The white sturgeon does not have scales but rather five rows of bony plates along the body. It has a large, underslung, sucking mouth, and its skeleton is cartilage rather than true bone. Sturgeon roe is better known as caviar. Though relatively few anglers fish for these behemoths, careful regulation of the fishery is necessary to prevent depletion of the white-sturgeon populations.

RANGE: The white sturgeon is found along the Pacific Coast from Monterey, California, to Alaska. They are also found inland in the largest of rivers, including the Columbia and Snake.

HABITAT: Some white sturgeon are entirely landlocked, but many spend much of their lives at sea and ascend large West Coast rivers to spawn. In large rivers they lie on the bottom in deep holes.

SIZE: The largest white sturgeon reported taken pulled the scales down to 1,800 pounds. Average size is difficult to determine.

FOOD: In freshwater the white sturgeon uses its vacuum-cleaner mouth to inhale crustaceans, mollusks, insect larvae, and all manner of other bottom organisms. Bait used by sturgeon anglers includes nightcrawlers, lamprey eels, cut bait, and even dried river moss.

Channel Catfish

COMMON NAMES: Channel catfish, fiddler.

SCIENTIFIC NAME: *Ictalurus punctatus.*

DESCRIPTION: This sizable member of the large catfish family (which includes bullheads) is undoubtedly the most streamlined, gamest, and most agile of the whole clan. In coloration the channel cat is steely blue on top and shades to white on the belly, though young ones may be silvery even along the back. It is the only spotted catfish (it has dark speckles on the sides, though these spots may be missing in large specimens) with a deeply forked tail.

RANGE: The channel catfish occurs from the Saskatchewan River and entire Great Lakes area southward into Mexico. Stocking has transplanted this fish far west and east of that natural range.

HABITAT: Channel catfish are found in lakes but are more common to rivers, especially large ones. They are likely to be found in faster, cleaner water than other catfish and seem to prefer a bottom composition of sand, gravel, or rock. Like all other catfish, they are bottom-feeders and are especially active at night.

SIZE: Channel cats are among the larger members of the catfish family, attaining weights of up to about 60 pounds. Average size is 1 to 5 pounds.

FOOD: The channel cat's varied menu includes just about anything he can get his jaws around—small fish, insects, crustaceans, worms, grubs, frogs, and many other aquatic food forms.

Blue Catfish

SCIENTIFIC NAME: *Ictalurus furcatus.*

DESCRIPTION: The blue is the largest member of the catfish clan. It has a deeply forked tail, but lacks the spots of the channel catfish. In color, the blue catfish is pale blue on the back, a lighter silvery blue on the sides, white on the belly. The most reliable way to tell the blue from other catfish is by the number of rays on its straight-edged anal fin (there are 30 to 36).

RANGE: The blue catfish is found mainly in the Mississippi River system but occurs south into Mexico and has been introduced into some rivers on the Atlantic Coast.

HABITAT: The blue is a catfish of large rivers and is likely to be found below the dams creating large impoundments, especially in the southern U.S. It prefers less-turbid waters than do most other catfish and seems to do best over bottoms of rock, gravel, or sand. It feeds in rapids or fast chutes.

SIZE: This heavyweight grows to well over 100 pounds. The average size, however, is 2 to 15.

FOOD: The blue catfish feeds primarily on small fish and crayfish. A favorite bait in some areas is a whole golden shad.

Brown Bullhead

COMMON NAMES: Brown bullhead, horned pout, speckled bullhead.

SCIENTIFIC NAME: *Ictalurus nebulosus.*

DESCRIPTION: Probably the most popular of the catfish—at least, it's the most often caught—the brown bullhead is a rather slender catfish with typical catfish features: sharp dorsal spine and sensitive barbels (the ''feelers'' projecting from the mouth area). The brown bullhead's chin barbels are dark brown or black. The tail has almost no fork, and the anal fin has 22 or 23 rays. The back is yellowish brown to light chocolate and has vague dark mottlings, the sides are lighter, and the belly is yellow to milky white.

RANGE: Brown bullheads occur from Maine and the Great Lakes south to Mexico and Florida, but stocking has greatly expanded this range.

HABITAT: Brown bullheads prefer relatively deep, weedy waters in lakes and slow-moving streams. They may be found over sand and gravel bottom and also over mud. They are almost exclusively bottom feeders.

SIZE: The brown bullhead seldom weighs more than 3 pounds, with its average size being 6 to 16 inches.

FOOD: Insect larvae and mollusks constitute the majority of the brown bullhead's menu, but it will eat almost everything from worms, small fish, and frogs to plant material and even chicken livers (a favorite catfisherman's bait).

Blue Catfish

Black Bullhead

Black Bullhead

COMMON NAMES: Black bullhead, horned pout.

SCIENTIFIC NAME: *Ictalurus melas.*

DESCRIPTION: Quite similar in appearance to the brown bullhead, the black bullhead is black to yellow-green on the back, yellowish or whitish on the sides, and bright yellow, yellow, or milky on the belly. Its chin barbels are dark or spotted, and its pectoral spines have no serrations. The body is chunky.

RANGE: The area in which the black bullhead is most numerous takes in New York, west to the Dakotas, and south to Texas. However, the fish has been introduced into most other areas of the U.S.

HABITAT: The black bullhead is a fish of muddy, sluggish, turbid streams and lakes. It seems to do well, in fact, in any kind of environment except cool, clear, deep water. It is a bottom-grubber.

SIZE: The largest black bullhead taken by sport fishing weighed 8 pounds, but this catfish seldom tops 2 pounds.

FOOD: Same as brown bullhead.

Carp

COMMON NAMES: Carp, common carp.

SCIENTIFIC NAME: *Cyprinus carpio.*

DESCRIPTION: This big, coarse, much maligned rough fish belongs to the minnow family and is related to the goldfish. In color the carp is olive to light brown on the back, golden yellow on the sides, and yellowish white on the belly. At the base of each of its large scales is a dark spot. On each side of the upper jaw are a pair of fleshy barbels, and the dorsal fin has a serrated spine. Though the carp is cussed out by most sport fishermen and often poisoned out of lakes and streams, he is taken by rod and line, bow and arrow, spear, ice gig, and set line, and he can put up a whale of a battle.

RANGE: Introduced into the U.S. in 1876, the carp has found its way into just about every area in the nation. He is also widely distributed through Europe and Asia.

HABITAT: The carp can live almost anywhere and under almost any conditions—except cold, clear waters. He is almost always found on the bottom, except during spawning, when schools of carp are often seen slashing about on the surface.

SIZE: Carp reach a maximum size of about 60 pounds, but average weight is 8 to 15 pounds.

FOOD: Carp are mainly vegetarians, feeding on aquatic plant life and plankton, though they also eat insects and are often caught by anglers on dough-balls, cornmeal, and such.

Alligator Gar

SCIENTIFIC NAME: *Lepisosteus spatula.*

DESCRIPTION: Exceeded in size in fresh water only by the western sturgeons, the alligator gar is the largest of the ancient gar family. It can be distinguished from its relatives by an examination of the teeth. Young alligator gars have two rows of large teeth on each side of the upper jaw; other gars have only a single row. The alligator gar has a long, cylindrical body that is olive-green or brownish green along the back and lighter below. The sides and rear fins have mottlings or large dark spots. Gars are of minor importance as sport fish, though they wage a wild no-holds-barred battle when taken on rod and line.

RANGE: The alligator gar is found mainly in the Mississippi and Ohio river systems as far north as Louisville, Kentucky, and St. Louis, Missouri and as far south as northeastern Mexico.

HABITAT: Alligator gars prefer sluggish rivers, lakes, backwaters and such over muddy, weedy bottoms. They often congregate in loose schools, usually near the surface, where they roll about.

SIZE: Largest reported alligator gar was 10 feet long and weighed 302 pounds. Average size is undetermined.

FOOD: Various kinds of fish, notably the freshwater drum (or gaspergou) are the principal food of alligator gars, though anglers catch them on wire nooses baited with minnows and on bunches of flosslike material that tangle tenaciously in the gar's teeth.

Longnose Gar

SCIENTIFIC NAME: *Lepisosteus osseus.*

DESCRIPTION: The longnose gar is the most common and most widely distributed of the entire gar family. Its name derives from its long, slender beak (nose). Other distinguishing characteristics are its overlapping diamond-shaped scales and the un-usual position of its dorsal fin—far back near the tail and almost directly above the anal fin. Coloration is similar to that of the alligator gar (which see).

RANGE: The longnose gar occurs from Quebec's St. Lawrence drainage west to the Great Lakes (excluding Superior) and as far as Montana, south along the Mississippi system and down into Mexico.

HABITAT: The longnose lives in much the same habitat as does the alligator gar, though it is more likely to be found swimming and feeding in flowing water—that is, where there is a moderate current.

SIZE: Smaller by far than the alligator gar, the longnose reaches a length of 4 to 5 feet.

FOOD: The longnose, like the alligator gar, feeds mostly on other fish, though it also eats plankton and insect larvae when young.

Muskellunge

COMMON NAMES: Muskellunge, maskinonge (and a variety of other spellings), muskie, pike, blue pike, great pike, jack, spotted muskellunge, barred muskellunge, tiger muskellunge.

SCIENTIFIC NAME: *Esox masquinongy.*

DESCRIPTION: Moody, voracious, and predacious, the muskellunge, largest member of the pike family, presents one of the greatest challenges of any freshwater fish. His adherents probably catch fewer fish per hour than do those who fish for any other freshwater species, and yet muskie fishermen are legion—and growing in number. The muskellunge—whose name means "ugly fish" in Ojibway dialect—is green to brown to gray in overall color, depending upon its geographical location. Side markings are usually vertical bars, though the fish may be blotched or spotted or lack any distinctive markings. The muskie has no scales on the lower part of cheek and gill covers; other members of the pike family have scales in those areas. There are three subspecies of the muskellunge: the Great Lakes muskie, the Ohio (or Chautauqua) muskie, and the tiger (or northern) muskie.

RANGE: The Great Lakes muskie is generally a fish of the Great Lakes basin area. The Ohio (Chautauqua) muskie occurs in New York's Chautauqua Lake and through the Ohio drainage. The tiger (northern) muskie is common in Wisconsin, Minnesota, and western Michigan. In overall distribution, the muskellunge is found as far north as the

James Bay and Hudson Bay drainages in northern Canada, across the northern U.S. from Wisconsin east to New York and Pennsylvania, and south into Tennessee, North Carolina, Georgia, and in much of the northern-Mississippi drainage. Stocking and propagation methods are greatly widening the muskie's range.

HABITAT: Muskies live in rivers, streams, and lakes, usually only in clear waters, though they may inhabit discolored water in the southern part of their range. They prefer cold waters but can tolerate water as warm as 70°F to 75°. Favorite hangouts for adult muskies are shoreline weed beds, particularly near deep water, and such items of cover as logs, stumps, and rocks. They are usually found in water shallower than 15 feet, though midsummer may find them as deep as 50 feet.

SIZE: Muskies reach weights of more than 100 pounds. However, the biggest rod-caught specimen weighed just shy of 70 pounds, and the average is 10 to 20 pounds.

FOOD: Muskies feed mainly on fish, including their own young as well as suckers, yellow perch, bass, and panfish. But they also eat crayfish, snakes, muskrats, worms, frogs, ducklings, squirrels, and just about anything else they can sink their ample teeth into.

Northern Pike

COMMON NAMES: Northern pike, pike, northern, snake, great northern, jackfish, jack.

SCIENTIFIC NAME: *Esox lucius.*

DESCRIPTION: This baleful-looking predator of the weed bed is of great importance as a sport fish. In color it is dark green on the back, shading to lighter green on the sides to whitish on the belly. Its distinctive side markings are bean-shaped light spots, and the fins are dark-spotted. The entire cheek is scaled, but only the upper half of the gill cover contains scales. The dorsal fin, as in all members of its family, is far to the rear of the body, almost directly above the anal fin.

RANGE: The pike is found in northern waters all around the globe. In North America it occurs from Alaska east to Labrador, and south from the Dakotas and the St. Lawrence to Nebraska and Pennsylvania. Stockings have extended this range to such

states as Montana, Colorado, North Carolina, and Maryland.

HABITAT: Over its entire range, the pike's preferred living conditions are shallow, weedy lakes (large and small); shallow areas of large, deep lakes; and rivers of moderate current. In summer pike are normally found in about 4 feet of water near cover, in fall along steep stormy shores.

SIZE: In the best Canadian pike lakes, rod-caught pike average 5 to 25 pounds, but in most waters a 10- to 15-pounder is a very good pike. Maximum weight is somewhat over 50 pounds.

FOOD: Pike are almost entirely fish-eaters but are as voracious and predacious as the muskie (which see) and will eat anything that won't eat them first.

Chain Pickerel

COMMON NAMES: Chain pickerel, jack, chainsides.

SCIENTIFIC NAME: *Esox niger.*

DESCRIPTION: This attractive pikelike fish with the chain-link markings is the largest of the true pickerels. Body color ranges from green to bronze, darker on the back and lighter on the belly. Its distinctive dark chainlike side markings and larger size make the chain pickerel hard to confuse with the other less-common pickerel (mud or grass pickerel and barred or redfin pickerel).

RANGE: The chain pickerel originally was found only east and south of the Alleghenies, but its range now extends from Maine to the Great Lakes in the north and from Texas to Florida in the south.

HABITAT: The pickerel is almost invariably a fish of the weeds. It lurks in or around weed beds and lily pads, waiting to pounce on unsuspecting morsels. It is usually found in water no deeper than 10 feet, though in hot weather it may retreat to depths of as much as 25 feet.

SIZE: Chain pickerel attain a maximum weight of about 10 pounds, but one of 4 pounds is bragging size. Average weight is 1 to 2½ pounds.

FOOD: Chain pickerel eat fish for the most part, although they will also readily dine on frogs, worms, crayfish, mice, and insects.

Redhorse Sucker

COMMON NAMES: Redhorse sucker, redhorse, northern redhorse, redfin, redfin sucker, bigscale sucker.

SCIENTIFIC NAME: *Maxostoma macrolepidotum.*

DESCRIPTION: Many anglers look on the entire sucker clan—of which the redhorse is probably the best known and most widely fished for—as pests or worse. And yet countless suckers are caught on hooks, netted, trapped, and speared every year, particularly in the spring, when their flesh is firm and most palatable. The redhorse, like all other suckers, has a large-lipped, tubelike, sucking mouth on the underside of its snout. Overall color is silver, with the back somewhat darker. The mouth has no teeth, and the fins lack spines.

RANGE: The redhorse is found east of the Rocky Mountains from the U.S. midsouth north to central and eastern Canada.

HABITAT: Unlike some of its relatives, the redhorse prefers clean, clear waters and is at home in large and medium-size rivers, even swift-flowing ones, and in lakes. These fish seem to prefer sandy shallows in lakes, deep holes in streams. As spawning runs begin in the spring, the redhorse congregates at the mouths of streams.

SIZE: The redhorse sucker's maximum weight is about 12 pounds. Most of the redhorses taken by anglers weigh 2 to 4 pounds.

FOOD: This bottom-feeding species eats various small fish, worms, frogs, crayfish, various insects (both aquatic and terrestrial), and insect larvae.

Splake

SCIENTIFIC NAME: (None).

DESCRIPTION: The splake is a trout hybrid created by crossing lake trout with brook trout. The name is a combination of *sp*eckled (brook) trout and *lake* trout. The first important crossing of these two trout species was done in British Columbia in 1946, and some of the new strain were stocked in lakes in Banff National Park in Alberta. The body shape of splake is midway between that of the brook trout and lake trout—heavier than the laker, slimmer than the brookie. Like the true lake trout, the splake's spots are yellow, but its belly develops the deep orange or red of the true brook trout (see Brook Trout and Lake Trout). Splake mature and grow faster than lake trout. Unlike many other hybrids, the splake is capable of reproducing.

RANGE: The splake's range is quite spotty, including a number of western-Canada lakes, at least one of the Great Lakes, and a few lakes in the northern U.S. Stockings are slowly increasing this range.

HABITAT: Similar to that of the true lake trout.

SIZE: As yet undetermined.

FOOD: Similar to that of lake trout.

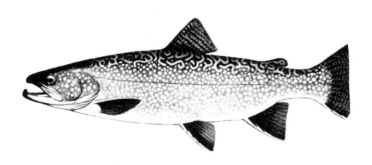

Splake

Tiger Trout

SCIENTIFIC NAME: (None).

DESCRIPTION: This hybrid is a cross between the female brown trout and the male brook trout. The tiger's most prominent physical characteristic is the well-defined vermiculations (wormlike markings) on back and sides. Lower fins have the white edges of the true brook trout. The tiger is an avid surface feeder and is considerably more aggressive than either of its parent species. Under hatchery conditions, only 35 percent of the tiger's offspring develop. The tiger occasionally occurs under natural conditions but does not reproduce.

RANGE: The tiger, being a hybrid, has no natural range, but stockings have introduced it into a few streams in the U.S. At least one state, New Jersey, has stocked this trout in its waters on an experimental basis.

HABITAT: Undetermined, but probably similar to that of the brook trout.

SIZE: Undetermined.

FOOD: Undetermined, but probably similar to that of the brook trout.

Rock Bass

COMMON NAMES: Rock bass, goggle eye, redeye, rock sunfish, black perch, goggle-eye perch.

SCIENTIFIC NAME: *Ambloplites rupestris.*

DESCRIPTION: The rock bass isn't a bass—it's one of the sunfishes. And though it isn't much of a fighter, it is fun to catch and is sometimes unbelievably willing to gobble any lure, bait, or fly it can get its jaws around. Basic color of the rock bass is dark olive to greenish bronze, with the belly lighter. The sides contain brownish or yellowish blotches, and a dark spot at the base of each scale produces broken horizontal streaks. The mouth is much larger than that of most other sunfishes, and the anal fin has six spines, while that of most of the other sunfishes has only three spines. There is a dark blotch on the gill flap.

RANGE: The rock bass occurs from southern Manitoba east to New England, and south to the Gulf states. Stockings have somewhat widened this range in recent years.

HABITAT: Rock bass prefer large, clear streams and lakes and are often found in the same waters as are smallmouth bass. As their name suggests, the more rocks and stones on the bottom, the better a fisherman's chances of finding rock bass. The species seems to prefer pools or protected waters to fast current or open waters.

SIZE: Top weight of rock bass is a bit more than 2 pounds. Most of those caught by fishermen are 6 to 10 inches long and weigh about ½ pound.

FOOD: A voracious eater, the rock bass eats crawfish, minnows and other baitfish, worms, adult and larval insect life, and the like.

Hickory Shad

SCIENTIFIC NAME: *Alosa mediocris (or Pomolobus mediocris).*

DESCRIPTION: The hickory shad—like its larger relative, the American shad—is a herring. In color it is gray-green above, with silvery sides and underparts. Behind the upper part of the gill cover is a horizontal row of dark spots, usually numbering about six. Spots on the upper rows of scales form faint horizontal lines. Upper jaw is shallow-notched, and lower jaw projects prominently. The hickory shad is not so important a food or sport fish as is the American shad.

RANGE: The hickory shad is found along the Atlantic Coast from the Bay of Fundy south to Florida.

HABITAT: An anadromous species (living in salt water but ascending freshwater rivers to spawn), the hickory shad's movements in the ocean are little-known. But in the spring it goes up the rivers, often the same rivers in which American shad spawn, though its runs usually precede those of the American shad.

SIZE: Though 5-pounders have been reported, the hickory shad seldom tops 2½ pounds in weight or 24 inches in length.

FOOD: The hickory shad feeds more on fish than does the American shad, and it is often caught by anglers using artificial flies and small spoons.

Freshwater Drum

COMMON NAMES: Freshwater drum, sheepshead, gray bass, gaspergou, white perch, croaker, crocus, jewelhead, grunter.

SCIENTIFIC NAME: *Aplodinotus grunniens.*

DESCRIPTION: This species is the only freshwater member of the drum (croaker) family, which has about three dozen saltwater members. The freshwater drum has a blunt head, rounded tail, long dorsal fin, and a humped back. Colors are pearl gray on back and upper sides, silvery on remainder of

Freshwater Drum

sides, and milky white on the belly. A rather faint lateral line runs all the way into the tail. These fish make a weird "drumming" noise which, when they feed near the surface on calm evenings, seems to come from everywhere. It is caused by repeated contractions of an abdominal muscle against the swim bladder. Another oddity: the otoliths, or ear bones, of freshwater drum were used as wampum by Indians, as lucky pieces, and to prevent sicknesses.

RANGE: Freshwater drum are found from Guatemala north through eastern Mexico and the Gulf states to Manitoba, northern Ontario, Quebec, and the Lake Champlain area. East to west, they range from the Atlantic Coast to the Missouri River drainage.

HABITAT: Found principally in large lakes and large, slow rivers, this species prefers modest depths (10 to 40 feet) and silty or muddy bottoms. It is a school fish, often congregating below large dams.

SIZE: Freshwater drum attain a maximum weight of about 60 pounds, but average size is 1 to 5 pounds.

FOOD: Primarily a bottom-feeder, this species feeds almost entirely on mollusks—clams, mussels, and snails—which it "shells" with its large, strong teeth. Other foods include crawfish and some baitfish.

SALTWATER SPECIES

Blue Shark

SCIENTIFIC NAME: *Prionace glauca.*

DESCRIPTION: This large shark species, which has a reputation as a man-eater, is distinguished by its abnormally long pectoral fins and by its bright-cobalt color (the belly is white). It has the long snout of many members of the large shark family, and the dorsal fin is set well back on the back, nearly at the midpoint.

RANGE: Blue sharks are found throughout the tropical and temperate waters of the world.

HABITAT: Though often seen in shallow waters on the U.S. Pacific Coast and on the surface in other northern areas, the blue shark is usually caught in deep water. It often roams in packs, while at other times it is found singly or in pairs.

SIZE: Blue sharks average less than 10 feet in length, but are reported to attain lengths of better than 20 feet. Largest rod-caught blue weighed 410 pounds.

FOOD: Blue sharks eat mainly mackerel, herring, squid, other sharks, flying fish, anchovies, and even such tidbits as seagulls and garbage deep-sixed from ships.

Mako Shark

COMMON NAMES: Mako shark, mackerel shark.

SCIENTIFIC NAME: *Isurus oxyrhynchus.*

DESCRIPTION: This huge, dangerous, fast-swimming, and hard-fighting shark is closely related to the white shark. It differs from the white mainly in the dorsal and pectoral fins, the tips of which are rounded in the mako, rather pointed in the white. In color the mako is dark blue to bluish gray above, shading to silver on the belly. The mako differs from the porbeagle shark in that its second dorsal fin is positioned a bit forward of the anal fin, while the porbeagle's second dorsal is directly above the anal.

RANGE: The mako is an inhabitant of the tropical oceans and the warmer areas of the Atlantic Ocean. It is not abundant in U.S. waters, though it is found as far north as Cape Cod. It seems to be most numerous around New Zealand.

HABITAT: Makos tend to stay near the surface in open-ocean areas.

SIZE: Makos reach lengths of better than 12 feet and weights of over 1,000 pounds.

FOOD: Staples of the mako's diet include tuna, mackerel, and herring. For some reason it often attacks, but seldom kills, swordfish.

White Shark

COMMON NAMES: White shark, great white shark, man-eater.

SCIENTIFIC NAME: *Carcharodon carcharias.*

DESCRIPTION: The white shark—enormous, vicious, and incredibly powerful—is one of the largest of all fish. Its usual colors are grayish brown, slate blue, or gray, while the belly is an off-white. Large specimens are sometimes a general off-white. The white shark is built blockier than the look-alike mako, having a much deeper body. The white has a pointed snout, triangular serrated teeth, and a crescent-shaped caudal fin.

RANGE: The white shark is found throughout the world in tropical and temperate waters, though it seems to prefer warm-to-temperate regions over tropics. It is not numerous anywhere.

HABITAT: White sharks generally stay well offshore and, as above, seem to prefer relatively cool waters.

SIZE: The white shark is a true behemoth; one specimen 36½ feet long has been captured. The weight of that fish must have been astronomical, considering that one white shark just 13 feet long weighed 2,100 pounds! Whites 20 feet long are not at all uncommon.

FOOD: White sharks eat such things as other sharks 4 to 7 feet long, sea lions, seals, sturgeon, tuna, sea turtles, squid, and refuse.

Porbeagle Shark

COMMON NAMES: Porbeagle shark, mackerel shark.

SCIENTIFIC NAME: *Lamna nasus.*

DESCRIPTION: The porbeagle is a blocky-bodied shark that closely resembles the mako, though it is much less game. Best way to distinguish the porbeagle from both the mako and the white shark is the location of the second dorsal fin—the porbeagle is the only one whose second dorsal is directly above the anal fin. In color the porbeagle shades from black to blue-gray on the back to white on the belly. Its anal fin is white or dusky.

RANGE: The porbeagle is found on both sides of the Atlantic as far south as the Mediterranean and Africa. On the U.S. Atlantic Coast it has been taken from South Carolina to the St. Lawrence Gulf. It is also found along most of the Pacific Coast.

HABITAT: The porbeagle is a fish of temperate waters. In warm waters it is found closer to shore and nearer the surface, but when the water cools it may head for depths as great as 80 fathoms.

SIZE: The porbeagle apparently reaches a maximum length of about 12 feet, though the largest definitely recorded stretched 10 feet. Largest rod-caught porbeagle weighed 465 pounds.

FOOD: Porbeagles thrive on school-type fish such as mackerel and herring and on bottom fish including cod, hake, and flounders.

Thresher Shark

SCIENTIFIC NAME: *Alopias vulpinus.*

DESCRIPTION: The thresher shark is nearly as large as the mako and is an excellent fighter, making breathtaking jumps and long runs. The thresher has one unique physical characteristic—its inordinately long upper lobe of the tail, or caudal fin, which is at least as long as the body. The thresher shark is dark gray, bluish, brown, or even black on the back and sides, while the belly is white, sometimes with a gray mottling.

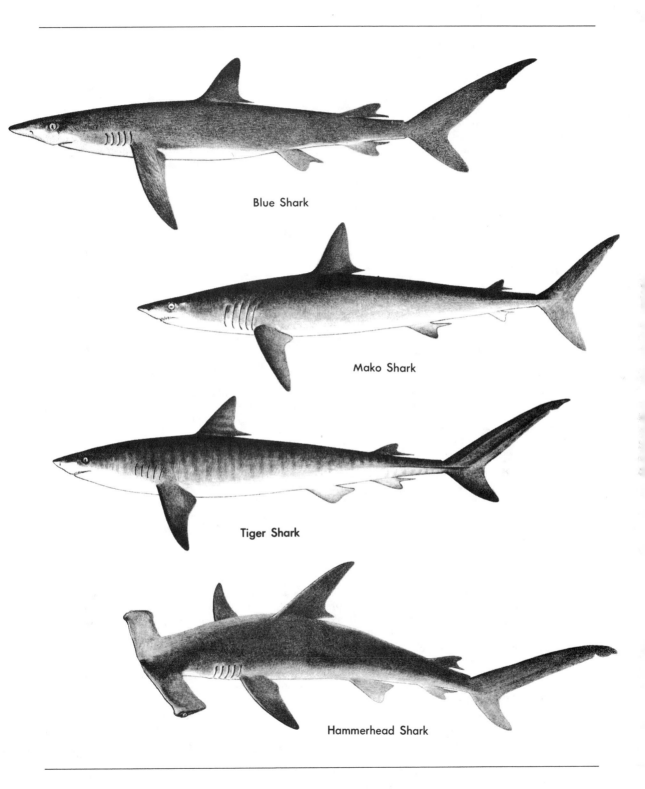

Blue Shark

Mako Shark

Tiger Shark

Hammerhead Shark

RANGE: Threshers are found from Nova Scotia to Argentina and from Ireland to the Cape of Good Hope. It occurs throughout the Mediterranean, in the Pacific from Oregon to Chile, and as far from the continental U.S. as Hawaii, Japan, and Australia.

HABITAT: The thresher is most at home at or near the surface in subtropical to temperate waters.

SIZE: Threshers reach lengths of 20 feet and weights of half a ton.

FOOD: The thresher uses its long tail to herd and injure such schooling fish as mackerel, menhaden, and bluefish.

Tiger Shark

SCIENTIFIC NAME: *Galeocerdo cuvieri.*

DESCRIPTION: One of the so-called requiem sharks, the aptly named tiger is often the culprit in attacks on swimmers. In color, it is usually a general steel gray or brownish gray with a white belly, though the young have bars and spots on back and upper sides. Upper lobe of the tail is long and slender, and the snout is short and sharp-pointed.

RANGE: Tiger sharks are found throughout the world's tropical and subtropical regions.

HABITAT: Though sometimes caught offshore, the tiger seems to be largely a coastal fish, and it occasionally comes into quite shallow waters. It stays near the surface.

SIZE: Tigers are reported to reach lengths of 30 feet. Maximum weight is unknown, but 13- to 14-footers tip the scales at 1,000 to about 1,500 pounds.

FOOD: Tiger sharks are omnivorous and cannibalistic. They eat their own kind, as well as fish of most species and crabs, lobsters, and even sea lions and turtles. Examinations of their stomachs have revealed such things as tin cans, parts of crocodiles, and even human remains.

Hammerhead Shark

COMMON NAMES: Hammerhead shark, hammerhead, great hammerhead.

SCIENTIFIC NAME: *Sphyrna mokarran.*

DESCRIPTION: There's no mistaking the hammerhead shark. Its small eyes are located at each end of its unique and grotesque head, which looks as if it had been modeled after the head of a huge mallet that had been pounded nearly flat. Gray or sometimes brownish gray on back and sides, off-white on the underparts, the hammerhead's dorsal fin is less erect than that of any of its Atlantic relatives. Though not officially classified as a gamefish, the hammerhead is a large and powerful adversary. Its hide makes fine leather, and its liver contains a high-grade oil.

RANGE: In the western Atlantic the hammerhead occurs from North Carolina to Argentina. It is found elsewhere in the tropical and subtropical areas of the Atlantic, as well as in the eastern Pacific and the Indo-Pacific.

HABITAT: Hammerheads often travel in schools and may be found both near shore and far offshore.

SIZE: Average size is difficult to determine, but hammerheads apparently reach a maximum length of about 18 feet and a maximum weight of considerably more than 1,600 pounds.

FOOD: Voracious and cannibalistic, the hammerhead eats just about anything unlucky enough to get in its way, including big tuna, tarpon, and other sharks.

Swordfish

COMMON NAMES: Swordfish, broadbill, broadbill swordfish.

SCIENTIFIC NAME: *Xiphias gladius.*

DESCRIPTION: The swordfish is one of the elite of saltwater fish, much sought by both commercial and sport fishermen. It is distinguished from the other billfish (sailfish and marlin) by its much-longer, flat bill (sword) and by its lack of scales and pelvic fins (the other billfish have both). The swordfish's dorsal and anal fins are sickle-shaped. Its color is usually dark brown or bronze, but variations of black to grayish blue are common. The belly is usually white, but the dark colors sometimes extend right down to the fish's undersides.

RANGE: Swordfish are migratory and are found worldwide in warm and temperate waters. Their occurrence in U.S. and adjacent waters extends in the Atlantic from Newfoundland to Cuba and in the Pacific from California to Chile.

HABITAT: Swordfish are open-ocean fish, usually feeding in the depths but often seen "sunning" on the surface.

SIZE: Maximum size of swordfish is a matter of some uncertainty, but specimens of nearly 1,200 pounds have been taken on rod and line. Average size is probably 150 to 300 pounds.

FOOD: Swordfish use their greatest weapon, the sword, to stun and capture such food as dolphins, menhaden, mackerel, bonito, bluefish, and squid.

Blue Marlin

SCIENTIFIC NAME: *Makaira nigricans.*

DESCRIPTION: This king of the blue water is probably the most highly prized of big-game fish, mainly because of its mammoth size and spectacular fighting abilities. In general coloration the blue marlin is steel blue on the back, shading to silvery white on the belly. In most specimens the sides contain light vertical bars, which are not nearly so prominent as those of the white marlin. The dorsal and anal fins are bluish purple and sometimes have dark blotches. The blue marlin's distinguishing physical traits include a relatively short dorsal fin and a relatively long anal fin, and a body shape that is considerably rounder than other billfish.

RANGE: Blue marlin are found in warm and temperate seas throughout the world. In U.S. and nearby waters they occur from the Gulf of Maine to Uruguay in the Atlantic, from Mexico to Peru in the Pacific.

HABITAT: Blue marlin are deep-water fish almost exclusively, and they are often seen cruising and feeding on the surface.

SIZE: Maximum size of blue marlin is something over 2,000 pounds, with the average being 200 to 500 pounds. Males seldom exceed 300 pounds, so those monsters often referred to as Big Daddy should really be called Big Mamma. Because the biggest blue marlin are thought to be in the Pacific, the International Game Fish Association separates these fish into two categories—Atlantic and Pacific.

FOOD: Blue marlin eat a broad range of fish life, including bluefish, mackerel, tuna, and bonito, as well as squid and octopus.

White Marlin

SCIENTIFIC NAME: *Makaira albida (or Tetrapturus albidus).*

DESCRIPTION: The white marlin is considerably smaller and less universal than the blue marlin. Its colors are a brilliant greenish blue on back and upper sides, changing abruptly to white at the lateral line. The sides have an irregular number of vertical bands of light blue or lavender. A unique feature of the white marlin is the rounded tips of its dorsal and anal fins. The body is slender and relatively flat-sided.

RANGE: The white marlin is limited to the Atlantic, occurring from Nova Scotia to Brazil and from the Azores to St. Helena Island and South Africa. Centers of concentration at differing times of year seem to be off Ocean City, Maryland, and near Venezuela.

HABITAT: Like the blue marlin, the white is a fish of warm and temperate waters and is a migrant.

SIZE: Most whites caught by fishermen weigh 40 to 60 pounds, but the species apparently reaches 160 pounds.

FOOD: The white is mainly a fish eater but will dine on anything it can capture.

Black Marlin

SCIENTIFIC NAME: *Makaira indica (or Istiompax indicus).*

DESCRIPTION: Possibly the largest of the marlins, the black is an ocean giant that is most easily distinguished from other marlins by the fact that its pectoral fins stick out at right angles from the body and are held rigidly in that position. The pelvic fins of the black marlin are shorter than those of other marlins, usually less than 1 foot long. The black marlin is seldom truly black, though its color varies greatly. Most are slate blue on the back and upper sides, shading to silvery white on the underparts. The sides occasionally exhibit pale blue stripes.

RANGE: Black marlin seem to be found almost exclusively in the Pacific and Indian oceans, being found as far north as southern California and Mexico. One area of abundance seems to be off the coast of Peru.

HABITAT: Little is known of the movements of the

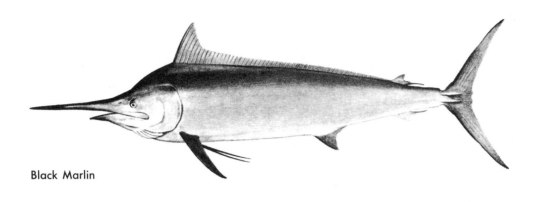

Black Marlin

black marlin, though it is certainly a fish of the open oceans, and evidence indicates that it migrates only short distances if at all.

SIZE: The record rod-caught black marlin weighed 1,560 pounds, but specimens of up to 2,000 pounds have been taken commercially. Average size is probably 300 to 500 pounds.

FOOD: Various fish species (a tuna of 158 pounds was found in a black marlin's stomach) and squid are the main items in the black's diet.

Striped Marlin

SCIENTIFIC NAME: *Makaira audax (or Tetrapturus audax).*

DESCRIPTION: Smaller than the blue and black marlins, the striped marlin, as its name suggests, is most easily distinguished by the stripes on its sides. These stripes vary both in number and in color, which ranges from pale blue to lavender to white. Body colors are steel blue on back and upper sides, shading to white on the bottom areas. The striped marlin also has a high, pointed dorsal fin, which is usually taller than the greatest depth of its body. Like all the other marlins, the striped variety puts up a breathtaking battle.

RANGE: Striped marlin are found in the Indian Ocean and in the Pacific from southern California to Chile.

HABITAT: Striped marlin are open-ocean fish. The

fairly well defined local populations seem to make short north-to-south migrations. Like all the other marlins, they are often seen feeding on the surface.

SIZE: The average rod-caught striped marlin weighs about 200 to 250 pounds, but the species grows to more than 500 pounds.

FOOD: Striped marlin feed on a wide variety of fish life (anchovies, bonito, mackerel, and many others), and on squid, crustaceans, octopus, and anything else that might get in their way.

Atlantic Sailfish

SCIENTIFIC NAME: *Istiophorus albicans.*

DESCRIPTION: The uncommonly beautiful sailfish probably adorn more den and living-room walls than do any other marine gamefish. They are spectacular fighters, hurling themselves high out of the water time and time again. You can't mistake the sailfish for anything else that swims—thanks to its enormous purple (or cobalt-blue) dorsal fin, which it often seems to flaunt at fishermen. Body colors range from striking blue on back and upper sides to silver-white below the well-defined lateral line. Side markings usually consist of a variable number of pale vertical bars or vertical rows of pale spots. The dorsal fin usually is marked with numerous black spots. A sailfish's pelvic fins are longer than those of other billfish.

RANGE: The Atlantic sailfish is commonly found

in the Atlantic Ocean from Cape Hatteras to Venezuela, with winter concentrations off the east coast of Florida. This species is also found off England, France, Africa, and in the Mediterranean.

HABITAT: Sailfish are most often seen—and are almost always caught—on or near the surface. However, studies of their preferred diet indicate that they do much of their feeding in middle depths, along reefs, and even on the bottom.

SIZE: Most Atlantic sailfish caught by sport fishermen weigh 30 to 50 pounds. Maximum size is probably a bit larger than the rod-and-reel record of 128 pounds, 1 ounce.

FOOD: According to studies made of the feeding habits of Atlantic sailfish in Florida waters, these fish feed mainly on a wide variety of fish life (tuna, mackerel, jacks, balao, needlefish, herring, and a few other species make up 83 percent of the Atlantic sail's diet). They also feed on squid and octopus.

Pacific Sailfish

SCIENTIFIC NAME: *Istiophorus greyi.*

DESCRIPTION: It is not known for certain whether the Pacific sailfish is truly a distinct species from the Atlantic sailfish, though it does grow considerably larger than the Atlantic variety. In most other important respects, the two fish are exactly alike. The only physical difference is that the Pacific sailfish's body colors tend to be somewhat more muted. It should be noted that in sport fishing for sailfish, marlin, and all other large pelagic gamefish, the trend today is toward releasing all fish that are not wanted for food (sailfish are not particularly good to eat) or mounting. (See Atlantic Sailfish).

RANGE: Pacific sailfish are found in the Pacific Ocean from about Monterey, California, south to Ecuador, and also in the vicinity of the Hawaiian Islands and elsewhere in the South Pacific.

HABITAT: See Atlantic Sailfish.

SIZE: Pacific sailfish put on a good deal more weight than their relatives in the Atlantic. Maximum weight is about 240 pounds, but the average rod-caught Pacific sail weighs from 60 to 100 pounds.

FOOD: See Atlantic Sailfish.

Bluefin Tuna

COMMON NAMES: Bluefin tuna, bluefin, horse mackerel.

SCIENTIFIC NAME: *Thunnus thynnus.*

DESCRIPTION: The bluefin is the king of the tunas, all of which are members of the mackerel family. Bluefins, from those of school size (15 to 100 pounds) to giants of nearly half a ton, have incredible strength and tenacity, and they are much sought by both sport and commercial fishermen. The bluefin has the blocky, robust body of a typical heavyweight. The head is rather small, and the snout is pointed. The bluefin has shorter pectoral fins than any of the American tunas. It has two dorsal fins—the forward one retractable and the rearward one fixed. Tail is sickle-shaped. In color the bluefin is steel blue on back and upper sides, shading to light gray or creamy white on lower parts. In small bluefins, the lower sides have vertical white lines.

RANGE: Bluefin tuna are found throughout the world, mostly in temperate and subtropical waters. In the western Atlantic they occur in abundance from the Bahamas north to the Labrador Current. In the Pacific they seem to be less abundant, being found in greatest numbers in the general area of Catalina Island.

HABITAT: The bluefin is generally a fish of the open ocean, though school-size bluefins occasionally come quite close to shore. In summer bluefins show up in large numbers from New Jersey to Nova Scotia, the smaller fish showing up first and closer to shore. Atlantic areas where bluefins tend to congregate and provide good fishing include the New York Bight, New Jersey, Block Island to Rhode Island, Cape Cod Bay, Wedgeport and St. Margaret's Bay in Nova Scotia, and Conception Bay in Newfoundland.

SIZE: For all practical fishing purposes, bluefins can be grouped in two size categories: school fish (those weighing 15 to 100 pounds) and adult fish (those weighing more than 100 pounds). The average schoolie weighs 30 to 50 pounds, while the giant bluefins attain maximum weights estimated to be 1,500 pounds or more. The rod-and-reel record is 1,496 pounds.

FOOD: Bluefin tuna feed on whatever is available, including a wide variety of fish (including herring, sand lance, hake, and even dolphin), as well as squid and crustaceans.

Yellowfin Tuna

COMMON NAMES: Yellowfin tuna, allison tuna.

SCIENTIFIC NAME: *Thunnus albacares.*

DESCRIPTION: Considerably smaller than the bluefin, the yellowfin tuna is a top sport and commercial fish, particularly in the Pacific. In color the yellowfin is steel blue or nearly black on back and upper sides, silvery white on lower parts. Characteristics that distinguish it from the bluefin are its much longer pectoral fins and the generous amount of yellow in most of the fins. The yellowfin is difficult to distinguish from some of the other tunas, but in large specimens the second dorsal fin and anal fin are much longer than those of any other tuna. The side markings of the yellowfin include a sometimes indistinct golden-yellow horizontal streak and white spots and vertical stripes on the lower sides.

RANGE: Yellowfins are found worldwide in tropical and subtropical waters.They are most numerous in the Pacific, where they are found widely off the coast of southern California and Baja California. They also range from the Gulf of Mexico north to New Jersey.

HABITAT: Yellowfin tuna are more southerly in general range than are bluefins. They are open-ocean fish, though there is some evidence that they do not make such long-range migrations as bluefins do.

SIZE: Yellowfins are thought to reach a maximum size of some 500 pounds. However, the rod-and-reel record is only 388 pounds, 12 ounces, and average size is less than 100 pounds.

FOOD: Same as bluefin tuna.

Big-Eye Tuna

COMMON NAMES: Big-eye tuna, Pacific big-eye tuna, Atlantic big-eye tuna.

SCIENTIFIC NAME: *Thunnus obesus.*

DESCRIPTION: Its eyes are not abnormally large, so it's difficult to determine how the big-eye tuna got its name. Its coloration is similar to that of its big brother, the bluefin, though its pectoral fins are longer. It is often hard to distinguish the big-eye from some of the other tunas. Its dorsal and anal fins are never greatly elongated (as in the large yellowfins), and the finlets running along back and belly from dorsal and anal fins to tail are yellow with black margins. Though Atlantic and Pacific big-eyes are the same species, the International Game Fish Association separates them for record-keeping purposes.

RANGE: Big-eye tuna range throughout the world in tropical and subtropical waters.

HABITAT: Big-eyes are fish of the open oceans and deep water, as witness the fact that many are caught by commercial longline fishermen.

SIZE: Big-eyes probably reach weights of 500 pounds and seem to grow somewhat bigger in the Pacific than in the Atlantic. Average size is about 100 pounds.

FOOD: Same as bluefin tuna.

Blackfin Tuna

SCIENTIFIC NAME: *Thunnus atlanticus.*

DESCRIPTION: Far more restricted in range than any of the other popular tunas, the blackfin is also one of the smallest members of the family. It is darker in color than the other tunas and has fewer gill rakers. The finlets behind the dorsal and anal fins are totally dark—not marked with yellow as are most of the other tunas.

RANGE: Blackfin tuna are found only in the western Atlantic Ocean, ranging from Cape Cod south to Brazil.

HABITAT: Blackfins are open-ocean, deep-water fish, like almost all the other members of the tuna family.

SIZE: The blackfin's top weight is probably not more than 40 pounds. The world-record rod-caught fish weighed 42 pounds. Average is probably about 10 pounds.

FOOD: The blackfin's diet is about the same as that of the other tunas, except that its prey is proportionately smaller.

Albacore

COMMON NAMES: Albacore, longfin tuna.

SCIENTIFIC NAME: *Thunnus alalunga.*

DESCRIPTION: The albacore is what you are likely to get when you buy a can of ''all-white-meat tuna.''

It is one of the tunas, and thus a member of the mackerel family. The albacore's most outstanding physical trait is its abnormally long pectoral (side) fins, which extend from behind the gills well past the second dorsal fin, ending about even with the third dorsal finlet. Coloring is an iridescent steel blue above, shading to silvery white on the belly. Fins are generally blue and bright yellow.

RANGE: Albacore are found in tropical, subtropical, and temperate waters in most parts of the world. In U.S. and adjacent waters they are primarily a Pacific species, being plentiful from southern British Columbia to southern California and Baja. In the Atlantic quite a few are caught off Florida, and they are occasionally found as far north as Massachusetts.

HABITAT: Albacore almost never come close to shore. They haunt deep, open waters and often feed near or on the surface. When on top, they can be seen smashing wildly into schools of frenzied baitfish.

SIZE: Albacore of up to 90 pounds have been taken in nets, and the record rod-caught fish went 88 pounds, 2 ounces. Average weight is 5 to 25 pounds.

FOOD: Albacore feed on a wide variety of fish, as well as squid and crustaceans.

Oceanic Bonito

COMMON NAMES: Oceanic bonito, bonito, skipjack, skipjack tuna, oceanic skipjack, striped tuna.

SCIENTIFIC NAME: *Euthynnus pelamis (or Katsuwonus pelamis).*

DESCRIPTION: The oceanic bonito is the most important member of the bonito group (which also includes the common, or Atlantic, bonito and the striped bonito, among others) and is the only bonito classified as a gamefish by the International Game Fish Association. The oceanic bonito is striking blue above and silvery below, with some shadings of yellow and red. It is unique in having four or more well-defined dark stripes running from the area of the pectoral fin to the tail along the lower part of the body.

RANGE: Oceanic bonito are found in tropical and subtropical waters throughout the world. In U.S. and adjacent waters, it is most common off the southern coasts.

HABITAT: All the bonitos are fish of offshore waters, though they come relatively close to shore if that is where their favorite food is. They are school fish and generally feed on or near the surface.

SIZE: The average weight of oceanic bonito is probably 10 to 18 pounds. Maximum is about 40 pounds.

FOOD: All the bonitos feed on a wide variety of fish, plus squid and crustaceans.

King Mackerel

COMMON NAMES: King mackerel, kingfish, cavalla, cero.

SCIENTIFIC NAME: *Scomberomorus cavalla.*

DESCRIPTION: Fast, strong, and good to eat is the king mackerel, largest member of the Spanish-mackerel family in U.S. waters. Its streamlined body—colored in iridescent bluish green above and shading to platinum below—seems built for speed, which the fish exhibits both in the water and above it in soaring leaps. The king's meandering lateral line and its lack of other side markings set it apart from most other fish. The lack of black in the rear part of the first dorsal fin distinguishes the king mackerel from other Spanish mackerels in our waters.

RANGE: Generally found from Brazil north to North Carolina and occasionally up to Cape Cod, the king mackerel is most numerous in the Gulf of Mexico and southern Atlantic.

HABITAT: King mackerel range in schools and usually stick to open water, though they sometimes hover near the outer reaches of bays, feeding on baitfish. March is the peak of the king-mackerel season for Florida anglers, while in the Gulf the fishing runs from spring into September.

SIZE: The average rod-caught king mackerel weighs 5 to 15 pounds, but the species apparently reaches a length of 5 feet and a weight of 100 pounds.

FOOD: King mackerel feed almost exclusively on smaller fish.

Wahoo

COMMON NAMES: Wahoo, queenfish, peto, ocean barracuda.

SCIENTIFIC NAME: *Acanthocybium solandri.*

DESCRIPTION: It is probably well that wahoo are neither as numerous as striped bass nor as large as bluefin tuna, for they are one of the wildest things with fins. They smash a trolled lure or bait with incredible force, make blitzing runs, and hurl themselves far out of the water (reports have it that wahoo have leaped over a fishing boat lengthwise!). The wahoo resembles no other fish, though it is shaped generally like the king mackerel. Its iridescent colors include blue or blue-green above, shading through coppery tints to silver below. The sides have narrow, wavy, dark, vertical bars. Older fish may lack the side markings.

RANGE: Wahoo range throughout the world in tropical and subtropical waters. In the Atlantic they stray as far north as the Carolinas but are most often caught off the Florida Keys, Mexico, and the West Indies.

HABITAT: Unlike most other mackerellike fish, wahoos are loners—that is, they do not range in schools. They live in deep water, often staying near the edges of deep dropoffs or along reefs.

SIZE: The average wahoo caught by anglers weighs 10 to 25 pounds, but the species is reported to hit 150 pounds.

FOOD: Wahoos eat various fish including flying fish, mackerel, mullet, as well as squid.

Cobia

COMMON NAMES: Cobia, crab-eater, ling, lemonfish, coalfish, black salmon, black bonito, cabio, cobio.

SCIENTIFIC NAME: *Rachycentron canadum.*

DESCRIPTION: The cobia is something of a mystery fish. Little is known of its wanderings or life history, and the species has no close relatives. In color the cobia is dark brown on the back and lighter brown on the sides and belly. A wide, black lateral band extends from snout to base of tail. Less-distinct dark bands are found above and below the lateral. The first dorsal fin is actually a series of quite short, stiff, wide spines that look nothing at all like a standard dorsal.

RANGE: The cobia is found in many of the world's tropical and warm-temperate waters. It occurs in the western Atlantic from Massachusetts to Argen-

tina, but its greatest abundance is from Chesapeake Bay southeast to Bermuda and in the Gulf of Mexico.

HABITAT: Young cobia are often caught in inlets and bays, but older fish seem to prefer shallower areas of the open sea. Cobias are almost invariably found around some kind of cover—over rocks, around pilings or bottom debris, and particularly under floating objects such as buoys, weeds, and other flotsam.

SIZE: Cobia reach top weights of over 100 pounds. Average size is 5 to 10 pounds in some areas, though in other areas, notably Gulf waters, 25- to 50-pounders are not uncommon.

FOOD: Cobias feed largely on crabs, though they also eat shrimp and small fish of all kinds.

Amberjack

COMMON NAMES: Amberjack, greater amberjack, horse-eye bonito.

SCIENTIFIC NAME: *Seriola dumerili.*

DESCRIPTION: Amberjacks are related to the pompanos and jacks, and more distantly to the tunas and mackerels. The amberjack is a stocky, heavy-bodied fish with a deeply forked tail, the lobes of which are quite slender. Body colors are blue-green or blue on the back, shading to silvery in the underparts. The fins have some yellow in them. A well-defined dark band runs upward from the snout to a point behind the eye. Mostly a solitary wanderer, the amberjack sometimes gathers in small groups in preferred feeding areas.

RANGE: Though occasionally found as far north as New England, the amberjack is primarily a fish of southern Atlantic waters from the Carolinas south to Florida and nearby islands. In the Pacific it is abundant from southern Mexico southward.

HABITAT: Reefs are the favorite habitat of amberjacks, though these fish often cruise for food at moderate depths—approximately 20 to 40 feet.

SIZE: The average rod-caught amberjack probably weighs 12 to 20 pounds, though ambers of up to 50 pounds are far from rare. Maximum size is about 150 pounds.

FOOD: Amberjacks prey on many smaller fish as well as on crabs, shrimp, crustaceans.

Pacific Yellowtail

COMMON NAMES: Pacific yellowtail, yellowtail, California yellowtail.

SCIENTIFIC NAME: *Seriola dorsalis.*

DESCRIPTION: A member of the amberjack family, the Pacific yellowtail is probably the most popular sport fish on the Pacific Coast. It is not of great commercial value. The yellowtail has a horizontal swath, ranging in color from brassy to rather bright yellow, running from eye to tail. Above the stripe the color is blue-green to green; below it the color is silvery. Fins are dusky yellow except the caudal fin (tail), which is bright yellow. The yellowtail is a tremendously powerful fighter.

RANGE: Yellowtails have been caught from Mazatlan, Mexico, through waters of Baja California, and north to the southern Washington coast. The world-record yellowtail was taken off New Zealand, but it is not known for sure whether it was of the same species as the Pacific yellowtail.

HABITAT: Yellowtails are fish of the mid-depths for the most part and are migratory. A preferred hangout is a kelp bed, and rocks often harbor yellowtails. Concentrations of yellowtails are at the Coronado Islands, around Catalina Island, and off San Clemente, Calif.

SIZE: Yellowtails reach weights of over 100 pounds, but average size is 8 to 25 pounds.

FOOD: Like many other voracious marine species, the yellowtail usually feeds on whatever is available. It seems to prefer sardines, anchovies, mackerel, squid, and crabs.

Jack Crevalle

COMMON NAMES: Jack crevalle, jack, common jack, cavally, cavalla, horse crevalle, toro.

SCIENTIFIC NAME: *Caranx hippos.*

DESCRIPTION: Probably the best-known member of a very large family, the jack crevalle is considered a fine gamefish by some anglers but a pest by others. The crevalle is short, husky, and slab-sided. It is yellow-green on the back and the upper sides, yellow and silvery on the lower areas. There is a dark mark on the rear edge of the gill cover, and the breast is without scales except for a scaled patch just forward of the ventral fins.

RANGE: The jack crevalle is found from Uruguay to Nova Scotia in the western Atlantic, and from Peru to Baja California in the eastern Pacific. It is most numerous from Florida to Texas.

HABITAT: The crevalle seems to prefer shallow flats, though large solitary specimens are often taken in deep offshore waters. It is a schooling species.

SIZE: Jack crevalles of better than 70 pounds have been caught, and 45-pounders are not uncommon in Florida waters. Average size is probably 2 to 8 pounds.

FOOD: Smaller fish are the main course of the jack crevalle, but shrimp and other invertebrates are also on the menu.

Rainbow Runner

COMMON NAMES: Rainbow runner, rainbow yellowtail, runner, skipjack, shoemaker.

SCIENTIFIC NAME: *Elagatis bipinnulatus.*

DESCRIPTION: The rainbow runner, an excellent gamefish, is a member of the jack family but doesn't look like most of the others. It is streamlined, not deep-bodied and chunky, and its coloration is striking. The back is a vivid blue or green-blue, while the lower areas and the tail are yellow. Along the upper sides is a broad dark-blue stripe, and below that are other, less-prominent blue stripes. Fins are greenish yellow. Finlets at rear ends of dorsal and anal fins distinguish the rainbow runner from the amberjack, which it somewhat resembles.

RANGE: Occurring in tropical waters worldwide, the rainbow runner is found in the Atlantic from Colombia to Massachusetts; in the Pacific it has been

Rainbow Runner

recorded from Peru and the Galapagos Islands to Baja California.

HABITAT: The wanderings of this fish, which is nowhere numerous, are little known. Trollers catch rainbow runners off Florida's east coast and in the Gulf of Mexico.

SIZE: Maximum size is about 30 pounds, but most rainbow runners caught go about 15 inches in length.

FOOD: Rainbow runners feed on smaller fish.

Permit

COMMON NAMES: Permit, great pompano, round pompano, palometa.

SCIENTIFIC NAME: *Trachinotus falcatus (or Trachinotus kennedyi).*

DESCRIPTION: The shy and wary permit, a much-prized gamefish, is the largest of the pompanos. Blocky and very deep-bodied (sometimes nearly half as deep as total body length), the permit's coloration varies greatly, especially in the young. Adults are generally bluish or gray on back, with the rest of the body being silvery. Very large ones may be almost entirely silvery with a green-blue tinge. Permit are far more numerous than many anglers think, but while they are often seen, they are much less often hooked and boated, for they put up a fight that is much more powerful than that of a bonefish. It usually takes at least a half-hour to tire a big permit.

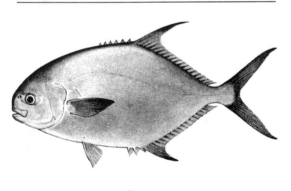

Permit

RANGE: In the Atlantic permit are found from Brazil to Massachusetts, in the West Indies, and in Bermuda. A Pacific variety is found from Ecuador to southern California. It is most abundant off southern Florida.

HABITAT: Permit are found from the surf out to deep water. They tend to stay in channels and deep holes but often come onto shallow tidal flats to feed, at which time their tails and backs can be seen above the surface.

SIZE: Permit reach weights of 50 pounds, but those caught by anglers probably average 15 to 25 pounds.

FOOD: Mainly bottom-feeders, permit prefer crabs and other invertebrates, plus small fish.

Bluefish

COMMON NAMES: Bluefish, chopper, tailor, snapper, jumbo.

SCIENTIFIC NAME: *Pomatomus saltatrix.*

DESCRIPTION: Savage, cannibalistic, delicious, abundant, willing—all those adjectives fit the bluefish, only member of the family Pomatomidae. In coloration, the bluefish is a rather dark blue on the back, shading through blue-gray and gray-silver to silvery on the belly. A fisherman getting his first look at a pack of blues attacking a horde of baitfish finds the sight hard to believe. The water boils white and then turns red and brown with the blood of the frenzied baitfish and the regurgitated stomach contents of the savage blues. Once hooked, the bluefish makes the angler fervently thankful that these fish don't reach the size of tuna, for blues are among the most powerful fighters in the sea.

RANGE: Blues are found in the western Atlantic from Massachusetts to Argentina, off the northwest coast of Africa, the Azores, Portugal, and Spain, and in the Mediterranean and Black seas. They are also found in the eastern Indian Ocean, the Malay Peninsula, Australia, and New Zealand.

HABITAT: Though primarily a deep-water species, particularly the large ones, bluefish often come right into the surf and sometimes go quite a distance up brackish-water rivers. Blues are rather erratic wanderers, though their general migration routes are fairly constant. They usually travel in large schools. In winter they are most numerous in Florida. As the waters warm, they head north to such bluefishing hotspots as the Carolinas, New Jersey, and New England. Tidal rips are top spots to look for blues.

SIZE: Bluefish average 2 to 5 pounds, though 15- to 20-pounders are not uncommon, and there was a 45-pounder taken off the coast of North Africa.

FOOD: Bluefish will eat anything they can handle—and some things that they can't, to which fact many a fisherman who has been bitten by a just-boated blue will attest. Menhaden is a bluefish's blue plate special, and other preferred foods are mullet, squid, and eels.

Dolphin

COMMON NAMES: Dolphin, bull dolphin, dorado, mahimahi.

SCIENTIFIC NAME: *Coryphaena hippurus.*

DESCRIPTION: The dolphin (a cold-blooded species that should not be confused with the warm-blooded dolphin, which is a mammal and a member of the porpoise family) is spectacular in both coloration and fighting ability. Purple and blue on the dorsal surface, iridescent green and yellow on sides and lower body, the dolphin's merging colors are enhanced by scattered blue dots. The head is extremely blunt, being almost vertical in large specimens (called bulls, though they may be either male or female). The dorsal fin extends from head nearly to tail. The dolphin is an explosive battler and an acrobatic leaper.

RANGE: Dolphins range widely in tropical and subtropical seas. In the western Atlantic they are found in relative abundance from North Carolina (particularly in or near the Gulf Stream) south into the Gulf of Mexico as far west as Texas. In the Pacific they range as far north as Oregon but are most numerous off southern California.

HABITAT: Dolphins are usually school fish, though large ones are often loners. They are fish of the open oceans; however, they lie under and cavort near various patches or bits of flotsam—floating grass, pieces of driftwood, and the like.

SIZE: The largest dolphin on record weighed 87 pounds. However, most rod-caught dolphins go 5 to 15 pounds.

FOOD: The food of dolphins includes a wide variety of smaller fish, squid, and crustaceans. In many parts of the dolphin's range, the flying fish forms a large portion of its diet, and the dolphin can often be seen soaring far out of the water in pursuit of a flying fish.

Tarpon

COMMON NAMES: Tarpon, silver king, sabalo.

SCIENTIFIC NAME: *Megalops atlantica.*

DESCRIPTION: The tarpon, considered the king of gamefish by the majority of those who have caught him, is a leaper to end all leapers. Tarpon jumps of 8 feet above the surface and 20 feet long have been measured. Tarpon are related to herring and shad and, oddly enough, to smelt and salmon. Usually blue or greenish black on the back, the tarpon's sides and underparts are a sparkling silver. Scales are very large, and there is a bony plate between the branches of the bottom jaw. The dorsal fin has no spines, but its last (rear) ray is abnormally extended and whip-like. Pectoral fins are quite low on the body. The tarpon's spectacular fighting tactics and hard, bony mouth make him difficult to subdue—one fish boated out of 20 strikes is about average success for a tarpon fisherman. The tarpon's only shortcoming is that he isn't much on the table. Most rod-caught tarpon are released.

RANGE: Tarpon are found on both sides of the Atlantic in tropical and subtropical waters. In the western Atlantic they stray as far north as Nova Scotia and range well south in the Gulf of Mexico. Main concentrations seem to be off southern Florida, Texas, and eastern Mexico.

HABITAT: Except in winter, when they apparently retreat to deeper water, tarpon are schooling fish of shallow waters. They frequent such places as mangrove flats, shoals, brackish bayous, cuts, inlets, and the lower reaches of coastal rivers. Sometimes they travel many miles upriver into fresh water. They are seldom far from the shore in summer.

SIZE: Though the rod-and-reel record is 283 pounds, tarpon reportedly attain weights in excess of 300 pounds. The average size of adult tarpon is probably 30 to 100 pounds. Tarpon of well over 100 pounds are subdued each year on fly rods!

FOOD: Tarpon feed on a variety of marine life including pinfish, mullet, needlefish, and other small fish, plus crabs and shrimp.

Bonefish

COMMON NAMES: Bonefish, ratfish, banana.

SCIENTIFIC NAME: *Albula vulpes.*

DESCRIPTION: What the tarpon is to leaping, the bonefish is to running. No one using sporting tackle can stop the blazing initial run of a hooked bonefish, which may tear 150 yards or more of line from a reel. The bonefish's body, built for speed, is torpedo-shaped. Colors are bronze or blue-green on the back, shading through bright silver on the sides to white on the belly. The sides occasionally have some dark mottlings. The bonefish is sometimes confused with the ladyfish, but telling them apart requires only a look at the mouth. The bonefish's upper jaw—a snout, really—is far longer than the lower, giving the fish a suckerlike look. The ladyfish has jaws of about equal length. Bonefish are related to tarpon.

RANGE: Bonefish are found in all tropical marine waters, being caught in such widely separated places as South Africa, Brazil, and Hawaii, where the biggest ones are found. By far the largest concentrations of bonefish in North America are around the Florida Keys and in the Bahamas.

HABITAT: Bonefish are a shallow-water species. They move onto very shallow tidal flats, sometimes in water only 6 inches deep, with the high tide to feed and then drop back into deeper water as the tide ebbs. On the flats is where fishermen, particularly fly fishermen, seek this ultrawary quarry.

SIZE: Bonefish probably reach a maximum weight of about 20 pounds or a bit more, but one of over 8 pounds is worth bragging about. Average size is about 4 to 6 pounds.

FOOD: Bonefish are primarily bottom-feeders, preying on crabs (particularly the hermit crab), shrimp, squid, sand fleas, and other crustaceans and mollusks.

Striped Bass

COMMON NAMES: Striped bass, striper, linesides, rock, rockfish, squidhound, greenhead.

SCIENTIFIC NAME: *Morone saxatilis.*

DESCRIPTION: The striped bass is one of the most popular of coastal gamefish. He fights well, and he "eats well." He is not likely to be mistaken for any other gamefish in his range, primarily because of his general shape, his side stripes (there are seven or eight horizontal dark stripes on each side), and the separation between the front and rear dorsal fins. Coloration is dark green to almost black on the back, silver on the sides, and white on the underparts. The striper is anadromous, living in the sea but ascending rivers to spawn.

RANGE: On the Atlantic Coast the striped bass is found from the Gulf of St. Lawrence south to the St. Johns River in Florida and in the Gulf of Mexico from western Florida to Louisiana. Introduced on the Pacific Coast in the 1880s, the striper is found there from the Columbia River south to Los Angeles, California. Center of the striper's range in the Atlantic is Massachusetts to South Carolina; in the Pacific it is in the San Francisco Bay area. Efforts to establish the striped bass in fresh water have been successful in such spots as the Santee-Cooper impoundment in South Carolina, Kerr Reservoir in North Carolina, some stretches of the Colorado River, and elsewhere.

HABITAT: Striped bass are almost exclusively coastal fish, seldom ranging more than a few miles offshore. Among the striper's favorite haunts are tidal rips, reefs, rocky headlands, jetties, bays, inlets, channels, canals, and reedy flats in tidal marshes.

SIZE: Most striped bass caught by anglers probably fall between 3 and 15 pounds, but many fish of 40 to 60 pounds are caught each year, most of them by trollers in the Cape Cod to Delaware range. The rod-and-reel record is a 78-pound, 8-ounce fish, caught in Atlantic City, New Jersey, but there are reliable records of a 125-pounder having been caught off North Carolina in 1891.

FOOD: The striper is a voracious feeder that preys on a wide variety of fish and invertebrates. The list includes herring, mullet, menhaden, anchovies, flounders, shad, silver hake, eels, lobsters, crabs, shrimp, seaworms, squid, clams, and mussels.

Snook

COMMON NAMES: Snook, robalo.

SCIENTIFIC NAME: *Centropomus undecimalis.*

DESCRIPTION: A fine fighter and excellent table fare, the snook is a much-sought prize of southern waters. In color the snook is brown, green, or brownish gold on the dorsal surface (back), shading to greenish silver on sides and becoming lighter on the belly. Distinctive traits include a depressed upper jaw and a jutting lower jaw, a somewhat humped back, and, probably most distinctive of all, a prominent dark lateral line that usually extends to and into the tail. The snook strikes a fishermen's offering with a startling smash but is an unpredictable feeder.

RANGE: Snook are found throughout tropical waters on the Atlantic and Pacific coasts, though they stray as far north as Delaware. They are plentiful along the Florida coasts and along the Gulf Coast in the U.S. and Mexico.

HABITAT: Snook are shallow-water fish that frequent such spots as sandy shores, mangrove banks, tidal bayous and canals, flats, bays, bridges and pilings, sometimes going upstream into fresh water. In cold weather they lie in deep holes.

SIZE: Snook probably average 2 to 5 pounds, but 10-pounders are not rare, and the top weight is better than 50 pounds.

FOOD: The voracious snook feeds on many varieties of fish, particularly mullet, but also eats crabs, shrimp, and crustaceans.

Great Barracuda

COMMON NAMES: Great barracuda, barracuda, cuda.

SCIENTIFIC NAME: *Sphyraena barracuda.*

DESCRIPTION: This toothy warrior is the subject of misunderstanding by both anglers and swimmers. Proven records of barracuda attacks on swimmers are relatively rare, though this fish, apparently out of curiosity, often approaches quite close to swimmers. Many fishermen write the 'cuda off as a poor fighter, but he usually puts on a powerful, acrobatic battle when hooked on sporting tackle. Shaped much like the freshwater pikes, the great barracuda is bluish gray or greenish gray on the back, silvery on the sides, whitish on belly. Dark, irregularly shaped blotches mark the sides, particularly toward the rear. Teeth are large and pointed. The 'cuda is a poor food fish and, in fact, may be poisonous.

RANGE: The great barracuda occurs in the American Atlantic from Brazil as far north as the Carolinas, though it occasionally strays north to Massachusetts. Centers of abundance are in Florida waters and in the West Indies.

HABITAT: Though barracuda are found in depths ranging from a couple of feet to 200 feet, they are mainly a shallow-water species. Preferred hangouts are reefs, flats, and around mangrove islands. The largest are usually found near offshore reefs.

SIZE: Known to reach a weight of better than 100 pounds and a length of 6 feet, the great barracuda probably averages 5 to 25 pounds. However, 50-pounders are not uncommon.

FOOD: Voracious in appetite, the barracuda feeds on a wide variety of smaller fishes, preying largely on whatever is most numerous in any given area. A favorite prey is mullet, though it will eat everything from puffers to small tuna.

Channel Bass

COMMON NAMES: Channel bass, red drum, redfish.

SCIENTIFIC NAME: *Sciaenops ocellata.*

DESCRIPTION: The name channel bass is actually a misnomer, for this species isn't a bass at all but rather a member of the croaker family. An important East and Gulf Coast gamefish, the channel bass is copper or bronze in overall body coloration. It can be distinguished from the black drum, which it resembles, by its lack of chin barbels and the presence, at the base of the upper part of the tail, of at least one large black spot. Food value of the channel bass varies with size. Small ones—often called puppy drum or rat reds—are fine eating, but large specimens have coarse flesh and are only fair eating.

RANGE: Channel bass are found along the Atlantic and Gulf coasts from Massachusetts to Texas.

HABITAT: These coastal fish are found off sandy beaches for the most part, moving shoreward as the tide rises to feed in holes, behind sand bars, and on flats. They are also found in such spots as the lee of mangrove islands, in sloughs, channels, and bayous.

SIZE: Channel bass reach weights of well over 80 pounds, though those of 50 pounds or more are relatively rare.

FOOD: Channel bass are bottom-feeders, eating mainly crustaceans, mollusks, and seaworms, though they sometimes prey on smaller fish, particularly mullet and mossbunker.

Weakfish

COMMON NAMES: Weakfish, common weakfish, gray weakfish, squeteague, yellowfin, tiderunner.

SCIENTIFIC NAME: *Cynoscion regalis.*

DESCRIPTION: The weakfish gets its name not from its fighting qualities, which are excellent, but rather from its quite delicate mouth, which is easily torn by a hook. This popular, streamlined gamefish is olive, green, or green-blue on the back and silver or white on the belly. The sides are quite colorful, having tinges of purple, lavender, blue, and green, with a golden sheen. The back and upper sides contain numerous spots of various dark colors. The lower edge of the tail is sometimes yellow, as are the ventral, pectoral, and anal fins. The weakfish is excellent table fare.

RANGE: This weakfish occurs along the U.S. Atlantic Coast from Massachusetts south to the east coast of Florida. Populations center around Chesapeake and Delaware bays, New Jersey, and Long Island.

HABITAT: Basically a school fish (though large ones are often lone wolves), these weakfish are a coastal species, being found in the surf and in inlets, bays, channels, and saltwater creeks. They prefer shallow areas with a sandy bottom. They feed mostly near the surface but may go deep if that is where the food is.

SIZE: The average size of weakfish seems to be declining. Today, most rod-caught fish go 1 to 4 pounds. Those early-fall ''tiderunners'' of past decades, fish of up to a dozen pounds, are seldom seen nowadays. Biggest rod-caught weakfish hit 19½ pounds.

FOOD: Weakfish eat sea worms, shrimp, squid, sand lance, crabs, and such small fish as silversides, killies, and butterfish.

Spotted Weakfish

COMMON NAMES: Spotted weakfish, spotted sea trout, speckled trout, trout, speck.

SCIENTIFIC NAME: *Cynoscion nebulosus.*

DESCRIPTION: This species is a southern variety of the common weakfish (see Weakfish), which it resembles. As its name might suggest, its markings (many large, dark, round spots found on sides and back and extending onto dorsal fin and tail) are far more prominent than those of the common weakfish. In general body coloration the spotted weakfish is dark gray on back and upper sides, shading to silver below. Like the common weakfish, the spotted variety has a projecting lower jaw and two large canine teeth at the tip of the upper jaw. It is a top food fish.

RANGE: The spotted weakfish occurs throughout the Gulf of Mexico, in Florida waters, and north to Virginia, though it is found as a stray as far north as New York. It is most abundant in the Gulf and in Florida.

HABITAT: Very much like that of the common weakfish.

SIZE: The average size of spotted weakfish is somewhat smaller than that of common weakfish. Most rod-caught spotted weaks fall in the 1- to 3-pound range. Maximum size is about 15 pounds.

FOOD: In many areas spotted weakfish feed almost exclusively on shrimp. They may also eat various smaller fish, particularly mullet, menhaden, and silversides, as well as crabs and sea worms.

California White Sea Bass

COMMON NAMES: California white sea bass, sea bass, white sea bass, croaker, white corvina.

SCIENTIFIC NAME: *Cynoscion nobilis.*

DESCRIPTION: Not a true sea bass, the California white sea bass is a relative of the weakfish of the Atlantic. It is a rather streamlined fish whose front and rear dorsal fins are connected. Body colors are gray to blue on the back, silvery on the sides, and white on the belly. The tail is yellow. The belly is somewhat indented from pelvic fins to vent. There is a dark area at the base of the pectoral fins.

RANGE: The California white sea bass has an extreme range of Alaska to Chile, but it is not often found north of San Francisco. Population center seems to be from Santa Barbara, California, south into Mexico.

HABITAT: The white sea bass seldom strays far offshore and is most often found in or near beds of kelp. Night fishing is often very productive.

SIZE: The white sea bass averages about 15 to possibly 25 pounds, though specimens of over 40 pounds are not uncommon. Maximum weight is a bit more than 80 pounds.

FOOD: White sea bass feed on a variety of small fish, plus squid, crabs, shrimp, and other mollusks and crustaceans.

California Black Sea Bass

COMMON NAMES: California black sea bass, giant black sea bass, giant sea bass.

SCIENTIFIC NAME: *Stereolepis gigas.*

DESCRIPTION: This large, blocky fish is a Pacific version of the Eastern sea bass. It is black or brownish black in general coloration, lighter on the underparts. Because of its size and color, the California black sea bass cannot be confused with any other species in its somewhat limited range.

RANGE: The California black sea bass is most numerous off Baja California and southern California, though it ranges north to central California.

HABITAT: The California black sea bass is strictly a bottom fish, being found in deep water, usually over rocks, and around reefs.

SIZE: The rod-and-reel record California black sea bass weighed 563 pounds, 8 ounces, which is probably about the maximum for the species. Average size is 100 to 200 pounds.

FOOD: California black sea bass feed on a variety of fish including sheepsheads, and on crabs and other mollusks.

Black Drum

COMMON NAMES: Black drum, drum, sea drum.

SCIENTIFIC NAME: *Pogonias cromis.*

DESCRIPTION: A member of the croaker family, the black drum is not so popular a gamefish as is the red drum. It is most easily distinguished from the red drum (channel bass) by the lack of a prominent dark spot near the base of the tail. Overall color of the black drum ranges from gray to almost silvery, usually with a coppery sheen. Young specimens usually have broad vertical bands of a dark color. Body shape is short and deep, the back is

arched, and the undersurface is somewhat flat. There are barbels on the chin.

RANGE: Black drums are an Atlantic species found from southern New England to Argentina, though they are rare north of New York. Centers of abundance include North Carolina, Florida, Louisiana, and Texas.

HABITAT: Usually found in schools, black drum prefer inshore sandy areas such as bays, lagoons, channels, and ocean surfs, and are often found near wharves and bridges.

SIZE: The black drum is known to reach a maximum weight of nearly 150 pounds. However, the average size is 20 to 30 pounds.

FOOD: Black drum are bottom-feeders, preferring clams, mussels, crabs, shrimp, and other mollusks.

Jewfish

COMMON NAMES: Giant sea bass, spotted jewfish, jewfish, spotted grouper, guasa.

SCIENTIFIC NAME: *Epinephelus itajara (or Promicrops itaiara).*

DESCRIPTION: Probably the largest of the groupers, the jewfish is not the gamest of fighters, but its weight alone makes up for that shortcoming. Overall color ranges from black to grayish brown, and back and sides are mottled. The upper sides contain dark spots. The tail is convex along the rear margin. The flesh of the jewfish is quite tasty. During World War II it was sold as "imported salt cod."

RANGE: The precise range of the jewfish seems uncertain. However, it is found in warmer waters of both the Atlantic and the Pacific and is most abundant in Florida waters and off the Texas Gulf Coast.

HABITAT: Despite its large size, the jewfish is most often found in relatively shallow water along the coast. It is at home under ledges and in reefs, in rocky holes, around bridges, and in deep channels.

SIZE: Though the rod-and-reed record is a 680-pounder, jewfish reach weights of at least 750 pounds. Average is probably 100 to 250 pounds.

FOOD: Jewfish feed on a great variety of small reef fish, including sheepsheads, and also feed on crabs and squid.

Blackfish

COMMON NAMES: Blackfish, tautog, oysterfish.

SCIENTIFIC NAME: *Tautoga onitis.*

DESCRIPTION: The blackfish is a member of the wrasse family, most of which are very brightly colored. The blackfish, however, is a drab gray or gray-brown with irregular black mottlings. Body shape is relatively long and quite plump. The snout is blunt, lips are thick, and the jaws hold powerful crushing teeth. Edge of the tail is straight. Dorsal fin is quite long and spiny. The blackfish's flesh is very tasty but for some reason is not much utilized. The blackfish is an accomplished bait-stealer.

RANGE: The blackfish is an Atlantic species found from Nova Scotia to South Carolina. It is most numerous from Cape Cod to Delaware Bay.

HABITAT: Blackfish are a coastal bottom species, preferring such lies as mussel beds, rocky areas both inshore and offshore, the outer edges of jetties and piers, and old wrecks. They are seldom found in water deeper than 60 feet.

SIZE: The average rod-caught blackfish weighs about 3 pounds, but 6- to 8-pounders are far from unusual, and the species reaches a maximum weight of about 25 pounds.

FOOD: Blackfish are bottom-feeders that eat such items as barnacles, mussels, crabs, snails, sea worms, shrimp, and even lobsters.

Sea Bass

COMMON NAMES: Sea bass, black sea bass, blackfish, humpback, black will.

SCIENTIFIC NAME: *Centropristes striatus.*

DESCRIPTION: The sea bass, though small, is one of the most popular of gamefish in its somewhat restricted range. It has a rather stout body shape, with a high back and a moderately pointed snout. The apex of each gill cover holds a sharp spine. The overall color is gray to brownish gray to blue-black, lighter on the fish's underparts. The sides are sometimes mottled and at other times appear to have light horizontal stripes formed by rows of dots. The dorsal fin also has rows of spots. Most distinctive trait of the sea bass is the elongated ray on the upper edge of the tail—it sticks out far to the rear of the rest of the tail. Sea bass are fine eating.

RANGE: Sea bass are found from Maine to northern Florida, but are most common from Cape Hatteras to Cape Cod.

HABITAT: Sea bass are bottom dwellers of coastal areas. Preferred depths seem to be 20 to 50 feet, though large sea bass are often found at depths of up to 100 feet, especially in winter. Sea bass like such spots as mussel beds, rocky areas, wrecks, pilings, bridges, offshore reefs and ledges, and rocky heads.

SIZE: Sea bass hit about 8 pounds maximum. Average is 1 to 3 pounds.

FOOD: Sea bass feed on smaller fish but prefer clams, mussels, crabs, shrimp, sea worms, and squid.

Atlantic Codfish

COMMON NAMES: Atlantic codfish, codfish, cod.

SCIENTIFIC NAME: *Gadus morhua.*

DESCRIPTION: This pot-bellied heavyweight of the northern Atlantic is the cause of many a runny nose among sport and commercial fishermen in the cold-weather months. The thick-bodied Atlantic cod seems to have two color phases: red and gray. In the red phase the fish may vary from orange to reddish brown. The gray phase ranges from black to greenish to brownish gray. The underparts are lighter, and the sides have many dark spots. The pale lateral line distinguishes the Atlantic cod from the haddock. The cod differs from the look-alike pollock in its longer chin barbel and the fact that its upper jaw projects past the lower (the opposite is true of the pollock). The cod's dorsal fin is in three spineless sections, and the anal fin, also spineless, has two sections—an unusual fin makeup.

RANGE: In the western Atlantic the cod is found from Greenland south to North Carolina. In the eastern Atlantic it ranges throughout the Baltic Sea, from northern Scandinavia east to some parts of Russia, and south to the Bay of Biscay.

HABITAT: Atlantic cod are schooling fish for the most part, bottom-feeders, and lovers of cold water. Though the young may be found in shallow water, cod generally prefer depths of 60 feet or more and are sometimes found down to 1,500 feet. Sport fishermen usually catch cod at the 50- to 300-foot levels. Cod migrate north and south to some extent, but most movement is from relatively shallow water, where they are likely to be found in winter, to the deeps, where they go in summer. Cod seem to prefer areas with a rocky or broken bottom and such places as wrecks.

SIZE: The average Atlantic cod taken by sport fishermen probably falls into the 6- to 12-pound category, but the rod-and-reel record is more than 80 pounds, and the species is known to exceed 200 pounds. Cod of up to 60 pounds are not unusual in the New Jersey to southern New England area.

FOOD: Atlantic cod feed on a variety of bottom life including various small fish (notably herring), crabs, clams, squid, mussels, snails, sea worms, and lobsters.

Pollock

COMMON NAMES: Pollock, Boston bluefish, green cod, coalfish.

SCIENTIFIC NAME: *Pollachius virens.*

DESCRIPTION: The pollock, in effect, lives under the shadow of its famous relative, the Atlantic cod. A better fighter than the cod (probably because it is generally taken from shallower water), it has a shorter chin barbel than its relative, and its lower jaw projects beyond the upper (the cod's upper jaw projects farther than the lower). The pollock is not spotted, as is the cod, and its tail is more severely forked. Pollock's colors range from dark olive green to brownish on upper parts, yellowish to gray on the lower sides, to silvery on the belly. Like the cod, its flesh is excellent eating.

Pollock

RANGE: Pollock range in the western Atlantic from the Gulf of St. Lawrence to Chesapeake Bay and in the eastern Atlantic from Iceland south to the Bay of Biscay.

HABITAT: In general, pollock are found in somewhat shallower water than are cod, and they are often caught at intermediate depths. Occasionally, usually during May at such points as Cape Cod's Race Point Rip, pollock come into shallow water near shore and can be taken on or near the surface.

SIZE: Most pollock caught by sport anglers weigh 4 to about 12 pounds. However, the species has a maximum weight of some 45 pounds.

FOOD: Pollock feed on a variety of fish—including herring and small cod—and on shrimp and some crustaceans and mollusks, as well as sea worms.

Summer Flounder

COMMON NAMES: Summer flounder, fluke, flatfish.

SCIENTIFIC NAME: *Paralichthys dentatus.*

DESCRIPTION: The summer flounder is one of 500-odd members of the flatfish family, a curious group. They begin life in an upright position and have an eye on each side of the head. As they grow, however, the body begins to "tilt," in some species to the right, in others to the left, and the eye on the downward-facing surface begins to travel to the upward-facing surface. Finally, the transformation is complete, and the fish spends the rest of its life on its side, with both eyes on the same side of the head (above and just to the rear of the point of the jaw). The summer flounder is white on the side that comes in contact with the ocean floor. The color of the upper surface depends on the physical makeup of the ocean floor, but is usually olive, brown, or gray, with prominent dark spots and some mottling. Body is flat and quite deep. Dorsal and anal fins are extremely long.

RANGE: The summer flounder occurs in the U.S. from Maine to South Carolina.

HABITAT: The summer flounder lives on the bottom, often buried in sand or mud. In summer it is found in shallow water, sometimes in depths of only a few feet, while in winter it moves offshore into as much as 50 fathoms of water. It frequents bays and harbors, the mouths of estuaries, and is often found around bottom obstructions such as wrecked ships.

SIZE: Most summer flounders caught by sport fishermen weigh 1 to 4 pounds, but the species' maximum size is probably close to 30 pounds.

FOOD: Summer flounders eat a wide variety of small fish, as well as sea worms, crabs, clams, squid, shrimp.

Winter Flounder

COMMON NAMES: Winter flounder, flatfish, blueback, blackback, black flounder, mud dab.

SCIENTIFIC NAME: *Pseudopleuronectes americanus.*

DESCRIPTION: One of the smaller members of the vast flatfish family, the winter flounder differs from the summer flounder in its smaller size and weight and in the fact that it is "right-eyed" (that is, has both eyes and the skin pigmentation on the right side of its head) while the summer flounder is "left-eyed." The winter flounder is white on the underside (the side on which it lies on the ocean floor), while on the other side the colors range from reddish brown to slate gray, usually with some dark spots. The mouth is small, and the lateral line is relatively straight. The winter flounder is widely sought for food by both sport and commercial fishermen.

RANGE: The winter flounder has an extreme range of Labrador south to Georgia, but is most common from the Gulf of St. Lawrence to Chesapeake Bay.

HABITAT: The winter flounder is found mostly in shallow water—as shallow as 1 foot, in fact—but is occasionally found at depths of up to 400 feet. It lies on the bottom, preferring sand or mud but accepting clay, gravel, and even a hard bottom. In the fall this species tends to move toward the shallows, while in spring the movement is toward deeper water.

SIZE: Winter flounders average from ½ to 1½ pounds in weight and 8 to 15 inches in length. Maximum size is about 8 pounds, and such heavyweights are often called snowshoes.

FOOD: Winter flounders eat such items as sea worms, crabs, shrimp, and minute crustaceans, as well as small fish and fish larvae.

Roosterfish

COMMON NAMES: Roosterfish, papagallo, gallo, pez de gallo.

SCIENTIFIC NAME: *Nematistius pectoralis.*

DESCRIPTION: The roosterfish—a relative of the jacks and pompanos, which it resembles at least in body shape—gets its name from the seven extremely long (far longer than the greatest body depth) spines of the forward dorsal fin, which vaguely resemble a rooster's comb. Body colors are green to gray-blue on upper areas, white to gold below. Two black stripes curve downward and then rearward from the forward dorsal fin, which itself has a white horizontal stripe. The roosterfish is a furious fighter and a fine table fish.

RANGE: Roosterfish are a Pacific species occurring from Peru as far north as southern California. They are particularly abundant in the Gulf of California.

HABITAT: Little is known of the movements and life history of the roosterfish. However, fishermen often catch them in sandy inshore bays and by trolling in open water. The fish are sometimes seen swimming on the surface, their dorsals erect and waving above the surface.

SIZE: Average size of roosterfish is estimated at 5 to 20 pounds. Maximum is probably about 130 pounds.

FOOD: The dietary preferences of the roosterfish aren't known in detail, but these fish certainly feed on most any small fish that are available. They strike artificial lures and plugs willingly.

Porgy

COMMON NAMES: Porgy, northern porgy, scup.

SCIENTIFIC NAME: *Stenotomus chrysops.*

DESCRIPTION: The porgy (most often called scup in some areas in its range) is what might be called a saltwater panfish. It has a somewhat ovate high-backed body with a small mouth and strong teeth. Basic body color ranges from silvery to brown, and there are usually three or four dark vertical bars on the sides. Dorsal fin is quite spiny. The porgy's flesh is highly palatable, and it is caught by both sport and commercial anglers, though in some areas rod fishermen consider the porgy a nuisance.

RANGE: The porgy (northern porgy) is found from Nova Scotia south to the Atlantic coast of Florida. In summer and fall it is quite abundant off the coasts of New England, New York, and New Jersey.

HABITAT: Porgies seem to prefer some bottom debris such as mussel beds. They live on or near the bottom in the middle depths of the Continental Shelf.

SIZE: Porgies average ½ to 2 pounds. Maximum size is about 4 pounds, and such individuals are often called humpbacks.

FOOD: Porgies feed mainly on small crustaceans, worms, mollusks, and occasionally on vegetable matter.

Spanish Mackerel

SCIENTIFIC NAME: *Scomberomorus maculatus.*

DESCRIPTION: This beautiful streamlined fish, though of modest size as mackerels go, is a magnificent fighter, making sizzling runs and soaring leaps. Body shape is rather compressed, and colors range from an iridescent steel blue or occasionally greenish on the dorsal surface to a silvery blue below. Side markings are mustard or bronze spots, quite large. Dorsal fin is in two sections, and there are dorsal and anal finlets. Its side spots, lack of stripes, and absence of scales on the pectoral fins distinguish the Spanish mackerel from the king mackerel and the cero.

RANGE: Spanish mackerel occur from Cape Cod south to Brazil but are never numerous in the northern part of their range. They are most plentiful from the Carolinas into the Gulf of Mexico.

HABITAT: This warm-water species is usually found in open waters, cruising about near the surface and slashing into schools of baitfish. They do, however, make occasional forays into the surf and into bays and channels in search of food.

SIZE: Spanish mackerel average 1½ to 4 pounds but reach a maximum weight of about 20 pounds. A 10-pounder is a very good one.

FOOD: Spanish mackerel feed primarily on a wide variety of small baitfish, and on shrimp. A favorite bait in some areas, particularly Florida waters, is a very small baitfish called a glass minnow.

Sheepshead

COMMON NAMES: Sheepshead, convict fish.

SCIENTIFIC NAME: *Archosargus probatocephalus.*

DESCRIPTION: Similar in shape and general appearance to the porgy, the sheepshead is a high-backed blunt-headed species whose bait-stealing abilities have frustrated countless fishermen. Its small mouth has a formidable set of rock-hard close-coupled teeth that are quite capable of demolishing a crab and biting through a light-wire hook. Basic color is silvery though the dorsal surface's color is closer to gray. Sides have five to seven dark vertical bands, spines of the dorsal fin are quite large and very sharp, and scales are large and coarse. Sheepsheads fight well and are excellent on the table.

RANGE: The sheepshead is found from Nova Scotia south to the northeastern Gulf of Mexico. It is far more numerous in the southern part of its range, particularly in Florida waters.

HABITAT: The sheepshead is a gregarious species that moves with the tides to wherever the food is plentiful. It is an inshore fish, taking up residence in bays and channels and around bridges, piers, pilings, and the like.

SIZE: Sheepsheads average 1 to about 5 pounds but may attain weights in excess of 20 pounds.

FOOD: Its teeth are a dead giveaway to this species' dietary preferences, which include crabs, mollusks, barnacles, and the like, as well as shrimp.

Pompano

COMMON NAMES: Pompano, common pompano, sunfish.

SCIENTIFIC NAME: *Trachinotus carolinus.*

DESCRIPTION: This high-strung, slab-sided character is the most abundant and most important member of the pompano family, which includes such fish as the much-prized permit. It has a small mouth, blunt head, and a relatively shallow body (body depth decreases proportionally with growth). Dorsal-surface colors range from gray-silver-blue to blue-green, and sides and underparts are silvery.

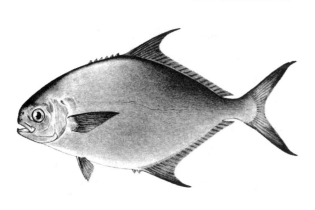

Pompano

short, high forward dorsal fin and a long, lower rear dorsal fin; and small barbels at the tip of the lower jaw. The corbina is a strong underwater fighter and an excellent food fish.

RANGE: The corbina is found from the Gulf of California north to Point Conception.

HABITAT: Primarily a target of surf fishermen, the corbina is an inshore species found primarily along sandy beaches and in shallow bays, moving into the surf line on the incoming tide.

SIZE: Corbina reach a maximum weight of about 8 pounds. Average size is 2 to 3 pounds.

Ventral surfaces are flecked with yellow. Dorsal fin is bluish, and most of the other fins are yellowish. The pompano is an epicurean's delight.

RANGE: The pompano is found from Brazil north to Massachusetts, and also in the West Indies and in Bermuda waters. It is particularly numerous in Florida and the Gulf of Mexico.

HABITAT: Pompano are inshore school fish, feeding on the bottom in shallow water in the surf, in channels and inlets and bays, and around bridges. They occasionally range well up into rivers with the tide.

SIZE: Pompano average about 2 pounds in weight, and maximum size is thought to be about 8 pounds.

FOOD: Pompano feed mostly on bivalve mollusks and on small crustaceans, notably a small beetlelike crustacean called the sand flea.

California Corbina

COMMON NAMES: California corbina, corbina, corvina, whiting, sea trout.

SCIENTIFIC NAME: *Menticirrhus undulatus.*

DESCRIPTION: The wary and unpredictable corbina, a member of the whiting group, is among the most popular of fish caught in inshore waters of the Pacific. Basic color is some shade of blue-gray, and identifying characteristics include a blunt snout; a

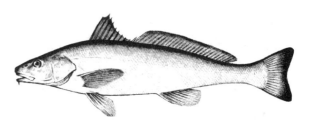

California Corbina

FOOD: Crabs of various kinds are the favorite food of the corbina, but it also feeds on clams, sea worms, and crabs.

Atlantic Croaker

COMMON NAMES: Atlantic croaker, croaker, hardhead, golden croaker.

SCIENTIFIC NAME: *Micropogon undulatus.*

DESCRIPTION: Most-common and most-prized of the eastern-U.S. members of the huge croaker family, the Atlantic croaker is a strong fighter and delicious eating. The croaker family gets its name from the sound—audible for quite a distance—it makes by repeated contractions of its swim bladder and a unique "drumming muscle." The Atlantic croaker has a small, tapered body; a short, high forward dorsal fin and a long, lower rear dorsal fin; and small barbels on the chin. Colors are brassy gold and silver, and upper parts of the body contain numerous dark spots that sometimes form slanting bars.

RANGE: The Atlantic croaker is found from Massachusetts south to Florida and west to Texas and eastern Mexico. In recent years, however, its numbers have declined in the northern part of the range. Center of abundance seems to be from the Carolinas to Florida and in the northern Gulf of Mexico.

HABITAT: Atlantic croakers are seldom found far from estuaries, preferring sandy shallows, shallow shell beds, sloughs, lagoons, and weedy flats. However, cold weather often sends the fish into deeper water.

SIZE: Atlantic croakers average ½ to about 2½ pounds and attain a maximum size of about 5 pounds.

FOOD: Predominantly bottom-feeders, Atlantic croakers feed on clams, crabs, sea worms, shrimp, snails, mussels, and sand fleas.

Red Snapper

SCIENTIFIC NAME: *Lutjanus blackfordi.*

DESCRIPTION: Most widely known for its eating qualities, the red snapper is among the best known of the more than 200 species of snappers found in the world's warm seas. The red snapper's color pattern (rose red overall, though paler red on underparts, with red fins and eyes, and a black spot

on each side), long pectoral fin, and more-numerous anal-fin rays distinguish this species from other snappers.

RANGE: The red snapper occurs from the U.S. middle-Atlantic and Gulf coasts southward throughout the tropical American Atlantic.

HABITAT: The red snapper's preference for deep waters—it is sometimes found as deep as 100 fathoms and seems most prevalent at 20 to 60 fathoms—detracts from its importance as a sport fish. It usually is found a few feet above a hard bottom.

SIZE: Most red snappers caught commercially run from 5 to about 30 pounds. Maximum size seems to be about 35 pounds.

FOOD: Red snappers eat baitfish and various deep-water mollusks and crustaceans.

Northern Whiting

COMMON NAMES: Northern whiting, whiting, northern kingfish, kingfish.

SCIENTIFIC NAME: *Menticirrhus saxatilis.*

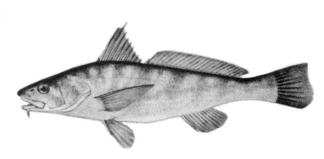

Northern Whiting

Red Snapper

DESCRIPTION: The northern whiting is one of four whitings (all members of the large croaker family) that inhabit the U.S. Atlantic and Gulf coasts. Basic color is silver-gray or silver-brown, and the upper part of the body contains rather indistinct dark vertical bands. Mouth is small, and there is a single chin barbel. The northern whiting is the only one of the four U.S. whitings in which the third and largest spine of the forward dorsal fin, when laid flat, reaches well past the beginning of the long and soft rear dorsal fin. The northern whiting is an excellent food fish.

RANGE: The northern whiting is found on the U.S. Atlantic Coast from Maine to Florida.

HABITAT: Northern whiting are usually found over a sandy bottom in the surf, shallow sloughs and bays, and, as the water cools, in depths as great as 100 feet or more.

SIZE: Averaging about 1 pound, the northern whiting reaches a maximum size of about 3 pounds and 18 inches in length.

FOOD: The northern whiting feeds mainly on small baitfish, sea worms, and small crustaceans.

PART 5
CAMPING

TENTS

Tents are manufactured in a variety of shapes and sizes. So whether you're just doing some backyard camping or heading for a couple of weeks in the mountains, there's probably a tent made for you and your family.

WALL TENTS

Many campers, particularly those who have spent time in the army, are familiar with the traditional wall tent. Its main advantages are that it has ample headspace, that it can house a wood-burning stove in cold weather, and that it readily sheds water off its inverted V roof.

A psychological benefit of the wall tent is that it somewhat resembles a small house in design, but upon closer examination, we see it is not quite as comfortable as it looks, nor is it very stable in wind.

There usually are no floors or windows, nor netting at the flap doors. Moreover, the walls tend to be so low that the only walking space is directly below the ridgepole. The large end pole that stands in the center of the doorway is another nuisance.

A wall tent is inexpensive and to erect it you only need two upright poles, a ridgepole, guy ropes, and pegs. Ventilation is poor in rainy weather, the tent offers little resistance to the wind, the door flaps leave myriad openings for insects and, if closed, make the tent's interior quite dark and warm. Auto campers appreciate the heavy wall tent as it can be pitched right next to their cars. But for those who wish to travel light, it is a poor choice.

The wall tent is generally available in sizes ranging from $6\frac{1}{2} \times 6\frac{1}{2}$ feet to 16×20 feet, although larger sizes are available from custom tent makers. The wall tent in these bigger custom sizes is favored by many big-game outfitters and guides. These tents are fitted with wood-burning stoves and chimneys. On average wall tents, however, the side walls run from 2 to 4 feet in height, but 3 feet is standard. Heights at the center are usually 7–$7\frac{1}{2}$ feet, adequate for the average adult.

This type of tent with a 7×9-foot floor space will provide sufficient room for two campers with gear. A trio of hunters will require at least a 9×12-foot wall tent for comfort.

WALL TENT

COTTAGE OR CABIN TENTS

If you're planning a long stay in an area and need plenty of space, the cottage or cabin tent just might be the answer.

This style of tent features vertical sides that give you more space for your gear than do tents with short side walls. The eaves are high and there are large windows with storm flaps. You've also got walking room to spare and sewn-in floors. Though the number of poles required to pitch it may approach 10, modern cottage tents generally employ light aluminum telescoping poles that are not difficult to handle. Guy lines are not required with most cottage and cabin tents, though the outside edges of the tent floor should be staked down. A large area of level ground is needed to put up the tent. An 8 × 10-foot tent can sleep four persons; a 9 × 12-foot, five to six.

UMBRELLA TENTS

The umbrella tent is best designed for the motorist who goes touring with his own shelter. A pyramid-shaped roof and straight sides distinguish this unit.

Wind resistance is exceptional and the vertical walls give you plenty of space for storing gear. The ample headroom lets you walk around without stooping, and, save the door awning, there aren't any large, flat surfaces that will hold rain or catch snow. A big door and one or more windows in the sides give good ventilation on warm evenings.

A sewn-in, waterproof floor keeps out drafts, bugs, and surface moisture, while a 4- to 6-inch doorsill strip in some models wards off snakes and small animals. With assembly time ranging from four to five minutes, this is a fine tent to have when a storm is approaching.

One of the main faults of the umbrella tent, however, is its pole arrangement. If it has but one pole (rare nowadays), you will need a small umbrella frame to hold the cloth straight. The center pole takes up entirely too much room inside, and its sole advantages are that you can reach up and slacken the umbrella frame when it rains, rather than having to go outside to loosen the stakes, and that useful shelves can be attached to the pole. Most current umbrella tents feature four aluminum poles, so if you're backpacking or canoeing, ignore this one.

Models come in interior- and exterior-pole styles. The former type can cause wear and capillary leaks due to metal rubbing against canvas. The latter is preferable as there is no center pole. Thus, there is more room inside. The exterior-pole setup is somewhat heavier and more expensive, however.

Another drawback is weight—30 to 65 pounds, depending on its size and method of pole support.

A couple can be accommodated by a 7 × 8-foot or an 8 × 8-foot model. Four persons would be better off in a 9½ × 9½-foot or 10 × 10-foot. Don't get anything bigger as it's unwieldy to pitch. You're better off with two small umbrella tents if the crew is large.

WEDGE TENTS

Although the Boy Scouts and the U.S. Army have taken a fancy to the wedge tent (also called the pup tent, "A" tent, Hudson Bay tent, or snow tent), it's not recommended if you're thinking of camping in any comfort. The wedge tent has no place to stand upright.

But there are several factors in this tent's favor: It's inexpensive, quite simple to erect, lightweight, sheds rain and snow rather well, and is quite stable (if properly pitched) on a windy day.

Heating this type of tent in cold weather is difficult, as a campfire inside is out of the question and a small heater can lead to asphyxiation if enough fresh air is not allowed into the tent.

A 5 × 7-foot tent of this style can sleep two people. Weight with stakes and poles approximates six pounds.

PYRAMID TENTS

For shedding rain and snow, the pyramid, or miner, tent is the best designed for the purpose. Also, when well pitched at the base and supported by an outside tripod of poles or a strong center pole, this tent can brave almost any windstorm.

A 7 × 7-foot tent of this style is adequate for sleeping and shelter, but buy the zipper-door type rather than the one with tie tapes as there will be less chance of leakage at the door.

Keep the doors open on hot days and use a reflector fire when the weather is brisk; wood stoves are not suitable in these small tents. Another flaw is that they are somewhat cramped, and an alcohol, gas, or oil stove can make the air stuffy.

BAKER TENTS

Similar to the wall tent except for one wall that is raised to form a front awning, the baker tent is quite roomy and is exceptional as a campfire tent. Temperatures can be far below the freezing point but this tent, provided it has a good fire in front of it, will keep you warm. Green logs or rocks can be stacked up behind the fire to reflect heat into the open tent.

Important: A waterproofing solution with fire-resistant chemicals should be used to treat the baker

TENT TYPES

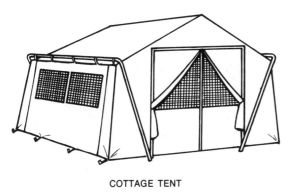

COTTAGE TENT

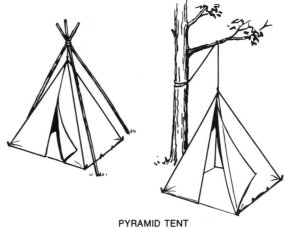

PYRAMID TENT

UMBRELLA TENT

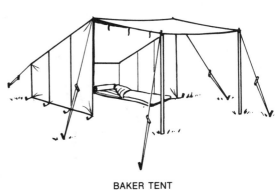

BAKER TENT

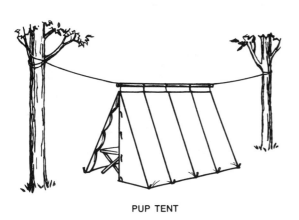

PUP TENT

FORESTER TENT

TENT TYPES (Continued)

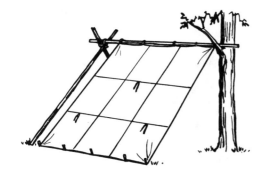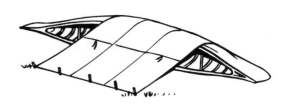

CANVAS LEAN-TO TARP

POP TENT

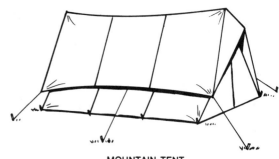

EXPLORER TENT　　　　　MOUNTAIN TENT

tent. Also, keep the fire at a reasonable level and the awning pitched high enough so that the two do not meet to create a hazard. As the roof is flat, a tight-woven fabric or a fine waterproofing is essential to help shed rain.

If you're looking for privacy, this tent is not for you. As the illustration on page 511 shows, the front is wide open and, if the porch is dropped down, ventilation is minimal. And besides that, in a driving rain the tent may have to be repositioned so as not to get the occupants wet.

Wind can be more harmful to a baker tent than it can to a wedge, pyramid, or wall tent. Therefore, face the tent away from prevailing winds and, if a storm is in the offing, anchor the tent with long stakes.

The open baker tent is poor protection from mosquitos and other biting flies. Cheesecloth or netting placed over the entrance can be helpful, but bed nets for each individual are more convenient and effective.

A 6×8-foot baker tent will sleep two campers comfortably, and perhaps three with a tight fit. A baker larger than 8×10 feet will render your fire virtually useless.

FORESTER TENTS

When there is a question of light weight and optimum warmth in cold weather, the forester tent is the best choice. The interior is so designed that the heat of a campfire will be well reflected throughout the entire unit. Pitching time is short, and the tent is stable if correctly pitched. It also sheds heavy rain and withstands high winds. The tent is small—typically 6 feet wide at the front and 8 feet deep. The shape of the interior is triangular, narrowing to a point at the back. Two campers will have sufficient sleeping room in this tent, but it is best for a lone camper who will have enough space for food and gear. During seasons when insects are a problem, individual bed nets are recommended for protection.

LEAN-TO SHELTERS

This shelter is not only the simplest one, but also the lightest and cheapest. It is merely a square sheet of fabric hemmed at the edges and provided with eyelets or loops through which supporting ropes are placed.

In the dry southwestern sections of the United States, outdoor enthusiasts have learned that a tent is rarely necessary from July through September. Thus, the popularity of the lean-to.

An 8×10-foot shelter, preferably waterproofed, can be set up in a variety of ways: draped over a

pole to resemble a pup tent, angled higher to create a baker tent type of shelter roof plus an awning, raised as a flat roof, etc.

If the fabric is untreated, it could leak at once—and badly, too. Also, the fabric may wilt or burn if placed too close to a fire. Other disadvantages are deterioration from intense sunlight and the tendency of some material to tear.

POP TENTS

The canvas igloo or dome tent is relatively new on the tent scene, and it can be assembled in a short time. Commercial models are usually waterproof and mildew resistant, with an exterior rib setup to aid in pitching. One model, 7 feet in diameter, will sleep two adults. But if you're a trio, a 9-foot diameter would prove more satisfactory. Not all styles permit you to stand upright, so sweeping out the sewn-in floor could prove a problem.

There appears to be some controversy as to this unit's stability in high winds. Some experts say it can be set up in sand without stakes and remain sturdy; others assert that unless the individual or his gear is present inside, the pop tent may blow over.

Zippered storm flaps on some creations will keep out wind and insects, and a window assists in cross-ventilation. A few models also feature an awning.

EXPLORER TENTS

The explorer tent has a number of advantages: it is lightweight, wind resistant, has adequate floor space, and, when checked thoroughly, bug-free.

This unit features a sewn-in floor as well as a large, netted front door that is shaped somewhat like a huge porthole.

In Canada and Alaska, mosquitos can be a problem. For this reason, many outdoors enthusiasts turn to the explorer tent when they're northward bound. Once the netting sleeve is tied shut—after shooing any tiny stragglers—you're in for a comfortable evening. The steep walls are designed to readily shed rain and to provide additional storage space. A 7×7-foot explorer tent sleeps one or two campers, and weighs a mere 10 to 12 pounds.

MOUNTAIN OR BACKPACK TENTS

In any weather except a very hot summer's day, the mountain tent (a form of backpacking tent) is a feasible proposition. But wintertime is the season when this tent really shows its stuff.

A stove—never an open wood fire—placed in the

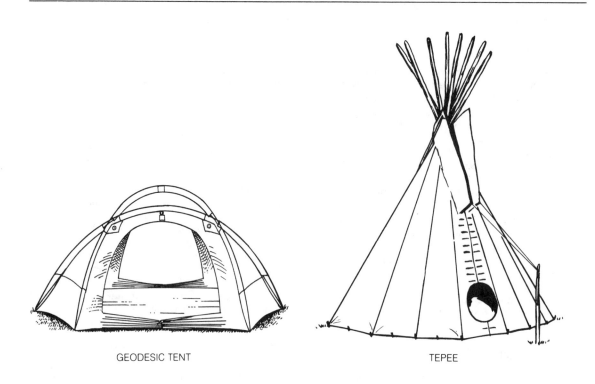

GEODESIC TENT   TEPEE

forepart of the tent will keep you warm in the coldest times. The vent at the peak of the tent must be opened before you light your stove, as the fumes can be lethal.

It is advisable with some models to take along one or two telescopic poles if the area you're camping in has no timber. This tent should be anchored to a point a minimum of 5 feet off the ground. Other styles, however, feature an exterior frame, a center pole or guy ropes that attach to pegs. The floor is sewn-in on most models. Front flaps are somewhat standard, and there usually is adequate screening to keep out insects.

GEODESIC TENTS

Newest in tents is the geodesic design, which simply means a domed framework of polygons in tension. There are no poles or structures inside the tent. The dome design is highly wind resistant and sheds rain and snow well. The tents are free-standing with minimal outside staking and pegging. Many of these new tents are made of breathable nylon taffeta with water-repellent polyurethane-coated nylon floors.

Setup is fast with the continuous shock-corded fiberglass frame pole system.

A typical geodesic dome tent that measures 8×7 feet has about 43 square feet of usable space, will sleep two or three persons and will weigh 10 to 11 pounds.

TEPEE TENTS

If you're staying in one spot for a long while, the tepee is a good choice. Unfortunately, marketed models are not as well designed as the original Indian tepees. Some do feature smoke-flaps, but they are smaller than those of the true tepee. The smoke leaves the tent at the point where the poles come together, rather than directly above the fire as in the early tepees. Tepees of old had several advantages. A weathertight seal would be created at the apex of the tent when the smoke-flaps were closed. Contemporary tepees do not feature this.

The floor is oval-shaped, and it is possible to stand upright within 3 feet of the front and 2 feet of the rear. As many as 15 people can be housed in an 18×21-foot tepee, but rather uncomfortably. Wind resistance is high despite the extensive wall area. The tepee is primarily for permanence, so the heaviness of the total unit (300 pounds including cover, lining, poles, and pegs), plus the extensive time needed for its erection, rule it out if you're constantly on the move.

TENT POLES

As most economy-minded campers are do-it-yourselfers, homemade tent poles are a good place to save money. Obtain a 2 × 2-inch board the same height as your tent. With a saw, cut the wood at a sharp angle into two equal pieces. Then affix a metal bracket to the angled end of each piece. The two halves will lock together firmly when necessary.

One commercial model features a metal sleeve that slides to lock the joint. Another factory-made tent pole is the adjustable Safetite aluminum upright that has a metal clamp instead of setscrews or nuts.

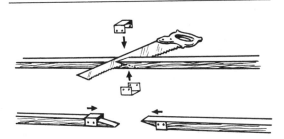

Homemade tent poles: After sawing 2 × 2-inch board in half at a 45-degree angle, screw metal brackets to the ends of each. When joined the two halves will lock together firmly.

This factory tent pole features a sliding metal sleeve that securely locks the joint.

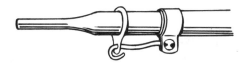

This commercial aluminum upright, known as Safetite, has no setscrews, no nuts to search for.

If this pole is lost, you can substitute a wooden or steel pole in its place. Even a broomstick will work in an emergency. Both styles are available in several sizes to suit your tenting needs. For ultimate ease of use, look for tent poles that are shock-corded together.

TENT PEGS

Just as tent poles can be homemade or purchased over the counter, the same goes for tent pegs, also known as tent stakes. The array available is large enough to satisfy any camper, as the following list indicates:

- Aluminum
- Plastic
- Steel
- Wood
- Metal spike
- Workshop wood
- Whittled branch

The auto camper can buy iron or aluminum tent pegs as weight makes little difference. The backpacker, on the other hand, must keep pack weight in mind. Therefore, he may resort to cutting his own wooden stakes. The softer the ground, the deeper the stakes must be buried. As a substitute for tent stakes, you can bury a bundle of stiff marsh grass,

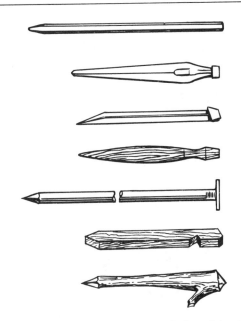

These tent pegs range from field-made (wood) to store-bought styles of steel, iron, and lightweight aluminum.

brush, or sticks in sand or dirt. In winter, blocks of ice or frozen snow will also make for a more rigid tent when you're out of pegs.

TENT FABRICS

Cotton. You may have heard the terms "canvas," "duck," and "balloon silk" mentioned when you were looking for a cotton tent. All three are various

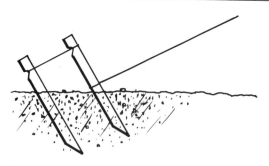

Tent pegs can be anchored in ground in this manner.

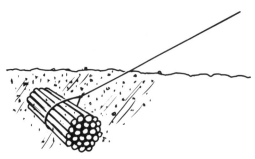

As a substitute for pegs, a number of small sticks can be buried in soft ground to secure tent. This is called the "deadman" technique.

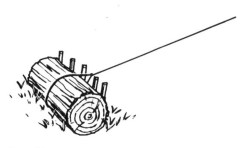

A small bundle of marsh grass or a log may be tied behind a row of short sticks to achieve the same purpose.

forms of cotton used in the manufacture of tents. Canvas and duck are a bit heavier than balloon silk—a long-fibered, high-quality cotton. Until World War II, practically every tent was made of cotton. Today, nylon, Dacron, and other synthetic fibers which have proven to be very lightweight are replacing cotton in tent manufacture.

Duck and canvas, if properly waterproofed, will shed water well, but are relatively heavy. The heavier the fabric, however, the stronger the tent. Conventional cotton tents are made in grades of 8, 10, and 12 ounces. The 8-ounce type is more fit for a hiking tent while the 12-ouncer would be required for a wall tent and the like. Another advantage is that cotton "breathes" well. Thus, there's no stuffiness.

The disadvantages of a mediocre cotton tent are several: It weighs more than the synthetic tents, and it may leak water and tear readily. Also, this material can only be dry-cleaned, as machine washing would destroy it.

Nylon. This synthetic has two prime advantages to the camper. It is relatively lightweight and is far less bulky to pack. Its disadvantages are that condensation forms in humid weather and, when the fabric is wet, the seams do not swell. This can lead to a clammy tent. Mountain tents and other styles valuable to the backpacker are often made of nylon.

Some nylon tents are waterproof, and some of the newer ones do breathe, as cotton does, but this material cannot be "breathable" and waterproof at the same time. Most of the nylon tents that breathe therefore come equipped with waterproof overhead flies (a cover suspended over the roof). Some nylon tents have cotton roofs—another solution to the same problem. And some are a blend of nylon and cotton.

Dacron. Like nylon, this synthetic is lightweight. In addition, it can be either dry-cleaned or machine washed. Unfortunately, it tends to be bulky when rolled up, and also is somewhat water-retentive.

Polyester. The newest tent fabric is spun polyester. This synthetic has nylon's strength, is lightweight, and breathes and repels water pretty much as cotton does. Like the other synthetics, polyester can be blended with cotton to achieve the desirable qualities of both fabrics.

Tents featuring blends of synthetic fibers and cotton are the most excellent of all for camping. They're highly water-repellent, strong, lightweight, and porous enough to provide maximum comfort. Probably the best way to locate these models is to look for the ultra-high price tags.

Flame-Resistant Tents. Regardless of fabric, more and more tents are now treated to be flame-resistant—sometimes called fire-retardant. It should be stressed that this treatment, though it is an excellent safety precaution, does not make the tents fireproof. A flame-resistant tent bears a label whose wording may vary slightly but whose message is clear: "*Warning. Keep all flame and heat sources away from this tent fabric*. This tent is made with flame-resistant fabric. . . . *It is not fireproof.* The fabric will burn if left in continuous contact with any flame source. The application of any foreign substance to the fabric may render the flame-resistant properties ineffective."

PITCHING A TENT

A tent is not a house. It's not even a small cabin. Pitch your tent in the wrong place and you could be in for a cold, wet night. Once you have selected a level site free of rocks and vegetation that might damage the tent floor or poke you in the back, you will have to deal with the two biggest campsite enemies: wind and water. In cold weather, you should find an area sheltered from the wind, but not at the bottom of a steep hill where you may get hit with frost-heaved rocks. If practical, pitch your tent facing east, so you can catch the morning sun.

It may be easier to drive a tent peg into soft ground, but that's also the type of terrain that holds moisture and dampness. Hard ground is better. Stay clear of dried riverbeds and gullies. In a sudden rain storm, they can quickly fill with water.

In bad weather, look for a site in the lee of a fallen tree or huge boulder. Don't ditch (dig a rain trench around your tent) unless you own the land. Most tents have sewn-in waterproof floors, so there is no need to destroy vegetation with a trench.

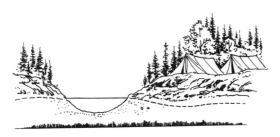

WATER TABLE: Avoid depressions or gullies that may be below the water table. If it rains, these areas will flood quickly.

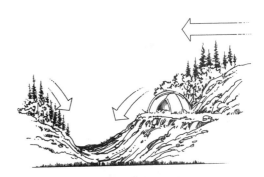

HILLY COUNTRY: Pick a level site part way up a slope where you will get wind protection, and cold air will naturally settle below you.

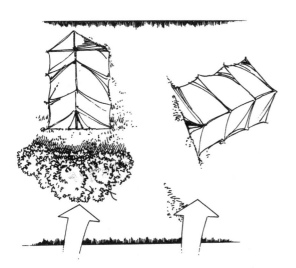

BAD WEATHER: Angle your tent to the wind or set it at an angle to the winds for best protection.

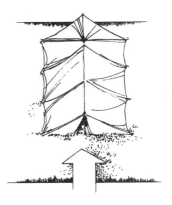

HOT WEATHER: Face your tent into the wind and let the breezes cool your camp and keep the bugs away.

CARE OF TENTS

Many tents have been in constant use for over 20 years. Others have been inadvertently destroyed by campers in a matter of days.

There is no reason why your tent, often the most expensive item of camping gear you own, cannot live a normal existence if you give it the proper care.

When you buy a tent, it is advisable to condition the canvas by pitching it for several days in the open air, and spraying it lightly with your garden hose to get it used to moisture.

A campfire should be kept safely away from your tent as well as downwind from it, as canvas is far from fireproof.

Canvas is vulnerable to mildew—a parasitic growth which develops in dampness. To prevent mildew from forming, your tent should be as dry as possible before you pack it. If you get caught in a heavy shower and must roll up a wet tent, you had better unroll it within three or four hours for a thorough drying. If you have D-rings on the outside of your pack, lash the tent to these rings and let it hang in a loose pile to dry. Occasionally change the tent's position to obtain as complete a drying as possible. Check seams, edges, reinforcements, and sod cloth for dampness, as the entire tent should be dry.

Needless to say, moisture is but one of the adversaries your tent faces. Trees, particularly in late spring, drop blossoms, along with an assortment of leaves, twigs, and sap. All can be damaging to the tent fabric, the waterproofing, and the dyes. Bombardment by birds is another hazard.

For these reasons, your tent should be kept as clean as possible. When you're finished tenting, spread out the material and brush it well on every side, particularly at wrinkles, seams, and the section of the floor by the door, where the most dirt accumulates. When you wash the tent, use soap and water.

Bird droppings shouldn't be allowed to harden, but if you're too late, you can work them loose and brush them off with a stiff brush. If you use a knife to remove droppings or dried pitch from the canvas, be sure the blade is dull and that you don't cut into the fabric. Any discolorations left behind can be removed with lighter fluid. But if the fabric has undergone wax treatment, forget it. The lighter fluid will remove the foreign matter and the wax as well. The use of brown soap and water is a less effective, but safer, method of treating discolorations.

Poles and stakes should be kept separate from the fabric when packing. Otherwise, you may be in for some damage. Guy ropes, however, can be placed inside the fabric when you're rolling it up, except for one rope. That piece should be used to tie up the completed roll. Rolling is more feasible than folding for your tent as the latter causes the fibers in the cloth to break.

Never dry a tent on the ground or let it hang outside till sundown. Absorbed moisture could cause mildew to begin. Optimum times to take down the tent are late morning or early afternoon, after the sun has done its work.

After a trip is completed and you're home again, pitch the tent and thoroughly hose it down. Then let it dry overnight, loosely packed.

When possible, try to open the tent on a daily

TENT MAKES AND MODELS

Coleman Guide Series Dakota is a three room tent that sleeps seven. Measures 15×7 feet. Coleman tents are built with double-coated taffeta nylon walls and poly/canvas roofs that guard against rain leakage.

RedHead Pine Lodge Dome Tent has three rooms and floor dimensions of 18×11 feet. The D-style door and two windows have no-see-um mesh. An awning over the door and hooded windows provide protection from rain and sun.

Peak 1 Apollo sleeps two people and has a floor size of 96×50-inches. Has a full coverage 2.3-ounce nylon taffeta fly that extends to create a vestibule area for gear storage.

Sunrise Cabin Tent is a two room model. Its 7-foot center height and 10×16-foot floor size sleeps 10 campers. The tent's steel truss-style frame is chain-corded for convenient set-up.

Eureka Shadowdance is a family cabin tent with near-vertical walls for a larger amount of usable space. It has four windows and a slide-opening twin track door. The model 10 is a 9½-foot square weighing 26 pounds. The model 12 is an 11½-foot square weighing 30 pounds.

Eureka Solitaire is a fiberglass-frame solo tent in a bivy shape. With its small folded size of 4×18 inches and storm cover, this tent is ideal for a survival pack or for spike-camp hunters.

Slumberjack's Bivy Shelter is a one-man, 2½-pound tent. Good for hunters, backpackers, canoeists, and any other sportsmen heading into remote areas and who may want a survival tent in their pack. It has a floor size of 38×90 inches.

---

basis to permit the air to circulate through it. This will dry up any moisture. If you store your tent, keep it in a dry, cool area, and loosely rolled so as to permit maximum circulation of air.

Avoid bumps and pressures against a pitched tent during rain. Such objects can cause slow leaks to spring in the material.

Temporary repairs on your tent can be made with small patches and patching cement. Adhesive tape can mend small tears for a while, but a sewing machine designed for canvas can do the repair work so it will last for the lifetime of the tent.

RECREATIONAL VEHICLES

Recreational vehicles today are designed with America's economy-oriented society in mind, and statistics indicate that an RV owner no longer need be a person with money to burn, though there are models for this type, too.

FOLDING CAMPING TRAILERS

Folding tent or camp trailers are collapsible tents on wheels that are towed by a car. The trailer usually opens up to form beds with foam mattresses on opposite sides of a camping or living area a foot or more off the ground. Erection in some models has been simplified through hydraulic or electric crank-up systems that work by merely pushing a button.

Tent trailers range in body length from 6 to 17 feet, and the standard width is 6½ or 7 feet. The lightweights scale 500 pounds but the heavyweights may register nearly 2,500 pounds or perhaps more when the load is full. Low price is the big draw for this RV.

Depending on how much you would care to spend for a tent trailer, there is a wide array of equipment, both standard and optional. Current styles usually feature huge screened windows to protect campers from insects; built-in refrigerators and kitchens; plastic tops; screen doors rather than zippered flaps; and wardrobes, toilets, and lighting arrangements. Optional gear on many models includes 12-inch wheels rather than 8-inchers, electric brakes, road covers for added protection, and boat or canoe carrying racks. Although camping trailers come equipped with brake lights, directional signals, standard clearance, and leveling jacks (all), use two safety chains rather than one, as this prevents the unit from swaying, or "fishtailing," to a dangerous degree.

It is wise to remember that you'll save by having the optionals put on prior to delivery rather than deciding on them several weeks afterward.

When it comes to advantages and disadvantages, the folding tent trailer has its share of each.

On the plus side, the rig has a low profile, permitting the driver a rear view through his center-mounted mirror that is very similar to what he would see if he were towing no rig at all. This same low profile lends itself to a reduction in wind resistance, simplifying the tasks of the driver.

The fact that the open rig is shaped like a tent is psychologically satisfying to a number of campers, as they can realistically enjoy the outdoor life under canvas, yet be far enough above the ground so that crawlers, creepers, and dampness aren't too close for comfort.

TENT TRAILERS

Coleman Laramie is a typical tent trailer. Closed, the entire unit measures 7 × 15 feet. Opened, the Laramie measures 22 feet. It features one double- and one queen-size bed. With a hitch weight of 164 pounds, it can be towed with a medium-size car. Interior has galley with sink and three-burner propane stove.

The light weight of the unit permits it to follow along rather inconspicuously, and it's simpler to park or back into a tight place than are the other RVs. Also, it can be used in numerous far-off and unpaved regions where the motor home and the travel trailer might not succeed. In addition, higher speeds are attainable and the effect on gasoline mileage is slight.

TRUCK CAMPERS

Truck campers fall into three categories. The big seller is the unit that can be installed in and readily removed from the bed of the pickup, leaving the truck free for countless other chores outdoors. The second most popular is the rig that is permanently installed on the chassis of the truck. The third is a basic roof or shell that clamps onto the truck bed. This unit will suffice if you only need one or two bunks and an area to sit down. The shell is adequate for two campers.

The first model mentioned is slid onto the truck when you're ready to use it. (The tailgate is either lowered or completely removed.) Other times, the camper can rest on tripods or jacks. The interior has standing room; a kitchen with a sink, a stove, and a refrigerator; a dinette that converts to a bed; plus space for storing groceries and clothing. A majority of these units also have an extended area over the cab to serve as sleeping quarters by night and storage space by day. The larger rigs may include a shower and toilet. Optionals include a radio, air-conditioning, a trailer hitch, a step bumper, and an auxiliary gas tank. One model even boasts an expanded rear door plus a ramp so that you can ride your ATV or snowmobile right up into the vehicle and tote it with you.

The camper—minus the truck—may weigh from 800 pounds to well over a ton. The length ranges from 6 to 12 feet.

The permanently mounted campers are often wider and longer than the other two styles because the bed of the truck is eliminated, and they're also superior in regard to self-containment. The chassis-mounts vary between 10 and 18 feet and weigh from 1,500 to 2,700 pounds. The legal maximum width is 8 feet, and these beauties often have that expanse. Formerly, most units were 6 feet wide.

The chassis-mounts are said to have better road-ability and easier driving over lengthy hauls than the non-permanent campers, but campers as a whole have some advantages over the other RVs.

Since the vehicle is basically a truck—perhaps 4-wheel-drive—it can negotiate roads that a motor home and a travel trailer couldn't begin to navigate. The non-permanent pickup camper leaves the truck for numerous other purposes.

If it's pouring outside, you can merely park the vehicle and proceed to prepare supper or simply relax. No problems with firewood and tent stakes.

PICKUP CAMPERS

Coachmen Ranger is a typical pickup camper. Unit is available in five floor plans and lengths of 10-12 feet. Power-operated stands make an easy task of setting the Ranger in your truck bed or leaving it at home. The Ranger has a furnace, a three-burner range, a cab over bed and can sleep up to five people.

Jayco 525 is a slide-in pickup camper with a 20-inch extended roof. An all-aluminum unit, it's available in 7, 8, and 9½ feet for full-size pickup trucks. (Jayco-AE Photo, Thayne Smith).

Riding in the camper coach is permissible while on the road, so the cab needn't be overcrowded. An intercom can even be installed to aid communication between the rear and the cab.

Now for the disadvantages:

Whenever you want to travel, you must take the entire camp with you. This necessitates securing gear and putting away all utensils and dishes.

Highway driving can occasionally be frightening. A gusty headwind or strong crosswinds can turn the rig into a huge sail, making the driver's job a difficult one—power steering or no!

When the time comes to store this vehicle, you might be in for some trouble. Several suburban regions prohibit parking on driveways, necessitating the rental of space or the use of your garage. With the unit measuring from 8½ to 10 feet in height when it is high enough on the jacks to be loaded, or on the pickup itself, you'll probably find that the ceiling of your garage isn't quite high enough. Take this into account before buying.

TRAVEL TRAILERS

The travel trailer is a permanent living area that features one or more rooms, and is mounted on two or four wheels, depending on its weight and size. Travel trailers range in length from 12 to 35 feet, with the 22-footer apparently the most popular according to sales figures. The array of vehicles is extensive, and there is a comparably wide range of prices. The interiors are usually plywood while the exteriors are aluminum. Foam insulation resides between the two, and the entire unit sits on a welded chassis of steel.

A 6-footer could stand up easily in the average trailer as the overall distance from floor to roof is 7 to 8 feet. The unit is rarely less than 7 feet wide, and often closer to the maximum of 8 feet.

With the accent on compact and subcompact automobiles in recent years, the trailer industry has followed the trend and produced a large selection of mini-travel trailers.

To be self-contained, a vehicle must be able to supply sewage disposal, water, and power. To do this, it must hold a minimum of 30 gallons of water; a holding tank for wastes; and enough bottled gas to take care of stove, heater, and refrigerator. The average travel trailer is conveniently self-contained, with sleeping space, heater, toilet, and shower. When it comes to optionals, you can have air-conditioning, television, stereo, and even a bathtub. With all of these comforts just behind the towing vehicle, it's easy to see why this RV is so popular.

The travel trailer also holds the upper hand over the pickup camper and the motor home in that you can park it and use the car or truck exclusively. With the other two, you have to drag your kitchen sink along wherever you go.

But there is less of an area where you *can* go if you want to take the trailer. It won't negotiate the same roads a pickup camper will, particularly if the latter is equipped with 4-wheel-drive.

And on the negative side . . .

Unless the trailer can be adjusted to a low silhouette to somewhat resemble a tent trailer, you may have some trouble driving it at first. Sway is a problem, often caused by poor distribution of weight over the axle of the trailer. To prevent it, try to place the bulk of the weight forward of the trailer's wheels. Also decrease front-tire pressure prior to your trip. It can speed up tire wear but may save your life. Use an equalizer hitch if the trailer weighs over a half-ton, to shift more weight to the car's front wheels.

Power steering seems to be the culprit in many trailer accidents as the inexperienced driver tends to oversteer once swaying begins.

As mentioned earlier in this chapter, you would be smart to have the correct options put on your car during assembly. Such items as oversize radiators, extra-blade fans, heavy-duty springs and shock absorbers, heavy-duty batteries and alternators, fade-resistant brake linings, etc., will cost you far more to put in after you've had the auto for a while.

Trailers can be used in winter, but you may want to store your own. If so, remember to do the following: Drain the complete water system, septic holding tank and the water heater. Also drain traps or pour alcohol into them. Remove the tires to prevent deterioration. If you want to leave the tires on, jack up the trailer to relieve the tires of weight. Also take the hubcaps off as they tend to rust quickly. When snow accumulates to over a few inches on the trailer roof, clear it off—but not with a shovel. A broom will do.

FIFTH-WHEEL TRAILERS

Fifth-wheel trailers—often just called fifth-wheelers—are the newest type of RV. The fifth wheel is the hitch, a modification of the fifth-wheel hitch used on tractor-trailer rigs. It goes over the axle of a pickup truck and is bolted to the frame, not just to the floor of the truck bed. The trailer itself has a cutout so that it can hang over the pickup's bed by about 7 feet, reducing the combined length of towing vehicle and trailer. A 29-foot fifth-wheeler, for example, extends only about 22 feet from the rear of the truck when it's hitched.

This design has several purposes. Most obviously, it provides extra interior trailer space in proportion

TRAVEL TRAILERS

This Starcraft double-entry camper is typical of travel trailers that can be more than 35 feet. This unit features a stove, heater and refrigerator. Optional features include air-conditioning, television, and other amenities.

Coachmen Catalina travel trailers range in length from 26 to 36 feet, and most come with slide-outs that increase the living area. Catalina sleeps up to six people in the 26-footer, and up to nine in the larger 36-footer.

to the rig's overall length. The objective is spacious luxury. The type of hitch also reduces trailer sway, helps insure against jackknifing, and makes for an extremely secure, safe coupling. In addition, hitching is easier. A big kingpin hangs down and couples to the hitch in the pickup bed. As you back the truck toward the kingpin, you can see it clearly, and this makes the connection easier than positioning a conventional coupler over a ball.

Fifth-wheelers come in a variety of lengths, from compact 18-footers to models as long as 35 feet. Most are in the 26- to 32-foot range. Some of the smaller ones can be towed by a half-ton pickup, but most need a three-quarter or one-ton pickup truck.

Although the construction techniques are pretty much the same as for travel trailers, the insulation tends to be better, the appliances bigger. Many fifth-wheelers are more like motor homes than travel trailers. The master bedroom, built into the overhang, may be big enough for a large double bed or twin beds. Some models have sliding glass patio doors and very spacious, open-looking interiors. And some have "tip-out" alcoves that crank out when parked at a campsite. Small couches or lounges fit to make the main floor less cluttered. Depending on size and interior features, fifth-wheelers sleep from four to eight persons. Like motor homes, they are, of course, expensive.

MOTOR HOMES

The motor home is a self-contained home on wheels, and the driver sits near facilities for dining, cooking,

sleeping, sanitation, water supply, and usually air-conditioning.

One manufacturer's standard equipment includes wall-to-wall foam padded nylon carpet, storage drawers, a four-burner stove with automatic oven, a dinette that converts into a bed, tinted windows, two skylight roof vents, a fire extinguisher, a bedroom privacy curtain, a cigarette lighter, four adjustable defroster vents, and many other worthwhile items. Optionals are quite numerous in many models. For the extra cost, you can include an AM-FM radio with four speakers, a trailer hitch, a dash-mounted water-tank gauge, wraparound windshield curtains, head- and armrests for driver and copilot, plus many other conveniences to make for a safer and more enjoyable excursion in your motor home.

The rigs measure from 17 to 30 feet in length, with the 20- to 24-foot models being the best sellers.

The interior of the unit is plywood with the outside constructed of molded fiberglass or aluminum. The counter and tabletops are made of material that can readily withstand any punishment.

Owing to the vehicle's enormous size and its overhang, you must travel on good roads. Parking also may be a problem, but this is not true in all cases. That same overhang, though, can come in very handy when you're launching a boat. And motor homes are excellent vehicles to trailer such craft behind.

One drawback of the motor home is its shoebox shape, but some new models are being aerodynamically designed so as to cut down on the hazards of wind.

FIFTH-WHEEL TRAILERS

Coachmen's Maxxum Fifth Wheels can range fom 30 to 39 feet and are designed to be hitch-mounted to the bed of a pickup truck. The exterior is seamless fiberglass with a one-piece seamless rubber roof. Interior has a slide-out room to increase living space.

MOTOR HOMES

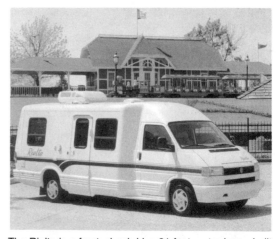

Winnebago Brave has a bus-style appearance and an optional slide-out room extension that increases interior area by 63 feet. Available on a Ford or Chevy chassis in six models from 25 to 33 feet.

The Rialta is a front-wheel-drive 21 foot motor home built by Winnebago. It has a Volkswagen-designed chassis and engine. Interior features a complete galley with microwave.

Jayco Mini-Motorhome is an all-fiberglass, 29-foot camper with a new wide-body design on a Ford chassis with a Ford 460 engine. It's totally self-contained with galley and generator. (Jayco-AE Photo, Thayne Smith).

If you store your motor home during the winter, remove water from every pipe in the system and leave valves in the *open* position. Also make certain that water is drained from the toilet and toilet holding tank, and follow this up with a thorough cleansing and deodorizing. LP gas-tank valves should be closed securely, as well as all windows and roof vents. The refrigerator should also be cleaned and emptied, and the door left open. Take out all food from the vehicle, as well as such items as fishing tackle which may leave undesirable odors. Give the vehicle a walk-through check on occasion, airing it out when possible. As tires are usually left fully inflated on the motor home, move the unit a couple of feet each week or so to avoid continuous stress on one section of the tire due to the total weight of the home being on it and the three to five other tires. Otherwise, jack up each wheel on occasion and slightly rotate it.

VAN CONVERSIONS

Van conversions, also called van campers, have become extremely popular. One reason is that some models cost little more than a full-size station wagon. Another is that they're easier to handle and park than some of the bigger camping rigs, and they can be used for everyday purposes around home, like an ordinary van or station wagon. Thus they combine the advantages of a super station wagon and "pocket" motor home. Many models provide not only sleeping bunks but a galley and even a shower and toilet, making them completely self-contained camping rigs.

The RV manufacturers convert all the standard van models—Chevrolet, Dodge, Ford, and GMC—using vans with both short and long wheelbases. Some RV companies stretch the width or length to provide jumbo interiors.

You can't stand up inside a standard van, so headroom is an important part of conversion. Most often, the roof is cut off and a raised fiberglass structure is substituted, resulting in more than 6 feet of interior height. However, the added frontal area can cause extra drag, and the increased height may make the vehicle slightly more susceptible to wind sway. Another approach is to increase headroom only in the galley area, by building a dropped floor

VAN CONVERSIONS

Coachmen Vans' Saratoga is a typical conversion van that offers most of the benefits of a motor home. It's built on a 19-foot Dodge chassis, and the interior features a complete galley with microwave. Twin sofas easily convert to a queen-size bed.

well. The disadvantage here is that you can stand straight only in that area—when preparing meals. Also, the floor well reduces ground clearance, which can be important on rough roads. A third way is to install an expandable top that lies almost flat (adding only about 4 inches to the van's height while driving) and can be popped up to provide headroom.

A typical interior might have a dinette that can be turned into a double bunk, plus another double bunk over the driver's cockpit. The galley generally contains a sink, range, and refrigerator or cooler. Models with a lavatory contain a chemical toilet, wash basin, and shower.

SNOWMOBILES

The snowmobile is the only vehicle available for traveling in remote, snow-covered regions. It's steered by ski-type runners up front and is propelled by a continuously running belt or track below the vehicle that grips the surface of the snow and sends the sled flying over it.

Low-priced models are compacts with engines averaging 225cc, but the big ones are known in the snowmobiler's lingo as "class 5 modifieds." The latter is the largest on the market, featuring a 350-pound toboggan with an 85-hp, 800cc engine. These machines hit 90 and beyond with little effort.

The track on the typical snowmobile measures 15 inches in width, and permits you to steer the vehicle by shifting your weight. Tracks, however, sometimes reach 30½ inches.

Snowmobiles can get into many areas where a car or an RV wouldn't stand a chance. Before the age of the snowmobile, conservation officers had to don their snowshoes. In times of accident or disaster in snowbound areas, help can get there quickly with a snowmobile to provide rapid medical assistance and transportation to hospital. For the outdoors enthusiast, the snowmobile offers enjoyment. He can go hunting, ice fishing, racing, or skijoring (skiing behind a snowmobile) with the rig.

Also, some people chase deer and other game animals with their snowmobiles. This practice, of course, is against the law.

Though a few snowmobiles on the market feature reverse transmission on an optional basis, most do not have standard reverse, making them somewhat dangerous. Accidents such as fatal or maiming collisions with automobiles, trains, pipes, fences, and the like also show the hazards of driving the vehicle.

Other disadvantages include its heavy weight; its often low, cramped size; and narrow cleats that often don't adhere to the ice and snow.

The heavier snowmobiles cannot negotiate all types of snow, but there are relatively new, lightweight models designed for better flotation on soft snow. Be careful with a heavier one, which may bog down. Also be sure to wear appropriate clothing for safety and warmth. Insulated snowmobile suits are recommended. So are helmets, goggles, and face masks. Some of the snowmobiles themselves have built-in safety features such as padded handlebars and breakaway windshields—excellent improvements.

In addition, the noise has been substantially reduced in recent years. Machines built since June 30, 1976, and certified by the Snowmobile Safety and Certification Committee of the International Snowmobile Industry Association emit no more than 73 decibels at 50 feet when traveling 15 miles an hour, and similarly certified machines produced since February 1, 1975, emit no more than 78 decibels at 50 feet when traveling *at full throttle.*

Polaris Indy Trail has a fan-cooled 488cc twin engine, toolless front shock spring pre-load adjustability, and an adjustable shock in back.

Polaris Indy XLT Special features long-travel suspension. It has a liquid-cooled 597cc engine, tool-less front spring pre-load adjustment, and torsion bar handling.

Snowmobiling has become more than a mechanized means of traveling over snow; it has become a sport (and almost a way of life in some regions). Trail systems have been developed in forest lands to accommodate snowmobilers without interfering with skiers or other winter-sports enthusiasts. Regulations have been established by states—and in some cases by the snowmobilers themselves—to promote safety. Some trails have stop signs, yield signs, and even information kiosks at strategic locations. Perhaps the most important improvements have come from the snowmobiling clubs, which have promoted responsible snowmobiling—not only in terms of safety but in terms of concern for wild animals and forest vegetation. When carried on in such a responsible manner, the sport is harmless to wildlife.

Obviously, the snowmobile season is rather short. Therefore, correct storage of your vehicle is essential.

Store it in a dry place, and block it off the ground to take the weight off the skis and track. Loosen the track tensioner. Drain the fuel tank and pour a quart of SAE 30 into the oil tank. Then roll the machine from side to side so the fuel-tank walls are well lubricated. Drain the carburetor. Take out the spark plug and pour a tablespoon of SAE 30 oil through the spark-plug hole. Turn the engine over four times by pulling the starter rope. Then replace the spark plug. Clean the outside of the engine and spread a thin film of oil over any of its exposed surfaces that could corrode.

ALL-TERRAIN VEHICLES

The snowmobiles' counterparts are the 2- and 4-wheel drive All-Terrain Vehicles (ATV), tough, knobby-tired vehicles designed to take sportsmen nearly everywhere off-road. Used properly, an ATV can safely take you into remote areas to hunt, fish, and camp.

If you are a farmer, guide, or outfitter, an ATV can also haul people and a trailer full of gear into a backcountry camp. It can also get downed game back to your cabin or rescue a lost hunter or hiker.

ATVs are available in a range of sizes with options ranging from front-load racks to rear cargo boxes and rifle scabbards. Most ATVs will carry loads up to 100 pounds on a front rack and up to 200 pounds on a rear load carrier. Many are two-wheel drives with a push-button four-wheel drive to engage four-wheel drive. ATVs can weigh from 400 to 800 pounds, depending on its power and utility. A typical sportsman's model will have a 4-stroke, liquid-cooled 500 engine, a DC outlet, disc brakes, and full steel skid plates to protect the bottom.

As with snowmobiles, ATVs sometimes suffer from a bad reputation because of the reckless antics of a few. ATVs, improperly used, can damage the environment by tearing up wet trails and by being ridden across steam beds and creeks. ATVs should also avoid livestock and wild game. Stressing game animals by driving too close can seriously sap their energy reserves when they may need it the most.

Ideally, ATV operators should not be under 18 years old. ATVs should be ridden only on designated roads and trails, and operators should wear hemmed and protective clothing. And, above all, operators should resist the urge to pioneer a new road or trail with an ATV.

Polaris Sportsman 500 has a 4-stroke, liquid-cooled 500 engine, shaft drive, and independent rear suspension with 9½ inches of travel. It has a 5.25-gallon fuel tank and push-button engage four-wheeled drive. Weighs 660 Pounds.

Polaris Sportsman 4 × 4 has a 2-stroke, liquid-cooled 400 engine, and 1⅜-inch rear shock. It also comes with E-Z shift gear selector and push-button engage four-wheel drive. Weighs 585 pounds.

CAMP BEDDING

SLEEPING BAG INSULATION

The warmest and lightest insulation used in today's sleeping bags is down, the breast feathers of a goose or a duck. Besides being quite soft and warm, down holds the heat generated by the body. It does not, fortunately, hold body moisture. This throwing-off process is known as "breathing," and prevents the bag from becoming uncomfortably clammy.

"Loft"—the height of a sleeping bag when fully fluffed and unrolled—is a good indication of the bag's insulating ability. A couple of synthetic fillers, PolarGuard and Hollofil, exhibit good loft and offer about two-thirds as much insulating efficiency as down per pound. Quallofil, a newer DuPont synthetic, has excellent loft, comes close to down in its insulating efficiency (and far surpasses down under wet conditions), and is almost as compactible as the finest goose feathers. There are 3-pound mummy-type sleeping bags with Quallofil insulation that have a temperature rating down to 5°F below zero. For certain purposes—canoe or boat camping, wet-weather camping, or camping from spring through fall, when the temperature isn't extremely cold—the synthetics have several advantages over down.

For one thing, down becomes almost useless as an insulator when it gets wet, and it dries slowly. Polyesters provide warmth even when wet, and they dry quickly. For another thing, down tends to shift around in a bag, making lumps and thin, cold spots unless extensive sewing "quilts" it in place. Polar-Guard is battlike and so doesn't shift and needs little quilting. Hollofil II needs almost as much quilting as down while Quallofil seems to need a bit less. Finally, the synthetics cost less, primarily because the raw materials are cheaper than down.

Even some of the polyester-and-acrylic combination fillers provide some warmth when wet, assuming that outside temperatures aren't extremely cold. And, like down, the newer polyesters retain body heat while allowing body moisture to escape and evaporate. Some synthetic-filled bags are more compressible than down—in spite of their good loft when fluffed out—and this can be another advantage when gear space is limited.

Other filler materials include wool, cotton (poplin), kapok, and Dacron. Except for Dacron, these insulators mat easily and aren't very resilient. Yet they may suffice in relatively thin, warm-weather bags, and such bags are comparatively inexpensive.

The label and/or packaging of a good sleeping bag usually states the weight of the filler and the temperature range or minimum temperature at which

Peak 1 Diamond Back, with Polarguard HV insulation, has a temperature rate down to 15 degrees. The bag is 33 × 80 inches and weighs 5½ pounds. Well-designed sleeping bag for backpackers.

the bag will keep you comfortable. Of course, with a bag which doesn't provide much insulation, you can wear extra sleeping clothes to add 20°F to 30° effectiveness to the bag. But it pays to buy a bag of good quality—both for warmth and durability—and to compare weights and comfort ranges before deciding which one to buy. Three pounds of one synthetic filler, for example, may keep you comfortable when the temperature dips to 30 degrees, while you'll need only about 2 pounds of down at that temperature. Consider the kind of camping you'll be doing and the price you can afford—and then shop aggressively.

STYLES

Sleeping bags come in two basic configurations—the rectangular bag and the mummy bag. A variation, designed for recreational vehicles, is called a station-wagon bag, but this is simply an oversize rectangular bag. The rectangular type is basically a three-season bag but is available in grades from summer-weight to heavy winter-weight. The mummy bag is intended primarily for cold weather; it fits more closely and cinches tight about head and shoulders, impeding exchange of inside and outside air.

Coleman Elk Hunter II is a rectangular sleeping bag with a 2 inch weather seal. It measures 39×84 inches, has a pack weight of 13 pounds, and a temperature rating down to 0 degrees. Good choice for deer camp where weight is not a factor.

Bass Pro Shops Outfitter Mummy Bag is made of a nylon shell with Quallofil insulation. Available in 32×84 or 38×92 inches, and at temperature rates of 0 or 15 degrees.

Except for a few huge station-wagon bags, the rectangular style is usually offered in a choice of three sizes. The junior (or small-adult) size often measures 33 × 68 inches. Most common is the adult size, 33 × 75 inches or 36 × 80 inches. The third size is extra-large—39 × 84 inches or 41× 86 inches—for large adults.

An important thing to remember when purchasing a sleeping bag is that two sizes are listed in the catalogs—the cut size and the finished size. Your best bet is totally to disregard the cut sizes as they indicate the size of the material prior to construction. The finished size is the figure you should concentrate on as it is the actual length and width of the completed bag. The finished size should be your guide. (Previous figures are all finished sizes.) Two sleeping bags may be paired together by opening and completely unzipping both. One should be placed atop the other so that the bottoms of both zippers meet. Then, simply connect each zipper at the point where the two meet. Double bags when used by two persons tend to be warmer than they are when used individually.

Such double bags have the same cover width on top as they do underneath. One manufacturer saw this problem recently and developed what is known

as the Four Seasons sleeping bag. The benefit is that the top cover is 1 foot wider than the bottom. The 50×76-inch bag is well insulated, and provides the sleepers with more room to move around because of its style. A junior bag is a waste of money; get an adult bag for your youngster as, with proper care, it will last him or her several years.

Rectangular bags in general are fine for car, canoe, and recreational-vehicle camping. But if you're backpacking, you'll probably have to put your faith in the mummy bag. You won't be making the wrong move, though.

As we've said, weight is an important consideration to the backpacker, and the mummy bag is designed with this in mind. It is widest at the shoulders—usually 33 inches—and tapers to about 19 inches at the feet. This tapering makes the bag fit like a robe, and that means additional warmth. Some mummy bags can keep the sleeper comfortable at zero and weigh only 3 or 4 pounds, half the weight of comparably warm oblong bags. Mummy bags are usually filled with down and have nylon covers.

Another valuable item for the backpacker is the stuff bag, into which he actually stuffs his sleeping bag. This method of storage saves wear on the bag through compression fatigue, and so helps to fluff it up when you're extracting it for use. Stuff bags usually are waterproof.

LINERS

Although a majority of sleeping bags on the market have an inner lining made of flannel, it is worthwhile to purchase an additional flannel liner. If you can carry the extra weight, an extra liner helps to regulate warmth during the night. Should it be warm when you fall asleep, you can take out the lining completely or use it folded underneath as a mattress pad. If the temperature drops substantially later on, the liner can be readily shifted so that you sleep between the layers or under both of them. This separate liner will stop drafts where the sleeper's head protrudes and will provide further insulation near the areas of the zipper and/or snap fasteners, where cold air may enter.

By purchasing a variety of liners, you can adjust your sleeping bag for practically any weather. That's the reason why a four-season camper usually relies on liners.

An advantage of the removable liner is that cleaning will be no problem, and the bag itself will remain unsoiled within. Tie-tabs on your sleeping bag are good for quickly attaching or removing such liners.

Liners are also made of synthetics and fleece. One manufacturer claims that its 3-pound liner consisting of 2 pounds of polyester fibers will add approximately 20 degrees to the minimum comfort range. Going a step further, another liner maker boasts that his product can convert a 3-pound Dacron sleeping bag, rated for 35°F, into a 5-pound bag that should keep the sleeper warm in zero temperatures.

In summer, when it may be too hot for a sleeping bag, you can sleep in the liner alone.

SHELLS FOR SLEEPING BAGS

It is important that sleeping bags breathe, letting body moisture escape. Otherwise, you wind up with a sauna effect.

Beware of any bag—especially a cheap one—advertised as waterproof. Such shells may be coated so they won't allow body vapors to pass through. On the other hand, some excellent waterproof shells, such as those made of a nylon and Gore-Tex laminate, do breathe while being impermeable to rain.

Economical "station-wagon" bags often have an inner shell of cotton flannel and an outer shell of heavy cotton. These bags are practical for warm-weather car-tenting or for use in a rec vehicle. But since they are heavy, bulky, and highly moisture-absorbent in relation to the warmth they provide, they are not suitable for backpacking or canoe camping.

Better bags filled with down or polyester usually have inner and outer shells made of nylon in ripstop or taffeta weaves. Both fabrics breathe. They also feel good next to the skin, wear well, resist mildew and fading, and are unaffected by machine washing.

There are also bivouac covers, which serve as mini-tents but drape over you and your sleeping bag like a sock—complete with mosquito netting. These covers normally have an airtight and waterproof underside and a waterproof (though breathable) topside made of materials such as Gore-Tex. Larger bivouac covers can house a couple of sleepers and their gear. Though more restrictive than tents, these covers are lighter and so get the nod from weight-conscious backpackers.

ZIPPERS

Zippers on mummy bags typically run three-quarter length or full-length down one side. A rectangular sleeping bag should be equipped with a heavy-duty zipper that runs completely down one side and across the bottom. This type of zipper permits you to open the bag completely for a thorough airing, and lets you zip together two matching sleeping bags. Two bags zipped together will accommodate two adults or up to four youngsters.

For both mummy and rectangular bags, zippers should have slides at both ends that allow you to ventilate the head and foot ends independently. Both slides should have finger tabs inside and out.

Zippers themselves may be made of metal, nylon, or other synthetics. Metal tends to feel colder in cold weather, work harder in all weather, and frost up in winter. A sleeping bag zipper should be large, whether it be of the conventional ladder design of most metal zippers or of the toothed-interlock or the continuous-coil designs used for synthetic zippers. Large zippers don't catch and abrade shell fabrics as readily as smaller, toothed zippers do—especially smaller metal-toothed zippers. Of all zippers, the continuous coil is easiest on fabric.

Most sleeping bags have a baffle panel—weatherstripping made of insulated material to prevent air from traveling through the zipper. This strip lies along the inner surface of the zipper, and, in better bags, may be from 1 to 1½ inches thick and from 3 to 4 inches wide. A cheaply made bag, needless to say, would have little or no weatherstripping and/or a short (30- to 36-inch) zipper that may tend to drag when the bag is closed or opened.

DRY-CLEANED BAGS

We stress proper airing of the sleeping bag, particularly when it has been dry-cleaned. An oft-told tale that bears repeating now deals with a teenager who had slept in a bag that had only recently been dry-cleaned and then left for 1½ days in a car trunk. The boy's parents found him in a coma after the first night. Eleven days later, he was dead. The hospital reports said death was due to the inhaling of perchloroethylene fumes that had been trapped within the insulation. The solvents used in dry-cleaning may leave behind long-lasting lethal fumes. A thorough airing is a must. The mummy bag, to be discussed in more detail further along, can literally turn into a shroud if not properly aired, because often only the sleeper's nose is exposed.

MATTRESS POCKETS AND CANOPIES

If there were ever two items in the camper's sleeping world that might be termed virtually vestigial, they are the mattress pocket and the canopy.

The former is built on some bags, yet its value is plainly in doubt. The intended purpose of the device is to act as a pocket for an inserted air mattress, but the mattress is extremely difficult to remove in the morning. Inserting the mattress into the bag is not a simple task, either. A better sleeping setup is to place the air mattress on a ground cloth or on smooth ground, the sleeping bag on top.

The canopy serves little purpose. It may act as a protective covering for the sleeping bag itself when rolled up or as a cloth panel to hold such items as eyeglasses or a flashlight which might come in handy during the night. But if the bag comes already equipped with a carrying case or stuff bag, the canopy is useless. It may ward off a light drizzle or gentle snow, but should a moderate or worse storm come up, offers no protection at all.

AIR MATTRESSES

An air mattress is not essential for sleeping in the outdoors, but it does add comfort. Most are made of nylon, which is lightweight enough for backpacking.

The chief drawback is that an air mattress can be used only at temperatures of about 45°F and higher unless you lay some insulation over the mattress. Otherwise, cold air in the mattress will convect body heat away. Another disadvantage is that air mattresses are subject to puncture as well as leakage from seams to valves. So a special patching kit should always accompany you on your travels.

Catalog listings of air mattresses often give both the deflated size and the inflated size. The latter is the one you should pay attention to, as that is what you will be sleeping on.

The average adult can be comfortably accommodated on a mattress measuring between 70 and 74 inches. A 6-footer would require the longest standard length—75 inches. A stout camper might need 32 inches of mattress across his back, but most

people can fit comfortably on 28- to 30-inchers with adequate elbow room.

There are two designs of air mattresses—the I-beam style and the tufted. The I-beam typically consists of five tubes that resemble steel construction beams when viewed from one end. The tufted design is wafflelike in appearance, and provides the sleeper with full support. It's more comfortable than the I-beam style, but is the more expensive of the two. When buying an air mattress, either I-beam or tufted, choose one with a metal valve, never the rubber or plastic type. The metal valves have screw tops.

If you sleep with a pillow, there's no need for you to do without one outdoors. Many sleeping bags

I-beam construction of this air mattress renders it less comfortable than the wafflelike pattern—and less expensive.

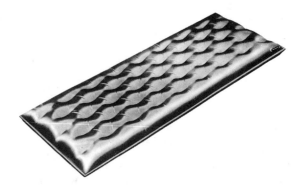

Air mattresses can range from poor to excellent in durability. One very good type is the tufted version, which boasts pliability and dependability even at 20° below zero.

come with built-in air pillows, or else the pillows—either filled with down, synthetic fibers, or air—can be bought separately.

There are many air mattresses made solely of plastic or rubber. Avoid them. Although plastic or rubber air mattresses are lighter than the recommended fabric-rubber combinations, they are delicate and tear easily.

Until recently, there were three ways to inflate an air mattress: with a hand pump, a foot pump, or your own lungs. Now there are also some cleverly designed self-inflating mattresses. If yours doesn't inflate itself, using your own lung power isn't very difficult, but the resulting moist vapor can condense and freeze in cold weather. A hand pump adds weight to your gear. Lightweight plastic foot pumps are popular; although they are bulky, they provide dry air quickly.

When you inflate an air mattress, keep it out of the sun. Otherwise, the heat will cause the air to expand, possibly breaking the mattress. Also, never use a gas-station air-pressure pump to inflate a mattress.

To deflate an air mattress, unscrew the metal cap, leaving the valve completely open. Then put a heavy object on the mattress to force air to escape more quickly. The last step is to slowly roll the mattress, beginning with the end opposite the valve, until all the air has been expelled.

When not in use, an air mattress should be blown up slightly and kept away from heat. Use it only for sleeping; it is not meant to be a surfboard. If the mattress does get wet, though, stand it up in an airy, shady place.

FOAM PADS

Sleeping pads are of two basic types: (1) hard, closed-cell foams and (2) soft, open-cell foams. The hard pads contain sealed bubbles that resist compression. The soft pads contain bubbles and a network of passages that allow air to escape when compressed.

Hard-foam pads are sold in thicknesses ranging from ⅜ to 1 inch and provide almost as much insulating loft as the pad's thickness. Soft-foam pads must be purchased four to five times as thick as hard foams to provide as much insulating loft when compressed under your body. Though more comfortable, soft-foam pads are bulkier to carry, and they absorb ground and body moisture—adding inconvenience and weight.

Both hard- and soft-foam pads can be purchased in various lengths and widths. To capitalize on the advantages of each type of pad, some manufacturers

Therm-a-Rest Camp Rest chair kit makes sitting or sleeping outdoors comfortable. Made of nylon oxford, the chair is 25-inches wide.

Therm-a-Rest Eco-Staytek is an "environmentally friendly" mattress woven from polyester fibers made from recycled plastic soda bottles. Available in two sizes: 20×72×1.5 inches and 3½-pound weight, and 20×47×1.5 inches and 2-pound weight.

laminate them together. Here, the top layer is soft foam for comfort, and the bottom layer is the hard foam for insulation and watertightness. Or you may see a soft-foam pad enclosed in a fabric cover. Better covers have a cotton upper surface, so that body moisture won't be trapped on top, and a lower surface of waterproofing-coated nylon.

Tough, young backpackers use hard foams almost exclusively. But age and desire for comfort usually lead even the toughest backpackers to combine the use of hard foam with either soft foam or an air mattress.

CANVAS COTS

A cot in your tent can waste floor space if you have a sloping-wall tent. Also, it's quite a task to set up alone. Canvas cots also tend to let cold air circulate beneath them, but some 6-inch-high models come equipped with down or Dacron batting. This insulation isn't compressed by the camper's weight while he sleeps, so it remains at peak efficiency. On the other hand, cots are comfortable, if weight and bulk are unimportant.

If you decide on a canvas cot, get a model that is about 12 or 14 inches off the ground so it can double as a tent seat.

FOOTGEAR

LEATHER BOOTS

The sturdiest boots are those constructed totally of leather, the best all-round material for four-season wear. Leather boots permit the feet to "breathe," giving off moisture that would otherwise tend to make the camper's feet hot and uncomfortable and cause blisters. Some manufacturers have treated boots with waterproofing compounds, but leather so treated seals in body heat and moisture.

The proper height for a boot is about 6 inches. A higher boot may constrict your leg muscles as well as restrict free circulation. Also, high boots are hot and heavy in summertime. The boot should also be uninsulated, for reasons we'll discuss shortly.

Avoid boots with leather soles and heels; they are not very water resistant. Leather soles wear quickly and slip on smooth rocks, pine needles, dry grass, and the like. Get boots with soles and heels of rubber or one of the tough synthetics. Rubber soles provide a good grip, and are flexible, long-lasting, and tough.

Many campers like boots with a platform, or straight-bottom, sole that has no heel. These soles are not recommended for mountain climbing. A heel permits you to hold back when you're descending a slope. Cleatlike treads (Vibram) are good if you hike on rocky trails.

Be certain that the tops of the boots are made of soft leather so that enough insulation is provided. The air space between the sock and the boot and the area around your foot should permit free, comfortable movement. In winter, a boot should keep cold air out and warm air in; that air space, if sufficient, will help achieve this dual purpose. The toe and heel should be hard, to give your feet the protection they need.

Some styles of leather boots are insulated. If the temperature is below freezing, and dry, such boots may be suitable for casual walking. But for all-round use, they are a poor choice. They become stuffy, heavy, and hot during strenuous activity, and when wet take a long time to dry. In cold weather you are better off with plain leather boots and several pairs of socks of varied weights which you can change if one pair becomes wet.

Before you try out your new boots on a hike, a thorough breaking-in is in order. Obviously, the spanking-new leather may be rather tough. That's why shoe grease should be applied, but not to any particular excess. Otherwise, your boots will become overly soft and all but worthless. Also, try short hikes at regular intervals with the new boots so that your feet will get accustomed to them. Bend your feet frequently to make each boot more pliable. Old-timers used to break in their boots by standing in a bucket of water till the boots were saturated, then walk around in them until they were dry.

Through proper care, you can add substantial life to your boots. When you're finished for the day and your boots are coated with mud, wash it off thor-

Irish Setter is a typical lightweight, upland, all-leather hunting boot. Made from water-repellent leather, the boot is ideal for early fall hunting.

oughly. Then fill them with wads of newspaper and place them in a warm, dry area (not above 100°F). When they're dry, rub some shoe grease into the leather to soften and waterproof it.

Another simple way to waterproof leather boots is to treat them with paraffin or a silicone-dressing spray. The method of waterproofing preferred by most outdoors enthusiasts is to use neat's-foot oil. (Keep the oil off rubber heels and soles as it may prove harmful to them.) Prior to application, wash the leather with warm water and mild soap. The purpose of this measure is to open the leather's pores for better absorption of the oil. Be sure the leather is still wet when you rub on the oil. A handy applicator is an old toothbrush as its bristles help get the oil deep into the seams.

For securing the boot to the foot, rawhide laces and eyelets have proved the best, with nylon strings running a close second. Some hikers prefer the quicker hooks, but they are not quite as reliable as laces. And if you get a cheap set of hooks, they'll break, rust, or bend in no time. Also, hooks often catch on twigs.

RUBBER AND LEATHER BOOTS

Though the all-leather boot is the best all-round boot for hiking, for wet weather many people prefer

shoepacs. These boots have a leather top and a rubber bottom and are the perfect choice for hiking in rain, swamplands, and wet snow. The leather tops shed moisture well if they're properly oiled or greased, and are flexible. As these tops aren't as airtight as they would be if they were of rubber composition, they provide good ankle support and a wide, roomy area for the foot. This air space lets you wear two pairs of socks—woolen over thermal—to withstand the cold down to 0°F. The rubber bottoms of shoepacs perform the all-important function of keeping the feet dry.

As you've noted, shoepacs are designed for the wet-weather enthusiast. That's why the neat's-foot oil treatment described earlier should be used to waterproof the boots. But be careful not to harm the rubber bottoms when applying the oil.

Manufacturers have developed shoepacs up to 18 inches in height, but a model from 8 to 12 inches should prove adequate. The extra inches will just hinder the circulation in your leg, and will add extra, unnecessary lacing and unlacing time to your chores outdoors.

RUBBER BOOTS (UNINSULATED)

The camper who fishes on his outings often finds himself pushing boats off beaches, and sloshing in

Cabela's rubber and leather lace-up boots and shoes have waterproof bottoms with non-slip tread. Upper is made of water-resistant cowhide. An all-around choice for outdoorsmen likely to encounter a variety of conditions.

water in his small craft. The top choice in footgear for this person is the uninsulated rubber boot.

The optimum choice is a boot about 12 or 13 inches high with no more than three eyelets at the top. The remainder of the boot is totally enclosed, protecting the feet from water.

In extreme cold, two pairs of socks—heavy woolen ones over thermal or athletic-type socks—are warmer than a single pair of heavy socks, and keep your feet dry and comfortable for quite a while.

When you shop for footgear, take along two pairs of socks to insure getting the proper size. You're better off learning about a too-snug fit in the store than when your feet begin to hurt on a cold day outside.

COMPOSITION BOOTS

The best news in recent years in outdoor footgear is the introduction of boots that combine several developments in modern technology, such as tough Cordura nylon and the waterproofing properties of Gore-Tex, a microporous membrane. The most popular boot of this type has a lug sole with leather toe and heel. The rest of the boot, however, is made of light Cordura nylon. The entire boot is lined with Gore-Tex, which makes it virtually waterproof. The resulting boot is frequently half the weight of a full leather boot. It requires very little break-in because the nylon sides mold more quickly to the foot than new leather. And the wearer can literally stand in water without getting wet.

For warm weather or early fall hunting and hiking, these boots are an excellent choice. If you expect to encounter colder temperatures, the same composition boots are also available insulated. Modern synthetic insulating materials such as Thinsulate and Insolite make them warmer per ounce of boot weight than any older type of insulation, yet they seem to "wick" away moisture. With proper socks, therefore, they don't tend to hold perspiration and make your feet feel uncomfortably clammy.

RUBBER BOOTS (INSULATED)

Insulated rubber boots are a good choice for ice fishing or sitting on a deer stand for lengthy periods—both of which are done in bone-chilling temperatures. These boots are much too heavy for conventional hiking, and even a lengthy walk will cause your feet to become clammy and sweaty. Another disadvantage is that if you should snag the outside layer, water may seep into the insulated lining. The proper procedure at this point is to squeeze out the moisture toward the area of the punctures until it is completely outside. Then prop open the tear with a twig or toothpick to let the insulation air out. Wait till all the moisture is removed before repairing the tear with a rubber-tube patch.

A final word on the insulated rubber boot: As mentioned, it can become clammy inside. By merely

Sorel's Manitoba is designed for temperatures as low as −25 degrees with its removable ThermoPlus inner boot. Made of natural rubber, a good choice for hunters who spend time in wetlands or other cold, wet conditions.

Dunham Bootmakers Big Sky is a lightweight boot made with waxed leather, DuPont Cordura nylon, and Gore-Tex Duratherm insulation. Sound design for hunters in cold winter conditions.

sprinkling talcum in the boot at night, you'll find that the clamminess will disappear, and your feet will slide in easier and not bunch up your socks uncomfortably.

Many campers wear boot liners inside waterproof boots. These add to the warmth and reduce clamminess. Most liners have an outer layer of cotton tricot to act as a blotter and an inner layer of insulating, moisture-resistant acrylic fiber. For a comfortable fit with liners, you may need slightly larger boots than you'd otherwise wear. When buying new boots, therefore, it's best to try them on over the liners.

LEATHER BOOTS (INSULATED)

Though not quite as waterproof as the insulated rubber boot, the insulated leather boot has some virtues. It generally gives more comfortable fit and provides better ankle support.

You can't remove the insulation for cleaning and drying, and you can't adjust the boot to rising temperatures. Thus boots tend to become hot, stuffy and heavy in warmer weather.

Most insulated leather boots are quite waterproof, but in wet weather over an extended period some moisture will seep inside. To further waterproof your boots, try the silicone-dressing sprays, paraffin, or the neat's-foot oil method described earlier.

HIPBOOTS AND WADERS

The duck hunter and the fisherman find themselves up to their knees—and often higher—in water. Hipboots or waders are an essential part of their equipment.

When the water is no more than knee-deep and a substantial amount of walking is required, hipboots will suffice. For the fisherman or marshland hunter, the uninsulated hipboot is best. It features the standard heavy-rubber foot that is welded to a top of strong fabric—usually a laminated nylon-rubber-nylon sandwich—with a thin inner bond of waterproof rubber. Although some models are manufactured with uppers of rubber-coated fabric, the welded ones are recommended. Though the price is just a bit higher, they're more flexible and far lighter.

The winter steelheader, fall surf fisherman, or duck hunter will find the insulated hipboot to be his best buy. The weather is usually bitter, and the core of insulation built into the shoe and ankle of the hipboot will keep him warm.

If you are a stream fisherman who wades on slick

Cabela's 5mm Boot-Foot Neoprene Waders have double layers of neoprene in knee area and 200-gram Thinsulate insulation in the boots. Available in brown felt sole, camouflage or brown lug, or sole.

rocks, felt-soled hipboots are required. They provide sure-footed, quiet movement. They wear quickly but can be replaced with special felt-sole kits available in sporting goods stores. These kits also can be used to apply felt soles to rubber-soled boots.

Waders are simply hipboots with waterproof tops that extend to the waist, or even to the chest. Some have stocking feet of thin rubber or a rubberized fabric, over which wading shoes are worn. Others have boot feet with waterproof uppers. The boot-foot style is simpler to put on, carry, and store; it is also less apt to develop leaks.

SNOWSHOES

When snow depths reach a foot or more, conventional boots are rendered virtually ineffectual. At such times snowshoes must be worn on outdoor treks. The purpose of the snowshoe is to distribute the weight of the body over a greater surface of snow than the shoe sole alone, thereby increasing support.

Snowshoes come in three basic styles—the Alaskan, the Michigan, and the bearpaw—plus several modifications of each of these styles.

The Alaskan is also known as the Yukon, pickerel,

SNOWSHOES

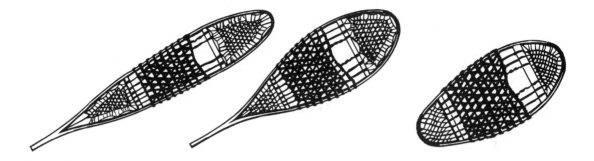

Left: For relatively open country with just traces of brush or timber, the Alaskan snowshoe will suffice. **Middle:** In areas of heavy brush, use the Michigan snowshoe. **Right:** When you need to make frequent turns, such as on hills or mountains, your best bet is to strap on a pair of bearpaws.

trial, or racing snowshoe. It's good for long-distance walking, even with a heavy load. Long and narrow, it has a conspicuous upward curl at the toe and a tail at the rear—a design suited to open country and powder snow with little timber or brush.

The "classic" style, the one that conforms to most pictures, is the Michigan, also known as the Maine or Algonquin snowshoe. It, too, has a tail, but tends to be wider and shorter than the Alaskan, and with less front curl—usually 2 inches or under—making it suitable for brushy country.

The bearpaw has no tail and little (or occasionally no) front curl. Its shape is more or less oval, but the forepart is often slightly wider than the rear. Shorter than the other types, it's good for hilly, brushy terrain, especially where abrupt turns are common. This is believed to be the most ancient of all snowshoe designs.

One modification, sometimes called the Green Mountain snowshoe, is narrower than the usual bearpaw and almost uniform in width. One advantage is that it's easy to learn to walk on and is very maneuverable. Another is that it's compact. Green Mountain snowshoes and more or less similar models are popular with snowmobilers and, indeed, are sometimes called snowmobile snowshoes.

Another variation, known simply as a modified bearpaw, has a short tail, which helps to prevent twisting. Still another, usually called the cross-country snowshoe, is a narrow, slightly elongated bearpaw (like the Green Mountain) with a tail that helps prevent twisting but isn't long enough to snag. Good for relatively even but somewhat brushy ter-

rain, it's essentially a cross between the bearpaw and the Alaskan.

The relatively new, nonwooden snowshoe frames are mostly of the same basic configuration as the bearpaw or Green Mountain but a bit more rectangular.

Traditionally, snowshoes are composed of frames made of ash—a tough and flexible wood—and rawhide webbing. The webbing must remain taut to

Sherpa Backcountry Tracker is a 9×34-inch mountain snowshoe. The binding withstands temperatures down to −42 degrees. Nylon decking is lightweight and polyurethane-coated.

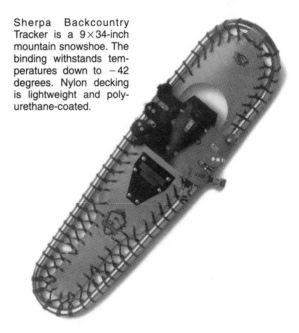

perform properly, and freezing weather does the trick. Thus, keep snowshoes far from the campfire and warm cabins. Moisture can dangerously stretch the webbing. Using spar varnish or polyurethane, you can give your webbing a protective, waterproof coat. Additional wrappings of rawhide near the snowshoe's toe can add to its life. As crusted snow usually affects the toe area first, this precaution should prove useful.

The size of the snowshoe depends on the weight of the snowshoer. The following chart will help you to determine the correct size for your boot.

Between seasons, remove and replace all broken, weak, or frayed webbing. Clean the entire snowshoe rapidly with soap and water to prevent any unnecessary stretch. Dry the pair a minimum of 36 hours if some or all of the rawhide has been replaced.

In recent years, several new materials for snowshoe frames have come into use, as have two new kinds of webbing. In addition to fine-grain ash, frames are now made of aluminum, magnesium, or synthetics. Frames of metal or plastic are durable, won't warp, and require no maintenance. On the other hand, wood has more esthetic appeal, won't usually crack in extreme cold, and doesn't readily cake with heavy snow. Wood remains the biggest seller.

BODY WEIGHT	MICHIGAN	ALASKAN	BEARPAW
35 to 50 lbs.	9″ x 30″	———	———
50 to 60	10″ x 36″	———	———
60 to 90	11″ x 40″	———	———
100 to 125	12″ x 42″	———	———
125 to 150	12″ x 48″	10″ x 48″	———
150 to 175	13″ x 48″	10″ x 56″	14″ x 30″
175 to 200	14″ x 48″	12″ x 60″	13″ x 33″
200 to 250	14″ x 52″	———	14″ x 36″

Instead of naked or varnished rawhide webbing, leading snowshoe makers now offer rawhide coated with polyurethane, which has superior moisture resistance. Most modern of all is nylon-coated neoprene lacing, which is very strong, doesn't stretch or absorb water, doesn't attract gnawing animals, and needs no seasonal varnishing or any other maintenance. With use, however, it does become abraded and hairy-looking, so a great many snowshoers prefer the tradition of rawhide combined with the protection of polyurethane.

As you may suspect, a device is needed to hold the snowshoe to your boot. The harness is a leather or leather-and-nylon strap arrangement which permits the toe to tilt downward and the heel to rise.

CAMP CLOTHING

WARM WEATHER

Underwear. The underclothing you wear at home or at work will suffice, although cotton boxer-type shorts, which cling less to your skin, are more comfortable than the jockey style. Two pairs of shorts and two T-shirts will last for a hike of less than a week, one set for wearing and one for washing. Drying in the sun ordinarily takes about two hours.

Though underwear can go for two days without a wash, the same *does not* go for your socks. A daily change and washing are necessary to health and comfort. Cotton wash-and-wear socks are recommended; wool may be too warm and scratchy. Light wool sweat socks with low boots are fine only in mountainous areas. In coastal regions that are flat and sandy, you may not need socks but simply sneakers. Prior to a day's hike, cut down on perspiration with a healthy sprinkle of foot powder or baby powder in your boots.

Waffle-weave underwear is intended for cooler temperatures, but the top part worn under a thin cotton shirt will keep you warm in an early-morning chill.

Outerwear. Khaki (cotton) pants are appropriately light and durable. Look for cuffless models that are an inch or so shorter than your regular pants, because cuffs tend to catch mud, water, stones, and twigs. Denims are also sturdy, but should be loose fitting for the active camper.

Allow extra room between your crotch and the top of your trousers, for bending and taking lengthy steps. Roomy pockets are important, but don't overfill them. Make sure the seams have been reinforced for longer wear.

Shorts are acceptable in hot areas, but they don't guard against underbrush and sunburn. A short-sleeved cotton shirt during the day is fine, but be careful of too much sun on your forearms. At night when mosquitos and other insects appear, you will need a long-sleeved cotton shirt. Shirttails which fall well below the waist are advisable. Have a sweater or sweatshirt on hand for the evenings.

As mentioned in another section, waterfowl down is the prime insulating material. But synthetics, such as Thinsulate, are acceptable and less expensive. A lightweight, quilted, insulated jacket that uses a good synthetic will keep the early-morning fisherman comfortably warm and dry all summer.

Headgear. A cotton hat like baseball players wear screens your head from the sun. Though the bill in the front shields your face from rain, you may need the additional protection of a light nylon, hooded jacket to cover your neck in a downpour.

COOL WEATHER

Underwear. On cool fall days when the temperature hovers around 40 degrees, leave on the warm-weather shorts and T-shirt, but add a one- or two-piece suit of cotton underwear with full sleeves and legs. Thermal-weave or waffle-weave underwear supplies greater warmth and more ventilation than the flat design. The weaving pattern consists of protrusions and hollow pockets close to the skin which trap body heat.

Two-layer underwear—often labeled Duofold—is another reliable insulated model. The smooth cotton layer facing the skin absorbs perspiration and passes it through the insulating air space to the outer layer of cotton, nylon, and wool. Moisture evaporates from the outer layer.

Wool socks are unparalleled for warmth. Make sure they extend a couple of inches over your boot tops. To prevent blisters on your feet, wear a thin pair of cotton socks underneath. The combination keeps your feet comfortable and free of moisture.

Outerwear. A good choice for cool weather is the heavy-duty work khakis simply called ''work clothes'' by most stores. As with summer outdoor pants, cuffless styles are best. Wear the inseam a few inches shorter than usual and look for reinforced seams. The cut of the pants should be full rather than ivy-league trim to facilitate climbing, bending, and the like. An extra inch between crotch and belt is also helpful.

If you prefer wool pants, get a lightweight pair. Twill fabric, which frequently consists of 65 percent Dacron polyester and 35 percent cotton, is a sturdy and less expensive alternative.

Loose-fitting trousers are important. A size larger at the waist may not be flattering, but with a heavy shirt, thicker undergarments, and a sweater to tuck in, it is a wise idea. A belt or suspenders are fine, and deep pockets on the trousers are also convenient.

Fall is a good time for lightweight wool or flannel shirts. These too should allow freedom of movement. Wool is warmer, and with a waffle-weave turtleneck worn underneath, you're ready for real cold. The shirttail should extend several inches below the waist so it doesn't slip out while you're moving. The buttons should be big so they are easy to handle with cold fingers.

A quilted, insulated jacket insures warmth if the insulating agent is down or a good-quality synthetic. The quilting prevents the insulation from bunching up. Excess moisture is absorbed and expelled through the insulation and fabric. Slip the jacket on whenever a shirt alone won't be enough. The jacket should have pockets and a strong, trustworthy zipper.

Down jackets are matchless for warmth and insulation, but prices are high. In cool weather, synthetics such as Thinsulate, PolarGuard, and Thermoloft are quite adequate. When available, choose garments with Gore's Windstopper fabric, which stops cold wind from penetrating, yet remains breathable.

Headgear. A billed cap of wool, cotton, or leather is the first choice.

The beret and the tam o'shanter are underrated as hats in the United States, but either one supplies a large amount of heat to your head, and body. Both styles can be pulled down to protect your ears, and each is compact, inexpensive, and long-lasting.

The watch cap—the type worn by merchant seamen—or the ski hat is acceptable. If it isn't too cool, they can be worn with the cuff doubled up, and in harsh cold, both can be pulled down to cover the neck, ears, and forehead.

COLD WEATHER

When temperatures drop to zero and below, your life may depend on the clothing you wear.

Underwear. The T-shirt and boxer shorts you wore in summer and fall should be the first clothes you put on. Follow with the full set of waffle-weave, quilted, or polypropylene underwear. The waffle-weave traps body heat and permits moisture to escape at the neck, a more rapid exit point than the underwear itself. The quilted underwear gives warmth by stopping the circulation of air inside your clothing. Polypropylene is a synthetic fiber with the softness of cotton and the wicking ability to pull moisture away from the body for evaporation.

Top-grade wool socks provide superior warmth and durability through many hard months and washings. Avoid colored wool, which may cause allergy, infect a blister, or discolor other clothing you may have thrown in your laundry pail.

A properly fitted sock is snug enough not to bunch about the toe or heel, but is not too tight to cause discomfort.

Wool socks reinforced with a strong synthetic such as Dacron or nylon last longer and are less expensive in the long run, but lose some advantage in ventilation, softness, and warmth. Socks made totally of nylon, Dacron, Orlon, or another synthetic are also not on a par with wool when it comes to softness and getting rid of moisture. Cotton socks are comfortable only till they're soaked with water or perspiration.

One large manufacturer features wick-dry socks that boast an inner surface of hydrophobic yarn to carry sweat away from your foot. The outer hydrophilic layer absorbs and holds the moisture. Some manufacturers offer battery-powered electric socks.

The wisest choice, however, is a pair of good-quality, wool hunting socks worn over a pair of cotton socks. Whatever the height of your boots, select socks which are 3-inches higher. Lap the extra material over the boot.

Outerwear. Cuffless wool pants and a lightweight wool shirt—with large buttons for ease of handling—furnish ample warmth when worn over the proper underwear. The advantage of wool to the camper who also hunts is that it is noiseless. And wool does a fine job of shedding and repelling water. Similar fabrics include Polartec and fleece.

Take along a quilted jacket insulated with down or one of the better synthetics. The camper who feels too restricted in a quilted jacket might choose a less cumbersome vest insulated with down or a good synthetic. A vest with a good zipper front, a button-down collar, and a flap pocket on either side is a treasure; more so when it is low enough in the rear to cover the kidneys. In extreme cold, the topmost outer garment can also be an oversize wool hunting shirt or jacket.

Heavy wool or leather gloves worn over a pair of cotton work gloves protect the hands. Although mittens may keep you somewhat warmer, they inhibit your ability to grasp triggers, utensils, and the like, such that gloves are a better choice.

Headgear. A wool hunting cap with earflaps along with a wool or cotton scarf is suitable. On a deer stand in a windy area, this combo is perfect. Place the scarf around the neck or over your head under the cap. Hoods tend to restrict head movement and muffle sounds coming from the sides and back, but a scarf can be quickly loosened when necessary.

The watch cap and ski hat tend to hamper peripheral vision. They are acceptable substitutes for the wool hunting cap, however, because they pull down completely to protect almost everything from the top of the head to the neck, revealing only the eyes, nose, and mouth.

RAINGEAR

There are two styles of rainwear: the rainsuit and the poncho. The rainsuit is a waterproof jacket and pants, while the poncho is a square of waterproof fabric with a hole for the head. The poncho does little to restrict the arms, but flares enough to protect the legs—when you are standing—and let in cooling air. A poor choice for the shotgunner because it tends to be clumsy and dangerous.

For sitting in a duck blind or boat most of the day, take a rainsuit. It should have drawstring pants and a hooded zipper jacket with elastic or snap-fastener wrists. These features will also keep out wind.

Though somewhat expensive, Neoprene-coated nylon fabric is a good buy in rainsuits. It's durable, waterproof, and lightweight, and doesn't stiffen so much in cold weather as do the popular and less expensive rubberized cotton suits. The inexpensive vinyl or plastic suits are worthless because they rip. Easily split seams, snagged material, and stiffness in cold weather are further drawbacks.

The backpacker, however, may find the poncho preferable to the rainsuit because of its lighter weight. A poncho with a rear flap will protect the pack as well.

Don't buy a cheap poncho. A good one slips on easily and doubles as a ground tarp, makeshift lean-to, or tent.

For fishing offshore or on lakes, however, the rainsuit is recommended. It keeps your entire body dry whether you are standing or sitting. Most serious outdoors enthusiasts own both the rainsuit and poncho.

No discussion of raingear would be complete without a special look at Gore-Tex, a form-fitting stretch material that keeps us from getting wet. What is Gore-Tex? The key to unique, waterproof, windproof, breathable performance characteristics of Gore-Tex fabric lies in the patented microporous membrane which is laminated to outer shell fabrics. The Gore-Tex membrane is composed of 100 percent expanded polytetrafluoroethylene. This is the same resin that DuPont's Teflon is composed of. The Gore-Tex membrane contains 9 billion pores per square inch, each 20,000 times smaller than a water drop but 700 times larger than a water vapor molecule. The membrane, therefore, effectively blocks wind and wet weather yet lets perspiration vapor pass through.

In two-layer Gore-Tex fabric the Gore-Tex membrane is laminated to one side of an outer shell fabric. In three-layer Gore-Tex fabric (for heavier uses) the membrane is sandwiched between a shell fabric and a tricot knit fabric. Because the Gore-Tex membrane is permanently bonded to fabrics it does not peel off or degrade after washing like most "waterproof" coatings or treatments. It is also not subject to contamination by body oils.

Today, outdoors enthusiasts will find Gore-Tex fabric in everything from rainwear, hunting gear, cycling gear, and dress outerwear to accessories such as waterproof boots, gloves, socks, and hats.

CAMP STOVES AND HEATERS

An open wood fire in a public campground is becoming a rare sight. For too long, careless campers have haphazardly cut down trees for fuel and left their fires unattended, causing costly forest fires which destroyed thousands of acres of woodland every year. As a result, most campgrounds today prohibit open fires. Even if they didn't, the lack of available wood would be a prohibition in itself.

Thus, the modern camper has been compelled to carry a stove on his camping trips, and in some ways has improved his lot. Certainly people who cook much are more at home with a stove than a wood fire. A stove does away with blackened cooking utensils, hot sparks, and eye-watering smoke.

WOOD STOVES

The Sheepherder's stove is the best known. But due to their weight and awkwardness, wood stoves in general are fading from the camping scene. The Sheepherder's stove is constructed of sheet metal and often features a small oven for baking, as well as several sections of piping to carry smoke outside the tent. An asbestos collar around the pipe where it passes through the tent is a necessity. Some models fold flat and have telescoping piping. Nevertheless, the wood stove is impractical for the average camper, particularly because modern tents are not equipped to handle stovepipes.

GASOLINE STOVES

With inexpensive white, unleaded gasoline a readily available commodity these days, the gasoline stove has become the leader among camp stoves. It's fine for year-round use as bitter-cold weather has little or no effect on gasoline.

The typical gasoline stove with just one burner weighs 2½ pounds and has a tank capacity of 2 pints of fuel, which should keep it burning approximately 3½ hours. For large families, there are two- and three-burner gasoline models that weigh up to 25 pounds.

The two-burner stove is the best choice for general camping. For large families, on a short outing one two-burner and one single-burner stove are better

GASOLINE AND KEROSENE STOVES

GASOLINE AND KEROSENE STOVES (Continued)

Left: Peak 1 Multi-Fuel Stove comes with a second generator that can be used to convert the appliance from a Coleman fuel burner to a kerosene-burning stove. The stove's multilevel ring keeps pots and pans level even if the stove is sitting on uneven ground. It will burn at high heat for 1½ hours and will simmer for 7 hours. **Center:** Peak 1 Feather 442 Dual Fuel gas stove burns both Coleman or unleaded fuel. The integral tank and precise flame means one fill-up should last through a typical weekend's cooking. **Right:** Coleman Electronic Ignition two-burner gas stove will burn Coleman fuel or unleaded gas. A good choice for all-season campers in areas where propane might not be readily available.

than a bulky three-burner stove. But for cabin or long-term camping, choose the three-burner model. The backpacker can get along with just one burner. Some backpacker models tip the scales at a mere 20 ounces and can fit in a large coat pocket. Hunters and fishermen who just want a quick pot of coffee or hot soup during the day appreciate the lightweight one-burner stoves.

PROPANE STOVES

Highly popular among warm-weather campers is the stove that runs on propane gas, also known as LP or liquified petroleum. In winter, propane stoves do not work well because the cold tends to reduce the temperature of the gas, thereby diminishing volatility and ultimately the vital heat output.

A 5-pound, single-burner stove is typical with the usually disposable 14.1-ounce cylinder of gas. A double-burner stove weighs about 12 pounds and often uses a separate cylinder for each burner. For extended stays in camp, many manufacturers make large-capacity, refillable tanks of propane that can be carried aboard a plane or packhorse.

As with gasoline stoves, we recommend a two-burner stove for general camping, and one single-burner and one double-burner model for larger families.

The advantages of propane gas over white gasoline are the ease with which it lights and its carrying convenience. Also, no pumping, priming, and pouring are necessary because the sealed containers of propane readily attach to the stove.

On the other hand, propane is not as easily available throughout the country as is gasoline. Before leaving home, take into account the length of your trip, whether or not you are carrying an ample supply of propane gas, and the proximity along your route of stores stocking propane. Another problem with propane is that you're never quite sure if you are running low. Thus it's a good idea to have two cylinders.

Getting down to economics, studies have shown that the average camp meal costs about a few cents to cook with gasoline, but approaches 50 cents when propane is used. With the advantages that propane stoves have in summer, many campers care little about the added expense. Another featherweight gas used in contemporary stoves is butane, also a liquified petroleum.

CANNED HEAT

Known commercially as Sterno, this is a solid, non-melting fuel that's odorless and safe, and burns clearly and steadily until totally consumed. You can extinguish it as many times as you like by simply

PROPANE STOVES

Peak 1 Micro Butane stove is a compact model at full weight of 12.2 ounces. The stove is rated at 13,000 BTU, and will burn on high for 20 minutes.

Peak 1 Backpack Butane stove has a built-in windscreen that can be swiveled to retract or extend pot supports. Its BTU is 14,000 and full weight is 21 ounces.

Peak 1 Apex II is a lightweight stove at 18.6 ounces. The stove features an Instant Lite for no pre-heating or waiting for it to warm before use. It runs on Coleman fuel or un-leaded gas, and is rated at 7,500 BTU.

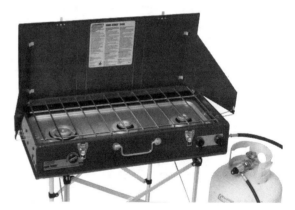

Coleman Guide Series Three-Burner Propane Stove. Ideal for extended boat or tent camping where weight is not a factor.

replacing the pry-off top. The touch of a match will quickly re-light it. Sterno is sold in two sizes. The 7-ounce can burns for 1½ hours while the 2⅝-ounce can lasts 45 minutes. A pint of water can be brought to a boil with Sterno in just 15 minutes, but canned heat is not intended for much else.

Stoves designed specifically for cans of Sterno can be purchased, ranging from stamped metal racks for 50 cents and under to two-burner models for about $2.

REFLECTOR OVEN

This device is used for baking bread, rolls, pies, muffins, cake, fish, and meat at your campsite. It is a simple, collapsible, lightweight (about 3 pounds) contraption made of sheet aluminum that reflects the heat of a stove or campfire onto the food. A stainless steel shelf provides the more even heating, but an aluminum shelf will suffice. A good shelf can handle up to 10 pounds of food.

Delectable rolls, muffins, baked bread, and even a roast can be prepared on this reflector camp oven. This super-light aluminum oven will comfortably accommodate a pair of 8-inch square pans.

The true Dutch oven is made of cast-iron and ranges in diameter from 5 to 16 inches. The flat lid is flanged to hold hot coals and the three stubby legs allow hot coals to be placed underneath.

DUTCH OVEN

If you could take only one pot on a camping trip, it would have to be the Dutch oven. Why? Because it does everything! In addition to helping create great one-pot dinners that require very little attention, it

can also be used to bake, grill, and stir-fry. Introduced to the Americans by Dutch traders, it was improved by Paul Revere, who added a flat top with turned-up edge (to hold coals) and three stubby legs (to sit over coals). It was the most important cooking pot for pioneers as they moved westward, and today it's an essential piece of gear for sportsmen, outfitters, camp cooks, and anyone else who enjoys preparing meals in the outdoors.

In fact, there's only one drawback to a good Dutch oven. It's heavy. An eight-quart pot may weigh nearly 20 pounds—it's obviously not for backpackers.

When buying a Dutch oven, avoid aluminum, steel, and glass-lined versions, since they don't distribute heat evenly and can cause your food to scorch. Instead, look for a cast-iron pot, which retains heat and distributes it equally throughout. And stick to the traditional oven, with flanged lid and legs.

All cast-iron Dutch ovens must be "seasoned" before being used for the first time. Wash the pot thoroughly with a mild dishwashing detergent to remove the wax coating used for protection in shipping. Rinse with hot water and dry with a paper towel. Grease the inside of the pot and the lid with pure vegetable shortening (do not use margarine or butter), then place in a 250° to 300° oven for 15 minutes. Remove the pot, carefully drain off any excess oil and return to the oven for another hour. Allow the pot to cool at room temperature. Your Dutch oven is now ready for use.

Your first step in cooking with it is to get some hot coals. You can get them in the traditional way from a campfire (a keyhole campfire is best) or you can cheat by using charcoal briquettes. In fact, many Dutch-oven recipes now specify the number of briquettes you'll need for the lid and beneath the pot.

With a Dutch oven, you can cook either above

ground or below ground. It may take some practice, but you can prepare a venison stew in a Dutch oven in the morning, bury it in hot coals and it will be ready for dinner when you return to camp in the evening. You can also use your Dutch oven to bake a batch of biscuits or an apple pie.

DUTCH-OVEN VENISON

6-pound venison roast
salt and pepper to taste
meat tenderizer
hot water
dry onion soup mix
Worcestershire sauce
cold water

Put salt, pepper, and meat tenderizer on venison roast. Make thick paste with hot water and dry onion soup mix, and coat entire roast. Sprinkle Worcestershire sauce over roast. Add one cup of cold water to Dutch oven, place roast in oven and cover. Place in hot coals, adding coals to the lid for approximately four to five hours. Serves 12. (Recipe from *Backcountry Cooking,* by Wayne Fears.)

BOX OVEN

Coleman manufactures a collapsible oven—the box oven—which has about the same capacity as the typical Dutch oven, and can be used with a gasoline stove for baking pies, biscuits, etc. This oven may be used on wood fires after some modifications have been made, provided it is always placed over the coals, never over the flame. Otherwise, your food will become smoked.

CAMP HEATERS

Called catalytic heaters because they use a catalyst—usually platinum—which burns the fuel (gasoline, propane, etc.), these heaters do not produce any flame, odor, or carbon monoxide.

Fairly new as camp gear, the catalytic heater provides an effective heat that can be regulated according to your needs. The heat output is measured in BTUs—British Thermal Units. Because of its safety, the catalytic heater is well ahead of other types on the market.

Coleman Electric Ignition Focus 15 Radiant Heater produces 15,000 BTU. Good choice for cabins and duck blinds.

CAMP LIGHTING

GASOLINE LANTERNS

For all-round use, the gasoline lantern is the most practical camp light. The fuel employed is white or unleaded gasoline (readily available throughout the United States), and it is fed from a pressure tank to relatively fragile mantles made of ash. A vapor given off by the gasoline collects in one or two mantles, and is ignited with a match. Should the lantern flare at this point, check for a generator leak. A wise move is to bring along a spare generator—they also tend to clog—and one or two extra mantles. They do add weight to the total unit, but you'll be in the dark without them should something go wrong.

Pumping a built-in tank device before lighting and at intervals during the burning should insure adequate candlepower. If the pressure drops and the light seems to dim or pulsate at times, bring this pump into play to correct the pressure.

The typical gasoline lantern is constructed of stainless steel and brass with a porcelain reflector (also called deflector) to provide ventilation and help direct the light in a wide circle or in one particular spot. A globe of clear Pyrex glass encircling the lit mantles is durable enough to withstand heat. The capacity of the fuel tank is normally two pints, enough for 10 to 12 hours of intense light. Before bedtime, turn off the fuel valve. The minute amount of vapor remaining in the mantles will give you enough light to get into your sleeping bag. The gasoline lantern is unaffected by wind, rain, and cold. It is a valuable piece of camp equipment, but its weight—often close to 10 pounds when you add in fuel—rules it out for the backpacker.

PROPANE LANTERNS

If your camping is usually confined to summer weekends, the propane-gas lantern is for you. There is no generator to clog and replace or liquid fuel to spill and perhaps taint your food. Working off light-

weight propane gas that is sold in a 14.1-ounce (usually throwaway) cylinder, this lantern can give you anything from a soft glow to a bright beam. Large-capacity propane tanks are also sold.

As with gasoline lanterns, one or more mantles are used to catch the gas vapors, but no pumping and priming are required. Porcelain reflectors are also featured to place the light where you want it. One propane cylinder can last from 10 to 15 hours, depending on how intense a light you require.

Since you never know how much gas remains in the cylinder, it is a necessity to take along a pair of cylinders, as well as extra mantles.

Weight is a problem with propane lanterns and backpackers should avoid them. But if you are traveling by auto, propane lanterns are suitable,

CAMP LIGHTING

Coleman 2000 NorthStar battery-powered electronic-ignition lantern burns white gas or unleaded gas. Holds two pints of fuel and will burn 14 hours on low setting, 17 hours on high. **Right:** Coleman Dual Fuel Lantern is a two-mantle model that will burn white or unleaded gas. Increased lighting is preferred for cabins and tents.

Right: Peak 1 Electronic Ignition Lantern weighs 26 ounces and outputs 80 watts for 4 hours. **Center:** The backpack-size Micro Lantern weighs 15¼ ounces and outputs 75 watts for 1 hour, 48 minutes. Both are fueled by a butane/propane mix. **Far Right:** Coleman NightSight Twin Tube Fluorescent Area Light. For campers who prefer to avoid fuels of any kind and look for ease of use, this battery-powered lantern provides one solution.

provided the weather isn't too cold. Otherwise, the pressure in the tank drops and you're lucky if you even get a dim glow.

BATTERY-POWERED LIGHTS

Flashlights are available in all stores stocking camp gear, but get the right kind. There are three- and four-cell models which throw a lot of light, but a two-cell flashlight is adequate. Also, anything larger than two cells means surplus weight. Choose a model with an angled head so that it can be hung on your belt or stood on end, leaving both hands free.

Besides being durable and water resistant, the flashlight should have a shiny or bright finish—perhaps with a luminous stripe painted on it—so it can be located easily. Some flashlights are colored olive-drab, making them a chore to find. Avoid them. A hang-up ring is also helpful, and a slightly recessed glass lens is close to shatterproof because of the protective lip.

Dry-cell batteries aren't too efficient when the weather turns cold; they'll throw a rather dim light. Your best bet is to warm them in your hands or place them under your sleeping bag at night.

You can even get some use out of dead batteries in an emergency by a crude method of recharging. Slowly warm them by the fire and punch holes in the sides. Add as much water as they'll hold, and return the batteries to the flashlight. Don't expect more than a couple minutes of feeble light, though.

When carrying your flashlight in your pack, tape the switch in the off position. Or else reverse one of the batteries in the tube. This will prevent ac-cidentally turning on the flashlight. Also, keep in mind that batteries last longer when they are burned for only short periods of time.

If you prefer a battery-powered lantern over a flashlight, you can get up to 50 hours of intense light if the weather is mild. These lanterns work on six-volt batteries and generally weigh about 5 pounds. If weight is not important, get the wide-beam rather than the searchlight model.

CANDLES

Primitive is the word for the candle as a light source, but it's 100 percent reliable and multi-purpose. It can be used to boil a pot of water, start a fire, mend a leaky spot in your tent.

No matter what kind of camper you are—back-packer through RVer—a few handy candles are a worthwhile investment. It must be stressed that the proper kind is the stearic-acid plumber's candle, made of animal fat. Paraffin candles that you may have at home for decorative purposes or maneu-vering about when a fuse blows are useless in camp. Paraffin will melt in a warm pack.

Never leave your tent unattended with a burning candle inside, even if it is in a candle lantern—as it should be.

And a final note of caution on the use of candles. Some modern waterproofing mixtures have proven to be flammable. If you are a backpacker and re-cently have waterproofed your small tent with a commercial product, carefully check the ingredients. Should any one of them be flammable, *do not* use a candle in your tent.

CAMP COOK KITS

For a party of four campers willing to accept the fact that filet mignon will not be on the menu, the most practical cook kit—in auto, tent, or trailer camping—is the commercial nesting set in which the pots, pans, plates, and cups fit inside one another.

The Boy Scout aluminum cook kit, a nesting set, is fine for a quartet of hungry campers. This model is the most compact package possible. A burlap cover bag is inexpensive and protects against dents and dirt. It consists of:

1 8-quart kettle
1 4-quart stewpot
1 2-quart stewpot
2 frypans with handles
1 spouted pot

4 plates
4 plastic cups

Extra plates and cups can be purchased for a group of more than four. Cups should be plastic rather than aluminum, since aluminum gets too hot to hold or drink from. Aluminum also lets liquids cool too quickly.

If you don't mind some additional weight there are commercial kits made of stainless steel. Much more durable than aluminum and simpler to clean, stainless steel is also heavier and more expensive. Make sure that the plates, frying pans, and cups are not too thin, as they too will become too hot or cold to handle.

Teflon keeps food from sticking and makes

Typical four-person aluminum nesting kit contains a 6-quart bucket with a cover that doubles as a 9¼-inch frypan; a 7⅞-inch fry pan; a 4-quart pot; a 2-quart pot; a coffeepot with cover; plus four plates and four plastic cups.

Peak 1 Solo Cook Kit comes with a frying pan and lid, 1-quart pot, bowl with lid, and cup. Weight of 1½ pounds and pack size of 4¾ × 6-inches makes the kit a good choice for backpackers.

The Coleman Kitchen offers a place for everything needed for outdoor cooking, including hooks for utensils, racks for spices, shelves for storage, and a removable sink. It weighs 35 pounds, carries like a suitcase, assembles with no tools and can be used with legs extended or folded.

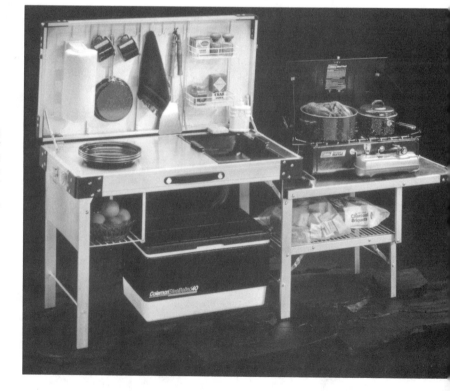

cleaning easier. Teflon-coated utensils require special tools to protect the thin coating from scratching, but if the added weight and bulk are no problem, these are excellent items.

In addition to knife-fork-and-spoon sets for each camper, the cook needs a tool kit. Again, use the Boy Scout model as a guide. It includes:

1 carving knife
1 paring knife
1 potato peeler
1 long fork
1 spoon
1 ladle
1 turner
1 bottle/can opener

The tools are encased in a cloth kit that can be hung up, and the total unit weighs just 1½ pounds.

The backpacker who must limit his supplies to a minimum may be included toward a more compact unit. A good choice is the Peak I Solo Cook Kit, which includes:

1 qt. pot
5½" frying pan
1 pt. bowl
1 cup mug

Examine any mess kit before buying it. It is best to discover a missing utensil in the store. Avoid gadgets from folding toasters to corn poppers to immersion heaters, advertised to simplify camp meals, until you are certain you need them. Begin with the basics and experiment.

To make cleaning easier, use all-purpose paper (toilet paper, for example) to wipe excess food out of your plate immediately after eating. Beware of slipshod washing, which can produce gastric upsets such as dysentery the next meal around.

A pair of lightweight cotton gloves may save the cook from getting burned, cut, or grimy. And while soap, towels, dishrags, and scouring pads (plastic, steel wool, or copper wire) add ounces to your gear, they also speed up the cleaning and drying process.

Aluminum foil, though not recommended as a cook kit in itself, proves quite useful as a supplementary item. As a pot liner, foil keeps foods from gumming up the pot. Wrapped around the bottom of the pot, it stops blackening from the fire. The same result can also be achieved by rubbing the pot's exterior with a bar of soap.

Paper plates and paper cups save time in cleaning up, but the choice is up to you.

The travel kitchen or chuckbox is recommended if you're camping in a motorized vehicle. Available assembled or in kits, these kitchens have five or six compartments to store separately items such as utensil kits, cleanup kits, nonperishable foods, and the like. Because of weight and bulk, the kitchen is inappropriate to horsepacking, canoeing (with portages), and backpacking trips. Many campers make wood-box arrangements with their own modifications after several years of camping.

Canteens come in various styles—round, oval, and a flask-shaped model that clips to the belt. All can be filled with practically any liquid and, if you care to, you can freeze the entire contents. Aluminum models are more rugged than plastic ones. Some feature a chained screw cap and most have a shoulder strap. Canvas covers ward off dirt and dents.

The main concern in purchasing a canteen is proper size. Many tenderfoot campers make the mistake of hauling along a canteen with a 4-quart capacity. That's a gallon, and awfully heavy to carry. For most daylong outings, a 1-quart model is sufficient. For weekends, a 2-quart canteen is advisable, particularly if potable water is a rarity in the area you are in. Water purification tablets are inexpensive and valuable if you're not sure how drinkable the water is.

CAMP TOOLS

HATCHETS

Way back when trees were plentiful, many campers wielded a full-length ax, relegating the smaller hatchet to novice woodchoppers. Nowadays, when wood is an all-too-precious resource, the hatchet has become the most common woodcutting tool at the campsite.

Invest extra money in a premium-quality hatchet. The one-piece styles are the best, with all-steel construction from the head to the bottom of the handle. A cheap hatchet, which may have loose headwork, might injure a nearby camper or shatter after several sessions of chopping. As perspiration can make a handle slippery, get a hatchet with a handle of rubber, wood, or leather laminations which will provide a secure grip.

Should you prefer a hatchet with a wood handle,

At left is a one piece all-steel ax with handle consisting of stacked leather rings. At right is a traditional wood-handle ax. With the one-piece construction at left, obviously there's no concern for a broken handle or a loose head.

HATCHET KNOW-HOW

Once a tree has been felled, strip the branches by always cutting with the slant of the branch.

make sure the handle is chemically bonded to the head. This process insures that it will rarely, if ever, come loose. Some choppers prefer wood handles because there isn't as much cushioning in them. Though the resultant shocks may be uncomfortable, they signify that you are chopping ineffectively. When the shocks cease, you will know you are handling your hatchet correctly.

Some hatchets feature neither the one-piece construction nor the bonded head. These models frequently use a wedge to secure the head to the handle. As this is far from safe, check this type of hatchet frequently during chopping.

Hatchets—also known as belt axes—come in a number of sizes and weights. The right choice obviously depends on your own needs. For all-round use, however, a hatchet with a 1-pound head and a handle about a foot long is an excellent choice. Slightly larger ones are preferred by some campers, and manufacturers have recently offered much smaller ones, as well. The light, very short-handled models, sometimes called backpackers' axes or hunters' axes, are fine for chopping kindling or the wood for a small campfire, and they can also be used to fashion wooden tent stakes (but then, so can a knife). They're useless for heavier work, though adequate for their intended purpose.

Despite its smaller size when compared to the ax, the hatchet is an important tool which needs special care. Never throw a hatchet. Besides ruining the bit and other important parts, you may injure someone.

Only use a hatchet to hammer metal stakes or nails if it is a half-hatchet, which features a regular

To create chip kindling for a fire, hold a branch on a chopping log and cut thin slivers from the bottom up.

To section a tree trunk, begin by chopping about halfway through one side. Then turn it over and start to chop through the other side.

hatchet blade at one end of the head and a tempered hammer head on the other end. A conventional hatchet used for such purposes soon becomes worthless.

A durable leather sheath with a sturdy leather buffer strip or rivets facing the cutting edge should be used to carry the hatchet. If you don't have a sheath handy, drive the blade into a stump or a log so it is not dangerously exposed. (Avoid the double-bitted hatchet on the market featuring blades at both ends of the head. It is dangerous except in the hands of a skilled chopper.)

To cut a piece of wood, use the contact method. Place the edge of the hatchet on the stick. Lift the two and then bring them down together hard on the chopping block. To split wood, place the hatchet edge in a crack. Again, lift the two and bring hatchet and stick down hard on the log or stump. Once contact has been made, slightly twist the hatchet hand to separate the pieces.

On a cold day, heat the hatchet slightly before putting it to work so it won't become brittle and crack.

To pass a hatchet to another person, hold it vertically, head down with the blade facing away from the two of you. Give the receiver more than enough room to grasp the top of the hatchet handle. When you are carrying it in camp, hold the hatchet firmly by its head, keeping the cutting edge away from you.

If not inside your pack while hiking, the hatchet should be strapped to the outside and sheathed. When the hike is a short one, sheath the hatchet and carry it on your belt on your right hip. Never strap it near the groin or kidney area.

AXES

Some chopping chores call for an ax. The camping trip, in this case, is usually for a week or more, and the work might include felling a tree or cutting firewood.

Among the many types of axes available, there are four common ones—the Hudson Bay single-bit, the Kentucky single-bit, the Michigan single-bit, and the Michigan double-bit.

Experienced choppers agree that a head that provides maximum steel-to-wood contact is best. This means the squarish Michigan-style head is preferred to the Hudson Bay or Tomahawk-type head, which has little steel-to-wood contact in proportion to the size of the bit. The tomahawk head has a lot of eye appeal and was popular with French Canadian trappers when weight was a big factor, but it's a poor design when compared with a Michigan head.

If you're selecting an ax for a permanent camp, your best bet is a full-size cabin ax, which usually has a 36-inch handle and a 3½- to 4-pound head. Stick with the Michigan head, which is the best design for nearly all situations. Avoid double-bit axes unless you're an experienced woodcutter. The dangers of using a double-bit ax far outweigh its advantages.

Fancy burl may be desirable in a shotgun stock, but not in an ax handle. You can, however, learn how to pick the best handle in your sports shop. Nearly all wood ax handles, incidentally, are made from hickory. First, eliminate handles with obvious flaws, such as knots in the wood. Next, narrow your selection down to handles that have straight grains

TYPES OF AXES

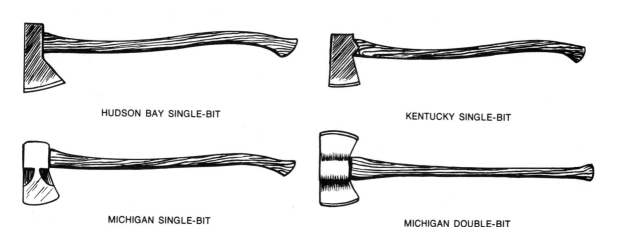

HUDSON BAY SINGLE-BIT

KENTUCKY SINGLE-BIT

MICHIGAN SINGLE-BIT

MICHIGAN DOUBLE-BIT

Altthough the Michigan style ax head, top, will split wood, the maul shown has a heavy head and wide wedge specially designed for splitting.

running the entire length. Now look at the cross-sectioned area of the handle butt. Make a quick count of the number of grains running across the butt and apply this rule: the fewer the grains, the stronger the handle. And grain should run roughly parallel to the long axis of the oval cross section. Avoid axes with painted wood handles. There's no telling how many flaws lie hidden under a coat of paint.

Handles are varnished for two reasons: (1) eye appeal, (2) protection from moisture during shipping and storage. Bare wood, however, affords a better grip. Your ax will be more comfortable to use if you remove the varnish from the handle.

Apply bright yellow, red, or bright blue paint to the ax head once you buy it. The paint will help locate the ax in weeds or brush if it is lost. The paint also assists in bonding the handle and head together. Last, if the paint cracks over the eye, it is a clear danger signal that the handle is loosening inside and may come off at any time.

The handle of an ax, no matter what size, should be made of seasoned hardwood with a grain that is both fine and straight. The handle itself should also be straight. Check to see that the "hang" of the ax is proper. Hang is determined by holding the ax in front of you and sighting down as though it were a rifle. If the center of the handle is in line with the cutting edge of the blade, the hang is correct.

Inspect the point where the handle fits the eye of the steel head, unless you have a one-piece model. If even the slightest gap shows there, look for another ax. An imperfect fit means the handle may work loose soon after continued chopping or pounding.

Several manufacturers use a chemical bond to anchor the ax handle to the head. This holds more securely than the wedges—either wood or steel—which conventionally attach the two parts. Wedges, however, are efficient.

If you want to avoid wood handles, pick one of the all-steel one-piece axes. With some cheap models, you'll experience a shock to the hands when chopping, but one manufacturer solved the problem with a nylon-vinyl grip.

There are a few important safety factors to keep in mind when you chop wood. First, check your ax for a loose head or a damaged handle. If the head continually comes loose, replace the handle. If you're on a trip, you can temporarily solve the problem by soaking the head in a bucket of water. The wood will swell and tighten against the head.

Before you start cutting, hold your ax at arm's length and turn a complete circle. Then move the ax slowly overhead in an arc. Clear away any limbs or brush that will be in your way and could deflect your ax during a swing. Also, no one should be within 30 feet of the person with the ax.

Check the cutting edge. A dull ax is a dangerous tool. A sharp ax will dig into wood, but a dull blade can bounce off and strike your leg.

Sharpening an ax is a two-stage job. You'll need a file, such as a Nicholson Black Diamond, and a round whetstone. (If there's any paint on the metal where you'll be filing, first remove it with sandpaper. Otherwise the paint will clog the file and the whetstone.)

Anchor the ax blade securely. If you're in the field, where there is no vise, drive a wood peg into

No loose ax heads or broken handles to worry about with Estwing's all-steel Camper's Ax. The nylon-vinyl handgrip on this 26-inch model assures a safe, sure grip. The leather sheath protects the 4-inch cutting edge.

HOW TO SHARPEN AN AX

Left: To sharpen a single-bit ax in the field, first drive a wood peg into the ground. **Right:** Brace the head against the peg. A log laid on the handle will help secure it. Wearing gloves and using a file, begin your stroke at the heel and file downward toward the toe. Keep the file about an inch from the edge.

Left: This is where the stroke ends. Don't file up. Instead, lift the file off. The desired stroke is nearly parallel to the ground. Repeat the filing until you get an even taper on both sides of blade. **Right:** Hone edge with a circular whetstone.

the ground and brace the single-bit head against it. A double bit can be driven into a log to hold it in position. When sharpening, wear gloves to protect your hands.

Start with the file, pushing it from toe to heel (top to bottom) of the blade, about 1 inch back from the

When splitting wood, aim for cracks already started in the log. There, wood fibers have already separated and so make splitting easier. Avoid knots; split around them.

edge. The purpose of this step is to cut some of the metal away from the blade so that the taper is uniform. Nearly all new axes have a blade that is too thick.

The photos on the previous page show the filing stroke in detail. When a good taper is achieved, a fine edge can be easily put on the bit with a round whetstone.

Don't tackle the entire job with only a whetstone, which may be fine for honing a knife. But a whetstone is not designed to cut enough metal from an ax head. The whetstone is only used for honing the bit after the blade has been taken down with a file. Don't use the file directly on the cutting edge; that's a job for the whetstone.

Perhaps the most common woodcutting job for the average camper is trimming limbs off downed trees and then chopping the limbs into firewood. Trimming these limbs is safe and easy if you follow this advice.

First, always trim toward the top of the tree, which will point the limbs away from your body. Keep the trunk between you and the limbs you're trimming. For example, stand on one side of the log and trim the far side first, then change positions. There's almost no chance of hitting your legs if there's a tree trunk between you and the blade.

If this is not possible and you have to stand on the same side as the ax, stand slightly forward of the limb you're trimming and swing the ax so that the blade strikes the limb behind your legs.

To cut a limb into campfire lengths, hold it firmly against a stump or log and chop it away from you at about a 45-degree angle. Using a three-quarter-length ax, you should have no trouble cutting limbs up to 1 inch in diameter with a single blow.

HOW TO SHARPEN A DOUBLE-BIT AX

Left: To sharpen a double-bit ax, embed one edge in a log and file the other edge, using downward strokes only. File far back from the edge, gradually thinning down the blade till a fanlike pattern appears. **Middle:** Then, take the ax in your hand and, with a whetstone, use circular strokes on one side. **Right:** Sharpen the other side by letting the head twist so the handle points downward.

To fell a tree, chop a notch about a third of the way into the side of the tree's natural lean. Then cut a second notch on the opposite side and about two inches above the first. The tree will fall in the direction of the lean.

Here are some final bits of advice when using an ax:

1. Always wear gloves when using and sharpening an ax.
2. Never carry an ax over your shoulder. Hold it close to the ax head, blade pointed downward and at your side. If you trip, hold it or throw it away from you.
3. Between cutting sessions, bury the blade of your ax in a log or lay it under a log so that no one could blunder into the blade.
4. Use a wood chopping block. Never cut on rock and other hard surfaces.
5. Never use the butt end of the ax head to drive anything heavier than a tent peg. Using it as a wedge or to drive wedges will weaken and perhaps crack the eye.
6. A split handle is best removed by sawing it off below the head and driving the rest of it out the top with a steel bar. You can also burn it out if you bury the blade in wet earth to protect the heat-tempered edge.
7. Logs will split more easily if you aim for the cracks in the top of a log you're about to split. They indicate weak sections. Avoid the knots; split around them.

CAMP SAWS

To cut wood neatly into particular sizes, the saw is the proper tool. An ax or a hatchet wastes a lot of wood, can't be too exact, and stands the chance of causing injury with flying chips or the blades them-

From Swen Products comes the noted Sven-Saw, a folding model weighing a mere pound. Folded saw is only 24 inches long and 1¾ inches wide, and fits in a backpack.

This little 9-ounce belt saw can handle big jobs such as quartering an elk and small tasks such as cutting branches. The 11-inch blade features both coarse and fine teeth, and sure-grip finger hold allows reasonable control. It comes with a top-grade cowhide belt that can also house a hunting knife.

Bow saw takes on this tree branch with ease. Blade is tempered chrome, and safety guard on the tubular-steel handle ensures a tight grip.

selves. Saws are precise, much faster than either ax or hatchet, and a camper can get the knack of using them with just a couple of minutes' instruction.

Lighter saws are suitable for camping, as the heavier models are impractical to carry along. There are three saws used by backpackers and other campers who must limit the bulk and weight of their packs—the bow saw, the folding saw, and the cable saw.

The collapsible bow-type saw, also known as the Swede saw, features a thin, narrow blade of flexible steel. This blade is held taut by a tubelike, jointed metal frame which can be taken apart and slipped into a case up to 1½ feet long. Several models are designed to carry spare blades.

A blade from 20 to 24 inches in length handles wood from 8 to 10 inches in thickness. Larger-diameter logs, however, require the use of a 30- or 36-inch blade.

Bow-saw frames come in U shapes and L shapes, but the former is recommended. The L-shaped models, though more compact, diminish the amount of blade that may be applied on the wood.

KNIVES

Selecting a quality hunting knife, never an easy task, is no longer quite so difficult. Even though a growing emphasis on knives in recent years has resulted in many fine models on the market, you can narrow down the selection by following a few simple rules.

First, there is no need for a hunting knife with a blade longer than 4½ inches. I've found that a straight blade or a slight drop-point design works best for most field chores. Remember that hunting knives frequently are used more for camp jobs than for dressing and skinning game.

Second, on a sheath knife, check the tang (the blade extension around which the handle is attached) and make sure it extends well up into or through the handle. This is the strongest design.

A new breed of camp tools that feature multiple tools in a compact system. **Gerber Multi-Plier Tool (Left):** Has 13 stainless steel tools available with blunt or needle-nose pliers and in satin or blackened finish. Features plier jaws that can be brought into working position with one hand. **Leatherman Super Tool (Center):** Has 10 locking stainless steel blades including a saw and a serrated knife. Weighs 9 ounces. **Schrade Tough (Right):** Measures 4¾ inches folded and weighs 8 ounces. Features 21 implements/structures including a plier jaw that serves as a regular plier, needle nose plier, vise and wire cutter.

KNIFE DESIGNS

Bowie-style with 6-inch blade and blood groove. Designed for heavy-duty all-round use. Generally too heavy for most tasks and with a longer blade than needed.

A standard design, somewhat heavy, with a 5-inch blade. A good choice if you want one knife for all jobs.

Short 3¼-inch drop-point blade design. Fine knife for small game and birds. Particularly good for the trophy hunter who must carefully skin out a head.

Straight 4-inch blade design for fish and small game. It has a fine point. Light, small, and a good choice as an all-round knife that will not be used for heavy-duty work.

Skinning knife. Has wide 4-inch blade with fine edge. Excellent for skinning big game, though limited in other tasks.

A good combination design that has features of a skinning knife but is helpful on small game as well. The blade on such a knife is usually 4½ inch.

Boning knife. For the hunter who butchers his own game, this knife is almost a must. Kept sharp, it will easily remove just about every bone in a big-game animal.

For fishermen only, this knife is usually about 10 inches overall and has a flexible blade for filleting, plus a fish scaler.

Buck Folding Hunter (left) and Ranger (right) are lockblade knives with rounded handles for easier grip and easy-sharpen blades.

KNIFE DESIGNS (Continued)

The Buck Zipper is a skinning-gutting knife. It has a sharp second blade precison-engineered into the main blade which virtually eliminates snagging. Available with wood or rubberized handle.

Schrade Outback is a lockback knife. Designed with stainless steel, this model has a Thermoplastic rubber handle.

FOLDING KNIFE BLADE DESIGNS

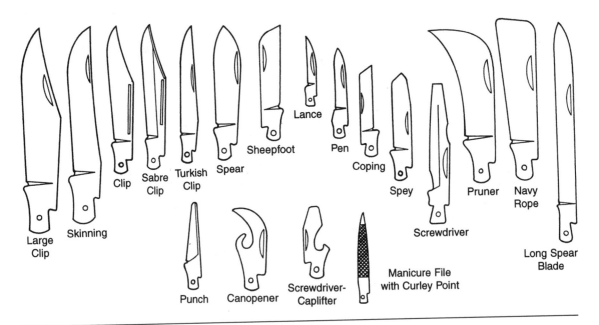

Large Clip

Skinning

Clip

Sabre Clip

Turkish Clip

Spear

Sheepfoot

Lance

Pen

Coping

Spey

Screwdriver

Pruner

Navy Rope

Long Spear Blade

Punch

Canopener

Screwdriver-Caplifter

Manicure File with Curley Point

Grip the knife in your hand. Does the handle extend a quarter inch or so beyond each side of your hand? If so, it fits your hand properly. If not, it doesn't fit and will probably be uncomfortable to use for extended periods.

Selection of blade steel is another consideration. Stainless steel is very hard, and will not sharpen easily with just a few quick strokes; but it is easy to maintain because it won't rust. Carbon steel, on the other hand, is easier to sharpen and will take an edge faster, but it generally requires more care than stainless does.

The choice of sheath-type or folding knife is pretty much a matter of personal preference. Many hunters prefer a folding knife. The reason is simple. A Buck Folding Hunter has a 4-inch blade, but it's still only

HOW TO SHARPEN A HUNTING KNIFE

Left: A good stone will last a lifetime, with some care. NEVER use it dry. And after the job is done, apply more oil to it and wipe clean. Oil floats steel particles above the surface, so they do not clog the stone. **Right:** Putting a good edge on a knife is not difficult. Use a Washita stone, preferably mounted, and clamp it to your work surface so it does not move. Oil the stone generously, spreading it over the entire surface.

 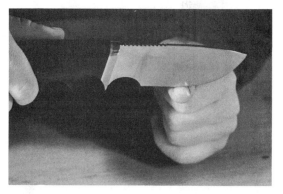

Left: Grip knife as shown, maintaining an angle of 15 degrees between back of blade and stone. Appying a hard steady pressure, draw the knife across the stone, beginning at the knife heel. Draw the knife across the stone as if you were taking a slice off top of the stone. As you come to the edge of the stone, lift the handle and sharpened point. Repeat these strokes 10 or 15 times on each side of the blade. Do not alternate strokes. Sharpen one side, then the other. A very dull knife may need more than 15 strokes. **Right:** You can check sharpness by drawing the blade across your fingernail. A well-sharpened knife will slide and not "grab."

If you have trouble maintaining angle during sharpening, sharpening devices will help. The tool clamps onto the blade, as shown. The clamp's guide bar, held flat against the stone during sharpening, ensures the desired 15-degree angle.

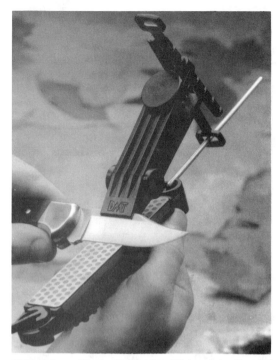

DMT Deluxe Aligner Sharpening Kit has four diamond whetstones for extra fine, coarse, and extra coarse sharpening. Pre-set guide rods adjust for seven different honing angles.

5 inches long when carried folded on a belt or in a pocket. For big skinning jobs at camp or home, though, most hunters like a sheath knife, also with a 4-inch blade.

What about sharpening a knife? A dull knife is both annoying and dangerous, especially in the woods where you may be rushing a field-dressing or skinning job. It's a good idea to carry a sharpening steel and a pocket-size whetstone to touch up the blade when it begins to dull. Many steels have two sharpening surfaces: a grooved side to put a uniform cutting edge on the blade and a smooth surface for final honing.

These steels are not designed to take an appreciable amount of metal from the edge, so on knives that are quite dull a stone must be used. For this job, you should carry a double-sided whetstone to get the edge back on your knife if it's badly dulled on bone or wood. Use a whetstone with a coarse 100 grit on one side and a medium-fine 240 grit on the other. Usually about 10 strokes per side on the medium-fine grit and 10 on the steel will sharpen a knife well enough to dress and skin a couple of deer.

A dirty stone will make sharpening a tough job.

If a stone is glazed smooth with dirt, wash and scrub it with kerosene or a detergent, then let it dry out thoroughly. Whetstones should never be used dry, however. If you're using the stone in the field, wet it with snow, spit on it, or even put carcass fat on it. The idea is to float steel filings above the surface of the stone, so that the stone's pores are not clogged. Some manufacturers produce stones that are already oil-filled. But for stones that do not have this feature it's important to use a generous amount of honing oil, and to bear down hard as you move the edge of the blade across the stone. The oil, in addition to floating the steel filings, allows the blade to move smoothly. Your stone will stay cleaner longer if you wash your knife completely before you sharpen it.

Keep in mind that any field sharpening steels or small whetstones are designed to put a quick edge on a knife. They will get you out of a tight spot, but don't expect them to put a lasting edge on your knife. For that final edge, you'll have to use better, mounted stones such as a Washita for sharpening and perhaps a Hard Arkansas for final honing.

The photos on page 559 show how to sharpen a knife correctly.

Once you have cleaned both the knife and the stone, oil the stone generously and spread the oil over the entire surface of the stone. A hard, steady pressure will be necessary as you begin to draw the edge of the knife across the stone, starting at the heel of the blade and ending each stroke by lifting the handle to sharpen the point. Alternate sides of the blade until you have made 10 to 15 strokes on each side. A fine, hard honing stone will give a keen edge, if you draw the knife as if you were taking a thin slice off the top of the stone.

A key factor in putting a good edge on any knife is maintaining a constant angle, usually 15 degrees, between the back of the blade and the stone. You can keep the angle constant for 30 or 40 strokes and then ruin all this work by changing the angle for the last six strokes. If this is your problem, pick up a device that will maintain this critical angle. Most devices are nothing more than a combination clamp and guide bar. Fit this onto your blade, hold the guide bar flat against the stone, and you can be sure of a constant angle.

The last step is stropping the knife against a piece of leather or cardboard. This is the only step in which you draw the edge backward with each stroke, instead of moving it forward as you did on the whetstone. Stropping lays down any roughness and "sets" the edge. You can check the sharpness by carefully pulling the edge toward you across your thumbnail. A well-sharpened knife will grab and stop. If it slips, it needs more strokes on the stone.

After getting a final edge on your knife, don't jam it back into its sheath unless you're going back in the field. Leather sheaths collect and hold moisture, which will rust a knife. The best way I know to store a knife is to oil it lightly, wrap it in waxed paper, and store it where no one will accidentally blunder against the edge or point.

BACKPACKS

Throughout this section on camping, there have been references to the backpacker, the camper who takes to the open air with all he needs on his back.

The backpacker is a keen weight watcher. He keeps in mind at all times that he should have with him the barest of essentials, and not one ounce more.

There are five basic pack designs. The type the individual camper needs depends upon the load he expects to carry as well as the distance he must carry it. The five designs are:

1. Day pack
2. Rucksack
3. Backpack and frame
4. Packbasket
5. Hip or waist pack

THE DAYPACK

The daypack, known to most campers as the knapsack, is pretty much what its name indicates—a pack which is useful on a daytime outing. It is little more than a rectangular canvas or nylon pack with shoulder straps which may or may not have side pockets, but never a metal frame.

When filling the daypack, place soft items—a poncho, a sweater—against the part of the pack that will press against your back. Also, don't load this pack too heavily as the total weight of the full pack will pull down uncomfortably on your shoulders and against your back.

For pack material, nylon is recommended for the adult camper as it is lightweight and waterproof.

DAYPACKS

Coleman Daypack with angled zipper and outer pouch. A good choice for day hunters, fishermen, and hikers.

JanSport Sole Survivor is a large-capacity daypack featuring a molded rubber bottom for water protection. Made of Cordura nylon, it has a front accessory pocket, front mesh pocket, and padded back.

DAYPACKS (Continued)

Fieldline Quadrant is 220 cubic inches. Features a full-opening front panel for cargo access, quick-release sternum and shoulder straps and waist belt, and a padded back for support. A durable choice for hunters.

Fieldline Pro-Guide Soft-Sided Tackle Box/Fanny Pack Combo. The main compartment is designed to hold three 3600 Plano tackle organizer boxes, while a smaller front pocket holds a wallet, keys or other personal items. It also has two side mesh pouches for ventilation for drying wet gear.

However, for youthful campers, who may carelessly toss their packs around, a canvas daypack can take more punishment and is less expensive. Some daypacks have waist straps as well as shoulder straps to take some weight off the shoulders.

THE RUCKSACK

The rucksack seems to fall midway between the daypack and the larger packs for carrying big loads on long outings. The backpacker who uses the rucksack is usually out for a full day and must cook a couple of meals in the field.

Unlike the daypack, the rucksack features one or two outside pockets as well as an inside or outside metal frame. This frame prevents the pack from sagging, and puts less tension on the back. These features make it preferable to the daypack in numerous ways.

A sleeping bag is too bulky to put inside a rucksack, but it can be rolled short and lashed to the top or rolled long into a horseshoe shape and lashed to the top and sides. This pack is ill suited for backpacking canned goods, steel traps, and other hardware that can bite into your back.

The rucksack should have web or leather shoulder

straps that are a minimum of 2 inches wide and thick enough so as not to curl into narrow bands from a heavy pack. These bands can cut mercilessly into your shoulders.

Strong buckles, snaps, and rings of bronze, brass or rustproof steel are essential. Beware of an over-

Trager Trapper Creek is a European military style rucksack. Made of 1000-denier Cordura nylon, this top-loading bag has leather accents and brass buckles.

abundance of tricky snaps, zippers, and buckles. They add to the cost, and usually just bring trouble.

Although such synthetics as nylon and Dacron are being used widely for rucksacks, a good choice is heavy canvas. The extra weight will seem inconspicuous, considering the padding to your back that canvas provides. Incidentally, a canvas pack is also simpler to waterproof and keep waterproof than one made of synthetic fibers.

BACKPACK AND FRAME

For the serious backpacker whose trips last from one to two weeks, the backpack and frame is the best choice.

The unit consists of a frame constructed of a light metal alloy, and a backpack with both shoulder straps and back supports. The frame is attached to the backpack.

FRAME PACKS

Coleman Dwight Schuh hunting pack. This three-way Polarfleece hunting pack was designed by bowhunter and author Dwight Schuh. Can carry three to five days worth of camping gear or remove the upper bag and use it as a daypack. The lower bag can also be used as a fanny pack.

The Dolomite, constructed of Cordura nylon, is designed for mountaineering and extended back-packing. Features load-carrying support, reinforced shovel pocket, and crampon patch on the exterior of the pack.

Peak 1 Ocala is a dual compartment backpack with a sleeping bag compartment, side water-bottle pocket and oversized pass-through pocket. It has dual front compression straps for load control and stability. Weighs 5.63 pounds.

This typical pack frame is made of aluminum alloy, with joints epoxied to form a bond as strong as the metal. Padded waist strap has sliding ring to fit hips of any size and exert continous pull on frame to prevent sway. Back bands are breathable mesh. Buckle is quick-release type. Neck opening between padded shoulder straps is adjustable.

Of all the frames, those made of magnesium are the best. They are lightweight and sturdy, but they are expensive. A practical choice is a frame of an aluminum alloy. It will have shoulder and waist straps, and on some models a nylon mesh to keep the load away from the back. This mesh allows air to circulate between pack and back.

As you need roominess for all of your equipment, the good backpack has five or six outside pockets for smaller, oft-used items. Inside the pack itself are two large compartments for larger items. Below the pack, on the frame, there is room to strap on a sleeping bag. Gear that won't fit inside the pack can be safely lashed to the frame.

Remember that backpack and frame can be removed from one another, permitting the packer to lash such bulky objects as an outboard motor to the frame for easy transportation.

There are certain things to look for in choosing such a backpack, some of which were mentioned earlier. The best choice for lightness would be a waterproof nylon backpack as it will keep the rain off your gear. Look for a top flap on the pack that is long enough to cover the top of the bag when it is full; heavy-duty, corrosion-proof zippers on the exterior side and back pockets that won't jam and will keep out dirt and rain; seams and pockets that can withstand rugged use, and shoulder and waist

straps that should be at least 2 inches wide so they won't curl up and cut you. Also, shoulder straps and harnesses for back support should be adjustable to allow for tightening and taking up slack as the load is increased or decreased.

Don't buy a pack just because it fulfills these requirements. Try on various models. The pack and frame should permit the load to be carried vertically with its center of gravity close to your back. In this manner the weight will be transferred to the legs, the most powerful part of the human body.

The backpack should weigh approximately 2 pounds, the pack frame 3 to 4 pounds. That means frame and pack together should weigh close to 5 pounds.

The total amount of gear and food carried depends on the individual. An average man can camp on his own for three days, using a good pack and frame, with carefully selected equipment and freeze-dried food weighing a total of 20 to 25 pounds. That same man can stay in the bush for up to two weeks if he carries a pack with 40 pounds of sustenance.

There is, of course, a limit to how much a person can comfortably carry over a certain period of time. The following limits (weight includes pack, frame, gear, meals) ought to be observed:

Men—35 to 40 pounds
Women—20 to 25 pounds
Children—15 pounds

Stray from these weight limits and you'll find backpacking a chore rather than a pleasure.

SUNDRY PACKS

A pack basket is one of the safest means of carrying breakable goods. This model is handwoven from selected seasoned white ash. Adjustable webbing harness and contour shape let it rest reasonably comfortably against your back.

THE PACK BASKET

The pack basket is an old-time favorite that seems to retain limited popularity because of tradition rather than utility.

Made of thin strips of wood from willow or ash logs, the pack basket is light and rigid. The construction protects the contents from breakage and the packer's back from rough or sharp objects inside. Trappers appreciate the basket for packing tools, axes, and traps. Canoeists favor it for packing odd-size canned goods and gear. Nevertheless, the basket is not recommended for general backpacking.

THE HIP OR FANNY PACK

This pack provides an ideal alternative for the person who doesn't like to carry a pack by means of shoulder straps. As the name implies, the pack rests on the hips and lower back, and easily carries whatever small gear a hunter, fisherman, or camper might bring along on a one-day trip.

HOW TO PACK A BACKPACK

How you load your pack is critical. A 50-pound pack may seem manageable when you start out, but it will wear you down quickly after a mile or so. Learn to trim your load. Get rid of those food boxes and cans. Repack everything in leakproof, sealable plastic bags. When you shop, look for dehydrated or freeze-dried foods.

How much weight you can carry depends on your size, strength, and appetite. With carefully selected gear and foods, an average man can camp for about three days with a backpack that will weigh 30 pounds. Here are some safe limits for maximum backpack weights.

MEN—35 to 40 pounds
WOMEN—20 to 30 pounds
CHILDREN—15 pounds

A few backpack trips and you will soon discover how little you actually need to camp in the woods.

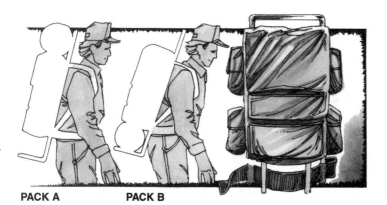

PACK A

PACK B

THE FRAME PACK. Combined weight of pack and frame should be about five pounds.

PACK A: When backpacking in flat country or rolling terrain, keep the weight in your backpack high, so that the center of gravity is on or above your shoulders (see arrow).

PACK B: When packing a load in rocky or steep country, load your pack low, so that the center of gravity is about the middle of your back.

THE RUCKSACK A typical rucksack, which sometimes comes with a small frame, can carry gear and food for a full day. When packing a rucksack, keep heavy gear next to your lower back to minimize sagging.

ROPES AND KNOTS

Ropes for camp use are made of either natural or synthetic materials. The natural fibers come in hemp, available in such types as manila and sisal, and in cotton strands of everyday cotton fiber which has been specially treated.

Synthetic fibers such as Dacron, nylon, and polypropylene often prove from 50 to 100 percent stronger than hemp or cotton rope of equal diameter. These waterproof synthetics do not swell or kink when they are wet. They are likewise unaffected by such hemp maladies as fungus, mildew, and dry rot.

A disadvantage of synthetics is the price. Cotton rope typically costs one-tenth the amount of most synthetic rope of the same diameter. Hemp costs are usually one-third those of synthetics. And knots made in synthetic rope do not hold as well as those in hemp or cotton. In the case of nylon rope, the stretch range may be up to 20 percent of the total length.

The following chart shows the approximate breaking strengths in pounds of dead weight of the various types of ropes:

DIAMETER	SISAL	MANILA	POLY-PROPYLENE	DACRON	NYLON
$1/4''$	480	600	1,050	1,600	1,800
$3/8$	1,080	1,350	2,200	3,300	4,000
$1/2$	2,120	2,650	3,800	5,500	7,100
$3/4$	4,320	5,400	8,100	11,000	14,200
1	7,200	9,000	14,000	18,500	24,600

The *safe working load* for a brand new rope is one-quarter the breaking strength. If the rope has been through average use, figure one-sixth of the breaking strength. Dropping the load or jerking the rope doubles the strain, and knots and splices diminish its strength, sometimes drastically.

To care for a hemp rope, remember that moisture causes damage. Keep this rope as dry as possible, whether you are storing it or using it. By hanging hemp or cotton rope in a dry, high, cool place, you protect it from harmful rodents. The sweat-salt traces left on a rope by human hands otherwise attract mice and rats with their ever-sharp teeth.

Synthetics need little protection from water but can be substantially weakened by acids, oils, and intense heat.

Now, let's tie some knots.

Whipping. The purpose of a whipping, using several turns of a strong thread, is to prevent the end of a rope from unraveling. Hold the thread taut during the wrapping turns. The section of the thread where the arrow points is given a half-dozen turns once

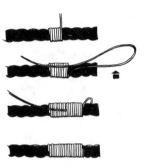

the pull-through loop has been formed. The loop should be pulled snug and the end trimmed. If the rope is synthetic, melt it with a cigarette lighter for a tighter seal. Hemp and cotton also seal more securely if dipped in a quick-setting glue.

Clove Hitch. To fasten a rope end to a tree, pole, post, or stake, use the clove hitch.

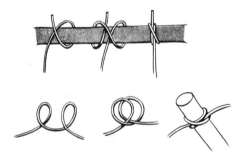

Square Knot. Also known as the reef knot, the square knot attaches two ends of the same rope, or joins two similar-size ropes or lines. The chances of this knot's slipping are nil.

Bowline. Easy to tie and untie, the bowline is best for such tasks as leading or hitching a horse with a rope around its neck. When you need to tie a loop around an object, the bowline will not slip.

Turns with Half Hitches. To make a simple knot for tying a rope end to a pole or ring, make two turns around the object, followed by a pair of half hitches. For additional strength, use more of each.

Guy-line Hitch. The guy-line hitch tightens tent and other guy ropes that need adjustment. Begin with two basic overhand knots, with the rope running through the top one. The bottom overhand knot will slide up or down to give or take slack on the guy line or tent rope. You needn't worry about tearing the tent fabric with this hitch.

Double Sheet Bend. When you are linking up a pair of ropes of varied diameters, try the double sheet bend. Make the simple loop in the thicker of the two ropes, using the thinner one for the turns. The

double sheet bend is preferable to the single style because it is safer and takes perhaps a second longer to finish up.

Carrick Bend. The carrick bend will join ropes to tow or support hefty loads. It doesn't jam and can be easily untied.

Timber Hitch. For towing logs or hitching to a pole or tree a rope that must sustain constant, strong pressure, the proper knot is the timber hitch. It ties in seconds and will not jam.

Horse Hitch. An infallible knot for tying a horse or boatline to a tree, pole, or ring is the horse hitch. The running end of the rope passed through a broad loop at the completion of the hitch will make it more secure.

Ring Knot. This knot works best when tied to a ring, such as a swivel end or a metal loop in a lure. If you are using slick monofilament fishing line, do not trim the loose end too closely or it may slip.

Slip Knot. The slip knot is simple and won't untie very quickly. A half hitch or two around the standing part of the rope or line will further bind this knot.

Water Knot. Any fisherman should be familiar with the water knot. Adequate for joining fishing lines, leaders, ropes, or small cords, the water knot begins with an overhand knot made loosely in the end of either line. Put the running end of the other line through it, and secure it using an overhand knot around the first line's standing part. Next, pull both overhand knots together. Half hitches on either side will tighten the knot. Trim the water knot carefully to prevent it from catching in your rod guides.

Figure-8 Knot. Tie the figure-8 knot just like the overhand knot, but give the loop a half-twist before the running end is passed through. Also an end knot, the figure-8 is slightly less compact than the overhand but significantly stronger.

Taut-Line Hitch. Primarily for tightening tent ropes, the taut-line hitch is actually a running loop that holds under strain.

Form a loop around the anchor. Then with the running end, make a pair of small turns around the standing part, spiraling it in the direction of the inside of the loop. A half hitch tied around the standing part, outside of the big loop, completes the loop knot.

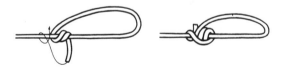

Bowline on a Bight. The bowline mentioned earlier has a variation called bowline on a bight which is especially useful for climbing.

Make an overhead loop and place the bight through it. Pull the bight downward to the end of the big loop formed by the running end. Then, separate the bight, putting the big loop through it. Slide

the running-end bight upward so it goes around the standing part. Pull it tight, and the knot is ready.

Spanish Bowline. Different from the bowline on a bight in that its two loops are separated, the Spanish bowline is another variation. It functions as an improvised seat and backrest.

A slip knot about twice the size of either of the completed loops is the first step. Give the loop a half-twist so the standing part crosses in the rear. Keep the running end of the slip knot tight against the standing part where they form parallel lines. At the same time, hold the turn at the back of the knot, and immediately slide the bight next to the running end outward. Stop when it forms a loop equal in size to the original slip knot.

The resulting X pattern should now be slid up the loops until both are rather small. Reach through the

pair from the back, taking the bight below the X and pulling it through. You will now have both loops and an X pattern between the two.

Butterfly Loop. When three persons are climbing, the person in the middle should be held with a fixed or butterfly loop. This loop also makes an excellent harness for dragging weighty loads.

Make a bight as big as you want the loop to be. Twist it one complete turn, forming a loose figure-8. Fold this double loop over the standing part to produce a pair of intertwined loops. Pass the tip of the original bight through the two loops where the overlapping takes place. Pull on the bight to tighten.

CAMPFIRES

To start a campfire, clear a site—always on rock or dirt—by removing all ground debris for at least 3 feet on all sides. This prevents any combustible material such as rubbish and underground roots from igniting and causing a possible forest fire. When using the top of a ledge for your fire, beware of small cracks through which hot coals might tumble into flammable material.

A good fire for cooking, lighting, or heat starts with tinder, thin sticks of kindling, and medium-size sticks of firewood. Stack them loosely or in pyramid fashion in that order. Now stand on the upwind side and light the tinder from there. This directs the flame upward and into the mass of tinder. Lighting from the downwind side leaves you little opportunity to direct the flame.

Once the tinder is well ignited, blow on it or fan the fire gently with your hat. The tinder will light the slim sticks which in turn will set the medium-size sticks ablaze.

Tinder, which forms the bottom layer of the fire, is any small-size fuel that ignites readily. Any scrap of dry paper will do, especially waxed paper and the like.

There are also wood sources of tinder. Birch bark that is stripped and wadded loosely, and dry cedar bark both perform well. Sagebrush bark, dead evergreen twigs still on the tree with brown needles intact,

FIREWOOD CHARACTERISTICS

Species	Heat Value	Ease of Splitting	Ease of Starting	Sparks
Alder	Medium/Low	Easy	Fair	Moderate
Apple	Medium/High	Difficult	Difficult	Few
Ash	High	Easy/Moderate	Fair/Difficult	Few
Aspen	Low	Easy	Easy	Few
Beech	High	Difficult	Moderate	Few
Birch	Medium	Moderate	Easy	Moderate
Cedar	Medium/Low	Easy	Easy	Many
Cherry	Medium	Easy	Difficult	Few
Cottonwood	Low	Easy	Easy	Moderate
Cypress	Low	Easy	Easy	Few
Dogwood	High	Difficult	Easy	Few
Douglas Fir	Medium	Easy	Easy	Moderate
Elm	Medium	Difficult	Moderate	Few
Fir, Grand Noble	Medium/Low	Easy	Easy	Moderate
Gum	Medium	Difficult	Moderate	Few
Hemlock	Medium/Low	Easy	Easy	Many
Hickory	Medium/High	Difficult	Difficult	Few
Juniper	Medium	Difficult	Fair	Many
Larch	Medium/High	Easy/Moderate	Easy	Many
Locust	Very High	Very Difficult	Difficult	Very Few
Madrone	High	Difficult	Difficult	Very Few
Maple-hard	High	Easy	Difficult	Few
Maple-soft	Medium	Easy	Fair	Few
Oak	Very High	Moderate	Difficult	Few
Pecan	High	Easy	Difficult	Few
Pine, Lodgepole	Low	Easy	Easy	Moderate
Pine, Ponderosa, White, Yellow	Medium/Low	Easy	Easy	Moderate
Pinyon	Medium	Easy	Easy	Few
Redwood	Low	Easy	Easy	Few
Spruce	Low	Easy/Moderate	Easy	Moderate
Sycamore	Medium	Difficult	Moderate	Few
Walnut	Medium/High	Easy/Moderate	Fair	Few
Willow	Low	Easy	Fair	Moderate

Courtesy of McCulloch

and dry, dead grass or weeds that are crushed into a ball are also effective.

Pitch is a primary burning agent which is found in the decayed trunks and upturned roots of woods such as spruce, pines, and fir. It also works efficiently as tinder when sliced up with the wood still attached. To tell if a wood contains pitch alert yourself to the resinous odor and weighty heft of the wood. Even heavy rains don't change the quality of pitch slabs as excellent tinder.

If you are handy with a knife and adept at whittling, you can make fuzz sticks (also known as fire sticks). Shave lengthy splinters from almost any dry, soft stick, leaving as many splinters attached as possible. When you have what resembles a tiny pine tree, thrust it upright into the ground and place some tinder around it. Set a match to the lower slivers, and you have a fine fire starter.

You can squirt a little kerosene, stove gasoline, or lighter fluid on the kindling as an alternative to gathering tinder. Be sure, however, to use these liquid fuels *prior to* striking your match to prevent an explosion. Kindling, which consists of thin, dry sticks, is ordinarily placed loosely in a teepee shape above the tinder, or crisscrossed on top of it.

The basic firewood is not added until both tinder and kindling are in place. This wood is necessarily heavier than the kindling, usually longer, and from 3 to 4, or possibly even 6, inches in thickness. Small logs or thick branches are prime sources of this firewood, which catches from the combustible material beneath to provide a strong and stable fire.

Woods vary in burning qualities. They "catch fire" primarily in relation to their dryness, cut size, and resin content. They give heat and good cooking coals primarily in relation to their density—the denser the wood, the more mass available for combustion.

Any dry (seasoned) wood will be good kindling if cut to finger thickness. Wood of conifers tends to catch fire more easily than that of deciduous trees because its high amounts of resin ignite at lower temperatures than the gases generated from wood fibers alone. But conifers tend to be smokier, and their resin pockets cause more popping and sparks.

If you are forced to burn unseasoned wood, as in a survival predicament, ash is one of the best because of its low moisture content "on the stump." For cooking, if very dry, the densest deciduous woods are best. These include the oaks, hickories, locusts, beech, birches, ashes, and hawthorns. Yet in parts of western states, you may find that conifers are the only woods available. In northwestern Canada and Alaska, birch and alder are about the only abundant, dense deciduous woods.

Oak and hickory rate as good wood, but remember that these hardwoods will quickly take the edge

off an ax or saw—something you may want to keep in mind if you're on an extended trip. And if sparks and smoke bother you, avoid the pines and spruces, tamarack, basswood, and chestnut.

HUNTER'S FIRE

Among the many possible arrangements of the basic campfire, the hunter's fire is a simple, dual-purpose one that provides hot coals for cooking along with heat and light.

TWO TYPES OF HUNTER'S FIRE

Start your fire as described earlier and wait for a bed of hot coals to form. At that point, place two green logs on either side of the fire to resemble a corridor. If this is done before the coals form, the fire will eventually eat right into the logs. Rocks can also be used to form a corridor. The camper out for a brief time or on a string of one-night stands on a pack trail or canoe route benefits most from this type of fire.

If the fire dies down, place a support under the ends of the logs to let more air in through the sides.

KEYHOLE FIRE

Like the hunter's fire, the keyhole fire supplies heat and light, and a place for cooking chores. Also for short-term use, this campfire consists totally of flat, small rocks arranged in a keyhole shape. It features a corridor 3 to 6 feet long and 1 foot wide, and a circle adjacent to the rectangle.

Begin the fire in the center of the corridor, and wait till you see that the surrounding rocks are hot and the trench is lined with a bed of coals. Using a piece of dry firewood, push the blazing wood to one end of the trench. The remainder stays at the other end for cooking. When the cooking coals seem to be losing their vigor, move some of the other coals to the cooking area.

KEYHOLE FIRE

Some campers prefer two keyhole fires rather than one, particularly for large groups of campers, so there are always a substantial amount of hot coals to work with.

TRENCH FIRE

When stoves and wood are nowhere to be found, and the pots you are using have no bails, set up a trench fire.

Dig a trench as deep as you need, parallel to the direction of the prevailing wind. Leave the upwind end open to provide an effective draft. If the trench

TRENCH FIRE

is very narrow, its sides may support the pots. Otherwise, you may need to use green sticks to hold up your cooking gear.

INDIAN FIRE

When wood fuel is at a premium and it is necessary to conserve what you have, try the Indian fire. Note

that five thick logs radiate outward from the center. Tinder should be placed at this midpoint. As the logs burn, push them gradually into the middle.

INDIAN FIRE

INDIAN FIREPLACE

If you have to contend with strong winds, the Indian fireplace is appropriate. Dig a hole that is a bit larger than your kettle, and build a small fire at the bottom. Using a forked shaped stick to support a straight stick with one end secured in the ground, hang the kettle over the hole. If you have enough fuel set the pot in the hole itself, but be sure there is adequate space at the bottom for air to circulate.

INDIAN FIREPLACE

The lower end of the stick for hanging the kettle doesn't have to be buried or driven into the ground if a heavy enough rock or log is handy. Just lay this weight on the end of the stick, or wedge the stick under it securely.

REFLECTOR FIRE

The reflector fire provides heat to a tent or an oven. A small raft of 1-inch-thick logs, rocks or sod, or aluminum foil will direct heat to the desired spot. A conventional fire built in front of the reflector safely warms up a baker tent or practically any other type of tent. The reflector oven using this fire lets you bake biscuits and such.

The reflector fire requires flames to project enough heat to a selected spot. Coals alone unfortunately radiate in all directions, making cooking more difficult.

REFLECTOR FIRE

DINGLE STICK

One of the simplest and most practical campfires utilizes the dingle stick, a device that holds a pot securely over a fire. The illustrations show two arrangements of the dingle stick. Be sure to choose a durable stick for either one.

DINGLE STICKS

SWEDISH FIRE LAY

An efficient fire for heating a single kettle, pot, coffeepot, or frying pan is the Swedish Fire Lay. It's especially convenient in confined spaces. Its foundation is a small fire with the sticks arranged in a star shape, like the basic Indian fire. Around this foundation, three split chunks of log, each about a foot long, are stood on end. Tilt the split logs in at the top, propping them against one another to form a pyramid. The heat travels up the logs to the top, and eventually they'll begin to burn. But even before they do, the top will be hot, and it serves as a base for the cooking utensil.

SWEDISH FIRE LAY

RAIN OR SNOW

Starting a fire in driving rain or snow is usually possible, and often easy. On rain-soaked ground, you can construct a foundation for the fire using slabs of bark, rocks, or broken limbs. On snow, build the foundation from thick pieces of green or punky and wet downfall. Avoid all fires beneath trees capped with snow, as the rising heat will melt the snow and possibly extinguish your fire.

The optimum wood under these conditions comes from standing dead trees. Most of the wood chopped from their insides will be dry enough to burn. Birch bark, pitch-saturated evergreen, and white ash are excellent choices, even when moist.

When you have gathered tinder, kindling, and firewood, look for a natural overhang—a rock ledge, for example. If none is available, improvise with a flat rock, a slab of bark, or a log propped up at an angle. A poncho, a canvas tarp, or a tent awning is even better.

Prepare the firewood, and search out a dry area to strike a match on. Your match case will probably be dry, and zippers and buttons on the inside of clothing will work in a pinch. Try scraping the match against your thumbnail, or even on the edge of your teeth as a last resort. Then, shield the initial fire until the heavy firewood is securely aflame. At that point, the fire stands little chance of being put out by the elements.

Make certain to carefully douse any fire you build with bucketful after bucketful of water when you are finished with it. Don't stop until every piece of wood and all coals are drenched. Then stir the coals till all sparks and steam are gone. A healthy mound of wet mineral soil guarantees that the fire is completely and safely extinguished.

CAMP FOODS AND MENUS

To plan nutritious camp menus, consider four basic questions: (1) How many meals of each type (breakfast, lunch, etc.) will there be? (2) Where will they be prepared—in a blind, on a mountainside? (3) How will the supplies be transported (backpack, RV, etc.)? (4) How many persons are in the group and what kind of appetites do they have?

Apply the answers to the three main groups of foods—carbohydrates, proteins, and fats—and determine the necessary amount of calories.

Calories supply energy. How many calories you need depends on your weight, your rate of metabolism, and how much work you are doing. Everyday camping chores use up about 3,000 calories per day, while backpacking requires 4,000 calories for the same period. Cold weather and a steep climb call for as many as 5,000 calories. When your intake of calories is less than your output, fat already stored by your body will be burned off. To prevent weight loss, it is necessary to consume a sufficient amount of calories daily.

The protein requirement depends primarily on body weight. A man weighing 130 pounds needs 60 grams of protein per day while a 175-pound man needs 80 grams. Proteins are essential because they build and repair body tissues. Good sources are cheese, meat, milk, eggs, and fish.

The accompanying tables of nutritional values of camp foods have been compiled by AlpineAire Foods, Mountain House, and Richmoor. These charts are invaluable in developing healthy camp menus.

A wide variety of dehydrated or freeze-dried foods is available through sporting goods stores, camp equipment dealers, and even supermarkets. Both processes take as much water out of the food as possible to permit lightweight packing and simple preparation.

Straight dehydration is an air-drying process wherein heat dries the food but leaves it flexible. Once the food is cooked, the water returns. Freeze-

drying, on the other hand, removes water by quick-freezing, and placement of the food in a vacuum chamber. The pressure drops in the chamber and heat is added. The ice then sublimates slowly, meaning it goes directly from solid to gaseous form with no intermediate liquid state. The resultant food is the same size, slighly paler, and far lighter. Soaking the food from 10 to 30 minutes brings on the flavor. Besides being odor-free, the freeze-drying process leads to finer taste and quality than standard dehydration.

The outdoor cook should stress simplicity, but variety is possible. Have cereal with dried fruit one day and pancakes with syrup the next. Lunches can go from cheese to sausage to peanut butter. Suppers can be more elaborate if you'd like, and precooked items are worthwhile in that respect. By adding water to certain foods, the camp chef can prepare delicous chicken or beef stew. And water is always available if you are near a stream or lake.

Consider prepackaging of such foods as sugar, salt, bacon, and flour. There's no need to lug along a box of salt or a bag of flour if you won't need much more than a quarter of the contents. Premeasure this food. Then pack and label it, specifying for which meal and which day it is intended.

Remember to include supplementary or trail foods. They are not a part of any set meal but may increase flavor (condiments, for example), add flexibility to the menu, or give rapid-fire energy. Supplementary foods are high in protein. Trail foods can substitute as lunch or emergency food when cooking a full meal is impractical. Often high in calories, fats, and carbohydrates, raisins, nuts, chocolate, bacon bars, and hard candy, for example, provide instant energy and keep the saliva flowing in your mouth so it doesn't become uncomfortably dry.

Keep in mind that fresh food is fine the first day out, but thereafter stick to foods that will not spoil quickly, if at all, on what might be a humid trail.

RICHMOOR

Item	Net Wt. Ozs.	Serving Size	# of Servings	Calories Total	Calories Fat	Total Fat	
No Cook Entrees—Serves 2							
Lasagna w/Meat Sauce	5	1¼ Cup (63.8g)	2	250	40	4g	7%
Spaghetti w/Meat Sauce	5¼	1¼ Cup (74.4g)	2	280	15	2g	3%
Beef Stroganoff	5	1¼ Cup (70.9g)	2	290	60	6g	10%
Beef Stew	3¾	1 Cup (53.1g)	2	210	25	2.5g	4%
Homestyle Chicken	4¾	1¼ Cup (63.7g)	2	240	15	2g	3%
Chicken & Rice	5¾	1¼ Cup (78g)	2	310	25	3g	4%
Sweet & Sour Chicken	6	1¼ Cup (92.1g)	2	340	10	1g	2%
Turkey Tetrazzini	5¼	1¼ Cup (81.5g)	2	320	55	6g	9%
Turkey Supreme	5	1¼ Cup (60.2g)	2	250	30	3.5g	5%
Breakfast Entrees—Serves 2							
Scrambled Eggs	2¼	½ Cup (32g)	2	200	110	12g	18%
Eggs w/Imitation Bacon	2½	½ Cup (39g)	2	190	110	12g	18%
Western Omelette	2¾	½ Cup (39g)	2	190	100	10g	15%
Hash Brown Potatoes	3¼	½ Cup (42.5g)	2	160	0	0g	0%
Blueberry Pancake Mix	5¾	6-5" cakes (81.5g)	2	330	90	10g	15%
Hash Browns O'Brien	3	½ Cup (46g)	2	160	0	0g	0%
Vegetables—Serves 2							
Peas	1	¼ Cup (14.2g)	2	50	0	0g	0%
Corn	1	¼ Cup (14.2g)	2	50	5	0.5g	1%
Green Beans	⅜	¼ Cup (5.3g)	2	15	0	0g	0%
Peas & Carrots	1¼	¼ Cup (19.5g)	2	70	0	0g	0%
Desserts—Serves 2							
Blueberry Cobbler	5¼	¾ Cup (78g)	2	330	60	6g	10%
Raspberry Cobbler	5½	¾ Cup (78g)	2	330	60	6g	10%
Apple Brown Betty	4½	¾ Cup (62g)	2	270	45	5g	8%
Applesauce	2¼	⅔ Cup (32g)	2	30	0	0g	0%
No Cook Entrees—Serves 4							
Beef Stew	7¾	1 Cup (54.9g)	4	210	25	2.5g	47%
Lasagne w/Meat Sauce	10¼	1¼ Cup (65.5g)	4	250	40	4g	7%
Beef Stroganoff	11	1¼ Cup (74.4g)	4	290	60	6g	10%
Spaghetti w/Meat Sauce	11	1¼ Cup (76.1g)	4	280	15	2g	3%
Homestyle Chicken	9½	1¼ Cup (65.5g)	4	240	15	2g	3%
Chicken & Rice	11½	1¼ Cup (77.9g)	4	310	25	3g	4%
Sweet & Sour Chicken	13	1¼ Cup (92.1g)	4	340	10	1g	2%
Turkey Tetrazzini	10½	1¼ Cup (79.7g)	4	320	55	6g	9%
Turkey Supreme	10¼	1¼ Cup (63.7g)	4	250	30	3.5g	5%
Breakfast Entrees—Serves 4							
Scrambled Eggs	3½	⅓ Cup (30g)	4	140	80	9g	14%
Eggs w/Imitation Bacon	4	⅓ Cup (30g)	4	140	80	9g	14%
Western Omelette	4¼	⅓ Cup (30g)	4	140	70	8g	12%
Blueberry Pancake Mix	11¼	6-5" cakes (81.5g)	4	330	90	10g	15%
Maple Syrup	6¼	½ Cup (44g)	4	180	0	0g	0%
Hash Browns O'Brien	6¼	½ Cup (44.2g)	4	160	0	0g	0%
Hash Brown Potatoes	6¼	½ Cup (46g)	4	160	0	0g	0%
Vegetables—Serves 4							
Corn	2	¼ Cup (14.2g)	4	50	5	0.5g	1%
Peas	2	¼ Cup (14.2g)	4	50	0	0g	0%
Green Beans	¾	¼ Cup (5.3g)	4	20	0	0g	0%
Peas & Carrots	2½	¼ Cup (19.5g)	4	70	0	0g	0%
Desserts—Serves 4							
Applesauce	3½	½ Cup (25g)	4	30	0	0g	0%
Fruit Cocktail	6	½ Cup (42.5g)	4	150	0	0g	0%
Raspberry Cobbler	11	¾ Cup (78g)	4	330	60	6g	10%
Blueberry Cobbler	11	¾ Cup (78g)	4	330	60	6g	10%
Strawberry Cheesecake	10½	⅔ Cup (81.5g)	4	350	60	6g	9%
Apple Compote	5¼	½ Cup (37.2g)	4	140	0	0g	0%
Chocolate Pudding	5¾	½ Cup (41g)	4	160	10	1g	2%
Banana Cream Pudding	5¾	½ Cup (41g)	4	160	5	0.5g	1%

Saturated Fat		Cholesterol		Sodium		Total Carbohydrate		Dietary Fiber		Sugar	Protein	Vit A	Vit C	Cal- cium	Iron
2g	11%	35mg	11%	710mg	30%	38g	13%	4g	17%	8g	15g	0%	10%	8%	15%
1g	4%	10mg	3%	750mg	31%	49g	16%	5g	20%	13g	17g	10%	15%	6%	10%
4g	19%	35mg	12%	820mg	34%	39g	13%	3g	11%	10g	19g	0%	6%	10%	10%
1g	6%	20mg	7%	734mg	31%	33g	11%	4g	18%	7g	13g	45%	15%	4%	15%
0.5g	3%	15mg	5%	720mg	30%	42g	14%	4g	15%	7g	13g	25%	15%	10%	8%
1g	4%	35mg	11%	660mg	27%	43g	14%	2g	10%	5g	16g	0%	6%	8%	30%
0g	0%	25mg	8%	620mg	26%	66g	22%	5g	21%	19g	18g	0%	15%	6%	15%
4g	18%	23mg	8%	780mg	33%	50g	17%	3g	12%	8g	18g	55%	8%	13%	8%
1g	5%	28mg	10%	750mg	15%	41g	14%	3g	10%	8g	15g	0%	10%	4%	8%
4g	20%	525mg	175%	300mg	13%	4g	1%	0g	0%	3g	16g	15%	2%	15%	10%
4g	20%	525mg	175%	230mg	10%	3g	1%	1g	4%	1g	16g	15%	0%	8%	15%
3g	15%	180mg	62%	400mg	17%	10g	3%	1g	4%	4g	17g	0%	10%	10%	10%
0g	0%	0mg	0%	35mg	1%	35g	12%	0g	0%	0g	4g	0%	15%	2%	4%
3g	15%	50mg	17%	990mg	41%	53g	18%	1g	4%	10g	6g	2%	0%	4%	6%
0g	0%	0mg	0%	35mg	1%	36g	12%	1g	4%	3g	4g	4%	45%	2%	20%
0g	0%	0mg	0%	0mg	0%	9g	3%	1g	4%	4g	3g	4%	20%	2%	6%
0g	0%	0mg	0%	10mg	0%	11g	4%	0g	0%	3g	2g	2%	4%	0%	2%
0g	0%	0mg	0%	0mg	0%	4g	1%	1g	4%	1g	1g	4%	8%	2%	4%
0g	0%	0mg	0%	75mg	3%	14g	5%	1g	4%	5g	3g	230%	20%	4%	6%
1.5g	6%	0mg	0%	530mg	22%	66g	22%	3g	12%	43g	2g	0%	20%	4%	15%
1.5g	6%	0mg	0%	530mg	22%	66g	22%	3g	12%	43g	2g	0%	20%	4%	15%
2.5g	13%	0mg	0%	180mg	8%	54g	18%	3g	12%	49g	1g	0%	10%	4%	6%
0g	0%	0mg	0%	0mg	0%	8g	3%	0g	0%	7g	0g	0%	0%	0%	0%
1g	6%	20mg	7%	734mg	31%	33g	11%	4g	18%	7g	13g	45%	15%	4%	15%
2g	11%	35mg	11%	710mg	30%	38g	13%	4g	17%	8g	15g	0%	10%	8%	15%
4g	19%	35mg	12%	820mg	34%	39g	13%	3g	11%	10g	19g	0%	6%	10%	10%
1g	4%	10mg	3%	750mg	31%	49g	16%	5g	20%	13g	17g	10%	15%	6%	10%
0.5g	3%	15mg	5%	720mg	30%	42g	14%	4g	15%	7g	13g	25%	15%	10%	8%
1g	4%	35mg	11%	660mg	27%	43g	14%	2g	10%	5g	16g	0%	6%	8%	30%
0g	0%	25mg	8%	620mg	26%	66g	22%	5g	21%	19g	18g	0%	15%	6%	15%
4g	18%	23mg	8%	780mg	33%	50g	17%	3g	12%	8g	18g	55%	8%	13%	8%
1g	5%	28mg	10%	750mg	15%	41g	14%	3g	10%	8g	15g	10%	0%	4%	8%
3g	15%	390mg	130%	220mg	9%	3g	1%	0g	0%	3g	12g	10%	2%	10%	8%
3g	15%	395mg	132%	170mg	7%	2g	1%	1g	4%	1g	12g	10%	0%	6%	10%
2.5g	13%	140mg	47%	300mg	13%	7g	2%	1g	4%	3g	11g	0%	8%	8%	8%
3g	15%	50mg	17%	990mg	41%	53g	18%	1g	4%	10g	6g	2%	0%	4%	6%
0g	0%	0mg	0%	110mg	5%	46g	15%	0g	0%	45g	0g	0%	0%	0%	0%
0g	0%	0mg	0%	35mg	1%	36g	12%	1g	4%	3g	4g	4%	45%	2%	20%
0g	0%	0mg	0%	35mg	1%	35g	12%	0g	0%	0g	4g	0%	15%	2%	4%
0g	0%	0mg	0%	10mg	0%	11g	4%	0g	0%	3g	2g	2%	4%	0%	2%
0g	0%	0mg	0%	0mg	0%	9g	3%	1g	4%	4g	3g	4%	20%	2%	6%
0g	0%	0mg	0%	0mg	0%	4g	1%	1g	4%	2g	1g	4%	8%	2%	4%
0g	0%	0mg	0%	75mg	3%	14g	5%	1g	4%	5g	3g	230%	20%	4%	6%
0g	0%	0mg	0%	0mg	0%	8g	3%	0g	0%	7g	0g	0%	0%	0%	0%
0g	0%	0mg	0%	40mg	2%	39g	13%	2g	8%	32g	1g	8%	2%	2%	4%
1.5g	6%	0mg	0%	530mg	22%	66g	22%	3g	12%	43g	2g	0%	20%	4%	15%
1.5g	6%	0mg	0%	530mg	22%	66g	22%	3g	12%	43g	2g	0%	20%	4%	15%
1.5g	8%	10mg	3%	540mg	23%	62g	21%	3g	12%	27g	10g	0%	15%	30%	8%
0g	0%	0mg	0%	240mg	10%	37g	12%	2g	8%	29g	0g	0%	0%	0%	2%
0.5g	3%	0mg	0%	370mg	15%	33g	11%	2g	8%	25g	6g	0%	4%	30%	4%
0.5g	3%	0mg	0%	350mg	15%	36g	12%	1g	4%	27g	5g	0%	4%	25%	0%

RICHMOOR (Continued)

Item	Net Wt. Ozs.	Serving Size	# of Servings	Calories Total	Calories Fat	Total Fat	
Apple Brown Betty	9	¾ Cup (62g)	4	270	45	5g	8%
Trail Mix							
WhaGuru Chew—Original	1⅛	1 Bar (31.8g)	1	160	110	12g	18%
WhaGuru Chew—Cashew Almond	1⅛	1 Bar (31.8g)	1	160	100	11g	17%
WhaGuru Chew—Sesame Almond	1⅛	1 Bar (31.8g)	1	160	100	11g	17%
Cinnamon Apple Chips	1½	½ Cup (21g)	2	70	0	0g	0%
Banana Chips	2¾	½ Cup (39g)	2	200	120	13g	20%
Miscellaneous							
Pilot Biscuits	7½	1¾ oz. (54g)	4	220	50	6g	10%
Freeze-Dried Beef	1	1½ oz. (14g)	2	60	15	2g	3%
Freeze-Dried Chicken	1	1½ oz. (14g)	2	60	5	0.5g	1%
Freeze-Dried Turkey	1	1½ oz. (14g)	2	60	15	1.5g	2%

*Percent Daily Values are based on a 2,000 calorie diet. Your Daily Values may be higher or lower depending on your calorie needs:

	Calories	2,000	2,500
Total Fat	Less than	65g	80g
Sat Fat	Less than	20g	25g
Cholesterol	Less than	300mg	300mg
Sodium	Less than	2,400mg	2,400mg
Total Carbohydrate		300mg	375mg
Dietary Fiber		25g	30g

MOUNTAIN HOUSE NUTRITIONAL CONTENTS

	Description			Nutrients per Serving			
				Calories		Fat/Grams	
Product	Pkg. Net Wt. (OZ)	Servings per Pkg	Serving Size	Total	From Fat	Total	Satur- ated
Breakfast Entrees							
Pork Sausage Patties	1.6	2	1 Pty	130	90	10	3.5
Cheese Omelette	2.4	2	½ cup	180	100	11	4.5
Eggs w/Bacon	2.2	2	½ cup	150	80	9	3.5
Precooked Eggs w/Bacon	2.6	2	½ cup	180	90	10	3
Granola w/BB & Milk	4.0	2	½ cup	250	80	9	3
Single-Serve Entrees							
Rice & Chicken	4.0	1	1 pouch	510	150	17	3
Spaghetti	2.8	1	1 pouch	330	90	10	4.5
Hearty Stew w/Beef	2.6	1	1 pouch	280	30	4	1.5
Strogan.Sauce & Beef	3.0	1	1 pouch	390	140	16	6
Lasagna	3.0	1	1 pouch	390	130	15	7
Sweet & Sour Pork w/Rice	3.8	1	1 pouch	480	120	14	4.5
Turkey Tetrazzini	2.7	1	1 pouch	340	120	13	3
Pasta Primavera	3.2	1	1 pouch	370	100	11	6
Double-Serve Entrees							
Chicken Stew	4.8	2.5	1 cup	240	80	9	2
Rice & Chicken	6.4	2.5	1 cup	310	90	0	2
Spaghetti w/Meat & Sauce	4.5	2.5	1 cup	210	60	6	3
Chicken ala King & Noodles	6.4	2.5	1 cup	300	90	10	2.5
Hearty Stew w/Beef	3.7	2.5	1 cup	160	15	2	1
Chicken Polynesian w/Rice	4.7	2.5	1 cup	220	35	4	1
Strogan. Sauce & Beef	4.8	2.5	1 cup	250	90	10	4
Beef Teriyaki w/Rice	5.8	2.5	1 cup	260	35	4	1
Chicken Teriyaki w/Rice	5.0	2.5	1 cup	220	20	2.5	1

Saturated Fat		Cholesterol		Sodium		Total Carbohydrate		Dietary Fiber		Sugar	Protein	Vit A	Vit C	Calcium	Iron
2.5g	13%	0mg	0%	180mg	8%	54g	18%	3g	12%	49g	1g	0%	10%	4%	6%
1g	8%	0mg	0%	60mg	3%	13g	4%	1g	4%	7g	4g	0%	0%	2%	4%
1g	5%	0mg	0%	60mg	3%	13g	4%	2g	8%	9g	4g	0%	0%	2%	6%
1g	5%	0mg	0%	60mg	3%	14g	5%	1g	4%	9g	3g	0%	0%	2%	4%
0g	0%	0mg	0%	60mg	3%	19g	6%	1g	4%	0g	1g	0%	0%	0%	2%
11g	55%	0mg	0%	0mg	0%	23g	8%	3g	12%	15g	1g	0%	4%	0%	2%
2g	10%	0mg	0%	220mg	10%	38g	12%	2g	8%	4g	4g	0%	0%	4%	0%
0.5g	3%	0mg	0%	180mg	8%	0g	0%	0g	0%	0g	11g	0%	0%	0%	6%
0g	0%	35mg	12%	15mg	1%	0g	0%	0g	0%	0g	13g	0%	0%	2%	0%
0g	0%	50mg	17%	25mg	1%	0g	0%	0g	0%	0g	12g	0%	0%	0%	2%

	Nutrients per Serving								% of Refer. Daily Intake					
Milligrams			Grams				Vitamins							
Cholesterol	Sodium	Carbos	Dietary Fiber	Sugars	Other Carb	Protein	A	C	Thiamin	Riboflavin	Niacin	Calcium	Iron
---	---	---	---	---	---	---	---	---	---	---	---	---	---
35	240	2	1	1	0	8	0	0	20	8	15	0	4
335	530	7	0	4	3	13	15	0	10	30	0	20	10
345	460	5	0	3	2	11	10	0	8	25	2	10	10
275	780	7	0	4	3	14	8	0	8	20	6	10	8
0	55	36	4	13	19	8	0	2	10	15	4	15	8
35	1840	74	3	3	68	14	4	0	15	4	20	4	10
25	1500	42	6	10	26	19	10	0	20	20	25	10	15
35	1690	44	5	9	30	18	15	20	15	25	25	8	15
25	1320	46	2	4	40	17	0	0	10	20	4	10	10
55	940	40	6	10	24	23	15	60	15	20	6	30	25
40	1330	70	3	25	42	18	0	40	20	15	20	4	8
70	1720	33	1	9	23	23	4	10	10	25	35	15	8
30	1070	56	4	14	38	14	8	80	20	25	10	2	6
35	1150	27	3	6	18	12	35	15	8	10	20	8	6
20	1110	44	2	2	40	9	2	0	10	2	15	2	8
15	960	27	4	6	17	12	8	0	10	10	15	6	10
75	1120	32	2	5	25	20	2	10	10	15	6	10	10
20	960	25	3	5	17	10	8	15	8	15	15	4	8
25	820	36	1	14	21	10	2	25	6	6	2	2	4
15	840	29	1	2	26	11	0	0	8	10	2	6	8
15	880	44	2	11	31	13	4	15	4	10	10	4	8
20	830	40	2	13	25	10	2	15	6	8	2	2	6

MOUNTAIN HOUSE NUTRITIONAL CONTENTS (Continued)

Product	Description Pkg. Net Wt. (OZ)	Servings per Pkg	Serving Size	Calories Total	From Fat	Fat/Grams Total	Satur- ated
Chili w/Beans & Beef	4.4	2.5	1 cup	200	45	5	2
Lasagna	4.8	2.5	1 cup	250	80	9	4.5
Chili Mac w/Beef	4.8	2.5	1 cup	240	70	7	3
Noodles and Chicken	4.7	2.5	1 cup	210	30	3.5	1
Sweet & Sour Pork w/Rice	6.1	2.5	1 cup	290	70	8	2.5
Turkey Tetrazzini	4.3	2.5	1 cup	220	80	8	2
Pasta Primavera	5.4	2.5	1 cup	250	60	7	4
Oriental Spicy Chicken Veg.	5.5	2.5	1 cup	230	40	4.5	1
Fisherman's Stew	4.4	2.5	1 cup	200	45	5	3
Mexican Rice & Chicken	5.4	2.5	1 cup	240	45	5	1.5
Four-Serving Entrees							
Rice & Chicken	12.7	5	1 cup	310	90	10	2
Spaghetti w/Meat & Sauce	9.0	5	1 cup	210	60	6	3
Hearty Stew w/Beef	7.5	5	1 cup	160	15	2	1
Strogan. Sauce & Beef	9.6	5	1 cup	250	90	10	4
Lasagna	9.6	5	1 cup	250	80	9	4.5
Pasta Primavera	10.8	5	1 cup	250	60	7	4
Vegetables							
Corn	1.1	2	½ cup	80	5	1	0
Green Beans	0.4	2	½ cup	25	0	0	0
Green Peas	1.5	2	½ cup	80	5	0.5	0
Snacks & Desserts							
Mixed Fruit Crisps	1.5	2	½ cup	120	0	0	0
Peach Fruit Crisps	1.5	2	½ cup	120	0	0	0
Pear Fruit Crisps	1.5	2	½ cup	120	0	0	0
Strawberry Fruit Crisps	1.0	2	⅓ cup	110	0	0	0
Nut Chocolate Lurps	3.0	1	1 pouch	480	270	30	10
Raspberry OREO Crumble	5.1	4	½ cup	150	25	3	0.5

AlpineAire Foods™ Nutritional Data

Information given below is per serving

Item	Calories Per Serving	Fat Grams	Sodium Mg.	Carbohydrate Grams	Protein Grams
5-Grain Fruit Nut Instant Cereal	270	1g	105	30	10g
Albacore Tuna with Noodles and Cheese	560	9g	770	40	12g
All American Roast Beef Hash	220	3.5g	1120	24	18g
Almond Chicken	340	7g	500	48	18g
Alpine Minestrone Soup	180	1g	35	25	17g
Apple Almond Crisp	270	4.5g	75	51	6g
Apple-Blueberry Fruit Cobbler	210	2g	170	45	3g
Applesauce with Cinnamon	120	1g	90	27	1g
Bandito Scramble	390	19g	1210	33	18g
BBQ Beef and Turkey with Beans	360	2.5g	1030	64	23g
Beef	60	1.5g	180	0	0g
Beef Rotini	340	4g	320	53	22g
Beef Stroganoff with Noodles	310	8g	1250	34	18g
Black Bart Chili with Beans	230	3g	1800	47	24g
Blueberries, whole, freeze-dried	60	.5g	0	12	0g
Blueberry Honey Granola with Milk	300	5g	190	49	15g
Blueberry Pancakes—Whole Grain	350	8g	580	63	9g

| | Nutrients per Serving | | | | | | Vitamins | | % of Refer. Daily Intake | | | | |
| Milligrams | | Grams | | | | | | | | | | | |
Choles-terol	Sodium	Carbos	Dietary Fiber	Sugars	Other Carb	Pro-tein	A	C	Thia-min	Ribo-flavin	Niacin	Cal-cium	Iron
15	1180	28	8	4	16	12	10	2	4	6	8	10	15
35	590	25	4	6	15	15	10	40	10	10	4	20	15
15	640	31	7	3	21	12	4	0	6	8	15	6	15
40	970	34	3	3	28	11	2	15	10	10	20	2	6
25	800	42	2	15	25	11	0	25	15	10	10	2	4
45	1080	21	1	6	14	14	2	6	8	15	20	10	6
20	730	38	3	9	26	9	6	50	10	15	8	2	4
20	1120	35	2	6	27	13	4	40	6	20	25	4	6
50	840	27	0	9	18	12	4	2	8	20	6	20	6
30	980	37	5	4	28	13	0	10	8	10	20	6	8
20	1110	44	2	2	40	9	2	0	10	2	15	2	8
15	960	27	4	6	17	12	8	0	10	10	15	6	10
20	960	25	3	5	17	10	8	15	8	15	15	4	8
15	840	29	1	2	26	11	0	0	8	10	2	6	8
35	590	25	4	6	15	15	10	40	10	10	4	20	15
20	730	38	3	9	26	9	6	50	10	15	8	2	4
0	0	17	2	2	13	2	0	2	4	4	4	0	2
0	0	5	2	1	2	1	4	20	4	4	0	2	4
0	65	12	5	5	2	5	6	25	15	6	2	2	6
0	20	28	2	24	2	1	2	6	2	2	2	0	2
0	40	28	2	24	2	1	2	8	2	2	6	0	4
0	15	29	3	26	0	1	0	4	2	2	2	0	2
0	0	25	2	21	2	1	0	110	2	2	2	2	2
0	105	39	3	31	5	13	0	0	10	10	20	6	15
0	75	31	2	22	7	1	0	10	2	0	2	2	8

AlpineAire Foods™ (Continued)
Nutritional Data

Information given below is per serving

Item	Calories Per Serving	Fat Grams	Sodium Mg.	Carbohydrate Grams	Protein Grams
Brown Rice and Chicken with Vegetable	310	.5g	960	41	22g
Cheddar Cheese Powder	130	15g	720	0	0g
Cheese Nut Casserole	360	17g	900	41	10g
Chicken	60	.5g	15	0	13g
Chicken Gumbo	280	2.5g	1620	42	16g
Chicken Primavera	240	1g	740	39	17g
Chicken Rotelle	330	7g	1080	40	19g
Chocolate Cheesecake Crunch	340	9g	200	18	6g
Chocolate Fondue with Strawberries	130	1.5g	40	26	2g
Corn	80	1g	0	17	3g
Country Bean and Beef Casserole	280	2.5g	830	42	22g
Cream of Broccoli Soup	120	6g	1230	15	3g
Creamy Potato and Cheddar Soup	180	8g	1390	25	3g
Date Pieces	40	0g	0	9	1g
Forever Young Macaroni and Cheese	400	11g	1460	49	30g
French Cut Green Beans Almondine	100	3g	800	12	4g
Garden Vegetables	70	0g	45	15	3g

AlpineAire Foods™ (Continued)
Nutritional data

Information given below is per serving

Item	Calories Per Serving	Fat Grams	Sodium Mg.	Carbohydrate Grams	Protein Grams
Hash Browns Reds and Greens	200	.5g	960	44	5g
Leonardo da Fettucine	310	8g	720	39	13g
Mashed Potatoes	180	.5g	70	41	4g
Mashed Potatoes and Country Gravy	260	1.5g	680	49	13g
Mexican Rice with Cheese	200	3.5g	700	34	4g
Mixed Bean Salsa Dip	360	15g	660	40	14g
Mixed Fruit Smoothie	120	.5g	25	26	3g
Mixed Fruit Yogurt Mousse	220	1.5g	210	22	4g
Mountain Chili	310	2g	1270	55	25g
Mushroom Pilaf with Vegetables	340	3g	770	65	13g
Mushrooms	40	.5g	5	7	3g
Pasta Roma	310	7g	830	41	14g
Peas	80	0g	140	14	5g
Pilot Bread Crackers	100	3g	130	18	2g
Pineapple Chunks	40	.5g	0	9	0g
Potatoes and Cheddar with Chives	210	8g	430	33	3.5g
Pure Maple Syrup	90	0g	0	23	0g
Rainbow Garden Pasta Salad	280	14g	330	33	5g
Ranch Omelet with Beef	370	25g	580	12	28g
Refried Mixed Beans with Cheese	340	15g	610	36	12g
Rice	110	.5g	5	22	3g
Santa Fe Black Beans and Rice	330	1g	1010	67	11g
Scrambled Eggs, freeze-dried	170	13g	250	9	44g
Scrambling & Omelet Eggs	300	21g	430	10	20g
Shrimp Alfredo	310	7g	870	38	15g
Shrimp Newburg	330	6g	620	47	11g
Sierra Chicken	310	1g	1550	43	21g
Spaghetti Marinara with Mushrooms	250	1g	320	51	13g
Strawberries, Whole, freeze-dried	50	.5g	0	11	1g
Strawberry Honey Granola with Milk	300	5	190	49	15g
Summer Chicken	300	7g	660	33	22g
Sweet and Sour Chicken with Noodles	310	1.5g	830	52	19g
Sweet Peach and Pecan Chicken	350	10g	580	46	19g
Teriyaki Turkey	260	2g	460	47	15g
Tomato Powder	90	0g	40	22	0g
Turkey	60	1.5g	25	0	12g
Turkey Romanoff	220	4g	500	30	16g
Vegetable Mix	240	7g	1130	34	11g
Western Style Tamale Pie with Beef	360	10g	1300	44	18g
Whole Wheat Pasta Stew	270	1g	690	54	11g
Whole Wheat Pasta Stew	280	7g	950	35	11g
Wild Rice Pilaf with Almonds	70	.5g	45	16	3g
Wild Tyme Turkey	350	10g	760	34	19g

ANIMAL-PROOF YOUR CAMP

If you're a hunter, fisherman, or camper, there is always the chance that you will encounter bears or other wild animals. How you behave may determine the outcome. Most advice on bears focuses on grizzlies, but the information can just as easily be applied to black bears and other wild animals. Most animals will avoid you, but there will always be the one that will break the rules.

If you're at a designated campsite, take all garbage with you. Don't leave it in a trash barrel to attract animals.

If you're a hunter, animal carcasses or parts of

carcasses should be stored at least 100 yards from any campsite or trail. In bear country, never sleep within 100 yards of any animal carcass.

If you encounter a grizzly, your behavior can affect the situation. The Wyoming Fish and Game Department advises that you should first try to slowly leave the area. Keep calm, avoid direct eye contact, back up slowly, and speak in a soft monotone. Never run and do not try to climb a tree unless you are sure that you have time and ability to climb at lest 10 feet before the bear reaches you. Grizzlies can run faster than you can.

If a grizzly charges, stand your ground. Bears often mock charge or run past you. If you're unarmed and a bear overpowers you, assume a cannonball position, covering your head and neck with your hands and arms. Stay in this position until you are sure the bear is gone.

GETTING IT RIGHT

In bear country, make sure that all food, beverages, and scented toiletries are stored out of reach of bears at night or when your camp is unattended during the day. Hang your food 10 feet off the ground and four feet from any vertical post, or store in inside a bear-resistant container, such as cars, pickup cabs or hard-sided campers. Coolers, pop-up campers, and tents are *not* bear resistant.

PART 6
SURVIVAL

Survival is the art of making efficient use of any available resource that can help sustain an individual. If a person is able to think clearly and objectively about an emergency situation—because he has prepared for it—he is far more likely to survive than those who panic and are unable to take full advantage of the resources that may be at hand.

To survive, five basic needs—Sustenance, Medical, Fire, Shelter, and Rescue—must be met. Few survival situations are identical, and not all of the needs must be met in every case. However, when thinking about and planning for survival, it is important to prepare for emergencies in which ALL of these needs must be met.

PLANNING AHEAD

It is ironic that many survival situations often strike the unexpected and ill prepared. The day-hiker, who is wearing nothing but shorts and a tee shirt, invariably is the one caught in the "unexpected" late spring snowstorm. Likewise, boats never seem to sink when there are enough life jackets to go around.

Planning and preparing for emergencies is more than carrying a survival knife into the woods with a compass on the end and three matches inside. Preparation requires investing time to be physically and mentally fit, and to thoughtful planning and intelligent selection of resources that will be available when you need them.

Mental preparation starts with the belief that it can happen to you. Nobody buckles their seatbelt with the intention of getting into an accident. It is foolhardy to head into the woods without enough gear to help you get through a day when Mother Nature throws you a curve.

The will to survive is influenced by skill, faith, and courage. The more practice, the more skill. The more skill, the greater the faith. The greater the faith, the more confident we are, and the more enjoyable our outdoor experiences can be.

PREPARING A SURVIVAL KIT

Preparation is the key. Far more is involved than simply buying a prepackaged "survival kit." It is unlikely that any single kit will meet YOUR specific needs.

Select the items for your survival kit based on their versatility, multi-functionality, and practicality. While improvising is not one of the five basic

needs of survival, it is an important process in bringing all these needs together. As an example, surgical tubing, selected as a tourniquet for the first aid kit, can be used in collecting water from an improvised solar still, drinking water from your water collection containers, or making a sling shot.

Buck Knives Field Knife has a 7⅛-inch blade with wire cutter, multi-purpose saw, bottle opener, screwdriver, and honing stone. For hunting, camping, and survival use, the M9 comes in a nylon sheath with an emergency honing stone.

DAYPACK/HIKER SURVIVAL KIT

The following items are recommended in a complete, quality daypack or hiker survival kit. These items have been selected for their versatility for all survival-related emergencies. No kit, however, can be entirely right for every situation. These items form the basic foundation on which you build after taking into account your activity and the environment. While the list may seem long, take into account that many of these items are small and light, and a number of the items (such as knives and saws) are tools you will want to take with you anyway for everyday use.

DAYPACK/HIKER SURVIVAL LIST

- 1 Gallon Water Bag or Container (Collapsible or Folded)
- Water Purification Tablets

- 3600 Calorie Non-Perishable Food Ration (Mainstay, Datrex, MRE, etc.)
- Hard Candy
- Container for Boiling Water
- Large Fixed-Blade Knife
- Pocket Knife, with locking blade
- Flint and Steel Fire Starter
- Fire Lighting Tinder
- Wind and Waterproof Matches (strike anywhere versions are best)
- Waterproof Match Case
- Lighter
- Flashlight with Spare Batteries
- 3 12-Hour High Intensity Cyalume Snap Lights
- Signal Mirror
- Whistle
- Compass
- Compact Strobe Light
- First Aid Kit (should include prescription medicines, large compresses, and be adequate for environment)
- Saw
- Multi-Person Emergency Tube Shelter
- Survival Bag
- Mylar Space Blanket Sleeping Bag
- Space Blanket
- Wool Gloves
- Wool Hat
- Dry Socks
- Emergency Poncho or Rain Jacket
- Cord or Rope
- Sewing Kit
- Multi-Tool (Schrade Tough, Leatherman Tool, etc.)
- Sharpening Stone
- Carry/Storage Bag (sealed for pilfer resistance)

OPTIONAL ITEMS

- Global Positioning System
- Fishing Kit
- Snare Wire
- Surgical Tubing

VEHICLE SURVIVAL KIT

The following items are recommended in a complete, quality vehicle survival kit. While items like jumper cables, tire chains, and road flares are not normally considered part of a vehicle survival kit, but rather safety items, far too many survival situations have started along the side of the road because they were not present. Be ready to improvise! For example, if your car overheats because of a ruptured hose, wait for the car to cool and fix the rupture with duct tape. This may not be the perfect fix but it can get you to the next town or nearest phone.

Remember also that your vehicle is poorly insulated and that as soon as you lose your power to run the heater or air conditioner, the car will become an ice box or oven. If you are using part of the car as shade, shelter, or wind block, don't forget to keep your fire well away from the vehicle. Getting outside the vehicle can greatly improve your survivability, but do not leave your vehicle or fail to cannibalize all of the resources it may offer. The thought of cannibalizing your car can be a disheartening thought when you think about their costs, but any vehicle can be replaced so don't fret too long. The mirrors make great signals; the hub caps can boil water; the tires can make a dark black, smoky signal fire; and the insulation in the seats can insulate you outside as well.

VEHICLE LIST

- Cellular Phone (a good recommendation for any traveler)
- Spare Tire
- Flash Light
- Jack
- Gas Can
- Spool 20 Gauge Wire
- Tire Chains
- Tire Flat Repair
- Ground Tarp
- Jumper Cables
- Tool Kit
- Tow Rope
- Road Flares (Red Cyalume 12-Hour Snap Lights also work well)
- Shovel
- Duct Tape
- 1 Gallon of Water
- Blanket
- Saw
- Emergency Poncho or Rain Jacket
- Wool Gloves
- Wool Hat
- Multiplier Tool (Gerber, Leatherman, etc.)
- Cord or Rope
- Large Emergency Tube Shelter/Tarp

- Mylar Emergency Space Blanket
- Sleeping Bags (during certain weather conditions)
- Water Storage Container
- Water Purification Tablets
- 6 Red, 12-Hour Cyalume Lights
- 6 12-Hour High Intensity Yellow Cyalume Lights
- 3600 Calorie Non-Perishable Ration (Mainstay, Datrex, MRE, etc.)
- Signal Mirror
- Whistle
- Compact Strobe Light
- First Aid Kit (should include prescription medicines, trauma dressings, and other large bandages)
- Surgical Tubing
- Large Fixed-Blade Survival Knife
- Pocket Knife, with locking blade
- Flint and Steel Fire Starter
- Fire-lighting Tinder
- Wind and Waterproof Matches (strike anywhere versions are best)
- Waterproof Match Case
- Lighter
- Compact Sewing Kit
- Holding Container (that can be sealed for pilfer resistance)

OPTIONAL ITEMS

- Global Positioning System
- Compact Backpacker's Tent

Sustenance, Medical, Fire, Rescue, and Shelter are the major categories of needs the survivor may have. Equally important, however, is thinking about these needs in the context of the environment that you will be in. A midsummer hike in the Grand Canyon requires different gear than a December snowshoe trip in the Rockies. As an example, carrying water to meet a subsistence need in the desert may make more sense than carrying water purification tablets—a logical choice when hiking in an area where water is plentiful. The need for water does not change, but how an individual prepares to meet that need does.

SUSTENANCE

Sustenance is the need for food and water which supplies our energy, increases our metabolism, regulates our temperature, and allows our minds to work rationally. Most healthy adults can miss a few meals without significant distress. However, even the healthiest adults can go no longer than a few days without water before they become delirious and lose vital body functions. While ready-to-eat low water rations make an excellent addition to many survival kits, far too much emphasis is placed on food and not nearly enough is placed on water, water storage, and water purification.

MAKING POTABLE WATER

Rainwater collected in clean containers or in plants is generally safe for drinking. However, you must purify water from lakes, ponds, swamps, springs, or streams, especially those near human habitation. When at all possible, you must disinfect all water obtained from vegetation or from the ground by using iodine or chlorine or by boiling.

You can purify water by:

- Using water purification tablets.
- Pouring 5 drops of 2% tincture of iodine in a canteen full of clean water, and 10 drops in a canteen full of cloudy or cold water. (Let the canteen of water stand for 30 minutes before drinking.)
- Boiling water for 1 minute at sea level, adding 1 minute for each additional 1,000 feet above sea level, or boil for 10 minutes no matter where you are.
- Using a commercial water purification device.

POTABLE DRINKING WATER SYSTEM DEVICES

Having to purify water is a bother. The only reason to carry any drinking water purifier at all is to protect your health against microbiological and chemical contaminants. Water-related health threats can occur any time you are in contact with water: drinking water directly, using water as a food or beverage ingredient, using water for washing, brushing teeth, or using water to clean cookware.

Primary exposure to drinking water contaminants occurs at the following times:

- When collecting raw water for purification . . . to avoid this threat, use a separate container for your raw water supply whenever possible. Be selective when possible. Choose a source least likely to be badly polluted.
- During purification . . . be careful to prevent dirty water from dripping or flowing into purified water.
- When storing your purifier either at meal or camp sites, or in your carry pack.
- Especially when handling the unit during storage, back washing, brushing, scraping, or other maintenance functions.

Remember, the primary microorganism of concern in most wilderness recreation areas are tough,

hardy cystic parasites that resist heat and cold—even freezing—drought, chlorine, iodine, and just about everything else. And while bacteria is relatively fragile and has very short life cycle, often less than a day, cysts can exist for months. All microorganisms of chief concern are invisibly small and cannot be seen, smelled, or detected in any quick and easy manner. Accordingly, you must rely on knowledge of your area and on common sense.

It is widely known, today, that Giardia and/or Cryptosporidia have been found in water supplies essentially in every country in the world. Therefore, you should always protect against parasitic cysts and insist on 100% reduction. Where one cyst can infect, a 99.9% reduction may not be good enough, especially when there is no known treatment for some cysts.

There have been essentially no water-borne typhoid, cholera, or hepatitis Type A epidemics in the U.S. for the last 50 years, so the likelihood of their occurrence from a U.S. wilderness water source is very low.

Pesticides, herbicides, and other chemicals can be present anywhere downwind or downstream from

General Ecology's First Need Base Camp System in use. The system purifies water to U.S. Public Health Service bacteria standards from virtually any non-saltwater, treatable source. Its high-flow-rate large-water capacity makes it good for small groups, extended expeditions, and families.

major agricultural and industrial areas even hundreds of miles away. These contaminants concentrate in streams, rivers, and lakes.

Asbestos fibers can be found in very high numbers of more than a million fibers per liter in most western and some eastern wilderness waters. Even though trace amounts of these chemicals won't make you ill today, no one wants to drink asbestos fibers if they can easily be avoided.

Micron ratings must be absolute to be meaningful, and precise measurements are essentially impossible to make. Micron ratings pertain only to the physical removal or straining of particles, so absolute micron ratings are only one means for evaluation of removal effectiveness. Removal of pesticides, herbicides, tastes, odors, most colors and solvents require other purification (separation) mechanisms. Many units, even those with very low micron ratings, have little or no ability to remove anything other than particles.

According to federal regulations all water purification devices are defined as being either pesticide or device products. Pesticide products rely on chemically poisoning organisms (pests), while devices rely on physically removing them. It's easy to tell whether a product is categorized as a pesticide or a device. All products must carry an EPA Establishment Regulation Number. Pesticide products, however, must carry two EPA registration numbers, one for the manufacturing establishment and one for the pesticide being used. So, decide if you want to use a device or a pesticide for your water purification needs, and be sure to check the label to choose the right type. In certain applications, it may be desirable to use a pesticide to preterit water. Complete removal of the pesticide is very desirable after enough kill time is allowed.

It is important to add that iodine resins are not effective against cysts.

All products being marketed today, carrying an EPA Establishment Registration Number, are deemed to meet all current, pertinent EPA and other federal regulations. Otherwise, they would not be permitted to be on the market.

SOLAR STILL FOR SAFE WATER

No matter how fresh and clean water may appear to be in that mountain stream or creek, you can never be sure that it isn't contaminated with chemicals and bacteria that make it unsafe for drinking. It is only common sense to *always* carry a container of water with your gear, especially in warm climates where dehydration is a danger. In a survival situation, a sportsman can get safe drinking water by

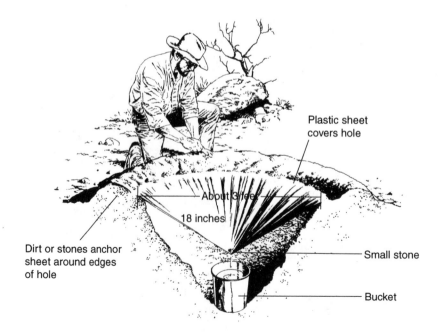

Plastic sheet covers hole

About 3 feet

18 inches

Dirt or stones anchor sheet around edges of hole

Small stone

Bucket

building a solar still, which will usually provide at least a pint of water every 24 hours. Here's how to use the sun to get safe drinking water:

Step 1 Dig a hole in the ground about two feet deep and three feet across.

Step 2 Place a clean bucket or pan at the bottom of the hole.

Step 3 Set a plastic sheet over the hole and hold it in place by piling stones or dirt around the edges.

Step 4 Place a small stone in the center of the plastic sheet, so that the water formed by condensation on

the sheet's sides is funneled down into the catch container.

HOW THE STILL WORKS

The sun causes condensation to form on the sides of the plastic sheet. As the water collects at the bottom of the sheet it drips into the bucket.

As an extra precaution, boil the water for 10 minutes or add a commercial water treatment tablet.

WILD PLANTS FOR FOOD

After water, food is your most urgent need. In a survival situation, you should always be on the lookout for wild foods and live off the land whenever possible. Plants are a valuable food source. Although they may not provide a balanced diet, they will sustain you even in the arctic where the heat-producing qualities of meat are normally essential. Many plant foods such as nuts and seeds will give you enough protein for normal efficiency. Roots, green vegetables, and plant food containing natural sugar will provide calories and carbohydrates that will give your body energy.

EDIBILITY OF PLANTS

Being able to recognize wild edible plants is important in a survival situation. There are certain factors you should keep in mind when collecting edible plants:

- Cultivated plants and wild plants growing in or near cultivated plants may have been sprayed with pesticides. So thoroughly wash whatever plants you collect.
- The surface of any plant food that grows or is washed in contaminated water is also contaminated. If you are going to eat the plant raw, wash it in water suitable for drinking.
- Some plants may have fungal toxins that are extremely poisonous. To lessen the chances that these toxins are present, collect fresh seeds, fruit, or leaves—not those that have fallen to the ground.
- Plants of the same species may differ in the amount of toxic or subtoxic compounds they con-

tain because of different environmental and genetic factors. One example of this is the foliage of the common chokeberry. Some chokeberry plants have high concentrations of cyanide compounds, other plants low concentrations.
- Some people are more susceptible than others to gastric upset from plants. If you are sensitive this way, avoid unknown wild plants. If you are extremely sensitive to poison ivy, avoid products from this family, including drinks made from sumacs, mangos, and cashews.
- There are some edible wild plants, such as acorns and water lily rhizomes, that are bitter. These bitter substances (usually tannin compounds) make them unpalatable. Boiling in several changes of water will help remove these substances.
- There are many valuable wild plants that have high concentrations of oxalate compounds. Oxalates usually produce a sharp burning sensation in your mouth. And they are bad for the kidneys. Boiling usually destroys these oxalates.
- The only way to tell if a mushroom is edible is by proper determination. Even then, some species are questionable. So do not eat mushrooms.

There are many, many plants throughout the world. Tasting or swallowing even a small portion of some can cause severe discomfort, extreme internal disorders, or death. Therefore, if you have the slightest doubt as to the edibility of a plant, apply the Universal Edibility Test before eating any part of it.

Before testing a plant for edibility, make sure that there are a sufficient number of the plants to make testing worth your time and effort. You need more than 24 hours to apply the edibility test.

Keep in mind that eating large amounts of plant food on an empty stomach may cause diarrhea or cramps. Two good examples of familiar foods that cause this problem are green apples and too many fresh berries. Even though you have tested plant food and found it safe, eat it in moderation with other foods.

You can see from the steps and time involved in testing edibility just how important it is to be able to identify edible plants.

UNIVERSAL EDIBILITY TEST

1. Test only one part of a potential food plant at a time.
2. Break the plant into its basic components— leaves, stems, roots, buds, and flowers.
3. Smell the food for strong or acid odors. Keep in mind that smell alone does not indicate if a plant is inedible.
4. Do not eat for 8 hours before starting the test.
5. During the 8 hours you are abstaining from eating, test for contact poisoning by placing a piece of the plant part you are testing on the inside of your elbow or wrist. Usually 15 minutes is enough time to allow for a reaction.
6. During the test period, take nothing by mouth except purified water and the plant part being tested.
7. Select a small portion of a single component and prepare it the way you plan to eat it.
8. Before putting the prepared part in your mouth, touch a small portion (a pinch) to the outer surface of the lip to test for burning or itching.
9. If after 3 minutes there is no reaction on your lip, place the plant part on your tongue, holding it there for 15 minutes.
10. If there is no reaction, thoroughly chew a pinch and hold it in your mouth for 15 minutes. DO NOT SWALLOW.
11. If no burning, itching, numbing, stinging, or other irritation occurs during the 15 minutes, swallow the food.
12. Wait 8 hours. If any ill effects occur during this period, induce vomiting and drink a lot of water.
13. If no ill effects occur, eat ½ cup of the same plant part prepared the same way. Wait another 8 hours. If no ill effects occur, the plant part as prepared is safe for eating.

CAUTION: Treat all parts of the plant for edibility, as some plants have both edible and inedible parts. Do not assume that a part that proved edible when cooked is also edible when raw. Test the part raw to ensure edibility before eating raw.

DO NOT eat unknown plants that:

- Have a milky sap or a sap that turns black when exposed to air.
- Are mushroomlike.
- Resemble onion or garlic.
- Resemble parsley, parsnip, or dill.
- Have carrotlike leaves, roots, or tubers.

PREPARATION OF PLANT FOOD

Although some plants or plant parts are edible raw, others must be cooked to be edible or palatable. Some methods of improving the taste of plant food are soaking, parboiling, cooking, or leaching. (Leaching is done by crushing food, placing it in some sort of strainer, and pouring boiling water through it.)

Leaves, Stems, and Buds. Boil until tender. Several changes of water help to eliminate bitterness.

Roots and Tubers. Boil, bake, or roast. Boiling removes harmful substances such as oxalic acid crystals.

Nuts. Leach or soak acorns in water to remove the bitterness. Although chestnuts are edible raw, they are tastier roasted or steamed.

Grains and Seeds. Parch to improve the taste, or grind into meal to use as a thickener with soups, stews, or to use as flour to make bread.

Sap. If the sap contains sugar, dehydrate it by boiling until the water is gone.

Fruit. Bake or roast tough, heavy-skinned fruit. Boil juicy fruit.

MEDICAL

The second basic need is Medical. One need not be a doctor to be prepared to meet basic medical and health needs. While there are good outdoor first aid kits available, make sure to take YOUR circumstances into account and supplement any kit with items you will need. This means taking sufficient quantities of any prescribed medicines, bringing extra contact lenses or pairs of glasses, and taking additional supplies (bug spray, antivenin, sea sickness medication) that are appropriate for the environment. (For medical treatment of any field emergencies see chapter on First Aid).

FIRE

It is often said that the presence of a fire means the survivor is going to make it. Although not an absolute truth, it certainly is the case that nothing can warm the soul, calm fear, and bring hope to a survivor more than a warm fire. In addition, fire is a resource that helps the survivor meet other needs from purifying water, to sterilizing bandages, to day and night signaling. Fire is a versatile and often essential survival resource. Cold weather, wind, and moisture are three enemies of the survivor. A good fire can help fight and prevail against them all. Unfortunately, most survival kits offer at best only mediocre fire-making implements, and firecraft seldom is given the attention it deserves in survival guides.

It takes skill to build a warming fire in the pouring rain, and for a small investment of time, learning this skill can help save your life. First, use good judgment when selecting fire-making implements for a survival kit, and think about how the tools you are selecting might fail under various conditions. For example, most lighters work poorly in extreme cold temperatures, can blow out in the wind, and last only as long as the butane fuel source. Most waterproof matches are waterproof only at the striking head and will stay lit for only 4-5 seconds.

In the hands of someone who has practiced with it, there is no better all-purpose fire-starting device than a large piece of flint and something to scrape it. Flints work effectively in the wind or rain and last a long time. Survival, Inc. manufactures two flint-based firestarter tools that are excellent choices for a survival kit.

Commercial fire starters or fuels, likewise,

Saber Cut flexible chain handsaw has a self-cleaning blade which cuts in both directions. The saw is packed in a molded foam case.

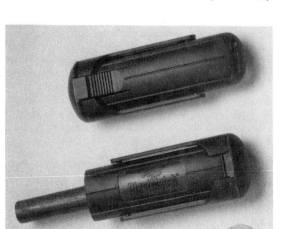

Blast Match is a fire-starter built around a flint bar more than 2 inches long and ½ inch in diameter. Allows users to generate a stream of sparks to start fires or light stoves in any weather. Can be operated with one hand.

should be chosen with care to ensure that they will work in wet weather. For those wanting to save a few pennies, a good homemade tinder is a 100% cotton ball saturated with Vaseline. Ten to 20 of these can be crammed into a waterproof match case or empty film canister.

Of course, good cutting tools can help immeasurably when you are preparing to make a fire. First, it makes sense to carry both a fixed-blade and a folding knife. A large fixed-blade knife is great for cutting into the heart of dry wood. A smaller folding locking-blade knife is good for preparing shavings and fire-starting materials. You should also always carry a good lightweight saw. Nothing works like a saw for quickly collecting dead, dry standing materials for fuel. The Ultimate Survival Saber Cut pocket chain saw is flexible and comes packed in a floating case. Good fixed-blade saws include the Sven Saw and the Sawvivor.

RESCUE

The survivor can dramatically improve his chances of being rescued if he knows, and can use, some basic signaling skills. Being seen or heard is the key. No person should ever venture off into the woods, go anywhere in their car, their boat, their plane, or engage in any other outdoor activity without a signal mirror and a whistle. You can't outscream the best whistles and even if you could you could not sustain the effort.

The signal mirror is second only to the radio or telephone for communicating your need for help. Unfortunately, outside of the military, who use signal mirrors religiously (including them in every survival kit), the general public has only limited

Star Flash signal mirror has a sight-through-the-lens targeting star which allows the user to aim the signal flash at the target. Visible for many miles.

Emergency Strobe is a hand-sized, battery powered personal strobe light that emits pulsing beacons of light 50 to 70 times per minute, for up to 16 hours. Visible up to 3 miles.

knowledge of the value of the signal mirror. A targetable signal mirror, such as the official Air Force Star Flash, that enables the survivor to aim the signal flash is the key.

Other widely available signaling devices include flashlights, strobe lights, and chem lights. High intensity 12 hour chem lights are a better choice in most instances than a flashlight, because they are lighter in weight and do not require batteries. A small string tied to the end of a chem light and spun in a circle over your head makes an excellent night signal that can be seen from a great distance. Moreover, when considering items to place in your home disaster kit, take into account that the spark from the switch of a flashlight can trigger an explosion in a gas-filled room, while a chem light poses no such danger.

With signaling and rescue devices, the key is to be seen. Bigger, louder, and more is better. A recognized international symbol of distress is a series of three signals. Three blasts of your whistle, three long honks of your car horn, three small fires (smoke or flame), or three shots from your rifle or shotgun are examples.

SHELTER AND PERSONAL PROTECTION

Shelter starts at the human body and works its way to protection overhead. Insect repellent falls within the category of shelter or personal protection, because protection from the elements means all of them: insects, wind, sun, heat, rain, snow, snakebite,

cold, and others. Clothing should be worn for the weather, workload, and activity, taking into account possible extremes and worse case scenarios. Would these clothes be sufficient to spend the night in, if you couldn't get back to camp or your vehicle? This

Space Emergency bag is made from durable and lightweight metalized polyester film. Folded, the bag measures 2 × 3 inches and weighs 3 ounces.

you. This might be true when used in perfect condition, but these blankets can tear in the wind and are open at the end. The best of the lightweight shelters are the Mylar (or equivalent) film sleeping bags. This is because you can get inside of them and trap the heat while minimizing the loss of heat through convection. Heat transfer in cold weather from the body is done by evaporation, radiation, convection, conduction, and respiration. Fifty percent of all body heat can be lost through the head alone. The better reflective type blankets are reinforced by polyethylene or polypropylene materials. These resist tearing and damage. Survival bags (over-sized and double strength garbage bags which go from head to toe) are widely available. This item in the survival kit makes an excellent emergency shelter to climb into, especially when used in conjunction with a Mylar space blanket sleeping bag. It is important to recognize, however, that these emergency shelters are not self-regulating and that they can become exceptionally hot and wet inside when moisture is not allowed to escape.

is the question you should be asking yourself as you prepare to set out.

Personal survival protection items like space blankets, emergency tube shelters, and others lead far too many people down the road to false security. Most space blankets come with the statement that they reflect up to 90% of your body heat back to

Sheltering not only effects the body directly, but is important in meeting other survival needs as well. It is very difficult to build a fire in the pouring rain if you cannot keep the material you are preparing dry, including your hands.

EMERGENCY TARP SHELTERS

Only your imagination limits the uses of tarps. They can protect you from foul weather, keep your sleeping bag dry on wet ground, make an emergency stretcher and lots more. Tarps are most useful, however, when made into shelters or makeshift tents. The most practical size tarp is 12 × 8 feet. When setting up any of the shelters shown here, you will

have to make strong tie-down points without puncturing the tarp. Place a small rock or pebble an inch or so from the edge, bunch the plastic tarp around it and tie your line around the neck. You can also use duct tape. Make small loops of line, pass the duct tape through the loop and tape it to both sides of the tarp.

A SIMPLE SHELTER provides protection in rainy weather. It can be set at any height, allowing campers to sit, stand or sleep. Clothespins will keep tarp taut on ridgepole. Use pebble tie-downs and pegs on corners.

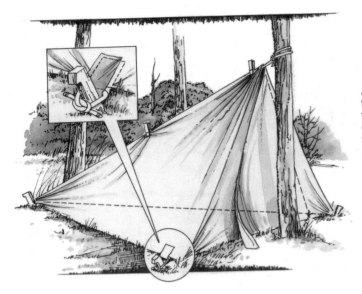

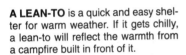

A MODIFIED MOUNTAIN shelter is ideal for hunters faced with a night in the woods. It's easy to set up and will totally enclose and protect a camper from foul weather. Always carry enough line to make a rope ridgepole.

A LEAN-TO is a quick and easy shelter for warm weather. If it gets chilly, a lean-to will reflect the warmth from a campfire built in front of it.

SURVIVING THE COLD

There is no way to beat the cold, but we can learn how to survive in it. High-tech manufacturing now offers us clothing that is insulated, waterproof, and windproof, but even with all of these advantages, there will always be someone who will get into trouble. Hypothermia is the cold-weather killer, and it is caused by exposure to wind, rain, snow or wet clothing. (For treatment of hypothermia see First Aid section.) Allow your body's core temperature

to drop below the normal 98.6°, and you will start to shiver and stamp your feet to keep warm. If these early signs are ignored, the next symptoms will be slurred speech, memory lapses, fumbling hands and drowsiness. If not treated quickly, hypothermia can kill its victim when body temperature drops below 78°, and this can happen within 90 minutes after shivering begins.

If you detect these symptoms in yourself or a friend, start treatment immediately. Get to shelter and warmth as soon as possible. If no shelter is

available, build a fire. Get out of wet clothing and apply heat to head, neck, chest and groin. Use body heat from another person. Give victim warm liquids, chocolate, or any food with a high sugar content. Never give a victim alcohol. It will impair judgment, dilate blood vessels, and prevent shivering, which is the body's way of producing needed heat.

You can also survive the cold by staying in shape and getting a good night's sleep before going outdoors. Carry candy, mixed nuts, raisins, and any other high-energy food. Stay as dry as possible and avoid overheating. Most important, dress properly. This means several layers of clothing and rain gear. And wear a wool hat with ear protection. An uncovered head can lose up to 50 percent of the body's heat.

SNOW BLINDNESS

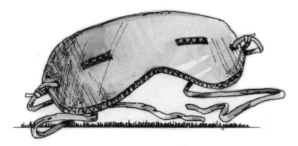

SNOW BLINDNESS is caused by the sun's reflection off snow, ice, or sand burning the corneas of the eyes. It is temporary, usually lasting 24 hours. Symptoms include red, watery, itchy eyes and pain when eyelids move. Snow blindness can be prevented by wearing sunglasses designed to cut ultraviolet radiation (UVR). If sunglasses are not available, make a snow mask by cutting narrow slits in cardboard and tying it to your head with string.

COOLING POWER OF WIND EXPRESSED AS "EQUIVALENT CHILL TEMPERATURE"

Wind Speed		Temperature (°F)																					
Calm	Calm	40	35	30	25	20	15	10	5	0	-5	-10	-15	-20	-25	-30	-35	-40	-45	-50	-55	-60
Knots	MPH	Equivalent Chill Temperature																				
3–6	5	35	30	25	20	15	10	5	0	-5	-10	-15	-20	-25	-30	-35	-40	-45	-50	-55	-65	-70
7–10	10	30	20	15	10	5	0	-10	-15	-20	-25	-35	-40	-45	-50	-60	-65	-70	-75	-80	-90	-95
11–15	15	25	15	10	0	-5	-10	-20	-25	-30	-40	-45	-50	-60	-65	-70	-80	-85	-90	-100	-105	-110
16–19	20	20	10	5	0	-10	-15	-25	-30	-35	-45	-50	-60	-65	-75	-80	-85	-95	-100	-110	-115	-120
20–23	25	15	10	0	-5	-15	-20	-30	-35	-45	-50	-60	-65	-75	-80	-90	-95	-105	-110	-120	-125	-135
24–28	30	10	5	0	-10	-20	-25	-30	-40	-50	-55	-65	-70	-80	-85	-95	-100	-110	-115	-125	-130	-140
29–32	35	10	5	-5	-10	-20	-30	-35	-40	-50	-60	-65	-75	-80	-90	-100	-105	-115	-120	-130	-135	-145
33–36	40	10	0	-5	-15	-20	-30	-35	-45	-55	-60	-70	-75	-85	-95	-100	-110	-115	-125	-130	-140	-150

Winds Above 40 Have Little Additional Effects.

Little Danger

Increasing Danger (Flesh may freeze within 1 minute)

Great Danger (Flesh may freeze within 30 seconds)

Danger of Freezing Exposed Flesh for Properly Clothed Persons

SURVIVING A SNOWSTORM

If you're a winter sportsman, you should know how to survive a snowstorm. First, always travel with a daypack stocked with survival gear, such as a knife, compass, map, waterproof matches, whistle, space blanket, water, high energy food, flashlight, spare socks and gloves.

During the winter, never hunt alone. It's also important to tell a friend where you are hunting and when you expect to return.

If travel in a snowstorm is hazardous, find shelter and don't venture far from a trail. Next, build a fire. It will give you light, warmth, dry clothing, a signal, hot food, and even drinking water from melted snow.

If you're driving off-road, don't leave your vehicle. It will provide shelter. To keep warm, use seat covers and carpeting. The stuffing from car seats makes tinder for a fire. Unhook the carburetor hose and you will be able to drain enough gasoline to start a fire.

IF YOU'RE STUCK in a snowstorm with huge drifts, you can build a snow cave. Snow is an effective insulation and will keep you warm in zero temperatures. Make sure your snow cave is air-vented.

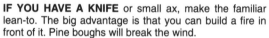

IF YOU HAVE A KNIFE or small ax, make the familiar lean-to. The big advantage is that you can build a fire in front of it. Pine boughs will break the wind.

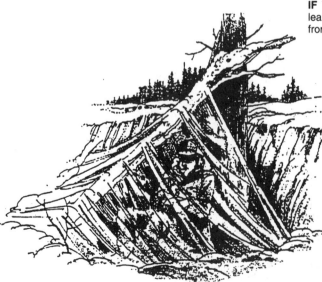

A TREE PIT IS THE EASIEST snow shelter to build. Find a tree and dig a hole in the snow next to it, then cover yourself with a piece of plastic or your space blanket draped over a small limb.

SURVIVING THE HEAT

To survive in a hot area, you must know about and be prepared for the environmental conditions you face. You must determine the equipment you will need, the tactics you will use, and how the environment will impact on them and you.

LOW RAINFALL

Low Rainfall is the most obvious environmental factor in a hot, arid area. Some desert areas receive less than four inches of rain annually, and this comes in brief torrents that quickly run off the ground surface. With the high desert air temperatures you cannot survive long without water. So in a desert survival situation, you must first consider "How much water do I have?" and "Where are other sources?"

A key factor in arid area survival is understanding the relationship between physical activity, air temperature, and water consumption. The body requires a certain amount of water for a certain level of activity at a certain temperature. For example, a man performing hard work in the sun at 110 degrees requires 5 gallons of water a day. Lack of the required amount of water causes a rapid decline in a person's ability to make decisions and to perform tasks efficiently.

Your body's normal temperature is 98.6 degrees. Your body gets rid of excess heat by sweating. The warmer your body becomes, whether caused by work, exercise, or air temperature, the more you sweat. The more you sweat, the more moisture you lose. Sweating is the principal cause of water loss. If a man stops sweating during periods of high air temperature and heavy work or exercise, he will have a heat stroke. This is an emergency that requires immediate medical attention.

Understanding how the air temperature and your physical activity affect your water requirements allows you to take measures to get the most from your water supply. These measures are:

- Find shade. Get out of the sun. Place something between you and the hot ground. Limit your movements.
- Conserve your sweat. Wear all your clothes, including tee shirt; roll the sleeves down; cover your head; and protect your neck with a scarf or similar item. This will protect your body from hot blowing, sand-laden winds and the direct rays of the sun. Your clothing will absorb your sweat, keeping it against your skin so that you gain its full cooling effect. By staying in the shade quietly, fully clothed, not talking, keeping your

mouth closed and breathing through your nose, your water requirement for survival drops dramatically.

- If water is scarce, do not eat. Food requires water for digestion. Eating food will use water that you need for cooling.

Thirst is not a reliable guide for your need for water. A person who uses thirst as a guide will only drink two-thirds of his daily requirement. To prevent this "voluntary" dehydration, use this guide:

- At temperatures below 100 degrees, drink 1 pint of water every hour.
- At temperatures above 100 degrees, drink 1 quart of water every hour.

Drinking water at regular intervals helps your body to remain cool, decreasing sweating. Even when your water supply is low, sipping water constantly will keep your body cooler and reduce water loss through sweating. Conserve your sweat by reducing activity during the heat of the day. DO NOT ration your water. If you attempt to ration your water, you stand a good chance of becoming a heat casualty.

INTENSE SUNLIGHT AND HEAT

Intense sunlight and heat are present in all arid areas. Air temperature can rise as high as 140 degrees during the day. Heat gain results from direct sunlight, hot blowing winds, reflective heat (the sun's rays bouncing off the sand), and conductive heat from direct contact with the desert sand and rock.

The temperature of desert sand and rock averages 30 to 40 degrees more than that of the air. For instance, when the air temperature is 110 degrees, the sand temperature may be 140 degrees.

Intense sunlight and heat increase the body's need for water. To conserve your body sweat and energy, you need a shelter to reduce your exposure to the heat of the day. Travel at night to minimize the use of water. You can survey the area at dawn, dusk, or by moonlight when there is little likelihood of mirage.

Temperatures may get as high as 130 degrees during the day and as low as 50 degrees at night in arid areas. The drop in temperature at night occurs rapidly and will chill a person who lacks warm clothing and is unable to move about. The cool evenings and nights are the best times to work or travel. If you plan to rest at night, you will find a wool sweater, long underwear, and a wool stocking cap extremely helpful.

Sunburn results from overexposing your skin to the sun's rays. So keep your body completely clothed, including gloves on your hands and a scarf around your neck. Use sunscreen liberally on any exposed areas of skin. Sun poisoning equals nausea and dehydration. In addition, burns may become infected, causing more problems.

Remember that:

- There is as much danger of sunburn on cloudy days as on sunny days, especially at high altitudes.
- Most sunscreens do not give complete protection against excessive exposure.
- The glare on the sand causes eyestrain, and wind-blown, fine sand particles can irritate the eyes and cause inflammation. Wear goggles and use eye ointments to protect your eyes.
- The combination of wind, sand, or dust can cause your lips and other exposed skin to chap. Use

chapstick and skin ointments to prevent or overcome this problem.

- Rest is essential in this environment. You need 20 minutes of rest for each hour in the heat and you need 6 hours of sleep each day.

SPARSE VEGETATION

Vegetation is sparse in arid areas. You will therefore have difficulty finding shelter. Seek shelter in dry washes or riverbeds with thicker growths of vegetation. Use the shadows cast from brush, rocks, or outcroppings. The temperature in shaded areas will be 20 to 30 degrees cooler than the air temperature. Finally, cover objects that will reflect light from the sun.

Prior to moving, survey the area for sites that provide cover. A problem you will have is estimating distance. The emptiness of a desert terrain causes most people to underestimate distance by three: What appears to be 1 mile away is really 3 miles away.

CROSSING DANGEROUS WATER

When you are in a survival situation in any area except the desert, you are likely to encounter a water obstacle. It may be in the form of a river, a stream, a lake, a bog, quicksand, quagmire, or muskeg. Whatever it is, you need to know how to cross it safely.

RIVERS AND STREAMS

A river or stream may be narrow or wide, shallow or deep, slow moving or fast moving. It may be snow-fed or ice-fed. Your first step is to find a place where the river is basically safe for crossing. So look for a high place from which you can get a good view of the river and find a place for crossing. If there is no high place, climb a tree. Check the river carefully for the following:

- A level stretch where it breaks into a number of channels. Two or three narrow channels are usually easier to cross than a wide river.
- Obstacles on the opposite side of the river that might hinder your travel. Try to select the spot from which travel will be safest and easiest.
- A ledge of rocks that crosses the river. This often indicates dangerous rapids or canyons.
- A deep or rapid waterfall or a deep channel—never attempt to ford a stream directly above or even close to such spots.

- Rocky places. Avoid these; you can be seriously injured from falling on rocks. An occasional rock that breaks the current, however, may assist you.
- A shallow bank or sandbar. If possible, select a point upstream from a shallow bank or sandbar so that the current will carry you to it if you lose your footing.
- A course across the river that leads downstream, so that you will cross the current at about a 45 degree angle.

RAPIDS

Crossing a deep, swift river or rapids is not as dangerous as it looks. If you are swimming across, swim with the current—never fight it—and try to keep your body horizontal to the water. This will reduce the danger of being pulled under.

In fast, shallow rapids, go on your back, feet first; fin your hands alongside your hips to add buoyancy and to fend submerged rocks. Keep your feet up to avoid getting them bruised or caught by rocks.

In deep rapids, go on your belly, head first; angle toward shore whenever you can. Breathe between wave troughs. Be careful of backwater eddies and converging currents as they often contain dangerous swirls. Avoid bubbly water under falls; it has little buoyancy. If you are going to ford a swift, treacherous stream, remove your pants and underpants so that the water will have less grip on your legs. Keep your shoes on to protect your feet and ankles from rocks and to give you firmer footing.

Tie your pants and important articles securely to the top of your pack. This way, if you have to release your pack, all your articles will be together. It is easier to find one large pack than to find several small items.

Carry your pack well up on your shoulders so you can release it quickly if you are swept off your feet. Not being able to get a pack off quickly enough can drag even the strongest of swimmers under.

Find a strong pole about 5 inches in diameter and 7 to 8 feet long to help you ford the stream. Grasp the pole and plant it firmly on your upstream side to break the current. Plant your feet firmly with each step, and move the pole forward a little downstream from its previous position, but still upstream from you. With your next step, place your foot below the pole. Keep the pole well slanted so that the force of the current keeps the pole against your shoulder.

If there are other people with you, cross the stream together. Make sure that everyone has prepared their pack and clothing as above. Have the heaviest person get on the downstream of the pole and the lightest person on the upstream end. This way, the upstream person will break the current, and the persons below can move with comparative ease in the eddy formed by the upstream person. If the upstream person is temporarily swept off his feet, the other persons can hold steady while he regains footing.

As in all fording, cross the stream so that you will cross the downstream current at a 45 degree angle. Currents too strong for one person to stand against can usually be crossed safely in this manner.

Do not be concerned about the weight of your pack as the weight will help rather than hinder you in fording the stream. Just make sure you can release the pack quickly if necessary.

SURVIVING IN COLD WATER

Spring and fall are traditional times for trout fishing and waterfowl hunting . . . and this means greater chances of accidentally finding ourselves in cold water. If you are suddenly the victim of a capsizing, you can survive a cold-water dunking if you follow a few survival rules.

First, don't panic. Clothing will trap body heat, so don't remove your clothes. If you are wearing a life jacket, restrict your body movements and draw your knees up to your body, a position that will reduce heat loss.

Don't try to swim or tread water. That will just pump out warm water between your body and cloth-

ing. Get into a protective posture and wait for a rescue. Here are body positions that will minimize heat loss and increase your chances for survival.

Group Huddle. Two or more persons in cold water should huddle together to conserve body heat. A small group in this position can extend survival time 50 percent longer than swimming.

Solo Survival. H.E.L.P. (Heat Escape Lessening Posture) is the body position that will minimize heat loss if you are alone. If you are wearing waders, keep them on, and assume a sitting position. The trapped air in your waders will help keep you afloat. Cover head and neck if possible.

PATHFINDING THE EASY WAY

There is nothing difficult about using a compass and map. If you're a sportsman, you need them to reach hotspots and to get in and out of the woods safely. Basic orienteering is quite easy to learn.

You should start with a topographic map as it contains a wealth of information. Topo maps have a scale of 1:24,000, which means that one inch on the map equals 24,000 inches (or 2,000 feet) in the field. It may be easier to visualize the area covered by such a map if the scale is translated as 2⅝ inches equals 1 mile.

The topo maps shown in the illustrations have a scale of 1:24,000. They show four important features: 1) man-made structures, 2) water, 3) vegetation, 4) elevation. Though the maps here are reproduced in black and white, these four symbols have distinct colors.

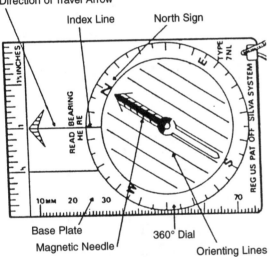

Parts of orienteering compass. Base plate and dial serve as protractor

Man-made features include roads, trails, and buildings. All are in black except some major highways, which may be in red. Water features are printed in blue, vegetation in green.

Elevation is represented by thin brown contour lines. A contour line is an imaginary line on the ground along which every point is at the same height above sea level. Follow a brown line on the map, and you'll find a number—for example, 100. Everything on that line is 100 feet above sea level. If the line next to it reads 200, then you have a rise

of 100 feet and a contour interval of 100 feet. (Generally, the contour interval is 20 feet.) This information is noted at the bottom of topographic maps.

Topo maps are easy to get; write to the U.S. Geological Survey, Map Distribution, Federal Center, Building 41, Box 25286, Denver, CO 80225, and request a Topographic Map Index of the state you're interested in, and a catalog of topographic maps. The index, free of charge, will describe how to select and order the right sections on quadrangles covering your area.

For topo maps of Canada or for a free index of those available, contact the Canada Map Company, 211 Yonge Street (Downstairs), Toronto, Canada M5B 1M4.

Now let's talk about compasses. A compass contains a magnetized steel needle that points toward magnetic north. The end of this needle will be black or red, stamped with the initial N, or shaped like an arrow.

The force that attracts this magnetized needle is the earth's magnetism. The earth is similar to a tremendous magnet, with one pole in the north, the other in the south. Compass needles always point toward magnetic north when at rest. The magnetic North Pole is about 1,400 miles south of the true North Pole.

That means you have two north directions to deal with—true north as it is shown on your map, and magnetic north as you find it with the compass. For the purposes of this article let's deal with magnetic north.

Most compasses fall into one of two categories: 1) conventional, which can be of watch-case, pin-on, or wrist-watch design, and 2) orienteering, which combines compass, protractor, and ruler. It has a magnetic needle, a revolving compass housing, and a transparent base plate (see accompanying sketches).

Carry two compasses in the field: a pin-on model for quick reference and an orienteering compass for cross-country traveling when map work is involved.

FINDING BEARINGS

To find a bearing with an orienteering compass, face the distant point toward which you want to know the direction. Hold the orienteering compass level before you, at waist height, with the direction-of-travel arrowhead pointing straight ahead.

Orient your compass by twisting the housing (without moving the base plate) until the needle lies over the orienting arrow on the inside bottom of the compass housing, with its north part pointing to the

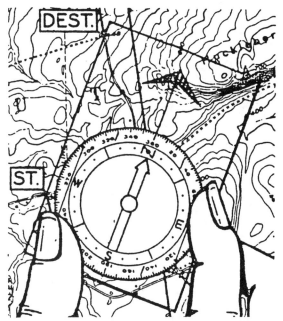

Step 1 in orienteering: on map line up compass with desired route from start (St.) to destination (Dest.)

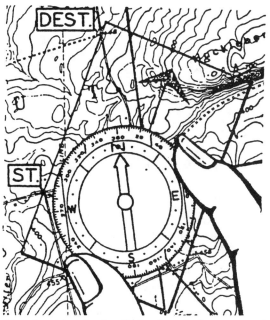

Step 2: set housing by aligning the orienting arrow and magnetic north. Hold base plate firmly against map

letter N on the top of the housing. What you've done is to make your compass show actual field directions.

Read the degrees of your desired direction—the bearing—on the outside rim of the compass housing at the spot where the direction line, as an index pointer, touches the housing. It's as easy as that with an orienteering compass.

FOLLOWING A BEARING

Suppose you're standing in a field and have decided to travel cross-country to a distant hilltop. Set your orienteering compass for the direction of the hilltop by holding your compass in your hand with the direction-of-travel arrowhead pointing to your destination. Twist the compass housing until the north part of the compass needle points to the letter N on the housing rim. Proceed in the direction in which the direction-of-travel arrowhead points.

If you lose sight of the distant hilltop, hold the compass in front of you, orient it, and sight a nearby landmark in the direction in which the arrowhead points. Walk to that point, then take a similar reading to another landmark—and so on until you reach the destination.

You can forget about degrees and figures when you use an orienteering compass. Your compass is set. Just orient it and proceed.

RETURNING TO ORIGINAL LOCATION

You have reached your destination and want to return home. How? Your orienteering compass is already set for your return journey.

When you went out, you held the compass with the direction-of-travel arrowhead at the front of the base plate pointing away from you toward your destination. The back of the base plate was in the opposite direction, pointing backward toward the spot from which you came. Make use of this fact.

Hold the compass level in your hand but with the direction-of-travel arrow pointing toward you instead of away from you. Orient the compass by turning your body (don't touch the compass housing) until the north end of the compass needle points to the N on the compass housing. Locate a landmark, and head for home. Your compass is set—simply use it backward.

Let's take a look at how to use a compass and map together. The difference or angle between magnetic north and true north is called declination, and it varies according to your geographic location. The degree of declination is indicated on topo maps. Fortunately, magnetic north is also indicated on topo maps, and you can use it to avoid the whole problem of declination and adjusting map bearings.

Instead of compensating for declination, simply

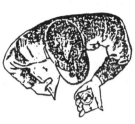

Step 3: in field, hold compass level. Turn yourself until needle points to N; follow direction-of-travel arrow

draw magnetic-north lines on your topo map. By using these lines instead of the true-north lines of the regular meridians, you make your map speak the same language as your compass. The settings you take on your compass using these lines do not require resetting to compensate for declination—the declination is already taken care of.

To provide your map with magnetic-north lines, draw a line up through the map on an angle to one of the meridian lines corresponding to the degrees of declination given on the map. Then draw other lines parallel to this line, one to two inches apart.

With your combined knowledge of map and compass, you can now travel from point to point: cabin to lake, camp to deer stand, and so on. It's done with three easy steps (see illustrations).

Step 1. On the map, line up your compass with your route. Place the orienteering compass on the map with one long edge of its base plate touching both your starting point and your destination, and with the base plate's direction-of-travel arrow pointing in the direction you want to go. Disregard the compass needle.

Step 2. On the compass, set the housing to the direction of your route. Hold the base plate firmly against

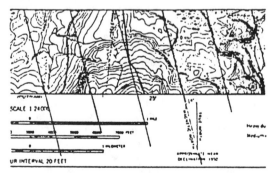

Make map speak compass language by drawing in magnetic-north lines. Lines coincide with degrees shown

the map. With your free hand, turn the compass housing until the orienting arrow on the bottom of the housing lies parallel to the nearest magnetic-north line drawn on your map, with arrow-point to the top. Disregard the compass needle. The compass is now set for the direction to your destination. By using the drawn-in magnetic-north line, you have compensated for any compass declination in the territory covered by your map.

Step 3. In the field, follow the direction set on the compass. Hold the compass in front of you, at waist height, with the direction-of-travel arrow pointing straight ahead. Turn yourself, while watching the compass needle, until the needle lies directly over the orienting arrow on the bottom of the compass housing, with the north end of the needle pointing to the letter N on the housing. The direction-of-travel arrow now points to your destination. Raise your head, pick a landmark, and walk to it. When you have reached it, again check the direction with your compass, on which you have been careful not to change the setting. Ahead is another landmark— and still another until you reach your destination. When it's time to return to your starting point, repeat Step 3, but keep the direction-of-travel arrow pointing toward you. Your compass is already set— simply use it backward to return home.

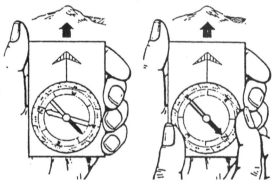

To find bearing, point direction-of-travel arrow to landmark, turn dial until needle is over orienting arrow. Read bearing at base of travel arrow

Applying what you've learned to hunting and fishing situations is not difficult. If you can follow a bearing, you can easily travel across strange country to a remote lake you've found on a topo map. You can hunt in any direction from camp and be confident about finding camp again. When it's time to head back, simply let your compass lead you safely back to camp. With a little practice, you'll be able to travel in the woods with complete confidence.

PART 7
BOATING

HULL DESIGN

The shape of a boat's hull is the biggest factor in how it will do its job for you. Hull design has always been the most intriguing subject among people who know boats and keep up with new developments, for changes in hull lines, skillfully conceived, have brought about some dramatic developments in how boats perform.

There are really just two types—displacement and planing hulls. But boat hulls in common use today are far from simple. In some, characteristics of the two types have been combined in order to get the best of both. Also, a variety of specific shapes have been designed to do certain things well that another shape cannot do. And there remain several traditional hull shapes that change little in the midst of a marine-design revolution, continuing to do a modest job well, and often at minimum cost.

Silverton Mainship 34 trawler exhibits a typically stable, seaworthy displacement hull.

DISPLACEMENT HULLS

Displacement hulls push through the water rather than on top of it, and therefore speed is limited. A round-bottomed, full-keeled displacement hull rides comfortably down in the water where wave and wind action have relatively little effect. The Indian canoe, the Viking ship, and the Great Banks fishing dory (a flat-bottomed boat) were all displacement-type hulls. They were narrow-beamed and pointed at both ends—for excellent reasons. They could be moved through the water more easily with only oars or sail for power; could be maneuvered in either direction; following seas had much less effect than on a flat stern; and a pointed trailing end dissipated suction created by the water displacement. Today we have squared-off sterns to provide useful space for motors and deck; but the displacement hull will probably be tapered back from a wide point amidships.

The seakindliness of a displacement hull is due principally to its low center of gravity. It rises with the swells, and a surface chop has little effect. A full-displacement hull with round quarters is less affected by beam seas (waves rolling in from one side or the other), while its full keel gives a good bite in the water, helping you to hold a course through winds and current. Because weight in a displacement hull is much less critical than in a planing hull, it can be sturdily, even heavily, built to take the worst punishment. Good examples of displacement hulls are those of trawlers, now popular in cruising.

Small displacement hulls are excellent for passing rocky river rapids and surviving the worst chop on a lake. In large boats, cabin space is lower in the water where it is more comfortable and secure-feel-

Tollycraft Cockpit Motor Yacht is a 43-footer with a semi-displacement hull and deep keel, designed for a soft, stable ride. Floorplan shows the interior features, furnishings, and storage facilities.

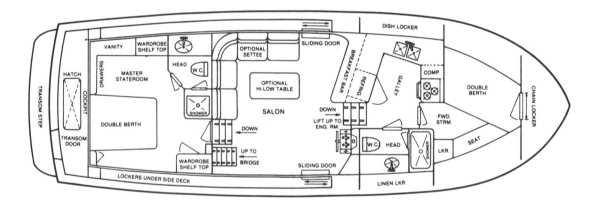

ing, especially on long cruises. On big water you might be annoyed at first by the constant roll; but the roll period is slower than the chop-chop surface banging of a planing hull on the same water, and never as sharp. What's more, the displacement hull will keep you dry in wave action that would soak you continually in a planing hull.

Just how limited is a displacement hull's speed? There is an actual formula. The square root of the waterline length times 1.5 equals possible speed. An 11-foot lake fishing boat might measure 9 feet at the waterline, for instance: the square root of 9 is 3; multiplied by 1.5, you get 4.5. That boat's probable maximum speed is 4½ mph. Load it deeper so the waterline is extended and you increase the possible top speed slightly. But there's no point in loading it down with a husky outboard, for you won't increase the speed significantly above the formula figure.

How narrow? Designers work on ratios of from

ROWING A BOAT

The correct way to row a boat is to use the arms and body together. Never sit straight upright and try to row with just your arms. Use your shoulders and the strength of your trunk. Long strong strokes with oars are more efficient and less tiring than short strokes. With a little practice, you will be able to maintain a course by pulling a little harder on one oar than on the other. You can pivot or turn a boat by pulling on one oar and pushing on the other. A pull on the right oar and a push on the left oar will turn the bow clockwise. Reverse the strokes to turn the bow counter-clockwise. You can slow down and stop a boat by dropping both oar blades in the water and holding them stationary. When rowing with outboard power, tilt the engine up and keep the weight forward to reduce transom drag.

1. WITH ONE PERSON on board, rowing should be from as close to amidships as possible to maintain straight tracking and a steady course in wind and currents.

2. IF YOU PREFER to see where you are heading, face forward and use a push stroke with your oars. Many river guides prefer this position.

3. WHEN FISHING with another person, the oarsman should move to a forward position to balance his angler in the stern. A good rowboat will always have two sets of oarlocks.

3½:1 up to 5:1, length to width. To some, this describes a "tippy" boat, tender when you step in or lean over.

While a small displacement hull such as a canoe or Maine guideboat can dump you of a sudden, then skitter away high and dry on top of the water while you try to grab it, a bigger displacement hull, say from 18 feet up, is as safe even for novices as anything in the water. And since speed is inherently limited, a small motor is in order. This makes for a safe, economical way to cruise or to fish all day in a limited distance. You just move along at a modest, steady rate, dry and comfortable in big water, though not so comfortable in a small displacement-type boat on calm water, where tippiness is tiresome. You conserve your resources and enjoy the boat's natural action, and the boat is always under control. That's the portrait of boating with a displacement hull.

Modified displacement hulls and semi-planing hulls are made so that the after-third or more of the bottom is flattened. A flat bottom toward the stern rides higher as speed is applied, instead of digging in and pushing the bow up, as will happen in a full-displacement hull. The flat section aft also reduces the tendency to roll. These boats have wider transoms, and can use bigger motors and run faster. You'll find modified round-bottomed hulls in small aluminum fishing boats as well as in deep-sea fishing boats, with a wide range of particular variations in design.

Round-Bottomed Cartoppers

Small aluminum fishing boats and fiberglass dinghies are often modified hulls that have round-bottom characteristics, yet they can move at high speed. You need a displacement hull for sitting on a choppy lake all day; nothing else will do. Using a motor of up to 25 hp, put the boat in the water and give it full speed. If the bow goes up and the stern digs in until you are depressed in a bowl the prop action makes in the water, reduce speed; it's a displacement hull, and your power is beyond the safe hull speed.

These boats have a rather full bow entry in relation to the beam, and there is a small keel. The middle and aft sections will be distinctly rounded, in contrast to the V-shaped cartop hull. If the sides taper toward the stern you will find it better for rowing.

CANOES AND KAYAKS

A camper or a fisherman who has never used a canoe to reach backwater havens is missing a rare wilderness experience. These silent boats can take you deep into remote areas that are hardly ever reached by most people.

Most canoes in the 16- to 17-foot range will work fine. Aluminum canoes are noisy, but they are also tough. Some space-age canoes of Kevlar and ABS plastic are so tough that they can take as much abuse as aluminum.

For most canoe camping and fishing, pick out a 17-footer. It will weigh about 60 to 70 pounds and hold nearly 800 pounds of gear and people. Don't plan on more than two people in a canoe this size.

If you're new to canoeing, pick a model with a keel, which will make it easier to paddle in a straight line for long distances. Whitewater models that have no keel (or a very shallow keel) are designed for fast maneuverability and not suitable for cruising. A good cruising canoe should have a beam of at least 36 inches and a center depth of 12 to 14 inches. The beam should be carried well into the bow and stern, so it can carry maximum gear and food.

Wood canoe paddles may look pretty, but you're better off with tough resilient fiberglass paddles. If you insist on wood, always carry a spare. For both bow and stern paddler, pick a paddle that reaches between your chin and eyes.

The kayak is a direct descendant of the sea-going kayaks of Eskimos of the Far North. The basic kayak is a slender closed-decked craft with a body-fitting cockpit and a waterproof skirt that seals the hatch around the paddler, who feels that he is "wearing the boat."

A two-bladed paddle propels the boat and a small rudder at stern assists in steering, making the kayak track straight, or holding the craft in position. The kayak is light, fast, and easy to handle in nearly all types of water.

Various models are designed for touring, whitewater, and sea kayaking. Whitewater kayaks are nearly always single cockpit crafts designed for high maneuverability and minimal effort in paddling upriver and downriver. Whitewater models are usually 13 to 15 feet long with beams of 23 inches or so. Skilled paddlers can run whitewater forward, backward, and even broadside in a kayak.

Touring kayaks, sometimes called expedition kayaks, are designed to carry one or two paddlers and range from 16 to 18 feet. Sea kayaks are bigger crafts with exceptional load capacities, as much as 900 pounds, and range from 18 to 22 feet in length with 30-inch beams. Some sea kayaks can accommodate three paddlers, and several manufacturers build collapsible kayaks for ease of storage for traveling kayakers.

CANOES AND KAYAKS

Mad River Synergy canoe is 15 feet long, 15 inches deep and weighs 50 pounds. A good choice for tandem paddlers, whitewater touring, and for solo paddlers who prefer bigger canoes.

Mad River Sunrunner canoe is 17 feet long and 12½ inches deep. Its hull design allows for enhanced cruising speed with minimal paddler effort, making it ideal for casual touring or extended adventures.

Northwest Kayaks' Seascape 2 is a 21-foot two-seater with a 30-inch beam. It weighs 95 pounds and has a load capacity of 850 pounds. A good choice for touring and family use. (Thomas Mishima Photography)

Wilderness Systems Alto, a 16-foot single kayak designed for paddlers looking for performance, responsiveness, and whitewater ability. Weighs 52 pounds.

INS AND OUTS OF CANOES

The cardinal rule for fishermen who use canoes: Don't Stand! Learn to cast, fight fish, and haul an anchor from a sitting position. Standing is one of the most common causes of people falling out of, or capsizing, canoes. Rule No. 2: Never swim away from your canoe if you get dumped. Most canoes have enough flotation to keep afloat until help arrives. Never be afraid of your canoe. I did some testing several years ago and I was amazed at how difficult it was to intentionally capsize or tip a canoe over from a sitting position. Getting in and out of a canoe, however, can be tricky unless you follow some basic procedures.

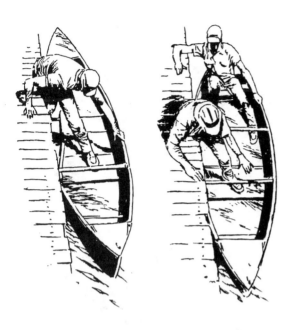

FROM THE DOCK When alone (left), hold dock with one hand and step into the canoe, make certain you step on the keel line so the canoe won't shift and slide away. With a friend (right), the stern paddler gets in first and steadies the canoe as bow paddler climbs aboard.

FROM THE SHORE Getting into a canoe from shore is a shaky deal unless someone steadies it. Launch canoe stern first, stern paddler gets into position while bow paddler steadies the craft (top). Stern paddler then steadies canoe (bottom) with paddle braced on the bottom and against gunwale. Bow paddler now steps aboard. Both push off.

This sequence (left to right) shows how to change positions safely. Bow man slides off seat and *sits* on bottom of the hull. Stern man, in a half crouch, holds both sides of canoe as he moves forward, over the bow man, and settles into the bow position. Bow man then moves to stern position in the same manner. Done smoothly, these moves will not rock the canoe.

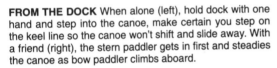

UNSWAMPING A CANOE

The most important rule in canoeing is, Don't Stand! Standing is the most common cause of people falling out of canoes, but the rule is often violated by sportsmen who are casting, fighting fish, or hauling an anchor. Equally important, if your canoe swamps, never leave it to try to swim toward shore.

Most modern canoes will keep you afloat, even when full of water. In fact, you can sometimes paddle a swamped canoe to shore with only your hands.

If another canoe swamps, here's how you can use your canoe as a rescue craft to get the swamped canoe back into service without having to beach it.

Step 1 The man overboard holds on to your canoe and steadies it as you roll the swamped canoe and simultaneously lift one end onto your gunnel.

Step 2 Work canoe across your gunnels so it's entirely out of the water, resting upside down across gunnels of your canoe. Allow water to drain out.

Step 3 Making certain the canoe is balanced across your gunnels, roll it over slowly. Swamping victim should still be in the water, steadying your canoe.

Step 4 Slide the empty canoe back into the water. Now it's ready to go. Steady the craft against your canoe, allowing the person in the water to pull himself aboard.

Punt, Pram, Johnboat

Anyone can build and care for a flat-bottomed boat. This is the least complicated and least costly hull shape, and the amateur can build a large craft on simple lines at low cost. Flat-bottomed hulls pound more than others, but while newcomers dislike their clumsy appearance and strictly functional design, serious boaters continue to choose them for hunting and fishing on quiet waters, for they make an excellent platform.

Punt, pram, and johnboat are often indistinguishable except in name. What might be called a pram down East and a punt on England's Thames could be called a johnboat in Missouri. These square-ended, flat-bottomed hulls are the most stable and best load carriers of all little boats. They are rather heavy handling, and are designed for use in quiet water, where their low sides and flat bottoms come into their own.

The true punt is made to be poled. Sides are straight, and both ends are identical, rising flat at about 45 degrees. The bottom slopes up slightly toward the ends. The pram has bowed sides, tapering forward, and the bottom rises toward the bow. The bow end rises at a rather shallow angle, and the stern end is broader. The pram is usually rowed or sailed, but may be powered with a small outboard or electric motor.

The johnboat, popular with outdoors enthusiasts, is made by a number of aluminum-boat manufacturers. The hull figure has nearly as many variations within the basic plan as the number of regions in which it has been built and used. For instance, in marshy country a coffin-shaped johnboat was built with stern wide enough only for one person; it tapered toward a slight flare forward, then in again toward a narrow bow. Sometimes the bow was decked over to cover parcels and goods. The bottom sloped up from the flare both fore and aft, easing the push through vegetation and making it easy to maneuver in open water. This version continues to be a useful fishing boat in marshland and bayous.

Modern aluminum johnboats range from 12 to 20 feet long. The bottom slopes up a bit forward from a low point directly in the midsection, and is rockered aft. Sides may be bowed somewhat forward and slope in toward the bottom. Three or four seats, with a wide bow seat, provide reinforcement in a broad-beamed hull that can carry a big load. Aluminum johnboats are rowed, poled, and powered.

Flat-Bottomed Skiff

Put a pointed bow on the flat-bottomed shape and you have a hull that gives sharper entry to oncoming waves and reduces the tendency to pound that is characteristic of the square-ended johnboat or pram. It also reduces stability, however.

For good rowing qualities a skiff is built with a relatively narrow stern; sides curve upward both fore and aft so that the tip of the bow and stern both clear the water slightly. The "active" bottom is the broad midsection. Such a boat is relatively easy to control and safe. For outboard power the stern is built wider and lower. Flat-bottomed skiffs 12 to 14 feet long are common in all parts of the country. In shorter lengths this hull is unstable, for the bow is too light.

The Dory

This hull is fun to handle and it's also a very competent one. You can take it through the surf or into fast, shallow rivers, for its two pointed ends and narrow bottom make it easy to row and control. Flaring, tall sides keep it dry inside, but this shape

DISPLACEMENT HULL DESIGNS

Alumacraft medium-sized johnboat with a rockered bottom forward and some flare in the midsection to keep it dry inside.

Little River Marine's Heritage Dory is a classic dory design reminiscent of the type of rowing craft that graced our waterways at the turn of the century.

is somewhat tender, especially in small sizes. For use with an outboard the design is modified by squaring off the stern. This presents a V-shaped transom—far from ideal for handling an outboard. Modern dory hulls have wider and lower sterns to improve handling with a motor. Mounting a small inboard engine amidships is the solution to powering the traditional double-end dory.

PLANING HULLS

They are built for speed. Given enough acceleration (called planing speed), the hull rises to the water's surface, levels off, and planes along the top. Design efficiency and possible power impose the only limits on its speed. The objective is to reduce wetted surface (friction) and the weight of the bow wave that a nonplaning hull pushes before it. To achieve this, a lightweight hull is important; but weight is related to power. A planing hull can have a wider beam; length-to-width ratios range from 2.5: to 3.5:1. Wider beam, especially in the aft sections, makes more space for the power plant. In relation to power carried, the hull is lightweight.

On plane, this hull is more nimble in handling, since a substantial part of it is airborne and steering action is quicker. The wider beam and hard chines (where bottom and sides meet) make for a more stable boat in calm water, though less so in a big roll.

But advantages in speed and handling bring penalties. A planing hull is more subject to wind and wave action—a surface chop can feel like a rock-strewn road at high speed. Big ocean waves can put you under; it's the tendency of an unmodified planing hull to cut through waves, rather than to rise with them. The lack of a useful keel on some planing hulls makes it hard to hold a course in heavy going. Aggravating these effects is the tendency of the bow to lift as more power is applied; the "active" hull on plane is aft, where the greatest weight is located in the broad beam and power plant. To overcome this, the designer may locate tanks in the bows, if there is space there. Power trim may adjust the planing angle to level. Or trim tabs may be added at the stern. These are metal wedges, preferably with an adjustable feature, that help to thrust the stern up and bow down at planing speed. When a planing boat holds a horizontal angle at plane, it is easier to steer, gives a drier ride, and rides better.

But it goes without saying that much boating is on quiet water, where the planing hull has few if any serious problems. In any case, not many planing hulls now made are the pure type—flat bottoms or simple Vs. We have adapted planing advantages to practical conditions, and come up with combinations

that are safe, fast, comfortable, and still easy to handle.

Cabin Dory

This is one flat-bottomed boat that is still being made in sizes of 20 feet or more. The explanation is that the dory hull's sloping sides and narrow bottom give it some of the features of a deep-V hull in handling rough water. On the Gulf and the Northeast and Northwest coasts you will see cabin boats with dory hulls made locally which have high bows running back to a flat, low stern, which is also wider than the stern of a displacement dory hull. The wide, flat section of bottom aft makes this a planing hull. But even at low speed it draws less water than a V-shaped hull and can be run in rough surf and shoal water where no other boats of the size would be safe.

V-Bottomed Skiff

The first design aimed to combine planing ability with the kinder qualities of the displacement hull was the simple V bottom, with flat planes rising from the keel to hard chines. By now, V-bottomed skiffs under 20 feet have slightly rounded chines to improve turning and reduce the slap of beam waves; the bottom aft is flattened; and the bow is deeper, with a sharp forefoot section. This makes a hull that is comfortable for all-day use on big lakes and bays, and can still plane off for a fast trip there and back. The bow deck line often has a wide flare overhanging the fine pointed bow. As the bow cuts the waves, the flare casts the spray aside, keeping you dry in moderate waves.

V-Bottomed Cartopper

Most cartop boats are planing hulls; to be light enough to qualify as a boat you can lift to a rack on top of the car, construction must be light. A planing hull is the logical type. Cartoppers that plane are usually modified-V hulls, though they may look round-bottomed at a glance. The bow is sharp, molding to a flat aft bottom with rounded chines and broad stern. If the shape tapers back to a narrower stern for easy rowing, you pay for it in reduced planing ability when you light up the outboard.

Deep-V Bottom

From a performance standpoint—when big demands are put on a hull—the best combination of displacement and planing hull traits is in the deep V. Invented by designer Ray Hunt, the deep-V bottom extends from a slightly rounded forefoot all the way to the stern. The V shape at the stern works well with inboard/outdrive power, where the lower

PLANING HULL DESIGNS

Grumman aluminum V-bottomed skiff with a 54-inch beam. This 12-foot 4-inch boat is suitable for cartopping.

Hydra-Sport 3000 is a 29½-foot member of the Hydra-Sports center console fleet. The integral transom also houses a livewell and bait station.

Grady-White 300 Marlin is a 30-footer rated for 500 horse-power outboards. Rigged for fishing, the Marlin has a tackle station and an 80-quart livewell.

Stratos Pro-Tournament 285 XL is a 19-foot bass boat with an 89-inch beam. It's equipped with bow and stern casting seats and a bow mounted electric motor.

Viking 35-foot Sport Fisherman, a modified deep V, is a canyon runner in nearly any sea.

Bertram Convertible is a 46-foot sportsfisherman with a 15-foot beam and an 800 gallon fuel capacity. Built with two staterooms, this Bertram will cruise to 30 knots with its 8V92 Detroit Diesel engines.

unit provides rudder action. Twin I/O installations put the propellers on either side of the V point and partially protected by it.

In a well-designed deep-V hull, the rounded, deep forefoot and full keel enable it to perform well in big waters, rising with the seas and rounding off a chop even at high speed. But how does such a hull rise on plane? With the help of longitudinal strakes, or steps in the bottom. As power is poured on, the strakes help the hull step up onto plane, while the V shape and flared bows part the wave tops and keep you reasonably dry. World ocean-racing records have been broken again and again with deep-V hulls.

Fishermen who went to deep-V hulls as a solution to heavy going when running far offshore in the Great Lakes and on the coasts found, however, that the original hull was anything but a nurse at slow trolling speeds. We often heard complaints of wallowing when the hull was off plane. To overcome hard steering and the elemental effects of a displacement-hull commerical fishing boat, some designs have been slightly flattened astern, with sharper chines for steadiness at slow speed. Others have cut off the point of the V beyond the forefoot in an effect related to the dory hull. Twin I/Os help in handling at trolling speeds on big water.

The Flats Boat

There was a time, many years ago, when flats boats were made by a handful of local builders. The boats weren't big and the hulls weren't very user-friendly in rough water. Those early boats just didn't perform well north of the bonefish flats. A lot has happened since those early years, and constantly evolving flats boat designs have now migrated north and west of the Florida flats.

What is a flat's boat? Essentially, it's a boat designed for shallow-water fishing, usually for bonefish and tarpon. It also has low freeboard, which means the wind won't blow it around and the low profile won't spook fish. The flats boat has a wide beam, which makes it exceptionally stable for two standing fishermen. The casting decks are flat fore and aft. The decks are also uncluttered with gear stored out of sight in hatches. Boat cleats and hardware are minimal to avoid line snagging. A poling platform is usually mounted over the outboard engine.

Flats boats are also fast. Some 18-footers are rated for outboards up to 150 horsepower. Flats boat can run at speeds of 50 mph or more and maneuver like sport cars. Typical sizes range from 16 to 18 feet.

Take a close look at a flats boat and its special features, and you suddenly realize that it also makes a great bass boat. But a flats boat is perfectly de-

Hewes Tournament 16-footer is a typical flats boat designed to run in shallow water in search of tarpon and bonefish. The poling platform at the stern affords good visibility and quiet maneuverability.

signed for salt-water anglers stalking tidal flats, and rivers, and barrier islands for striped bass, bluefish, weakfish, bonefish, and tarpon.

The Sea Skiff

This boat is often described as round-bottomed, but in fact it is usually a combination of V-hull and displacement-hull design. Forward, a rounded bilge

This 28-footer is a typical Jersey sea skiff, showing a dramatically wide V bow and flare.

Ranger F24 Cherokee Pontoon is 24 feet long with a 102-inch beam. With a horsepower range of 60-115, the boat is good for a variety of watersports.

helps it rise with waves and pound less in a chop. The bottom, with rounded chines, slants to a shallow V to form a keel, and flattens aft. The Jersey sea skiff, a remarkably practical and able hull for fishing in bigger waters, will taper to a narrower stern than many planing hulls have. This raises the planing speed, but makes it a safer boat for getting home and running inlets when the following sea may present the most trouble. Sea skiffs are usually planked with lapstrake. The strakes help lift the hull to reach plane when power is applied, and reduce roll in big water. But this also increases the total wetted surface or drag on the hull. Wood lapstrake hulls have great pliability and shock resistance, which admirably suits fishing the coasts. Today, nearly all skiff designs of this type are custom built.

Multiple Hulls

You've heard them called tri-hulls, cathedral, trihedral, gullwing and more. The basic principle is the catamaran, adding stability to a hull by means of a secondary hull. In the catamaran, the secondary hull is called an outrigger. A trimaran has two outriggers—one on each side of the load-bearing hull.

This idea, applied to modern fiberglass and aluminum boat design, has just about taken over boat manufacture in the 15–30 foot class. First, it has brought unbelievable stability to the small boat, even in rough water. Second, it has made the entire deck usable; you can fight a big fish standing on the gunwales or bows of such a boat without rocking it dangerously. The deck area is actually increased up to 100 percent, since a much wider beam in the same length is possible, with a bowline topside that is more square than pointed. This makes a boat that is useful all over. For families and for fishermen and hunters who tend to concentrate on matters other than boat handling when the fun and action warms up, it has great value.

You can see why the multiple-hull design has brought about a revolution in small boats. Naturally the hulls are unified—built in a single structure,

MULTIPLE-HULL DESIGNS

Montauk 17, like other Boston Whaler models under 18 feet in length, utilizes a tri-hull design (which was pioneered by Whaler) to provide maximum stability and cargo capacity in a relatively small sport boat.

Grady-White's 26-foot Tigercat walkaround cabin catamaran was designed for big water sportsfishing enthusiasts. The twin-hull design affords stability and handles rough water exceptionally well.

while the Polynesian and East Indian catamaran and trimaran boats had hulls joined with wood poles bound at each hull. Between keel points are sculptured hollow spaces, where air is trapped when the boat is on plane, making a cushion against the chop and providing a lifting effect. In a tri-hull design the middle hull is deepest (often with a deep-V bow and forefoot line), and the side hulls are minor points interrupting the rise of the V toward the waterline, sometimes acting as deep chines.

This hull is slower to plane than the other V hulls, for the multiple points tend to push a bow wave ahead of the boat until planing speed is reached. Also, wetted area is greater, holding the hull off plane until considerable power pushes it up. It's also a heavy hull compared to others of the same length.

Obviously it takes more gas to operate. You have to reckon the greatly increased useful deck area and stability against these drawbacks.

A second revolution that has become as big as the multiple-hull takeover is the boom in bass boats with multiple-hull characteristics. These bass boats, made of fiberglass, aluminum, or Kevlar, are mostly 14- and 16-foot boats with two- or three-point molded hulls. The difference is that the beam is quite narrow, requiring less power and making them practical in weedy waters and in the brush-filled shorelines of reservoir lakes. The sledlike hull points of the bottom are only a few inches lower than the flat areas between. This hull is potentially very fast, but that's hardly the purpose in a bass boat.

BOAT CONSTRUCTION

The material of which a boat is made and the way that material is used in building a boat has a direct effect on its cost, strength, weight, buoyancy, and durability. Commercial builders have turned mostly to fiberglass and aluminum hulls because they are easier to mass-produce. And people are buying them because the man-made materials need less upkeep than wood. But there are still wood-boat builders in business today, and some of the woodworking techniques are worth noting.

WOOD

It's hard to appreciate the work and time needed to keep a wood boat in good shape until you have stripped a hull down to clean, bare board, repaired rot and loose fastenings, filled and sanded it all smooth, then fiberglassed, repainted, and refinished it inside and out.

Wood is a natural material. It feels good, absorbs sound, absorbs shock, and can be worked and repaired by anyone. An important advantage over fiberglass and aluminum is that wood is naturally buoyant. Wood burns, but it's less flammable—especially the hardwoods—than most think.

Generally, round-bottomed, wood displacement hulls are built on temporary molds with ribbands connecting to delineate the shape. Structural members are bent to the molds. Planking is lined up and secured by the structure. V-bottomed, planing hulls are generally built on sawn frames (sawn lumber firmly joined at angles where the contour changes).

Here, the frames make permanent molds to which the planks or plywood is attached.

But wood boats take their characteristics from the way the hull is covered as well as from the hull shape. Structural features, weight, strength, and to an extent water characteristics go hand in hand with the planking method. Some of the methods have been almost abandoned in favor of simpler and cheaper ones, but are described because valuable older hulls made with great skill are still available.

Plywood

The advantages of building with marine-grade plywood are economy, simplicity, and availability of the material. Most amateur boat builders, especially those who build from kit plans, use plywood. There are fewer fastenings, and the tricky work of fitting plank lines into a pleasing boat shape is largely avoided. Of course, plywood serves best in boats with rather simple design, since it won't take compound bends. The dory, with flat bottom and flat-curved sides, is a good example. In bigger boats plywood is used with hard chines and flat bottoms for flat-V designs.

One big-boat builder starts with a frame of white oak ribs, over which sheets of plywood are laid from sheer to sheer as a tough and tight inner hull. Over the inner hull another of solid mahogany planks is built in carvel fashion.

Don't be alarmed when you see fist-size patches in marine plywood: voids in the core have been filled. When used in exterior hull covering, the

Left: Construction of a wood offshore boat shows mahogany planking being fastened to steam-bent frames with silicon bronze screws. Stem (big bow timber at right), knee, and keel are solid oak. Planing hulls, with flat bottom section toward stern, are often built inverted, later righted for inside construction and fittings. **Right:** Sawn frames are used in construction of modified-V hull of 26-foot Mackenzie Cuttyhunk bass boat. All timbers are seasoned white oak.

seams, which expose the laminations, must be thoroughly treated and sealed, and the surface fiberglassed to protect the end-grain exposed in all plywood. Repair is simpler than in any other wood boat. Maintenance is relatively easy, but must be regular. Delamination of the wood plies can result from spray collecting in the bilges as well as from outside the hull, so many plywood boats are fiberglassed both inside and out.

Plywood is also used in sawn strips for other planking methods.

Carvel

This is a tighter and stronger form of carvel planking, originated thousands of years ago. Planks are laid edge to edge to form a smooth hull. Simple carvel planking is fastened only to ribs or frames, which must be closely spaced and therefore make a boat heavier. Calking is put between planks, the exterior edges of which are grooved slightly to hold the calk. In water, planks swell into the calk for tightness; out of water (and this goes for planks above the waterline) drying tends to open seams. A simple carvel-built boat is not a very dry one, and requires seasonal work to keep shipshape.

Batten-Seam

This is a tighter and stronger form of carvel planking. Staunch battens are notched into the frames, and planks are laid so that seams fall at the centers of battens. This closes the seams from be-

hind, and planks are shaped so that seams are tight when laid, without calking on the exterior. Pliable batten compound is spread on battens and plank edges, and planks are screwed along the edges through the battens into frames.

Lapstrake

A favorite method for building boats that are very light and strong, its other names are clinker-built or clinch, referring to clinched nails traditionally used in fastening. Planks are overlapped, resembling clapboard on a house. The effect looks "boaty." Relatively thin, wider planks can be used, and are fastened to each other along the overlap and also through frames where they occur. Frames can be wider spaced than in most other construction. Seam compound is applied to the overlap before fastening.

Lapstrake building is an expert's job; planking must be painstakingly lined up with the boat's shape, without stealers (which are cut to fit awkward places in carvel construction, where their use in the flat skin does not destroy appearance). Repairing damage to lapstrake is also an expert's job.

Strip Planking

This is a popular and successful way for amateurs to build wood boats, but it requires too many fastenings to be the choice of professional builders. Narrow strips (about 1¼ inch for a 20-foot boat) are used in planking. Another variation of carvel, it combines light weight with great strength, long life, and minimum maintenance compared to ordinary carvel planking. The narrow planks will not often warp or lift, which happens even with professionally built carvel boats when planking that is too wide and thin has been used.

Tight, strong seams are achieved by shaping the edges, one side concave, the other convex. Edges are covered with marine glue as a plank is laid, the plank is clamped tight in place and edge-nailed through the width of two planks and into a third. Only each third or fourth plank is fastened through frames. Fewer and lighter frames reduce weight and save interior space, as in lapstrake planking. All the fastenings in strip planking make it hard to repair; the job should be turned over to a skilled worker.

Diagonal Planking

Strong, true, and trim boats are produced this way. An amateur can handle it successfully in its simpler forms. For instance, a single layer of ¼-inch diagonal strips can be applied to plywood

transverse frames for very small and light boats, such as a shallow duckboat. Strips are laid at 45 degrees to the centerline, glued and fastened to each frame at the crossing point. The edge of each strip is glued before the next is laid, and clamped in place for fastening to frames. In this lightweight construction, fiberglassing the hull both inside and out is imperative for watertightness and strength.

In larger and heavier boats, planks are laid tight in two layers and overlapped. This is an easy way for an amateur to build a dinghy-shaped boat. The keel, sheer, and longitudinal frames make the bones in this construction without transverse framing, except in offshore boats. Double-planking compound, available in marine stores, is laid between layers of planks. An unusually strong, lightweight hull results.

Professionals build double-diagonal hulls. One method is to plank in two layers laid at opposite 45-degree angles. Another is to lay the first layer at the angle, the second straight fore and aft as in strip planking. The first layer is fiberglassed; and you will

KINDS OF PLANKING

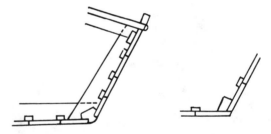

Batten-seam construction: Battens are notched into frames and seal planking seams from inside. At **left,** construction for bigger boats. **Right:** Simpler work often seen in home-made rowboats.

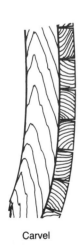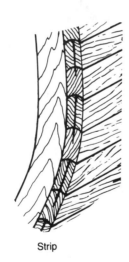

Carvel   Strip

Left: Carvel planking is grooved for caulking, which is driven between planks. In larger boats, screw holes may be counterbored and wood-plugged, keeping the smooth carvel look and keeping the fasteners tightly seated, as well. **Right:** In strip planking, tight, strong seams have concave-convex edges. Edges are glued as the planks are clamped in place. Then the planks are edge-nailed. The frames are fastened from the inside.

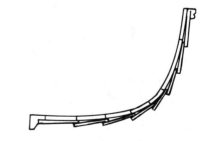

Lapstrake (clinker) planking may be as simple or detailed as you bargain for. Strakes are fitted from the garboard at the keel upward.

find older boats whose first layer has been covered with construction canvas and glued before laying the second layer of planking.

About Wood

Whether you are buying or building a wood boat, characteristics of different woods should be compared to qualities you need in a boat. Things to consider are decay resistance, impact and flex strength, dry weight, and suitability to various parts of the boat and to various sizes of boat. Before buying, read about wood and wood-boat construction in detail. Talk to those who really know about marine woods and construction, such as a local boat builder and a lumber dealer who specializes in boat lumber. To build a wood boat, regardless of size, always start with a set of plans that have been used in building a number of successful boats.

ALUMINUM

Light weight, low cost, and low maintenance make aluminum a popular and useful material, especially in small boats such as cartoppers. Another important quality often overlooked: it won't burn. These boats

Building a Starcraft stern drive on production line includes welding as well as riveting of some seams. The worker here uses a pneumatic riveter on the exterior while his partner backs it inside. The rocker device for turning hull to working angles is required. Aluminum hulls are lightweight, low cost, and easy to repair.

can be noisy, and poorly made aluminum hulls will "pong" as panels flex under pressure and temperature change. Some makers use sound-deadening rubber-based paints, asbestos, and other coatings on the inside. In larger hulls, a layer of flotation is sandwiched between two aluminum skins, providing safety and quiet, too. It may surprise you, but an unpainted and uninsulated aluminum boat is not hot, but cool: sun rays are radiated through the metal into the water.

Aluminum boat building came of age with development of the 5000 and 6000 series of marine aluminum, which contain no copper. The 5000 series is alloyed with magnesium and manganese, the 6000 series with magnesium and silicon. Corrosion is not a problem, even in salt water, if the boat is built with marine aluminum. A reputable maker will declare this in a label on the boat.

Electrolysis presents a real danger to aluminum hulls in salt water, however. Copper, steel, nickel, or chromium, for instance, will cause electrolytic decay in aluminum in the presence of an electrical current in salt water. Motor ignitions and electronic gear and lighting systems must be properly grounded by a qualified technician to avoid this danger. For this reason, aluminum boats sell better in freshwater areas.

Aluminum hulls may be welded or riveted, and frequently both fastening methods are used. Stretch-forming presses make almost any hull form possible. Smooth, structurally sound extrusions provide strength needed in keels, stringers and ribbing, transom and gunwales. You will dent an aluminum hull oftener than crack and rip it open, but even at the worst, it is surprisingly easy to repair. If you don't like the look of aluminum you can paint it, but then you have a surface that has to be maintained beyond anti-fouling.

FIBERGLASS

Seamless, impervious to marine parasites, rot, or electrolysis, fiberglass is popular because it needs little maintenance or caution in use in either fresh or salt water. Lamintated fiberglass has great strength and versatility. Because it can be molded in any shape, it has aided development of hull shapes that are more useful and popular, such as the cathedral hulls. If made with a good gel coat, the slick surface is faster in the water.

You should realize that fiberglass itself is heavier than water and will sink like a stone unless flotation is built in or added to the construction. Also, fiberglass will burn—or rather, it will smoke and smolder to destruction unless precautions are taken. Interest is increasing in the use of fire-retardant resins such as Hetron, which has been successfully in lifeboats of the Canadian Navy and Department of Transportation, and by Uniflite, a large U.S. boat builder.

A well-made fiberglass boat will be totally free of leaks, but it's a common misconception that fiberglass *can't* leak and that therefore any fiberglass boat will be securely dry. In careless production, pinhole leaks will occur because resin has been unevenly applied to the glass cloth and mat, resulting in dry patches in the glass where water can enter. These places are also weak.

Fiberglass boats are production boats now, of necessity; the cost and complexity of molds, skills, and technology have made custom- or amateur-built boats rather rare. Building methods are by contact or hand layup, matched-metal die molding, and spray-up.

Contact or Hand Layup

Quality construction of larger and more valuable boats is by this method. A male mold is carefully made of wood, the details complete. On this, a female mold is formed of plastic materials. Laminations are laid, outside in. First, the gel coat: This is the outside surface of the boat and is an epoxy or polyester resin in which desired color is mixed, but without fiberglass body. Next comes a layer of fiberglass mat made of random fibers woven together, very porous but a suitable base for the finish just laid. Into this is laid polyester resin with a mohair or nylon roller, binding the fibers and creating a bond to the gel coat. Depending on required strength and weight of the hull, additional layers of fiberglass cloth, woven rovings (cord-twisted fiberglass for strength) are laid, and the reverse order—cloth, mat, and inside gel coat. All layers are rolled or painted with resin to bond them together and to the next layer. The exact composition and number of laminations may be varied to suit design requirements. When layup is complete, the laminate is cured at atmospheric temperature. When the resin hardens, it permanently bonds the fiberglass in a tough sheet.

The roller or brush work with resin is most important. Too much laid on will result in weakness in any lamination because a bulk of resin will be unstructured—without fiberglass. Too little anywhere will result in a dry patch that may become porous, delaminate and leak, as noted above.

Foam planks, balsa wood, or plywood can be laid at the core to add strength and built-in flotation, and these cores also help to reduce noise and vibration. In bigger boats, the core is laid with resin I-beams joining laminations on either side at intervals to give structure to this sandwich construction. Some builders avoid any wood in the construction to dispel fear of rot and parasites. Others swear by the shock resistance and flex of wood in the core.

The big advantage of contact or "hand" layup is that the whole hull or deck is visible at one time. Defects such as air bubbles or dry patches can be seen and remedied before proceeding. Sometimes a hull mold is made in halves to aid this; a large wheel is often built into the mold platform to roll the lamination into accessible positions as it proceeds.

Extra layers of lamination needed at chines, keel, stem, and transom are applied according to design needs. Stringers and stiffening of fiberglass or plywood may be bonded in place as the schedule proceeds, and bulkheads and motor mounts in larger craft laid after the glass hull is complete. Even hardware may be fastened and bedded in during glassing.

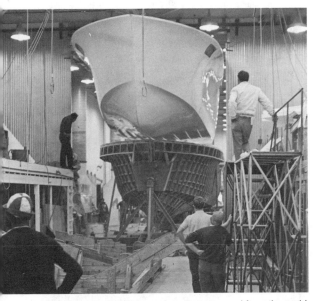

The hull of a fiberglass cruiser, just removed from the mold, was made by hand layup of laminations. Its fine gel coat glistens in the light and will help the boat slip through the water. Complex shapes that are possible in fiberglass molding are apparent in this photo.

Matched-Die Molding

This method is used in large-volume production of fiberglass hulls under 20 feet. A fiberglass preform is made on a shaped vacuum screen placed over a metal male mold. The female mold is pressed onto it, heat applied, and the hull (including any core and ribs) is quickly fused into a unit. Voids and flaws cannot be seen during fabrication, but techniques of reputable builders are advanced and there are few rejects.

In some production lines, fiberglass fibers and catalyzed resin are shot with a chopper gun into a female mold and cured at atmosphere.

Other Plastics

Boat building with other plastics and other methods is developing. One new process for molding polyethylene increases rigidity without increasing weight, and also provides inherent flotation. The solid skin and cellular core are molecularly one piece (no laminations) formed in low-pressure injection molding. A number of different plastics can be used in this method.

FERRO-CEMENT

Back in the 1970s, this method of boat building stimulated considerable interest in the industry. But it was never developed and little, if any, activity in ferro-cement boats exists today. Let's take a look at these cement boats.

Why build a boat of cement? Costs ran from half to three-quarters of other materials. And ferro-cement boats seem to last forever. They are practically maintenance-free, without seams and impervious to rot and insects, and of course are fireproof. Resistance to shock and abrasion is said to be excellent. Penetration of a ferro-cement hull by severe impact is practically unknown. Collision and grounding may cause local damage with limited cracks. Leakage is easy to control, and repair is made by hammering out a bulge and sealing cracks with epoxy or patching cement.

It sounds heavy? Not necessarily so: Ferro-cement, wood, fiberglass, and steel boats of 35 to 45 feet all weigh about the same. Above 45 feet, ferro-cement boats are usually lighter; below 35 feet, they're usually heavier than boats of other materials. Under 20 feet, using conventional methods, the weight per foot is prohibitive.

A ferro-cement boat can be built of any shape that steel reinforcing can be formed to. Vertical frames of steel pipe or bar are shaped on plans or plywood forms, then stringers are welded to space and hold the frames rigidly, and vertical bars of smaller size added. Six to eight layers of chicken wire, half on each side of the rod structure, are stapled on to hold firmly when loaded with mortar. Galvanized chicken wire is used conventionally, but good results with square welded mesh have recently been reported. Two layers are used on each side, with stringers of only a quarter inch. This reduces structural bulk, and the finished hull thickness does not exceed half an inch and weighs only 8 or 9 pounds per square foot. Using this method, boats of less than 20 feet may be entirely practical in ferro-cement.

Type I portland cement, the common building material, is suitable for use in fresh water. In salt water, Type II is needed to withstand sulphate action.

Air-entrained mortar produces the best results. This is mortar made with countless tiny air bubbles from a chemical agent in the mix. It flows on smoother, and when hardened is a safety factor in freezing temperatures. Only sand—no gravel—is used in the mix.

Plastering the hull requires two workers. One on the inside pushes the mortar through the structure while one on the outside smoothes the surface. The quality of the work depends on leaving no voids while filling the mesh, and working rapidly without dry joints (wet on dry concrete). A cement hull can be epoxied to reduce surface drag.

Bulkheads and cabin are usually ferro-cement as well. The reinforcement for these structures may be welded into the hull structure, or brackets which have been welded to the hull structure can be bolted to brackets welded to the inserted structures, which in that case are made separately. Engine mounts may be laid on plates welded into the hull structure. Stress-bearing hardware should be welded to the structure before cementing.

Most of the boats made with ferro-cement in the U.S. were sailboats. Before the technique could be applied to power boats, however, the ferro-cement concept faded out.

FABRIC

Wood-Canvas

Making a wood-canvas canoe is started by shaping white cedar ribs around a canoe form. Red cedar planking is clinch-nailed to these, then mahogany gunwales are attached. Seamless canvas, Dacron, or a reinforced plastic is used for the outside skin. Seats are framed with ash; seat-bottoms are cane. Thwarts are separate, not embodied in the seats. A small keel may extend the entire bottom length for directional stability, or may be omitted on white-water canoes. Coats of waterproof varnish are laid on exposed wood surfaces, and the entire exterior is brushed with a high-gloss enamel to reduce water friction. Such a canvas canoe will stand many years of hard use.

Duckboats, kayaks, and portable canvas-covered rowboats are made by similar methods.

Inflatables

Serviceable inflatables are made by laminating nylon on both sides with neoprene or Hypalon, which toughen the fabric, resist aging, and withstand petroleum and sun, as well as abrasion. Thick patches reinforce wear and chafing points. The neoprene-nylon ply is tremendously strong for its weight, and a boat made of it can take collision and grounding on rocks better than any other hull.

The secret to the serviceability of a quality inflatable is its low air pressure—only 2 or 3 pounds. It inflates quickly, but leaks, if any, are slow—usually very small breaks that are easy to repair. A good inflatable is made with at least three buoyancy chambers, any of which will keep the boat afloat.

In the bigger sizes, over 20 feet, these inflatables are extremely tough and rigid. Some models, rigged with twin outboard motors, are used for rescue work by the Coast Guard in coastal offshore waters.

Serviceability, almost no maintenace, and portability are the reasons for the popularity of most of these inflatables.

Quicksilver Sport Model QS 330 is a rigid hull inflatable boat rated for up to 15 horsepower outboards.

MARINE MOTORS

Naturally your choice of power should be matched to the boat you select. Don't feel limited, however, to what you see already mounted. The great variety of motor designs and horsepower ratings available, and the versatility of these motors, give you options that boaters have never had before. You can customize your boat-motor rig precisely to your own preferences—if you inform yourself before you buy.

An offshore fishing boat, for instance, doesn't have to be powered by a 4-cycle inboard engine, though it's traditional. It's common now to see unusually seaworthy deep-V hulls in the 25-foot range heading offshore with either twin outboard engines or a single huge outboard up to 275 horsepower with a dependable V-6 or V-8 engine.

Similarly, a 14-foot bass boat doesn't necessarily "take" a 10-hp trolling motor; depending on the boat's power rating, you can mount a huskier outboard for covering distance *plus* a small gas or electric troller—or you can do with the troller and a pair of oars. And for that matter, you don't have to paddle your own canoe; a 2-hp gas or electric motor will do it for you handsomely.

The motor to buy is the one that you particularly want and that is safe and sensible for your use. Power your boat adequately, but take care not to overpower it. Check the BIA plate and the maker's specs for recommended and maximum power rating for that boat.

OUTBOARD

The outboard is a self-contained power unit that, happily, does not require through-hull fittings. It is lightweight in relation to horsepower produced and it can be installed or removed quickly and inexpensively.

Mounted outside the boat, its fuel and vapor can be kept safely out of bilges and cabin; deck space is clear of engine or hatches. You have positive steering with outboard power—the whole motor turns, and the propeller thrust is in the direction that will help turn the boat, instead of at an angle to a rudder. The outboard tilts up for shallow running, beaching, or trailering. There are no underhull fittings that have to be protected at all costs.

A large outboard presents something of an obstacle to fishing lines; and the propeller, out from the hull, can be a hazard to divers and skiers. Mounted on the transom, the outboard is an unbalanced weight that is trimmed by adjusting the position of its thrust relative to the plane on which the boat is moving—but it *can* be trimmed, whereas an inboard-powered boat must have its load trimmed instead.

Trim is easy to understand if boaters remember that at normal running speeds the outboard propeller shaft should be parallel to the surface. Some boats, however, obtain optimum planing attitude with the

OUTBOARD MOTORS

Left: Yamaha Saltwater Series range from 115-250 horsepower. Has an oxygen-density sensor that monitors combustion and adjusts the fuel/air ratio for fuel efficiency and reduced emissions. **Center:** Suzuki 40 HP features a power tilt and trim switch in the throttle control which allows boaters to adjust trim. Push-button tilt operation makes storage and trailering easy. A 2-cylinder model with a 6.6 gallon fuel tank. **Right:** Yamaha 50 hp four-stroke outboard's large 4-cylinder displacement and accelerator pump design give it quick acceleration and a smooth ride while trolling.

Left: Mariner 9.9 HP Four Stroke has a drain funnel for draining crankcase oil from engine. Tiller handle models feature shift-in-handle for ease of operation. **Center:** Twin Johnson 225 horsepower Oceanrunners power this 33-foot ocean fishing machine. Outboard engines have a freshwater flushing port that allows you to flush out harmful saltwater with an ordinary garden hose without running the engine. **Right:** Mercury 90-hp 3-cylinder motor is a quiet, powerful outboard with oil injection, a battery-charging alternator, a 6-gallon fuel tank and electric starter. It's popular for fishing and is also a good engine for water-skiers since it holds well on high-speed turns.

This Mako 262 full transom model is rigged with twin Yamaha Saltwater Series 150 hp outboards. Yamaha Saltwater Series outboards are available with counter-rotation. The two propellers turn in opposite directions to prevent steering torque and listing. This helps keep an even keel and true course. It also allows the boat to turn in its own length when one motor is put in forward and one in reverse.

HOW OUTBOARD TRIM AFFECTS PLANING

Bow too low
Trim outboard out

Bow too high
Trim outboard in

Boat and outboard
properly trimmed

Porpoising

(boat bottom 3° to water)

Trim is easy to understand if you remember that at normal running speeds the outboard propeller shaft should be parallel to the surface. Some boats, however, obtain optimum planing attitude with the motor trimmed out slightly past this point. When trimmed out too far the boat will not operate efficiently. Courtesy Mercury Outboards

motor trimmed out slightly past this point. When trimmed out too far the boat will not operate efficiently. The bow may plane too high or too low.

Boaters should have their outboards "tucked" under (trimmed in) when starting. This forces the bow down and the stern up, and the boat pops up on plane much quicker.

As the engine is trimmed out the bow rises and more of the boat clears the surface. With reduced drag (less friction between boat and water), the boat gains speed. Once on plane at wide-open throttle, the outboard should be running in the middle of the recommended RPM range.

On bigger outboards, the power trim control button is on the end of the throttle control. With one finger, the boater can trim the engine for best performance. The operator can easily adjust the engine for optimum boat attitude as boat load or water conditions change. Power trim improves acceleration and helps get a boat on plane quicker. It also means top-end speed advantages.

Outboard manufacturers now produce engines up to 250 horsepower. Surprisingly enough, these big outboards with V-6 engines are more fuel-efficient per horsepower than smaller motors. A 250-hp outboard, for example, burns less gas at cruising speed than twin 150s. Some manufacturers also produce special outboard engines for saltwater use. Yamaha, for example, builds a saltwater series with outboards ranging from 115 to 250 horsepower.

ELECTRICS

The small, silent electric trolling motor purred along unnoticed by all but the most devoted fishermen and hunters until a few years ago, when it took off. Why? Better designs have made electric trollers more versatile; there are more models to match boats that people buy; and the new permanent-magnet motors are more efficient—that is, they run longer on a battery charge. These motors are also slimmer and they pass through water and weeds with less resistance.

Because models and characteristics are changing rapidly, partly due to the newfound popularity, we'll go into some detail about how they work and what features are important. All electrics are easy to start

This bass boat has a bow-mounted electric outboard with foot control that allows a fisherman to work a shoreline quietly and effectively without disturbing fish.

ELECTRIC MOTORS

Mercury Thruster T2000 is a transom model that delivers 20 pounds of thrust. Has two speed settings, 30-inch shaft and weighs 12 pounds. Ideal for anglers who rent small boats or who fish waters where gas outboards are prohibited. (Move to electric file)

MotorGuide's Voice-Activated Control gives you verbal command of its trolling motors. Just speak into the microphone clipped to your shirt, and the motor responds to your directions, such as, "off," "on," "left," "right," "stop," "forward," and so on.

MotorGuide's Lazer Series electric motors range from 41-55 pounds of thrust and are typically bow mounted.

and operate. Endearing traits include low cost, light weight (the least is 6 pounds—plus storage battery), and near-silent running. Electric is the ideal power for quiet waters, where silence and small movement are important to the careful fisherman and hunter.

Nearly all electric motors are rated in pounds of thrust ranging from 8 pounds to 72 pounds.

The penalty? Slow speed (about 3½ mph with a canoe and one man and gear, 2½ mph with a cartopper); and the storage battery, which gives you about four hours continuous trolling time on one charge.

But it's unlikely that you'll ever run an electric continuously for that long. In the careful sport it suits, your electric will be turned off frequently, and with experience you'll learn how to conserve a battery charge. If you are casting or staked out with

decoys, it's not hard to get a full day's sport from one battery with full charge. Trolling is another matter; then a second battery and your own battery charger are good investments.

How much current a motor draws, of course, determines how many hours of running time you can get on a battery charge. Several things affect this. The permanent-magnet motor, and quality manufacture of switches and windings, are definite advantages. Speed is a big factor in current draw—electrics are most efficient at low speed settings. If your motor draws six amps to move your boat at 1½ mph, it might draw 16 to 18 amps to go 2½ mph. Also, some motors are designed with a higher speed range than others and will take more from your battery throughout the range.

Most models house the motor in a pod underwater, connected to the propeller by direct drive. A sturdy control shaft from 20 to 50 inches long mounts to the boat's gunwale, transom or bow, and controls are located at the top. This motor position eliminates transmission gears, gives quieter operation, and leaves only the control head at the top to get in the way of action. Waterproof shaft seals and tough motor housings take care of the once-important problem of a wet motor resulting from hitting rocks and logs.

For regular use in water that is filled with weeds and obstructions, some boaters prefer electrics that have the motor on top of the shaft, with the tiller and controls attached to the motor housing. A flexible-cable drive permits a curved shaft that tends to shed weeds and slip over obstacles, with only the propeller at the end to hang up. A problem in this design is that the drive cable may whip against the sleeve when turning at top RPM. The cable has to be set at exact length to avoid this.

The ultimate convenience is a remote foot-pedal control that's available with many top-of-the-line models. All remotes give you no-hands steering and on-off motor. Depress the pedal and the motor goes. Roll the ball of your foot over the pedal and three switches can activate a servo motor on the shaft that will give you right, middle, or left "rudder."

A variable speed control, which comes with remote-controlled models, is realized to full advantage only if you can control it from a remote box placed on the seat beside you.

Remote controls radically change the weight and cost features of electrics, however. Weight is increased two or three times, price is increased drastically. Plug-in remotes, which let you detach the controls from the mounted motor unit, keep it a manageable package to tote to the car.

Most electrics can be mounted on the transom, on either side of the boat, or at the bow. Canoes give you an even choice, but most boats handle best with the electric attached to the transom. It's hard to hold a true course when it's attached on a midship gunwale, and at the bow—unless you have a remote control—you have to sit in the most uncomfortable place in the boat in order to run it.

Many experienced hands prefer bow mounting because they can see the direction of steering while looking ahead, and because this gives them more exact steering, since the motor leads the boat.

Other things to look for on electrics: Make sure the shaft length fits the freeboard of your boat, especially at the bow. The prop should be 6 inches down in the water for its best bite. Brackets and tilt-control hardware must be well designed, so that the unit does not wobble or shift. Also, it should permit you to swing or bring the motor inside the boat readily for moving out fast with your regular outboard power.

INBOARD (GASOLINE)

The typical inboard engine's similarity to an auto engine brought it to popularity and keeps it there. When our cars come to be powered by rotaries and turbines, so will inboard boats. Inboard engine blocks are manufactured by car or truck engine makers, then are converted to marine use. It is always possible to make repairs locally because it's the commonest type of engine we have.

The 4-cycle inboard is heavier than a comparable outboard, requires permanent installation, and keeps fuel and vapor inside the boat. It also occupies a lot of space. But it's lighter on gas and oil, the lubricating oil system puts out less smog and takes less maintenance, and muffling and insulation can control its noise.

A major advantage is the inboard motor's location amidships, where the hull is capacious and weight is best handled. With fixed, through-hull propeller shaft and separate rudder, however, an inboard installation presents rather delicate bottom gear that must always be protected. Since the shaft runs at a downward angle to clear the prop action, its thrust is less efficient, pushing at an upward angle.

The V drive helps to beat these drawbacks. This may also permit a lower engine location right against the stern, an advantage on some smaller inboard boats. Penn Yan improved on this design with a tunnel section in the hull to protect the propeller, a design favored by the insurance companies. Another solution is the popular inboard/outdrive.

The first and last word about inboards is to the skipper: Keep critical attention on good ventilation and fuel fixtures, and on the quality and condition of fuel lines.

DIESEL

You'll see diesels now in many sport-fishing boats under 50 feet that could not have accommodated this heavy machinery 20 years ago. Compact designs and lighter metals in the high-compression cylinder walls have put them in hearty competition with gasoline engines in some categories.

While the diesel burns only half as much fuel as its gasoline counterpart, and diesel fuel costs less, the diesel doing the same job weighs a third more and initial cost is twice as much. But with a diesel you can increase your cruising range with the same gallonage, or reduce fuel carried to save weight. Because this fuel is less volatile, you have a safer boat. On a still day, however, diesel exhaust odor

DIESEL ENGINE

These photos show both sides of the Volvo Penta Model TAMD 70E inboard diesel marine engine. This is a heavy-duty turbocharged and aftercooled model with six in-line cylinders, overhead valves, single-lever control for both speed regulation and gear changing, and a maximum operating range of 2,300 to 2,500 rpm.

PARTS OF AN OMC STERN DRIVE ENGINE

OMC Cobra Outdrive, seen here in a cutaway view, is a stern drive with an exclusive 56° tilt angle that raises the propeller to the surface, making the changing of props easier. It has a large drive coupler, reported to handle up to twice the torque managed by some other units. Another detail is the position of its water pump, located for easy access and service even when the boat is in the water.

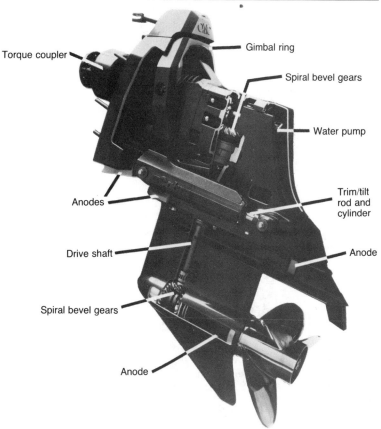

STERN DRIVE ENGINE

Mercruiser 525SC shows typical stern drive construction placing the engine and weight in front of the stern. These engines are also typically freshwater cooled.

JET DRIVE ENGINE

Left: Yamaha 105 is a jet drive with loop charging, offset crankshaft for balance and an oil injection system that eliminates the need to premix gas and oil. Its jet drive design ensures the jet pump stays above the bottom of the boat for shallow water travel. **Right:** Mercury Sport Jet 95 XR is an inboard jet drive. It's a 2-stroke, 3-cylinder in-line engine with a 75.1 cubic inch displacement.

will mix your joys. This engine makes sense if you use your boat hundreds of hours each year for extended cruising and chasing gamefish.

STERN DRIVE

The stern drive, or inboard/outboard, as you might know it, is an inboard 4-cycle engine mounted at the stern with an outboard drive. The propeller of a stern drive drives parallel with the boat, and the lower unit of the outdrive turns, giving positive prop steering as with an outboard motor. There is no separate rudder. Power lift is much favored, as is an automatic kickup release that may save the lower unit when it hits an obstacle.

Stern drives are popular on smaller cruisers and open boats, for it is a compact inboard power arrangement that is feasible even where there is insufficient space for underdeck installation. The stern drive is a heavy machine to be located at the transom on small boats. It is a successful match with fast, deep-V hulls, for the point of the V helps to protect the propeller, and prop steering combines with the keel action of the V bottom to reduce side-slip in turns and maneuvers. It is more expensive than a straight inboard engine, but obviously more versatile.

JET DRIVE

Here is another exciting design that has become a practical buy for the boater. Water-jet propulsion is most efficient at high speeds, and having fast acceleration the big market is for water skiers.

Any inboard engine can be used with a jet pump. The engine is linked by direct drive to a high-speed impeller, and a water jet is forced out a nozzle to propel the boat. With the nozzle gate raised, the jet pushes the boat forward. With gate down, the jet is deflected downward and forward to reverse the boat.

Jet boats used to spin out at high speeds. To improve directional stability, manufacturers have put a small rudder under the jet nozzle and keels one inch deep on either side of the impeller screen on the boat's bottom.

Any jet intake can be clogged eventually by thick weeds, but the impeller shrugs off sand, and passes small gravel without harm.

The latest innovation incorporates water-jet drive into conventional outboard fishing motors to permit operation in water too shallow for a prop. Initially, a jet conversion unit had to be purchased, but now it's a standard propulsion system in some models. A crankshaft-driven impeller draws water through an intake grill, and the water is jetted rearward at high pressure, like the compressed air in a jet aircraft engine. When the motor is put in reverse, a cup swings over the jet stream, channeling it in the opposite direction. The throttle, shift and of course steering are conventional.

BOATS FOR FISHING

You'll catch more fish and enjoy it more if you suit your boat and motor combination to the type of fishing you do. A good rule is: Small boats for sheltered waters; big, beamy boats for big waters. But that is only the beginning. Most of us want a boat that will handle more than one type of fishing sport well, so that what we look for is the best combination of qualities. If you analyze your needs and preferences and decide what is really important, you'll be able to select a boat-motor combination with confidence.

BOATS FOR SHELTERED WATERS

Trout ponds, little bass lakes and such are not called quiet waters because nothing happens there. They *are* quiet, and the noise you make there will be the loudest heard all day unless it's moose country. Therefore it is sensible to use the quietest boat you can find. If you stay within about 12 feet in length, with narrow beam, the size of your shadow will be reduced, and boat action will be in scale with the surroundings. Canvas and inflatable canoes, latex-painted aluminum canoes or skiffs, or an inner-tube rigged with a web seat fit quiet waters perfectly. You can put these into the water soundlessly, with little more than a ripple. If you want to catch fish here, and keep the fishing good, make your outfit as simple as possible. Leave the outboard at home, bring only a paddle or pole, and be proud of your inexpensive rig. You've matched nature, and that is the sportsman's art.

For small rivers and streams the canoe, lightweight johnboat, or car-top boat are time-honored choices and cannot be beat. They have narrow beams and move easily against the current. Add a

FISHING BOATS

Coleman Crawdad provides a low, stable, easily rowed fishing platform. Primarily designed for fishing small lakes and ponds, it can also be used as a drift boat on large, placid rivers.

MirroCraft Vision Series, Aggressor XL & Outfitter XL. The Vision Series line of 16- and 17-foot aluminum boats was created in response to environmental concerns. Features a Lake Saver filtration system and clean running Yamaha F50 four stroke outboard. Also has three removable seats with built-in pedestal bases, 80-quart livewell and 19-gallon gas tank.

small outboard and you're in clover. The johnboat is probably more comfortable for two fishermen and gear when casting and moving for long hours, but experience with a canoe will win you by its easy movement, light weight, and silence. A length of 15 feet or more gives enough space for two casting rods and is safer, unless you are an expert.

When you put into lakes only a few miles across, many types of boats suit the action. First, observe the wave action, wind, and depth; then take a good look at the boats commonly used there. They probably suit those conditions remarkably well.

If the surface is usually quiet, consider a boat that will give you platform space with shallow draft, such as the johnboat or pontoon boat. If your sport is fishing bass and crappies out of the brush and weeds, look for a boat with narrow beam that is easy to push and pry loose; the canoe or johnboat does it well.

The most popular boat in America today may well

be the bass boat. The phenomenal boom in this new breed, rather long, narrow, and up on sled runners, is well deserved because it fits the sport so well. The hull, developed on southern lakes, is a cross between the johnboat and tri-hull. It is very stable, yet rises quickly to the top of the water and moves fast when you want to cross the lake. With its shallow draft you can get in almost anywhere there is water that holds fish. Seats are designed for all-day fishing, rod-holders are located where you want them—it's all thought out. The typical bass boat today is built of fiberglass or Kevlar or a combination of both materials. These boats can range from 15 feet to 20 feet and can handle outboard motors up to 225 horsepower. The hulls are designed to handle almost any kind of water and speeds. There are only two drawbacks: weight and price. Both are big. You'll need a trailer for these rigs.

The favorite all-rounder, however, is the aluminum fishing boat. Successful makes are designed to adapt to the widest variety of conditions. With flotation built in they are good in fairly rough water, are lightweight and easy to handle, can be stored anywhere, and certainly cost little for the service they give. You see them on all inland waters, whatever the area and fishing sport. They come from 12 feet up; probably the most serviceable length is 14 feet. A 10-hp outboard is the common power match, but they will take huskier pushers if that's what you need.

For remote waters where the approach is on foot, look at inflatables. You backpack in, then inflate at the water's edge with a CO_2 cartridge or foot pump. Inflatables handle rather badly, but they are very stable and surprisingly tough, and are a lot of fun. They can also handle small outboard motors. Other candidates are small canoes, kayaks, and canvas boats, but most of these take two persons to tote.

FLOAT-TRIP BOATS

Several schools of thought about boats for float trips are all cogent and tend to follow regional custom—not for custom's sake, but because water conditions vary considerably. A broad, fairly slow river without rapids will usually see shallow-draft boats that maneuver slowly but offer comfort and convenience in their broad-beamed stability. Johnboats, large inflatables, pontoon boats, and river-style houseboats fit these conditions. Such boats have broad front ends that are inefficient in meeting waves or cutting much speed, but those aren't the needs. All you need is enough power to push a heavy bow wave upstream when you return. Knowing your stream, the weight and size of the boat will help you determine how much power you need.

Typical johnboat designs come in 14-, 16-, and 18-foot lengths.

For fast rivers with rapids and white waters, the needs are more demanding. First you need a hull that will withstand a lot of punishment; it must be built strong to survive bumping hard into rocks, logs, and gravel bottoms without damage. Flotation must be positive—sufficient to support the craft, occupants and load if swamped. Maneuverability is very important, as is a bow design that will lift and throw off white water. Light weight is necessary so that portages will be easy. The choice is usually a canoe for rivers where narrow bends and fast water between rocks make maneuverability essential. Expert white-water canoeists prefer craft under 15 feet, with round bottoms and no keel for quicker handling. However, since a canoe of this design won't hold much, the choice for float trips is usually a bigger canoe with high ends.

Inflatables are usually chosen for big, fast rivers. A big inflatable has great stability and is forgiving when you bounce it off banks and obstructions; and it's roomy enough to let you relax when the going is straight. But maneuvering a big inflatable is a real problem. Some experienced float men add a broad, shallow tiller for steering. On some rivers this is essential. Don't plan on powering your boat on fast streams, but arrange for transport at the lower end.

BOATS FOR OPEN WATERS

Big lakes, river estuaries, coastal bays, inlets, and off the beaches: size and seaworthiness are absolutely essential here. The bigger the water, the greater are potential dangers and need for a capable hull that will bring you safely back through all weather, yet serve you comfortably in routine use

Stratos 1850 CC is an 18½-foot center console with a 150 horsepower Johnson. Ideally designed for coastal bays and big lakes. Under the right sea conditions, this boat can also fish the beaches.

and help you to catch more fish. Open waters are not the places for a flat-bottomed 12-foot skiff. Look at what is being used. You will see deep bow points, rounded chines on smaller boats, probably with flat planing surface aft, and enough freeboard to keep dry when the wind comes up. If your waters commonly have a sharp chop, as in many Great Lakes locations, you will need more freeboard, and the hull shape should ride comfortably in those conditions. Too much freeboard can be a curse, however, making fish handling difficult and presenting a big profile to the wind, causing eternal drifting.

Fishermen who run out to the reefs on the Great Lakes to anchor and drop a line for perch want a boat that gives a comfortable seat for hours on end, riding the waves without slapping and shipping water. The man who trolls for lake trout or coho salmon prefers a competent running boat that also provides a good platform for fighting and landing the fish, with a bow shape that will handle the waves when they rise, and that can move off fast to change locations and make the run home.

Calm days on open waters—and many big lakes a fraction of the size of the Great Lakes fit the case—are deceptive. The water looks calm when you start out in the morning. By noon you are occupied with sunburn and poor fishing, so that when the wind and big waves come up at 3 P.M. you're taken by surprise. Getting back to shore can be dangerous if you are out in a 12- or 14-footer with a 10-hp motor. Think in terms of 16 feet and more length, with plenty of beam in relation to length. For big inland lakes and coastal bays you will need a motor of 25 hp and up. For trolling the ocean beaches a motor or twin motors from 85 hp up are indicated.

Now you have to plan your boat more carefully for the sport. For trolling in such waters you need a broad, clear stern for handling the lines. For casting, you should consider a boat that provides a good casting platform both fore and aft.

OFFSHORE BOATS

Perhaps the most versatile boats we have are the center-console deep-V boats. Deep bows permit them to handle the seas, but this slopes into a moderately flat mid and stern bottom that permits them to plane easily and ride over the flats without scraping. This design is also very stable for its seaworthiness. These boats are best described as inshore-offshore boats, great for fishing coastal bays and reefs, for running the inlets, and going offshore—weather permitting—into really big-water country.

But it is increasingly common to see these boats, some of them outboard powered, offshore on calm days. Big twin motors are mounted on a broad transom. This kind of rig, of course, costs only a fraction of the outlay for an all-out sport-fishing boat, and is much easier and simpler to handle—at least until the going gets rough. The limited fuel supply that can be carried and the modest size (about 20 to 30 feet) impose a limit on how far you can run offshore.

The all-out sport-fishing boats, which sail in all kinds of weather and offshore seas, are a breed apart from the others. Until you have handled a boat on the ocean, following the fish on really big water, it's hard to imagine what is required of a boat in these conditions. Not only are these boats bigger (from 25 to 55 feet), with deeper hulls and more beam, but they are built to take tremendous forces. Big power is needed, as well as great reliability and fuel economy, and a frequent choice is twin diesels.

Layout is most important to the offshore sport fisherman in order to handle the boat efficiently when baiting and after hooking a big fish so that it is not broken off or lost due to a slack line, but boated in a minimum of time. (With an inadequate boat or inept skipper, it can take hours to boat a good billfish; in that time, tackle and equipment break down, people have accidents brought about by fatigue, and the boat itself can be endangered.) The steering station should give the captain a clear view of the cockpit and stern as well as forward. The cockpit will be clear of all tackle and equipment except the fighting chairs, with a clean rail from the

deckhouse all around the stern. Sport-fishing boats are being built now with engine hatches under the cabin floor for easy access.

Big sport-fishing boats with gas turbine power have created a new experience in the offshore sport. Instead of having to shout above the engine roar, you can communicate in normal tones. This is very important when the action is fast. Giving and getting a command promptly can make all the difference. On turbine-powered boats there is only a whisper of sound from the engine plant, and all vibrations are reduced to a fraction. Being able to hear other sounds on the ocean, too, is a great help in tournament fishing. For day-after-day running out on the blue water, the turbine-powered boat is tops.

BASS BOATS

Ranger 238S Cherokee is 18½ feet long with a 96-inch beam. Horsepower ranges from 115-175. Available in single or dual console models. Ideal for big waters.

Tracker Pro Team 18 DC is a dual-console aluminum bass boat. Features dry storage compartments, three-across seating and large lockable boxes. A good choice for budget-minded bass fishermen.

OFFSHORE BOATS

Pro-Line Bimini Cuddy 3400 marries a high performance design with an efficient fishing layout. This 35-foot center console will take outboard power up to 675 horsepower. Twin 200-quart fish boxes and a 50-gallon recirculating transom baitwell will keep you in fishing action all day.

Regulator 26 can run offshore at 50+ miles per hour with twin 200 horsepower outboards. This 26-footer is rigged strictly for fishing with 5-foot-long fish boxes and a 50-gallon livewell.

Pursuit 3000 Offshore is a 34-footer with a 12-foot beam. With a fuel capacity of 250 gallons, this boat can easily work offshore waters. Will handle up to 660 horsepower.

Luhrs Tournament 320 Open is a 35-footer with a 13-foot beam. It has a fuel capacity of 340 gallons for serious offshore and canyon fishing. Center console design is rare in boats this size.

BOATS FOR HUNTING

Any boat is potentially a hunting boat. If you have a fishing boat, it will probably serve your hunting needs well. Every boat discussed in this section has been used successfully in hunting, even the big sport fishermen.

If hunting is your sole game, you may want a specialized boat such as a duckboat. There are good reasons, however, for having a boat that will do several things well. If you must travel far on water to reach your hunting ground, you need outboard speed to save time. If you usually hunt in protected waters, you may still want to go to the big lakes or the shore to hunt. You may want to spend the night in your boat on some trips. You may like more than one kind of boat hunting—float hunting for deer, for small game, waterfowling.

If you already own a good-size fishing boat and trailer, a good solution for the all-round hunter is to get an additional, specialized hunting boat. On the water, you can use the big boat to cover distance, then use it as your "lodge," where you make your meals, keep supplies, and bed down overnight. Towing the small hunting boat behind, you can hop in when you're ready to hunt and have a small, maneuverable boat that is quiet and easy to handle, able to get in close and keep a low profile.

FLOAT HUNTING

Any of the flat-bottomed, low-sided boats such as the johnboat make practical float hunters. These boats have tremendous load-carrying capacity for their size, so that two hunters and their gear, including camping equipment and tent, are no problem at all. And I have seen two deer laid across the gunwales of a johnboat in addition to everything else, and there was still enough freeboard to move slowly back upstream to the car.

The stability and broad beam of these boats is another reason for their popularity with float hunters. You can stand to shoot with confidence, take a wide stance, and move around easily. Besides, bird dogs like them, while they dislike tippy and confining boats.

The flat bottom is ideal for setting up the frame of a blind, and you can pop up a small aluminum-framed tent there for overnight shelter if you're in marshland. "Waiting hour after hour in cold, cramped quarters" just doesn't describe the experience of hunters in a johnboat. There's plenty of room for sleeping bags plus a heater to ease the wait.

Big inflatables are also popular with float hunters.

They are comfortable to lounge around in while floating or waiting it out. But the flexible construction means that you should kneel or sit to shoot. A big plus is the light weight of an inflatable, making portages easy, and you can turn it over on shore for a blind, propping up one side for gunning while you stay in the shadow.

An outboard of 10 to 20 horsepower is suitable for either of these types. You have to be guided by the boat's size, the load you carry, distances you have to motor upstream and the strength of the current, and of course the maximum-hp rating of the boat.

Important: Check out your state's hunting laws before you shoot from a boat. Some states require that you have the outboard tilted up and not operating when you shoot. Others will not permit shooting from a boat equipped with a motor.

DUCKBOATS

These suit any hunting for shy game, especially in a small hunting ground such as island country, where you need something stealthy to succeed. Double-enders are most popular: a small duckboat, canoe, or kayak. If you can, leave the motor at home and use paddles or oars; work around your base, and move your base often. If you need a motor to cover distance and reach fallen game before the current takes it, think of a really small outboard. An electric trolling motor is preferred by some hunters because it never breaks the quiet.

The decked-over double-ender will keep you dry and snug, but the limitation is tight space. There is room for only one hunter and little else. You'll have to return to camp oftener unless you're a Spartan who knows the art of traveling ultralight.

Small hunting canoes afford more space. If you use a canoe, treat yourself to detachable buoyant pontoons. This makes shooting more secure and the whole thing more relaxed. A well-made aluminum canoe with reinforced ends is great for forcing a low lie in the marsh, and also for breaking through the thin sheet of ice in late fall. You would wreck a wooden or canvas canoe doing this unless you cover the ends with aluminum or plastic sheet.

Take the trouble to paint your aluminum canoe before you go hunting. There's nothing like blazoning the horizon with sunrays reflected from a mirror finish to earn you a birdlaugh. Camouflage paint colors should be chosen to suit the seasonal color of your hunting grounds.

The gunning craft shown in these two photos is simply called The Duck Boat. It's constructed of fiberglass with a rigid foam core in the hull plus foam flotation fore, aft, and under 7-foot side shelves. Rated for a 10-hp motor, it will take a 600-pound load. When fully loaded with two men, gear, a dog, and up to six dozen decoys, it draws only 3 inches of water and has 23 inches of freeboard. With its built-in camo-patterned Cordura nylon blind raised, it keeps hunters dry in wind and choppy water. Grassing loops and rails can be used to turn it into a fully grassed stand-up shooting platform.

Left: This fiberglass double-ender is suitable for gunning on waters where layout boats or the old Merrymeeting sculls are used. It has a side-mount for small gasoline or electric outboard. **Right:** Most aluminum cartop boats can accommodate two gunners, plus dog, decoys, and gear. This 12-foot 4-inch boat has lockable under-the-seat storage and is available with dead-grass camouflage paint.

BOATS FOR CAMPING

Boat camping is a natural way to extend your enjoyment of fishing, hunting, and life in the outdoors. Instead of having to backtrack to your starting point toward the end of the day, just when things are going well, you can put ashore at the first suitable site if you are prepared for camping. If your boat is big enough, you can anchor and camp aboard. Still another version of boat camping is to trailer or cartop a boat to your base camp and extend your range from there by means of the boat.

For those whose primary pleasure is camping, a boat gets you away from crowded, metropolis-like campgrounds. Going camping by boat gives you a private preserve in the outdoors, brings you closer to unspoiled nature, and increases your alternatives for camping locations tenfold.

CAMPING WITH SMALL BOATS

When you camp with a canoe, kayak, cartopper, inflatable, johnboat, or other really small boat, you can pack your supplies and tent or sleeping bags in the boat, travel through the wilderness on water, then make your camps ashore. This style suits many lake chains and small rivers. With careful packing, there is room for your supplies and gear, two adults, or a couple and small child in this size of boat.

When you plan your trip, make a list based on roughing it, with the minimum of equipment, only one change of clothing, backpack-style tentage, concentrated and freeze-dried foods, and a streamlined fishing or hunting outfit. There is a distinct pleasure in traveling light, and as the experience progresses, you'll be glad to have discovered a simple way to camp. Portages will be light, and if you get a dunking the damage is not irreparable.

A canoe for camping should be from 16 to 18 feet long and fairly narrow to make paddling easier. If you are going to camp on a lake, use a canoe with a keel. This will help you hold your course easily in a wind. With canoe ends slightly rockered you can adjust course fairly easily even with a heavy load. For canoe camping on a river, avoid a canoe with much of a keel, and stick to the camping length. Loaded with gear, a canoe with a keel will catch rocks and snags too often for comfort. The camping length, as opposed to shorter white-water canoes, will keep handling easy. There is a lot in favor of using a small motor on a canoe for camping. In that case, choose a canoe with full rather than fine ends so the motor will not cause the ends to dig in.

If you find yourself in hostile territory when night falls, with posted land on both sides of you, don't give up. You can make do for one night by wedging the canoe between rocks or submerged logs, heat your stew with a sterno stove, and crawl into your sleeping bags where you are.

A cartop boat will increase your load capacity, and by using an outboard you will extend your range considerably compared to paddling, or drifting. Don't forget that you will have to carry enough gas to make it between refueling points. Determine gas-pump locations in advance, and make sure you can get to them from the water's edge. Cartop fishing boats are ideal for light camping, but avoid flat-bottomed skiffs, which lack stability needed for long water routes with a big load.

Inflatable boats are excellent for drift camping on a large river. Four people can camp with a 16-foot inflatable; this boat can carry big loads, and the relatively wide beam makes it easy to load and stay aboard for long hours without getting cramped. At night you can use an inflatable as a lean-to over your sleeping bags and avoid carrying a large tent.

A full-size johnboat of 16 feet or so is too big and heavy to cartop, but it's a good candidate for trailering or loading in the back of a truck, your gear already packed in the boat. The johnboat design is excellent for boat camping, as it can carry great loads for its size. Small aluminum johnboats do suit cartopping, however, and driving is faster and easier with your boat on the car's roof than trailing behind the vehicle.

FAMILY RUNABOUTS

When the family with a new runabout gets over its novelty and has learned to water ski, going camping with the boat is an interesting next stage. This is an imaginative and ambitious way to use the family's recreational resources.

Since runabouts have more beam and weight capacity than a fishing boat or canoe of the same length, you are not quite so limited in the amount of gear and supplies aboard. Often there is enough space to do simple cooking aboard and bed down. Runabouts from 16 to 19 feet suit camping best. You can use the runabout to go greater distances at better speeds with its greater horsepower capacity. If the boat is really not big enough to eat and sleep aboard, use its range to reach choice campsites, with more variety.

A family boat of 18 or 19 feet is generally big enough for four people and even a couple of small children in addition to live aboard, more or less, if they are good organizers. Boats of this size have several advantages: You can travel on large open waters such as the Great Lakes, large river estuaries, and the Inland Waterway, moving in close along shore on weather days or to camp for the night, and also pass through fairly shallow places when you have to. Many families enjoy camping vacations in the Florida Keys aboard large runabouts. These boats are a size that can be trailered at fair highway speeds so that reaching a distant vacation area is not a big problem.

Many makers offer camper tops as options for family runabouts. These vary considerably in quality of materials, workmanship, and design for prices that are universally high. Shop with your eyes open when buying a runabout if you think you will use it for camping. A good camper top is made of high-grade nylon with double seams, double zippers, tough plastic windows and nylon-mesh screening. Designs that have at least one large area with stand-up height are most useful. Tight closure all around is usually achieved with plastic rubber channel

Bayliner 1950 Capri is an 18-footer with a standard Mercruiser stern drive. The bow rider design gives it maximum utility for all-around family use.

Baja's Islander 232 is a runabout powered for more speed than most family boats in this category.

which presses together, and strong grommets and double-reinforced eyelets anchor the camper top to the boat. If you cannot get a camper top to suit you with the boat you want to buy, shop around for a good tent maker who will make the top to your specifications.

Optional camper built-ins are a good investment if they are efficiently designed and well made. A fold-up alcohol stove with two burners stows out of the way in a side storage space under the gunwales. Deluxe double lounge seats with comfortable padding and vinyl covering are made to fold down to make a bed for one person. Removable seats can be lifted out to make more space on deck for sleeping bags.

HOUSEBOATS AND CRUISERS

Whether this should be called camping is decided by your own point of view and how you go about

it. If you want to camp, you'll do so, and some families are inveterate campers even in a 50-foot houseboat with automatic laundry and electric stove. The lure of building a campfire ashore, and pup-tenting for the young along the way, is very attractive when you have a boat with shallow draft that can nudge shore when you like. With a small houseboat or pontoon boat, camping is still a natural extension of what you can do with such a boat. Here planning is more relaxed because you can keep more aboard. People who like camping in a travel trailer or motor home will find this scale to their taste.

Houseboats and small cruisers are used extensively on big rivers, along the shores of the Great Lakes, and on other open waters where you can keep in touch with shore and duck in if the weather

Maxum 3900 SCR is a 43-foot cruiser with a 13½-foot beam. Cockpit includes lounge seating, wet bar, and helm station. Cabin has full galley and two double berths.

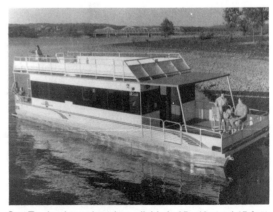

Sun Tracker houseboat is available in 35-, 40-, and 45-foot versions. These cruisers offer comfortable beds, sleeper sofas, and fully equipped galleys and showers.

Cobia Odyssey 226 Sport Deck is a hybrid design showing distinct signs of both pontoon boat and runabout. A good choice for family boating.

blows up. These hulls have fairly shallow drafts customarily, so that you have many options in where you go.

One pleasure with a houseboat or small cruiser is to nose up to a river bank or anchor near shore, then have a barbecue ashore, follow the deerpaths, explore islands, and walk the beaches. You can tow a small dinghy or stow it on the cabin roof for fishing and going ashore. Some houseboats and cruisers carry a bicycle to run into towns along the way for groceries, laundry, and mail.

BUYING A NEW OR A USED BOAT

NEW BOATS

Before you start shopping for a boat, do some careful reasoning with yourself.

• Where are you going to use the boat? In fresh or salt water, big waters or small, calm waters? It makes an enormous difference in what kind of boat you need. Do you want a boat specially suited to one location and use—or do you want a versatile boat you can use in a number of different locations?
• How big a boat do you need? That depends on the size of the water, the distances you'll go, and how many people will be aboard. Just you and a fishing and hunting partner—or the whole family plus friends now and then? Between choosing a boat that's too small and one that's bigger than minimal needs, it makes sense to buy a bigger boat. But you can buy too much boat—too much for you to handle, and maintain, and too much out of your wallet.
• Where will you keep it? In a marina, on a trailer, or in a public mooring? Learn the terms—you might decide you can live with a smaller or lighter boat.
• Where will you store it in off-season? You're lucky if you can store it at home. Boatyards charge by length and type of boat, so learn the going rates, and what service they will give you.
• Does your choice have a BIA plate—a metal plate attached to the hull that certifies the Boating Industry Association has determined these figures: maximum horsepower rating, number of adult persons or maximum total weight it can carry on calm water, and total net load of persons, motor and gear properly located aboard.
• Questions to ask about small fishing boats: What kind of flotation does it have? Is flotation impervious

to alcohol and petroleum products? Is it located in the gunwales or high enough to keep the boat upright if swamped, or under seats, floor, or in the bow too low, so the boat will turn bottom up? Will the boat stay afloat with a normal load, or support only the hull weight when flooded?
• Is it round-bottomed or V-bottomed? Will it sit comfortably in the water you use it on, hour after hour? Is there enough freeboard (height of sides above the waterline) for your waters? Is the transom dangerously low, or is there a well closed off by a bulkhead to keep the boat dry and safe?
• What is the gauge thickness of an aluminum hull, and how are seams finished—welded, riveted, or both? Are seams reinforced? Can you find cast or stiff extruded aluminum at the bow and keel? Are edges and corners smooth and rounded?
• Is the transom reinforced with strong corner plates? Is an outboard pad built in, or do you have to add one? Do you know how to do it? Do splash rails really keep water out of the boat? Does the whole hull have fairly stiff integrity when it's lifted, or does it twist and pong too much?
• Want to cartop your boat? Then it has to be light enough to heft up by yourself or with one person helping. A boat of 11 or 12 feet that weighs from 85 to 100 pounds is right for one-man cartopping. Boats that weigh up to 130 pounds need two to cartop.
• Look for these things in a fiberglass boat: The gel coat (glassy smooth outer surface) should be free of checks, hairline cracks, bubbles, thick and thin places. Study the dark side of the boat, looking toward brighter light: Can you see pinholes of light coming through? Then the layup has been resin-starved. Are there bare, rough spots where the gel coat is absent and unhardened fabric is exposed?

Insufficient resin or epoxy will produce delamination and leaks. Too much resin unsupported by fiberglass will produce weak places that can crack and break. The smoother and more even the gel coat, the faster your boat will be in the water, and the less work it will need to clean.

• Inquire in detail about fiberglass construction. Is the boat made by hand layup or by production-line mold pressing? The latter should cost less. Is wood or fiberglass used in the stringer (structural reinforcement) system? Where is the flotation? Is it molded in or added on? Are transom, bow, keel, and deck joints reinforced with extra laminations? Is hardware bolted through the hull with backing plates, or bolt-anchored into structural members? Both are satisfactory. Screwed-on hardware will eventually work loose in fiberglass hulls.

• When buying a wood boat, look for planks that are long, with fewer ends that water can find a way into, and that can work loose from fastenings. Joints in hull planks should be butted or joined at a flat angle and blocked inside, not joined on a frame. Butts must be staggered, never in line vertically. Butt blocks should overlap the butt seam at least half an inch, rounded away from the plank to drain well. These details are signs of quality construction, especially important if you are buying from an individual builder.

• Except in canoes and small rowboats, look for relatively thick, narrow planks. Economy building with the opposite dimensions results in magnified swelling with warping at the seams and rapid permeation of the thin walls. This can mean great danger in an aging boat.

• Fastenings in a wood boat should be stainless steel, bronze, or other noncorrosive alloy, for even the best-sealed boat collects moisture inside that will get to the fastenings. Rust and eventual rot of the wood pursue iron or galvanized fittings like an infection.

• Want to trailer your boat? Make sure there's a trailer on the market that fits your boat well; the manufacturer will tell you. Otherwise, you'll have to buy one custom-made.

• The bigger the boat, the more you need to know before buying. In boats of 16 to 20 feet you have the widest variety of hull types, carrying capacity, construction value, horsepower capacity, and price. In this range you should definitely know the speed and power you'll need. Should you plan on one motor, or two—say, a big outboard stern drive, plus a small trolling motor? Figure this in price.

• Look at through-hull fittings. They must be completely sealed and lipped in a professional manner to avoid delamination, rot, and leaks.

• On any boat, what options and equipment do you need? Find out what is standard in the purchase price, and what you will have to buy besides. This can change the look of the total figure.

• Will your choice depreciate fast or slowly? The value of well-made aluminum or fiberglass boats will depreciate slowly after the first 18 months. And they are easy to keep new-looking for years. The same is not true of many wood boats. This makes a difference if you expect to trade your boat periodically for a better one.

• Finally, do you know how to handle the boat you are buying? If it's your first, by all means enroll in a U.S. Power Squadron course in small-boat piloting and seamanship. You'll get more out of the course if you have just bought your own boat and can practice what you learn.

USED BOATS

Many of the points to look for when buying a new boat apply to finding a good buy in a used boat, with the difference that by the time you see them, original faults are more obvious. The trick in buying real value for your money in a used boat is to check out points that are not so obvious.

• Where has the boat been stored? Covered and enclosed storage is best. If stored exposed, look for signs of freezing damage (expanded seams, splits at fastenings, braces, and joints). And look for rust and corrosion, including the power plant.

• Was it used in fresh or salt water? If in salt, look thoroughly for borer damage to wood hulls. Look for electrolysis damage to metal hulls and all exterior metal parts, including fastenings (rivets and screws). Inspect the motor's lower unit and prop for electrolysis and corrosion. The seller is justified in asking from 10 to 30 percent more for a boat used only in fresh water.

• Is the hull hooked? The hook is a dread ailment that can afflict an otherwise sound wood or fiberglass hull. It is an unwanted curve, usually concave, in the bottom centerline of the boat resulting from improper support during storage. Using the wrong trailer can do this. Best to buy a small boat that has been stored bottom up and covered.

• What's the condition of hull fastenings and hardware? They tell a tale. Too many loose rivets and screws indicate the hull has taken too much stress and perhaps abuse, or that maintenance has been slack.

• Inspect the transom carefully. Here's where careless use and original construction weakness are bound to turn up. Are the joints with the sides and bottom sound, or are there signs of cracking, splits, and separation? Can the transom pad be replaced without damaging the boat?

• Take the cover off. Is it clean? Signs of prolonged overheating probably indicate heavy use for water-skiing, hard acceleration, and big overload. Turn it on and watch for thick smoke. Fill the grease port on the lower gear, take the rig for a spin, and look again. If the grease is gone, look out. The gears may be badly worn. A badly knicked propeller indicates hard, careless use.

• Pitted surface on an aluminum hull shows electrolysis. Don't buy that boat. But dents, or just a few broken rivets, mean little. You can knock out the dents and restore a few rivets. Loose rivets all over can't be repaired—the holes are too wide.

• Crazing of the surface on a fiberglass boat's gel coat may only tell its age, with little effect on quality. But cracks are serious. Look for signs of delamination at the transom, bow, and joints on a fiberglass boat. If serious, it's hard to restore and you'd better look further.

• In wood hulls, beware of signs of rot, borers, and poor original construction that will come to light after several years. Stick an icepick into the transom wood, near joints, and around the keel. Inspect closed underfloor bilge areas, where rot is frequent. Warped or loose boards indicate poor and inexpert

maintenance, or economy-type construction. Too many loose fastenings mean a costly overall repair job, and perhaps rot around the fastenings.

• Look inside the hull, in the point of the bow, at transom corners, and under floorboards for signs of collision damage, just as you'd look at the frame and undersides of a car body. Are repairs well made? Any signs of rot or leaking around them? They should be sounder and tighter than the rest of the hull.

• Don't pass up a used boat just because it has a hole punched in it, unless there are signs of rot that gave way. A simple hole—even a large one—can mean a big bargain to you that might be easily repaired. Aluminum and fiberglass are easier to patch than wood.

• If a used boat costs several thousand dollars, as big ones do, buy only subject to a clean bill from a professional boat surveyor. He can find things that you can't and advise you on the extent of damage and deterioration.

• Finally, know who you're doing business with. Make sure you can come back, though it's just for information. All you want from the seller is a fair deal and not a steal.

BOATING ELECTRONICS

Once you have selected your boat, you will need to rig it. And this means learning the basics of marine electronics.

Basic electronic gear ensures the safety of your boat and passengers. A radio will summon help in case of an accident, and a depthsounder will help keep you out of trouble in unfamiliar waters. Once you've met the basic safety requirements, however, you'll quickly discover that electronics can be interesting and useful—whether cruising or fishing.

It's easy to pick out rod holders and similar accessories, but electronic equipment is a different story. If you make the wrong choice there, you could be out hundreds of dollars and stuck with something that doesn't perform as needed. Let's take a look at some of the electronics to consider.

DEPTHSOUNDERS

Portions of text courtesy of Lowrance Electronics Inc.

The word "sonar" is an acronym for SOund, NAvigation, and Ranging. It was developed during World War II as a means of tracking enemy submarines.

With sonar an electrical impulse is converted to

a sound wave and transmitted into the water. When this sound wave strikes an obstacle, it rebounds. Sound transmitted through water travels at approximately 4,800 feet per second, compared with 1,100 fps through air. And since the speed of sound in water is a known constant, the time lapse between the transmitted signal and the received echo can be measured and the distance to the obstacle determined. An electronic sonar unit can both send and receive sound waves, as well as time, measure, and record them.

A depthsounder's transducer sends a high-frequency sound wave through the water. (This sound wave is inaudible to fish as well as humans.) When the echo returns, the transducer picks it up and reconverts it to electrical energy. The unit times the interval and flashes a red signal on the dial. Since the dial is calibrated, the signal shows the distance between the transducer and the obstacle that returned the echo.

Types of Depthsounders
The four most popular depthsounders are flashers, paper recorders, liquid crystal displays, and video sonars. The flashers are the cheapest and work out well for boaters who are content just to cruise. The

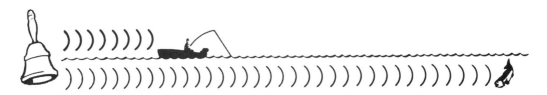

Sound travels 4800 feet per second in water, more than four times as fast as sound travels in air.

biggest disadvantage of flashers, however, is that they have no recording features. If a fisherman does not constantly monitor his flasher, he may well pass over fish and not see them. Recorders, on the other hand, do not require this constant monitoring. Here's how all four function on the water.

The Flasher Depthsounder. The transducer, mounted on the transom or hull, transmits sound waves into the water. At the same time, a high-intensity neon bulb whirls at constant speed behind the dial on a disc driven by an accurately governed motor. The bulb lights up every time the transmitter fires. This provides a visual reference point on the dial which is used as a starting point to measure depth, and as an indication the flasher is on and operating. Even though the neon bulb actually flashes, the flashing occurs so frequently that it appears to be a nearly constant light.

The bulb also flashes at the point on the dial that indicates the depth. The point is indicated by the length of time required for the sound waves to reach the bottom and return, and this is why a regulated motor speed is so important.

In addition, echoes returned from any object in the water between the surface and bottom fire the bulb too. Since these echoes are also timed, they show the exact depth of any fish—or any number of fish. And because the sound waves from the transducer descend in a cone pattern, they tell, within a matter of a few feet, the location of fish, as well as their depth.

Remember, the signal at zero on the dial shows continuously and serves as a visual reminder that the flasher is on. Always interpret the depth of the water and depth of the fish by starting with the surface as zero and counting down.

The Chart-Recorder Depthsounder. When a chart recorder is operating, an electronically regulated motor drives a lightweight belt at the edge of the recording paper. A stylus is attached to this belt. When the stylus is at the top of the paper, a small mark

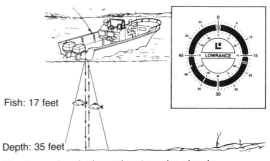

Fish: 17 feet

Depth: 35 feet

Depthsounders both send and receive signals.

is burned onto the paper. This is called the zero mark, and represents the water surface. The stylus continues to move down the edge of the paper while the sound pulse is traveling through the water. When an echo is detected, the stylus burns another mark on the paper. The depth of the object that reflected the echo can be read in feet by comparing its location on the paper to the depth scale printed on the paper.

The paper speed is controlled by a variable-speed motor. During one revolution of the stylus belt, a very narrow mark will be made by the flexible stylus, but the paper will move a small amount before the next revolution. Each mark will blend into the one before so that a composite "picture" of the target will be made, one tiny mark at a time.

The Liquid-Crystal-Recorder Depthsounder. In principle, the liquid crystal recorder, or graph, works like a paper recorder, except that these "paperless recorders" utilize liquid crystal squares, called pixels, on a display screen. When an impulse or electronic signal is sent to the screen, it hits the liquid and turns it so the tiny square shows black on the screen. A continuing series of signals will literally draw a picture of the bottom or any object or fish

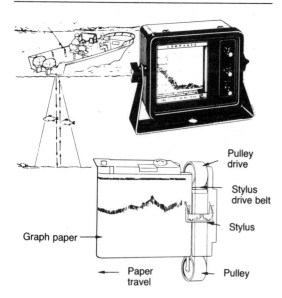

Recorders both send and receive signals and record them on graph paper.

between the bottom and the boat. Some of the latest liquid crystal recorders, or graphs, have features that border on the amazing. Some have memories with playback. Others have a split screen that shows two segments of the water. And many have optional fish alarms and water temperature readouts.

The Video-Sonar Depthsounder. Instead of using chart paper or liquid crystal squares, an underwater video sonar produces a sharp clear black-and-white or color picture on a CRT (cathode ray tube) screen. The imaging principle is the same as that of a television picture. With color video sonars, the screen shows signal intensity by color difference, making it easier to distinguish individual fish from structure and the bottom. With black-and-white video sonars, the unit provides a constant view of the bottom, underwater structure, drop-offs, schools of fish, and even single fish in distinct, easy-to-identify shades of gray.

Uses for Depthsounders

Though most fishermen believe the primary use for a depthsounder is to find fish, there are many others. Since a depthsounder tells depth accurately, it can be used for making contour maps of lakes, bays, saltwater areas, or large streams. It is useful in navigation because it warns you when you are approaching shallow water. It will find the deep holes in rivers. It is useful in salvage operations be-

cause it will accurately show a sunken boat on the bottom. It even tells what kind of bottom your boat is passing over. And divers use it to study the depths before descending.

It tells the depth of the water accurately. But since everything it reports is shown by signals on the dial or screen, the amount it can tell is limited by your ability to interpret these signals. The more skillful you become at reading the signals, the more your depthsounder will tell you about the mysterious world beneath the surface.

MARINE RADIOS

If you are a boater, the U.S. Coast Guard advises that you know your marine communications system well because it can be your sole means of rescue. A radio system that is properly installed and correctly used is one of the best forms of life insurance a boater can buy.

Basically, a communications system is comprised of the transceiver (transmitter/receiver unit) and an antenna. The distance a communications system can send and receive messages is determined by the height of the system's antenna, the transceiver's wattage and sensitivity, and the propagation characteristics of the frequency being used. Propagation characteristics relate to the ability of radio waves to travel through the air and their interaction with the environment.

In selecting a radio for your boat, you should consider many factors. How will the boat be used? For business or pleasure, or both? Will it be operated on inland waters or lakes? Will it be operated in U.S. coastal waters? If so, how far offshore? Regardless of the area, what coastal stations exist, or are planned? And how far apart are they? What frequencies do they monitor?

Types of Marine Radio Systems

The boating public has three communications systems, or bands, from which to choose: the 2–3 Megahertz (MHz) Radiotelephone band, the Very High Frequency-Frequency Modulated (VHF–FM) Maritime Mobile band, and Citizens Band (CB). Note: CB is *NOT* strictly a marine communications band and may be operated from ships, boats, cars, trucks, and fixed land stations.

In making your decision, you should know that the 2–3 MHz and the VHF–FM bands have been officially designated and internationally recognized as "marine" communications bands. For this reason, the Coast Guard, and maritime rescue organizations throughout the world, continuously monitor the distress frequencies of these bands.

The Coast Guard also monitors the emergency

DEPTHSOUNDERS

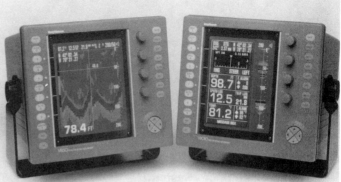

Top Left: Apelco 560 Fishfinder/Plotter will read depth ranges to 1,900 feet. The transducer can also look forward up to 600 feet in front of the boat. Ideal for anglers who troll ledges, the cruising boater looking for safe anchorage and divers searching for a favorite wreck. **Top Right:** Raytheon V850 (left) and V8010 (right) Color Fishfinders/Plotters. The V850 has 500-watt operation to read fish in waters up to 5,000 feet deep. Electronic charting is also a standard feature on both units. This enables fishermen to have both a sounder plus a complete navigational instrument. **Bottom Left:** Lowrance X-45 offers three-beam technology. It searches downward as well as outward on both the left and right sides of the boat. The X-45 displays the entire three-beam underwater view on the screen.

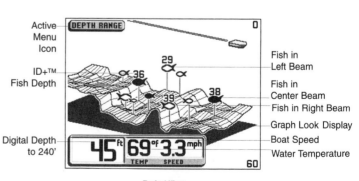

Humminbird Wide 3D Paramount is an LCD depthsounder with the capability of reading down to 240 feet, 1,000 feet with optional 2D transducer. Also features speed and temperature readouts. Accompanying matching illustration identifies various features in detail.

DEPTH SOUNDERS (Continued)

Humminbird Jimmy Houston Pro Flasher (left) and the WP60 In-Dash (right) are flasher-type fish-finders. Both units will provide high-speed readings to speeds up to 75 miles an hour. The In-Dash 60 features a 16-degree transducer and will read down to 120 feet.

GPS (Global Positioning System)

Magellan GSC 100 is a global two-way e-mail satellite communicator. In addition to GPS capability, the model sends and receives e-mail messages to any internet e-mail address.

Garmin GPS Map 220 is a 16-color LCD with built-in world maps to 64 nautical miles. Utilizes G-chart cartridges for detailed mapping and worldwide coverage. Features 500 waypoints. The waterproof unit measures 5.8 inches high, 9 inches wide, and 3 inches deep.

Garmin GPS 45 Personal Navigator is a 9-ounce hand-held GPS receiver with 250 waypoints and 20 reversible routes with 30 waypoints each. Battery life of the GPS 45 is 10-20 hours.

Lowrance Global Map 2000 combines mapping and GPS navigation with sonar capability. Global Map 2000 comes complete with a built-in background map of the entire world with detailed emphasis on the 48 states, the Hawaiian Islands, southern Canada, the Caribbean, and the Virgin Islands.

Humminbird GPS NS 10 has built-in digital maps to help orient you to your surroundings. Features 249 waypoints and 99 routes with a one button emergency position store. Also includes alarms for anchor, off course and arrival. Built-in simulator and AC adaptor makes off boat instruction easy. Features disc antenna (right).

Raytheon Nav 598 GPS/Loran can switch back and forth between GPS, Loran and plotting functions at the touch of a button. In the plot mode, routes can be recorded and marked with up to 500 waypoints which can be entered into memory as Lat/Lon range and bearing.

TYPES OF COMMUNICATIONS SYSTEMS AVAILABLE TO BOATERS

	2-3 MHz Radiotelephone	VHF-FM Maritime Mobile Band	Citizens Band
Power Output	50-150 watts	1-25 watts	4 watts
Range	50-150 miles	10-15 miles (Ship-to-Ship) 20-30 miles (Ship-to-Shore)	3-10 miles
Primary Use	Coastal Communications	Ship-to-Ship Ship-to-Shore (line of sight)	Private, 2-way communications on land, sea, and air.
Distress Frequency	2182 kHz (Upper Sideband)	156.8 MHz (channel 16)	Channel 9
Does Coast Guard monitor distress frequency?	Yes	Yes	Yes, but on a "not-to-interfere" basis.
Is marine information available over the system?	Yes. On 2670 kHz, after a preliminary call over 2182 kHz. Info. available: Weather forecasts in some areas, weather warnings, navigational safety info.	Yes. On 157. 1 MHz (channel 22) after a preliminary call over 156.8 MHz. Info. available: weather forecasts and warnings and navigational safety info. in some areas. The National Weather Service broadcasts weather info. continuously on some VHF-FM channels.	No.

OTHER SOURCES OF INFORMATION: More detailed information on FCC licenses, radiotelephone equipment and its usage, frequencies, locations of distress guards, marine weather and emergency procedures is contained in the Radiotelephone Communication for Marine Services (RTCM) handbook "How to Use Your Marine Radiotelephone." The free handbook is available by writing to: RTCM, P.O. Box 19087, Washington, D.C. 20036.

MARINE RADIOS

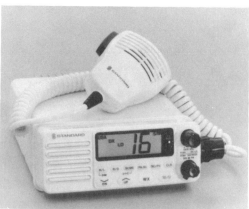

Left: SMR SeaLab 5100 is a flip-style, hand-held VHF radio. The compact, 6-inch-high model features a full five-watt output. Covers all US and international channels, 10 weather channels, and all channel scanning. **Center:** Standard Horizon Omni is a full 25-watt VHF radio with a six-watt PA hailer. At the touch of an emergency button, when interfaced with a Loran GPS or SatNav position receiver, the Omni automatically sends a continuous digital "mayday" message on channel 70 with your precise location to the Coast Guard. **Right:** Humminbird DC5 hand-held VHF radio has five watts of power for receiving and transmitting on all US and international channels, plus 10 weather channels. The Humminbird DC5 is waterproof and completely submersible.

Left: Apelco 501 Plus VHF hand-held radio features five full watts of power and a low battery indicator. The 501 Plus also has SCAN feature, which stops on all or selected channels with traffic. Transmits on 53 channels and receives on 92 channels, including 10 weather channels. **Right:** Raytheon's Ray 201 and Ray 202 scanning VHF-FM marine radios. These models transmit and receive on all US and international channels, plus 10 weather channels.

channel for Citizens Band radio, but this is on a "not-to-interfere" basis, with its primary responsibility for monitoring distress frequencies on the recognized marine bands. In other words, if the Coast Guard receives a distress call over the 2–3 MHz and VHF–FM bands, it may cease monitoring CB in order to devote its entire efforts to respond to the emergency. However, if the Coast Guard receives a distress call over the CB emergency channel, it will respond immediately, but it will not cease monitoring the distress frequencies of the designated marine communications bands.

Marine weather forecasts are available from the National Weather Service on VHF–FM. Also, in some areas the Coast Guard will broadcast weather information on both 2–3 MHz and VHF–FM. You should contact the National Weather Service, your marina, or your boating equipment store for information on which channel serves the area you will be boating in.

The most popular marine communication system in use today is the VHF-FM, and this popularity is reflected in the wide variety of VHF–FM radios available to boaters. The modern VHF-FM radio is compact, waterproof, and sometimes digital. Some have automatic scanning features. If you prefer not to install a radio permanently in your boat with an antenna, you can select a handheld portable model with rechargeable batteries. The price tag will pretty much determine the number of features in a radio. Keen competition in the international market has driven the price down to several hundred dollars for a perfectly reliable boat radio. Do some shopping and price/feature comparisons before making your selection.

How to Use a Marine Radio

With the number of radio-equipped boats continuing to increase, it is important that each boater observe the following basic procedures:

1. Prior to going out on the water, make sure your equipment is operating properly. Obtain a radio check. To do this you must call a specific station on a working frequency and, after establishing contact, ask "how do you hear me?" Radio checks on 2182 kHz are prohibited by law. And on VHF–FM Channel 16, they are strongly discouraged. The Coast Guard will not respond to a radio check on CB Channel 9.

2. Be courteous. Always listen to see if the channel is clear before transmitting. Try not to cut into someone else's conversation.

3. When transmitting, always identify your boat by name and call sign.

4. Distress frequencies can be used to establish contact with another station, but after establishing contact you must shift to a working frequency unless you are in distress or have knowledge of a distress.

5. Complete all conversations as soon as practical. Don't tie up a frequency with "chit-chat."

6. Federal Communications Commission regulations require that boats equipped with 2–3 MHz and VHF–FM radiotelephone maintain a listening watch on 2182 kHz or Channel 16, respectively, if the radio is turned on.

7. Tell what is wrong.

8. Tell what kind of assistance you need.

9. Give the number of people who are aboard your boat and, if any are injured, their condition.

10. Give the estimated seaworthiness of your boat.

11. Give a description of your boat—length, type, color, number of masts, etc.

12. Tell which channel or frequency you will be listening on.

13. End your message with: "This is (your boat's name and call sign). Over."

14. Wait for a response. If no answer, repeat your call. If still no answer, try another channel or frequency.

Note: If the Coast Guard, or another rescue organization, responds to your call, you may be asked many questions that seem unnecessary. Every question is important, since each item of information increases your chances of rescue. If you are in immediate danger, help will be dispatched while the information is being taken.

THE GLOBAL POSITIONING SYSTEM (GPS) AND LORAN

WHAT IS GPS?

The Global Positioning System is a constellation of satellites which orbit the earth twice a day, transmitting precise time and position (latitude, longitude, and altitude) information. With a GPS receiver, users can determine their location anywhere on earth. Position and navigation information is vital to a broad range of professional and personal activities, including boating, fishing, surveying, aviation, vehicle tracking and navigation, and more.

The complete system consists of 24 satellites orbiting about 12,000 miles above the earth, and five ground stations to monitor and manage the satellite constellation. These satellites provide 24-hour-a-day coverage for both two- and three-dimensional positioning anywhere on earth.

Development of the GPS satellite navigation system was begun in the 1970s by the U.S. Department of Defense, which continues to manage the system, to provide continuous, worldwide positioning and navigation data to U.S. military forces around the globe. However, GPS has an even broader civilian, commercial application. To meet these needs, GPS offers two levels of service, one for civilian access and the second encrypted for exclusive military use. The GPS signals are available to an unlimited number of users simultaneously.

HOW DOES GPS WORK?

The basis of GPS technology is precise time and position information. Using atomic clocks (accurate to within one second every 70,000 years) and location data, each satellite continuously broadcasts the time and its position. A GPS receiver receives these signals, listening to three or more satellites at once, to determine the user's position on earth.

By measuring the time interval between the transmission and the reception of a satellite signal, the GPS receiver calculates the distance between the user and each satellite. Using the distance measurements of at least three satellites in an algorithm computation, the GPS receiver arrives at an accurate position fix.

The position information in a GPS receiver may be displayed as longitude/latitude, military grid, or other system coordinates. Information must be received from three satellites in order to obtain two-dimensional (latitude and longitude) fixes, and four satellites are required for three-dimensional (latitude, longitude, and altitude) positioning.

Each satellite continuously broadcasts two signals, L1 and L2. The L1 frequency contains the C/A code which provides Standard Positioning Service (SPS) for worldwide civilian use. The encrypted P-code is broadcast on both the L1 and L2 frequency, resulting in the Precise Positioning Service (PPS) for military use. The SPS signal will provide a civilian user an accuracy of better than 25 meters. Because they are so accurate, civilian GPS receivers using the SPS signal are sometimes subjected to Selective Availability (SA) interference by the United States Government, to maintain optimum military effectiveness of the system. When engaged, SA inserts random errors in the data transmitted by the satellites. As a result, SPS signal accuracy can be reduced to 100 meters.

However, using a technique called differential GPS (DGPS), the user can overcome the effect of SA interference and increase the overall accuracy of the GPS receiver. With DGPS, one GPS receiver unit is placed at a known location and the position information from that receiver is used to calculate corrections in the position data transmitted by the satellites. This corrected information is then transmitted to other GPS receivers in the area. The resulting real-time accuracy is in the 10-meter range.

GPS receivers provide positioning, velocity, and navigation information for a variety of purposes. Anyone who needs to know the precise time or the exact location of people or objects will benefit from GPS. In turn, this information can be used in charting and mapping, plotting a course, navigating from point to point, tracking vehicle movement, locating previously identified sites, or any number of similar functions.

LORAN

Portions of text courtesy of National Marine Electronics Assn.

Loran-C is a radionavigation system operating on a frequency of 100 kHz. It uses shore-based transmitters, which broadcast signals hundreds of miles in all directions. The transmitting stations are organized into chains covering geographical regions. An on-board Loran-C receiver calculates its location by measuring the time differences in signals received from three or more stations in a chain.

Loran is an acronym standing for **LO**ng **RA**nge Navigation. The modern Loran-C system grew out of an earlier system called Loran-A, which was developed during World War II to meet military requirements. Based on successful wartime experience with Loran-A, the system was expanded during the postwar years. By the end of the 1960s, there were more than 80 Loran-A transmitters serving tens of thousands of mariners.

Loran-A had limitations, however, and work soon began on a successor system that would have longer range and better accuracy. Thus Loran-C was born.

In 1974, the U.S. government, following an exhaustive survey of all available systems, designated Loran-C as the offical government-provided radionavigation aid for the Coastal Confluence Zone. The U.S. Coast Guard embarked on a dramatic expansion of the system. As the Loran-C system grew, Loran-A was slowly phased out, and by the early 1980s the changeover was complete.

Loran-C coverage now exists along the entire

PRINCIPLES OF LORAN-C

Figure 1: Broadcast from master and secondary stations.

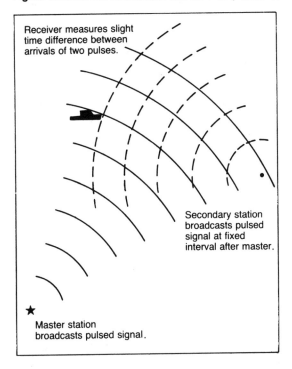

Receiver measures slight time difference between arrivals of two pulses.

Secondary station broadcasts pulsed signal at fixed interval after master.

Master station broadcasts pulsed signal.

Figure 2: Hyperbolic lines of constant time difference.

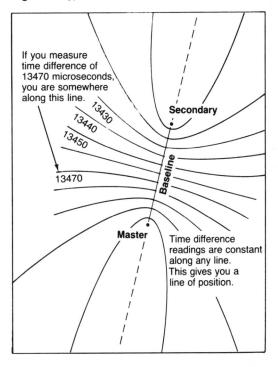

If you measure time difference of 13470 microseconds, you are somewhere along this line.

13430
13440
13450
13470

Secondary

Baseline

Master

Time difference readings are constant along any line. This gives you a line of position.

Figure 3: A Loran-C fix.

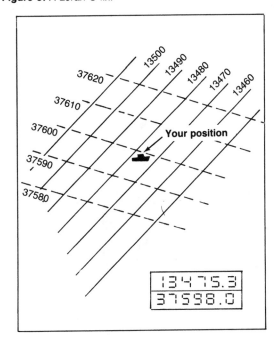

13500
13490
13480
13470
13460
37620
37610
37600
37590
37580

Your position

```
13475.3
37598.0
```

U.S. and Canadian coastline at least 200 miles to sea, as well as in the Great Lakes region and in many other parts of the world.

While the basic principles of Loran-C may be confusing at first, remember that the main purpose of Loran is to fix your position anywhere on the water in any kind of weather. This means you can drift or troll all day out of sight of land, then fix your position and compute a direct course home. By reversing the process, this also means you can return to the exact location the next day to catch the big ones that got away. All you need are a pair of numbers to plot your course. And if you get into trouble, give your Loran numbers to the Coast Guard and they can get to you fast and directly.

RADAR

RADAR means **RA**dio **D**etection **A**nd **R**anging. Basically, it's an electronic device that provides ranges and bearings as well as visual pictures of boats, planes, land and so on. Radar is extremely valuable to boaters on the water in times of low visibility, such as fog and at night.

Radar operates much the way a depthsounder

RADAR UNITS

Left: Raytheon Compact RL9 LCD Radar measures 8 inches wide, 7½ inches high, and 2½ inches deep. Has a range up to 16 miles and can also be used to view electronic charts on the radar display. **Center:** Furuno 821/841 LCD Radar has an 8-inch diagonal screen and a range up to 36 nautical miles. Can be interfaced with a GPS or Loran-C to read your navigational information right on the radar screen. **Right:** SI-TEX T-150 LCD radar has a 7-inch display screen and 12 programmable ranges up to 16 miles. To monitor fishing hotspots, the Position-Pick-Off Control can display the Lat/Lon coordinates of any boat on the screen.

does, except that the transmission is through air rather than water. A radar unit transmits pulses of super-high frequency radio waves that are reflected by objects in the distance. The time it takes for the radio wave to go out and the echo to return is the measure of the distance to the object.

There are four components to a radar set:

1. The transmitter, which transmits radio waves in brief impulses.
2. The antenna, which radiates the impulses and collects the returning echoes.
3. The receiver, which picks up the returning echoes.
4. The screen, which produces a visual display of the objects in the path of the radar signals.

Makers of modern radar units for small boats have managed to combine these four components into two units: The transmitter and antenna in one unit, and the receiver and screen in another.

As with other marine electronics, stiff competition has also driven down the price of radar. Radar, at one time, was found only on big private yachts or commercial vessels. Today, it is not uncommon to see radar on small fishing boats in the 25-foot range. There's no doubt that radar can give you a much greater edge of safety.

RADIO DIRECTION FINDERS

There was a time when radio direction finders (RDF) were considered a valuable navigational aid for small boats. An angler just rotated his antenna on his RDF, picked up the two strongest signals from the

Aqua Meter Radio Direction Finder is a radio receiver with rotatable antenna designed to pick up strongest radio signals to fix a position.

U.S. Coast Guard's radio beacon system or the standard AM radio broadcast band and triangulated his position. There was just one catch. Positional accuracy was always questionable with a RDF. When affordable, compact Loran-C came along with its unbelievable accuracy, the RDF faded from popularity. Radio directional finders are still useful, however, and some anglers still carry them as a backup for their Loran. Of course, RDFs are invaluable if you have no other navigational aids on your boat.

EPIRB

EPIRBs (Emergency Position Indicating Radio-beacons) are electronic devices that transmit signals that can guide rescuers to your disabled boat. If you regularly go far offshore, especially beyond 20 miles or so, where you will be stretching the range of your VHF radio, it's wise to carry a Class A or EPIRB. In an emergency, this device will transmit a continuous signal on two aircraft frequencies. High-flying aircraft can pick up these signals as far away as 200 miles. More important, Coast Guard planes are equipped with automatic direction finders for EPIRB frequencies.

The latest development in EPIRBs is the Class C units, which became available in the early 1980s. The Class C EPIRB is designed for use in coastal waters to about 30 miles offshore. A Class C will send its signal on VHF channels 16 and 15, the channels constantly monitored by the Coast Guard. A brief signal is transmitted on Channel 16, then the signal is switched to Channel 15 for a longer period of time for verification and direction finding. A complete cycle of these alternating signals continues

ACR Miniature Class B Emergency Position Indicating Radio Beeping (EPIRB), the Mini B2, transmits simultaneously on 121.5 MHz (civilian) and 243.0 MHz (military) search and rescue homing frequencies. A good choice for recreational boaters who want the security of an emergency beacon on their craft.

for 24 hours on both channels 16 and 15. All EPIRBs are battery powered and must be capable of transmitting a signal for 48 hours. These units are also designed to float and transmit signals in case of a sinking boat.

ANCHORS, MOORINGS, AND ROPES

An anchor is essential to safe boat operation, yet many boat liveries where small fishing boats are rented put their boats out without either anchor or lines. When you know the importance of having an anchor, you will insist on having an effective one aboard even on a normally calm lake, and enough anchor line to give safe scope. In addition to safety, an anchor is necessary to hold position in a breeze or current when fishing and hunting. For the boater, a boat is half useless without a good anchor.

The major misconception about anchors is that the heavier the anchor, the more it will hold. This is not the case. The key is the meaning of *hold*. An

anchor does not function by weighing down but by holding onto the bottom effectively. A concrete block weighing twenty pounds may roll on a sloping bottom and slide on a hard bottom as the breeze tugs at the boat. Finally, with luck, it may come up against a flat-sided rock, where it might hold until the breeze shifts. In the same situation, a Danforth or a kedge anchor weighing only three pounds will probably hold the boat fast after kedging only several feet until its sharp flukes find a grip in the bottom.

Many small boats are equipped with mushroom-type anchors. These have a solid, weighty feel—even the small ones. Regardless of the direction in

TYPES AND PARTS OF ANCHORS

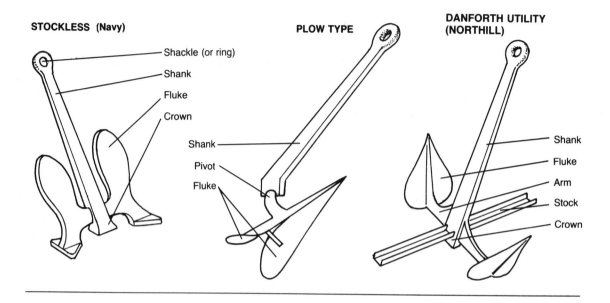

STOCKLESS (Navy)

— Shackle (or ring)

— Shank

— Fluke

— Crown

PLOW TYPE

Shank —

Pivot —

Fluke —

DANFORTH UTILITY (NORTHILL)

— Shank

— Fluke

— Arm

— Stock

— Crown

MUSHROOM ANCHOR WEIGHTS

LENGTH OF BOAT	POWER:	SAIL: (Racing)	SAIL: (Cruising)
25'	225 lbs.	125 lbs.	175 lbs.
35'	300 lbs.	200 lbs.	250 lbs.
45'	400 lbs.	325 lbs.	400 lbs.
55'	500 lbs.	450 lbs.	550 lbs.

which they are pulled, the lip of the cup will drag in contact with the bottom and possibly hold. But when they hook a bottom snag or settle in mud, the weight of the cast-iron mushroom plus the weight of the bottom becomes a formidable load to haul up through the water.

Since anchor weight and size suitable to a boat of a given size vary widely according to the anchor design and to local conditions, no guidelines can be given that apply to all anchor types in common use. (Remember that concrete blocks and cans with cast-in concrete are among the commonest of small-boat anchors). However, guidelines for Danforth and mushroom-type anchors are provided in the accompanying tables.

A mushroom anchor may be adequate on a protected lake with a firm bottom, but on a fast-moving stream this anchor will be ineffective. On a large,

open water, a concrete block or another type of simple, heavy anchor can be a hazard. When the wind blows, the anchor will roll until the boat is in water deeper than the length of the anchor rope. The anchor then becomes a load on the bow, dipping deeper in the trough of waves than it should.

A number of anchor designs for pleasure boats have been developed which are effective by application rather than weight. One of the best is the Danforth. This anchor will hold on a hard bottom and can be retrieved on a rock-filled bottom. Most have trip features for releasing the anchor when it gets caught on the bottom.

The length of the anchor line is an important factor in effective anchoring. In calm waters, twice the depth of the water is enough line. This assumes you are in the boat and can bring it easily to shore if a sudden storm comes up or your motor gives out. In open waters, your anchor line should be three to five times the depth of the water. For riding overnight or when the boat is unattended, you need seven times the depth. Obviously the reason is holding power. If the length of the line plus the anchor design permit the pull to be applied horizontally against the anchor's purchase on the bottom, it will help it to hold. On boats 17 feet and larger, a short length of strong chain next to the anchor will help the an-

ANCHORS

Left: Mushroom anchors depend on weight to a large extent for holding the boat. A well-made mushroom anchor has holes cast in the cup to let water and mud drain; still, it is a job to haul one of these from deep water with mud or marl bottom. **Center:** Cadmium-plated folding anchor weighs only 2 pounds. Its four flukes lock open and will hold on most bottoms. It's suitable for canoes and small boats. **Right:** This lightweight Danforth anchor is made in various sizes for boats from 10 feet up. When the anchor line is attached to the sliding ring on the shank, a snagged anchor can be drawn out backwards by backing boat across anchor. This arrangement is perfect for use on snag-filled bottoms.

SUGGESTED DANFORTH ANCHOR SIZES

LENGTH OF BOAT	BEAM		STANDARD SIZES			HI-TENSILE SIZES	
	SAIL	POWER	WORKING	STORM	LUNCH	WORKING	STORM
10 ft.	4 ft.	4 ft.	2½	4	Hook	5	5
15 ft.	5 ft.	5 ft.	4	8	—	5	5
20 ft.	6 ft.	6 ft.	8	13	—	5	12
25 ft.	6½ ft.	7 ft.	8	13	5	12	12
30 ft.	7 ft.	9 ft.	13	22	5	12	18
35 ft.	8 ft.	10 ft.	22	22	5	18	18
40 ft.	9 ft.	11 ft.	22	40	5	18	28
50 ft.	11 ft.	13 ft.	40	65	12	28	60
60 ft.	12 ft.	14 ft.	65	85	12	60	90

chor hold its bite and reduce chafing of the rope against the rocks and the anchor itself.

The best way to free most anchors that are stuck in the bottom is by pulling straight up. If you find you cannot do this, try snubbing the line until it runs vertically down to the snagged anchor. Take a bite around the cleat to hold the line tight, then rock the boat fore and aft, or let wave action do this until the anchor is worked free. The force of the boat's motion is greater than you can apply by hand.

When anchoring on large or windy waters, reckon the directions of wind and wave action before setting anchor. If you have a choice of anchoring on a lee or windward shore, choose the lee. Then your boat won't be blown or washed onto the rocks by morn-

MOORINGS

Three-anchor mooring
with Danforth anchors

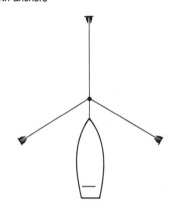

Fore-and-aft mooring
for crowded anchorage

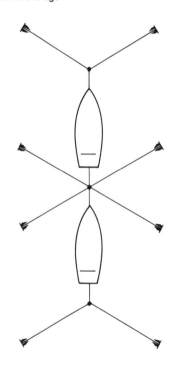

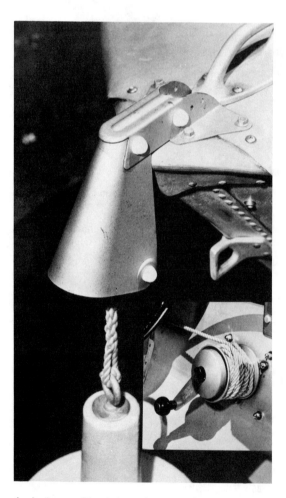

Anchoring small boats is made easy and quick for the lone sportsman with a hand-operated winch and bow pulley.

ing. In a popular mooring place, set your anchor so that you have several boat lengths between you and other craft. Then if a storm arises, even the worst fury won't cause damage.

Many fishermen like to drag or tow their anchor when drift fishing in windy, deep waters. This is somewhat of a hazard to the anchor and line, and the anchor must be fully hauled to start the motor again to regain the best position. You might prefer instead to store a sea anchor or two for the purpose. This is a canvas bucket that acts as a drag. It is attached with a halter to a light nylon line that can be hauled in easily.

HOW TO SET A MOORING

An anchored mooring is cheaper than a dock, and in many crowded public facilities it is the only choice. The authorities may stipulate the minimum mooring that is acceptable. You may want to improve on this, particularly if you have a valuable boat. In any case, remember that your boat might do damage if it drags its mooring or breaks loose—and the responsibility is yours.

On soft bottoms, heavy iron mushroom-type moorings are often used successfully. Chain is attached from the mooring anchor to a floating buoy, where the boat is tied, usually with a snap hook on a short line from the bow. Even a big mushroom mooring can be pulled through the mud if a really hard storm or hurricane blows, however, and it is

against this occasional danger that you must prepare when setting a permanent mooring. A single mooring anchor assumes adequate scope on the line to hold in a blow; but scope of this length is impossible in crowded anchorages. Therefore, three anchors are sometimes used, set in an equilateral triangle with only one boat-length of extra scope to the buoy (see diagram). An alternative in the most crowded locations is fore-and-aft anchoring, with two anchors to each buoy, and each boat tied to the buoy both fore and aft of it.

ANCHOR LINES AND STRENGTH

Synthetic fibers have produced ropes that are a blessing to boatmen. The new ropes are somewhat more expensive than manila and linen rope, but they are stronger for their size, lighter, more comfortable to handle, do not rot or mildew, and are easy to work. One drawback is that they resist bite in tying; therefore knots must be positive. Granny knots and loose knots are out. Elasticity is always a factor to be considered when using any line for anchoring or tying a boat at a dock. Nylon rope is more than four times as elastic as manila when loaded repeatedly; Dacron is about 50 percent more elastic than manila, but is more sensitive than nylon to abrasion from the side. Here, courtesy of Plymouth Yacht Ropes, are comparative strengths for common boating ropes:

ROPES: COMPARATIVE STRENGTH AND WEIGHT

		MINIMUM TENSILE STRENGTH (LBS.)*			AVERAGE TENSILE STRENGTH (LBS.)			
Circ.	Dia.	Ship Brand Manila	Yacht Manila	Linen Yacht	Nylon and Gold Line	"Dacron"	Poly-ethylene	Poly-propylene
9/16"	3/16"	450	525	600	1100	1050	690	1050
3/4"	1/4"	600	688	1020	1850	1750	1150	1700
1"	5/16"	1000	1190	1520	2850	2650	1730	2450
1-1/8"	3/8"	1350	1590	2090	4000	3600	2400	3400
1-1/4"	7/16"	1750	1930	2700	5500	4800	3260	4300
1-1/2"	1/2"	2650	2920	3500	7100	6100	4050	5300
1-3/4"	9/16"	3450	3800	4350	8350	7400	5000	6400
2"	5/8"	4400	4840	5150	10500	9000	6050	7600
2-1/4"	3/4"	5400	5940	7100	14200	12500	9000	10000
2-3/4"	7/8"	7700	8450	9400	19000	16000	12000	13000
3"	1"	9000	9900	12000	24600	20000	15000	16500
3-1/2"	1-1/8"	12000	13200	——	34000	21500	18500	19500
3-3/4"	1-1/4"	13500	14850	——	38000	24500	21000	22000
4-1/2"	1-1/2"	18500	——	——	55000	36000	29000	31500

For the approximate average tensile strength, add 20% for Ship Brand and Yacht Manila Ropes; 20% for Linen Yacht Rope.

CORDAGE FIBER PROPERTIES—TYPICAL VALUES

	Manila	Sisal	Cotton	Nylon	Polyester	Polypropylene	Polyethylene	Aramid[2]	Extended Chain P/E[2]
STRENGTH:									
• Breaking tenacity-dry (grams/denier)	5–6.0	4–5.0	2–3.0	7.8–10.4	7.0–10.5	6.5	6.0	18–26.5	30[f]/35[g]
• Wet strength compared to dry strength	Up to 120%	Up to 120%	Up to 120%	85–90%[1]	100%[-][1]	100%	105%	95%	100%
• Shock load absorption ability	Poor	Poor	Very Poor	Excellent	Very Good	Very Good	Fair	—	Fair
WEIGHT:									
• Specific gravity	1.38	1.38	1.54	1.14	1.38	.91	.95	1.44	.97
• Able to float	No	No	No	No	No	Yes	Yes	No	Yes
ELONGATION:									
• Percent at break	10–12%	10–12%	5–12%	15–28%	12–15%	18–22%	20–24%	1.5–3.6%	2.7[f]/3.5[f]
• Creep (extension under sustained load)	Very Low	Very Low	—	Moderate	Low	High	High	Very Low	Moderate
EFFECTS OF MOISTURE:									
• Water absorption of individual fibers	Up to 100%	Up to 100%	Up to 100%	2.0–8.0%	<1.0%	None	None	3.5–7.0%	None
• Resistance to rot, mildew and deterioration due to marine organisms	Poor	Very Poor	Very Poor	Excellent	Excellent	Excellent	Excellent	Excellent	Excellent
DEGRADATION:									
• Resistance to U.V. in sunlight	Good	Good	Good	Good	Excellent	Fair (Black is best)	Fair (Black is best)	Fair[e]	Fair
• Resistance to aging for properly stored rope	Good	Good	Good	Excellent	Excellent	Excellent	Excellent	Excellent	Excellent
ROPE ABRASION RESISTANCE:									
• Surface	Good	Fair	Poor	Very Good	Best	Good	Fair	Fair[e]	Very Good
• Internal	Good	Good	Good	Excellent	Best	Good	Good	Good	Excellent
THERMAL PROPERTIES:									
• High temperature working limit	300°F	300°F	300°F	250°F	275°F	200°F	150°F	350°F	150°F
• Low temperature working limit	-100°F	-100°F	-100°F	-70°F	-70°F	-20°F	-100°F	-100°F	-200°F
• Melts at	—	—	Chars 300°F	420–480°F	490–500°F	330°F	285°F	800°F (Begins to decompose)	297°F
CHEMICAL RESISTANCE:									
• Effect of acids	Will disintegrate in hot diluted and cold concentrated acids	Same as Manila	Same as Manila	Decomposed by strong mineral acids; resistant to weak acids	Resistant to most mineral acids; disintegrate by 95% sulphuric acid	Very Resistant	Very Resistant	Resistant to most weak acids. Strong acids will attack, particularly at high temperatures or concentrations	Very Resistant
• Effect of alkalis	Poor resistance; will lose strength where exposed	Same as Manila	May swell but will not be damaged	Little or none	No effect cold; slowly disintegrate by strong alkalis at the boil	Very Resistant	Very Resistant	Resistant to most weak alkalis. Strong alkalis will attack, particularly at high temperatures or concentrations	Very Resistant
• Effect of organic solvents	Fair resistance for fiber, but hydrocarbons will remove protective lubricants on rope	Good resistance	Poor resistance	Resistant, soluble in some phenolic compounds and in 90% formic acid	Generally unaffected; soluble in some phenolic compounds	Soluble in chlorinated hydrocarbons at 160°F	Same as polypropylene	Resistant to most ketones, alcohols, oils, hydrocarbons	Same as polypropylene

Source: Kordage Institute Technical Service

[1]Grades with special overfinishes are available to enhance wet strength properties.   [3]Excellent when jacketed.   [4]Based on DuPont Kevlar® data.   [6]Based on Allied/Signal Spectra® data—type 900.
[5]Based on Spectra® data—type 1000.   [2]Based on Allied/Signal Spectra® data.

RECOMMENDED ANCHOR LINES FOR POWER CRAFT

	ANCHOR	OVER-ALL LENGTH OF BOAT					
		Under 20'	20'–25'	25'–30'	30'–40'	40'–50'	50'–65'
Length of	Light	100'	100'	100'	125'	150'	180'
Anchor Lines	Heavy		150'	180'	200'	250'	300'
Diameter if	Light	3/8"	3/8"	1/2"	9/16"	3/4"	7/8"
Nylon	Heavy		1/2"	9/16"	3/4"	1"	1 1/8"
Diameter if	Light	1/2"	1/2"	5/8"	3/4"	1"	1 1/4"
1st Class Manila	Heavy		5/8"	3/4"	1"	1 3/8"	1 1/2"
Diam. if Plymouth	Light	7/16"	7/16"	9/16"	5/8"	7/8"	1"
Bolt Manila	Heavy		9/16"	5/8"	7/8"	1 1/8"	1 1/4"

EASY ANCHOR RETRIEVAL

This simple-and-easy method of pulling up your anchor is a boon to bad backs and big boats. Learn this technique and the hard work is done by an inflated net ball, the kind usually found on commercial fishing boats. The only equipment you will need is a stainless-steel anchor ring, heavy-duty stainless snap, five or six feet of nylon, and the net ball. The box (upper right) shows all of the elements of an anchor-retrieval system properly rigged.

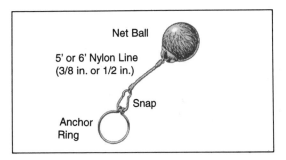

Step 1—When you are ready to haul your anchor, take the anchor retrieval rig and snap the ring on your anchor line. Start your boat.

Step 2—Run your boat at a slow speed in a direction slightly to either side of the anchor line. Watch your anchor line, so you do not run over it. When the anchor line comes alongside, fasten the line to a rear cleat and keep the boat moving in the same direction.

Step 3—The net ball will slide down the anchor line and disappear. When it pops back up with the anchor, keep going to make sure the anchor ring rides all the way down the anchor chain to the blades. When you stop the boat, the net ball, anchor, and anchor line will be floating on the surface for an easy pickup.

The following chart shows the suggested ball sizes.

Ball	Anchor/chain
NB-40	40 pounds
NB-50	75 pounds
NB-60	130 pounds
NB-75	240 pounds

BOAT KNOTS

Part of the fun in owning a boat is in learning and using boat knots. Most of the knots commonly used in boating are illustrated in the Camping section of this book. Here are ways to make knots and splices needed for anchoring and mooring your boat.

SHORT SPLICE

This is the strongest of splices for joining ends of two pieces of rope, but it cannot be used to run through a pulley due to the bulk of the splice.

1. Lash rope about twelve diameters from each end (A). Unlay the strands up to the lashings. Whip strands to prevent untwisting and put together as in diagram **above,** alternating the strands from each end. Pull up taut.

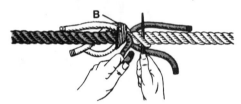

2. Now tie down all the strands temporarily (B). Take off the lashing from one side of the rope and raise one strand on this side, using a fid. Take the middle strand of the opposite side. Tuck it over one strand and under the raised strand. Pull it up taut.

3. Tuck against the twist or "lay" of the rope. What happens is that the tuck goes over one strand, under the second, and out between the second and third.

4. Roll the rope toward you. Pick up the second strand. Repeat the same operation. Then do it again with the third strand. You have now made one full tuck.

To taper the splice, first make one more tuck just like the first one. Then make the third tuck the same way, but first cut off ⅓ of the yarns from the strands. For the fourth tuck, cut off ½ the remaining yarn.

For the untapered short splice, you do not cut the strands. You just make three more tucks, exactly like the first one.

5. Take both lashings (which were applied in No. 1 and No. 2) off the other side of the rope. Repeat above operations.

6. To finish, cut off ends of strands, leaving about one or two inches protruding.

To Splice Nylon Rope—The above procedure applies to splicing of nylon and other synthetic ropes except that one additional full tuck should be used.

LONG SPLICE

Slightly weaker than the Short Splice, but it allows the rope to run freely through a properly sized pulley and causes less wear at the point of splicing.

1. Unlay the end of each rope about 15 turns and place the ropes together, alternating the strands from each end, as shown **above.**

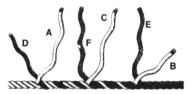

2. Start with any opposite pair, unlay one strand and replace it with strand from the other part. Repeat operation with another pair of strands in the opposite direction as shown.

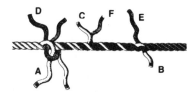

3. Now tie each pair of opposing strands, as B and E above, with an overhand knot, tuck each strand twice, as in the Short Splice, and then twice more. Or, halve each strand (see A and D) and tie with an overhand knot before tucking. By this latter method a smaller splice results—but at a considerable sacrifice of strength.

4. Roll and pound well before cutting strands off close to rope.

EYE OR SIDE SPLICE

The Side Splice is also called the Eye Splice because it is used to form an eye or loop in the end of a rope by splicing the end back into its own side.

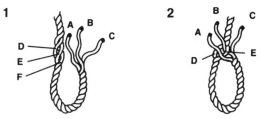

1. Start by seizing the working end of the rope. Unlay the three strands A, B, and C to the seizing and whip the end of each strand. Then twist the rope slightly to open up strands D, E, and F of the standing part of the rope, as indicated **above left.**

2. The first tuck is shown **above right.** The middle strand is always tucked first, so strand B is tucked under strand E, the middle strand of the standing part.

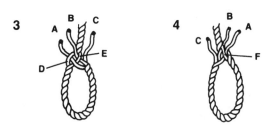

3. The second tuck is now made, as shown **above left.** Left strand A of the working end is tucked under strand D, passing over strand E.

4. Illustration **above right** shows how the third tuck is made. In order to make strand F easy to get at, the rope is turned over. Strand C now appears on the left side.

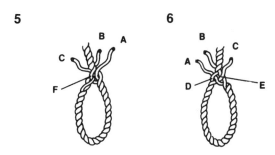

5. Strand C is then passed to the right of and tucked under strand F, as shown **above left.** This completes the first round of tucks.

6. Illustration **above right** shows the second round of tucks started, with the rope reversed again for ease in handling. Strand B is passed over strand D and tucked under the next strand to the left. Continue with strands A and C, tucking over one strand and then under one to the left. To complete the splice, tuck each strand once more.

7. The finished Eye Splice is shown **above.** Remove the temporary seizing and cut off the strand ends, leaving at least ½ inch on each end. Roll splice back and forth under your foot to even up and smooth out the strands.

FIGURE EIGHT KNOT

This knot can be tied simply and quickly. Used in the end of a rope to temporarily prevent the strands from unlaying, it does not jam as easily as the overhand knot and is therefore useful in preventing the end of a rope from slipping through a block or an eye.

BOWLINE

The bowline is often used for temporary anchor knots. It never jams or slips if properly tied.

DOUBLE BOWLINE

To Tie: Make an overhand loop with the end held toward you, exactly as in the ordinary Bowline. The difference being that you pass the end through the loop *twice* —making *two* lower loops, A and B. The end is then passed *behind* the standing part and down through the first loop again as in the ordinary Bowline. Pull tight. Used as a seat sling, the outside loop B goes under the person's arms, and the inside loop A forms the seat.

BOWLINE IN BIGHT

Here's a useful knot to know when you want to attach tackle to, say, the middle of a line when both ends of it are made fast. To Tie: Grasp the rope where you want the new knot, shape it into a loop in one hand and strike this against the two lines leading to the loop, held in the other hand. Then complete the first bight used in tying a regular Bowline. Now, open the loop after it has passed through the bight and bring the whole knot through it. Pull the loop tight over the standing part.

RUNNING BOWLINE

Tie the regular Bowline around a loop of its own standing part. This makes an excellent slip knot, commonly used to retrieve spars, rigging, etc. And with lighter rope or twine, it's good for tightening to begin package tying.

SURGEON'S KNOT

This knot is usually tied with twine. It is a modified form of the Reef Knot, and the extra turn taken in the first tie prevents slipping before knot is completed.

FISHERMAN'S BEND

An important knot because of its strength and simplicity it is used for making the end of a rope fast to a ring, spar, or anchor, or for a line to a bucket. More secure when the end is tied as shown.

REEF KNOT

Probably the most useful and popular of all knots, this is also known as the Square Knot. Used to join two ropes or lines of the same size, it holds firmly and is easily untied.

TIMBER HITCH

Very useful for hoisting spars, boards, or logs. Also handy for making a towline fast to a wet spar or timber. This knot holds without slipping and does not jam.

FISHERMAN'S KNOT

This is probably the strongest known method of joining fine lines such as fishing lines. Simple to tie and untie.

CLOVE HITCH

This is the most effective quick way to tie a boat line to a mooring post. It can be tied in the middle or end of a rope but it is apt to slip if tied at the end. To prevent slipping, make a half-hitch in the end to the standing part.

SHEET BEND

Used aboard a boat for joining small or medium-sized ropes. Sometimes used for attaching the end of a rope to an eye splice.

TYING LINE TO A CLEAT

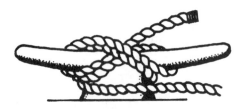

This is the correct method for tying line to a cleat. The half hitch which completes the fastening is taken with the free part of the line. The line can then be freed without taking up slack in the standing part.

KNOTS FOR POLYPROPYLENE CORD

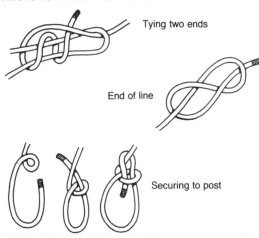

Tying two ends

End of line

Securing to post

TO PREVENT TWISTED ROPE FROM UNRAVELING WHEN CUT

1. Nylon, polyester, and polypropylene: Tape the rope around circumference as illustrated. Cut in the middle leaving tape intact on either side. When cutting these synthetic fibers with a pocket knife or scissors, fuse the cut ends by match-flame to prevent untwisting.

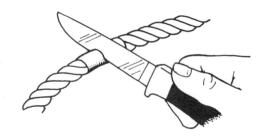

Tape is unnecessary if a "hot knife" is used. Heat will melt and fuse the cut ends.

2. Manila and sisal: Tape the rope as illustrated **above**. Cut in the middle so that each end remains permanently taped. Natural fibers do not fuse with heat.

PREPARING FOR WINTER STORAGE

This work is necessary to keep your boat serviceable and to protect your investment in it. If you live where you can enjoy year-round boating, there are important semi-annual maintenance jobs that you will recognize. If you can store your boat at home the job will be greatly simplified, but if you store it in a boatyard you may have to work within the yard's schedule. In deciding whether to store your boat outside or in a heated garage, for instance, there are two dangers that must be avoided: formation of ice on the boat, and continual dry heat. Small aluminum boats are affected less than wood, fiberglass, or fabric ones. Hard freezing and ice can pop fastenings, open seams, split and check the surface, and cause permanent warp in straight lines. Dry heat

for long periods can destroy the resins in woods (including wood stringers and outfittings in other than wood boats) and dry out calking and seam compounds. If you store your boat outdoors in natural humidity conditions, keep it covered so that water cannot collect and form ice. Indoors or out, free ventilation is essential so that condensation can evaporate.

• First, make sure your boat is properly cradled for storage. If you have a trailer that fits your boat you have no problem. Level the trailer on chocks, wheels off the ground. If you own a small aluminum boat, it will store well turned face down, resting on the strongly built gunwales. If you must build a cradle for a larger boat, make accurate templates and cut cradle supports for transom, engine bed, construction center, and stem at least.

• Clean the bottom and outside hull entirely of algae, fungi, and barnacles. This must be done immediately, before they harden and dry fast. At this time you'll get a good look at the condition and know what repairs have to be made before spring launching.

• Scrub down the entire boat inside, starting at the top. Flush and clean out bilges with bilge cleaner. Flush out freshwater tanks, fish and bait boxes, and freshwater lines with disinfectant solution and let them dry. Remove all traces of salt water, polish, clean, and spray on preservative.

• Wash canvas tops, curtains, and rope lines with mild soap and rinse with fresh water. Spray with preservative before storing in a dry place.

• Treat serious rust at once. Clean down to bare metal or remove and replace. Reputty fastenings, spray fixed hardware with clear vinyl, spray moving hardware with light machine oil.

• Make sure every corner of the boat, every fitting and joint, is dry, clean, and free of fungi. Treat inside corners in a wood boat with dry-rot compound. Put dessicants wherever needed. Air the boat by opening all hatches on each dry, bright day.

Follow motor storage procedures given in the owner's manual. Cover these points particularly:

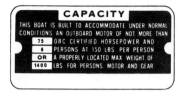

Some boats have a metal capacity plate, usually mounted near the operator's position.

• Flush cooling system with fresh water and rust inhibitor, then drain system well.

• Disconnect fuel lines and run idle until out of fuel.

• Disconnect battery, wipe connectors and terminals clean, then follow maker's battery storage procedures.

• Clean carburetor bowl with automotive carburetor cleaner or lacquer thinner. Slosh the cleaner fluid around in a portable gas tank and pour out through the fuel lines and drain it well. This removes gummy substance left by fuel.

• Remove spark plugs with a spark-plug wrench, squirt lubricating oil into each cylinder, then turn crankshaft by hand to distribute the oil. Replace spark plugs.

• Leave motor head and lower unit clean of heavy dirt, rust, and grease deposits. Wipe the head and lower unit with an oily cloth.

• Make sure lower unit grease reservoir is left full.

PREPARING FOR SPRING LAUNCHING

Most owners start too late, missing a month or two of good boating before they are ready to launch. Use the post-holiday winter quiet to do inside work you want to accomplish: Build cabinets, a fish box, circulating bait well, other basement shop jobs. Keep your eye on the old girl throughout the winter if she's stored outside. At the first robin, go down and look her over, head to foot. Make an estimate of nobs, tools, and materials you'll need. First, do the outside hull—everything it needs to give you a safe and trouble-free season. A wood hull should be sanded down to clean, bare wood, whether you are restoring just a place or two where needed or refinishing the complete hull. Peeling and cracking on top indicates trouble underneath. Down to bare wood, you may discover the source. Sand the wood smooth, fill cracks and holes and over fastenings, replace damaged boards, and dust clean before starting to paint.

Marine paints will take ten times the abuse and

last three times longer than they did twenty years ago; but they have their price. Proceed carefully until you know what to do. Get paint-maker's recommendations and specifications for your hull. Polyester paints will give you an amazingly tough coat when properly applied, but you will probably do better with an epoxy-based paint over fiberglass. Talk to your dealer and other owners. If you want to paint an originally unpainted aluminum boat, get the boat-maker's specifications; certain paints can't be used.

Before you paint a bare fiberglass hull or cabin, think twice. You will not be able to sand and strip it as you did the wood hull before. To repaint, you have to leave the first paint or risk damaging the gel coat. Most owners for this reason try to bleach out discolorations and stains. Spots can be scoured and buffed. Ask for recommended materials at a marine store. Damaged spots can be patched with fiberglass. Best overall treatment is to wax well with a marine-grade wax and sail on. If you must paint it, use steel-wool which will give tooth for the paint, and use paints recommended by the manufacturers.

Any surface must be absolutely clean before re-painting.

On cabin woods, spar varnish is usually used; it's tough and looks boaty. Oiled and waxed cabin wood is serviceable and looks more homey. Whatever your choice, on high-wear places that scuff and go bare quickly, use a good grade of clear plastic vinyl on top, renewed every spring.

If you find mildew or water inside, note how they got in and repair the damage. Next fall you will use more dessicant in some corners, buy a better tarp, or add weatherstripping to your windows. Neutralize foul odors before you launch; it's easy. Try the su-permarket.

Flush out all freshwater systems again with dis-infectant, fill the tanks, and turn on the pressure. A drip is a leak. Fix it before you sail and you'll have a drier, safer boat. Check all through-hull fit-tings. If you find any sign of leaking or rot, restore the watertight fit and get the best advice you can to make it permanent.

Here, from the service experts at Outboard Ma-rine Corporation (the Johnson Outboards and Ev-inrude Motors people) are some important steps to follow to get your motor ready to go after winter storage:

1. Check the level of lubricant in the lower unit and make sure it's filled to the proper level. If it appears oil has been leaking, have a service expert check this out since it could indicate the lower seals and gaskets need replacing. And if you didn't do this before off-season storage, drain the gearcase and refill it with the manufacturer's recommended lubricant.

Gearcase lube is available in a variety of con-tainers, from small tubes to gallons (complete with a hand-operated pump for clean, efficient applica-tion). So whether you have a small motor or a large one, one motor or a fleet of them, lubricant is avail-able in the size you need.

2. If your motor has a power trim or power tilt unit, check the level of fluid in the system's res-ervoir, and refill it with the manufacturer's rec-ommended fluid, as needed.

3. Check your spark plugs. Your outboard can't start quickly and run efficiently if the plugs aren't sparking. Remove them, clean them, and make sure they are gapped to specification. Also make sure the spark-plug terminal connections and wiring are clean, unfrayed, and snug-fitting.

4. Check the boat's battery. Make sure it's filled with water and fully charged. Clean the terminal posts and connectors so they are free of corrosion.

5. If there was unused fuel left in the tank and engine over the winter, it should have been treated with a fuel conditioner before storage. If the fuel *was* conditioned, all you need to do in the spring is make sure fuel-system clamps and fittings are tight and not leaking. Also check for cracked, worn, or aged fuel lines and replace as necessary.

However, if *no* fuel conditioner was added before storage, clean the fuel-pump filter before adding fresh fuel. Although they vary from brand to brand, most outboard fuel filters are designed for easy cleaning. Check your owner's manual for instruc-tions. Of course, all the old, untreated fuel should be drained from the tank and disposed of properly before new, fresh fuel is added. If you have an out-board with an oil injection system, check to make sure the oil tank is filled. Also check your owner's manual for any special maintenance the oil injection system might require.

6. Many boaters use a fuel conditioner for win-ter storage, but then neglect its in-season use. Used in much smaller quantities during the boating sea-son, outboard fuel conditioners help keep the car-buretor clean, reduces plug fouling, and reduces moisture in the fuel system. A note of caution: Use only fuel conditioners designed for marine use in your boat, not automotive additives or conditioners, which can do your motor more harm than good.

7. Check your propeller. A little ding in the prop can make a big dent in your boat's performance. If the propeller is nicked, gouged or bent, take it to your dealer or a prop shop for repair. If the prop is too far gone, invest in a new one. Stainless pro-pellers offer much greater durability than most alu-minum props.

Here's a safety tip: before removing your pro-peller, always shift your motor to neutral and re-move the key from the ignition switch to prevent the motor from accidently starting. If you have trouble loosening the propeller nut, try wedging a piece of 2×4 between the prop blade and the anti-ventilation plate to keep the prop from turning.

Before replacing the propeller, lube the prop shaft with grease as specified in your owner's manual. Also check around the base of the prop shaft for monofilament fishing line which may have become wrapped around the shaft. Look closely—old mono-filament might look like a plastic washer. Be sure to check your owner's manual for any special in-structions and torque specifications before installing the propeller.

8. While you're checking the prop, also check the bottom of the boat. For clean, efficient running the hull must be clean and efficient, too. Now's the time to remove any leftover barnacles or dried-up marine algae or weeds.

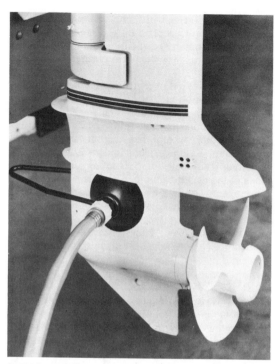

A running test can be performed at home with a flushing device. Attach and flush with fresh water (garden hose). While water is running and with engine in neutral, start motor. Make sure water tell-tale is streaming from engine. Warm it up while in neutral. Do not exceed 2,000 RPM (slightly above idle). Re-examine for fuel leaks.

9. Spring is also a good time to touch up any scrapes or scratches in your motor's paint job. Most manufacturers offer factory-matched colors in easy-to-use spray paint cans. If you're touching up the lower unit, be careful not to clog the water intake screen with paint. This could lead to motor overheating. Also, don't make the mistake of painting over the sacrificial zinc anodes on your motor. They won't work if they're covered with paint. While you're inspecting the motor, check the anodes. If they are more than 50 percent destroyed, replace them with new ones. If you boat in salt water or brackish water, the anodes are supposed to dissipate as they protect your motor.

10. After the mechanical work is done, give your motor (and boat) a good cleaning. Remove all the dirt and grime collected over the winter. Use an engine degreaser to clean up your outboard's powerhead. As a final touch, give the motor a coat of automotive wax or polish. This will help it sparkle and protect the finish from the sun and water.

11. After the motor's all cleaned up, consult the lubrication section of your owner's manual. Most motors require a shot of lubricant on the throttle linkage or other moving parts on the engine. On motors with remote steering, the steering cable ram should be greased before the start of each season and periodically thereafter. Once again, check the owner's manual for detailed instructions.

Final Notes: If your motor needs more than the normal preseason preparation, some manufacturers now offer do-it-yourself repair kits designed for the nonexpert to service such parts as magneto ignitions, water pumps, and carburetors.

Before you head out for the water, make sure you've replaced any tools you normally carry in the boat, like a wrench for the prop nut or spark plugs. During the winter, you may have borrowed that wrench to fix the snowblower!

A preseason checkup like this is easy, even for the most unmechanical of boaters. But the checkup will go a long way towards a season full of boating fun, not service woes.

BOAT TRAILERS

What size boat is trailerable? That is really a conundrum. The answer depends on how much you are willing to put into trailering. Each year's new-boat announcements include a large cabin cruiser with the claim, " . . . and it can be trailered!" The fact is that it actually *can* be trailered, but it may be a professional transport job. You will need a heavy-duty custom-built trailer, and should have a heavy-duty truck to make it go. And then it might do the boat no good. It's not a consumer proposition.

Then there are the very small boats you see rattling around on a trailer that weighs twice as much. A newcomer to boating has bought a special bargain offer of a boat and trailer combined, when he should have been advised to cartop his boat or load it in the back of a wagon. Trailering is no sport unless you really need a trailer; then it can be an asset.

Common boat sizes for regular trailering are 14 to 20 feet. It is true that some 12-footers weigh more than 120 or 130 pounds, weight that can be lifted to the top of a car easily by two people. If you buy a

Trailering a boat on rough roads poses few problems if the tow-car's suspension and clearance are adequate. Before setting out, check shocks and springs on both vehicles.

same time? You will probably get a better fit for your boat if you do. The maker can supply information about trailer specifications for current-model hulls, and the dealer will probably carry trailers that suit.

But if you live near the water, why have a trailer? First, you save on mooring fees and winter storage. Second, your boat will be a much bigger asset if you can take it along on vacations, trail it to another water when you want to fish and hunt or camp away from home. Keeping a boat on its trailer in your yard, you can keep bottom fouling cleaned off instead of facing a big job once or twice a year. Make it part of your routine when washing and waxing the car, and you will have a hull that is always in good shape. Keep a tarp over the boat and motor when it's idle on the trailer. When it sits in your own yard, there's no worry about vandalism at mooring.

CHOOSING A TRAILER

The best advice is to get a trailer one size bigger than your present boat requires. This will accommodate the occasional extra-heavy load you will pack in it. If you get a trailer larger than that, your boat will not be properly supported and the trailer will be awkward to tow, bouncing around because the boat is not heavy enough to hold it on the road.

Proper hull support is essential in a trailer. This is where the boat maker's advice is important. Three critical points are: full support at the transom, at the bottom forefoot, and at the construction center, either where greatest weight is built in amidships or

heavy 12-footer or a light 14-footer, consider buying a one-man boat loader that will make cartopping practical. On the other end of the range, boats over 20 feet (and some less) commonly have a deep bow, broad beam, and big weight that make all sorts of problems in trailering. For a starter, most state and all federal highways have a width limit of 8 feet; beyond that you'll need a special permit and arrangements to travel.

If you are going to buy a boat in the prime size range for trailering, should you get a trailer at the

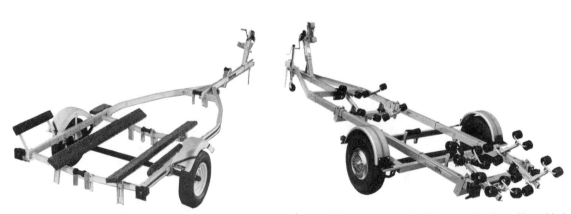

Left: Holsclaw lightweight trailer for boats up to 16 feet long. It has a 1,600-pound capacity. This type of trailer, with padded siderail guides, can be backed all the way into the water so that a boat can be run onto it without first dragging the craft out of the water onto the launch ramp. **Right:** Tee-Nee Trailer for boats up to 19 feet long can handle a 2,500-pound load. It features a full system of keel rollers to guide, position, and help secure the boat.

under the engine stringers in an inboard boat. You must avoid a trailer mismatch that will, over a period of time, cause the hull to hook or rocker. A well-engineered trailer for a boat of 500 pounds or more will have pairs of strong, securely set rollers on good bearings at frequent intervals for the entire bottom length.

Regardless of size, the trailer must enable you to back down to the water and launch your boat efficiently without getting the trailer-wheel hubs in the water. This may mean that you will need a tilt bed. If so, make sure the tilt operates easily fully loaded, and that the pivots are built to last.

Winch quality is important for heavier boats. Wobbly or ill-fitting crank, wheel, and ratchet won't do. For a boat of 1,500 pounds or more you might consider adding an electric winch. It saves a lot of knuckle busting, and it will be well made mechanically so that slips won't occur.

Trailer suspension, wheel mounts, and general construction should be spelled out by the trailer maker. Study these and get full information from the dealer about use and maintenance. Leaf springs are good on a heavy trailer; a soft ride is not important, while good support is. If you trail 3,500 pounds or more load, tandem wheels are needed.

You will have to look up state laws on trailers for your region, then equip your trailer and the tow vehicle according to the most exacting of these. Should you have brakes on the trailer the laws specify over what weights trailer brakes are required; but you may decide you want breaks even if yours is below the limit. In that case look into electric brakes that operate in tandem with your car's foot pedal but can be operated independently with a hand control. Quality trailer brakes are practically foolproof, make driving safer and easier, and reduce wear on the tow vehicle's rear suspension and tires.

Insist on a frame-mounted hitch, even though the salesman may try to give you a shallow hitch bolted to the body pan when you buy that new wagon. As for bumper-mounted hitches, they are dangerous. With a frame-mounted hitch you will be able to step up in weight over a big range without additional expense, and you'll trail your present boat without worry. You will need an umbilical electric hookup to your car's electrical system for trailer lights and

brakes or other accessories. Cable, clamps, and plugs come in a package at reasonable price. On your car you'll need "western" type rearview mirrors—big rectangular ones mounted on arms on each side that let you see around the trailer. For a trailer load of 3,000 pounds or more you should have an equalizing hitch that compensates a big load in normal travel and substantially reduces danger in a crash stop.

LOADING YOUR BOAT AND TRAILER

Most makers recommend loading with five to seven percent more weight ahead of the trailer axle. This prevents fishtailing and gives you good load control. If you are going on an extended trip with camping and sporting gear loaded inside the boat (you and your family will be happy to get it out of the car), watch the weight distribution, weigh big items as they are loaded, and don't under any circumstances exceed the maker's maximum weight limit. Your trailer will be designed to haul your boat and motor with the correct load in front of the axle. Additional weight inside the boat should maintain this distribution, or the position of the boat on the trailer bed should be adjusted accordingly. A well-made trailer will let you do this.

TRAILER MAINTENANCE

Wheel bearings are the critical point. When traveling, stop every few hours to feel for excessive heat at the hubs. If the news is bad, let them cool off, then creep to the nearest service station and have them repack the wheel bearings. Have the bearings inspected before each trip, and have them repacked at the start of each season.

Keep the hitch and mount free of rust, repaint each season with metal paint on clean metal, and grease moving joints on an equalizing hitch only as the maker specifies. You'll find that a well-made boat trailer will last at least as long as the boat if it's well cared for. And you will be delighted when you learn how much extra gear you can take along trailered in the boat.

ON THE ROAD AND LAUNCHING

The U.S. Coast Guard makes the following recommendations for trailering a boat. Heeding their advice will ensure your safety on the road and at the launch ramp.

PRE-DEPARTURE CHECKS

• Make a complete check of the trailer and towing vehicle. Inspect tires for tread wear, inflation, and

condition. Examine the hitch and associated safety devices, check brakes on both vehicles.
• Check radiator coolant, fluid level in the transmission and engine oil level.
• Check tightness of wheel lugs. Repeat this periodically during the trip.
• Equip towing vehicle with large rearview mirrors on both sides. Check the inside rearview mirror. The boat and the load should be low enough so that it does not obstruct the view.
• Check shocks and springs on both vehicles.
• Load tools, emergency equipment, and foul-weather gear in a readily accessible location in the towing vehicle.
• Check the load on the trailer. It must be loaded correctly from front to rear, and from side to side for best balance.
• Couple the trailer to the tow vehicle and observe the attitude of the tow vehicle. Check trailer lights.
• Check wheel bearings on the trailer.
• Check all tie-down straps.

UNDERWAY

Once underway never forget that you have a boat behind you. This sounds foolish but when you're wheeling along at highway speeds, it is all too easy to lose a feel for the tow—until you have to pass, turn, or brake. Always start slowly, in low gear, and take the car up through the gears gently. Think twice about passing other vehicles—but if you decide to pass, don't delay. Be alert for signs restricting trailers. Remain sensitive to unusual sounds or handling factors, and if there's anything that seems at all unusual, pull over immediately and check. In fact, you should pull over and check the entire rig every hour or so—check for high temperatures in the wheel bearings, slackening tie-downs, lights, tire pressure, and car engine temperature.

• Never let anyone ride in the trailer while moving. It is dangerous, and illegal in many states.
• Observe speed limits. In many states the speed limit for cars towing a trailer is lower than for the car traveling by itself.
• Maintain a greater following distance between your vehicle and the one in front of you. With the trailer you need much more room to stop.
• When traveling over bumpy roads or crossing railroad tracks, slow down. Going too fast may cause the tow vehicle to bottom out and the hitch to scrape, causing damage to both the car and the trailer.
• Large trucks and buses create considerable turbulence which may cause the trailer to fishtail. Keep a firm grip on the steering wheel and tension on the

hitch ball. If there is a manual lever which will operate the trailer brakes separately from those on the car, a quick application of the trailer brakes may slow the trailer sufficiently to eliminate sway.

LAUNCHING

Launching will be the critical part of your trailer-boating expedition. It's embarrassing, as well as expensive, to safely travel many highway miles just to do something dumb at the moment of truth. Before going to the ramp, check with the marina operator or others to determine if there are any unusual hazards, such as a drop-off at the end of the ramp. You should prepare your boat for launching away from the ramp so that you don't hold up other boaters. This is known as "Ramp Courtesy." Preparations for launching should include: raising the lower unit to avoid scraping; installing the drain plug; releasing the tie-downs; and disconnecting or removing the trailer's stop and directional lights.

When launching or recovering, never turn the car's engine off, and keep the parking brake set while you work the boat off the trailer. Only the driver should be in the towing vehicle during launching and recover. One or two observers can help the driver watch the trailer and traffic. Keep everyone else away from the launching ramp. It is also prudent to use a tire stop to avoid an unexpected dunking of trailer and car.

Many trailer-boat owners' worst moments have occurred at busy launching ramps because they have not practiced backing their rig. Before you attempt a launching, you should put in a couple of hours in a deserted parking lot learning how to back your rig through a maze of cardboard boxes.

A helpful hint when backing is to place your hand on the bottom of the steering wheel and move the wheel in the direction you want the trailer to go. *Do not oversteer.*

If you have an unwieldy trailer, you may want to get an auxiliary front bumper hitch which will make close-quarters maneuvering much simpler as well as keeping the drive wheels of the towing vehicle on higher, drier ground.

Make sure you *never, never* cast off all the lines from the boat before launching. Someone on shore must have a line that is made fast to the boat. The line makes it easy to shove the boat off the trailer and then pull the boat to a dock or boarding platform or back to the trailer at a wide, busy launching ramp. Above all, take the time necessary to launch safely; but as soon as the boat is afloat, move the vehicle and the trailer to the parking lot and the boat to the dock for loading. Don't loiter.

Always try to avoid getting the trailer hubs in the

water. If you can not avoid dunking them, at least let them cool first. If you don't the sudden cooling may crack or chip the bearings, or suck them full of water. One way to pass the time, if you are a sailor, is to step the mast in the parking lot while waiting to launch. However, make sure that there are no low power lines or other overhead obstructions between you and the launching ramp. Unfortunately, a few boaters are electrocuted every year because their rigging comes in contact with overhead electrical wires.

BACKING A TRAILER

Backing a boat trailer down a tight, slick launch ramp can be tricky, and a busy ramp is not the place to learn. Practice in an empty parking lot on a Sunday morning: You'll be able to go at your own pace . . . without an impatient audience.

When backing the trailer, keep in mind that you're pushing it, not pulling it. No big deal when you back straight up—you just have to keep the wheels of the tow vehicle perfectly straight. But when it's time to turn, everything is reversed: Turning the steering wheel to the right will turn the rear end of the tow vehicle to the right, causing the trailer to turn left, and vice versa.

STEERING TIP

Placing your hand on the bottom of the steering wheel simplifies the process of backing up: Pull the wheel to the right, the trailer heads right, and vice-versa.

1. Keep the tow vehicle and trailer straight and close to the ramp when getting into position. Remember that you will be steering in reverse.

2. When your trailer is in position to be backed onto the ramp, turn the steering wheel sharply in the direction opposite the intended path of the trailer.

3. As the trailer begins to move down the ramp, start to turn your steering wheel to the left (in the illustrated example above), which will push your trailer to the right. If possible, have a second person to assist you with hand signals.

4. As soon as your trailer is lined up correctly on the ramp, straighten your wheels and follow the trailer as you back it down the ramp for your launch. While waiting your turn on the ramp, watch other launchings to gauge the effects of wind and current.

RETRIEVAL

Retrieving your boat is similar to launching and should be done with the same courtesy by reversing the procedures for launching. Unload your boat at the dock and keep it there until the trailer is ready to move down the ramp. Move the boat to the trailer and *raise* the lower unit. Winch the boat on to the trailer and secure it. Finally, move the towing vehicle and trailer with boat to the parking area for loading, housekeeping, and of course other general maintenance chores.

STORAGE

To prevent water from accumulating in the boat, remove the drain plug and tilt the trailer and the boat enough to allow drainage. This should be done for even short-term storage.

When storing the boat on its trailer for any length of time, get the weight off the wheels. Cinder blocks under the tongue and four corners of the frame of the trailer should be adequate support, shimmed up if necessary by boards. Once the trailer frame is jacked up, you should check to be sure that the boat itself is evenly supported. Be forewarned: the frame itself can easily be bent out of its normal shape by excessive jacking at a corner.

SAFE BOATING

Boaters don't have a clean record when it comes to accidents afloat. Do you know why? It has little to do with the perquisites of fishing and hunting, but much to do with neglecting to control the boat and guard personal safety aboard. A sportsman who has not schooled himself in basic boating safety and safe habits will forget about it when the action gets lively. Here's your chance to start right.

BASIC TOOL KIT

Every boat must be equipped to get home on its own. The exact selection of tools, spare parts, and supplies necessary must be suited to your boat and motor and to problems you are most likely to encounter.

- Ordinary pliers
- Vice-grip pliers
- Diagonal-cutting pliers
- Long-nose electrician's pliers
- Screwdrivers
- Spark-plug wrench to fit
- Combination open-end and box wrenches in sizes ⅜ to ¾ inch
- Sharp knife

SPARE PARTS

- Spark plugs of correct specifications
- Distributor cap, rotor, condenser, point set
- Fuel pump and filter
- Oil filter
- Water-pump impeller
- V-belts to match each size used

- Spare fuel lines, cocks, and fittings
- Gaskets and hoses
- Bailing-pump diaphragm
- Fuses and bulbs to double for each used

ALL-PURPOSE KIT

- 50-ft. chalk line
- Molly screws and pot menders for small cracks and holes
- Nails, screws, bolts and nuts, washers
- Hose clamps
- Electrical tape
- Insulated wire
- Cotter pins
- Packing
- Elastic plastic bandage material
- Small blocks of wood that can be carved
- Machine oil

OUTBOARD MOTOR TROUBLESHOOTING CHECKLIST

- Check gas supply and tank pressure; squeeze bulb several times.
- Check to be sure propeller is not wrapped in weeds, line, or net. If line is wrapped around prop, try slow reverse to loosen it; then cut off pieces until you can pull the rest free.
- Look for loose ignition wire at battery terminals.
- Remove ignition wire from any spark plug, crank the motor; spark should jump from wire end to engine head; if no spark, check back to ignition switch.

Every boat should carry basic safety, emergency, and handling equipment. On the left is a hand-operated pump, on the right a first-aid kit and boat hook (for taking a line that's thrown). Note fire extinguisher held by woman.

• If you have a hot spark, look into fuel feed; pull gas feed line off from side of outboard; blow through line until you hear bubbles in tank.
• Clean the carburetor bowl and fuel filter.
• Did you remember to add oil to gas tank in right proportion?

SAFE BOATING PROCEDURES

First, it is important to know your boat. Get familiar with its equipment and discover its limitations. If it's a livery rental, check it over completely before you push off.

Make a habit of checking off safety equipment aboard. First, locate the safety items required by law. Then compare your optional equipment with the Coast Guard's list of recommended equipment in the same section.

Count the life preservers, and make sure that each passenger has one that will keep him afloat in the water.

Check the fuel supply, the condition of the tank and feed line. Make sure the spark is strong and

LIFE JACKETS

Left: Children's collar vest has a grab-loop and a crotch strap with a quick-release buckle to prevent it from slipping off when a child or infant is pulled from the water. The design of the vest, coupled with the a special floating collar, keeps the wearer's head up out of the water. Filled with polyethylene foam, vests of this type are approved by the Coast Guard. **Center:** Typical high-impact vest is a PFD (personal flotation device) that combines modern styling with safety features offering extra protection in the event that someone is bucked out of a boat moving at high speed. Because a victim might hit the water (or some solid object) hard enough to cause severe injury, the vest has a foam-filled neck brace and rib padding. Thigh straps prevent it from riding up in a fast-moving boat or being blown right off by impact. This vest has a 100-mph impact rating. **Right:** Most fishing vests employ flotation material inside a nylon shell. Adjustable side-straps can be secured to the fisherman's belt to keep the vest from riding up, and flap pockets can hold a supply of the items an angler may want to reach quickly.

regular. Take along at least 1½ times as much fuel as you estimate you will need. If you run into heavy waves, your boat will take more fuel to go the same distance.

Carry a map you can read—a proper chart if the water is a large one—and a compass that is reliable near machinery.

Put tackle, guns, decoys, nets and other gear where they are secure and won't clutter walkways and footing. There is a bonus for the sportsman who keeps everything in place on board: He always knows where to find it when the action gets hot.

Gasoline vapors are explosive and will settle in the low areas of a boat. Keep doors, hatches, ports, and chests closed during fueling, stoves and pilot lights off, electrical circuits off, and absolutely no smoking! Keep the fill nozzle in firm contact with the fill neck to prevent static spark. Don't spill, for you'll have to dry it up before starting the engine. Do not use gasoline appliances aboard—they're lethal risks. Use alcohol and other less volatile, unpressurized fuels.

After fueling, ventilate thoroughly before pressing the starter. One minute is the minimum safe ventilation time. Big boats should be ventilated longer, with effective blowers operating and all ports opened. Keep your fuel lines in perfect condition and the boat's bilges clean.

Electrical equipment, switches, and wiring are some prime sources of boat fires and explosions. Avoid knife switches or other arcing equipment aboard. Keep batteries clean and ventilated.

Do not overload your boat. Make sure you have safely adequate freeboard before casting off. Look ahead to water conditions and weather changes you might encounter.

Keep an alert lookout. If you have a boat over 20 feet, name your mate and agree he'll keep lookout any time you can't. You have more to watch than other boats and shallow water. Watch for obstructions such as big rocks and floating logs.

Swimmers are hard to see in the water. Running through swimmers or a swimming area is the most sensitive violation a boat can make. If in doubt, give beaches and rafts a wide swing.

Your wake is potent. You can swamp small craft such as a canoe or rowboat, damage shorelines and shore property, disturb sleepers, and ruin fish and wildlife sport for hours by running fast through small passages and shallows.

Learn the Rules of the Road and obey them at all times. Copies are available free from the Coast Guard. Most collisions are caused by those "one-time" violations.

Make sure at least one other person aboard knows how to operate the boat and motor in case you are disabled or fall overboard.

Know a plan of action you will take in emergencies—man overboard, a bad leak, motor won't run, collision, bad storm, or troublesome passenger.

Storm signals and danger signs are often informal. Learn to read the weather, and keep alert to what passing boats are trying to tell you.

Wear your life preserver—or at least make sure children and nonswimmers wear theirs. In any case, don't sit on life preservers.

STORM WARNING SIGNALS

SMALL CRAFT

DAYTIME: Red Pennant.

NIGHTTIME: Red Light over White Light.

Indicates: Forecast winds as high as 33 knots and sea conditions considered dangerous to small-craft operations.

GALE

DAYTIME: Two Red Pennants.

NIGHTTIME: White Light over Red Light.

Indicates: Forecast winds in the range 34-47 knots.

STORM

DAYTIME: Square Red Flag with Black Square Centered.

NIGHTTIME: Two Red Lights.

Indicates: Forecast winds 48 knots and above no matter how high the wind speed. If the winds are associated with a tropical cyclone (hurricane), storm warnings indicate forecast winds of 48-63 knots.

HURRICANE

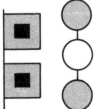

DAYTIME: Two Square Red Flags with Black Squares Centered.

NIGHTTIME: White Light between Two Red Lights.

Indicates: Forecast winds of 64 knots and above, displayed only in connection with a hurricane.

In a capsizing, remember that you are safer if you stay with the boat, where you can be seen. It will help you stay afloat until help arrives.

Under Coast Guard legislation, it is illegal for anyone to build, sell, or use a craft that does not conform to safety regulations. Check with your dealer, and check with yourself to make sure your boat measures up.

SMALL BOAT, BIG WATER

The best way to stay out of trouble on open water is to learn how to read the wind and current. The National Weather Service issues marine forecasts every six hours (sometimes more frequently), with details of winds and seas. If you have a VHF radio, Channels WX-1, WX-2, and WX-3 broadcast these weather conditions continuously. Matching the wind forecast with the chart below will give you a good idea of the seas you can expect to encounter.

But such forecasts are regional, and local conditions can be radically different—thunderstorms, for instance. You can determine the distance in miles of an approaching thunderstorm by counting the interval between seeing a lightning flash and hearing its accompanying thunder in seconds, then dividing by five. For example, if it takes 10 seconds to hear the thunder, the storm is two miles away.

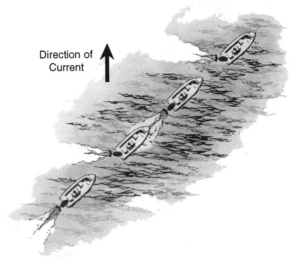

Direction of Current

1. QUARTERING A FOLLOWING SEA

Quartering may be the only solution to crossing a following sea. Your speed, however, must be faster than the waves running at your stern. You'll have to make corrections with each wave you meet. As you cross the crest, wave action tries to turn a quartering boat broadside by pushing its stern into the trough between it and the next wave crest. You must power your boat into the direction of the trough to properly point your bow toward the next crest. (Note direction of outboard and prop in illustration.) Never allow wave action to push your boat parallel to the trough.

WIND/SEA RELATIONSHIPS

	Velocity	Conditions
Calm Conditions	0–3 knots	Sea like a mirror
	4–6 knots	Ripples, less than 1 foot
	7–10 knots	Smooth wavelets, 1 to 2 feet
	11–16 knots	Small waves, 2 to 4 feet
Small Craft Warning	17–21 Knots	Moderate waves, 4 to 8 feet, whitecaps
	22–27 knots	Large waves, 8 to 13 feet, spray
	28–33 knots	High waves, 13 to 20 feet, heaped seas, foam from breaking waves
Gale Warning	34–40 knots	High waves, 13 to 20 feet, foam blown in well-marked streaks
	41–47 knots	Seas rolling, reduced visibility from spray, waves 13 to 20 feet
Storm Warning	48–55 knots	White seas, very high waves, 20 to 30 feet, overhanging crests
	56–63 knots	Exceptionally high waves, 30 to 45 feet
Hurricane Warning	More than 63 knots	Air filled with foam, sea white, waves over 45 feet

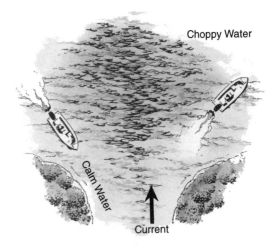

Choppy Water

Calm Water

Current

2. MOUTH OF RIVER OR INLET

Wherever a current enters a body of water—this is true for river mouths as well as ocean inlets—you can expect to find relatively calm water at the edge of the intruding flow. Usually this calm transition zone is marked by surface wave action. When running any inlet, always ride the back of the wave in front of you. Never power over its crest, or drift far enough back to be picked up by the crest of the following wave.

But that knowledge won't help much if you don't have time to get to safety. Besides, odds are you're going to get caught on the water eventually. Knowing how to handle difficult seas in a small boat is insurance all sportsmen should have.

COAST GUARD APPROVED EQUIPMENT

For safe boating under most conditions, you are required by federal law to carry "Coast Guard Approved" equipment aboard your craft. Coast Guard Approved Equipment simply means that it has been approved by the Commandant of the U.S. Coast Guard and has been determined to be in compliance with U.S. Coast Guard specifications and regulations relating to materials, construction and performance.

Here are Coast Guard recommendations for the most essential lifesaving equipment you must have on board under federal law.

Fire Extinguishers

Each approved fire extinguisher is classified by a letter and a Roman numeral according to the type of fire it is designed to extinguish and its size. The letter indicates the TYPE OF FIRE:

A—Fires of ordinary combustible materials.
B—Gasoline, oil and grease fires.
C—Electrical fires.

Extinguishers approved for motorboats are hand-portable, of either B-I or B-II classification or their U.L. equivalents, and have the following characteristics:

Coast Guard Classes	UL listing	FOAM (Gals.)	CO$_2$ (LBS.)	DRY CHEM (LBS.)	HALON (LBS.)
B–I	5B	1.25	4	2	2.5
B–II	(6B)*	2.5	15	10	10
—	10B	—	10	2.5	5

*UL rating 6B is no longer issued.

Fire extinguishers must be carried on ALL motorboats that meet one or more of the following conditions:

- Inboard engines.
- Closed compartments under thwarts and seats where portable fuel tanks may be stored.
- Double bottoms not sealed to the hull or which are not completely filled with flotation materials.
- Closed living spaces.
- Closed stowage compartments in which combustible or flammable materials are stored.
- Permanently installed fuel tanks. There is no gallon capacity to determine if a fuel tank is portable. However, if the fuel tank is secured so it cannot be

moved in case of a fire or other emergency, then the Coast Guard considers the tank permanently installed. In addition, if the weight of the fuel tank is such that persons on board cannot move it in case of a fire or other emergency, then the Coast Guard considers it permanently installed.

Dry chemical fire extinguishers without gauges or indicating devices must be inspected every six months. If the gross weight of a carbon dioxide (CO_2) fire extinguisher is reduced by more than 10% of the net weight, the extinguisher is not acceptable and must be recharged.

Check extinguishers regularly to be sure that gauges are free and nozzles clear.

Fire extinguisher requirements are classified by the size of the vessel:

1. *Boats less than 26 feet in length* with NO fixed fire-extinguishing system installed in machinery spaces, must have at least one Type B–1 approved hand-portable fire extinguisher. When an approved fixed fire-extinguishing system is installed in machinery spaces, no Type B–1 extinguisher is required. If the construction of the boat does not permit the entrapment of explosive or flammable gases or vapors, no fire extinguisher is required.

2. *Boats 26 feet to less than 40 feet* in length must have at least two Type B–1 or at least one Type B–2 approved hand-portable fire extinguisher. When an approved fixed fire-extinguishing system is installed, one less Type B–1 extinguisher is required.

3. *Boats 40 feet to not more than 65 feet* in length must have at least three Type B–1 or at least one Type B–1 PLUS one Type B–2 approved portable fire extinguisher. When an approved fixed fire-extinguishing system is installed, one less Type B–1 extinguisher is required.

Note: Coast Guard Approved extinguishers carry the following label: "Marine Type USCG Approved, Size . . ., Type . . ., 162.208/," etc. UL listed extinguishers not displaying this marking are also acceptable, provided they are of the above sizes and types and carry a minimum UL rating of 5–B:C.

Personal Flotation Devices (PFDs)

Personal Flotation Devices must be Coast Guard Approved and are classified by "Type" according to performance.

Boats Less Than 16 Feet in length must be equipped with one Type I, II, III, or V PFD for each person aboard.

Boats 16 Feet and Larger must be equipped with one Type I, II, III or V for each person aboard PLUS one Type IV.

Type I— A Type I PFD is any approved wearable device that is designed to turn most *unconscious* persons in the water from a face-down position to a vertical or slightly backward position. The Type

I PFD has the greatest required buoyancy: the adult size provides a minimum buoyancy of 22 pounds and the child size provides a minimum bouyancy of 11 pounds. The Type I PFD provides the most protection to its wearer and is most effective for all waters, especially during offshore and ocean cruising, where there is the probability of a delayed rescue.

Type II— A Type II PFD is any approved wearable device designed to turn its wearer in a vertical or slightly backward position in the water. The turning action is not as pronounced as with a Type I, and the device will not turn as many persons under the same conditions as a Type I. An adult-size device provides a minimum bouyancy of 15½ pounds, the medium child size provides a minimum of 11 pounds and the infant and small child sizes provide a minimum bouyancy of 7 pounds.

Type III— A Type III PFD is any approved wearable device designed so the wearers can place themselves in a vertical or slightly backward position. While the Type III has the same buoyancy as the Type II PFD, it has little or no turning ability. The Type III PFD comes in a variety of styles, colors and sizes and many are designed to be particularly useful when water skiing, sailing, fishing, hunting, or engaging in other water sports. Several of this type will also provide increased hypothermia protection.

Type IV— A Type IV PFD is any approved device designed to be thrown to a person in the water and grasped and held by the user until rescued. It is *not* designed to be worn. The most common Type IV devices are buoyant cushions and ring buoys.

Type V— A Type V PFD is any PFD approved for restricted use.

All PFDs that are Coast Guard Approved bear one of the above designations. All PFDs must be in good and serviceable condition and of an appropriate size for the persons who intend to wear them. Wearable PFDs must be *readily accessible* and throwable devices must be *immediately available* for use.

Includes Special Use Devices. Approved only for the activities listed on the label. Some are approved specifically for whitewater rafting, board sailing, etc.

A water skier, while being towed, is considered on board the vessel for the purposes of compliance with the PFD carriage requirements.

Note: Canoes and kayaks, regardless of length, must carry one approved PFD of any type for each person on board. A Type V PFD may be carried in lieu of any PFD, but only if that Type V PFD is approved for the activity in which the boat is used.

INFLATABLE PFD

The new inflatable vests will be classified into one of four categories:

*Type I—*Minimum 34 lbs. buoyancy. Two independent cartridges with both manual and automatic inflation mechanisms.

*Type II—*Minimum 34 lbs. buoyancy. Single cartridge with manual and automatic inflation.

*Type III—*Minimum 22½ lbs. buoyancy. Single manual inflation mechanism.

*Type V—*22½–34 lbs. buoyancy, depending on style. Single manual inflation mechanism.

Inflatables contain a CO_2 cartridge that inflates the vest. Automatic models inflate upon contact with water; the manual models require the wearer to pull a ripcord to activate inflation. This cartridge must be properly installed and replaced with a new one after the vest has been inflated. The new standards require indicators that show whether the CO_2 cartridge is properly installed and ready for use.

When inflated, inflatable life jackets provide greater buoyancy than traditional jackets and do a better job keeping a victim's head out of the water, especially important when the victim is unconscious. They also contain an oral inflation tube so a victim can maintain buoyancy in the water for an extended period of time.

Visual Distress Signals

All recreational boats, when used on coastal waters, the Great Lakes, territorial seas, and those waters connected directly to the Great Lakes and the territorial seas, up to a point where a body of water is less than 2 miles wide must be equipped with Visual Distress Signals. Boats owned in the United States operating on the high seas must also be equipped with Visual Distress Signals. The following are excepted from the requirements for day signals and only need to carry night signals when operating at night:

• Recreational boats less than 16 feet in length.
• Boats participating in organized events such as races, regattas, or marine parades.
• Open sailboats less than 26 feet in length not equipped with propulsion machinery.
• Manually propelled boats.

Pyrotechnic Visual Distress Signals must be Coast Guard Approved, in serviceable condition and stowed to be readily accessible. They are marked with a date showing the serviceable life, and this date must not have been passed. Launchers produced before January 1, 1981, intended for use with approved signals are not required to be Coast Guard Approved.

USCG Approved Pyrotechnic Visual Distress Signals and Associated Devices include:

• Pyrotechnic red flares, hand-held or aerial
• Pyrotechnic orange smoke, hand-held or floating
• Launchers for aerial red meteors or parachute flares

Non-Pyrotechnic Visual Distress Signaling Devices must carry the manufacturer's certification that they meet Coast Guard requirements. They must be in serviceable condition and stowed to be readily accessible. This group includes:

• Orange distress flag
• Electric distress light

No single signaling device is ideal under all conditions and for all purposes. Consideration should therefore be given to carrying several types. For example, an aerial flare can be seen over a long distance on a clear night, but for closer work, a hand-held flare may be more useful.

Handling and Storage

Pyrotechnic devices should be stored in a cool, dry location and must be readily accessible in case of an emergency. Care should be taken to prevent puncturing or otherwise damaging their coverings. A watertight container, such as a surplus ammunition box, painted red or orange and prominently marked "DISTRESS SIGNALS" is recommended.

If young children are frequently aboard your boat, careful selection and proper stowage of visual distress signals becomes especially important. If you elect to carry pyrotechnic devices, select devices that are in tough packaging and that would be difficult to ignite accidentally.

Coast Guard Approved pyrotechnic devices carry an expiration date. This date cannot exceed 42 months from the date of manufacture and at such time the device can no longer be counted toward the minimum requirements.

Types: A wide variety of signaling devices, both pyrotechnic and nonpyrotechnic, can be carried to meet the requirements of the regulation.

Boats less than 16 feet operating in coastal waters and certain other exempted boats listed on the previous page need only carry night signaling devices when operated at night. All other recreational boats must carry both night and day signaling devices.

Note: If pyrotechnic devices are selected, a minimum of three must be carried. Any combination can be carried as long as they add up to three signals for day use and three signals for night use. Three day/night signaling devices meet both requirements.

The following is an illustration of the variety and combinations of devices which can be carried in order to meet the requirements:

1. Three hand-held red flares (day and night).
2. One electric distress light (night).
3. One hand-held red flare and two parachute flares (day and night).
4. One hand-held orange smoke signal, two floating orange smoke signals and one electric distress light (day and night).

APPROVAL NUMBERS

Number Marked on Device	Device Description
	NIGHT USE ONLY
161.013	Electric Distress Light for Boats
	DAY USE ONLY
160.022	Floating Orange Smoke Distress Signal (5 minutes)
160.037	Hand-Held Orange Smoke Distress Signal
160.057	Floating Orange Smoke Distress Signal (15 minutes)
160.072	Orange Distress Signal Flag for Boats
	NIGHT AND DAY USE
160.021	Hand-Held Red Flare Distress Signal
160.024	Parachute Red Flare Distress Signal (37mm) (These signals require use in combination with a suitable launching device.)
160.036	Hand-Held Rocket-Propelled Parachute Red Flare Distress Signal
160.066	Red Aerial Pyrotechnic Flare Distress Signal for Boats (These devices may be either meteor or parachute-assisted type. Some of these signals may require use in combination with a suitable launching device.)

All distress signaling devices have both advantages and disadvantages. The most popular, because of cost, are probably the smaller pyrotechnic devices. Pyrotechnics make excellent distress signals, universally recognized as such, but they have the drawback that they can be used only once. Additionally, there is the potential for both injury and property damage if pyrotechnics are not properly handled. Pyrotechnic devices have a very hot flame and the ash and slag can cause burns and ignite materials that burn easily. Projected devices, such as pistol-launched and hand-held parachute flares and meteors, have many of the same characteristics of a firearm and must be handled with the same caution and respect.

Under the Inland Navigation Rules, a high intensity white light flashing at regular intervals from 50–

For the boater who wants that extra margin of safety, this Olin 12-gauge Alert/Locate Kit includes 12-gauge launcher with three 12-gauge meteors, three orange smoke signals, three hand-held red flares.

The distress flag must be at least 3 × 3 feet with a black square and ball on an orange background. It is accepted as a day signal only and is especially effective in bright sunlight. The flag is most distinctive when waved on something such as a paddle or boat hook or flown from a mast.

The electric distress light is accepted for night use only and must automatically flash the international SOS distress signal (· · · — — — · · ·). Flashed four to six times each minute, this is an unmistakable distress signal, well known to most boaters. The device can be checked anytime for serviceability if shielded from view.

Red hand-held flares can be used by day, but are most effective at night or in restricted visibility such as fog or haze. Only hand-held flares made after October 1, 1980 are approved by the Coast Guard for use on recreational boats. When selecting such flares, look for the Coast Guard approval number and date of manufacture. Make sure that the device does not carry the markings, ''Not approved for use on recreational boats.''

70 times per minute is considered a distress signal. Therefore, strobe lights used in inland waters shall only be used as a distress signal.

The hand-held and the floating orange smoke signaling devices are good day signals, especially on clear days. Both signals are most effective with light to moderate winds because higher winds tend to keep the smoke close to the water and disperse it, which makes it hard to see.

REQUIRED NONAPPROVED EQUIPMENT

Sound Signaling Devices for Vessels Less Than 20 Meters (65.6 ft)

1. Vessels 12 meters (39.4 ft.) or more in length but less than 20 meters (65.6 ft.) must carry on board a power whistle or power horn and a bell.

2. Vessels less than 12 meters (39.4 ft.) need not carry a whistle, horn, or bell. However, the navi-

LIGHTING OPTIONS FOR POWER DRIVEN VESSELS (See text) ————

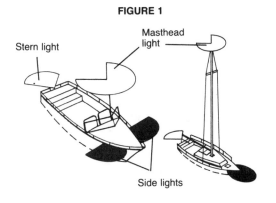
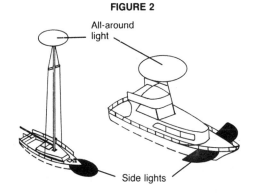

Note: A sailing vessel operating under machinery alone, or under sail and machinery power, is considered a power-driven vessel.

LIGHTING OPTIONS FOR SAILING VESSELS AND VESSELS UNDER OARS (See text) ⎯⎯

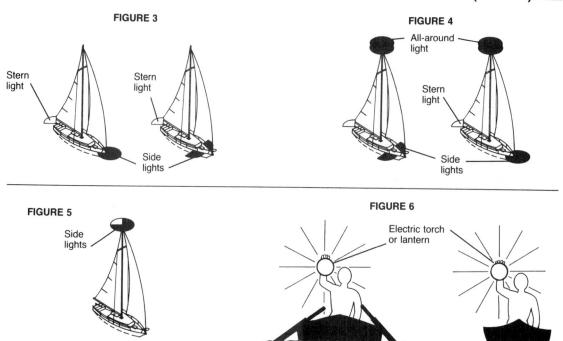

FIGURE 3

Stern light

Stern light

Side lights

FIGURE 4

All-around light

Stern light

Side lights

FIGURE 5

Side lights

FIGURE 6

Electric torch or lantern

gation rules require sound signals to be made under certain circumstances, and you should carry some means for making an efficient signal when necessary.

Ventilation

No person may operate a boat built after July 31, 1980 that has a gasoline engine (for whatever use) unless it is equipped with an operable ventilation system that meets the Coast Guard standards.

For boats built after April 25, 1940, and before August 1, 1980 (with engines using gasoline as fuel and other fuels having a flash point of 110°F or less) the following is required: At least two ventilation ducts fitted with cowls or their equivalent for the purpose of properly and efficiently ventilating the bilges of every engine and fuel tank compartment. There shall be at least one exhaust duct installed so as to extend to the lower portion of the bilge and at least one intake duct installed so as to extend to a point at least midway to the bilge or at least below the level of the carburetor air intake.

For boats which were built after July 31, 1978, but prior to August 1, 1980, there is no requirement for ventilation of the fuel tank compartment if there is no electrical source in the compartment and if the fuel tank vents to the outside of the boat.

The operator of a vessel is required to keep the system in operating condition.

Navigation Lights

Required on Boats Between Sunset and Sunrise: Recreational boats operating at night are required to display navigation lights between sunset and sunrise. Although most recreational boats in the United States operate in waters governed by the Inland Navigation Rules, recent changes to the rules have made the general lighting requirements for both the Inland and International rules basically the same. The differences between them are primarily in the options available.

RANGE AND ARC OF VISIBILITY OF LIGHTS

VESSELS LESS THAN 20 METERS

| | Visible Range in Miles | | |
Light	Less than 12 meters	12 meters or more	Arc in Degrees
Masthead light	2	3	225
All-round light	2	2	360
Sidelights	1	2	112.5
Sternlight	2	2	135

1. A power-driven vessel less than 20 meters (65.6 ft.), shall exhibit navigation lights as shown in Figure 1. If the vessel is less than 12 meters (39.4 ft.) in length, it may show the lights in either Figure 1 or Figure 2.

2. On a vessel less than 12 meters (39.4 ft.) in length, the masthead light must be 1 meter (3.3 ft.) higher than the sidelights. If the vessel is 12 meters or more in length and less than 20 meters (65.6 ft.) the masthead light must not be less than 2.5 meters (8.2 ft.) above the gunwale.

3. A power-driven vessel less than 50 meters in length may also carry, but is not obligated to, a second masthead light abaft of and higher than the forward one.

4. A power-driven vessel less than 7 meters (23.0 ft.) in length and whose maximum speed cannot exceed 7 knots may, *in International waters only,* in lieu of the lights prescribed above, exhibit an all-round white light, and shall, if practicable, also exhibit sidelights.

Sailing Vessels and Vessels Under Oars
1. A sailing vessel less than 20 meters (65.6 ft.) in length shall exhibit navigation lights shown in either Figure 3 or Figure 4. She may combine the lights in a single lantern carried at the top of the mast as shown in Figure 5.

2. A sailing vessel less than 7 meters (23.0 ft.) in length shall, if practicable, exhibit those lights prescribed for sailing vessels less than 20 meters, but if she does not, she shall have ready at hand an electric torch or lighted lantern showing a white light which shall be exhibited in sufficient time to prevent collision (see Figure 6).

3. A vessel under oars may display those lights prescribed for sailing vessels, but if she does not, she shall have ready at hand an electric torch or lighted lantern showing a white light which shall be exhibited in sufficient time to prevent collision (see Figure 6).

Lights Used When Anchored
Power-driven vessels and sailing vessels at anchor must display anchor lights. However, vessels less than 7 meters in length are not required to display anchor lights unless anchored in or near a narrow channel, fairway or anchorage or where other vessels normally navigate.

An anchor light for a vessel less than 20 meters in length is an all-round white light visible for 2 miles exhibited where it can best be seen. A vessel less than 20 meters in Inland waters when at anchor in a special anchorage area designated by the Secretary of Transportation, does not require an anchor light.

Day Shapes

Required on Boats Between Sunrise and Sunset: A vessel proceeding under sail when also being propelled by machinery, shall exhibit forward, where it can best be seen, a conical shape, apex downwards (see Figure 7), except that for Inland Rules, a vessel less than 12 meters in length is not required to exhibit the dayshape.

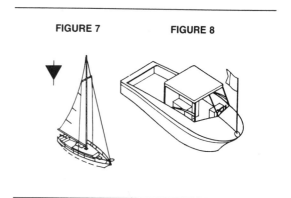

FIGURE 7   **FIGURE 8**

LOADING YOUR BOAT

There are several things to remember when loading a boat: distribute the load evenly; keep the load low; don't overload; don't stand up in a small boat; and consult the "U.S. Coast Guard Maximum Capacities" label. On boats with no capacity label, use the following formula to determine the maximum number of persons your boat can safely carry in calm weather:

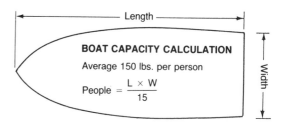

The length of your vessel is measured in a straight line from the foremost part of the vessel to the aftermost part of the vessel, parallel to the centerline, exclusive of sheer. Bowsprits, bumpkins, rudders, outboard motors, brackets and similar fittings are not included in the measurement.

FLOAT PLAN ⎯⎯⎯⎯

File a float plan. Tell someone where you are going and when you plan to return. Tell them what your boat looks like and other information that will make identifying it easier should the need arise. Make copies of the following Float Plan and leave it with a reliable person who can be depended upon to notify the Coast Guard, or other rescue organization, should you not return as scheduled. Do not, however, file float plans with the Coast Guard.

1. NAME OF PERSON REPORTING AND TELEPHONE NUMBER.

2. DESCRIPTION OF BOAT. TYPE _____ COLOR_____

    TRIM _____ REGISTRATION NO. _____

    LENGTH _____ NAME _____ MAKE_____

    OTHER INFO. _____

3. PERSONS ABOARD _____

NAME	AGE	ADDRESS & TELE. NO.
_____	___	_____
_____	___	_____
_____	___	_____

4. ENGINE TYPE_____ H.P. _____

    NO. OF ENGINES_____ FUEL CAPACITY _____

5. SURVIVAL EQUIPMENT: (CHECK AS APPROPRIATE)

    PFDs _____ FLARES _____ MIRROR _____

    SMOKE SIGNALS _____ FLASHLIGHT _____ FOOD _____

    PADDLES _____ WATER _____ OTHERS _____

    ANCHOR _____ RAFT OR DINGHY _____ EPIRB _____

6. RADIO YES/NO TYPE_____ FREQS. _____

7. TRIP EXPECTATIONS: LEAVE AT _____(TIME)

    FROM _____GOING TO _____

    EXPECT TO RETURN BY _____(TIME) AND IN

    NO EVENT LATER THAN _____

8. ANY OTHER PERTINENT INFO. _____

9. AUTOMOBILE LICENSE _____ TYPE _____

    TRAILER LICENSE _____ _____COLOR AND MAKE OF

    AUTO _____

        WHERE PARKED _____

10. IF NOT RETURNED BY _____(TIME) CALL THE

    COAST GUARD, OR _____(LOCAL AUTHORITY)

    TELEPHONE NUMBERS _____

    _____

    _____

WATER SPORTS ⎯⎯⎯⎯⎯⎯⎯⎯⎯⎯

PERSONAL WATERCRAFT

All personal watercraft are officially considered power boats by the U.S. Coast Guard and others. No matter how simple they are to ride, under the law, they have the same requirements for registration, regulation, and come under the same laws as other power boats. Technically, PWC are termed "Class A Inboard Boats" (boats less than 16 feet in length) by the U.S. Coast Guard.

What makes personal watercraft different from other boats on the water? The main difference is the innovative jet drive propulsion system. With this drive system, a PWC does not have an exposed propeller like most motor boats on the water today.

Personal watercraft are smaller boats powered by an inboard engine and a jet pump mechanism—but they are still boats. Your boat's capabilities and limitations are a little bit different from other boats on the water. Your boat can operate in more shallow water and is quickly and easily maneuvered. You can accelerate quickly, but you may be more af-fected by waves, turbulence, and obstructions than larger craft.

There are several types of personal watercraft on the market. They vary in performance, stability, and the amount of skill necessary to operate them. Some are ridden in a sitting position while others are rid-den while kneeling or standing. Some have the ca-pacity for one person while others can carry up to three people. One thing all personal watercraft have in common is that they are designed to allow the operator to fall safely overboard and reboard the boat with little risk if safety guidelines are followed. This reduced risk is because the jet propulsion sys-tem in personal watercraft replaces the rudder and propeller on the outside of the hull.

The jet drive used in a personal watercraft is somewhat similar to the jet drive on modern air-craft. The unit is pushed through the water by the action of a jet pump driven by the engine. To give you an idea how the jet drive in your personal wa-tercraft works, think about a balloon. Just as the air exiting a released balloon pushes the balloon in the

Yamaha WaveRunner III was the first three passenger, sit-down watercraft ever introduced. Powered with a 55-horsepower engine. A good choice in personal watercraft for family use.

Kawasaki 1100STX is a three-passenger watercraft that offers good handling for solo riders or with two or more passengers aboard, and the ability to tow waterskiers and others. It has a 107cc 3-cylinder engine with 120 horsepower.

opposite direction around the room, the water leaving the jet pump pushes the personal watercraft through the water.

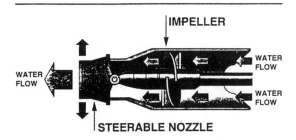

The pump works by drawing water into the housing ahead of the impeller. The impeller (a type of precision propeller contained within the housing) pressurizes the water and forces it in a stream toward the back of the personal watercraft. The force of the exiting water pushes the boat in the opposite direction.

Although you will not have to worry about hurting yourself from an exposed propeller, there are some precautions you should take with the jet pump on your personal watercraft.

- Keep hands and feet, as well as hair and clothing, away from the pump intake.
- When checking the pump intake for possible obstructions make sure the engine is off.
- Don't operate your boat in shallow water (less than 24 inches).
- Anything stirred up from the bottom, such as sand or vegetation, can be sucked into the jet pump and damage your PWC, as well as possibly injuring someone if particles are expelled out of the pump.

Most personal watercraft have a steerable nozzle at the rear of the pump housing that is controlled by the handlebars. The steering control directs the stream of water to the left or right. When the steering control is turned to the right, the steerable nozzle also turns to the right. As throttle is applied, the force of the water stream, pointed right, then pushes the back of the boat to the left, which causes the craft to turn to the right.

For safety purposes, the most important thing to remember about steering is that you must have power to the pump in order to maintain steering control. If you allow the engine to return to idle or shut off during a turn, the craft will continue in the same direction as it was moving at the point the power was cut, regardless of the steering input from the operator.

Reverse is available on some types of personal watercraft. This is accomplished by a "clam-shell" type device which moves over the directional nozzle and reverses the water flow allowing the personal watercraft to "back-up." This mechanism is not a brake and should not be regarded as such.

If you take a spill, most personal watercraft have one of the following options:

* The engine will run at idle speed while the boat circles slowly so that the operator can board as it circles past. It is important that the idling speed be properly set.

* An engine stop lanyard is attached to the operator's wrist or PFD and shuts off the engine when the operator falls off. For this reason, it is essential that the lanyard is always properly attached to the watercraft and the operator.

Swim to your personal watercraft, reboard carefully, reattach the lanyard (if applicable), restart your engine and continue your ride. If the watercraft has turned upside down, follow the instructions in your owner's manual and turn the watercraft upright. If your personal watercraft has stalled or will not restart, do not attempt to swim to shore. Stay with your vessel and continue to wear your personal flotation device.

WATER SKIING

Portions of text and photos, courtesy of the American Water Ski Association

For many skiers nothing quite compares with the thrill of their first ski ride. Learning to water ski is akin to learning to ride a bike. Both are essentially balance skills and once you get the hang of it the going is easy.

Before you start make sure you have:

* a properly-fitted personal flotation device (jacket or vest-type) that fits snugly yet comfortably and fastens securely.
* appropriate-size skis with adjustable binders.

While any boat can be used to tow a waterskier, some boats are better equipped than others. This ski boat, for example, has a large rearview mirror for the driver to observe the skier, as well as an observer in the stern of the boat. Note that the towline is also attached to a pylon in the center of the boat, which allows more efficient planing of the boat while towing a skier.

Polaris SL 900 has a 3-cylinder 900 engine that delivers over 100 horsepower. The seat features a stability hump to keep the rider in place.

Skis typically come in sizes—adult skis usually are 60–70 inches in length and junior skis for children usually 40–50 inches in length. They should be mounted with appropriately sized adjustable bindings. The size ski you choose depends on your weight and boat speed.

The longer and the wider the skis the better support at slower speeds. However, larger skis are more awkward to control when positioning the skis for the start, because of their greater buoyancy. Shorter sizes are preferred for smaller people and children.

The first step also requires you and the boat crew to learn and understand the basic American Water Ski Association (AWSA) hand signals.

It is advisable to learn these signals during the "first step," but don't overload. If you are learning with experienced people in the boat, #4—*Back to Dock* and #7—*I'm OK,* (after a fall) will suffice at this stage.

DRY LAND PRACTICE

All skiing skills should first be practiced on dry land. The basic body position is simple—knees bent; arms straight; head up. Remember these key elements. Of course there is more to it than just these three basic points, but this is a good start on dry land.

- Put on your flotation device and fasten it firmly yet comfortably and then
- Put on your skis by:

  1. First wetting the ski bindings and your feet.
  2. Bending down and holding the heel binding to one side so it is flat.
  3. Sliding your foot into the front binding as far as possible.
  4. Raising your heel slightly and with both hands grasping the heel piece and pulling it over your heel.

Wet bindings and feet, then hold heel binding flat and slide foot into front binding.

Raise heel slightly and with both hands pull heel piece over your heel.

AWSA, HAND SIGNALS

1. Speed-Up: The "thumbs-up" gesture is used to indicate the skier would like the speed increased.

2. Slow Down: The "thumbs-down" gesture is used to indicate the skier would like the speed decreased.

3. Turn: When either the skier or the driver wants the boat turned, a circle motion with the arm over the head with one finger in the air is used. It is usually followed by

pointing in the direction of the turn.

4. Back to Dock: A pat on the head indicating that the skier would like to return to the starting dock.

5. Cut Motor/Stop: A slashing motion with the hand across the neck indicates the boat is to stop immediately. This signal can be used by the skier, driver or observer.

6. OK: If the newly set speed or boat path is good then the skier uses the OK signal—an "O" made with the index finger and thumb. This signal can also be used between skier and observer to indicate that signals given by one of them has been received by the other.

7. "I'm OK" after a fall: This is the most important signal which indicates that a skier is OK after falling. It consists of both hands clasped over the head.

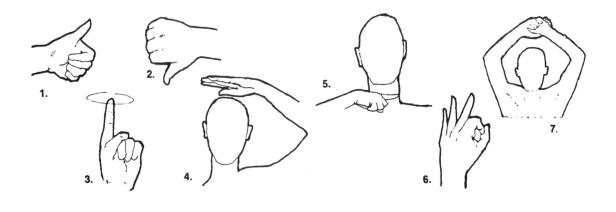

Wetting the bindings and your feet will ease putting on your skis, as your foot will slide rather than stick to the rubber binder.

Properly equipped, you are now ready for the start.

1. Assume a sitting "cannonball" position, knees pulled into the chest, heels in close to buttocks, on the tails of the skis.
2. Arms straight, extending forward on either side of the knees.
3. Head up, feet about shoulder-width apart.

Practice this position until you can assume it naturally.

With the towline firmly held by an instructor or

assistant, we can simulate and practice the start method on dry land. It is important to understand that the person holding the rope is doing the job of the towboat and will pull you to the skiing position. It must be emphasized that the boat will do all the work, you need only keep your knees bent, arms straight and head up.

• The person holding the line pulls firmly but gradually.
• As the pull increases you should rise slowly using the legs only, keeping your feet flat in the binders.
• Keep rising until you are in the correct, basic body position explained earlier, knees bent, arms straight, head up, back straight.

For dry land practice, assume cannonball position with knees pulled into chest, buttocks on tails of skis, and arms straight.

An assistant pulls the towline gradually but firmly. As pull increases, skier should rise slowly using only his legs, keeping feet flat in bindings.

Skier keeps rising until reaching basic body position—knees bent, arms straight, head up, back straight.

If your arms are bent at any time during this exercise it means you pulled on the rope, and on the water a fall backward would likely occur.

During dry land practice if you have a tendency to "pull" up rather than "rise" up with the legs, correct it immediately. Think of the arms as merely a link with the towboat, an extension of the tow rope. Practice this exercise until you have mastered the basics and are confident in their execution.

There are several indicators you might use to determine if you are starting correctly:

1. The amount of force (pull) required to pull you to the skiing position.

   - If a lot of force is needed you are resisting the pull by leaning back against it. Allow the boat (instructor) to *pull you* to a skiing position.
   - If too little force is needed you should "stand up" more slowly, allowing the boat to do the work.

2. Once you are in the "skiing position" drop the line suddenly. If you topple backward you are leaning too far back. Stand upright with your knees bent, arms straight and head up. When the handle is placed in your outstretched hands you will be in the correct skiing position.

By this point you should have realized the key to on-water success is very simply arms straight, knees bent, head up, and let the boat do the work.

ON THE WATER

Provided you have learned the techniques thoroughly in dry land practice, the next step on the water will be easy. If possible, a shallow sand beach is ideal for this "next step."

- Position yourself in approximately chest-deep water.
- Assume the same position that you practiced on land, sitting back on the skis, knees tight against the chest with arms straight on the outside of the knees.
- Skis shoulder width apart, rope between skis.
- When the rope is taut and you are ready, signal the driver to proceed. Caution: Be sure you are well clear of the rope and that the rope is taut without any loops that might entangle you.

As the power increases you will experience the same pull as you did during dry land practice. This time, however, you will be moving through the water.

In the water, bring skis together and rotate body into a cannonball position, with knees against chest, arms straight on the outside of knees, and towline between skis.

Don't be in too great a hurry to stand up. As the speed increases lift up with your legs. Chances are you will be skiing on the first attempt or shortly thereafter.

Before we move on to other skills and start methods, let's analyze some of the basics to this point. In simplest terms: knees bent centers your weight over the skis and allows you to absorb any wakes or other rough water; arms straight keeps the upper body square and prevents pulling on the rope; head up helps keep the back straight and upper body position correct.

If you have trouble with your start, refer to the following error and correction guide:

Symptom	Error	Correction
1. Fall backwards or slack rope	Pulling in with arms	Keep arms straight
2. Fall to the side	Uneven weight distribution	Both knees equally bent, balanced position in water
3. Fall forward	Standing up too quickly—straight legs	Rise gradually, knees bent
4. Plowing	Weight too far back chest away from knees	Weight forward, knees close to chest
5. Riding on back of skis	Did not use legs to stand up as boat accelerated	Stand up sooner when boat accelerates at start
6. Loss of balance	Body too stiff	Bend knees, bend slightly forward at waist
7. Legs separate at start	Loss of basic start position	Place arms outside knees, tuck knees up at chest

DEEP WATER START

Once you have mastered the first step and are successful in getting up on skis, you should learn and practice the deep water start method.

The actual start technique is no different than that already learned. What is different is that now you must put your skis on in deep water. For many beginners this can be the most difficult step. The method is similar to that used on dry land except that now the skis are not stationary and they have a tendency to float to the surface, a fact that more often than not will roll you over onto your side or stomach with your skis cocked at odd angles behind you. The following simple procedure will overcome this common dilemma.

Enter the water, wearing a flotation device, with both skis close by.

• Bend one knee up to chest.
• Hold ski on either side near binding.

- Bend the heel of the binding to one side, insert foot as far as possible (wiggling the toes helps).
- Grasp the heel piece with both hands and pull up.
- Put the second ski on in the same manner.

Once the skis are on you can maintain balance by a fanning motion with the hands and by keeping the knees bent tight to the chest.

Should you lose control as the skis float or attempt to float, simply relax, float on your side, and bend both knees tight to your chest. Once you have brought the skis together in this manner it is relatively easy to submerge them and rotate your body into an upright "cannonball" position.

In the "cannonball" position, balance can easily be maintained with the fanning motion of the hands. Relax and wait for the tow rope. A word of caution—*never* have the towline around your body! If the towboat has, as is common practice, circled around you to put the rope within reach, lift the rope over your head and have it in front of your body, never behind. Take care to avoid any loops that might entangle you and never signal the driver to accelerate until you are sure the line is taut and you are well clear.

Once you are comfortable and ready, signal the driver to move forward by the command "in gear." (Movement of the boat at this point is strictly at the skier's command. The driver should never assume the skier is ready until signaled so.)

As the rope tightens, you will start to move forward. When you are ready command the driver to "hit it." This command indicates to the driver you are ready to ski. From here on the start is no different than that already learned.

You will be sitting back on the skis, knees bent tight to your chest; arms straight outside your knees; ski tips out of water about shoulder width apart with the rope between the skis.

As the boat accelerates simply rise up, keeping knees bent, arms straight, head up and back straight. Keep your weight evenly distributed over both skis.

TURNING

In order to turn (steer) you simply lean in the direction you wish to go. To increase the degree or angle of the turn, lean into the turn and apply increased pressure on the outside ski of the turn. Practice this first inside the boat's wake until you are comfortable and confident with turning the skis.

WAKE CROSSING

The key to crossing the wake is to cross as quickly and at as sharp an angle as possible. This is accom-

When crossing a wake, do it quickly and at as sharp an angle as possible.

plished by beginning the approach from the inside opposite wake when crossing outside the boat's wake, and from as wide as possible when returning to inside the boat's wake.

Crossing with one ski and then the other at a shallow angle will result in a fall. The knees act as shock absorbers and must be bent to absorb the wake.

LANDING

Probably the simplest stage in learning to water ski is the landing. The easiest way is to simply release the handle and sink slowly into the water—*simply release the handle*, never throw the rope.

You should always stay behind the boat when finishing a ski ride. Never ski toward a dock or beach. Always glide parallel to the dock or beach and as the speed diminishes sink slowly into the water. With a little practice and experience this will be accomplished in reasonable proximity to the landing area, be it a dock or beach.

One important safety practice you should learn is how to "apply the brakes." If for any reason you must stop more quickly than anticipated, sit down on the tails of the skis, or even lie down backwards while dragging your hands in the water as brakes.

THE DOCK START

The dock start is similar to the deep water start but differs in that it is a quicker start with a firm, progressive acceleration and a transition from the dock to water.

With your skis and properly-fastened flotation device on, move to the dock's edge and extend the ski tips as far over the water as balance allows. Now sit to one side of the skis and then slide them off the dock into the water. You should now be sitting as close to the edge of the dock as possible, facing the stern of the towboat.

Sitting on the edge of the dock with your ski tips out of water, lean slightly away from the boat with knees bent and arms bent slightly to absorb the pull.

As the boat idles slowly away from the dock and the slack is taken up, you must be prepared to resist the boat's pull and maintain the start position. A major precaution again is to be certain you are clear of the tow rope before you give the command to "hit it."

At this point there is some timing and team work required that comes with practice and experience. Learn the dock start with an experienced driver! As the last coil in the line starts to pay out, give the command to "hit it" and as the rope tightens, transfer your weight from the dock to the skis, keeping your knees bent and the towline held at waist level. The team work is that the driver must apply just the right amount of power at exactly the moment you shift from dock to skis. If you have trouble with the dock start, analyze the symptom, detect the error, and apply the correction.

Symptom	Error	Correction
1. Fall forward	Transferred weight too soon or too quickly, legs too straight, did not resist pull	Transfer weight as boat pulls skier off dock, bend knees, resist pull
2. Fall backward	Legs too straight, rope too high, pulled in with arms, weight on tails of skis	Bend knees, rope waist high, keep arms locked, keep weight over feet

Proper position for a dock start. Sit on edge of dock with ski tips out of water and lean slightly away from the boat.

As slack in towline is taken up, skier gives command "Hit It!" Skier now shifts from dock to skis. Timing and teamwork requires practice for this maneuver.

PART 8
ARCHERY &
BOWHUNTING

TYPES OF BOWS

Archery as a sport today is practiced in a variety of ways. There are archers who prefer to shoot at conventional targets; roving archers who ramble through woodlands testing their skill on tree stumps and other natural targets; field archers who roam a course shooting at targets that simulate hunting conditions. Then there are bowhunters, some of whom have taken every game animal from the groundhog to the bull elephant with well-placed arrows. An interesting offshoot of bowhunting is bowfishing, in which a harpoon-type rig is used to shoot coarse fish.

Like the hunter who uses various types of guns designed for different species of game, the bowhunter also uses various types of bows according to his sport. While there are differences among bows—those designed for championship performance on the target range, others for plinking and roving, and still others for hunting big-game animals—foremost to remember when purchasing any bow is its draw or pull weight, that is, the amount of strength required to pull the string back to full draw. "Overbowing" is the cardinal sin of the beginner.

COMPOUND BOWS

The acceptance of compound bows—especially for hunting deer and other good-size game—has been so pronounced that some manufacturers make no other type or else make only a few recurve models. This newest concept in archery was invented by H. W. Allen of Billings, Missouri, and most compounds are manufactured under license from Mr.

Allen. A compound bow looks a bit strange but is simple in operation. Attached to its relatively short, stout limbs is a small pulley system. A conventional bowstring is connected to two strands of cable that run over the wheels—an idler pulley plus an eccentric pulley at each end of the limbs—in the manner of a block and tackle. This device solves bow-weight problems, vastly increases the power and accuracy of an arrow, and eases the draw and release.

To understand some of the reasons, consider how energy is applied in a firearm. A rifle produces greater bullet velocity than a handgun because the rifle's longer barrel applies gas pressure for a longer distance, thus increasing the foot-pounds of energy exerted on the projectile. The eccentric pulleys on a compound's limb tips accomplish the same thing by applying maximum pull weight for a greater number of inches. With an ordinary recurve bow, the pressure decreases steadily from the instant of release as the bowstring moves forward. With a compound, the peak pull-weight poundage is about at mid-draw. Thus, as the bowstring moves forward, the pressure increases to a peak before decreasing. This substantially raises the foot-pounds of energy applied to the arrow.

Also, with a conventional bow the release pressure must overcome the inertia not only of the arrow but of the bowstring and the moving part of each limb. In a compound, limb-tip travel is reduced from about 8 inches to 3 and inertia is greatly reduced. In a conventional bow with a 50-pound pull weight, 50 pounds must propel the weight of the limbs 8 inches while also propelling the arrow and center of the string 20 inches to the string-rest position.

689

PARTS OF BOWS

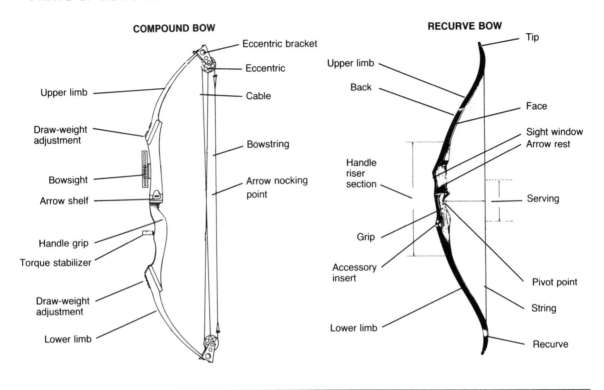

COMPOUND BOW

- Eccentric bracket
- Eccentric
- Upper limb
- Cable
- Draw-weight adjustment
- Bowstring
- Bowsight
- Arrow nocking point
- Arrow shelf
- Handle grip
- Torque stabilizer
- Draw-weight adjustment
- Lower limb

RECURVE BOW

- Tip
- Upper limb
- Back
- Face
- Sight window
- Arrow rest
- Handle riser section
- Serving
- Grip
- Accessory insert
- Pivot point
- String
- Lower limb
- Recurve

With the pulleys and three strands (bowstring plus two strands of cable), the same pull results in three times the power—150 pounds.

Due to the action of the eccentric pulleys, the pull weight reaches a maximum and then relaxes—eases off—somewhat before full draw is reached. This reduces finger strain and muscle fatigue at full draw, making a compound bow easier to shoot well. The same principle also permits the use of lighter arrows. A compound with a 50-pound peak setting will hold at full draw at approximately 40 pounds, so an arrow spined for a 40-pound pull is about right. (Manufacturers include arrow-matching instructions with their bows, and these instructions should be followed.) The lighter arrows, released in the compound manner, have a flatter trajectory—a bonus advantage.

In many compound bows, draw lengths can be adjusted somewhat, and peak weight can be adjusted within a 10-pound range. Target compounds are usually 56 to 58 inches long. Hunting models generally range from 38 to 50 inches, and bows to be used for both purposes are about 50 inches long.

The weight of these bows ranges from about 3½ to 4¼ pounds. They're made in either a one-piece style or in the take-down style. The cables are steel. The handle risers may be magnesium or hardwood. In top-quality bows, the limbs are laminated wood and fiberglass. Less expensive models may be solid fiberglass. Even these, however, are more costly than high-quality bows of conventional design.

CROSSBOWS

The basic design of the crossbow is centuries old, but a major change has been made in recent years. We now have compound crossbows which incorporate the pulley system of the conventional compound bow. Older crossbows were impossible to draw manually and employed a crank for cocking them. The modern compound crossbow, however, has a draw weight of around 125 pounds (from 100 to 175 pounds on various models), and can be drawn by hand. It has either a stirrup or bipod stand at the front end. The archer plants his feet on this and pulls the bowstring up into cocking position.

COMPOUND BOWS

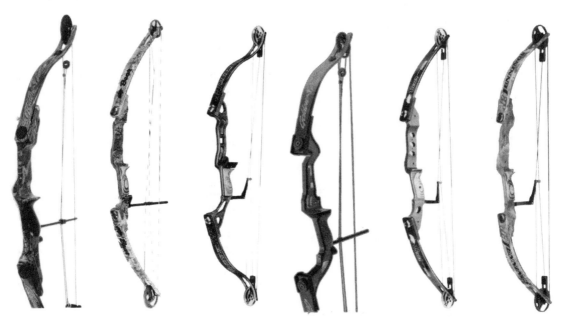

Typical compound bows: Golden Eagle Falcon Flame, Bear Fury, Jennings Aurora, Golden Eagle Revolution, Bear Odyssey, Jennings Quest. In a compound bow a small pulley system, similar to a block and tackle, is attached to the limbs: Conventional bowstring is connected to cable run over idler and eccentric pulleys at each end. This system solves weight problems, increases arrow power and accuracy, and eases draw and release. Tournament bows are generally longer and heavier than hunting models. The lengths for target compounds range from 56 to 58 inches, compared to 48 to 50 inches for hunting models. Dual-purpose bows are about 51 inches long.

Nearly all modern crossbows have many features in common: They have shoulder stocks, mechanical "trigger" releases, and sights. Crossbows are also drawn and cocked in advance. They are easier to master than conventional bows because all functions are mechanical.

The crossbow is currently the subject of much controversy among hunters. Most bowhunters agree that the crossbow is far too mechanized to be called a primitive weapon and should not be allowed in the field with other bowhunters. In fact, most states ban the use of crossbows for hunting.

Typical modern crossbow is the Bear Lightning Crossbow. This crank-style cocking device attaches to the stock for quick loading.

RECURVE BOWS AND STRAIGHT BOWS

Conventional bows are of two basic types—straight or long bow and recurve. The straight bow, as its name implies, has straight limbs. Such bows were once standard. Today, few are sold, but there are archers who enjoy the ancient and classic style, and some of these people make their own straight bows. The limbs of a recurve bow curve back and then, near the tips, curve forward.

The modern recurve bow is popular because it casts an arrow at greater speed with less draw weight than older styles. A relatively short recurve bow has excellent cast and is also maneuverable in brush, so models measuring 50 to 60 inches are popular for hunting. Longer bows—some of them 64 to 70 inches—are more stable, easier to draw, and

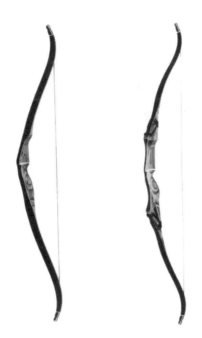

smoother to release, so long models are used for target shooting. A bow for both purposes will have a compromise length.

Wood alone is still used in making some bows—primarily inexpensive models. Lemon and hickory are the most common woods. Hickory withstands cold better than lemon wood, but neither material produces the best cast. Various metals (especially tubular aluminum) have also been used by bowyers. Aluminum bows are unaffected by temperature changes but, again, the cast is poor. Solid fiberglass is used, too. It's impervious to weather but lacks the shooting qualities of ''composite'' bows, which are now most common. These are laminations of two or more different materials—metal, wood, fiberglass, and various synthetics. The laminated composite bows produce excellent cast and are, in general, better than any other type.

Typical modern recurve bows: Bear Kodiak Magnum (Left) and Fred Bear Take Down. A modern recurve bow casts an arrow at greater speed with less draw weight than older styles. Recurves are made both in one-piece and take-down models, from wood, metal, or solid fiberglass.

BOW SELECTION AND CARE

DRAW WEIGHT

For tournament shooting (as well as plinking), select a bow that you can easily bring to full draw and hold for 10 seconds without shaking unduly. A little tremor is all right, but if you are forcing yourself to hold the bow at full draw, it is too heavy for you. An accompanying chart shows recommended draw weights for men, women, and youngsters.

A hunter should use a bow with as much draw weight as he can shoot comfortably. This will give an arrow the speed needed for penetration on game. It will also produce flatter trajectory—hence, more hits on game at unknown distances. Moreover, the faster an arrow arrives, the less chance a game animal has to ''jump string'' (dodge the arrow). For hunting deer, a recurve bow should have a minimum draw weight of about 50 pounds, even if your state's game laws set a somewhat lower minimum, and a compound bow should have a minimum peak weight of 50 to 55 pounds. With a little practice, an average man can usually shoot a bow 5 or 10 pounds heavier than that with ease.

Of course, a lighter draw weight is adequate for smaller game, and a heavier draw is required for game larger than deer. Recommended weights are listed in the accompanying chart. With a compound

RECOMMENDED DRAW WEIGHTS FOR TARGET SHOOTING

	20 lb. & under	20 lb.	25 lb.	30 lb.	35 lb.	40 lb.	40 lb. & over
Children 6-12	X	X					
Teen (Girl)		X	X				
Teen (Boy)		X	X	X			
Ladies			X	X	X		
Men				X	X	X	

RECOMMENDED DRAW WEIGHTS FOR HUNTING

Game	Rabbit and Squirrel	Coyote and Fox	Deer and Bear	Elk	Moose
30–40	X				
40–50	X	X			
50–60	X	X	X		
60–70	X	X	X	X	X
70–80	X	X	X	X	X

DRAW WEIGHT

Drawing shows why the compound bow is easy to hold at full draw and release smoothly. Peak draw weight is reached when archer has drawn bow string only partway back. Weight then eases down as string comes back to let-off point, so less strength is needed to pull it back and hold it steady.

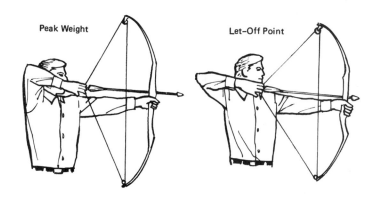

Peak Weight

Let-Off Point

bow, the draw weight is the peak weight—the amount you must pull through before the weight decreases at full draw. With a recurve bow, draw weight is the number of pounds it takes to draw the bowstring back to 28 inches. For each inch of draw above or below 28 inches, add or subtract 2 pounds to determine the approximate weight of your personal draw length.

BOW HANDLING

Remember these "don'ts" when handling a bow. A bow at full draw, according to the manufacturer's

specifications, is usually considered to be 8/10 broken. For example, if you have a bow that is designed for 30-inch arrows and pulls 50 pounds at full draw, at that particular point it is 8/10 broken. If you drew the bow past the 30-inch mark, you would subject it to serious stress that could cause it to break.

Another way to shatter a bow is to pull to full draw without an arrow and release the string. Under no circumstances release a bowstring without an arrow in the bow or attempt to overdraw the bow.

Quality bows can also be broken or have limbs twisted by incorrect stringing techniques. String a bow carefully and you'll have it for years. Perhaps

HOW TO STRING A RECURVE BOW

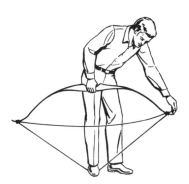

Left: Bow stringer places identical stress on both limbs. Slip leather pockets over bow tips, place foot over center of cord, and pull up. Bowstring will slip into nock. **Center:** Lacking a bow stringer, one way to string a bow is to brace the tip against your instep, holding the bow as shown, and flex it by applying opposite pressure with each hand. Then slide the bowstring into the nock. **Right:** Third method of stringing bow is to insert right leg between string and bow, hooking tip over shoe, and use thigh as a fulcrum to flex the bow as you slip string into nock.

the most efficient way to string a bow is with a bow stringer, a device designed to place identical stress on both limbs as in actual shooting. It also eliminates the possibility of the bow accidentally jumping out of your hands and causing injury to yourself or by-standers. The bow stringer is a stout length of nylon cord with leather pockets fitted at both ends which are slipped over the bow tips. By placing your foot over the center of the cord, the bow is readily raised and the limbs bent, permitting the string to be slipped into the nock. To prevent the bowstring from slipping off the opposite nock when stringing, place an elastic band or bow-tip protector over the lower nock and secure the string in place.

There are special bow stringers available for compound bows, but restringing a compound bow, especially if the cables have come off the wheels, is usually a job for an archery pro shop.

Without the assistance of a bow stringer, there are two acceptable ways to string your bow, and they are shown in the accompanying illustrations.

Once the bow has been strung, brace height is an important consideration. Brace height is the distance from the bowstring to the deepest cut in the handle on the face of the bow, below the arrow shelf. Proper brace height for a particular bow is given in the manufacturer's specifications; but this is not a rigid figure, and by altering it slightly some archers find that they shoot better. Brace height can be altered by twisting the bowstring to shorten it or by untwisting it to lengthen it. Care, however, should be used not to twist the string excessively, for this will damage it, and ultimately the bow.

The proper brace height for your bow depends entirely on your shooting style and the conditions under which you are shooting. There is no brace height which will give you maximum performance every time. For example, as your bow "warms up" during a sustained shooting session, the string will have a tendency to stretch. Conversely, after a period of idleness, the string will return to its original

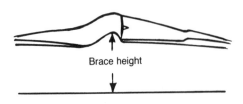

Correct brace height, given with manufacturer's specifications, is measured from bowstring to handle.

DETERMINING ARROW LENGTH

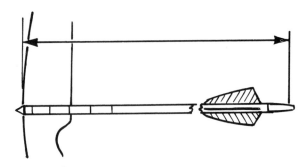

Correct arrow length can be determined by using a measuring arrow marked in inches. At full draw, your correct arrow length is the point at which the arrow stops in relation to the front of the arrow shelf.

Spread measurement

Drawing length

Alternate method of determining correct arrow length: Measure your arm spread and choose the correct arrow from the table below.

Spread Measurement	Arrow Length
57"-59"	24"-25"
60-62	25-26
63-65	26-27
66-68	27-28
69-71	28-29
72-74	29-30
75-77	30-31

length. For this reason it is important that you "tune" your bowstring before and during every shooting session.

Proper brace height for your bow and your individual shooting style will give you the least amount of wrist slap, string noise, and vibration, and an arrow that does not wobble in flight.

BOW CARE

When not shooting a recurve bow, always keep your bow unstrung and hang it vertically or lay it across pegs supporting both limbs. Keep you bow in a case when transporting it, to protect it from damage. When using a bow during rain or snow, coat it generously with high-grade automobile or furniture wax to protect its finish, and wipe it dry after a day afield in bad weather. Prior to sustained periods of storage, apply a generous coat of wax to protect the bow's finish. In cold weather, "flex" the bow several times to warm it up before shooting.

Another important consideration is the nocking point that is added to the bowstring serving. A nocking point is nothing more than a small piece of tape, attached to the bowstring at right angles to the bow to prevent the arrow from slipping up and down or off the bowstring, to aid in consistent shooting. To locate the nocking point, place an arrow on the bowstring as you would when actually shooting the bow, and add the nocking point above, below, or on both sides of the arrow on the string serving. This is essential for the bowhunter, who hasn't time to position his arrow correctly on the string when he sights game. With a nocking point, he can quickly feel and place his arrow in the exact position every time.

Most bows manufactured today are weighed-in at a given draw length. For example, a bow will be marked 55 pounds at 28 inches. This simply means the manufacturer has weighed the bow when it has been drawn back to 28 inches, the standard length of most arrows. But if the bow is drawn less than 28 inches or more than 28 inches its pull decreases and increases accordingly. If you use a 28-inch arrow and desire a 55-pound bow, then the bow marked 55 pounds at 28 inches is for you. On the other hand, if you draw a 26-inch arrow, a bow measured and weighed for a 28-inch draw will lose 2 pounds per inch. Hence, despite the fact the bow is marked 55 pounds, at your 26-inch draw it will only pull some 51 pounds. Conversely, if you use a 29-inch arrow, the pull will be increased by 2 pounds to 57.

Proper arrow measurement for your individual requirements varies greatly with every archer. Proper arrow measurement techniques are shown in the accompanying illustration.

ARROWS

The single most important piece of archer's equipment is the arrow. Any bow of a reputed manufacturer will probably perform well, but not so with an arrow. Purchase a bow within your price range, but under no circumstances should you buy the least expensive arrows.

Matched arrows are a set of eight or one dozen, absolutely straight and of identical length. Each is perfectly round and made of the same material. They are fletched exactly alike, and all balance at the same point. All are of equal weight and have the same spine (stiffness) for your particular bow.

The nomenclature of the arrow, the "archer's messenger," is shown in the accompanying illustration. The arrow is composed of a shaft, nock, fletching, crest, and point. Fiberglass, graphite, and aluminum arrow shafts are beginning to replace the traditional wood in popularity.

Wood arrow shafts come in several varieties. The arrow constructed of a single piece of wood is termed the "self" arrow. The "footed" arrow is a self arrow whose forward segment has a section of extreme hard wood carefully spliced to it. This design fortifies the foreshaft against weakening and breakage. The diameter of a wood arrow shaft is usually $\frac{9}{32}$ inch, $\frac{5}{16}$ inch or $\frac{11}{32}$ inch, depending on the draw weight of your bow. Light women's and children's bows ordinarily use the $\frac{9}{32}$-inch shaft. Men's target shafts are $\frac{5}{16}$ inch in diameter. Most hunting arrows constructed of wood are $\frac{11}{32}$ inch in diameter.

The nock is a simple notch in the end of the arrow, or a specially designed plastic contrivance, which holds the arrow on the bowstring. It should be deep enough to keep the arrow on the string and wide enough to permit an easy fit on the string without crowding. In former years, nocks were made of such items as horn and fiber, but today cellulous plastic that is easily die-cast and as tough as nails is common nock material. It is readily fitted to the arrow shaft by means of an 11-degree tapered hole inside the nock itself. The nock end of the shaft is tapered and with cellulous cement it is quickly and efficiently glued to the shaft.

PARTS OF AN ARROW

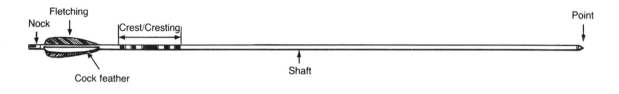

Plastic nocks are available in a wide variety of colors and sizes. To replace them, burn them off with a match. The plastic nock burns quickly without damaging the wood. Many plastic nocks contain a small knob or marker which is aligned with the cock feather to permit an archer easy reference by feel during rapid shooting. With this marker reference, the archer simply feels for the eruption on the nock and immediately knows the cock feather is in line.

The fletching of feathers on the arrow keeps it stable in flight. "Fletcher" is the old English name for a man who attaches feathers to an arrow, hence arrow feathers are known by that term. Most feathers are added to the arrow shaft somewhere between one-quarter to one-half inch below the nock. The size of the feathers is directly proportional to the arrow head or point used. In target shooting some use a feather of some 2½ inches in length and not over a half-inch in height at any given point. Hunting arrows that contain large and heavy broadhead blades have a fletching of some 4 to 6 inches in length.

Standard fletching consists of three individual feathers, spaced 120 degrees apart. The "cock" feather, or odd colored feather, is the one positioned at right angles to the bow. The odd color tells the archer how to place the arrow to the bow. In addition to the cock feather are usually a brace of hen or identically colored feathers. Feathers on one arrow are mainly of turkey right and left wing feathers. It makes no difference which feather is used, right or left, but in constructing a matched set of arrows either all rights or all lefts are used.

Today, many bowhunters prefer all feathers to be the same color. Solid orange, white or yellow are most often used because they are more easily detected in flight in the early dawn or twilight hours.

There are many methods of arrow fletching. The feathers can be added to the shaft in a straight line. Most archers prefer to add them to the shaft in a slight spiral, for spiral fletching allows the arrow to rotate in flight, creating more stability. Many archers today also prefer four and six fletched arrow shafts, again, for better stability. The basic arrow in wide use today is the three-feather fletched version.

The prime concern with all fletching, however, is uniformity: the feathers must be all right or all left wing, of uniform equal thickness, and carefully fletched to the arrow. Most feathers are not more than a half-inch high at any given point. A feather of greater height retards the flight. On the other hand, an arrow whose feathers are too low will vastly reduce stability and cause wobbling in flight.

In former years swan and goose wing quills were in common use, and today there are some plastic feathers, but turkey feathers still dominate the field. At one time arrow feathers were cut to length and attached to the shaft by tying them with sinew, but today a wide variety of fletching jigs perform this task. The feather is "base ground" before it is applied to the shaft. Base grinding means that the quill itself is ground until a mere wisp remains to hold the feather to the quill itself. The feathers are glued to the shaft by means of cellulous cement. A feather burner burns the feather to shape once the feather is attached to the arrow.

The arrow crest is a distinguishing mark added to the arrow for quick identification.

Woods used for the construction of arrow shafts over the years consisted of Norway pine, Douglas fir, birch, and Port Orford cedar.

Port Orford cedar comes from the West Coast forests in the United States and from the mountain region north of Palestine, where it is known as the cedars of Lebanon. Port Orford cedar has an extremely straight grain and provides the finest spine of any wood material.

All woods have a tendency to warp, however. Hence the introduction of other materials in recent years. Aluminum provides a uniformity that wood cannot equal and it is unaffected by wide temperature changes.

Aluminum arrows today are selected by tournament archers for their uniformity and outstanding precision performance. While some bowhunters choose aluminum shafts for hunting, most prefer the fiberglass shaft that appeared after World War II. The development of quality fiberglass arrows followed.

Aluminum tends to be too noisy afield and is invariably rendered useless once it strikes an animal, tree, or rock. The fiberglass arrow shaft lacks these drawbacks. It is unaffected by temperature changes, can be produced to exacting specifications, and will not warp or bend out of shape, the most common fault of other materials. The rugged fiberglass arrows are capable of deep penetration in game animals and are thus most widely used by bowhunters throughout the world.

Although fiberglass arrows cost about twice as much as high-grade wooden arrows, their quality and durability make them a good buy for many archers. Their shafts are tubular. The fiberglass is wrapped around a metal mandrel which is removed after construction. These arrows are made in suitable sizes for bow weight and draw length. The sizes are numbered from 1 through 12, whereas wooden arrows are lettered from A through K. (Aluminum arrows are also numbered.) Some glass hunting arrows are available with inserts that allow the use of either broadheads or field points on the same shaft.

A matched set of arrows must be carefully adjusted in weight and spine to the individual bow and carefully matched in length to your individual draw length. Spine or "stiffness" of an arrow is of utmost importance. An arrow with too soft a spine tends to shoot to the right of the point of aim. Conversely, too stiff a spine deflects the arrow to the left of the point of aim. The spining of arrows is difficult to comprehend. Formerly archers merely flexed arrow shafts in their hands to determine stiffness. Today the various arrow shaft manufacturers have developed formulas which quickly and easily determine arrow spine.

When an arrow is released from a bow, the weight of the bowstring and the friction against the bow handle bends the arrow slightly to the right. As the string moves forward, it violently draws the arrow shaft to the left. As the arrow leaves the string the shaft recovers stability by straightening, or by bending toward the right until it has fully corrected itself and assumed a straight course. An arrow must be spined exactly to the individual bow weight if it is to bend uniformly and recover quickly. Too weak a spine will send the arrow to the right; too stiff, and it will shoot to the left.

The weight of individual shafts is important. Although the exact weight of the arrows is not critical, every arrow in a matched set must weigh within a few grains of the others for uniform shooting. The lightest arrows possible are best for tournament shooting, while slightly heavier shafts are more suitable for field and hunting.

The method for determining correct arrow length for individual requirements was discussed in the preceding section. When purchasing arrows you must know your proper arrow length and obtain a complete set that is further matched in weight and spine to your individual bow.

Various types of arrows draw to different lengths. The target arrow with its target point is usually drawn to the end of the pile. Field and broadhead-blade points, however, can be added to an arrow shaft by increasing the shaft length by three-quarters of an inch. This is usually done to prevent the bowhunter with a razor-sharp broadhead blade from mistakenly overdrawing.

Most quality wood, aluminum, graphite, and fiberglass arrows in use today have either tapered ends or some type of insert for the attachment of arrow points. Thus an archer who purchases one set of matched arrows can quickly add field points to his shaft (which would weigh the same as the broadhead you plan to use during the hunting season) for between-season field practice on the target butt. When hunting seasons open, it is simple to remove the field points and add broadhead blades. Many matched field-hunting arrows sets are often fitted with six arrows using field points and six fitted with broadhead blades. Passing the point over an open

ARROW POINTS

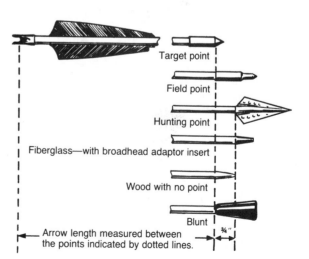

Target point

Field point

Hunting point

Fiberglass—with broadhead adaptor insert

Wood with no point

Blunt

¾"

Arrow length measured between the points indicated by dotted lines.

Various arrow points draw to different lengths.

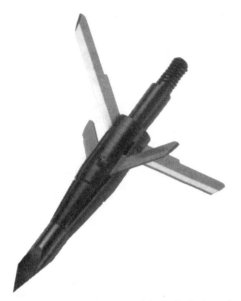

The Satellite Scorpion Broadhead is typical of modern broadhead design. Upon impact, the .030-inch-thick blades expand open to a 1½-inch or 1⅞-inch cutting diameter broadhead.

small feathers and have light target points. These arrows are intended for shooting into a straw-type mat or target butt.

The field, roving, and hunting arrows are basically the same. They are usually more ruggedly constructed than the target arrow, though of similar materials to withstand great abuse. They are heavier and contain larger fletching to permit more stability in flight. The roving or field arrow uses a point that should weigh the same as the broadhead blade the hunter anticipates using during the hunting seasons. The field or roving arrow, then, is primarily a practice arrow for the bowhunter since it weighs exactly the same as the hunting arrow. Roving or field arrows become hunting arrows merely by changing the points to broadheads and vice versa.

The flu-flu arrow is used for hunting or wing shooting where the archer is required to shoot his arrow skyward. The flu-flu arrow has abnormally high fletching to retard its flight. The high feathers prevent the arrow from traveling more than 30 to 50 yards. The point is usually a blunt or small-game type and is ideal where small game and especially squirrel hunting are legal with the bow and arrow. Flu-flu's are also used by enterprising bird hunters who have the courage to attempt wing shooting for

flame, being careful not to burn the shaft itself, will remove it easily from the shaft.

Among the many arrow types designed for special purposes, there are only a few the archer should be concerned with. These are the target arrow, field or roving arrow, hunting arrow, and flu-flu and fish arrows.

Most high-quality target arrows are now made of lightweight aluminum alloy. They are fletched with

Archer practices with flu-flu arrows in preparation for upland-bird season. Blunt points are most effective on gamebirds.

Flu-flu arrows with high fletching to retard flight are used for wing-shooting and hunting small game.

upland gamebirds. Blunt points are far superior to all other type points for small-game hunting. Broadhead blades used so efficiently by bowhunters on big-game animals will not stop the small gamebirds and animals as will the blunt. The blunt stuns the small bird or animal, allowing the archer quick recovery of his quarry.

Another arrow type in wide use today is the fish or harpoon arrow. Bowfishing with the bow and arrow for coarse fish such as carp and suckers is a challenging sport. The fish arrow must be heavy in order to penetrate the water's depths, hence heavy-solid fiberglass arrows are appropriate. The conventional turkey feathers must also be replaced, and today rubber-type arrow fletching appears on most fishing arrows. The fish arrow contains a removable barbed fish point. For further details on this sport, see the chapter on bowfishing.

All arrows require some care in use and storage. Most arrows are best stored in the boxes they came in. Never stack wood arrows haphazardly in an inaccessible corner of the closet, as they will warp. Keeping arrows in a quiver is fine with fiberglass or aluminum, but wood arrows must be stored to avoid warpage.

During sustained periods of storage, watch arrow fletching carefully to prevent moth damage. It is also a good idea to lightly oil field, blunt, broadhead, and fish points. Wood arrow shafts should be waxed

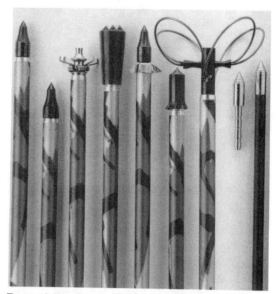

Types of Arrowheads: (From left) **Screw-In Field Point. 3D Field Point:** Specially designed to reduce damage to 3D targets. **Judo Point:** Good choice for small-game hunters. Small spring arms snag on grass, brush, or ground on impact to flip your arrow up vertically to reduce loss. **Bludgeon:** Tough plastic tips deliver high-shocking power on small game. Design prevents arrow from snaking under grass or sticking in stumps. **Adder Point:** Good design for turkeys and small game. **Game Nabber:** Allows good penetration on tough small game but resists sticking into trees. **Snaro Bird Point:** Good design for taking game birds in flight. Wide wire loops increase impact and prevent arrow loss. **Glue-In Points:** These glue-in points eliminate the need for outserts, and make it easier to remove arrows from 3D targets.

with a good grade auto wax before use in the field. Fiberglass and aluminum require no other care. In extremely damp or rainy weather, coat arrow fletching with a silicote-based liquid or spray to keep it from becoming matted to the shaft.

BOWSTRINGS

One of the least expensive items in the archer's kit, yet one of the most important, is the bowstring. A string that is too long or constructed of fewer strands than required to sustain the pull weight can cause severe damage to a quality bow.

The bowstring is subjected to extreme wear at three points—the nocking position of the arrow and

the nock point at the bow tips. A bowstring should be checked carefully prior to each shooting stint for any signs of fraying or excessive wear. At the slightest indication of wear, the string should be immediately replaced.

Through the years bowstrings have been made from a wide variety of materials including rawhide,

Dwight Schuh photo

Quality bowstrings are inexpensive and of prime importance to accurate shooting. The bowman should never venture to the target butt or hunting field without an extra.

sinew, linen or flax, hemp, fortisan (a synthetic rayon yarn), Dacron, and Kevlar. Dacron is most universally accepted by modern archers. Bowstrings are composed of a number of strands in accord with bow weight.

Inexpensive bowstrings used for children's lightweight target bows are made of hemp and have a single loop. The single loop string has the one advantage of being suited to any bow length, since it can be tied to one nock of the bow at any length desired. However, quality bowstrings are made of top-grade Dacron, with double loops, and are manufactured to exact dimensions.

Although some archers make their own strings to suit their bows, top-grade bowstrings can be purchased so inexpensively today that it is hardly worth the time or effort required to make a string.

The double-loop Dacron bowstring is composed of a varied number of strands for varied pull weights and averages some 3 inches shorter than the bow it was constructed for. Hence the pull and length of the bow are important numbers to remember when purchasing bowstrings. Most quality bows manufactured today are marked with the draw weight at a particular arrow length as well as its overall length.

For example, a bow marked 50 lbs @ 28–60 inches simply means that it will draw 50 pounds at a 28-inch draw length and measures 60 inches in overall length. Therefore, when purchasing a bowstring for this bow simply remember its draw weight of 50 pounds and the bow's overall length—60 inches. Manufacturers invariably build into the bowstring the necessary compensation for overall length, and the bowstring marked 60 inches is actually not 60 inches, but some 3 inches shorter.

A new bowstring has a tendency to stretch and can stretch almost an inch after hard use. Keep this point in mind, for after a day spent shooting with a new string it will have stretched enough to reduce the brace height of your bow.

If you find the string has stretched to a point where your bow's brace height is too low, the bowstring can be shortened by merely twisting it several turns. Be careful, however, not to twist the string excessively or you could cause excessive wear and damage to the string itself. Usually several turns is sufficient to bring the new string back to brace height.

After sustained periods of shooting, the bowstring should be rewaxed. Apply gently an additional layer of wax and briskly rub into the string with a piece of brown wrapping paper. The paper, quickly moved over the surface of the string, tends to melt the wax and permit it to penetrate into the individual strands.

To prevent excess wear to the string, a serving, consisting of cotton thread, is added to the string at both nocking points and where the arrow is fitted to the string. The serving at the arrow nock position is of such a length to cover the string where the arrow is fitted and where the archer places his fingertips.

String serving, especially at the arrow nock position, takes severe wear. At any sign of fraying, the serving should be renewed with the aid of a string serving tool.

Of prime importance, every bowstring should have an arrow nocking point to permit the arrow to be placed on the bowstring in exactly the same location every time and to prevent the arrow from sliding off, or up and down, the string.

Remember, however, that the nocking point should not be positioned on the bowstring until after the string has been used several times to eliminate all possible stretch. There are numerous commercially produced nocking points in use today, but a suitable nocking point can be quickly made by simply wrapping the nock point location with a piece of tape or several turns of serving thread.

There are several other necessary items that can and should be fitted to the bowstring, especially when in the hunting field. The bowstring should be fitted with brush buttons and string silencers (*see* Accessories). Brush buttons are fitted to the bowstring at the bow's nock points to prevent brush and leaves from catching between string and bow. String silencers, usually constructed of pieces of rubber and attached to the bowstring at midpoint between the serving and nocking area, are also added to eliminate excessive string noise that can spook game in the field.

In conclusion, remember that bowstrings are cheap insurance and can easily mean the difference between success and failure in the field or on the range. Always carry a few extra strings with you as added insurance whenever you are shooting.

ARCHERY ACCESSORIES

SHOOTING GLOVES

To prevent the string from irritating the drawing fingers and to assist in releasing it smoothly and without creep, some sort of leather protection is required. Fitted on the three fingers of the archer's drawing hand, this protection is available either as a three-finger shooting glove or a tab. Most shooting gloves are of the skeleton type, with leather finger stalls or tips that fit over the three drawing fingers. These are available in either right- or left-handed models, in varied sizes.

The shooting glove provides ample all-round protection to the archer's drawing hand and is widely accepted among archers in both the hunting and target fields. However, there is another group of archers who prefer the three-finger tab over the glove simply because they have better "feel" of the bowstring when using the tab.

The tab is cheaper than the glove. Constructed of cordovan leather, tabs are available to fit one or two fingers of the shooting hand. They are slotted to permit the arrow nock to pass. The tab affords excellent protection for the balls of the fingers, but not for the inside of the fingers. In recent years tabs have been made with finger separators. In any case, you will require some sort of finger protection for the bowstring drawing hand. The choice is up to the individual.

ARM GUARDS

The next item of importance so essential for the archer is some sort of protection for the wrist and lower forearm of the bow arm. When a bowstring is released it may strike the inside of the archer's forearm, and without some sort of protection for this tender portion of the anatomy, the arm can become severely and dangerously bruised.

The arm guard buckles or snaps about the wrist of the bow arm. It is made of cordovan leather, with a few steel stays sewed between the leather and lining for added protection.

SHOOTING GLOVES

Three-finger archery glove

Three-finger shooting tabs

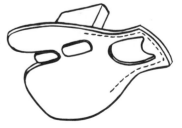

ARM GUARDS

Hunting arm guard

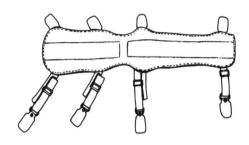

Target arm guard

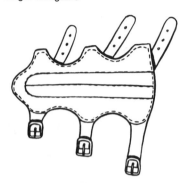

QUIVERS

Aside from the shooting glove or tab and the arm guard the archer needs something to carry his arrows afield or to the target range—a quiver. Quivers that hold anywhere from a half dozen to a few dozen arrows are available in many styles, each designed for a specific purpose.

The ground quiver, a metal stake with an attached metal ring, is stuck in the ground to hold arrows when shooting from a stationary position on the target field. The ground quiver is popular with the target archer. Center-back and shoulder quivers are used by bowhunters. Belt and pocket quivers are used by both tournament and field archers. In recent years, bowhunters have adopted the bow quiver, which attaches directly to the bow itself.

The shoulder quiver is the traditional bowhunter's

QUIVERS

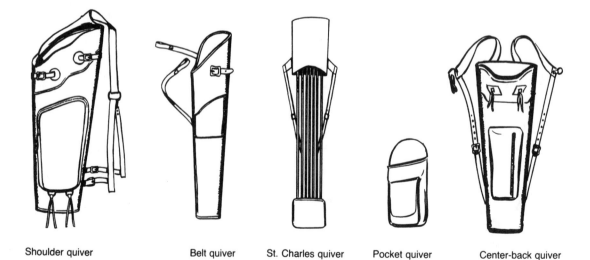

Shoulder quiver   Belt quiver   St. Charles quiver   Pocket quiver   Center-back quiver

Bow quiver, which holds arrows at the ready, is widely used in the hunting field.

Dwight Schuh photo

quiver. It is available in either right- or left-hand models, permitting the archer to reach back with his bowstring hand, grasp the nock end of the arrow, and with a forward swing draw the arrow from the quiver. The only drawbacks to the shoulder quiver are that, in the hunting field, the arrows projecting from the quiver tend to catch on tree limbs or rattle freely and spook game.

The center-back quiver was developed to help eliminate the problem of arrows getting caught in brush. The quiver fits the center of the archer's back, the protruding arrows nesting neatly behind his head.

Used widely by target archers, belt and pocket quivers are smaller than back and shoulder models, holding at the most a half-dozen arrows.

The bow quiver, attached directly to the bow, provides the fastest delivery and also ample protection for the arrows. Most quality quivers are equipped with some sort of metal shield to cover the broadhead blades. Without a shield to protect the blades, a bow quiver can be a dangerous piece of equipment with exposed razor-sharp broadheads.

Bow quivers are constructed to hold four to six arrows; some as many as eight.

BOWSIGHTS AND BOW SCOPES

Bowsights, especially bow scopes, are relative newcomers to archery. The early archer used no mechanical sighting aids—he aimed "instinctively." The modern archer, however, has a wide variety of bowsights to choose from. Archery tournaments are divided into two divisions, the instinctive and the freestyle. It is the freestyle group that uses the bowsight.

Bowsights and scopes have become highly sophisticated, and many have micrometer windage and elevation adjustment knobs, prisms, and aperture inserts, as well as a variety of post sighting points for shooting at varied yardages.

It is interesting to note that both schools—freestyle and instinctive—have turned in equally creditable scores in the hunting field. The bowsight used for hunting is usually made with a number of sighting posts; each post is sighted for a given or known range for a particular bow.

STABILIZERS

The torque stabilizer is perhaps one of the more recent innovations in the field of tournament or target archery, and is gradually gaining in popularity in the hunting field. The torque stabilizer does exactly

Bear and Jennings Balancing Act Stabilizer System is unique in that it has moveable weight discs, allowing the archer to adjust the bow's balance point according to personal shooting style.

BOWSIGHTS

Golden Eagle Orion VersaSight is designed to fit any make or model bow. Features a vertical adjustment of over one inch, providing shooters with the capability of quickly changing their set-ups.

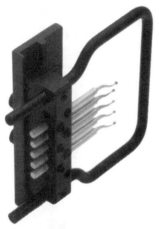

Golden Eagle Adjustable Constellation 1001. This compact sight adjusts vertically over one inch. All pins move simultaneously as the sight is moved up or down.

High Country Ultra Tuff Bead Sight. Five fluorescent beads on the center wire are mounted loose enough to move easily by hand, but tight enough to remain fixed with high energy bows.

what its name implies—it stabilizes the bow when the string is released. Miniature torque stabilizing inserts are fitted into tourney bows, to absorb the forward shock and thrust of the bowstring.

Torque stabilizers are fitted to the bow face just below the bow handle and vary in length according to the archer's preference. This stabilizing unit quickly dampens vibration. It further provides the tournament archer with additional weight for added stability, permitting a far more steady hold and smoother follow-through after the arrow has been released. But above all the stabilizer absorbs the

bow's recoil energy and greatly assists the archer in achieving accuracy.

OTHER EQUIPMENT

Brush Buttons. Although not required by the target archer, the bowhunter and field archer should add brush buttons to their bowstrings to prevent snagging the bow in brush and undergrowth when afield. The brush button is made of soft rubber and is quickly added to the bowstring at both string nocking points on the bow.

Silencers. Bowstring silencers are also a requisite for the bowhunter. Bowstrings have an uncanny ability to "twang" when released, which can quickly spook game. The string silencers, fitted to the bowstring midway between the string serving and the nocking points, reduce such noise. A simple pair of string silencers can be easily made simply by attaching a portion of a rubber band to the string. However, quality string silencers are available at a nominal price.

Mechanical Release. A trigger device that releases the bowstring cleanly and exactly the same every shot. Popular with target archers, but considered somewhat impractical for hunters and even unethical in some areas. There are a variety of designs, but all operate pretty much the same way. The archer holds the release in his string hand and clips it to his string. At full draw, he "pulls" a trigger, usually a button, and the string is released. His finger never touches the string.

Camouflage. The sheen and sparkle of a highly polished bow can readily startle game. The glitter can be eliminated by the addition of some sort of cam-

Hunter rattling up a buck during bow season. A hunting bow should be covered with camouflage material to prevent polished limbs from glaring in the sun and spooking game.

OTHER EQUIPMENT

Left: Brush buttons attached to bowstring near each nock prevent bow from snagging on undergrowth. **Right:** Bowstring silencers eliminate "twang" in field that spooks game.

OTHER EQUIPMENT (Continued)

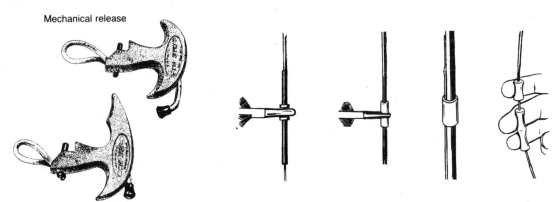

Mechanical release

Above left: Mechanical release is a trigger device that releases the bowstring cleanly and uniformly every shot. **Center and right:** Various types of nocking points for guiding the arrow onto the bowstring at the same spot each time.

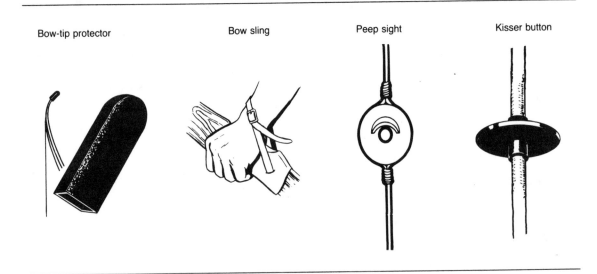

Bow-tip protector   Bow sling   Peep sight   Kisser button

ouflage, such as a cloth sock slipped over the limbs of the bow. Camouflage tape is also used, but if you use it remember to wax your bow well to prevent damage to the finish when the tape is removed. Many hunting bows are also available with a camouflage finish.

Bow Stringer. The bow stringer is another important piece of equipment. A quality bow that is not strung properly will wear quickly and warp, eventually even break. However, the bow stringer eliminates this problem. Made of a stout length of nylon rope

and a pair of leather bow-tip protectors, the stringer quickly, efficiently, and safely strings the bow.

Bowstring Nocking Points. These are added to the bowstring to permit positioning the arrow in the same spot each time and to prevent the arrow from slipping off the string when afield. A number of archery manufacturers produce varied nocking points at a nominal price.

Bow-tip Protectors. Made of soft rubber, the bow-tip protector prevents scuffing the bow when stringing, keeps bow tips in good condition, and holds the bowstring in place when stringing.

Bow Sling. Used primarily by tournament archers, the bow sling provides perfect balance and holds the bow in shooting position, giving the archer confidence that his bow cannot fall.

Peep Sight. A disc device with a small hole in the center. It is mounted on the bowstring and used to help the shooter line up sights on his bow more accurately.

Kisser Button. This device is used primarily by target archers to assure consistency of draw. Attached to the bowstring, it touches the archer's lip when at full draw to signal you are at proper draw.

Archery Targets. Available in 24-inch, 36-inch, and 48-inch sizes, archery target matts are often made of Indian cord grass covered with burlap. Conventional "ringed" target faces as well as animal faces are available. Using a proper archery target is essential for the preservation of your arrows. Shooting quality arrows into a rock-studded field can quickly ruin them. On the other hand, broadhead hunting arrows should not be used when shooting at the conventional archery matt since a few well-placed broadheads can quickly destroy the target.

HOW TO SHOOT

Shooting the modern bow and arrow, as with all other forms of shooting sports, requires patience and endless practice in order that the basic techniques required to strike a target consistently become instinctive. No shooter can expect to pick up a trap or skeet gun for the first time and break 25 straight targets on the claybird layouts. Neither can the neophyte archer expect to place all his arrows in the gold or drop a buck deer as it approaches his stand in the twilight hours without acquiring the fundamentals of shooting: stance, nocking, aiming, release, and follow-through.

STANCE

Proper stance is essential in archery. Shooting the bow and arrow differs from other forms of shooting in that considerable strength and effort are required. Hence the shooting stance must not only be comfortable, the feet must be correctly positioned in order that the body be properly braced.

Stand with your feet about 15 inches apart and at right angles to the target. You must be comfortable, and if you can feel more comfortable with a slightly wider stance, take it. But remember not to stand with your feet too close together since such a stance creates strain and invariably results in poor aiming techniques and sloppy shooting.

After finding the best shooting stance for yourself, remember it well and stick to it; do not vary the position. Consistency is the key to success.

STANCE

Correct shooting stance is important in achieving accuracy with the bow and arrow. Stand at right angles to the target with feet spread to assure a firm, yet balanced position.

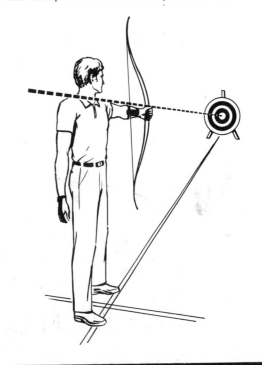

NOCKING

Nocking simply means placing the arrow on the bowstring. Foremost to remember is that the arrow must be fitted to the bowstring in exactly the same place each time, hence the use of a string "nocking point" which assures the archer of the correct position.

Before the introduction of center-shot bows and those with built-in arrow rests, the archer used his hands as an arrow rest, but this made for inconsistent shooting since he could not place his hand exactly in the same position every time. The arrow rest on most modern bows eliminates this age-old problem.

Once you have correctly positioned the string nocking point on the bowstring you are ready to place (nock) the arrow. With the bow firmly, but not tightly, held in the left hand at the left side grasp an arrow in the quiver with the thumb and forefinger of the right hand. (All instructions assume a right-handed archer.)

With one motion, as you remove the arrow from the quiver, bring the bow to waist height in a hor-

NOCKING

Arrow should be positioned on the rest and nocked at the same point each time. A nocking point should be added to the bowstring to permit accurate placement of the arrow.

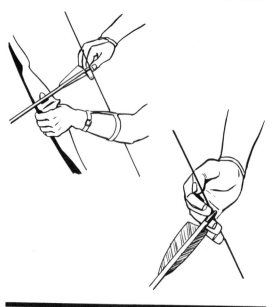

izontal position, and place the arrow across the bow. Center the arrow on the bowstring at the predetermined nocking point with the fingers of the right hand, holding the arrow firmly at the bow handle with the forefinger of the left hand. Place the first three fingers of the right hand on the bowstring, one finger above the arrow nock, the second two fingers below. You need not grasp the nock tightly.

DRAWING

Prior to starting the draw, cock your head toward the target, breathe deeply and relax, bringing the bow and fitted arrow into shooting position by extending your left arm forward with the elbow pointing slightly to the left and with the bow vertical or cocked slightly to the right. (The target and tournament archer prefers to keep his bow vertical; the bowhunter tends to cant it to the right.) Be certain that the bow hand, and especially the forearm, is not in the path of the bowstring, otherwise it could be struck as the arrow is released.

Now you are ready to draw back the bowstring to full-draw position. It is at this point that the beginner may encounter the problem of the arrow slipping from the arrow rest. This happens when the archer tries to apply pressure to the bowstring by curling his fingers around it, causing the string to roll to the left and the arrow to slip off the bow handle.

The bowstring should be grasped only with the pads of the three fingers of the drawing hand, with the hand, wrist, and forearm in a straight line. This way, the string will be rolled to the right and keep the arrow on its shelf.

As you bring the bow to full draw, keep the elbow of the drawing arm at right angles to the body. Such a position will bring the muscles of the shoulder and upper back into play and make drawing the bow much easier. Remember to push with the left shoulder and pull with the right side of the body. The chest, shoulders, and back will do the work.

Bring the bowstring back to full draw to the position near cheek or chin, being certain the string is "anchored" at the same point each time. Tournament archers invariably use the low anchor point with the bowstring hand resting just below the chin and the string touching the nose. On the other hand, the bowhunter likes to be closer to his line of sight and usually prefers the high anchor point with the second finger of the drawing hand anchored at the corner of the mouth. Some bowhunters anchor just below the eye as well. Again, the exact anchor point depends primarily on your individual preference and shooting style. But remember, once the anchor point has been established, do not vary it.

DRAW

The full draw position. With the three fingers of the drawing hand, and the aid of the back, shoulder, and chest muscles, the bowstring is drawn to an anchor point near the chin.

If you are a right-handed archer and you have established that your shooting eye is the right eye, then shoot with both eyes open. In all kinds of shooting, most top-notch shooters use both eyes. Closing one eye merely limits your vision. However, if your left eye is your shooting eye, learn to shoot left-handed.

Many tournament archers use a small rubber button, called a "kisser," fitted to the bowstring to determine full draw. It is positioned on the string at the correct anchor point for the individual archer and centered between the lips. With the anchor point under the chin, the bow should be held vertical. The bowhunter, on the other hand, with his higher anchor point, tilts both his head and bow.

AIMING

You are now at the full-draw position, relaxed, with the bow held firmly and the arrow resting snugly in the anchor position. You are now ready to aim.

There are three basic methods of aiming, each designed for a specific form of shooting. These include the bowsight method, the point-of-aim, and the instinctive style.

The instinctive style is without doubt the oldest method of aiming a bow and arrow. It is extremely accurate and consistent up to a distance of 40 yards. At ranges of 20 to 25 yards it is deadly, hence it is the method most used by bowhunters.

In instinctive aiming, your foremost attention is directed to the target while you see the arrow shaft indirectly. Concentrating on the target, your indirect vision automatically adjusts and compensates for elevation and windage. Foremost to remember is that everything must be done in exactly the same manner each time you draw, sight, and release an arrow. Your anchor point must be constant; the arrow must be drawn to its exact full length each time and positioned exactly on the bowstring and on the arrow rest. Uniformity is the key. Instinctive

ANCHOR

The low anchor position (*left*) and the high anchor position (*right*). Choice of position depends on individual preference.

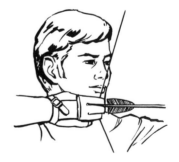

AIMING METHODS

Aiming with a bow sight. Archer's eye becomes the rear sight; bow sight is itself the front sight.

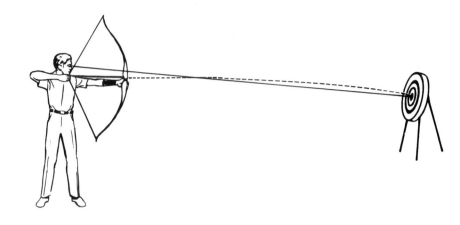

AIMING METHODS

Point-of-aim method. Archer aims at a predetermined spot below or above the target, depending on range. Eye acts as rear sight, arrow tip as front sight.

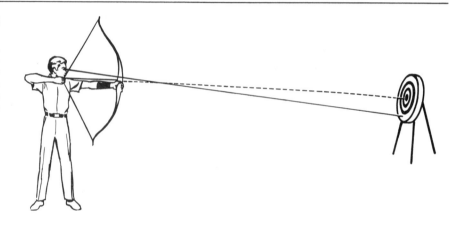

Instinctive aiming. Archer's vision is concentrated on the target. He sees arrow shaft indirectly and automatically adjusts for elevation and windage.

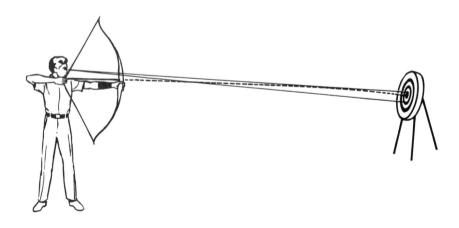

shooting comes from practice and more practice, but once you begin using this method you will be surprised at how swiftly you will become proficient.

The second most popular method, commonly used by target archers, is the point-of-aim method. As shown in the diagram, using the point-of-aim system the archer does not aim at the center of his target, but at a predetermined location below or above the target according to its range. Unlike instinctive shooting, the anchor point usually is located directly under the chin with the bowstring touching lips and nose, the bow held in the vertical position.

With the point-of-aim method the eye acts as the rear sight and the point of the arrow acts as the front sight. Through trial and error, the archer determines the exact trajectory of his arrow for the particular bow he is shooting and adjusts his "sights" accordingly. The average target bow of about 40-pounds draw usually shoots dead on at 80-yards range. At more than 80 yards the archer sights at an object above the point of intended impact; short of 80 yards he would center on a point below the target.

Target archers using the point-of-aim technique usually have a small stake which they push into the ground for a point-of-aim when the aim is below the target. The point-of-aim method is widely used by target archers, but it is ineffective for bowhunters since the exact range must be known.

The third method of aiming is with a bowsight. When using a bowsight, the archer's eye becomes the rear sight and the bowsight itself becomes the front sight.

The simplest form of sight is nothing more than a pin or marker of sorts attached to the bow just above the handle that is adjusted for windage and elevation by moving it up or down, to the right or left.

The refined bowsight has adjustment knobs for windage and elevation, and is quickly adjusted. Remarkable scores have been compiled by archers using such a sight. However, like the point-of-aim method, the bowsight must be adjusted to a given range before it becomes effective.

THE RELEASE

Hold the bold at full draw just long enough to be certain your aim is correct, then relax your fingers, permitting the bowstring to slip smoothly away. Any undue movement of the three fingers of the drawing hand will cause "creep," which can greatly affect the accuracy of the release. Another common fault among neophyte archers is what is termed "plucking" the string—pulling or drawing the bow hand

away from the string. This is sure to spoil your aim. Again, the exact manner of release rests with the individual archer.

FOLLOW-THROUGH

Your arrow is away, speeding toward its target. At the moment the arrow is released, the tension in your body, created during the draw and sighting, is totally relaxed. At this point you must follow through.

A proper follow-through is just as essential to accuracy as any other step in correct shooting. At the moment of release the shooting hand and right shoulder move backward slightly. The bow should slip loosely in the bow hand, but the bow arm should be kept extended and the shooting hand held firmly at the anchor point. Follow-through is essential to prevent a relaxation of shooting stance just before the release of the arrow.

FOLLOW-THROUGH

Proper follow-through is essential for accuracy. The bow arm should remain extended, and the shooting hand should be held firmly at the anchor point.

BOWHUNTING

Within the last several decades, bowhunters in North America have taken moose, deer, and the three species of bears. In Africa, bowhunters have felled rhino, elephant, Cape buffalo, leopard, and lion. Clearly, bowhunting as a sport has become enormously popular, to the extent that every state has set aside a special game season for bowhunters.

Among all our game, deer are still the favorite of the bowhunter—especially whitetails. For it has been said that if a bowhunter can successfully bag a whitetail deer, he can easily take any other game animal in the world.

Bowhunting requires more patience and perseverance than firearm hunting. The bowhunter must be within relatively close range to be assured a hit in a vital area. And he must be certain that his arrow has a clear path to its target, for the slightest twig or hidden branch can quickly deflect a shaft.

Dwight Schuh photo

The bow is a short-range weapon capable of killing every type of game, but it is especially popular for deer.

To be assured a positive hit in the vital area of an animal the size of a deer, the bowhunter would be wise not to shoot at any deer beyond a range of 45 yards. While it's true deer have been bagged with the bow and arrow at far greater distances, it is by its very nature a short-range weapon. Limit your distance before you loose an arrow; your chance of a successful hit and a clean kill will be vastly enhanced.

TRAIL WATCHING

The bowhunter after deer employs varied hunting methods. Most bowhunters prefer ''runway''

watching—finding a well-worn deer trail and sitting motionless several yards away to wait for a deer to amble by. Others like to stillhunt, that is, to walk up a deer. Some bowhunters also like to hunt in teams of three or four, and there are others who ''drive'' deer, emulating the firearm deer hunter in many sections of the East.

Trail watching calls for several preseason trips to your favorite deer area. Deer are creatures of habit, and when not pushed or spooked prefer to select the easiest route between bedding, watering, and feeding grounds. They move from these areas usually twice a day, at dusk from ridgetop bedding grounds down to feed and water, returning to the high country at dawn along specific runways. Trails used by deer can be easily recognized: they are well-worn and often contain tracks and droppings. By carefully selecting a good vantage point several yards off the main trail, with a clear path to the target area, the bowhunter's opportunity for success is greater than in other methods of hunting.

A good location for the bowhunter is near an apple orchard. Whitetails love apples and will travel many miles to find them. If you can find such a spot, es-

Dwight Schuh photo

A tree stand may be uncomfortable but is a good vantage point from which to watch for game. Safety-conscious hunters secure themselves to their perches with belts.

Three typical tree stands (From left): Trax America Penthouse ladder stand with rain roof, Warren and Sweat Future Series, and Trax America Comfort Rest. Mechanical tree stands permit the bowman to climb a tree trunk, and also provide a steady platform.

pecially with fruit-laden trees, you're in luck. Look for well-used trails leading into the orchard and choose a stand that will afford you a good shot as the deer enter the orchard. Better yet, select a good apple tree that will afford a comfortable position and climb into the tree.

Of utmost importance when trail watching is that the archer must remain motionless and be well hidden or camouflaged. This may sound easy, but it's not. Deer are most easily spooked by motion, and a bowhunter who slaps at buzzing insects or squirms restlessly will never see a deer.

One way to avoid detection when trail watching is to use a tree stand or a blind. If a blind is properly constructed with material from the surrounding area, the bowhunter is perfectly concealed and can readily move about without being detected by the deer. The blind can be constructed several yards from a well-used runway at ground level or in a tree.

Perhaps one of the handiest items for the bowhunter to carry afield, if he anticipates constructing a blind, is a spool of monofilament fishing line. He can wind several yards of line between two trees, then carefully interweave brush and foliage. Burlap bags are also useful in blind construction. Remember to construct the blind so that it provides good visibility and offers complete freedom of movement

when the bow is brought to full draw.

Tree stands include everything from a limb to an elaborately constructed platform. The advocates of the tree stand reason that usually deer do not look up, and if a blind is placed in a tree, often a deer will approach at close range. In fact, tree-stand hunting is considered so effective that in some states it is outlawed.

The most effective time of day for trail watching is at dawn and late twilight when deer move between feeding-watering and bedding grounds. During the day, when deer are not pushed or spooked, they will simply bed down and refuse to move. However, if there are a number of hunters in the woods, deer will be kept moving and the runway method then can be effective throughout the midday hours. But usually trail watching is only productive from daybreak to 9 A.M. and again from 3 P.M. to dark.

Remember to take account of the wind. When you are stationed along a runway, the wind should never be blowing at your back in the direction you expect the deer to come. Your scent will be carried to the deer. Keep the wind in your face, and deer approaching you will not detect your presence. You can also use some of the commercial or natural scents to neutralize or mask human scent. Or even a buck lure made from glandular secretions.

STILLHUNTING AND STALKING

While not as effective as trail watching, stillhunting and stalking are more thrilling, steeped as they are in the traditions of the longbowhunters of yesteryear. The stillhunter prowls silently through the woods, hoping to sight a deer. Upon sighting a deer, he then stalks to within bow range. This is often a good tactic during the daylight hours when the deer are bedded down.

Wind direction plays the most important role in stillhunting. Always hunt with the wind in your face. If you sight a deer, only move when the animal's head is down in feeding position. Never attempt to approach a deer when its head is erect and ears are cocked—it will immediately spook. But when the deer brings its head down, you can move toward it, instantly freezing again as it snaps its head upward again. Make use of every bit of cover. Watch for other deer in the general area, too. You can be stalking one animal only to be startled when another snorts a few yards away.

THE MYSTERY OF DEER SCENTS

Every deer season there will be many bowhunters who will go into the woods and start squirting all sorts of deer scents around their stands, on their boots, or wherever. They will try to mask their human odor with food or animal scents. Or perhaps, they may spray a little sex scent to draw a buck within range. There's no doubt that these deer scents will work, but unless you know what you're doing, you may well scare off a buck before he even gets within hundreds of yards of your stand.

Understanding this whole business of deer scents is not difficult if you think about it logically. You can start by learning the three classifications of deer scents: 1) cover or masking scents, 2) attracting scents, and 3) food lures or scents. Let's take them one by one. You will see why all of them will not work all of the time.

The cover scents are designed to mask human odor, and they can be used any time around your treestand or hunting area. These cover or masking scents include skunk essence, cattle scent, earth, pine, cedar, fox urine, and interdigital gland scent. There may be more cover scents available, but these are the most common.

The major cover or masking scents are fox and skunk, but even these should be selected carefully. Skunk essence may not be the best choice because it is an alarm scent and could alert deer that something is wrong. Fox scent is good, but you will still have to choose between red fox and gray fox. Use red fox scent in farm land, where they are most common. In mature timber, however, go with the gray fox, an animal that you will rarely see in farm fields or hedge rows.

Regardless of what cover scent you choose, it is very important that you use it sparingly. A deer will pick up the scent hundreds of yards away. Use too much scent and you risk the chance of spooking a deer.

Attracting scents make up the next major classification of scents. There are only three types of attracting scents that you should know about. The first is estrus, which is the scent of a doe in heat. This, obviously, cannot be used all the time. Hunters should use it only during the rut (mating season). You can get approximate dates of the rut in your region from your state wildlife biologists. The dates, however, are never exact. In the East, for example, from Southern Canada to Georgia, the rut will run from November 1 to December 10, with the peak from November 1 to November 5. Use estrus scent around your stand or on your boot pad. With this scent, you are trying to attract a buck within range.

The next attractant is called interdigital gland scent, which comes from the bottom of a deer's foot or between the hooves. A deer leaves this scent in its tracks; and it is how one deer locates another, or how a doe finds its fawn. This is the ideal scent for the hunter who prefers to move quietly through the woods. Put it on your boot pad when you're still hunting and walking to your tree stand.

Interdigital gland scent also works well as a cover or masking scent. It's critical that you use only three or four drops of this scent and never use any of it on your body. A felt boot pad tied to your laces is ideal.

The last attractant is buck urine, which is used to draw bucks by making them think another buck has moved into their territory. It is also the scent to use when making a mock scrape, which is a buck's way of leaving his calling card in his area.

Finally, there are the food lures. These include such scents as apple, acorn, corn, and grape, to name a few. The most common mistake with food lures is using them in areas where the food and scent may be completely foreign to deer. You would not, for example, use corn scent in a swamp or acorn scent in an orchard. Food lures should be used in areas where deer will be able to identify the scent, and seek it out as a food source.

Always remember that a deer's sense of smell is his key to survival. Therefore, our most common scents should be avoided. If you're deer hunting, don't use scented soaps, shampoos, laundry detergents, or after-shave lotions. Never wear your hunting boots in your house, garage, or gas station, where they will pick up odors that don't belong in the woods. There are plenty of soaps and chemicals especially designed to neutralize human scent. This may all seem like a lot of work, but it will be worth it when a buck walks up to your stand.

DRIVING

Another effective way of hunting deer is by driving. Though not one of the more popular methods of bowhunting, deer driving is productive during the midday hours. For a drive to be successful, several hunters must work in close agreement with one another and be intimately familiar with the territory they plan to hunt.

In a properly organized deer drive several bowhunters take stands along varied known escape routes of deer in a particular piece of woodlot, while several others move through the woodlands "pushing" any deer that is in the cover to the waiting hunters. Successful drives have been managed with only five or six hunters; eight to 10 bowhunters make an ideal group.

In a successful deer drive, the elected drivers move toward the standers as silently as possible. In this way even the drivers have an occasional opportunity of getting a shot. Often a wary old buck won't move ahead of the driver, but instead will quarter and cut back through the drive, and the alert driver will then have an opportunity for a shot. When posting standers, remember to place one or two hunters on the flanks, since a wary whitetail will often attempt to slip through or out the flank of a drive. With flanker standers this possibility is eliminated and will usually produce a shot for the hunter.

The successful deer drive should be planned with extreme care. A captain of the hunt should be elected. He is the one who should know the area most intimately. Standers should be spaced sufficiently far apart so that they will not interfere with each other. Drivers should also be placed sufficiently far apart, but in as parallel line as possible to the standers and be extremely cautious and aware of the other hunters in the area. When possible, deer should be driven crosswind.

Driving deer does have one disadvantage. Often a driven deer will come bounding through the forest at top speed, an almost impossible target for the bowhunter. A whitetail deer at top speed is moving at about 40 miles per hour. To hit such a rapidly moving target, the bowhunter would have to "lead" his target by 12 feet at 10 yards; 24 feet at 20 yards;

and 35 feet at 30 yards. Such a running target should not be taken for it is almost impossible to strike the vital area of a running deer under such conditions. Unless you are extremely close to a moving deer do not attempt a shot; invariably the deer will be struck far back and will escape.

At some point during your bowhunting days, you're going to release an arrow at an animal only to have it "jump the string." How many times have you heard a bowhunter remark that his arrow was flying directly at the deer's chest area, but it jumped aside and the arrow flew harmlessly by?

While we doubt that the deer saw the arrow coming toward it, jumping the string is nothing more than an instinctive reflex action. Compared with a rifle bullet, an arrow is comparatively slow in flight; and the twang of a bowstring, or the whispering of the arrow as it moves in flight, is sufficient to cause a deer to jump.

SMALL GAME

Although bowhunters have hunted the world for trophy big-game animals, small-game and varmint hunting is also popular. It's a year-round sport; during the legal hunting season the bowhunter can seek small game, while the remainder of the year he can devote to varmints.

The woodchuck is the ideal bowhunter's game since it requires the utmost stalking skill to approach

Woodchuck is ideal off-season target for the bowhunter.

ANATOMY OF A DEER

Drawing shows location of deer's vital organs. Also note placement of major arteries. Arrow kills by hemorrhage.

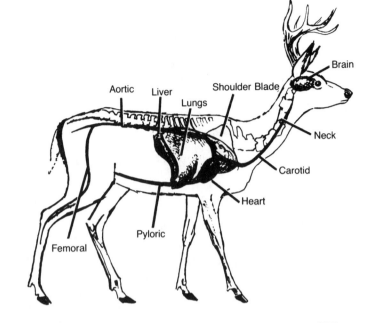

If a buck walks beneath your tree stand, aim between shoulder blades to penetrate the vital area.

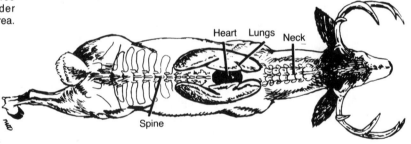

the wary animal and considerable shooting finesse to bring it to bag. While most small-game targets should be hunted with blunt field arrows, the woodchuck requires broadheads.

Woodchucks venture from their dens during the early morning and late evening hours, spending the remainder of the day comfortably snoozing in the cooling depths of their dens. Consequently the bowman must be afield during the early morning and late twilight hours. Some hunters prefer to wait motionlessly within a few yards of a den for the 'chuck to appear. Others prefer to stalk the 'chuck, attempting to get as close as possible before loosing an arrow. Both methods are successful, although the hunter who stalks his game will undoubtedly sight more animals.

Woodchucks emerge from their dens in early spring and spend the remainder of the summer stuffing themselves with clover in preparation for their long winter's sleep, giving the hunter several months of the year to stalk his quary. The successful 'chuck hunter can be assured that come deer season he won't miss too many bucks.

Other small game eagerly sought by bowhunters include rabbits and squirrels, quail, ringneck pheasants, turkeys, and grouse. While successful wing shooting has been enjoyed by a few professionals, the average hunter would find it difficult to hit birds on the wing.

The flu-flu arrow must be used when hunting squirrels in trees. This is an arrow shaft fletched with sufficient feathers to retard its flight. Such shafts will not travel much beyond 50 yards and can be readily recovered. The broadhead blade, while perfect for big-game animals, does not work as well on small game. The blunt point or field point should be used when hunting small game. There are a number of small-game points currently available, ranging from empty rifle or pistol cartridge cases to specially manufactured blunts, which produce a great deal of shocking power. A fine commercially manufactured small-game point in wide use today is termed the "rubber blunt."

Since small-game hunting seasons vary from state to state, as well as regulations pertaining to legal weapons, be sure to check your local game laws before venturing afield with the bow and arrow. For example, in most states the prospective bowhunter must compete with the firearm hunter since there are few states which offer special small-game seasons specifically for archers. But hunting small-game with the bow and arrow is a keenly satisfying pastime and in the long run will enhance your skills as an archer and provide hours of relaxing enjoyment afield before and after the big-game hunting seasons.

WHERE TO HIT BIG GAME

The most important factor in killing big game quickly and cleanly is arrow (or bullet) placement. You'll minimize the chance of losing wounded game if you take time to study the animals you hunt and learn the location of vital organs, as well as where to aim in order to hit those vital organs when the animal is seen at different angles.

The accompanying drawings show the anatomy of a deer—the most popular game for bowhunters— and the aiming points that are important. Remember that an arrow kills by hemorrhage. A bowhunter should note especially the location of main arteries.

A neck shot should not be attempted except at close range, and even then it's only a fair choice. An arrow in the neck may possibly damage the spinal column and cause the deer to drop quickly,

but you don't want to gamble on that. If you hit a big artery such as the carotid, bleeding will be profuse and you may not have to track the deer far. However, your chance of causing major hemorrhaging is better if you can place the arrow *low* in the neck (in the brisket area) or in the chest cavity.

The best shots should really be described in terms of vital areas rather than vital organs. The forward one-third of a deer's body is a vital area since it houses heart, lungs, several major arteries, spine, and shoulder. An arrow penetrating one of the organs will bring down a deer (though not as quickly as a bullet). When possible, try for the heart. If you miss, the arrow has a good chance of hitting one of the other vital organs—particularly the lungs. Even though a lung-shot deer may not drop because of shock (since an arrow produces little shock by comparison with a bullet), the animal will die through hemorrhaging.

In this case, however, the deer may travel a good distance, so tracking is even more important for the bowhunter than for the rifle hunter. If you're not sure where your arrow struck, the blood may tell you. If you spot blood on brush a few feet off the ground and to the side of the tracks, it's coming from the side of the deer—a good indication of a lung hit. Frothy blood also signifies a lung hit. Bright red blood usually means a heart or lung shot. Brownish-yellow blood, particularly if you see white hair in it, means the deer is gut-shot. This is unfortunate. A gut-shot deer can travel a long way, and you'll just have to stick with the track.

If you're in a tree stand, shooting down as a buck walks below, less of the vital area will be exposed than when you have a broadside shot. The best place to aim then is between the shoulder blades. An arrow there may penetrate heart, lungs, or arteries. A shot at a quartering animal should not be quite the same as a broadside shot, either. When a deer is quartering away, your point of aim should be somewhat farther back on the body. A straight-traveling broadhead will penetrate from that rearward point forward into the vital area.

BOWFISHING

Most bowhunters have learned that the hunting seasons are brief and that they must either turn to target archery or to the sport of bowfishing.

In fresh water the most popular species sought by bowhunters is the carp, which can attain heavy-weight proportions. Other species hunted are suckers, buffalofish, squawfish, dogfish and gar. In salt

water, stingrays, skates, barracuda, and sharks all offer sport.

The tackle required to convert to bowfishing consists of a few inexpensive items—a bow reel, some line, and a few bowfishing arrows.

A bow reel is nothing more than a special large spool to which at least 50 feet of stout nylon line is attached. The bow reel itself is easily and quickly fastened to the bow with tape and can be easily removed when the big-game hunting season arrives. Some bow reels manufactured today do not require taping to the bow, but have a bracket which can be instantly attached or removed from the bow. Most bow reels contain a small catch built into the reel spool to keep the line from peeling off when making shots at extreme angles. Some bows are mounted with conventional spincast reels.

For most freshwater fishing, 36-pound-test nylon line can handle most fish bowhunters will encounter, but for those enterprising bowhunters who take to salt water seeking larger species, then nylon line to 100-pound test is in order. Any bow you use for big-game hunting will suffice for bowfishing.

Arrows must be of solid fiberglass for durability. A fish weighing in excess of several pounds can easily roll on an arrow once it is struck and snap a wood shaft or bend an aluminum one. The solid, glass arrow also has the extra weight required to drive it into the water. From a husky hunting bow a solid fiberglass arrow can often be driven to depths of 10 feet and more.

Conventional feather fletching is out for the bowfisherman since feathers can quickly be ruined in water. The bowfishing arrow is therefore manufac-

Bohning Warhead II Fish Point is a typical fish arrow. The War Head's blades are 3½ inches wide when fully extended.

tured with rubber fletching, and if you are shooting at extremely close range, even this can be eliminated. However, since most bowfishing arrows are equipped with rubber fletching, the bowfisherman should use them.

The solid fiberglass fishing arrow is equipped with some sort of barbed or harpoon head which is not permanently fastened to the arrow shaft. Instead, the head slips over the end of the arrow and is attached to a line that runs through a small hole in

Bowfishing gear can be simple and inexpensive: a bow reel, line, and a few bowfishing arrows. Bow reel is a special large spool with 50 or more feet of stout nylon line attached. It is usually taped to the bow and can be easily removed when the big-game hunting season arrives. **Right:** Young woman drawing this compound is about to shoot a carp. Popular accessories for both compounds and recurve bows include fishing reels and lines. Arrow is fiberglass with barbed, or harpoon, head.

the shaft just above the nock, then down the length of the shaft and is tied to the hole in the harpoon head itself.

Once a fish is struck, it is easy to handline it in. However, when seeking large, heavy fish, some bowhunters prefer to eliminate the bow reel and attach the line directly to a fishing rod and reel. When using the rod and reel, strip some 20 yards of line through the rod guides and carefully coil it on the bottom of the boat or in a small tub or bucket, and attach the forward end of the line to the arrow.

Arrow points or harpoon heads vary widely. For greatest penetration, the single barbed point is best, but the double barbed rig is needed for big fish, especially in salt water.

Foremost to remember when shooting fish underwater is to aim low. Your view underwater is affected by light refraction and when fish are working under the water's surface and viewed at an angle your quarry is always lower than it appears to be. A few shots taken at such targets will quickly show the bowhunter where he should aim his arrow.

Polaroid sunglasses should be worn when bowfishing to help you see the quarry. The best time is midday, when the sun warms the surface and brings the fish up within easy view. Without polarizing sunglasses you will be at a loss to spot fish.

Carp provide outstanding sport for the bowhunter, especially during early spring and summer when, heavy with roe, they move into the shallows of rivers and lakes to spawn. Many southern bowhunters also find action hunting garfish—the shortnose gar, which rarely exceeds 3 feet in length; the longnose gar, which usually attains a length of 5 feet; and the giant alligator gar, which can attain a length of 8 feet and a weight in excess of 300 pounds. Hot summer evenings are best for hunting large gars. Bowhunters paddle slowly through the water searching with a flashlight for these prehistoric giants. They always

Best way to bowfish is to use a boat and cruise until you spot your quarry.

use a wire leader between the harpoon head and line.

In salt water, the bowfisherman can choose from a wide variety of fish. Fast and furious action can be found by searching the flats in back-bay country for skates and stingrays. Rays are powerful and once harpooned can tow a boat with ease. When seeking large rays, remember to add additional line to the bow reel to allow for their powerful, surging run.

Bowfishing has become so popular in recent years that most states now have special seasons for taking rough fishes. Check local regulations for most states require that a bowman have a fishing license.

ARCHERY AND BOWHUNTING ORGANIZATIONS

There are numerous archery organizations in the United States whose purpose is to regulate competition and bring together archers from all parts of the world. Here are the principals:

NATIONAL ARCHERY ASSOCIATION OF THE U.S.A.

Undoubtedly the oldest archery association, the N.A.A. was organized in 1879; its first president was the famous bowman Maurice Thompson.

The National Archery Association was formed primarily to provide the rules and regulations for local, state, regional and national tourneys. It also conducts qualifying U.S. tryouts for the international F.I.T.A. team selections. A member of the Olympic Association, N.A.A. sponsors interscholastic, collegiate, and other archery programs, and is the United States representative to the international body of archery, the F.I.T.A. Headquarters address for the N.A.A. is 1951 Geraldson Drive, Lancaster, PA 17601.

NATIONAL FIELD ARCHERY ASSOCIATION

The N.F.A.A. was formed in the late thirties by a group of West Coast archers who were tired of the formal type of shooting promoted by N.A.A. and wanted competition that simulated field or hunting conditions. Thus the first field course was developed with targets at varying ranges. In 1946, the newly organized N.F.A.A. held its initial National Field Tourney in Michigan.

The N.F.A.A. conducts and oversees state, regional, and national field tourneys as well as a host of mail tournaments. Headquarters is Route 2, Box 514, Redlands, CA 92373.

FEDERATION INTERNATIONALE DE TIR À L'ARC

This is the international body governing world archery. The organization was founded in 1931 and today comprises 36 nations. It conducts many tourneys to establish world archery records. Since World War II, the F.I.T.A., has conducted international archery tournaments every two years. Their rules are identical to those of the National Archery Association. For information, contact: Via Passione, 420122, Milano, Italy.

FRED BEAR SPORTS CLUB

The FBSC's main purpose is to help save the sport of hunting from being outlawed. It serves as a national clearing house on antihunting information and rumors. It provides state or local support, when requested, from a nationally based bowhunting organization. The FBSC attempts to educate the general public on the contribution of hunters and fishermen to proper wildlife management and conservation. The FBSC has also devised indoor and field rounds for bowhunters. For more information, contact the club at: Dept. TBS, Rural Route 4, Gainesville, FL 32601.

PROFESSIONAL ARCHERS ASSOCIATION

The Professional Archers Association is just what the name implies—a group of pros who shoot for money and who are organized to teach the sport.

To become a P.A.A. professional instructor, an applicant must be 18 years of age, must pass a writ-ten exam, and must meet the other requirements as set by the P.A.A. Constitution.

The Professional Archers Association headquarters is 4711 S. Brennan Road, Hemlock, MI 48626.

AMERICAN INDOOR ARCHERY ASSOCIATION

The A.I.A.A. comprises members who are interested in the betterment of their sport—indoor shooting both on an individual and league basis. The A.I.A.A. has in recent years develped several indoor rounds designed solely for the indoor archer, plus a score of novelty events. A.I.A.A. headquarters is P.O. Box 174, Grayling, MI 49738.

POPE AND YOUNG CLUB

Like its brother, the famed Boone and Crockett Club, the Pope and Young Club was organized to promote conservation, the highest ethics of sportsmanship, and to establish world records for game taken with the bow and arrow.

The Pope and Young Club, organized in 1957, took its name from two world-famous bowhunters, Dr. Saxton Pope and Arthur Young. An extremely exclusive club, it limits its membership to 100 regulars and only a handful of associates. To qualify for membership in this elite bowhunting group one must, in fair chase, have bagged three different species of North American big-game animals with the bow and arrow, with one scoring in the trophy class by Pope and Young standards.

Pope and Young further has a number of Official Measurers scattered throughout the country in order to find and score record-class trophies taken by bowhunters. To be listed in the Pope and Young record book an archer does not have to be a member of this organization. If he has a trophy, taken in fair chase and during the legal bow and arrow hunting season, his trophy will be recognized, provided it meets Pope and Young standards for qualification. Pope and Young Club headquarters is Route 1, Box 147, Salmon, ID 83467.

NATIONAL BOWHUNTER EDUCATION FOUNDATION

It is the policy of the N.B.E.F. (National Bowhunter Education Foundation) to continually assist states in establishing sound bowhunter education programs. These programs shall be conducted using the prescribed curriculum and materials as provided by the N.B.E.F. Once the program has been fully and properly implemented the N.B.E.F. will relinquish all administrative responsibilities to the state wildlife agency. If the state wildlife agency does not wish to administer the program, the leading bowhunter and/or archery organization will be requested to do so. The N.B.E.F. will not acknowledge certification of students other than those taught using the curriculum and training materials developed by the N.B.E.F. All proceeds from sale of training materials developed by the N.B.E.F. is used for the purchase of additional materials, program development, research, continued training of program participants and the international advancement of bowhunter training. The N.B.E.F. headquarters is Route 6, Box 199, Murray, KY 43071.

PART 9
HUNTING DOGS

PROFILES OF BREEDS

Beagle

HISTORY: While the origin of the Beagle is not definitely known, this small hound was widely bred in England before it was imported into the United States between 1860 and 1870.

There was a great deal of breeding among the various strains of Beagles brought into America to develop a small strong hound capable of hunting small game in all types of cover. Unfortunately, so much of this breeding took place during the late 1800s that problems arose as to what constituted the perfect Beagle. This was finally settled by the founding of the American-English Beagle Club in 1884, an organization that set the standards for the ideal Beagle.

For the most part, these standards are the same as those presently set forth by the National Beagle Club of America. Today, the Beagle is the most popular of all the hound breeds.

DESCRIPTION: The most common color combination of the Beagle is black, white, and tan, though many good Beagles may show up in any hound color.

Here, briefly, are some of the physical characteristics to look for in a purebred Beagle.

The head (skull) should be long and domed toward the rear. Cranium should be broad. Eyes large, set well apart, and brown or hazel in color.

The muzzle should be medium in length and straight, with a square cut at the nose. The nostrils open and large.

Ears should be set low, close to the head, and long enough to reach nearly the end of the dog's nose when drawn out. A good Beagle's ears are also rounded at the tips, with the forward edges of the ears angling slightly toward the cheeks.

The jaws are level and throat free of folds of skin.

BEAGLE

722

Shoulders are muscular and slope cleanly. The chest broad and deep. Shoulders and chest should not be overly muscular, which would interfere with freedom of action when working thick cover or chasing cottontails.

The back is muscular and short. The ribs well spread, giving the hound plenty of lung room. Legs are short and straight, with feet round and firm. Pads should be full and hard. Hindquarters should be strong and well muscled, giving the Beagle plenty of propelling power.

The tail is set high with a slight curve, but not so curved as to turn forward over the back. The tail should have a brush and give the appearance of being a bit short for the size of the Beagle. The coat is of medium length with a close hard texture.

SIZE: Beagles generally stand 11 to 15 inches tall at the shoulder. A good Beagle will not exceed 15 inches. Beagles generally fall into two size categories: 13- or 15-inch class, the measurement referring to height at the highest point of the shoulder. Choice of size class is generally a matter of personal preference. Weight, depending on size, ranges from 20 to 40 pounds.

HUNTING ABILITY: There is no doubt that the Beagle is a born hunter and a good gundog. His specialty is rabbits, and few, if any, breeds can beat him at routing out his quarry. He has a keen nose, and when he "opens up" on a rabbit, his combination bawl and cry is music to the ears of the hunter.

The Beagle is also an enthusiastic and hardy worker and will not hesitate to work through thick briar patches to hunt out small game. He learns his lessons quickly, and generally all the training he needs is exposure to rabbits. When he sees a cottontail he almost instinctively knows what to do and takes up the chase. This makes the Beagle a good choice for the hunter who does not have the time for extensive training sessions with his dog.

By no means is the Beagle limited to chasing rabbits. He makes an excellent squirrel dog. When it comes to pheasants, he is second only to the pointing breeds and spaniels. In fact, the Beagle is worth his salt on just about every kind of upland game. A Beagle from good hunting stock may flush, locate, and retrieve downed birds.

For the hunter whose budget cannot carry the expense of a high-priced professionally trained dog, the Beagle is strongly recommended. He does not need much kennel room and is quick to adjust to all climates. The little hound is a faithful companion and topnotch hunter in the field and well worth the low cost of feeding and housing him.

DISPOSITION: In addition to his excellent hunting ability, the friendly little Beagle makes a fine family dog and companion for children. A loyal and merry little hound, the Beagle will usually lick the hand of a child who pulls his tail or twists his ear. His happy and affectionate disposition makes him a favorite choice for a family pet.

Basset

HISTORY: The Basset Hound's history is a long one, dating back to medieval times. Originating in France, the breed's ancestry includes the old French bloodhound and the now-extinct St. Huberts hound.

According to legend, the Basset resulted from attempts to develop a dog that pursued game surely but very slowly, the only pace that the French aristocracy—terribly debauched and badly out of physical shape—could follow. Bassets were brought to England in the late 1860s and later to America, where they were crossed with other Bassets that reached America by way of Russia. From those breedings have come the American Basset Hound.

DESCRIPTION: It's been said that the Basset has the coloring of a foxhound, the head of a bloodhound, the legs of a Dachshund, and the body of a barnyard bull. There's no mistaking this breed, thanks to his inordinately long ears, heavy folds of skin around the entire head, and deep-set, incredibly sad, brown eyes.

BASSET

A Basset should meet the following physical standards:

Head should be quite large, skull narrow and long, with a characteristic point. Head, in short, should resemble that of a bloodhound. Folds of skin should wrinkle perceptibly when the dog puts his nose to the ground.

Nose should be strong and not snippy. Ears should be long enough so that they can be folded well over the tip of the nose.

Neck should be powerful, shoulders sloping, and forelegs short, extremely strong, and heavy-boned. Rib cage should be well-rounded, chest broad and powerful, hindquarters muscular and heavy-boned.

The coat should resemble that of the Beagle: dense, fairly short, and of medium texture. Any good hound color is permissible, but most Bassets have some version of the tricolor combination (black, tan, and white).

SIZE: Bassets, like Beagles, stand 10 to 15 inches at the highest point of the shoulder, with the average height about 13 inches. Bassets, however, are much heavier than Beagles, some of them weighing as much as 80 pounds. Average weight is probably about 50 pounds. The Basset is heavy-boned and appears to weigh much less than he actually does.

HUNTING ABILITY: The Basset is second only to the Beagle as a rabbit and hare hunter, and his nose is as keen as any other hound's with the exception of the bloodhound. Bassets also will run pheasants and grouse, and some have even been taught to retrieve. They can easily be trained to tree game and so make fine coon, possum, and squirrel dogs.

The Basset runs game much slower and more painstakingly than does a Beagle, and many hunters prefer that kind of a chase. And most Bassets do not give tongue (bark) so readily on a scent trail as do most Beagles. The Basset's voice is much deeper and more resonant than the smaller hound's.

If the Basset has a hunting fault, it is that it will often stay quite close to the hunter until it strikes a scent trail. Most Beagles, on the other hand, range well out from the hunter and search widely for scent.

DISPOSITION: As the Beagle is merry and affectionate, the Basset is sadly dignified and extremely friendly. Though it is not as outwardly affectionate as the Beagle, the breed is hard to beat as a family dog, house pet, and hunting companion.

Black and Tan

HISTORY: The Black and Tan—generally recognized as a coonhound, though it can be trained to run everything from possums to cougars—is the oldest of the coonhound breeds. The history of the Black and Tan (and that of most of the other trail and tree hounds) is cloudy at best, for early breeding records, when they were kept at all, were vague and inaccurate. However, it has been pretty well established that the foundation stock of the modern Black and Tan came from an old Virginia foxhound strain known as the Virginia Black and Tan (or Ferguson-Virginia Black and Tan). As the strain was developed, primarily to run possums and raccoons, record-keeping procedures and breeding practices improved, and the modern Black and Tan came to be recognized as a breed. It is one of six trail-hound breeds recognized by the United Kennel Club and the only one recognized by the American Kennel Club.

DESCRIPTION: In looks, performance, and voice, the Black and Tan is the ideal of what a coon hunter is looking for in a dog. It has a houndlike appearance and yet is built for speed and agility.

The body is relatively short but quite powerful, particularly in hindquarters and in the broad chest. The back is almost level, the stern long and tapering. Legs are straight, strong, and well-boned, and the feet are well-knuckled and heavily padded.

The Black and Tan has probably the most attractive head of any of the trail hounds. It is broad and evenly rounded, the muzzle is deep and squared off, and the dark-brown eyes are large and clear. The ears are quite long (when spread, they should

BLACK AND TAN

measure tip to tip about the same as the dog's shoulder height) and set low on the head. The coat is a little shorter and the hair somewhat finer than that of the other trail hounds. Colors are jet black over the entire body, except for tan areas over the eyes and on chest, feet, and stern. Some white on the chest is permitted.

SIZE: As trail hounds go, the Black and Tan is of medium size. Males stand 24 to 26 inches at the withers, females 22 to 24 inches. Weight should always be proportionate to an animal's bone structure and height. Males should not exceed 60 pounds, females should not weigh more than 40.

HUNTING ABILITY: Born to hunt, the Black and Tan has a full-choke nose, great determination, and durability. It is versatile, too. Though it is most often used to run raccoons and foxes, the Black and Tan is often put on the trail of deer, bears, boar, bobcats, lynx, and cougars.

The Black and Tan, particularly those used exclusively on coons, works almost entirely by foot scent (scent secreted by glands in or near the feet of the animal being pursued). He is fast on the trail—an important factor in getting a predator up a tree. He has a magnificent voice and seems to enjoy using it. The Black and Tan's treeing instinct is as strong as that of any hound.

DISPOSITION: The Black and Tan is quite affectionate, though less showily so than the Beagle. It is not quarrelsome with other dogs and takes readily to being run in a pack. It is a rather shy breed and reacts with equal sensitiveness to praise and discipline. And yet it is more than willing to engage in a tooth-and-fang battle with coons, bobcats, and even larger game.

Bluetick

HISTORY: The Bluetick has a relatively short breed history, being recognized as a distinct breed (by the United Kennel Club) only since the 1940s. But its ancestry—though a matter of some conjecture, as with most hounds—is a long one.

Some dog fanciers claim that the Bluetick (and all other coonhound breeds except the Plott hound) branches from Black and Tan stock. Others say it is an offshoot of the English Coonhound. However, many authorities are of the opinion that the Bluetick's progenitor was the French Gascony Bluetick, used widely as a deer and boar hound in France and England as far back as the 13th century. The Gas-

cony hounds were widely acclaimed for their impressive voice, appearance, and performance. The Bluetick is one of the six recognized coonhound breeds.

DESCRIPTION: The Bluetick's name describes his color, which is unique. The highly attractive coat, in most individuals, is almost solidly ticked with black, which appears blue against the white background. The Bluetick usually has a black head, some black spots on the body, and some tan trim. The coat is similar in texture to the Black and Tan's, but is somewhat heavier.

The Bluetick is quite "houndy" in general appearance. Many are quite strong and large, powerfully muscled, with massive head, while others are somewhat smaller and lighter, being bred for speed on the trail.

Often the Bluetick's body is longer, in relation to height, than that of the Black and Tan. Shoulders and chest are broad and powerful, hindquarters are heavily muscled, and legs are straight and substantially boned. Feet are well padded.

Despite its heft and muscle, a Bluetick should move gracefully and effortlessly. A good one can leap a 5-foot-high fence almost without breaking stride.

The Bluetick's head resembles the Black and Tan's but may be a bit heavier and have longer ears.

BLUETICK

SIZE: Blueticks exhibit some variance in size. They reach larger maximum sizes than any of the other tree hounds, some of them exceeding 100 pounds, though the official standard limits a Bluetick's weight to between 45 and 80 pounds. Most of those heavyweights are tough old cougar and bear-hunting hounds.

Average height ranges a minimum of from 21 inches at the withers for females to a maximum of 26 inches for males.

HUNTING ABILITY: Like the Black and Tan, the Bluetick has an excellent nose and a clear bawling voice. It is a top cold-trailer (that is, it is capable of picking up and following a scent trail that is many hours old) and has a highly refined treeing instinct.

Also like the Black and Tan, the Bluetick is used to pursue a wide variety of game, including raccoons, foxes, bobcats, bears, and cougars. Once he has his quarry up a tree, the Bluetick will hold it there for hours or even days, if necessary, until the hunters reach the scene.

Like most hounds, the Bluetick needs little formal training, learning most of his lessons "on the job."

DISPOSITION: The Bluetick in general has the typical hound personality: friendly, affectionate, even-tempered. Like trail hounds as a whole, however, they can be standoffish with strangers.

English Coonhound

HISTORY: Anyone who tries to pin down the genealogy of any hound breed or strain has cut himself a mighty big slice of trouble. With no other hound breed is this fact truer than with the English Coonhound. The breed's actual origins are lost in the mists of antiquity. However, it was first recognized as a distinct breed—and formally registered—in 1900. At that time the individual members were dogs with heavy blue or red ticking (spotting or dotting). Today, however, the breed will accept registered Treeing Walkers and Blueticks (the English and the Bluetick share common ancestors), grade (unregistered) dogs of those types, and English-type dogs with blue or red ticking into its registry files. In fact, you may even hear English Coonhounds called redticks. And you may well have to take an owner's word that his hound is an English Coonhound, a Bluetick, or a Treeing Walker. The English is one of the six recognized coonhound breeds.

DESCRIPTION: Because of its melting-pot background and present-day registration confusion, it is

difficult to categorize the description of the English Coonhound. Many individual dogs recognized as Blueticks, for example, are nearly identical in conformation to many individuals recognized as English Coonhounds.

In general, however, the English standard today calls for a smaller, lighter dog than the Bluetick standard.

The ideal English is a medium-size dog with typical hound porportions. It has a broad rib cage and chest and generally appears to be built for speed and stamina.

The head is broad across the skull, muzzle is square, and ears are set relatively low and are of medium length. Eyes are large and widely set. The big, flaring nostrils indicate good scenting capabilities.

As for coat color, the English can be any good hound color or combination of colors, including blue ticking, red ticking, black and white, tan and white, and tricolor. Among the members of the breed, those dogs of red ticking and blue ticking are more numerous than English of any other color.

SIZE: English Coonhounds range in height at the shoulders from 21 inches (for the smallest females) to 25 inches (for the tallest males). Weights depend upon height for the most part; an average English in the 24-inch category would weigh approximately 60 pounds.

HUNTING ABILITY: The English (and all other coonhounds, for that matter) differs from other trail or predator hounds mainly in his ability to put an animal up a tree. And the English is as good at that as any other coonhound breed.

A hound's working ability is what determines his worth—or lack of it—to a hunter. The English, because of the many different hound types involved in its genealogy and present makeup, may exhibit any of a great number of working characteristics, none of which can be said to be typical of the breed.

For example, some English are good cold-trailers but work slowly on the trail. Some others are wide-working "drifting" types. Because of this great variety in working traits among this breed, it is wise for any prospective buyer to know exactly what he wants and to become thoroughly familiar with the individuals on the dog's pedigree and with the animal's parents.

DISPOSITION: All hounds are good-natured animals, and the English Coonhound is no exception. He laps up praise and petting and yet takes discipline well. He is at home either in the house or outside in the roughest of weather.

Redbone

HISTORY: The Redbone—one of six coonhound breeds recognized by raccoon hunters everywhere and by such organizations as the United Kennel Club, American Coon Hunters Association, and American Hound Association—originated back in the 19th century, when breeders of the Redbone strain of foxhounds began to feel that their dogs were too slow and methodical on the trail. As a result, these dogs were switched from running foxes to running raccoons. Their ability at chasing the smaller and slower game was quickly recognized, and the Redbone was recognized as a distinct coonhound breed in about 1900 by the U.K.C.

Since that time the Redbone has increased in favor among raccoon hunters, mainly because of the work of such well-known breeders as Brooks Magill, R. J. Blakesley, and W. B. Frisbee.

DESCRIPTION: The Redbone's most distinctive physical characteristic is its coat, which is a solid deep red, though some white on the brisket or feet isn't objectionable.

The Redbone's build complements his beautiful coat. The body is large and quite powerful, with long, straight legs, strong hindquarters, and a tail carried smartly. The head is not so typically "houndy" as that of the Bluetick and the Black and Tan. Ears are set somewhat higher on the head, muzzle and skull are a bit lighter. However, some Redbones have extremely long ears and a heavy head—particularly those of R. J. Blakesley's Northern Joe strain.

Not every red-colored hound is a Redbone, but most are.

SIZE: The Redbone's size and weight—though perhaps more uniform—are typical of most trail hounds. Shoulder height ranges from 21 inches for females to a maximum of 26 inches for males. Weights are proportionate to shoulder heights, but maximum is about 90 pounds and average is 45 to 75 pounds.

HUNTING ABILITY: An excellent voice that might even be described as sweet, a good cold nose, tenaciousness, and an acute treeing ability—those traits describe the Redbone as a hunter.

The breed's cold nose (the ability to pick up and follow an old scent trail) has caused some breeders to shy away, reasoning that a dog with a medium nose would waste less time on a bad track. However, the cold-trailing ability is much prized by many breeders and hunters.

In general, Redbones bark only occasionally while the trail is cold, but their barking picks up in tempo and intensity as the trail gets warmer. This fact, which makes it easy for the listening hunter to determine the freshness of the track, cannot be said of all trail hounds. Some Blueticks and Black and Tans, for example, will give tongue so often, even on a cold track, that they can be accused of babbling, a fault in a hound.

When a Redbone pushes a coon or other quarry up a tree, its voice changes from a bawl to a chop.

The Black and Tans and the Blueticks have sometimes been criticized as being somewhat lacking in fighting ability. Not so the Redbone, which is a real scrapper, though that trait, while important if the dog is chasing bears or big cats, is not so important when the quarry is coons.

DISPOSITION: The Redbone has a kindly demeanor and, like most hounds, makes a fine family pet and companion. Also like most hounds, when he is on the trail his mind and body are totally committed to the chase, so the hunter is wasting lungpower if he attempts to call the dog in. In general, the Redbone lives to hunt, is easily taught, and is tractable.

Treeing Walker

HISTORY: The Treeing Walker, one of the six recognized coonhound breeds, almost certainly is an offshoot of the Walker strain of foxhound, though Bluetick blood may also be present. The Walker

TREEING WALKER   REDBONE

foxhound is the result of 50 years of careful breeding from the same stock of hounds by two Kentucky sportsmen and neighbors, George Washington Maupin and John W. Walker. Eventually the Maupin-Walker dogs were outcrossed to the legendary Tennessee Lead (a hound that was said to have been literally stolen from a pack of Tennessee hounds that was in the process of running a deer) and two imports from England—Rifler and Marth. Those three dogs proved to be excellent fox hunters, and their offspring, crossed again with other English imports, eventually came to be known as Walker foxhounds.

It has been theorized that the first Treeing Walkers were working Walker foxhounds that, because of advanced age, lack of speed on trail, and a well-developed treeing instinct, gave up on foxes and took to treeing raccoons.

The Treeing Walker was recognized as a distinct breed in the mid-1940s.

DESCRIPTION: The Treeing Walker looks much like the Walker foxhound. A wide range of coat colors is permissible, but the most popular and predominant combination is a white background with black spots and tan markings. The saddle is often black. Hair is of medium length and texture.

The head is fairly long, and the skull is slightly domed and broad. The brown or hazel eyes are houndlike and set well apart. The ears are set moderately low, and when stretched out they should reach nearly to the tip of the nose.

Neck is of medium length and rises free from muscular shoulders. Throat is free from folds of skin. Chest is deep, ribs well sprung. Back is moderately long, muscular, and strong. Forelegs are straight and well-boned, and pasterns are short and straight.

If there is a notable difference in appearance between the Treeing Walker and the Walker foxhound, it is that the Treeing Walker is a bit "houndier." Of the other coonhound breeds, the one that most closely approaches the Treeing Walker in looks is the English.

SIZE: Weight scales for the Treeing Walker run 50 to 75 pounds for males, 40 to 65 pounds for females. Recommended shoulder height for males is 25 inches, for females 21 inches.

HUNTING ABILITY: Due probably to its foxhound ancestry, the Treeing Walker's hunting traits include good range, speed, and general aggressiveness. Those characteristics—plus his reputation as a "drifter"—set the Treeing Walker apart from most of the other coonhound breeds. A drifter is a dog that doesn't hesitate to range away from the line when the track gets tough, rather than puzzle things

out at close quarters. Many hunters don't like this trait in a hound, but there's no quarreling with the fact that it produces game. The opposite of a drifter is a "straddler," a dog that sticks to the track like glue. Black and Tans, Blueticks, and, to a lesser extent, English and Redbones are known to be straddlers. Treeing Walkers are not the best at cold-trailing, but their treeing instinct is highly developed.

DISPOSITION: The Treeing Walker's temperament is much like that of most of the other coonhound breeds: not quite so gentle and affectionate as the Beagle but more so than say, the Plott Hound. The breed takes discipline well, and training is simply a matter of exposing the animal to the game he is expected to run. Like most hounds of all types, the Treeing Walker is quite healthy and does not demand much in the way of living conditions. It must be remembered, however, that any dog worth his salt in the field merits proper care.

Plott Hound

HISTORY: In 1750 a man named Jonathan Plott brought to the mountains of North Carolina from his native Germany a pack of hounds, offspring of generations of dogs used to hunt the big and tough German wild boars. These dogs proved to be proficient at hunting black bears, numerous then in the Carolina mountains. For 30 years Plott kept the strain pure and free from any outcross, selecting his breeding stock carefully.

In 1780 Henry Plott took over the pack from his father and decided to introduce into the strain some blood from a line of Georgia bear hounds called "leopard" or "spotted-leopard" dogs. Only that one cross took place, and the Plott family descendants—who are still breeding Plott Hounds today—vehemently deny rumors of subsequent crossings of Plotts with Black and Tans, Bloodhounds, and other breeds.

In 1946 the United Kennel Club recognized the Plott Hound as a distinct breed. It is generally recognized as a coonhound breed, though its widest use until recent years had been as a bear and boar hound in the Great Smoky Mountains of Tennessee and North Carolina.

DESCRIPTION: In color the Plott is brindle (brindle is a mixture of gray and yellowish brown, with darker streaks) with a black saddle and sometimes white points. The coat is thicker, heavier, and provides more protection from the elements than that of any of the other trail hounds.

The Plott is of medium height. Its head is rather large and blocky, and the jaws are those of a fighter.

PLOTT HOUND

The body has a wiry but well-balanced appearance, though it is not so heavily muscled or boned as is that of the Bluetick or Black and Tan. The build is something like that of a husky pointer. Ear length tends to vary (see "Hunting Ability").

Agility is one of the Plott Hound's strong points; he moves with the grace of a cat.

The Plott's voice is not the most attractive of the trail hounds. The chop, in particular, is higher in pitch than that of the other trail hounds.

SIZE: This breed's standard calls for males to weigh no more than 60 pounds and females to weigh no less than 40 pounds. Despite the standard, the breed's weight is on the average somewhat less than that of the other trail hounds. Some individuals, on the other hand, reach 90 pounds.

The Plott's height ranges from 21 inches at the shoulder for bitches to 25 inches for males.

HUNTING ABILITY: The Plott is a tough character, as befits a dog bred to battle boars and bears. The breed is also used to hunt wolves, cougars, bobcats, coyotes, deer, and various small game including raccoons.

The breed's hunting ability seems to depend upon whether an individual dog is of the long-eared or short-eared "type," both of which were developed by the Plott family. The short-eared type is generally considered to be faster and a more efficient fighter of dangerous game, and so it is usually preferred by bear and boar hunters. The long-eared type is said to have a better voice, to be a better cold-trailer, and to be more "open" on trail. There also seems to be a sort of "happy-medium-type" Plott, which is gaining favor among hunters.

DISPOSITION: Because theirs is a relatively tough life—most of them live in the mountains under rugged conditions and often find themselves within striking distance of an animal that can fight back—the Plott's temperament is less gentle and affectionate than that of most other hounds.

In fact, Plotts may be downright quarrelsome, and owners have learned the folly of keeping several in the same pen, for these dogs have a tendency to fight.

American Foxhound

HISTORY: The Foxhound is the oldest sporting dog in the U.S., dating back to early Colonial times. The year 1650 is the date generally accepted as the Foxhound's introduction into the U.S. In that year a friend of Lord Baltimore's, Robert Brooke, brought to Maryland from England a hound pack used primarily on foxes.

Foxhunting's popularity—and that of the hounds bred for the purpose—spread from Maryland to Virginia, Pennsylvania, New Jersey, New York, New England, and throughout the South in the ensuing 150 years. Among the sport's adherents were George Washington, Thomas Jefferson, Alexander Hamilton, and John Marshall. Washington, in fact, was given seven "staghounds" by the Marquis de Lafayette. Though these large French dogs did not take well to foxhunting, their blood, and to a greater extent the blood of English and Irish hounds imported by foxhunters in the Southeast U.S., went into the development of the Foxhound we know today.

For all intents and purposes, however, the American Foxhound was developed within the past 150 years and is largely the result of the breeding practices of a number of families, most of them in the South. Those practices have brought about the recognition by foxhunters of some 20 or so strains of Foxhounds (foxhunters are prone to regard these strains as breeds, but they are actually strains, a strain being a line of dogs showing similar characteristics as a result of selective breeding).

The Foxhound strains include the Walker, Trigg, and July—by far the most popular—as well as the Brooke, Birdsong, Goodman, Travis, Buckfield, Robinson, Wild Goose, Arkansas Traveler, Avent,

Hudspeth, Tucker, Hampton-Watts-Bennett, Shaver, Bywaters, Whitlock Shaggie, Trumbo, Sugar Loaf, Cook, Byron, Gossett, and New England Native.

The history of many of these strains is lost in antiquity, usually because of slipshod or nonexistent record-keeping practices. Among those that are known are the following:

• *Walker*—(See Treeing Walker).
• *Trigg*—Dr. T. Y. Henry, a grandson of Patrick Henry, kept at his Virginia home a pack of hounds that had fine reputations as fox chasers. On a trip south for his health, Henry met Col. George L. F. Birdsong of Georgia. A friendship developed that resulted in Birdsong's acquiring the entire Henry pack when Henry found that in Florida, his new home, the dogs couldn't resist chasing the deer that were abundant there. Birdsong crossed his dogs with a Maryland hound and then began corresponding with Col. Haiden C. Trigg of Kentucky, who was looking for some new blood with which to put some speed into his pack of slow-moving black-and-tan hounds. Birdsong sent three of his hounds to Trigg, who thereupon began the breeding process that was to give rise to the strain of foxhounds that today bear his name.
• *July*—A Mr. Miles G. Harris of Georgia secured a fine hound named July from a hunter in Maryland. This dog, of Irish derivation and believed to be related to dogs bred by Dr. Henry of Virginia, was crossed on Col. Birdsong's hounds. Hounds tracing back to that breeding and others by Georgia hunters, are today known as Julys (or Georgia Julys).
• *Buckfield*—In about 1858 a Canadian peddler is said to have brought to the town of Buckfield, Maine, a red and blue-mottled bitch that looked like a cross between a foxhound and an Irish Setter. This dog was mated with a black stumptailed hound owned by another passer-through described as a tramp. Result of this mating was Bose, a compact, red, shaggy bitch and a topnotch foxhunter. She is supposedly the fountainhead of the Buckfield strain.
• *Robinson*—A man named B. F. Robinson of Kentucky developed this strain by breeding Irish hounds to hounds from some of the established Maryland packs. The strain that resulted bears his name.
• *Goodman*—One W. C. Goodman obtained some of the Robinson dogs and crossed them with some of his own dogs, which were of the Maupin-Walker type. Most individuals of this strain were excellent fox dogs.
• *Wild Goose*—These are Tennessee hounds originally developed in Virginia in the 1830s by John Fuquay and C. S. Lewis and later brought to Tennessee by Lewis.

• *Arkansas Traveler*—Judge C. Floyd Huff of Hot Springs, Arkansas, owned some "Missouri" hounds that were somewhat lacking in size and bone. To build them up, he introduced some blood from English hounds and some from a pack of Kentucky dogs. The results were the Arkansas Traveler strain, dogs that set a fast pace in that state and Louisiana.
• *Avent*—These dogs were the result of a mixture of Ferguson Virginia Black and Tans, dogs called "Bachelors," and native hounds that had enjoyed much success around Avent's home town of Hickory Valley, Tennessee. The Avent dogs were hunted widely in South Carolina, in the Mississippi Delta (on bears), in the West (for wolves and coyotes), and even in Africa (for lions and other big game).

DESCRIPTION: Speed, endurance, and toughness are a Foxhound's trademarks, and his physical attributes should reflect those trademarks.

Because there are so many strains, it is all but impossible to use specifics in describing the typical Foxhound. But since most Foxhounds, regardless of strain, are related, a general picture of this breed can be painted.

A Foxhound can be expected to be sturdily built overall, but the body should not be so heavy that the dog's speed or endurance is impeded. Legs should be strong and straight, feet catlike, chest and hindquarters powerful, ribs well-sprung.

The head should be proportionate to the rest of

AMERICAN FOX HOUND

the body—that is, not too large or too small—cleanly formed, and must not have loose skin as in the Bassett. Ears should be of medium length (when extended outward they should reach nearly to the tip of the nose) and should be set rather low on the head. Eyes are dark brown.

The coat should be of typical hound length and hard-textured. The predominant Foxhound colors are similar to those of Beagles and Bassets, but there is a great variation in colors, which include black and tan, orange and white, solid red, and many others.

SIZE: Because of the great variety in Foxhound types, there is considerable variation in the size of these dogs. In general, however, males should be no taller than 25 inches at the shoulder nor shorter than 22 inches. Females average an inch shorter. Weights range, on the average, from 50 to 65 pounds. Too much weight tends to reduce the dog's speed and stamina.

HUNTING ABILITY: The American Foxhound is unsurpassed in speed, courage, endurance, and tenacity. It is far rangier and a better producer of game than its English ancestors.

In effect, the American Foxhound's hunting ability is measured by the kind of hunting he is asked to do. There are two major forms of fox hunting practiced in the U.S.

In the South the sport of fox hunting is rooted almost entirely in the chase. The foxes, usually hunted at night, are not shot, but rather are highly valued for their ability to lead hound packs on runs that are fast, merry, loud, and usually long. For this kind of sport the hound must be inordinately fast, hard-driving, and capable of following hot scent that may be floating some distance from the actual track. He must be able to range out well in order to hit the scent of a moving fox (these dogs are expected to find their own foxes).

In the North foxes are most often hunted on snow during the day, and the object is for the hounds to run the fox around to hunters who station themselves at likely crossings. The foxes are usually shot, for their fur value or for bounty. Dogs for this form of the sport must have cold-trailing ability, for they are seldom put down until a track is found by the hunters, and the track may be an old one. Competition is lacking for the most part, for only one or two dogs are usually put on a track—at least until the fox is up and running, at which time other hounds may be released. Speed is less important in these northern dogs than is a loud and clear voice. Such a voice serves to let the owner know the direction of the chase and also prods the fox.

It should be noted that American Foxhounds are used to run game animals ranging from rabbits to cougars.

DISPOSITION: The American Foxhound's appealing and friendly facial expression is a key to his temperament, in most individuals. He is relatively gentle, takes well to training (though little formal training, other than obedience work, is needed) and discipline, and possesses the common-sense sagacity that all hounds seem to have in one degree or another. He is also greatly adaptable, being able to work out different conditions of terrain, weather, and quarry. And yet he can be cantankerously independent.

English Springer Spaniel

HISTORY: The word "spaniel" has its origins in the Roman term for Spain: Hispania. But there is no concrete proof that this type of dog originated in Spain. It is known, though, that spaniels have been in existence for thousands of years. In New York's Metropolitan Museum there is a figure of a spaniel-like dog that dates back to about 3000 B.C.

Starting in about 1800, spaniel-type dogs were classified in three rather loose categories that were based mainly on size. Dogs of under 14 pounds were called lap (or comforter) spaniels, those of 14 to 28

ENGLISH SPRINGER SPANIEL

pounds were called cocker spaniels, and those weighing more than 28 pounds were called springer, English, or field spaniels.

The English Springer Spaniel that we know today apparently dates back to about 1812, when the Boughey family of Shropshire, England, began to keep a relatively pure line of these dogs. The first trials for Springers, run under the auspices of the sporting Spaniel Club, were held in England in 1895. The larger and faster Springers began to dominate the trials, outhunting the cocker, Clumber, and field spaniels, and sportsman esteem for the Springer grew.

The generally agreed-upon date for the introduction of the purebred Springer into America is 1907, but the breed did not take hold until a Manitoba dog fancier, Eudore Chevrier, began to import and train large numbers of these dogs in about 1921.

The English Springer Field Trial Association was formed in 1924, and the first trials were held that same year. A standard for the breed was devised, and the American Kennel Club approved it in 1932.

DESCRIPTION: The English Springer Spaniel is a flushing dog—that is, he hunts the ground ahead of his master—but within shotgun range—and puts gamebirds into flight, rather than points them.

The Springer's coat is flat and somewhat wavy (but not curly), of medium length, and dense enough to provide protection against water, weather, and briary vegetation. There is a fringe of wavy hair on throat, brisket, chest, and bell. Coat colors include liver and white (the most prevalent), liver and tan, black and white, black and tan, tan and white, black and white and tan, and others. Unacceptable color combinations are red and white, and lemon and white.

The ears are long and set on at about eye level. The tail is docked. The feet are webbed for swimming and for work in muddy and swampy areas. Toes are well-arched, and pads are deep and horny. The body is muscular and relatively heavily boned.

In general, the Springer's physical conformation should give him speed, agility, and endurance.

SIZE: The Springer is a medium-size hunting dog. Weights range from 45 to 50 pounds for males and from 42 to 47 pounds for females. Shoulder height ranges from 18 to 22 inches.

HUNTING ABILITY: Being a flushing dog rather than a pointing dog, the Springer must work within range of his master's gun. The breed has a natural tendency to work close and so is easily taught to flush gamebirds.

Many Springers, given the proper training, also make at least passable retrievers and can learn to

mark the spots where shot birds fall. They are top-notch bird finders and fetchers in thick cover and in swamps, and they can handle rough weather well.

The Springer will hunt any gamebird, but it is far more popular with hunters who seek birds that tend to run rather than fly (such as pheasants and desert quail) than it is with men who hunt tight-sitting game (bobwhite quail and the like). In fact, the recent upsurge in Springer popularity in America is due mainly to the rise of the pheasant as the top gamebird in the northern U.S. Running birds are right down a Springer's alley, while they tend to corrupt the performance of a pointing dog.

DISPOSITION: The Springer's temperament is gentle, particularly with children, and friendly. The breed adapts well to various maintenance conditions—that is, it is as much at home in the home as in the kennel. It takes well to training and discipline.

Cocker Spaniel

HISTORY: At one time, beginning in the early 19th century, all spaniel-type dogs were classified according to size, with the cockers (14 to 28 pounds) ranking between the lap spaniels (under 14 pounds) and the field spaniels (over 28 pounds). The name ''cocker'' comes from the woodcock, which the cockers were bred to hunt.

But the Cocker Spaniel as a distinct breed is generally believed to have originated with a dog named Obo, whelped in England in 1879. Obo, 10 inches tall at the shoulder and weighing 22 pounds, led directly to the separate registration of Cockers in the English stud book, beginning in 1893. The first field trial for Cockers was held in 1899.

Many English Cockers were imported to America, where a separate strain, the American Cocker, was developed. The fountainhead of that strain is said to have been a dog named Braeside Bob.

The first major Cocker trial held in the U.S. was run in 1924 under the auspices of the Cocker Spaniel Field Trial Club of America. Field trials were largely responsible for maintaining the breed's value as hunting dogs, but that value declined markedly, particularly with the onset of World War II, which had the effect of almost entirely eliminating Cocker field trials. Trials were resumed after the war, but by then the breed was largely relegated to bench shows and pet status. Very few cockers are seen in the game coverts today.

DESCRIPTION: The Cocker, like the Springer Spaniel, is a breed that flushes, rather than points, gamebirds.

The modern Cocker Spaniel is actually two dogs:

COCKER SPANIEL

the American Cocker and the English Cocker. The American Cocker is perhaps the most beautiful of all the spaniels. It has a rounded skull, large and rather prominent eyes, and long ears that are placed at eye level or a bit lower. The leather of the ears reaches to the muzzle when they are outstretched.

The American's body is rather short, with a much broader chest than in other spaniels. The top line slopes from the withers to the croup. Feet are strong and compact, with thick pads.

The American Cocker comes in three varieties, based mainly on color. The three are black, any other solid color (but including black and tan), and parti-colors. The black variety usually has a thicker coat and feathering than the other color types.

The English Cocker's muzzle is slightly longer than the American's, and there is not the excess of hair as in the American black variety. Colors vary, including many self colors (all black, all liver, and all red) and parti-colors, as well as roan colors of blue, red, orange, liver, and lemon. The English Cocker is leggier than the American.

SIZE: The English Cocker is somewhat heavier than the American Cocker, ranging from 28 to 34 pounds for the males, 26 to 32 pounds for the females. The American Cocker should weigh no less than 22 pounds and no more than 28 pounds.

HUNTING ABILITY: As stated above, the Cocker Spaniel today is far more popular as a bench-show animal and house pet than as a hunter of gamebirds.

Therein lies the breed's major disadvantage, as far as hunters are concerned—it is difficult to find a good hunting strain of Cocker Spaniel.

If an interested hunter can find a dog whose recent ancestry contains good hunting and field-trial stock, he is on the right track. The hunter should then try to determine whether the dog has the following desirable characteristics: courage, a well-developed instinct for following bird scent, willingness to work, and tractability. The dog should like the water (particularly if the hunter wants the dog to do some waterfowl retrieving) and should be willing to charge right in to get a bird even though the water may be cold or rough. And the dog should be willing to work all kinds of cover with enthusiasm and fair speed.

In general, the English Cocker is a better bet than the American as a hunting dog. That is partly due to the fact that in England Cockers are required to prove their worth in a field trial before they can become eligible to qualify as a bench champion, a practice that has prevented the widespread deterioration of the hunting instinct that has plagued the American Cocker.

The Cocker, being the smallest of the spaniels, is not so effective in heavy cover or in water work. The Cocker is not as fast or as effective a hunter as the Springer Spaniel. It is, however, faster than the Clumber or Sussex spaniels and so is generally preferred over those breeds.

DISPOSITION: Good Cockers—especially those that are to be used for hunting—should have a happy, bubbly type of disposition. In recent years, however, many Cockers have been extremely high-strung and nervous, given to urinating on the floor because of excitement and to biting people for little reason. Shyness and hysteria are other character faults, but those, like the others, may well be on the way out, thanks to the efforts of breeders.

Cockers from good hunting stock are alert and take correction in stride.

American Water Spaniel

HISTORY: The American Water Spaniel is one of only a very few hunting-dog breeds that was developed entirely in the U.S. Though it has been in existence as a recognizable type for almost 100 years, the American Water Spaniel was not recognized officially until 1920, when the United Kennel Club accepted a Wisconsin dog for registration as an American Water Spaniel. The Field Dog Stud Book sanctioned the breed in 1938, and the American Kennel Club followed suit in 1940.

The breed's development was centered in the

pheasant belt of the Midwest and in New England. One of the men largely responsible for that development was a Wisconsin physician and surgeon, Dr. F. J. Pfeifer, whose Curley Pfeifer was the first American Water Spaniel registered with the U.K.C. Dr. Pfeifer's kennels contained as many as 130 of these dogs at one time.

It was Dr. Pfeifer's opinion that the breed was the result of a cross between the English Curly-Coat Retriever and the Field Spaniel. In all probability there was also some Irish Water Spaniel blood. The breed's original purpose was to retrieve ducks shot by hunters in small skiffs.

DESCRIPTION: Once called the American *Brown* Water Spaniel because of its rich liver color, this breed's coat is closely curled or deeply waved, but not kinky. The hair is quite dense, to give protection in water and heavy cover.

The forehead is covered with short smooth hair and lacks the tuft or topknot that is characteristic of the Irish Water Spaniel. The American's tail is covered with hair while the Irish's tail is ratlike.

There apparently are two strains within the American Water Spaniel breed. One type is small, compact, and somewhat benchlegged, while the other is quite a bit larger and longer-legged. The larger strain is preferred by jumpshooters.

SIZE: The American Water Spaniel stands 15 to 18 inches at the shoulder and weighs 25 to 45 pounds. It is compact and built close to the ground.

HUNTING ABILITY: The American Water Spaniel is a natural hunter and over the years has maintained all the "hunt" that was originally bred into him. That is probably due to the fact that this breed has not attracted the attention of dog-show people.

The American is essentially a flushing dog, though it is occasionally classified as a retriever. It can be trained to quarter about in the uplands in front of the hunter, to scent and chase up upland game, to drop to shot, and to retrieve upon command. Its main use in the uplands is on birds that tend to run rather than fly, such as pheasants and various Western quail.

The American is a fair waterfowl retriever but can't compare to the various retriever breeds for that purpose, though it is a tougher water breed than any of the other spaniels.

The American doesn't rank as tops in any facet of hunting-dog work. On the other hand, he is an excellent choice as a multipurpose dog, capable of both flushing game and fetching it and able to perform moderately well in a duck blind. And the American will hunt anything from pheasants, grouse, and woodcock to rabbits and squirrels.

DISPOSITION: The American Water Spaniel is likable, friendly, intelligent, even-tempered, and tractable. He is a natural hunter and a quick learner, and he seldom possesses personality quirks. He takes well to training and discipline and adapts well to varying conditions of terrain and weather. Though he has an appealing way about him, the American, more so than most other spaniels, seems to be distrustful of strangers.

Welsh Springer Spaniel

HISTORY: No one knows exactly when the Welsh Springer Spaniel first came upon the dog scene, though it is known to be an ancient breed indeed. As one might expect, the breed was developed in Wales but found its way into England and Scotland and eventually to America and such far-flung lands as India, Australia, and Siam. The breed standards were drawn up by the Welsh Springer Spaniel Club of England and later adopted by the American Kennel Club.

DESCRIPTION: The Welsh Springer Spaniel—in contrast to the Cocker and English Springer, which may be a wide variety of colors—is red and white only. The coat is flat and thick and silky, and it has a soft understory that provides protection from bri-

AMERICAN WATER SPANIEL

WELSH SPRINGER SPANIEL

ary cover and from rugged water and weather conditions.

Ears are quite hairy and set low on the head. Legs are straight and fringed with hair. Tail is plumed.

SIZE: The Welsh Springer is a bit smaller than the English Springer and a great deal larger than the Cocker Spaniel. The Welsh ranges in weight from 35 to 45 pounds.

HUNTING ABILITY: The Welsh Springer is a flushing-type rather than a pointing dog. Its importance as a hunting breed is limited, however, and very few of these dogs are seen in the game coverts.

Nonetheless, the Welsh Springer can be taught to hunt in front of the gun like other flushing spaniels, though his training, particularly obedience training, may be more difficult and time-consuming than for any of the other spaniels.

If this breed has a strong point, it is probably that it is able to work under temperature extremes, particularly on land (it is not able to stand very cold water, as retrievers can). It is capable of hunting upland game when the weather is quite warm.

The Welsh Springer has an acutely tuned nose and is a willing worker. However, his working pace is somewhat slower than that of the English Springer.

DISPOSITION: The Welsh Springer Spaniel has a pleasant and even temperament. He is kind and

gentle with children, is fiercely loyal, and is dependable. His training may take more time than with some other breeds, but he takes discipline well.

Clumber Spaniel

HISTORY: The first mention, in print, of the Clumber Spaniel was an 1807 article that appeared in a British publication, Sporting Magazine. An engraving with the article showed part of a painting in which a number of long, low, heavy-bodied dogs surrounded the gamekeeper of the estate—called Clumber House—of the Duke of Newcastle, Henry Clinton. The spaniel-like dogs, which the magazine article called ''springers, or cock-flushers,'' were said to have been a gift of the Duke of Noailles of France. The gamekeeper, William Mansell, was said to have ''studied to increase, unmixed, this peculiar race of flushers.''

Clumbers dominated the early field trials held for spaniels, despite the fact that at least one authority—the American dog writer James Watson, thought the breed was of ''little use'' in the field because of its slowness. But then the Cockers and Springers became faster, and the Clumbers began to lose favor.

Clumbers never became popular in America, mainly because no ''specialty'' club was ever formed to espouse the breed. No trials are held.

DESCRIPTION: The Clumber might be said to be the Basset Hound of the bird-dog set. Slow-moving, short-legged, and heavy-bodied, it gives the appearance of being very powerful. The head is large and massive, with relatively short ears. Neck is long and thick, and the shoulders are heavily muscled. The back is long, broad, and straight, free from droop or bow. Legs are short but heavy-boned, and the feet are large.

The coat is straight and silky, not too long but very dense, and has long and abundant feather. White predominates in the coat color, which varies from lemon and white to orange and white, with the body having almost no lemon or orange. Ears are (or should be) solid lemon or solid orange. Muzzle and legs are ticked.

SIZE: Today's Clumber Spaniel is somewhat larger than the English Springer, standing 17 to 18 inches tall at the shoulder but weighing 55 to 65 pounds for males, 35 to 50 pounds for bitches.

HUNTING ABILITY: Clumbers were bred as ''retired gentlemen's shooting dogs'' and were used in restricted areas such as turnip patches and truck gardens and in small game preserves with large

CLUMBER SPANIEL

populations of birds. In such places the slow-moving, close-working Clumber was a major advantage. However, most American conditions of cover, terrain, and game require a dog that works at a much faster pace and covers a good amount of ground. That is the main reason the Clumber has never found wide favor in this country. He is so rare here, in fact, that finding a good one is extremely difficult.

Nonetheless, the Clumber is a topnotch game-flusher and will retrieve well if trained properly. Because of his light coat, he is said to be unparalleled as a hot-weather hunter.

DISPOSITION: One of the Clumber's advantages (perhaps the only advantage, so far as many American hunters are concerned) is that he is about the most easily trained of all the spaniels. He takes training and discipline well, remembers his lessons, and does not have to be retrained. Though some early accounts of the breed's temperament called these dogs "naturally ill-tempered" and said they "would not work for every person," such temperament quirks have apparently been bred out.

Tolling Dog

You won't find the Tolling Dog listed in any of the American breed registries. It is "officially" recognized only by the men who use these dogs—and they are used in a most intriguing way.

In Europe, especially France and England, and in Nova Scotia (the only place in North America where these dogs are known to be used) dogs are used to "toll"—or lure—waterfowl. In Europe the dogs—belonging, apparently, to no specific breed—were trained to run up and down a stream bank at the confluence of the stream with a larger body of water. The antics of one of these dogs would arouse the curiosity of ducks sitting offshore on the larger body of water, and they would swim closer to investigate. Eventually, if things worked out as planned, the birds would wind up trapped inside a funnel-shaped net stretched across the stream's outlet. As the birds would move in, the dog would put on his show farther up the shore, thus drawing the birds in closer and closer to the shore and the net.

In Nova Scotia, the Tolling Dog is used in a similar fashion, except that he draws waterfowl in to a hunter's shotgun. The hunter finds a lake that is harboring a respectable number of ducks. He then builds a blind or uses natural camouflage on the shore, preferably on an outjutting point or on an island. The dog puts on his act on the shore near the blind, occasionally barking sharply. For some reason the ducks cannot overcome their curiosity, and they come within range of the hunter.

The Nova Scotia Tolling Dog is bred more or less true to type and looks like a red fox in size, coat texture, and color. (It is claimed that foxes use similar tactics to lure waterfowl and other birds.) As might be expected, Tolling Dogs are far from numerous.

Labrador Retriever

HISTORY: There is little doubt that the Labrador originated in the Canadian province of the same name, probably from a strain of dog bred in and around St. John's. The breed's greatest development, however, took place in England and began when the Second Earl of Malmesbury imported some of the dogs from Newfoundland (Labrador). The Third Earl of Malmesbury is given the credit for giving the breed its name and keeping it relatively pure. It is generally agreed, though, that some early English breeders introduced some blood from other retrievers, notably the flat-coat and curly-coat types.

In 1903 the Labrador was recognized as a breed by the English Kennel Club, and in 1906 Labradors were first entered in English field trials.

Labradors first appeared in the U.S. in the late 1920s, and the first licensed Labrador field trial in this country was held in 1931, in Orange County, New York. And Labradors swept the first three

LABRADOR RETRIEVER

placements in the first all-retriever-breed trial, held in 1934 at East Setauket, New York. Since that time the Labrador has outdistanced all other retriever breeds in popularity among hunters and field-trialers. That popularity is due in large measure to such early breeders as J. F. Carlisle and Averell Harriman. About 65 percent of all retriever registrations today are Labradors.

DESCRIPTION: The Labrador's overall appearance is that of a strongly built, close-coupled, and active animal. In comparison with the Flat-Coat and Curly-Coat retrievers, the breeds which the Lab most resembles, he is wider in the head and through the chest, and wider and more powerful in loins and hindquarters. Generally the Lab is shorter of leg than other retrievers and of a more solid build.

The Lab's skull is broad and has a slightly pronounced brow, and the head is clean-cut and free from any fleshiness. Jaws are long and powerful, not snippy. Ears hang rather close to the head and well back, are set somewhat low, and should not be large and heavy. Eyes are brown, yellow, or black.

Neck is long and powerful, shoulders long and sloping. Legs are straight from shoulder to ground, and feet are compact, with well-arched toes and well-developed pads.

The tail, almost totally free of feathering but clothed all around with short, thick hair and having a rounded look, is quite thick near the base but tapers gradually toward the tip.

The coat is short, very dense, and without waviness. The coat color is generally all black, though other solid colors—yellow being the most abundant—are permissible, as is a white spot on the chest.

SIZE: The standard for Labrador Retrievers calls for shoulder heights as follows: 22½ to 24½ inches for males, 21½ to 23½ inches for females. Average weights of Labs in working condition are 60 to 75 pounds for males and 55 to 70 pounds for bitches.

HUNTING ABILITY: The Labrador well deserves its position of preeminence among retrievers. It is the No. 1 choice of hunters who want a dog that will fetch birds on both land and water. The Lab takes naturally to water and to the job of retrieving, at which he is at his best. Properly trained—and this breed takes training very well—the Lab will sit or lie quietly in a boat or blind or walk at heel until ordered to retrieve.

The Lab is probably best known for his waterfowl work. His rugged build and constitution, and his short but protective coat, enable him to withstand extremes of heat or cold. He is second in toughness only to the Chesapeake Bay Retriever.

Though retrieving downed gamebirds is his specialty, the Labrador has phenomenal scenting powers and can also be trained to quarter ahead of the hunter and flush upland game, including pheasants, grouse, quail, woodcock, and the like. When working upland coverts, the Lab is quick, stylish, and aggressive—traits that also endear him to field-trialers. He will also trail wounded and running birds such as pheasants.

And Labradors, because of their tractability and trainability, are often used as seeing-eye dogs.

Finally, Labradors have compiled an enviable record in retriever field trials, topping all other breeds in numbers of dogs entered and in placements won.

DISPOSITION: Even-tempered, likable, friendly—all describe the Labrador. He makes an excellent pet for the hunter's family, though the more aggressive individuals of this breed may be too rough for small children (however, the most aggressive Labs are usually the best hunters). The Lab is very easily trained and quite intelligent, takes discipline without cringing or quitting, and is never mean. Some Labs (like some dogs of any breed) tend to be roamers when left to their own devices.

Golden Retriever

HISTORY: The Golden Retriever is directly descended from a strain of very large light-colored dogs known as Russian Trackers. These animals were part of a circus troupe touring England in 1860. A certain nobleman, Sir Dudley Majoribanks, saw the dogs and was so impressed that he bought the entire group of eight.

Sir Dudley bred the dogs for 10 years without outcrossing. But in 1870, feeling that the dogs—which weighed as much as 100 pounds—were too large and cumbersome to be hunters, he crossed the Russian Trackers with the bloodhound. The outcross reduced the size of the breed, improved its scenting abilities, and gave the coat a somewhat darker color and a finer texture. In 1911 these dogs were recognized as a distinct breed by the English Kennel Club, and at about that same time the Golden Retriever Club of England was formed.

It was about the turn of the century when the first Goldens came to North America, brought to Vancouver Island, British Columbia by British army personnel. The breed spread rapidly on the Pacific Coast, even as far as Alaska. One of the breeders most responsible was Bart Armstrong, of Winnipeg, Manitoba. The Golden was recognized by the Canadian Kennel Club in 1927 and by the American Kennel Club in 1932.

DESCRIPTION: From puppyhood, when he is a round little ball of yellow fluff, through adulthood, the Golden Retriever is a beautiful animal. The gorgeous coat—rich red overall (it must not be too light, like cream, or so dark as, say, the red of an Irish Setter)—and soft, honest facial expression give the

GOLDEN RETRIEVER

Golden an attractiveness few other breeds can match.

Standard for the Golden Retriever calls for a broad skull set on a clean and muscular neck. Muzzle is powerful and wide. Eyes are dark and set well apart, kindly in expression, and have dark rims.

The coat may be either flat or wavy, and it is dense and water resistant, with a good undercoat.

Ears are small and well set on. Feet are round and catlike, not splayed. Forelegs are well-boned and straight, hind legs strong and muscular. Tail is straight, not curled at the tip or carried over the back.

Body in general is well-balanced, short-coupled, and deep through the chest. Shoulders are well laid back and long in the blade.

SIZE: Ideal weights for Golden Retrievers in top working condition are as follows; 65 to 68 pounds for males, 55 to 60 pounds for bitches. Shoulder heights average 23 to 24 inches for males, 20½ to 22 inches for bitches.

HUNTING ABILITY: The Golden's status as the second most popular retrieving dog in the U.S. attests to the breed's ability as a bird finder/fetcher.

The Golden ranks behind the Chesapeake and the Labrador as a straight retriever of downed waterfowl, particularly under rigorous conditions. Icy water is easily absorbed by the Golden's silky coat, so he does not perform his best under most waterfowling situations (in warmer climates, however, the Golden makes a fine waterfowl retriever).

The Golden seems to be at his best on dry land. He hunts well in front of the upland gunner, quartering nicely and hunting an area thoroughly and methodically. He marks downed birds well and, of course, is an accomplished fetcher.

The Golden isn't as good as the Labrador in the upland coverts, lacking the Lab's speed, style and aggressiveness. But he tops the Chesapeake in that department.

The Golden, on the other hand, is about the most reliable of all bird-fetchers when it comes to nonslip retrieving. (A nonslip retriever is a dog that walks at heel or sits quietly at the handler's side until ordered out to retrieve.)

The Golden's coat can be a problem, for it collects burrs in the uplands, mud in the marshes. The coat requires considerable attention.

DISPOSITION: There is no more affectionate breed than the Golden Retriever. He thrives on verbal and physical praise, is wonderfully understanding and gentle with children, and makes the best pet of any of the retriever breeds.

The Golden is exceptionally intelligent and tractable. He is eminently trainable too—provided that the trainer uses patience and a soft hand. Too much two-fisted discipline can turn this otherwise docile and biddable animal into an obstinate sulker that will refuse to learn or work.

Chesapeake Bay Retriever

HISTORY: It is generally agreed that the Chessie, as this breed is affectionately known, descended at least partly from the Newfoundland dog of some 150 years ago. It therefore shares a common heritage with the Labrador.

It is said that an English brig was wrecked off the shores of Maryland in 1807. Aboard the vessel—and rescued—were two Newfoundland puppies, a dingy red male and a black female, that became the property of local breeders. These dogs were reported to have extraordinary retrieving ability.

Stories vary on the development of the breed from that point. Some have it that the two Newfoundland dogs were crossed with yellow and tan coonhounds. Another story, amusing but absurd, says that a Chesapeake bitch was mated to an otter! Still another account, possibly the true one, is that the Newfoundland dogs were crossed with English water poodles.

The Chessie's popularity grew rather rapidly, and by 1918, when the American Chesapeake Club was founded, the breed had become the No. 1 duck dog not only in the Chesapeake area but also in such places as Manitoba, Minnesota, and along the Mississippi Flyway. The breed was recognized by the American Kennel Club in 1931.

DESCRIPTION: Beauty, it is said, is in the eye of the beholder. Under that premise the Chesapeake is the apple of the eye of many a duck and goose hunter. But actually the Chessie is a sort of homely animal. And Chesapeake breeders have resisted efforts to beautify the breed—an attitude that, from the hunter's standpoint, is very fortunate, since a breed's "beautification" is usually accompanied by a drastic decline in its hunting abilities.

The Chessie's most unusual traits are his dense and oily coat (which enables this dog to be oblivious to the coldest water), yellow eyes, rather long tail, and his color, which ranges from a light shade quite reminiscent of dead grass to chocolate brown.

Skull is broad, muzzle is powerful, and the ears are rather small and set well up on the head. The thick and muscular neck appears to be too short for the body. Shoulders are powerful, and chest strong, deep, and wide.

CHESAPEAKE BAY RETRIEVER

Hindquarters are especially powerful, for swimming. Legs are of medium length, well-boned, and straight. The feet appear abnormally large.

SIZE: Male Chesapeake Bay Retrievers weigh from 65 to 75 pounds on the average, females 55 to 65 pounds. Shoulder heights are 23 to 26 inches for males, 21 to 24 inches for females.

HUNTING ABILITY: The Chesapeake is unparalleled as a water retriever of ducks and geese in rugged wintry weather. There are a number of reasons for this standing.

For one, the Chessie has an unbounded love for the water, the icier the better. He hits the water with abandon, which can be somewhat disquieting to occupants of a floating blind.

For another, the dog's coat—heavy, woolly, and oily—prevents his skin from ever getting wet and accounts for his ability to withstand bitter cold water. A couple of shakes, and the coat is freed of ice and water.

The Chessie has great strength, stamina, and aggressiveness. These dogs have been known to fetch more than 200 ducks in one day under the most inhuman weather conditions and to swim a mile to retrieve a single bird.

The Chessie is possessed of a fine memory. A well-trained one can mark and recall the falls (locations of downed ducks) of as many as six birds at a time.

If the Chesapeake has a fault in the area of waterfowl retrieving, it is that some individual Chessies tend toward hard-mouth, the practice of clamping the teeth so tightly on a bird being retrieved that the bird's flesh is marked or damaged. Training can overcome that problem.

The Chesapeake does have a place in the uplands, but that place is as a nonslip retriever (a dog that stays at heel until ordered out to fetch) rather than as a flusher of game.

DISPOSITION: The Chesapeake's temperament is a good deal less even than is the Labrador's. The Chessie does not take to strangers well, and he is something of a rugged individualist. He doesn't make as good a pet as most of the other hunting breeds, and he is inclined to fight when put into a kennel with other dogs. His enthusiasm can make him difficult to train. But such enthusiasm, when linked with drive and aggressiveness, is what makes for a topnotch hunting dog.

Irish Water Spaniel

HISTORY: In Ireland in the early part of the 19th century, there existed two distinct strains of water spaniels. The north-of-Ireland strain was small, parti-colored, and had a wavy coat. In the south of Ireland, around the River Shannon bogs, was a larger dog with a curly coat. This larger dog is thought to be the progenitor of the dog we know today.

The Irish Water Spaniel as it is presently known is directly traceable to one Justin McCarthy, who in 1850 was actively breeding Irish Water Spaniels, using the larger strain with the curly coat. His most famous dog was Boatswain, whose name is found in the pedigree of one of the early dogs registered in the American Stud Book.

These dogs apparently first appeared in the U.S. in the 1860s. However, the first official registrations appeared in 1878 in the stud book of the National American Kennel Club, forerunner of the American Kennel Club. The breed is one of the first retrievers to be imported into this country.

The Irish, bred to work the thick cover and cold waters of Ireland's bogs, came into great favor among U.S. market hunters, especially in the Midwest, and its fame spread to both the East and West coasts. The Irish's popularity probably was never greater than in the early 1920s, but that popularity began to fall off as that of the other retriever breeds increased, mostly because the Irish could not hold their own in field trials with the other breeds. Today the Irish is seldom seen in the duck marshes.

DESCRIPTION: The Irish Water Spaniel is the largest of all the spaniels. He is a rather heavy-boned animal whose solid-liver coat is composed of tight, crisp ringlets. The face, however, is smooth and free of any long or curly hair. The leg hair gives the dog the appearance of wearing pantaloons and should not look like the feathering of a setter.

One of the breed's most noticeable physical characteristics is its almost ratlike tail—the reason this breed is sometimes called the rattail. Actually, the tail isn't hairless. It is covered with short, smooth hair—except near the root, where the hair is much longer and curly.

Head is cleanly chiseled, skull rather large with a prominent dome, eyes dark hazel and browless. Ears are long, lobular, and set low on the head. Neck is long, shoulders sloping and clean, chest deep but not too wide between the legs. Body overall is of medium length. Feet are large, thick, and well clothed with hair both above and between the toes.

SIZE: Irish Water Spaniels develop slowly, both physically and mentally. They may not reach physical maturity until the age of two years. Generally, males weigh 55 to 65 pounds and stand 22 to 24 inches at the shoulder. Females weigh 45 to 58 pounds and stand 21 to 23 inches at the shoulder.

HUNTING ABILITY: The Irish has a few things going for him. His thick, ropy, oily coat enables him to withstand the rigors of a typical duck-shooting situation: frigid water, wind, sleet, mud, and the like. He is leggy enough to work in heavy marsh cover and such. And he loves the water and is a strong swimmer. If he's properly (and patiently) trained he

IRISH WATER SPANIEL

can become a proficient retriever of waterfowl—particularly in jump-shooting situations in wadable marshes—and nonslip retriever in the uplands. And if you're very lucky, he might develop a knack for flushing game ahead of the upland shooter.

It must be said, on the other hand, that the Labrador, the Golden, and the Chesapeake can be expected to do the job of retrieving better, faster, and easier than the Irish. The Irish is no great shakes in routing out and flushing upland game. And his coat, though it offers him fine protection, is an abomination from the hunter's standpoint, for it seems to form mats and pick up burrs as if by magic. And the comings and goings of an Irish in a duck blind can all but inundate the occupants with water and mud.

To top it off, the Irish is far more difficult to train than is any of the other retriever breeds.

DISPOSITION: The Irish Water Spaniel's temperament is an odd but often engaging melange of clownishness, perversity, stubbornness, desire to please, and even theatricality. The Irish tends to be loyal to a master but suspicious of strangers. He thrives on affection and companionship but will not stand abuse. His training calls for an inordinate amount of patience and the ability to coax rather than force. Once the Irish learns a lesson, though, he learns it well and remembers it.

Flat-Coat Retriever

HISTORY: The Flat-Coat derives from the original water dogs of Newfoundland, probably from a cross between the St. John's and the Labrador strains. It is also likely some blood from the Gordon and Irish Setters and possibly even the Russian Tracker (fountainhead of the Golden Retriever) was used to advantage in the development of the Flat-Coat.

The earliest-known Flat-Coat was an animal displayed at a show in Birmingham, England, in 1860 by a man named Braisford. This dog looked a good deal like a Labrador but was larger and its coat was much heavier and longer-haired. This dog was an excellent water dog and also performed well on upland gamebirds such as pheasants.

The breed was stabilized and developed under the hand of such breeders as Dr. Bond Moore of Wolverhampton, England. Before the Labrador's popularity began to soar, Flat-Coats served as gamekeepers' dogs over much of England. They are still used on estates and moors, mostly as retrievers.

Though recognized by the American Kennel Club, the Flat-Coat has never gained much popularity in the U.S. and is seldom seen in field trials. None has become a field-trial champion.

DESCRIPTION: The Flat-Coat Retriever is possessed of a distinctive coat that is dense, sleek, and fine-haired (the breed was once called the Wavy-Coat Retriever, but as the breed was developed the hair straightened). Color is either all black or all liver, though a small white spot on the chest is not unusual.

The head is long and nicely molded, while the skull is flat and somewhat broad. The dark-brown or hazel eyes convey an intelligent expression. Ears are relatively small and well set on close to the side of the head.

Neck is long, chest deep and fairly broad, and the back short, square, and well-ribbed, with muscular quarters. Forelegs are perfectly straight and well-boned down to the feet, which are round and strong. The limbs should be well-feathered when the animal is in full coat.

SIZE: The Flat-Coat Retriever stands 21½ to 24 inches at the shoulder and weighs between 60 and 75 pounds.

HUNTING ABILITY: Because the Flat-Coat has never mustered much support in the U.S. and is far from numerous here, its ability to cope with conditions of cover, terrain, and game common in the U.S. has not really been put to the test. It must be said, however, that the Flat-Coat's work in field trials has never measured up to that of the Labrador, Chesapeake, and Golden retrievers.

FLAT-COAT RETRIEVER

The Flat-Coat is a fine retriever, particularly of upland gamebirds. He is a strong swimmer and loves water work, including marking, fetching, and delivering.

Because the Flat-Coat's silky hair absorbs water, this breed is not at its best under cold-water conditions. It is also far from the best at hunting for and rousting out birds in front of the gun.

The breed was once notoriously hard-mouthed, but that is no longer true.

DISPOSITION: The Flat-Coat has an even, pleasant disposition; he is unsurpassed as a companion. He is intelligent, tractable, and rugged. Though he may occasionally exhibit a hard-headed or stubborn streak, he takes training and discipline well.

Curly-Coat Retriever

HISTORY: Though the precise origin of this animal is beclouded by time, it is known that the Curly-Coat is the oldest of all breeds that are now called retrievers. It is likely that this breed stemmed from a cross of the St. John's Newfoundland with the Irish (or English) Water Spaniel, despite the fact that the Curly-Coat lacks the Irish's topknot. Some poodle blood was undoubtedly introduced in order to increase the tightness of the curl.

The Curly-Coat has existed as a true breeding strain since 1855. It was first shown on the bench and run in field trials in 1859, in England, and was acknowledged by the international shows in 1864, when it was given a separate classification.

Beginning in about 1890 Curly-Coats were extensively exported to New Zealand and Australia, where they are today a very popular breed. The first Curly-Coats were brought to the U.S. in 1907. The breed is recognized by the A.K.C.

DESCRIPTION: The Curly-Coat Retriever is indeed a handsome animal. He is named for the mass of crisp, tight curls that cover his body from the occipital crest of the head to the point of his tail. The color is either black or dark-liver, with a bit of white on the chest not overly unusual.

The head is long and well-proportioned, skull not too flat. Eyes are black or brown and rather large; ears are rather small and set on low, lying close to the head, and are covered with short curls.

Shoulders are deep and muscular, the chest not too wide but quite deep, and the body rather short, muscular, and well-ribbed. The legs are quite long, the forelegs being straight. Feet are compact. The tail is moderately short and carried fairly straight.

CURLY-COAT RETRIEVER

The Curly-Coat has the longest legs and lightest build of all the retriever breeds.

SIZE: Height and weight are not vitally important in the Curly-Coat; in fact, the breed standard gives neither maximum nor minimum figures for height or weight. On the average, however, the Curly-Coat stands 24 inches at the shoulder and weighs 65 to 75 pounds.

HUNTING ABILITY: It is surprising that the Curly-Coat has never found favor among U.S. hunters, for he is a fine water dog and would make any waterfowler happy with his abilities to mark and remember the locations of shot birds, to fetch them unerringly, and to deliver them.

This breed's love for the water is almost a mania, and his thick coat enables him to swim for hours in the bitterest water. The dog will dive for crippled ducks, which often hold onto submerged vegetation with their bills and would die there and otherwise be lost to the hunter.

The Curly-Coat will also do the job in the uplands, though not so capably as in the marshes. In the uplands he is best suited as a nonslip retriever—a dog that stays at his master's side until he is sent out to retrieve. The Curly-Coat is seldom used to hunt out in front of the gun.

That thick coat that provides such good protection in rugged weather is also a shortcoming, for it picks up mud, burrs, and the like and requires considerable care of the owner.

The breed once had a reputation for being hard-mouthed, but that is no longer true.

DISPOSITION: Eager to please, steady, and affectionate are three adjectives that fit the Curly-Coat. He is intelligent, has a gentle temperament, and makes a splendid companion. His field traits include eagerness, endurance, and a good nose. He is easy to train and takes discipline in stride.

Pointer

HISTORY: The Pointer (formerly known as the English Pointer) dates back as far as the 14th or 15th century. Its exact origins are not known, though many fanciers of the breed believe that the first Pointers came from Spain. However, equally reliable records indicate that dogs of similar conformation and traits existed at about the same time in France, Belgium, Portugal, and other European countries. The French ''Braque''—described as a dog that ''stops at scent and hunts with the nose high''— was such an animal.

There can be little doubt, however, that England is the nation most responsible for the breed as we know it today. Among the English nobility whose breeding practices helped the Pointer to soar in popularity were Thomas Webb Edge, John Legh, Lord Combermere, the Earl of Sefton, Thomas Statter, Lord Derby, and George Moore. The fountainheads of the breed in England were such dogs as Brockton's Bounce, Statter's Major, Whitehouse's Hamlet, and Garth's Drake.

The 19th-century Pointer in England was a large, relatively slow, big-boned animal that was ideal for hunting slow-flying, tight-sitting grouse, birds that were raised domestically and freed in rather restricted hunting areas. But such dogs were far from ideal for hunting in the United States, where the birds were wild and scattered.

Since the mid-19th century the breed has undergone a drastic change, thanks to the efforts of such dog fanciers and breeders as T. H. Scott, S. A. Kaye, U. R. Fishel, C. H. Foust, and A. G. C. Sage. Sage's Alabama plantation, called Sedgefields, has long been famous as a trial grounds.

The Pointer today is fast, agile, and wide-ranging, able to seek out birds and pin them. Such qualities were passed down from such famous U.S. Pointers as Mary Montrose, Becky Broomhill, and Ariel, each of which won the National Championship three times.

Most top hunting Pointers are registered with the Field Dog Stud Book, while most show-type Pointers are on the list of the American Kennel Club.

DESCRIPTION: The Pointer is a beautiful animal, the epitome of what a bird dog should look like. Streamlined, and with a build that bespeaks speed and endurance, he carries his head high.

The Pointer's skull is long and moderately wide, with the forehead rising well at the brows. Muzzle is long, square, straight. Ears are thin and silky, long enough to reach just below the throat when hanging normally. Eyes are soft and dark. Neck is long, clean, and firm.

Shoulders are long and oblique, with the tops of the blades close. Chest is deep, and as wide as the shoulders will permit. Ribs are well-sprung. Back is strong, with a slight rise to the tops of the shoulders. Tail is straight, strong, and tapered, carried level or just above the line of the back.

Quarters are very muscular, legs moderately short but well-boned. Feet are round, deep, and well-padded, with well-arched toes.

The coat is short, flat, and firm. Coat color ranges from liver and white (the most common) to black and white, lemon and white, or solid white, any of which is highly visible in the field.

SIZE: The Pointer is a medium to fairly large animal, as bird dogs go. Average weight is 50 to 65 pounds, though some small specimens, particularly bitches, may weigh as little as 35 pounds and some large males may hit 80 pounds. Shoulder height is 24 to 25 inches.

HUNTING ABILITY: The Pointer is at present the ''top dog'' among the pointing breeds, both in the field and in trials, and that stature is well earned.

POINTER

This breed is fast, enduring, and has a great nose and sometimes uncanny bird sense (the ability to recognize and home in on birdy-looking cover and to anticipate what birds are going to do and react to it).

The Pointer's strong suit is quail, particularly bobwhites, on which he has no peer. There are few sights in the hunting world that can match that of a stanch Pointer locked up in a statuesque point over a covey of bobwhites.

But this dog has also proven himself on pheasants, one of the most demanding assignments for any bird-dog breed. He will also work well on any of the western quail and on woodcock and grouse, though closer-working breeds are usually preferred for the latter two species.

The Pointer has a deeply ingrained and well-defined instinct to hunt and to point. He has a rugged constitution and can withstand long hours in hot weather, a factor that has made him extremely popular in the southern U.S. Some other breeds, however, are better able to stand bitter-cold weather.

DISPOSITION: The Pointer has a temperament that might best be termed reserved. Though he is not unresponsive to gentle and kind treatment, he cannot truthfully be called affectionate. He is not much for hand-licking. In fact, he sometimes assumes an air of indifference toward people other than his master. That aloofness may be attributed to the fact that the Pointer—most individuals, at any rate—just lives to hunt gamebirds, and unless he's doing that job he's not happy. Of course, in the Pointer, as in any other dog breed, you may find an individual dog that seems to be the rule-proving exception.

The Pointer's rugged disposition is an asset, as far as training is concerned. The breed will tolerate a considerable amount of force by a trainer without becoming balky or allowing itself to be made into a "mechanical" dog lacking style and dash.

English Setter

HISTORY: The English Setter dates back at least as far as the 16th century. Etchings and other illustrations of that time show a pointing dog that looks very much like the English. The breed in all probability originated in Spain, from a cross between a Spanish pointing dog with one or more spaniel-type dogs. The early setters were known as "setting spaniels" because they "set" (pointed) their game. One of the earliest dog writers called the setter "a spaniel improved."

Many setter strains were developed in England, among them Featherstone, Lovat, Southesk, Na-

worth Castle, Seafield, and Laverack. Edward Laverack, the first major breeder of the English Setter, set the breed's type during a period of some 35 years of demanding inbreeding.

In the 1870s or 1880s Laverack and R. Purcell-Llewellin imported some outstanding setters to North America. The Llewellin strain, established from Laverack stock, became very popular in the U.S. (see Llewellin Setter).

During the English Setter's early days in this country, the breed was all but untouchable in field trials. In fact, the Setter's performance was so superior to that of the Pointer (whose ascendancy had not yet begun) that putting the two into head-to-head competition was not considered sporting. The Pointer has since, of course, surpassed his longer-haired rival. The first National Bird Dog Championship, held in 1896, was won by a Setter—Count Gladstone IV. Other famous English Setters include Count Noble (whose name is found in the pedigrees of many of today's Setters), Druid, Sport's Peerless, and Florendale Lou's Beau.

DESCRIPTION: The English Setter is a graceful and handsome animal, alert and agile. In general build he is not so heavily muscled, particularly in the hindquarters, as the Pointer, and his chest is not so broad. Following are the standards for the breed:

The head is long and lean, not so broad and square as that of the Pointer, and the dome tends more toward an oval shape. Muzzle is long and square, but not so square (particularly in trial dogs) as the Pointer's. Ears are set low and well back and are of moderate length, and they are covered with silky

ENGLISH SETTER

hair. Eyes are dark brown and project an intelligent and mild expression.

Neck is long and lean. Shoulder blades stand moderately close at the tops. Chest is deep but not overly wide. Ribs are well-sprung. Back is strong and either straight or sloping upward slightly to shoulders. Legs are strong, straight, well-boned, and muscular. Feet are closely set and strong, with tough pads and well-arched toes that are covered with thick, short hair.

Tail is straight and tapers to a fine point, and its feathering is straight and silky but not bushy.

Field and trial English Setters should not be overly tall and thin, as are many show Setters, for this conformation detracts from the ruggedness needed for field work.

The Setter's coat is long and flat and without curl. Colors vary, but they include white and black; white, black, and tan; white and orange; white and chestnut; blue belton; orange belton; and others. Among the most popular color combinations is white with a mixture of black, tan, lemon, and orange.

SIZE: Similar in size and weight to the Pointer, the English Setter ranges in average weight from 50 to 60 pounds, with some small bitches weighing as little as 35 pounds and large males weighing up to about 75 pounds. Average height at the shoulders is 24 to 25 inches.

HUNTING ABILITY: The English Setter is the only pointing dog that rivals the Pointer in drive, speed, nose, and bird sense. Though the Setter has not even approached the Pointer in field-trial accomplishments, the two are not so far apart in performance for the general hunter.

Though the Pointer is the generally acknowledged king of quail country, meaning the southern U.S., many quail hunters prefer the English Setter because he tends to work a bit closer to the gun.

Just as the Pointer, because of his short hair, is better able to withstand hot-weather conditions, the Setter, because of his long hair, is unquestionably better than the Pointer under the rigors of winter hunting. The Setter is also better able to cope with briars and other tough cover, again because of his thick and protective coat.

That long hair, on the other hand, can pose a maintenance problem for the Setter owner. Burrs and matted hair may take hours to remove. Some Setter fanciers suggest that this problem can be reduced by trimming the feathering on a dog's underparts, tail, and ears.

English Setters are particularly adept at handling pheasants. A top Setter will even circle ahead of a running pheasant to pin it and prevent it from flushing wild. Too, a Setter is more apt to keep in touch with the hunter than is a Pointer.

In midwestern and northern states, the Setter does more than a passable job of water work, hauling pheasants and Hungarian partridge out of potholes and performing similar damp duties.

A prospective dog buyer—and this advice applies not only to English Setters but to all other hunting-dog breeds—should be certain that any dog in which he is interested comes from ancestors that have proven their worth as hunting dogs.

DISPOSITION: The English Setter is not a tough nut, as are many pointers. He literally thrives on attention and affection, and he will dispense those same feelings. The Setter is seldom timid, but he is sensitive, and a trainer would do well to keep that fact in mind. Too much force can cow a Setter or make him a sulker, and the breed cannot take too much punishment.

The Setter takes well to gentle, unhurried training tactics, and he learns his lessons well, being less apt to forget or disregard them than is the Pointer. He is also more likely to become a one-man dog than is a Pointer.

It pays for a hunter to make a companion of an English Setter. The dog is sure to meet the man more than halfway.

Irish Setter

HISTORY: The Irish Setter, a product of the British Isles, was not always the solid-mahogany-red animal that we know today. Most of the original Irish were red and white, though the red predominated.

The development of the Irish Setter rather closely paralleled that of his English cousin (see English Setter). The Irish dogs, a bit more rough and rugged, were much prized by hunters, for they performed many tasks, ranging from seeking out and pointing such upland gamebirds as woodcock, grouse, and quail, to the retrieving of waterfowl from the most frigid of waters.

The Irish Setter's heyday in the U.S. began, for all intents and purposes, in 1876, when one of the early imports, an Irish named Erin, won an important stake at the Tennessee State Sportsmen's Association field trials, only the third trial series ever held. The Irish won a surprising number of placements in early trials—surprising because of the small number of Irish Setters entered in the competitions.

A dog named Elcho might well be considered the fountainhead of the breed in the U.S. Elcho—imported from Dublin by Charles H. Turner of St.

Louis—won fame in bench shows. Most of today's Irish Setters are traceable to Elcho.

The breed's outstanding beauty has led directly to a decline in its field capabilities, and thus to a drop in popularity among hunters. In the early part of the 20th century (and continuing even today) many breeders became interested in bench shows and so bred into many Irish Setters physical characteristics that improved the breed's already handsome looks but were a handicap in the hunting field. That factor, plus the rapid rise in the popularity of the Pointer and other bird-dog breeds, has shunted the Irish into the background in hunter popularity.

DESCRIPTION: The Irish Setter is generally hailed as the most beautiful of all the sporting breeds. It should be noted, however, that physical characteristics can vary considerably from hunting to show stock.

The physical standards are of interest mainly to dog fanciers who are concerned with show animals and in many instances do not accurately describe Irish Setters from good hunting stock.

In general, the hunting Irish is a dog with a powerful build, being well-boned and quite muscular, particularly in the quarters. Head is good and broad. The coat is rather heavy, flat, and silky. Coat color is a deep mahogany, often with white areas on chest, feet, and face.

Show breeding produces such characteristics as a rather snippy or narrow head, slim hips, weak quarters, long legs, and a lack of roundness in the rib cage, a shortcoming that usually causes a dog to lack endurance.

Basically, the Irish Setter is an English Setter with a red coat.

SIZE: The Irish Setter, being of somewhat slighter build than the English Setter or the Pointer, will weigh a bit less. An average Irish of normal height will be about 55 pounds. Shoulder height ranges from 25 to 26 inches.

HUNTING ABILITY: Though field excellence is hard to find in today's Irish Setter breed as a whole, there are still a few breeders who concentrate on hunting ability. If you can find a dog from good hunting stock, you might well find yourself stuck on this breed.

A good hunting Irish has a nose that is the equal of that of any other breed. He is rugged, sturdy, and enduring and can handle bitter weather with the best of them. He has a deeply ingrained pointing instinct, though many field trialers dislike the Irish's tendency to point with a rather low tail, a factor that takes away from the stylishness of a point.

Few Irish Setters display the dash or the wide range of the English Setter or Pointer, but the Irish generally does his job in a businesslike manner, covering the terrain thoroughly. Above all, the Irish almost always keeps in visual touch with the hunter—that is, he hunts for the gun, not for himself.

The coat is a drawback. That dark red of the Irish is more difficult to see in thick cover than is that of the English or the Pointer, which have some white.

DISPOSITION: The Irish Setter is an extremely affectionate animal that thrives on attention. Of all the pointing breeds, he is the most likely to become a "one-man dog" and may, in fact, hunt only for his master.

The Irish has long carried a reputation for being stubborn and hard to handle. That may have been true of some of the early imports into this country, but it does not apply to the Irish of today.

However, it is true that patience and kindness, rather than force and abuse, should be the bywords of the trainer of an Irish. The breed is eager to please, a factor that can also be used to a trainer's advantage.

German Shorthaired Pointer

HISTORY: The basic original stock from which the German Shorthair evolved was an early Spanish

IRISH SETTER

pointing dog, probably crossed with the Braque, an early French pointing animal. Later a cross with the Bloodhound added to the breed's nose, and still later Foxhound blood was added to improve the speed and endurance (though this infusion may well have detracted from the dog's bird sense).

A strange mixture? It would be for American hunting conditions, but the German breeders, who followed a rigorous selective-breeding program, knew what they wanted—a multipurpose dog suitable for hunting on German shooting preserves. These preserves held many varieties of game, both feathered and furred, and the ideal dog had to have a good nose and trailing ability for such game as rabbits and foxes, pointing instinct and bird sense for upland gamebirds such as grouse and woodcock, and the size, strength, and courage to handle such big game as wild boar and deer.

The German Shorthair filled the bill as well as any dog in existence.

The German Short-Haired Pointer Club of America, with headquarters in Minneapolis, did much to further the development of the breed in this country. The breed is slowly becoming quite popular in the U.S., probably because it is a jack-of-all-trades.

DESCRIPTION: Good individuals of this breed are extremely attractive animals. In general, they are relatively tall and quite strong, slightly lower in the hips than in the shoulders. The legs are straight, and the overall build is powerful.

GERMAN SHORTHAIRED POINTER

The German Shorthair's head is similar in conformation to that of the Pointer, except that it is longer, a bit narrower, and not so squared off at the muzzle. The ears are quite long and often quite houndlike, and they are set lower on the head than are a Pointer's.

Shoulders are muscular and moderately wide, chest deep and wide, ribs well-sprung.

The tail is docked, or cut, to approximately one-third of its original length and is carried almost straight out behind.

Coat is short, flat, and firm. Its texture is somewhat heavier than the Pointer's. Color is all liver or different combinations of liver and white that may involve ticking, spotting, or both.

SIZE: German Shorthair males weigh 55 to 70 pounds, females 45 to 60. Shoulder heights range from 23 to 25 inches in males, 21 to 23 inches for females. However, specimens of this breed tend to be taller and heavier than other pointing breeds. For example, a Shorthair standing 26 inches at the shoulder is not at all uncommon.

HUNTING ABILITY: The German Shorthair as a bird dog has an excellent nose, medium range, and moderate speed. His head is generally carried rather low, and he tends to crouch while on point (actions that are not stylish), and his somewhat bulky build prevents him from being as fast as the Pointer and English Setter.

However, while those factors make the Shorthair a poor choice for pheasants in big fields or for such open-country birds as sharptailed grouse, they make him eminently practical for the man who hunts woodcock, ruffed grouse, and quail in heavy cover. And the Shorthair, despite his relatively thin coat, will retrieve shot waterfowl, even from bitter water.

DISPOSITION: The German Shorthair has a mild and even temperament. He is seldom quarrelsome, though he can certainly hold his own in a fight. This dog is tractable and not overly difficult to train—provided he has the natural instincts to begin with.

The Shorthair does exhibit a tendency to be possessive, and dogs of that type make very good watchdogs. The Germans prize this quality highly, calling it "sharpness," but some hunters consider it a shortcoming.

Gordon Setter

HISTORY: Tradition has it that some two centuries ago the Duke of Gordon heard reports of a dog, owned by a shepherd in the highlands of Scotland, that was an accomplished finder of game. The Duke acquired the dog, a Collie-type bitch named Maddy, and crossed it with the setters that were kept at Gordon Castle. The result was what we know today as the Gordon Setter.

But the Gordon may have had even earlier origins. It is possible that the breed was developed from a "black and fallow setting dog" that was described in print as early as the first half of the 1600s.

In 1842 a man named George Blunt brought Rake and Rachel, both bred at Gordon Castle, to the U.S. Unlike today's Gordons, these animals were white with black-and-tan markings. The two dogs were bred, and a resulting puppy wound up, via Daniel Webster, in the hands of Henry Clay, who apparently had no great love of dogs but who seems to have been won over by the beguiling pup.

In the 1880s a lighter, more streamlined Gordon was brought to the U.S. It proved to be a hunting and show animal.

There was a time—the late 1800s—when the Gordon Setter knew few peers as a bird-finding hunting dog. But the English Setter, Pointer, and, to a lesser degree, Irish Setter—bred for speed and other qualities needed to handle the decreasing amount of game in this country—soon outstripped the Gordon in popularity.

DESCRIPTION: The Gordon Setter is a bird dog of great beauty. Its body symmetry and proportions are similar to those of other setters, except that the Gordon is a slight bit heavier and often has slightly shorter legs.

The Gordon's beauty is rooted in its heavy coat of smooth, silky hair. The color is jet black, except for mahogany markings above the eyes and on chops, ear linings, chest, belly, and feather. The coat should be as free from white hair as possible. Feathering should be generous on legs, underparts, and tail.

The Gordon is wide across the forehead and has a fairly long muzzle. Nose is big and broad. Eyes are dark brown and have a wise look. Chest is deep, and ribs are well sprung. Forelegs are big-boned and straight, hind legs muscular.

Feet have close-knit, well-arched toes, plenty of hair between the toes, and generous pads. The tail is relatively short (should not reach below the hocks) and is carried horizontally or nearly so.

SIZE: The Gordon is a bit heavier than the other setters, ranging in weight from 45 to about 75 pounds. Shoulder height varies from 23 to 27 inches. The official standard for the breed allows considerable range in size, to suit sportsmen in various parts of the U.S.

GORDON SETTER

HUNTING ABILITY: The Gordon Setter is rarely seen today in the hunting fields. His decline in popularity since the late 19th century can be ascribed to a number of factors, chief among them being that few breeders made any effort to widen the breed's range and increase its speed, as was done with the English Setter and the Pointer. Good range and speed are qualities that more and more hunters are demanding, because of the increasing scarcity of gamebirds. Also, the Gordon lacks the dash, determination, and stylishness of the English Setter and Pointer.

The above is not meant to imply that the Gordon is a poor hunter. He has an excellent nose and a good pointing instinct, and his heavy coat enables him to handle the heaviest of cover. (On the other hand, that same coat, because of its black and mahogany coloration, tends to make the dog hard to see in heavy cover.)

Though the Gordon is a slow hunter, he is also a sure hunter and tends to keep in touch with the hunter. Those factors make the Gordon a good choice for the man who hunts ruffed grouse and woodcock.

The Gordon is quite trainable, and is easily broken to retrieving. He makes a good retriever from land or water.

DISPOSITION: The Gordon Setter's most endearing quality is his loyalty. He forms such a strong attachment to his owner or handler that he may not hunt for anyone else. That loyalty, however, should not be allowed to become so pronounced that, for example, the dog finds it impossible to readjust to his owner after spending some time under the whistle of a trainer.

The Gordon is responsive to training, eager to please, and wary of intruders. He jealously guards his human family and is regarded as a "most-pettable" dog.

Llewellin Setter

HISTORY: The Llewellin Setter is not a distinct breed but rather one of the many strains of the English Setter (see English Setter). But it attained such a high degree of popularity that it once was accorded virtual—if not official—breed status among hunters. The Field Dog Stud Book recognizes the Llewellin as a distinct strain of English Setter. The American Kennel Club does not distinguish between the various setter strains.

The Llewellin had its beginnings in England in about 1825, when one Edward Laverack began a rigorous setter-breeding program. Using a bitch from a strain said to have been kept pure for 35 years, he produced some noteworthy hunting animals.

In 1871 another Englishman, R. Purcell Llewellin, while attending a field trial, bought a pair of male setters—Dan and Dick, offspring of parents named Field's Duke and Statter's Rhoebe—and later bred them to Laverack bitches that he already owned. This was the foundation of the Llewellin strain.

Llewellin, aided greatly by his kennel manager, G. Teasdale Buckell, did much to develop and popularize the strain that bears his name.

American sportsmen were greatly impressed with the hunting capabilities of the Llewellin Setters and imported many of the animals to this country. (Oddly, the fountainheads of the Llewellin strain, Field's Duke and Statter's Rhoebe, never amounted to much as field dogs.)

Among the early Llewellin imports to the U.S. was Count Noble, a prepotent dog and a great trial winner. When Noble died, he was mounted, and the mount is now on display at the Carnegie Museum in Pittsburgh.

Another import was Gladstone, whose work in trials and in the field did much to promote setter popularity in the U.S. Gladstone was the loser in a well-publicized two-day quail hunt in which he was worked against a "native" (American-bred) setter named Joe Jr.

The Llewellin Setters took the U.S. by storm. In the strain's heyday the ownership of a true Llewellin was a matter of great prestige. But that heyday was short-lived, and the ascendancy of the Pointer rel-

egated the Llewellin to the status of an also-ran. Today very few true Llewellins are found in the hunting fields.

DESCRIPTION: Same as English Setter, with the following exception:

Some dog fanciers incorrectly assume that any lightly marked blueticked setter is a Llewellin. However, color and physical appearance are invalid criteria. The Field Dog Stud Book recognizes as members of the Llewellin strain only those animals that are traceable back, without outcross, to the Duke-Rhoebe-Laverack origins.

SIZE: Same as English Setter.

HUNTING ABILITY: Same as English Setter.

DISPOSITION: Same as English Setter.

Weimaraner

HISTORY: The Weimaraner, one of the Continental pointing breeds, originated nearly a century and a half ago in Weimar, Germany, where the Grand Duke Charles Augustus held court. The court was a gathering place for the sporting gentry of Germany.

The demands of those hunters were high: they wanted a dog that would trail land game, fetch from water, and point upland birds—and also to be a companion. Toward that end they used a number of dog strains, none of which is known for certain. However, the old German bloodhound was probably one. That bloodhound, called the schweisshunde, was a sort of super-bloodhound and a source of most of that country's hunting breeds.

For many years Germans guarded the Weimaraner jealously, treating it almost as a national dog. This careful supervision even extended so far as to cause the passage of a law making it a legal offense for a commoner to own a Weimaraner.

The breed was introduced in the U.S. in 1929, when a man named Howard Knight of Providence, R.I., imported two of the animals. No breed has ever been given such a welcome or so much publicity. Claims of the Weimaraner's field prowess and high intelligence included "Smartest Dogs in the World." It was even said that they could perform such feats as answering the telephone and taking care of children.

That publicity, unfortunately, proved to be the breed's undoing. He became greatly popular with the general public, and unsound breeding programs. including programs aimed mainly at producing show stock, resulted. Only recently has the Weimaraner

WEIMARANER

shown signs of overcoming the pressures of its early days in the U.S. The breed was recognized by the American Kennel Club in 1944.

DESCRIPTION: The Weimaraner has been dubbed the "Gray Ghost" because of his distinctive overall gray color, which may vary all the way from a bright or silvery gray, through a yellowish gray, to a dark or blue-gray. The nickname also accrues from the dog's silent manner of movement. In texture the breed's coat is short, flat, and dense, and it gives a sleek or velvety appearance. The woolly undercoat protects the animal from rough weather.

The Weimaraner's back should be firm and level, not sagging—a fault seen in many individuals of the breed some years ago. The body in general is quite large and extremely muscular, and the build is much like that of the German Shorthaired Pointer.

The tail is docked to about one-third to one-half of its normal length, docked length being about 1½ inches just after birth and about 6 inches at maturity. Docking, incidentally, has a utilitarian purpose—if the tail were left its normal length, it would whip about in heavy cover and be cut by briars.

The Weimaraner's eyes also are rather distinctive, being blue-gray or amber but appearing to change color with varying light conditions.

SIZE: The Weimaraner is a big dog, taller and heavier than the German Shorthair. Shoulder height averages 24 to 26 inches for males, 22 to 25 inches for bitches. Average weights are 65 to 85 pounds for males, 55 to 75 pounds for bitches.

HUNTING ABILITY: The Weimaraner has managed to survive the overpublicity of its first quarter-century in the U.S., and today serious efforts are being made toward the reestablishment of the breed as a working gun dog.

In general, the Gray Ghost has a well-developed pointing instinct and is fairly staunch. It has good bird sense and a strong penchant for retrieving. It loves the water.

The Weimaraner is not a fast worker in the field. He is more of a stalker and in fact might even be legitimately called a pussy-footer (a trait due probably to his bloodhound origins). This characteristic makes him a good choice for both pheasants and ruffed grouse and for some of the western and southwestern gamebirds that like to run rather than fly.

The breed's water work is not outstanding. He will do an acceptable job on short retrieves along waterways, for example, but for ambitious retrieves on open water or mud flats, where he must follow hand signals, the Weimaraner is not the best choice.

It has been said that the Weimaraner tends toward being hard-mouthed (holding retrieved game so tightly in his teeth that he marks or pierces the skin). This tendency, too, may be ascribed to the breed's bloodhound ancestry.

DISPOSITION: The Weimaraner is a garrulous, friendly fellow. He has a good temperament, being tractable and taking well to training. He is also quite intelligent—one individual, Grafmar's Ador, won his obedience degree at the tender age of six months and was at that time the youngest dog ever to accomplish that feat.

The breed learns its lessons not only early but also well. He also adapts well to the home, making an excellent family pet and a topnotch watchdog.

Brittany Spaniel

HISTORY: The distant ancestors of the Brittany Spaniel—and those of all other pointing-dog breeds—lived in Spain, where they were used to "set" (point) upland game. Further development of these breeds took place in France and began more than 1,000 years ago.

Some dog historians believe that the Brittany Spaniel as we know it today is distantly related to the red and white setter, original ancestor of the Irish Setter. Whether or not that is true, the first tailless ancestor of today's Brittany is a pup that resulted from the crossing of a white-and-lemon woodcock-hunting dog brought to France's Brittany area by an Englishman, and a white-and-mahogany bitch owned by a Frenchman. The pup developed into a topnotch hunting dog and was much in demand as a stud.

The breed's early development was mainly the result of the efforts of a French breeder and sportsman, Arthur Enaud. He used an Italian pointer and the French Braque (also a pointing dog) as outcrosses, thereby improving the bloodlines. The use of outcrosses was then discontinued, and Enaud adhered closely to selective breeding practices, firmly establishing the breed's type.

It is thought that the first Brittany Spaniels brought to the U.S. arrived here in 1912. However, it was not until 1934–36 that the first sizable importations were made and efforts were intensified to establish the breed here. A prime mover in those efforts was Louis Thebaud.

Since that time the Brittany has become well-known in this country and well respected for his abilities in the hunting field.

DESCRIPTION: The Brittany is unique among spaniels—for a number of reasons. For one, he is often called "the spaniel that looks like a setter." For another, he is often born without a tail.

The Brittany's head is much like that of the English Setter, except that it is shorter, a bit wider across the dome, shorter and higher set in the ears, and a little lighter in the muzzle. While most of the other pointing breeds have dark-brown eyes, the Brittany's eyes are a deep amber. They convey an expression of extreme alertness, intelligence, and tractability.

The coat is a good deal like that of the setter, but is heavier and either quite smooth or slightly wavy. The Brittany's coat should not be so heavily feathered or so silky as that of the Setters. Coat color in the Brittany is liver and white or orange and white, preferably with roan ticking. The white usually predominates.

Overall, the Brittany is small, closely knit, and strong, with well-fringed thighs, muscular shoulders, deep chest, broad and strong hindquarters. Tail is naturally short, but docking is occasionally needed to keep it to a length of 4 inches.

SIZE: The Brittany is the smallest of all the pointing-dog breeds. The shoulder height ranges from 17 to 19¾ inches, and weight averages 35 to 45 pounds.

HUNTING ABILITY: The Brittany is the only spaniel with a highly developed pointing instinct, and it is almost always considered as a pointing breed. The Britt is also the widest-ranging of all of the spaniels. In fact, its range is only slightly shorter than that of Pointers and Setters. And the Brittany has the ability to adapt his range to the type of terrain he is hunting, staying close to the gun in thick cover and moving well out there in open country. He is at his best, however, in thick stuff and will keep in touch with the hunter. Thanks to his spaniel ancestry, he can easily be trained to fetch.

As a result of that fine admixture of characteristics, the Britt can be used on woodcock and ruffed grouse, on pheasants and other open-country birds such as quail and sharptailed grouse, and to retrieve shot game from land or water.

The Brittany has fine bird sense, pointing intensity, and style. He also has good speed. His coat provides fine protection from brambles and other rugged cover, and because of its coloration it is easily seen.

A good indicator of the Brittany's increasing favor among hunters is the fact that more and more Britts are being entered in field trials today.

DISPOSITION: The Brittany is quite friendly, highly intelligent, extremely alert, and very tractable. He makes a fine companion for the one-dog hunter as well as an excellent family pet. Though not really timid, the Britt is rather sensitive, so rough handling or harsh treatment should be avoided. Gentle coercion is the ticket during training sessions.

BRITTANY SPANIEL

Wirehaired Pointing Griffon

HISTORY: In 1874 E. K. Korthals, a young Dutchman living near Haarlem, Holland, became preoccupied with creating a new breed of hunting dog, a dog that would have a keen nose, ability to trail, an instinct to point birds, and the ruggedness to enable it to withstand rigorous conditions. The young man's father, a wealthy banker, apparently became so angered with his quest that the younger Korthals was obliged to leave home.

It was in Germany, and later in France, that much of Korthals' breed development took place (in France the Wirehaired Pointing Griffon is known today as the Korthals Griffon). Korthals—using woolly-haired, rough-coated, and short-haired animals as basic stock—came up with a harsh-coated animal. It is generally believed that the blood of the otterhound, setter, pointer, and probably a large spaniel were used. The result was a useful—and unusual—hunting animal.

DESCRIPTION: The Wirehaired Pointing Griffon's most striking physical characteristic is his unique coat, which, though short-haired, is best described as unkempt. It is made up of harsh bristles, a good deal like those of a wild boar. The bristles form on the dog's head a "moustache" and heavy eyebrows. Coat colors are mixed: steel gray, gray-white, and chestnut—never black.

The skull is long and narrow, the muzzle square. The large eyes are iris-yellow or light brown. Ears are of medium size, set rather high. Nose is always brown. Neck is rather long, shoulders long and sloping. Ribs are slightly rounded. Forelegs are straight and muscular and have short wiry hair, as do the hind legs, which are well developed. Feet are round, firm, well-formed. Tail is bristly and has no plume, and it is usually docked to one-third of its normal length.

SIZE: The Wirehaired Pointing Griffon has an average shoulder height of 19½ to 23½ inches. Weight averages about 56 pounds.

HUNTING ABILITY: Though the Wirehaired Pointing Griffon has been known in the U.S. since 1901, it has never acquired even a modicum of popularity with American hunters. It is seldom seen here. The reasons are many. For one, the breed is too slow to be suitable for many gamebird-hunting situations in this country. For another, the breed's coat and color fail to appeal to U.S. hunters.

The Griffon is not the best choice if the game to be hunted is such open-country birds as quail and

WIREHAIRED POINTING GRIFFON

Hungarian partridge. He is much better suited to heavy-cover work on such targets as woodcock and ruffed grouse. He is an excellent retriever on both land and water, being a strong swimmer and having a rough coat that affords excellent protection from frigid water and briary cover.

Despite those strong points, however, the Wirehaired Pointing Griffon is unable to compete on even terms with many of the established pointing breeds.

DISPOSITION: Because so few Wirehaired Pointing Griffons exist in the U.S. today, an accurate rundown on the breed's temperamental and mental makeup is difficult. However, these dogs are known to be quite intelligent. They learn their lessons well and take readily to training. It is safe to say that the breed is highly unlikely to have any behavioral quirks that would make it unsuitable as a hunting companion in the field or as a family pet.

Vizsla

HISTORY: More than 500 years ago, certain Magyar tribes, then the ruling element in Hungary, set about to develop a dog that would hunt all the many varieties of game that abounded in that country. Then (as now in most of Europe) dogs were expected to take game as it came—that is, be capable of trailing hare, wild boar, bears, and deer, as well as pointing and retrieving feathered game.

The result of that development was the Vizsla (properly pronounced "Veesh-lah"), also known as the Magyar Vizsla. Little is known about the early development of this breed, except that a generous amount of hound blood (probably bloodhound) was used. The early Vizsla differed only slightly from the other Continental pointing breeds (German Shorthair, German Wirehair, Brittany Spaniel, and Weimaraner).

Though famed in Hungary and elsewhere in Europe, the Vizsla was little known until after World War I, when fanciers of the breed formed clubs, held trials, and did much to publicize the breed. Col. Jeno Dus of the Hungarian Cavalry, genealogy registrar and breed supervisor, also did much to further the cause of the Vizsla in the U.S.

The Vizsla was recognized by the American Kennel Club in 1960. Many Vizslas are registered with the Field Dog Stud Book.

DESCRIPTION: No conformation standards have been set up for this breed, but in general the Vizsla is an average-size short-haired pointing dog having a neat, sleek appearance.

The Vizsla is often called the Yellow Pointer because of his sedge-colored (rich yellow or yellowish brown) coat. The coat is smooth and easily cared for. The tail, like that of all the other Continental breeds, is normally docked to one-third of its standard length. This is to prevent it from being cut and torn by briars and other rough cover.

SIZE: The Vizsla is about the same size as other shorthaired pointing dogs, standing about 25 inches

VIZSLA

high at the shoulder and having an average weight of about 70 pounds.

HUNTING ABILITY: The Vizsla—and the other Continental pointing breeds—has enjoyed a considerable increase in popularity among U.S. hunters in recent years. The breed's versatility in the field is the principal reason.

In the good old days—when game was plentiful, limits were generous, and hunting country was abundant—hunters sought rather specialized game dogs: a wide-ranging quail dog, an open-country pheasant dog, a close-working grouse dog. But today game is scarcer, hunting country is more restricted, and limits are lower. It's not practical for today's hunter to limit himself to one kind of game. He wants a dog that will help him get pheasants, quail, grouse, and woodcock, and maybe fetch ducks and even run a rabbit. The Vizsla is—or at least can be—such a dog.

The key to the development of any multipurpose dog is its training. Only by positive training in control and field work can a dog be made to handle many varieties of game satisfactorily.

No dog can be expected to excel in all forms of hunting. But the Vizsla will, if brought along patiently, find, point, and retrieve gamebirds. Training procedures should cover one kind of game at a time.

Generally, the Vizsla performs better as a close worker in heavy cover than he does as a wide-ranging animal in open country. Consequently, he is better on ruffed grouse and woodcock than on pheasants and quail. He is most popular in the midwestern U.S.

Field trials have done much to improve the field work of the Vizsla. The parent organization, the Vizsla Club, holds a national Vizsla trial each year.

DISPOSITION: The Vizsla's temperament is much like that of most of the Continental pointing breeds. He is quietly friendly, intelligent, and alert. He learns his lessons well, but the trainer must be sure that his pupil knows what is expected of him and how he (the dog) should do it. Many Vizslas do not take kindly to strangers, but they are not vicious. The breed makes a good home companion.

German Wirehaired Pointer

HISTORY: Much speculation and assumption is involved in tracing the origins of most dog breeds, and the German Wirehair is no exception. It is known, however, that this breed's development began in Germany about 1870, when it was known as the Deutsche Drahthaar.

According to historical accounts, the early Wirehairs represented a combination of the Wirehaired Pointing Griffon, the Deutsche Stichelhaar, and the Pudel-Pointer (those dogs being three other wire-coated German pointing breeds), as well as the German Shorthaired Pointer. It is likely that the German Wirehair's makeup also includes the blood of a strain of terrier.

The German Wirehair was first brought to the U.S. in about 1920. It was known as the Drahthaar until the American Kennel Club recognized it in 1959 (the Field Dog Stud Book recognized the breed some years earlier).

The first Wirehair to win an A.K.C.-licensed field trial was Haar Baron's Mike, who won the German Pointing Dog National in 1959. However, the individual Wirehair that probably had the most to do with publicizing the breed was Herr Schmardt v. Fox River. Owned by an Illinois couple, Mr. and Mrs. A. H. Gallagher, Schmardt was widely hunted in the Midwest, placed in many trials, and took part in numerous hunting-dog demonstrations. Mr. Gallagher was a prime mover in the German Drahthaar Pointer Club of America.

DESCRIPTION: The German Wirehaired Pointer resembles the German Shorthaired Pointer except for its coarse coat and whiskered face. Essentially a pointing dog in general type, the Wirehair is usually an aristocratic-looking animal of sturdy build, lively manner, and an intelligent, determined expression. That facial expression, on the other hand, can sometimes appear almost monkeylike.

The Wirehair's coat is straight, harsh, wiry, and rather flat-lying. Its color is best described as grizzle (gray), with sizable patches of liver or brown on the head and body. Rare individuals are self-colored (solid) brown.

The eyebrows are heavy, and there is a short beard and whiskers. The undercoat ranges from dense to quite thin, depending upon the season, and is sometimes absent. The tail is usually docked to one-third of its normal length.

The better Wirehairs are trim and agile, rather than blocky, though some individual specimens are heavy-boned and plodding.

SIZE: According to the American Kennel Club standard, the German Wirehair ranges in shoulder height from 22 to 26 inches. Weight averages 55 to 65 pounds.

HUNTING ABILITY: Like most of the other Continental pointing breeds, the German Wirehair is best described as a general-purpose hunting dog that points and retrieves. He is agile, has a fine nose, and he will work relatively close to the hunter, though he will move out there a fair distance if the situation calls for it. He is essentially taught his manners on game and just as quickly picks up the knack of fetching shot birds, including waterfowl.

What gamebirds will the breed work best? That depends on the individual dog and on his training. But generally, the breed does best in relatively thick cover on tight-sitting birds. Because of the coat's color, however, the Wirehair is a bit hard to see in heavy cover.

In general, the Wirehair has a bit more range than the Shorthair and a good deal more than the Weimaraner and Brittany Spaniel. The Wirehair's gait is freer and more flowing than that of the Weimaraner and the Shorthair.

For water work and in rugged cover, the Wirehair's rough coat gives him an edge over the other German breeds. And he has the drive and stamina to hunt hard all day. The Wirehair's coat dries out very fast. On the other hand, that coat tends to pick up a great quantity of burrs and dirt.

DISPOSITION: The German Wirehair is intelligent, sensitive, and inherently clownish, having quite a sense of humor. He is quick to learn, has a retentive memory, and is eager to please.

Like most intelligent dogs, however, the Wirehair requires firm (but not harsh) and consistent discipline. He is easily bored and will become mischievous if left to his own devices.

The Wirehair tends to be aloof or suspicious with strangers. But to those humans he knows he is ingratiatingly affectionate. He makes a good house dog and family companion.

GERMAN WIREHAIRED POINTER

PART 10

FIRST AID

FIRST AID

Let's suppose that you and a companion are well out in the woods on a fishing, hunting, or camping trip and one of the following mishaps occurs:

Your friend is bitten by a snake that escapes before either of you can identify it. Could you tell from the bite itself whether or not the snake was a poisonous species? If it was, what would you do?

Your companion suffers a severe fall and begins to act strangely. You fear that he may be going into shock. How do you tell for sure? How do you treat it?

You've made an ambitious hike on snowshoes on a brilliantly sunny day after a heavy snowfall the night before. Your eyes begin to burn and smart, your forehead aches, and you can't seem to stand the glare from the glistening snow—all symptoms of snow blindness. What do you do?

A toothache comes on suddenly and savagely. The nearest dentist is hours away by foot and car. Is there anything you can do to ease the pain?

The outdoor sports—as proved by studies made by American insurance companies—are among the safest of pastimes. But accidents do happen, and a knowledge of first aid procedures is especially important to outdoors enthusiasts, whose favorite haunts are seldom down the street from the doctor's office or within arm's reach of a telephone.

Most accidents or maladies suffered in the outdoors are minor. But if a serious injury should occur, these actions should be taken, in the order given:

1. Give urgently needed first aid immediately: stop severe bleeding, restore breathing, treat for poisoning, treat for shock. Keep the victim lying down.

2. Examine the victim as carefully—and calmly—as you can, and try to determine the extent of his injuries.

3. Send someone for help if possible. If not, try signaling with a rifle (three quick shots are a widely recognized distress signal) or by building a smoky fire.

4. Take necessary first aid steps for secondary injuries, making patient as comfortable as possible and moving him only if absolutely necessary.

This chapter will give detailed step-by-step procedures for every first aid situation the outdoors person is likely to run into. It should be remembered, however, that these procedures, though vitally important, aren't the only form of first aid. The victim's mental distress also needs treatment. A reassuring word, a smile, your obvious willingness and ability to help—all will have an encouraging effect. The knowledgeable first-aider also knows what *not* to do and thereby avoids compounding the problem by making errors that could be serious.

The procedures and instructions that follow reflect recommendations of the American National Red Cross, the American Medical Association, the United States Department of Agriculture, and of course respected physicians.

BLEEDING

External Bleeding. If a large blood vessel is severed, death from loss of blood can result in 3 to 5 minutes. So it is vital to stop the bleeding at once. Always do so, if possible, by applying pressure directly over the wound.

Use a clean cloth—a handkerchief, an item of clothing, or whatever else is near at hand. Use your bare hand if nothing else is available, and then, once the bleeding is under control, apply a cloth. Put on additional layers of cloth, and when the covering is substantial, bandage snugly with strips of cloth cut from a bedsheet, neckties, or similar materials. Don't remove the bandage. If it becomes saturated with blood, put on more layers of cloth, and perhaps tighten the dressing directly over the wound.

If you are sure that no bones are broken, try to raise the bleeding area higher than the rest of the body.

If extremely quick action is needed, or if the above method fails to stop the flow of blood, you may be able to diminish the flow by pressing your fingers or the heel of your hand at one of two pressure points. One of these is located on the inner half of the arm midway between elbow and armpit; pressure applied here will reduce bleeding in the lower area of the arm. Pressure on the other point, located just below the groin on the front, inner half of the thigh, will reduce bleeding on the extremity below that point.

Internal Bleeding. Often caused by a severe fall or a violent blow, bleeding within the body can be difficult to diagnose, though it may be revealed by bleeding from the nose or mouth when no injury can be detected in those organs. Other symptoms may include restlessness, nausea, anxiety, a weak and rapid pulse, thirst, paleness, and general weakness.

The first treatment procedure is to use pillows, knapsacks, folded clothes, or something similar to raise the victim's head and shoulders if he is having difficulty breathing. Otherwise, place him flat on his back.

Keep him as immobile as possible, and try to have him control the movements caused by vomiting. Turn his head to the side for vomiting.

Do not give stimulants, even if the bleeding seems to stop.

If victim loses consciousness, turn him on his side, with head and chest lower than hips.

Medical care is a must. Get the victim to a doctor or hospital as soon as possible.

Nosebleed. Nosebleeds often occur "for no reason," while at other times they are caused by an injury. Most of them are more annoying than serious. It

THREE WAYS TO REDUCE EXTERNAL BLEEDING

Left: To control heavy bleeding, apply pressure directly over wound using clean cloth. Another way to stop heavy bleeding is to apply pressure to one of two main pressure points: inner part of arm between elbow and armpit (**center**), and just below groin on inner part of thigh (**right**).

occasionally happens, though, that the bleeding is heavy and prolonged and this can be dangerous.

The person should remain quiet, preferably in a sitting position with his head thrown back or lying down with head and shoulders raised.

Pinch the victim's nostrils together, keeping the pressure on for 5 to 10 minutes. If bleeding doesn't stop, pack gauze lightly into the bleeding nostril and then pinch.

Sometimes the application of cold wet towels to the face will help.

Use of Tourniquet. According to The American National Red Cross, the use of a tourniquet to stop bleeding in an extremity is "justifiable only rarely." Because its use involves a high risk of losing a limb, a tourniquet should be applied only if the bleeding seems sure to cause death.

Use only a wide, strong piece of cloth—never a narrow strip of material such a rope or wire. Wrap the cloth around the upper part of the limb above the wound, and tie a simple overhand knot (half a square knot). Place a short stick on the knot, and tie another simple overhand knot (that is, complete the square knot) over the stick. Twist the stick just enough to stop the bleeding. Loosen the binding (untwist stick) for a few seconds every 15 minutes.

Once the bleeding has been controlled, keep the victim quiet and warm. If he is conscious and can swallow easily, give him some water or maybe some weak tea—no alcoholic drinks. If he is not conscious, or if abdominal or other internal injuries are suspected, do not give him any fluid.

ARTIFICIAL RESPIRATION

Artificial respiration, now commonly called *resuscitation,* is the technique of causing air to flow into and out of the lungs of a person whose normal breathing has stopped. Causes of stoppage of normal breathing include inhalation of water, smoke, or gas, electric shock, choking, and drug overdose. In most instances, death will result within 6 minutes unless artificial respiration is administered.

The treatment may also be needed if breathing does not stop completely but becomes slow and shallow and the victim's lips, tongue, and fingernails turn blue. If you're in doubt, give artificial respiration—it is seldom harmful and can save a life.

Before beginning any of the artificial respiration methods described below, check the victim's mouth and throat opening for obstructions; remove any foreign objects and loose dentures.

APPLYING A TOURNIQUET

Since a tourniquet can cause the loss of the affected limb, it should be applied only when no other means will reduce blood flow enough to prevent the victim from bleeding to death. **Left:** Wrap strong, wide cloth around limb above wound, and tie a simple overhand knot. **Center:** Place a short stick on the knot and tie another overhand knot over the stick, and twist stick to stem bleeding. **Right:** Bind stick with ends of tourniquet, but be sure to loosen it every 15 minutes.

Mouth-to-Mouth. Place the victim on his back. Put one hand under the victim's neck. At the same time, place the other hand on his forehead and tilt the head back.

Using the hand that was under the neck, pull the victim's chin up, thereby insuring a free air passage. Take a deep breath, place your mouth over the victim's mouth, trying to make the seal as airtight as possible, and pinch the victim's nostrils closed. Blow into the victim's mouth until you see his chest rise.

Lift your head from the victim, and take another deep breath while his chest falls, causing him to exhale. Repeat the process. For the first few minutes, do so as rapidly as the victim's lungs are emptied. After that, do it about 12 times per minute.

If the victim is an infant or small child, use the same procedure, but place your mouth over both the mouth and nose, and force air into his lungs gently.

HEART STOPPAGE (CPR)

If artificial respiration produces no response in an injured person, it may mean that his heart has stopped beating. You can make a fairly certain diagnosis by checking his pulse at the wrist and holding your ear to the victim's chest. If you feel no pulse

MOUTH-TO-MOUTH RESUSCITATION FOR ADULTS

Lift victim's neck with one hand and tilt the head back by holding top of the head with other hand.

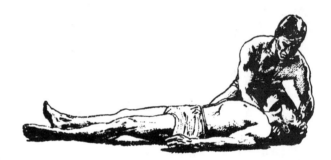

Pull victim's chin up with the hand that was lifting the neck. This insures a free air passage.

Take a deep breath, place your mouth over victim's mouth and pinch his nostrils. Breathe into his lungs until you see his chest rise. Remove your mouth and let him exhale. Repeat cycle as rapidly as victim's lungs empty themselves first few minutes, then 15 times per minute.

MOUTH-TO-MOUTH RESUSCITATION FOR A CHILD

Lift victim's neck with your right hand and with your left lift his lower jaw so that it juts out.

Place your mouth over the victim's *mouth and nose,* making a leakproof seal, and force air into his lungs gently until you see the chest rise and you feel the lungs expand.

CHEST COMPRESSIONS

Heart stoppage: employing the extended chest compressions (CPR), using weight of upper part of your body.

and hear no heartbeat, you will have to use external heart massage (Cardiopulmonary Resuscitation—CPR) in addition to artificial respiration.

Here are the warning signs of a heart attack:

1. Pressure; feeling of "fullness"; squeezing or pain in the center of the chest lasting more than two minutes.
2. Pain radiating to shoulders, neck, jaw, arms or back. Tingling sensation down left arm.
3. Dizziness, weakness, sweating, or nausea. Pale complexion and shortness of breath.

If the victim's heart and breathing have stopped, begin CPR. The technique involves mouth-to-mouth resuscitation, which delivers air to the lungs, and chest compressions, which help circulate the blood.

MOUTH-TO-MOUTH RESUSCITATION

Remember the ABCs: airway, breathing, and circulation, in that order.

Airway. If there are no head, neck, or back injuries, gently tilt the victim's head and raise the chin.

This will lift the tongue and ensure a clear air passage. Check for breathing by placing your ear over the victim's mouth and feeling for any exhalation.

Breathing. If the person is not breathing, pinch his nose, take a deep breath, and place your mouth over his. Breathe into his lungs two times slowly—1½ to 2 seconds each time. If victim's chest does not rise, re-tilt head and repeat the cycle at the rate of 12 times per minute, until the victim can breathe on his own.

Circulation. Check for a pulse. Keeping the victim's head tilted, place your index and middle fingers on the victim's Adam's apple, and then slide your fingers down to the next "ridge" on the neck. This is where you'll find the carotid artery. Press firmly to determine if there's a pulse. If there isn't one, proceed with chest compressions.

CHEST COMPRESSION

Postitioning yourself perpendicular to the victim, place the heel of one hand on the lower third of the victim's sternum (breastbone). Place your other hand on top of the first one. Press down firmly with both hands about 1½ to 2 inches and then lift both hands to let the chest expand. Repeat at a rate of 80 to 100 compressions a minute. The mouth-to-mouth breathing should continue at the rate of two steady lung inflations after every 15 chest compressions.

CHOKING

More than one person has died from choking on a fish bone, an inadvertently swallowed hard object, a piece of food that went down the "wrong pipe," and the like. Anything that lodges in the throat or air passages must be removed as soon as possible. Here's how to do it:

If the victim is conscious, give him four back blows between the shoulder blades. If the victim is lying down—roll him on his side, facing you with his chest against your knee. If the victim is sitting or standing—you should be behind and to one side of him. If the victim is an infant—face him on your forearm, head down. Make sharp blows with the heel of your hand on the spine, directly between his shoulder blades.

If this doesn't remove the object, and the victim is standing or sitting, employ the Heimlich maneuver: (**1**) Stand behind the victim and wrap your arms around his waist. (**2**) Place the thumb side of your fist against the victim's upper abdomen, just below the rib cage. (**3**) Grasp your fist with your other hand and press into the victim's abdomen with two or three quick upward thrusts.

If the victim is in a lying position, do this: (**1**) Place him on his back and kneel close to his side.

CHOKING: BACK BLOWS

If the choking victim is conscious, give four back blows between the shoulder blades in hopes of dislodging the obstruction. If this doesn't work, employ the Heimlich maneuver.

CHOKING: HEIMLICH MANEUVER

If the choking victim is standing and back slaps do not dislodge the obstruction, apply the Heimlich maneuver shown here and described in accompanying text.

LYING ABDOMINAL THRUST

If the choking victim is lying down, assume the position shown and perform the steps described in text.

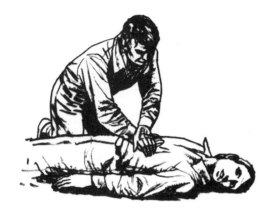

(2) Place your hands, one on top of the other, with the heel of the bottom hand in the middle of the abdomen, just below the rib cage. (3) Rock forward so that your shoulders are directly over the victim's abdomen and press toward the victim's diaphragm with a quick forward thrust. (4) Don't press to either side.

If the victim is unconscious, tilt the head back and attempt to give the victim artificial respiration. If this fails, give the victim four back blows in rapid succession. If the object has still not been forced out of the air passages, then stand behind the victim, put both your fists into his abdomen, and give eight upward thrusts.

Finally, if none of these methods works, you should insert your index finger deep into the victim's throat, using a hooking action to try to dislodge the object.

SMALL CHILD: Put one arm around the youngster's waist from behind, and lift him up so that his head and upper torso are leaning toward the ground. With your free hand, give him several sharp taps between the shoulder blades. When the object has been dislodged, clear his throat with your fingers, and pull the tongue forward.

INFANT: Hold him up by the ankles, head hanging straight down. Open his mouth, pull his tongue forward, and the object will likely fall out. If not, give him a tap or two on the back.

SHOCK

Medical (traumatic) shock is a depressed condition of many bodily functions and is usually caused by loss of blood following a serious injury (a burn, wound, fracture, exposure, and the like). However, some degree of shock can result from even minor injuries and from psychological shock.

Prolonged shock can result in death even if the injury causing it would not be fatal otherwise. In every health emergency, the possibility of shock should be considered. Signs of shock include the following: vacant and lackluster eyes and dilated pupils, shallow or irregular breathing, weak or seemingly absent pulse, skin that is pale and moist and cooler than it should be, nausea, perspiration, restlessness, thirst, and unconsciousness.

Symptoms usually develop gradually and may not be apparent at first. Even if a severly injured person exhibits none of the signs, shock is a real danger, and the following steps should be taken:

Keep the victim lying down, preferably with his head lower than the rest of his body. *Exception:* If there is difficulty in breathing, the head and chest should be elevated.

Raise his legs 8 to 12 inches. *Exception:* Do not raise the legs if there is a head injury, if breathing difficulty is thereby increased, or if the patient complains of pain during the raising process. If you are in doubt about the correct position, keep the victim lying flat.

HOW TO TREAT FOR SHOCK

In most cases, treatment for shock includes keeping the victim warm and elevating the feet. But there are exceptions, as described in accompanying text.

Keep the victim warm. If the weather is cold or damp, cover him and put a blanket underneath as well. Do not overheat; keep him just warm enough to prevent his shivering.

Fluids can have value in shock, but don't give the victim liquids unless medical help will be delayed at least an hour. If the victim is conscious and able to swallow, give him water that is neither hot nor cold—a few sips at first and then increasing the amount. If medical help will be considerably delayed, give the victim half-glass doses (at 15-minute intervals) of a solution made by adding 1 teaspoon of salt and ½ teaspoon of baking soda to 1 quart of water. Do not give any fluids if the victim is only partly conscious, if an abdominal injury is suspected, or if he is nauseated.

FEVER

A rise in body temperature is a signal that something is amiss internally. There are many causes of fever, infection being the most common. In fact, fever is one of the body's defense mechanisms against infection. But if the fever reaches 104°F or higher, it may become a danger in itself. Here's what to do:

Get the victim into bed, and take his temperature if possible.

Send for a doctor.

Sponge the victim's body with cool or lukewarm water, treating one part of the body at a time and keeping the other parts covered.

Apply an ice bag or cool cloths to his head.

If he is conscious and there is no evidence of abdominal injury, give him some cold water to drink.

ORAL POISONING

If the victim has ingested poisonous material and is unconscious or otherwise unable to tell you what it was, you may be able to ascertain the source by the odor on his breath, discoloration on his lips or mouth, or a telltale container nearby.

Speed is vital in treating the victim of poisoning. You must take the following steps quickly, before the body has a chance to absorb much of the poison:

If you know the antidote (antidotes are printed on containers of almost all potentially dangerous materials) and if it is at hand, give it at once.

If not, dilute the poison by giving the victim four or more glasses of milk or water.

Call a doctor or hospital if possible.

Induce vomiting by sticking your finger into the victim's throat or by making him drink a glass of warm water into which have been mixed 2 tablespoons of salt. *Exceptions:* Do not induce vomiting if the victim is unconscious, has pain or a burning sensation in mouth or throat, has swallowed a petroleum product (gasoline, kerosene, white gas, or the like) or any acid or any alkali (caustic soda, an ammonia solution, and so on).

When the vomiting begins, position the victim face down, with his head lower than his hips, to prevent the expelled material from getting into his lungs.

If you can't identify the poison, save some of the vomitus for subsequent examination by a physician or hospital laboratory.

SNAKEBITE

It is doubtful whether any other first aid situation is more feared and less understood than snakebite. And there is little agreement, even among leading authorities, about its treatment.

About 6,500 humans are bitten by poisonous snakes in the U.S. each year. Of those, only about 350 are hunters or fishermen. And the death rate is very low, an average of 15 persons annually in the entire country. Most of those bites occur south of an imaginary line drawn from North Carolina to southern California. More than half occur in Texas, North Carolina, Florida, Georgia, Louisiana, and Arkansas.

There are four kinds of poisonous snakes in the U.S. Three are of the pit-viper variety: rattlesnakes, copperheads, and cottonmouth moccasins. The fourth, the coral snake, is a member of the cobra family. The pit vipers are so named because they have a small deep depression between the eyes and the nostrils. The coral snake has broad red and black bands separated by narrow yellow bands, giving rise to the saying, "Red on yellow, kill a fellow."

The bite of a poisonous snake—except for the coral snake, which chews rather than bites—is in the form of fang punctures of the skin. If you are bitten by a snake that leaves two U-shaped rows of tooth marks on your skin, relax—it is almost certainly a nonpoisonous snake. The bite of a nonpoisonous snake produces little pain or swelling.

Symptoms of the bite of a venomous snake include immediate pain, swelling and discoloration in the area of the wound, general weakness, nausea and vomiting, a weak and rapid pulse, dimming of vision, faintness, and eventually unconsciousness.

Most medical authorities now agree that the preferred treatment for snakebite is antivenin administered as quickly as possible after the bite. If a snakebite victim is within a two-hour drive of a medical facility, get the person there as fast and as calmly as possible. Keep the bite location immoble, even if you have to splint it. Also keep the bitten body part below the level of the heart. A snakebite victim may walk up to a half-hour before symptoms start. If the distance is longer to transportation, the victim should be carried. If you are alone, you should still be able to walk several hours before symptoms start. If possible, kill the snake and take the head with you. Use caution: The head of a snake can still bite through reflex action up to one hour after it is killed.

Most bites, however, occur in the field, often

NORTH AMERICAN POISONOUS SNAKES

2. EASTERN DIAMONDBACK Body has dark diamonds with light borders along a tan or light brown background. Diamonds gradually change to bands in the tail. Habitat is lowland thickets, palmettos, flatwoods.

1. COTTONMOUTH Eastern cottonmouths as well as Florida and Western cottonmouths are frequently confused with nonpoisonous water snakes. Cottonmouths have dark blotches on an olive body and broad, flat heads.

3. CORAL SNAKE Dangerously poisonous, but its small mouth prevents it from biting most parts of the body. Red and black rings wider than interspaced yellow rings. Habitat is open woods in East and loose soil and rocks in West.

4. COPPERHEAD Large chestnut brown cross bands on a pale pinkish or reddish-brown surface with a copper tinge on head. Habitat in North is wooded mountains and stone walls; lowland swamps, and wooded suburbs in South.

5. WESTERN DIAMONDBACK Light brown to black diamond-shaped blotches along light gray, tan and sometimes pink background. Also has black and white bands of about equal width around tail. Habitat includes woods, rocky hills, desert and farmland.

6. TIMBER RATTLER AND CANEBRAKE RATTLER In the South, dark streak from canebrake's eye to mouth. Dark chevrons and rusty stripe along midline. In the North, timber rattler has yellowish body and dark phase in parts of its range. Habitat for the canebrake is lowland brush and stream borders. The timber rattler prefers rocky wooded hills.

many miles from a road, so the victim cannot always get antivenin quick enough. Survival in such cases depends upon the first aid steps taken by the victim and his companions. And here is where the disagreement among medical authorities is most prevalent.

The best and most up-to-date tactics for treating snakebite seem to be those advocated by Dr. Clifford C. Snyder, chairman of the Division of Plastic Surgery at the University of Utah and chief of surgery at the Veterans Hospital in Salt Lake City. Dr. Snyder is rated among the world's foremost authorities on snakebite.

Here's what to do, according to Dr. Snyder, if a poisonous snakebite occurs in a remote area where medical help is not readily available.

Avoid exertion and excitement. Sit down, and try to calm yourself. Panic could bring on shock.

Kill the snake if you can. Take it with you when you leave, for identification later.

Apply a constricting band—belt, tie, shirtsleeve, or handkerchief—between the bite and the heart. If the bite is on a leg or arm, put the constricting band 2 to 3 inches above the bite. But be sure it is above the swelling. Use no constricting band if the bite is on the face. *The constricting band should be loose enough so that you can insert a finger beneath it without force.* Any tighter, and it may cut off blood circulation. Such a loose band can be left in place for an hour without harm. Don't loosen it every few minutes, as many handbooks suggest (periodic

SNAKEBITE TREATMENT

Make a linear ½-inch incision through each fang mark and parallel with the affected finger or limb. Gently force venom from the incisions, using finger pressure or a suction device.

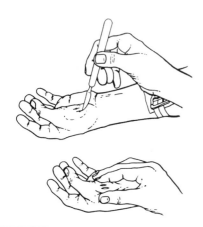

loosening tends to actually "milk" venom from the bite into the body, according to Dr. Snyder's studies.)

Sterilize the fang wounds with a sponge soaked in alcohol.

Using a scalpel, or a knife sterilized in flame, make ½-inch linear incisions through each fang mark—the cuts should extend ¼ inch past each puncture. Deepen the cut through skin and fat, but do not cut into muscle, tendon, or nerve. *Do not use cross incisions through fang marks,* as suggested in some publications.

Squeeze venom gently from the incisions with the fingers. Do so for 30 to 60 minutes or for as long as it takes to get the victim to a doctor. Do not use oral suction.

If ice is handy, put some into a towel, shirt, or other such makeshift "bag," and apply it to the area of the bite—but for no longer than one hour. Keeping the wound cool will slow absorption. Do not *pack* the limb in ice or bind the ice tightly to the skin. Be sure to remove the ice gradually—sudden removal can result in rapid uptake of the venom.

In an emergency, antivenin can be injected in the field, but the instructions printed on each package must be followed rigidly, and the required test for allergy (many persons are allergic to the horse-blood serum from which antivenin is prepared) must have proven negative.

Get the victim to a doctor or a hospital as soon as possible but without exertion on his part.

Alcoholic beverages, Dr. Snyder points out, are worse than useless to the snakebite victim. They are likely to speed the uptake of the venom.

Outdoors people would do well to take along a snakebite kit on all trips into a terrain known to contain poisonous snakes. Such a kit should include the following items: (**1**) constricting band, (**2**) two surgical prep sponges presaturated with alcohol and protected in aluminum foil, (**3**) a disposable scalpel in foil, (**4**) one kit of antivenin. The sponges and scalpel can be bought at a drug store.

COPING WITH BUGS

The outdoors is a great place, but bugs can turn a pleasant day into a nightmare. You can fight back! There are five bugs that will give you the most trouble: mosquitoes, black flies, no-see-ums, deerflies, and ticks. Mosquitoes, the worst of the bunch, are most active at dawn and dusk. Mosquitoes are attracted to dark colors, so wear light-colored clothing. Black flies draw blood. Male black flies use blood for food, and the female needs blood to complete her breeding cycle. Common throughout Canada and the northern United States, black flies bite

HOW TO BATTLE THE BUGS

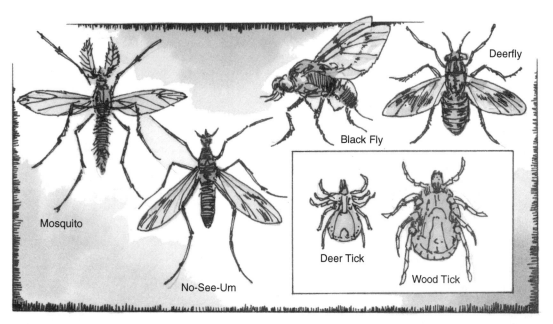

Deerfly

Black Fly

Mosquito

No-See-Um

Deer Tick

Wood Tick

MOSQUITOES home in on warmth, carbon dioxide, and the odor of human skin. Your best weapon is a repellant on your skin that will set up a barrier that will confuse the mosquito's sensors.

BLACK FLIES are inactive at night but a problem during the day. You will rearely feel the bite. The first thing you may notice is the blood. If you get bitten and begin to itch, coat bites with alcohol or witch hazel.

DEERFLIES are found anywhere in the Northern woods, and both sexes can inflict painful bites. Use a headnet and tape cuffs, but be aware that deerflies can also bite through clothing.

NO-SEE-UMS are troublesome because it is difficult to protect yourself from them. They can fit through headnets, screens, clothing—almost anything. A repellent helps, but the only sure cure is a stiff wind.

DEER TICKS pose a Lyme disease threat. They are half the size of the common wood tick and orange-brown with a black spot near the head. Symptoms of Lyme disease include red ring-shaped rash, fever, chills, headache, stiff joints, and fatigue. Learn how to identify ticks and remove them from your body with tweezers. Don't burn, twist or crush a tick on your body.

as soon as they land and they zero in on the face, hairline, wrists, and ankles. Peak period is the spring and the early summer. Aside from using a repellent, you should wear a hat, tuck pants into socks, tape cuffs around ankles, and wear long sleeves. No-see-ums are so small you can't see them, but they hurt when they bite. You find no-see-ums along lakes, beaches, and marshes. The deerfly is another painful biter and will attack the face, legs, arms, and neck. Once again, wear light-colored clothes. The tick, because of the threat of Lyme disease, is our most dangerous pest. Wear light-colored clothes, tuck pants into socks, and avoid wooded areas, high grass, and use a tick repellent. The most effective repellent against these bugs contains DEET.

BEE STINGS

Stinging insects are seldom more than an annoyance, even if they hit the target on your hide. Some people, however, are highly allergic to the stings of certain insects. If you or a member of your party has had a severe reaction to a bee sting in the past and is again stung, take the following steps:

Use a tight constricting band above the sting if it is on an arm or leg. Loosen the band for a few seconds every 15 minutes.

Apply an icepack or cold cloths to the sting area.

Get the victim to a doctor as soon as possible.

For the average bee-sting victim, these procedures will suffice:

Remove the stinger with tweezers.

Make a paste of baking soda and cold cream (if it is available), and apply it to the sting area.

Apply cold cloths to help ease the pain.

If there is itching, use calamine lotion.

SPIDER AND SCORPION BITES

Scorpions are most common in the southwestern U.S. and are found in such spots as cool and damp buildings, debris, and under loose banks. Most species of scorpions in the U.S. are nonpoisonous; few of their stings are dangerous.

The biting spiders in the U.S. include the black widow, the brown widow, and the tarantula. The brown widow—its abdomen has a dull-orange hourglass marking against a brown body—is harmless in almost all cases. The tarantula is a large (up to 3 inches long, not including the legs) and hairy spider, but despite its awesome appearance its bite is almost always harmless, though it may cause allergic reactions in sensitive persons. The black widow—the female's body is about ½ inch long, shiny black, usually with a red hourglass marking on the underside of the abdomen—has a poisonous bite, but its victims almost always recover.

The symptoms of these bites may include some swelling and redness, immediate pain that may—especially with a black-widow bite—become quite severe and spread throughout the body, much sweating, nausea, and difficulty in breathing and speaking.

First aid procedures are as follows:

Keep the victim warm and calm, lying down.

Apply a wide constricting band above the bite, loosening it every 15 minutes.

Apply wrapped-up ice or cold compresses to the bite area.

Get medical help as quickly as possible.

CHIGGER AND TICK BITES

The irritation produced by chiggers, which are the larval stage of a mite, results from fluid the tiny insects inject. Chiggers do not burrow under the skin, as is often suggested.

Since chiggers do not usually attach themselves to the skin until an hour or more after they reach the body, bathing promptly after exposure, using a brush and soapy water, may eliminate them. Once the bites have been inflicted, application of ice water may help. The itching and discomfort can be relieved

REMOVING TICK WITH TWEEZERS

Since ticks may carry any of various disease vectors, it's important to remove embedded ticks promptly to lessen chances that you will be infected.

by applying calamine lotion or a paste made of baking soda and a little water.

Ticks—flat, usually brown, and about ¼ inch long—attach themselves to the skin by making a tiny puncture, and they feed by sucking blood. They can thereby transmit the germs of several diseases, including Rocky Mountain spotted fever and Lyme disease. A newer strain, Granulocytic Ehrlichiosis, has flu-like symptoms nearly identical to Lyme disease. Protecting yourself from Granulocytic Ehrlichiosis is the same as with Lyme disease.

If you have been in a tick-infested area, be sure to examine your clothes and body for the insects, paying particular attention to hairy areas. Removing ticks promptly is insurance against the transmission of any germs they may be carrying since that process seldom begins until 6 hours or so after the insect attaches itself and begins to feed.

Use tweezers to remove a tick, but don't yank—that may cause the tick's head or mouth parts to break off and remain in the flesh. Pull it gently, taking care not to crush the body, which may be full of germs. If it can't be pulled off gently, cover the entire tick with heavy oil, which closes off its breathing pores and may make it disengage itself.

THE DEER HUNTER AND LYME DISEASE

Not very long ago, a lucky deer hunter would simply roll up his sleeves and field-dress his buck with no concern for his safety. It's a much different story today because of the comparatively new threat of picking up Lyme disease from a deer tick on your buck.

A deer tick is a speck of a bug, but unnoticed on your body, its bite can infect you with a spirochete bacteria that produces the crippling Lyme disease. Deer ticks are found on a wide variety of wild and domestic animals, but about 75 percent of the deer ticks live on whitetail deer. This means that deer hunters have a greater risk of Lyme disease than most other sportsmen.

Hunters should take certain precautions in the woods. Most hunters will be wearing high boots, but you should start tucking in the bottom of your pant legs. If you prefer to wear your pants stagged outside your boots, so your pants shed rain and snow outside your boots rather than inside, use masking tape to close off your cuffs. Before you go into the woods, spray yourself with a good tick repellent. There are several on the market that will do the job, especially if it contains the ingredient DEET.

After a day of deer or small-game hunting, check your body for ticks. The bite of a deer tick is painless, so you may never know you've been bitten unless you look for a tick or signs of a bite. Look wherever you have hair. Check your scalp, the back of your neck and head. Two favorite spots are your armpits and groin. It's important to check everywhere.

If you find a tick, don't panic. Grab the tick as close to the skin as possible and pull outward slowly and steady. Don't twist or jerk the tick out, which may break off parts of the tick in your skin. Squeezing is also risky because you may release bacteria into your body.

We know that it takes at least several hours for a deer tick to release its bacteria into your bloodstream, so it's critical to remove the tick as quickly as possible. When the tick is out, wash and disinfect the bite area thoroughly. If you see signs of redness or a rash, call a doctor immediately.

Many old hunters have field-dressed bucks with bare hands and may frown on the idea of wearing surgical gloves. But Lyme disease is a serious threat and can result in headaches, fever, muscle weakness, and an arthritic condition that can persist for years. Surgical gloves can give you a degree of protection.

There is no doubt that if you're handling a deer carcass you are in a high risk situation. Deer ticks thrive on warm blood. Once an animal cools, these deer ticks will lose interest and jump on the closest warm body . . . and that may be you.

Don't load a deer into the back of a van and leave camp with the heater on full blast. This is a high risk situation. The hunters may well arrive at home with a few ticks in residence on their bodies. Therefore, the best place to transport a deer is on the roof of your vehicle or the open bed of a pickup truck, where it will cool properly and the deer ticks can drop off without finding a warm human body to infect.

Finally, the best solution is to hang the deer outside, whenever possible, for at least 12 hours or overnight. The ticks should have left the carcass by then.

POISON IVY, POISON OAK, AND POISON SUMAC

We cannot escape from poison ivy, poison oak, and poison sumac. There are virtually no areas in the United States in which at least one of these plants does not exist. Poison ivy is found throughout the country, with the possible exception of California and Nevada. Poison oak occurs in the southeastern states, and a western variety exists in the West Coast states. Poison sumac grows in most of the states in the eastern one-third of the country.

If you're lucky, you may be one of the 50 percent of the population who are not sensitive to these poisonous plants. If you are not lucky, however, and you've already had a few run-ins with poison ivy, oak, or sumac, you better know how to identify it and learn where it grows. Poison ivy grows along streams, lakes, and on sunny hillsides. It can also grow as a shrub, a small tree, or vine.

If you want to avoid poison ivy and poison oak, beware of low or vinelike three-leaved plants, which in fruit have creamy white berries. Poison sumac has ivory to grayish white berries. Poison sumac likes wet ground, so you are less likely to come in contact with it if you keep your boots dry.

Urushiol is the sticky, colorless oil that comes from the leaves and stems of poison ivy that, when it gets on our skin, causes the poison oak and poison sumac irritation. Urushiol in poison ivy is nearly the same in poison oak and poison sumac. If you're sensitive to one, you're sensitive to all of them.

If you don't wash the poison sap off your skin quickly, you will develop a rash within a couple of days. The rash will eventually produce swollen patches with blisters that will break and ooze.

POISONOUS PLANTS

Poison Ivy

Poison Oak

Poison Sumac

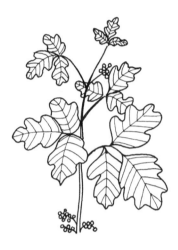

Poison ivy and poison oak: Beware of low or vinelike three-leaved plants, which in fruit have creamy white berries. Poison sumac has ivory to grayish white berries; but since poison sumac likes wet ground, you'll be less likely to come in contact with it if you keep your boots dry.

Healing will take about two weeks, no matter what you do, but here is some advice to ease the intense itching and promote healing. The best medicine against poison ivy is cortisone, if given within the first 24 hours. Oral prednisone will also help. If you are sensitive to poison ivy, take a supply of cortisone along on your trips.

Here are other remedies that will at least relieve some of the symptoms:

1) Cool compresses with Burow's solution will ease itching and speed up the drying process. Apply them for 15 minutes three or four times a day.
2) Calamine lotion will also relieve the itching.
3) Oatmeal baths are helpful. Add a cup of Aveeno oatmeal to the tub and soak in it for 15 minutes two or three times a day.
4) Aloe vera will aid in skin healing. Apply the lotion twice a day.
5) Oral antihistamines will help eliminate the itch-

ing, but antihistamine lotions don't help. Don't use anesthetic sprays and lotions may actually sensitize the skin and irritate the rash.
6) If you're very sensitive to poison ivy, try Ivy Shield, an organic clay barrier that will give 95 percent protection to the skin.
7) If you come in contact with poison ivy, shower with soap and water immediately.

The best protection is learning how to identify these plants and avoid them. The shiny leaves grow in groups of three, so try to remember "leaves of three, beware of me."

THERMAL BURNS

Burns are classified according to degree. In first-degree burns, the skin is reddened. In second-degree burns, blisters develop. Third-degree burns result in destruction of tissue and the cells that form new skin. Another important factor in determining the seriousness of any burn is the extent of the affected area.

The following first aid procedures have the primary objectives of treating shock (a major hazard that can quickly cause death in severely burned persons), relieving pain, and preventing contamination.

Here is how to treat relatively minor first- and second-degree burns:

For first-degree burns, medical treatment is usually not required. To relieve pain, apply cold water applications to the affected area or submerge the burned area in cold water. A dry dressing may be applied, if desired.

For second-degree burns (minor), immerse the burned parts in cold water (not ice water) or apply freshly ironed or laundered cloths that have been wrung out in ice water until the pain subsides. Immediate cooling can reduce the burning effect of heat in the deeper layers of skin. Never add salt to ice water; it lowers the temperature and may produce further injury. Gently blot the area dry with sterile gauze, a clean cloth, a towel, or other household linen. Don't use absorbent cotton. Apply dry, sterile gauze or a clean cloth as a protective dressing. Don't break blisters or remove shreds of tissue, and don't use an antiseptic preparation, ointment, spray, or home remedy on a severe burn.

Because the degree of a burn is often difficult to determine at first, it pays—except with obviously minor burns—to seek medical help.

Here is how to treat extensive second- and third-degree burns:

If a doctor or hospital is within easy reach, cover the burn with a sterile (or at least clean) dressing, treat for shock (procedures for shock appear elsewhere in this section), and rush the victim to the doctor or a hospital.

If the burn occurs in a remote area, take the following steps:

Remove all clothing from the burn area, cutting around any cloth that may adhere to the flesh and leaving it there (trying to remove it may well worsen the wound).

Apply a sterile dry dressing to the entire burn area. Do not treat a serious burn with any substance; that is, don't apply ointment, antiseptic, oil, or anything similar. Cover the dressing with at least six more layers of dressing (or clean tightly woven cloth material). Try not to rupture blisters.

Bandage the dressings in place. Make the bandage snug enough to protect the burned area from possible contamination from the air but not so tight as to cut off circulation.

Treat for shock, if medical help will be delayed

for more than an hour. Give the victim the shock solution: 1 teaspoon of salt and 1 teaspoon of baking soda in 1 quart of water.

Arrange for medical help as quickly as possible, notifying authorities that plasma may be needed.

Don't try to change the dressing. That is a job for a doctor.

SUNBURN

Not everyone is aware of this genuine health hazard from the solar system. The National Cancer Institute estimates 600,000 malignancies a year as a direct result of careless exposure to the sun. Of that number, close to 7,000 people will die from malignant melanoma, the most deadly skin cancer.

The sun is the bad guy, causing at least 90 percent of all skin cancers. Fortunately, the sun warns its victims with early symptoms. Those symptoms include those fashionable tans we see around town and which we usually ignore.

The sun produces two different types of UV rays, both harmful to the skin. Beta rays (UVB) can cause skin cancer. Alpha rays (UVA) cause both skin cancer and premature wrinkling of the skin. The easiest and most effective way of protecting yourself from these rays is through the use of a good sunscreen that is rated with a SPF (sun protection factor) of at least 15.

There are sunscreens with ratings of SPF 35 and higher. In most cases, a rating of SPF 15 is all that is necessary for daily use. With a SPF 15, a person can stay in the sun 15 times longer than without any protection at all.

Some doctors claim that regular use of a SPF 15 for the first 18 years of life may reduce the risk of skin cancer by 78 percent. For this reason, it's extremely important for parents to remember to keep small children out of direct sunlight, especially between 10 a.m. and 3 p.m., when the sun is the strongest and can do the most damage to the skin.

Choose a waterproof SPF 15 sunscreen containing PAPA and benzopheno (oxybenzone) to screen ultraviolet rays. Apply it liberally an hour or two before you go out in the sun, and reapply it every two or three hours, especially after swimming and sweating. Some newer sunscreens are formulated to last all day, even after swimming.

Your skin type is also an important factor. If you're a Type I or II, which means fair skin, blond, and blue eyed, you will need more skin protection and a doctor should check you for skin cancer at least once a year. At the other extreme is Type V and VI, which includes Middle Easterners, Indians, and Blacks, who will burn only after heavy exposure.

If you spend a lot of time in the sun, you should know about the types of skin cancers and how to detect them early. There are three kinds of skin cancers: basal cell, squamous cell carcinomas, and malignant melanoma.

Basal cell carcinoma is the most common skin cancer (about 80 percent) and is seldom deadly. It usually appears on the neck, head, face, and hands. It may be as small as a pinpoint or as large as an inch. It may also crust and bleed.

Squamous-cell carcinoma is the second most common and looks like a raised pink wart. If left untreated, it can spread to other parts of the body.

Malignant melanoma is the least common, but most deadly skin cancer. It usually appears quickly on the upper back or legs. It can be brown-black or multi-colored. Malignant melanoma grows fast and spreads to other organs.

If you spend a lot of time in the sun, check your skin regularly. Look at the back of your hands and your face. Look for scaly, rough patches of skin. Are there any white spots or red nodules with scales? If you see anything that looks suspicious, see your doctor. Most of the time, skin cancers are easily and successfully removed.

CHEMICAL BURNS

Chemical burns—from acid, alkali, lime, petroleum products, cleansing agents, and the like—are unusual in the outdoors, but do happen occasionally.

For such burns on exposed skin, the first step is to immediately flush the area with water, thereby lessening the pain and probably reducing the extent of the skin damage. Thereafter, treat as you would a thermal burn.

If a noxious chemical gets into an eye, flush the eye with water at once. Do so by having the victim

CHEMICAL BURN IN EYE ⎯⎯⎯⎯⎯

Pull down upper eyelid and then look upward.

Pull skin under eye gently downward.

Flush with boiled, salted water.

lie down with his head tilted slightly to one side. Pour the water into the corner of the eye nearest the nose so that it flows across the entire eye and out the other corner and does not enter the unaffected eye.

Cover the eye with a sterile compress, bandage it into place, and get the victim to medical help as fast as possible.

SUNSTROKE

Sunstroke is extremely dangerous. Aged people are the most susceptible. The usual symptoms are headache, dry skin, and rapid pulse. Dizziness and nausea may occur, and in severe cases the victim may lapse into unconsciousness. Body temperature soars, sometimes as high as 109°F.

Medical help, as soon as possible, is a must. Until it arrives, do the following.

Undress the victim, and sponge the body freely with cool water, or apply cold cloths, the objective being to reduce body temperature to a tolerable level of 103°F or below. If you have no thermometer, check the victim's pulse; a pulse rate of 110 or below usually means a tolerable body temperature.

When the body temperature lowers to 103°F, stop the sponging or cool-cloth treatment for about 10 minutes. If the temperature again starts to rise, resume the sponging.

If the victim is conscious and can swallow, give him as much as he can drink of a saltwater solution (1 teaspoon of salt to 1 quart of water).

Later, cover according to the victim's comfort.

HYPOTHERMIA

Hypothermia is one of the major causes of death among outdoor people, and it will strike anyone who is not prepared to handle extreme weather conditions. Hypothermia is caused by exposure to high winds, rain, snow, or wet clothing. A person's normal core (inner body) temperature is 98.6. When the body begins to lose heat, early stages of hypothermia will be apparent. The person will start to shiver and stamp his feet.

If these early signs of hypothermia are ignored, the next stage of symptoms will be uncontrollable spells of shivering, slurred or slow speech, memory lapses, fumbling hands, and drowsiness. If not treated quickly, hypothermia will likely kill its victim when body temperature drops below 78 degrees and this can happen within 90 minutes after shivering begins.

If you're outdoors and detect any of these symptoms in yourself or a friend, start treatment immediately. First, get to shelter and warmth as soon as

HYPOTHERMIA'S EFFECTS ON THE BODY

When extreme cold causes the body to lose its interior heat, these symptoms occur as temperature drops:

99 to 96 degrees:
Shivering becomes intense; ability to perform simple tasks is slowed.

95 to 91 degrees:
Skin tone pales; shivering turns violent and speech is impaired.

90 to 86 degrees:
Muscular rigidity replaces shivering; thinking is dulled considerably.

85 to 81 degrees:
Victim becomes irrational and may drift into stupor; pulse is slow.

80 to 78 degrees:
Unconsciousness occurs; reflexes cease to function.

Below 78 degrees:
Condition may be irreversible; death is likely at this point.

---

possible. If no shelter is available, build a fire. Get out of wet clothing and apply heat to the victim's head, neck, chest, and groin. Use chemical heat packs if you have them. If not, use body heat from another person. If you have a sleeping bag, the victim should be placed in it with another person.

As the victim begins to recover, give him warm liquids, chocolate, or any other high-sugar content foods. Never give a hypothermia victim alcohol. It will only impair judgement, dilate blood vessels, and impair shivering (the body's way of producing heat).

If you're in a boat and capsize into cold water, don't take off your clothing; it will help trap heat. When you wear a life jacket, draw knees up to your body, which will reduce heat loss. If there are several people in the water, huddle together so you can conserve heat. Survival in cold water depends on the water temperature. If water temperature is 32.5 degrees, survival time may be under 15 minutes. If water is over 80 degrees, survival time is indefinite.

Preventing hypothermia is a lot easier than treating it. First, stay in shape and get a good night's sleep before going outdoors. Always carry candy, mixed nuts, raisins, or some other high-energy food. Stay as dry as possible and avoid getting overheated. Wet clothing will lose 90 percent of its insulating qualities and will rob the body of heat.

Stop and rest often—most important, dress properly. This means several layers of clothing to form an insulating barrier against the cold. Carry rain gear and use it when the first drops fall. Wear a wool hat with some kind of ear protection. Several manufacturers now make wool knit caps with a Gore-Tex lining, which will keep your head and ears dry in a downpour. It's a fact that uncovered head can lose up to 50 percent of the body's heat.

You should also carry a survival kit with a change of clothing, waterproof matches, and candy bars or other high-energy snacks.

FROSTBITE

Frostbite is the freezing of an area of the body, usually the nose, ears, cheeks, fingers, or toes.

Just before the actual onset of frostbite, the skin may appear slightly flushed. Then, as frostbite develops, the skin becomes white or grayish yellow. Blisters may develop later. In the early stages the victim may feel pain, which later subsides. The affected area feels intensely cold and numb, but the victim is often unaware of the problem until someone tells him or he notices the pale glossy skin. First aid treatment is as follows:

Enclose the frostbitten area with warm hands or warm cloth, using firm pressure. Do not rub with the hands or with snow. If the affected area is on fingers or hands, have the victim put his hands into his armpits.

Cover the area with woolen cloth.

Get the victim indoors or into a warm shelter as soon as possible. Immerse the frostbitten area in warm—not hot—water. If that is not possible, wrap the area in warm blankets. Do not use hot-water bottles or heat lamps, and do not place the affected area near fire or a hot stove.

When the frostbitten part has been warmed, encourage the victim to move it.

Give the victim something warm to drink.

If the victim must travel, apply a sterile dressing that widely overlaps the affected area, and be sure that enough clothing covers it to keep it warm.

Medical attention is usually necessary.

SNOW BLINDNESS

The symptoms of this winter malady include a burning or smarting sensation in the eyes, pain in the eyes or in the forehead, and extreme sensitivity to light. First aid steps include the following:

Get the victim into a shelter of some kind, or at least out of the sun.

Apply cold compresses to the eyes.

Apply mild eye drops. Mineral oil is a suitable substitute.

Have the victim wear dark glasses.

SUN AND EYES

If you're a fisherman or a boater, you are probably already aware of the punishing effects of the sun's glare on your eyes. In fact, the effect of glare on the surface of the water can be 25 times brighter than the light level indoors. For most activities, sunglasses should be able to absorb about 60 percent of the sun's rays. For fishing or boating, however, sunglasses should be darker, absorbing at least 80 percent of the sun's rays. Bausch & Lomb suggests this simple in-store test for lens darkness: Look in a mirror with the sunglasses on. If the lenses are dark enough, you will have some difficulty seeing your eyes. This test does not work for photochromic sunglasses because they would be at their light stage indoors. If you are a fisherman, you should select sunglasses with Polarizing lenses, which are usually made by sandwiching Polarizing film between layers of dark glass or plastic. They eliminate reflections on the surface of the water and allow fishermen to see beneath the surface. Sunglasses come in a variety of lens colors, but most eye-care professionals recommend green, gray, or brown for outside activities.

EFFECTS OF SUN RAYS

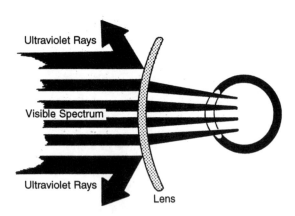

Ultraviolet (UV) rays, hidden in the sun's rays, can be irritating and dangerous, causing both short and long-term harmful effects on the eyes. Industry standards require that sunglasses designed for water sports should absorb up to 95 percent of UV rays. Make sure that the sunglasses you select are ones that afford UV protection.

CUTS, ABRASIONS, AND BRUISES

Minor mishaps frequently involve one of these three injuries. With abrasions (the rubbing or scraping off of skin) and small cuts, the emphasis should be on preventing infection.

Immediately clean the cut or abrasion and the surrounding area with soap and warm water. Don't breathe on the wound or let fingers or soiled cloth contact it.

If there is bleeding, put a sterile pad over the wound and hold it there firmly until the bleeding stops. Then apply an antiseptic, if available, and apply a fresh sterile pad, bandaging it in place loosely.

A bruise results when small blood vessels under the skin are broken, causing discoloration of the skin and swelling, which is often painful.

First aid may be unnecessary if the bruise is minor. If it is more severe, apply an ice pack or cold cloths to reduce the swelling and relieve the pain. Bruises on an extremity can be made less painful if the limb is elevated.

BONE DISLOCATIONS

A dislocation results when the end of a bone is displaced from its normal position in the joint. The surrounding ligaments and other soft tissue always suffer some damage. Fingers, thumb, and shoulder are the areas most often affected.

Symptoms include severe pain, swelling, and loss of movement. Unless a dislodged bone is properly relocated and cared for, dislocations of the bone may occur repeatedly and eventually cause considerable disability.

Relocating a seriously dislodged bone should be done only by a doctor. The first aider's primary concerns here are to prevent further injury and to see to the victim's comfort.

The dislocated part should be kept as immobile as possible. Apply cold compresses, and get the victim to a doctor.

If an elbow or shoulder is dislocated, use a loose sling to keep the part immobile during transport. If the dislocation is in the hip, transport the victim on

DISLOCATED HIP

Dislocated joints should be kept immobile and protected until the victim can be transported into the hands of a doctor.

DISLOCATED FINGER

Far from medical help, you might with a gentle pull attempt to restore a dislocated finger to its socket.

a wide board or on a stretcher that has been made rigid, and use blankets or clothing as a pad to support the affected-side leg in whatever position the victim finds most comfortable.

If the dislocation is in a finger and medical help is far away, you might try pulling—very cautiously—on the finger in an attempt to bring the bone back into place. If a gentle pull does not work, do not persist. And do not try this on a dislocated thumb—the problem is more complicated at this joint, and further injury may result.

BONE FRACTURES

There are two kinds of bone fractures (breaks). In a simple fracture the broken bone does not push through the skin. In an open fracture the skin is broken and a wound extends from the skin to the fracture area.

It is often difficult to tell whether or not a bone has been broken. If the first-aider was not there when the injury was suffered, he should ask the victim to tell him exactly what happened and then check the injured area for physical evidence.

Symptoms of a break include tenderness to the touch, difficulty or pain in moving the injured part, swelling, skin discoloration, and deformity.

If you're not sure, treat the injury as a break. Never try to reset a broken bone yourself. Your basic objectives are to prevent further injury, treat for shock if necessary, and make the patient as comfortable as possible until medical help arrives.

With any break, handle the victim gently. Careless handling will increase the pain and may also increase the severity of shock and cause jagged bone ends to damage muscle, nerves, blood vessels, and skin.

First aid procedures for various kinds of breaks are as follows:

Arm or Leg. If medical help will arrive shortly, don't move either the broken limb or the victim.

If there is bleeding, cut away as much clothing as necessary, place a sterile pad or a piece of clean cloth over the wound, and apply firm pressure. Bandage the pad in place.

If the patient must be moved, position the limb as naturally and comfortably as possible, and put on two splints. Boards, poles, metal rods, or any other firm objects—even a thick layer of newspaper folded to the proper shape and firmness—will do. Splints must be long enough to extend beyond the joints above and below the break. Use soft material as padding between the limb and the splints. Fasten the splints in place with bandage material (or handkerchiefs, cloth strips, etc.) at a minimum of three places: adjacent to the break, near the joint above the break, and near the joint below the break.

FRACTURED ARM

FRACTURED LEG

Check the splints every 15 minutes or so. If swelling of the limb has caused tightening of the bandaging so that circulation is cut off, loosen the bindings accordingly.

Apply cold packs to the fracture.

Get victim to medical help.

Skull. Skull fracture symptoms include unconsciousness, mental confusion or dazedness, variation in size of eye pupils, and bleeding from mouth, ears, or nose.

Keep victim lying down. If his face has normal color or is flushed, prop up his head and shoulders. If his face is pale, try to position him so that his head is slightly lower than the rest of his body.

If there is an open scalp wound, apply a sterile gauze pad, and bandage it in place.

If the victim must be moved, transport him in a prone position.

FRACTURED SKULL

Never leave the victim alone, even during transport. If he begins to choke on blood, lower his head and turn it to one side so that the blood can drain from mouth and throat.

Neck and Back. If the victim can't readily open or close his fingers or grip anything firmly, his neck may be broken. If finger movement seems normal but he can't move feet or toes, the back may be broken. If he is unconscious and you suspect a spinal injury, treat as if the neck were fractured.

FRACTURED NECK OR BACK

Do not let the victim move his head.

Cover him with blankets.

Watch his breathing closely. If breathing stops, begin mouth-to-mouth resuscitation, but do not move his head as you do so.

Medical help should be brought to the scene if at all possible. If a move is absolutely necessary, extreme caution is a must, for a slight twist or jerk can be fatal to the victim of a broken neck or spine. Pad the head at the sides to prevent movement. Tie the victim's hands across his chest, and tie his head and body rigidly to the stretcher, which should itself be rigid. Put a pad under the neck.

Pelvis. The pelvis is a basin-shaped bone that connects spine and legs. It also encloses or protects many important organs; therefore a fracture of the pelvis is a serious injury that requires careful handling. Evidence of damage to organs or blood vessels includes difficulty in urinating or blood in the urine.

Treat for shock, which may be severe.

Bandage the knees together; bandage ankles together.

Keep victim lying down, either with legs flat on ground or with knees flexed up and pads positioned under the knees, whichever position is most comfortable for the patient.

FRACTURED PELVIS

If the victim complains of pain when his lower extremities are moved, apply splints to the extremity.

If victim must be moved, transport him in a prone position on a rigid stretcher.

Rib. Symptoms include pain in the break area and shallow breathing (deep breathing causes pain). A broken rib sometimes punctures a lung, causing the victim to cough up frothy bright-red blood.

If the broken rib has punctured the skin, infection

must be guarded against. Apply a dressing that is airtight.

Keep victim lying down and calm.

If the skin is not punctured, apply one or more wide bandages around the chest, thereby restricting rib motion. One of the bandages should cross the area of the injury. The knot or knots should be on the side of the chest opposite the break. Put a folded cloth under the knots. If the bandages cause pain, remove them.

FRACTURED RIB

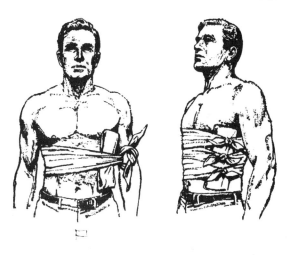

If the broken rib seems to be depressed—that is, pushed down into the chest cavity, do not apply bandages.

If victim must be moved, transport him in prone position.

Nose. Most nose-break victims have a noticeable wound—at least a bruise. There is usually some swelling and discoloration, and sometimes the shape of the nose is altered. Broken nose bones must be treated properly, or permanent deformity and breathing difficulties may result.

If there is bleeding, hold the lower end of the nose between thumb and forefinger and press the sides of the nose against the septum (middle partition) for about five minutes. Avoid any side-to-side movement. Release pressure gradually. Apply cold cloths. Have the victim sit up, hold his head back, and breathe through his mouth.

If there is a wound, apply a sterile protective dressing, and tape it into place. Or bandage the

FRACTURED NOSE

dressing in place with strips of clean cloth tied around the head.

The nose-break victim should see a doctor as soon as possible.

Jaw. In a fracture of the lower jaw, the upper and lower teeth often do not line up properly. There may

FRACTURED JAW

be mild bleeding of the gum near the break, and jaw movement will cause pain. Speaking and swallowing are usually difficult.

Lift the lower jaw gently so that the lower and upper teeth meet.

Position the middle of a wide strip of clean cloth under the chin, and tie the ends on top of the head, thereby supporting the jaw.

If the victim begins to vomit, remove the cloth bandage at once. Support the jaw with your hand. Replace the bandage when the vomiting stops.

Collarbone. Victim of this break will usually assume the following position: shoulder bent forward, elbow flexed, forearm across the chest and supported by the hand on the opposite side. There may be swelling, local tenderness, and possibly some deformity.

Use a sling—wide enough to extend from elbow to wrist—to support the arm on the injured side. Adjust the sling so that the hand is slightly above the level of the elbow.

FRACTURED COLLARBONE

Tie another bandage, not so wide, so that it encircles the injured-side arm and the chest, snugging the arm against the side of the body. Don't tie the bandage so tight that it interferes with circulation.

Try to keep the victim's shoulders erect.

Elbow. One symptom is swelling above the elbow joint. Leave the arm in the position in which the victim holds it. Protect the joint from movement.

If the arm is held straight, put on a single splint that extends from fingertips to armpit. Position the splint on the palm side of the arm. Tie it on securely, but do not wrap any of the bindings around the elbow area.

If the arm is bent, put it in a sling, and use an around-the-chest bandage to bind the arm to the side of the body.

Wrist or Forearm. A break in one of the two bones in the forearm is quite common. The break is usually near the wrist. A break in one of the eight small wrist bones is sometimes thought to be only a sprain. With a break in either place, the fingers and thumb can be moved freely, though movement may cause some pain.

FRACTURED ELBOW

FRACTURED FOREARM OR WRIST

Put on a padded splint that extends from palm to elbow.

Put the arm in a sling arranged so that the fingers are about 4 inches higher than the elbow.

The fingers should remain uncovered so that they can be watched for swelling or discoloration. If either of those signs occur, carefully loosen the splint, the sling, or both.

Finger. Put a splint on the finger, immobilizing it. Support the hand with a sling. Don't treat this injury casually: get the victim to a doctor. Permanent deformity can result if proper treatment isn't given.

Kneecap. Prompt and proper treatment of this injury is a must, because flexion of the knee can pull apart the pieces of a broken kneecap (patella).

Gently straighten the victim's leg.

Put on a splint on the underside of the leg. The splint should be inflexible, about 6 inches wide, and long enough to reach from the buttocks to just below the heel. Tie the splint in place firmly, but not so tight that circulation is impeded (check the ties every

FRACTURED KNEECAP

half-hour or so). Do not make any of the ties over the kneecap itself.

Transport victim in prone position.

Foot or Toe. Remove the victim's shoe and sock quickly—swelling may be extremely rapid. Cut away the footwear if necessary.

Apply clean dressings padded with cotton. Or tie a small pillow, folded blanket, or something similar around foot and bottom of leg.

Caution victim against movement of foot, ankle, or toes.

FRACTURED TOE OR FOOT

SPRAINS

Sprains are injuries to the soft tissues that surround joints. Ligaments, tendons, and blood vessels are stretched and sometimes torn. Ankles, fingers, wrists, and knees are the areas most often affected.

Symptoms include pain when the area is moved, swelling, and tenderness to the touch. Sometimes a large area of skin becomes discolored because small blood vessels are ruptured.

It is often difficult to tell whether the injury is a sprain or a fracture. If in doubt, treat as a fracture. Otherwise, take the following steps:

Elevate the injured joint, using pillows, or something similar. A sprained ankle should be raised about 12 inches higher than the torso. For a wrist or elbow sprain, put the arm into a sling.

Apply an ice pack or cold cloths to reduce swelling and pain. Continue the cold treatment for half an hour.

ANKLE SPRAIN

If a sprain victim is far from help and must walk, loosen or untie his shoelaces to allow for swelling and then begin a wrap as shown.

Following wrap procedures described in accompanying text, support the injured area.

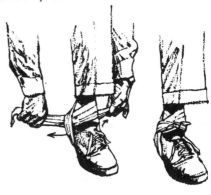

Always have a sprain X-rayed. There may indeed be a fracture or a bone chip.

If the victim of a sprained ankle is far from help and must walk, make the following preparations: 1) untie the shoelaces to allow for swelling, but do not take off the shoe; 2) place the middle of a long bandage (a folded triangular bandage is best) under the shoe just forward of the heel; 3) bring the ends of the bandage up and back, crossing them above (at the back of) the heel; 4) bring ends forward around ankle, and cross them over the instep; 5) bring ends downward toward the heel, and slip each end beneath the wrap that comes up from each side of the heel; 6) bring ends all the way around the ankle again, pull on them to produce the desired tension, and tie square knot in front.

PUNCTURE WOUNDS

A puncture wound results when a sharp object—knife, needle, branch end, or the like—penetrates the skin and the tissue underneath. The first-aider's primary objectives here, and in all other wounds, are to prevent infection and control bleeding.

Puncture wounds are often unusual in that they may be quite deep and the bleeding, because of the small opening in the skin, may be relatively light. The lighter the bleeding, generally, the lesser the chance that germs embedded by the penetrating object will be washed out. This means that the danger of infection is greater in puncture wounds than in other types.

The danger of tetanus (lockjaw) infection is also greater in puncture wounds.

First aid procedures are as follows:

If the bleeding is limited, try to increase the flow by applying gentle pressure to the areas surrounding the wound. Do not squeeze hard, or you may cause further tissue damage.

Do not probe inside the wound. If a large splinter or a piece of glass or metal protrudes from it, try to remove it, *but do so with extreme caution.* If the sliver cannot be withdrawn with very gentle pressure, leave it where it is, or you may cause further damage and severe bleeding.

Wash the wound with soap and water.

Apply a sterile pad, and bandage it in place.

Get the victim to a doctor for treatment, including a tetanus shot if necessary.

GUNSHOT WOUNDS

Tetanus is a special problem in gunshot wounds. First aid steps are as follows:

Stop the bleeding (see ''Bleeding,'' elsewhere in this section).

Apply a sterile pad, and bandage it in place.

If there is a fracture or a suspected fracture, immobilize the part (see ''Bone Fractures'' elsewhere in this section).

Treat for shock (see ''Shock'' elsewhere in this section).

Get the victim to a doctor quickly. A tetanus shot may be needed.

FISHHOOK REMOVAL

A doctor's care—and a tetanus shot, if needed—are recommended for anyone who has had a fishhook embedded past the barb in the flesh. In many cases, however, medical help is not within easy reach. The severity of the injury and the size of the hook determine what action the first-aider should take.

If the hook has penetrated only up as far as the barb or slightly past it—and if it is not in a critical spot such as the eye—you should be able to pull or jerk it out. Then clean the wound, and treat it as you would any other superficial wound (see ''Cuts, Abrasions, and Bruises,'' elsewhere in this section).

If the hook has penetrated well past the barb and is not in a critical area, there are two recommended methods of removal:

1) Force the hook in the direction in which it became embedded so that the point and barb exit through the skin. Try to make the angle of exit as shallow as possible. This can be quite painful, so the victim should anchor the affected part as solidly as possible before the process is begun. Using wire cutters or a similar tool, cut the hook in two at a point on the shank just before the bend. Remove the two pieces.

2) Have the victim anchor the affected part solidly. Take a 12- to 18-inch piece of strong string (30-pound-test fishing line is ideal), and run one end around the bend of the hook as if you were threading a needle. Bring the two ends together, and tie them in a sturdy knot. With thumb or forefinger, push down (toward the affected part) on the shank of the hook at the point where the bend begins. This disengages the barb from the tissue. Maintaining that pressure, grasp the line firmly at the knotted end, and give a strong yank. The finger pressure on the shank should reduce flesh damage to a minimum as the barb comes out the same way it went in. Do not use this method if the hook is a large one.

If bleeding is minimal after either of these procedures, squeeze the wound gently to encourage blood flow, which has a cleansing effect. Put on a sterile dressing, and get medical help.

If the hook is a large one and is deeply embedded, or if it is in a critical area, do not try to remove it.

PUSH-THROUGH HOOK REMOVAL

Force hook in direction in which it became imbedded.

Cut off barb with wire cutter.

Remove the two pieces of the hook.

BACK-OUT HOOK REMOVAL

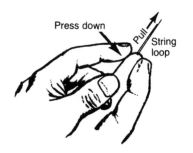

Press down

Pull

String loop

Cover the wound, hook and all, with a sterile dressing, and get the victim to a doctor.

EYE INJURIES, FOREIGN BODY IN EYE

For first aid purposes, eye injuries fall into three categories: 1) injury to eyelids and soft tissue above the eye, 2) injury to the surface of the eyeball, 3) injury that extends into tissue beneath the eyeball surface.

In category 1, treament involves putting on a sterile dressing and bandaging it in place. If the injury is in the form of a bruise (the familiar "black eye"), the immediate application of cold cloths or an ice pack should halt any bleeding and prevent some swelling. Later, apply warm wet towels to reduce discoloration.

FOREIGN BODY IN EYE

Step 1: Pull the upper eyelid down over the lower one and hold it there, instructing the victim to look upward.

Step 2: If Step 1 doesn't work, have the victim force the lower lid skin downward as shown and inspect for the foreign object. Remove the object per text.

Step 3: Flush the eye with sterilized saltwater, as described in text.

Category 2 injuries usually occur when a foreign body lodges on the surface of the eyeball. To remove the object, pull the upper eyelid down over the lower one, and hold it there for a moment, instructing the victim to look upward. Tears will flow naturally and may wash out the object.

If that doesn't work, put two fingers of your hand on the skin just below the victim's lower eyelid, and force the skin gently downward, thereby exposing the inner area of the lower lid. Inspect the area closely, and if the object is visible, lift it out carefully, using a corner of a clean handkerchief or a small wad of sterile cotton that has been moistened with water and wrapped around the end of a toothpick.

If the foreign object can't be seen, it can sometimes be flushed out. Boil some water, add table salt (¼ teaspoon to an average glassful), and let the salt water cool to about body temperature. With the victim lying down, tilt his head toward the injured side, hold his eyelids open with your fingers, and pour the liquid into the inner corner of his eye so that it runs across the eyeball and drains on the opposite side.

Category 3 eye injuries are extremely serious. Never attempt to remove an object that has penetrated the eyeball, now matter how shallow. Apply a sterile compress or clean cloth, cover it with a loose bandage, and get the victim to a doctor at once.

BOILS

A boil—a round, reddened, and usually painful elevation in the skin—is mostly dead tissue and germ-laden pus. Actually, it is an attempt by the body to keep an infection localized.

Do not squeeze a boil, or you may spread the infection. If the boil is very painful or appears to be spreading, apply hot wet compresses. These may reduce the pain and cause the boil to come to a head more quickly.

When the boil comes to a head and discharges its contents, do not touch the escaping pus. Soak it up thoroughly with a gauze pad or clean cloth, thereby preventing infection of the surrounding skin. Cover the boil with a sterile dressing.

BLISTERS AND FOOT CARE

There was a time when we were told, "*never* take brand-new boots on a hunting trip." That's no longer a hard and fast rule. Leather boots still require a break-in period, but composite boots that are synthetic do not require extensive breaking in.

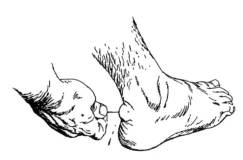

1. Blisters demand attention. If you get a small blister, don't break it. Simply protect it with a bandage. If it's a big, painful blister, however, you should break it. Use an alcohol wipe and sterile pin. Break the blister but don't remove protective skin. When the blister has drained, coat it with a first-aid cream and cover it.

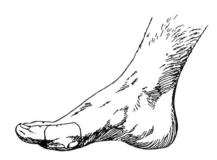

2. Prevent blisters by using Elastoplast, which stretches, or Moleskin, which has no stretch. Both products can be cut to fit. On long hikes, use Elastoplast around your heel, bunion area, and any other part of your foot that you know is blister-prone.

3. Air out boots at the end of the day. Open laces and turn down collars. In the morning, sprinkle the inside of the boots with baby powder. Your socks will slide into the boot and not bind.

Opinions vary, but most sportsmen prefer eight-inch-high boots for hunting; six-inch boots are the favorite for hiking.

Besides boots, there are other ways to protect your feet in the field. You should always wear two pairs of socks. The first pair to go on your feet should be lightweight, preferably polypropylene to wick away perspiration. The second should be heavyweight, to warm and cushion your feet. In addition to providing warmth, two pairs of socks rub against each other—not against your feet.

Finally, give your feet a break. On your next trip, occasionlly take off your boots and socks and rest your feet on a log.

INFECTED WOUNDS

One of the primary objectives in any first aid situation is the prevention of infection, but the first aider is sometimes called on to treat a wound that has already become infected. Symptoms of infection include swelling, redness (including red streaks emanating out from the wound), throbbing pain, and a "hot" feeling in the infected area.

First aid steps are as follows:

Keep the victim lying down and as comfortable and calm as possible.

Apply heat to the area with hot water bottles, or put warm, moist towels or cloths over the wound dressing. Change the wet packs often enough to keep them warm and cover them with a dry towel wrapped in plastic, aluminum foil, or waxed paper to hold in the warmth and to protect bedclothing.

Continue applying the warm packs for 30 minutes. Then remove them and cover the wound with a sterile dressing for another 30 minutes. Apply the warm packs again. Repeat the whole process until medical care can be obtained.

EPILEPSY

In a full-blown epileptic attack, the victim becomes pale, his eyes roll, and he falls down, usually with a hoarse cry. He may turn blue, bite his tongue, and froth at the mouth. Head, arms, and legs jerk violently, and he loses consciousness.

First aid steps are as follows:

Do not try to restrain the victim's convulsions or thrashing; that phase of the attack will pass, usually within a few minutes.

Try to protect him against injury by moving away nearby objects.

To prevent him from biting his tongue, try to place an appropriate object (wad of cloth, piece of thick rubber, piece of a book cover) between upper and lower teeth in one side of the mouth. Be sure that

the object does not obstruct his breathing.

Give the victim no stimulants.

When the attack subsides, let the patient rest undisturbed.

APPENDICITIS

The principal symptom is pain in the lower right part of the abdomen and sometimes over the entire abdominal region. Nausea and vomiting may be present, as may a mild fever. Constipation often occurs and is sometimes thought to be the cause of the victim's discomfort. Do not give a laxative if appendicitis is suspected—it will increase the danger that the appendix will rupture.

Have the patient lie down, and keep him comfortable.

Do not give him any food or water.

An ice pack placed over the appendix area may relieve pain. Do not apply heat to the appendix area.

Get medical help as soon as possible.

DIARRHEA

Diarrhea is a common malady among outdoorsmen. Its causes are often associated with change: during an extended hunting or fishing trip, for example, the sportsman's eating and drinking habits are often much different than what they are at home. Attacks of diarrhea usually subside once the body adapts to those changes.

Paregoric is helpful in combating diarrhea, as are many of the products designed for that purpose and sold in drugstores. If you or your companions are particularly subject to attacks of diarrhea, see a doctor and ask him to prescribe a drug, preferably in tablet form, that will combat the problem during trips afield.

EARACHE

An earache is usually a sign of an infection, so the sufferer should seek medical attention as soon as feasible.

The following first aid procedures should give some relief:

Treat with either heat or cold. There is no way to predict which will work best, but try cold first, putting an icepack or cold compress over the ear. If that doesn't work, try a hot-water bottle or hot compresses.

For further relief, put a few drops of warm mineral oil in the affected ear, if it is not ruptured.

Caution the sufferer against blowing his nose hard, which probably will increase the pain and may spread the infection.

TOOTHACHE

First aid procedures are as follows:

Inspect the sufferer's mouth under the strongest light available.

If no cavity is visible, place an ice pack or cold compress against the jaw on the painful side. If that doesn't provide relief, try a hot-water bottle or hot compress.

If a cavity can be seen, use a piece of sterile cotton wrapped on the end of a toothpick to clean the cavity as thoroughly as possible.

Oil of cloves, if available, can give relief. Pack it gently into the cavity with a toothpick. Do not let the oil touch the tongue or the inside of the mouth—the stuff burns.

TRANSPORTING THE SERIOUSLY INJURED

The first-aider's principal objectives in transporting a seriously injured person are to avoid disturbing the victim unnecessarily and to prevent injured body areas from twisting, bending, or shaking.

Transportation is a vital factor, and it requires proper planning by the first-aider and proper preparation of the victim. The rescuers must make every effort to remain calm and mentally alert.

In some situations, however—such as an auto accident, fire, and the like—there is not time for planning or preparation; the victim must be moved from the danger area, or he may suffer further injury.

If such a victim must be pulled to safety, the pull should be along the length of his body (that is, head-first or feet-first), not sideways. The danger of compounding the injury during pulling is reduced if a blanket or something similar can be placed beneath him so that he can "ride" the blanket.

If a victim must be lifted to safety, the rescuers should try to protect all parts of his body from the tensions of lifting. The body should be supported at a minimum of three places along its length, not jacknifed (lifted by head and feet only). Keep the body as straight as possible.

Once a victim is moved to safety, further transportation is inadvisable unless absolutely necessary. The first-aider should make every effort to get medical help to the scene. If the injury occurs deep in the backwoods, it may be possible to arrange for a doctor to come in via float plane or helicopter.

If there is no way to get medical help to the scene and the victim must be carried to a cabin, farmhouse, or road, a stretcher of some sort is a must. A well-padded folding-type cot will serve adequately. If no cot is available, a serviceable stretcher can be made by inserting two sturdy poles inside a buttoned coat or a couple of buttoned heavy-duty shirts, or by wrapping a blanket around two poles as shown in the accompanying drawing.

The victim must be properly prepared for a long carry. In addition to being given the first aid treat-

STRETCHER MADE OF POLES AND BLANKET

STRETCHER MADE OF POLES AND BUTTONED COAT

PULLING VICTIM TO SAFETY

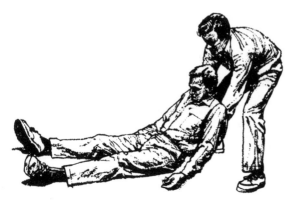

ments called for by his particular injury, he may need a period of rest before the ordeal of transportation. Broken bones and other injured areas should be made as immobile as possible. Loosen any tight clothing, and in general make the victim as comfortable as you can.

Care is the watchword when loading a victim onto a stretcher. It is best if at least three persons take part in the loading. The victim should be lying on his back with his feet tied together if feasible. Place the stretcher next to the victim.

The loaders should position themselves facing the victim's uninjured side, one loader at the head, another at the midsection, the third at the feet. Each loader should kneel on the knee nearest the victim's feet. Arms are positioned under the victim as follows: loader at head cradles the victim's head and shoulders with one arm and puts the other arm under the lower back; loader at midsection supports back and area just below the victim's buttocks; the third loader's arms support the victims thighs and calves.

One loader gives the command, "Lift," and all three together bring the victim up onto their knees, supporting him there without putting undue strain on the victim's body. One loader pulls the stretcher under the victim, and then all three, again on command, lower the victim down gently.

Provide enough blankets to keep the victim warm during the carry. Place padding wherever it's needed. (If victim's injury is to the back of the head, he should be positioned on his side.) Tie the victim to the stretcher firmly enough to prevent him from slipping or rolling but not so tightly as to interfere with blood circulation. Be sure that none of the bindings exert pressure on the injured area.

Ideally, there should be four stretcher-bearers,

LOADING VICTIM ONTO STRETCHER

Loaders should be on victim's uninjured side, all kneeling on knee nearest victim's feet.

Loader in command moves stretcher under victim and victim is lowered to stretcher.

At command "Lift," loaders raise victim gently to their knees.

Victim is covered and tied to stretcher. If possible, there should be a bearer at each end and at each side.

one at each end and one on each side. It's best to carry the victim so that he can see where he is going. In most cases, the head should be a bit lower than the rest of the body; however, the head should be elevated if there is a head injury or difficulty in breathing.

Woods trails can be treacherous, so stretcher-bearers should be especially alert for roots and other snags, rocks, slippery mud, and the like. If the carriers should lose their balance, the victim can incur further injury.

Bearers should watch the victim closely for signs of shock, discomfort, breathing difficulties, and other problems. Check the dressings periodically, and change or adjust them if necessary.

FIRST AID KITS

Improvisation is an ability that most outdoors people seem to develop naturally. But an improvised dressing for a wound, for example, is a poor second best to a prepackaged, sterile dressing. Any first aider can function more effectively if he has the proper equipment.

A first aid kit—whether it is bought in a drug store or medical-supply house or is put together by the individual—should meet the following requirements:

Its contents should be complete enough for the purposes for which it will be used.

The contents should be arranged so that any component desired can be located quickly and without removing the other components.

Each component should be wrapped so that any unused portion can be repacked and thereby prevented from leaking, becoming soiled, and so on.

How and where the kit will be used are the main factors to consider when assembling a first aid kit. The three kits described below should fill the needs of most outdoor situations:

POCKET KIT: (Suitable for one-day, overnight, or short term backpacking trips in areas not far from medical help.)

- 1 × 1-inch packaged sterile bandages (2)
- 2 × 2-inch packaged sterile bandages (2)

- 2 × 2-inch packaged sterile gauze pads (2)
- Roll of adhesive tape
- Band-Aids (10)
- Ammonia inhalant (1)
- Tube of antiseptic cream
- Small tin of aspirin (or 12 aspirins wrapped in foil)

ALL PURPOSE OUTDOORS FIRST AID KIT: (Suitable for general outings.)

- 4-inch Ace bandages (2)
- 2-inch Ace bandages (2)*
- 2 × 2-inch sterile gauze pads (1 pkg.)*
- 5 × 9-inch combine dressing (3)
- Triangular bandage (1)
- Sterile eye pads (2)
- ½-inch adhesive tape (5 yards)
- Assorted Band-Aids (1 pkg.)*
- Betadine liquid antiseptic
- Yellow mercuric oxide ointment (eyes)*
- Bacitracin (ointment)
- Tylenol (aspirin substitute)
- Dramamine (motion sickness)
- Sunscreen
- Snakebite kit*
- Insect repellent
- Single-edge razor blade
- Tweezers (flat tip)
- Small scissors
- Eye patch
- Needle
- Matches in waterproof container
- Needle-nose pliers with cutting edge
- First aid manual

Add these items if going into remote area for extended period:

- Tylenol with codeine (pain killer)**
- Antibiotic (Tetracycline)**
- Lomotil, 2.5 mg. (cramps, diarrhea)**
- Antihistamine tablets
- Phillips Milk of Magnesia (antacid, laxative)

*Items, in lesser quantities, recommended for a small first aid kit for day trips.
**Requires prescription.

PART 11

OUTDOOR

INFORMATION SOURCES

U.S. FISH AND GAME DEPARTMENTS AND STATE PARK COMMISSIONS

United States

ALABAMA
Division of Game and Fish
64 N. Union St.
Montgomery, AL 36130

Department of Conservation and Natural
  Resources
Division of Parks
64 N. Union St.
Montgomery, AL 36130

ALASKA
Department of Fish and Game
P.O. Box 25526
Juneau, AK 99802

ARIZONA
Game and Fish Department
2221 W. Greenway Rd.
Phoenix, AZ 85023-4312

ARKANSAS
Game and Fish Commission
2 Natural Resources Dr.
Little Rock, AR 72205

Department of Parks and Tourism
1 Capitol Mall
Little Rock, AR 72201

CALIFORNIA
Department of Fish and Game
1416 9th St.
Sacramento, CA 94244

Department of Parks and Recreation
1416 9th St.
Sacramento, CA 94244

COLORADO
Division of Wildlife
6060 Broadway
Denver, CO 80216

CONNECTICUT
Department of Environmental Protection
79 Elm St.
Hartford, CT 06106-5127

DELAWARE
Division of Fish and Wildlife
89 Kings Hwy.
P.O. Box 1401
Dover, DE 19903

FLORIDA
Game and Freshwater Fish Commission
620 S. Meridian St.
Tallahassee, FL 32399-1600

Division of Recreation and Parks
3900 Commonwealth Blvd.
Tallahassee, FL 32399-3000

GEORGIA
Game and Fish Division
205 Butler St., SE
Atlanta, GA 30334

Department of Natural Resources
205 Butler St., SE
Atlanta, GA 30334

HAWAII
Division of Forestry and Wildlife
1151 Punchbowl St.
Honolulu, HI 96813

IDAHO
Fish and Game Department
600 S. Walnut
Box 25
Boise, ID 83707

ILLINOIS
Department of Conservation
Lincoln Tower Plaza
524 S. 2nd St.
Springfield, IL 62701

INDIANA
Division of Fish and Wildlife
402 W. Washington St.
Indianapolis, IN 46204

Department of Natural Resources
402 W. Washington St.
Indianapolis, IN 46204

IOWA
Department of Natural Resources
Wallace State Office Bldg.
Des Moines, IA 50319-0034

KANSAS
Department of Wildlife and Parks
900 SW Jackson St.
Topeka, KS 66612-1233

KENTUCKY
Department of Fish and Wildlife Resources
1 Game Farm Rd.
Frankfort, KY 40601

Department of Parks
Capital Plaza Bldg.
Frankfort, KY 40601

LOUISIANA
Department of Wildlife and Fisheries
P.O. Box 98000
Baton Rouge, LA 70898-9000

Office of State Parks
P.O. Box 44426
Baton Rouge, LA 70804

MAINE
Department of Inland Fisheries and Wildlife
284 State St. Station 41
Augusta, ME 04333

Bureau of Parks and Recreation
State House, Sta. 22
Augusta, ME 04333

MARYLAND
Department of Natural Resources
Forest, Park and Wildlife Services
Tawes State Office Bldg.
Annapolis, MD 21401

MASSACHUSETTS
Department of Fisheries and Wildlife
100 Cambridge St.
Boston, MA 02202

Division of Forests and Parks
100 Cambridge St.
Boston, MA 02202

MICHIGAN
Department of Natural Resources
Box 30028
Lansing, MI 48909

MINNESOTA
Division of Fish and Wildlife
Department of Natural Resources
500 Lafayette Rd.
St. Paul, MN 55155

MISSISSIPPI
Department of Wildlife, Fisheries, and Parks
Southport Mall
P.O. Box 451
Jackson, MS 39205

MISSOURI
Department of Conservation
P.O. Box 180
Jefferson City, MO 65102

Division of Parks and Recreation
P.O. Box 176
Jefferson City, MO 65102

MONTANA
Department of Fish, Wildlife and Parks
1420 E. 6th
Helena, MT 59620

NEBRASKA
Game and Parks Commission
P.O. Box 30370
2200 N. 33rd St.
Lincoln, NB 68503

NEVADA
Department of Wildlife
Box 10678
Reno, NV 89520

Division of State Parks
Capitol Complex
123 W. Nye Ln.,
201 S. Fall St.
Carson City, NV 89710

NEW HAMPSHIRE
Fish and Game Department
2 Hazen Dr.
Concord, NH 03301

Division of Parks
172 Pembroke Rd.
P.O. Box 1856
Concord, NH 03302

NEW JERSEY
Division of Fish, Game and Wildlife
CN 400
Trenton, NJ 08625

NEW MEXICO
Game and Fish Department
P.O. Box 25112
Santa Fe, NM 87504

State Park and Recreation Division
141 E. DeVargas St.
P.O. Box 1147
Santa Fe, NM 87504

NEW YORK
Division of Fish and Wildlife
Department of Environmental Conservation
50 Wolf Rd.
Albany, NY 12233

NORTH CAROLINA
Wildlife Resources Commission
Archdale Bldg.
512 N. Salisbury St.
Raleigh, NC 27604

NORTH DAKOTA
State Game and Fish Department
100 N. Bismarck Expressway
Bismarck, ND 58501

OHIO
Division of Wildlife
Department of Natural Resources
Fountain Square
Columbus, OH 43224

OKLAHOMA
Department of Wildlife Conservation
1801 N. Lincoln
P.O. Box 53465
Oklahoma City, OK 73152

Tourism and Recreation Department
2401 N. Lincoln
Suite 500
Oklahoma City, OK 73105

OREGON
Department of Fish and Wildlife
P.O. Box 59
Portland, OR 97207

State Parks Department
1115 Commercial St., NE
Salem, OR 97310-1001

PENNSYLVANIA
Fish Commission
P.O. Box 67000
Harrisburg, PA 17106-7000

Game Commission
2001 Elmerton Ave.
Harrisburg, PA 17110-9797

Bureau of State Parks
Dept. of Environmental Resources
Public Liaison Office
Box 2063
Harrisburg, PA 17105-2063

RHODE ISLAND
Department of Environmental Management
Division of Fish and Wildlife
83 Park St.
Providence, RI 02908

SOUTH CAROLINA
Wildlife and Marine Resources Department
Rembert C. Dennis Bldg.
Box 167
Columbia, SC 29202

State Commission of Forestry
Box 21707
Columbia, SC 29221

SOUTH DAKOTA
Department of Game, Fish and Parks
523 E. Capitol
Pierre, SD 57501-3182

TENNESSEE
Wildlife Resources Agency
P.O. Box 40747
Ellington Agricultural Center
Nashville, TN 37204

Department of Conservation
Division of Parks and Recreation
401 Church St.
Nashville, TN 37243

TEXAS
Parks and Wildlife Department
4200 Smith School Rd.
Austin, TX 78744

UTAH
Division of Wildlife Resources
1596 W. N. Temple
Salt Lake City, UT 84116

Division of Parks and Recreation
1636 W. N. Temple
Salt Lake City, UT 84116

VERMONT
Fish and Game Department
103 S. Main St.
Waterbury, VT 05671

Department of Forests and Parks
Waterbury Complex, 10 S.
Waterbury, VT 05671

VIRGINIA
Commission of Game and Inland Fisheries
Box 11104
4010 W. Broad St.
Richmond, VA 23230

Division of Parks
203 Governor St.
Suite 306
Richmond, VA 23219

WASHINGTON
Department of Fish and Wildlife
600 N. Capitol Way
Olympia, WA 98501

State Parks and Recreation Commission
7150 Cleanwater Lane
P.O. Box 42650
Olympia, WA 98504

WEST VIRGINIA
Division of Natural Resources
1900 Kanawha Blvd. East
Charleston, WV 25305

WISCONSIN
Department of Natural Resources
Box 7921
Madison, WI 53707

WYOMING
Game and Fish Department
5400 Bishop Blvd.
Cheyenne, WY 82006

CANADIAN FISH AND GAME AGENCIES

ALBERTA
Fish and Wildlife Division
9th Floor, South Tower
Petroleum Plaza
9945-108 St.
Edmonton, Alberta
Canada T5K 2C6

BRITISH COLUMBIA
Ministry of Environment
Fish and Wildlife Branch
780 Blanshard
Victoria, BC
Canada V8V 1X4

MANITOBA
Department of Natural Resources
Fisheries and Wildlife Branch
Legislative Bldg.
Winnipeg, Manitoba
Canada R3C 0V8

NEW BRUNSWICK
Department of Natural Resources
Fish and Wildlife Branch
P.O. Box 6000
Fredericton, NB
Canada E3B 5H1

NEWFOUNDLAND
Wildlife Division
Bldg. 810
Pleasantville
P.O. Box 8700
St. Johns, Newfoundland
Canada A1B 4J6

NORTHWEST TERRITORIES
Fish and Wildlife Management
Yellowknife, NWT
Canada X1A 2L9

NOVA SCOTIA
Department of Lands and Forests
Director of Wildlife
P.O. Box 698
Halifax, NS
Canada B3J 2T9

ONTARIO
Ministry of Natural Resources
Division of Fish and Wildlife
Whitney Block Parliament Bldgs.
Toronto, Ontario
Canada M7A 1W3

PRINCE EDWARD ISLAND
Fish and Wildlife Division
Box 2000
Charlottetown, PEI
Canada C1A 7N8

QUEBEC
Fish and Game Branch
Place de la Capitale, 150 Boul.
Rene-Levesque Est.
Quebec
Canada G1R 4Y1

SASKATCHEWAN
Department of Parks and Renewable Resources
Fisheries and Wildlife Branch
3211 Albert St.
Regina, Saskatchewan
Canada S4S 5W6

YUKON
Department of Renewable Resources
Fish and Wildlife
Box 2703
Whitehorse, Yukon Territory
Canada Y1A 2C6

U.S. NATIONAL PARKS AND FORESTS

PARK REGIONAL OFFICES

NATIONAL PARKS
National Park Service
1849 C Street, NW
MS-1013
Washington, D.C. 20240
(202) 208-4747
For Campground Reservations call:
Bestinet (800) 365-2267
Yosemite (800) 436-7275

SOUTHEAST REGIONAL OFFICE
National Park Service
75 Spring St., S.W.
Atlanta, GA 30303

MIDWEST REGIONAL OFFICE
National Park Service
1709 Jackson St.
Omaha, NB 68102

SOUTHWEST REGIONAL OFFICE
National Park Service
P.O. Box 728
Old Santa Fe Trail
Santa Fe, NM 87501

WESTERN REGIONAL OFFICE
National Park Service
P.O. Box 36063
450 Golden Gate Ave.
San Francisco, CA 94102

NORTH-ATLANTIC REGIONAL OFFICE
National Park Service
15 State St.
Boston, MA 02109

NATIONAL CAPITOL REGIONAL OFFICE
National Park Service
1100 Ohio Drive, S.W.
Washington, D.C. 20242

MAIN OFFICE
National Park Service
Department of the Interior Bldg.
Washington, D.C. 20240

MID-ATLANTIC REGIONAL OFFICE
National Park Service
143 S. Third St.
Philadelphia, PA 19106

PACIFIC NORTHWEST REGIONAL OFFICE
National Park Service
1920 Westin Bldg.
2001 6th Ave.
Seattle, WA 98121

ROCKY MOUNTAIN REGIONAL OFFICE
National Park Service
P.O. Box 25287
Denver, CO 80225

ALASKA REGIONAL OFFICE
National Park Service
2525 Gambell St., Rm. 107
Anchorage, AK 99503

FOREST HEADQUARTERS

The following headquarters offices will supply booklets covering activities in their regions.

NATIONAL FORESTS
National Forest Service
U.S. Department of Agriculture
Office of Information
P.O. Box 96090
Washington, D.C. 20090
(202) 205-1760

NORTHERN REGION
National Forest Headquarters
Federal Bldg.
P.O. Box 7669
Missoula, MT 59807

ROCKY MOUNTAIN REGION
National Forest Headquarters
11177 W. 8th Ave.
Box 25127
Lakewood, CO 80225

SOUTHWESTERN REGION
National Forest Headquarters
Federal Bldg.
517 Gold Ave. S.W.
Albuquerque, NM 87102

INTERMOUNTAIN REGION
National Forest Headquarters
Federal Office Bldg.
324 25th St.
Ogden, UT 84401

CALIFORNIA REGION
National Forest Headquarters
630 Sansome St.
San Francisco, CA 94111

PACIFIC NORTHWEST REGION
National Forest Headquarters
319 S.W. Pine St.
P.O. Box 3623
Portland, OR 97208

EASTERN REGION
National Forest Headquarters
633 W. Wisconsin Ave.
Milwuakee, WI 53203

NATIONAL REFUGES
U.S. Fish & Wildlife Service
Public Affairs Office
1849 C Street, NW
Publication Dep. WEB
Room 130
Washington, D.C. 20240
(703) 358-1711

SOUTHERN REGION
National Forest Headquarters
Suite 800
1720 Peachtree Rd., N.W.
Atlanta, GA 30367

ALASKA REGION
National Forest Headquarters
Federal Office Bldg.
Box 1628
Juneau, AK 99802

BLM RECREATION SITES
Bureau of Land Management Public Affairs
Office
1849 C Street, NW
MS-5600/MIB
Washington, D.C. 20240
(202) 452-5121

TRAVEL INFORMATION

Organizations and agencies listed below will supply free travel information on request. The highway commissions in every state and all the provinces of Canada will also send road maps. Information usually includes directory of accommodations, campgrounds, and points of interest.

UNITED STATES

ALABAMA BUREAU OF TOURISM & TRAVEL
P.O. Box 4309, Dept. TIA
Montgomery, AL 36103-4309
(205) 242-4169
Toll-free: 1-800-ALABAMA

ALASKA DIVISION OF TOURISM
P.O. Box 110801, TIA
Juneau, AK 99811-0801
(907) 465-2010

ARIZONA OFFICE OF TOURISM
1100 W. Washington
Phoenix, AZ 85007
(602) 542-8687

ARKANSAS TOURISM OFFICE
1 Capitol Mall, Dept. 7701
Little Rock, AR 72201
(501) 682-7777
Toll-free: 1-800-NATURAL

CALIFORNIA OFFICE OF TOURISM
P.O. Box 9278, Dept. TIA
Van Nuys, CA 91409
(916) 322-2881
Toll-free: 1-800-TO CALIF

COLORADO TOURISM BOARD
P.O. Box 38700
Denver, CO 80238
(303) 592-5410
Toll-free: 1-800-COLORADO

**CONNECTICUT DEPARTMENT OF ECONOMIC
DEVELOPMENT, TOURISM DIVISION**
865 Brook St.
Rocky Hill, CT 06067
(203) 258-4355
Toll-free: 1-800-CT BOUND

DELAWARE TOURISM OFFICE
99 Kings Highway
Box 1401, Dept. TIA
Dover, DE 19903
(302) 739-4271
Toll-free: 1-800-441-8846

FLORIDA DIVISION OF TOURISM
126 W. Van Buren St., FLDA
Tallahassee, FL 32301
(904) 487-1462

GEORGIA DEPARTMENT OF INDUSTRY, TRADE, & TOURISM
P.O. Box 1776, Dept. TIA
Atlanta, GA 30301
(404) 656-3590
Toll-free: 1-800-VISIT GA

HAWAII DEPARTMENT OF BUSINESS, ECONOMIC DEVELOPMENT, & TOURISM
P.O. Box 2359
Honolulu, HI 96804
(808) 586-2423

IDAHO DIVISION OF TOURISM DEVELOPMENT
700 W. State St., Dept. C
Boise, ID 83720
(208) 334-2470
Toll-free: 1-800-635-7820

ILLINOIS BUREAU OF TOURISM
100 W. Randolph, Suite 3-400
Chicago, IL 60601
(312) 814-4732
Toll-free: 1-800-223-0121

INDIANA DEPARTMENT OF COMMERCE TOURISM AND FILM DEVELOPMENT DIVISION
1 N. Capitol, Suite 700
Indianapolis, IN 46204-2288
(317) 232-8860
Toll-free: 1-800-289-6646

NEVADA COMMISSION OF TOURISM
Capitol Complex, Dept. TIA
Carson City, NV 89710
(702) 687-4322
Toll-free: 1-800-NEVADA 8

NEW HAMPSHIRE OFFICE OF TRAVEL AND TOURISM DEVELOPMENT
P.O. Box 856, Dept. TIA
Concord, NH 03302
(603) 271-2343

NEW JERSEY DIVISION OF TRAVEL AND TOURISM
20 W. State St., CN 826, Dept. TIA
Trenton, NJ 08625
(609) 292-2470
Toll-free: 1-800-JERSEY 7

NEW MEXICO DEPARTMENT OF TOURISM
1100 St. Francis Dr.
Joseph Montoya Building
Santa Fe, NM 87503
(505) 827-0291
Toll-free: 1-800-545-2040

NEW YORK STATE DEPARTMENT OF ECONOMIC DEVELOPMENT
One Commerce Plaza
Albany, NY 12245
(518) 474-4116
Toll-free: 1-800-CALL NYS

NORTH CAROLINA DIVISION OF TRAVEL AND TOURISM
430 N. Salisbury St.
Raleigh, NC 27603
(919) 733-4171
Toll-free: 1-800-VISIT NC

NORTH DAKOTA TOURISM PROMOTION
Liberty Memorial Building,
Capitol Grounds
Bismarck, ND 58505
(701) 224-2525
Toll-free: 1-800-HELLO ND

OHIO DIVISION OF TRAVEL AND TOURISM
P.O. Box 1001, Dept. TIA
Columbus, OH 43211-0101
(614) 466-8844
Toll-free: 1-800-BUCKEYE
(Continental U.S., Ontario, Quebec)

OKLAHOMA TOURISM AND RECREATION DEPARTMENT
TRAVEL & TOURISM DIVISION
500 Will Rogers Bldg., DA92
Oklahoma City, OK 73105-4492
(405) 521-3981
Toll-free: 1-800-652-6552
(Information requests only)

OREGON ECONOMIC DEVELOPMENT DEPARTMENT, TOURISM DIVISION
775 Summer St., NE
Salem, OR 97310
(503) 373-1270
Toll-free: 1-800-547-7842

PENNSYLVANIA BUREAU OF TRAVEL MARKETING
130 Commonwealth Dr.
Warrendale, PA 15086
(717) 787-5453
Toll-free: 1-800-VISIT PA

RHODE ISLAND TOURISM DIVISION
7 Jackson Walkway, Dept. TIA
Providence, RI 02903
(401) 277-2601
Toll-free: 1-800-556-5404

SOUTH CAROLINA DIVISION OF TOURISM
Box 71, Room 902
Columbia, SC 29202
(803) 734-0235

IOWA DIVISION OF TOURISM
200 E. Grand, TIA
Des Moines, IA 50309
(515) 242-4705
Toll-free: 1-800-345-IOWA

KANSAS TRAVEL & TOURISM DIVISION
400 W. 8th St., 5th Floor, Dept. DIS
Topeka, KS 66603-3957
(913) 296-3009
Toll-free: 1-800-252-6727

KENTUCKY DEPARTMENT OF TRAVEL DEVELOPMENT
2200 Capitol Plaza Tower, Dept. DA
Frankfort, KY 40601
(502) 564-4930
Toll-free: 1-800-225-TRIP

LOUISIANA OFFICE OF TOURISM
Attn: Inquiry Department
P.O. Box 94291, LOT
Baton Rouge, LA 70804-9291
(504) 342-8119
Toll-free: 1-800-33-GUMBO

MAINE OFFICE OF TOURISM
189 State St.
Augusta, ME 04333
(207) 289-5711
Toll-free: 1-800-533-9595

MARYLAND OFFICE OF TRAVEL AND TOURISM
217 E. Redwood St., 9th Floor
Baltimore, MD 21202
(410) 333-6611
Toll-free: 1-800-543-1036

MASSACHUSETTS OFFICE OF TRAVEL AND TOURISM
100 Cambridge St., 13th Floor
Boston, MA 02202
(617) 727-3201
Toll-free: 1-800-447-MASS
(for ordering vacation kit only, U.S. only)

MICHIGAN TRAVEL BUREAU
P.O. Box 30226
Lansing, MI 48909
(517) 373-0670
Toll-free: 1-800-5432-YES

MINNESOTA OFFICE OF TOURISM
375 Jackson St., 250 Skyway Level
St. Paul, MN 55101
(612) 296-5029
Toll-free: 1-800-657-3700

MISSISSIPPI DIVISION OF TOURISM
P.O. Box 22825
Jackson, MS 39205
(601) 359-3297
Toll-free: 1-800-647-2290

MISSOURI DIVISION OF TOURISM
P.O. Box 1055, Dept. TIA
Jefferson City, MO 65102
(314) 751-4133
Toll-free: 1-800-877-1234

TRAVEL MONTANA
Room 259
Deer Lodge, MT 59722
(406) 444-2654
Toll-free: 1-800-541-1447

NEBRASKA DIVISION OF TRAVEL AND TOURISM
301 Central Mall S., Rm. 88937
Lincoln, NE 68509
(402) 471-3796
Toll-free: 1-800-228-4307

SOUTH DAKOTA DEPARTMENT OF TOURISM
711 E. Wells Ave.
Pierre, SD 57501-3369
(605) 773-3301
Toll-free: 1-800-843-1930

TENNESSEE DEPARTMENT OF TOURISM DEVELOPMENT
P.O. Box 23170, TNDA
Nashville, TN 37202
(615) 741-2158

TEXAS DEPARTMENT OF COMMERCE, TOURISM DIVISION
P.O. Box 12728
Austin, TX 78711-2728
(512) 462-9191
Toll-free: 1-800-88-88-TEX

UTAH TRAVEL COUNCIL
Council Hall/Capitol Hill
Dept. TIA
300 N. State St.
Salt Lake City, UT 84114
(801) 538-1030

VERMONT TRAVEL DIVISION
134 State St., Dept. TIA
Montpelier, VT 05602
(802) 828-3236

VIRGINIA DIVISION OF TOURISM
1021 E. Cary St., Dept. VT
Richmond, VA 23219
(804) 786-4484
Toll-free: 1-800-VISIT VA

WASHINGTON, D.C. CONVENTION AND VISITORS ASSOCIATION
1212 New York Ave. NW.
Washington, D.C. 20005
(202) 789-7000

WASHINGTON STATE TOURISM DEVELOPMENT DIVISION
P.O. Box 42513
Olympia, WA 98504-2513
(206) 586-2088, (206) 586-2012
Toll-free: 1-800-544-1800

WEST VIRGINIA DIVISION OF TOURISM & PARKS
2101 Washington St. East
Charleston, WV 25305
(304) 348-2286
Toll-free: 1-800-CALL-WVA

WISCONSIN DIVISION OF TOURISM
P.O. Box 7606
Madison, WI 53707
(608) 266-2161
Toll-free in state: 1-800-372-2737
Out of state: 1-800-432-TRIP

WYOMING DIVISION OF TOURISM
I-25 at College Dr., Dept. WY
Cheyenne, WY 82002
(307) 777-7777
Toll-free: 1-800-225-5996

PUERTO RICO TOURISM COMPANY
P.O. Box 5268, Dept. TH
Miami, FL 33102
Toll-free: 1-800-866-STAR, Ext. 17

U.S. VIRGIN ISLANDS DIVISION OF TOURISM
P.O. Box 6400, VITIA
Charlotte Amalie, St. Thomas,
USVI 00801
(809) 774-8784
Toll-free: 1-800-372-8784

CANADA

GENERAL
Canadian Government Office of Tourism
235 Queen St., 4th Floor East
Ottawa, Ontario
Canada K1A 0H6

ALBERTA
Travel Alberta
Edmonton, Alberta
Canada T5J 2Z4

BRITISH COLUMBIA
Ministry of Tourism
1117 Wharf St.
Victoria, British Columbia
Canada V8W 2Z2

MANITOBA
Department of Tourism
Box 5077
Legislative Bldg.
Winnipeg, Manitoba
Canada R3C 0V8

NEW BRUNSWICK
Department of Tourism
Fredericton, New Brunswick
Canada E3B 5C3

NEWFOUNDLAND—LABRADOR
Department of Tourism
Tourist Services Division
St. John's, Newfoundland
Canada A1C 5R8

NOVA SCOTIA
Department of Tourism
Halifax, Nova Scotia
Canada B3J 2M7

ONTARIO
Ontario Travel
Queen's Park
Toronto, Ontario
Canada M7A 2E5

PRINCE EDWARD ISLAND
Department of Tourism
Tourist Services
Charlottetown, Prince Edward Island
Canada C1A 7M5

QUEBEC
Department of Tourism
Place de la Capitale, 150 E. Saint Cyrille Blvd.
Quebec, Quebec
Canada G1R 2B2

SASKATCHEWAN
Department of Tourism
Extension Services
1825 Lorne St.
Regina, Saskatchewan
Canada S4P 3V7

NORTHWEST TERRITORIES
TravelArctic
Government, Northwest Territories
Yellowknife, Northwest Territories
Canada X1A 2L9

YUKON
Department of Tourism
Box 2703
Whitehorse, Yukon Territory
Canada Y1A 2C6

MEXICO

Mexican National Tourism Council
405 Park Ave.
New York, NY 10022

OUTDOOR RECREATION ORGANIZATIONS ⸻

The following organizations can provide advice and information. They are listed under their specialty.

SHOOTING
The Clay Pigeon Shooting Association
107 Epping New Rd., Buckhurst Hill
Essex, England 1G9 5TG

Connecticut Travelers Sporting Clays Association
91 Park Lane Rd.
New Milford, CT 06776

Federation Internationale de Tir Aux Armes
   Sportives de Chasse
10 Rue de Lisbonne Paris
75008 France

The International Shooting Union
Bavariaring 21, D-80336
Munich 1, Germany

International Sporting Clays Federation
5 Brighton Parade, Southport 4215
Queensland, Australia

National Sporting Clays Association
5931 Roft Rd.
San Antonio, TX 78253

New England Sporting Clays Association
441 Rose Hill Rd.
Peace Dale, RI 02879

Sporting Clays of America
9 Mott Ave.
Suite 103
Norwalk, CT 06850

US Shooting Team, Office of Junior Development
P.O. Box 3207
Brentwood, TN 37024-3207

USA Shooting
One Olympic Plaza
Colorado Springs, CO 80909

Women's Shooting Sports Foundation
1505 Hwy. 6 South, Suite 101
Houston, TX 77077

International Handgun Metallic Silhouette
   Association
Box 1609
Idaho Falls, ID 83401

National Bench Rest Shooters Association, Inc.
5735 Sherwood Forest Dr.
Akron, OH 44319

National Muzzle Loading Rifle Association
P.O. Box 67
Friendship, IN 47021

National Rifle Association of America
1600 Rhode Island Ave., N.W.
Washington, D.C. 20036

National Shooting Sports Foundation
1075 Post Road
Riverside, CT 06878

National Skeet Shooting Association
P.O. Box 28188
San Antonio, TX 78228

Amateur Trapshooting Association
P.O. Box 458
Vandalia, OH 45377

HUNTING

Boone and Crockett Club
250 Station Dr.
Missoula, MT 59801

Ducks Unlimited
1 Waterfowl Way
Memphis, TN 38120

Foundation for North American Big Game
P.O. Box 2710
Woodbridge, VA 22193

National Trappers Association
15412 Tau Rd.
Marshall, MI 49068

National Wild Turkey Federation
Box 530
Edgefield, SC 29824

Safari Club International
5151 E. Broadway, Suite 1680
Tucson, AZ 85711

FISHING

American Littoral Society
Sandy Hook Marine Laboratory
Box 117
Highlands, NJ 07732

Atlantic Salmon Federation
P.O. Box 429
St. Andrews, New Brunswick
Canada E0G 2X0

American Sportfishing Association
1033 North Fairfax St., Ste. 200
Alexandria, VA 22314

Federation of Fly Fishers
P.O. Box 1595
502 S. 19th, Suite #1
Bozeman, MT 59771

Future Fisherman Foundation
1033 N. Fairfax St., Suite 200
Alexandria, VA 22314

International Game Fish Association
(for spinfishing and saltwater fly records)
1301 E. Atlantic Blvd.
Pompano Beach, FL 33060

Izaak Walton League of America
1701 N. Ft. Myer Dr.
Suite 1100
Arlington, VA 22209

Stripers Unlimited, Inc.
P.O. Box 45
South Attleboro, MA 02703

Trout Unlimited
501 Church St., N.E.
Vienna, VA 22180

CAMPING AND HIKING

American Camping Association
Bradford Woods
Martinsville, IN 46151

American Hiking Society
P.O. Box 20160
Washington, D.C. 20041-2160

Appalachian Trail Conference
P.O. Box 807
Harpers Ferry, WV 25425

National Campers and Hikers Association, Inc.
7172 Transit Road
Buffalo, NY 14221

National Recreation and Park Association
3101 Park Center Dr.
Alexandria, VA 22302

North American Family Campers Association
P.O. Box 328
Concord, VT 05824

Recreation Vehicle Dealers Association (RVDA)
RV Rental Association (RVRA)
RV Aftermarket Association (RVAM)
3930 University Drive
Fairfax, VA 22030
(703) 591-7130

Recreation Vehicle Industry Association (RVIA)
1896 Preston White Drive
P.O. Box 2999
Reston, VA 22090-0999
(703) 620-6003
Western Office:
1748 West Katella Suite 108
Orange, CA 92667-3429
(714) 532-1688

National Association of RV Parks and
   Campgrounds (ARVC)
8605 Westwood Center Drive
Suite 201
Vienna, VA 22182-2231
(703) 734-3000

Canadian Recreation Vehicle Association
670 Bloor St. West, Suite 200
Toronto, Ontario CANADA M6G 1L2
(416) 533-7800
FAX: (416) 533-4795

ARCHERY

American Cross Bow Association
P.O. Box 72
Huntsville, AL 72740

American Indoor Archery Association
R.R. 4, 4600 S.W. 41st Blvd.
Gainesville, FL 32601

Archery Manufacturers and Merchants
   Organization
2622 C-4 NW 43rd St.
Gainesville, FL 32606

Boat/U.S.
880 South Pickett St.
Alexandria, VA 22304

Bowhunters Who Care
38 Stires Lake, P.O. Box 269
Columbus, NE 68601

Fred Bear Sports Club
Rural Route 4, 4600 S.W. 41st Blvd.
Gainesville, FL 32601

National Archery Association
1750 E. Boulder St.
Colorado Springs, CO 80909

National Bowhunters Educational Foundation
Rt. 6, Box 199
Murray, KY 43071

National Crossbow Association
3605 Hewn Lane
Linden Knoll, 721
Wilmington, DE

National Field Archery Association
31419 Outer I-10 Rt. 2
Box 514
Redlands, CA 92373

Professional Bowhunters Society
25233 TR 192
Coshocton, OH 43812

Pope and Young Club
Route 1, Box 147
Salmon, ID 83467

BOATING

American Power Boat Association
17640 E. 9 Mile Rd.
East Detroit, MI 48021

American White Water Affiliation
146 N. Brockway
Palatine, IL 60067

National Marine Manufacturers Assn.
401 N. Michigan Ave.
Chicago, IL 60611

Outboard Boating Club of America
2550 M St. NW
Washington, DC 20037

United States Canoe Association
2509 Kackapoo Dr.
Lafayette, IN 47905

Index